UNDERSTANDING AND MANAGING

Organizational Behavior

Second Edition

Jennifer M. George
Texas A & M University

Gareth R. Jones
Texas A & M University

ADDISON-WESLEY

An imprint of Addison Wesley Longman, Inc.

Reading, Massachusetts • Menlo Park, California • New York • Harlow, England
Don Mills, Ontario • Sydney • Mexico City • Madrid • Amsterdam

For our parents,

Agnes and Harvey George

and

Mona and Iori Jones

and our children,

Nicholas and Julia George-Jones

Executive Editor: Michael Roche
Assistant Editor: Ruth Berry
Editorial Assistant: Adam Hamel
Production Supervisor: Heather Bingham
Marketing Manager: Julia A. Downs
Senior Marketing Coordinator: Joyce E. Cosentino
Supplements Editor: Karen Stevenson
Design Manager: Regina Hagen
Project Coordination and Text Design: Electronic Publishing Services Inc., NYC
Cover Designers: Jeannet Leendertse and Regina Hagen
Cover Photo: Image © 1998 PhotoDisc Inc.
Photo Researcher: Electronic Publishing Services Inc., NYC
Manufacturing Manager: Sheila Spinney
Electronic Page Makeup: Electronic Publishing Services Inc., NYC
Printer and Binder: World Color/Taunton

Library of Congress Cataloging-in-Publication Data
George, Jennifer M.
     Understanding and managing organizational behavior / Jennifer M.
     George, Gareth R. Jones; annotations by William C. Sharbrough. —
     2nd. ed.
          p.   cm.
     Includes bibliographical references and index.
     ISBN 0-201-35063-7
     1. Organizational behavior.   2. Organizational effectiveness.
     I. Jones, Gareth R.   II. Title.
     HD58.7.G454   1999
     658.3–dc21   98-22611
                                                      CIP

ISBN 0-201-35063-7
REPRINT
345678910—RNT—010099

Brief Contents

Detailed Contents

The Role of Performance Appraisal in Motivation 254

Encouraging High Levels of Motivation and
Performance 255   Providing Information for Decision Making 256   Developing a Performance Appraisal System 257
Potential Problems in Subjective Performance Appraisal 264

Pay as a Motivation Tool 265

Merit Pay Plans 265   Should Merit Pay Be Based on
Individual, Group, or Organizational Performance? 267
Should Merit Pay Be in the Form of a Salary Increase or a
Bonus? 268   Examples of Merit Pay Plans 269   The Ethics
of Pay Differentials and Comparable Worth 270

Motivation Through Career Opportunities 271

The Nature of Careers 272   Types of Careers 273   Career
Stages 273

Career Challenges for the 1990s and Beyond 279

Ethical Career Management 280   Career Management
That Supports Diversity 280   Career Management in an
Era of Dual-Career Couples 282

Summary 283

Organizational Behavior in Action 284

CHAPTER 9   Stress and Work-Life Linkages 290

Opening Case: Balancing Work and Home Life 290

The Nature of Stress 291

Individual Differences and Stress 292   Consequences
of Stress 294

Sources of Stress 299

Personal Stressors 300   Job-Related Stressors 303
Group- and Organization-Related Stressors 306   Stressors
Arising Out of Work-Life Linkages 310

Coping With Stress 310

Problem-Focused Coping Strategies for Individuals 311
Emotion-Focused Coping Strategies for Individuals 313
Problem-Focused Coping Strategies for Organizations 316   Emotion-Focused Coping Strategies for
Organizations 319

Summary 322

Organizational Behavior in Action 324

PART II   GROUPS AND ORGANIZATIONAL PROCESSES

CHAPTER 10   The Nature of Work Groups and Teams 330

Opening Case: High Performing Teams at Nucor 330

Introduction to Groups 331

Types of Work Groups 332   Group Development Over
Time: The Five-Stage Model 335

Characteristics of Work Groups 337

Group Size 338   Group Composition 339   Group
Function 341   Group Status 341   Social Facilitation 341

PART III   INTERGROUP RELATIONS AND THE ORGANIZATIONAL CONTEXT

Preface

Encouraged by the favorable reception and level of support that greeted the first edition of *Understanding and Managing Organizational Behavior*, we have revised the second edition of our book in significant ways based on the reactions and suggestions of both users and reviewers. As with the first edition of our book, our goal has been to show students how an understanding of organizational behavior can help them to better appreciate and manage the complexities and challenges associated with working in modern organizations. To achieve this goal, we have continued to strive to ensure that our book (1) is comprehensive, integrated, and makes important theories accessible and interesting to students; (2) is current, up-to-date, and contains expanded coverage of issues of contemporary significance such as ethics, diversity, and global management; and (3) uses rich, real-life examples of people and organizations to bring key concepts to life and provide clear managerial implications. In particular, enthusiasm for our end-of-chapter experiential exercises contained in the Organizational Behavior in Action sections at the end of each chapter has led us to expand this material and to add an Internet Exercise as well as a closing case for analysis. We want students to catch the excitement of organizational behavior as a fluid, many-faceted discipline with multiple levels of analysis, and we have revised all the parts and content of our book with this in mind.

Comprehensive and Integrated Coverage

Most of the chapters of our book have been significantly revised either to incorporate the most recent theoretical advances in organizational behavior or to change the way the material is presented in accordance with feedback from users and reviewers. As with the first edition, however, we have been careful to organize the material in an integrated way so that each part of the book builds on the previous parts, and inside each part, each chapter builds on the material in earlier chapters in a clear and logical fashion. In this way, students develop an integrated and cohesive understanding of organizational behavior. The comprehensive and integrated coverage in *Understanding and Managing Organizational Behavior* includes the following highlights.

- The book opens with an account of organizational behavior in Chapter 1 that demonstrates its real-world relevance and outlines the key challenges managers face in todays global environment: diversity, ethics, competitive advantage, and global issues.

- An up-to-date treatment of personality and ability and their implications for modern organizations is provided in Chapter 2, with detailed coverage of the Big Five Model of Personality. New to this edition is coverage of emotional intelligence.

- In Chapter 3 we present a new model that explains clearly to students the relationship between work values, attitudes, and moods and their implications for such organizational behaviors as citizenship behavior. Also new are our identification of two types of organizational commitment—affective commitment and continuance commitment—and our examination of the determinants and potential consequences of affective commitment.

- In Chapter 4 we use a unique approach in examining diversity from the perspective of perception and attribution, which are fundamental individual processes that operate in every organization. New to this edition is coverage of sexual harassment and ways to combat it.

- Chapter 5 presents extensive coverage of recent approaches to learning, such as vicarious learning, self-control, and self-efficacy. New to this edition is coverage of organizational learning and the learning organization.

- We have written three chapters on motivation (Chapters 6, 7, and 8), and we have now reorganized the motivation model to present an even more integrated approach to understanding work motivation—one of the most important challenges in organizational behavior. First, we present the overall model of motivation, going on to explain how the different theories of motivation are related and complementary and to offer an in-depth treatment of procedural justice theory. Then, building on basic theories of motivation, we discuss job design, goal setting, performance appraisal, pay, and careers as motivation tools. Our inclusion of social information processing theory and our discussion of the limits to goal setting continue to be innovative, as is our analysis of ethical career management, career management that supports diversity, and career management in an era of dual-career couples. New to this edition is coverage of contingent workers and 360-degree performance appraisals.

- Two chapters (Chapters 10 and 11) set forth integrated coverage of groups as the basic building blocks of organizations. After describing the nature of work groups and the ways in which groups control their members, we focus on what makes for effective work groups in organizations. The discussion of process losses and gains, social loafing, and important types of groups, such as the top management team, self-managed work teams, and R&D teams, are innovations.

- At the intergroup and organizational level of analysis we provide a two-chapter (Chapters 15 and 16) integrated treatment of organizational design, organizational structure, and organizational culture. After discussing the basic building blocks of organizational structure and culture, we provide an up-to-date account of the three most important factors affecting the design of structure and culture: the organizations environment, strategy, and technology. This discussion includes coverage of cross-functional team structures and ethical cultures.

- The whole chapter (Chapter 17) we have provided on all aspects of managing global organizations proved very popular with our reviewers. We want students to see how differences in attitudes, values, ethics, and ways of doing business in different countries present many challenges for managers. New coverage of cross-cultural differences in communication and understanding of linguistic styles is presented in Chapter 13. The last chapter of the book (Chapter 19) continues to provide what we believe to be the most current treatment of organizational change in any organizational behavior textbook on

the market. This chapter offers an in-depth treatment of restructuring, reengineering, total quality management, and other approaches to improving organizational effectiveness in todays increasingly competitive global environment.

Extensive Learning System

We believe that no other organizational behavior textbook has the range of learning features for students that ours has. These features—some integrated into the text and some at the end of each chapter or part—ease the students way through the study of organizational behavior. These features were crafted so that instructors can actively involve their students in the chapter material. They provide an interactive approach to teaching organizational behavior that helps students understand and appreciate the complexity of the challenges facing managers and workers in todays business environment. The following list highlights the wide range of learning features available in our text.

OPENING CASE

The student enters the chapter via an in-depth, real-world example of people and organizations that focuses attention on the upcoming chapter issues.

RUNNING GLOSSARY

To address the abundance of terminology that an introductory student needs to assimilate, we have included a running glossary that provides a definition for every key term in the book.

ADVICE TO MANAGERS

In each chapter we have included two or more managerial summaries called *Advice to Managers,* where the practical implications of key organizational behavior theories and concepts are clearly outlined. These take-home lessons extend the chapter material into the realm of application in ways that students can actually use when they enter the workplace.

INSIGHT BOXES

Understanding and Managing Organizational Behavior reflects all the current and pressing concerns facing organizations and their managers and workers today. We have created interesting real-world examples geared to the subject matter of the chapter to engage the student and bring these concerns to life. These *Insights* are not mere summaries of academic studies or contrived situations, but are stories from the front line of todays businesses. They are different from similar features in most other textbooks in that they are directly integrated into the text material to highlight and illustrate the most significant points. We have deliberately set up these features this way because our experience has shown that students are more likely to read material that is seamlessly woven into the fabric of the chapter rather than set apart. Each chapter contains several Insights directly related to the text material.

ORGANIZATIONAL BEHAVIOR IN ACTION

The sections entitled *Organizational Behavior in Action* are found at the end of each chapter and include a wide range of activities to help students build the skills they will need as future managers and workers. We have carefully developed the features within these modules with both large and small classes in mind, as well as individual and group assignments. Our overriding goal is to help students appreciate that there are no absolute answers to organizational behavior issues and that they must instead learn how to analyze particular situations, compare alternative courses of action, and generate options for solution.

TOPICS FOR DISCUSSION AND ACTION

A collection of thought provoking questions serve as a review of the chapter material.

BUILDING DIAGNOSTIC SKILLS

This experiential feature engages students by challenging them to explore, analyze, and diagnose actual organizational behavior based on what they have just learned in the chapter. This exercise leads students to draw on their own experience base to apply theories diagnostically to real situations from their own lives and to organizations and companies they select.

RESEARCH ON THE INTERNET: A MANAGER'S TOOL

Each chapter contains two Internet exercises that students can use to do research on the World Wide Web. One is specific, asking students to complete a particular assignment; the other is general, asking students to do their own research. For example, the specific exercise at the end of Chapter 3 has students visit the Haliburton Company home page and examine its Summary Code of Business Conduct; the exercises provide guidance for examining and discussing this code.

The general task asks the student to discover an Internet site where an organization has attempted to increase employee job satisfaction and engender positive feelings about the company; the student is then asked to discuss the effectiveness of the companys initiatives.

TOPICS FOR DEBATE

This experiential feature is cast in a debate format and asks students to develop their own arguments as they examine chapter content from two different perspectives. Our experience has shown that debates, rebuttals, and questions from the audience fire up students involvement and imagination and spark a high level of class participation.

EXPERIENTIAL EXERCISE

In this group based exercise, students divide into groups and explore together the chapter material by focusing on a practical OB task, problem, or issue. To complete the assignment, students must use all their knowledge and experience and work in a group situation—a dynamic that they are sure to encounter in the workplace. These exercises are all original and have been tested by the authors.

MAKING THE CONNECTION

Students collect real-world examples of people and organizations from newspapers like *The Wall Street Journal* and magazines like *Fortune* and *Business Week* to answer questions related to the chapter material. This feature represents a more advanced assignment that works especially well when the instructor requires students to subscribe to key business publications. The goal is to develop students critical thinking skills and help them see how OB principles apply to business organizations in the news.

CLOSING CASE

Each chapter contains a closing case that can be used to stimulate class discussion of the chapter content. For example, Chapter 9 includes a case on Xerox utilization of flexible working hours as a vehicle for combating stress. Each case includes questions that require students to apply some immediate hands-on managerial analysis of the situation.

Teaching Package

Instructors Resource Manual. Prepared by Amit Shah of Frostburg State University and Sonia Goltz of Northern Michigan University, the Instructors Resource Manual contains many valuable materials for faculty. Suggested course outlines, sample assignments, and detailed information about how to use and integrate the text features will assist instructors in preparing both lectures and class discussions. Detailed chapter outlines, lecture support, and analysis of both introductory and end-of-chapter cases are prepared for each chapter, as well as additional applications and teaching suggestions. Detailed answers to the end-of-chapter Discussion Questions complement the multiple choice questions in the Test Bank.

Test Bank. Prepared by Amit Shah of Frostburg State University and Scott Sherman, each chapter of the Test Bank includes 100-120 True-False, Multiple Choice, Short Answer, Fill-in-the-Blank, and Essay questions. The range of elements covered by the questions includes the chapter material as well as the Organizational Insights and all Cases. For each question, the correct answer and the page number(s) where the answer can be found are referenced. Misleading words and phrases, such as all of the above and none of the above, as well as trivia-type questions, have been eliminated.

Computerized Test Bank and Network Testing (TestGen EQ with QuizMaster). The test generation software for Windows in fully networkable. TestGen EQ's graphical interface enables instructors to view, edit, and add questions; transfer questions to tests, and print tests in various fonts and forms. Search and sort features let the instructor quickly locate questions and arrange them in a preferred order. QuizMaster will grade tests automatically, and provide detailed feedback analysis. Both these programs are components of the Instructor's CD-ROM.

FastFax Testing. As an additional service to instructors using this text, FastFax testing is available through our Glenview Software Products and Services Group. This group will create tests based on instructions from the professor and send a hard copy of the test to the professor via fax or mail within two days. To receive more information, or forms for requesting tests, please contact your local sales representative.

PowerPoint Presentation Package. An extensive set of PowerPoint slides has been prepared to accompany *Understanding and Managing Organizational Behavior.* The selection of slides includes text illustrations and additional lecture material.

Instructor's CD-ROM. This Windows based CD-ROM contains the computerized test bank, PowerPoint pre-

sentation, and Instructor's Manual. This innovative, user-friendly electronic supplement is now a programmed CD-ROM.

Videos. A collection of video segments are available to qualified adopters. The segments, which relate to issues discussed in the chapters, includes interesting and engaging footage of actual workers, managers, and companies. The Instructors Manual contains a Video Guide that explains how the instructor can link the topic of each video segment to the corresponding textual material. The guide contains summaries, key topics covered, companies discussed, and other information to facilitate use of the videos.

The George & Jones Web Site. A dynamic Web site has been created to extend and amplify the content in *Understanding and Managing Organizational Behavior.* The World Wide Web is transforming the ways in which we teach and learn, and its instant accessibility allows us to provide you with more timely information. Visit our Web site at http://hepg.awl.com and select the keyword George/Jones from the keyword pull-down menu.

Acetates. A collection of color acetates contains selected figures, tables, and graphs from the text.

Acknowledgments

Finding a way to coordinate and integrate the rich and diverse body of literature on organizational behavior is no easy task. Neither is it easy to present the material in a way that students can easily understand and enjoy, given the plethora of concepts, theories, and research findings in existence. In writing *Understanding and Managing Organizational Behavior,* we were fortunate to have had the assistance of several people who have contributed greatly to the books final form. We are grateful to our editor, Mike Roche, for helping us to present the chapter material in a way that ensures its integrated flow within and between the books chapters; he has also ably coordinated the books progress and provided us with timely feedback and information from professors and reviewers that allowed us to shape the book to meet the needs of its intended market. We also want to acknowledge the contributions of Ruth Berry and Karen Stevenson, whose efforts can be seen in the comprehensiveness of the package of materials that accompanies *Understanding and Managing Organizational Behavior.* We are also grateful to Electronic Publishing Services Inc. for providing the copyediting and improving the readability of our manuscript, Heather Bingham for coordinating the production process, and Anthony Calcara and Linda Harms of Electronic Publishing Services Inc. for providing us with excellent production support. We are also grateful to the many reviewers and colleagues who provided us with detailed feedback on the chapters and with perceptive comments and suggestions for improving the manuscript:

Cheryl Adkins, *Louisiana State University*
Deborah Arvanites, *Villanova University*
Wendy S. Becker, *Pennsylvania State University*
Robert Bontempo, *Columbia University*
W. Randy Boxx, *University of Mississippi*
Dan Brass, *Pennsylvania State University*
Diane Caggiano, *Fitchburg State University*
Shawn Carraher, *Indiana State University*
Russell Coff, *Washington University*
John L. Cotton, *Marquette University*
Anne C. Cowden, *California State University,* Sacramento
Lucinda Doran, *The Hay Group*
Mark Fearing, *University of Houston*
Dave Fearon, *Central Connecticut State University*
Steve Grover, *Indiana University*
Bob Gulbro, *Jacksonville State University*
Jennifer Halpern, *Cornell University*
Sandra Hartman, *University of New Orleans*
Thomas C. Head, *Tennessee State University*
Brooks C. Holtom, *University of Washington*
Bruce Johnson, *Gustavus Adolphus College*
Diane Kellogg, *Bentley College*
Mary Kernan, *University of Delaware*
Andrew Klein, *Keller Graduate School of Management*
Karen Maher, *University of Missouri,* St. Louis
Stephen Markham, *North Carolina State University*

Gary McMahan, *University of Southern California*
Janet Near, *Indiana University*
Tim Peterson, *University of Tulsa*
Allayne Pizzolatto, *Nicholls State University*
Peter Poole, *Lehigh University*
Elizabeth Ravlin, *University of South Carolina*
Diana Reed, *Drake University*
Susan Rhodes, *Syracuse University*
Peter Richardson, *Southwest Missouri State University*
Sandra Robinson, *New York University*
Goli Sadri, *California State University,* Fullerton
David M. Savino, *Ohio Northern University*
Chris Scheck, *Northern Illinois University*
Marian C. Schultz, *University of West Florida*
William Sharbrough, *The Citadel*
Eric Stephan, *Brigham Young University*
Charlotte Sutton, *Auburn University*
Charles N. Toftoy, *The George Washington University*
John Todd, *University of Arkansas*
John P. Wanous, *The Ohio State University*
Susan Washburn, *Stephen F. Austin State University*
Judith Y. Weisinger, *Northeastern University*
Frank Wiebe, *University of Mississippi*
Joseph P. Yaney, *Northern Illinois University*

Thanks are also due to Ken Bettenhausen, University of Colorado at Denver; David Bowen, Arizona State University, West; and Art Brief, Tulane University.

Finally, we are grateful to our children, Nicholas and Julia, for providing us with much fun and joy while we were engaged in the hard work of writing our book, and for continuing to do so as we work together on new projects.

J.M.G. - G.R.J.
College Station, TX

Why is a picture of two space shuttle astronauts on the front cover of a book about organizational behavior? Visit the George and Jones *Understanding and Managing Organizational Behavior* Web site at http://hepg.awl.com (Keyword: georgejones) to find out.

Organizational Behavior and Management

1

OPENING CASE

How George Fisher Manages at Kodak

In 1994, George Fisher, the well-respected former chief executive officer (CEO) of Motorola, took control of the ailing Kodak Company (www.kodak.com). He took the helm of a company whose declining performance had led to billion dollar losses and the layoff of over 100,000

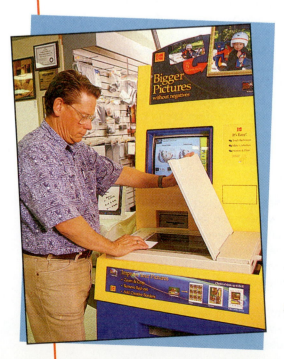

employees, which had resulted in a demoralized and anxious workforce. Kodak's problems had been largely due to its inability to innovate new photographic and imaging products and keep up with the challenge of global competition. The task facing Fisher was to develop a plan of action to apply the new product development skills he had learned while head of Motorola to speed the development of new, high-quality photographic and imaging products at Kodak to give Kodak a competitive advantage.[1]

Many analysts thought that Fisher faced an impossible task, but he took the challenge in his stride. Fisher decided that, if he was to succeed, he had to find a new way to change the behavior and attitudes of Kodak's employees and change it fast. After studying the way his new employees worked, he decided that, to galvanize them into action, he needed to establish specific, challenging goals, often called "stretch goals," for employees to encourage them to come up with new ideas for performing their jobs more effectively. Next, he gave employees more responsibility for meeting those goals and told them not to be afraid to take risks to create new products. He also decided to form Kodak's employees into product teams composed of employees from different functions or departments so that they could combine their skills to speed the development of exciting new imaging products.[2]

To make sure that employees did change their behaviors, Fisher also started a program that was new for the conservative company: linking pay to performance. In the past, Kodak employees had become used to a pay system that paid them a bonus of between 5% and 15% of their base salaries no matter how the company performed. Fisher decided that in the future all bonuses would be linked to employees, groups, and the company achieving their specific improvement goals. Moreover, to make sure that the people most responsible for contributing to meeting these goals received the most rewards, he instituted a 360-degree performance review of Kodak's managers, a review in which a manager's superior, peers, and subordinates have a say in assessing that manager's level of performance.

As you can imagine, Kodak's already nervous employees were surprised and stressed by this new system of managing organizational behavior. However, Fisher is well known for his easygoing and approachable management style and for being highly supportive of his managers. He encourages them to take risks and provides positive feedback and advice even when things are not going well or even when they fail. Moreover, to increase his accessibility to employees, he established an e-mail system by which any employee can e-mail him, and he responds personally to each one. Thus, employees have come to realize that Fisher has their, and the company's, long-term interests at heart, and that they must change their behavior and adjust to the realities of the new competitive global marketplace if Kodak is to survive and they are to keep their jobs.

Overview

At Kodak, George Fisher actively seeks input and advice from employees and goes to great lengths to get to know them and let them know he supports their activities and is listening to their concerns. Fisher strives to understand and appreciate how and why his employees behave as they do, and he uses this knowledge to try to improve their performance and well-being, and thus the performance of Kodak itself. To these ends, Fisher has taken the following steps:

- He works hard to involve employees in the running of the business and encourages them to find new ways to speed product development, raise quality, and increase revenues.

George Fisher, CEO of Kodak.

• He sets specific challenging goals for people and groups to achieve and links superior performance to rewards by paying employees bonuses so that they share in the profits of the business.
• He tries to create a work setting in which employees can work hard to further their organization's goals and interests.

As Fisher's actions suggest, a solid understanding and appreciation of how people behave in organizations, and what causes them to behave the way they do, is the first step in managing organizational behavior effectively.

In this chapter, we define organizational behavior and its relationship to management, and we demonstrate how for managers and employees alike a working knowledge of organizational behavior is essential for helping an organization to meet its goals. We discuss the functions, roles, and skills of management and describe how understanding organizational behavior is necessary for a manager to be effective. We also discuss four contemporary challenges to the management of organizational behavior. By the end of this chapter, you will understand the central role that organizational behavior plays in determining how effectively an organization and its members achieve their goals.

What Is Organizational Behavior?

To begin our study of organizational behavior, we could just say that it is the study of behavior in organizations and the study of the behavior of organizations, but such a definition reveals nothing about what this study involves or examines. To reach a more useful and meaningful definition, let's first look at what an organization is. An **organization** is a collection of people who work together to achieve a wide variety of goals. The goals are what individuals are trying to accomplish by being members of an organization (earning a lot of money, helping promote a worthy cause, achieving certain levels of power and prestige, enjoying a satisfying work experience). The goals are also what the organization as a whole is trying to accomplish (providing innovative goods and services that customers want, getting candidates elected, raising money for medical research, making a profit to reward stockholders, managers, and workers). Police forces, for example, are formed to achieve the goals of providing security for law-abiding citizens and providing police officers with a secure, rewarding career while they perform their valuable service. Paramount Pictures was formed to achieve the goal of providing people with entertainment while making a profit, and in the process, actors, directors, writers, and musicians receive well-paid and interesting work. George Fisher agreed to take control of Kodak not only to provide customers with high-quality imaging products, but also to provide himself with power, wealth, and a satisfying work experience.

Organizations exist to provide goods and services that people want, and the amount and quality of these goods and services are products of the behaviors and performance of an organization's workers—of top managers, of highly skilled workers in sales or research and development, and of the workers who actually produce or provide the goods and services.

Organizational behavior is the study of the many factors that have an impact on how individuals and groups respond to and act in organizations and how organizations manage their environments. Understanding how people behave in an organization is important because most people, at some time in

Organization
A collection of people who work together to achieve individual and organizational goals.

Organizational behavior
The factors that affect how individuals and groups act in organizations and how organizations manage their environments.

their life, work for an organization and are directly affected by their experiences in it. People may be the paid employees of small mom-and-pop operations or large Fortune 500 firms, the unpaid volunteers of a charitable organization, the members of a school board, or entrepreneurs who start new businesses. No matter what the organizational setting, however, people who work in organizations are affected significantly by their experiences at work.

Most of us think we have a basic, intuitive, commonsense understanding of human behavior in organizations because we all are human and have been exposed to different work experiences. Often, however, our intuition and common sense are wrong, and we do not really understand why people act and react the way they do. For example, many people assume that happy workers are productive workers—that is, that high job satisfaction causes high job performance—or that punishing someone who performs consistently at a low level is a good way to increase performance, or that it is best to keep pay levels secret. As we will see in later chapters, all these beliefs are either false or are correct only under a narrow set of circumstances, and applying these principles can have negative consequences for workers, managers, and organizations.

The study of organizational behavior provides guidelines that both managers and workers can use to understand and appreciate the many forces that affect behavior in organizations and to make correct decisions about how to motivate and coordinate people and other resources to achieve organizational goals. Organizational behavior replaces intuition and gut feeling with a well-researched body of theories and systematic guidelines for managing behavior in organizations.

The study of organizational behavior provides a set of tools—concepts and theories—that help people to understand, analyze, and describe what goes on in organizations and why. Organizational behavior helps people understand, for example, why they and others are motivated to join an organization, why they feel good or bad about their jobs or about being part of the organization, why some people do a good job and others don't, why some people stay with the same organization for thirty years and others seem to be constantly dissatisfied and change jobs every two years. In essence, organizational behavior concepts and theories allow people to correctly understand, describe, and analyze how the characteristics of individuals, groups, work situations, and the organization itself affect how members feel about and act within their organization (see Fig. 1.1).

FIGURE 1.1

What Is Organizational Behavior

Organizational behavior
Provides a set of tools that allow:

People to understand, analyze, and describe behavior in organizations

Managers to improve, enhance, or change work behaviors so that individuals, groups, and the whole organization can achieve their goals

The ability to use the tools of organizational behavior to understand behavior in organizations is one reason for studying this topic. A second reason is to learn how to use and apply these concepts, theories, and techniques to improve, enhance, or change behavior so that individuals, groups, and the whole organization can better achieve their goals. For example, a salesperson working in Neiman Marcus in Houston has the individual goal, set by his sales manager, of selling $5,000 worth of men's clothing per week. In addition, he and the other members of the men's clothing department have the group goal of keeping the department looking neat and attractive and of never keeping customers waiting. The store as a whole (along with all the other stores in the nationwide Neiman Marcus chain) has the goals of being profitable by selling customers unique, high-quality clothes and accessories and providing excellent service. As you can see, these goals are interrelated. By being helpful to customers, the salesperson's behavior contributes to attaining (1) his personal sales goal, (2) the department's goal of never keeping customers waiting, and (3) the organization's goals of being profitable and providing excellent service.

Recall from the opening case that Kodak's goal is to attract customers by providing them with innovative, high-quality imaging products. To achieve this goal, George Fisher has had to find ways to speed the development of new products while keeping quality high. Kodak has been improving its ability to achieve these goals because of the way Fisher encourages his employees to work hard and well and because of his concern for their well-being. A key challenge for all managers, and one that we address throughout this book, is how to encourage organizational members to work effectively and happily for their own benefit, the benefit of their work groups, and the benefit of their organization. How does Fisher at Kodak try to meet this challenge? He requires workers to work hard individually and in teams to meet their goals, and he ensures that workers benefit directly from their hard work by giving them bonuses so that they share in Kodak's profits. Now that change is becoming a way of life for many organizations, it is extremely important for managers to be constantly on the alert to find new ways to motivate and coordinate employees to ensure that their goals are aligned with organizational goals.

LEVELS OF ANALYSIS

Our examples of how managers can use organizational behavior tools to understand and alter behavior signal the three levels at which organizational behavior can be examined: the individual, the group, and the organization as a whole. A full understanding of organizational behavior is impossible without a thorough examination of the factors that affect behavior at each level.

Much of the research in organizational behavior has focused on the way in which the characteristics of individuals (such as personality and motivation) affect how well people do their jobs, whether they like what they do, whether they get along with the people they work with, and so on. In Chapters 2 through 9 we examine individual characteristics that are critical for understanding and managing behavior in organizations: personality and ability, attitudes and values, perception and attribution, learning, motivation, and stress and work-life linkages (see Fig. 1.2).

The effects of group characteristics and processes (such as communication and decision making) on organizational behavior also need to be understood. A **group** is two or more people who interact to achieve their goals.

 Group
Two or more people who interact to achieve their goals.

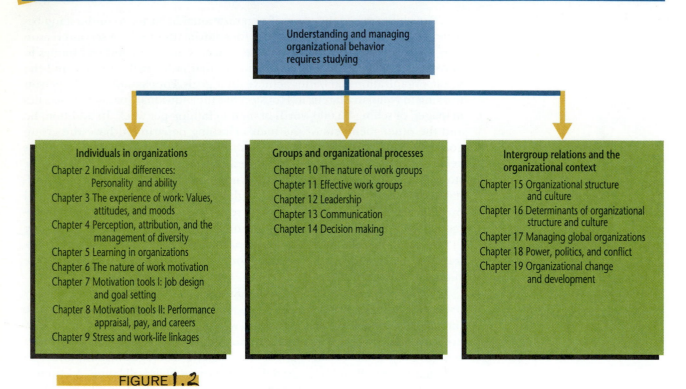

FIGURE **1.2**

Components of Organizational Behavior

Team
A group in which members work together intensively to achieve a common group goal.

A **team** is a group in which members work together intensively to achieve a common group goal. The number of members in a group, the type and diversity of team members, the tasks they perform, and the attractiveness of a group to its members all influence not just the behavior of the group as a whole but also the behaviors of individuals within the group. For example, a team can influence its members' decisions on how diligently they should do their jobs or how often they are absent from work. Chapters 10 through 14 examine the ways in which groups affect their individual members and the processes involved in group interactions such as leadership, communication, and decision making.

Many studies have found that characteristics of the organization as a whole (such as the design of an organization's structure and its culture) have important effects on the behavior of individuals and groups. An organization's structure controls how people and groups cooperate and interact to achieve organizational goals. The principal task of organizational structure is to encourage people to work hard and coordinate their efforts to ensure high levels of organizational performance. An organization's culture controls how the individuals and groups interact with each other and with people (such as customers or suppliers) outside the organization. Organizational culture also shapes and controls the attitudes and behavior of people and groups within an organization and influences their desire to work toward achieving organizational goals. Chapters 15 through 19 examine the way organizational structure and culture affect performance and also examine how factors such as the changing global environment, technology, and ethics impact work attitudes and behavior.

ORGANIZATIONAL BEHAVIOR IN ACTION: AN EXAMPLE

The way in which individual, group, and organizational characteristics work together to affect behavior within an organization is illustrated in the way General Motors (GM) and Toyota cooperated to reopen a car assembly plant in Fremont, California—a plant that GM had previously closed because of its poor performance. (See Insight 1.1.)

Insight 1.1

Organizational Behavior

A New Approach at NUMMI

In 1963, GM opened a car plant in Fremont, California, thirty-five miles east of San Francisco. The plant was a typical assembly-line operation where workers performed simple, repetitive tasks on cars that moved steadily past them on conveyer belts. From the beginning, the plant experienced many problems that reduced its performance. Worker productivity was low, and the quality of the assembled cars was poor. Worker morale was also low, drug and alcohol abuse were widespread, and absenteeism was so high that hundreds of extra workers had to be employed just to make sure that enough workers were on hand to operate the plant. To try to improve the plant's performance, GM managers tried many things, such as changing the workers' jobs, increasing the speed of the production line, and instituting penalties for absenteeism. None of these actions seemed to work, and, seeing no chance of improving performance, GM closed the plant in 1981.

In 1983, GM and Toyota announced that they would cooperate to reopen the Fremont plant. GM wanted to learn how Toyota operated its efficient production system, and Toyota wanted to know whether it could achieve a high level of productivity by using Japanese management techniques on U.S. workers. In 1984 the new organization, New United Motors Manufacturing Inc. (NUMMI), reopened in Fremont under the control of Japanese management. By 1986 productivity at NUMMI (www.toyota.ca) was higher than productivity at any other GM factory, and the plant was operating at twice the level it had operated at under GM management. Alcohol and drug abuse had virtually disappeared, and absenteeism had dropped to near zero. A new approach to managing organizational behavior had brought about this miracle—which has continued to this day.

At the NUMMI factory, Toyota divided the workforce into 350 self-managed teams consisting of from five to seven people, plus a team leader, and made the group rather than the individual workers responsible for the performance of the team's assigned task. Each worker was trained to do the jobs of the other team members, and workers regularly rotated jobs, so their work experiences were less repetitive and boring. In addition, each worker was taught procedures for analyzing the jobs within the team and was encouraged to find ways to improve the way tasks were done. Team members timed each other using stopwatches and continually attempted to find better ways to perform their jobs. In the old plant, GM had employed eighty managers to perform this analysis. Now, in the new plant, self-managed work teams not only perform job analysis but also take responsibility for monitoring product quality.

With all workers divided into self-managed teams, what role do managers play in the new factory? At NUMMI a manager's job is defined explicitly in terms of providing workers with support. In the new work system, the manager's role is not to directly monitor or supervise team activities but to find new ways to facilitate team activities and give a team advice on how to improve work procedures. In setting up NUMMI's organization, the plant's upper management gave each team the authority to make its own decisions; however, team members and management are jointly responsible for coordinating and controlling work activities to maintain and improve organizational performance.

Why did employees buy into this new work system? A number of factors came into play, all of which increased worker well-being: NUMMI's no layoff policy, extensive worker training, and the use of flexible work groups, which give workers, not managers, control over how things are done on the production line. Apparently, most NUMMI workers still consider assembly-line work a "lousy job" but feel it's the best job they can expect to get, and in the new work system they at least have some control over what they do.[3] At NUMMI the new approach to managing behavior has increased performance and well-being for workers and the organization, an increase that continues to this day.

At the reopened Fremont plant, action to improve performance was possible only when managers realized the need to rethink the way they managed organizational behavior at all three levels of analysis. First, upper management changed organizational-level characteristics by moving from a system in which managers analyzed and controlled jobs and work processes to one in which self-managed teams controlled all aspects of a given task. At the group level, each team was given the authority and responsibility for designing group members' tasks and for monitoring and controlling members' behavior. At the individual level, work-group members became responsible for learning a wider range of tasks and for monitoring their own performance level so that performance could be increased at all levels in the plant. As the NUMMI story shows, the effective management of organizational behavior requires managers and workers alike to consider the impacts and effects of individual, group, and whole-organization characteristics as they try to achieve organizational goals.

DISCIPLINES THAT SHED LIGHT ON ORGANIZATIONAL BEHAVIOR

The realization that characteristics of individuals, groups, and the whole organization all affect behavior in organizations emerged from a series of research studies in many different academic disciplines. Here we examine the various disciplines that have enriched our knowledge of organizational behavior and have made it such a critical area of study in business and management.

Psychology. Many of the most important contributions to organizational behavior have come from psychology, the study of the feelings, thoughts, and behaviors of individuals and groups. Psychologists have created many theories to improve the ability to explain and predict individual behavior. Psychology's findings on personality, attitudes, learning, motivation, and stress have been applied in organizational behavior to understand work-related phenomena such as performance, job satisfaction, commitment, absenteeism, turnover, and worker well-being and to improve organizationally important processes such as performance appraisal, goal setting, and the design of jobs and reward systems.

Sociology. Sociology studies the structure and function of the social foundations of a society—its political, economic, educational, and religious bases. Sociologists who have studied the structure and function of work organizations and their effect on individual and group behaviors have been very influential in the study of organizational behavior. Especially important are studies that have investigated the relationship between organizational characteristics and performance.

Social Psychology. Social psychology, a subfield of psychology and sociology, focuses on understanding the behavior of individuals in social groups and settings such as families, work groups, and organizations. Many of organizational behavior's concepts and theories about groups and the processes of communication, decision making, conflict, and politics are rooted in theories originally developed by social psychologists. Organizational behavior researchers who were principally interested in social behavior in work settings refined, modified, and expanded on these concepts and theories. These organizational behavior theories have given rise to many techniques for improving group performance, improving the decision-making process, and managing conflict and politics in organizational settings, to name just a few.

Other Disciplines. Several other disciplines have contributed to our understanding of the different aspects of behavior in organizations. Political science has helped us to understand how differences in preferences and interests lead to conflict and power struggles between groups within organizations. Economics has helped organizational behavior researchers to appreciate how competition for scarce resources both within and between organizations leads organizations to try to increase their efficiency and productivity. Anthropology has shed light on the way organizations develop different cultures and systems of beliefs and values. All these disciplines help us to understand the many dimensions of organizational behavior.

Organizational Behavior and Management

A working knowledge of organizational behavior is important to individuals at all levels in the organization because it helps them to appreciate the work situation and how they should behave to achieve their own goals (such as promotion or higher income). But knowledge of organizational behavior is particularly important to managers. A significant part of a manager's job is to use the findings of organizational behavior researchers, and the tools and techniques they have developed, to increase **organizational effectiveness,** the ability of an organization to achieve its goals. A **goal** is a desired future outcome that an organization seeks to achieve.

Organizational effectiveness
The ability of an organization to achieve its goals.

Goal
A desired future outcome that an organization seeks to achieve.

Management
The process of planning, organizing, leading, and controlling an organization's human, financial, material, and other resources to increase its effectiveness.

Manager
A person who is responsible for supervising the use of an organization's resources to achieve its goals.

Top-management team
High-ranking executives who plan a company's strategy so that the company can achieve its goals.

Management is the process of planning, organizing, leading, and controlling an organization's human, financial, material, and other resources to increase its effectiveness. A **manager** is a person who is responsible for supervising the use of an organization's resources to achieve its goals. Lou Gerstner, chief executive officer of International Business Machines Corp. (www.ibm .com), for example, is IBM's top manager and ultimately responsible for how effectively all 150,000 of IBM's employees and other resources are utilized. The sales manager of IBM's southern region, who controls 300 salespeople, is also a manager, as is the manager (or supervisor) in charge of an IBM computer service center who supervises 5 service technicians.

Managers at all levels confront the problem of understanding and managing the behavior of their subordinates. Gerstner has to manage IBM's **top-management team,** high-ranking executives who plan the company's strategy so that it can achieve its goals. The sales manager has to manage the sales force so that it sells the mix of mainframe, mini, and personal computers that best meet customers' information-processing needs. The service manager has to manage technicians so that they respond promptly and courteously to customers' appeals for help and quickly solve their problems. (Traditionally, IBM has been well known for its high-quality customer service and responsiveness.)

Each of these managers faces the common challenge of finding ways to help the organization achieve its goals. A manager who understands how individual, group, and organizational characteristics affect work attitudes and behavior can begin to experiment to see whether changing one or more of these characteristics might increase the effectiveness of the organization and the individuals and groups it consists of. The study of organizational behavior helps managers meet the challenge of improving organizational effectiveness by providing them with a set of tools:

- A manager can work to raise a person's self-esteem or beliefs about his or her ability to accomplish a certain task in order to increase the worker's productivity or job satisfaction.
- A manager can change the reward system to change workers' beliefs about the extent to which their rewards depend on their performance.
- A manager can change the design of a person's job or the rules and procedures for doing the job to reduce costs, make the task more enjoyable, or make the task easier to perform.

MANAGERIAL FUNCTIONS AND ROLES

As we mentioned above, the four principal functions or duties of management are planning, organizing, leading, and controlling human, financial, material, and other resources to allow an organization to achieve its goals.[4] As our examples showed, managers knowledgeable about organizational behavior are in a good position to improve their ability to perform these functions (see Fig. 1.3).

Planning. In **planning,** managers establish their organization's strategy— that is, they decide what organizational goals to pursue and how best to allocate and use resources to achieve them. Planning is a complex and difficult task because a lot of uncertainty normally surrounds the decisions managers need to make. Because of this uncertainty, managers face risks when deciding what actions to take. A knowledge of organizational behavior can help improve the quality of decision making, increase the chances of

Planning
Deciding what organizational goals to pursue and how best to allocate and use resources to achieve them.

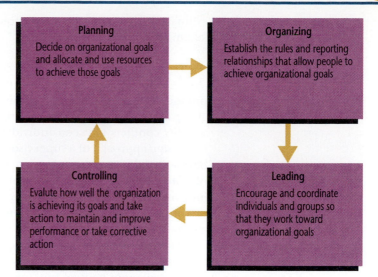

FIGURE 1.3

Four Functions of Management

success, and lessen the risks inherent in planning and decision making. First, the study of organizational behavior reveals how decisions get made in organizations and how politics and conflict affect the planning process. Second, the way in which group decision making affects planning, and the biases that can influence decisions, are revealed. Third, the theories and concepts of organizational behavior show how the composition of an organization's top-management team can affect the planning process. The study of organizational behavior, then, can improve a manager's planning abilities and increase organizational performance.

Organizing.   In **organizing,** managers establish a structure of work relationships that dictate how organizational members are to cooperate to achieve organizational goals. Organizing involves grouping workers into groups, teams, or departments according to the kinds of tasks they perform. At IBM, for example, service technicians are grouped into a service operation department, and salespeople are grouped into the sales department. In the NUMMI example, we saw how workers were grouped into self-managed work teams. Organizational behavior offers many guidelines on how to organize employees (the organization's human resources) to make the best use of their skills and capabilities. In later chapters we discuss various methods of grouping workers to enhance communication and coordination while avoiding conflict or politics.

Leading.   In **leading,** managers encourage workers to do a good job (work hard, produce high-quality products) and coordinate individuals and groups so that all organizational members are working to achieve organizational goals. The study of different leadership methods and of how to match leadership styles to the characteristics of the organization and all its components is a major concern of organizational behavior.

Controlling.   In **controlling,** managers monitor and evaluate individual, group, and organizational performance to see whether organizational goals are being achieved. If goals are being met, managers can take action to maintain and improve performance; if goals are not being met, managers must take corrective action. The controlling function also allows managers to

 Organizing
Establishing a structure of work relationships that dictate how members of an organization are to cooperate to achieve organizational goals.

 Leading
Encouraging and coordinating individuals and groups so that all organizational members are working to achieve organizational goals.

Controlling
Monitoring and evaluating individual, group, and organizational performance to see whether organizational goals are being achieved.

evaluate how well they are performing their planning, organizing, and leading functions.

Once again, the theories and concepts of organizational behavior allow managers to understand and accurately diagnose work situations in order to pinpoint where corrective action may be needed. Suppose the members of a group are not working effectively together. The problem might be due to personality conflicts between individual members of the group, to the faulty leadership approach of a supervisor, or to poor job design. Organizational behavior provides tools managers can use to diagnose which of these possible explanations is the source of the problem, and it enables managers to make an informed decision about how to correct the problem. Control at all levels of the organization is impossible if managers do not possess the necessary organizational behavior tools.

The way in which Betty Wagner transformed her company after the loss of its major customer, IBM, vividly demonstrates not only the importance of the management control function but also the way successful planning, organizing, and leading depend on a manager's ability to take quick corrective action. (See Insight 1.2.)

Insight 1.2

Management

All Change at Cavalier

In 1978, Betty Wagner, a community college graduate, joined Cavalier Gage & Electronic, based in Poughkeepsie, New York, as a secretary. The company is a fabricator of small metal parts and a manufacturer of printed circuit boards. Wagner's energy and enthusiasm caught the attention of Cavalier's founder, Dominic Cavalieri, who rapidly promoted her up the ranks of the company. In 1988, Cavalieri decided that he wanted to pursue other ventures and sold his business to Wagner, who became its president.

Cavalier's major customer was IBM, and the company had enjoyed good, steady profits from dealing with IBM over the years. In the early 1990s, however, IBM dropped a bombshell for Cavalier when it announced that it would no longer buy Cavalier products because of a recession in the mainframe computer market. In one year Cavalier's sales plummeted from over $5 million to $2 million and the company faced a crisis—just as Wagner was due to have a baby. Only two days after giving birth to her daughter, Betty Wagner was back at her desk trying to find a new way to manage her company that would allow it to survive.[5] She was forced to immediately lay off 25 percent of her employees to cut payroll costs. It was obvious to Wagner, however, that she needed to completely reevaluate the way her company was managed in order to decide what corrective action should be taken.

The magnitude of the problems led her to realize that just trying to control the situation was not enough. She needed a new approach to

Betty Wagner, CEO of Cavalier Gage & Electronic profiled in Insight 1.2, is pictured here back at her desk two days after the birth of her daughter. Using Cavalier's popular new participative team approach to management, Wagner is working to increase her company's prosperity.

planning, organizing, and leading, and she needed it quickly. The first thing she did was to change her leadership approach from one where she called the shots to one where she sought the involvement of lower-level managers. She sat down with her managers, opened the company's books, and showed them how fragile the company's situation was; and together they worked out a new approach to planning and organizing the company's resources.

The management team decided to devise a strategy to use and improve the company's skills in manufacturing so that Cavalier could create new products for new customers. To speed the product development process, the management team adopted a new approach to organizing. Managers began to work as a group to coordinate their activities, and they discovered that by sharing information and knowledge they could eliminate many unnecessary tasks and substantially reduce the time and cost of developing new products. As a result of the new team approach, for example, Cavalier was able to reduce the bidding time on new contracts from two days to less than an hour—a time savings that allowed managers to pursue another part of their strategy: finding new customers.

This new management approach has been continually refined by Cavalier's managers, who are always on the lookout for new ways to improve their control over the company's activities so that quality increases and costs fall. Since the crisis, Cavalier has won over twenty-five new contracts, which have gone a long way to make up for the loss of IBM's business. Wagner has been able to rehire many of the workers she was forced to lay off, and she hopes to continue to do so as Cavalier's performance continues to increase.

Role
A set of behaviors or tasks a person is expected to perform because of the position he or she holds in a group or organization.

Skill
An ability to act in a way that allows a person to perform well in his or her role.

MANAGERIAL ROLES

Managers perform their four functions by assuming specific roles in organizations. A **role** is a set of behaviors or tasks a person is expected to perform because of the position he or she holds in a group or organization. One researcher, Henry Mintzberg, has identified ten roles that managers play as they manage the behavior of people inside and outside the organization (such as customers or suppliers).[6] (See Table 1.1.)

MANAGERIAL SKILLS

Just as the study of organizational behavior provides tools that managers can use to increase their ability to perform their functions and roles, it can also help managers improve their skills in managing organizational behavior. A **skill** is an ability to act in a way that allows a person to perform well in his or her role. Managers need three principal kinds of skill in order to perform their organizational functions and roles effectively: conceptual, human, and technical skills.[7]

TABLE **1.1**

Managerial Roles Identified by Mintzberg

Type of Role	Examples of Role Activities
Figurehead	Give speech to workforce about future organizational goals and objectives; open a new corporate headquarters building; state the organization's ethical guidelines and principles of behavior that employees are to follow in their dealings with customers and suppliers.
Leader	Give direct commands and orders to subordinates; make decisions concerning the use of human and financial organizational resources; mobilize employee commitment to organizational goals.
Liaison	Coordinate the work of managers in different departments or even in different parts of the world; establish alliances between different organizations to share resources to produce new products.
Monitor	Evaluate the performance of different managers and departments and take corrective action to improve their performance; watch for changes occurring in the industry or in society that may affect the organization.
Disseminator	Inform organizational members about changes taking place both inside and outside the organization that will affect them and the organization; communicate to employees the organization's cultural and ethical values.
Spokesperson	Launch a new organizational advertising campaign to promote a new product; give a speech to inform the general public about the organization's future goals.
Entrepreneur	Commit organizational resources to a new project to develop new products; decide to expand the organization globally in order to obtain new customers.
Disturbance handler	Move quickly to mobilize organizational resources to deal with external problems facing the organization, such as environmental crisis, or internal problems facing the organization, such as strikes.
Resource allocator	Allocate organizational resources between different departments and divisions of the organization; set budgets and salaries of managers and employees.
Negotiator	Work with suppliers, distributors, labor unions, or employees in conflict to solve disputes or to reach a long-term contract or agreement; work with other organizations to establish an agreement to share resources.

Conceptual skills
The ability to analyze and diagnose a situation and to distinguish between cause and effect.

Human skills
The ability to understand, work with, lead, and control the behavior of other people and groups.

Technical skills
Job-specific knowledge and techniques.

Conceptual skills allow a manager to analyze and diagnose a situation and to distinguish between cause and effect. Planning and organizing require a high level of conceptual skill, as do the decisional roles discussed above. The study of organizational behavior provides managers with many of the conceptual tools they need to analyze organizational settings and to identify and diagnose the dynamics of individual and group behavior in these settings.

Human skills enable a manager to understand, work with, lead, and control the behavior of other people and groups. How managers can influence behavior is a principal focus of organizational behavior research, and the ability to learn and acquire the skills that are needed to coordinate and motivate people is a principal difference between effective and ineffective managers.

Technical skills are the job-specific knowledge and techniques that a manager requires to perform an organizational role—for example, in manufacturing, accounting, or marketing. The specific technical skills a manager needs depend on the organization the manager is in and on his or her position in the organization. The manager of a restaurant, for example, needs cooking skills to fill in for an absent cook, accounting and bookkeeping skills to keep track of receipts and costs and to administer the payroll, and artistic skills to keep the restaurant looking attractive for customers.

Effective managers need all three kinds of skills—conceptual, human, and technical. The lack of one or more of these skills can lead to a manager's downfall. One of the biggest problems that entrepreneurs who found their own businesses confront—a problem that is often responsible for their failure—is lack of appropriate conceptual and human skills. Similarly, one of the biggest problems that scientists, engineers, and others who switch careers and go from research into management confront is their lack of effective human skills. Management functions, roles, and skills are intimately related, and in the long run the ability to understand and manage behavior in organizations is indispensable to any actual or prospective manager.

Challenges for Organizational Behavior and Management

In the last ten years, the number of women and minorities assuming managerial positions in the workforce has increased by over 25 percent. Similarly, in the last decade, companies have come under increasing scrutiny because of ethical concerns about the safety of the products they produce and their employment policies toward the people who make those products, both in the United States and abroad. Organizations have also been facing increased global competition from low-cost countries like Malaysia and China, and technological change has significantly reduced the employment opportunities for U.S. manufacturing workers. Xerox, IBM, GM, and most other Fortune 500 companies have downsized their workforces, employing over 10 percent fewer workers in 1995 than they did in 1985. During the same period, the movement to a service economy has opened new opportunities for people in service jobs, but those jobs are relatively low paid compared to skilled manufacturing jobs. The social, cultural, and technological changes taking place in the world today pose many challenges for the men and women whose jobs require them to manage organizational behavior:

- How to manage human resources to give an organization a competitive advantage.

- How to develop an ethical organizational culture.
- How to manage work-force diversity.
- How to manage organizational behavior when an organization expands internationally and operates at a global level.
- How to manage advanced information technologies that affect the tasks and jobs of all employees—both managers and workers.

We introduce these four challenges here in Chapter 1 and examine them throughout the rest of the book.

Challenge 1: Managing Human Resources to Gain a Competitive Advantage

The ability of an organization to produce goods and services that its customers want is a product of the behaviors of all its members—the behaviors of its top-management team, which plans the organization's strategy; the behaviors that middle managers use to manage and coordinate human and other resources; and the behaviors of first-line managers or supervisors and production workers. An organization seeking to obtain a **competitive advantage**—that is, the ability to outperform competitors or other organizations that provide similar goods and services—can do so by pursuing any or all of the following goals: (1) increasing efficiency, (2) increasing quality, (3) increasing innovation and creativity, (4) increasing responsiveness to customers.[8] The study of organizational behavior can help managers achieve these goals, each of which is a part of managing human resources to gain a competitive advantage (see Fig. 1.4).

Competitive advantage
The ability to outperform competitors or other organizations that provide similar goods and services.

INCREASING EFFICIENCY
Organizations increase their efficiency when they reduce the amount of resources such as people and raw materials or the amount of time they need to produce a quantity of goods or services. For example, McDonald's Corporation recently developed a fat frier that not only reduces (by 30 percent) the amount of oil used in the cooking process but also speeds up the cooking of

FIGURE **1.4**

How to Manage Human
Resources to Gain a
Competitive Advantage

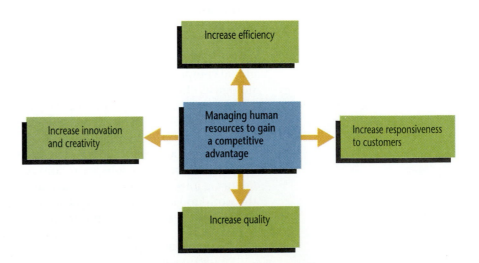

french fries. In today's increasingly competitive environment, organizations are trying to increase efficiency by finding ways to better utilize and increase the skills and abilities of their workforce. Many organizations train their workforce in new skills and techniques, such as those needed to operate increasingly computerized assembly plants. Similarly, cross-training workers so that they learn the skills necessary to perform many different tasks and finding new ways of organizing workers so that they can use their skills more efficiently are major parts of the effort to improve efficiency. Many organizations, like NUMMI, are creating self-managed work groups that are collectively responsible for finding cost-reducing ways to perform their jobs.

INCREASING QUALITY

The challenge from global organizations such as Japanese car manufacturers, German engineering companies, and Italian design studios has also increased pressure on U.S. companies to improve the skills of their workforces so that they can increase the quality of the goods and services they provide. One major trend in the attempt to increase quality has been the introduction and expansion in the United States of the total quality management (TQM) techniques developed in Japan. In an organization dedicated to TQM, for example, workers are often organized into teams or quality control circles that are given the responsibility to continually find new and better ways to perform their jobs and to monitor and evaluate the quality of the goods they produce (just as in the NUMMI plant). Many organizations pursuing TQM have also sought to improve product quality by forming **cross-functional teams** in which workers from different functions such as manufacturing, sales, and purchasing pool their skills and knowledge to find better ways to produce high-quality goods and services. TQM involves a whole new philosophy of managing behavior in organizations, and we discuss this approach in detail in Chapter 19 when we discuss organizational change and development.

Cross-functional teams
Teams consisting of workers from different functions who pool their skills and knowledge to produce high-quality goods and services.

INCREASING INNOVATION AND CREATIVITY

U.S. companies are among the most innovative companies in the world, and encouraging innovative and creative behavior in organizations is a special management challenge. Typically innovation takes place in small groups or teams, and to encourage it, an organization and its managers give control over work activities to team members and create an organizational setting and culture that reward risk taking. Understanding how to manage innovation and creativity is one of the most difficult challenges that managers face. It especially taxes managers' human skills, because creative people tend to be among the most difficult to manage. George Fisher was actively sought out to take control of Kodak because he possesses skills that can improve an organization's ability to be innovative and creative.

INCREASING RESPONSIVENESS TO CUSTOMERS

Because organizations compete for customers, training workers to be responsive to customer needs is important for all organizations but particularly for service organizations. Organizations like retail stores, banks, and hospitals depend entirely on their employees performing behaviors that result in high-quality service at reasonable cost. As the United States has moved to a service-based economy (in part because of the loss of manufacturing jobs), managing behavior in service organizations has become an increasingly important area of study.

NEW WAYS TO INCREASE PERFORMANCE

Investing in employee skills and abilities to increase organizational performance is not the only way U.S. corporations have responded to an increasingly competitive global environment. To reduce costs and increase efficiency, some companies have responded by reengineering and restructuring their organizations. **Reengineering** involves a complete rethinking and redesign of business processes to increase efficiency, quality, innovation, or responsiveness to customers. A company that engages in reengineering examines the business processes it uses to produce goods and services (such as the way it organizes its manufacturing, sales, or inventory), and the way its business processes interact and overlap, to see whether a better way of performing a task can be found.[9]

A company that engages in **restructuring** makes a major change in an organization's structure, such as eliminating a department or reducing the number of layers of management, to streamline the organization's operations and reduce costs. Restructuring and reengineering often result in many workers being laid off. The smaller workforces that remain are retrained to increase efficiency; they learn how to perform at a higher level, and they learn new skills. Organizational behavior researchers have been interested in the effects of layoffs not only on workers who lose their jobs but also on employees who remain in the organization. GM and IBM are among the organizations that have laid off hundreds of thousands of employees in the last ten years in their efforts to increase organizational performance.

To reduce costs, many organizations do not rehire laid-off workers as full-time employees even when demand for their products picks up; instead, they employ part-time workers who can be given lower wages and fewer benefits. It has been estimated that 20 percent of the U.S. workforce today consists of part-time employees who work by the day, week, month, or even year for their former employers. Part-time workers pose a new challenge for managers' human skills because part-time workers cannot be motivated by the prospect of rewards such as job security, promotion, or a career within an organization.

Organizations are also engaging in an increasing amount of **outsourcing.** Many organizational tasks are performed not within the organization but on the outside, by freelancers. A **freelancer** is an independent individual who contracts with an organization to perform specific services. Freelancers often work from their homes and are connected to an organization by computer, phone, fax, and express package delivery. Because freelancing is expected to increase as organizations outsource more and more of their tasks to reduce costs, managers will face new kinds of problems in their efforts to manage organizational behavior.

Reengineering, restructuring, downsizing, hiring part-time workers, and outsourcing are just a few of the many new ways in which organizations are utilizing human resources to reduce costs and compete effectively against domestic and global competitors. Several organizational behavior researchers believe that organizations in the future will increasingly become composed of a "core" of organizational workers who are highly trained and rewarded by an organization and a "periphery" of part-time or freelance workers who are employed when needed but will never become true "organizational employees." In the years ahead, managing an organization's human resources to increase performance wili be a continuing challenge.

Reengineering
A complete rethinking and redesign of business processes to increase efficiency, quality, innovation, or responsiveness to customers.

Restructuring
Altering an organization's structure by such actions as eliminating a department.

Outsourcing
Acquiring goods or services from sources outside the organization.

Freelancer
A person who contracts with an organization to perform specific services.

Teamwork led to innovation at Davidson Interiors, a division of Textron. One team innovated a new product called Flexible Bright, a coating that makes plastic look exactly like chrome but, unlike chrome, does not rust or scratch. Here, members of the team are shown holding grilles coated with the new product, which Ford is using in its new Lincoln models and will eventually use in other car models too.

The way in which Black & Decker responded to the need to increase performance to regain its competitive advantage illustrates many of these issues. The Competitive Advantage Insights in this and other chapters show how managers use the tools of organizational behavior to increase efficiency, quality, customer responsiveness, and innovation. (See Insight 1.3.)

Insight 1.3 **Competitive Advantage**

Black & Decker's Turnaround

Black & Decker (www.blackanddecker.com), a well-known maker of tools and small appliances, experienced a crisis in the 1980s. The company, which is based in Towson, Maryland, had become so preoccupied with marketing and financial issues that its management had lost sight of the need to develop its traditional strengths in manufacturing. As a result, the company started to lose its competitive advantage. Costs were high because the company was using an inefficient technology and carrying a huge inventory of component parts. Quality was falling because the company was using outdated machinery and equipment to manufacture its products. Customer responsiveness was low because the company took from eight to ten weeks to fill customer orders. Innovation was low because the company failed to incorporate recent technological developments such as microprocessors into its products.

In 1984 a new CEO, Nolan Archibald, took control of Black & Decker and immediately began a reengineering program to turn the company around and restore its competitive advantage. He changed the work processes used to develop and manufacture products. He grouped managers and workers together into small teams to find and implement new, efficient ways of manufacturing products. Each team had five or six members, including a supervisor and a manufacturing engineer. The teams recommended that Black & Decker switch to a new, computer-controlled, flexible manufacturing technology, which would allow workers to rapidly produce different kinds of product as and when customers ordered them. In addition, the new technology would allow workers to closely monitor and control product quality and increase efficiency.

The new manufacturing process has saved over $200 million a year, and greater control over the work system has allowed workers to increase product quality and respond to customer demands in just one week. Innovation has quickened at Black & Decker in the 1990s, and the rate of successful new product development has increased as the company works closely with its customers to try to meet their needs.

Challenge 2: Developing Organizational Ethics and Well-Being

 Ethics

Rules, beliefs, and values that specify what is right or wrong behavior and the ways in which managers and workers should behave.

Well-being

The condition of being happy, healthy, and prosperous.

An organization's **ethics** are rules, beliefs, and values that specify what is right or wrong behavior and the ways managers and workers should behave when confronted with a situation in which their actions may help or harm other people inside or outside an organization.[10] Ethical behavior enhances the **well-being** (the happiness, health, and prosperity) of individuals, groups, and the organization, and sometimes the environment in which they operate.[11] Ethical behavior can enhance well-being in several ways.

Ethics establish the goals that organizations should pursue and the way in which people inside organizations should behave to achieve them.[12] For example, one goal of an organization is to make a profit so that it can pay the managers, workers, suppliers, shareholders, and others who have contributed their skills and resources to the company. Ethics specify what actions an organization should engage in to make a profit. Should an organization be allowed to harm its competitors by stealing away their skilled employees or by preventing them from obtaining access to vital inputs? Should an organization be allowed to produce inferior goods that may endanger the safety of customers? Should an organization be allowed to take away the jobs of U.S. workers and transfer them overseas to workers in countries where wages are $5 per day? What limits should be put on organizations' and their managers' attempt to make a profit? Who should determine those limits?

The devastating effects of a lack of ethics is illustrated by what happened in a factory in North Carolina when management acted unethically and put profit before employee well-being. The Ethics Insights in this and other chapters show how managers respond to the ethical challenge. (See Insight 1.4.)

Insight 1.4

Ethics

Tragedy in North Carolina

In 1991 a huge fire at a North Carolina chicken-processing plant resulted in the death of twenty-five employees. Employees could not escape the blaze because management had illegally locked all the exits to prevent employee theft, which had been reducing the plant's profits. Although stealing chickens was not ethical behavior, there were other ways to prevent it, such as by putting alarms on doors or by stationing guards at the exits.

In 1992, the plant's owner, Andrew Cox, entered a plea bargain with the state of North Carolina and was sentenced to fifteen years in prison. The company also faces over $1 million in fines, its plants in North Carolina and Georgia have been shut down, and the company is bankrupt as a result of the tragedy. Survivors of the blaze lobbied for the federal government and state of North Carolina to hire more inspectors to enforce laws that govern safe work practices so that such a tragedy will never happen again.

Social responsibility
An organization's duty or obligation toward individuals or groups outside the organization that are affected by its actions.

In addition to defining right and wrong behavior for employees, ethics also define an organization's **social responsibility,** its duty or obligation toward individuals or groups outside the organization that are directly affected by its actions.[13] Organizations and their managers must establish an ethical code that describes acceptable behaviors and must create a system of rewards and punishments to enforce ethical codes.

Different organizations have different views about social responsibility. To some organizations, being socially responsible means performing any action as long as it is legal. Other organizations do more than the law requires and work to advance the well-being of their employees, customers, and society in general.[14] Ben & Jerry's Homemade, Inc., for example, contributes a significant percentage of its profits to support charities and community needs and expects its employees to be socially active and responsible. Green Mountain Coffee Roasters seeks out coffee-growing farmers and cooperatives that do not use herbicides and pesticides on their crops, that control soil erosion, and that treat their workers fairly and with respect in terms of safety and benefits. Green Mountain also contributes a share of its profits for health and education in Costa Rica and other countries from which it buys coffee beans.

Not all organizations are willing or able to undertake such programs, but all organizations need codes of conduct that spell out fair and equitable behavior if they want to avoid doing harm to people and other organizations. Developing a code of ethics helps organizations protect their reputation and maintain the goodwill of their customers and employees.

In November 1992 the NBC program Dateline broadcast a story about GM pickup trucks with "sidesaddle" fuel tanks that, reporters claimed, made the trucks vulnerable to catching fire during side-impact accidents. Unknown to viewers, NBC rigged the truck fire after side-impact crashes failed to produce a fire. Small rockets attached to the truck ignited the fire shown here, which was far less severe than it appeared to be. As a result of this unethical reporting, several people associated with the program lost their jobs.

The challenge confronting managers is to create an organization in which members resist the temptation to engage in illegal or unethical acts that promote their own interests at the expense of the organization or promote the organization's interests at the expense of people and groups outside the organization. Workers and managers have to recognize that their behavior has important effects not only on other people and groups inside and outside the organization but also on the organization itself. The well-being of organizations and the well-being of the society of which they are a part are closely linked and are the responsibility of everyone.[15] (How to create an ethical organization is an issue that we discuss in detail in Chapter 3 but also throughout the text.)

Challenge 3: Managing a Diverse Workforce

Diversity
Differences among people resulting from age, gender, race, ethnicity, religion, sexual orientation, socioeconomic background, and capabilities or disabilities.

The third principal challenge is to understand how the diversity of a workforce affects behavior, performance, and well-being. **Diversity** is differences among people resulting from age, gender, race, ethnicity, religion, sexual orientation, socioeconomic background, and capabilities or disabilities. If an organization or group is composed of people who are all of the same gender, ethnicity, age, religion, and so on, the attitudes and behavior of its members are likely to be very similar. Members are likely to share the same sets of assumptions or values and will tend to respond to work situations (projects, conflicts, new tasks) in similar ways. By contrast, if the members of a group differ in age, ethnicity, and other characteristics, their attitudes, behavior, and responses are likely to differ.

In the last twenty years, the demographic makeup of employees entering the workforce and advancing to higher-level positions in organizations has been changing. Partly as a result of affirmative action and equal employment opportunity legislation, the number of minority employees entering and being promoted to higher-level positions has increased.[16] By the year 2005, African American and Hispanic employees are expected to make up over 25 percent of the workforce, and the percentage of white male employees is expected to decrease from 51 percent to 44 percent.[17] At the same time, the number of women entering the workforce has also been increasing, and by the year 2000 women are expected to make up 40 percent of the U.S. workforce.[18] Finally, because of increased internationalization, diversity is evident not just among Americans but also among people born in other nations who come to the United States to live and work. They are expected to contribute significantly to these totals by 2005.[19]

The increasing diversity of the workforce presents three challenges for organizations and their managers: a fairness and justice challenge, a decision-making and performance challenge, and a flexibility challenge (see Fig. 1.5).

FAIRNESS AND JUSTICE CHALLENGE

Jobs in organizations are a scarce resource, and obtaining jobs and being promoted to a higher-level job is a competitive process. Managers are challenged to allocate jobs, promotions, and rewards in a fair and equitable manner. As diversity increases, achieving fairness can be difficult, at least in the short run, because many organizations have traditionally appointed white male employees to higher organizational positions. Also, seniority plays a role and many minorities are recent hires.[20] Rectifying this imbalance by actively recruiting and promoting increasing numbers of women and minorities can lead to difficult equity issues because this attempt to fix the traditional imbalance reduces the prospects for white male employees. An increase in diversity can thus strain an organization's ability to satisfy the aspirations of its workforce, creating a problem that, in turn, directly affects the workforce's well-being and performance. Organizations must learn to manage diversity in a way that increases the well-being of all employees, but deciding how to achieve this goal can pose difficult ethical problems for managers.[21]

FIGURE 1.5

The Challenge Posed by a
Diverse Workplace

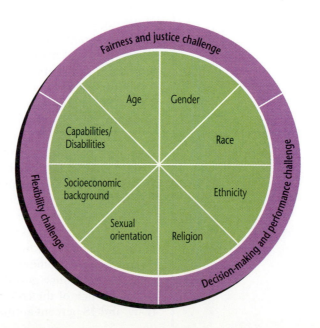

DECISION-MAKING AND PERFORMANCE CHALLENGE

Another important challenge posed by a diverse workforce is how to take advantage of differences in the attitudes and perspectives of people of different ages, genders, or races in order to improve decision making and organizational performance.[22] Many organizations have found that tapping into diversity reveals new ways of viewing traditional problems and provides a means for an organization to assess its goals and ways of doing business. Coca-Cola, for example, in an attempt to increase its top managers' abilities to manage a global environment, has deliberately sought to recruit top managers of different ethnic backgrounds. Its CEO came from Cuba originally, and other top managers are from Brazil, France, and Mexico. To increase performance, organizations have to unleash and take advantage of the potential of diverse employees. Hoechst Celanese has been a leader in exploiting the advantages of a diverse workforce. The Diversity Insights in this and other chapters, particularly in Chapter 4, describe the management of diversity in organizations. (See Insight 1.5.)

Insight 1.5  **Diversity**

Hoechst Celanese's Approach to Diversity

Hoechst Celanese Corp. of New Jersey (www.celanese.com) makes chemicals, fibers, and film and is the seventy-fifth largest industrial company in the United States, having over $7 billion in sales and 32,000 employees. Under chief executive officer Ernest H. Drew, Hoechst has embarked on a major program to increase the diversity of its employees. Drew wants half of Hoechst's top twenty-seven executives to be drawn from minorities and women by the year 2000. To achieve this goal, half of the organization's professional entry-level jobs go to women and minorities, who are then encouraged to take positions in line management—in actual manufacturing or marketing—from which Hoechst's future top managers are currently drawn. In contrast, minorities and women in many organizations simply go into staff positions like personnel, legal affairs, or accounting—areas from which few top managers typically are selected.

Why has Hoechst undertaken this program? According to CEO Drew, "We're doing it because we want to have the most successful competitive company. It's not a social thing; this gets results."[23] Drew and Hoechst pursue total quality management and use self-managed teams to develop and make products.

Drew found that the quality of decision making was better in teams composed of employees with different characteristics and backgrounds. He remarked, "It dawned on me that what you get with diversity is a different viewpoint coming in and a much broader analysis of the solutions than you get from a group that's fairly narrow in its makeup." Drew attributes much of the company's 8 percent annual increase in productivity, and 18 percent annual return on capital, to its diversity program.

Does the new approach to diversity hurt the pool of white male employees from whom the company's managers traditionally came? The answer is no. According to Drew, 89 percent of the company's managers are still white males. In any case, Drew expects the competitive advantage that Hoechst obtains from its approach to diversity to result in so much growth and expansion that many new jobs will be created, and, in the end, everybody will benefit.

Two other significant performance issues confront organizations with a diverse workforce. First, research has found that many supervisors do not know how to manage diverse work groups and find it difficult to lead diverse groups of employees. Second, supervisors are often uncertain about how to handle the challenge of communicating with employees whose cultural backgrounds result in assumptions, values, and even language skills that differ from the supervisors'.[24] Various racial or ethnic groups may respond differently to the demands of their job responsibilities or to the approaches that leaders use to manage relationships in work groups. Age and gender differences can also cause problems for managers, such as when younger employees find themselves in a position of authority over older and perhaps more experienced employees. Similarly, some men find it difficult to report to or be evaluated by women. The mixing of generations, such as the baby-boomer (1946–1964) and the baby-bust (1965–1976) generations, can also cause problems (as we discuss in Chapter 4).

If diversity produces conflict and distrust among organizational members, individual, group, and organizational performance suffers and organizations must take active steps to solve diversity-related problems.[25] For example, if the skills and talents of women and minorities are not being fully utilized because older white males cannot (or refuse to) recognize them, an organization will suffer a significant loss of potential productivity. To reduce such losses, many organizations have instituted cultural diversity programs to improve personal

IBM, like Hoechst Celanese, has a commitment to diversity. IBM's workforce diversity staff ensures that IBM responds equitably to the needs of its employees regardless of their race, religion, age, status, or sexual orientation.

and group relationships, to promote cultural sensitivity and acceptance of differences between people, and to promote skills for working in multicultural environments.[26]

FLEXIBILITY CHALLENGE

A third diversity challenge is to be sensitive to the needs of different kinds of employees and to try to develop flexible employment approaches that increase employee well-being. Examples of some of these approaches include the following:

- New benefits packages customized to the needs of different groups of workers, such as single workers with no children and families, homosexuals in long-term committed relationships, and workers caring for aged parents.
- Flexible employment conditions (such as flextime) that give workers input into the length and scheduling of their workweek.
- Arrangements that allow for job sharing so that two or more employees can share the same job (to take care of children or aged parents, for example).
- Designing jobs and the buildings that house organizations to be sensitive to the special needs of disabled or handicapped workers (and customers).
- Creating management programs designed to provide constructive feedback to employees about their personal styles of dealing with minority employees.
- Establishing mentoring relationships to support minority employees.
- Establishing informal networks among minority employees to provide social support.

The Xerox Corporation, for example, has undertaken major initiatives to increase diversity by increasing the proportion of women and minorities it recruits and promotes. Xerox has also established a sophisticated support network for minority employees. Managing diversity is an ongoing activity that has important implications for organizations, particularly as diversity is forecast to increase as more and more women and minority employees enter the workforce.

Challenge 4: Managing the Global Environment

The challenge of managing a diverse workforce increases as organizations continue to expand their operations internationally. Thus managing in the global environment is the fourth challenge that we focus on. Global companies like GM, Toyota, PepsiCo, and Sony all face similar problems of effectively managing diversity across countries and national boundaries.[27] In Chapter 17, we discuss the global organization and take an in-depth look at problems of managing behavior in global organizations. Here, we summarize some of the main issues involved in this increasingly important task—issues that we also discuss in most other chapters.

First, there are the considerable problems of understanding organizational behavior in global settings.[28] Evidence shows that people in different countries may have different values and views not only of their work settings but also of the world in general. It has been argued, for example, that Americans have an individualistic orientation toward work and the Japanese people have a collectivist orientation. These individual orientations reflect cultural differences, which affect people's behavior in groups, their commitment and loyalty to the organization, and their motivation to perform.[29] Understanding the differences between national cultures is important in any attempt to manage behavior in global organizations to increase performance.

Second, the management functions of planning, organizing, leading, and controlling become much more complex as an organization's activities expand across the globe. On the planning dimension, decision making must be coordinated between managers at home and managers in foreign countries who are likely to have different views about what goals an organization should pursue. The way managers organize the company and decide how to allocate decision-making authority and responsibility between managers at home and abroad is one of the most significant functions of global managers.[30]

On the leadership dimension, managers must develop their management skills so that they can learn to understand the forces at work in foreign work settings. They must also tailor their leadership styles to suit differences in the attitudes and values of workforces in different countries. There is considerable evidence that the problems managers have in managing diversity inside their home countries are compounded when they attempt to manage in different national cultures.[31] Finally, controlling involves establishing the evaluation, reward, and promotion policies of the organization and training and developing a globally diverse workforce.

All management activities are especially complex at a global level because the attitudes, aspirations, and values of the workforce differ by country. For example, most U.S. workers are astonished to learn that in Europe the average shop-floor worker receives from four to six weeks of paid vacation a year. In the United States a comparable worker receives only one or two weeks. Similarly, in some countries promotion by seniority is the norm, but in others level of performance is the main determinant of promotion and reward. The way in which global organizations attempt to understand and manage these and

Levi Strauss discovered that two of its Bangladeshi suppliers were employing children under the age of 14 in violation of International Labor Organization standards. Rather than requiring the contractors to fire the children, many of whom were the sole breadwinners in their families, Levi Strauss chose to pay for their educations. They persuaded the suppliers to continue to pay the children's wages while they were in school and to guarantee that their jobs would be waiting for them when they became of age.

other problems can be seen in the way the Ford Motor Company adopted a global approach to car design. The Global View Insights in this and other chapters, particularly in Chapter 17, examine the topic of managing global organizations. (See Insight 1.6.)

Insight 1.6

A Global View

Ford's New Global Approach

Ford Motor Company (www.ford.com) used to organize its design activities by country. Managers in Ford design studios in Cologne, Germany; Dearborn, Michigan; Dunton, England; Hiroshima, Japan; Melbourne, Australia; Turin, Italy; and Valencia, California, reported to the product development chiefs in their own countries. Each studio developed its own approach to design, championed its own design, and often refused to share information with other design teams, keeping new designs secret to protect its own interests. Language problems and cultural differences made communication between design teams difficult, and design managers outside the United States felt their efforts were not fairly rewarded because U.S. top management paid most attention to Ford's U.S. design managers.

This competition among design teams hurt Ford's corporate performance. The competition among designers increased the costs of developing cars. Furthermore, opportunities to achieve cooperation to produce innovative designs were being lost. Recognizing these problems, Ford's chief design manager, Jack Telnack, moved to change the way the design teams were organized.[32] All the design studios—except for the Melbourne studio, which reports to Ford's chief designer in Hiroshima—now will report to Telnack in the United States. He is responsible for organizing and leading their efforts to increase performance. Telnack intends to use state-of-the-art video teleconferencing systems, fiber optics, and other electronic and computer media to bring the design teams face to face and to motivate and coordinate their activities. His goal is to mold them into one unit to speed innovation and product development. Telnack also plans to transfer designers from country to country to improve their design skills, capitalize on diversity, and enable them to learn about the needs of customers in other countries. This kind of global outlook is very important in an age in which cars are beginning to look the same the world over and the design of a new car must appeal to a global customer.

SUMMARY

Organizational behavior is a developing field of study, and researchers and managers face new challenges to their understanding of, and ability to manage, work behavior. In this chapter, we made the following major points:

1. Organizational behavior is the study of factors that impact how individuals and groups respond to and act in organizations and how organizations manage their environments. Organizational behavior provides a set of tools—theories and concepts—to understand, analyze, describe, and manage attitudes and behavior in organizations.

2. The study of organizational behavior can improve, and change individual, group, and organizational behavior to attain individual, group, and organizational goals.

3. Organizational behavior can be analyzed at three levels: the individual, the group, and the organization as a whole. A full understanding is impossible without an examination of the factors that affect behavior at each level.

4. A significant part of a manager's job is to use the tools of organizational behavior to increase organizational effectiveness—that is, an organization's ability to achieve its goals. Management is the process of planning, organizing, leading, and controlling an organization's human, financial, material, and other resources to increase its effectiveness. Managers perform their functions by assuming ten types of roles. Managers need conceptual, human, and technical skills to perform their organizational functions and roles effectively.

5. Four challenges face those seeking to manage organizational behavior: how to use human resources to gain a competitive advantage, how to develop an ethical organization, how to manage a diverse workforce, and how to manage organizational behavior as an organization expands internationally.

Organizational Behavior in Action

TOPICS FOR DISCUSSION AND ACTION

1. Why is a working knowledge of organizational behavior important to managers? How can such information increase a manager's effectiveness?
2. Why is it important to analyze the behavior of individuals, groups, and the organization as a whole to understand organizational behavior in work settings?
3. Recall a manager you have known, and evaluate how well that person performed the four functions of management: planning, organizing, leading, and controlling.
4. Think of a manager you have known or read about, and describe instances when that manager seemed to play some of the ten managerial roles identified by Mintzberg.
5. Select a restaurant, supermarket, church, or some other familiar organization, and describe how the organization tries to increase efficiency, quality, innovation, and responsiveness to customers.
6. How can information about organizational behavior help organizations manage their human resources to obtain a competitive advantage?
7. What are organizational ethics, and why is ethics such an important issue facing organizations today?
8. Why is diversity an important challenge facing organizations today?
9. What special challenges does managing behavior on a global scale pose for managers?
10. Find a manager and ask what challenges he or she is confronting now and may confront in the future.

BUILDING DIAGNOSTIC SKILLS

Behavior in Organizations

Think of an organization—a place of employment, a club, a sports team, a musical group, an academic society—that provided you with a significant work experience, and answer the following questions.

1. What are your attitudes and feelings toward the organization? Why do you think you have these attitudes and feelings?
2. Indicate, on a scale from one to ten, how hard you worked for this organization or how intensively you participated in the organization's activities. Explain the reasons for your level of participation.
3. How did the organization communicate its performance expectations to you, and how did the organization monitor your performance to evaluate whether you met those expectations? Did you receive more rewards when you performed at a higher level? What happened when your performance was not as high as it should have been?
4. How concerned was your organization with your well-being? How was this concern reflected? Do you think this level of concern was appropriate? Why or why not?

5. Think of your direct supervisor or leader. How would you characterize this person's approach to management? How did this management style affect your attitudes and behaviors?
6. Think of your coworkers or fellow members. How did their attitudes and behavior affect yours, particularly your level of performance?
7. Given your answers to these questions, how would you improve this organization's approach to managing its members?

RESEARCH ON THE INTERNET: A MANAGER'S TOOL

Specific Task

Each organization has its own unique approach to management and organizational behavior. To discover Wal-Mart's distinctive approach, enter its website, click on corporate information, and then click on Wal-Mart culture. (www.mart.com/corporate/culture.shtml)

1. What do the stories about Wal-Mart's culture suggest about the company's approach to management and organizational behavior?
2. What do the stories say about Wal-Mart's approach to managing its human resources to gain a competitive advantage?

General Task

Search for the website of a company that describes its managers' approach to utilizing human resources or the way they address one of the four management challenges identified in the chapter. What is their approach, or what is the main challenge they are facing?

TOPICS FOR DEBATE

Now that you understand the nature of organizational behavior and management, and the kinds of issues they address, debate the following topics:

Debate One

Team A. Organizations should do all they can to promote the well-being of people and groups inside and outside the organization.

Team B. Organizations exist to make a profit. As they earn money for their shareholders, all they should do to promote social well-being is to follow government laws and regulations.

Debate Two

Team A. The best way to increase organizational performance is to clearly specify each worker's position and the relationships among positions.

Team B. The best way to increase organizational performance is to give workers the flexibility to define and negotiate their own positions.

EXPERIENTIAL EXERCISE

A Question of Ethics

Objective

Your objective is to uncover and understand the factors that allow you to determine whether behavior in organizations is ethical.

Procedure

1. The class divides into groups of from three to five people, and each group appoints one member as spokesperson, to present the group's findings to the whole class.

2. Each member of the group is to think of some unethical behaviors or incidents that he or she has observed in organizations. The incidents could be something experienced as an employee, a customer, or a client, or something observed informally.
3. The group identifies three important criteria to use to determine whether a particular action or behavior is ethical. These criteria need to differentiate between ethical and unethical organizational behavior. The spokesperson writes them down.
4. When asked by the instructor, the spokespersons for each group should be ready to describe the incidents of unethical behavior witnessed by group members and the criteria developed in Step 3.

MAKING THE CONNECTION

At the end of most chapters is a "Making the Connection" exercise that requires you to search newspapers or magazines in the library for an example of a real company that is dealing with some of the issues, concepts, challenges, questions, and problems dealt with in the chapter. The purpose of the exercise for this chapter is to familiarize you with the way in which managers make use of organizational behavior to increase organizational effectiveness.

Find an example of an organization in which managers made use of organizational behavior concepts or theories to deal with one of the four challenges discussed in Chapter 1: gaining a competitive advantage, organizational ethics, diversity in the workforce, or globalization.

CLOSING CASE

How Herb Kelleher Manages at Southwest Airlines

In 1973 Herb Kelleher founded Southwest Airlines in Dallas, Texas. From the start chief executive officer (CEO) Kelleher adopted a unique approach to managing his airline. To avoid competition with major airlines, he planned a strategy based on low-price fares and flights between a limited number of southwestern cities, such as Phoenix, Los Angeles, and Dallas.

To keep Southwest's prices low, Kelleher had to keep costs low, something he accomplished by organizing and leading his employees in an innovative way. At Southwest, every employee has a specific job (pilot, flight attendant, baggage handler, and so on), but whenever employees have free time, they are expected to help other employees. If the need arises, for example, pilots check in passengers and flight attendants help load baggage. As a result, it takes Southwest just ten to fifteen minutes to turn around a plane (other airlines typically need an hour). Southwest's planes thus make many more flights a day than do the planes of its competitors, and those additional flights increase its revenues.

Kelleher's unique approach to leadership is the envy of other CEOs. He is a hands-on manager who works closely with employees to find cost-saving solutions to problems. Moreover, as CEO, Kelleher acts as a figurehead to his employees, personifying Southwest's dedication to the well-being of its employees and customers.

Kelleher's sincere concern for creating a good working relationship with his employees came from studying the behavior of other leaders, particularly his father, who was a general manager at Campbell Soup Co. Kelleher believes managers should have an active interest in their employees, and Southwest has many innovative programs through which employees meet with managers and develop strong personal relationships. For example, at Southwest's Dallas headquarters Kelleher holds weekly cookouts at which employees join with him to celebrate the company's success. He also holds frequent ceremonies to mark events in the airline's history and employees' promotions to higher ranks in the organization.[33] Kelleher's well-known sense of humor and penchant for pranks (he has been known to dress up as Elvis Presley or the Easter Bunny) have endeared him to employees and customers alike. In fact, he insists on a sense of humor in his employees, who often work in fancy dress and play jokes on passengers to enliven their flights. Southwest employees return Kelleher's commitment to them by going the extra mile for the organization and performing above and beyond the call of duty to support its goals. Their happiness at being part of the Southwest organization is further reflected in low absenteeism and low turnover.

As a part of his organizing and leadership approach, Kelleher puts his money where his mouth is and rewards employees for high performance and for helping the organization meet its goals. Although pay levels and benefits at Southwest are similar to those at other airlines, Kelleher has established a generous profit-sharing plan in which 15 percent of Southwest's net profits are returned to its workers. The airline also offers good pension benefits and has never had a layoff.[34]

Kelleher's concern for Southwest's performance is shown in the way he closely controls and monitors costs and productivity and takes corrective action quickly when it is needed. All expenditures over $1,000 require his direct approval, for example, and he constantly searches for new ways to increase efficiency and customer service. Workers, realizing that increased performance protects their jobs at a time when most other airlines are laying off employees, also work hard to sustain and increase performance and find new ways to satisfy customers.

At Southwest, all of Herb Kelleher's actions are designed to improve employees' work attitudes and behaviors and to increase the performance and well-being of employees and customers alike. A recent article in Fortune magazine suggested that Kelleher might be the best CEO in America because his management style has made Southwest consistently profitable while American, Continental, and other major airlines have been losing billions of dollars.[35]

Discussion Questions
1. What management functions and roles is Herb Kelleher performing that make him such a successful manager?
2. How easy would it be for other CEOs to manage like Kelleher?

Individual Differences: Personality and Ability

2

Craig Barrett's Conscientiousness Pays Off

When Craig Barrett was recently named president of Intel (www.intel.com), he was the first person outside of Intel's founders, Gordon Moore, Robert Noyce, and Andrew Grove, to hold such a high position in the company.[1] What seems to set Barrett apart from other top managers at Intel is his conscientious nature combined with an enthusiasm for taking risks and embracing new experiences.

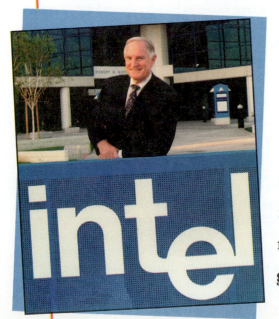

One of Barrett's claims to fame at Intel is his manufacturing expertise, which analyst Daniel Klesken suggests turned "Intel from a 50-pound weakling in chip manufacturing into a 500-pound gorilla."[2]

Barrett is extremely conscientious regarding every aspect of the manufacturing process, is careful and persevering, and pays close attention to detail. A friend of Barrett's recalls how when their families were on a camping trip in Montana and the proprietor of the cabin they were staying at served them homemade berry wine, Barrett gathered the necessary information to determine how much berry wine could be produced on a daily basis.

Conscientiousness and attention to detail have served Barrett well at Intel. For example, his innovative Copy Exactly program, designed to improve quality and reduce variability in microprocessors, helped convince major customers such as Dell Computer Corp. that they could rely on Intel to manufacture and supply the Intel-designed chips featured in their computers. The principle underlying Copy Exactly is that all Intel plants use identical equipment and procedures throughout the manufacturing process so that their finished products will be uniform and of high quality.

Barrett's high level of conscientiousness is complimented by his diverse interests and openness to new experiences. He was a tenured professor at Stanford University prior to joining Intel over twenty years ago. He is a fly-fishing enthusiast who owns a 350-acre ranch in Montana and commutes from his home in Phoenix to Intel's headquarters in Santa Clara, California. While insiders note that Barrett is not as exuberant as Intel's CEO Andrew Grove, his methodical and analytical nature have helped Intel develop into the manufacturing giant it is in the microprocessor industry.[3]

Overview

Each member of an organization has his or her own style and ways of behaving. Effectively working with others requires an understanding and appreciation of how people differ from one another. Craig Barrett, for example, is detail-oriented and conscientious, qualities that have contributed to his success at Intel. In order to effectively work with Barrett, it is important that Barrett's subordinates, coworkers, and superiors understand what he is like and what is important to him.

In this chapter we focus on **individual differences,** the ways in which people differ from each other. Managers need to understand individual differences because they have an impact on the feelings, thoughts, and behaviors of each member of an organization. Individual differences affect, for example, job satisfaction, job performance, job stress, and leadership. Organizational members interact with each other on a daily basis, and only if they understand each other are their interactions likely to result in high levels of satisfaction and performance.

Individual differences may be grouped into two categories: personality differences and differences in ability. We focus on the nature, meaning, and determinants of personality and on the ways that personality and situational factors combine to influence feelings, thoughts, and behavior in organizations. We discuss specific personality traits that are particularly relevant to organizational behavior. We then turn our attention to differences in ability. After describing various types of ability, we discuss the key issue for managers: how ability can be managed to ensure that workers can effectively perform their jobs.

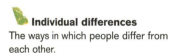

Individual differences
The ways in which people differ from each other.

The Nature of Personality

People's personalities can be described in a variety of ways. Some people seem to be perfectionists; they can be critical, impatient, demanding, and intense. Other kinds of people are more relaxed and easygoing. You may have friends or coworkers who always seem to have something to smile about and are fun to be around. Or perhaps you have friends or coworkers who are shy and quiet; they are hard to get to know and may sometimes seem dull. In each of these examples, we are describing what people are generally like without referring to their specific feelings, thoughts, and behaviors in any specific situation. In formulating a general description of someone, we try to pinpoint something that is relatively enduring about the person, something that seems to explain the regularities or patterns we observe in the way the person thinks, feels, and behaves.

Personality is the pattern of relatively enduring ways in which a person feels, thinks, and behaves. Personality is an important factor in accounting for why workers act the way they do in organizations and why they have favorable or unfavorable attitudes toward their jobs and organizations. Personality has been shown to influence career choice, job satisfaction, stress, leadership, and some aspects of job performance.

DETERMINANTS OF PERSONALITY: NATURE AND NURTURE

Why are some workers happy and easygoing and others intense and critical? An answer to this question can be found by examining the determinants of personality: nature and nurture.

Personality is partially determined by **nature,** or biological heritage. The genes that you inherited from your parents influence how your personality has been unfolding. Although specific genes for personality have not yet been identified, psychologists have studied identical twins in an attempt to discover the extent to which personality is inherited.[4]

Because identical twins possess identical genes, they have the same genetic determinants of personality. Identical twins who grow up together in the same family have the same permissive or strict parents and similar life experiences. If the twins have similar personalities, it is impossible to identify the source of the similarity because they have not only the same genetic makeup but similar life experiences.

In contrast, identical twins who are separated at birth and raised in different settings (perhaps because they are adopted by different families) share the same genetic material but often have very different life experiences. Evidence from research on separated identical twins and other studies suggests that approximately 50 percent of the variation we observe in people's personalities can be attributed to nature—to genetic factors (see Fig. 2.1).[5] Thus, about half of the variation we observe in workers' personalities in organizations reflects the distinctive ways of thinking, feeling, and

Personality

The pattern of relatively enduring ways in which a person feels, thinks, and behaves.

Nature

Biological heritage, genetic makeup.

FIGURE 2.1

Nature and Nurture: The Determinants of Personality

Nurture
Life experiences.

behaving they inherited from their parents. The other 50 percent reflects the influence of **nurture,** or life experiences.

Personality develops over time, responding to the experiences people have as children and as adults. Factors such as the strictness or permissiveness of a child's parents, the number of other children in the family, the extent to which parents and teachers demand a lot from a child, success or lack of success at making friends or getting and keeping a job, and even the culture in which a person is raised and lives as an adult are shapers of personality.

Because about half of the variation in people's personalities is inherited from their parents and thus is basically fixed at birth, it comes as no surprise that personality is quite stable over periods of time ranging from five to ten years. This does not mean that personality cannot change; it means that personality is likely to change only over many years. Thus the impact of any specific work situation or crisis on a worker's personality is likely to be felt only if the situation continues for many years. An important outcome of this fact is that managers should not expect to change workers' personalities in the short run. In fact, for all practical purposes, managers should view workers' personalities as relatively fixed in the short run.

Personality, nevertheless, is an important individual difference that managers and other organizational members need to take into account in order to understand why people feel, think, and act as they do in organizations. For example, realizing that a worker complains a lot and often gets upset because of his or her personality will help a manager deal with this type of subordinate, especially if the person's job performance is acceptable.

PERSONALITY AND THE SITUATION

Because personality accounts for observable regularities in people's attitudes and behaviors, it would seem reasonable to assert that it would account for such regularities at work. A substantial body of literature in psychology and a growing set of studies in organizational behavior suggest that personality *is* useful for explaining and predicting how workers generally feel, think, and behave on the job.[6] Personality has been shown to influence several work-related attitudes and behaviors, including job satisfaction (Chapter 3), the ability to handle work-related stress (Chapter 8), the choice of a career (Chapter 8), and leadership (Chapter 12).[7] Because of personality, some people, like Craig Barrett in the opening case, are very conscientious about most things they do and thus perform at a higher level than do those who are not so conscientious, as we discuss later in this chapter.[8]

However, in addition to personality, the organizational situation also affects work attitudes and behaviors. In some organizations, strong situational constraints and pressures (such as job requirements or strict rules and regulations) force people to behave in a certain way, regardless of their personalities.[9] For example, a worker on an assembly line manufacturing bicycles must put handlebars on each bicycle that passes by. A bike passes by every 75 seconds, and the worker has to be sure that the handlebars are properly attached to each bicycle within that time frame. It doesn't matter whether the worker is shy or outgoing; regardless of his or her personality, the worker has a specific task to perform day in and day out in the same manner. Because the worker is not free to vary his or her behavior, personality is not useful for understanding or predicting job performance in this situation.

Consider another example. Workers at McDonald's and other fast-food restaurants follow clearly specified procedures for preparing large quantities of burgers, fries, and shakes and serving them to large numbers of customers. Because each worker knows exactly what the procedures are and how to carry them out (they are spelled out in a detailed manual), the food is always prepared in the same manner, regardless of the workers' personalities.

As those two examples show, in organizations where situational pressures on workers' behavior are strong, personality may not be a good predictor of on-the-job behavior. When situational pressures are weak, however, and workers have more choice about how to perform a job, personality plays a more important role, and what a person can put into his or her job performance will sometimes depend on the kind of person he or she is. For instance, a statewide English curriculum requires English teachers to teach Shakespeare's *Macbeth* to high school seniors, but the curriculum does not specify exactly how the play is to be taught. A teacher who is outgoing and has a flair for the dramatic may bring the play and its themes to life by dressing up in period costumes and acting out scenes. A teacher who is less outgoing may simply ask students to take turns reading aloud from the play or ask them to write a paper on how Shakespeare reveals a certain theme through the play's dialogue and action.

By now it should be clear to you that both personality and situational factors affect organizational behavior.[10] It is the interaction of personality and situational factors that determines how people think, feel, and behave in general and, specifically, how they do so within an organization (see Fig. 2.2). Robert Greene, for example, is an executive in an advertising agency who is responsible for coming up with advertising campaigns and presenting them to the agency's clients. Greene is a creative, achievement-oriented person who has good ideas and has developed the agency's most successful and lucrative campaigns. But Greene is also shy and quiet and cannot always effectively communicate his ideas to clients. Greene's personality and the situation combine or interact to determine his overall performance. He performs well when working on his own or with his team to develop advertising campaigns, but in interpersonal situations such as when he presents his campaigns to clients, he performs poorly. A manager who understands this interaction can capitalize on the personality strengths (creativity and achievement orientation) that propel Greene to develop successful advertising campaigns. The manager can also guard against the possibility of clients having a negative reaction to Greene's shyness by teaming him up for presentations with a gregarious executive whose strong suit is pitching campaigns to clients. If Greene's manager did not understand how Greene's personality and the situation interacted to shape Greene's performance, the

FIGURE 2.2

The Interaction of Personality
and Situational Factors

advertising agency might lose clients because of Greene's inability to relate to them effectively and convince them of the merits of his campaigns.

Effective managers recognize the various ways that personality and situation interact to determine feelings, thoughts, attitudes, and behaviors at work. An understanding of workers' personalities and the situations in which they perform best enables a manager to help workers perform at a high level and feel good about the work they are doing. Furthermore, when workers at all levels in an organization understand how personality and situation interact, good working relationships and organizational effectiveness are promoted.

PERSONALITY: A DETERMINANT OF THE NATURE OF ORGANIZATIONS

Attraction-selection-attrition (ASA) framework
The idea that an organization attracts and selects individuals with similar personalities and loses individuals with other types of personality.

Ben Schneider, a prominent organizational researcher at the University of Maryland, has come up with an interesting view of the way in which personality determines the nature of whole organizations. He calls his schema the **attraction-selection-attrition (ASA) framework.** Schneider proposes that the "personality" of a whole organization is largely a product of the personalities of its workers. He suggests that individuals with similar personalities tend to be attracted to an organization (*attraction*) and hired by it (*selection*), and that individuals with other types of personality tend to leave the organization (*attrition*). The interplay of attraction, selection, and attrition results in some consistency or similarity of personalities within an organization, and this "typical" personality determines the nature of the organization itself.[11]

ASA processes operate in numerous ways. When organizations want to hire new employees, they implicitly size up the extent to which prospective hires fit in with the organization—that is, the extent to which their personalities match the personalities of current members. This sizing up is especially likely to occur in small organizations. Larry Pliska, who heads up Planterra, a Michigan company that sells plants and trees, hires all new managers himself so that he can be sure they relate to and support his philosophy for the company. John Schaeffer, founder of the California company Real Goods Trading, conducts most of the final interviewing and does most of the hiring for his company in an attempt to find what he calls "even-tempered" workers.[12]

What are the implications of the ASA framework? We would expect, for example, that people who are creative and like to take risks would be attracted to entrepreneurial organizations and would be likely to be hired by such organizations. Individuals who do not have this orientation either would not seek jobs with these organizations or would be likely to leave them. Over time, ASA processes may result in these organizations being composed of large numbers of creative risk takers who, in turn, give the organization its entrepreneurial nature. The entrepreneurial nature of the organization, in turn, influences employees' feelings, thoughts, and behavior and reinforces their own propensity for risk taking. It is important to realize that although ASA processes can strengthen an organization, they can also lead an organization to perform poorly or fail. This negative outcome occurs when most members of the organization view opportunities and problems in the same way and, as a result of their shared point of view, are resistant to making needed changes.

TO MANAGERS

The Nature of Personality

◆ Acknowledge and appreciate that workers' feelings, thoughts, attitudes, and behaviors are partially determined by their personalities, which are difficult to change. Realize that you might need to adjust your own feelings and actions to work effectively with others.

◆ When you are trying to understand why workers have certain attitudes and behave in certain ways, remember that attitudes and behaviors are determined by the interaction of an individual's personality and the situation in which the individual works.

◆ When feasible, structure an individual's work situation to fit his or her personality. A good match is likely to result in positive attitudes and behaviors.

◆ Encourage an acceptance and appreciation of the diverse personalities in your organization.

The Big Five Model of Personality

When people describe other people, they often say things like "She's got a lot of personality," meaning that the person is fun loving, friendly, and outgoing, or "He's got no personality," meaning that the person is dull and boring. In fact, there is no such thing as a lot of personality or no personality; everyone has a specific type of personality.

Because personality is an important determinant of how a person thinks, feels, and behaves, it is helpful to distinguish between different types of personality. Researchers have spent considerable time and effort trying to identify personality types. One of the most important ways that researchers have found to describe personality is in terms of traits. A **trait** is a specific component of personality that describes particular tendencies a person has to feel, think, and act in certain ways, such as shy or outgoing, critical or accepting, compulsive or easygoing. In the opening case, Craig Barrett of Intel, was described as being conscientious and open to new experiences; as you will learn, conscientiousness and openness to experience are actually two personality traits. Thus, when we speak of a person's personality, we are really referring to a collection of traits that describe how the person generally tends to feel, think, and behave.

Researchers have identified many personality traits, and most psychologists agree that the traits that make up a person's personality can be organized in a hierarchy. The "Big Five" model of personality places five general personality traits at the top of the trait hierarchy: extraversion, neuroticism, agreeableness, conscientiousness, and openness to experience (see Fig. 2.3).[13]

Trait
A specific component of personality.

FIGURE **2.3**

The Hierarchical
Organization of Personality
Source: Adapted from R. R. McCrae and P. T. Costa, "Discriminant Validity of NEO-PIR Facet Scales," *Educational and Psychological Measurement,* 52, pp. 229–237. Copyright 1992. Reprinted by permission of Sage Publications, Inc.

The "Big Five"
dimensions of
personality

| Extraversion | Neuroticism | Agreeableness | Conscientiousness | Openness to experience |

 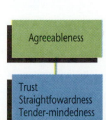  

Specific traits
related to the
"Big Five"

| Positive emotions
Gregariousness
Warmth | Anxiety
Self-consciousness
Vulnerability | Trust
Straightfowardness
Tender-mindedness | Competence
Order
Self-discipline | Fantasy
Actions
Ideas |

Each of the Big Five traits is composed of various specific traits. Extraversion (the tendency to have a positive outlook on life), for example, consists of specific traits such as positive emotions, gregariousness, and warmth. The Big Five and the specific traits lower in the hierarchy are universal. They can be used to describe the personalities of people regardless of their age, gender, race, ethnicity, religion, socioeconomic background, or country of origin.

Each of the general and specific traits represents a continuum along which a certain aspect or dimension of personality can be placed. A person can be high, low, average, or anywhere in between on the continuum for each trait. Fig. 2.4 shows a profile of a person who is low on extraversion, high on neuroticism, about average on agreeableness and conscientiousness, and relatively high on openness to experience. To help you understand what a Big Five personality profile means, we describe the extremes of each trait below. Keep in mind that a person's standing on the trait could be anywhere along the continuum (as in Fig. 2.4).

EXTRAVERSION

Extraversion, or **positive affectivity,** is a personality trait that predisposes individuals to experience positive emotional states and feel good about themselves and about the world around them. Extraverts—people high on the extraversion scale—tend to be sociable, affectionate, and friendly. Introverts—people low on the extraversion scale—are less likely to experience positive emotional states and have fewer social interactions with others. At work, extraverts are more likely than introverts to experience positive moods, be satisfied with their jobs, and generally feel good about the organization and those around them. Extraverts also are more likely to enjoy socializing with their coworkers. They may do particularly well in jobs requiring frequent social interaction, such as in sales and customer relations positions. An example of a personality scale that measures a person's level of extraversion is provided in Fig. 2.5.

Extraversion
The tendency to experience positive emotional states and feel good about oneself and the world around one; also called positive affectivity.

FIGURE 2.4

A Big Five Personality Profile
This is the profile of a person who is low on extraversion, high on neuroticism, about average on agreeableness and conscientiousness, and relatively high on openness to experience.

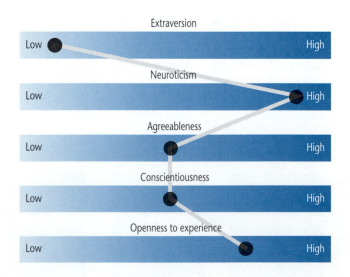

Instructions: Listed below is a series of statements a person might use to describe her or his attitudes, opinions, interests, and other characteristics. If a statement is true or largely true, put a "T" in the space next to the item. If the statement is false or largely false, mark an "F" in the space.

Please answer *every statement*, even if you are not completely sure of the answer. Read each statement carefully, but don't spend too much time deciding on the answer.

_____ 1. It is easy for me to become enthusiastic about things I am doing.

_____ 2. I often feel happy and satisfied for no particular reason.

_____ 3. I live a very interesting life.

_____ 4. Every day I do some things that are fun.

_____ 5. I usually find ways to liven up my day.

_____ 6. Most days I have moments of real fun or joy.

_____ 7. I often feel sort of lucky for no special reason.

_____ 8. Every day interesting and exciting things happen to me.

_____ 9. In my spare time I usually find something interesting to do.

_____ 10. For me life is a great adventure.

_____ 11. I always seem to have something pleasant to look forward to.

Scoring: Level of extraversion or positive affectivity is equal to the number of items answered "True."

FIGURE 2.5

A Measure of Extraversion or Positive Affectivity

Source: A. Tellegen, *Brief Manual for the Differential Personality Questionnaire,* unpublished manuscript, University of Minnesota, 1982. Reprinted with permission.

Neuroticism

The tendency to experience negative emotional states and view oneself and the world around one negatively; also called negative affectivity.

NEUROTICISM

In contrast to extraversion, **neuroticism,** or **negative affectivity,** reflects people's tendency to experience negative emotional states, feel distressed, and generally view themselves and the world around them negatively. Individuals high on neuroticism are more likely than individuals low on neuroticism to experience negative emotions and stress over time and across situations. Individuals who are high on neuroticism are more likely to experience negative moods at work, feel stressed, and generally have a negative orientation toward the work situation. Often, the term *neurotic* is used in the media and popular press to describe a person who has a psychological problem. Neuroticism, however, is a trait that all normal, psychologically healthy individuals possess to a certain degree.

Individuals high on neuroticism are sometimes more critical of themselves and their performance than are people low on neuroticism. That tendency may propel them to improve their performance, so they may be particularly proficient in situations, such as quality control, that require critical thinking and evaluation. Individuals high on neuroticism may also exert a needed sobering influence in group decision making by playing devil's advocate and pointing out the negative aspects of a proposed decision. Individuals low on neuroticism do not tend to experience negative emotions and are not as critical and pessimistic as their high-neuroticism counterparts. An example of a personality scale that measures neuroticism is provided in Fig. 2.6.

Instructions: Listed below is a series of statements a person might use to describe her or his attitudes, opinions, interests, and other characteristics. If a statement is true or largely true, put a "T" in the space next to the item. If the statement is false or largely false, mark an "F" in the space.

Please answer *every statement*, even if you are not completely sure of the answer. Read each statement carefully, but don't spend too much time deciding on the answer.

_____ 1. I often find myself worrying about something.

_____ 2. My feelings are hurt rather easily.

_____ 3. Often I get irritated at little annoyances.

_____ 4. I suffer from nervousness.

_____ 5. My mood often goes up and down.

_____ 6. I sometimes feel "just miserable" for no good reason.

_____ 7. Often I experience strong emotions—anxiety, anger—without really knowing what causes them.

_____ 8. I am easily startled by things that happen unexpectedly.

_____ 9. I sometimes get myself into a state of tension and turmoil as I think of the day's events.

_____ 10. Minor setbacks sometimes irritate me too much.

_____ 11. I often lose sleep over my worries.

_____ 12. There are days when I'm "on edge" all of the time.

_____ 13. I am too sensitive for my own good.

_____ 14. I sometimes change from happy to sad, or vice versa, without good reason.

Scoring: Level of neuroticism or negative affectivity is equal to the number of items answered "True."

FIGURE 2.6

A Measure of Neuroticism or Negative Affectivity

Source: A. Tellegen, *Brief Manual for the Differential Personality Questionnaire,* unpublished manuscript, University of Minnesota, 1982. Reprinted with permission.

The Walt Disney Company looks for special people to "delight" Disney customers. The organization recruits people who are enthusiastic, outgoing, and responsible. After completing their training each new recruit—or "cast member"—receives a name tag from Mickey Mouse, to celebrate his or her entry into the company.

Agreeableness
The tendency to get along well with others.

AGREEABLENESS

Agreeableness is the trait that captures the distinction between individuals who get along well with other people and those who do not. Likability in general, and the ability to care for others and to be affectionate, characterize individuals who are high on agreeableness. Individuals low on agreeableness are antagonistic, mistrustful, unsympathetic, uncooperative, and rude. A low measure of agreeableness might be an advantage in jobs that require a person to be somewhat antagonistic, such as a bill collector or a drill sergeant. Agreeable individuals generally are easy to get along with and are "team players." Agreeableness can be an asset in jobs that hinge on developing good relationships with other people. (See Insight 2.1.)

Insight 2.1

Personality

Agreeableness Leads to Advertising Coup

Ogilvy & Mather, a New York advertising agency, recently scored a major victory. IBM (www.ibm.com) chose Ogilvy & Mather as the sole agency to manage all its domestic and international advertising, which amounts to more than $400 million a year. Was Ogilvy & Mather chosen because it has an established global network to manage advertising around the world and is renowned for its advertising expertise? In part, yes. Insiders, however, also attribute this major coup to the good relationships that Rochelle Lazarus, president of Ogilvy & Mather's North American unit, had developed with key decision makers at IBM over the years. Together, Ogilvy & Mather's reputation, Lazarus's professional credentials, and her long-term friendships with Louis Gerstner (IBM CEO) and Abby Kohnstamm (IBM vice president of corporate marketing) landed the IBM account for the agency.

Lazarus appears to have a high level of agreeableness. She is straightforward and trusting and thus is able to understand people and develop good relationships with them. Others, in turn, trust her. If the comments of people who know her are true, Lazarus's concern for others is sincere. As one Ogilvy & Mather client put it, "She makes a client feel understood."[14]

In a field that some say is built on relationships, Rochelle Lazarus's agreeableness has not only business advantages (the winning of major accounts) but personal advantages as well. Indeed, Lazarus spends about three quarters of her time interacting with clients and has lunch with former or current clients everyday. She says, "I enjoy people. . . . If some who are clients left their jobs tomorrow and went to some company that had no advertising potential, that doesn't mean I wouldn't stay in touch. . . . I just love the people I love."[15]

Conscientiousness
The extent to which a person is careful, scrupulous, and persevering.

Openness to experience
The extent to which a person is original, has broad interests, and is willing to take risks.

CONSCIENTIOUSNESS

Conscientiousness is the extent to which an individual is careful, scrupulous, and persevering. Individuals high on conscientiousness are organized and have a lot of self-discipline. Individuals low on conscientiousness may lack direction and self-discipline. Conscientiousness is important in many organizational situations and has been found to be a good predictor of performance in many jobs in a wide variety of organizations.[16] Roger Salquist, entrepreneur and CEO of the successful Calgene Incorporated, is known for his attention to details. In trying to win U.S. Food and Drug Administration (FDA) approval for his genetically altered tomato, for instance, Salquist made over twenty-five trips to Washington, D.C., and was relentless in his efforts to provide the FDA and other agencies with all the scientific data he could in support of the safety of his tomato. Salquist's conscientiousness paid off because the FDA agreed that no special labeling or testing would be necessary for genetically engineered foods such as Calgene's new tomato.[17] In the opening case, it is clear that Craig Barrett of Intel also is high on conscientiousness.

OPENNESS TO EXPERIENCE

The last of the Big Five personality traits, **openness to experience,** captures the extent to which an individual is original, open to a wide variety of stimuli, has broad interests, and is willing to take risks as opposed to being narrow-minded and cautious. Recall the diverse interests of Craig Barrett in the opening case, such as fly fishing, and the risk he took when he gave up his job as a tenured professor at Stanford University to join Intel. For jobs that change frequently, require innovation, or involve considerable risk, individuals who are open to experience may have an advantage. For openness to experience to be translated into creative and innovative behavior in organizations, however, the organization must remove obstacles to innovation. Entrepreneurs, who are often characterized as risk takers,[18] frequently start their own businesses because the large organizations that employed them placed too many restrictions on them and gave them too little reward for innovation and risk taking. (See Insight 2.2.)

Diversity

Openness to Experience in Action

Some workers who are high on openness to experience find that large organizations are very risk-averse and will not allow them to be as creative and innovative as they would like to be. This dilemma may be especially problematic for minorities who because of discrimination do not ascend the corporate ladder at the same pace as their white counterparts.[19] Typically, as workers get promoted to more responsible positions in organizations, they are allowed and often expected to be more innovative.

A growing number of young African American professionals who want to be creative and innovative are taking matters in their own hands and starting their own businesses. Ricardo Cumberbatch, who was a loan officer at the Bank of Montreal in New York, left his banking job to start his own company, Coastal Communications of America Inc., which provides pay telephone service in six states and has around $1 million per year in revenues.

Carole Riley worked in advertising for ten years at Time Warner Inc. Riley had always wanted to do something innovative, so she quit her job to open a McDonald's franchise in Harlem. Not content to follow McDonald's traditional ways of doing things, Riley changed the typical McDonald's uniform and had it made out of brightly colored West African Kente cloth, hung paintings and drawings by African American artists in her restaurant, and scheduled events to appeal to African American customers, such as Sunday gospel concerts called McPraising. Top management at McDonald's liked what Riley was doing and asked her to open another McDonald's restaurant in Harlem. Riley's two Harlem restaurants are now part of C. H. Riley Enterprises Inc. (of which she is president) and have combined revenues of almost $4 million.[20]

Although openness to experience clearly is an advantage for entrepreneurs and in jobs that require innovation, organizations also need people to perform jobs that do not allow much opportunity for independent thinking. In addition, sometimes organizations are afraid to take the risks that workers high on openness to experience may thrive on.

CONCLUSIONS

Research suggests that the Big Five traits hold considerable promise for increasing our understanding of work-related attitudes and behaviors and thus our understanding of organizational behavior. As we discuss in more detail in Chapter 9, for example, negative affectivity is useful in understanding stress in the workplace.[21] Researchers have found that individuals high on negative affectivity are more likely to indicate that there are significant stressors in the workplace and to experience stress at work. Research has also shown that individuals high on positive affectivity are more likely to feel good at work and be satisfied with their jobs and are likely to perform well in jobs (such as management and sales) that require social interaction.[22]

As you have undoubtedly recognized from our discussion of the Big Five traits, there is no such thing as a good or bad personality profile. Each person is unique and has a different type of personality that may be suited to different kinds of organizational situations. Good managers need to understand and learn to deal with people of all personality types.

Other Organizationally Relevant Personality Traits

Several other specific personality traits are relevant to understanding and managing behavior in organizations (see Fig. 2.7).

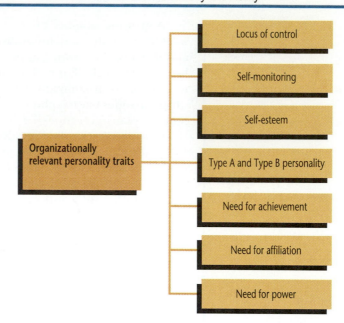

FIGURE *2.7*

Personality Traits Specifically
Relevant to Organizations

External locus of control

Describes people who believe that fate, luck, or outside forces are responsible for what happens to them.

Internal locus of control

Describes people who believe that ability, effort, or their own actions determine what happens to them.

Self-monitoring

The extent to which people try to control the way they present themselves to others.

LOCUS OF CONTROL

People differ in how much control they believe they have over the situation they are in and over what happens to them. Some people think they have relatively little impact on their surroundings and little control over important things that happen in their lives. Others believe that they can have a considerable impact on the world around them and on the path their lives take. The locus of control trait captures this difference among individuals.[23]

Individuals with an **external locus of control**—externals—tend to believe that outside forces are largely responsible for their fate, and they see little connection between their own actions and what happens to them. Individuals with an **internal locus of control**—internals—think that their own actions and behaviors have an impact in determining what happens to them. When people with an internal locus of control perform well, they are likely to attribute their performance to qualities within themselves, such as their own ability or effort. When people with an external locus of control perform well, they are likely to attribute their performance to external forces such as luck, the effects of powerful people, or simply the fact that the task was easy. In organizations, internals are more easily motivated than externals and do not need as much direct supervision because they are more likely to believe that their work behaviors influence important outcomes such as how well they perform their jobs and the pay increases, praise, job security, and promotions they receive.

SELF-MONITORING

Self-monitoring is the extent to which people try to control the way they present themselves to others.[24] High self-monitors want their behavior to be socially acceptable and so are attuned to any social cues that signal appropriate behavior in a situation. High self-monitors strive to behave in a situationally appropriate manner. For example, they don't yell, stamp, and whistle at a symphony concert, as they would at a football game. They are also good at managing the impressions that others have of them. In contrast, low self-monitors are not particularly sensitive to cues indicating acceptable behavior, nor are they overly concerned about behaving in a situationally appropriate manner. For example, they may act bored in a meeting with the president of an organization, tell customers about the merits of a competing product, or voice their concerns about working long hours in a job interview. People who are low self-monitors are guided by their own attitudes, beliefs, feelings, and principles and are not too concerned about what others think of their behavior.

High self-monitors are more likely than low self-monitors to tailor their behavior to fit a given situation. Thus high self-monitors may perform especially well in jobs such as sales or consulting, which require workers to interact with different types of people on a regular basis. In addition, because high self-monitors can modify their behavior to be appropriate for the individual or group they are interacting with, they may be particularly effective when an organization needs someone to communicate with an outside group whose support is being sought, such as when nonprofit organizations and universities try to secure donations from wealthy individuals.

Low self-monitors are more likely than high self-monitors to say what they think is true or correct and are not overly concerned about how others will react to them. Thus low self-monitors may be especially adept at providing organizational members with open, honest feedback (particularly when it's negative) and playing devil's advocate in decision-making groups. A scale that measures self-monitoring is provided in Fig. 2.8.

SELF-ESTEEM

Self-esteem
The extent to which people have pride in themselves and their capabilities.

Self-esteem is the extent to which people have pride in themselves and their capabilities. Individuals with high self-esteem think they are generally capable and worthy people who can deal with most situations. Individuals with low self-esteem question their self-worth, doubt their capabilities, and are apprehensive about their ability to succeed in different endeavors.

Self-esteem has several implications for understanding behavior in organizations.[25] Self-esteem influences people's choices of activities and jobs. Individuals with high self-esteem are more likely than individuals with low self-esteem to choose challenging careers and jobs. Once they are on the job, individuals with high self-esteem may set higher goals for themselves and may be more likely to tackle difficult tasks. High self-esteem also has a positive impact on motivation and job satisfaction. It must be kept in mind, however, that people with low self-esteem can be just as capable as those with high self-esteem in spite of their doubts about their abilities.

TYPE A AND TYPE B PERSONALITY

Type A
A person who has an intense desire to achieve, is extremely competitive, and has a strong sense of urgency.

Type B
A person who tends to be easygoing and relaxed.

In the popular press, you will often hear someone referred to as a "Type A" or read that "Type A personalities" are prone to high blood pressure. Individuals who are **Type A** have an intense desire to achieve, are extremely competitive, have a sense of urgency, are impatient, and can be hostile.[26] Such individuals have a strong need to get a lot done in a short time period and can be difficult to get along with because they are so driven. They often interrupt other people and sometimes finish their sentences for them because they are so impatient. More relaxed and easygoing individuals are labeled **Type B.**

Given the Type A drive to get so much done, Type A's would seem to be ideal workers from the organization's perspective, especially in situations

Instructions: Please indicate the extent to which each of the following statements is true or false for you personally.

_T_ 1. I find it hard to imitate the behavior of other people.

_T_ 2. At parties and social gatherings, I do not attempt to do or say things that others will like.

_T_ 3. I can only argue for ideas that I already believe.

_F_ 4. I can make impromptu speeches even on topics about which I have almost no information.

_T_ 5. I guess I put on a show to impress or entertain others.

_F_ 6. I would probably make a good actor.

_T_ 7. In a group of people, I am rarely the center of attention.

_F_ 8. In different situations and with different people, I often act like very different persons.

_F_ 9. I am not particularly good at making other people like me.

_F_ 10. I'm not always the person I appear to be.

_T_ 11. I would not change my opinions (or the way I do things) in order to please someone or win their favor.

_T_ 12. I have considered being an entertainer.

_F_ 13. I have never been good at games like charades or improvisational acting.

_F_ 14. I have trouble changing my behavior to suit different people and different situations.

_F_ 15. At a party I let others keep the jokes and stories going.

_F_ 16. I feel a bit awkward in public and do not show up quite as well as I should.

_K_ 17. I can look anyone in the eye and tell a lie with a straight face (if for a right end).

_T_ 18. I may deceive people by being friendly when I really dislike them.

Scoring: Individuals high on self-monitoring tend to indicate that questions 4, 5, 6, 8, 10, 12, 17, and 18 are *true* and that questions 1, 2, 3, 7, 9, 11, 13, 14, 15, and 16 are *false.*

FIGURE 2.8

A Measure of Self-Monitoring
Source: S. Gangestad and M. Snyder, " 'To Carve Nature at Its Joints': On the Existence of Discrete Classes in Personality," *Psychological Review,* 1985, 92, pp. 317–349. Copyright 1985 by the American Psychological Association. Reprinted with permission.

where a lot of work needs to be done in a short time. Because Type A's can be difficult to get along with, however, they may not be effective in situations that require a lot of interaction with others. Consistent with this observation, one study found that Type A managers were more likely to have conflicts with their subordinates and with coworkers than were Type B managers.[27] Type A workers are not particularly good team players and often work best alone. In addition, Type A's may get frustrated in long-term situations or projects because they like to see results.

Another important difference between Type A and Type B individuals has contributed to the attention in the popular press this trait has received. Type A individuals are sometimes more likely than Type B's to have coronary heart disease. In fact, two heart doctors identified this trait after they realized that many of their heart attack patients were very impatient, sometimes hostile, and always in a hurry and watching the clock. Some research suggests that a tendency toward hostility is particularly responsible for Type A's heart problems.

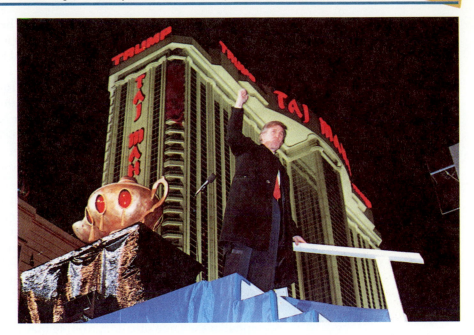

Donald Trump, controversial property developer and owner of the Taj Mahal casino in Atlantic City, appears to possess many of the attributes of a Type A personality. He is known to be competitive and has a strong drive to succeed. His subordinates find him a demanding boss and difficult to get along with.

NEEDS FOR ACHIEVEMENT, AFFILIATION, AND POWER

David McClelland has done extensive research on three traits that are present in all people to varying degrees: the need for achievement, the need for affiliation, and the need for power.[28]

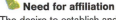

Need for achievement
The desire to perform challenging tasks well and to meet one's own high standards.

Individuals with a high **need for achievement** have a special desire to perform challenging tasks well and to meet their own personal standards for excellence. They like to be in situations in which they are personally responsible for what happens, like to set clear goals for themselves, are willing to take personal responsibility for outcomes, and like to receive performance feedback. Not surprisingly, such individuals are often found in jobs that help them to satisfy their strong desire to achieve. Indeed, McClelland has found that entrepreneurs and managers are especially likely to have a high need for achievement. In one study, for example, McClelland found that ten years after graduation, undergraduates who had shown a high need for achievement were more likely to be found in entrepreneurial occupations than were those who had shown a low need for achievement.[29] In addition, effective managers often have a strong goal orientation and tend to take moderate risks, a finding that is consistent with the profile of an individual with a high need for achievement.

Need for affiliation
The desire to establish and maintain good relations with others.

Individuals with a high **need for affiliation** are especially concerned about establishing and maintaining good relations with other people. They not only want to be liked by others but also want everyone to get along with everyone else. As you might expect, they like working in groups, tend to be sensitive to other people's feelings, and avoid taking actions that would result in interpersonal conflict. In organizations, individuals with a high need for affiliation are especially likely to be found in jobs that require a lot of social interaction. Although they make good team players, a manager might not want a group to be composed primarily of individuals with a high need for affiliation because the group might be more concerned about maintaining good interpersonal relations than about actually accomplishing the group's tasks. Individuals with a high need for affiliation may also be less effective in situations in which they need to evaluate others because it may be hard for them to give negative feedback to a coworker or a subordinate, a task that might disrupt interpersonal relations.

 **Need for power**
The desire to exert emotional and behavioral control or influence over others.

Individuals with a high **need for power** have a strong desire to exert emotional and behavioral control or influence over others.[30] These individuals are especially likely to be found in situations, such as in managerial jobs and leadership positions, that require one person to exert influence over others. Individuals with a high need for power may actually be more effective as leaders than those with a low need for power. In a study of the effectiveness of former presidents of the United States, for example, Robert House of the University of Pennsylvania and his colleagues found that a president's need for power predicted presidential performance or the president's effectiveness in office.[31] The levels of the presidents' need for power were assessed by analyzing their inaugural speeches for thoughts and ideas reflective of a high need for power.

When two individuals with strong needs for power both try to be influential in the same situation, trouble may ensue. The bankruptcy of a famous architectural firm, Johnson/Burgee Architects, and the personalities of the two principal architects who built and later destroyed the firm provide an interesting insight into the workings of the need for power. (See Insight 2.3.)

Insight 2.3 — **Personality**

Dueling Needs for Power

Philip Johnson is a renowned American architect who has designed many famous buildings, including AT&T's (www.att.com) headquarters in New York and the Pennzoil Center in Houston (www.pennzoil.com). In 1969 Johnson invited John Burgee (a competent architect but less well known than Johnson) to become his sole partner. They called their firm Johnson/Burgee Architects, and it thrived for many years.

From the 1980s to the early 1990s, however, trouble was brewing, in part because of both men's strong need for power. Johnson, the more famous of the two, sought to maintain his celebrity status. He tried to maintain tight control over the firm's design work and wanted Burgee to focus on managerial tasks and project administration. Because architectural design is the source of much of the status, glory, and recognition in architectural work, and Johnson was the guru of design, Johnson's name came to be associated with the firm's crowning achievements.

Burgee was not content to play second fiddle to Johnson. Burgee's own need for power led him to take steps to gain more control and influence within the firm and to raise his status in the architectural community. Because Johnson was aging and had recurrent health problems,

Burgee periodically eliminated Johnson's name from the name of the firm on company letterhead and reports and relegated Johnson to the status of a consultant. When Johnson continued to receive most of the attention from the architectural community, Burgee sought to limit Johnson's influence within the firm by, for example, specifying which projects he could and could not work on and asking him to direct any inquiries from the media to a public relations firm. Eventually, Burgee asked Johnson to leave the firm. Johnson's departure led several major clients to leave the firm. These problems, plus the loss of a lawsuit against the firm brought by another architect whom Burgee had asked to leave, resulted in the firm filing for Chapter 11 (bankruptcy).[32]

This saga illustrates an important point. It is often difficult for two individuals with a very strong need for power to try to run the same show. Johnson, the founder of the firm, had very strong influence and control over it, and his and the firm's reputation and status were one in the same. Because this set of circumstances helped to satisfy his need for power, he strove to maintain the status quo. Burgee, however, was not content to leave the reins of influence in Johnson's hands. Once Burgee gained experience and knowledge, his need for power propelled him to try to take over the firm. Burgee wanted not only power and influence over the firm itself but also the status and reputation that go with such power. With two men, each with a strong need for power, trying to reign over the same domain, disaster was bound to strike.

What combination of the needs for achievement, affiliation, and power results in higher managerial motivation and performance? Although it might seem that high levels of all three are important for managerial effectiveness, research by Michael Stahl suggests that managers should have a high need for achievement and power.[33] A high need for affiliation might not necessarily be a good quality in managers because they may try too hard to be liked by their subordinates instead of trying to lead them to higher performance levels. Stahl's findings on managerial effectiveness primarily apply to lower- and middle-level managers. For top executives and managers, the need for power appears to be the need that dominates all others in determining their success.[34]

HOW PERSONALITY IS MEASURED

We have been discussing the various traits that make up an individual's personality without much mention of how to determine an individual's standing on any of these traits. By far the most common and cost-effective means of assessing the personality traits of adults is through scales developed to measure personality. To complete these scales, individuals answer a series of questions about themselves. Figures 2.5, 2.6, and 2.8 provide examples of scales that measure positive affectivity, negative affectivity, and self-monitoring. Personality scales like these are often used for research purposes—for example, to determine how people who vary on these traits respond to different work situations. Although the use of such scales always runs the risk of respondents intentionally distorting their answers to portray themselves in a desirable fashion, research suggests that this is not a significant problem.[35]

TO MANAGERS

Personality Traits

- Realize and accept that some workers are more likely than others to be positive and enthusiastic because of their personalities. Similarly, realize and accept that some workers are more likely than others to complain and experience stress because of their personalities.
- Provide an extra measure of direct supervision to workers who don't take the initiative to solve problems on their own and always seem to blame someone or something else when things go wrong.
- Provide additional encouragement and support to workers with low self-esteem who tend to belittle themselves and question their abilities.
- Realize and accept that Type A individuals can be difficult to get along with and sometimes have a hard time working in teams.
- Let subordinates who seem overly concerned about other people liking them know that sometimes it is necessary to give honest feedback and be constructively critical (such as when supervising others).

 Ability
The mental or physical capacity to do something.

The Nature of Ability

While looking at individual differences and the way they affect the attitudes and behaviors of workers, we must look not only at each worker's personality but also at the *abilities, aptitudes,* and *skills* the worker possesses. Those terms are often used interchangeably. In our discussion, however, we focus on **ability,** which has been defined as "what a person is capable of doing."[36] Ability has important implications for understanding and managing organizational behavior. It determines the level of performance a worker can achieve, and because the effectiveness of an organization as a whole depends on the performance levels of all individual workers—from janitors and clerks to upper managers and the CEO—ability is an important determinant of organizational performance. Two basic types of ability affect performance: cognitive or mental ability and physical ability.

COGNITIVE ABILITY

Psychologists have identified many types of cognitive ability and grouped them in a hierarchy. The most general dimension of cognitive ability is *general intelligence.*[37] Below general intelligence are specific types of cognitive ability that reflect competence in different areas of mental functioning (see Fig. 2.9). Eight types of cognitive ability identified and described by psychologist Jum Nunnally, whose work was based in part on the pioneering work of L. L. and T. G. Thurstone in the 1940s, are described in Table 2.1.[38]

PHYSICAL ABILITY

People differ not only in cognitive ability but also in physical ability. Two types of physical ability are motor skill and physical skill.[39] *Motor skill* is the ability to physically manipulate objects in an environment. *Physical skill* is a person's fitness and strength. E. A. Fleishman has devoted considerable attention to identifying and studying physical ability and has concluded that there are eleven basic motor skills (such as reaction time, manual dexterity, and speed

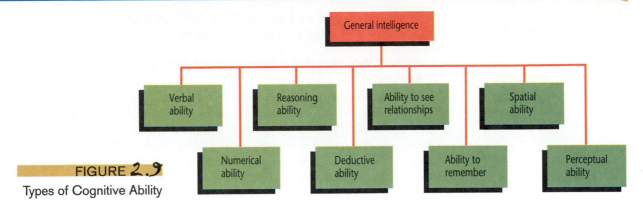

FIGURE **2.9**

Types of Cognitive Ability

TABLE **2.1**

Cognitive Abilities

Ability	Description	Examples of Jobs in which the Ability Is Especially Important
Verbal ability	Ability to understand and use written and spoken language	Comedians, teachers, lawyers, writers
Numerical ability	Ability to solve arithmetic problems and deal with numbers	Waiters, investment bankers, engineers, accountants
Reasoning ability	Ability to come up with solutions for problems and understand the principles by which different problems can be solved	Therapists, interior designers, car mechanics, computer software designers
Deductive ability	Ability to reach appropriate conclusions from an array of observations or evaluate the implications of a series of facts	Medical researchers, detectives, scientists, investigative reporters
Ability to see relationships	The ability to see how two things are related to each other and then apply this knowledge to other relationships and solutions	Anthropologists, travel agents, consultants, wedding planners
Ability to remember	Ability to recall things ranging from simple associations to complex groups of statements or sentences	Translators, salespeople, managers researchers
Spatial ability	Ability to determine the location or arrangement of objects in relation to one's own position and to imagine how an object would appear if its position in space were altered	Air traffic controllers, architects, clothing designers, astronauts
Perceptual	Ability to uncover visual patterns and see relationships within and across patterns	Professional photographers, airplane pilots, cruise ship captains, landscape designers

Based, in part, on J.C. Nunnally, *Psychometric Theory,* 2nd ed. (New York: McGraw-Hill, 1978).

of arm movement) and nine physical skills (such as static strength, which includes the ability to lift weights and stamina).[40]

WHERE DO ABILITIES COME FROM AND HOW ARE THEY MEASURED?

Like personality, both cognitive ability and physical ability are determined by nature and nurture (see Fig. 2.10). General intelligence is determined by the genes we inherit from our parents (nature)[41] and by situational factors (nurture). Standardized tests such as the GMAT (General Management Aptitude Test) or the SAT (Scholastic Aptitude Test) are designed to measure certain basic aptitudes and abilities that people are probably born with, but we know that people's scores on these tests change over time and that situational changes such as repeated training on practice exams can improve performance on the tests. Moreover, an individual may be genetically endowed with superior intelligence, but if that person grows up in a severely impoverished environment (characterized by poor nutrition, parents who are drug abusers, or irregular attendance at school), his or her scores on standard intelligence tests will probably suffer.

Both nature and nurture also determine physical ability. Height, bone structure, limb length, and relative proportions are genetically determined and cannot be changed. Through practice and training such as weight lifting and aerobic exercise, however, people can enhance some of their physical and motor skills.

Researchers have developed many accurate paper-and-pencil measures of cognitive ability, so managers can often rely on the results of tests that have been shown to be useful indicators of the underlying ability they are measuring. These tests can be used to ensure that prospective employees have the types of ability necessary to perform a job, to place existing employees in different jobs in an organization, to identify individuals who might need additional training, and to evaluate how successful training programs are in raising ability levels (we discuss each of these issues in the next section). Before using any of these tests, however, managers have to make sure that the tests are ethical and do not unfairly discriminate against different kinds of employees. Some tests of cognitive ability have been criticized for being culturally biased. Critics say that they ask questions that, because of differences in the test takers' ethnic backgrounds, may be relatively easy for members of certain groups to answer and more difficult for members of other groups to answer.

Physical ability can be measured by having a person engage in the relevant activity. Managers who need to see whether a prospective employee is strong enough to deliver, unpack, and set up heavy appliances could ask the individual to lift progressively heavier weights to determine the level of his or her static strength. New York City evaluates the physical ability of prospective sanitation workers by having them pick up trash bags and toss them into garbage trucks.

FIGURE 2.10

Nature and Nurture: The Determinants of Cognitive and Physical Abilities

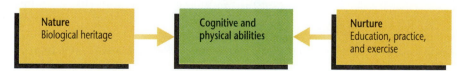

Cognitive and physical abilities can degenerate or become impaired because of disease, drug or alcohol abuse, excessive levels of stress, or fatigue. In many organizations it is important to accurately assess ability level to know what a worker is capable of doing, and it is also necessary to know when and why ability may be impaired on the job. (See Insight 2.4.)

Insight 2.4

Ethics

Curbing Unethical Behavior: Testing for Ability Impairment

When organizations test ability levels, they assume that workers will perform their jobs using their highest level of ability. This assumption, however, is not always valid. Workers' abilities can be impaired by any number of factors, and such impairment may increase risk in certain types of jobs (such as transportation and medical treatment). For example, when the oil tanker Exxon Valdez ran aground, use of alcohol by the ship's captain was implicated, and numerous train derailments and collisions have been attributed to substance abuse by train operators. It is unethical for workers to perform their jobs with their abilities impaired, because they not only may hurt themselves but also may cause injury to other members of the organization and to the general public.

The connection between the use of alcohol or drugs and the impairment of a person's ability is usually straightforward. But there are cases in which the causes of impairment are much more subtle. Are the abilities of the medical intern who has just completed an eighteen-hour shift in the emergency room impaired by excessive fatigue and stress? Are the driving skills of the moonlighting taxicab driver who is also a single parent impaired by the heavy demands placed on her in her two jobs and at home?

Organizations' traditional response to potential impairment on the job is to test workers for substance abuse by means of urine analysis. Such testing may detect the presence of drugs and alcohol, but it does not tap into impairment due to other sources such as excessive fatigue. Another problem with urine tests is that it usually takes at least two to three days to get the results. In response to those problems, Essex Corporation (www.essexcorp.com) and other firms have developed "fitness for duty" performance tests to determine whether workers can safely perform their jobs. Some of these tests involve the use of computer terminals and games that measure accuracy and reaction time against a worker's baseline score. Although the accuracy of these tests has yet to be determined, the need for them is expected to increase. At least 4.5 million transportation workers in safety-relevant jobs are already required to take drug tests, and at least 1.5 million interstate truck drivers already undergo alcohol testing.

Given the magnitude of the impairment problem, some firms have already begun experimenting with the new performance tests. Domino's Pizza (www.dominos.com) has begun testing some of its truck drivers, warehouse workers, and dough makers with a test called Factor 1000 marketed by Performance Factors Inc. At the beginning of each workday, employees play a video game that assesses hand-eye coordination by testing their ability to center a swinging pointer on the screen of a computer. Workers who fail the test on any given day are reassigned to jobs where they cannot hurt themselves or anyone else. Three failures within ninety days result in a worker's agreeing to counseling. A California gasoline and diesel fuel company, R. F. White Co., reports a considerable reduction in accidents and errors since it started using the Factor 1000 test four years ago.

Factor 1000 is a relatively simple test. Other tests are more complicated. Essex Corporation's Delta system, for example, has twenty tests that measure reasoning, judgment, and spatial perception. Such tests can be costly, but proponents counter that they are preferable to the indignities of urine testing. Even unions seem to be split on the issue of performance testing. Some claim that organizations might use it as an excuse to get rid of certain types of workers (for example, older workers). Others view the tests as an improvement over alternatives such as urine analysis.[42] What does seem clear is that the impairment of abilities is an ethical issue that managers need to confront in any jobs where safety is a consideration.

EMOTIONAL INTELLIGENCE: A NEW KIND OF ABILITY

A new kind of ability, emotional intelligence, has been identified by psychologists that is not so much concerned with cognitive or physical capabilities but rather with emotional capabilities. *Emotional intelligence* is the ability to understand and manage one's own feelings and emotions and the feelings and emotions of others. People differ in terms of the extent to which they know how they are feeling, know why they are feeling that way, and are able to manage their feelings. Similarly, people differ in terms of the extent to which they understand how other people are feeling and why, and are able to influence or manage other people's feelings. Emotional intelligence describes these individual differences.[43]

Research on emotional intelligence is in its early stages. However, it is plausible that emotional intelligence may facilitate job performance in a number of ways, and a low level of emotional intelligence may actually impair performance. For example, psychologist Martin Seligman found that salespeople at Metropolitan Life who were high on optimism (an aspect of emotional intelligence) sold considerably more insurance policies than salespeople who were less able to manage their feelings and think positively.[44] For Sir Rocco Forte, CEO of Forte Hotels, the ability to understand how customers feel and determine what they want is key to excellent customer service.[45]

As a final example, consider the case of Jane, who was hired by George McCown of McCown Dee Leeuw, a buyout company in Menlo Park, California, to help determine which companies are good purchase opportunities. Jane was highly intelligent with excellent numerical skills and a top-notch educational background. McCown sent Jane to visit a company he was interested in purchasing. After visiting the company and performing various calculations, Jane advised McCown to buy the company because the numbers looked good. McCown, however, decided to visit the company himself, and he was glad he did. As he puts it, "I could tell in the first two minutes of talking to the CEO that he was experiencing serious burnout. The guy was being overwhelmed by problems. On paper, things looked great. But he knew what was coming down the line. Jane had missed those cues completely." Evidently, Jane's low level of emotional intelligence prevented her from understanding how and why the CEO of the targeted company was feeling; cues her boss was able to pick up on. Jane is no longer with McCown Dee Leeuw.[46]

The Management of Ability in Organizations

Although we have mentioned the many types of ability that people possess, only a few abilities are likely to be relevant for the performance of any particular job. Managerial work, for example, requires cognitive ability, not very many physical abilities, and probably some degree of emotional intelligence, whereas being a shelf stocker in a grocery store or a car washer requires mainly physical ability. A brain surgeon, for instance, must rely on cognitive and physical abilities when performing highly complicated and delicate operations.

For managers, the key issue regarding ability is to make sure that workers have the abilities they need to perform their jobs effectively. There are three fundamental ways to manage ability in organizations to ensure that this matchup happens: selection, placement, and training.

SELECTION

Managers can control ability in organizations by selecting individuals who have the abilities the organization needs. Managers have to identify the tasks they want the worker to accomplish. Then managers need to identify which abilities are needed to accomplish these tasks. Once these abilities are identified, managers need to develop accurate measures of these abilities. The key question at this point is whether a person's score on the ability measure actually predicts performance on the task in question. If it does not, there is no point in using the ability measure as a selection device, and it would be unethical to do so. An organization that uses an inappropriate measure and rejects capable applicants leaves itself open to potential lawsuits for unfair hiring practices. But if the ability measure does predict task performance, then managers can use it as a selection tool to ensure that the organization has the mix of abilities needed to accomplish organizational goals.

PLACEMENT

Once individuals are selected and become part of an organization, managers must accurately match each worker to a job that will capitalize on his or her abilities. Again, managers need to identify the ability requirements of the jobs to be filled, and they need accurate measures of these abilities. Once these measures are available, the aim is to place workers in positions that match their abilities. Placement, however, involves more than just assigning new workers to appropriate positions. It is also an issue in horizontal moves or promotions within the organization. Obviously, an organization wants to promote only its most able workers to higher-level positions.

Large companies, like General Electric, Arthur Andersen, and Wal-Mart are well-known for the time and money they spend training their new employees so that they can perform at the high level these organizations require.

TRAINING

Selection and placement, as ability management techniques, are concerned with *nature* aspects of ability. Training acknowledges that *nurture* also contributes to ability levels. Training can be an effective means of enhancing workers' abilities. We often think that the goal of training is to improve workers' ability beyond the minimum level required. Frequently, however, organizations use training to bring workers' skills up to some minimum required level. (See Insight 2.5.)

Competitive Advantage

Training in the Basics: Workplace Literacy and Reading, Writing, and Arithmetic

To gain a competitive advantage, organizations often need to use new and advanced technology to lower costs and increase quality, efficiency, and performance. Companies that use advanced technology often find that their workers' abilities and skills are deficient in a number of ways. In the factories of the past, workers could get by with sheer physical strength and stamina; but those days are gone forever, and automation and computer technology require higher levels of skill. Many U.S. workers lack even basic abilities in reading, writing, and arithmetic. The Work in America Institute estimates that about 30 million workers in the United States are illiterate. Ford Motor Company, General Motors, and Chrysler have invested millions of dollars in training initiatives, and the need for more training is one issue on which union officials and management agree.[47]

The need for training became obvious at Collins & Aikman, a carpet firm, when it computerized its factory to remain competitive.[48] Workers started to tell managers that they couldn't work with computers. Managers soon realized that they had significantly underestimated the number of workers needed to keep the factory running, because workers who could read and perform necessary calculations were covering for those who could not. A little probing indicated that about a third of the factory's workforce had not completed high school.

Rather than resorting to drastic measures such as abandoning the new technology or moving production overseas where labor costs are cheaper, Collins & Aikman decided to equip the workers with the skills they needed to be competitive. An adult education instructor was hired to teach classes two days a week on every shift; the classes covered reading, writing, science, social studies, and math. Workers, some of them older, were at first apprehensive about taking classes, but the instructor's warmth and agreeableness soon overcame their misgivings and embarrassment over their own shortcomings.

So far, Collins & Aikman's investment seems to be paying off. Productivity is up, returns due to poor quality are down, and workers are feeling more confident about their new jobs. Worker morale and even health seem to have improved (judging by the number of sick days taken), and even workers' children may be benefiting because their parents are encouraging them to stay in school.[49] Such programs are not without their drawbacks, however. Intensive training can put a lot of demands on workers who may already be at their limit because of their work and home responsibilities. It can be pretty difficult to do homework in the evening after a full day's work in the office and an early evening of taking care of the children and other household responsibilities.

Training is seen by some as the key to the struggle of the United States to maintain its competitiveness in the global economy. Indeed, the United States may learn from looking at training initiatives in other countries such as Germany and Japan. (See Insight 2.6.)

Insight 2.6

A Global View

Training Abroad

If America is to maintain its competitiveness in the global economy, training needs to be one of its top priorities. Given the dramatic and rapid changes in technology and other areas, workers need to be able to change jobs and careers several times in their working lives. The jobs of the future will increasingly demand that workers be knowledgeable, have technological skills, be able to communicate, and be flexible. The primary and secondary school systems in the United States, however, are not preparing students for these realities, and many companies think that the primary responsibility for training does not reside with corporate America.[50]

The United States invests only about half of the amount of money that Japan and Germany invest in worker training (on a per capita basis).[51] Moreover, America does little to help workers with their career planning. In contrast, Germany has intensive apprenticeship and skill enhancement programs. In fact, it is useful to look to Germany's experiences in training to try to gain some insight into what America might need to do to maintain its global competitiveness.[52]

Take, for example, the case of Andreas Mayr, a 17-year-old German mechanic. He is proficient in college-level math, physics, and chemistry and has experienced few problems in handling a complex production line after two years as an apprentice. German companies spend around $17 billion annually on apprentice training and $18 billion on the retraining of existing workers. Once students finish secondary school, those not going on to college apply to companies for apprenticeships. This system ensures that workers have the skills that companies need, and eventually it results in a highly skilled and flexible workforce. During their apprenticeship, workers spend one or two days a week in classes at a career school (similar to a junior college in America) and the remainder of the week in an organization where a very skilled worker teaches them how to operate machinery, work with computers, and perform other tasks. Training can be costly (up to $75,000 per year per trainee), but it seems to be paying off in a skilled workforce.[53] It appears that the United States will have to beef up its training of workers both in basic and in advanced skills if it is to remain globally competitive. More than likely, government initiatives at the primary and secondary school levels and an increased commitment by corporate America to skills training will be needed.

SUMMARY

The two main types of individual differences are personality differences and ability differences. Understanding the nature, determinants, and consequences of individual differences is essential for managing organizational behavior. Because people differ so much from each other, an appreciation of the nature of individual differences is necessary to understand why people act the way they do in organizations. In this chapter, we made the following major points:

1. Personality is the pattern of relatively enduring ways in which a person feels, thinks, and behaves. Personality is determined both by nature (biological heritage) and nurture (situational factors). Organizational outcomes that have been shown to be predicted by personality include job satisfaction, work stress, and leadership effectiveness. Personality is not a useful predictor of organizational outcomes when there are strong situational constraints. Because personality tends to be stable over time, managers should not expect to change personality in the short run. Managers should accept workers' personalities as they are and develop effective ways to deal with people.

2. Feelings, thoughts, attitudes, and behaviors in an organization are determined by the interaction of personality and situation.

3. The Big Five personality traits are extraversion (positive affectivity), neuroticism (negative affectivity), agreeableness, conscientiousness, and openness to experience. Other personality traits particularly relevant to organizational behavior include locus of control, self-monitoring, self-esteem, Type A and Type B personality, and the needs for achievement, affiliation, and power.

4. In addition to possessing different personalities, workers also differ in their abilities, or what they are capable of doing. The two major types of ability are cognitive ability and physical ability.

5. Types of cognitive ability can be arranged in a hierarchy with general intelligence at the top. Specific types of cognitive ability are verbal ability, numerical ability, reasoning ability, deductive ability, ability to see relationships, ability to remember, spatial ability, and perceptual ability.

6. There are two types of physical ability: motor skills (the ability to manipulate objects) and physical skills (a person's fitness and strength).

7. Both nature and nurture contribute to determining physical ability and cognitive ability. A third, recently identified, ability is emotional intelligence.

8. In organizations, ability can be managed by selecting individuals who have the abilities needed to accomplish tasks, placing workers in jobs that capitalize on their abilities, and training workers to enhance their ability levels.

Organizational Behavior in Action

1. Why is it important to understand that both nature and nurture shape a worker's personality?
2. What are some situations in which you would *not* expect workers' personalities to influence their behavior?
3. What are some situations in which you would expect workers' personalities to influence their behavior?
4. Is it good for organizations to be composed of individuals with similar personalities? Why or why not?
5. A lawyer needs to score high on which of the Big Five personality traits? Why?
6. What are some jobs or situations in which workers high on agreeableness would be especially effective?
7. When might self-monitoring be dysfunctional in an organization?
8. What levels of the needs for achievement, power, and affiliation might be desirable for an elementary school teacher?
9. What types of cognitive ability are especially important for an upper-level manager (such as the president of a division) to possess? Why?
10. Think of a job for which emotional intelligence might be an especially important ability for the jobholder to possess. Find someone in your local community who has this kind of job and interview them to determine the extent to which they actively try to manage their own emotions or the emotions of others at work.

BUILDING DIAGNOSTIC SKILLS

Characteristics of People and Jobs

Choose a job that you are very familiar with—a job that you currently have, a job that you used to have, or the job of a close family member or friend. Or the job could be one that you have been able to observe closely during your interaction with an organization as a customer, client, or patient. For the job of your choosing, respond to the following items.

1. Describe the job, including all the tasks that the jobholder must perform.
2. Choose two of the Big Five personality traits that you think would have the most impact on the jobholder's feelings, thoughts, attitudes, and behaviors. Explain why you think these traits might be particularly important for understanding the jobholder's reactions.
3. Identify three of the organizationally relevant personality traits that you think would impact performance on this job, and explain why you think they are likely to be important.
4. Which of the jobholder's behaviors are primarily determined by the situation and not personality?
5. What cognitive abilities must the jobholder possess?

6. What physical abilities must the jobholder possess?
7. How can selection and placement be used to ensure that prospective job-holders have these abilities?
8. How can an organization train jobholders to raise levels of these abilities?

RESEARCH ON THE INTERNET: A MANAGER'S TOOL

Specific Task

Dell Computer Corporation is one of many companies who try to ensure that their employees' characteristics and abilities are well-suited to their jobs. Scan Dell's website (www.dell.com) to learn more about this major producer of personal computers. Then, click on "Careers" (great2b@dell) and then click on 3 ("What can you do"). Complete the survey as honestly as possible. Then click on "Result." Review your career suggestions. Do you think these are good career suggestions for you given your personality and abilities? Why or why not?

General Task

Think of a well-known, large corporation that you are familiar with. Go to the website of this company. Scan the website to learn more about the company. Then, find and read any information on the website about the company's CEO (or another top manager who is profiled on the website). From what you have read, which personality traits does this top manager seem to be high on? Which abilities does he or she seem to possess?

TOPICS FOR DEBATE

Personality and ability have major implications for how people feel, think, and behave in organizations. Now that you have a good understanding of these individual differences, debate the following issues.

Debate One

Team A. Organizations should select or hire prospective employees on the basis of their personality traits.

Team B. Organizations should *not* select or hire prospective employees on the basis of their personality traits.

Debate Two

Team A. Organizations should view the ability levels of their members as relatively fixed. The management of ability should focus on selection and placement.

Team B. Organizations should view the ability levels of their members as changeable. The management of ability should focus on training.

EXPERIENTIAL EXERCISE

Individual Differences in Teams

Objective

In organizations like Merck & Co., the pharmaceuticals giant, and Microsoft Corporation, the leading producer of computer software, research scientists or computer programmers often work together in small teams on complex, path-breaking projects to create new drugs or computer software. Team members interact closely, often over long time periods, in order to complete their projects. Individual differences in personality and ability provide teams not only with valued resources needed to complete their projects but also with potential sources of conflict and problems. Your objective is to understand how individual differences in personality and ability affect people's behavior in teams.

Procedure

The class divides into groups of from three to five people, and each group appoints one member as spokesperson, to present the group's findings to the whole class. Each group discusses how the personalities and abilities of team members may impact team performance and may cause conflict and problems. Using the knowledge of personality and ability gained in this chapter, each group answers the following questions.

1. Do certain personality traits make people good team members? If so, what are they and why are they important? If not, why not?
2. Is it more effective for teams to be composed of members who have different personality types or similar personality types?
3. What kinds of abilities make people good team members?
4. Should team members have similar or different kinds and levels of abilities?

When all the groups are finished discussing these issues, the spokespersons take turns presenting their groups' findings to the rest of the class, and the instructor lists the findings on the board.

MAKING THE CONNECTION

Find an example of a manager who has helped or hurt his or her organization in an important way. For example, the manager may have helped the organization to develop new and successful products or find new customers, or the manager may have behaved in an unethical fashion or driven customers away. What personality traits may have influenced this manager's behavior? What abilities may have contributed to this manager's success or failure?

CLOSING CASE

Procter & Gamble's "Wrecking Ball"

Edwin L. Artzt, former chairman of Procter & Gamble (www.pg.com), made revolutionary changes in how this consumer products giant markets its products. Perhaps most dramatic, however, were the internal changes he brought about—changes that have earned him the nickname "Wrecking Ball."[54]

Many of these changes reflect Artzt's personal style and way of managing. Artzt has no patience for what he views as substandard performance. Stories abound of his demanding and harsh treatment of subordinates.

When Artzt was dissatisfied with the way managers were marketing Noxzema skin cream, he indicated his disgust by asking them, "How could you people be so stupid to get into this mess?" He railed at them for more than half an hour until someone reminded him that Procter & Gamble had just acquired Noxzema and the managers in question had been assigned to that product for less than two months.

When Artzt had a disagreement with managers in Taiwan concerning the launching of the Oil of Olay product line in that geographic market, he was reported to have called them "stupid" and "imbecilic" and supposedly went so far as to suggest that "You'd better be right, because if you're not, you're all going to be cleaning toilets."

Dissatisfied with the lack of foreign sales of the domestically successful shampoo product Pert Plus, Artzt railed against managers who claimed they lacked manufacturing capabilities and suggested they use a tent to produce the product. One manager involved in this incident said that Artzt certainly got them to increase production of Pert Plus and thus helped propel Procter & Gamble into the arena of global marketing.

Artzt appears to be just as demanding of himself as he is of the managers who report to him. During his forty-year climb up the corporate ladder at Procter & Gamble, he has worked in practically every division of the company. He approaches his work with exceptional intensity and pays close attention to detail. Artzt has been characterized as a workaholic who turns out vast quantities of work and gets involved in all aspects of a product such as Old Spice, from advertising plans to the color of packaging. He has been known to call his subordinates in the middle of the night about work-related problems, and he reads the 120 reports a month that they prepare.

Managers' reactions to Artzt were mixed. Those who tired of Artzt's browbeating left Procter & Gamble and took positions elsewhere. Some of those who remained claim that Artzt pushes them to do their best. Others fear that his harshness prompts subordinates to concentrate on doing what he wants rather than coming up with their own creative ideas.

The marketing changes that Artzt wrought at Procter & Gamble also have gotten mixed reviews. On the one hand he has been commended for getting rid of unprofitable products such as Citrus Hill orange juice and expanding Procter & Gamble's international sales and cosmetic lines. More than half of Procter & Gamble's sales are now from countries other than the United States, making it a truly global organization.[55] On the other hand, Artzt's strategy of everyday low pricing had raised some eyebrows. In any case, his ability as a marketer is generally hailed, and the numbers confirm it.[56] In 1994, Procter and Gamble made $2.2 billion in profits, its highest level in twenty-one years.[57]

When Artzt retired in 1995 (he remains a member of the board of directors), his job was split into two positions, and veteran Procter & Gamble managers John Pepper and Durk Jager were named Chairman and CEO, respectively. Pepper is a well-liked manager who tries to get along with his subordinates, involves others in decision making, often considers how his decisions will affect other people such as employees and stockholders, and occasionally seems shy. Jager, Artzt's protégé, is more like Artzt than Pepper. He tends to be impatient, abrasive, and intimidating.[58] At the time of their appointments, there was much skepticism about how these two managers with such different personalities could ever get along and run a huge corporation. Surprisingly enough, Jager and Pepper seem to be getting along, Pepper focusing on long-term growth while Jager concentrates on the actual day-to-day running of Procter & Gamble. While Jager is still relatively impatient, Pepper's more mellow nature seems to have rubbed off on him, resulting in his being a bit easier to get along with.[59]

Questions for Discussion
1. When he was chairman of Procter & Gamble, why did you think Edwin Artzt acted the way he did?
2. Why did managers who reported to Artzt have different reactions to his demanding and sometimes harsh treatment?
3. Why do you think Pepper and Jager are working well together despite their different personalities and styles?

The Experience of Work: Values, Attitudes, and Moods

3

OPENING CASE

Meaning and Contentment on the Job

A decade of layoffs and downsizings have made many employees aware of the fact that their jobs may not be secure. Prior to the widespread layoffs in the 1980's and 1990's, workers who were performing monotonous, routine jobs at least could rest assured that their jobs and economic  well-being were secure. Layoffs and downsizings have not only diminished workers' levels of job security but also have often increased the work demands placed on those workers who remain in a company after a layoff. Some managers are responding to this decrease in security and increase in work demands by helping their employees find more meaning, contentment, and even fun on the job. They are striving to help their employees enjoy and derive meaning from the actual work they perform, promote job satisfaction, and make work more fun.

Take the case of Doreen Dickey, who gets paid $9.00 an hour to scrape and sand leftover sealant on the seats of restaurant chairs manufactured by Foldcraft Corp. in Kenyon, Minnesota. When Dickey first took this job, she thought it would be mind-numbing and boring. However, managers at Foldcraft asked for Dickey's input on how to improve the processes she used on her job and sent her on an educational trip to Guatemala and El Salvador to visit and learn about manufacturing and factory work in these Central American countries. While her day-to-day work may still be somewhat boring, Dickey takes pride in what she does and sees why her job is important.[1]

Foldcraft is not alone in trying to build more meaning and satisfaction into jobs of rank-and-file workers. For example, managers at Web Industries, a Massachusetts manufacturing company, allow assembly-line workers to take breaks from their work to read intellectually stimulating books. Managers at Silicon Graphics, Inc., a computer manufacturer based in California, give fifty employees a year Spirit awards for such things as creativity or seeking solutions to problems. Winners of Spirit awards not only have the privilege of joining a management advisory board for a year but also enjoy a paid Hawaiian vacation for two.

Pat Sullivan, a legal secretary in California, found her own way to feel good on the job. Her job is often stressful, performing secretarial duties for attorneys who always seem to be in a rush. Sullivan set aside a part of her desk for some of her favorite treasured possessions. When she feels stress setting in, she focuses on a small painting or holds a treasured keepsake for a few minutes to keep things in perspective.[2]

Some managers are trying to lighten up the workplace and promote positive feelings and job satisfaction by deliberately building in time for activities on the job that are fun. The communications company Sprint (www.sprint.com), recently held a Fun at Work day for its 3,000 employees in regional offices. Part of the day's activities included the employees dividing up into teams and trying to take the funniest photographs of themselves. As Sprint executive Margery Tippen puts it, "We believe employees who have fun feel appreciated, come together as a team, and are more productive, which ultimately benefits our customers."[3] Other companies are hiring humor consultants to help managers inject fun and humor into the workplace. All in all, more meaning, job satisfaction, and plain old fun may be just what over-stretched and insecure workers need.

Overview

What people think and feel about work in general, and about their jobs and organizations in particular, affects not only how they behave at work but also their overall well-being—how happy, healthy, and prosperous they are. In the opening case, we described how a sense of meaning, job satisfaction, contentment, and even fun may be advantageous for organizations and their members and may help workers deal with increasing levels of demands at work and lower levels of job security. In this chapter we focus on the thoughts and feelings that determine how people experience work and the ways in which these thoughts and feelings affect organizational behavior. We discuss work values, attitudes, and moods—the different types of thoughts and feelings people have about work in general, and about their jobs and organizations in particular. We describe the nature and consequences of two of the most widely studied work attitudes: job satisfaction and organizational commitment. By the end of this chapter you will have a good appreciation of the range of thoughts and feelings central to the experience of work and the implications of these thoughts and feelings for understanding and managing organizational behavior.

Work Values, Attitudes, and Moods

The thoughts and feelings people have about work, their jobs, and their organizations determine how they experience work. Some thoughts and feelings are fundamental and broad; they are concerned not so much with aspects of a particular job or organization but with the nature of work in general. These thoughts and feelings, called *work values,* are relatively long lasting. Other thoughts and feelings are more specific. Those that are focused directly on a person's current job or organization, called *work attitudes,* are not as long lasting as work values. *Work moods*—that is, how people feel while they are performing their jobs from day to day, hour to hour, and even minute to minute—also determine how people experience work. Below, we describe each of these determinants of how people experience work.

THE NATURE OF WORK VALUES

Work values
A worker's personal convictions about what outcomes one should expect from work and how one should behave at work.

Work values are a worker's personal convictions about what outcomes one should expect from work and how one should behave at work.[4] Outcomes that people might expect to obtain through work include a comfortable existence with family security, a sense of accomplishment and self-respect, or social recognition and an exciting life. Ways people think they should behave at

This social worker is on a routine visit to a poor Chicago family. Social workers tend to have intrinsic work values and are motivated by the desire to care for and protect other people.

work include being ambitious, being imaginative, and being obedient, self-controlled, and respectful to one's supervisor.[5] Work values also guide *ethical behavior* at work; some people's work values stress the importance of being honest, trustworthy, and helping others whenever possible. Work values are the most general and long-lasting feelings and beliefs people have that contribute to how they experience work.

Why are work values important for understanding and managing organizational behavior? They reflect what people are trying to achieve through and at work. A worker who thinks that he should learn new things on the job, for example, will be unhappy working as a cashier in a supermarket because once he has learned how to use the cash register, there will be little opportunity for any further learning. His unhappiness may, in turn, cause him to be less helpful to customers or more likely to look for another job.

The work values that researchers in organizational behavior have identified generally fall into two broad categories: intrinsic work values and extrinsic work values (see Table 3.1).[6]

Intrinsic Work Values.   **Intrinsic work values** are values that are related to the nature of the work itself. Workers who desire to be challenged, learn new things, make important contributions, and reach their full potential on their jobs have intrinsic work values. These workers want challenging jobs that use all of their skills and abilities and provide them with responsibility and autonomy (the ability to make decisions) while at the same time providing opportunities for personal growth. In the opening case, Silicone Graphics' efforts to support and encourage creativity may help some workers achieve their intrinsic work values. Even on relatively monotonous jobs, some elements of intrinsic work values may be important, as they were for Doreen Dickey in the opening case, who has a sense of pride in her work and its importance. People who personally value and desire intrinsically interesting work often assume that everyone else does too, but this is not necessarily the case.

Intrinsic work values
Work values that are related to the nature of work itself.

Extrinsic Work Values.   Rather than valuing features of the work itself, some workers have **extrinsic work values,** values that are related to the consequences of work. Workers whose primary reason for working is to earn money,

Extrinsic work values
Work values that are related to the consequences of work.

TABLE 3.1
A Comparison of Intrinsic and Extrinsic Work Values

Intrinsic Work Values	Extrinsic Work Values
Interesting work	High pay
Challenging work	Job security
Learning new things	Job benefits
Making important contributions	Status in wider community
Reaching full potential at work	Social contacts
Responsibility and autonomy	Time with family
Being creative	Time for hobbies

for example, have extrinsic work values. They see work primarily as a means of providing economic security for themselves and their families. These workers value their work not for its own sake but for its consequences. Other extrinsic work values include a job's status in the organization and in the wider community, social contacts provided by the job, and the extent to which a job enables a worker to spend time with his or her family, pursue a hobby, or volunteer for a worthy cause.

The Relationship Between Extrinsic and Intrinsic Work Values.   Because working is the way most people make a living, there is an extrinsic element to most people's work values, but many people have both extrinsic and intrinsic work values. Extrinsic and intrinsic work values differ in their relative importance from one person to another. An elementary school teacher who likes teaching but quits her job to take a higher-paying position as a sales representative for a computer company has stronger extrinsic than intrinsic work values. A social worker who puts up with low pay and little thanks because he feels that he is doing something important by helping disadvantaged families and their children has stronger intrinsic than extrinsic work values.

When making changes in the workplace, managers need to take into account workers' values. Managers may try to increase workers' motivation by making their work more interesting, giving workers more freedom to make their own decisions, or expanding the number of activities a worker performs (see Chapters 6, 7, and 8 for details on motivation). A manager might try to increase the motivation of a computer sales representative by requiring her to call on different types of customers and by giving her the responsibility for setting up the equipment a customer purchases.

The success of such approaches to increasing motivation, however, depends on the extent to which the change in a worker's job relates to the worker's values. Making the work of the computer sales representative more interesting and challenging may do little to increase her motivation if her strong extrinsic work values result in her being motivated primarily by the money she earns. Indeed, these efforts may actually backfire if the sales representative thinks she is working harder on her job but not receiving any additional financial compensation. Workers who are extrinsically motivated may be much more responsive to financial incentives (such as bonuses) and job security than to changes in the work itself.

Because work values reflect what workers are trying to achieve through working, they hold the key to understanding how workers will react to different events in the workplace and to understanding and managing organizational behavior. Managers need to be especially sensitive to the work values of their subordinates when making changes in jobs, working hours, or other aspects of the work situation.

THE NATURE OF WORK ATTITUDES

Work attitudes
Collections of feelings, beliefs, and thoughts about how to behave in one's job and organization.

Work attitudes are collections of feelings, beliefs, and thoughts about how to behave that people currently hold about their jobs and organizations. More specific than values, work attitudes are not as long lasting as values because the way people experience their jobs and organizations often changes over time. Such changes are due in part to changes in the work situation, such as being given or denied a promotion. Moreover, workers often change jobs and organizations. Such work changes often result in attitude changes; work values, in contrast, can and often do remain constant from job to job and organization to organization. Two work attitudes that have especially important implications for organizational behavior are job satisfaction and organizational commitment.

Job satisfaction is the collection of feelings and beliefs that people have about their current jobs. People's levels or degrees of job satisfaction can range from extreme satisfaction to extreme dissatisfaction. In addition to having attitudes about their jobs as a whole, people also can have attitudes about various aspects of their jobs—such as the kind of work they do; their coworkers, supervisors, or subordinates; their pay.

Organizational commitment is the collection of feelings and beliefs that people have about their organization as a whole. Levels of commitment can range from being extremely high to extremely low, and people can have attitudes about various aspects of their organization—such as the organization's promotion practices, the quality of the organization's products, and the organization's stance on ethical issues.

Work attitudes like job satisfaction and organizational commitment are made up of three components: feelings, the affective component; beliefs, the cognitive component; and thoughts about how to behave, the behavioral component (see Fig. 3.1).[7] For example, the *affective component* of a social worker's attitude is the worker's *feelings* about his or her job or organization. The *cognitive component* is the worker's *beliefs* about the job or organization. (He or she believes the job is meaningful and important.) The *behavioral component* is the worker's *thoughts about how to behave* in his or her job or organization. Each component of a work attitude influences and tends to be consistent with the other components.

Because job satisfaction and organizational commitment are key determinants of the experience of work and are central to understanding and managing organizational behavior, we explore these two work attitudes in depth later in the chapter. At this point, however, it is interesting to explore how work attitudes like job satisfaction vary across countries. (See Insight 3.1.)

> **Job satisfaction**
> The collection of feelings and beliefs that people have about their current jobs.

> **Organizational commitment**
> The collection of feelings and beliefs that people have about their organization as a whole.

FIGURE 3.1

Components of Work Attitudes

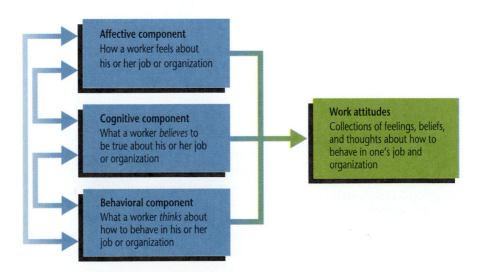

A Global View

Work Attitudes: Some Cross-Cultural Comparisons

Louis Harris and Associates conducted a worldwide poll of job satisfaction levels for Steelcase, an office furniture maker. Although the popular press might lead you to believe that the Japanese are more satisfied with their jobs than Americans are, this is not the case. For example, only 17 percent of Japanese office workers were very satisfied with their jobs, the lowest rate of any of the fifteen countries included in the Harris survey. By contrast, 43 percent of the surveyed U.S. workers indicated that they were very satisfied. U.S. workers were also more satisfied than workers in Canada and the European Union.[8]

Also illuminating were responses to questions regarding different aspects of the workers' jobs and employing organizations. Forty percent of U.S. workers indicated that their managers were honest and ethical, but only 16 percent of Japanese workers attributed those qualities to their managers. Japanese workers were also less satisfied than their U.S. counterparts about pay and benefits, job challenges, recognition, and their employer's responsiveness to family needs. The next time you read laments about low morale in American industry, keep these cross-cultural comparisons in mind. The grass is not necessarily greener on the other side.

THE NATURE OF WORK MOODS

Work moods
How people feel at the time they actually perform their jobs.

Work moods are how people feel at the time they actually perform their jobs. Some workers tend to feel excited and enthusiastic at work, others feel anxious and nervous, and still others feel sleepy and sluggish. Much more transitory than values and attitudes, work moods can change from hour to hour, day to day, and sometimes minute to minute. Think about how your own moods have varied since you woke up today or about how your moods today differ from how you felt yesterday. Then you will have some idea about the fluctuating nature of work moods.

Although people can experience many different moods at work, moods can be categorized generally as positive or negative. When workers are in *positive moods,* they feel excited, enthusiastic, active, strong, peppy, or elated. When workers are in *negative moods,* they feel distressed, fearful, scornful, hostile, jittery, or nervous. Sometimes workers' feelings are neither strongly positive nor negative; they may simply experience less intense feelings, such as being drowsy, dull, and sluggish or calm, placid, and relaxed.[9] The extent to which workers experience positive, negative, and less intense moods at work is determined by both their personalities and the situation.

Recall from Chapter 2 that workers who are high on the personality trait of *positive affectivity* are more likely than other workers to experience positive moods at work, and workers who are high on the trait of *negative affectivity* are more likely to experience negative moods at work. A wide range of situational factors also affect work mood—major events and conditions such as receiving a promotion (or a demotion) and getting along well with one's coworkers, and relatively minor conditions such as how pleasant the physical surroundings are.[10] If you stop and think a minute about the different factors that influence your own moods—weather, pressures of school or family life, your love life, and so on—you will see that many of them have the potential to influence a worker's mood on the job. Many circumstances that are not work related can impact mood at work. Getting engaged, for example, may put a worker in a very good mood both on and off the job, but having a big argument with one's spouse may put a worker in a very bad mood.

Researchers have just begun to explore the consequences of mood at work for organizational behavior, but preliminary research suggests that mood at work has important consequences for understanding and managing organizational behavior. Workers in positive moods at work, for example, are more likely to be helpful to each other and to those around them, including clients and customers, and may also be less likely to be absent from their jobs.[11] One study found that salespeople who were in positive moods at work provided higher-quality service to customers in a department store than did salespeople who were not in positive moods.[12] Another study found that the extent to which leaders (in this case, managers of small retail stores) experienced positive moods was related to the performance levels of their subordinates (the salespeople in the stores).[13] (Leadership is the subject of Chapter 12.) Research has also found that positive moods tend to promote creativity, but negative moods may result in members of an organization being especially accurate in their judgments (such as when appraising the performance of subordinates).[14]

Preliminary studies like those described above suggest that work moods have important effects on organizational behavior. Moreover, because managers and organizations can do many things to promote positive moods—for example, giving people attractive offices to work in, giving praise when it is deserved, providing workers with opportunities for social interaction, and incorporating fun and humor into the workplace—work moods are receiving additional attention from researchers and managers alike. Furthermore, workers like Pat Sullivan in the opening case are taking steps themselves to ensure that they feel good on the job.

RELATIONSHIPS BETWEEN WORK VALUES, ATTITUDES, AND MOODS

Work values, attitudes, and moods capture the range of thoughts and feelings that make up the experience of work. Each one of these determinants of the experience of work has the potential to affect the other two (see Fig. 3.2). Because work values are the most stable and long lasting, they can strongly affect both work attitudes and work moods. A person whose work values emphasize the importance of being ambitious, for example, may have negative work attitudes toward a job as a bus driver and may often be in a bad mood while driving the bus if he or she has been told that there is no possibility for promotion.

Work attitudes can affect work moods in a similar fashion. A salesperson who is very satisfied with his or her job and loves interacting with customers

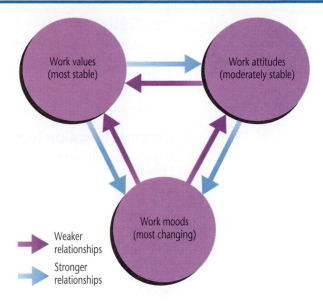

FIGURE 3.2

Relationships Between Work
Values, Attitudes, and Moods

may often be in a good mood at work. In this case, work attitudes (job satisfaction) affect work moods (positive moods).

In the long run—over a few years—work values might change in response to work attitudes and moods, even though attitudes and moods are not as long lasting as work values. A person whose work values stress that work is a way to make a living and not a source of personal fulfillment might find a job as a nurse so rewarding and exciting that he or she is usually in a good mood at work and, over time, develops positive attitudes toward the job. Eventually, the person's work values may change to include the importance of doing something that helps other people. But a worker who has experienced bad moods at work on and off for the past few months (perhaps because of a supervisor who is dishonest and unpleasant to be around) may realize that the job is not meeting his or her expectations and may feel a decline in job satisfaction. In this case, even though moods are more transitory than attitudes, moods affect attitudes.

TO MANAGERS

Work Values, Attitudes, and Moods

- Do not assume that most workers have strong intrinsic work values just because you do.
- Realize that any attempt you make to improve attitudes (such as job satisfaction and organization commitment), motivation, or performance will be most effective when the change you implement is consistent with workers' values. For example, making a job more challenging may do little to motivate a worker who is primarily motivated by the money earned. In fact, this worker may be less motivated by such a change if she or he feels that the newly challenging job should pay more than the old job because it is more difficult.
- Make the work environment pleasant and attractive to help promote positive moods.

Job Satisfaction

Job satisfaction (the collection of feelings and beliefs that people have about their current jobs) is one of the most important and well-researched work attitudes in organizational behavior. Why is job satisfaction viewed as so important by managers and researchers? It has the potential to affect a wide range of behaviors in organizations and to contribute to workers' levels of well-being.

DETERMINANTS OF JOB SATISFACTION

What causes different workers to be satisfied or dissatisfied with their jobs? Four factors affect the level of job satisfaction a person experiences: personality, values, the work situation, and social influence (see Fig. 3.3).

Personality.   Personality, the enduring ways a person has of feeling, thinking, and behaving (see Chapter 2), is the first determinant of how people think and feel about their jobs or job satisfaction.[15] An individual's personality influences the extent to which thoughts and feelings about a job are positive or negative. A person who is high on the Big Five trait of extraversion, for instance, is likely to have a higher level of job satisfaction than a person who is low on this trait.[16]

Given that personality helps to determine job satisfaction and that personality is, in part, genetically determined, researchers have wondered whether there may be genetic influences on job satisfaction. Richard Arvey of the University of Minnesota and his colleagues explored the extent to which

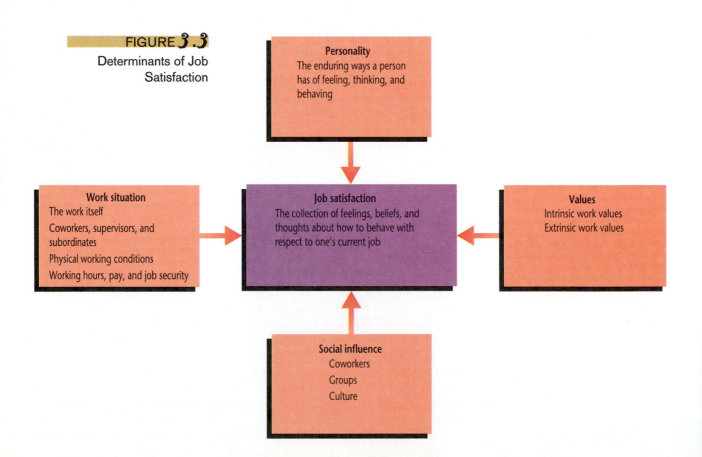

FIGURE **3.3**
Determinants of Job Satisfaction

Personality
The enduring ways a person has of feeling, thinking, and behaving

Work situation
The work itself
Coworkers, supervisors, and subordinates
Physical working conditions
Working hours, pay, and job security

Job satisfaction
The collection of feelings, beliefs, and thoughts about how to behave with respect to one's current job

Values
Intrinsic work values
Extrinsic work values

Social influence
Coworkers
Groups
Culture

workers' levels of job satisfaction were inherited from their parents.[17] They studied thirty-four identical twins who were raised apart from an early age. The twins shared the same genetic makeup but were exposed to different situational influences in their developmental years and later in life. For each pair of twins, the researchers measured the degree to which one twin's level of job satisfaction was the same as the other twin's level.

The researchers found that genetic factors accounted for about 30 percent of the differences in levels of job satisfaction across the twins in their study. Another interesting finding was that the twins tended to hold jobs that were similar in complexity, in motor skills needed, and in the physical demands of the work. This suggests that people seek out jobs that are suited to their genetic makeup. In other words, people's personalities (which are partially inherited) predispose them to choose certain kinds of jobs.

What do these findings mean for managers? Essentially, they suggest that part of job satisfaction is determined by workers' personalities, which an organization or manager cannot change in the short run. Does this mean that managers should not worry about the job satisfaction levels of their subordinates or that it is pointless to try to improve levels of job satisfaction? Definitely not. Although it certainly is impressive that genetic factors account for 30 percent of the differences in levels of job satisfaction, 70 percent of the variation in job satisfaction remains to be explained. It is this 70 percent that managers can influence. Thus managers should be concerned about job satisfaction because it is something that is within their power to influence and change.

Values.   Values have an impact on levels of job satisfaction because they reflect workers' convictions about the outcomes that work should lead to and how one should behave at work. A person with strong intrinsic work values (those related to the nature of the work itself), for example, is more likely than a person with weak intrinsic work values to be satisfied with a job that is interesting and personally meaningful (such as social work) but that also requires long working hours and doesn't pay well. A person with strong extrinsic work values (those related to the consequences of work) is more likely than a person with weak extrinsic work values to be satisfied with a job that pays well but is monotonous.

The Work Situation.   Perhaps the most important source of job satisfaction is the **work situation** itself—the tasks a person performs (for example, how interesting or boring they are), the people a jobholder interacts with (customers, subordinates, supervisors), the surroundings in which a person works (noise level, crowdedness, temperature), and the way the organization treats the jobholder (working hours, job security, the extent to which pay and benefits are generous or fair). Any aspect of the job and the employing organization is part of the work situation and can affect job satisfaction.

Most people would be more satisfied with a job that pays well and is very secure than with a job that pays poorly and exposes the worker to the ever-present threat of a layoff. Some of the theories of job satisfaction that we consider later in the chapter focus on the way in which specific situational factors affect job satisfaction.

Social Influence.   The last determinant of job satisfaction is **social influence,** or the influence that individuals or groups have on a person's attitudes and behavior. Coworkers, the groups a person belongs to, and the culture a person grows up in and lives in all have the potential to affect workers' levels of job satisfaction.

Work situation
The work itself, working conditions, and all other aspects of the job and the employing organization.

Social influence
The influence that individuals or groups have on a person's attitudes and behavior.

Social influence from *coworkers* can be an important determinant of a worker's job satisfaction because coworkers are usually always around, often have similar types of jobs, and often have certain things in common with a worker (such as educational background). Coworkers can have a particularly potent influence on the job satisfaction levels of newcomers to a job or organization. Workers who are new on the job have had very limited direct experience with the job, so they don't really know what to make of it and might not be sure whether they like it. Newcomers who are surrounded by coworkers who are dissatisfied with their jobs are more likely to be dissatisfied themselves than are newcomers who are surrounded by workers who enjoy and are satisfied with their jobs.

A worker's level of job satisfaction is also influenced by the *groups* he or she belongs to. The family a child grows up in, for example, can affect how satisfied the child is with his or her job as an adult. A worker who grows up in a wealthy family might be dissatisfied with a job as an elementary school teacher because the salary places out of reach the high standard of living he or she enjoyed while growing up. A teacher raised under more modest circumstances might also desire a higher salary but might not be dissatisfied with his or her teaching job because of its pay level.

A wide variety of groups can impact job satisfaction. Workers who belong to certain religious groups are likely to be dissatisfied with jobs that require working on Saturdays or Sundays. Unions can have powerful effects on the job satisfaction levels of their members. Belonging to a union that thinks that managers are not treating workers as well as they should, for example, might cause a worker to be dissatisfied with a job.

The *culture* a person grows up in and lives in may also affect a worker's level of job satisfaction. Workers who grow up in cultures (like the American culture) that emphasize the importance of individual achievement and accomplishment are more likely to be satisfied with jobs that stress individual accomplishment and provide rewards for individual achievement, such as bonuses and pay raises. Workers who grow up in cultures (like the Japanese culture) that emphasize the importance of doing what is good for everyone (for example, for the members of one's work group or department) may be less satisfied with jobs that stress individual competition and achievement. In fact, cultural influences may shape not just job satisfaction but the attitudes workers have about themselves, as indicated in Insight 3.2.

Insight 3.2

A Global View

I Am Who My Culture Says I Am

An American may introduce a lecture with a joke that displays both his knowledge and his wit, but a Japanese lecturer in the same position would more likely start off apologizing for his lack of expertise. According to Dr. Hazel Markus of the University of Michigan and Dr. Shinobu Kitayama of the University of Oregon, these two contrasting styles reflect how Americans and Japanese view themselves, which is, in turn, based on the values of their respective cultures.[18]

Consistent with American culture, the American lecturer views and portrays himself as independent, autonomous, and striving to achieve; this makes him feel good and makes his American audience comfortable. In contrast, Japanese culture stresses the interdependence of the self with others; the goal is to fit in, meet one's obligations, and have good interpersonal relations. The Japanese lecturer's more self-effacing style reflects these values; it demonstrates that he is but one part of a larger system and emphasizes the connection between himself and the audience.

Markus and her colleagues have been conducting some interesting research that further illuminates the effects of culture on attitudes about the self. They have asked Japanese and American students to describe themselves using what the researchers call the "Who Am I" scale. Americans tend to respond to the scale by describing personal characteristics (such as being athletic or smart). Japanese students, however, tend to describe themselves in terms of their roles (such as being the second son). These responses again illustrate that Americans view themselves in terms of personal characteristics and Japanese view themselves in terms of social characteristics, such as their position in their family.[19] This is a simple yet powerful demonstration of how the culture and society we grow up in influences our attitudes, even attitudes as fundamental as our attitudes about ourselves.

Theories of Job Satisfaction

Theories or models of job satisfaction are numerous. Each of them takes into account one or more of the four main determinants of job satisfaction (personality, values, the work situation, and social influence) and specifies in more detail exactly what causes one worker to be satisfied with a job and another worker to be dissatisfied. Here, we discuss four of the most influential theories: the facet model, Herzberg's motivator-hygiene theory, the discrepancy model, and the steady-state theory. These different theoretical approaches to job satisfaction are complementary. Each helps us to understand various aspects of job satisfaction. Each theory highlights factors that managers need to consider when trying to understand the satisfaction levels of their subordinates. Each theory also describes important issues that managers face when trying to change the work situation to increase job satisfaction.

THE FACET MODEL OF JOB SATISFACTION

Job facet
One of numerous components of a job.

The facet model of job satisfaction focuses primarily on work situation factors by breaking a job into its component elements, or **job facets,** and looking at how satisfied workers are with each facet. Many of the job facets that researchers have investigated are listed and defined in Table 3.2. A worker's overall job satisfaction is determined by summing his or her satisfaction with each facet of the job.

As Table 3.2 indicates, workers can take into account numerous aspects of their jobs when thinking about their levels of job satisfaction. The facet

TABLE 3.2

Job Facets That Play a Part in Determining Job Satisfaction

Job Facet	Description
Ability utilization	The extent to which the job allows one to use one's abilities
Achievement	The extent to which a worker gets a feeling of accomplishment from the job
Activity	Being able to keep busy on the job
Advancement	Having promotion opportunities
Authority	Having control over others
Company policies and practices	The extent to which they are pleasing to the worker
Compensation	The pay the worker receives for the job
Coworkers	How well one gets along with others in the workplace
Creativity	Being free to come up with new ideas
Independence	Being able to work alone
Moral values	Not having to do things that go against one's conscience
Recognition	Praise for doing a good job
Responsibility	Being accountable for decisions and actions
Security	Having a secure or steady job
Social service	Being able to do things for other people
Social status	The recognition in the wider community that goes along with the job
Human relations supervision	The interpersonal skills of one's boss
Technical supervision	The work-related skills of one's boss
Variety	Doing different things on the job
Working conditions	Working hours, temperature, furnishings, office location and layout, and so forth

Source: From D. J. Weiss et al., *Manual for the Minnesota Satisfaction Questionnaire,* 1967. Minnesota Studies in Vocational Rehabilitation: XXII, © 1967 University of Minnesota. Reproduced by permission of Vocational Psychology Research.

model is useful because it forces managers and researchers to recognize that jobs affect workers in multiple ways. However, managers who use this model to evaluate the work situation's effect on job satisfaction always need to be aware that, for any particular job, they might inadvertently exclude an important facet that strongly influences a worker's job satisfaction. The extent to which an employing organization is "family friendly," for example, is an important job facet for more and more workers. (See Insight 3.3.)

Insight 3.3

Diversity

Family-Friendly Policies and Benefits: An Up-and-Coming Job Facet

Given the increasing diversity of the workforce and the increasing numbers of women, dual-career couples, and single parents who need to balance their responsibilities on the job and at home, family-friendly organizational policies and benefits are becoming important to more and more workers. For Robert Maser, a 24-year-old graduate of the University of South Carolina's international business program, an important job facet is the extent to which his job allows him to balance his career and family life.[20] When Maser, a husband and the father of a 2-year-old son, was in the job market, he made it clear to prospective employers that spending time with his family was important to him. After IBM (www.ibm.com) indicated that it tried to help workers achieve a balanced lifestyle through its policies and benefits, Maser decided to join IBM.

A decade or two ago, concerns such as Maser's would never have been mentioned to recruiters in job interviews, but today more and more workers are indicating that the extent to which their employer is family-friendly is an important facet of a job. Some workers desire flexible working hours; others want on-site child care facilities or provisions for time off to care for dependents. Christian Kjeldsen, vice president for headquarters resources at Johnson & Johnson (www.jnj.com), suggests that "work and family policies are now being viewed as a competitive tool."[21] The Families and Work Institute, a work-family think tank, expects this trend to strengthen, judging from recent surveys.

Family-friendly policies are particularly important for organizations in industries facing a tight labor market. For example, Lancaster Laboratories, a company located in Lancaster, Pennsylvania, had a hard time attracting analytical chemists until it started its family care programs. Now workers are joining Lancaster rather than its competitors because its on-site day care center allows workers to bring their children to work with them and even join them for lunch. Family programs also help companies to retain their employees. Terry McMahon, a senior systems analyst at Fel-Pro Inc., is frequently contacted by headhunters who offer him tempting positions with other companies using advanced technologies. He acknowledges that he sometimes gets restless for a change, but he remains with Fel-Pro because of the peace of mind he has from knowing his two sons are being cared for in Fel-Pro's child care center.

As these accounts indicate, a sizable portion of the workforce values family-friendly policies and benefits as an important job facet, and organizations are responding to this need. Companies such as Johnson & Johnson, IBM, Aetna Life & Casualty, and Corning have adopted family policies to help them recruit and retain workers and reduce worker stress. These policies range from family care leave and sick days to on-site child care centers, flexible work schedules, work-at-home programs, job sharing, and school-holiday programs.[22] Such benefits are likely to become even more important in the future.

Another issue that must be considered by managers using facet models of job satisfaction is that some job facets may be more important than others for any given worker.[23] Family-friendly policies, for example, are important for workers with dependents, but they clearly are less important for workers who are single and intend to remain so. Compensation and security may be key job facets that determine the level of job satisfaction of a single woman who has strong extrinsic work values. At the other end of the spectrum, a 55-year-old high-ranking official retired from the military who is receiving a generous military pension may have strong intrinsic work values and be primarily concerned with finding a post-retirement job that has high levels of ability utilization, achievement, and creativity.

Frank Courtney, a Harvard University graduate, was the butt of jokes when he accepted a position with U.S. Steel while many of his classmates were accepting positions with more prestigious and glamorous companies. Working in heavy industry, however, provided Courtney with a job facet he truly desired: responsibility. At U.S. Steel, he had the responsibility for overseeing the production and shipping of hundreds of tons of steel while his buddies in the more glamorous legal and financial industries were spending a lot of their time making photocopies.[24]

HERZBERG'S MOTIVATOR-HYGIENE THEORY OF JOB SATISFACTION

One of the earliest theories of job satisfaction, Frederick Herzberg's motivator-hygiene theory, focuses on the effects of certain types of job facets on job satisfaction. Herzberg's theory proposes that every worker has two sets of needs or requirements: motivator needs and hygiene needs.[25] *Motivator needs* are associated with the actual work itself and how challenging it is. Job facets such as interesting work, autonomy on the job, and responsibility satisfy motivator needs. *Hygiene needs* are associated with the physical and psychological context in which the work is performed. Job facets such as the physical working conditions (for example, the temperature and pleasantness of the surroundings), the nature of supervision, pay, and job security satisfy hygiene needs.

Herzberg proposed the following theoretical relationships between motivator needs, hygiene needs, and job satisfaction:

1. When motivator needs are met, workers will be satisfied; when these needs are not met, workers will not be satisfied.
2. When hygiene needs are met, workers will not be dissatisfied; when these needs are not met, workers will be dissatisfied.

According to Herzberg, a worker could experience job satisfaction and job dissatisfaction at the same time. A worker could be *satisfied* because *motivator needs* are being met by, for example, having interesting and challenging work yet *dissatisfied* because *hygiene needs* are not being met because of, for example, low job security. According to the traditional view of job satisfaction, satisfaction and dissatisfaction are at opposite ends of a single continuum, and workers are either satisfied or dissatisfied with their jobs. Figure 3.4(a) illustrates the traditional view. Herzberg proposed that dissatisfaction and satisfaction are two *separate dimensions,* one ranging from satisfaction to no satisfaction and the other ranging from dissatisfaction to no dissatisfaction. Figure 3.4(b) illustrates Herzberg's view. A worker's location on the satisfaction continuum depends on the extent to which motivator needs are met, and a worker's location on the dissatisfaction continuum depends on the extent to which hygiene needs are met.

Many research studies have tested Herzberg's formulations. Herzberg himself conducted some of the early studies that supported the theory. He relied on the *critical incidents technique* to collect his data. Herzberg and his colleagues interviewed workers and asked them to describe a time when they felt particularly good about their jobs and a time when they felt particularly bad about their jobs. After collating responses from many workers, they made the following discovery: Whenever workers related an instance when they felt good about their job, the incident had to do with the work itself (it was related to their *motivator needs*). Whenever they described an instance when they felt bad about their job, the incident had to do with the working conditions (it was related to their *hygiene needs*). These results certainly seemed to support Herzberg's theory.

When other researchers used different methods to test Herzberg's theory, however, the theory failed to receive support.[26] Why did studies using the critical incidents technique support the theory? As you will learn in Chapter 4, people have a tendency to want to take credit for the good things that happen to them and blame others or outside forces for the bad things. This basic tendency probably accounts for workers describing good things that happened to them as being related to the work itself, because the work itself is something a worker can take direct credit for. Conversely, working conditions are mostly

FIGURE 3.4

Two Views of Job Satisfaction

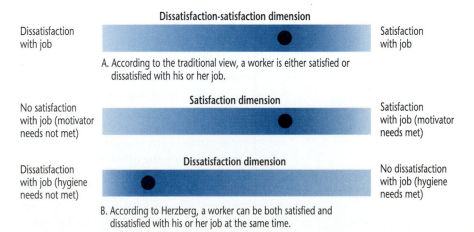

Dissatisfaction-satisfaction dimension

Dissatisfaction with job

Satisfaction with job

A. According to the traditional view, a worker is either satisfied or dissatisfied with his or her job.

Satisfaction dimension

No satisfaction with job (motivator needs not met)

Satisfaction with job (motivator needs met)

Dissatisfaction dimension

Dissatisfaction with job (hygiene needs not met)

No dissatisfaction with job (hygiene needs met)

B. According to Herzberg, a worker can be both satisfied and dissatisfied with his or her job at the same time.

outside the control of a worker, and it is human nature to try to attribute bad things to situations that are beyond one's control.

Even though research does *not* support Herzberg's theory, the attention Herzberg paid to motivator needs and to work itself as determinants of satisfaction helped to focus researchers' and managers' attention on the important topic of job design and its effects on organizational behavior (discussed in detail in Chapter 7). Nevertheless, managers need to be aware of the lack of research support for the theoretical relationships Herzberg proposed.

THE DISCREPANCY MODEL OF JOB SATISFACTION

The discrepancy model of job satisfaction is based on a simple idea: To determine how satisfied they are with their jobs, workers compare their job to some "ideal job."[27] This "ideal job" could be what one thinks the job should be like, what one expected the job to be like, what one wants from a job, or what one's former job was like. According to the discrepancy model of job satisfaction, when workers' expectations about their "ideal job" are high, and when these expectations are not met, workers will be dissatisfied. As indicated in Insight 3.4, new college graduates may be particularly prone to having overly high expectations for their first jobs.

Insight 3.4   **Job Satisfaction**

Great Expectations

A frequent lament of college recruiters is the excessively high expectations of the students they interview.[28] According to discrepancy models of job satisfaction, these students are bound to experience some job dissatisfaction when their new positions fail to meet their high hopes.

Martin Fives, a personnel manager at Rite Aid Corporation (www.riteaid.com), says that many of the college students he interviews expect to find jobs in which they will spend all their time managing and not actually *doing* work themselves. Recruiters also complain that many students have inflated egos. They read about figures for average salaries and then think that they should earn at least the average and probably above it. This thinking is obviously not realistic, but it is consistent with the tendency we all have to think that we are above average.

Given these high expectations, few college graduates find jobs that meet their hopes. Ralph Barsiano, a college recruiter from IBM in Boston, indicates that with approximately a million new graduates on the market each year and companies all trying to identify the top 10 percent of them, the other 90 percent have to do a great job of selling themselves to try to land a top entry-level position. Barsiano and other college recruiters advise new graduates to concentrate on gaining as much work experience as they can, rather than being disappointed when it looks as if their expectations may not be met.[29]

Some researchers have combined the facet and discrepancy models of job satisfaction.[30] For each of the job facets described in Table 3.2, for example, we could ask workers how much of the facet they currently have on the job and how much of the facet they think their job should have. The difference between these two quantities would be the workers' level of satisfaction with the facet. For example, a worker who indicates that she thinks she should have a lot of autonomy on her job but reports that she currently has limited autonomy would be dissatisfied with the autonomy facet of her job. After determining satisfaction levels for each of the job facets in this manner, the total of all of the responses would give an overall satisfaction score.

Discrepancy models are useful because they take into account that people often take a comparative approach to evaluation. It is not so much the presence or absence of job facets that is important but rather how a job stacks up against a worker's "ideal job." Managers need to recognize this comparative approach and should ask workers what they want their jobs to be like. This information can help managers make meaningful changes to the work situation to raise subordinates' levels of job satisfaction.

THE STEADY-STATE THEORY OF JOB SATISFACTION

The steady-state theory suggests that each worker has a typical or characteristic level of job satisfaction, called the steady state or equilibrium level. Different situational factors or events at work may move a worker temporarily from this steady state, but the worker will return eventually to his or her equilibrium level[31] (see Fig. 3.5). For example, receiving a promotion and raise may temporarily boost a worker's level of job satisfaction, but it eventually will return to the equilibrium level. The finding that job satisfaction tends to be somewhat stable over time[32] supports the steady-state view. The influence of personality on job satisfaction also is consistent with the steady-state approach. Because personality, one of the determinants of job satisfaction, is stable over time, we would expect job satisfaction to exhibit some stability over time.

The steady-state theory suggests that when managers make changes in the work situation with the hope of raising workers' levels of job satisfaction, they need to determine whether resulting increases in job satisfaction are temporary or long lasting. Some researchers have found, for example, that when

FIGURE 3.5

Job Satisfaction as a Steady State
A worker's level of job satisfaction fluctuates above and below the equilibrium level as events increase or decrease job satisfaction.

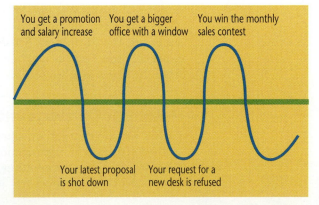

Events that increase job satisfaction

You get a promotion and salary increase

You get a bigger office with a window

You win the monthly sales contest

Equilibrium level of job satisfaction

Events that decrease job satisfaction

Your latest proposal is shot down

Your request for a new desk is refused

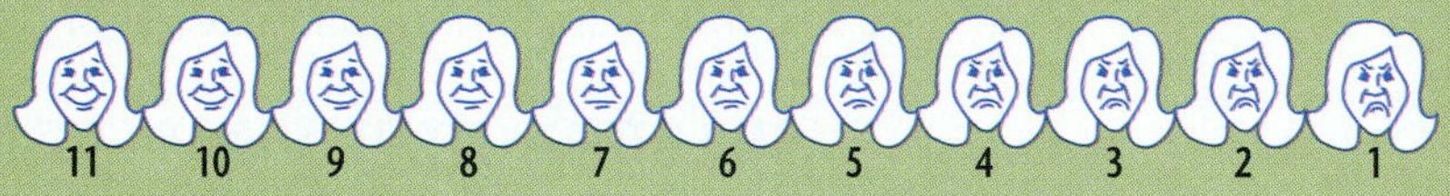

FIGURE 3.6

Sample Items From Popular Measures of Job Satisfaction

Source: (A) From D. J. Weiss et al., Manual for the Minnesota Satisfaction Questionnaire, 1967, Minnesota Studies in Vocational Rehabilitation: XXII. Copyright 1967 University of Minnesota. Reproduced by permission of Vocational Psychology Research. (B) From R. B. Dunham and J. B. Herman, "Development of a Female Faces Scale for Measuring Job Satisfaction," *Journal of Applied Psychology,* 1975, 60, pp. 629–631. Copyright 1975 by the American Psychology Association. Reprinted with permission.

A. Sample items from the Minnesota Satisfaction Questionnaire

Workers respond to each of the items by checking whether they are:

☐ Very dissatisfied
☐ Dissatisfied
☐ Can't decide whether satisfied or not
☐ Satisfied
☐ Very satisfied

On my present job, this is how I feel about . . .
1. Being able to keep busy all the time.
2. The chance to be "somebody" in the community.
3. The way my job provides for steady employment.
4. My pay and the amount of work I do.
5. The freedom to use my own judgment.
6. The chance to work by myself.
7. The chance to develop close friendships with my coworkers.
8. The way I get full credit for the work I do.
9. The chance to help people.
10. My job security.

B. The faces scale

Workers select the face that best expresses how they feel about their job in general.

11   10   9   8   7   6   5   4   3   2   1

changes are made in the nature of the work itself (such as making jobs more interesting), levels of job satisfaction increase temporarily (for example, for six months) but then return to their former levels.[33] To decide on the most effective ways to sustain an increase in job satisfaction, it is also important for managers to determine *how long* it takes workers to return to their equilibrium levels. Changes in some job facets, for example, may lead to longer-lasting changes in job satisfaction than changes in other facets.

MEASURING JOB SATISFACTION

There are several measures of job satisfaction that managers can use to determine the job satisfaction levels of their subordinates and that researchers can use in studies of job satisfaction. A manager who discovers that most workers are dissatisfied with the same few job facets and that as a result overall levels of job satisfaction are low can use this information to determine where to make changes in the work situation to raise satisfaction levels. Researchers can use these measures to learn more about the causes and consequences of job satisfaction. Most of these measures ask workers to respond to a series of questions or statements about their jobs. Among the most popular scales are the Minnesota Satisfaction Questionnaire (based on a facet approach),[34] the Faces Scale,[35] and the Job Descriptive Index.[36] Sample items from the first two of these scales appear in Fig. 3.6.

Potential Consequences of Job Satisfaction

Earlier we said that job satisfaction is one of the most important and most studied attitudes in organizational behavior. One reason for the interest in job satisfaction is that whether a worker is satisfied with his or her job has significant consequences not just for the worker but for coworkers, man-

TO MANAGERS

Job Satisfaction

- Realize that some workers are going to be more satisfied than others with the same job simply because they have different personalities and work values. Also realize that you can take steps to increase levels of job satisfaction because it is determined not only by personality but also by the work situation.
- Try to place newcomers in work groups whose members are satisfied with their jobs.
- Ask workers what facets of their jobs are important to them, and do what you can to ensure that they are satisfied with these facets (for example, by providing on-site child care for workers who indicate that being a member of a family-friendly organization is important to them).
- Because job satisfaction has the potential to impact workers' behaviors in organizations and their well-being, use existing scales such as the Minnesota Satisfaction Scale or the Faces Scale to periodically survey your subordinates' levels of job satisfaction. When levels of job satisfaction are low, follow the advice in the preceding step.
- Recognize that workers' evaluations of job facets, not what you think about them, determine how satisfied workers are and that changing some facets may have longer-lasting effects on job satisfaction than changing others.

agers, groups, teams, and the organization as a whole. In this section we consider several potential consequences of job satisfaction: job performance, absenteeism, turnover, organizational citizenship behavior, and worker well-being.

DOES JOB SATISFACTION AFFECT JOB PERFORMANCE?

Intuitively, most people (including managers) believe that job satisfaction is positively associated with job performance—that is, that workers who are more satisfied with their jobs will perform at a higher level than those who are less satisfied. Many studies have been conducted to see whether this piece of conventional wisdom is valid. Surprisingly, the results indicate that job satisfaction is *not* strongly related to job performance; at best, there is a very weak positive relationship. One recent review of the many studies conducted in this area concluded that levels of job satisfaction accounted for only about 2 percent of the differences in performance levels across workers in the studies reviewed.[37] For all practical purposes, then, we can conclude that job satisfaction is *not* meaningfully associated with job performance.

Although this finding goes against the intuition of many managers, it is not that surprising if we consider when work attitudes such as job satisfaction *do* affect work behaviors. Research indicates that work attitudes (such as job satisfaction) affect work behaviors only when workers are free to vary their behaviors and when a worker's attitude is relevant to the behavior in question.

Are most workers free to vary their levels of job performance to reflect how satisfied they are with their jobs? Probably not. Organizations spend considerable time and effort to ensure that members perform assigned duties dependably regardless of whether they like their jobs or not. As you will see in later chapters, organizations develop rules and procedures that workers are expected to follow, and to ensure that these rules are followed organizations reward workers who perform at acceptable levels and punish or dismiss workers who do not. Such rules, procedures, rewards, and punishments are situational pressures that propel workers to perform at acceptable levels.

If chefs in a restaurant, for example, lower the quality of the meals they prepare because they are dissatisfied, customers will stop coming to the restaurant, and the restaurant will either go out of business or the owners will replace the chefs. Similarly, firefighters will not keep their jobs if, because of their levels of job satisfaction, they vary the number of emergencies they respond to. Secretaries who, because of dissatisfaction, cut back on the quality or quantity of letters they type are likely to be reprimanded or even fired and certainly will not be offered a promotion.

In order for a work attitude (job satisfaction) to influence behavior, the attitude must be relevant to the behavior in question (job performance). Sometimes workers' levels of job satisfaction are not relevant to their job performance. Suppose a security guard is satisfied with his job because it is not very demanding and allows him to do a lot of outside reading while on the job. Clearly, this worker's job satisfaction is not going to result in higher levels of performance because the reason for his satisfaction is that the job is not very demanding.

Because of strong situational pressures in organizations to behave in certain ways and because a worker's level of job satisfaction may not be relevant to his or her job performance, job satisfaction is *not* strongly related to job performance. Some research, however, suggests that the direction of influence between these two factors (satisfaction and performance) may be reversed: Job performance may lead to job satisfaction. Job performance may contribute to workers being more satisfied with their jobs only if workers are fairly rewarded for a good performance. The relationship between job performance and rewards, the importance of equity or fairness, and the implications of these issues for understanding and managing organizational behavior are covered in more detail in Chapters 6, 7, and 8 on motivation.

ABSENTEEISM

Absenteeism can be very costly for organizations. It is estimated that approximately a million workers a day are absent from their jobs. In a year, absenteeism costs companies in the United States approximately $40 billion.[38] Not surprisingly then, many researchers have studied the relationship between absenteeism and job satisfaction in an attempt to discover ways to reduce absenteeism. Research focusing on this question has indicated that job satisfaction has a weak negative relationship with absenteeism—that is, workers who are satisfied with their jobs are less likely to be absent.

Richard Steers and Susan Rhodes have provided a model of absenteeism that helps explain these results.[39] They propose that employee attendance (the opposite of absence) is a function not only of workers' motivation to attend but also of their ability to attend (see Table 3.3). Job

TABLE 3.3
Determinants of Absence from Work

Motivation to Attend Work Is Affected By	Ability to Attend Work Is Affected By
Job satisfaction	Illness and accidents
Organization's absence policy	Transportation problems
Other factors	Family responsibilities

satisfaction is only one of many factors that affects *motivation* to attend. As we discussed earlier, it is likely that work moods contribute to motivation to attend; workers who experience positive moods on the job are more likely to want to come to work.[40] A worker's *ability* to go to work is influenced by illness and accidents, transportation problems, and family responsibilities. Because of the variety of situations and factors that affect absence from work, it is not surprising that the relationship between satisfaction and absence is relatively weak.

Absenteeism is a behavior that organizations can never eliminate, but they can control and manage it. To do so, organizations should not have absence policies that are so restrictive that they literally force workers to come to work even if they are ill. Organizations may even want to recognize that a certain level of absence (perhaps from a high-stress job) is indeed functional. Many companies, such as the General Foods Corporation, have acknowledged this possibility by including "mental health days" or "personal days" in their absence policies. These days, which workers can take off at their discretion, do not count as unexcused absences and do not reduce the workers' numbers of sick and vacation days.

TURNOVER

Turnover is the permanent withdrawal of a worker from the employing organization. Job satisfaction shows a weak-to-moderate negative relationship to turnover—that is, high job satisfaction leads to low turnover. Why is this relationship observed? Workers who are satisfied with their jobs are less likely to quit than those who are dissatisfied, but some dissatisfied workers never leave, and others who are satisfied with their jobs eventually move on to another organization. Moreover, unlike absenteeism, which is a *temporary* form of withdrawal from the organization, turnover is *permanent* and can have a major impact on a worker's life. Thus the decision to quit a job is not usually made lightly but is instead the result of a carefully thought-out process.

When in the turnover process does job satisfaction play an important role? According to a model of the turnover process developed by Bill Mobley, job satisfaction triggers the whole turnover process (see Fig. 3.7).[41] Workers who are very satisfied with their jobs may never even think about quitting; for those who are dissatisfied, it is the dissatisfaction that starts them thinking about quitting.

At this point, the individual evaluates the benefits of searching for a new job and the costs of quitting. These costs could include any corporate benefits that

Turnover
The permanent withdrawal of a worker from the employing organization.

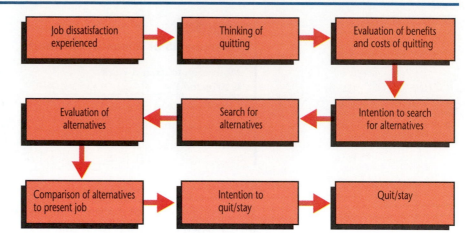

FIGURE **3.7**

Mobley's Model of
the Turnover Process

Source: Adapted from W. H. Mobley,
"Intermediate Linkages in the
Relationship Between Job Satisfaction
and Employee Turnover," *Journal
of Applied Psychology,* 1977, 6, pp.
237–240. Copyright 1977 by the
American Psychological Association.
Reprinted with permission.

are linked to seniority (such as vacation time and bonuses), the loss of pension and medical plans, and a reduced level of job security (which is often based on seniority in the organization). On the basis of this cost/benefit evaluation, the individual may decide to search for alternative jobs. The person evaluates and compares these alternatives to the current job and develops an intention to quit or stay. The intention to quit eventually leads to turnover behavior. Hence, although job satisfaction or dissatisfaction is an important factor to consider because it may trigger the whole turnover process and start a worker thinking about quitting, other factors come into play and help to determine whether a worker actually quits. (Mobley's model applies neither to workers who impulsively quit their jobs when they have a rough time nor to workers who quit their jobs before even looking for alternatives.)

Just as in the case of absenteeism, managers often think of turnover as a costly behavior that must be kept to a minimum. There are certainly costs to turnover, such as the costs of hiring and training replacement workers. In addition, turnover often causes disruptions for existing members of an organization, it may result in delays on important projects, and it can cause problems when workers who quit are members of teams.

Although these and other costs of turnover can be significant, turnover can also have certain benefits for organizations. First, whether turnover is a cost or benefit depends on who is leaving. If poor performers are quitting and good performers are staying, this is an ideal situation, and managers may not want to reduce levels of turnover. Second, turnover can result in the introduction of new ideas and approaches if the organization hires newcomers with new ideas to replace workers who have left. Third, turnover can be a relatively painless and natural way to reduce the size of the workforce through *attrition,* the process through which people leave an organization of their own free will. Attrition can be an important benefit of turnover in lean economic times because it reduces the need for organizations to make major cuts in, or *downsize,* their workforces. Finally, for organizations that promote from within, turnover in the upper ranks of the organization frees up some positions for lower-level members to be promoted into. Like absenteeism, turnover is a behavior that needs to be managed but not necessarily reduced or eliminated.

ORGANIZATIONAL CITIZENSHIP BEHAVIOR

Although job satisfaction is not related to job performance, new research suggests that it is related to work behaviors that are of a more voluntary nature and not specifically required of workers. **Organizational citizenship behavior** (OCB) is behavior that is above and beyond the call of duty—that is, behavior that is not required of organizational members but is nonetheless necessary for organizational survival and effectiveness.[42] Examples of OCB include helping coworkers; protecting the organization from fire, theft, vandalism, and other misfortunes; making constructive suggestions; developing one's skills and capabilities; and spreading goodwill in the larger community. These behaviors are seldom required of organizational members, but they are important in all organizations. Helping coworkers is an especially important form of OCB when it comes to computing in the workplace. (See Insight 3.5.)

> **Organizational citizenship behavior**
> Behavior that is not required but is necessary for organizational survival and effectiveness.

Insight 3.5 Competitive Advantage

Using Computers Effectively

More and more companies are using computers to increase efficiency and cut costs, increase product quality, and improve service to customers. Indeed, personal computers are standard equipment in most offices. A sizable portion of the workforce, however, still does not know what to do when the screen goes blank.[43] Many workers are proficient in using their PCs for the everyday tasks they encounter on the job, but they are often at a loss when something goes wrong or they need to do something new. Some workers turn to computer professionals for help (who are compensated for their time), and others turn to computer-literate coworkers. In the computing age, the helping-coworkers form of organizational citizenship behavior is especially important for smooth organizational operations.

Stanley Labak, one of the world's leading sonar engineers, is employed by Marine Acoustics Inc. of Rhode Island and is the unofficial PC guru for his company. Whenever anyone's hard disk crashes or individuals encounter some other PC problem, Labak is often the first person to be called for help. Although he thinks it is good to help others in the company, he also has to be careful so that too much of his time is not consumed by attending to every PC-related problem that comes up.

Helping coworkers with their PC problems may be vital to organizational effectiveness and may prevent PCs from becoming unused office ornaments, but it bears a cost. A study conducted by Nolan, Norton, & Co. (a consulting unit of KPMG Peat Marwick) of ten large U.S. corporations (Ford, Xerox, and Sprint Communications Company, among them) found that the time workers spend helping others with their PC problems costs from \$6,000 to \$15,000 a year for every PC a company uses.[44] The companies involved in the study were surprised about the amount of "informal helping" that was going on. Managers realized that mutual support occurred, but they tended to underestimate the extent of PC-related help giving.

Workers have considerable discretion over whether or not they engage in acts of organizational citizenship behavior. Most workers' job descriptions do not require them to come up with innovative suggestions to improve the functioning of their departments. Nevertheless, workers often make valuable innovative suggestions, and it may be that workers who are most satisfied with their jobs are most likely to do so. Once again, because these behaviors are voluntary—that is, there are no strong situational pressures to perform them—it is likely that they are influenced by attitudes such as job satisfaction. As we saw earlier, work moods are also likely to have some impact on these behaviors. Workers who are in positive moods are especially likely to perform forms of OCB, such as helping customers or suggesting new ideas.[45]

Dennis Organ of Indiana University suggests that satisfied workers may be likely to perform these behaviors because they seek to give something back to an organization that has treated them well.[46] Organ notes that most people like to have fair exchanges with the people and organizations for which they work. Because of this desire, workers who are satisfied may seek to reciprocate or give something back to the organization by engaging in various forms of OCB.

Because the various forms of organizational citizenship behavior are not formally required of workers, they may not be formally recognized by the organization's reward and incentive systems. Often, managers may not even be aware of these behaviors or may underestimate their occurrence (as in the case of workers helping others with their PC problems). This lack of awareness does not mean, however, that managers cannot recognize and acknowledge OCB that does occur.

John Brady, president of John Brady Design Consultants, developed a simple yet innovative method to acknowledge OCB. At the start of each year he

These Midland, Texas, police officers regularly engage in organizational citizenship behavior by volunteering their time to promote the Texas Special Olympics for physically and mentally disabled people.

TO MANAGERS

gives each of his eighteen employees a jar containing twelve marbles. Throughout the year, workers give marbles to others who have helped them in some way or have accomplished some out-of-the-ordinary feat. In this way, workers are recognized for the OCB that occurs and are proud of the marbles they accumulate over the year, even though they may receive no more tangible rewards (such as a bonus) for performing these behaviors.[47]

Similarly, Texas A&M University recognizes OCB by publishing accounts of OCB in the *Human Resources Newsletter* distributed periodically to all employees of the university. A special section of the newsletter titled "We Caught You Doing Something Right" chronicles instances of OCB that have taken place during the past few months. Here is a sample entry: "Michael Jackson, who works in the Library, was caught coming in on his own time to review work for a cooperative grant-funded project involving 18 Texas academic libraries. By voluntarily contributing his time, Michael has enabled the Texas Documents to the People Project to stay on schedule."[48]

WORKER WELL-BEING

Worker well-being

How happy, healthy, and prosperous workers are.

Worker well-being—how happy, healthy, and prosperous workers are—is the last potential consequence of job satisfaction we consider. Unlike absenteeism and turnover, this consequence focuses on the worker rather than the organization. If you count the number of hours of their adult lives that workers spend on the job, the number is truly mind-boggling: A worker who puts in an 8-hour day, works five days a week, and has two weeks off a year for vacation works approximately 2,000 hours a year. Over a forty-year period (from age 25 to 65), this worker clocks in some 80,000 hours on the job. (These figures don't even touch on the amount of time workers spend thinking about their jobs during their time off.) Being dissatisfied with one's job for a major portion of one's working life almost certainly adversely affects well-being and general happiness. Consistent with this observation, research suggests that job satisfaction contributes to overall well-being in life.[49]

Organizational Commitment

Whereas job satisfaction is feelings and beliefs that individuals have about specific jobs, organizational commitment is feelings and beliefs about the employing organization as a whole. Researchers have identified two distinct types of organizational commitment, affective commitment and continuance commitment. **Affective commitment** exists when workers are happy to be members of an organization, believe in and feel good about the organization and what it stands for, are attached to the organization, and intend to do what is good for the organization. **Continuance commitment** exists when workers are committed not so much because they want to be but because they have to be; the costs of leaving the organization (for example, loss of seniority, job security, pensions, and medical benefits) are too great.[50] As you might imagine, affective commitment generally has more positive consequences for workers and organizations than continuance commitment.

DETERMINANTS OF AFFECTIVE COMMITMENT

A wide range of personality and situational factors have the potential to affect levels of affective commitment. For example, workers may be more committed to organizations that behave in a socially responsible manner and contribute to society at large. It is easier to believe in and be committed to an organization that is doing good things for society rather than causing harm, such as by polluting the atmosphere. Ben & Jerry's Homemade, the ice cream company, encourages worker commitment through socially responsible corporate policies and programs that support protection of the environment and contributions to the local community.[51] The Body Shop, which manufactures and sells organic beauty products, engenders commitment from its employees by supporting protection of the environment and animal rights. Workers may also be more likely to be committed to an organization that shows that it cares about its employees and values them as individuals. Managers cannot expect workers to be committed to an organization if the organization is not committed to workers. Moreover, some managers and workers alike would argue that organizations have an ethical obligation to show a certain level of commitment to their employees. (See Insight 3.6.)

Affective commitment
The commitment that exists when workers are happy to be members of an organization, believe in and feel good about the organization and what it stands for, are attached to the organization, and intend to do what is good for the organization.

Continuance commitment
The commitment that exists when it is very costly for workers to leave an organization.

Insight 3.6   **Ethics**

Commitment Is a Two-Way Street

It may seem pretty obvious that an organization that wants committed workers should demonstrate some degree of commitment to its workers. In addition, the well-being of organizational members often hinges on an organization's commitment to them, and some organizations view such commitment as an ethical imperative. Time and time again, however, we hear examples of committed workers who are disappointed by their organization's lack of commitment to them. Juanita Lewis, for example, was a committed employee of Delta Air Lines—so committed, that she worked thirty-six hours straight for Delta without a break after a plane crash, and for free! But when Lewis had some medical and family problems, her supervisor at Delta was unsupportive. Eventually, Lewis was fired by Delta because she refused to relocate at her own expense.[52]

Many companies, however, are beginning to realize that they need to show their employees that they are committed to them if they want high levels of commitment from their workers. Even such seemingly trivial things like office layout may signal an organization's level of commitment to workers. Frank Becker, a professor at Cornell and an office design expert, was recently visiting Sweden, where he was taken aback because all offices were the same size. This design is in sharp contrast to the norm in the United States, where office size corresponds to one's position in the corporate hierarchy. Becker asked one of his Swedish hosts how they could get away with giving an engineer the same size office as a secretary. He in turn was asked, "How can we hire a secretary and expect her to be committed to our company when, by the size of the office we give her, we tell her she's a second-class citizen?"[53] One definition of an ethical organization is that it is a fair organization that values and shows that it cares about all of its members.

Union Carbide's (www.unioncarbide.com) old company headquarters on Park Avenue in New York City was one of the most status-conscious offices around. Each rank in the hierarchy had different kinds of supplies, furniture, and office layout. When the company moved to Danbury, Connecticut, workers were asked how their new building should be designed and outfitted. The employees' input resulted in all offices being the same size and in the abolishment of executive parking spaces and dining rooms. Workers are happier in the new layout and also appear to be more productive.

Stanley Gault, Rubbermaid's CEO, demonstrated his commitment to workers by giving up an hour's sleep to be at work at 5 o'clock in the morning to meet with a worker who really needed to talk to him and got off his shift at 5 a.m. Open-door policies such as Gault's are another way in which managers can show their commitment to workers. Such policies, which are rarely abused, help to ensure that top managers are aware of, and can respond quickly to, potential problems and ethical issues in their organizations.[54]

POTENTIAL CONSEQUENCES OF AFFECTIVE COMMITMENT

Managers intuitively believe that workers who are committed to an organization will work harder, and research has found affective commitment to have a weak positive relationship with job performance.[55] However, affective commitment (like job satisfaction) may be more highly related to organizational citizenship behavior (OCB), which is above and beyond the call of duty. Because these behaviors are voluntary, they tend to be more directly related to workers' attitudes toward an organization. When affective commitment is high, workers are likely to want to do what is good for the organization and thus perform OCBs. However, when continuance commitment is high, workers are not expected to go above and beyond the call of duty because their commitment is based more on necessity than a belief in what the organization stands for.

Affective commitment also shows a weak, negative relationship to absenteeism and lateness. A stronger negative relationship exists between affective commitment and turnover. Workers who are committed to an organization are less likely to quit; their positive attitude toward the organization itself makes them reluctant to leave.[56]

TO MANAGERS

Organizational Commitment

- Adopt socially responsible policies and programs such as supporting protection of the environment and helping out the community in which your organization is located.
- Be committed to your employees by, for example, showing concern for their well-being, helping them when they have hard times, and soliciting their input on decisions that will affect them.

SUMMARY

Work values, attitudes, and moods have important effects on organizational behavior. Work values (a worker's personal convictions about what outcomes one should expect from work and how one should behave at work) are an important determinant of on-the-job behavior. Job satisfaction and organizational commitment are two key work attitudes with important implications for understanding and managing behaviors such as organizational citizenship behavior, absenteeism, and turnover. Work moods also are important determinants of behavior in organizations. In this chapter, we made the following major points:

1. Work values are people's personal convictions about what one should expect to obtain from working and how one should behave at work. Work attitudes, more specific and less long lasting than values, are collections of feelings, beliefs, and thoughts that people have about how to behave in their current jobs and organizations. Work moods, more transitory than both values and attitudes, are people's feelings at the time they actually per-

form their jobs. Work values, attitudes, and moods all have the potential to influence each other.

2. There are two types of work values. Intrinsic work values are values related to the work itself, such as doing something that is interesting and challenging or having a sense of accomplishment. Extrinsic work values are values related to the consequences of work, such as having family security or status in the community.

3. Two important work attitudes are job satisfaction and organizational commitment. Job satisfaction is the collection of feelings and beliefs that people have about their current jobs. Organizational commitment is the collection of feelings and beliefs that people have about their organization as a whole. Work attitudes have three components: an affective component (how a person feels about his or her job), a cognitive component (what a person believes about his or her job), and a behavioral component (what a person thinks about how to behave in his or her job). People can have work attitudes about specific aspects of their jobs

and organizations and about their jobs and organizations as a whole.

4. People experience many different moods at work. These moods can be categorized generally as positive or negative. When workers are in positive moods, they feel excited, enthusiastic, active, strong, peppy, or elated. When workers are in negative moods, they feel distressed, fearful, scornful, hostile, jittery, or nervous. Workers also experience less intense moods at work, such as feeling sleepy or calm. Work moods are determined by both personality and situation and have the potential to influence organizational behaviors ranging from absence to being helpful to customers and coworkers to creativity to leadership.

5. Job satisfaction is one of the most important and well-researched attitudes in organizational behavior. Job satisfaction is determined by personality, values, the work situation, and social influence. Facet, discrepancy, and steady-state models of job satisfaction are useful for understanding and managing this important attitude.

6. Job satisfaction is not strongly related to job performance because workers are often not free to vary their levels of job performance and because sometimes job satisfaction is not relevant to job performance. Job satisfaction has a weak negative relationship to absenteeism. Job satisfaction influences turnover; workers who are satisfied with their jobs are less likely to quit them. Furthermore, workers who are satisfied with their jobs are more likely to perform voluntary behaviors, known as organizational citizenship behavior, that contribute to organizational effectiveness. Job satisfaction also has a positive effect on worker well-being.

7. Organizational commitment is the collection of feelings and beliefs that people have about their organization as a whole. Affective commitment exists when workers are happy to be members of an organization and believe in what it stands for. Continuance commitment exists when workers are committed to the organization because it is too costly for them to leave. Affective commitment has more positive consequences for organizations and their members than continuance commitment. Affective commitment is more likely when organizations are socially responsible and demonstrate that they are committed to workers. Workers with high levels of affective commitment are less likely to quit and may be more likely to perform organizational citizenship behavior.

Organizational Behavior in Action

TOPICS FOR DISCUSSION AND ACTION

1. How would you describe a person you know who has strong intrinsic and extrinsic work values?
2. Why might two workers with the same job develop different attitudes toward it?
3. On what kinds of jobs might the moods that workers experience be particularly important for understanding why they behave as they do?
4. Why are attitudes less long lasting than values, and why are moods more transitory than attitudes?
5. What specific standards might people use to determine their satisfaction with different facets of their jobs?
6. Why is job satisfaction not strongly related to job performance?
7. Should managers always try to reduce absenteeism and turnover as much as possible? Why or why not?
8. In what kinds of organizations might organizational citizenship behaviors be especially important?
9. What specific things can an organization do to raise levels of affective commitment?
10. In what kinds of organizations might affective commitment be especially important?

BUILDING DIAGNOSTIC SKILLS

Understanding Your Own Experience of Work

1. Describe your work values. Are they predominantly extrinsic or intrinsic?
2. How would your work values impact your reactions to each of these events at work?
   a. Getting promoted
   b. Being reassigned to a position with more responsibility but receiving no increase in pay
   c. Having to work late at night and travel one week a month on a job you find quite interesting
   d. Having a stressful job that pays well
   e. Having an exciting job with low job security
3. Describe your mood over the past week or two. Why have you felt this way? How has your mood affected your behavior?
4. What facets of a job are particularly important determinants of your level of job satisfaction? What standards do you (or would you) use to evaluate your job on these dimensions?
5. Toward what kind of organization are you most likely to have affective commitment? Toward what kind of organization are you most likely to have continuance commitment?
6. How might your affective commitment to an organization affect your behavior?

7. What forms of organizational citizenship behavior are you especially likely to perform and why? What forms of organizational citizenship behavior are you least likely to perform and why?

RESEARCH ON THE INTERNET: A MANAGER'S TOOL

Specific Task

Halliburton Company is one of the many corporations that stress the importance of behaving in accordance with ethical values. Review Halliburton's web site (www.halliburton.com) to learn more about this company. Then, click on "About Halliburton" and then click on "Summary Code Business Conduct." Review the various documents available and, in particular, read "Letter to All Halliburton Company Employees" from Dick Cheney, chairman of the board. Which ethical values does Halliburton endorse and emphasize? What are the various steps that Halliburton has taken to ensure that its employees can behave in accordance with these ethical values?

General Task

A growing number of companies are trying to boost levels of job satisfaction and promote positive feelings among their employees. Find the web site of such a company. What steps is this company taking to boost job satisfaction, promote positive moods, or simply incorporate more fun into the workplace? Do you think this company's initiatives would be effective at other companies? Why or why not?

TOPICS FOR DEBATE

Work values, attitudes, and moods have important implications for understanding and managing organizational behavior. Now that you have a good understanding of work values, attitudes, and moods, debate the following issues.

Debate One

Team A. Work attitudes are more important than work values for understanding and managing organizational behavior.

Team B. Work values are more important than work attitudes for understanding and managing organizational behavior.

Debate Two

Team A. Because job satisfaction is not related to job performance, managers do not need to be concerned about it.

Team B. Managers *do* need to be concerned about job satisfaction even though it is not related to performance.

EXPERIENTIAL EXERCISE

Promoting Organizational Citizenship Behavior

Objective

Organizations work most effectively when their members voluntarily engage in organizational citizenship behaviors. It is likely that you have witnessed some kind of organizational citizenship behavior. You may have seen this behavior performed by a coworker or supervisor where you work. You may have seen this behavior when you were interacting with an organization as a customer or client. Or someone in your university (a faculty or staff member or a student) may have gone above and beyond the call of duty to help another person or the university as a whole. Your objective is to identify instances of OCB and think about how managers can promote such behavior.

Procedure

Each member of the class takes a few minutes to think about instances of organizational citizenship behavior that he or she has observed and makes a list of them. The class then divides into groups of from three to five people, and each group appoints one member as spokesperson, to present the group's conclusions to the whole class. Group members do the following:

1. Take turns describing instances of organizational citizenship behavior they have observed.
2. Discuss the similarities and differences between each of these instances of organizational citizenship behavior and suggest some reasons why they may have occurred.
3. Compile a list of steps that managers can take to promote organizational citizenship behavior.

Spokespersons from each group report the following back to the class: four examples of organizational citizenship behavior that group members have observed and three steps that managers can take to try to promote OCB.

MAKING THE CONNECTION

Find an example of an organization that recently made some changes that have the potential to improve workers' attitudes or moods. Why did this organization make these changes? Why do you think these changes might improve workers' attitudes or moods?

CLOSING CASE

What Do Baby-Busters Want from Work?

Baby-boomers in professional and managerial careers are often said to be consumed by work. They have strived not only for traditional incentives—money, job titles, security, a climb up the corporate ladder—but also for interesting and challenging work. The new generation of professionals, the baby-busters (born around 1965), is posing some interesting challenges for their baby-boomer managers because of their different orientation toward working. What the busters seek to achieve through working is causing them to do things, such as turning down promotions, that were virtually unheard of in the past.[57]

What do baby-busters want from their jobs? These young individualists want interesting and challenging work, as did the boomers, but they do not want to make personal concessions or sacrifices for their employers. They have other interests that are just as important to them as work—leisure activities, the pursuit of their desired lifestyle, and family life. The baby-busters have no qualms about telling their managers that they do not want to work more than forty hours a week because they want to pursue a hobby or learn a new language. They also value their personal relationships. The busters are less willing than adults in prior generations, such as their parents, to sacrifice time with spouses and family to pursue the goal of corporate advancement. Essentially, they are seeking balance in their lives. For them, work is not necessarily the dominating factor.

It is important to keep in mind that among both the boomers and the busters, individuals differ in what they desire from working. All boomers are not absorbed by working, and some have actually stepped off the fast track to pursue careers that do not demand so much time, energy, or personal sacrifice. Similarly, some busters are just as consumed by working as their boomer managers. However, there does seem to be a fundamental difference in how these two generations of workers view work in general and their jobs in particular.

The younger generation's orientation toward work not only leads the baby-busters to do the unexpected in corporate America but also causes their managers to reflect on the best way to motivate and manage them. Angela Azzaretti, a professional in her twenties with Caterpillar (www.caterpillar.com), recently turned down two promotions. Her decision would have been strongly frowned on in previous generations. Linda Persico, an engineer with Ford Motor Company (www.ford.com), is engaged to be married. She says that her relationship with her future husband comes before her career. Aaron Evans, a sales manager with Intel (www.intel.com) in his twenties, is currently enjoying the comforts of his relatively high salary and job perks, but he is thinking about retiring in a couple of years to teach high school. His thinking: If he is going to work hard in sales, he wants to make a lot of money because he knows that at some point he will want to make a change. Rick Watkins left a promising job with investment banking giant Merrill Lynch (www.ml.com) because of its excessive hours. He currently works for the lower-key but successful Susquehanna Investment Group, where forty-hour weeks enable him to pursue one of his important hobbies: playing golf. As these baby-busters' choices and decisions illustrate, they are a breed apart from their predecessors.[58] Upper-level management may need to change some of the rules of the game to attract, retain, and motivate these independent thinkers whose lives do not necessarily revolve around work.

Questions for Discussion
1. What are the baby-busters trying to achieve through work?
2. Is it realistic to expect to have interesting and challenging work and an equally interesting and challenging life outside of work?
3. Which situational factors would be especially likely to lead to baby-busters being satisfied with their jobs?
4. What can managers and organizations do to encourage affective commitment among baby-busters?

Perception, Attribution, and the Management of Diversity

4

OPENING CASE

Why the Glass Ceiling and the Brick Wall?

Data gathered from a variety of sources indicate that women are not promoted as readily as men and have limited access to high-level management jobs. In some organizations, an invisible barrier—a sort of glass ceiling—prevents women from advancing as rapidly and as far up the corporate ladder

as men do.[1] A recent study by Catalyst, a nonprofit research organization in New York, found that women hold only about 10 percent of the top jobs in the 500 largest companies in the United States.[2] Although some women have made it to the very top of their organizations, such as Gail McGovern of AT&T and Carol

Bartz of Autodesk Inc., Catalyst found that women occupy only 2.4 percent of the chairman, president, CEO, and executive vice president positions in the largest 500 corporations.[3] Even in forward-thinking Silicon Valley, women lead only 5.6 percent of the 1,686 high-tech companies.[4] Why is this the case?

Discrimination is one of the biggest barriers to women's climbing the corporate ladder. No matter how qualified or experienced a female executive may be, upper-level managers—most of them white males—sometimes consider her capabilities inferior to those of a man simply because she is a woman. Moreover, male CEOs tend to groom successors who are like themselves and thus rarely pick a woman for such a role. So, not surprisingly, women are less likely than men to be chosen to participate in management training programs essential for upper-level corporate success. Participation in executive training seminars run by the nation's leading business schools is often an important prerequisite for high-level managers. Nationwide, only about 5 percent of the people enrolled in these programs are women.

Supporting the idea that women are perceived differently from men in corporate America is evidence that men continue to earn more money than women even when they have exactly the same qualifications, years of experience, and number of promotions and relocations, and when the women have not taken any time off from work for personal reasons. Moreover, women often experience a more subtle form of discrimination that senior researcher Anita Borg at Digital Equipment Corp. (www.digital.com) in Palo Alto, California, calls the "invisible woman syndrome," the tendency for women's opinions, ideas, and inputs to be disregarded, given short shrift, or ignored.[5] It seems that some men continue to view women as sweethearts, wives, daughters, and secretaries rather than as professional equals and colleagues. This view affects how male managers perceive and treat women in the workplace.[6]

Frustrated by the glass ceiling, some professional women quit their corporate jobs to start their own businesses. Kim Polese, founder and CEO of the Web company Marimba Inc. (www.marimba.com) recently suggested that, "If you really want to shoot to the top, you probably have to start your own business."[7] Before starting her own company, Polese was a product manager at Sun Microsystems, where she named and promoted the popular Java programming language.[8] Often, however, women who try to start their own businesses have not left their troubles behind but have instead traded a glass ceiling for a brick wall.[9] Investment manager Adela Cepeda, for instance, recently left her job at a Wall Street firm when it became clear that she would never be promoted to managing partner. Cepeda started her own investment company, Abacus Financial Group, which has outperformed the bond-index average and now has approximately $40 million in assets.[10] The success of her venture was not smooth, however. Cepeda encountered numerous problems, some of them apparently stemming from the fact that she is a woman. When she tried to get financing for her company, for example, bank officials were condescending and told her to try to get funding from her family. Male clients also have been leery of trusting a woman for investment decisions.

Many female entrepreneurs have encountered the brick wall. Women sometimes have unequal access to credit and financing, are excluded from bidding on or getting government contracts, and have problems in their day-to-day interactions with customers, clients, and suppliers. Despite having produced the popular *Carmen Sandiego* software while an employee of Broderbund Software Inc., Janese Swanson had trouble finding financing for her new venture, Girl Tech, a San Rafael, California, producer of electronic products for girls. She recently summed up her experience this way: "I went in with a doctorate, a track record, and a stellar business plan showing a hole in the marketplace. Everywhere I went, I heard no's."[11] Lynn Wilson, who founded the architecture firm of Lynn Wilson Associates International (Miami, Florida), says she has to be very careful when she interacts with construction crews and subcontractors who don't want a woman telling them what to do. In all of these cases, women in business are being seen as less competent and capable than their male counterparts even though their qualifications are comparable.[12]

Overview

Often, two people in an organization with the same qualifications are viewed differently. One may be seen as much more capable than another even though there is no objective basis for this distinction—the "more capable" person doesn't perform at a higher level. The opening case shows, for example, that women in business settings are sometimes seen as less capable and competent than men even when they have identical qualifications.

As another example of the way people can view things differently, think of the last group meeting you attended and the different ways in which people in the group interpreted what went on in the meeting. One person might have seen the final decision as the result of an impartial consideration of all alternatives, but another person might have seen it as the result of a powerful member imposing her or his will. Similarly, what might have appeared to be a reasonable, lively discussion to one person was a noisy, incomprehensible free-for-all to a second, and deeply offended a third. Although it seems obvious that there is an "objective" reality out there—that is, a reality that exists independent of each person who observes or describes it—descriptions of reality differ, depending on who is doing the describing. Each of us sees and interprets the same people, objects, and events differently.

In this chapter, we look at how perception and attribution help people organize, make sense of, and interpret what they observe. We discuss why equally qualified members of an organization are perceived differently, as in the opening case, and why people who attend the same meeting might have different interpretations of what went on, and even why two people who watch the same movie may come away with very different views about it. A major focus of this chapter is the role of perception and attribution in the effective management of diverse employees. Throughout the chapter, we give examples of how managers can enhance their ability to manage diverse employees by paying attention to the way they perceive and judge other people.

Perception and attribution are of fundamental importance in understanding and managing organizational behavior because all decisions and behaviors in organizations, such as the management of diversity, are influenced by how people interpret and make sense of the people and the events around them. Decisions about who should be hired, fired, transferred, or promoted and decisions about how to encourage organizational members to be more productive, to be more helpful to coworkers, or to perform otherwise desirable organizational behaviors are all based on managers' interpretations of the situations they face. Managers at all levels of an organization who understand how perception and attribution shape such interpretations are in a good position to try to ensure that their decisions help rather than harm the organization and its members. Understanding perception and attribution actually helps people at all levels of an organization be effective in their jobs and in their interactions with others.

The Nature of Perception

 Perception
The process by which individuals select, organize, and interpret the input from their senses.

Perception is the process by which individuals select, organize, and interpret the input from their senses (vision, hearing, touch, smell, and taste) to give meaning and order to the world around them.[13] Through perception, people try to make sense of their environment and the objects, events, and other people in it. Perception has three components (see Fig. 4.1):

1. The *perceiver* is the person trying to interpret some observation that he or she has just made, or the input from his or her senses.
2. The *target of perception* is whatever the perceiver is trying to make sense of. The target can be another person, a group of people, an event, a situation, an idea, a noise, or anything else the perceiver focuses on. In organizational behavior we are often concerned with *person perception,* or another person as the target of perception.
3. The *situation* is the context in which perception takes place—a committee meeting, the hallway, the office coffee machine, and so on.

Characteristics of all three components influence what is actually perceived.

People tend to think that perception is a simple phenomenon. They believe that there is an objective reality—a reality that exists independent of who observes or describes it—and that as long as their senses are not impaired (as long as they see clearly, hear well, are not intoxicated, and so on), perception is simply the understanding of this objective reality. People who believe in objective reality tend to believe that their own perceptions are accurate depictions of that reality. They believe that they perceive the true nature of the target (see Fig. 4.1) and behave as if this were the case.

Accurate perceptions
Perceptions that are as close as possible to the true nature of the target of perception.

The perceptual process, however, does not always yield **accurate perceptions**—perceptions that are as close as possible to the true or objective nature

FIGURE 4.1

Components of Perception: Perceiver, Target, and Situation

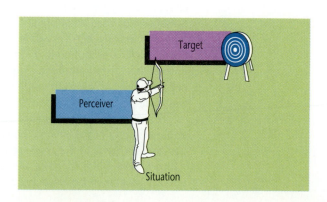

of the target. Even people who are trying to be totally "objective"—that is, to have accurate perceptions—often act and base decisions on an interpretation of reality that is subjective—that is, based on their own thoughts, feelings, and experiences. As a result, interpretations of reality vary among individuals. What is seen depends on who is doing the looking.

The fact that perception is not always accurate has significant implications for understanding and managing organizational behavior. Virtually every decision that a manager makes—decisions about hiring, firing, compensating organizational members, and so on—depends on the perceptions of the decision maker, and accurate perceptions are the prerequisite for good decisions. When perceptions are inaccurate, managers and other members of an organization make faulty decisions that hurt not only the workers involved but also the organization. Why are accurate perceptions of such fundamental importance in organizational behavior in general and in managing diverse employees in particular? The answer to this question touches on issues of motivation and performance, fairness and equity, and ethical action.

Motivation and Performance. Recall from Chapter 1 that a major responsibility of managers at all levels is to encourage organization members to perform behaviors that help the organization achieve its goals and to perform these behaviors as best they can. In essence, managers need to make sure that subordinates are motivated to perform at a high level. Because motivation and performance are of such fundamental importance in organizations, in Chapters 6, 7, and 8 we discuss them in detail and the organizational behavior tools that managers can use. However, in order to use these tools and motivate their subordinates, managers need to understand diverse subordinates and see them as they really are. The more accurately managers perceive subordinates, the better able they are to motivate them. For example, a manager who accurately perceives that a subordinate is independent and resents close supervision will be more likely to give the subordinate the breathing room he or she needs. Similarly, if a manager accurately perceives that a subordinate who shies away from difficult tasks has the necessary ability but is low on self-esteem (one of the personality traits discussed in Chapter 2), the manager will be more likely to assign to the subordinate tasks of an appropriate level of difficulty while at the same time providing the encouragement and support the subordinate needs. Accurate perceptions also help managers relate to each other and enable members at all levels to work together to achieve organizational goals.

Fairness and Equity. Suppose a manager supervises a diverse group of twenty subordinates, and every six months the manager has to decide how well each subordinate performed and how big a bonus each subordinate deserves. When the manager makes these decisions, it is extremely important that his or her perceptions of each subordinate's performance are as accurate as possible. If the manager's perceptions are inaccurate, the wrong decisions will be made, and diverse employees will feel that they are not being fairly treated, perhaps even that they have been discriminated against. Some of the high performers may receive lower bonuses than some of the mediocre performers and will feel that they are not being fairly or equitably treated. As you will see in Chapter 6, to be motivated to perform at a high level, workers need to feel that they are being fairly and equitably treated. High performers who are not fairly treated because of the inaccurate perceptions of their supervisors may resent their supervisors and the organization and may be more likely to lower their efforts. Why should they bother to try so hard when their efforts are not being recognized? Similarly, as suggested by the opening case, if a male manager fails to promote competent women because he mistakenly perceives women to be less competent than men, his unfair treatment hurts not only the women themselves but the organization as a whole because it is denied the opportunity to take advantage of the abilities of some of its female members. Ultimately, some high-performing women may leave the organization to seek fairer treatment elsewhere; this turnover will further weaken the organization. It is therefore extremely important for managers' perceptions to be accurate, so that managers can make fair and equitable decisions and effectively manage a diverse workforce.

Ethical Action.   We mentioned in Chapter 1 that the workforce is becoming increasingly diverse, and members of an organization often interact with others who may be different from them in age, race, gender, ethnicity, and other characteristics. Accurately perceiving diverse members of an organization and their abilities, skills, and performance levels is not only a legal requirement but also an ethical necessity. To ensure that such individuals are given the opportunities and rewards they deserve, to avoid illegal discrimination, and to ensure ethical behavior, perceptions must be accurate. Careful attention to the way managers perceive and judge diverse employees is an ethical and legal necessity.

As you can see, the process of perception is central to organizational behavior. Managers and all other members of an organization must be aware of and attuned to the factors that cause them to perceive things in particular ways. Managers and other participants in organizational life who understand what perceptions are, how they are formed, and what influences them are in a good position to ensure that their perceptions are as accurate as possible. Accurate perceptions enable members of an organization to make decisions that benefit the organization and all its members and are fair and ethical.

Characteristics of the Perceiver

Have you noticed that several people can observe the same person or event and come away with different interpretations of what they saw? That suggests that something about the perceiver may influence perception.

Perceivers do not passively process information. Their experience or knowledge (*schemas*), their needs and desires (*motivational states*), and their feelings (*moods*) filter information into their perceptions of reality (see Fig. 4.2). We now consider the way each of these characteristics of the perceiver affects perception.

SCHEMAS: THE PERCEIVER'S KNOWLEDGE BASE

When John Cunningham, a project manager at the engineering firm Tri-Systems Inc., was assigned to a new supervisor (a retired Air Force colonel), he did not gather a lot of information before forming an impression of him. Instead he took whatever information was at hand (however incomplete) and developed his own view or perception of his new boss. Simply knowing that his new supervisor used to be in the military was enough to convince Cunningham that he had a pretty good handle on what the retired colonel was like. Cunningham's supervisor in his last position had served in the armed

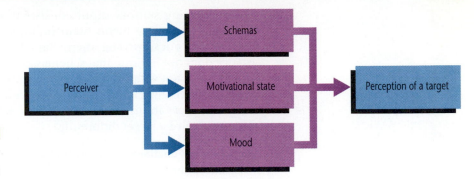

FIGURE 4.2

Characteristics of the Perceiver
That Affect Perception

🌱 **Schema**

An abstract knowledge structure that is
stored in memory and makes possible
the organization and interpretation of
information about a target of perception.

forces, and Cunningham had found him bossy and opinionated. To a neutral
observer, such limited information (the supervisor's military background)
hardly seems sufficient to support an assessment. But for Cunningham, the
equation was simple: His new ex-military supervisor would be opinionated
and bossy just as his other one had been.

Like Cunningham, we all interpret the world around us on the basis of
limited information. In large part, we rely on past experience and the knowledge we have gathered from a variety of sources to interpret and make sense
of any new person or situation (the *target of perception*) we encounter. Our past
experiences are organized into **schemas,** abstract knowledge structures that
are stored in memory and allow people to organize and interpret information
about a given target of perception.[14] Once an individual develops a schema for
a target of perception (such as a former military person), any new target related to the schema activates it, and information about the target is processed
in a way consistent with information stored in the schema. Thus schemas determine the way a target is perceived.

Schemas help people interpret the world around them by using their past
experiences and knowledge. Think about the last time you went to a party
where there were many people you didn't know. How did you decide whom to
talk to and whom to try to avoid? Without realizing you were doing so, you probably relied on your schemas about what different types of people are like to
form your perceptions and decide with whom you wanted to spend some time.

John Cunningham's schema for "ex-military supervisor" indicates that
"ex-military supervisors are bossy and opinionated." Because his new boss was
in the military, Cunningham perceives him as bossy and opinionated. All
perceivers actively interpret reality so that it is consistent with their expectations, which are, in turn, determined by their schemas.[15] In the opening case,
for example, business executives whose schemas for "CEOs" tell them that
"CEOs are men" will be unlikely to see qualified female executives as potential CEO material.

Schemas also influence the sensory input we pay attention to and the input we ignore. Once a schema is activated, we tend to notice information that
is consistent with the schema and ignore or discount information that is inconsistent. Because of his schema, Cunningham is especially attuned to any
information that indicates that his new supervisor is bossy and opinionated
(the boss has already rearranged the office layout), but Cunningham tends to
ignore information to the contrary (the boss solicits and listens to other people's suggestions).

By selecting sensory input consistent with existing schemas and discounting or ignoring inconsistent input, we reinforce and strengthen the schemas. It is not surprising, then, that schemas are resistant to change.[16] Resistance does not indicate that schemas never change; if they never changed, people could not adapt to changes in their environment. Schemas are, however, slow to change, and people need to encounter a considerable amount of contradictory information before their schemas are altered and they are able to perceive a target differently.

Are Schemas Functional?   Many times we jump to the wrong conclusions and form inaccurate perceptions of other people based on our schemas, especially when we have limited information about the target. Schemas, nevertheless, are functional for perceivers. We are continually bombarded with so much sensory input, so many potential targets of perception, that we cannot possibly take them all in and make sense of each one. Schemas help us make sense of this confusing array of sensory input, help us choose what information to pay attention to and what to ignore, and guide our perception of often ambiguous information. In this way, schemas help members of an organization learn about and adapt to the complex environment inside and outside the organization.

Schemas can be dysfunctional, however, if they result in inaccurate perceptions. Cunningham's new supervisor may not be at all bossy or opinionated but may instead be an accessible, competent, and talented manager. Cunningham's schema for "ex-military supervisor," however, causes him to perceive his boss in a different, and negative, light. Thus Cunningham's schema is dysfunctional because his inaccurate perceptions color his interactions with his new boss.

Inaccurate perceptions can also be dysfunctional for the target of perception. The opening case indicates that some men in business have schemas that fit successful female professionals into a pigeonhole marked "wife, mother, daughter." When a man with such a schema encounters a woman in an organization, the schema is activated, and the man perceives the woman as less competent and capable in a business context than she actually is. This incorrect perception can hurt the woman's future prospects when she is passed up for promotion or denied access to financing to start her own business.

Schemas can guide perceptions in a functional way, but we have to guard against the common tendency to jump to incorrect conclusions based on our past experiences.[17] John Cunningham clearly did not have enough information to have an accurate perception of his supervisor, and he should have refrained from making a judgment until he saw how his supervisor actually behaved on the job.

Stereotype
A set of overly simplified and often inaccurate beliefs about the typical characteristics of a particular group.

Stereotypes: An Example of a Dysfunctional Schema.   A **stereotype** is a set of overly simplified and often inaccurate beliefs about the typical characteristics of a particular group. We all are familiar with stereotypes based on highly visible characteristics such as race, gender, nationality, or age, and we are aware of the damage they can do.[18] Stereotypes are dysfunctional schemas because they are often based on inaccurate information about individuals' interests, beliefs, capabilities, behaviors, and so on. Stereotyped individuals are assigned to the schema only because they possess a single distinguishing characteristic.

As soon as a person is encountered and stereotyped, the perceiver assumes that the person has the characteristics associated with the stereotype.

The perceiver pays attention to information consistent with the stereotype and ignores inconsistent information. Because objective reality (what the person is really like) rarely matches subjective reality (what the perceiver *thinks* the person is like), stereotypes can be dysfunctional and damaging for the perceiver, the target, and the organization.

Stereotypes based on race, gender, and age have been responsible for discrimination in society in general and in the workplace in particular. As a result of the negative effects of such stereotypes, it is illegal to discriminate against people because of their race, gender, or age, and organizations that do so may face lawsuits. (See Insight 4.1.)

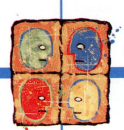

Insight 4.1

Diversity

Age Stereotypes Take Their Toll on Older Workers

The U.S. workforce is getting older, and more and more older workers are finding themselves reporting to supervisors younger than they. Some of these young supervisors have stereotype schemas that cause them to perceive older subordinates as rigid, unwilling to change, and lacking up-to-date skills and capabilities.

Assistant manager John Kolterman (age 63) and another assistant manager (age 52) were fired from their jobs at a Wal-Mart (www.wal-mart.com) store in Ruskin, Florida, by their young supervisor. Kolterman had helped Wal-Mart successfully open several new stores, and previous supervisors often had rated his performance and leadership capabilities highly. Prior to being fired, he had received a pay raise.

In the age discrimination lawsuit that Kolterman filed against Wal-Mart, he claimed that his young supervisor told him that "he wouldn't be able to adapt to the coming changes" and frequently called him "Pops" or "Old Man." After the firings, the supervisor is alleged to have told other employees that "they were going to get some younger assistant managers that were go-getters." However, officials at Wal-Mart claim that the firings were simply part of a companywide cut in assistant managers.[19]

Age stereotypes often lead to inaccurate perceptions of older workers, but they may be hard to dispel because of the few times when they contain a grain of truth. For example, Io Oakes was fired from her job as head of the interior design group at a Boston architectural firm. Although Oakes was 50 years old at the time of the firing, it was not age discrimination that led to her dismissal but rather the fact that she had not kept up to date with changing technology and lacked computer skills. Oakes, however, subsequently demonstrated that she could learn computer-assisted architectural design, regardless of her age. After learning how to use computers, she started her own company.[20]

Workers and managers have to guard against stereotypical thinking about different types of organizational members. One way to do so is to encourage members of an organization to think about characteristics that really affect job performance and not irrelevant characteristics such as age or race. Managers should be careful to evaluate older workers in terms of their skills, capabilities, and performance levels—can they use computers; are they willing to learn how to use computers; are they among the top performers in the organization—rather than simply noting that they are 50 or 60 years old and assuming that they are "over the hill." Similarly, older workers need to be aware of the skills, capabilities, and performance levels of younger workers, rather than simply noting that they are young enough to be their children and assuming that they are still "wet behind the ears." Discriminating against or treating workers differently because of their gender, age, or race is not only illegal but also unethical.

THE PERCEIVER'S MOTIVATIONAL STATE

Perceiver's motivational state
The needs, values, and desires of a perceiver at the time of perception.

The **perceiver's motivational state**—the perceiver's needs, values, and desires at the time of perception—influences his or her perception of the target. Perceivers see what they want to see, hear what they want to hear, and believe what they want to believe, because of their motivational states. A simple yet ingenious experiment has demonstrated the effects of the perceiver's motivational state. Participants are shown a series of meaningless abstract pictures and are asked what objects and shapes they perceive in them. The images they see depend on their motivational states. Those who are hungry, for example, are motivated to see food and actually do indicate that they perceive images of food in the abstract pictures.[21]

Like schemas, motivational states can result in inaccurate perceptions and faulty decision making. Suppose a manager does not get along with a hardworking, productive subordinate. The subordinate is a thorn in the manager's side, and the manager would welcome any opportunity to justify recommending that the subordinate be transferred to another position or even dismissed. What is likely to happen when the manager must evaluate the subordinate's performance on some relatively subjective dimensions such as cooperation and being a good team player? Even if the subordinate actually deserves to score high, the manager may rate the person low.

Organizational members need to be aware that their own needs and desires influence their perceptions and can result in faulty decisions that have negative consequences for the organization. One way managers can guard against this outcome is to base perceptions on actual behaviors they have observed a person perform. Managers also can take other steps to increase the accuracy of their perceptions. They can be aware of their own motives, concentrate on perceiving how people actually perform, and refrain from assuming how someone probably behaved when they did not directly observe his or her behavior.

THE PERCEIVER'S MOOD

Perceiver's mood
How a perceiver feels at the time of perception.

The **perceiver's mood**—how the perceiver feels at the time of perception—can also influence perception of the target. In Chapter 3, we discussed how work moods (people's feelings at the time they perform their jobs) influence organizational behavior. People's moods also affect their perception of a target.

Marie Flanagan, a fashion designer for a clothing manufacturer, was so excited about the new line of women's suits she finished designing late one afternoon that she could hardly wait to show her sketches to her supervisor Phil Kraus the next day. But when Flanagan saw Kraus in the hallway the next morning, he barely grunted hello, and later that morning his secretary told Flanagan that Kraus was in a terrible mood. Despite her eagerness to find out what Kraus thought of her new line, Flanagan decided to wait until he was in a better mood before showing him her sketches. She reasoned that even if the new line was a potential winner, Kraus was likely to find fault with it because of his bad mood. She realized that people's moods influence their perceptions and judgments. When workers are in a positive mood, they are likely to perceive their coworkers, supervisors, subordinates, and even their jobs in a more positive light than they would when they are in a negative mood.[22]

Characteristics of the Target and Situation

We defined *perception* as the process whereby people select, organize, and interpret the input from their senses to give meaning and order to the world around them. This input comes from the targets of perception in the situations in which they are perceived. Thus, just as characteristics of the perceiver influence perceptions, so too do characteristics of the target and of the situation (see Table 4.1).

How do characteristics of the target influence perception? Consider two job applicants (targets of perception) who have similar qualifications and are equally capable. An interviewer (the perceiver), however, perceived one applicant much more positively than the other because of the way each acted during the interview. One applicant tried to make a good impression by volunteering information about his past accomplishments and achievements and behaving in a confident and business-like fashion. The other was low key

TABLE 4.1

Factors That Influence Perception

Characteristics of the Perceiver	Characteristics of the Target	Characteristics of the Situation
Schemas: The perceiver's knowledge base	Ambiguity: A lack of clearness or definiteness that makes it difficult to determine what a person, place, or thing is really like	Additional information: Situational information that the perceiver uses to interpret the target
Motivational state: The perceiver's needs, values, and desires at the time of perception	Social status: A person's real or perceived position in society or an organization	Salience: The extent to which a target stands out among a group of people or things
Mood: The perceiver's feelings at the time of perception	Use of impression managment: A person's efforts to control others' perceptions of him or her	

and mentioned his achievements only when he was specifically asked about them. The difference in behavior caused the interviewer to perceive one applicant as more capable than the other.

Here is an example of how the situation influences perception. Suppose you (the perceiver) see one of your friends (the target) having a beer at a party (the situation). You might perceive that he is having a good time. Now suppose you see the same friend having a beer before his 9 a.m. class (another situation). You perceive that he has a drinking problem.

In this section, we consider the ambiguity and social status of the target and impression management by the target. We then discuss how characteristics of the situation influence perception by providing additional information for the perceiver to use to interpret the target. Managers and other members of an organization who are aware of the ways in which various target- and situation-related factors influence perception are well positioned to ensure that their perceptions of people, things, and events are as accurate as possible.

AMBIGUITY OF THE TARGET

The word *ambiguity* refers to a lack of clearness or definiteness. It is difficult for a perceiver to determine what an ambiguous target is really like. As the ambiguity of a target increases, it becomes increasingly difficult for perceivers to form accurate perceptions. It is also more likely that different perceivers will differ in their perceptions of the target.

Four managers are jointly responsible for choosing new locations for fast-food restaurants for a national chain. Certain locations (for example, those across the street from a large university) are sure winners and others (for example, those difficult to enter and leave because of traffic congestion) are sure losers. Such locations are relatively unambiguous targets of perception. Each of the four managers perceives them accurately and they agree with each other about the desirability of those locations.

When the nature of a target is clear, different perceivers have little difficulty forming similar perceptions of the target that are close to its real nature. But when a target is ambiguous, the perceiver needs to engage in a lot more interpretation and active construction of reality to form a perception of the target. The suitability of some of the locations that the four managers must evaluate is ambiguous. Will a restaurant located in a once-prosperous but now-failing shopping mall that is being renovated do well? Will a restaurant located on the outskirts of a small town in a rural area attract enough customers to earn a profit? The managers' perceptions of the desirability of such locations tend to be less certain than their perceptions of less ambiguous locations, and they often find themselves disagreeing with each other.

The more ambiguous a target is, the more potential there is for errors in perception. Thus, when targets are ambiguous, members of an organization should not be overly confident about the accuracy of their perceptions, and they should acquire as much additional information as they can to help them form an accurate perception. When looking at ambiguous restaurant locations (to continue our example), the four managers collect a lot of information—estimates of the performance levels of other fast-food restaurants in the vicinity, traffic patterns at meal times, population growth in the area, spending patterns of likely patrons—in order to make a decision based on accurate perceptions.

Social status
A person's real or perceived position in society or in an organization.

SOCIAL STATUS OF THE TARGET

Social status is a person's real or perceived position in society or in an organization. In the minds of many people, targets with a relatively high status are perceived to be smarter, more credible, more knowledgeable, and more responsible for their actions than lower-status targets. Organizations often use a high-status member to make an important announcement to other members of the organization or to the public at large because the audience is likely to perceive the announcer as credible because of his or her status. A lower-status member of the organization who is more knowledgeable than anyone else about the issue at hand is likely to lack credibility because of his or her status.

To ensure that women and members of minority groups enjoy equal footing with white men and have the social status they deserve in an organization, and to conform with legal requirements, many organizations have adopted affirmative action programs. These programs, however, sometimes perpetuate the perception problems and stereotypes they were meant to overcome. Women and minority group members are sometimes perceived as having relatively low status in the organization because they were affirmative action hires—people hired not because of their own merits but because of their gender or minority status. Their affirmative action status causes other members of the organization to perceive and treat them as second-class citizens. This situation occurred at Monsanto.[23] (See Insight 4.2.)

Is this touch an innocent and supportive one, or is it threatening and an instance of sexual harassment? Because physical contact between coworkers can always be misinterpreted, it should be avoided.

Insight 4.2

Affirmative Action Can Lower Status of Women and Minorities

Colton Isadore, a supervisor at Monsanto Co.'s (www.monsanto.com) Chocolate Bayou chemical company, is against hiring quotas for women and minority group members. His opinion may be somewhat surprising given that Isadore is an African American and Monsanto is a champion of affirmative action. However, affirmative action programs and the use of quotas in hiring have had some unintended consequences for the people they were designed to help, and Isadore fears white backlash from a quota system.

A vigorous supporter of affirmative action since the 1970s, Monsanto has hired relatively high proportions of women and minorities. In the late 1980s and early 1990s, however, a puzzling trend was noticed: relatively high voluntary turnover rates among the affirmative action workers. The chemical company was succeeding at hiring women and minorities but seemed to have difficulty retaining them.

Concerned about this trend, the company started a series of exit interviews to determine why these workers were leaving. What managers found was disturbing. Fully 100 percent of the minorities who left indicated that they had had trouble dealing with their supervisors and had wanted more job responsibility. A comparison of minorities and whites who voluntarily left the company revealed that 30 percent more minorities than whites thought their bosses were unfair and arbitrary. Such complaints were also heard from departing women. For example, 20 percent more women than men who left Monsanto felt that pay and promotion decisions were unfair. A large proportion of the women who had already found new jobs indicated that they would have better career advancement opportunities with their new employers.

These findings were surprising to top managers but not to rank-and-file workers. What appears to have taken place is that affirmative action programs had lowered the social status of some of the women and minorities who were hired. Viewed and treated as second-class citizens, capable and talented minorities and women did not get the feedback and developmental assistance they needed to progress in the company and often felt that they did not fit in.

After uncovering these problems, Monsanto began an innovative series of "how to manage diversity" programs aimed at helping managers to deal with groups of subordinates from all walks of life. In diversity training workshops, for example, participants are made aware of gender and race stereotypes and are shown how they may even unintentionally hold and perceive others in terms of these stereotypes. In the thirteen-day "Consulting Pairs" program, employees receive intensive training to serve as in-house consultants to other members of the organization on race and gender issues. Pairs of same-race or same-gender participants who have completed the training then spend between 10 to 20 percent of their time in the next eighteen months helping other workers deal with diversity issues such as how a white subordinate feels reporting to an African American supervisor for the first time. The pairs are also charged with uncovering unintended race and gender stereotypes in company policies and job assignments and helping new supervisor-subordinate teams get off on the right foot.[24]

We can learn two important managerial lessons from Monsanto. First, being labeled "affirmative action hire" can adversely affect a worker's status in the organization and thus influence how others perceive and behave toward that worker. Whether or not such workers leave the organization, both the organization and the employee involved suffer. The organization suffers because it is not fully utilizing these workers' capabilities: They probably are not receiving the training they need and are not being promoted when they should be. Individual employees suffer because they are not being treated fairly. The second managerial lesson is that organizations should manage diversity and create innovative programs to help eliminate bias in the workplace and the second-class status that women and minorities may inadvertently acquire.

IMPRESSION MANAGEMENT BY THE TARGET

Impression management
An attempt to control the perceptions or impressions of others.

Impression management is an attempt to control the perceptions or impressions of others.[25] Just as a perceiver actively constructs reality through his or her perceptions, a target of perception can also play an active role in managing the perceptions that others have of him or her.

People in organizations use several impression management tactics to affect how others perceive them. They are especially likely to use these tactics when interacting with perceivers who have power over them and on whom they are dependent for evaluations, raises, and promotions.[26] Subordinates, for example, use impression management tactics on their supervisors to a greater extent than supervisors use them on subordinates. Nevertheless, impression management is a two-way street and is engaged in by individuals at all organizational levels as they interact with superiors, peers, and subordinates as well as with suppliers, customers, and other people outside the organization. Table 4.2 describes five common impression management tactics: behavioral matching, self-promotion, conforming to situational norms, appreciating or flattering others, and being consistent.

Conforming to situational norms—the informal rules of behavior that most members of an organization follow—is a particularly important impression management tactic.[27] Situational norms can pertain to working past the traditional 5 p.m. quitting time to impress the boss, disagreeing with others in meetings to be seen as important, or even dressing to make a good impression.

People differ in the extent to which they conform to situational norms and engage in other forms of impression management. In Chapter 2, we discussed how people who are high on the trait self-monitoring are especially concerned about behaving appropriately. It is likely, therefore, that people who are high on self-monitoring are more likely than individuals who are low on self-monitoring to engage in impression management tactics such as conforming to situational norms.

TABLE **4.2**

Impression Management Tactics

Tactic	Description	Example
Behavioral matching	The target of perception matches his or her behavior to that of the perceiver.	A subordinate tries to imitate her boss's behavior by being modest and soft-spoken because her boss is modest and soft-spoken.
Self-promotion	The target tries to present herself or himself in as positive a light as possible.	A worker reminds his boss about his past accomplishments and associates with coworkers who are evaluated highly.
Conforming to situational norms	The target follows agreed-upon rules for behavior in the organization.	A worker stays late every night even if she has completed all of her assignments because staying late is one of the norms of her organization.
Appreciating or flattering others	The target compliments the perceiver. This tactic works best when flattery is not extreme and when it involves a dimension important to the perceiver.	A coworker compliments a manager on his excellent handling of a troublesome employee.
Being consistent	The target's beliefs and behaviors are consistent. There is agreement between the target's verbal and nonverbal behaviors.	A subordinate whose views on diversity are well known flatters her boss for her handling of a conflict between two co-workers of different racial backgrounds. When speaking to her boss, the target looks her boss straight in the eye and has a sincere expression on her face.

Sources: C. N. Alexander, Jr., and G. W. Knight, "Situated Identities and Social Psychological Experimentation," *Sociometry,* 1971, 34, pp. 65–82; S. T. Fiske and S. E. Taylor, *Social Cognition* (Reading, Mass.: Addison-Wesley, 1984); K. J. Gergen and M. G. Taylor, "Social Expectancy and Self-Presentation in a Status Hierarchy," *Journal of Experimental Social Psychology,* 1969, 5, pp. 79–92; D. Newston and T. Czerlinsky, "Adjustment of Attitude Communications for Contrasts by Extreme Audiences," *Journal of Personality and Social Psychology,* 1974, 30, pp. 829–837; B. R. Schenkler, *Impression Management: The Self-Concept, Social Identity, and Interpersonal Relations* (Monterey, Calif.: Brooks/Cole, 1980); M. Snyder, "Impression Management," in L. S. Wrightsman, ed., *Social Psychology in the Seventies* (New York: Wiley, 1977).

Conforming to situational norms can often be difficult for people operating in the international arena. Common courtesies and gestures that are taken for granted in one culture or country may be frowned on or downright insulting in another. The common hand signal for "OK" that is used in the United States, for example, is considered obscene in Brazil, Ghana, Greece, and Turkey and means "zero" or "worthless" in France and Belgium. As another example, in the United States it is considered polite to ask a man how his wife is, but in Arab countries this inquiry is considered indiscreet.[28]

Outright deceit can be used in impression management but is probably not that common. Ingrained moral or ethical codes prevent most people from deliberately misrepresenting themselves or lying.[29] In addition, the chances of being found out are often pretty high. Claiming on an employment application, for example, that you attended a certain school or worked for a company though you never did is neither honest nor smart. Most impression management is an attempt to convey as positive an impression as possible without lying about one's capabilities, achievements, and experiences. People are especially likely to engage in impression management when they are likely to benefit from it. The reward may be desirable job assignments, promotions, raises, or the good opinions of others.

INFORMATION PROVIDED BY THE SITUATION

The situation—the context or environment surrounding the perceiver and the target—provides the perceiver with additional information to use in interpreting the target. Consider the situation Marci Sloan was in when she started a new job as supervisor of salespeople in a large department store. The department store had just begun a push to increase the quality of customer service, and Sloan's boss impressed on her that improved service to customers should be a major priority for her department. On her first day on the job, Sloan decided to spend as much time as she could unobtrusively observing her salespeople in action, so she could get a good idea of the level of service they were routinely providing.

The levels of service offered by the four salespeople she was able to observe varied considerably. In forming her perceptions of these salespeople, however, she relied not only on the behavior she observed but also on the situation in which the behavior occurred. One key factor was how busy the department was when she observed each salesperson. She observed two of them in the morning when business was slow. Each person only handled two customers, but one salesperson provided significantly more service than the other. She observed the other two salespeople in the late afternoon, the busiest time of day for the department. Both had a continual stream of customers. One salesperson handled more customers than the other, but the slower salesperson gave each customer more personal attention. Clearly, Sloan could not rely solely on the behavior of the salespeople in forming her impression of the customer service they were providing. She also had to consider all the additional information that the situation provided.

The salience of individual minority members of the Supreme Court has steadily decreased over time as the number of minority members has increased. Sandra Day O'Connor, the first woman on the Supreme Court, became far less salient after Ruth Bader Ginsberg joined her on the bench. Clarence Thomas remains the Court's only African-American justice.

STANDING OUT IN THE CROWD: THE EFFECTS OF SALIENCE IN A SITUATION

 Salience
The extent to which a target of perception stands out in a group of people or things.

In considering how the situation affects perception, we need to focus on one factor that is particularly important: the **salience** of the target in the situation—that is, the extent to which the target stands out in a group of people or things. We have all experienced the effects of salience. Have you ever been the only student in a room full of professors, the only man in a group of women, or the only African American in a room full of white people? A salient individual is very conspicuous and often feels self-conscious and believes that everyone is watching his or her every move. That assessment is pretty accurate too. The other people in the group or room do pay more attention to the salient person, for he or she indeed does stand out. Salience, in and of itself, *should not affect* how a target is perceived. After all, a man is the same person regardless of whether he is in a room full of men or women. But remember that perception is a subjective process, and because of that subjectivity, salience *does affect* how a target is perceived. Table 4.3 lists some situational factors that cause a target to stand out.

What are the consequences of salience for perception in organizations? Consider the experiences Mary Schwartz has had as the only female partner in a small consulting firm. Her male colleagues treat her as their equal, and she gets along well with each of them, but she still feels the effects of her salience. These effects take the form of extreme evaluations and stereotyping.

Extreme Evaluations.   Schwartz noticed that her male colleagues' reactions to her various accomplishments and mishaps on the job seemed to be extreme. She recently landed a major new account for the firm and received such lavish praise that she became embarrassed. Likewise, when she was unable to attend an important meeting because of a family problem, it was made clear to her that she had lost favor in everyone's eyes.

TABLE **4.3**

Causes of Salience

Cause	Description	Examples
Being novel	Anything that makes a target unique in a situation	Being the only person of a particular age, sex, or race in a situation; wearing jeans when everyone else is dressed in business clothes
Being figural	Standing out from the background by virtue of being bright or illuminated, changing, moving, sitting or standing in a prominent place, or seeming to be complex	Being in a spotlight; moving more than others in a group; sitting at the head of the table; wearing bright clothes
Being inconsistent with other people's expectations	Behaving or looking in a way that is out of the ordinary	A normally shy person who is the life of the party; a salesperson who insults a customer; a man or woman who is exceptionally attractive

Sources: S. T. Fiske and S. E. Taylor, *Social Cognition* (Reading, Mass.: Addison-Wesley, 1984); R. M. Kanter, *Men and Women of the Corporation* (New York: Basic Books, 1977); L. Z. McArthur and E. Ginsberg, "Causal Attribution to Salient Stimuli: An Investigation of Visual Fixation Mediators," *Personality and Social Psychology Bulletin,* 1981, 7, pp. 547–553; L. Z. McArthur and D. L. Post, "Figural Emphasis and Person Perception," *Journal of Experimental Social Psychology,* 1977, 13, pp. 520–535; C. Wolman and H. Frank, "The Solo Woman in a Professional Peer Group," *American Journal of Orthopsychiatry,* 1975, 45, pp. 164–171.

Schwartz's experience is not unique. Individuals who are salient are often perceived in more extreme terms (positive or negative) than inconspicuous members of a group. They are also seen as being especially influential or responsible for what happens to them and to the groups they belong to.[30]

Stereotyping. On several occasions Schwartz felt that her male colleagues were unintentionally stereotyping her as a "typical woman." They frequently called on her to enlighten them about the "woman's point of view" on various matters, such as how to deal with a female client or subordinate. On several occasions, Schwartz was tempted to tell her colleagues that all women are not alike and to point out that she had more in common with them even though they were men than she had in common with their female subordinates or clients.

Individuals who are salient, like Schwartz, are often perceived in terms of whatever is causing their salience: They are stereotyped.[31] Perceivers consider the thoughts, feelings, and behaviors of salient individuals to be more consistent with their distinguishing feature than would be the case if they were not salient. Perceivers often also view them as being representative of all people who are like them on the salient characteristic. Salience due to gender—for example, being the only woman in a group of men—is just one form of salience that impacts perceptions of organizational members. Salience due to race also has particularly powerful effects on perception. (See Insight 4.3.)

Insight 4.3

Diversity

Salience Takes Its Toll on African Americans in Corporate America

Although there are more African Americans in management positions today than there were several years ago, African American managers still experience the effects of their relative salience. African American managers are still a small minority (in 1990, only 5.2 percent of the managers in firms with at least a hundred employees were African American) and thus are often perceived in an extreme and a stereotypical manner.

A. Bruce Crawley, an African American manager at the First Pennsylvania Corp. bank has had a hard climb up the corporate ladder during his twenty-two-year tenure. When he was assistant advertising director, he created a sales promotion that helped to generate $73 million in bank deposits. His boss, however, tried to take credit for this promotion, and Crawley had to work hard to get the recognition due him. Crawley took his case to James Bodine, who at the time was president of the bank. Bodine recalls thinking that Crawley was very talented but was having problems because he is an African American and because some upper managers perceived him as an antagonistic proponent for African American rights. Crawley finally won the promotion to advertising director that he was seeking and received subsequent promotions to bank vice president and senior vice president. But each move was delayed, and his climb up the corporate ladder was slower than the climbs of his white peers.

It appears that some of Crawley's behaviors evoked extreme responses among white managers because of Crawley's racial salience. For example, Crawley adopted an aggressive and driving style—a style used by many of the senior managers at the bank. But when he behaved this way, they advised him to be more congenial if he wanted to get ahead. Crawley, however, was not content to be meek and mild because that was not the behavior his colleagues were using to get ahead.

Noland Joiner, an African American senior consultant at Arthur Andersen & Co., has also learned that being salient causes an individual to be on his or her guard. He sometimes feels that he has to watch everything he says and does. Joiner says that he is perceived as not being serious if he relaxes too much, but if he attempts some strong corporate maneuvering, he is perceived to be stabbing people in the back. Knowing that others perceive you differently because of your race eventually takes its toll on performance, according to Joiner.[32]

Some companies are taking steps to overcome some of these problems for African Americans and other minorities. Levi Strauss & Co. (www.levi.com), which has been proactive in this area, is among the most ethnically and culturally diverse organizations in the United States. In 1991, 56 percent of Levi Strauss's employees in the United States were minority group members. CEO Robert B. Haas has been hard at work to eliminate the "glass ceiling" (discussed in the opening case) that keeps many women and minorities from top-management positions. Levi Strauss spends $5 million a year on "Valuing Diversity" educational programs, which seek to change the way employees at all levels in the organization, including senior managers, think about and view minorities.[33]

Biases and Problems in Person Perception

We have been describing what perception is, how and why perceptions are formed, and the powerful effects they have on organizations and their members. Throughout this discussion, we emphasized the importance of accurate perceptions. Accurate perceptions enable managers to evaluate subordinates' performance accurately and make fair and ethical decisions about whom to hire and promote. They also enable members of an organization to understand and get along with each other and with clients, customers, and other people outside the organization.

You might think that once members of an organization are armed with this knowledge of perception (as you are now), their perceptions would be greatly improved and they would do a better job of seeing other people (targets) as they really are. Unfortunately, biases and problems in person perception limit the accuracy of perception, and dramatic improvement does not always come about.

A **bias** is a systematic tendency to use or interpret information about a target in a way that results in inaccurate perceptions. When bias and problems in person perception exist, perceivers form inaccurate perceptions of a target. In turn, when perceptions are inaccurate, decisions are likely to be inappro-

Bias

A systematic tendency to use or interpret information in a way that results in inaccurate perceptions.

TO MANAGERS

priate: An incompetent subordinate gets promoted, or a competent job candidate receives a negative rating from an interviewer. Managers, coworkers, and subordinates who are aware of biases and problems in person perception are in a good position to prevent them from having an effect on their perceptions and subsequent behavior and decisions. We have already examined how stereotypes can bias perception. In this section we look at primacy, contrast, and halo effects and other common biases (see Table 4.4).

PRIMACY EFFECTS

Despite the old saying "You can't judge a book by its cover," you have probably heard or learned firsthand how important first impressions are. Scientific evidence, however, supports the folk wisdom of the adage. **Primacy effect** is the biased perception that results when the first pieces of information that people have about some target have an inordinately large influence on their perception of the target.

Primacy effects are a common problem in interviews. Research has found that many interviewers decide in the first few minutes of an interview whether a job candidate is a good prospect, then spend the rest of the interview confirming their initial judgment by selectively paying attention to information that is consistent with that judgment and discounting or ignoring inconsistent information. An interviewer who falls victim to the primacy effect may turn down qualified interviewees who fail to perform well in the first minute or two of an interview because they are nervous.

Primacy effects can also be a problem in the perception and evaluation of long-time members of an organization. The manager of a subordinate who starts out on the fast track but then begins to slide downhill may fail to perceive the subordinate's performance problems because of the primacy effect. The manager's perception of the subordinate's current level of performance is biased by the subordinate's early success. As a result of this faulty perception, the manager will fail to give the subordinate the feedback and coaching necessary to get the subordinate back on track. Organizational members who are aware of primacy effects can be on guard not to let their first impressions distort their perceptions.

Primacy effect
The biased perception that results when the first information that a perceiver has about a target has an inordinately large influence on the perceiver's perception of the target.

TABLE **4.4**

Biases and Problems in Person Perception

Source of Bias	Description	Example
Primacy effects	The initial pieces of information that a perceiver has about a target have an inordinately large effect on the perceiver's perception and evaluation of the target.	Interviewers decide in the first few minutes of an interview whether or not a job candidate is a good prospect.
Contrast effect	The perceiver's perceptions of others influence the perceiver's perception of a target.	A manager's perception of an average subordinate is likely to be lower if that subordinate is in a group with very high performers rather than in a group with very low performers.
Halo effect	The perceiver's general impression of a target influences his or her perception of the target on specific dimensions.	A subordinate who has made a good overall impression on a supervisor is rated as performing high-quality work and always meeting deadlines regardless of work that is full of mistakes and late.
Similar-to-me effect	People perceive others who are similar to themselves more positively than they perceive those who are dissimilar.	Supervisors rate subordinates who are similar to them more positively than they deserve.
Harshness, leniency, and average tendency	Some perceivers tend to be overly harsh in their perceptions, some overly lenient. Others view most targets as being about average.	When rating subordinates' performances, some supervisors give almost everyone a poor rating, some give almost everyone a good rating, and others rate almost everyone as being about average.
Knowledge of predictor	Knowing how a target stands on a predictor of performance influences perceptions of the target.	A professor perceives a student more positively than she deserves because the professor knows the student had a high score on the SAT.

Contrast effect
The biased perception that results when perceptions of a target person are distorted by the perceiver's perception of others.

CONTRAST EFFECTS

Contrast effect is the biased perception that results when perceptions of a target person are distorted by the perceiver's perception of others in the situation. A manager's perception of a subordinate whose performance is average is likely to be less favorable if that subordinate is in a group of very high performers than it would be if that subordinate were in a group of average or low performers. An average job applicant will be perceived more favorably by an interviewer if he or she is preceded by two or three below-average applicants rather than by two or three above-average applicants. Both the manager and the interviewer in those examples are victims of the contrast effect. The subordinate's and the job applicant's performance and capabilities are not changed at all by the behavior of other workers and applicants.

Halo effect

The biased perception that results when the perceiver's general impression of a target distorts his or her perception of the target on specific dimensions.

HALO EFFECTS

A **halo effect** occurs when the perceiver's general impression of a target distorts his or her perception of the target on specific dimensions.[34] A subordinate who has made a good overall impression on a supervisor, for example, may be rated as performing high-quality work and always meeting deadlines (specific dimensions of performance) even though the person's work is full of mistakes and is usually late. Because of the halo effect, the subordinate will not receive the feedback necessary to improve performance on the specific dimensions in question. Halos can be negative too: A supervisor who has a negative overall impression of a subordinate may mistakenly perceive that the subordinate is uncooperative and spends too much time on the telephone.

SIMILAR-TO-ME EFFECTS

It is a fact of life that people tend to like others who are similar to themselves. In organizations, this "birds of a feather" or "like likes like" tendency can create problems because people tend (often unconsciously) to perceive those who are similar to themselves more positively than they perceive those who are dissimilar. During a performance appraisal, for example, supervisors may rate subordinates who are similar to them more positively than they deserve.[35] Likewise, interviewers may evaluate potential candidates who are similar to themselves more positively than they rate candidates who are dissimilar. Similar-to-me effects can be particularly problematic for women and minority group members trying to climb the corporate ladder. As indicated in the opening case, male CEOs tend to groom as their successors men who are like themselves and thus may not perceive a woman as a viable successor. The effects of the similar-to-me bias are not confined to top-level executives, however. (See Insight 4.4.)

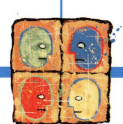

Insight 4.4   **Diversity**

Helping Those Who Are Like Oneself

Mentoring is a process through which an experienced member of an organization (the mentor) provides advice and guidance to a less experienced member (the protégé) to help the less experienced person learn the ropes and do the right things to advance in the organization. Young minority managers sometimes find that they aren't being mentored by white senior colleagues. Ilene Wasserman, of the Cincinnati-based Kaleel Jamison Consulting Group, which specializes in helping organizations manage a diverse workforce, says that senior managers typically try to mentor someone who reminds them of themselves when they were younger—someone who, as she puts it, is a "clone."

Mixed-race mentor-protégé relationships are rare. Benson Rosen, a management professor at the University of North Carolina at Chapel Hill, indicates that white managers sometimes feel uncomfortable dealing with minorities and may slight them (often unintentionally) in various ways, such as failing to invite them to functions and giving them performance feedback that is less constructive than the feedback they give white subordinates. LaVon Stennis, a young African American lawyer who worked for a large corporation in Nebraska, found it difficult to relate to her white male superiors, so it was unlikely that any of them would serve as her mentor. These observations do not mean that white men cannot mentor minorities or that minorities do not want to receive help from white managers. Rather, they suggest that all members of an organization (regardless of race, gender, or other characteristics) need to be aware that the similar-to-me bias might predispose them to help members who are similar to them. In his study, Rosen found that white women were more likely than white men to mentor minorities of either gender.[36]

The similar-to-me bias also rears its ugly head in organizations when the subject is promotions. Ken Martin, a managing director of the Hay Group consulting firm, says that male managers have traditionally promoted individuals who were similar to themselves. However, the Civil Rights Act passed at the end of 1991 (which updates the Civil Rights Act of 1964 prohibiting discrimination on the basis of race, color, creed, or gender) may be influential in curtailing this practice. The 1991 act allows victims of discrimination in organizations to receive punitive damages and a jury trial. The majority of recent employment discrimination cases involve charges of unfair promotion and dismissal actions, not unfair hiring practices.

Many organizations fear lawsuits and are following the leads of firms such as Xerox, AMR Corp., and Baxter International Inc., which have been proactively trying to halt the effects of the similar-to-me bias in promotion decisions. Xerox (www.xerox.com), for example, known for its efforts in trying to advance the careers of minorities, created an informal network of six female top executives to help come up with ways to prevent women from being passed over for promotion. As a result of some of the network's activities, "male" definitions of success that in the past were used to judge management potential (such as "an intense desire to win") have been abandoned and gender-neutral definitions (such as "an intense desire to succeed") are being used. Xerox has also started a policy of always including a woman on teams that make promotion decisions and career-development plans.[37]

The similar-to-me bias is especially important to overcome today, given the increasing diversity in organizational membership. In a workforce that includes many women and members of minority groups, managers and subordinates have more frequent contact with people who are dissimilar to themselves in race, age, gender, and nationality. When evaluating others who are different, people must try to be as objective as possible and avoid the similar-to-me trap.

Members of an organization also have to be on the lookout for the similar-to-me bias when interacting with people from other cultures. For example, when researchers from three global organizations—Siemens AG of Germany, Toshiba Corporation of Japan, and IBM—joined forces at IBM's East Fishkill, New York, facility to work together to develop a revolutionary computer chip,

The founders and top management of Fairchild demonstrate the "similar-to-me" effect in this 1960 photograph taken in the company's lobby.

the similar-to-me bias struck. Some of the researchers tried to interact primarily with people from their own culture. Some of the Japanese researchers, for instance, tried to work mainly with other Japanese, rather than with the Germans or the Americans, whom they perceived as "so different."[38]

HARSHNESS, LENIENCY, AND AVERAGE TENDENCY BIASES

When rating subordinates' performances, some supervisors tend to be overly harsh, others overly lenient. Others tend to rate everyone as being about average. Any of these tendencies is problematic for two reasons. First, the supervisor does not correctly perceive the variations in the performance of his or her subordinates. As a result, high performers do not receive appropriate recognition and rewards for their superior accomplishments, and low performers do not receive the constructive feedback they need to improve performance.

The second reason these biases are problematic is that they make it difficult to evaluate and compare the performance of subordinates who have different supervisors. A subordinate who has received relatively poor ratings from a harsh supervisor may be just as accomplished as a subordinate who has received average or high ratings from a lenient one. Evaluations biased in this manner can result in faulty decision making about pay raises and promotions. These biases can also operate in classroom settings. One professor, for example, gives mostly A's in a course in which another professor maintains a C+ class average. Students in the first professor's class may be content, but those in the other professor's class are likely to feel that they are not being fairly treated.

KNOWLEDGE-OF-PREDICTOR BIAS

To decide whom to hire, how to assign jobs to newly hired and existing members of an organization, and whom to promote, organizations measure people's standing on different predictors of performance. Depending on the job in question, the indicators used to determine how well a person will be able to accomplish work activities in the future can range from educational background and prior work experiences, to performance on standardized tests, to performance on certain critical job-related tasks.

Knowledge-of-predictor bias
The biased perception that results when knowing a target's standing on a predictor of performance influences the perceiver's perception of the target.

Self-fulfilling prophecy
A prediction that comes true because a perceiver expects it to come true.

If coworkers, managers, or others in the organization know what a person's standing on a predictor of performance is, the information may bias their perceptions of the person. This problem is known as **knowledge-of-predictor bias.** If a professor knows, for example, that a student has scored highly on some predictor of academic performance such as the SAT or the GMAT, this knowledge may lead the professor to perceive the student more positively than he or she deserves. This bias could also work to the disadvantage of a person who scored poorly on the predictor.

Sometimes, knowledge-of-predictor bias results in a **self-fulfilling prophecy**—a prediction that comes true because a perceiver expects it to come true—such as when an initially false definition of a situation results in behaviors that eventually cause the false definition to become true.[39] The classic demonstration of this phenomenon took place in a classroom setting in the 1960s. At the beginning of the school year, teachers were told that a few of their students were potential "late bloomers" who, given the proper encouragement, should excel. In fact, these students had been randomly selected from the class rosters and were no different from their peers. Later on in the school year, however, the "late bloomers" were indeed doing better and had even improved their scores on standardized IQ tests compared to their earlier performance and the performance of the other children in the class.[40] What was responsible for the change? The teachers in the study probably gave the "late bloomers" more attention, encouragement, and feedback, and had higher expectations of them, all of which resulted in their improved performance. The teachers may have also looked more at these students and made encouraging body gestures toward them. In this way, knowledge of a predictor (in this case, a false predictor) resulted in behavior changes that caused that prediction to become true. Research has also shown that when an interviewer conveys negative expectations to a job applicant simply through nonverbal body language, the applicant performs poorly.[41] This situation hurts both the applicant and the organization; the applicant won't get the job, and the organization may lose a potentially capable member.

Sometimes self-fulfilling prophecies can occur in an entire work group. A group of construction workers, for example, may be very responsible and perform highly when their supervisor has high expectations and treats them with respect. The same workers, however, may act lazy and perform at a low level when they have a supervisor who has low expectations and a derogatory attitude toward them.

Attribution Theory

Through the process of perception, people try to make sense of their environment and the people in it. Sometimes, however, just making sense of a target does not produce good understanding. To return to an earlier example, if you see your friend drinking beer before a 9 a.m. class, you perceive that he has a drinking problem. This perception may lead you to wonder why he has the drinking problem. In answering the why question, you attribute your friend's behavior to a certain cause. Your explanation of his behavior is an **attribution.**

Attribution theory describes how people explain the causes of their own and other people's behavior. Attribution theory is interested in why people be-

Attribution
An explanation of the cause of behavior.

Attribution theory
A group of theories that describe how people explain the causes of behavior.

TO MANAGERS

Biases in Person Perception

- Be careful not to let your first impressions have too strong an effect on your perceptions of others. Avoid categorizing workers—that is, fitting them to a schema—until you have sufficient information to form an accurate perception.
- When evaluating or interviewing a series of individuals, do not let your evaluations of preceding individuals influence your ratings of those that follow.
- Be careful not to be lenient in your perceptions of people who are similar to you and overly harsh to those who are dissimilar.
- If you tend to rate most of your subordinates very negatively, very positively, or just about average, stop and think whether each individual truly deserves the rating he or she received.
- Share organizational members' standing on predictors of performance only with people who need this information for decision making. Be careful not to let this information bias your own perceptions.

have the way they do and what can be done to change their behavior. Consider the case of Martin Riley, a newly hired production worker at Rice Paper Products. Riley worked at a much slower pace than his coworkers; he always seemed to be lagging behind the other members of his production team. The big question in his supervisor's mind was why. Attribution theory focuses on how the supervisor and how Riley himself explain the cause of Riley's lackluster performance.

In organizations, the decisions that are made and the actions that are taken are based on attributions for behavior. Only when these attributions are accurate (that is, only when the real cause of a behavior has been determined) are good decisions likely to be made and appropriate actions taken. In a job interview, for example, whether a qualified applicant who is quiet and fails to ask questions receives an offer often depends on the interviewer's attributions for this behavior. Is the applicant a shy person who takes a while to warm up to new people? Was the applicant suffering from a bad case of nerves? Is the applicant not really interested in the job? If the interviewer makes the last attribution for the applicant's behavior, an offer will probably not be forthcoming. If that attribution is inaccurate, however, and the applicant was simply nervous, then the organization may be missing an opportunity to hire one of the best applicants for the job.

Similarly, supervisors' reactions to high or low performance by subordinates often depend on the attributions the supervisors make. A supervisor who attributes a subordinate's high performance to exceptional ability may give the subordinate increasingly challenging assignments and eventually recommend a promotion. If the subordinate's high performance is attributed to luck, however, no changes may be made in the subordinate's assignments. In either case, if the attributions are incorrect, problems are likely to result: The subordinate will be overwhelmed by challenging assignments or will not receive the challenges he or she thrives on. When subordinates perform poorly, supervisors are likely to provide additional on-the-job training if they attribute poor performance to a lack of knowledge rather than to laziness. If laziness is the real cause, however, training is not likely to improve performance.

Smooth day-to-day interactions among members of an organization often hinge on the extent to which people's attributions are accurate. If a coworker snaps at you a couple of times one day and you correctly attribute the coworker's behavior to the personal problems he is having at home, these small incidents are not going to damage your relationship. But if you incorrectly attribute this behavior to the coworker's dislike for you, you may start avoiding him and treating him in a cold and distant manner, which will cause your relationship to deteriorate.

INTERNAL AND EXTERNAL ATTRIBUTIONS

Internal attribution
An attribution that assigns the cause of behavior to some characteristic of the target.

People generally attribute someone's behavior to internal and external causes (see Fig. 4.3). An **internal attribution** assigns the cause of behavior to some characteristic of the target and assigns credit or blame to the individual actor. Martin Riley's supervisor at Rice Paper Products might attribute Riley's poor performance to personal limitations: (1) Riley lacks the ability to perform at a higher level; (2) Riley is not making an effort to work faster; (3) Riley has a low need for achievement. Attributions to ability, effort, and personality are the most common internal attributions that people make.

External attribution
An attribution that assigns the cause of behavior to outside forces.

However much people like to feel that they are in control of what happens in their lives, outside forces often play a decisive role in determining behavior. An **external attribution** assigns the cause of behavior to factors outside the individual. The most common external attributions are to task difficulty and luck or chance. A salesperson who has just landed a major contract, for example, may have been successful because her company is the sole provider of a particular product in a certain geographic region or because the customer was in a particularly good mood at the time of negotiations. In the first case, the salesperson's success is attributed to the easiness of the task; in the second case, it is attributed to luck.

Whether attributions for a behavior are internal or external is an important determinant of how people respond to the behavior. If the supervisor of the salesperson mentioned above correctly attributes the landing of the major contract to external causes such as an easy task or luck, getting this contract may have little impact on the supervisor's decisions about the salesperson's job assignments and suitability for promotion. But if the super-

FIGURE 4.3

Types of Attributions

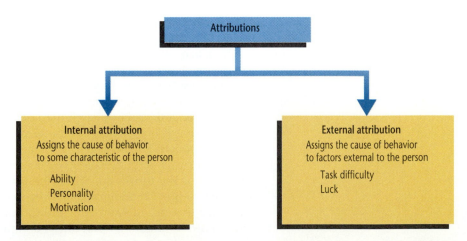

visor incorrectly attributes the behavior to an internal cause such as ability, the supervisor might promote this salesperson instead of another one who is more deserving but covers a more difficult territory.

The attributions people make for their own behavior also influence their own subsequent actions. A worker who fails on a task and attributes this failure to a lack of ability may be likely to avoid the task in the future or exert minimal effort on it because he feels that his lack of ability will almost certainly guarantee a negative outcome. Conversely, attributing failure to a lack of effort may lead the worker to try harder in the future on the same task. As another example, a worker who succeeds on a task and attributes the outcome to luck is unlikely to be affected by her success, whereas attributing the success to her ability or effort will increase her confidence.

ATTRIBUTIONAL BIASES

The attributions people make for their own and for other people's behaviors can have powerful effects on their subsequent actions. Like perceptions, however, attributions may sometimes be inaccurate because of certain biases. Here we consider three of these biases: the fundamental attribution error, actor-observer effect, and self-serving attributions (see Table 4.5).

The Fundamental Attribution Error. Behavior is often caused by a combination of internal and external factors, but situational factors are the sole determinants of behavior in certain circumstances. Regardless of how capable and motivated a worker might be, for example, if the worker does not have the proper resources to accomplish a task, she or he will not be able to perform at a high level. No matter how hard a waiter tries to have customers enjoy their meals, they are bound to be dissatisfied if the restaurant serves poorly prepared food. Despite the fact that external factors often determine behavior, people have a very strong tendency to attribute other people's behavior to internal factors. Because this tendency to overattribute other people's behavior to internal rather than to external causes is so basic to human nature, it has been called the **fundamental attribution error.**[42]

Why does the fundamental attribution error occur? Researchers have offered two explanations. According to the first, which concentrates on perception of the target's behavior, when we observe a person behaving, we focus on the person, and the situation is simply the background for the behavior. Because

Fundamental attribution error
The tendency to overattribute behavior to internal rather than to external causes.

TABLE 4.5
Attributional Biases

Bias	Description
Fundamental attribution error	The tendency to overattribute behavior to internal rather than to external causes
Actor-observer effect	The tendency to attribute the behavior of others to internal causes and to attribute one's own behavior to external causes
Self-serving attribution	The tendency to take credit for successes and avoid blame for failures

the person is the focus of our thinking and the situation receives little attention, we tend to think that something about the person prompted the behavior. According to the second reason for the occurrence of the fundamental attribution error, we often are simply unaware of all the situational factors that may be responsible for the behavior we observe.

Because of the tendency to overattribute other people's behavior to internal causes, managers are likely to think that a subordinate's behavior is due to some characteristic of the subordinate rather than to the situation. Similarly, subordinates are likely to think that their supervisors' behavior is determined by internal rather than by external causes. Suppose a manager must lay off 30 percent of his or her staff because of a major decline in the organization's performance. Those who are laid off (and those who remain) may be likely to attribute this action to the manager's hardheartedness and lack of concern for the well-being of others rather than to economic necessity.

People who manage diverse employees need to be especially aware of the fundamental attribution error and try to avoid it. Just as perceptions can be inaccurate as a result of stereotypes, so too can attributions. Inaccurate stereotypes about women, older workers, or African Americans, for example, may cause members of an organization to inappropriately attribute behavior to internal causes such as gender, age, or race when behavior is actually caused by an external factor. If an older worker has difficulty getting new computer software to run, the worker's supervisor may fall victim to the stereotype that older workers have difficulty learning new things and inaccurately attribute this behavior to the worker's age even though the real cause of the problem is that the computer has insufficient memory to handle the new software (an external cause).

The Actor-Observer Effect.   We make attributions not only for the behavior of other people but also for our own behavior. Researchers comparing these two types of attributions uncovered an interesting phenomenon: the **actor-observer effect.** The actor-observer effect is the tendency to attribute the behavior of others to internal causes (the fundamental attribution error) and to attribute one's own behavior to external causes.[43] We tend to think that other people's behavior is relatively stable from situation to situation because it is due to their very nature, but we think that our own behavior varies from situation to situation.

What causes this bias? According to one explanation, when we are behaving, we focus not on our behavior but rather on the situation we are in. Because we are totally aware of the external, situational pressures that we face, we see them as key. Because we are less aware of external pressures or factors that another person is dealing with, we are likely to see his or her behavior as internally driven.

Self-Serving Attribution.   Suppose you get promoted at work. Chances are, you attribute this outcome to your superior abilities and the excellent job you have been doing. Now suppose that one of your coworkers gets the promotion that you have been expecting. You probably think that your supervisor has been unfair or that some political maneuvering has taken place. This example illustrates **self-serving attribution,** the tendency to take credit for successes and avoid blame for failures.[44] The considerable amount of research conducted on this phenomenon suggests that accepting the credit for success is more common than avoiding blame for failure.[45] Furthermore, people are most likely to accept the blame for failure when it is due to something they can control in the future, such as by working harder or planning their time better.[46]

Actor-observer effect
The tendency to attribute the behavior of others to internal causes and to attribute one's own behavior to external causes.

Self-serving attribution
The tendency to take credit for successes and avoid blame for failures.

Attributions

- Make sure your attributions for other people's behavior are as accurate as possible.
- Consider external factors that may be responsible for other people's behavior, such as inadequate resources or supplies, an exceptionally difficult task, or chance occurrences.
- Consider internal factors that may be responsible for your own behavior, such as your personality, your strengths and weaknesses, and your level of motivation.
- Be aware of the tendency in yourself and in others to take credit for successes and avoid blame for failures.

Self-serving attribution can also bias one's perception of friends and spouses and even organizations.[47] People are more likely to attribute the good things that happen to their spouses to internal causes and the bad things that happen to their spouses to external causes.[48] When your organization makes a record contribution to the United Way, you are likely to attribute this generosity to the organization's being socially responsible (an internal cause). But when your organization is cited for polluting the environment, you may attribute its problems to external circumstances such as the unavailability or high cost of alternative ways to dispose of waste (an external cause).

Effectively Managing a Diverse Workforce

Throughout this chapter we have discussed how accurate perceptions and attributions are necessary to effectively manage a diverse workforce and the many issues involved in ensuring that perceptions and attributions are as accurate as possible. Effective management of a diverse workforce is necessary for an organization to perform at a high level, gain a competitive advantage, make fair decisions, and be ethical. In this section, we explore three steps organizations can take to promote accurate perceptions and attributions and effectively manage diverse employees: securing the commitment of top management to diversity; diversity training; and education. We also discuss the steps organizations can take to eliminate and prevent sexual harassment.

SECURING TOP-MANAGEMENT COMMITMENT TO DIVERSITY

Ernest H. Drew, CEO of Hoechst Celanese, is a prime example of a top manager who is committed to diversity and whose diversity crusade has achieved tangible payoffs for his organization (see Insight 1.5). Drew travels around the country meeting with workers and managers at Celanese production plants, emphasizing the importance of diversity. As he puts it, "When the CEO meets with employees, it signals diversity is important."[49]

In addition to meeting face to face with workers and managers, Drew has taken other steps to secure the commitment of top managers to diversity. At Celanese, managers' salaries and bonuses are based on four criteria: financial performance, customer satisfaction, environmental and safety improvements, and workforce diversity. Because having and maintaining a diverse workforce is on equal footing with the traditional performance criteria, managers can readily see that diversity not only is an important organizational goal but also benefits them personally. Celanese aims to have at least 34 percent of its employees at all levels be women and minorities by the year 2001 because that is the percentage of women and minorities who are projected to be graduating with relevant degrees from the colleges at which Celanese recruits.[50]

Another way in which top managers' commitment to diversity is secured at Celanese is through the requirement that all top managers join and participate in two organizations in which they themselves are a minority. This gives managers firsthand experience in how it feels to be a minority, helps break down stereotypes, and lets managers know the ways in which diverse members of an organization are similar to each other. Drew is a member of the overseeing boards for Hampton University (a historically black college) and SER–Jobs for Progress (a Hispanic organization). Realizing the value of this experience, one Celanese vice president has joined three such organizations, including the board of historically black Florida A&M University.[51]

What is the likely outcome when top managers are committed to diversity? Their commitment helps ensure that their perceptions of and their attributions for the behavior of diverse members of an organization will be as accurate as possible and that they will understand and see diverse employees as they really are. Top-management commitment to diversity also helps to promote accurate perceptions and attributions throughout an organization. When supervisors support diversity, subordinates are more likely to be committed to diversity and less likely to rely on stereotypes.

DIVERSITY TRAINING

Diversity training can facilitate the management of a diverse workforce. There are many diversity training programs with many different objectives—for example:

- Making explicit and breaking down organizational members' stereotypes that result in inaccurate perceptions and attributions.
- Making members aware of different kinds of backgrounds, experiences, and values.
- Showing members how to deal effectively with diversity-related conflicts and tensions.
- Generally improving members' understanding of each other.

Diversity training programs can last hours or days and can be run by consultants or existing members of an organization with expertise in diversity. Small organizations are more likely to rely on consultants; larger organizations often have diversity managers. Fifty percent of Fortune 500 organizations, for example, have diversity managers on staff.[52]

Diversity training can include but is not limited to:

1. Role-playing in which participants act out appropriate and inappropriate ways to deal with diverse employees.
2. Self-awareness activities in which participants' own prejudices and stereotypes are revealed.
3. Awareness activities in which participants learn about others who differ from them in lifestyle, culture, sexual orientation, gender, and so on.

Cardiac Concepts Inc., a Texas medical laboratory that performs cardiovascular tests, helped to reduce conflict among workers with diverse ethnic backgrounds by using a training program in which pairs of participants from different ethnic backgrounds made lists of the stereotypes held about each other.[53] New York City–based consultant Richard Orange, who conducts diversity training programs for several Fortune 500 companies, often takes top managers to see films and plays such as *Angels in America, Thelma and Louise, Malcolm X,* and *Philadelphia* to increase managers' awareness of different lifestyles, cultures, and points of view and to give them a starting point for discussing their own feelings about diversity.[54]

Many diversity programs are successful, but others do not change the ways in which people perceive and treat each other in organizations. It appears that diversity training is most likely to be successful when it is ongoing or repeated (rather than a single session), when there are follow-up activities to see whether the training has accomplished its objectives, and when it is supplemented by other diversity-related activities in an organization, such as events focused on celebrating diversity. IBM's Systems Storage Division in San Jose, for example, sets aside one day a year as Diversity Day. On that day, employees dress in traditional ethnic clothing and share authentic dishes with their coworkers.[55]

EDUCATION

Sometimes effectively managing diversity requires that members of an organization receive additional education to make them better able to communicate and work with diverse employees and customers. The Kentucky state government, for example, realized that it was unable to provide employment opportunities for people with hearing impairments and could not provide high-quality service to hearing-impaired citizens wanting to use state-provided services and programs. The Americans with Disabilities Act (passed by Congress in 1990 and put into effect in 1992) requires organizations to be responsive to and accommodate people with disabilities (including deafness or hearing impairments).[56]

After considerable research, the Kentucky state government developed a three-stage program to improve its responsiveness to people (both customers and potential employees) who are hearing impaired or deaf. First, state employees chosen for the program participate in a one-day workshop that educates them about deaf culture and background. Second, employees attend a four-day workshop in which they learn some of the basics of American Sign

Modern organizations are composed of widely diverse people and groups. AT&T has seven caucuses to represent the interests of its minority employee groups, including African Americans, Latinos, Asians, gays, and women.

Language (the most often used form of signing and a visual language that deaf people use to communicate). Finally, employees attend a week-long workshop on advanced American Sign Language.[57]

Visible top-management commitment, training, and education are just some of the specific ways in which organizations can promote effective management of a diverse workforce—an ethical and effectiveness imperative. As we have discussed throughout this chapter, effectively managing diversity begins with the recognition that organizational members' perceptions and attributions need to be as accurate as possible, regardless of the age, race, gender, ethnic background, religion, sexual orientation, or other characteristic of the target of perception.

SEXUAL HARASSMENT

After extensive study, the U.S. Army has indicated that sexual harassment exists throughout its ranks.[58] Unfortunately, sexual harassment is not just an Army problem but also a problem that many other organizations have had to face, such as Chevron Corporation.[59] There are two distinct types of sexual harassment: quid pro quo sexual harassment and hostile work environment sexual harassment. **Quid pro quo sexual harassment** is the most obvious type and occurs when the harasser requests or forces a worker to perform sexual favors in order to receive some opportunity (such as a raise, a promotion, a bonus, or a special job assignment) or avoid a negative consequence (such as demotion, dismissal, a halt to career progress, or an undesired assignment or transfer).[60] **Hostile work environment sexual harassment** is more subtle and occurs when organizational members are faced with a work environment that is offensive, intimidating, or hostile because of their sex.[61] Pornographic pictures, sexual jokes, lewd comments, sexually oriented comments about a person's physical appearance, and displays of sexually oriented objects are all examples of hostile work environment sexual harassment. Hostile work environments interfere with organizational members' abilities to perform their jobs effectively and are illegal. Chevron recently settled a $2.2 million lawsuit with four employees who experienced a hostile work environment by, for example, receiving violent pornography through the company's mail system and being asked to deliver pornographic videos to Chevron workers in Alaska.[62]

Organizations have a legal and ethical obligation to eliminate and prevent sexual harassment, which can occur at all levels in an organization. Some organizations, such as NBC, include segments on sexual harassment in their diversity training and education programs.[63] At a minimum, there are several key steps that organizations can take to combat the sexual harassment problem.[64]

- *Develop a sexual harassment policy supported by top management.* This policy should (1) describe and prohibit both quid pro quo and hostile work environment sexual harassment, (2) provide examples of types of behaviors that are prohibited, (3) outline a procedure employees can follow to report sexual harassment, (4) describe the disciplinary actions that will be taken for instances of sexual harassment, and (5) describe the organization's commitment to educating and training organizational members about sexual harassment.
- *Clearly communicate the organization's sexual harassment policy throughout the organization.* All members of an organization should be familiar with the organization's sexual harassment policy.

Quid pro quo sexual harassment
Requesting or forcing a worker to perform sexual favors in order to receive some opportunity or avoid a negative consequence.

Hostile work environment sexual harassment
Creating or maintaining a work environment that is offensive, intimidating, or hostile because of a person's sex.

- *Investigate charges of sexual harassment with a fair complaint procedure.* A fair complaint procedure (1) is handled by a neutral third party, (2) deals with complaints promptly and thoroughly, (3) protects victims and treats them fairly, and (4) treats alleged harassers fairly.
- *Take corrective action as soon as possible once it has been determined that sexual harassment has taken place.* The nature of these corrective actions will vary depending upon the severity of the sexual harassment.
- *Provide sexual harassment training and education to all members of the organization.* Many organizations have such training programs in place, such as Du Pont, NBC, Corning, Digital Equipment, and the US Navy and Army.[65]

SUMMARY

Perception and attribution are important topics because all decisions and behaviors in organizations are influenced by how people interpret and make sense of the world around them and each other. Perception is the process by which individuals select, organize, and interpret sensory input. Attribution is an explanation of the cause of behavior. Perception and attribution thus help to explain how and why people behave in organizations and how and why they react to the behavior of others. In this chapter, we made the following major points:

1. Perception is the process by which people interpret the input from their senses to give meaning and order to the world around them. The three components of perception are the perceiver, the target, and the situation. Accurate perceptions are necessary to make good decisions and to motivate workers to perform at a high level, to be fair and equitable, and to be ethical.

2. The perceiver's knowledge base is organized into schemas, abstract knowledge structures stored in memory that allow people to organize and interpret information about a given target of perception. Schemas tend to be resistant to change and can be functional or dysfunctional. A stereotype is a dysfunctional schema because stereotypes often lead perceivers to assume erroneously that targets have a whole range of characteristics simply because they possess one distinguishing characteristic (such as, race, age, or gender). In addition to the perceiver's schemas, his or her motivational state and mood also influence perception.

3. Characteristics of the target also influence perception. Ambiguous targets are subject to a lot of interpretation by the perceiver; the more ambiguous the target, the more likely perceivers are to differ in their perceptions of it. The target's social status also affects how the target is perceived. Through impression management, targets can actively try to manage the perceptions that others have of them.

4. The situation affects perception by providing the perceiver with additional information. One particularly important aspect of the situation is the target's salience—that is, the extent to which the target stands out in a group of people or things.

5. Biases and problems in person perception include primacy effects, contrast effects, halo effects, similar-to-me effects, harshness, leniency, and average tendencies, and knowledge-of-predictor bias. Inaccurate perceptions resulting from these biases can lead to faulty decision making.

6. Attributions are important determinants of behavior in organizations because how members of an organization react to other people's behavior depends on what they think caused the behavior. Attribution theory focuses on understanding how people explain the causes of their own and others' behavior. Common internal attributions for behavior include ability, effort, and personality. Common external attributions for behavior include task difficulty and luck or chance. Like perceptions, attributions can be inaccurate as a result of several biases, including the fundamental attribution error, the actor-observer effect, and self-serving attribution.

7. Three ways in which organizations can promote accurate perceptions and attributions and effectively manage diverse employees are securing top management's commitment to diversity, diversity training, and education. Organizations also need to take steps to eliminate and prevent both quid pro quo and hostile work environment sexual harassment.

Organizational Behavior in Action

TOPICS FOR
DISCUSSION
AND ACTION

1. How do schemas help members of an organization make sense of each other and of what happens in the organization?
2. Are stereotypes ever functional for the perceiver? Why or why not?
3. Why might a supervisor be motivated to perceive a subordinate's performance as being poor when it really is not?
4. How might managers' moods affect organizational decision making?
5. In what ways might impression management be functional in organizations? In what ways might it be dysfunctional?
6. Can and should workers who are salient try to reduce their salience?
7. Why do perceptual biases exist?
8. Why might a supervisor make internal attributions for a subordinate's poor performance?
9. Why are attributions important determinants of behavior in organizations?
10. Why might members of an organization disagree about the nature of hostile work environment sexual harassment?

**BUILDING
DIAGNOSTIC
SKILLS**

Understanding Perceptions and Attributions in Group Meetings

Think of the last meeting or gathering that you attended. It could be a meeting that took place at the organization you are currently working for, a meeting of a club or student organization you are a member of, a meeting of a group you have been assigned to for a project in one of your classes, or any other recent gathering that involved more than two people.

1. Describe your perceptions of what took place during the meeting, and explain why events unfolded as they did.
2. Describe the characteristics and behavior of the other people who were present at the meeting, and explain why they acted the way they did.
3. Describe how you think you were perceived by other people during the meeting, and explain why you behaved as you did.
4. After you have completed activities 1 through 3, pick another person who participated in the meeting, and arrange to meet with her or him for around fifteen minutes. Explain to the person that you want to ask a few questions about the meeting for one of your classes.
5. When you meet with the person, ask her or him to be as accurate and honest as possible. Remind the person that your get-together is part of an assignment for one of your classes, and assure that person that answers to your questions are confidential. While the person is answering you, take careful notes, and do not attempt to correct anything that is said. Just listen and take notes. Ask the person to respond to each of these questions (one by one):
   a. How would you describe what took place during the meeting, and why do you think it took place?

       b. How would you describe the characteristics and behavior of the other people who were present at the meeting, and why do you think they behaved as they did?

       c. How would you describe the reasons why I behaved as I did during the meeting?

6. Compare your own descriptions from activities 1 through 3 with the descriptions you obtained from activities 4 and 5. In what ways were your perceptions and attributions similar to those of the other person? In what ways were they different?

7. Use the knowledge you have gained from Chapter 4 to explain why there were differences in your and the other person's perceptions and attributions and why there were similarities. Be specific.

RESEARCH ON THE INTERNET: A MANAGER'S TOOL

Specific Task

Citibank, one among many companies that value diversity, has taken active steps to ensure that diverse organizational members are given the opportunities they deserve and strives to effectively manage diversity in order to gain a competitive advantage. Scan Citibank's web site (www.citibank.com) to learn more about this company and its diversity-oriented initiatives. Then click on "About Citibank," then on "College/University opportunities," then on "You & Citibank."

1. What steps is Citibank taking to provide opportunities to diverse organizational members?

2. In what ways does Citibank see the effective management of diversity as key to gaining a competitive advantage?

General Task

Many organizations have made a strong commitment to the effective management of diversity for both business and ethical reasons. Find the web site of such a company. How is this company demonstrating its commitment to diversity? What specific initiatives has this company taken to support and effectively manage diversity?

TOPICS FOR DEBATE

Perception and attribution have major effects on the decisions that are made in organizations and on how members of an organization respond to each other's behavior. Now that you have a good understanding of perception and attribution, debate the following issues.

Debate One

Team A. There is not much that managers can do to reduce the negative effects of perceptual problems and biases in organizations.

Team B. Managers can take active steps to reduce the negative effects of perceptual problems and biases in organizations.

Debate Two

Team A. The accuracy of organizational members' attributions for behavior is more important than the fact that the behavior took place.

Team B. Whether or not a behavior is performed is more important than the accuracy of the attributions that are made for it.

EXPERIENTIAL EXERCISE

Managing Diversity

Objective

Your objective is to gain firsthand experience in some of the issues involved in managing diversity.

Procedure

The class divides into groups of from three to five people, and each group appoints one member as spokesperson, to present the group's recommendations to the whole class. Each group plays the role of a team of diversity consultants who have been called in by a high-tech company in the computer industry to help effectively manage diverse employees. Here is the scenario.

Nick Hopkins is the team leader of a group of ten programmers who are developing innovative software to be used in architectural design. The team is composed of seven men and three women. Hopkins thought that everything was going pretty smoothly in his team until the following two recent events. First, one of the women, Cara Lipkin, informed him that she would be resigning to work for a competing organization. Hopkins asked Lipkin why she decided to make this change, and she answered at length.

"I can't exactly explain it," she said, "but I never really felt that my contributions were valued by the team. I know you always appreciated the work I did and appraised my performance highly, but somehow I didn't really feel a part of things. In the long run, I was afraid that my prospects in the company might not be as good as other people's because I didn't seem to be included in certain activities and discussions. To give you what will probably sound like a really silly example, last month I overheard several of my team members planning a deep-sea fishing trip; I kept waiting to be included but never was. As another example, I sometimes feel like the last person people will come to for help with a programming problem."

The second event troubling Hopkins was as follows: Bob Risoto, another team member who at the time was unaware of Lipkin's resignation, complained that the women on the team always seemed to stick together.

"It's like they've got their own little clique going," Risoto said. "They go to lunch together. They talk to each other but not really to the rest of the team. When I have a programming problem that I think one of the women on the team would be able to help me with, for some reason I often feel hesitant to seek out her advice. Maybe it's just my fault. I don't know."

Hopkins has met with you (in your role as a team of diversity consultants) and asked you to help him effectively manage diversity as a team leader. He has indicated that he thought everything was going smoothly, but it evidently isn't and he wants to take some concrete steps to improve matters. Develop a concrete plan of action to help Hopkins effectively manage diversity in his team.

Once your group has developed a plan, the spokesperson for the group will present the group's recommendations and the rationale behind them to the rest of the class.

MAKING THE CONNECTION

Find an example of an organization that has taken steps to improve the accuracy of its members' perceptions of diverse employees. What steps has this organization taken? How have organizational members responded to these diversity initiatives?

Lessons from Texaco

In late 1996 Texaco Inc. (www.texaco.com) settled a race-discrimination law-suit on behalf of 1,400 employees for $176.1 million. The case, originally filed by six African American employees, had dragged on since 1994 with no clear resolution in sight until audio tapes were discovered of high-level Tex-aco managers making disparaging and derogatory comments about African Americans and discussing the shredding of documents relevant to the lawsuit, such as information on the hiring of minorities. While the statements made on these tapes were shocking, particularly as some of them were made by high-level managers, racial discrimination in the oil industry is not uncom-mon, according to diversity experts, and Shell Oil Co. and BP Oil Co. have also had suits filed against them.[66]

Some experts suggest that the reason there is still discrimination against African Americans and other minorities despite many of the diversity initia-tives of organizations is that, in the eyes of top managers and boards of di-rectors, the effective management of diversity is not as urgent or important as other initiatives more closely linked to the bottom line. The Texaco settle-ment has prompted some boards of directors of large corporations to re-think their stance on diversity. B. Kenneth West, a member of Motorola's board of directors likens the Texaco settlement to a "wake-up call for think-ing boards."[67]

In the wake of the settlement, for the first time, Chase Manhattan Bank's entire board of directors met with top managers and discussed the bank's ef-forts to increase the number of women and minorities in top management po-sitions. Some board members such as Robert J. Brown, who is on the boards of Duke Power Co., First Union Corp., and Sonoco Products Inc., now believe that directors themselves need diversity training. At Texaco, some directors ac-knowledge that they didn't spend too much time thinking about diversity as long as everything seemed to be going all right and reports indicated progress in minority hirings and promotions.[68]

Some boards of directors and top managers have taken a more proactive stance toward diversity. At Gannett Inc., director Andrew F. Brimmer is chair-man of the personal-practices committee, which evaluates the extent to which managers at different levels meet their diversity goals, which in turn can af-fect the managers' bonuses. At Ciridian Corp., 10 percent of top managers' bonuses are based on their diversity-related efforts.[69]

Allstate Insurance Co. (www.allstate.com) is one company that has taken active steps to ensure a commitment to diversity at all levels of management and actually monitors the results of this commitment. Allstate surveys its 50,000 employees four times a year to determine, among other things, if di-verse employees are receiving the development and promotion opportunities they should be. Based on results of the survey, each manager is scored on a diversity index that tracks the extent to which the manager is unbiased in his or her interactions with diverse customers, respects employees regardless of their race or gender, and encourages and maintains a working environment that is sensitive to diversity-related issues. Managers' merit bonuses are par-tially determined by their scores on the index. Perhaps it's not surprising that 21 percent of Allstate's managers are minorities while the comparable na-tional average is about 10 percent.[70]

Questions for Discussion

1. Why would managers at Texaco make disparaging comments about African Americans?

2. How can racial discrimination be eliminated in organizations?

3. What is the role of the Board of Directors in supporting diversity?

4. How might large settlements like the Texaco settlement influence organizations' diversity initiatives?

Learning in Organizations

5

Starbucks and the "Bean Stock"

Howard Schultz, CEO of Starbucks (www.occ.com/starbucks/), bought the company in 1987 and transformed a local Seattle, Washington, chain of six coffee stores into a national, publicly owned company with more than 25,000 employees (which Starbucks refers to as partners) and more than 1,300 stores. Star-

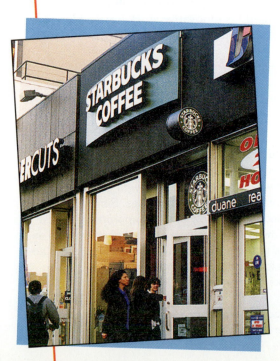

bucks sales and profit growth have been phenomenal, and the company has changed the way that Americans think about coffee. Starbucks stores range from coffee carts in crowded city streets to intimate coffee bars to full-sized restaurants that sell espressos and cappuccinos as well as coffee by the pound, coffee-making equipment, and food items.[1]

Throughout Starbucks' rapid growth, Schultz has emphasized the importance of rewarding partners for the contributions they make to Starbucks and ensuring that they have the necessary training to be effective. In 1991, when Starbucks was still a privately owned company, Schultz and other top managers came up with an innovative type of reward to encourage partners to behave in ways that would contribute to Starbucks' growth and profitability. Starbucks made all partners partners by granting them stock options, which could be turned into stock when the company went public. If the company did well, partners themselves would benefit, as their options would be worth more money. Called "Bean Stock," the options caused partners to behave in ways that would increase Starbucks' sales and profitability. Partners thought of new ways to lower costs and increase sales ranging from staying overnight on Saturdays when traveling on business to lower the cost of airfares to finding better ways to communicate with customers. Starbucks went public in 1992, and partners have since been rewarded for their efforts. For example, an employee who earned $20,000 a year in 1991 received options that had a value of $50,000 in 1996.[2]

Starbucks also provides extensive customer service training to partners to ensure that they are knowledgeable, confident on the job, and feel capable of making decisions on their own to better serve customers. Store managers teach classes on topics such as coffee history and coffee brewing at home, and partners must take a minimum of 24 hours of training. Partners learn how to take orders and prepare various coffees in a company training room rather than on the job (as in most restaurants) so that they can fully absorb what they are learning without the stress of waiting on real customers and so that customers receive the excellent service they have come to expect of Starbucks.[3]

Schultz seems to be doing all the right things at Starbucks. His efforts to ensure that partners learn to perform behaviors that will contribute to Starbucks' sales and profitability and his innovative stock option plan to reward all partners for their contributions to Starbucks' success certainly seem to be paying off.

Overview

When you first started college, you needed to learn how to register for courses, how to find out what books you needed, where to buy your books, how to drop and add classes, how to find your way around campus, how to use your college's computer systems, and how to behave in your classes. Similarly, when people join organizations, they need to learn how to dress appropriately, how much time to take off for lunch, how to use machinery and equipment such as computers and fax machines, how to perform their assigned duties, how to address their supervisors, and what to do when problems arise. In the opening case, we described how Starbucks partners need to learn how to take orders and make coffee.

Learning is a fundamental process in organizations because organizational members have to learn how to perform the tasks and duties that make up their jobs. Although learning is particularly important to newcomers (discussed in more detail in Chapter 10), it is also important for experienced members at all levels of the hierarchy because they are frequently called on to do things they haven't done before.

Experienced organizational members often have to learn how to perform new tasks and use new technology and equipment as the nature of their jobs changes. Similarly, as they receive promotions, they have to learn how to interact with new supervisors, subordinates, and coworkers and how to apply new organizational policies and procedures (such as how pay raises are determined and when they are given). Furthermore, once employees learn new behaviors, the organization needs to ensure that the new behaviors continue; otherwise, any performance gains will be lost.

In this chapter, we discuss the principles of learning and how managers and other members of an organization can best put them to use to promote and maintain a wide variety of desirable organizational behaviors, including the consistent provision of high-quality customer service and performing a job at a high level. The principles of learning also form a basic underpinning for our discussion of work motivation in Chapters 6, 7, and 8. By the end of this chapter, you will have a good appreciation of why learning is essential for understanding and managing organizational behavior.

The Nature of Learning

 Learning

A relatively permanent change in knowledge or behavior that results from practice or experience.

Learning is a relatively permanent change in knowledge or behavior that results from practice or experience.[4] There are several key points in this definition. First, with learning comes *change*. Your knowledge of how to do things in college changed through the learning that took place during your first few weeks as a freshman. So too does the behavior of a new worker at Starbucks change as he or she takes classes on brewing coffee and practices taking orders and making coffee.

Second, the change in knowledge or behavior has to be *relatively permanent,* or long lasting. If, the first time you registered for classes, you told a friend who knew the ropes what classes you wanted to take, and your friend did all the paperwork for you, learning did not take place because there was no permanent change in your knowledge of how to register.

The third key aspect of the definition is that learning takes place as a result of practice or through the *experience* of watching others. Think back to when you were learning how to drive a car. Only through practice did you eventually learn such things as how to make a three-point turn and parallel park. Similarly, through practice or experience, secretaries learn how to use new software packages, financial analysts learn the implications of new tax laws, engineers learn how to design more fuel-efficient automobiles, and flight attendants learn how to serve meals on airplanes.

Two major theories about learning are operant conditioning and social learning theory. Each theory emphasizes a different way in which people learn in organizations and in life in general, and learning takes place in the ways described by each theory. In the rest of this chapter, we describe these two learning theories and why they are key to an understanding of learning in organizations. We also discuss the importance of an organization as a whole, adopting a learning mentality or organizational learning.

Operant Conditioning: Increasing the Probability of Desired Behaviors

Operant conditioning is one of the key ways in which learning takes place. Much of what we know about it can be attributed to the work of psychologist B. F. Skinner.[5] **Operant conditioning** is learning that takes place when the learner recognizes the connection between a behavior and its consequences (see Fig. 5.1).[6] An individual learns to engage in specific behaviors (such as being responsive to customers' needs) in order to receive certain consequences (such as a bonus). This type of learning is called *operant* conditioning because individuals learn to operate on their environment, to behave in a certain way to achieve certain consequences.

You have probably learned that if you study hard, you will receive good grades, and if you keep up with your reading throughout the semester, you will not be overburdened during finals week. Thus you have learned how to *operate* on your environment to achieve your desired goals. In organizations, operant conditioning focuses on associations between work behaviors (such as job performance, absenteeism, and lateness) and consequences provided by a worker's environment (a supervisor, coworkers, or the organization as a whole): *desired* consequences such as pay and verbal praise, and *undesired* consequences such as reprimands.

In addition to individuals' learning the connection between a behavior and its consequences, another factor—antecedents—plays a supporting role in operant conditioning. Antecedents are instructions, rules, goals, advice from other members of an organization, and anything else that helps workers realize what behaviors they should and should not perform and lets them know what the likely consequences are for different behaviors. Antecedents play an educational role by letting workers know what the organizational consequences are (such as a pay raise or a promotion) for different behaviors (performing at a high level or impressing the division president during a presentation) and

Operant conditioning
Learning that takes place when the learner recognizes the connection between a behavior and its consequences.

FIGURE **5.1**
Operant Conditioning

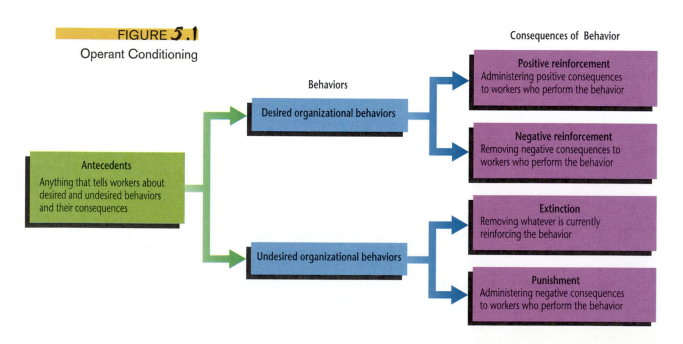

Service organizations such as United Parcel Service (UPS), which are committed to providing high quality customer service, go to great lenghts to develop formal rules to teach and reinforce desired behaviors from their employees, such as the UPS driver pictured here.

thus what behaviors they should perform.[7] For example, a rule (the antecedent) that three latenesses result in the loss of one vacation day (the consequence) lets employees know what will happen if they are continually late (the behavior).

Operant conditioning focuses on how organizations can use consequences to achieve two outcomes. One is increasing the probability that workers perform desired behaviors such as satisfying customers and coming to work on time. The other is decreasing the probability that workers perform undesired behaviors such as taking home office supplies and making lengthy personal telephone calls at work. In the next section, we focus on the use of operant conditioning to promote desired behaviors in organizations; then we describe how operant conditioning can be used to discourage undesired behaviors.

ENCOURAGING DESIRED BEHAVIORS THROUGH POSITIVE AND NEGATIVE REINFORCEMENT

Reinforcement

The process by which the probability that a desired behavior will occur is increased by applying consequences that depend on the behavior.

In operant conditioning, **reinforcement** is the process by which the probability that a desired behavior will occur is increased by applying consequences that depend on the behavior in question. One of a manager's major responsibilities is to ensure that subordinates learn and continue to perform desired behaviors consistently and dependably. In operant conditioning terms, managers need to increase the probability that desired organizational behaviors occur. For example, managers may want to encourage their subordinates to sell more products, assemble computer components faster, attend work more regularly, make more consistent use of safety equipment such as helmets, ear plugs, and goggles, or provide higher-quality customer service. Similarly, professors may want to encourage students to come to class, actively participate in class discussions, or turn in assignments on time.

Identifying Desired Behaviors.   The first step in the use of reinforcement is to identify desired behaviors to be encouraged or reinforced, such as using safety equipment or participating in class (see Fig. 5.1). Correctly identifying these behaviors is not as easy as it might seem.

To an outside observer, for example, paying a commission on sales seems a logical way to encourage salespeople to learn to satisfy customers. In this example, making sales is the behavior that is the focus of the reinforcement effort. However, this approach may result in short-run sales but will not necessarily lead to satisfied, loyal, long-term customers. Salespeople may adopt a "hard sell" approach, pushing customers to buy items that do not really satisfy their needs. Thus the behaviors that result in satisfied long-term customers—behaviors such as building long-term relationships and making sure customers buy what is right for them—have not been identified correctly. What has been identified is the amount of actual sales, which may lead to a hard-sell approach.

Similarly, a professor who wants to encourage students to participate in class might reason that students have to regularly attend class in order to participate. The professor thus decides to reinforce attendance by making it worth 5 percent of the course grade. Most students do come to class, but they do not actively participate because the behavior the professor has reinforced is attendance, not actual participation. The professor has not correctly identified the desired behavior.

When desired behaviors are identified correctly, the second step in the reinforcement process is to decide how to reinforce the behavior. In operant conditioning, there are two types of reinforcement: positive and negative.[8]

Positive reinforcement
Reinforcement that increases the probability of a desired behavior by administering positive consequences to workers who perform the behavior.

Positive Reinforcement.   **Positive reinforcement** increases the probability that a behavior will occur by administering positive consequences to workers who perform the behavior. These positive consequences are known as *positive reinforcers*. To use positive reinforcement to facilitate the learning of desired behaviors, managers need to determine what consequences a given worker considers to be positive. Potential positive reinforcers include rewards such as pay, bonuses, promotions, job titles, interesting work, verbal praise, time off from work, and awards. Managers can determine whether these rewards are

At company ceremonies, employees are often given awards in recognition of their outstanding performance. Such awards are important sources of positive reinforcement for employees and are used widely by all kinds of organizations.

positively reinforcing for any given worker if that worker performs desired behaviors in order to obtain these rewards.

It is important to keep in mind that individuals differ in what they consider to be a positive reinforcer. A worker who is independently wealthy, for example, may not view financial rewards as a positive reinforcer but may consider interesting work very reinforcing. In contrast, a worker with many financial needs and few financial resources may have exactly opposite preferences. Similarly, getting full credit for 5 percent of a course grade for regular class attendance might be a powerful positive reinforcer for a student who is hoping to make the dean's list but may not be a positive reinforcer for a student who is content with a B or C in the course. Thus, in using positive reinforcement to increase the probability of desired behaviors in organizations, managers need to take into account individual preferences for different consequences.

With a little creative thinking, organizations can use reinforcement to promote the learning and performance of a wide variety of desirable behaviors. Many companies, for example, are trying to get their employees to give equal opportunities to an increasingly diverse workforce yet are having a hard time getting a specific handle on the best ways to accomplish this objective. Positive reinforcement for diversity efforts may be one strategy that organizations can use to promote the learning of ways to encourage and support diversity. (See Insight 5.1.)

Insight 5.1   **Diversity**

Promoting Diversity Through Positive Reinforcement

Few managers would disagree about the importance of managing diversity, but there is much uncertainty about how to achieve this goal. Some organizations at the cutting edge of diversity management are using positive reinforcement to promote diversity-related efforts. In fact, Barbara Dean, editor of the *Cultural Diversity at Work* newsletter, says that the extent to which organizations link pay and other rewards to the management of diversity is one indicator of how advanced an organization is in its diversity efforts.

Colgate-Palmolive (www.colgate.com) is one organization that uses positive reinforcement (primarily in the form of pay increases) to support diversity. At Colgate-Palmolive, pay is linked to diversity through the firm's Executive Incentive Compensation Plan. According to the plan, incentive compensation (such as a yearly bonus) depends on the extent to which managers achieve certain predetermined objectives, one of which (for managers in the United States) is the support of diversity. Colgate's diversity efforts in the United States have focused primarily on giving equal opportunities to women, African Americans, and Hispanics by having managers recruit and hire these workers, and once hired, give them meaningful job assignments and opportunities for advancement and promotion in the company. Robert Burg, vice president of global compensation, indicates that tying pay to diversity efforts works at Colgate-Palmolive, and the company is currently working on a similar plan for its global operations. Other companies actively promoting the learning of ways to support diversity through similar kinds of efforts include Corning and Quaker Oats.[9]

Negative reinforcement
Reinforcement that increases the probability of a desired behavior by removing a negative consequence when a worker performs the behavior.

Negative Reinforcement.   As in the case of positive reinforcement, subordinates experiencing negative reinforcement learn the connection between a desired organizational behavior and a consequence, but the consequence is not a positive one that a worker wants to obtain; instead, it is a negative consequence that the worker wishes to remove or avoid. **Negative reinforcement** increases the probability that a desired behavior will occur by removing a negative consequence when a worker performs the behavior. The negative consequence that is removed is called a *negative reinforcer.* If you live away from home and your parents complain that you don't call them enough, their complaining is a negative reinforcer if it makes you call home more often. By calling home, you are able to avoid the negative consequence of your parents' complaints.

Just as with positive reinforcement, managers need to take into account that individuals differ in what they consider to be a negative reinforcer. A manager who tells workers that they will be laid off unless they increase their sales is using negative reinforcement to encourage workers to sell more. The threat of unemployment is the negative consequence (the negative reinforcer) that can be removed only by selling more goods. A manager who continually nags a subordinate for having a sloppy office and only lets up when the subordinate straightens up the office is trying to get the subordinate to learn to have a tidier office through the use of negative reinforcement. In these cases, for learning to take place, the workers in question must consider unemployment and the supervisor's nagging to be negative consequences they wish to avoid.

When positive and negative reinforcement are used to promote the learning of desired behaviors, it is important for the consequences to be equivalent in magnitude to the desired behavior. For example, even if pay is a positive reinforcer for a worker, a small increase in pay (a $5 weekly bonus) might not be significant enough to cause the worker to perform a desired behavior (make follow-up calls to all new customers). In the same way, 5 percent of the course grade might not be a big enough reinforcer to cause chronically absent students to come to class, and a professor's complaints in class might not be a big enough negative reinforcer to get some students to participate in class discussions (and by doing so, stop the professor from complaining).

Administering the Reinforcers.   As the third step in the reinforcement process, managers administer the positive or negative reinforcer to the worker. Managers who pay salespeople a commission on sales, give workers a bonus for increasing the rate at which they assemble computer components, verbally praise workers for wearing safety equipment, and give workers with perfect attendance an award are all engaging in positive reinforcement, assuming that the commission, the bonus, the verbal praise, and the award, respectively, are valued by the workers in question. Similarly, professors who give students 5 percent of a course grade for attendance, give students extra-credit points for doing a research project, and praise students who make valuable contributions to class discussions are engaging in positive reinforcement if students value these outcomes. Through positive reinforcement, people (workers as well as students) learn that if they perform a desired behavior, they will receive a positive consequence or reinforcer. In organizations, workers learn the connection between behaviors the organization wants them to perform and consequences they want to obtain.

When managers use negative reinforcement, workers learn the connection between a desired behavior and a consequence they wish to avoid. A worker who cleans up his or her office (the desired behavior) to stop the nagging of a supervisor (the negative reinforcer) has learned that the office must be tidy to bring the nagging to a halt.

In the opening case, you saw how Starbucks positively reinforces its employees through its stock option plan. If employees find new ways to cut costs and increase sales, the value of Starbucks stock will increase, making their stock options more valuable. Telephone operators, engineers, and even company presidents are often positively reinforced through increases in pay and bonuses that are contingent on their performance of desired behaviors, such as efficiently handling customers, designing environment-friendly ways to dispose of waste, and increasing organizational performance.

USING REINFORCEMENT APPROPRIATELY

In general, positive reinforcement is better for workers, managers, and the organization as a whole than negative reinforcement. Negative reinforcement often has unintended side effects and makes for an unpleasant work environment. Continually having the threat of unemployment looming over their heads, for example, can be very stressful for workers and may prompt some good workers to seek employment elsewhere. Likewise, a supervisor who continually berates subordinates may be resented and looked down on. Even if positive and negative reinforcement are equally successful in encouraging desired behaviors, the person or organization providing the reinforcement is likely to be viewed much more positively when positive reinforcement is consistently used.

In using reinforcement to promote the learning of desired behaviors in organizations, managers need to exercise some caution: When certain behaviors receive extensive reinforcement and others do not, workers may tend to focus on the former and ignore the latter. As we discussed earlier, if salespeople are paid solely on a commission basis, they may focus on making quick sales and in doing so may not perform the behaviors (follow-up calls, service reminders, and so on) necessary for building long-term customer satisfaction. Similarly, managers have to be careful to identify the right behaviors to reinforce. As we see in Insight 5.2, managers can make some serious mistakes in their use of reinforcement. If they are not careful to reinforce the right behaviors, they can end up with a disaster on their hands.

Insight 5.2

Ethics

Sears Inadvertently Reinforces Unethical Behavior

In the early 1990s Edward Brennan, chairman of Sears, Roebuck (www.sears.com), tried to revitalize his organization's lackluster performance by promoting an emphasis on sales and profits throughout the retailer's operations. The compensation of workers at Sears Tire & Auto Centers, for example, was to be based in the future on the number of auto repairs that customers authorized. Positive reinforcers such as sales commissions and quota systems and rewards for different types of repairs were used to promote repairs and sales. Negative reinforcement was used as well. Workers who did not sell enough faced the threat of being fired, and the only way to eliminate this threat was by making sales. Workers started to feel pushed to the limits and sometimes felt that their livelihood depended on their sales performance rather than on providing high-quality repair and maintenance services to customers. Essentially, Sears was trying to get its employees to learn to make and sell more auto repairs through the use of positive and negative reinforcement.

Did this radical program work? Not according to Sears's customers. Ruth Hernandez of California said that when she went to a Sears Tire & Auto Center to get new tires for her car, the mechanic indicated that she also had to replace the car's struts, for an additional $419. Hernandez went to another car center for a second opinion and was told that the struts on her car were fine. Irate, she went back to Sears, and the original mechanic said that he had been wrong. Other complaints similar to this one were received by the California Consumer Affairs Department, which, after an extensive investigation, charged that Sears was making unnecessary auto repairs in its Tire & Auto Centers. Similar charges were filed against Sears Tire & Auto Centers in New Jersey, Florida, and Alabama. Sears faced more than ten lawsuits for unethical behaviors that customers indicated occurred in the centers. Perhaps most damaging to the company was the bad publicity Sears received from this scandal in newspapers, magazines, and radio and television news programs. Sales at the centers dropped once the public became aware of the charges of fraud levied against Sears.[10] Realizing that his efforts at promoting sales and profits had backfired, Brennan abandoned commissions, sales quotas, and product-specific sales goals in all of the Tire & Auto Centers.[11]

What went wrong at Sears? Essentially Sears went overboard and made some significant mistakes in trying to promote sales through the use of positive and negative reinforcement. Employees were negatively reinforced for unethical behavior—they avoided being fired by selling unnecessary auto repairs to customers. Thus, although Sears was reinforcing sales, it was not reinforcing good, honest customer service; in fact, it was reinforcing the opposite and promoting customer dissatisfaction. Sears employees were learning to be dishonest and to perform repairs that weren't needed; when they engaged in these behaviors, they received positive and negative reinforcement. Essentially, Sears's inappropriate use of the operant conditioning techniques of positive and negative reinforcement led its workers to learn the wrong behaviors and to act unethically.

As Sears's problems suggest, the use of reinforcement has to be carefully thought out in advance. In particular, managers must identify the appropriate behaviors to reinforce for the right kind of learning to take place. It would have made more sense, for example, for Sears to reinforce mechanics for properly diagnosing auto problems, making repairs in a timely manner, and treating customers with respect and dignity. Another problem with Sears's use of reinforcement was its reliance on negative reinforcement and the threat of job loss. Organizations should not put people in desperate situations in which their employment and economic well-being depend on outcomes that are not entirely under their direct control.

REINFORCEMENT SCHEDULES

Managers using reinforcement to encourage the learning and performance of desired behaviors must choose whether to use continuous or partial reinforcement. When reinforcement is *continuous,* a behavior is reinforced every time it occurs. When reinforcement is *partial,* a behavior is reinforced intermittently. Continuous reinforcement can result in faster learning than can partial reinforcement. But if the reinforcement for some reason is curtailed, continuously reinforced behaviors will stop occurring more quickly than will partially reinforced behaviors.

Practical considerations often dictate whether reinforcement should be continuous or partial. A manager who is trying to encourage workers to use safety equipment, for example, may find continuous reinforcement infeasible. If she has to continually monitor her subordinates' use of safety equipment, she will never be able to get any work done herself.

Managers who decide to use partial reinforcement can choose from four schedules of partial reinforcement.[12] With a *fixed-interval schedule,* the period of time between the occurrence of each instance of reinforcement is fixed or set. An insurance agent whose supervisor takes him out to lunch at a fancy restaurant on the last Friday of the month if he has written a large number of policies during the month is being reinforced on a fixed-interval schedule. Once the supervisor has taken the agent out to lunch, a month will pass before the supervisor takes him out again for performing well. If in any given month the agent writes only a few policies, the supervisor does not treat him to lunch.

With a *variable-interval schedule,* the amount of time between reinforcements varies around a constant average. The owner of a car wash company who every so often watches each employee work on a car and praises those who do a good job is following a variable-interval schedule. The owner may watch and reinforce a given worker once a week, once every three weeks, or once a month, but over a six-month period the average amount of time between reinforcements is two weeks.

With a *fixed-ratio schedule,* a certain number of desired behaviors must occur before reinforcement is provided. Workers who are paid $5 for every three circuit boards they assemble are being reinforced on a fixed-ratio schedule. Many piece-rate pay plans currently in use at companies like Lincoln Electric follow a fixed-ratio schedule.

With a *variable-ratio schedule*, the number of desired behaviors that must occur before reinforcement varies around a constant average. A manager who allows a worker to leave early after she has stayed late for several evenings is following a variable-ratio schedule of reinforcement. Sometimes the manager allows the worker to leave early after working two late evenings, at other times after four late evenings, but over time the average is three evenings.

The choice of a schedule of partial reinforcement often depends on practical considerations: the particular behavior being encouraged, the type of reinforcer being used, the nature of the worker's job. The specific type of schedule chosen is not as important as the fact that reinforcement is based on the performance of desired behaviors: Learning takes place only when the provision of a reinforcer depends on performance of a desired behavior.

SHAPING

Sometimes, a desired behavior is unlikely to occur on its own or at any given point in time because an individual does not have the skills and knowledge necessary to perform the behavior or because the behavior can only evolve out of practice or experience. Consider, for example, a worker who is learning to drive a bus in New York City. At the beginning of her training by the firm's driving instructor, the worker is unlikely to drive the bus properly and thus cannot be reinforced for this desired behavior. The instructor can use reinforcement to *stimulate* learning, however, by reinforcing successively closer approximations to the desired behavior (in this case, the proper handling of the bus in city traffic).

TO MANAGERS

Reinforcement

- Administer rewards only when workers perform desired behaviors or close approximations of them.
- When using reinforcement, make sure you identify the right behaviors to reinforce (that is, those that help the organization achieve its goals).
- Because job performance is likely to vary across workers, administer rewards so that high-performing workers receive more rewards than low-performing workers. All workers who are at a given level in an organization or who hold a particular job should not receive identical rewards unless there is no way for you to accurately distinguish among their performance levels.
- Do not assume that a given reward will function as a positive reinforcer for all workers. Take into account individual preferences for different rewards.
- Make sure the consequences of a behavior are equal to the behavior. Very small pay increases given for a substantial increase in performance may not change a worker's behavior because the size of the reinforcement does not match the magnitude of the desired behavior change.
- Make sure that workers know (through antecedents such as rules, procedures, goals, and instructions) what reinforcers are available for desired behaviors. Managers often assume that such details are common knowledge, but workers (especially newcomers) often lack clear information about how and when they will be reinforced.

Suppose the worker initially jumps the curb when making left turns, but after her sixth trip she makes a turn that, although still too wide, does not jump the curb. Even though the behavior was not at its ideal level because the turn was a bit wider than it should have been, this behavior is positively reinforced by verbal praise from the instructor to increase the probability that it will occur again.

The reinforcement of successive and closer approximations to a desired behavior is known as **shaping**.[13] Shaping is particularly effective when workers need to learn complicated sequences of behavior. When it is unlikely that workers will be able to perform the desired behaviors all at once, managers reinforce closer and closer approximations to the desired behavior, to encourage workers to gradually acquire (learn) the skills and expertise needed to perform at an adequate level.

Shaping
The reinforcement of successive and closer approximations to a desired behavior.

Operant Conditioning: Reducing the Probability of Undesired Behaviors

Just as managers need to ensure that workers learn to perform desired behaviors dependably, they also need to ensure that workers learn *not* to perform undesired behaviors. Examples of undesired behaviors in organizations include (among hundreds of others): excessive horsing-around in group meetings, dangerous operation of heavy equipment such as bulldozers and cranes, and excessive absenteeism. Universities sometimes want students to learn not to perform undesired behaviors such as excessive drinking at on-campus parties and local bars and loud conversations in the library. Two main operant conditioning techniques reduce the probability of undesired behaviors: extinction and punishment (see Fig. 5.1).

EXTINCTION

According to the principles of operant conditioning, all behaviors—good and bad—are controlled by reinforcing consequences. Thus any behavior that occurs is performed because the individual is receiving some form of reinforcement for it. If managers wish to decrease the probability that an undesired behavior will occur, they need to first determine what is currently reinforcing the behavior and then remove the source of reinforcement. Once the undesired behavior ceases to be reinforced, its frequency diminishes until it no longer occurs. This process is called **extinction.**

Extinction
The lessening of undesired behavior by removing the source of reinforcement.

Suppose every time a manager has a group meeting with his subordinates, one of his subordinates, Sam, always tells jokes and generally fools around. At first the manager thinks Sam's joking is harmless, but soon he realizes that the meetings are taking twice as long as they should, that certain items on the agenda are getting short shrift because time runs out, and that the other group members have stopped taking the meetings seriously. After attending a management development seminar on operant conditioning, the manager realizes that Sam's fooling around in the group meetings must be due to some sort of reinforcement he is receiving. At the next meeting, the manager observes what happens when Sam engages in his usual routine: Everyone (including the manager) laughs when Sam starts telling jokes, and Sam generally receives a lot of attention throughout the meeting.

After the meeting, the manager meets with each of the other group members individually, discusses the issue with them, and asks them to try to refrain from laughing or paying much attention to Sam when he jokes in the group meetings. To the manager's surprise, some of his subordinates were also concerned about the way the meetings had been going and were happy to follow his plan. At the next meeting, all the group members behave politely to Sam but refrain from laughing at his jokes or paying a lot of attention to him when he fools around. Sam is shocked at what happens but soon adjusts, and over the course of this and subsequent meetings his behavior changes dramatically.

This example illustrates that extinction can be a relatively painless way to reduce the occurrence of undesired behaviors. The supervisor had considered talking directly to Sam or criticizing his disruptive behavior at the next group meeting. Eliminating Sam's positive reinforcement for horsing around probably did less to hurt his feelings and disrupt his otherwise good relationships with his supervisor and coworkers than these other approaches would have done.

PUNISHMENT

Managers do not have the time to wait for extinction to lessen or eliminate some undesired behaviors. Certain behaviors are so detrimental or dangerous that managers need to reduce their occurrence immediately. Just as a parent cannot rely on extinction to stop a child from touching a hot stove, a manager cannot rely on extinction to eliminate highly undesirable behaviors in the workplace, such as sexual harassment or failing to follow safety rules. Under such circumstances, a manager can try to eliminate undesired behavior by using **punishment**—by administering a negative consequence when the undesired behavior occurs.

In operant conditioning, punishment and negative reinforcement are often confused. Students, employees, and managers alike think that these two techniques for managing behavior are similar or have the same result. However, they differ from each other in two important ways. First, punishment *reduces* the probability of an *undesired* behavior; negative reinforcement *increases* the probability of a *desired* behavior. Second, punishment involves administering a *negative* consequence when an *undesired* behavior occurs; negative reinforcement entails removing a *negative* consequence when a *desired* behavior occurs. Table 5.1 summarizes the effects of the different operant condition-

Punishment
The administration of a negative consequence when undesired behavior occurs.

TABLE **5.1**

Operant Conditioning Techniques

Technique	How Consequence Is Administered	Effect on Behavior	Example
Positive reinforcement	Positive consequence is given when desired behavior is performed	Increases probability of desired behavior	Worker is praised for cleaning up workstation
Negative reinforcement	Negative consequence is removed when desired behavior is performed	Increases probability of desired behavior	Supervisor complains about messy workstation and stops only when worker cleans it up
Extinction	Positive consequence is removed when undesired behavior is performed	Decreases probability of undesired behavior	Coworkers refrain from laughing when worker tells disruptive jokes in group meetings
Punishment	Negative consequence is given when undesired behavior is performed	Decreases probability of undesired behavior	Worker is criticized for telling disruptive jokes in group meetings

ing techniques that managers can use to encourage the performance of desired behaviors and eliminate undesired behaviors.

Managers need to take into account that people differ in what they consider to be punishment. If being scolded by a supervisor after coming to work late is a source of punishment for one worker, that worker will try as hard as possible not to be late after receiving a scolding. But a worker who hardly gives the scolding a second thought will come to work late again the next day. Some forms of punishment that organizations typically use are verbal reprimands, reductions in pay, elimination of privileges (such as personal days a worker can take off at his or her discretion), and temporary suspension. Organizations sometimes use a system of progressive punishment to try to curtail an undesired behavior; the more a worker engages in the behavior, the stricter the punishment becomes. (See Insight 5.3.)

Insight 5.3   Learning

Progressive Punishment Stops Excessive Absence at Allen-Bradley

Out-of-control absenteeism was causing big problems at the Allen-Bradley Co. (www.ab.com) facility in Fullerton, California. Costs were rising, productivity was falling, and an unfair burden was being placed on employees who came to work every day. Absenteeism records showed that about 15 percent of the employees were responsible for most of the absenteeism. The company lacked any clear-cut attendance control policy, and there was no formal means of disciplining workers for excessive absence.

When Jeff Stinson joined the Fullerton facility as human resources manager, he realized that something needed to be done to stop the excessive absenteeism. After carefully analyzing the current situation and various options, Stinson and his colleagues decided that their best bet might be to develop a system of punishment to curtail excessive absenteeism. Then, after excessive levels of absence were curtailed, perhaps the company might consider some kind of reward system for good attendance.

The human resources department at Allen-Bradley devised a carefully thought-out system of progressive punishment for excessive absenteeism and tardiness. Some absences were excluded from the system and thus were not subject to any sort of punishment or disciplinary action: the first 40 hours (5 days) of personal excused time (including any sick leave), approved leaves of absence, absences due to military obligations, time off because of the death of a loved one, workers' compensation leave, and time off for jury duty, vacations, and holidays. Absences and lateness that did not fall into any of these categories were subject to a point system. Serious absence infractions were assigned more points than less consequential ones. For example, an unnotified absence carried six points, whereas simply being late to work one day carried one point. Points for other absence-related infractions were clearly specified.

Progressive punishment for excessive absenteeism and lateness was administered in this way. A worker with any unexcused absence or lateness was counseled by his or her supervisor. An accumulation of 6 points resulted in a documented verbal warning, 9 points in a formal written warning, 12 points in a three-day suspension, and 15 points in termination. Employees were able to remove points from their records after twelve months had elapsed from the time the points in question were incurred. Allen-Bradley took great pains to communicate the new policy clearly to all affected workers, and everyone started with a clean slate. All absence problems incurred before the new policy was put into place were forgiven.

Did this system of progressive punishment eliminate excessive absence at Allen-Bradley? Yes, dramatically. After the new program had been in place for two years, absenteeism was down 83.5 percent, 4,591 hours, for a savings of approximately $60,000. The program also resulted in some problem workers leaving Allen-Bradley voluntarily. As they accumulated an excessive amount of points, these workers chose to leave the company because they knew that termination was around the corner.

Supervisors and workers alike have many positive things to say about the program, and everyone likes having a formal policy and procedure to follow. Currently, Stinson and his colleagues are at work developing a system of positive reinforcement to promote good attendance.[14]

NBA basketball star Dennis Rodman (pictured left) has been suspended and fined for, among other things, kicking a courtside photographer, skipping practice, and head-butting a referee. Karl Malone (pictured right), the Utah Jazz all-star forward, has cultivated a "good guy" image and maintains a strong work ethic and conditioning program that has made him a "role-model" player for his coach, Jerry Sloan.

Punishment can have some unexpected side effects and should be used only when necessary. Punishment not only has the potential to threaten workers' self-respect but can also create so much resentment and negative feelings toward the punisher and the organization as a whole that a worker may want to retaliate and choose to engage in even more undesired behaviors. Thus, when punishment is used, managers want to eliminate the undesired behavior but do not want to create excessive hostility or negative feelings. For example, Allen-Bradley's punishment to curtail excessive absenteeism was directed solely at the undesired behavior and was used in a clearly specified and objective manner to avoid the surfacing of any of these negative feelings.

The following guidelines can help to ensure that punishment has its intended effect and does not generate negative side effects:

- Try to downplay the emotional element involved in punishment. Remember that you are punishing not the person but the person's performance of an undesired behavior.
- Make sure the chosen negative consequence is indeed a punishment for the individual in question, and punish the undesired behavior immediately.[15] Make sure workers know why they are being punished.
- Try to avoid punishing in front of others. Although public punishment might seem to be a good idea because it might serve as a warning to other workers, it is likely to humiliate the individual being punished, reduce the worker's esteem in the eyes of coworkers, and make coworkers uncomfortable. Remember: The key goal in using punishment is to eliminate an undesired behavior, not a person's self-respect.

When a manager does not follow those guidelines, not only is the individual who is being punished likely to suffer, but so too are his or her coworkers, the manager, and the whole organization. (See Insight 5.4.)

Insight 5.4

Learning

CEO Fired for Inappropriate Use of Punishment

CEO William J. Fife has been credited with turning around the fortunes of Giddings and Lewis Inc. (www.giddings.com), a manufacturer of automated factory equipment for companies like GM, Boeing, and Ford. This once-troubled company is now riding high. Fife increased sales at Giddings and Lewis by emphasizing customer responsiveness throughout the company. Fife himself would fly anywhere in the United States to solve a customer problem. He seemed to be doing all the right things, but unfortunately there was a dark side to his reign as CEO.

Periodically, Fife met with top managers at Giddings and Lewis to review sales and profitability data for the products they were responsible for. When he was displeased with a manager's figures, he verbally attacked and abused the manager in front of the others. These punishing attacks seemed endless. The other managers would become very embarrassed and uncomfortable. If an attacked manager tried to fight back or justify his or her figures, this response only prolonged the punishment.

The managers realized that Fife's inappropriate use of punishment was damaging their working relationship with him and threatening the continued success of Giddings and Lewis. They informed the board of directors of their concerns, and after considering the problem, the board asked Fife to resign.[16]

Advice
TO MANAGERS

Extinction and Punishment

- Remember that all behaviors, good and bad, are performed because they are reinforced in some way. Undesired behaviors can be eliminated by determining how the behavior is being reinforced and removing the reinforcer.
- When feasible, use extinction rather than punishment to eliminate undesired behaviors.
- When you need to use punishment, make sure workers know exactly why they are being punished.
- Downplay the emotional element in punishment, punish immediately after the undesired behavior occurs, and do not punish in front of others.

Operant Conditioning in Practice: Organizational Behavior Modification

The systematic application of the principles of operant conditioning for teaching and managing important organizational behaviors is called **organizational behavior modification,** OB MOD for short. OB MOD has been successfully used to improve productivity, attendance, punctuality, safe work practices, and other important behaviors in a wide variety of organizations such as Emery Air Freight, Michigan Bell, Connecticut General Life Insurance, General Electric, Standard Oil of Ohio, Weyerhaeuser, and B. F. Goodrich. OB MOD can be used to encourage the learning of desired organizational behaviors as well as to discourage undesired behaviors.

> **Organizational behavior modification**
>
> The systematic application of the principles of operant conditioning for teaching and managing important organizational behaviors.

THE BASIC STEPS OF OB MOD

Organizations that successfully use OB MOD to encourage their members to learn and perform desired behaviors and to learn not to perform undesired behaviors follow five basic steps (see Fig. 5.2).[17]

Step 1.   Identify the behavior to be learned. OB MOD works best for behaviors such as attendance and punctuality, the use of safety equipment, making sales, and assembling circuit boards—behaviors that are observable, objective, and countable. The work behaviors also should be relevant to the job and to organizational performance. For example, one of the behaviors that managers at Emery Air Freight identified at this step of the OB MOD process was "container utilization." Emery frequently uses containers to transport freight. If containers go out only partly filled, a major expense is incurred; for this reason, the containers must be packed to capacity when they are brought to the airport. Thus, Emery wanted employees to learn to fill the containers as close to capacity as possible.

Step 2.   Measure the frequency with which the behavior identified in Step 1 actually occurs prior to any intervention. At Emery Air Freight, the warehouse workers who packed the containers, and their managers, thought that the containers were pretty full when they were brought to the airport. But when Emery's managers performed Step 2 of the OB MOD process, they discovered that the average container shipped was only 45 percent full.

Step 3.   Perform a functional analysis. A functional analysis determines the antecedents of the behavior identified in Step 1 and the consequences of the behavior. At Emery, upper management's functional analysis determined that there were few if any antecedents prompting workers to fill containers to their capacity and no reinforcers to encourage this behavior because workers and managers alike were unaware of the extent of container utilization.

Step 4.   Develop a strategy to change the frequency of the behavior, make it known to all the employees it affects, and apply it fairly and uniformly. The available strategies are taken directly from operant conditioning principles and include positive reinforcement, negative reinforcement, punishment, and extinction. Upper management at Emery decided that the workers who packed the containers should keep checklists of their own container utilization. That procedure would provide them with immediate feedback on their performance. The workers' managers were instructed to

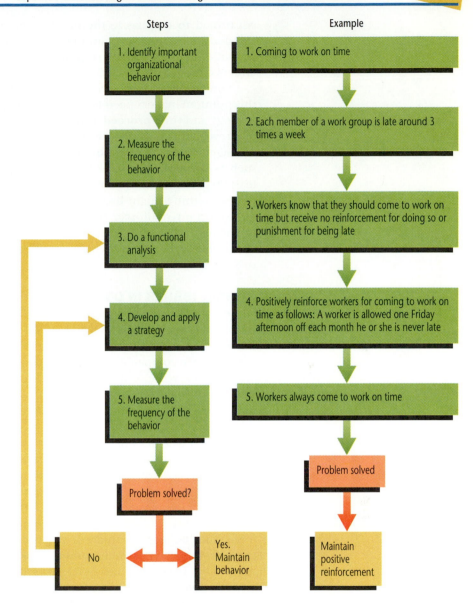

Steps

1. Identify important organizational behavior

2. Measure the frequency of the behavior

3. Do a functional analysis

4. Develop and apply a strategy

5. Measure the frequency of the behavior

Problem solved?

No

Yes. Maintain behavior

Example

1. Coming to work on time

2. Each member of a work group is late around 3 times a week

3. Workers know that they should come to work on time but receive no reinforcement for doing so or punishment for being late

4. Positively reinforce workers for coming to work on time as follows: A worker is allowed one Friday afternoon off each month he or she is never late

5. Workers always come to work on time

Problem solved

Maintain positive reinforcement

FIGURE 5.2

Steps in OB MOD

Source: Adapted from F. Luthans and R. Kreitner, *Organizational Behavior Modification and Beyond* (Glenview, Ill.: Scott, Foresman, 1985).

use verbal praise as a positive reinforcement when workers packed their containers close to capacity.

Step 5. Measure the frequency of the behavior. At Step 5, the frequency of the behavior is measured again to determine whether workers have learned to perform the desired behavior more frequently or the undesired behavior less frequently so that the problem is solved. The same measure of the behavior used in Step 2 should be used in Step 5. At Emery, the problem was clearly solved: Container utilization improved dramatically, saving the company approximately $2 million over a three-year period.[18]

Once a problem has been solved by OB MOD, managers need to maintain the gains they have achieved by, for example, continuing to reinforce desired behaviors. When Emery realized its problem was solved, managers continued to emphasize the importance of container utilization (an antecedent), and workers continued to keep checklists of their own container utilization and receive verbal praise from their supervisors for packing containers close to capacity (reinforcing consequences).

Sometimes, however, Step 5 reveals that the problem is not solved. At this point, managers need to go back to Step 4 and develop and apply a new strategy and then proceed again to Step 5. At Emery, for example, if Step 5 had revealed that container utilization was still hovering around 50 percent, managers would have gone back to Step 4 and developed another strategy, such as giving workers weekly bonuses when they packed their containers at least 90 percent full five days in a row. On occasion, when managers suspect that something might have been missed in the functional analysis, such as an important reinforcer of an undesired behavior or an antecedent that might be confusing workers and causing them to perform the wrong behavior, managers may actually want to go back to Step 3, and then proceed to Steps 4 and 5.

ETHICAL ISSUES IN OB MOD

Some controversy surrounds the use of OB MOD in organizations. Proponents point out that OB MOD is a useful way to manage important organizational behaviors. Evidence indicating that OB MOD has been successfully used by some companies to, for example, increase productivity and cut down on accidents, waste, and absenteeism is certainly consistent with this view. Opponents of OB MOD complain that it is overly controlling. These critics say that managers who explicitly manipulate consequences to control behavior rob workers of their dignity, freedom of choice, and individuality. They also believe that treating workers in such a cut-and-dried fashion may, over time, rob them of their capacity or willingness to use their own initiative to respond appropriately to changing conditions.

Moreover, workers who are managed in such a fashion may refrain from performing important organizational behaviors that are not part of their job duties—that is, the organizational citizenship behaviors discussed in Chapter 3 (such as helping coworkers or coming up with new and good ideas)—because these behaviors often cannot be assigned in advance and appropriately reinforced. These voluntary behaviors are essential for organizational survival and effectiveness but may not be covered by an organization's formal system of rewards because they are performed voluntarily. When workers are managed according to the principles of operant conditioning, they may become so reinforcement oriented that they refrain from doing anything that is not reinforced.

As with most ethical questions, there is no clear-cut answer to the ethical dilemma posed by OB MOD, and there are counterarguments to each of the anti–OB MOD positions. In response to the criticism that OB MOD robs workers of their freedom of choice and individuality, for example, OB MOD proponents might assert that whether a worker performs a behavior is ultimately his or her own choice, and that operant conditioning takes into account individuality in its consideration of individual preferences for different reinforcers. It is important to be aware of the issues raised by this debate and to think through its implications for your own perspective on the pros and cons of OB MOD.

Social Learning Theory

Although operant conditioning accurately describes some of the major factors that influence learning in organizations, certain aspects of learning are not covered in this theory. To get a more complete picture of how members of an organization learn, we now turn to **social learning theory.** Albert Bandura, one of the principal contributors to social learning theory, suggests that any attempt to understand how people learn must take into account the impact on learning not only of reinforcement and punishment but also of a person's feelings and thoughts. Social learning theory acknowledges the importance of the person in the learning process by taking cognitive processes into account.[19]

Cognitive processes are the various thought processes that people engage in. When people form attributions (see Chapter 4), for example, they are engaging in a cognitive process to determine why a person has performed a specific behavior. From the perspective of social learning theory, workers actively process information when they learn.

Suppose you study hard yet are doing poorly in one of your classes. A friend of yours doesn't seem to put in as much time as you do yet is maintaining a B+ average in the class. You think you are just as smart as your friend and notice how your friend studies for the class: He takes detailed notes in class, highlights the chapters and then summarizes the key points, and goes to see the professor whenever he's confused. You start doing this yourself, your grades improve, and you think you can salvage a B in the course after all. This example demonstrates how cognitive processes impact learning. In learning how to do well in the class, your thoughts about your poor performance and about your friend's relatively good performance, your observations of how your friend studies for the class, your belief that you are just as smart as your friend, and your decision to copy your friend's approach to studying were the cognitive processes you engaged in to learn how to perform well in the class.

In addition to stressing the importance of cognitive processes, social learning theory emphasizes three factors that influence learning in organizations:[20] vicarious learning, self-control, and self-efficacy (see Fig. 5.3). Social learning theory suggests that learning can take place vicariously—that is, through observation of how other people behave. Social learning theory acknowledges that workers can engage in self-control, or learn on their own and manage their own behavior. Social learning theory emphasizes the importance of self-efficacy, or people's beliefs about whether they can perform a desired behavior. Each factor entails cognitive processes—the thoughts people have when they watch and imitate others, the thoughts involved in learning on one's own, the thoughts people have about their own capabilities.

LEARNING FROM OBSERVING OTHERS: THE ROLE OF VICARIOUS LEARNING

Vicarious learning occurs when one person (the learner) learns a behavior by observing another person (the model) perform the behavior. The learner observes the effect of the model's behavior on the environment (is it reinforced?), and when an appropriate situation arises, the learner imitates the model's behavior.

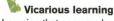 **Social learning theory**
A learning theory that takes into account that thoughts and feelings influence learning.

Cognitive processes
Thought processes.

Vicarious learning
Learning that occurs when one person learns a behavior by watching another person perform the behavior.

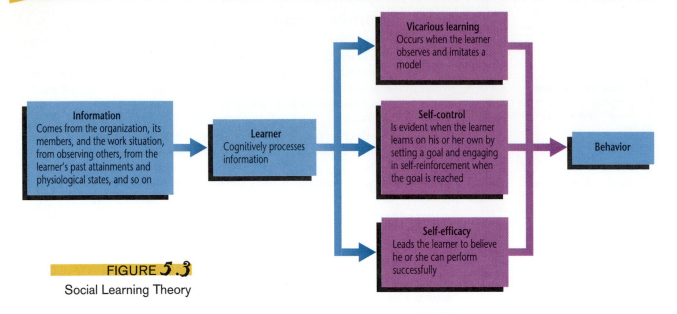

FIGURE 5.3

Social Learning Theory

Several conditions must be met for vicarious learning to take place:[21]

- The learner must observe the model when the model is performing the behavior.
- The learner must accurately perceive the model's behavior.
- The learner must remember the behavior.
- The learner must have the skills and abilities necessary to perform the behavior.
- The learner must see that the model receives reinforcement for the behavior in question. If the model is not reinforced (or is punished) for the behavior, there is obviously no incentive for the learner to imitate the behavior.

As this list reveals, various cognitive processes—such as attention, perception, and memory—are involved in vicarious learning.

A substantial amount of the learning that takes place in organizations occurs vicariously. Training new recruits, for example, involves considerable amounts of vicarious learning. Formal training sessions often rely on demonstrations of appropriate behaviors by experienced workers and role playing during which workers observe others performing right and wrong behaviors. Retail organizations sometimes use films of experienced salespeople providing high-quality customer service to help train new salespeople in these desired behaviors. For these films to be effective, it is essential for the model (the experienced salesperson) to be reinforced for the high-quality service behaviors. Often the reinforcement is the customer's decision to purchase something. Similarly, restaurants often have inexperienced waiters and waitresses follow and observe the behaviors of an experienced coworker for a few days prior to serving their first customers. By watching others, new recruits learn appropriate on-the-job behaviors.

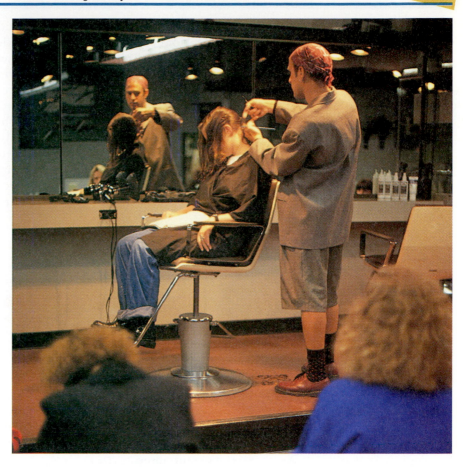

Students at a beautician's school learn proper hair-cutting techniques vicariously, by observing a skilled hairdresser in action. The students then take this learning and apply it in practice sessions.

Vicarious learning also plays an important role in the day-to-day functioning of most organizations. Organizational members continually observe others and often try to remember behaviors that result in reinforcement. These behaviors can range from relatively routine matters such as when to arrive at work, how long to take for lunch, and when to leave, to subtle issues such as the best way to present a report to upper-level management or how to conduct oneself in a business meeting.

Vicarious learning is also an important means of acquiring behaviors that are complicated and have a high cost of failure. Much of the learning that takes place through operant conditioning is a result of trial and error: The learner engages in a variety of behaviors and learns to repeat those that are reinforced and abandon those that are not. For some kinds of work, however, an organization simply cannot afford the costs of trial-and-error learning. No one would want to be at the mercy of a medical intern who is learning open-heart surgery by means of trial and error; the costs (a few dead patients) of learning in this manner are just too high. In such situations, vicarious learning is essential. A learner who has all the necessary knowledge, skills, and abilities can learn quite complicated sequences of behavior by carefully observing the behaviors and outcomes of others with more experience.

In organizations, there are many potential models available for members to imitate. However, only a few of these models will be used to acquire new behaviors vicariously. To take advantage of vicarious learning in organizations, managers should ensure that good performer models are available for newcomers and existing organizational members to learn from. Models that are most likely to be imitated by others tend to be (1) organizational members who are highly competent in the modeled behavior and may even have a reputation for being an expert, (2) individuals with high status in the organization, (3) models who receive reinforcers that the learner desires, and (4) models who engage in desired behaviors in a friendly manner.[22] Individuals very high up in an organization's hierarchy can sometimes be important models for workers to imitate. (See Insight 5.5.)

Insight 5.5

Learning

CEOs as Models

Rosabeth Moss Kanter, former editor of the *Harvard Business Review* and a leading researcher and consultant on organizational behavior issues, suggests that one of the ways CEOs can be more effective is by serving as models for their employees. What CEOs do and what they choose to learn can have powerful effects on what takes place at lower levels in the organization.

For example, when Arnold Hiatt, chairman of the Stride Rite shoe company (www.nauticom.net/www/majes/), was traveling from Korea to Hong Kong, he saw a tab on the back of a little girl's shoe that helped her put the shoe on by herself. This simple observation was the impetus for an innovative product. What did Stride Rite employees learn from their CEO's behavior? They learned that creative ideas can be triggered in a variety of ways and that one should always be on the lookout for different ways of doing things.

Kanter suggests that CEOs can be most effective as role models by actually engaging in desired behaviors instead of trying to teach workers about them. David Dworkin, head of BhS, a British retailing company, exemplified this approach when he wanted to emphasize to sales associates the importance of new technology in increasing his company's level of customer service. Rather than delivering the traditional lecture with overhead transparencies or films on the new technology, Dworkin brought home his important message by actually learning how to operate advanced cash registers with some other top managers.[23]

CEOs should always be aware that their status and expertise make them important behavior models for others in their organizations.

Self-control

Self-discipline that allows a person to learn to perform a behavior even though there is no external pressure to do so.

Self-reinforcers

Consequences or rewards that individuals can give to themselves.

MANAGING ONE'S OWN BEHAVIOR: THE IMPORTANCE OF SELF-CONTROL

Social learning theory acknowledges that people can learn on their own by using **self-control**—that is, by learning to perform a behavior even though there is no external pressure to do so. Several conditions indicate that a person is using self-control:[24]

An individual must engage in a low-probability behavior.   A low-probability behavior is a behavior that a person would ordinarily not want to perform. This condition distinguishes individuals exhibiting self-control from those engaging in activities they enjoy. For example, Sylvia Crano, an administrative secretary, has had a new software package for graphics sitting on her desk for the past six months. She hates learning how to use new software and, fortunately, her boss hasn't put any pressure on her to learn the new software. Taking the initiative to learn how to use the new software is a low-probability response for Crano. If she bites the bullet and comes in one Saturday to learn it, Crano will be exhibiting self-control.

Self-reinforcers must be available to the learner.   **Self-reinforcers** are any consequences or rewards that individuals give to themselves. Potential self-reinforcers include buying oneself a present, eating a favorite food, going out to a movie, getting some extra sleep, and going out with friends. Sometimes self-reinforcement comes simply from a feeling of accomplishment or achievement. In the past, when Sylvia Crano has accomplished a particularly difficult task, she has rewarded or reinforced herself by buying a new CD or having lunch with a friend.

The learner must set goals that determine when self-reinforcement takes place.   When self-control takes place, people do not indiscriminately reward themselves but set goals that determine when they will self-reinforce. How do people determine these goals or standards? Essentially, they rely on their own past performance, the performance of others on similar kinds of tasks, or some socially acquired performance standard. Crano's goal was to complete the new software's tutorial program and to use the new software to reproduce some graphs she had done previously.

The learner must administer the reinforcer when the goal is achieved.   Crano allowed herself to have lunch out with her friend only when she was able to use the new software to reproduce her existing graphs.

All people engage in self-control and self-reinforcement to learn behaviors on and off the job. These activities can range from the relatively mundane (such as cutting short a lunch hour to learn how to send and receive e-mail) to the more involved (learning how to appropriately give subordinates negative feedback). Managers need to be aware that self-control takes place at work, especially when individuals are interested in and care about their work. When opportunities for self-control are present and workers engage in it, managers do not need to take as active a role in controlling behavior and consequences because workers are taking responsibility for learning and performing desired behaviors themselves. In such cases, the managers' efforts at control may be not only redundant but counterproductive because they may irritate and anger those who are self-controlled. Instead of trying to control those who do not need to be controlled, managers would be wise to focus their efforts on those who do.

Workers who manage their own behavior through self-control are often said to be self-managing. Sometimes, however, workers may need a bit of coaching and guidance to become truly self-managing. Managers can provide the training and support workers need to develop self-management skills and put them to use. Some organizations explicitly recognize this need and have formal programs in place to teach self-management. (See Insight 5.6.)

Insight 5.6   Competitive Advantage

Facilitating Self-Management at National Semiconductor

Like most large organizations, National Semiconductor (www.national .com) has always spent a considerable amount of time and money trying to select and hire only the most capable of new college graduates. The organization was successful at attracting highly qualified young people, but it seemed to take these new hires too long to make substantial contributions to the company without extensive guidance, coaching, and supervision by their managers. To remedy this problem, National Semiconductor created an innovative College Hire Assimilation Program (CHAP) to help new hires to become productive on their own more quickly.

One aspect of CHAP focuses on new hires' self-management of their own careers. National Semiconductor believes that responsibility for career planning and management should rest primarily with the worker, but the company recognized that newcomers often lack the knowledge and skills they need to manage their own careers effectively. To help new college hires acquire the knowledge and develop the skills to manage their own careers, National Semiconductor developed the CHAP adviser program.

Each new hire is assigned to an experienced manager in his or her group who is not the new hire's supervisor. The adviser and the new hire meet periodically to formulate specific objectives that will help the new hire meet his or her career goals. These specific goals might entail specific types of assignments or tasks that new hires should seek out to help them reach their career aspirations. Throughout this process, the new hire is in control, and the experienced manager is an adviser who helps the new hire to begin to manage his or her career.

The objectives that the new hires set for themselves must be realistic and obtainable and must enable them to contribute as much as they can to the organization. For example, a process engineer who wants to learn more about product engineering might set a goal of selecting a product engineering project to work on and then becoming responsible for and completing the project.[25]

BELIEFS ABOUT ONE'S ABILITY TO LEARN: THE ROLE OF SELF-EFFICACY

Self-efficacy
A person's belief about his or her ability to perform a particular behavior successfully.

Social learning theory also emphasizes the importance of **self-efficacy**—a person's belief about his or her ability to perform a particular behavior successfully—in the learning process. One secretary may believe that she can learn how to use a new software package on her own, and another may have strong doubts about his ability to learn new software without taking a formal training course. Self-efficacy has powerful effects on learning because people try to learn only those behaviors that they think they will be able to perform successfully.[26] Recall from the opening case how Starbucks trains employees so that they are knowledgeable, confident, and feel that they can successfully make decisions on their own to improve customer satisfaction. Self-efficacy affects learning in three ways:[27]

Self-efficacy influences the activities and goals that individuals choose for themselves. Workers with a low level of self-efficacy may never try to learn how to perform challenging tasks because they think they will fail at them. Such workers tend to set relatively low goals for themselves. Conversely, an individual with high self-efficacy is likely to try to learn how to perform demanding tasks and set high personal goals. Consistent with this reasoning, research has found that individuals not only learn but also perform at levels consistent with their self-efficacy beliefs. You learn what you think you are capable of learning.

Self-efficacy affects learning by influencing the effort that individuals exert on the job. Workers with high self-efficacy generally work hard to learn how to perform new behaviors because they are confident that their efforts will be successful. Workers with low self-efficacy may exert less effort when learning how to perform complicated or difficult behaviors, not because they are lazy but because they don't think the effort will pay off. Their lack of confidence in their ability to succeed causes them to think that exerting a lot of effort is futile because they are likely to fail anyway.

Self-efficacy affects the persistence with which a person tries to master new and sometimes difficult tasks. Because workers with high self-efficacy are confident that they can learn how to perform a given task, they are likely to persist in their efforts even in the face of temporary setbacks or problems. Conversely, workers with low self-efficacy who think they are unlikely to be able to learn a difficult task are likely to give up as soon as an obstacle appears or the going gets a little tough.

Because self-efficacy can have such powerful effects on learning in organizations, it is important to identify the sources of self-efficacy. Bandura has identified four principal sources.[28]

Past performance is one of the most powerful sources of self-efficacy. Workers who have succeeded on job-related activities in the past are likely to have higher self-efficacy for such activities than workers who have failed. Managers can boost low levels of self-efficacy by ensuring that workers can and do succeed on certain tasks. "Small successes" boost self-efficacy and enable more substantial accomplishments in the future. At Starbucks, it is likely that the self-efficacy of new employees for serving customers increases once they have successfully taken orders and made coffee in training sessions.

Vicarious experience or observation of others is another source of self-efficacy. Seeing coworkers succeed at a particular task may heighten the observer's self-efficacy. Conversely, seeing coworkers fail is likely to discourage the observer.

Verbal persuasion—that is, trying to convince people that they have the ability to learn and succeed at a particular task—can give rise to self-efficacy. Research has shown that the greater managers' confidence is that their subordinates can succeed at a particular task, the higher is the level at which subordinates actually perform.[29]

Individuals' readings of their internal physiological states is the fourth source of self-efficacy that Bandura identified.[30] A person who expects to fail at some task or to find something too demanding is likely to experience certain physiological symptoms: pounding or racing heart, feeling flushed, sweaty hands, headaches, and so on. The particular symptoms vary from individual to individual but over time become associated with doing poorly. If the symptoms start to occur in any given situation, self-efficacy for dealing with that situation may plummet.

Consider the case of Michael Pulinski, who was facing an important job interview. Pulinski really wanted to get this job and had spent a considerable amount of time preparing for the interview. He was familiar with the company and had prepared good questions to ask the interviewer about the job. He also had thoroughly rehearsed answers to typical interview questions

TO MANAGERS

(such as "Where do you see yourself in five years?") and had bought a new suit for the occasion. The day of the interview, Pulinski got up feeling quite good and was actually looking forward to the interview and to demonstrating that he was the right candidate for the job. He arrived to the interview a little early and paged through a recent copy of *Business Week* in the reception area. As he was thinking about how much this job meant to him, he started getting nervous. He could feel his face getting flushed, his hands were sweaty, and his heart started pounding in his chest. Pulinski's self-efficacy plummeted. Because of these physical symptoms, he decided that he was much too nervous to make a good impression in the interview. Unfortunately, his low self-efficacy resulted in his not doing well in the interview and failing to get a job offer.

The Learning Organization

Not only is it important that individuals learn to perform behaviors that contribute to organizational effectiveness, but also that the organization as a whole adopts a learning mentality. **Organizational learning** is the process through which managers instill in all members of an organization a desire to find new ways to improve organizational effectiveness.[31] Recall from the opening case how Starbucks encouraged its employees to find new ways to cut costs and increase sales by rewarding them through its stock option plan. Learning organizations like Starbucks invest in such initiatives and make sure that their members actually do have the knowledge and skills to continuously learn. Learning organizations also take steps to make sure that new ideas are acted upon and knowledge is shared throughout the organization.

Learning theorist Peter Senge has identified five key activities central to a learning organization.[32]

Organizational learning
The process through which managers instill in all members of an organization a desire to find new ways to improve organizational effectiveness.

- *Encourage personal mastery or high self-efficacy.* In order for members of an organization to strive to find new ways of improving organizational effectiveness, they must have confidence in their ability to do so.
- *Develop complex schemas to understand work activities.* Recall from Chapter 4 that schemas are abstract knowledge structures. In order for members of an organization to learn new ways to cut costs or increase revenues, they must have an appreciation of not only their own jobs but also how the work they do affects the work of others and the organization as a whole.
- *Encourage learning in groups and teams.* New discoveries often take place in groups and teams. Members of groups and teams need to strive to find new ways of doing things and manage the learning process by, for example, increasing the self-efficacy of group members who may question their own capabilities.
- *Communicate a shared vision for the organization as a whole.* Members of an organization need guidance in terms of what they should be striving for. For example, should they be striving to cut costs or should they focus more on increasing customer satisfaction even at the expense of higher costs?
- *Encourage system thinking.* Organizations are systems of interrelated parts. What one part of the organization does or learns affects other parts of the organization. Organizational members must be encouraged to think

in these terms and address how their individual actions and their actions in groups and teams influence other parts of the organization.

Organizational learning is especially important for organizations in environments that are rapidly changing. As John Browne, CEO of British Petroleum, puts it: "Learning is at the heart of a company's ability to adapt to a rapidly changing environment. It is the key to being able both to identify opportunities that others might not see and to exploit those opportunities rapidly and fully."[33]

SUMMARY

Two approaches to learning are offered by operant conditioning and social learning theory. Organizational learning complements these approaches by stressing the importance of a commitment to learning throughout an organization. In this chapter, we made the following major points:

1. Learning is a relatively permanent change in knowledge or behavior that results from practice or experience.

2. In operant conditioning, the learner behaves in a certain way to achieve certain consequences. Antecedents let workers know which behaviors are desired, which should be avoided, and what the consequences are for performing different behaviors.

3. In operant conditioning, there are two ways to promote the learning of desired behaviors in organizations: positive reinforcement and negative reinforcement. Positive reinforcement increases the probability that a behavior will occur by administering positive consequences to workers who perform the behavior. Negative reinforcement increases the probability that a desired behavior will occur by removing a negative consequence if a worker performs the behavior. Positive reinforcement is generally preferred over negative reinforcement.

4. Reinforcement can be continuous or partial. Partial reinforcement can be administered according to one of four schedules: fixed interval, variable interval, fixed ratio, and variable ratio. The choice of reinforcement schedules in organizations is often influenced by practical considerations such as the nature of the behavior, job, and reinforcer in question. Shaping, or reinforcing progressively closer approximations to a desired behavior, can be used to encourage behaviors that are unlikely to occur on their own.

5. In operant conditioning, there are two ways to reduce the probability of undesired behaviors in organizations: extinction and punishment. Extinction, removing the source of reinforcement for an undesired behavior, can take time. Punishment, administering a negative consequence when an undesired behavior occurs, is sometimes needed to eliminate detrimental behaviors quickly. Punishment can have some unintended negative side effects (such as resentment) and should be used with caution.

6. The systematic application of the principles of operant conditioning to managing organizational behavior is known as organizational behavior modification (OB MOD). OB MOD works best for managing behaviors that are specific, objective, and countable, such as productivity, attendance, punctuality, and safe work practices.

7. Social learning theory acknowledges that cognitive processes affect learning. Social learning theory adds to our understanding of learning in

organizations by taking into account the role of vicarious learning, self-control, and self-efficacy.

8. In order for vicarious learning to take place, the learner must pay attention to the model, accurately perceive the model's behavior, remember the behavior, and have the skills and abilities necessary to perform the behavior; the model must also receive reinforcement for the behavior. Models who are most likely to be imitated by workers are competent or expert, have high status, receive positive reinforcers that the learner desires, and model behaviors in a friendly manner.

9. In order for self-control (taking the initiative to learn desired behaviors on one's own) to take place, the following conditions must be satisfied: An individual must engage in a low-probability behavior, self-reinforcers must be available, the learner must set performance standards or goals, and reinforcers must be self-administered when the goal is attained.

10. Self-efficacy (beliefs about one's ability to perform particular behaviors successfully) influences the tasks workers choose to learn and the goals they set for themselves. Self-efficacy also affects workers' levels of effort and persistence when learning difficult tasks. Past performance, observations of others, verbal persuasion, and physiological states are determinants of self-efficacy.

11. Organizational learning is the process through which managers instill in all members of an organization a desire to find new ways to improve organizational effectiveness.

Organizational Behavior in Action

TOPICS FOR
DISCUSSION
AND ACTION

1. Why might an organization prefer to use positive reinforcement rather than negative reinforcement?
2. How can a manager use the principles of operant conditioning to stop workers from bickering and fighting with each other?
3. Why do some organizations use punishment more often than others?
4. Is OB MOD ethical? Why or why not?
5. In what ways are the behaviors of managers controlled by the principles of operant conditioning?
6. On what kinds of jobs might vicarious learning be especially prevalent?
7. When might workers be especially likely to engage in self-control?
8. How might social learning theory help explain how managers learn?
9. Why do some capable members of an organization have low levels of self-efficacy?
10. What steps can organizations take to promote organizational learning?

BUILDING
DIAGNOSTIC
SKILLS

Learning Difficult Behaviors

Think about the last time you finally succeeded at something that had been giving you trouble. It could be a particularly troublesome class that you managed to pull through with a decent grade or a difficult project at work that you finally were able to finish satisfactorily.

1. Describe the specific behaviors that gave you trouble.
2. What antecedents prompted you to perform these behaviors?
3. What were the reinforcing consequences for performing these behaviors successfully?
4. Would you have been punished if you had not finally succeeded? If you would have been punished, how would you have felt about being punished?
5. Did you use vicarious learning to try to solve your problem? If you did, which model did you use and why? If you did not, why not?
6. Did you use self-control to try to solve your problem? If you did, what goal did you set for yourself, and what was your self-reinforcer? If you did not use self-control, why not?
7. Describe your level of self-efficacy when you first started out, when you were having a particularly troublesome time, and when you finally succeeded.
8. What do you think your level of self-efficacy will be for similar tasks in the future? Why do you think your self-efficacy will be at this level?

RESEARCH ON
THE INTERNET:
A MANAGER'S
TOOL

Specific Task

Many organizations strive to ensure that their members have the necessary knowledge and skills to effectively perform their jobs and have high self-efficacy. One such organization is Ford. Scan Ford's website (www.ford.com/us/) to learn more about this major manufacturer of automobiles and Ford's learning-related initiatives. Then click on "Inside Ford," then on "Government Policies," then on "Ford Competitiveness Efforts," and then on "Our People."

1. What steps is Ford taking to ensure that its employees learn how to perform their jobs effectively?
2. How might Ford's various initiatives boost employees' levels of self-efficacy?

General Task

Many organizations are striving to be learning organizations and encourage learning to take place on a continual basis throughout the organization. Find the website of such a company. How does this company encourage organizational learning? Why does this organization view organizational learning as a critical ingredient for organizational effectiveness?

TOPICS FOR DEBATE

Learning is the way in which all members of an organization acquire behaviors that are necessary for the organization to achieve its goals. Now that you have a good understanding of learning, debate the following issues.

Debate One

Team A. OB MOD robs workers of their dignity and should be used only when absolutely necessary.

Team B. OB MOD works to everyone's advantage and should be used whenever possible.

Debate Two

Team A. Social learning theory is more useful than operant conditioning for understanding and managing organizational behavior.

Team B. Operant conditioning is more useful than social learning theory for understanding and managing organizational behavior.

EXPERIENTIAL EXERCISE

Managing the Learning Process

Objective

Your objective is to gain experience in applying learning principles and theories and understanding the challenges involved in managing the learning process.

Procedure

The class divides into groups of from three to five people, and each group appoints one member as spokesperson, to present the group's findings to the whole class. Here is the scenario.

You are a group of supervisors who are responsible for teaching production workers how to operate a new, computerized production process. The new process requires employees to work in small teams, and each team member's performance influences the performance of the team as a whole. Prior to this major change, employees did not work in teams but performed simple, repetitive tasks that required few skills.

To operate the new production process, workers are required to learn new skills to perform their now-more-complicated jobs, and they are currently receiving formal training in a classroom setting and on-the-job instruction in their teams. Some workers are responding well to the changes, are doing well in training and instruction, and are performing up to expectations in their teams. Other workers are finding it difficult to adapt to their changed jobs and to teamwork and have been slow to acquire the necessary new skills. In addition, there have been reports of high levels of conflict among members of some teams. As a result, the overall performance of the teams is suffering and below expectations.

As the group of supervisors responsible for ensuring a smooth transition to the new production process and high performance in the production teams, do the following:

1. Develop a plan of action based on the principles of operant conditioning to facilitate learning and high team performance. Be specific about how operant conditioning techniques (positive reinforcement, negative reinforcement, punishment, and extinction) could be used to promote team members' learning desired behaviors, working well together, and performing at a high level.
2. Develop a plan of action based on the principles of social learning theory (vicarious learning, self-control, and self-efficacy) to facilitate learning and high team performance. Be specific about how social learning theory could be used to promote team members' learning desired behaviors, working well together, and performing at a high level.
3. Decide whether the two plans of action that you developed should be combined for the most effective learning to take place. Explain why or why not.

MAKING THE CONNECTION

Find an example of a company that recently used positive or negative reinforcement to try to change employees' behavior. What behaviors was the company trying to change? What reinforcers were used, and how were they administered? Was the company successful in changing behavior? Why or why not?

CLOSING CASE

Putting the Customer First

Because customer satisfaction is an important goal for a large variety of organizations, such as retail stores, restaurants, hospitals, and even companies that manufacture cars and appliances, providing high-quality customer service is one of their top priorities. To increase customer service and satisfaction, managers try to get employees to put customers first by encouraging employees to learn better ways to satisfy customers' needs.

General Electric, Reynolds Metal, Chrysler, Du Pont, and other companies have recognized that all workers in all areas and at all hierarchical levels must learn to be customer oriented to meet the organization's commitment to increasing customer satisfaction. Chrysler Corporation (www.chrysler.com), for example, has acknowledged that high sales figures alone are no indication that customers are satisfied. To promote the goal of customer satisfaction and to get dealers to learn that it is now a top priority, Chrysler recently started paying extra money to dealers who receive top ratings from customers on customer satisfaction surveys.

The current focus on customer satisfaction has important implications for how organizations reward service providers, such as salespeople. Theories about how people learn suggest that service providers will learn desirable behaviors only if they are appropriately rewarded for them—that is, if organizations tie rewards to the provision of high-quality customer service. Traditional incentives such as sales commissions encourage salespeople to adopt a hard-sell approach. This approach focuses the salesperson's attention on making an immediate sale and not necessarily on attracting customers back and ensuring their repeat business. To combat this short-term focus, the front-runners in the customer service race are changing their reward structures to encourage salespeople to learn how to think long-term and retain satisfied customers. Craig Ulrick of the William & Mercer Consulting Company indicates, for example, that rewarding salespeople for customer satisfaction is the biggest trend in sales compensation. Consistent with this trend, the Universal credit card unit of American Telephone & Telegraph Co. (AT&T) monitors customer satisfaction, and all of the unit's employees from phone operators to the president receive bonuses based on meeting customer satisfaction goals.[34] By doing this, AT&T is encouraging employees to learn new behaviors that will result in increased customer satisfaction.

Even physicians are being urged to learn how to increase customer (patient) satisfaction, and some are being compensated for doing so. Take the case of family doctor David Badolato, who works for the health maintenance organization (HMO) U.S. Healthcare Inc. (www.ushc.com) in Fort Washington, Pennsylvania. One month he received a bonus of 19 percent of his U.S. Healthcare pay, an amount based on his patients' responses to a questionnaire. Badolato's bonus resulted from his being available for emergencies, providing clear explanations of treatments, and generally showing concern for his patients' needs. By tying bonuses to being responsive to patient needs, U.S. Healthcare helps Badolato and others like him to learn important customer service behaviors. Many managed health care programs and HMOs, such as FHP International Corp. and AvMed–Santa Fe, also use incentive pay to improve the quality of care provided by their physicians. AvMed–Santa Fe, for example, pays doctors a bonus for quality service ranging from 5 to 15 percent of their base pay, depending on the scores they receive on patient surveys and reviews of office records (which show things such as whether a doctor has extended office hours to serve patients who work during the day). Basing doctors' pay on their performance may also be expanded by some of these organizations to include other areas and issues, such as not relying too heavily on Caesarean sections for births.[35] Essentially, these organizations are trying to get doctors to learn how to give patients the time and attention they need by rewarding doctors for increasing patient/customer satisfaction.

Questions for Discussion

1. Why might paying salespeople a commission on the amount of goods they sell result in quick sales and dissatisfied customers?
2. How could salespeople be rewarded for increasing customer satisfaction?
3. How might physicians respond to being rewarded on the basis of patient satisfaction?
4. Is there a tradeoff between providing high quality medical care and patient satisfaction? Why or why not?

The Nature of Work Motivation

6

Creating Best Selling Games at Square Co.

Square Co. is a leading producer of computer games in Japan for use with machines for Sony Computer Entertainment's Playstation. Square has a knack for creating high-quality, best-selling games. Fourteen of its games have sold over 1 million copies in Japan, with the Final Fantasy VII game selling more than 3 million copies. These sales figures attest to the high quality of Square's games; in Japan, a game is considered to be a best-seller if it sells over 300,000 copies.[1] How does Square do it? Square's success is at least partially attributable to the high motivation of its designers. Only creative game

designers are hired, people who really enjoy their work for its own sake. Managers at Square then take steps to make sure that designers really do have reason to enjoy the work they do. Square's office areas are spacious yet functional and are designed to encourage the sharing of information and ideas among game designers. Moreover, designers are encouraged to take all the time they need to come up with revolutionary new ideas for games. Managers think nothing of designers taking time to visit museums or parks in order to come up with the spark of a new idea. With the idea in mind, designers and their coworkers then put forth high levels of effort throughout the two-year design process to make the idea a successful new game.[2]

Designers also receive rewards they value for their efforts. Once a game is completed and ready to be marketed and sold, its designers are rewarded with a two-month vacation. Square's designers' pay is linked to the volume of the sales of the games they create, and they also receive paid overseas trips. Linking pay to sales is not a common practice in Japan, but managers at Square think it is only fair that designers reap some of the benefits of their efforts.[3]

Recently, Square Co. expanded globally and established Square USA (www.sqla.com). Square USA has offices in Marina Del Ray, California, and Honolulu, Hawaii, and a $10 million graphic research facility in Honolulu.[4] Offices in Square USA, like their counterparts in Japan, are designed to facilitate creativity and enjoyment of the design process. As in Japan, Square USA only recruits and hires employees who are highly motivated by the kind of work they do and are at the top of their fields. Employees, in turn, benefit from being in a highly charged and motivating work environment, working alongside the best in the field to develop their skills. Square USA's employees are also granted considerable autonomy and freedom and are rewarded for their efforts.[5] All in all, Square seems to be doing all the right things to ensure that its employees are highly motivated to create best-selling computer games.

Overview

As the case of Square Co. suggests, the motivation of organizational members to make important contributions to their jobs and organizations can have a major impact on organizational effectiveness. Motivation is central to understanding and managing organizational behavior because it explains why people behave as they do in organizations. Just as your own motivation determines how many classes you take, how hard you study for exams, and the amount of time and effort you spend on research projects, so too does motivation determine the extent to which organizational members perform at a high level and help the organization achieve its goals. Motivation explains, for example, why one worker wants and tries to do a good job while another worker with the same abilities couldn't care less. Motivation also explains why some students strive for A's and study much harder than others, who are content with maintaining a solid B average.

In this chapter we examine work motivation. We focus on the important distinctions between motivation and performance and between intrinsic and extrinsic motivation. We discuss several specific theories of work motivation—need theory, expectancy theory, equity theory, and procedural justice theory. Each theory seeks to explain why people behave as they do in organizations and suggests ways of increasing worker motivation and performance. An understanding of motivation is of utmost importance for organizational effectiveness. Managers need to ensure that workers choose to act in ways that help the organization achieve its goals and avoid behaving in ways that injure or hinder the pursuit of organizational objectives.

What Is Work Motivation?

Motivation is a frequently used but poorly understood term. Over 140 definitions have been provided over the years,[6] and noted scholars of work motivation have said that trying to define *motivation* often gives them "a severe stomachache."[7] This remark may be a bit of an exaggeration, but it underscores the need to get a firm grasp of what motivation is before we try to understand its role in understanding and managing organizational behavior.

Motivation is important because it explains why workers behave as they do. **Work motivation** can be defined as the psychological forces within a person that determine the direction of a person's behavior in an organization, a person's level of effort, and a person's level of persistence in the face of obstacles.[8] Because motivation involves psychological forces within a person, many of the topics that we cover in prior chapters are relevant to understanding motivation: personality and ability (Chapter 2), values, attitudes, and moods (Chapter 3), and perception and attribution (Chapter 4).

The three key elements of work motivation are direction of behavior, level of effort, and level of persistence (see Table 6.1).

Work motivation
The psychological forces that determine the direction of a person's behavior in an organization, a person's level of effort, and a person's level of persistence.

TABLE **6.1**

Elements of Work Motivation

Element	Definition	Example
Direction of behavior	Which behaviors does a person choose to perform in an organization?	Does an engineer take the time and effort to convince skeptical superiors of the need to change the design specifications for a new product to lower production costs?
Level of effort	How hard does a person work to perform a chosen behavior?	Does an engineer prepare a report outlining problems with the original specifications, or does the engineer casually mention the issue when he or she bumps into a supervisor in the hall and hope that the supervisor will take the advice on faith?
Level of persistence	When faced with obstacles, roadblocks, and stone walls, how hard does a person keep trying to perform a chosen behavior successfully?	When the supervisor disagrees with the engineer and indicates that a change in specifications is a waste of time, does the engineer persist in trying to get the change implemented or give up despite his or her strong belief in the need for a change?

Direction of Behavior.   Which behaviors does a person choose to perform? On any job, the jobholder can engage in many behaviors (some appropriate, some inappropriate). *Direction of behavior* refers to which of the many potential behaviors that a worker could perform the worker actually performs. Whether a stockbroker in an investment banking firm illegally manipulates stock prices, whether managers focus their efforts exclusively on advancing their own careers at the expense of their subordinates' development, and whether an engineer takes the time and effort to convince skeptical superiors of the need to change the design specifications for a new product in order to lower production costs—all reflect behaviors that people *choose* to perform.

As those examples illustrate, workers can be motivated in *functional* ways that help an organization achieve its goals or in *dysfunctional* ways that hinder an organization from achieving its goals. In looking at motivation, managers want to ensure that the direction of their subordinates' behavior is functional for the organization. They want workers to be motivated to come to work on time, perform their assigned tasks dependably, come up with good ideas, and help others. They do not want workers to come to work late, ignore rules concerning health and safety, or pay lip service to quality.

Level of Effort.   How hard does a person work to perform a chosen behavior? It is not enough for an organization to motivate workers to perform desired functional behaviors; the organization must also motivate them to work hard at these behaviors. If, for example, an engineer decides to try to convince skeptical superiors of the need for design changes, the engineer's level of motivation determines the lengths to which he or she will go to convince them of the need for change. Does the engineer just mention the need for the change in casual conversation, or does the engineer prepare a detailed report outlining the problems with the original specifications and describing the new, cost-saving specifications that are needed? In the opening case, designers and other employees at Square Co. are motivated to exert high levels of effort in order to create best-selling games.

Level of Persistence.   When faced with obstacles, roadblocks, and stone walls, how hard does a person keep trying to perform a chosen behavior successfully? Suppose the engineer's supervisor indicates that a change in specifications is a waste of time. Does the engineer persist in trying to get the change implemented, or does the engineer give up even though he or she strongly believes in the need for a change? Likewise, if a factory worker's machine breaks down, does the worker simply stop working and wait for someone to come along to fix it, or does the worker try to fix the machine or at least alert others about the problem?

THE DISTINCTION BETWEEN MOTIVATION AND PERFORMANCE

Because motivation determines what workers do and how hard and diligently they do it, you might think that a worker's motivation to do a job is the same as the worker's job performance. In fact, motivation and performance, though often confused by workers and managers alike, are two distinct aspects of behavior in an organization. *Performance* is an evaluation of the results of a person's behavior: It involves determining how well or poorly a person has accomplished a task or done a job.[9] *Motivation* is only one factor among many that contributes to a worker's job performance. The performance of a screen-

Although Michael Eisner, the CEO of The Walt Disney Company, has received hundreds of millions of dollars in salary and bonuses as a result of helping that company perform highly, he works as hard or even harder today to keep his company at the top. Clearly, Eisner is intrinsically motivated to help his company succeed.

writer for a television series, for example, is the extent to which viewers find his scripts to be informative, entertaining, and engaging. Similarly, a research scientist's performance is the extent to which her research advances knowledge, and a physician's performance is the extent to which the physician provides high-quality care to patients.

What is the relationship between motivation and performance? All else equal, one would expect a highly motivated screenwriter to write better scripts than a poorly motivated screenwriter. All else, however, is not always equal because so many other factors affect performance—factors such as personality and ability (see Chapter 2), the difficulty of the task, the availability of resources, working conditions, and chance or luck. A screenwriter who is highly creative, for example, may quickly turn out high-quality scripts even though his or her motivation to do so is not high. A physician in Somalia who is highly motivated to provide high-quality medical care may have a difficult time providing it because of a lack of supplies and inadequate facilities.

In summary, because motivation is only one of several factors that can affect performance, a high level of motivation does not always result in a high level of performance. Conversely, high performance does not necessarily imply that motivation is high: Workers with low motivation may perform at a high level if they have a great deal of ability. Managers have to be careful not to automatically attribute the cause of low performance to a lack of motivation or the cause of high performance to high motivation (see Chapter 4). If they incorrectly assume that low performance stems from low motivation, managers may overlook the real cause of a performance problem (such as inadequate training or a lack of resources) and fail to take appropriate actions to rectify the situation so that workers can perform at a high level. Similarly, if managers assume that workers who perform at a high level are highly motivated, they may inadvertently fail to take advantage of the talents of exceptionally capable workers: If workers perform at a high level when their motivation levels are low, they may be capable of making exceptional contributions to the organization if managers devote their efforts to boosting their motivation.

INTRINSIC AND EXTRINSIC MOTIVATION

Another distinction important to a discussion of motivation is the difference between the intrinsic and extrinsic sources of work motivation. **Intrinsically motivated work behavior** is behavior that is performed for its own sake; the source of motivation is actually performing the behavior.[10] A professional violinist who relishes playing in an orchestra regardless of the relatively low pay and a millionaire CEO who continues to put in twelve-hour days because of enjoyment of the work are intrinsically motivated by their work. Designers at Square Co., in the opening case, are intrinsically motivated; they really enjoy creating new computer games. Workers who are intrinsically motivated often remark that their work gives them a sense of accomplishment and achievement or that they feel that they are doing something worthwhile.

Extrinsically motivated work behavior is behavior that is performed to acquire material or social rewards or to avoid punishment.[11] The behavior is performed not for its own sake but rather for its consequences. The operant conditioning theory of learning discussed in Chapter 5 essentially deals with how consequences (positive and negative reinforcers

Intrinsically motivated work behavior
Behavior that is performed for its own sake.

Extrinsically motivated work behavior
Behavior that is performed to acquire material or social rewards or to avoid punishment.

and punishment) can be used to generate extrinsically motivated behavior. Examples of rewards that may be a source of extrinsic motivation include pay, praise, and status (discussed in detail in Chapter 8). Both extrinsic and intrinsic motivation can play key roles in promoting innovation in organizations. (See Insight 6.1.)

Insight 6.1 Motivation

Extrinsic and Intrinsic Motivation Contribute to Innovation

Jaron Lanier, a musician, computer programmer, and entrepreneur in his early twenties, founded VPL Research Inc. in Palo Alto, California, in 1984, to develop software for virtual reality. Virtual reality uses computers and software to create a three-dimensional environment that users can access by donning special gloves and goggles. Virtual reality gives users the sense of actually being in this environment instead of simply watching it. For example, virtual reality can be used to permit medical students to perform surgery on virtual patients, allow individuals building a home to choose different designs and fittings and then walk around the home they have chosen, and give teenagers the opportunity to fulfill their dream of being a rock star.[12]

Given the allure and many potential uses for this new technology, VPL grew rapidly. Sales rose from $600,000 in 1989 to $6 million in 1991. Lanier's technical genius was, however, not matched by his ability to run a company, and he lost control of VPL to a French company, Thomson-CSF. How did this setback affect Lanier? Although it obviously was not what he had planned for, his intrinsic motivation did not suffer, as evidenced by the following remark: "I just love doing this stuff. Someday I'll probably get rich from it, but if I don't, no big deal." After losing control of VPL, Lanier, then in his thirties, and several key VPL employees founded a new California-based software company called Domain Simulations.[13]

Intrinsic motivation can play a key role in innovation (as in the case of Jaron Lanier), and so too can extrinsic motivation. Some companies explicitly recognize the importance of extrinsic motivation and devise novel award programs to provide extrinsic rewards for desired innovative and risk-taking behaviors.

United Electric Controls Co. created its Valued Employee Program to motivate workers to contribute ideas for improvements to the company's operations. If the company implements an idea contributed by an employee, the employee receives $100 at a monthly presentation in the factory and is entered into drawings for various gifts including an annual grand prize of a seven-day Caribbean cruise. Although the program is clearly oriented toward extrinsic motivation, some workers indicate that participating in the program has made them enjoy their work more because they are on the lookout for ways to improve things.

GTE Data Services' Spirit of the Best Program is geared toward motivating workers to engage in entrepreneurial behaviors that improve either customer satisfaction or business performance. Coworkers or supervisors can nominate individual workers for the award. Winners receive $500 and a paid trip for themselves and their spouses to the prestigious four-day Personal Best conference, and their pictures and accomplishments are featured in the organization's magazine, Quest. Award-winning behaviors include helping the company to cut costs and coming up with a creative way to complete a specific project on time and under budget.[14] Although the possibility of obtaining the various rewards from the Spirit of the Best program is a source of extrinsic motivation for many GTE workers, the program also has the potential to boost intrinsic motivation if workers start enjoying their jobs more.

As those examples suggest, a worker can be extrinsically motivated, intrinsically motivated, or both. When workers are primarily extrinsically motivated and doing the work itself is not a source of motivation, it is especially important for an organization and its managers to make a clear connection between the behaviors the organization wants workers to perform and the outcomes or rewards workers' desire.

You may be wondering whether there is any connection between intrinsic and extrinsic motivation and the intrinsic and extrinsic work values

Teaching is a relatively low-paying profession, but teachers are often intrinsically motivated by interacting with students and stimulating them to explore and expand their creativity.

TO MANAGERS

Introduction to Motivation

● Keep in mind that motivation determines what behaviors workers choose to perform, how hard they work, and how persistent they are in the face of difficulties.
● Do not equate motivation with performance. Motivation is only one of several factors that contribute to determining performance.
● To better understand the source of your subordinates' work motivation, determine whether your subordinates are extrinsically or intrinsically motivated.

we described in Chapter 3. Workers who have intrinsic work values desire things such as challenging assignments, the opportunity to make important contributions to their jobs and organizations, and the opportunity to reach their full potential at work. Workers with extrinsic work values desire some of the consequences of working, such as earning money, having status in the community, social contacts, and time off from work for family and leisure. It stands to reason that workers with strong intrinsic work values are likely to want to be intrinsically motivated at work, and those with strong extrinsic work values are likely to want to be extrinsically motivated at work.

Why People Do What They Do: Theories of Work Motivation

We have explored what motivation is, where it comes from, and how it is related to the performance of behaviors in an organizational setting. But we have not considered what motivates people, why they become motivated, and how they sustain their motivation. In Insight 6.1, for example, we did not ask questions about what causes Jaron Lanier to love his work in computer programming and virtual reality so much. Nor did we discuss why and how Lanier decided to put so much time and effort into starting VPL Research Inc. and, once he lost control of this company, why and how he was motivated to start another new company. Likewise, we did not try to explain why a student might strive to make the dean's list or how the student maintains a 3.9 average across a wide variety of classes.

Theories about work motivation provide answers to such questions by explaining why workers behave as they do in organizations. The key challenge facing managers in terms of motivation is how to encourage workers to contribute inputs to their jobs and to the organization. Managers want workers to be motivated to contribute inputs (effort, specific job behaviors, skills, knowledge, time, and experience) because inputs influence job performance and, ultimately, organizational performance. Workers are concerned with obtaining outcomes from the organization—extrinsic outcomes (pay and job security) and intrinsic outcomes (a feeling of accomplishment from doing a good job or the pleasure of doing interesting work). These key concerns of managers and workers are at the heart of motivation. As indicated in Fig. 6.1, we can graphically depict these concerns in an equation: Inputs—Perfor-

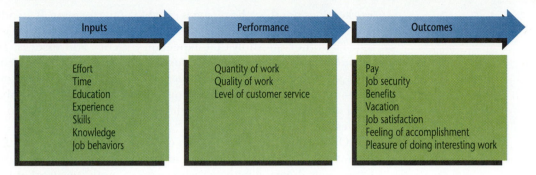

FIGURE 6.1

The Motivation Equation
Need theory, expectancy
theory, equity theory, and
procedural justice theory
address different questions
about the relationships shown
in this equation.

mance—Outcomes. Each of the four motivation theories covered in this chapter—need theory, expectancy theory, equity theory, and procedural justice theory—addresses different questions about the relationships in this equation.

The four theories that we describe in this chapter (and the motivation tools that we cover in the next two chapters) are *complementary* perspectives. Each theory addresses different questions about motivation in organizations. The various theories do not compete with each other, and you should not waste time trying to decide which is best. To get a good understanding of motivation in organizations, you need to take into account all four theories.

QUESTION ANSWERED BY NEED THEORY

Need theory focuses on the outcome side of the equation and on this question: *What outcomes is an individual motivated to obtain from a job and an organization?* The principal message of need theory is that workers have needs that they are motivated to satisfy in the workplace,[15] and that to determine which outcomes will motivate workers, a manager must determine which needs workers are trying to satisfy.

Once a manager has determined what needs a worker is trying to satisfy, the manager must make sure that she or he can control (administer or withhold) those outcomes that satisfy the worker's needs and make it clear to the worker that receiving the outcomes depends on performing desired behaviors. Then the manager must administer the outcomes to the worker contingent on the worker's performing desired organizational behaviors. In this way, the worker satisfies her or his needs while also contributing important inputs to the organization.

QUESTIONS ANSWERED BY EXPECTANCY THEORY

Expectancy theory addresses two questions about motivation. One question is, *Does the individual believe that his or her inputs (such as effort on the job) will result in a given level of performance?* Expectancy theory proposes that regardless of which outcomes are available, workers will not be motivated to contribute their inputs to the organization unless they believe that their inputs will result in achieving a given level of performance. Workers' beliefs about the relationship between their inputs (such as effort) and the performance level they reach are thus central to understanding motivation. Put simply, if a worker does not think he or she is capable of performing at an adequate level even with maximum effort, motivation to perform at that level will be zero.[16]

The other question that expectancy theory addresses is, *Does the individual believe that performance at this level will lead to obtaining desired outcomes (pay, job security, and a feeling of accomplishment)?* The second key part of expectancy theory indicates that workers will be motivated to obtain a given level of performance only if that level of performance leads to desired outcomes.[17]

Only when the answer to both of these questions is yes will the individual be motivated to contribute effort and other inputs on the job. According to expectancy theory, a manager who wants to motivate a worker to perform at a certain level first must make sure that the worker believes he or she can achieve the performance level. Then the manager must make sure that the worker believes he or she will receive, and actually does receive, desired outcomes once the performance level has been achieved.

QUESTION ANSWERED BY EQUITY THEORY

Equity theory focuses primarily on the relationship between inputs and outcomes and addresses this question: *Are outcomes perceived as being at an appropriate level in comparison to inputs?* The theory proposes that from past experience or observation of others, workers will have a sense of what level of inputs should result in a certain level of outcomes.[18]

To motivate workers to contribute inputs that the organization needs, managers need to administer outcomes to workers based on their inputs. Moreover, managers need to ensure that different workers' outcome/input *ratios* are approximately equal so that workers who contribute more inputs receive more outcomes and vice versa.

QUESTION ANSWERED BY PROCEDURAL JUSTICE THEORY

Procedural justice theory addresses this question about motivation: *Are the procedures used to assess inputs and performance and to distribute outcomes perceived as fair?* Procedural justice theory proposes that workers will not be motivated to contribute their inputs unless they perceive that fair procedures will be used to distribute outcomes in the organization. Procedures relevant to the distribution of outcomes include those used to assess the level of inputs a worker contributes to the organization, to determine the level of performance obtained, and to actually distribute outcomes.

When these procedures are not perceived as fair, motivation suffers because *all* the relationships in the motivation equation (see Fig. 6.1) are weakened: The relationship between inputs and performance is weakened when they are not assessed in a fair manner, and the relationship between performance and outcomes is weakened when the procedures to assess performance and distribute outcomes are not fair.

Figure 6.2 summarizes the questions addressed by each of the four approaches. Each approach has different implications for what managers should do to achieve a high level of motivation in their subordinates. Maintaining workforce motivation is central to an organization's success, for it determines whether individuals will contribute the inputs the organization needs to be effective.

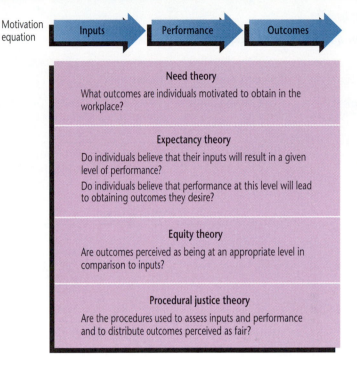

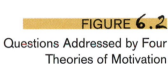

FIGURE 6.2

Questions Addressed by Four
Theories of Motivation

Need theory

A group of content theories about work
motivation that focus on workers' needs
as the sources of motivation.

Need

A requirement for survival and well-
being.

Need Theory

Although we just described need theory as if it is only one theory, **need theory** is actually a group of theories about work motivation. Collectively, these theories explain what motivates workers to behave in certain ways by focusing on workers' needs as the sources of motivation. Need theories propose that workers seek to satisfy many of their needs at work and that their behavior at work is therefore oriented toward need satisfaction.

A **need** is a requirement for survival and well-being. To determine what will motivate a worker, a manager first must determine what needs a worker is trying to satisfy on the job (needs vary from worker to worker) and then must ensure that a worker can satisfy his or her needs by engaging in behaviors that contribute to organizational effectiveness. The two theories that we discuss next, Abraham Maslow's and Clayton Alderfer's, describe several specific needs that workers try to satisfy through their work behaviors and discuss the order in which workers try to satisfy these needs. In previous chapters, we discussed two other need-based approaches to understanding behavior in organizations: David McClelland's work on the needs for achievement, affiliation, and power (see Chapter 2) and Frederick Herzberg's motivator-hygiene theory (Chapter 3).

MASLOW'S HIERARCHY OF NEEDS

Abraham Maslow, a psychologist, proposed that human beings have five universal needs that they seek to satisfy: physiological needs, safety needs, belongingness needs, esteem needs, and self-actualization needs. Descriptions of these needs and examples of how they are met in organizations are provided in Table 6.2. Maslow proposed that these needs can be arranged in a

TABLE **6.2**

Maslow's Hierarchy of Needs

	Need Level	Description	Examples of How Needs Are Met or Satisfied in an Organization
Highest-Level Needs	Self-actualization needs	The needs to realize one's full potential as a human being	By using one's skills and abilities to the fullest and striving to achieve all that one can on a job
	Esteem needs	The needs to feel good about oneself and one's capabilities, to be respected by others, and to receive recognition and appreciation	By receiving promotions at work and being recognized for accomplishments on the job
	Belongingness needs	Needs for social interaction, friendship, affection, and love	By having good relations with coworkers and supervisors, being a member of a cohesive work group, and participating in social functions such as company picnics and holiday parties
	Safety needs	Needs for security, stability, and a safe environment	By receiving job security, adequate medical benefits, and safe working conditions
Lowest-Level Needs (most basic or compelling)	Physiological needs	Basic needs for things such as food, water, and shelter that must be met in order for an individual to survive	By receiving a minimum level of pay that enables a worker to buy food and clothing and have adequate housing

hierarchy of importance, with the most basic or compelling needs—physiological and safety needs—at the bottom.[19] These basic needs must be satisfied before an individual seeks to satisfy needs higher up in the hierarchy. Maslow argued that once a need is satisfied, it is no longer a source of motivation.

There are many ways in which organizations can help workers who are at different levels in Maslow's hierarchy satisfy their needs while at the same time helping the organization achieve its goals and a competitive advantage. Some organizations, for example, help satisfy workers' esteem needs by providing special recognition for outstanding accomplishments. (See Insight 6.2.)

Insight 6.2   **Competitive Advantage**

Unocal Helps Satisfy Scientists' Esteem Needs

Managers at Los Angeles–based Unocal Corporation (www.unocal.com) realized that research scientists need to feel good about their accomplishments and to receive recognition and appreciation. One way Unocal has attempted to help satisfy these esteem needs is through the establishment of Creativity Week. Creativity Week was instituted by the Unocal Research Center, which employs scientists to create innovative ways to discover and develop energy resources and transform them into usable products such as fuel and electricity and to work on chemicals research. Creativity is very important at the research center, and Unocal scientists and management alike recognize the importance of acknowledging the scientists' accomplishments and the company's appreciation for superior innovation.

During Creativity Week, scientists whose year-long projects not only involved considerable creative effort but also benefited the company are singled out and called up onto a stage where their accomplishments are described. The researchers' colleagues applaud their achievements, and the researchers receive a cash award and plaque. A grand-prize winner is announced and receives a substantial bonus.

The Inventor's Wall of Fame provides another opportunity to recognize scientists for their accomplishments. Unocal has been very successful in obtaining patents and licenses for its inventions. Scientists who have obtained more than five patents for the company are honored during Creativity Week with plaques, statues, and other prizes. Scientists who have obtained more than ten patents receive an additional acknowledgment: Their names are added to the Inventor's Wall of Fame. As Greg Wirzbicki, Unocal's head patent attorney, indicates, "The reaction of the inventors to being recognized was very positive. . . . It really meant a lot to them. One retiree listed on the Wall of Fame came in just to see his name, despite having to make a long journey with great difficulty."[20] All in all, the various activities of Creativity Week are a relatively easy way for Unocal to help satisfy researchers' esteem needs and encourage innovation.

According to Maslow's theory, unsatisfied needs are the prime motivators of behavior, and needs at the lowest levels of the hierarchy take precedence over needs at higher levels.[21] At any particular time, however, only one set of needs motivates behavior, and it is not possible to skip levels. Once an individual satisfies one set of needs, he or she tries to satisfy needs at the next level of the hierarchy, and this level becomes the focus of motivation.

By specifying the needs that contribute to motivation, Maslow's theory helps managers determine what will motivate any given worker. A simple but important lesson from Maslow's theory is that workers differ in the needs they try to satisfy at work and that what motivates one worker may not motivate another. What does this conclusion suggest? To have a motivated workforce, managers must identify which needs each worker is seeking to satisfy at work, and once these needs have been identified, the manager's job is to ensure that the worker's needs are satisfied if he or she performs desired behaviors.

ALDERFER'S ERG THEORY

Clayton Alderfer's existence-relatedness-growth (ERG) theory is also a need theory of work motivation. Alderfer's theory builds on some of Maslow's thinking but reduces the number of universal needs from five to three and is more flexible in terms of movement between levels.[22] Like Maslow, Alderfer also proposes that needs can be arranged in a hierarchy. The three types of needs in Alderfer's theory are described in Table 6.3.

Whereas Maslow assumes that lower-level needs must be satisfied before a higher-level need is a motivator, Alderfer lifts this restriction. According to ERG theory, a higher-level need can be a motivator even if a lower-level need is not fully satisfied, and needs at more than one level can be motivators at any time. Alderfer agrees with Maslow that as lower-level needs are satisfied, a worker becomes motivated to satisfy higher-level needs. But Alderfer breaks with Maslow on the consequences of need frustration. Maslow says that once a lower-level need is satisfied, it is no longer a source of motivation. Alderfer proposes that when an individual is motivated to satisfy a higher-level need but has difficulty doing so, the person's motivation to satisfy lower-level needs will increase.

To see how this process works, let's look at the case of a middle manager in a manufacturing firm whose existence and relatedness needs (lower-level needs) are pretty much satisfied. Currently, the manager is motivated to try to satisfy her growth needs but finds this hard to do because she has been in the same position for the past five years. She is very skilled and knowledgeable about all aspects of the job, and the wide variety and number of her current responsibilities leave her no time to pursue anything new or exciting. Essentially, the manager's motivation to satisfy her growth needs is being frustrated because of the nature of her job. According to Alderfer, this frustration will increase the manager's motivation to satisfy a lower-level need such as relatedness. As a result of this motivation, the manager becomes more concerned about interpersonal relations at work and continually seeks honest feedback from her colleagues.

THE RESEARCH EVIDENCE

Because Maslow's and Alderfer's theories were among some of the earliest approaches to work motivation, they have received a considerable amount of attention from researchers. Although they seem logical and intuitively appealing and many managers like them, by and large these theories have tended *not* to

TABLE 6.3

Alderfer's ERG Theory

	Need Level	Description	Examples of How Needs Are Met or Satisfied in an Organization
Highest-Level Needs	Growth needs	The needs for self-development and creative and productive work	By continually improving skills and abilities and engaging in meaningful work
	Relatedness needs	The needs to have good interpersonal relations, to share thoughts and feelings, and to have open two-way communication	By having good relations with coworkers, superiors, and subordinates and by obtaining accurate feedback from others
Lowest-Level Needs	Existence needs	Basic needs for human survival such as the need for food, water, clothing, shelter, and a secure and safe environment	By receiving enough pay to provide for the basic necessities of life and by having safe working conditions

TO MANAGERS

receive support from research.[23] There appear to be at least two major difficulties with the theories. First, it may be unreasonable to expect a relatively small set of needs ordered in a particular fashion to apply to all human beings. Second, it may be unrealistic to expect that all people become motivated by different types of needs in a set order (that is, that the satisfaction of higher needs is sought *only* when lower-level needs have been satisfied).

Studies of U.S. workers generally do not support the main tenets of Maslow's and Alderfer's theories, and it is likely that international studies conducted in other cultures would yield even less support. Even though the conclusions of the theories have not been supported, however, managers can still learn some important lessons about motivation from the work of Maslow and Alderfer. Some of these lessons are summarized in our Advice to Managers.

Expectancy Theory

Expectancy theory
A process theory about work motivation that focuses on how workers make choices among alternative behaviors and levels of effort.

Need theories try to explain *what* motivates workers. Expectancy theory focuses on *how* workers decide which specific behaviors to perform and *how much* effort to exert. In other words, **expectancy theory** is concerned with how workers make choices among alternative behaviors and levels of effort.[24] With its emphasis on choices, expectancy theory focuses on workers' perceptions (see Chapter 4) and thoughts or cognitive processes (Chapter 5).

To understand the overall focus of expectancy theory, consider the *direction of behavior* of an experienced nurse who has just taken a job at a new hospital. Which behaviors could she choose to perform? Does she spend time casually chatting with patients, or does she limit her interactions to those directly pertaining to medical care? Does she discuss her patients' symptoms and complaints with their physicians in detail, or must doctors rely on her written records? Does she readily help other nurses when they seem to have a heavy load, or does she provide assistance only when asked?

Once the nurse chooses what she will do, she also needs to decide how much *effort* to exert on the job. Should she push herself to do as much as she can even if doing so means foregoing some of her authorized breaks? Should she do just enough to adequately perform her job requirements? Should she minimize her efforts by taking longer breaks, referring her most difficult patients to her supervisor, and avoiding conversations with patients and physicians?

Also, with what level of *persistence* should she report her fears that a junior doctor has made a misdiagnosis? Should she mention it to some of her more senior coworkers? Should she tell her supervisor? If her supervisor does nothing about it, should she raise the issue with the head nurse in charge of her unit? If the head nurse is unconcerned, should she discuss her fears with a more senior doctor?

Expectancy theory seeks to explain how workers go about making these various decisions. Because these choices determine what workers do on the job and how hard they work, they have profound effects on organizational effectiveness. By describing how workers make these choices, expectancy theory provides managers with valuable insights on how to get workers to perform organizationally functional behaviors and how to encourage workers to exert high levels of effort when performing these behaviors.

Because of its profound organizational implications, expectancy theory is among the most popular theories of work motivation. The theory, which was originally developed by Victor Vroom in the 1960s, assumes that workers are essentially pleasure seeking[25]—that is, they are motivated to receive positive outcomes (such as a weekly paycheck, a bonus, or an award) and to avoid negative outcomes (such as getting reprimanded, fired, or demoted). It also assumes that workers are rational, careful processors of information and use information about their jobs, abilities, and desires to decide what they will do on the job and how hard they will do it.

Expectancy theory identifies three major factors that determine a worker's motivation: valence, instrumentality, and expectancy.[26]

VALENCE: HOW DESIRABLE IS AN OUTCOME?

Workers can obtain a variety of outcomes from their jobs—pay, job security, benefits, feelings of accomplishment, the opportunity to do interesting work, good relationships with coworkers, promotions. For any individual, the desirability of each outcome is likely to vary. The term **valence** refers to the desirability of an outcome to an individual worker. Valence can be positive or negative and can vary in size or magnitude. If an outcome has *positive valence,* a worker prefers having the outcome to not having it. If an outcome has *negative valence,* a worker prefers not having the outcome. For most workers, getting a raise is likely to have positive valence, and being fired is likely to have negative valence. The magnitude of valence is how desirable or undesirable an outcome is for a worker.[27] Maslow's and Alderfer's need theories suggest that workers will find outcomes that satisfy their needs to be especially attractive or valent. In the opening case, some highly valent outcomes for the designers in Square Co. include the opportunity to do interesting and creative work, a pleasant work environment, two months off when a game is completed, and pay.

Some motivation problems occur because highly valent outcomes are unavailable to workers. To determine what outcomes might motivate a worker, managers must determine what outcomes a worker desires, or the valence of different outcomes for the worker.

INSTRUMENTALITY: WHAT IS THE CONNECTION BETWEEN JOB PERFORMANCE AND AN OUTCOME?

In our discussion of learning and operant conditioning in Chapter 5, we emphasized how important it is for outcomes (or *consequences* as they are called in operant conditioning) to be given to workers on the basis of their performance of desired behaviors. Like operant conditioning, expectancy theory

Valence
In expectancy theory, the desirability of an outcome to an individual.

Instrumentality

In expectancy theory, a perception about the extent to which performance of one or more behaviors will lead to the attainment of a particular outcome.

proposes that outcomes should be directly linked to desired organizational behaviors or to overall levels of job performance.

Instrumentality, the second key determinant of motivation according to expectancy theory, is a worker's perception about the extent to which performing certain behaviors or performing at a certain level will lead to the attainment of a particular outcome. In organizations, workers are going to engage in desired behaviors and be motivated to perform them at a high level only if they perceive that high performance and desired behaviors will lead to positively valent outcomes such as a pay raise, a promotion, or sometimes even just a pat on the back.

Just like valence, instrumentality can be positive or negative and varies in size or magnitude. Instrumentality, the *perceived* association between a certain level of job performance (or the performance of certain behaviors) and the receipt of a specific outcome, can be measured on a scale from –1 to +1. An instrumentality of –1 means that a worker perceives that performance (of a certain behavior or at a certain level) definitely *will not result* in obtaining the outcome. An instrumentality of +1 means that a worker perceives that performance *definitely will result* in obtaining the outcome.

An advertising executive, for example, perceives that if she obtains three new major corporate accounts this year (and holds on to all of her existing accounts), her performance definitely *will result* in her receiving a hefty year-end bonus (an instrumentality of +1) and definitely *will not result* in her being asked to relocate to one of the agency's less prestigious locations (an instrumentality of –1). The magnitude of instrumentalities between the extremes of –1 and +1 indicates the extent of the perceived association or relationship between performance and outcome. An instrumentality of zero means that a worker perceives *no* relationship between performance and outcome. Let's continue with the example of the advertising executive. She perceives that there is some possibility that if she performs at a high level she will be given a promotion (an instrumentality of 0.3) and a larger possibility that she will obtain a bigger office (an instrumentality of 0.5). She perceives that her medical and dental benefits will be unaffected by her level of performance (an instrumentality of zero).

In trying to decide which behaviors to engage in and how hard to work (the level of job performance to strive for), the advertising executive considers the *valences* of the outcomes that she perceives will result from different levels of performance (how attractive the outcomes are to her) and the *instrumentality* of performance at a certain level for attaining each outcome (how certain it is that performance at that level will result in obtaining the outcome). In this way, both instrumentality and valence influence motivation.

Instrumentalities that are in fact high and that workers believe are high are effective motivators. Managers need to make sure that workers who perform at a high level do in fact receive the outcomes that they desire—outcomes with high positive valence. In the opening case, Square Co. maintains high instrumentalities by giving designers two months off when they successfully complete a game and partially linking their pay to the sales of the games they create. Managers also need to clearly communicate instrumentalities to workers by letting them know what outcomes will result from various levels of performance.

Sometimes workers are not motivated to perform at a high level because they do not perceive that high performance will lead to highly valent outcomes (such as pay raises, time off, and promotions). When workers think that good performance goes unrecognized, their motivation to perform at a high level tends to be low.

When workers do not believe that performance is instrumental to obtaining valent outcomes, management can take steps to rectify the situation and ensure that performance leads to highly valent outcomes for as many workers as possible. (See Insight 6.3.)

Insight 6.3

Motivation

Increasing Instrumentality at Diamond International

Labor relations were at an all-time low at Diamond International Corporation's cardboard egg carton production plant in Palmer, Massachusetts. Low motivation, low productivity, a series of layoffs, and other problems plagued the plant. Concerned about the situation, management decided to conduct an informal survey of plant workers. One survey question asked whether the workers thought they were rewarded for doing a good job. Approximately 79 percent of those surveyed indicated that they thought they were not.[28] This answer told management that workers were *not* motivated to perform at a high level because performance was *not* seen as leading to desired outcomes. The instrumentality of job performance for obtaining positively valent outcomes or rewards was close to zero for a majority of the surveyed workers.

Management established the 100 Club to correct this situation by rewarding good performance. The 100 Club provides workers with positively valent outcomes for performing their jobs and other required behaviors at an acceptable and predetermined level. Workers who meet their productivity goals, are punctual, and have satisfactory safety records receive a certain number of points. Once they obtain 100 points, they become members of the 100 Club and receive a jacket on which the company and club logos are embossed. As club members accumulate more points, they earn more gifts. Accumulating points, joining the 100 Club, receiving a jacket, and accumulating additional points to earn more gifts are positively valent outcomes for many workers at the plant. Workers perceive that performing their jobs at an acceptable level is instrumental for obtaining these outcomes, and thus they are motivated to do so.

The results of introducing the 100 Club were spectacular. During its first year, the club helped to boost productivity 14.2 percent and reduce quality-related errors 40 percent. Diamond International was so impressed with the results of the club that it instituted 100 Clubs in several of its other plants.[29] All in all, it appears that the 100 Club was successful in boosting motivation by increasing the instrumentality of job performance for obtaining desired outcomes.

EXPECTANCY: WHAT IS THE CONNECTION BETWEEN EFFORT AND JOB PERFORMANCE?

Even though a worker perceives that a pay raise (a highly valent outcome) will result directly from high performance (instrumentality is high), the worker still may not be motivated to perform at a high level. To understand why motivation is low even when instrumentalities and valences are high, we need to consider the third major factor in expectancy theory: expectancy.

Expectancy is a worker's perception about the extent to which his or her effort will result in a certain level of job performance. Expectancy varies from 0 to 1 and reflects the chances that putting forth a certain amount of effort will result in a certain level of performance. An expectancy of 0 means that a worker believes there is no chance that his or her effort will result in a certain level of performance. An expectancy of 1 signifies that a worker is absolutely certain that his or her effort will lead to a certain level of performance. Expectancies between 0 and 1 reflect the extent to which a person perceives that his or her effort will result in a certain level of performance.

Workers are going to be motivated to perform desired behaviors at a high level only if they think they can do so. If they think they actually *will perform* at a high level when they work hard, their expectancy is high. No matter how much the advertising executive in our earlier example wants the pay raise and promotion that she thinks will result from high performance, if she thinks she cannot possibly perform at the necessary level, she will not be motivated to perform at that level. Similarly, no matter how much a student wants to pass a course, if she thinks she will flunk no matter how hard she studies, she will not be motivated to study. Expectancy is similar to the concept of self-efficacy, discussed in Chapter 5, which captures the idea that workers are not always certain that their efforts will be successful or result in a given level of performance.

If motivation levels are low because workers do not think their efforts will pay off in improved performance, managers need to let workers know that they can perform at a high level if they try hard. In addition, organizations can boost worker's expectancies by helping them improve their skills and abilities. Organizations often use training to boost expectancy. The Andersen companies, Arthur Andersen & Co. and Andersen Consulting, are great believers in training. (See Insight 6.4.)

Expectancy

In expectancy theory, a perception about the extent to which effort will result in a certain level of performance.

Insight 6.4

Motivation

Boosting Expectancy at Arthur Andersen

In 1989 Arthur Andersen split its operations into two operating units. Arthur Andersen & Co. (www.arthurandersen.com) provides corporate clients with business, audit, and tax services. Andersen Consulting helps corporate clients use information-based (computer) technologies. Because these units sell their employees' skills, abilities, and talents to corporations in need of some form of assistance, the units spend approximately 5.5 percent of their revenues on training (over $300 million per year).[30]

Most new employees at the Andersen companies receive three weeks of professional training prior to starting their jobs. After that, they receive, on average, 138 hours of training per year. Some of the training takes place at the St. Charles Center for Professional Education, a school owned and operated by Andersen and located on a 150-acre campus outside Chicago. At the St. Charles Center, new recruits and experienced professionals attend classes on topics ranging from elementary auditing to the latest developments in technology.[31]

To assess the success of the training programs, Andersen evaluates its training on several dimensions (such as participant reactions, knowledge acquired, and job performance) and is always on the lookout for ways to improve its training programs.[32] Andersen's commitment to training helps ensure that Andersen professionals have the necessary skills to serve clients effectively and helps the professionals believe that they can perform at a high level if they exert a high level of effort. In other words, training boosts employees' expectancies that they can do a good job.

THE COMBINED EFFECTS OF VALENCE, INSTRUMENTALITY, AND EXPECTANCY ON MOTIVATION

In order for a worker to be motivated to perform desired behaviors and to perform them at a high level, the following conditions are necessary (see Fig. 6.3):

- *Valence* must be high: The worker desires outcomes the organization has to offer.
- *Instrumentality* must be high: The worker perceives that she or he must perform desired behaviors at a high level to obtain these outcomes.
- *Expectancy* must be high: The worker thinks that trying hard will lead to performance at a high level.

If just one of these three factors—valence, instrumentality, or expectancy—is zero, motivation will be zero. Our advertising executive must perceive that

FIGURE 6.3

Expectancy Theory

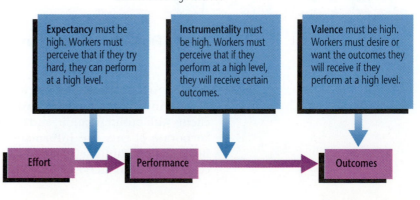

(1) she is likely to receive desired (positively valent) outcomes if she performs at a high level and (2) she can perform at a high level if she tries (she has high expectancy).

High performance in an organization depends on what a worker does and how hard he or she does it. According to expectancy theory, in trying to decide what to do and how hard to do it, workers ask themselves questions such as these:

- Will I be able to obtain outcomes I desire? (In expectancy theory terms: Is the valence of outcomes that the organization provides high?)
- Do I need to perform at a high level to obtain these outcomes? (In expectancy theory terms: Is high performance instrumental for obtaining these outcomes?)
- If I try hard, will I be able to perform at a high level? (In expectancy theory terms: Is expectancy high?)

Only when workers answer yes to each of these three questions are they motivated to perform at a high level and to try hard to perform desired behaviors as best they can. Expectancy theory suggests not only that rewards should be based on performance and that workers should have the abilities necessary to perform at a high level, but also that managers must make sure that workers accurately perceive this to be the case.

Expectancy theory is a popular theory of motivation and has received extensive attention from researchers. Some studies support the theory and others do not,[33] but by and large the theory has been supported.[34]

TO MANAGERS

Expectancy Theory

- Determine what outcomes your subordinates desire. More specifically, identify outcomes that have high positive valence for your subordinates in order to motivate them to perform at a high level. Clearly communicate to subordinates what behaviors or performance levels must be obtained for them to receive the valent outcomes.
- Once you have identified desired outcomes, make sure that you have control over them and can give them to subordinates or take them away when warranted.
- Let subordinates know that obtaining their desired outcomes depends on their performing at a high level (raise instrumentalities). Administer the highly valent outcomes only when subordinates perform at a high level (or engage in desired organizational behaviors).
- Do whatever you can to encourage workers to have high expectancies: Express confidence in subordinates' abilities, let them know that others like themselves have been able to perform at a high level, and give them guidance in terms of how to perform at a high level (for example, by being better organized, setting priorities, or managing time better).
- Periodically assess workers' beliefs concerning expectancies and instrumentalities and their valences for different outcomes by directly asking them or administering a survey. Using these assessments, make different outcomes available to workers, clarify instrumentalities, or boost expectancies when necessary.

Equity Theory

The equity theory of work motivation was developed in the 1960s by J. Stacy Adams (*equity* means "fairness"). Equity theory is based on the premise that a worker perceives the relationship between *outcomes,* what the worker gets from a job and organization, and *inputs,* what the worker contributes to a job and organization.[35] Outcomes include pay, fringe benefits, job satisfaction, status, opportunities for advancement, job security, and anything else that workers desire and receive from an organization. Inputs include special skills, training, education, work experience, effort on the job, time, and anything else that workers perceive that they contribute to an organization. According to **equity theory,** however, it is *not* the objective level of outcomes and inputs that is important in determining work motivation. What is important to motivation is the way a worker perceives his or her outcome/input ratio compared to the **outcome/input ratio** of another person.[36]

This other person, called a *referent* by Adams, is simply another worker or group of workers perceived to be similar to oneself. The referent could also be oneself at a different place or time (for example, in a previous job), or it could be one's expectations (for example, one's beliefs about what the outputs and inputs of an entry-level accountant's job should be). Regardless of the referent a worker chooses, it is the *worker's perceptions* of the referent's outcomes and inputs that are compared, not any objective measure of actual outcomes or inputs.

EQUITY

Equity exists when an individual's outcome/input ratio equals the outcome/input ratio of the referent (see Table 6.4). Because the comparison of the ratios is what determines the presence or absence of equity (not the comparison of absolute levels of outcomes and inputs), equity can exist even if the referent receives more than the individual who is making the comparison.

Consider the case of two financial analysts who have been working at the same corporation for two years. At the end of the two years, analyst A gets promoted, but analyst B does not. Can both analysts consider this situation to be equitable? The answer is yes: Equity exists if analyst A and analyst B perceive

Equity theory
A process theory about work motivation that focuses on workers' perceptions of the fairness of their work outcomes and inputs.

Outcome/input ratio
In equity theory, the relationship between what a worker gets from a job (outcomes) and what the worker contributes to the job (inputs).

TABLE **6.4**

Conditions of Equity and Inequity

	Individual	Referent	Example
Equity	$\dfrac{\text{Outcomes}}{\text{Inputs}}$ =	$\dfrac{\text{Outcomes}}{\text{Inputs}}$	A financial analyst contributes more inputs (time and effort) to her job and receives proportionally more outcomes (a promotion and a pay raise) than her referent receives.
Overpayment inequity	$\dfrac{\text{Outcomes}}{\text{Inputs}}$ >	$\dfrac{\text{Outcomes}}{\text{Inputs}}$ (greater than)	A financial analyst contributes the same level of inputs to her job as her referent but receives more outcomes than the referent receives.
Underpayment inequity	$\dfrac{\text{Outcomes}}{\text{Inputs}}$ <	$\dfrac{\text{Outcomes}}{\text{Inputs}}$ (less than)	A financial analyst contributes more inputs to her job than her referent but receives the same outcomes as her referent.

that their respective outcome/input ratios are equal or proportional. If both analysts perceive that analyst A generally worked more hours than analyst B, for example, that added input (overtime) will account for analyst A's additional outcome (the promotion).

When workers perceive that the worker's and the referent's outcome/input ratios are proportionally equal, they are motivated either to maintain the status quo or to increase their inputs to receive more outcomes.

INEQUITY

Inequity, or lack of fairness, exists when outcome/input ratios are not proportionally equal. Inequity creates tension and unpleasant feelings inside a worker and a desire to restore equity. Inequity motivates the individual to try to restore equity by bringing the two ratios back into balance.

There are two basic types of inequity: overpayment inequity and underpayment inequity (see Table 6.4). **Overpayment inequity** exists when an individual perceives that his or her outcome/input ratio is greater than that of a referent. **Underpayment inequity** exists when a person perceives that his or her outcome/input ratio is less than that of a referent.

Consider the case of Steve and Mike, who are janitors in a large office building. Steve is a conscientious worker who always gets to work on time and keeps his areas of the building spotless. Mike is often late, takes long lunch hours, and often "forgets" to clean some of his areas. Steve and Mike receive the same level of pay, benefits, and other outcomes from their employer. According to equity theory, if both workers have accurate perceptions and choose each other as a referent, Mike should perceive *overpayment inequity,* this perception creates tension within Mike (perhaps it makes him feel guilty), and Mike is motivated to restore equity or make the ratios equal. Steve, in contrast, perceives *underpayment inequity.* Because Steve is contributing more than Mike yet receiving the same level of outcomes, he too experiences tension (anger) and is motivated to restore equity.

WAYS TO RESTORE EQUITY

There are several ways by which equity can be restored in situations such as the one involving Steve and Mike.[37]

1. *Workers can change their inputs or outcomes.* When workers perceive underpayment inequity, for example, they can restore equity by reducing inputs such as effort. In the case of the two janitors, Steve could restore equity by cutting back on his inputs—by coming to work late, taking longer breaks, and working less conscientiously. An underpaid worker could also try to change his or her outcomes by asking for a raise.

2. *Workers try to change their referents' inputs or outcomes.* Steve might complain to his supervisor about Mike's coming to work late and not doing a very good job, in the hope that the supervisor will alter Mike's inputs (perhaps by getting him to show up on time or do a better job) or Mike's outcomes (cutting his pay or threatening his job security). Or Mike might encourage Steve to relax and not be such a grind.

3. *Workers change their perceptions of inputs and outcomes (either their own or the referents').* Mike could restore equity by changing his perceptions about his inputs. He could start to think that his area is larger or harder to clean than Steve's or that he works faster, so his and Steve's ratios are really proportional after all. As this example illustrates, workers who

Overpayment inequity
The inequity that exists when a person perceives that his or her outcome/input ratio is greater than the ratio of a referent.

Underpayment inequity
The inequity that exists when a person perceives that his or her outcome/input ratio is less than the ratio of a referent.

perceive overpayment inequity are especially likely to change their perceptions (rather than their actual inputs or outcomes) to restore equity. This is why overpaid workers often do not feel guilty for very long.

4. *Workers can change the referent.*[38] A worker may decide that the original referent does not allow for an appropriate comparison and thus select another one. Steve might recall hearing that Mike is a relative of one of the managers in the company and conclude that he is not the most suitable basis for comparison. Conversely, Mike might decide that Steve is clearly an extraordinary, almost superhuman janitor and select someone else to compare himself to.

5. *Workers leave the job or organization or force the referent to leave.* The most common example of this approach is employee turnover, and, not surprisingly, leaving the organization is most prevalent in situations of underpayment inequity. Thus Steve might be motivated to look for a job elsewhere.

Sometimes when workers experience underpayment inequity, they go one step further to restore equity. As indicated in Insight 6.5, some workers in Japan are restoring equity by not only leaving their organization but also leaving their country, and some workers in the United States are appealing to the legal system to help them restore equity and increase their outcomes.

Insight 6.5 A Global View

Restoring Equity in Japan and the United States

Professional women in Japan often face underpayment inequity. Although they may have the same qualifications as Japanese men, they often find it hard to obtain the professional jobs they are trained for. Even if they do find a suitable position, they often do not receive the respect, status, and pay to go along with it and are not likely to receive important and challenging job assignments. Recently, college students who are already facing these problems in their job-search efforts took to the Tokyo streets to demand equitable treatment for women in the Japanese workforce and voiced their concerns to Japanese labor minister Manso Hamamoto.[39]

Some professional Japanese women already in the workforce are seeking to restore equity not only by leaving their organizations but by leaving Japan altogether. Tired of not getting the respect, status, job assignments, promotions, and pay they deserve, increasing numbers of Japanese women are moving to Hong Kong. There, in professional positions in large banks and insurance companies, they are treated much more equitably.

In the United States, some workers are taking a different approach to restoring equity by seeking help from the legal system. For example, sex, age, and race discrimination charges have been recently made against the large investment banking firm Kidder Peabody & Co.[40] Employees have complained that the firm has underpaid them, denied them promotions, and in some cases fired them even though their contributions or inputs to the firm have been comparable to those of other workers who did not receive these negative outcomes.

These employees, seeking to restore equity, have brought their complaints to the U.S. Equal Employment Opportunity Commission (EEOC), which has the power to bring discrimination cases to federal court. Women who used to work at Kidder Peabody complain that they were excluded from consideration for high-level positions, paid less than men doing similar jobs, and verbally harassed. Elizabeth Sobol, who used to be a managing director at Kidder Peabody, indicated that it was the norm rather than the exception for women to be underpaid relative to men. African American employees and those over the age of 40 also have complained of unfair treatment.[41]

In some cases, the workers who felt they were unfairly treated have brought their complaints not only to the EEOC but also to the New York Stock Exchange. Cathy Cumberpatch was a vice president when she was dismissed from the firm in 1990. She complained to the New York Stock Exchange that when she worked at Kidder Peabody, she was underpaid relative to male colleagues who had inputs similar to hers. In an arbitration proceeding, the New York Stock Exchange ruled that Kidder Peabody had to pay Cumberpatch $94,000 in damages plus cover her legal expenses. Although this amount was less than the $1 million she had originally sought, it helped to restore some equity for Cumberpatch.

Kidder Peabody disputes some of the allegations made against it but is nevertheless trying to rectify matters by paying more attention to the equitable treatment and the hiring and promoting of women and minorities.[42]

THE EFFECTS OF INEQUITY AND THE RESEARCH EVIDENCE

Both underpayment inequity and overpayment inequity are dysfunctional for organizations, managers, and workers. In the case of overpayment, although workers are sometimes motivated to increase their inputs to restore equity (an effort that is functional for the organization), they are more likely to be motivated to change their perceptions of inputs or outcomes (an effort that is dysfunctional because there is no *actual* increase in the level of inputs contributed by the overpaid workers). In the case of underpayment, capable and deserving workers may be motivated to reduce their inputs or even leave the organization, both of which are dysfunctional for the organization.

All in all, motivation is highest when equity exists and outcomes are distributed to workers on the basis of their inputs to the organization. Workers who contribute a high level of inputs and receive in turn a high level of outcomes are motivated to continue to contribute inputs (that is, to perform at a high level). Workers who contribute a low level of inputs and receive a low level of outcomes know that if they want to increase their outcomes, they must increase their inputs.

TO MANAGERS

Like expectancy theory, equity theory is a popular theory of motivation and has received extensive research attention. Also, as in the case of expectancy theory, although there have been some nonsupportive results, by and large the research evidence supports the main ideas of equity theory.[43]

Procedural Justice Theory

Because equity theory focuses on the fair distribution of outcomes across workers to encourage high levels of motivation, it is often called a theory of *distributive* justice. Another dimension of fairness in organizations, *procedural* justice, is also important for understanding worker motivation. **Procedural justice theory,** a relatively new approach to motivation, is concerned with the perceived fairness of the procedures used to make decisions about the distribution of outcomes (it is *not* concerned about the actual distribution of outcomes).[44] Procedural decisions pertain to how performance levels are evaluated, how grievances or disputes are handled (if, for example, a worker disagrees with a manager's evaluation of his or her performance), and how outcomes (such as raises) are distributed across workers. In procedural justice theory, as in equity theory, workers' *perceptions* are key; workers' reactions to procedures depend on how they *perceive* the procedures rather than on what the procedures actually are.

Procedural justice theory holds that workers are going to be more motivated to perform at a high level when they perceive the procedures used to make decisions about the distribution of outcomes as fair. Workers will be more motivated, for example, if they think that their performance will be accurately assessed. Conversely, if workers think that their performance will not be accurately assessed because the supervisor is not aware of their con-

> **Procedural justice theory**
> A process theory about work motivation that focuses on workers' perceptions of the fairness of the procedures used to make decisions about the distribution of outcomes.

tributions to the organization or because the supervisor lets personal feelings affect performance appraisals, they will not be as strongly motivated to perform at a high level. Procedural justice theory seeks to explain what causes workers to perceive procedures as fair or unfair and the consequences of these perceptions.

CAUSES OF PROCEDURAL JUSTICE

According to procedural justice theory, two factors are important in determining workers' perceptions of the fairness of procedures.[45] One factor is the interpersonal treatment of workers—that is, how workers are treated by distributors of outcomes (usually their managers). It is important for managers to be honest and courteous, to respect the rights and opinions of workers, and to provide workers with timely feedback about how they are doing.[46] It is also important for managers to allow workers to contribute their own viewpoints, opinions, and perspectives to the decision-making process.[47]

The other factor that determines perceptions of procedural justice is the extent to which managers explain their decisions to workers.[48] For example, managers can explain to workers (1) how they assess inputs (including time, effort, education, and previous work experience), (2) how they appraise performance, and (3) how they decide how to distribute outcomes (such as promotions) across workers. (Performance appraisal and the distribution of outcomes in organizations are discussed in detail in Chapter 8.)

By treating workers with respect and courtesy, providing feedback, considering workers' viewpoints, and carefully explaining the manner in which decisions are made, managers can help ensure that perceptions of procedural justice are high. In addition, procedural justice is more likely to be high when members of an organization make decisions and behave in an ethical manner. Organizations can take active steps to promote ethical decision making and motivate people to behave ethically. (See Insight 6.6.)

Insight 6.6   **Ethics**

Promoting Ethical Conduct at Texas A&M

At its September 1994 meeting, the board of regents for the Texas A&M University System (TAMUS) focused on promoting ethical decision making and behavior by all of its thousands of employees. A major focus of the board's efforts was the development of principles of ethical conduct to guide employees' decision making and behavior. These principles, which were quickly communicated to employees in the November–December 1994 TAMUS newsletter, state the following:

System employees should:

1. Not hold financial interests that are in conflict with the conscientious performance of their official duties and responsibilities.

2. Not engage in any financial transaction in order to further any private interest using nonpublic information which they obtain in the course of their employment.

3. Put forth honest effort in the performance of their duties.

4. Make no unauthorized commitments or promises of any kind purporting to bind TAMUS or any of its components.

5. Not use their public offices for private gain.

6. Act impartially and not give preferential treatment to any private or public organization or individual.

7. Protect and conserve public property and not use it for other than authorized activities.

8. Not engage in outside employment or activities, including seeking or negotiating for employment, that conflict with official duties and responsibilities.

9. Promptly disclose waste, fraud, abuse, and corruption to the appropriate authorities.

10. Adhere to all laws, regulations, and policies that provide equal opportunity for all persons regardless of race, color, religion, sex, national origin, age, or disability.

11. Endeavor to avoid any actions that would create the appearance that they are violating the law or the ethical standards of TAMUS.[49]

CONSEQUENCES OF PROCEDURAL JUSTICE

Researchers have just begun to explore the specific consequences of procedural justice for work motivation. However, one can get a good handle on some of the possible consequences by considering the implications of procedural justice for the expectancy and equity theories of motivation.

Recall that expectancy theory asserts that individuals are motivated to work hard when they believe that (1) their effort will result in their achieving a satisfactory level of performance (expectancy is high) and (2) their performance will lead to desired outcomes such as pay or a promotion (instrumentality and valence of outcomes are high). Suppose, however, that an organization has a problem with procedural justice and its workers do *not* perceive that the procedures used to distribute outcomes are fair. More specifically, suppose workers believe that the performance appraisal system is inaccurate and biased, so that performing at a high level does *not* ensure a good performance appraisal and performing poorly has been known to result in an average performance rating. In this organization, workers may believe that they are capable of performing at a high level (their expectancy is high), but they cannot be sure that they will receive a high performance rating because the appraisal system is unfair (procedural justice is low). Workers will *not* be motivated to exert a lot of effort on the job if they think their performance will *not* be accurately and fairly assessed and they will *not* receive the outcomes they think they deserve.

From the perspective of equity theory, motivation will also suffer when perceptions of procedural justice are low. Workers may believe that their inputs to the organization are not going to be fairly assessed or that outcomes will not be distributed based on relative inputs. Under these circumstances, workers will not be motivated to contribute inputs, for there is no guarantee that their inputs will result in the outcomes they think they deserve.

It appears that perceptions of procedural justice may be especially important when outcomes like pay and benefits are relatively low—that is, when there are few rewards to give to workers. Some preliminary research suggests that individuals who obtain a medium or high level of outcomes view their outcomes as fair *regardless* of the fairness of the procedures that were used to distribute them but view a low level of outcomes as fair only when they were obtained as a result of fair procedures![50] In sum, although a lot of work still needs to be done in the area of procedural justice, it nevertheless appears to be an important factor to consider in understanding motivation in organizations.

SUMMARY

Work motivation explains why workers behave as they do. Four prominent theories about work motivation—need theory, expectancy theory, equity theory, and procedural justice theory—provide complementary approaches to understanding and managing motivation in organizations. Each theory answers different questions about the motivational process. In this chapter, we made the following major points:

1. Work motivation is the psychological forces within a person that determine the direction of the person's behavior in an organization, the person's level of effort, and the person's level of persistence in the face of obstacles. Motivation is distinct from performance; other factors besides motivation (for example, ability and task difficulty) influence performance.
2. Intrinsically motivated behavior is behavior performed for its own sake. Extrinsically motivated behavior is behavior performed to acquire material or social rewards or to avoid punishment.
3. Need theory, expectancy theory, equity theory, and procedural justice theory are complementary approaches to understanding motivation. Each answers different questions about the nature and management of motivation in organizations.
4. Need theories of motivation identify the needs that workers are motivated to satisfy on the job. Two major need theories of motivation are Maslow's hierarchy of needs and Alderfer's existence-relatedness-growth theory.
5. Expectancy theory focuses on how workers decide what behaviors to engage in on the job and how much effort to exert. The three major concepts in expectancy theory are valence (how desirable an outcome is to a worker), instrumentality (a worker's perception about the extent to which a certain level of performance will lead to the attainment of a particular outcome), and expectancy (a worker's perception about the extent to which effort will result in a certain level of performance). Valence, instrumentality, and expectancy combine to determine motivation.
6. Equity theory proposes that workers compare their own outcome/input ratio (the ratio of the outcomes they receive from their jobs and from the organization to the inputs they contribute) to the outcome/input ratio of a referent. Unequal ratios create tension inside the worker, and the worker is motivated to restore equity. When the ratios are equal, workers are motivated to maintain their current ratio of outcomes and inputs or raise their inputs if they want their outcomes to increase.
7. Procedural justice theory is concerned with the perceived fairness of the procedures used to make decisions about inputs, performance, and the distribution of outcomes. How managers treat their subordinates and the extent to which they provide explanations for their decisions influence workers' perceptions of procedural justice. When procedural justice is perceived to be low, motivation suffers because workers are not sure that their inputs and performance levels will be accurately assessed or that outcomes will be distributed in a fair manner.

Organizational Behavior in Action

TOPICS FOR DISCUSSION AND ACTION

1. Why might a person with a very high level of motivation perform poorly?
2. Why might a person with a very low level of motivation be a top performer?
3. Why do people differ in the types of needs they are trying to satisfy at work?
4. Why might workers differ in their valences for the same outcomes?
5. Why might perceptions of instrumentality be relatively low in an organization?
6. Why might a very capable worker have low expectancy for performing at a high level?
7. How does the choice of a referent influence perceptions of equity and inequity?
8. Is inequity always dysfunctional for an organization? Why or why not?
9. Why might fair procedures be perceived as being unfair by some workers?
10. What steps can organizations take to encourage procedural justice?

BUILDING DIAGNOSTIC SKILLS

Peak Motivation Experiences

Think about the last time you felt really motivated to do well at some activity: in one of your classes, at work, in some kind of hobby or leisure activity (such as playing golf, running, or singing).

1. Describe the activity, and indicate how you felt while engaged in it.
2. Was your motivation extrinsic, intrinsic, or both?
3. What needs were you trying to satisfy by this activity?
4. What outcomes did you hope to obtain by performing this activity well?
5. Did you think it was likely that you would attain these outcomes if you were successful?
6. How would you characterize your expectancy for this activity? Why was your expectancy at this level?
7. Did you ever compare what you were putting into the activity and what you were getting out of it to the input and outcome of a referent? If not, why not? If so, how did you feel about this comparison, and how did it affect your behavior?
8. Did thoughts of procedural justice ever enter your mind and affect your motivation?

RESEARCH ON THE INTERNET: A MANAGER'S TOOL

Specific Task

Texas Instruments is one among many companies that have taken active steps to create and maintain a motivated workforce. Go to Texas Instruments' website to learn more about this company (www.ti.com). Then click on "Employment" and then on "Working@TI." Review the material that is shown. Then click on "Compensation and Financial Benefits."

1. What outcomes does Texas Instruments provide its employees to help ensure that they are highly motivated?
2. How does Texas Instruments link these outcomes to the contribution of important inputs and performance?

General Task

Many organizations take active steps to ensure that their employees are fairly treated. Find the website of such a company. What steps is this organization taking to ensure that its employees perceive that they are being fairly treated? How is this organization promoting distributive justice? How is this organization promoting procedural justice?

TOPICS FOR DEBATE

Motivation explains why members of an organization behave as they do and either help or hinder the organization from achieving its goals. Now that you have a good understanding of motivation, debate the following issues.

Debate One

Team A. Intrinsic motivation is more important than extrinsic motivation for organizational effectiveness.

Team B. Extrinsic motivation is more important than intrinsic motivation for organizational effectiveness.

Debate Two

Team A. Equity and justice cannot be achieved in the workplace.

Team B. Equity and justice can be achieved in the workplace.

EXPERIENTIAL EXERCISE

Motivating in Lean Economic Times

Objective

Your objective is to gain experience in confronting the challenges of (1) maintaining high levels of motivation when resources are shrinking and (2) developing an effective motivation program.

Procedure

The class divides into groups of from three to five people, and each group appoints one member as spokesperson, to present the group's recommendations to the whole class. Here is the scenario.

Each group plays the role of a team of top managers in a magazine publishing company that has recently downsized and consolidated its businesses. Now that the layoff is complete, top management is trying to devise a program to motivate the remaining editorial and production workers, who range from rank-and-file workers who operate printing presses to upper-level employees such as magazine editors.

As a result of the downsizing, the workloads of most employees have been increased by about 30 percent. In addition, resources are tight. A very limited amount of money is available for things such as pay raises, bonuses, and benefits. Nevertheless, top management thinks the company has real potential and that its fortunes could turn around if employees could be motivated to perform at a high level, be innovative, and work together to regain the company's competitive advantage.

Your group, acting as the top management team, answers the following questions.

1. What specific steps will you take to develop a motivation program based on the knowledge of motivation you have gained from this chapter?
2. What key features will your motivation program include?
3. What will you do if the program you develop and implement does not seem to be working—if motivation not only does not increase but sinks to an all-time low?

When your group has completed those activities, the spokesperson will present the group's plans and proposed actions to the whole class.

MAKING THE CONNECTION

Find an example of an organization that uses outcomes such as pay and bonuses to motivate employees to perform at a high level. What behaviors is this organization trying to encourage? How does this organization use outcomes such as pay and bonuses to promote high motivation and performance?

CLOSING CASE

Troubles at a Whirlpool Plant

Productivity was going from bad to worse at the Whirlpool Corporation (www.whirlpoolcorp.com) plant at Benton Harbor, Michigan. In response to declining productivity, the appliance maker had already closed a major part of the plant. A small tooling and plating shop (which stamped metal into parts for washing machines and dryers) was the only part of the plant that remained open, and now poor quality and productivity threatened its future.

What was going wrong? Concerned managers' conversations with workers seemed to indicate that some of the plant's productivity problems were due to low levels of worker motivation. One worker told managers that when machines broke down, workers stopped what they were doing and simply waited for someone to come along and fix the broken machines rather than try to solve the problem themselves. Moreover, even though it was known that the plant was having problems with quality, managers discovered that workers weren't concerned about quality and hid substandard parts from quality inspectors rather than try to improve the situation themselves. Things were so bad that managers from Whirlpool headquarters announced to workers that the tooling and plating shop would be shut down unless productivity improved.

The announcement got the attention of some workers. They realized that their job security was in jeopardy unless the plant became more productive. In addition to making this announcement, Whirlpool management realized it had to make radical changes to try to raise levels of worker motivation to increase quality and productivity. To establish a new feeling of cooperation between managers and workers and to try to secure the plant's future, managers adopted a gain-sharing plan: If the plant became more productive and quality increased, workers would benefit by receiving a share of the increased earnings. Because quality has such an important effect on productivity, workers also received additional training to increase their skills and boost their confidence.

These changes have had a dramatic effect on worker motivation. Since they have been instituted, productivity at the Benton Harbor plant has increased over 19 percent, and workers' pay rates have gone up approximately 12 percent. Many workers are more motivated, and the future of the plant looks secure. But, although there is no doubt that the situation at the plant has dramatically improved, some workers complain that because *all* workers receive the *same* amount of money from productivity gains, unproductive workers tend to benefit from the efforts of those who are more productive.[51] The hard workers argue that if bonuses were based on individual performance and not on plant performance, productivity and quality would increase even more. Thus managers at the plant face a new challenge: how to motivate high-performing workers to continue doing such a good job.

Questions for Discussion
  1. Why were there so many problems at the Benton Harbor plant?
  2. How might the new gain-sharing plan affect the motivation of top performers in the plant?

Motivation Tools I: Job Design and Goal Setting

7

Motivating Factory Jobs

In the past, the idea that managers could make factory work highly motivating for employees was viewed as more or less an impossible goal to achieve. Factory jobs primarily involved employees performing routine, manual tasks which tended to be repetitive and boring. Clichés that employees should "check your brains at the factory door because you won't need them on the job" were descriptive of many factory settings. However, the need to lower costs and raise

product quality to respond to increased global competition has led managers to seek new ways to make factories more efficient and effective. In the process, managers have utilized new computer-based and automated technologies and work layouts that lower costs and increase quality while making factory workers' jobs more motivating.

Take the case of Fred Price, who works at Northeast Tool & Manufacturing Co., a tool-and-die factory in North Carolina. When not working metal, he schedules orders and fills the role of supervisor. Price is also receiving specialized training to increase the depth and range of his knowledge and skills. A powerful computer on the shop floor helps workers like Price keep track of what's going on. Rusty Arant, Price's manager, says of the computer: "I crammed it with memory because I want these guys to be managing the business from the shop floor."[1]

Adlai John Warner, a factory worker at Acme Metals Inc. (www.acmemetal.com) in Illinois, found his boring and monotonous job transformed when Acme invested in a major redesign of the mill to incorporate new, cutting-edge technology. Warner and 130 other Acme employees were paid to take nine months of full-time training in a variety of areas, including mathematics, metallurgy, computers, and the new technology adopted by the mill. Factory workers like Warner now need to make rapid decisions on the factory floor with wide-sweeping ramifications, a far cry from the days when little thought was involved in their work.[2]

In addition to adopting new computer technology, managers have also been experimenting with changes in the work layout to try to improve motivation and performance. Traditionally, factories have used a mass production system in which workers are positioned along a straight or linear production line that can be hundreds of feet long. As a result, the speed of the production line controls how fast employees work, and each employee works separately. To try to raise motivation and performance, managers have been experimenting with new work layouts such as spirals, Ys, and 6s, that give employees more input into the work process and make their jobs more motivating. At a Sony (www.sony.com) camcorder plant in Kohda, Japan, for example, Sony dismantled its previous mass production system in which fifty workers worked sequentially to build a camcorder, and replaced it with a spiral arrangement forty feet long in which only four workers perform all the operations necessary to assemble camcorders. Sony says the new system is 10 percent more efficient than the old system. Why? Because it allows the most efficient workers to set their own goals and perform at a higher level. In the United States, it has been estimated that 40 to 70 percent of large companies have been experimenting with new work layouts that typically use new computer-controlled technology and make jobs more motivating.[3]

Additionally, increased domestic and global competition is resulting in factory workers striving to reach ever more difficult quality and effectiveness goals. At Northeast Tool, for example, quality levels must not only be high, but metal products must have precise tolerances obtained through statistical quality control techniques in order for Northeast to win contracts from companies such as Siemens and BMW.[4]

Overview

Changes in the design of jobs and work processes, such as those being made at Northeast Tool, Acme Metal, and Sony, are dramatically changing the nature of factory work. Workers are being required to develop and use more skills than ever before, and they experience higher levels of autonomy because they are responsible for managing many aspects of the work process. Extensive use of computers in factories provides workers with immediate feedback on how they are doing, feedback that allows them to monitor quality and production levels and correct problems before they get out of hand. Jobs are also being perceived as much more important in the wider scheme of things, and factory workers have a better appreciation of how their efforts contribute to their organization's success.

In Chapter 6, we examined the nature of work motivation and four approaches to understanding motivation in organizations. Building from this foundation, in Chapters 7 and 8 we focus on several motivation tools—job design, goal setting, performance appraisal, pay, and careers—that managers can use to promote high levels of motivation and the achievement of organizational objectives. The prime objective of these motivational tools is to ensure that (1) workers are motivated to contribute their inputs to their jobs and to the organization and (2) these inputs result in acceptable job performance, which in turn allows the organization to achieve its goals.

To take a simple example, the survival and profitability of a Burger King restaurant hinges on workers' performing their jobs in an acceptable fashion (preparing meals in accordance with company standards, promptly waiting on customers, and keeping the restaurant clean). If workers do not perform their jobs acceptably and, for instance, take twenty minutes to prepare a Whopper, ignore customers to engage in personal conversation, and fail to clear off dirty tables, many disgruntled customers will decide to take their business to McDonald's or Wendy's. This loss of customers will make it harder (if not impossible) for the restaurant to achieve its goals of serving large numbers of customers and being profitable. Likewise, the survival and profitability of Northeast Tool, Acme Metal, and Sony in the opening case depend on factory workers being motivated to contribute their own inputs (effort, time, and skills) to learning and using the new, computer-based technology. Factory workers like Price and Warner are motivated by the opportunity to learn and use new skills, autonomy and responsibility, and realizing how important their work is for the success of the organization as a whole. The challenging effectiveness and quality goals their organizations set further spur them on.

In this chapter, we discuss job design, a major tool that managers can use to facilitate intrinsic motivation. We explore goal setting as a way to motivate workers to contribute appropriate levels of inputs to their jobs and to ensure that these inputs result in acceptable levels of performance. In terms of the motivation equation, introduced in Chapter 6 (see Fig. 6.2) and restated in Figure 7.1, job design and goal setting are motivation tools used primarily to ensure that workers are motivated to contribute inputs to the organization. In the next chapter, we focus on the other three motivation tools shown in Figure 7.1: performance appraisal, pay, and career opportunities.

Job design

The process of linking specific tasks to specific jobs and deciding what techniques, equipment, and procedures should be used to perform those tasks.

Job Design: Early Approaches

Job design is the process of linking specific tasks to specific jobs and deciding what techniques, equipment, and procedures should be used to perform those tasks. The tasks that make up a secretary's job, for example, include answering the telephone, filing, typing letters and reports, and scheduling meetings and appointments. The techniques, equipment, and procedures the secretary uses to accomplish these tasks may include using a personal computer and one or more word-processing software packages to type documents and prepare graphs, using an answering machine to take calls, and keeping a weekly appointment book to schedule and keep track of meetings.

In general, managers design jobs to increase motivation and encourage workers to perform well, enjoy their work, and receive the outcomes available to those who perform at an acceptable level. Job design influences the level of inputs that workers are motivated to contribute to their jobs and to the organization (see Fig. 7.1). When workers are motivated to contribute a high level of inputs (to work harder, more efficiently, and more creatively) and perform their jobs more effectively, organizational effectiveness increases.

In the next sections, we examine scientific management, job enlargement, and job enrichment—three early approaches to job design. Each has implications not only for how *new* jobs should be designed but also for how *existing* jobs can be redesigned to improve motivation and performance. Some of the approaches can also be used to design a job so that performing the job will promote job satisfaction (discussed in Chapter 3), an outcome that many workers desire along with pay, promotion, and the other rewards a job can bring.

SCIENTIFIC MANAGEMENT

In 1911, Frederick W. Taylor published one of the earliest approaches to job design, *The Principles of Scientific Management.*[5] Taylor was concerned that workers were slacking off and not performing as highly as they should on their

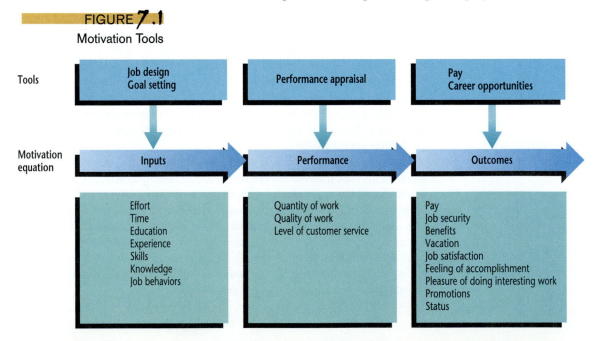

FIGURE **7.1**

Motivation Tools

Scientific management
A set of principles and practices designed to increase the performance of individual workers by stressing job simplification and specialization.

Job simplification
The breaking up of the work that needs to be performed in an organization into the smallest identifiable tasks.

Job specialization
The assignment of workers to perform small, simple tasks.

Time and motion studies
Studies that reveal exactly how long it takes to perform a task and the best way to perform it.

jobs. **Scientific management,** a set of principles and practices stressing job simplification and specialization, was developed by Taylor to increase the performance of individual workers. Taylor started with this premise: There is one best way to perform any job, and management's responsibility is to determine what that way is. He believed that following the principles of job simplification and job specialization would help managers determine the best way to perform each job. **Job simplification** is the breaking up of the work that needs to be performed in an organization into the smallest identifiable tasks. Jobs are then designed around these narrow tasks. **Job specialization** is the assignment of workers to perform small, simple tasks. Workers specialize, or focus exclusively, on those tasks.

Many fast-food restaurants employ the principles of job simplification and specialization. The jobs of food preparers in the popular and successful Subway chain of sandwich shops show the effects of simplification and specialization. One person puts the meat on a sandwich, another person puts on the trimmings (such as lettuce, tomatoes, and condiments), and another person collects the money from customers. Because of the simplification and specialization, Subway restaurants can make large numbers of "custom" sandwiches in a short period of time. The effectiveness of this job design is easily illustrated by watching what happens at a Subway shop when specialization is reduced because one or more workers are unavailable (because, for example, they are on the telephone or are replenishing supplies). The other workers perform their own jobs plus the job of the temporarily absent worker, and it generally takes much longer to serve a customer. A cashier who fills in for the "trimmings" worker, for example, must wash his or her hands after handling a customer's money before trimming another sandwich (in keeping with Subway's cleanliness policy).

Advocates of scientific management conduct time and motion studies to determine the one best way to perform each narrow task. **Time and motion studies** reveal exactly how long it takes to perform a task and the best way to perform it—for example, what body movements are most efficient for performing the task. Workers are then instructed in precisely how to perform their tasks.

Workers at Subway, for example, learn exactly how to slice the roll for a sandwich, how to place the meat on a sandwich, and how to add the trimmings. Because these tasks are simple, workers quickly learn to perform them correctly. Because managers know (from the time and motions studies) exactly how long it should take to perform each task, they know how much output (on average) they can expect a worker to produce. Subway knows, for example, how many sandwiches can be made and how many customers can be served in each shop per hour. By clearly specifying exactly what a worker should do on the job, exactly how a task should be done, and exactly how long the task should take, scientific management ensures that worker inputs result in acceptable performance levels.

In the scientific management approach to job design, pay is the principal outcome used to motivate workers to contribute their inputs. Pay is often linked closely to performance by a piece-rate pay system in which workers are paid a set amount of money for performing a certain number of tasks. For example, a worker might be paid $5 for every eight sound mufflers that he or she attaches to computer printers.

Scientific management has been instrumental in helping organizations to improve worker effectiveness and productivity. The early assembly lines

To increase efficiency, a candy factory supervisor orders an increase in the speed of the production line in this well-known episode of **I Love Lucy.** Unable to keep up, Lucy and Ethel resort to eating the candy or hiding it in their hats, suggesting that increasing production line speed is not always the best way to increase output.

that made the mass production of affordable automobiles possible reflected scientific management principles. These principles still guide some mass production assembly lines in use today. Eventually, however, some disadvantages of designing jobs according to the principles of scientific management became apparent. Many problems stemmed from the fact that workers are intelligent human beings who have the capacity to be intrinsically as well as extrinsically motivated and who also like to have control over their work.

Recall from Chapter 6 that *extrinsically* motivated behavior is behavior performed to acquire rewards (such as pay) or to avoid punishment, and *intrinsically* motivated behavior is behavior performed for its own sake. Workers who are intrinsically motivated enjoy performing their jobs; the motivation comes from the work itself. Scientific management focuses exclusively on extrinsic motivation and ignores the important role of intrinsic motivation. This narrow focus results in several disadvantages for workers and the organizations trying to motivate them.

First, workers may feel that they have lost control over their work behaviors. With its careful, exact specification of how a simple, repetitive, specialized task should be performed, and how long it should take, scientific management leaves no room for workers to feel that they have some control over their actions. Second, workers tend to feel as if they are part of a machine and are treated as such. Because they view their work as depersonalized, meaningless, and monotonous, their job satisfaction may decline. This decline, in turn, can lead to decreases in the quality of work life and potential increases in absenteeism and turnover. Finally, workers have no opportunity to develop and acquire new skills. These three drawbacks of simplified and specialized jobs are part of the reason Subway and other fast-food restaurants experience high levels of turnover: Workers leave to find more interesting and demanding work.

JOB ENLARGEMENT AND JOB ENRICHMENT

The first widespread attempt to counteract some of the disadvantages of designing jobs according to principles of scientific management was job enlargement, a movement that started in the late 1940s and continued through the 1950s.[6] **Job enlargement** is increasing the number of tasks a worker performs but keeping all of the tasks at the same level of difficulty and responsibility. Job enlargement is often referred to as *horizontal job loading* because the content of a job is expanded but the difficulty remains constant. For example, one might enlarge the job of assembly-line workers who attach the paper tray to a computer printer by also requiring them to attach the sound muffler and the toner cartridge. The workers now do more tasks of equal difficulty with no increase in the level of responsibility.

Proponents of job enlargement thought that increasing the number of tasks performed on a job might increase intrinsic motivation. The job enlargement approach to job design was put into effect at a number of companies, including IBM, Maytag, and AT&T.[7] Some companies reported success in the form of increased worker productivity and satisfaction, but at others the effects of job enlargement were not clear-cut. This mixed success is not surprising, for jobs that are enlarged may still be simple and limited in how much control and variety workers have. Even though they no longer do one simple task, workers performing several simple tasks (each of which may quickly lose its appeal) may still be bored.

In response to the limited effects of job enlargement on work motivation, job enrichment emerged in the 1960s. **Job enrichment** is designing jobs to provide opportunities for worker growth by giving workers more responsibility and control over their work. Job enrichment is often referred to as *vertical job loading* because workers are given some of the responsibilities that used to belong to their supervisors, such as planning how to go about completing a project or checking the quality of one's work. Herzberg's motivator-hygiene theory (discussed in Chapter 3) was a driving force in the movement to enrich jobs. Recall that Herzberg's theory suggested that workers' motivator needs are satisfied by things such as having autonomy on the job and being responsible for one's work and that workers are satisfied with their jobs only when these needs are met.

Managers can enrich jobs in a variety of ways. The following are some of the most common:[8]

- *Allow workers to plan their own work schedules:* For example, when possible, allow a secretary to determine when he or she does various tasks such as typing, filing, and setting up meetings and how much time to allow for each activity.
- *Allow workers to decide how the work should be performed:* If a manager wants a secretary to prepare a new company brochure or filing system, the manager may let the secretary decide how to design the brochure or filing system.
- *Allow workers to check their own work:* Instead of insisting that the secretary give a draft of the brochure to the manager to check for errors, the manager holds the secretary responsible for producing a top-quality, error-free brochure.
- *Allow workers to learn new skills:* A secretary may be given the opportunity to learn bookkeeping and some basic accounting procedures.

Job enlargement
Increasing the number of tasks a worker performs but keeping all of the tasks at the same level of difficulty and responsibility; also called horizontal job loading.

Job enrichment
Increasing a worker's responsibility and control over his or her work; also called vertical job loading.

As illustrated in Insight 7.1, sometimes jobs can be both enlarged and enriched: A worker is given more tasks to perform and more responsibility and control on the job.

Insight 7.1

Job Design

Enlargement and Enrichment Dramatically Change Trucking

Herman Willoughby's job was transformed nine years ago when he started setting up Xerox Corporation's quarter-ton copy machines. Willoughby is a truck driver employed by Ryder Systems Inc. (www.ryder.com) in Orlando, Florida. Willoughby used to just deliver the copy machines, but his job was enlarged to include setting them up. He became so proficient at setting up the copiers that now he can set up many different models and types.

Because Willoughby proved that he was able and willing to take on additional responsibilities, his job has also been enriched in a number of ways. He checks every copier he assembles to make sure it is in perfect working order and copying at exactly the right level of darkness. He trains workers in how to use copiers and their new and advanced features (such as document shrinking and two-sided copying). He even calls and tries to satisfy disgruntled customers.

Willoughby's job has been so transformed that driving the truck is now just one of many tasks he performs. Similarly, many truck drivers now have computers, satellites, and fax machines in their 18-wheelers and are responsible for faxing bills to customers, following up on bills that haven't been paid on time, and providing training and assistance to customers in how to use a new machine or piece of equipment they are delivering.[9] The drivers' jobs have been enlarged and enriched by the addition of responsibility and autonomy.

Like job enlargement, job enrichment is aimed at increasing intrinsic motivation so that workers enjoy their jobs more. When workers are given more responsibility, they are more likely to feel competent and to feel that they have control over their own work behaviors. Not all workers, however, want the additional responsibility that job enrichment brings, and job enrichment can sometimes have disadvantages for the organization as a whole. Enriching some jobs can be very expensive for an organization and may be impossible to do. On other jobs, enrichment may result in less efficiency. One of the reasons Subway sandwich shops are able to make large numbers of sandwiches to order is because of job simplification and specialization. Enriching the jobs of Subway workers might increase the time it takes to serve customers, an outcome that would reduce organizational effectiveness.

Research evidence on the effects of job enrichment has been mixed. Although workers seem to be more satisfied with enriched jobs, it is not clear whether workers with enriched jobs are actually more motivated and perform at a higher level.

Job Design: The Job Characteristics Model

The job enlargement and job enrichment movements came about in part because of some of the negative effects observed when jobs were designed according to the principles of scientific management. Both movements attempted to increase workers' levels of intrinsic motivation to perform their jobs, in the hope that workers who found their jobs more interesting and meaningful would be more motivated to perform at higher levels and be more satisfied. Satisfied workers would mean less turnover and absenteeism. The **job characteristics model** proposed by Richard Hackman and Greg Oldham in the 1970s built on these early approaches but went further. Based on the work of A. N. Turner and P. R. Lawrence, Hackman and Oldham attempted to identify exactly which job characteristics contribute to intrinsically motivating work and what the consequences of these characteristics are.[10]

The job characteristics model is one of the most popular approaches to job design. Hackman and Oldham sought to provide a detailed and accurate account of the effects of job design on motivation, performance, job satisfaction, and other important aspects of organizational behavior. Like the job enlargement and enrichment approaches, the job characteristics model focuses on what makes jobs intrinsically motivating. When workers are intrinsically motivated by their jobs, Hackman and Oldham reasoned, good performance makes them feel good. This feeling motivates them to continue to perform at a high level, so good performance becomes self-reinforcing.[11]

Job characteristics model
An approach to job design that aims to identify characteristics that make jobs intrinsically motivating and the consequences of those characteristics.

L.L. Bean, the mail order catalog clothing company, is well known for its high level of customer service, such as its policy of allowing customers to return clothing with which they are unsatisfied with no questions asked. The key to its success is the way it motivates its employees. As a part of their regular jobs, L.L. Bean employees are expected to manage all customer accounts and deal personally with customer complaints. Their pay is directly linked to their customers' statisfaction.

CORE JOB DIMENSIONS

According to the job characteristics model, any job has five core dimensions that impact intrinsic motivation: skill variety, task identity, task significance, autonomy, and feedback. The higher a job scores on each dimension, the higher the level of intrinsic motivation.

Skill variety

The extent to which a job requires a worker to use different skills, abilities, or talents.

1. **Skill variety** is the extent to which a job requires a worker to use a number of different skills, abilities, or talents. Workers are more intrinsically motivated by jobs that are high on skill variety.

   High variety: In the opening case, we described how the jobs of factory workers are increasing in skill variety due to the prevalence of sophisticated and computer-based technology. Workers now use a variety of skills, including computer skills, mathematics, statistical control, and quality control, in addition to skills related to whatever they are producing, such as metal products.

   Low variety: The jobs of workers in a Subway restaurant have a low level of skill variety. All the workers need to know is how to slice rolls and put meat and trimmings on sandwiches.

Task identity

The extent to which a job involves performing a whole piece of work from its beginning to its end.

2. **Task identity** is the extent to which a job involves performing a whole piece of work from its beginning to its end. The higher the level of task identity, the more intrinsically motivated a worker is likely to be.

   High identity: A carpenter who makes custom wood cabinets and furniture has high task identity. The carpenter designs and makes cabinets and furniture from start to finish.

   Low identity: For a factory worker assembling computer printers, task identity is low if the worker only attaches the paper tray.

Task significance

The extent to which a job has an impact on the lives or work of other people in or out of the organization.

3. **Task significance** is the extent to which a job has an impact on the lives or work of other people in or out of the organization. Workers are more likely to enjoy performing their jobs when they think their jobs are important in the wider scheme of things.

   High significance: Medical researchers and doctors experience high levels of task significance as their work promotes the health and well-being of current and future patients.

   Low significance: The job of a worker who dries off cars after the cars go through a carwash has low task significance because the worker doesn't think it has much impact on other people.

Autonomy

The degree to which a job allows a worker the freedom and independence to schedule work and decide how to carry it out.

4. **Autonomy** is the degree to which a job allows a worker the freedom and independence to schedule work and decide how to carry it out. High autonomy generally contributes to high levels of intrinsic motivation.

   High autonomy: From the opening case, it is clear that factory workers' levels of autonomy are on the rise. They are increasingly being responsible for scheduling work and making important decisions on the shop floor.

   Low autonomy: A worker at the Internal Revenue Service who opens tax returns and sorts them into different categories has a low level of autonomy because she or he must work at a steady, predetermined pace and follow strict guidelines for sorting the returns.

Feedback

The extent to which performing a job provides a worker with clear information about his or her effectiveness.

5. **Feedback** is the extent to which performing a job provides a worker with clear information about his or her effectiveness. Receiving feedback has a positive impact on intrinsic motivation.

High feedback: Computer-based technology in factories often gives factory workers immediate feedback on how well they are doing, and this information contributes to their intrinsic motivation.

Low feedback: A worker who reshelves books in the New York City Public Library rarely receives feedback as he or she performs the job and is often unaware of when he or she makes a mistake or does a particularly good job.

Sometimes redesigning some of a job's core dimensions can help reduce costs in an organization, improve customer relations, and help an organization gain a competitive advantage. (See Insight 7.2.)

Insight 7.2   Competitive Advantage

Two Core Dimensions Change at Aetna

Today, many companies are experimenting with reengineering, the widespread redesign of jobs and critical processes in an organization to increase efficiency, cut costs, increase customer satisfaction, and gain a competitive advantage. Often, reengineering focuses on improving critical organizational processes such as the way insurance claims are handled or how customer orders and complaints are processed.[12] Reengineering and the job redesign that accompanies it frequently result in higher levels of core job dimensions such as autonomy and task identity.

Filing a claim with an insurance company, for example, can be an exercise in frustration. After making an initial call to notify the company of an accident, customers must wait for days, weeks, and sometimes even months for their claims to be settled. Because many different employees are involved in processing the claim, there are many opportunities for delay, and no one person is ever sure of exactly where in the pipeline the claim is. As delays continue and questions go unanswered, customer annoyance increases. Reengineering the handling of insurance claims can be accomplished by reducing the number of steps and employees involved in processing the claim and by giving one or a few employees more autonomy to make decisions. Levels of task identity also increase because the same employee is more likely to handle a claim from start to finish.

Aetna Life & Casualty (www.aetna.com) has made major changes in the ways it processes insurance claims and in the design of jobs within its claim-processing units. Under its new system, a customer whose car has been stolen calls an 800 number. In a single phone call, the customer is told where to pick up a rental car and who will be handling the claim at Aetna, and the customer is given an appointment with a claims adjuster. Under Aetna's old system, this procedure would have taken from two to five days.

Levels of autonomy and task identity are likely to be higher under the new system because workers have more discretion to make decisions and can handle most claims from start to finish. According to the job characteristics model, these increases in autonomy and task identity should have positive effects on the intrinsic motivation of claim processors. The CEO of Aetna, Ronald Compton, expects such changes to help the company dramatically cut its costs and gain a competitive advantage. In any case, customers appear to be delighted with the new system. Aetna has been receiving fan mail from satisfied customers![13]

According to the job characteristics model, when managers consider the five core dimensions of a job, it is important for them to realize that *workers'* perceptions of the core dimensions (not the actual reality or a manager's perceptions) are the key determinants of intrinsic motivation. As we discussed in Chapter 4, two people can watch the same movie or take part in the same group meeting and have very different perceptions of what they have experienced. One person might hate a movie that another person loved, and one group member might perceive that a group meeting was a noisy, incomprehensible free-for-all while another perceives that a reasonable and lively discussion took place. In like manner, two workers may have the same job yet perceive it differently so that, for example, one worker perceives the job to be high on task significance while another perceives it to be low on this dimension.

THE MOTIVATING POTENTIAL SCORE

To measure workers' perceptions of their jobs on each of the core dimensions, Hackman and Oldham developed the *Job Diagnostic Survey*. The scales used to measure the five dimensions are shown in Figure 7.2. Once a worker completes each of these scales for his or her job, it is possible to compute the job's motivating potential score. The **motivating potential score (MPS)** is a measure of the overall potential of a job to foster intrinsic motivation. MPS is equal to the average of the first three core characteristics (skill variety, task identity, and task significance) multiplied by autonomy and feedback, as indicated in Figure 7.2. Since the *Job Diagnostic Survey* provides for each of the core dimensions a score ranging from a low of 1 to a high of 7, the lowest MPS possible for a job is 1 and the highest MPS possible is 343 (7 x 7 x 7). The lowest MPS score that Hackman and Oldham have observed was 7 for a typist in an overflow typing pool who waited at her typewriter all day for the occasional jobs she received when the regular typing pools got overloaded. The highest score was 300 for a management consultant. Hackman and Oldham suggest that an average motivating potential score for jobs in U.S. corporations is around 128.[14]

The *Job Diagnostic Survey* can be used to identify the core dimensions that are most in need of redesign in order to increase a job's motivating potential score and thus a worker's intrinsic motivation. Figure 7.3 shows a survey profile for a gardener who works for a landscape company. The gardener is a member of a three-person crew that provides landscape services to residential and commercial customers. The crew is headed by a landscape supervisor who assigns individual tasks (such as cutting grass, preparing flower beds, or planting trees) to crew members at each job site. As indicated in Figure 7.3, the gardener's levels of task identity and autonomy are especially low and should be the main focus of any redesign efforts. Currently, the supervisor assigns very

Motivating potential score (MPS)
A measure of the overall potential of a job to foster intrinsic motivation.

FIGURE **7.2**

Measures of the Five
Core Characteristics From
Hackman and Oldham's Job
Diagnostic Survey
Source: J. R. Hackman and G. R.
Oldham, *Work Redesign,* copyright
1980 Addison-Wesley Publishing Co.,
Inc., Reading, Mass. Reprinted with
permission.

specific and unrelated tasks to each crew member: At a particular site, the gardener might plant some flowers, cut some borders, and plant a tree. The supervisor also tells the crew members exactly how to do each task: Put the daisies here and the marigolds around the border.

To increase task identity and autonomy, the supervisor could change the way he assigns tasks to crew members: The supervisor could make each crew member responsible for a major aspect of a particular landscaping job and, after providing some basic guidelines, give the crew member the autonomy

Skill variety

1. How much *variety* is there in your job? That is, to what extent does the job require you to do many different things at work, using a variety of your skills and talents?

1	2	3	4	5	6	7
Very little; the job requires me to do the same routine things over and over again.			Moderate variety			Very much; the job requires me to do many different things, using a number of different skills and talents.

2. The job requires me to use a number of complex or high-level skills.

How accurate is the statement in describing your job?

1	2	3	4	5	6	7
Very inaccurate	Mostly inaccurate	Slightly inaccurate	Uncertain	Slightly accurate	Mostly accurate	Very accurate

3. The job is quite simple and repetitive.*

How accurate is the statement in describing your job?

1	2	3	4	5	6	7
Very inaccurate	Mostly inaccurate	Slightly inaccurate	Uncertain	Slightly accurate	Mostly accurate	Very accurate

Task identity

1. To what extent does your job involve doing a *"whole"and identifiable piece of work*? That is, is the job a complete piece of work that has an obvious beginning and end? Or is it only a small *part* of the overall piece of work, which is finished by other people or by automatic machines?

1	2	3	4	5	6	7
My job is only a tiny part of the overall piece of work; the results of my activities cannot be seen in the final product or service.			My job is a moderate-sized "chunk" of the overall piece of work; my own contribution can be seen in the final outcome.			My job involves doing the whole piece of work, from start to finish; the results of my activities are easily seen in the final product or service.

2. The job provides me the chance to completely finish the pieces of work I begin.

How accurate is the statement in describing your job?

1	2	3	4	5	6	7
Very inaccurate	Mostly inaccurate	Slightly inaccurate	Uncertain	Slightly accurate	Mostly accurate	Very accurate

3. The job is arranged so that I do *not* have the chance to do an entire piece of work from beginning to end.*

How accurate is the statement in describing your job?

1	2	3	4	5	6	7
Very inaccurate	Mostly inaccurate	Slightly inaccurate	Uncertain	Slightly accurate	Mostly accurate	Very accurate

Task significance

1. In general, how significant or important is your job? That is, are the results of your work likely to significantly affect the lives or well-being of other people?

1	2	3	4	5	6	7
Not very significant; the outcomes of my work are *not* likely to have important effects on other people.			Moderately significant			Highly significant; the outcomes of my work can affect other people in very important ways.

2. This job is one where a lot of people can be affected by how well the work gets done.

How accurate is the statement in describing your job?

1	2	3	4	5	6	7
Very inaccurate	Mostly inaccurate	Slightly inaccurate	Uncertain	Slightly accurate	Mostly accurate	Very accurate

(Continued)

Task significance (continued)

3. The job itself is *not* very significant or important in the broader scheme of things.*

How accurate is the statement in describing your job?

1	2	3	4	5	6	7
Very inaccurate	Mostly inaccurate	Slightly inaccurate	Uncertain	Slightly accurate	Mostly accurate	Very accurate

Autonomy

1. How much *autonomy* is there in your job? That is, to what extent does your job permit you to decide *on your own* how to go about doing your work?

1	2	3	4	5	6	7
Very little; the job gives me almost no personal "say" about how and when the work is done.			Moderate autonomy; many things are standardized and not under my control, but I can make some decisions about the work.			Very much; the job gives me almost complete responsibility for deciding how and when the work is done.

2. The job gives me considerable opportunity for independence and freedom in how I do the work.

How accurate is the statement in describing your job?

1	2	3	4	5	6	7
Very inaccurate	Mostly inaccurate	Slightly inaccurate	Uncertain	Slightly accurate	Mostly accurate	Very accurate

3. The job denies me any chance to use my personal initiative or judgment in carrying out the work.*

How accurate is the statement in describing your job?

1	2	3	4	5	6	7
Very inaccurate	Mostly inaccurate	Slightly inaccurate	Uncertain	Slightly accurate	Mostly accurate	Very accurate

Feedback

1. To what extent does *doing the job itself* provide you with information about your work performance? That is, does the actual *work itself* provide clues about how well you are doing — aside from any "feedback" coworkers or supervisors may provide?

1	2	3	4	5	6	7
Very little; the job itself is set up so I could work forever without finding out how well I am doing.			Moderately; sometimes doing the job provides "feedback" to me; sometimes it does not.			Very much; the job is set up so that I get almost constant "feedback" as I work about how well I am doing.

2. Just doing the work required by the job provides many chances for me to figure out how well I am doing.

How accurate is the statement in describing your job?

1	2	3	4	5	6	7
Very inaccurate	Mostly inaccurate	Slightly inaccurate	Uncertain	Slightly accurate	Mostly accurate	Very accurate

3. The job itself provides very few clues about whether or not I am performing well.*

How accurate is the statement in describing your job?

1	2	3	4	5	6	7
Very inaccurate	Mostly inaccurate	Slightly inaccurate	Uncertain	Slightly accurate	Mostly accurate	Very accurate

Scoring: Responses to the three items for each core characteristic are averaged to yield an overall score for that characteristic.

Items marked with a " * " should be scored as follows: 1 = 7; 2 = 6; 3 = 5; 5 = 3; 6 = 2; 7 = 1

$$\text{Motivating potential score} = \left(\frac{\text{Skill variety + Task identity + Task significance}}{3}\right) \times \text{Autonomy} \times \text{Feedback}$$

to decide how to accomplish this aspect of the job. On one job, for example, the gardener might be responsible for preparing and arranging all of the flower beds (the result is in high task identity). After the supervisor tells the gardener about the customer's likes and dislikes, the gardener would be free to design the beds as he sees fit and work on them in the order he wants (high autonomy). As a result of these changes, the MPS of the gardener's job would rise from 20.4 to 100 (see Fig. 7.3).

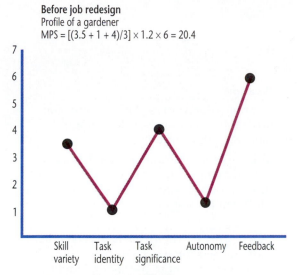

Before job redesign
Profile of a gardener
MPS = [(3.5 + 1 + 4)/3] × 1.2 × 6 = 20.4

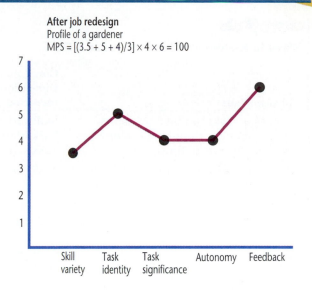

After job redesign
Profile of a gardener
MPS = [(3.5 + 5 + 4)/3] × 4 × 6 = 100

FIGURE 7.3

Sample Job Diagnostic
Survey Profiles

Jobs can be redesigned in a variety of ways to increase levels of the five core dimensions and the MPS. Common ways to redesign jobs are described in Table 7.1.

CRITICAL PSYCHOLOGICAL STATES

Hackman and Oldham proposed that the five core job dimensions contribute to three critical psychological states that determine how workers react to the design of their jobs: experienced meaningfulness of the work, experienced responsibility for work outcomes, and knowledge of results.

First, workers who perceive that their jobs are high in skill variety, task identity, and task significance attain the psychological state of experienced meaningfulness of the work. **Experienced meaningfulness of the work** is the degree to which workers feel their jobs are important, worthwhile, and meaningful. The second critical psychological state, **experienced responsibility for work outcomes,** is the extent to which workers feel that they are personally responsible or accountable for their job performance. This psychological state stems from the core dimension of autonomy. The third critical psychological state, **knowledge of results,** is the degree to which workers know how well they perform their jobs on a continuous basis; it stems from the core dimension of feedback. Figure 7.4 summarizes the relationships among the five core dimensions, the three critical psychological states, and work and personal outcomes (discussed next).

WORK AND PERSONAL OUTCOMES

Hackman and Oldham further proposed that the critical psychological states result in four key outcomes for workers and their organizations: high intrinsic motivation, high job performance, high job satisfaction, and low absenteeism and turnover (see Fig. 7.4).

1. *High intrinsic motivation:* One of the major outcomes of job design is intrinsic motivation. When jobs are high on the five core dimensions, workers experience the three critical psychological states and are intrinsically motivated. When intrinsic motivation is high, workers enjoy

Experienced meaningfulness of the work
The degree to which workers feel their jobs are important, worthwhile, and meaningful.

Experienced responsibility for work outcomes
The extent to which workers feel personally responsible or accountable for their job performance.

Knowledge of results
The degree to which workers know how well they perform their jobs on a continuous basis.

TABLE **7.1**

Ways to Redesign Jobs to Increase MPS

Change Made	Core Job Dimensions Increased	Example
Combine tasks so that a worker is responsible for doing a piece of work from start to finish.	Skill variety Task identity Task significance	A production worker is responsible for assembling a whole bicycle, not just attaching the handlebars.
Group tasks into natural work units so that workers are responsible for performing an entire set of important organizational activities rather than just part of them.	Task identity Task significance	A computer programmer handles all programming requests from one division instead of one type of request from several different divisions.
Allow workers to interact with customers or clients, and make workers responsible for managing these relationships and satisfying customers.	Skill variety Autonomy Feedback	A truck driver who delivers photo copiers not only sets them up but also trains customers in how to use them, handles customer billing, and responds to customer complaints.
Vertically load jobs so that workers have more control over their work activities and higher levels of responsibility.	Autonomy	A corporate marketing analyst not only prepares marketing plans and reports but also decides when to update and revise them, checks them for errors, and presents them to upper management.
Open feedback channels so that workers know how they are performing their jobs.	Feedback	In addition to knowing how many claims he handles per month, an insurance adjuster receives his clients' responses to follow-up questionnaires that his company uses to measure client satisfaction.

Source: Based on J. R. Hackman, "Work Redesign," in J. R. Hackman and J. L. Suttle, eds., *Improving Life at Work* (Santa Monica, Calif.: Goodyear, 1976).

performing a job for its own sake. Good performance makes workers feel good, and this positive feeling further motivates them to continue to perform at a high level. Poor performance makes workers feel bad, but this feeling may motivate them to try to perform at a high level. In other words, because good performance is self-reinforcing (performance is its own reward), motivation to perform well comes from inside the worker rather than from an external source such as the praise of a supervisor or the promise of pay.

2. *High job performance:* Jobs high in the five core dimensions, which lead to high levels of the three critical psychological states, motivate workers to perform at a high level.

3. *High job satisfaction:* Hackman and Oldham reasoned that workers are likely to be more satisfied with their jobs when the critical psychological states are high, because workers will have more opportunities for personal growth and development on the job.

4. *Low absenteeism and turnover:* When workers enjoy performing their jobs, Hackman and Oldham reasoned, they will be less likely to be absent or quit. (Also, recall from Chapter 3 that satisfied workers are less likely to be absent or quit.)

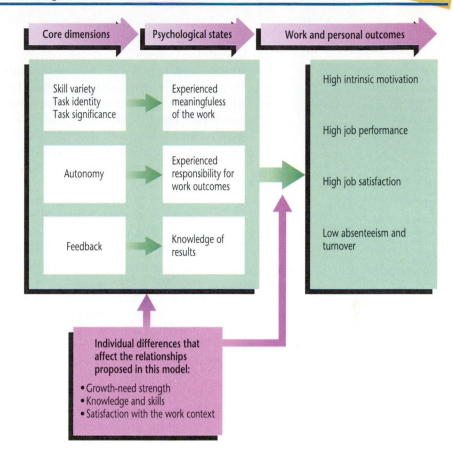

FIGURE 7.4

The Job Characteristics Model
Source: Adapted from J. R. Hackman
and G. R. Oldham, *Work Redesign,*
copyright 1980 Addison-Wesley
Publishing Co., Inc., Reading, Mass.

THE ROLE OF INDIVIDUAL DIFFERENCES IN WORKERS' RESPONSES TO JOB DESIGN

The job characteristics model acknowledges the role that individual differences play in determining how workers respond to the design of their jobs. To see how individual differences interact with job design, let's look at the case of three sales managers, each of whom manages a different department in a department store. Mary Catalano, the manager of women's shoes, is a competent manager, eager to learn more about different aspects of retailing, and serious about her career. Ron Richards, the manager of men's shoes, is still mastering the responsibilities of his first supervisory position and has had a rough time. Roberta Doran has an MBA in marketing and manages the china department. She is a competent manager but always complains about how low retailing salaries are compared to salaries she could be making in other types of organizations.

To increase the motivating potential score of each manager's job, the department store has recently redesigned each job. In the past, the managers' main responsibility had been to supervise the sales teams in their respective departments. After the redesign, their responsibilities were increased to include the purchasing of merchandise (increases in skill variety and task significance), the hiring and firing of salespeople (increases in skill variety and task significance), and accountability for the profitability of their respective departments (increases in task identity, autonomy, and feedback).

As you might expect, Catalano, Richards, and Doran have responded in different ways to the redesign of their jobs and the resulting increase in motivating potential score. The job characteristics model helps to explain why workers may respond somewhat differently to an increase in some of the core characteristics of their jobs. The model identifies three types of individual differences that affect the relationships between the core dimensions and the psychological states and the relationships between the psychological states and the outcomes (see Fig. 7.4). The nature of those relationships depends on the growth-need strength, knowledge and skills, and satisfaction with the work context of the individual worker.

1. *Growth-need strength* is the extent to which an individual wants his or her work to contribute to personal growth, learning, and development. When an individual wants his or her job to fuel personal growth, both relationships in the model (core dimensions–psychological states and psychological states–outcomes) are stronger. Such individuals are expected to be especially responsive both to increased levels in the core dimensions and to the critical psychological states. In our example, Mary Catalano is likely to have the most favorable response to the job redesign because she is most eager to learn what there is to learn about her chosen career.

2. *Knowledge and skills* at an appropriate level enable workers to perform their jobs effectively. When workers do not have the necessary knowledge and skills, the relationships depicted in Figure 7.4 may be weak, nonexistent, or even negative. In our example, Ron Richards was barely keeping his head above water before the increases in the core dimensions of his job. Once the job is redesigned, he may become frustrated because his lack of knowledge and lack of skills prevent him from performing well. As a result, his intrinsic motivation and job satisfaction will probably suffer, and he will be unable to perform the more complicated job.

3. *Satisfaction with the work context* describes how satisfied workers are with extrinsic outcomes (such as pay, benefits, job security, and good relationships with coworkers) they receive from their jobs. Hackman and Oldham reasoned that when workers are dissatisfied with their work context, they spend much of their energy trying to deal with their dissatisfaction with the context and are not able to appreciate and respond to the potential for intrinsic motivation on their jobs.[15] When satisfaction with the work context is high, the relationships depicted in Figure 7.4 are expected to be strong; when context satisfaction is low, they are expected to be weak. In our example, Roberta Doran's dissatisfaction with her pay is intensified by the job redesign because she must now take on additional responsibilities but will receive no extra pay. (In terms of the equity theory that we discussed in Chapter 6, Doran sees her outcome/input ratio as being more unfavorable than it was before the job redesign because her inputs are going up but she is not receiving any additional outcomes.) Instead of increasing intrinsic motivation and job satisfaction, the changes in Doran's job make her even more dissatisfied with her pay, and she spends much of her time complaining, thinking about how to improve matters, and looking for another job.

Although the job characteristics model has focused on characteristics of individuals that affect relationships between the core dimensions and the psychological states and relationships between the psychological states and the outcomes, cultural differences may also have an impact on these relationships. American workers may be used to a certain amount of autonomy at work, but workers in other countries often have, and expect to have, very little freedom and independence on the job. Chinese workers, for example, may be motivated by core job dimensions such as autonomy, but it might take a little time and effort to convince them that they can really make decisions on their own. (See Insight 7.3.)

Insight 7.3 A Global View

Increasing Autonomy in China

William E. O'Brien is general manager of the operations in China of Minneapolis-based H. B. Fuller Co. Fuller owns and runs a joint-venture factory in China; its joint-venture partner is a Chinese banking organization, Guangdong International Trust & Investment Corp. The factory makes adhesives that are used in products ranging from cardboard boxes to packages of cigarettes.

The 42-year-old O'Brien seems an ideal candidate for managing the factory. He is fluent in Chinese, has lived in China for several years, is married to a Chinese woman, and has a good understanding of Chinese customs and culture. Running a factory in China, however, can be pretty complicated. So far O'Brien has faced several challenges, including not being able to get a shipping company to transport the factory's products down the Pearl River to Hong Kong and the new factory's walls crumbling because of structural problems with the building.

O'Brien has taken those challenges in stride and has focused a lot of his efforts on motivating the thirty-two workers in the factory. Before O'Brien took over as general manager, the workers had looked to management to make all decisions and solve all problems no matter how big or small. In the communist Chinese culture, it seems that managers often think they need to be involved in everything that goes on in an organization. At first, O'Brien couldn't be away from the factory for more than a day or two because he was afraid things would grind to a halt if he wasn't there to tell workers what to do. He remembers being "called out of meetings to take an urgent telephone call, and it would be some guy saying a piece fell off one of our machines and asking what he should do."[16]

O'Brien realized that the smooth functioning of the factory and the motivation of its workers hinged on providing workers with more autonomy. He did all he could to convince workers that they could make decisions on their own, and he gave them the authority to make many of the day-to-day decisions that came up in the course of their work. Lucy

Liu, a 27-year-old worker in purchasing at the factory, indicates that "This environment encourages us to work harder. . . . Mr. O'Brien makes us feel responsible." O'Brien's efforts seem to be paying off: The factory started to make a profit three years ahead of the Fuller Co.'s target date.[17]

THE RESEARCH EVIDENCE

Many research studies have tested different components of the job characteristics model since Richard Hackman and Greg Oldham originally proposed it. A recent review of this literature conducted by Fried and Ferris identified almost 200 studies. Fried and Ferris's overall conclusion from their review is that there is modest support for the model.[18] Some of their specific findings are as follows:

1. It is not clear that exactly five dimensions (the five core job dimensions) best describe the job design of all jobs.
2. Research shows that job dimensions have the most significant effects on intrinsic motivation and on job satisfaction; the effects on actual work behaviors (such as job performance, absenteeism, and turnover) are not as strong.
3. Simply adding the scores for the job characteristics might be a better way of calculating the motivating potential score than using the multiplicative formula proposed by Hackman and Oldham.

TO MANAGERS

Job Characteristics Model

- Realize that increasing subordinates' intrinsic motivation decreases your need to closely supervise subordinates and frees up your time for other activities. To increase levels of intrinsic motivation, increase levels of a job's five core dimensions (skill variety, task identity, task significance, autonomy, and feedback).
- To increase levels of job satisfaction, increase levels of the five core dimensions.
- Do not redesign jobs to increase levels of the five core dimensions if workers do not desire personal growth and development at work.
- Before any redesign effort, make sure that workers are satisfied with extrinsic job outcomes (pay, benefits, and job security). If workers are not satisfied with these factors, try to increase satisfaction levels prior to redesigning jobs.
- Make sure that workers have the necessary skills and abilities to perform their jobs. Do not redesign jobs to increase levels of the core dimensions for workers whose skills and abilities are already stretched by their current jobs.
- Periodically assess workers' perceptions of the core dimensions of their jobs as well as their levels of job satisfaction and intrinsic motivation. Take appropriate action when necessary.

The results of this review of the job characteristics model as well as other reviews and studies[19] lead to these overall conclusions: Workers tend to prefer jobs that are high in the five core dimensions in the model, they tend to be more satisfied with these types of jobs, and they have higher levels of intrinsic motivation. Thus job design can contribute to the quality of work life and may also have some indirect effects on absenteeism and turnover through its effects on job satisfaction. In addition, when workers' intrinsic motivation is high, managers do not need to supervise them as closely as they do when intrinsic motivation is low, because workers are internally motivated to perform well. The need for less supervision may free up some management time for other activities. Nevertheless, it is not clear that job performance will actually be higher when core dimensions are high.

Job Design: The Social Information Processing Model

The job characteristics model is complemented by another approach to job design, the social information processing model developed in 1978 by Gerald Salancik and Jeffrey Pfeffer.[20] According to the **social information processing model,** factors other than the core dimensions specified by Hackman and Oldham influence how workers respond to the design of their jobs. Salancik and Pfeffer propose that how workers perceive and respond to the design of their jobs is influenced by *social information* (information from other people) and by workers' own past behaviors. The following example highlights the social information processing model.

Joseph Doherty and Robert Cantu have recently received their law degrees from Columbia University and accepted associate positions with the same prestigious Wall Street law firm. They work in different sections of the corporate law department and report to different partners in the firm, for whom they do a lot of research and grunt work. The design of their jobs and the extrinsic outcomes (pay and perks) that they receive are similar. About half of their work is interesting and challenging, and the other half is tedious. They are expected to put in between sixty and seventy hours each week and are well paid, receiving $75,000 a year.

Despite these and other similarities, Doherty's and Cantu's reactions to their jobs are different. Doherty still can't believe his luck at landing a job that is so interesting and challenging. He enjoys his work and thinks nothing of the long hours; his high salary is the icing on the cake. Cantu complains that he didn't spend four years in college and three years in law school (never mind the year spent studying to pass the bar exam) to spend half of his time at work running errands for the partners of a law firm. He resents the fact that he is not able to deal directly with corporate clients (this job is reserved for the partners) even though he is the one who does most of the work on their cases. In his view, his high salary barely makes up for the long working hours.

Doherty is both intrinsically motivated by and very satisfied with his job. The opposite is true for Cantu, whose motivation (both intrinsic and extrinsic) is low and dissatisfaction is high. Why do they have such different reactions to jobs that are similar on most dimensions?

Social information processing model
An approach to job design based on the idea that information from other people and workers' own past behaviors influences workers' perceptions of and response to the design of their jobs.

THE ROLE OF THE SOCIAL ENVIRONMENT

Salancik and Pfeffer's social information processing model suggests several reasons Doherty's and Cantu's reactions are so different. First, the model proposes that the social environment provides workers with information about which aspects of their job design and work outcomes they should pay attention to and which they should ignore. Here, *social environment* means the other individuals with whom workers come into contact at work. A worker's social environment thus includes coworkers, supervisors, and the other members of a work group. Second, the model suggests that the social environment provides workers with information about how they should evaluate their jobs and work outcomes.

Doherty and Cantu belong to two different work groups, each of which has three other associates in it. In Doherty's work group, there is one other new associate and two experienced associates who have been with the firm for several years. Rumor has it that the experienced associates are soon to be promoted to the position of managing attorney. From day one, these two associates impressed on Doherty and the other newcomer to the group the valuable experience they would obtain if they did their jobs well. They acknowledged the dullness of the grunt work but made light of it and instead stressed the considerable autonomy the new associates had in conducting their research. These two associates are very satisfied with their jobs and are intrinsically motivated. Interestingly enough, the long hours expected of all the associates never became a topic of conversation in this group. Doherty's social environment emphasizes the importance of the valuable experience he is obtaining from his job, points out the considerable autonomy he has, and suggests that this job provides high levels of intrinsic motivation and job satisfaction.

Cantu's work group is also composed of one other newcomer and two experienced associates who have been with the firm for several years. These two associates, however, do not expect to be promoted, and both are on the job market. They are bitter about their experiences in the law firm and warn Cantu and the other newcomer that they can look forward to being "the personal slaves" of the partners for the next several years. They also complain that most of the work they had to do when they first joined the firm didn't require someone with a law degree and that the long hours were simply inhumane. Given the type of social environment Cantu encountered, his dissatisfaction with his new job and his lack of intrinsic and extrinsic motivation are hardly surprising. If two seasoned veterans evaluate the job so negatively, why should he think any differently?

The different social environments that Doherty and Cantu encounter focus their attention on different aspects of their jobs and work outcomes and also suggest how they should evaluate these factors.

The increasing reliance of organizations on contingent workers has some interesting implications for social environments at work. **Contingent workers** are employees organizations hire or contract with on a temporary basis to fill needs for labor which change over time. Contingent workers have little job security and loyalty towards their organizations because they know their employment is on a temporary, as-needed basis.[21] Contingent workers often face a different social environment on the job than that experienced by regular workers.

Contingent workers
Employees organizations hire or contract with on a temporary basis to fill needs for labor which change over time.

THE ROLE OF PAST BEHAVIORS

The social information processing model proposes another reason why Doherty and Cantu view their similar jobs so differently: Workers' past behaviors have implications for how they view their current jobs and work outcomes. Doherty made considerable sacrifices to get through law school. He worked at night as a waiter to supplement the $60,000 worth of student loans he took out to pay his tuition and living expenses over the three-year period. His hectic schedule made his social life practically nonexistent. Cantu, in contrast, did not have to take out any loans or work to pay for law school. His father, an attorney, always assumed that Cantu would follow in his footsteps. In fact, Cantu was not overjoyed by the prospect of going to law school but couldn't find a decent job with his BA in anthropology. His parents were pleased that he decided to attend Columbia law school and thought nothing of paying the high tuition and living expenses involved.

Because Doherty freely chose to become a lawyer, made a lot of sacrifices to attend law school, and will be paying off his debts from law school for the next several years, his intrinsic motivation is high, and his attitude toward his job is extremely positive. Having such a good job justifies all the sacrifices Doherty has made. Cantu didn't have many options after graduating from college, was pressured by his parents to become a lawyer, and did not have to sacrifice much at all to attend law school. In terms of his past behaviors, Cantu has much less to justify because he didn't have much choice, nor was he required to make many sacrifices.

The social information processing model thus identifies a second factor that affects workers' reactions to the design of their jobs: Workers' past behaviors have implications for their evaluations of their current jobs, their levels of intrinsic motivation, and their levels of job satisfaction, especially when these behaviors are freely chosen and involve certain personal sacrifices.

To sum up, the social information processing model points to the importance of the social environment and past behaviors for an understanding of how workers react to the design of their jobs[22] and helps explain why two workers with the same job and outcomes may have very different levels of motivation and satisfaction. As you might expect, research has found that both the objective features of a job (the job's actual design in terms of the five core dimensions in the job characteristics model) and a worker's social environment and past behavior all interact to affect levels of motivation and satisfaction.[23] Research has found that the social environment is an especially potent source of information when workers with limited information and experience

TO MANAGERS

Social Information Processing Model

- Place newcomers into work groups whose members like their jobs, are intrinsically motivated, and are satisfied.
- Avoid placing newcomers into work groups whose members are disgruntled and dissatisfied.
- When you assign workers to supervise or help train a newcomer, pick workers who are satisfied with and intrinsically motivated by their jobs and who are high performers.

are new to a job or to an organization. Once workers have gained firsthand experience with their jobs, the social environment may play less of a decisive role in molding reactions, and the actual design of the job itself may become more important.

Job Design Models Summarized

Scientific management, job enlargement, job enrichment, the job characteristics model, and the social information processing model—each theory highlights different aspects of job design that are important to consider in understanding work motivation. The main features and motivational focus of each approach are recapped in Table 7.2.

Scientific management advocates job simplification and job specialization, and its key goal is maximizing performance. Scientific management implicitly assumes that extrinsic motivation is the primary determinant of performance and provides no opportunity for intrinsic motivation. Proponents believe workers can be motivated to contribute inputs to their jobs and organizations if pay is closely linked to performance by means of piece-rate pay sys-

TABLE 7.2

Approaches to Job Design

Approach	Main Features	Motivational Focus
Scientific management	Work simplification Specialization Time and motion studies Piece-rate pay	Extrinsic
Job enlargement	Horizontal job loading (increase number of tasks with no increase in difficulty and responsibility)	Intrinsic
Job enrichment	Vertical job loading (increase responsibility and provide worker with opportunities for growth)	Intrinsic

Job characteristics model	Core job dimensions
	  Skill variety
	  Task identity
	  Task significance
	  Autonomy
	  Feedback
	Motivating potential score
	Critical psychological states
	  Experienced meaningfulness of the work
	  Experienced responsibility for work outcomes
	  Knowledge of results
	Work and personal outcomes
	  Intrinsic motivation
	  Job performance
	  Job satisfaction
	  Absenteeism and turnover
		Intrinsic

Social information processing model	Emphasis on social environment (what aspects to consider and how to evaluate a job) Emphasis on implications of past behaviors (on how jobs and outcomes are perceived)	Extrinsic and intrinsic

tems. Jobs designed according to the principles of scientific management tend to be boring, monotonous, and dissatisfying.

Job enlargement and *job enrichment* focus on expanding the simple jobs created by scientific management (enlargement, through horizontal loading; enrichment, through vertical loading) to promote intrinsic motivation.

Building from those early responses to some of the problems of designing jobs according to principles of scientific management, Hackman and Oldham proposed the *job characteristics model,* which specifies the dimensions of jobs that lead to high levels of intrinsic motivation. When workers are intrinsically motivated, they contribute inputs to their jobs because they enjoy the work itself. According to this model, how jobs are designed along five core dimensions can impact intrinsic motivation, job performance, job satisfaction, and absenteeism and turnover.

The *social information processing model* makes the important point that how workers view their jobs and their levels of intrinsic and extrinsic motivation are affected not just by the objective nature of the job but also by the social environment at work and the workers' own past behaviors.

As we mentioned at the beginning of this chapter, the primary aim of the different approaches to job design is to try to ensure that workers are motivated to contribute their inputs (time, effort, knowledge, and skills) to their jobs and organizations. Approaches like scientific management that stress extrinsic motivation advocate designing jobs to be very efficient and closely linking pay and performance. Approaches that stress intrinsic motivation (for example, the job characteristics model) suggest designing jobs in such a way that performing them will be interesting and enjoyable. Regardless of whether the motivational focus is intrinsic, extrinsic, or both, job design affects the level of motivation primarily by influencing the level and amount of inputs that workers contribute to their jobs and organizations.

Goal Setting

Goal
What an individual is trying to accomplish through his or her behavior and actions.

A **goal** is what an individual is trying to accomplish through his or her behavior and actions.[24] Goal-setting theory, like the different approaches to job design, focuses on how to motivate workers to contribute inputs to their jobs (see Fig. 7.1). Goal-setting theory also stresses the importance of ensuring that workers' inputs result in acceptable levels of job performance.

Edwin Locke and Gary Latham, the leading figures in goal-setting theory and research, suggest that the goals workers try to attain at work have a major impact on their levels of motivation and performance. Just as you might have a goal to get an A in this course or to find a good job or a nice apartment, workers have goals that direct their behaviors in organizations. Salespeople at Dillard's department stores, for example, have weekly and monthly sales goals they are expected to reach, and telephone operators have goals for the number of customers they should assist each day. CEOs of organizations such as IBM, Chrysler, and Acme Metal strive to meet growth, profitability, and quality goals.

Goal-setting theory
A theory that focuses on identifying the types of goals that are most effective in producing high levels of motivation and performance and why goals have these effects.

Goal setting is used in organizations not just to influence the level of inputs that workers are motivated to contribute to their jobs and organizations but also to help ensure that inputs are directed toward furthering organizational goals. **Goal-setting theory** explains what types of goals are most effective in producing high levels of motivation and performance and why goals have these effects.

WHAT KINDS OF GOALS LEAD TO HIGH MOTIVATION AND PERFORMANCE?

According to goal-setting theory, there are two major characteristics of goals that, when appearing together, lead to high levels of motivation and performance. One is specificity; the other is difficulty.

Specific goals lead to higher performance than do vague goals or no goals. Specific goals are often quantitative, such as a salesperson's goal of selling $600 worth of merchandise in a week, a telephone operator's goal of assisting twenty callers per hour, or a CEO's goal of increasing monthly and annual revenues by 10 percent. Vague goals are much less precise than specific goals. A vague goal for a salesperson might be "Sell as much as you can." A vague goal for a CEO might be "Increase revenues and quality."

Difficult goals lead to higher motivation and performance than do easy or moderate goals. Difficult goals are goals that are hard (but not impossible) for most workers to reach. Practically all workers can achieve easy goals. Moderate goals can be achieved, on average, by about half of the people working toward the goal.

The major proposition of goal-setting theory is that goals that are both specific and difficult lead to higher motivation and performance than do easy, moderate, vague goals or no goals at all.[25] Results from many research studies conducted in a wide variety of organizations support this proposition. Although most studies have been conducted in the United States, research conducted in Canada, the Caribbean, England, Israel, and Japan suggests that specific, difficult goals lead to high levels of motivation and performance in different cultures as well.[26]

Specific, difficult goals lead to high motivation and performance whether the goals are set by managers for their subordinates, by workers for themselves, or by managers and workers together. When managers set goals for subordinates, it is important that the subordinates accept the goals—that is, agree to try to meet them. It is also important that workers are committed to attaining goals—that is, want to attain them. Sometimes managers and workers may set goals together (a process often referred to as allowing subordinates to *participate* in goal setting) to boost subordinates' acceptance of and commitment to the goals. High self-efficacy also helps ensure that workers will be motivated to try to reach difficult goals. Recall from Chapter 5 that self-efficacy is a person's belief that she or he can successfully perform a behavior. Workers with high self-efficacy believe that they can attain difficult goals, and this belief contributes to their acceptance, commitment, and motivation to achieve those goals. Finally, goal setting seems to work best when workers are given feedback about how they are doing.

WHY DO GOALS AFFECT MOTIVATION AND PERFORMANCE?

Why do specific, difficult goals lead to consistently higher levels of motivation and performance than easy or moderate goals or vague goals such as "Do your best"? There are several reasons, and they are illustrated in the case of Mary Peterson and Allison Rios, who are the division managers of the frozen desserts and frozen vegetables divisions, respectively, of a food-processing company. Both divisions overran their operating budgets the previous year and one of Peterson's and Rios's priorities for the current period is to cut operating expenses. When Peterson and her supervisor, the vice president who oversees the dessert division, met to decide Peterson's goals for the year, they agreed that she should aim to cut operating expenses by 10 percent. Rios met with the vice president of the vegetables division on the same issue, and they decided on a goal of reducing operating expenses by 25 percent. At year end, even though Peterson met her goal of reducing expenses by 10 percent and Rios failed to meet her goal, Rios's performance was still much higher than Peterson's because she had reduced expenses by 23 percent.

Why did Rios's more difficult goal motivate her to perform at a level higher than the level that Peterson felt she herself needed to achieve? First, Rios's difficult goal prompted her to direct more attention toward reducing expenses than Peterson felt she needed to expend. Second, it motivated her to put forth more effort than Peterson felt she had to put forth. Rios spent a lot of time and effort working out ways to reduce expenses; she developed more efficient inventory and product distribution systems and upgraded some of her division's production facilities. Peterson devoted much less attention to reducing expenses and focused exclusively on cutting back inventories. Third, Rios's difficult goal motivated her to create a plan for achieving her goal. The plan outlined the cost savings from each change she was proposing. Peterson, confident that she could reach her goal through improved inventory management, did not do much planning at all. Fourth, Rios's difficult goal made her more persistent than Peterson. Both Rios and Peterson changed their inventory-handling procedures to try to cut costs, and they originally decided to focus on reducing their inventories of both raw materials and finished product. The former, however, was much easier than the latter to cut back. Peterson, confident that she could attain her easy goal, decided to maintain her finished-product inventories as they were and focus solely on reducing the raw-materials inventories. Rios also encountered problems in reducing her finished-product inventory but persisted until she was able to come up with a viable plan to do so.

To sum up, specific, difficult goals affect motivation and performance by:

- Directing workers' attention and action toward goal-relevant activities.
- Causing workers to exert higher levels of effort.
- Causing workers to develop action plans to achieve their goals.
- Causing workers to persist in the face of obstacles or difficulties.[27]

It is important to note that research shows that goal setting affects motivation and performance even when workers are *not* given any extra extrinsic rewards for achieving their goals. Not surprisingly, however, specific, difficult goals tend to have more powerful effects on performance when some financial reward *is* given for goal attainment. Goal setting can operate to enhance both intrinsic motivation (in the absence of any extrinsic rewards) and extrinsic motivation (when workers are given extrinsic rewards for achieving their goals).

Because goals work so well to direct worker attention and effort toward goal attainment, goals may also lead workers to *not* perform activities that are *not* related to the worker's specific goal attainment (recall the discussion of organizational citizenship behavior in Chapter 3) but are important for organizational effectiveness. Research has found, for example, that workers with specific, difficult goals may be less likely to help a coworker who is having a problem because such action might interfere with the achievement of their goals.[28] Helping a coworker takes time and effort that could otherwise be used

Goal Setting

- Be sure that a worker's goals are specific and difficult whether set by you, by the worker, or by both of you.
- Express confidence in your subordinates' abilities to attain their goals, and give subordinates regular feedback on the extent of goal attainment.
- When workers are performing difficult and complex tasks that involve learning, do not set goals until the workers gain some mastery over the task.

to attain goals. A telephone operator who spends time explaining how to use a new electronic directory to a coworker, for example, might fail to meet her own goal of assisting twenty callers per hour because of the fifteen minutes she spent helping her coworker.

LIMITS TO GOAL-SETTING THEORY

Although goal-setting theory has received extensive research support for a variety of jobs and organizations, some recent research suggests that there may be certain limits on the theory's applicability. Research suggests that there are two circumstances under which setting specific, difficult goals will not lead to high motivation and performance:

1. *When workers lack the skills and abilities needed to perform at a high level:* Giving a worker the goal of writing a computer program to calculate production costs will not result in high levels of motivation and performance if the worker does not know how to write computer programs.
2. *When workers are given complicated and difficult tasks that require all of their attention and require a considerable amount of learning:* Good performance on complicated tasks depends on workers being able to direct *all* of their attention to learning the task at hand. When workers are given difficult goals for such tasks, some of their attention will be directed toward trying to attain the goal and away from actually learning about the task. Under these circumstances, assigning a specific, difficult goal actually *reduces* performance.[29] Once the task has been mastered, goal setting will then have its customary effects.

Ruth Kanfer and Philip Ackerman of the University of Minnesota explored the effects of goal setting on the performance of Air Force personnel who were learning the complicated, difficult tasks involved in becoming an air traffic controller.[30] During the early stages of learning this task, assigning goals to the recruits resulted in lower levels of performance because it distracted some of their attention away from learning how to direct air traffic and toward trying to achieve the goal. Once the recruits had developed a certain level of mastery over the task, setting specific, difficult goals did enhance performance.

MANAGEMENT BY OBJECTIVES

Some organizations adopt formal systems to ensure that goal setting actually takes place on a periodic basis. **Management by objectives (MBO)** is a goal-setting process in which a manager meets periodically with the manager who is his or her supervisor to set goals and evaluate the extent to which previously

Management by objectives (MBO)
A goal-setting process in which a manager meets with his or her supervisor to set goals and evaluate the extent to which previously set goals have been achieved.

set goals have been achieved.[31] The objective of MBO is to make sure that all goals that are set contribute to organizational effectiveness. Most MBO programs are usually reserved for managers, but MBO can also be used as a motivational tool for nonmanagers. Although the form and content of MBO programs varies from organization to organization, most MBO programs have three basic steps: goal setting, implementation, and evaluation (see Fig. 7.5).[32]

1. *Goal setting:* The manager and the supervisor meet and jointly determine the goals the manager will try to achieve during a specific period such as the next six or twelve months. In our earlier example, Allison Rios, the division manager for frozen vegetables, met with the vice president to whom she reports, and together they decided that she should work throughout the coming year toward the goal of reducing operating expenses by 25 percent.
2. *Implementation:* The manager is given the autonomy to decide how to meet the goals in the specified time period. Progress toward goal attainment is periodically assessed and discussed by the manager and her or his supervisor. In our example, Rios came up with several ways to cut expenses, including the development of more efficient inventory and product distribution systems and upgrading the production facilities. Rios made and implemented these decisions on her own and periodically met with her supervisor to review how her plans were working.
3. *Evaluation:* At the end of the specified time period, the manager and supervisor again meet to assess the extent of goal attainment, discuss why some goals may not have been attained, and set goals for the next period.

The success of a management by objectives program depends on the appropriateness and difficulty of the goals that are set. Clearly, the goals should focus on key dimensions of a manager's performance such as cutting operating expenses, expanding sales, or increasing the profitability of a division's product line. And, as we've seen, goals should be specific and difficult. Finally, for MBO to work, a certain amount of rapport and trust must exist between managers and their supervisors. A manager who doesn't trust her supervisor, for example, might fear that if some unforeseen, uncontrollable event prohibits her from attaining a difficult goal, the supervisor will penalize her (for example, by not giving a raise). To avoid this situation, the manager may try to set easy MBO goals. Managers and supervisors must be committed to MBO and be willing to take the time and effort needed to make it work.

FIGURE 7.5

Basic Steps in Management by Objectives

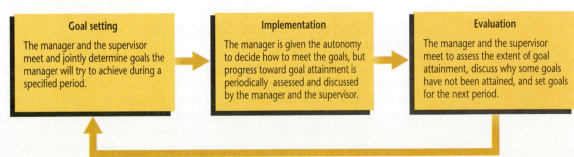

Goal setting	Implementation	Evaluation
The manager and the supervisor meet and jointly determine goals the manager will try to achieve during a specified period.	The manager is given the autonomy to decide how to meet the goals, but progress toward goal attainment is periodically assessed and discussed by the manager and the supervisor.	The manager and the supervisor meet to assess the extent of goal attainment, discuss why some goals have not been attained, and set goals for the next period.

Some organizations use MBO programs to ensure that different parts of the organization work toward the same goal of organizational effectiveness or profitability so that there is no duplication of effort across units. The company-wide goal of maximizing productivity prompted the Upjohn Company to adopt a company-wide MBO program. (See Insight 7.4.)

Insight 7.4

Competitive Advantage

Management by Objectives at the Upjohn Company

The Upjohn Company (www.pharmacia.se/), a major U.S. pharmaceutical corporation, uses MBO at the subunit level (for example, hair growth research) to help direct the activities of subunit managers and gain a competitive advantage. Subunit managers who participate in the program are required to set six- and twelve-month productivity improvement goals for their respective subunits. These goals need to be difficult yet attainable and clearly related to organizational effectiveness. The goals must also be related to the goals of the next higher unit of which the subunit is a part and must not conflict with the goals of any other Upjohn subunits. Once these goals have been established, subunit managers create action plans for achieving them.

Subunit managers also determine how the productivity of their respective units will be assessed. Each subunit manager selects three or four productivity measures that will be used to assess the extent to which the subunit goals have been attained. Although the subunit managers determine which measures are most appropriate, they are required to include a quality measure, a timeliness measure, and a cost measure.[33]

The MBO program at Upjohn helps to keep subunit managers on track by directing their efforts toward increasing productivity and cutting costs—key ingredients for gaining a competitive advantage. The MBO program also helps to ensure that efforts are coordinated across units, for upper-level managers can easily determine whether one subunit's goals conflict with another's.

Goal Setting and Job Design as Motivation Tools

Recall from Chapter 6 that motivating workers to contribute their inputs (which include their time, effort, and skills) to their jobs is a key challenge in an organization. Goal-setting theory suggests that one way to meet this challenge is to set specific, difficult goals. Workers exert more effort for such goals than they do for easy or vague goals, and they are more likely to persist in the face of obstacles. In addition to motivating workers, goals focus worker inputs in the right direction so that the inputs result not only in acceptable levels of job performance but also in the achievement of organizational goals.

Together, job design and goal setting address some of the many questions managers face in the realm of motivation: How can I make my subordinates more interested in doing a good job? What is the best way to assign specific tasks to each of my subordinates? How can I get my subordinates to care about their work? How can I achieve increases in performance and quality necessary for the organization to achieve its goals? In terms of the motivation equation (Inputs $\rightarrow$ Performance $\rightarrow$ Outcomes), job design and goal setting focus primarily on how to motivate workers to contribute their inputs to their jobs and organizations (see Fig. 7.1).

SUMMARY

Job design and goal setting are important tools of motivation. The ways in which jobs are designed and the types of goals that are set can have profound effects on worker motivation and performance and the extent to which an organization is able to achieve its goals. In this chapter, we made the following major points:

1. One of the earliest systematic approaches to job design was scientific management, which stresses job simplification and job specialization. Scientific management focuses on extrinsic motivation and can result in an efficient production process. It also may result in high levels of job dissatisfaction.

2. Job enlargement and job enrichment focus, respectively, on the horizontal and the vertical loading of jobs. Each attempts, by raising levels of intrinsic motivation, to overcome some of the problems that arise when jobs are designed according to the principles of scientific management.

3. The job characteristics model also focuses on intrinsic motivation. The model proposes that five core dimensions (skill variety, task identity, task significance, autonomy, and feedback) lead to three critical psychological states (experienced meaningfulness of the work, experienced responsibility for work outcomes, and knowledge of results) that in turn lead to several outcomes (intrinsic motivation, job performance, job satisfaction, and low absenteeism and turnover). Individual differences (growth-need strength, knowledge and skills, and satisfaction with the work context) affect the key relationships in the model. Research suggests that intrinsic motivation and job satisfaction do tend to result from the core characteristics and psychological states as proposed by the model; however, job performance is not necessarily affected.

4. The social information processing model suggests that the social environment provides workers with information about which aspects of their job design and work outcomes they should pay attention to and how they should evaluate them. This information influences motivation. In addition, workers' past behaviors have implications for how they view their current jobs and current levels of motivation, particularly when these past behaviors were freely chosen or entailed personal sacrifices.

5. Goal-setting theory and research suggests that specific, difficult goals lead to higher motivation and performance than do easy goals, moderate goals, vague goals, or no goals. Specific, difficult goals influence motivation and performance by directing workers' attention toward goal-relevant activities, influencing effort expenditure, influencing levels of persistence, and causing workers to develop action plans. When workers are performing very complicated and difficult tasks that require all of their attention and a considerable amount of learning, specific, difficult goals should not be set until the workers have mastered the tasks.

Organizational Behavior in Action

TOPICS FOR DISCUSSION AND ACTION

1. Why might an organization want to design jobs according to the principles of scientific management?
2. When might workers be dissatisfied with jobs that are enlarged or enriched?
3. Why might some workers not want their jobs enriched?
4. How might a manager redesign the job of a person who delivers newspapers to raise levels of the core job dimensions identified by the job characteristics model?
5. Can principles of scientific management and the job characteristics model both be used to design a job? Explain.
6. Why do individual differences affect the relationships in the job characteristics model?
7. Why does the social environment influence workers' responses to the design of their jobs?
8. What kinds of goals should be set for a supermarket cashier?
9. Why do people try to attain difficult goals?
10. When might specific, difficult goals result in low levels of performance?

BUILDING DIAGNOSTIC SKILLS

Extrinsic and Intrinsic Motivation

Pick two people you know pretty well (such as friends or relatives) who are working. Try to pick one person who is primarily extrinsically motivated by his or her job and another person who is primarily intrinsically motivated (or both intrinsically and extrinsically motivated). Informally meet with each of these people, and ask them about their jobs (especially, what their jobs entail, the social environment at work, and their work goals, if any). Then do the following:

1. Describe each person's job.
2. Is either job designed according to the principles of scientific management? If so, how?
3. Describe each job in terms of the five core dimensions of the job characteristics model.
4. Describe each person in terms of the individual differences in the job characteristics model.
5. How are the people's social environments at work similar? How are they different?
6. Is either person assigned goals? If so, what kinds of goals?
7. What do you think accounts for the extrinsic motivation and the intrinsic motivation of the people you have chosen?

RESEARCH ON THE INTERNET: A MANAGER'S TOOL

Specific Task

3M is one among many companies which strives to design jobs to be intrinsically motivating. Go to 3M's website (www.3m.com) and learn more about this company. Then click on "3M Careers" and then on "Working At 3M."

1. What features does 3M try to incorporate into the design of its jobs?
2. Which kinds of employees do you think would be highly motivated by these jobs?

General Task

Many organizations use specific, difficult goals to motivate their employees to perform at a high level and contribute to the attainment of organizational goals. Find the website of such a company. What goals does this company encourage its employees to achieve? Is it likely that striving to reach these goals would result in intrinsic motivation, extrinsic motivation, or both? How might the achievement of these goals contribute to organizational effectiveness?

TOPICS FOR DEBATE

Job design and goal setting are two major motivation tools that managers can use to increase motivation and performance. Now that you have a good understanding of job design and goal setting, debate the following issues.

Debate One

Team A. Managers should try to avoid designing jobs according to the principles of scientific management whenever possible.

Team B. Designing jobs according to the principles of scientific management can help an organization achieve its goals and should be used whenever appropriate.

Debate Two

Team A. Practically all members of an organization should be given specific, difficult goals to achieve.

Team B. Specific, difficult goals should be given only to certain members of an organization.

EXPERIENTIAL EXERCISE

Increasing Autonomy

Objective

Your objective is to gain experience in redesigning a job to increase worker autonomy.

Procedure

Assume the role of a manager in charge of a group of artists who draw pictures for greeting cards. You currently assign the artists their individual tasks. Each artist is given a particular kind of card to work on (one works on birthday cards for female relatives, one on birthday cards for children, and so on). You inform each artist of the market research that has been done on his or her particular category of cards. You also communicate to each artist your ideas about what you would like to see in the cards he or she creates. The artists then produce sketches based on this information. You review the sketches, make changes, sometimes make the decision to abandon an idea or suggest a new one, and eventually give the artists the go-ahead to proceed with the drawing.

You thought everything was working pretty smoothly until you accidentally overheard one of your subordinates complaining to another that you are stifling his creativity. This exchange brought to mind another troubling incident. One of your artists who had drawn some of the company's best-selling cards quit a few months ago to work for a competitor. You began to wonder whether you have designed the artists' jobs in the best way possible.

You decide to administer the *Job Diagnostic Survey* to your subordinates. They complete it anonymously, and you are truly shocked by the results. Most of your subordinates indicate that their jobs are low on autonomy. Being an artist yourself, you are disturbed by this outcome because you see autonomy as being a necessary ingredient for creativity.

1. Develop an action plan to increase levels of autonomy in the artists' jobs. Although you want to increase autonomy, you also want to make sure that your group creates cards that are responsive to market demands and customer taste.
2. The class divides into groups of from three to five people, and each group appoints one member as spokesperson, to present the group's recommendations to the whole class.
3. Group members take turns describing their own specific action plans for increasing autonomy in the artists' jobs while making sure the cards are responsive to market demands and customer taste.
4. Discuss the pros and cons of the different alternative action plans, and create an action plan that group members think will best increase autonomy while at the same time meeting the organizational goal of creating best-selling cards.

When your group has completed those activities, the spokesperson will present the group's action plan to the whole class.

MAKING THE CONNECTION

Find an example of a company that uses goals to motivate its workers. What kinds of jobs do the workers in this company have? What kinds of goals does the company use?

CLOSING CASE

Motivating Company Presidents at Dover Corporation

Dover Corporation (www.dovercorporation.com) seems to be doing something right when it comes to motivating upper-level managers. Dover Corporation owns over fifty different businesses operating in several different states and foreign countries and has annual revenues of over $4 billion.[34]

Most of the businesses are in the manufacturing sector and produce industrial equipment such as gas pumps and flow meters. Unlike other Fortune 500 companies, Dover has no organization-wide sales, marketing, personnel, or legal departments and no private dining rooms and jets for top managers. Five high-level executives oversee all of Dover's operations. One of Dover's keys to success appears to be how it motivates the presidents of its different businesses.

Those presidents have considerable autonomy in running their individual companies.[35] As former Dover Chairman Gary Roubos indicated, "We don't just let a company president run his own business; we insist he do so—on his own." Roubos went on to suggest that running a Dover business is "the next best thing to owning your own" because company presidents have full responsibility for an entire business.[36] Current Dover CEO Thomas L. Reece put it this way, "We try to stay out of the way."[37]

Dover sets specific, ambitious yearly goals for its company presidents: a 25 percent after-tax return on capital, a 20 percent pretax profit margin, and a 15 percent growth in income. Although some of the businesses fail to reach these difficult goals, company presidents are given clear feedback on how they are doing, and Dover's businesses are generally successful. Each month, quarter, and year, Dover circulates an "honor roll" of the businesses that were successful in achieving at least one of these goals.

At Dover, the pay levels of the company presidents depend on the extent to which they have met each of the three performance goals over the past three years.[38] By basing pay on the past three years' performance, Dover helps to ensure that unforeseen events beyond a president's control (a natural disaster or an economic recession) will not have an inordinate effect on a president's pay. By setting difficult goals, Dover is able to strongly motivate the presidents of its various companies to perform at high levels and make Dover Corporation the success it is.

Questions for Discussion
1. Why does Dover Corporation give its presidents so much autonomy in running their businesses?
2. What effect do the ambitious yearly goals have on the presidents' levels of motivation?

Motivation Tools II: Performance Appraisal, Pay, and Careers

8

A New Career Program at Siemens

When Heinrich von Pierer became CEO of the German electronics giant Siemens (www.siemens.de), the company was in trouble. With over $46 billion of sales from its 350 different divisions and 402,000 employees, Siemens is Germany's equivalent of America's General Electric. In the 1990s, Siemens was suffering greatly from increased global competition from large U.S. and Japanese electronics companies. Over fifty of

its divisions were losing money, and 150 were barely breaking even. Von Pierer's goal was to turn Siemens around so that it could compete effectively in the global marketplace.

On becoming CEO, von Pierer recognized that his major objective would be to change the way things have been done at Siemens. Over time, at Siemens as at American companies such as IBM and General Motors, top managers made all important decisions, and the thousands of middle managers in the organization's hierarchy carried out their directives. As a result, middle managers had little motivation to take risks and do things differently to improve Siemens's performance. Von Pierer recognized that he had to find new tools to motivate Siemens's middle managers—to energize them to find new and better ways for Siemens to achieve its goals and to motivate them to take risks.

As a first step, he created a career program that transformed the company's old practice of forcing talented junior managers to wait years before they could assume responsible middle- or top-management positions. Von Pierer announced that Siemens would select 500 of the company's best junior managers and put them on a fast track to the top. Junior managers in their twenties and thirties were told that if they were selected for the new program *and* if they performed well subsequently, they would be promoted into top-management positions by they time they were 35 to 45. (In the past, top-performing junior managers ordinarily had to wait until they were 50 or 60 years old before being promoted into top management.) Older middle managers were told that new, high performance standards were being adopted and that they would have to meet these tougher standards if they wanted to be promoted into top-management positions. This new career program sent a signal throughout Siemens that major change was on the way.

Selection into the fast-track career program entailed several steps. First, a junior manager had to receive a favorable performance appraisal from his or her boss. At the second step, a handpicked team of highly capable top managers reviewed the performance appraisals of all the highly rated junior managers and selected those whom they judged to be the most talented. At the third step, these junior managers attended a high-powered training camp at Siemens's management training center in Germany's Black Forest. There, in small teams, the junior managers were put through a rigorous testing and evaluation program in which Siemens's top managers and psychologists evaluated candidates on several dimensions, including creativity, knowledge, and leadership ability. Finally, junior managers who performed well and were evaluated positively at the center were selected to be among the 500 fast-track managers.

Junior managers in the new career program are given many challenging tasks and opportunities for growth in their climb to the top. They also have their performance constantly evaluated by top managers and are given frequent feedback on how they are doing. In fact, the performance appraisal process spans the ten years or so it will take for the fast-track managers to reach top-management positions. Fast-track managers also receive substantial rewards for high performance on an ongoing basis. They have been informed that if they receive favorable performance appraisals, their starting salary in the fast-track program could be increased by as much as 30 percent a year. Thus the potential salary increases of top performers in the program over a three-to-five-year period, for example, could be enormous.[1]

The new career program has already had dramatic effects on motivation at Siemens. Junior managers in the program are motivated to be top performers and to find innovative ways to help Siemens compete in the global marketplace. While helping Siemens achieve its goals, these managers also receive valued personal outcomes in the form of high pay, promotions, and successful careers. Because the program is ongoing and more junior managers will be periodically selected for it, those not yet in the program are highly motivated to perform well so that they might be chosen. As these aspiring "fast-trackers" strive to stand out from their coworkers, they also help Siemens achieve its goals of becoming the biggest and most profitable electronics company in the world.[2]

Overview

In addition to job design and goal setting (covered in Chapter 7), managers have other tools to promote motivation and the achievement of organizational goals. In this chapter, we focus on three of these tools: performance appraisal, pay, and careers. Like job design and goal setting, these tools also have the objective of motivating workers to contribute time, effort, creativity, knowledge, and other inputs to their jobs. These tools also ensure that inputs result in acceptable (or high) levels of job performance and the achievement of organizational goals.

Think about how students would feel if an instructor evaluated their performance as follows: Writing an excellent research paper resulted in a C, doing well on an exam did not guarantee an A or a B as a test grade, and students who participated the most in class received only a C for participation. In addition to being angry with the instructor about the unfair treatment they were receiving, students would no longer be motivated to do well in the course because they knew that their performance was not being accurately appraised. Similarly, workers' motivation depends on the accurate appraisal of their performance by their supervisors, as we emphasized in Chapter 6. At Siemens, performance appraisals are used to select junior managers for the fast-track career program, determine their pay raises, and evaluate their progress in the program. In order for Siemens to make the right decisions and motivate junior managers, performance appraisals must be as accurate as possible.

Once performance has been accurately appraised in an organization, the next step to attain and sustain high levels of motivation and performance is to allocate desired outcomes to workers on the basis of their performance. The need to distribute outcomes based on performance was one of the main messages in our discussions of learning in Chapter 5 and motivation in Chapter 6. Two of the outcomes that many workers desire are pay and career opportunities. Siemens uses pay and career opportunities to motivate managers in the fast-track career program and those who are trying to get into it.

In terms of the motivation equation introduced in Chapter 6 and restated in Figure 8.1, performance appraisal focuses on the performance part of the equation, and pay and career opportunities are two of the major outcomes desired by organizational members. By the end of this chapter, you will understand how organizations should appraise and reward their members to encourage high levels of motivation and performance.

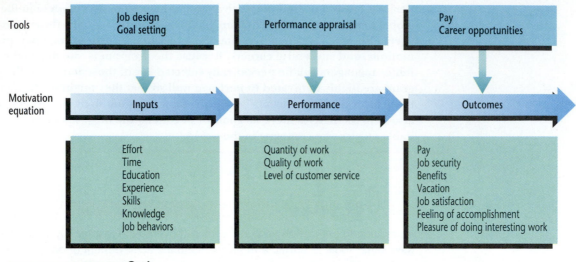

FIGURE 8.1

Motivation Tools

The Role of Performance Appraisal in Motivation

Almost all of the theories and approaches to motivation that we have covered so far assume that managers can accurately *appraise*—that is, evaluate—their subordinates' performance and contributions to their jobs and to the organization. In expectancy theory (see Chapter 6), two of the main determinants of motivation are *expectancy* (the perceived connection between effort and performance) and *instrumentality* (the perceived connection between performance and outcomes such as pay, praise, and career opportunities). Workers are likely to have high levels of expectancy, instrumentality, and thus motivation only if their managers can accurately appraise their performance.

According to equity theory, workers will be motivated to perform at a high level only if they perceive that they are receiving outcomes in proportion to their inputs or contributions to their jobs and to the organization. Accurately appraising performance is necessary for determining workers' contributions. From the perspective of equity theory, then, workers will be motivated to perform at a high level only if their performance can be and is accurately appraised.

Procedural justice theory suggests that the procedures that are used to appraise performance must be perceived as fair in order for motivation to be high. If workers think that managers' appraisals are biased or that irrelevant information is used in evaluating performance, workers' motivation is likely to suffer. More generally, no matter which approach managers use to motivate workers, workers will be motivated to contribute their inputs to the organization and perform at a high level only if they think that their managers can and do appraise their performance accurately.

Because motivation and performance have so great an impact on organizational effectiveness, many researchers have focused on how to appraise performance in organizations. **Performance appraisal** has two overarching goals:

- To encourage high levels of worker motivation and performance.
- To provide accurate information to be used in managerial decision making.[3]

Performance appraisal

Evaluating performance to encourage worker motivation and performance and to provide information to be used in managerial decision making.

These goals are interrelated because one of the principal ways that managers motivate workers is by making decisions about how to distribute outcomes to match different levels of performance.

ENCOURAGING HIGH LEVELS OF MOTIVATION AND PERFORMANCE

As we mentioned above, all the approaches to motivation we discussed in Chapter 6 depend on the accurate assessment of a worker's performance. An accurate appraisal gives workers two important pieces of information: (1) the extent to which they are contributing the appropriate level of inputs to their jobs and to the organization and (2) the extent to which they are focusing their inputs in the right direction on the right set of tasks. Essentially, performance appraisal gives workers *feedback* that contributes to intrinsic motivation.

A positive performance appraisal lets workers know that their current levels of motivation and performance are both adequate and appreciated. In turn, this knowledge makes workers feel valued and competent and motivates them to sustain their current levels of inputs and performance. Many workers consider a good performance appraisal an important outcome or reward in itself.

An inadequate performance appraisal tells workers that their performance is unacceptable and may signal that (1) they are not motivated to contribute sufficient inputs to the job, (2) they cannot contribute certain inputs that are required (perhaps because they lack certain key abilities), or (3) they are misdirecting their inputs, which in and of themselves are at an adequate level.

The case of Susan England, Ramona Michaels, and Marie Nouri, salespeople in the women's clothing department of a large department store, illustrates the important role of performance appraisals in encouraging high levels of motivation and performance. England, Michaels, and Nouri have just met individually with the department supervisor, Ann Rickels, to discuss their latest performance appraisals. The performance of all three sales clerks was assessed along four dimensions: quality of customer service, dollar amount of sales, efficient handling of transactions (for example, processing sales and returns quickly to avoid long lines), and housekeeping (for example, keeping merchandise neat on shelves and racks and returning "try-ons" from the dressing rooms to the racks).

England received a very positive evaluation on all four dimensions. This positive feedback on her performance helps sustain England's motivation because it lets her know that her efforts are appropriate and appreciated.

Michaels received a positive evaluation on the customer service dimension but a negative evaluation on sales, efficiency, and housekeeping. Michaels tried very hard to be a good performer and provided exceptionally high levels of service to the customers she served. Rickels noted, however, that even though her shifts tended to be on the slow side in terms of customer traffic, there was often a long line of customers waiting to be served and a backlog of clothes in the dressing room to be restocked. Rickels judged Michaels's sales performance to be lackluster. She thought the problem might be that Michaels's attempts to help individual customers arrive at purchase decisions were consuming most of her time. Discussions with Michaels confirmed that this was the case. Michaels indicated that she was working as hard as she could, yet she knew that her performance was lacking on three of the four dimensions. She confessed to feeling frustrated that she couldn't get everything done even though she always seemed to be busy. Michaels's negative performance evaluation let her know that she was misdirecting her inputs. The time and effort she was spending to help customers were preventing her from performing her other job duties. Even though Michaels's performance evaluation was negative, it helped sustain her level of motivation (which had always been high) because it showed her how she could become a good performer.

Nouri received a negative evaluation on all four dimensions. Because Nouri was an experienced salesperson who had the necessary skills and abilities, the negative evaluation signaled Nouri and her manager that Nouri's level of motivation was unacceptable and in need of improvement.

PROVIDING INFORMATION FOR DECISION MAKING

As mentioned earlier, the second goal of performance appraisal is to provide information for managerial decision making. Part of Rickels's job as supervisor of the women's clothing department, for example, is training the salespeople in her area and making decisions about pay raises and promotions.

On the basis of the performance appraisals, Rickels decides that England should receive a pay raise and is most deserving of a promotion to the position of senior sales associate. The performance appraisals let Rickels know that Michaels needs some additional training in how to provide an appropriate level of customer service. Finally, Rickels decides to give some counseling to Nouri because of the negative evaluation of her performance. Rickels knows that Nouri is looking for another job and doesn't expect to remain with the department store for long. Rickels lets Nouri know that as long as she remains in the department, she must perform at an acceptable level to receive the outcomes she desires—pay, not having to work in the evenings, and good working relationships with the other members of the department.

In this example, performance appraisal is used to decide how to distribute outcomes like pay and promotions equitably and how to improve the performance of workers who are not performing as highly as they should be. Performance appraisal can also be useful for other aspects of decision making. For example, information from performance appraisal may allow managers to more effectively use the talents of organizational members, group people into high-performing work teams, and assign specific tasks to individual workers. Performance appraisals also can alert managers to problems in job design or shortcomings in an organization's approach to motivation and the distribution of outcomes.

Finally, performance appraisal provides workers and supervisors with information for career planning. By helping managers identify a worker's strengths and weaknesses, performance appraisal sets the scene for meaningful discussions about the appropriateness of a worker's career aspirations and about how a worker can best progress toward those career goals. Performance appraisal may also signal areas in which workers need to improve and skills they may need to develop to meet their career goals. Siemens in the opening case uses performance appraisals to select junior managers for its fast-track career program and to evaluate the progress of those selected.

DEVELOPING A PERFORMANCE APPRAISAL SYSTEM

Managers can use the information gained from performance appraisal for two main purposes:

- *Developmental purposes* such as determining how to motivate a worker to perform at a high level, evaluating which of a worker's weaknesses can be corrected by additional training, and helping a worker formulate appropriate career goals.
- *Evaluative, decision-making purposes* such as deciding whom to promote, how to set pay levels, and how to assign tasks to individual workers.

Regardless of which purpose is most important to a manager, there are a number of choices that managers need to make in developing an effective performance appraisal system. In this section, we discuss four of these choices: the extent to which formal and informal appraisals are to be used, what factors are to be evaluated, what methods of appraisal are to be used, and who is to appraise performance (Fig. 8.2).

Choice 1: The Mix of Formal and Informal Appraisals. When a performance appraisal is formal, the performance dimensions and the way workers are evaluated on them are determined in advance. IBM, GE, Siemens, and most other large organizations use formal appraisals, which are usually conducted on a fixed schedule (such as every six months or once a year).[4] In a meeting between the worker whose performance is being appraised and the person doing the evaluating, the worker is given feedback on his or her performance. Feedback contributes to intrinsic motivation.

Sometimes workers want feedback on a more frequent basis than that provided by the formal system. Similarly, managers often want to use performance feedback to motivate subordinates on a day-to-day basis. If a worker is performing poorly, for example, a manager might not want to wait until the next six- or twelve-month performance review to try to rectify the problem. In these situations, an informal performance appraisal, in which managers and subordinates meet informally to discuss ongoing progress, can meet the needs of both workers and managers. Informal appraisals vary in form and content and range from a supervisor commending a worker for doing an outstanding job on a project to criticizing a worker for slacking off and missing a deadline.

FIGURE 8.2

Choices in Developing an Effective Performance Appraisal System

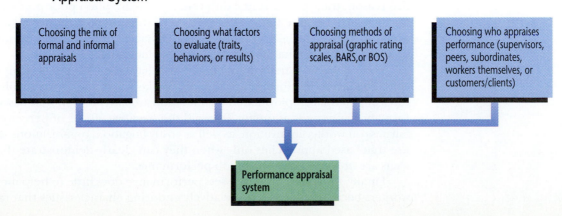

| Choosing the mix of formal and informal appraisals | Choosing what factors to evaluate (traits, behaviors, or results) | Choosing methods of appraisal (graphic rating scales, BARS, or BOS) | Choosing who appraises performance (supervisors, peers, subordinates, workers themselves, or customers/clients) |

Performance appraisal system

Informal performance appraisals are beneficial. Because they often take place right after desired or undesired behaviors occur, workers immediately have a good idea of what they are doing right or wrong. As you learned in Chapter 5, workers will learn to perform desired behaviors and learn not to perform undesired behaviors only when it is clear to them that consequences such as praise (for a desired behavior) or a reprimand (for an undesired behavior) result from performing the behavior in question. The smaller an organization is, the more likely it is to rely exclusively on informal performance appraisals.

Ideally, an organization should rely on both formal and informal performance appraisals to motivate its members to perform at a high level and to make good decisions. The formal appraisal ensures that performance gets assessed periodically along the dimensions important to an organization. Because many managers and workers believe that formal performance appraisals should not yield any "surprises," however, ongoing informal appraisals should be part of an organization's performance appraisal system. A worker who is performing poorly should not have to wait six months or a year to find out; likewise, good performers should be told that they are on the right track, as at Siemens in the opening case. Informal performance appraisals are important for motivation and performance on a day-to-day basis because they identify and rectify problems as they arise. Although managers in small organizations may not want to spend time and money on the development of a formal system and managers of large organizations may spend less time than they should appraising performance informally, in most cases the motivational benefits of using formal and informal appraisals outweigh the costs.

Choice 2: What Factors to Evaluate.   In addition to varying in degree of formality, performance appraisals can also vary in content. Traits, behaviors, and results are the three basic types of information that can be assessed.[5]

When traits are used to assess performance, personal characteristics (such as personality, skills, or abilities) that are deemed relevant to job performance are evaluated. A division manager of a large corporation may be evaluated on personal initiative, farsightedness, and the ability to identify and promote managerial talent. A hotel reservations clerk may be evaluated on patience, politeness, and the ability to keep calm when under pressure.

Using traits to assess performance has several disadvantages. First, recall from Chapter 2 that the *interaction* of individual differences such as personality traits or abilities and situational influences usually determines behavior. For this reason, traits or individual differences *alone* are often poor predictors of performance because the possible effects of the situation are not taken into account. Traits may be good indicators of what a worker is like but not very good indicators of what the worker actually does on the job.

Second, because traits do not necessarily have clear-cut relationships with actual behaviors performed on the job, workers and law courts involved in cases of potential employment discrimination are likely to view trait-based performance appraisals as unfair. To avoid the negative effects of perceived unfairness on worker motivation, as well as costly litigation, organizations should use trait-based approaches only when they can clearly demonstrate that the traits are *accurate* indicators of job performance.

Finally, the use of traits to assess performance does little to help motivate workers because it focuses on relatively enduring characteristics that cannot be changed in the short term, if at all. For example, telling a division manager that she lacks initiative or a hotel reservations clerk that he is impatient does not give either worker much of a clue about how to do the job differently.

When *behaviors* are used to appraise performance, the focus is on the actual behaviors or actions a worker displays on the job: What a worker does is appraised, not what the worker is like. A division manager's behavior might be appraised in terms of the extent to which she has launched successful new products and scrapped unprofitable existing products. A hotel reservations clerk might be assessed on the extent to which he gathers all the information needed to make accurate reservations that accommodate guests' requests and the extent to which he satisfactorily explains unmet requests to guests.

Relying on behaviors to assess performance is especially useful when how workers perform their jobs is important, because it lets them know what they should do differently on the job. For example, telling a hotel reservations clerk that he should explain why a certain request can't be met and should answer guests' questions calmly and clearly regardless of how many people are in line waiting to check in gives the clerk a lot more direction than simply telling him he needs to be more patient, polite, and calm.

One potential problem with relying on behaviors to assess performance is that sometimes the *same* level of performance can be achieved through *different* behaviors. For example, two managers may be equally effective at launching new products and scrapping unprofitable ones even though one reaches decisions through careful, long-term research and deliberation while the other relies more on gut instincts. To overcome this problem, performance appraisals sometimes focus on the results of behaviors rather than on the behaviors themselves.

When *results* are used to appraise performance, the focus is not on what workers do on the job but on the *effects* of their behaviors or their actual output. The performance of a hotel clerk might be assessed in terms of the number of reservations handled per day and on guests' satisfaction ratings with their check-in experience. Recall from Chapter 7 that at the Dover Corporation, the performance of company presidents is assessed by their companies' performance on three dimensions: return on capital, pretax profit margins, and growth in income. When there are many ways to achieve the same results and which avenue a worker chooses is not important, results can be a useful way of assessing performance.

As with the other two approaches, however, using results alone to assess performance has disadvantages. Sometimes results are not under a worker's control: A division's profitability might suffer because sales were lost when foreign trade regulations changed unexpectedly. A day's worth of reservations might be lost because of a computer malfunction. Workers may also become so results oriented that they become pressured into unethical practices such as overcharging customers or failing to perform important organizational citizenship behaviors such as helping coworkers. Recall that mechanics at Sears Tire & Auto Centers were so results oriented because of Sears's push to increase sales and profits in the early 1990s that they made unnecessary repairs to customers' cars (see Insight 5.2).

Sometimes, organizations can use both behaviors and results to appraise workers' performance, as in the case of USAA, the large insurer. (See Insight 8.1.)

Insight 8.1

Competitive Advantage

USAA Appraises Both Behaviors and Results

In an effort to increase performance levels of white-collar employees and gain a competitive advantage, many companies are developing new and improved ways of appraising performance. Some of these appraisal systems combine the assessment of behaviors and results. For example, USAA, an insurance and investment management firm, has developed a performance appraisal system called the Family of Measures (FOM) to assess the performance of each of its 14,000 employees on a monthly basis.

The FOM focuses on quantity of performance, quality of performance, timeliness, and customer service because these are key goals for most USAA workers. To assess individual performance, managers develop specific measures related to these objectives for each job in the company. Some of the measures assess results; others assess behaviors. In the telephone sales department, for example, representatives are evaluated in terms of two *results* measures (number of policies sold and accuracy of price quotes) and two *behavior* measures (amount of time spent on paperwork and politeness to customers on the telephone).

Supervisors use individual employee FOM scores to determine promotions and bonuses. When appropriate, individual FOM scores are combined into team scores, as in the case of a group of sales representatives who work together. Each team is given a name (for example, "Success Express" and "Top Guns"), and the FOM scores for the team are computed on a monthly basis. Teams performing exceptionally well in any given month receive public recognition in USAA.[6]

USAA is a very successful company, and part of its competitive advantage is probably attributable to its state-of-the art FOM performance appraisal system, which motivates employees to perform at high levels.

As USAA's experience suggests, it is a good idea to appraise both behavior and results when both dimensions of performance are important for organizational effectiveness. In most sales jobs, for example, the results of a salesperson's behavior (number of items sold) are crucial, but the kinds of behaviors employed (treating customers courteously and politely and processing transactions efficiently) are often equally important. Because traits generally have less direct bearing on performance in many kinds of jobs, they are not as useful in performance appraisal.

Choice 3: Methods of Appraisal. Regardless of the approach to performance appraisal (formal or informal) and the types of information assessed (traits, behaviors, or results), the measures managers use to appraise performance can be of two types: objective or subjective. **Objective measures** such as numerical counts are based on facts. They are used primarily when results are

Objective measures
Measures that are based on facts.

the focus of performance appraisal. The number of televisions a factory worker assembles in a day, the dollar value of the sales a salesperson makes in a week, the number of patients a physician treats in a day, and the return on capital, profit margin, and growth in income of a business are all objective measures of performance.

Subjective measures are based on individuals' perceptions, and can be used for appraisals based on traits, behaviors, and results. Because subjective measures are based on perceptions, they are vulnerable to many of the biases and problems that can distort person perception (discussed in Chapter 4). Because there is no alternative to the use of subjective measures for many jobs, researchers and managers have focused considerable attention on the best way to construct subjective measures of performance.

Typically, when subjective measures are used, managers identify specific dimensions of performance (traits, behaviors, or results) that are important in a job. Then they develop some kind of rating scale or measure to assess an individual's standing on each dimension. Various rating scales can be used. Three of the most popular types are graphic rating scales, behaviorally anchored rating scales, and behavioral observation scales (see Fig. 8.3). Graphic rating scales can be used to assess traits, behaviors, or results. Behaviorally anchored rating scales and behavioral observation scales focus exclusively on behaviors.

When a **graphic rating scale** is used, the rater—the person responsible for the performance appraisal—assesses the performance of a worker along one

Subjective measures
Measures that are based on individual perceptions.

Graphic rating scale
A subjective measure on which performance is evaluated along a continuum.

FIGURE 8.3

Examples of Subjective Measures of Performance

A. Graphic rating scale

How courteous is this salesperson toward customers?

●	●	●	●	●
Very discourteous	Discourteous	Neither discourteous nor courteous	Courteous	Very courteous

B. Behaviorally anchored rating scale

1	2	3	4	5	6	7
Ignores customers who need help	Keeps customers waiting unnecessarily	Fails to thank customers for purchases	Answers customers' questions promptly	Completes transactions in a timely manner	Greets customers pleasantly and offers assistance	Always tries sincerely to help customers locate items to suit their needs

C. Behavioral observation scale

	Almost never				Almost always
Sincerely thanks customers for purchases	1	2	3	4	5
Pleasantly greets customers	1	2	3	4	5
Answers customers' questions promptly	1	2	3	4	5

or more continua with clearly specified intervals. As indicated in Figure 8.3(a), for example, level of customer service may be assessed by rating a salesperson in terms of how courteous she or he is to customers on a five-point scale ranging from "very discourteous" to "very courteous." Graphic rating scales are popular in organizations because they are relatively easy to construct and use.[7] One potential disadvantage of these scales is that different raters may disagree about the meaning of the scale points. For example, what is "very discourteous" behavior to one rater may be only "discourteous" to another.

A **behaviorally anchored rating scale (BARS)** attempts to overcome that problem by careful definition of what each scale point means. Examples of specific work-related behaviors correspond to each scale point.[8] Figure 8.3(b) is an example of a BARS for rating the performance of a salesperson on the dimension of courtesy to customers. One potential problem with behaviorally anchored rating scales is that sometimes workers exhibit behaviors corresponding to more than one point on the scale. For example, a salesperson may thank customers for their purchases but otherwise tend to ignore them. A BARS can also take a considerable amount of time and effort to develop and use.

A **behavioral observation scale (BOS)** overcomes the BARS problem of workers exhibiting behaviors corresponding to more than one scale point by not only describing specific behaviors (as does a BARS) but also asking raters to indicate the frequency with which a worker performs the behaviors, as shown in Figure 8.3(c).[9] A BOS, however, tends to be even more time-consuming than a BARS for raters to complete.

These are just a few of the types of scales that are available for subjective appraisals of performance. As we indicated, each scale has its advantages and disadvantages, and it is not clear at this point that any one type is better to use than another. The BARS and BOS can be a lot more time-consuming to develop and use than graphic rating scales, but they can be more beneficial for giving feedback to workers because they appraise more precise behaviors.

Choice 4: Who Appraises Performance?   We have been assuming that supervisors are the people who appraise their subordinates' performance. This is usually a fair assumption. In most organizational settings, supervisors are responsible for performance appraisal because they are generally the most familiar with their subordinates' behavior and are responsible for motivating subordinates to perform at acceptable levels. Sometimes, however, self-appraisals, peer appraisals, subordinate appraisals, customer/client appraisals, and multiple raters are also used to appraise performance.

Self-appraisal may offer some advantages, because a worker is likely to be familiar with his or her own level of performance. But most people consider themselves to be above average, and no one likes to think of himself or herself as a poor performer, so a self-appraisal is likely to be inflated.

Peer appraisals are appraisals given by a worker's coworkers. Peers are often very familiar with performance levels, yet they may be reluctant to provide accurate appraisals. A worker may not want to give his friend a poor rating. A worker may not want to give her coworker too good a rating if she thinks this rating will make her look bad in comparison. Nevertheless, peer ratings can be useful, especially when workers are members of teams and team performance depends on each member being motivated to perform at a high level. Under these circumstances, team members are motivated to provide accurate peer ratings because the whole team suffers if one member performs poorly. By accu-

---

◗ Behaviorally anchored rating scale (BARS)
A subjective measure on which specific work-related behaviors are evaluated.

◗ Behavioral observation scale (BOS)
A subjective measure on which the frequency with which a worker performs a behavior is indicated.

rately appraising each other's performance, team members can help motivate each other to perform well and can make sure that all members do their share of the work. It is for this reason that many professors who assign group projects have group members appraise each other's performance on contributing to the final project. Peer ratings help to ensure that no group members get a "free ride" and take advantage of hard-working students in the group.

Subordinate appraisals are appraisals given to a manager by the people he or she supervises. Subordinates rate the manager on, for example, leadership behaviors. In order for subordinates to feel free to give an accurate appraisal (especially a negative one), it is often desirable for the appraisals to be anonymous so that subordinates need not fear retaliation from their supervisors. Many universities use anonymous student evaluations to appraise the quality of instructors' classroom teaching.

Customer/client appraisals are another source of performance information. Recall from Chapter 5 that some health maintenance organizations such as U.S. Healthcare and AvMed–Sante Fe evaluate their physicians' performance, in part, on the basis of scores they receive on patient surveys. These surveys measure whether doctors are available for emergencies, provide clear explanations of treatments, and show concern for patients' needs.

The advantage of using these other sources of information is that each source may be familiar with important aspects of a worker's performance. But because each source has considerable disadvantages if used exclusively, some organizations rely on 360-degree appraisals. In a **360-degree appraisal,** a worker's performance is evaluated by a variety of people who are in a position to evaluate it. A 360-degree appraisal of a manager, for example, may include evaluations made by peers, subordinates, superiors, and clients or customers who are familiar with the manager's performance. The manager would then receive feedback based on evaluations from each of these sources. When 360-degree appraisals are used, managers have to be careful that each evaluator

360-degree appraisal
A performance appraisal in which a worker's performance is evaluated by a number of people who are in a position to evaluate the worker's performance such as peers, superiors, subordinates, and customers or clients.

TO MANAGERS

is familiar with the performance of the individual he or she is evaluating. While 360-degree appraisals can be used for many different kinds of workers, they are most commonly used for managers. (See the closing case for more information on 360-degree appraisals.)

POTENTIAL PROBLEMS IN SUBJECTIVE PERFORMANCE APPRAISAL

Recall from Chapter 4 that a number of problems and biases can result in inaccurate perceptions of other people in an organization. These problems and biases (recapped in Table 8.1) can be particularly troublesome for subjective performance appraisals. Awareness of these perception problems

TABLE 8.1

Problems and Biases in Person Perception That May Result in Inaccurate Performance Appraisals

Problem or Bias	Description	Example of Problem or Bias Leading to an Inaccurate Performance Appraisal
Stereotypes	A type of schema (abstract knowledge structure stored in memory) built around some distinguishing, often highly visible characteristic such as race, gender, or age.	A 35-year-old supervisor gives a 60-year-old engineer a negative performance appraisal that indicates that the engineer is slow and unwilling to learn new techniques although this is not true.
Primacy effect	The initial pieces of information that people have about a person have an inordinately large effect on how that person is perceived.	A subordinate who made a good first impression on his supervisor receives a better performance appraisal than he deserves.
Contrast effect	People's perceptions of a person are influenced by their perception of others in an organization.	A subordinate's average level of performance is appraised more harshly than it should be by her supervisor because all the subordinate's coworkers are top performers.
Halo effect	People's general impressions of a person influence their perceptions on specific dimensions.	A subordinate who has made a good overall impression on a supervisor is appraised as performing high-quality work and always meeting deadlines although this is not true.
Similar-to-me effect	People perceive others who are similar to themselves more positively than they perceive those who are dissimilar.	A supervisor gives a subordinate who is similar to her a more positive performance appraisal than the subordinate deserves.
Harshness, leniency, and average tendency biases	When rating their subordinates' performance, some supervisors tend to be overly harsh, some overly lenient. Others tend to rate everyone as about average.	An exceptionally high-performing secretary receives a mediocre performance appraisal because his supervisor is overly harsh in rating everyone.
Knowledge-of-predictor bias	Perceptions of a person are influenced by knowing the person's standing on a predictor of performance.	A computer programmer who scored highly on cognitive and numerical ability tests used to hire programmers in an organization receives a more positive performance appraisal than she deserves.

can help to prevent them from leading to an inaccurate appraisal of some-one's performance.

Pay as a Motivation Tool

The accurate assessment of performance is central to the goals of motivating workers to perform at acceptable levels and improving the effectiveness of managerial decision making. One area of decision making that often has profound effects on the motivation of all members of an organization, managers and workers alike, is the distribution of outcomes—pay, benefits, vacations, perks, promotions and other career opportunities, job titles, offices, and privileges. In this section we focus on the outcome that is one of the most powerful of all motivation tools: pay. Pay can be used not only to motivate people to perform highly but also to motivate them to join and remain with an organization. At Siemens in the opening case, pay is used to motivate fast-track managers to do well in the new career program.

The principles of operant conditioning discussed in Chapter 5 and all approaches to motivation covered in Chapter 6 suggest that outcomes should be distributed to workers *contingent* on their performing desired organizational behaviors:

- Operant conditioning theory suggests that to encourage the learning of desired organizational behaviors, positive reinforcers or rewards should be distributed to workers contingent on performance.
- Need theory suggests that when pay is contingent on performance, workers are motivated to perform because performance will help satisfy their needs.
- Expectancy theory takes into account that pay is an outcome that has high valence (is highly desirable) for most workers and that instrumentality (the association between performance and outcomes) must be high for motivation to be high.
- Equity theory indicates that outcomes (pay) should be distributed in proportion to inputs (performance).
- Procedural justice theory suggests that the methods used to evaluate performance and distribute pay need to be fair.

From a learning and motivational perspective, the message is clear: Whenever possible, pay should be based on performance.[10]

MERIT PAY PLANS

Merit pay plan
A plan that bases pay on performance.

A plan that bases pay on performance is often called a **merit pay plan.** When pay is not based on merit, it might be based on the particular job a worker has in an organization (all workers who have this job receive the same pay) or on a worker's tenure in the organization (workers who have been with the organization for a longer period of time earn more money). Merit pay, however, is likely to be much more motivational than pay that is not based on performance.

Merit pay plans tend to be used most heavily at the upper levels in organizations (as in the case of company presidents at the Dover Corporation),[11] but basing pay on performance has been shown to be effective for workers at lower levels in an organization's hierarchy. The experience of New Balance in motivating its workforce illustrates this point. (See Insight 8.2.)

Insight 8.2   **A Global View**

Merit Pay at New Balance and Around the World

Many manufacturers of athletic shoes, including Nike, have moved most of their production facilities overseas because of low input costs in other countries and because of production quality problems in the United States. New Balance Inc. (newbalance.com), with U.S. sales of approximately $135 million,[12] has bucked this trend and not only manufactures most of its shoes in the United States but also locates some of its factories in inner cities from which other manufacturers have fled. One such city is Lawrence, Massachusetts, a former factory town with high levels of poverty and unemployment. New Balance's Lawrence factory employs 180 workers and is located in a part of town in which abandoned buildings have been the frequent targets of arsonists and people are afraid to walk or to park their cars because of the crime problem.

The odds certainly seem to be against New Balance having a successful factory in such a setting, yet James Davis, chairman of New Balance, claims that the workers at the Lawrence factory are twice as productive as their counterparts overseas. What is New Balance's secret? At least part of the organization's success lies in the merit pay plan it has adopted to help motivate factory workers.

At New Balance, pay is based on the number of defect-free athletic shoes workers produce. Approximately 70 percent of the workers' pay depends on the quality of the shoes they produce, so the system has been very successful in promoting product quality. New Balance also devotes considerable resources to training. The training helps workers develop skills to improve product quality. Proper training combined with an effective merit pay plan helps New Balance manufacture high-quality shoes at competitive costs while at the same time giving jobs to workers who really need them.[13]

Merit pay is not an important motivation tool only in the United States. It is being used with increasing frequency in many other countries. In 1979, only 8 percent of companies in Great Britain used some form of merit pay, but in 1994, 75 percent of British companies used merit pay to motivate their members. On average, 40 percent of an upper manager's pay in Britain is based on performance. Merit pay is also increasing in popularity in Japan. Honda, for example, based 40 percent of its managers' pay on performance in 1992, and in 1994 their pay totally depended on their performance levels. Similarly, at Nissan, 85 percent of managers' salaries is based on their performance levels. Merit pay also is increasing in popularity in Germany, and even the pay of some European government workers or civil servants (such as those in Britain) is based in part on their performance levels.[14]

SHOULD MERIT PAY BE BASED ON INDIVIDUAL, GROUP, OR ORGANIZATIONAL PERFORMANCE?

One of the most important choices managers face in designing an effective merit pay plan is whether to base merit pay on individual, group, or organizational performance. The following guidelines, based on the theories of learning and motivation discussed in previous chapters, can be used to make this choice:

1. When individual performance can be accurately assessed (for example, the number of cars a salesperson sells, the number of insurance policies an insurance agent writes, a lawyer's billable hours), the maximum motivational impact is obtained from basing pay on individual performance.[15]

2. When workers are highly interdependent—when what one worker does affects the work of others—and individual performance levels cannot be accurately assessed, an individual-based pay-for-performance plan is not a viable option. In this case, managers can implement a group or organization-level pay-for-performance plan in which workers' pay levels depend on how well their group or the organization as a whole performs. It is impossible, for example, to accurately assess the performance of individual members of a group of carpenters who jointly design and construct large, elaborate pieces of custom furniture. Together they produce pieces of furniture that none of them could construct alone.

3. When organizational effectiveness depends on individuals working together, cooperating with each other, and helping each other out, group- or organization-based pay-for-performance plans may be more appropriate than individual-based plans.[16] When a team of research scientists works together in a laboratory to try to come up with a cure for a disease such as AIDS, for example, it is essential for group members to share their insights and findings with each other and to be able to build off each other's findings.

American Express CEO Harvey Golub applied these principles in his efforts to improve the performance of division managers in the company's flagship credit card unit. (See Insight 8.3.)

Insight 8.3

Pay

Using Pay to Encourage Teamwork at American Express

When Harvey Golub became president of American Express (www.americanexpress.com) and CEO of its credit card unit, American Express Travel Related Services Co. (TRS), he faced an intimidating task. TRS had experienced some tough times due to competition from lower-fee bank cards, merchants who had balked at AmEx's relatively high fees, and fleeing customers. Although Golub had a strategy for improving TRS performance, he admitted that he was not certain what the new TRS would actually look like.[17]

Golub has made many changes at TRS.[18] One key realization he has had is that more cooperation is needed among managers in the green, gold, platinum, and corporate card divisions. In the past, these divisions operated like individual businesses, and upper-level managers' pay (in the form of bonuses) was based on their own division's performance. To change the orientation of the division managers and get them to work together as a team for the good of TRS, Golub changed the pay structure of division managers. Their bonuses are no longer based on division profitability but rather are based on the profitability of TRS as a whole.19 This change has motivated the division managers to cooperate with each other to improve TRS performance.

Sometimes it is possible to combine elements of an individual and group or company-wide plan to get the benefits of both. Lincoln Electric, for example, uses a combination individual- and organization-based plan.[20] Each year Lincoln Electric establishes a bonus fund, the size of which depends on the whole organization's performance that year. Money from the bonus fund is distributed to workers on the basis of their individual levels of performance. Lincoln Electric workers are motivated to cooperate and help each other because when the firm as a whole performs well, everybody benefits by receiving a larger bonus at year-end. Workers are also motivated to perform at a high level individually because their individual performance determines their share of the fund.

SHOULD MERIT PAY BE IN THE FORM OF A SALARY INCREASE OR A BONUS?

There are two major ways to distribute merit pay: salary increases and bonuses. When salary increases are used, individual salaries are increased by a certain amount based on performance. When bonuses are used, individuals receive a lump-sum amount (in addition to their regular salary) based on performance. Bonus plans such as the one used by Lincoln Electric tend to have a greater impact on motivation than do salary increase plans, for three reasons.

First, an individual's current salary level is based on performance levels, cost-of-living increases, and so on from the day the person started working in the organization; thus the absolute level of one's salary is based largely on factors not related to current performance. Increases in salary levels based on current performance tend to be small (for example, 6 percent) in comparison to the total amount of the salary. Second, current salary increases may be only partially based on performance, such as when across-the-board cost-of-living raises or market adjustments are given to all workers. Third, organizations rarely cut salaries, so salary levels across workers tend to vary less than do performance levels. Bonus plans overcome some of the limitations of salary increases because a bonus can be tied directly and exclusively to performance and because the motivational effect of a bonus is not diluted by the other factors mentioned above. Bonuses can vary considerably from time period to time period and from worker to worker, depending on performance levels.[21]

EXAMPLES OF MERIT PAY PLANS

Two clear examples of individual-based merit pay plans are piece-rate pay and commission pay. In a *piece-rate pay plan,* a worker is paid for each unit he or she produces, as in the cases of a tailor who is paid for each piece of clothing he sews or alters or a factory worker who is paid for each television she assembles. With commission pay, often used in sales positions, salaries are a percentage of sales. Salary levels in *full commission plans* fluctuate directly in proportion to sales that are made. Salespeople in a *partial commission plan* receive a fixed salary plus an amount that varies with sales. The maximum motivational impact is obtained when pay is based solely on performance, as in a full commission plan. Workers operating under such a plan, however, are not likely to develop any kind of team spirit. (See Insight 8.4.)

Insight 8.4

Pay

High Sales, High Pay, But Low Camaraderie at Re/Max

Since it was founded approximately twenty years ago by David Liniger, Re/Max International Inc. (www.remax.com) has grown to become one of the largest real estate brokerage firms in the United States. Liniger opened the first Re/Max office in 1973, and the firm now boasts 1,800. Of its competitors, only Century 21 boasts a bigger sales volume, but Re/Max agents' average annual sales are approximately $2.6 million, considerably higher than the $1 million sold on average by Century 21 agents. In the real estate industry, Re/Max is a force to be contended with.

What sets Re/Max apart from its competitors is its unique pay plan for real estate agents. Most real estate firms use a partial commission plan to pay their agents: Agents receive a salary and split their commissions (which are typically around 6 percent) with the firm. Re/Max uses a full commission plan: Agents receive no salary, keep their entire commission for themselves, and pay Re/Max approximately $18,000 a year to cover the firm's expenses. At Re/Max, pay is based solely on performance; at Century 21 and other firms, it is only partially based on performance. Re/Max's pay plan is effective in motivating agents to sell real estate because they essentially receive all of the benefits from their sales. Moreover, the potential for higher earnings with Re/Max has enabled Re/Max to attract some of the best agents in the country away from competing firms.[22]

Some agents, however, do not thrive under the Re/Max system, which generates a very individualized approach to selling real estate. Each agent is out to maximize his or her own sales, and there is little camaraderie or team spirit among agents working out of the same office. Some agents compare working out of a Re/Max office to working in a shark tank. Other agents are not pleased about having to pay the $18,000 annual fee regardless of the state of the economy and the local real estate market.[23] In any case, Re/Max's unique pay plan has contributed to its having one of the most productive real estate sales forces in the industry.

Clearly, when pay is based solely on individual performance, as at Re/Max, workers are motivated to perform at a high level, and organizations may be able to attract and retain top performers because they will receive maximum levels of pay. But such plans can result in workers adopting a highly individualized approach to their jobs and failing to take the time or effort to work together as a team.

Pay plans that are linked strictly to organizational performance are often called *gain-sharing plans*. Workers in organizations that have these kinds of plans are given a certain share of the profits that the organization makes or a certain share of the expenses that are saved during a specified time period. Gain sharing is likely to encourage camaraderie and a team spirit among workers because all organizational members stand to benefit if the organization does well. However, because pay is based on organizational rather than on individual performance, each individual may not be so motivated to perform at the high level he or she would have achieved under a pay plan based on individual merit.

One kind of gain-sharing plan is the *Scanlon plan*, developed by Joseph Scanlon, a union leader at a steel and tin plant, in the 1920s.[24] This plan focuses on reducing costs. Departmental and organization-wide committees are established to evaluate and implement cost-saving suggestions provided by workers. Workers are motivated to make suggestions, participate on the committees, and help implement the suggestions because a portion of the cost savings realized is distributed back to all workers.

Another kind of gain-sharing pay plan is *profit sharing*. Workers participating in profit-sharing plans receive a certain share of an organization's profits. Approximately 16 percent of workers in medium and large companies and 25 percent of workers in small firms receive some form of profit sharing. Rutgers University economist Douglas Kruse estimates that productivity tends to increase from 3 to 5 percent when companies institute profit sharing. Profit-sharing plans that give workers their share of profits in cash tend to be more successful than programs that use some sort of deferred payment (such as contributing workers' shares of profits to their retirement funds).[25] If an organization has a bad year, then no money may be available for profit sharing regardless of individual or group performance levels.

THE ETHICS OF PAY DIFFERENTIALS AND COMPARABLE WORTH

It is well established that women earn less money than men. Women earn approximately 74 cents for every dollar earned by men.[26] Some of the gender gap in rates of pay may be due to overt discrimination (women with qualifications and performance levels equal to those of men being paid less than men for the same jobs) or to the fact that some men have more experience or better qualifications. But there is another reason for these discrepancies in pay.[27] This subtle form of discrimination works as follows: Jobs that women have traditionally held (such as nurse, teacher, secretary, and librarian) have lower pay rates than jobs that men have traditionally held (such as carpenter, upper manager, doctor, and construction worker), even though the jobs may require similar levels of skill (albeit different skills) and may be of equal value to an organization.

Pay

- To have high levels of motivation, pay should be based on performance whenever possible.
- When individual performance can be appraised accurately and cooperation across workers is adequate, pay should be based on individual levels of performance because this results in the highest levels of individual motivation.
- When individual performance cannot be appraised or when a higher level of cooperation across workers is necessary, pay should be based on group or organizational performance.

Comparable worth
The idea that jobs of equivalent value to an organization should carry the same pay rates regardless of differences in the work and the personal characteristics of the worker.

Pay differentials between men and women have the potential to adversely affect the motivation of high-performing women who perceive that they are not receiving as much pay as the job is worth. From the perspective of equity theory, women who perceive themselves as contributing levels of inputs equivalent to those of their male counterparts but receiving lower levels of outcomes (in particular, pay) may be motivated to reduce their inputs (perhaps by exerting less effort) to restore equity. More critical than their effects on motivation, pay differentials based on gender, age, race, ethnic background, or any other nonperformance characteristic are unethical.

The principle of **comparable worth** suggests that jobs of equivalent value to an organization should carry the same pay rates regardless of differences in the nature of the work itself and regardless of the personal characteristics of the persons performing the work.[28] Pay rates should be determined by factors such as effort, skill, and responsibility on a job and not by whether one type of person or another usually performs the job. The gender, race, or ethnic background of jobholders is an irrelevant input that managers should not consider when they establish pay rates for different positions. When pay rates are determined by comparable worth, it is more likely that all members of an organization will be motivated to perform at a high level because they are more likely to perceive that they are being paid on an equitable basis.

Although comparable worth makes a lot of sense in principle, it has been hard to put into practice. Organizations have resisted basing salaries on comparable worth because pay levels for some jobs would have to be raised (organizations rarely lower pay rates). On a more fundamental level, however, determining what the value or worth of a job is to an organization and comparing this value to that of other very different types of jobs is difficult. Such comparisons are often value laden and the source of considerable disagreement. Even so, comparable worth is an ethical issue that managers need to be aware of and is a goal worth striving for.

Motivation Through Career Opportunities

There are outcomes in addition to pay that members of an organization are motivated to obtain from their jobs and organizations. One of these outcomes, career opportunities, is related not just to the specific job a person holds today but to the jobs a person expects to perform or advance to over the course of his or her entire career. Siemens, in the opening case, uses its fast-track career program and the promise of promotion to senior management positions to motivate junior managers to perform at a high level.

Career opportunities often do include such things as being in a fast-track management program or getting a promotion, but they can include other specific career-related outcomes such as having the opportunity to do the kind of work you really want to do, receiving career-relevant experiences and training, and having exposure to people who can help you advance your own career. Many of these career opportunities impact levels of intrinsic motivation because they help people pursue the kind of work they enjoy.

Sometimes it is possible to give workers the chance to do what they love even when they are performing a job that is not directly related to their career aspirations. At a restaurant called Applause in New York City, many aspiring singers and actors take what they hope are temporary jobs waiting tables to support themselves because Applause allows waiters and waitresses to sing and entertain customers while serving meals. The restaurant thus gives aspiring singers and actors the chance to do what they love, to gain experience in performing before a live audience, and to gain exposure to customers (who might include talent scouts, directors, and producers) who can further their careers.

Both organizations and individual workers should try to manage careers. When careers are effectively managed, organizations make the best use of their members' skills and abilities, and workers are motivated to perform at a high level and tend to be satisfied with their jobs, all of which help an organization achieve its goals. To use career opportunities as a motivation tool (as both Siemens and Applause do), managers must understand what careers are, how people progress through them, and how careers can be managed by workers and by organizations.

THE NATURE OF CAREERS

Career

The sum of work-related experiences throughout one's lifetime.

A **career** can be defined as the sum of work-related experiences throughout one's lifetime.[29] A career includes the number and types of jobs a person has had as well as the different organizations a person has worked for.

Why are individuals concerned about their careers? A career can have major effects on a person's economic and psychological well-being. At a basic economic level, work provides most people in modern society with the income they need to support themselves and their loved ones and to pursue personal interests such as hobbies and leisure activities. From this economic perspective, career opportunities are an important source of *extrinsic motivation* for workers. As a source of psychological well-being, work can provide personal fulfillment and give a sense of meaning and purpose to people's lives. From this psychological perspective, career opportunities are an important source of *intrinsic motivation*.

Why are organizations concerned with the careers of their members? Effectively managing careers helps an organization to motivate its members to achieve individual and organizational goals and perform at a high level. Effective career management in an organization means that there will be well-qualified workers at all levels who can assume more responsible positions as needed to help the organization achieve its goals. Organizations can help motivate their members through career management by helping members develop the knowledge, skills, abilities, and other inputs needed for high levels of performance and by rewarding high performers with career opportunities such as valuable experience and training, choice job assignments, and promotions.

TYPES OF CAREERS

Although every individual's career is unique, careers fall into four general categories: steady-state careers, linear careers, spiral careers, and transitory careers.[30]

Steady-State Careers. A steady-state career reflects a one-time commitment to a certain kind of job that is maintained throughout one's working life.[31] Workers with steady-state careers can become very skilled at, and intrinsically motivated by, the work they do and often see themselves as experts. A family doctor who sets up a medical practice in her hometown when she finishes her medical training and keeps the same practice throughout her career until she retires at age 70 has a steady-state career.

Linear Careers. In a linear career, a person progresses through a sequence of jobs, and each job entails progress over the prior one in terms of responsibility, skills needed, level in the hierarchy of an organization, and so on.[32] Workers can stay with the same organization or move from company to company as they pursue linear careers. Edwin L. Artzt, former chairman of Procter & Gamble, started working for Procter & Gamble over forty years ago in a low-level job and worked his way up the corporate ladder through each of the corporate divisions to assume the top position.[33]

Unlike Artzt, who has stayed with the same organization, Michael Lorelli, president of PepsiCo's Pizza Hut International division, started his linear career with an entry-level job in the marketing department at Clairol. After two years he was promoted to the position of product manager and helped Clairol successfully deal with a potential crisis produced by claims that hair dyes cause cancer. He then moved on to Playtex and helped that organization expand internationally. After a successful stint at Playtex, Lorelli signed on at PepsiCo as senior vice president for the marketing of Pepsi-Cola. He then headed the company's eastern U.S. Pepsi-Cola division prior to assuming his current position as president of Pizza Hut.[34]

Spiral Careers. In a spiral career, a person holds different types of jobs that build on each other but tend to be fundamentally different.[35] An associate professor of management with a spiral career leaves university teaching and research to head up the human resources department at a large company, then, after working at that job for ten years, leaves to start a consulting company.

Transitory Careers. A person with a transitory career changes jobs frequently, and each job is different from the one before it.[36] After graduating from college, Paul Jones worked as the manager of a hardware store for two years, then worked in a bank for a year, and is currently training to become a police officer.

Many of the career opportunities that organizations provide to motivate their members reflect the idea that people should be given the opportunity to assume more responsible positions as they gain knowledge and experience. Thus linear careers are the most relevant for understanding and managing organizational behavior. This is clearly true at Siemens in the opening case. In the remainder of this chapter, therefore, we focus on linear careers.

CAREER STAGES

Although each linear career is unique, a linear career usually follows a certain progression through a number of stages. Each stage is associated with challenges to be met and tasks to be tackled. Researchers disagree about the exact

Michael Lorelli's linear career has taken him to the presidency of Pizza Hut International. Only 42 years old, the ambitious Lorelli hopes to rise higher in America's corporate hierarchy.

number of career stages; here we discuss five stages found in most linear careers (see Fig. 8.4).[37]

Preparation for Work.   During the first stage, individuals must decide what kind of career they want and learn what qualifications and experiences they need to obtain a good career-starting job.[38] Critical tasks faced in the preparation stage involve acquiring the necessary knowledge, skills, education, and training either from formal classroom education or from on-the-job apprenticeships or other programs.

Personality, ability, attitudes, and values are among the factors that impact initial career choice.[39] Individuals who are high on the Big Five dimension of extroversion (see Chapter 2), for example, may tend to gravitate toward careers (such as sales) that require significant amounts of social interaction with others. Individuals with exceptional numerical ability may lean toward a career in engineering. A person who has extrinsic work values (Chapter 3) and values work for its consequences may choose a law career that might result in a high income for years to come. But a person who has intrinsic work values and values work for its own sake may choose a nursing career that might lead to feelings of personal accomplishment and fulfillment.

Organizational Entry.   During the second stage, people try to find a job that will be a good start to their chosen career. People in the entry stage find out as much as they can about potential jobs and organizations from various sources, including business newspapers and magazines, college placement offices and career/job fairs, company-sponsored information and seminars, and personal contacts.

FIGURE 8.4

Career Stages

| Preparation for work | → | Organizational entry | → | Early career | → | Midcareer | → | Late career |

Once job seekers have gathered this information, they want to become jobholders. Getting an interview with an organization that you are interested in is sometimes as simple as signing up with a company representative visiting on campus or getting the friend of a friend to put in a good word for you with his wife, who is a manager at the company.

Once an interview is scheduled, it is crucial to make the most of it. Finding out as much as possible about the company, doing practice interviews, thinking of interesting questions to ask the interviewer, and thinking of good answers to frequently asked questions (such as, Where do you see yourself in five years? Why do you want to be an accountant?) are things job applicants can do to increase their prospects. In Chapter 4, we discussed many of the factors that affect perception and thus affect both how interviewers perceive job applicants and how job applicants can actively influence the perception process through impression management. We also explained how perception is distorted by biases like the primacy effect, which leads interviewers to make an initial decision about someone in the first few minutes of the interview and then spend the rest of the interview selectively hearing and seeing things that confirm that initial impression. In an interview, then, job applicants must make a good impression from the minute they walk in the door.

In addition to selling themselves to an organization, applicants also need to find out as much information as they can about the job they are seeking, their career prospects with the organization, and the organization as a whole, to make a good choice. Sometimes what people think a job or an organization will be like is very different from what they actually experience on the job. A new assistant to the division president might find, to her dismay, that her job is really a secretarial position and not the start to the management career she envisions.

Organizations should provide applicants with accurate information about the job in question, about their career prospects, and about the organization as a whole. Sometimes, in an effort to attract outstanding applicants who might have several job offers, members of an organization might be tempted to paint a rosy picture of what their organization has to offer. This practice can lead new hires to experience disappointment and negative attitudes, both of which might prompt them to quit. Research has found that organizations that use realistic job previews can reduce turnover. A **realistic job preview** gives applicants an accurate picture of the job and the organization by including both positive features (such as high levels of autonomy and excellent benefits) and negative ones (long working hours and slow advancement).[40]

Realistic job preview
Occurs when an organization gives job applicants an accurate picture of the job and the organization by including both positive features and negative ones.

Early Career. The early career stage starts once a person has obtained a job in a chosen career. There are two distinct steps in this stage. The first step is *establishment,* during which newcomers are motivated to learn how to perform their jobs, what is expected of them, and more generally how to fit in (see Chapter 10). The second step is *achievement.* Once newcomers have mastered their jobs and know the organization, they are motivated to accomplish something worthwhile and make a significant contribution to the organization. Achievement can mean different things to different people. For some, achievement is synonymous with moving up the corporate ladder; for others, it can mean becoming an expert in a certain area or devising creative solutions to difficult problems.[41]

Organizations can do several things to help ensure that members are motivated to achieve individual, group, and organizational goals. In Chapters 6 and 7, we discussed how organizations motivate members to perform at a high level and how jobs should be designed to result in high levels of motivation and achievement. Managers need to make sure that workers think that they are able to achieve difficult goals (have high expectancy) and that instrumentality is high—that is, workers think they will and actually do receive desired outcomes such as pay and career opportunities like promotions when they actually achieve their goals.

According to equity theory, managers must also distribute outcomes (pay, status, choice job assignments, promotions, and other career opportunities) to workers based on their inputs to the organization (ability, education, experience, time, and effort). Earlier in this chapter we saw the important role that performance appraisal can play in motivation by providing workers with feedback. Accurate performance appraisals help workers assess their own levels of achievement, determine how to improve in the future, and more generally assess their career progress.

In addition to identifying where and how they can make the most valuable contributions to an organization, individuals can advance their careers during the achievement step by seeking out a mentor (see Chapter 4) and setting their own career goals. Getting help from a mentor has been found to increase levels of pay and pay satisfaction and the rate of promotion for protégés.[42] Although it has commonly been assumed that mentors seek out protégés, protégés can and do seek out mentors. One recent study found that workers who had an internal locus of control, were high on self-monitoring, and were low on negative affectivity (Chapter 2) were most likely to seek out and obtain help from a mentor. Moreover, the mentoring clearly benefited the workers in terms of salary levels and the extent to which the protégés felt good about their accomplishments and the progress they were making.[43]

Some organizations have formal mentoring programs that assign experienced members to newcomers. Often, however, mentoring is an informal process in which mentors and protégés seek each other out because of some common interest or bond. One researcher who interviewed successful working women found that 77 percent of them had received help from a mentor. Jennie Coakley received extensive help from her mentor, Ronnie Andros, when she began teaching the fifth grade at Columbia Elementary School in Fairfax County, Virginia. Andros helped Coakley cope with many of the challenges new teachers face. For example, Andros clarified official rules and procedures, introduced Coakley to important school administrators, and gave Andros tips about how to obtain textbooks.

Mentors are often in the same organizations as their protégés, but sometimes protégés can obtain help from mentors outside their organizations. For example, Lee Cooke was the office manager of the American Automobile Association in Washington, D.C., when he met his mentor at a local Rotary club meeting. Lee's mentor was an orchid breeder, and their relationship eventually led Lee to land a position with the American Orchid Society in West Palm Beach, Florida.[44]   •

In addition to seeking out the help of a mentor, workers can also advance their careers by formulating career goals. In Chapter 7 we said that goals are useful motivation tools because they help to focus workers' attention and effort in the right direction. Career goals are the experiences, positions, or jobs that workers would like to have in the course of their careers.[45] **Career goals** are good guides for achievement because they help workers decide what activities to concentrate on to advance their careers. (See Insight 8.5.)

Career goals
The experiences, positions, or jobs that workers would like to have in the course of their careers.

Insight 8.5

Diversity

Career Goals Key to Success

Sharon Hall, who at age 37 is general manager of Avon Products' (www.avon.com) personal-care products group, has relied on career goals to help her make significant achievements. Diverse workers such as Hall (she is an African American) sometimes experience obstacles due to inaccurate stereotypes and discrimination, but Hall's determination and strong career goals have resulted in her having the kind of career she wants.

When Hall attended Morris Brown College in Atlanta, her goal was a career in marketing. At the organizational entry stage of her career, her goal was to start her career with Procter & Gamble. Once she set this goal, she was relentless in her pursuit. Even though she learned that Procter & Gamble was planning on hiring only MBAs just as she was about to receive her bachelor's degree, Hall learned as much as she could about the company and tried her hardest to get an interview with Procter & Gamble's on-campus recruiter. When she found that the recruiter's schedule was completely booked, Hall asked him to call her if any of the scheduled interviewees was late, so that she could take their place. Hall got the call and so impressed the recruiter with her enthusiasm and knowledge about Procter & Gamble that the company offered her a job as a brand assistant.

While learning a great deal about marketing during her first two years on the job, Hall realized that she would not be happy remaining at Procter & Gamble and working her way up the corporate ladder. She reassessed her career goals and decided that her objectives were to obtain an MBA, work for the management consulting organization Booz Allen & Hamilton for a couple of years, and then get a senior management position at a large organization. She received a fellowship at the University of Southern California, where she received her MBA, and went on to work for Booz Allen.

At Booz Allen she had three major goals: (1) to learn as much as she could about global marketing; (2) to improve her analytical skills; (3) to get the experiences she needed to get a high-paying job with a large organization. After two years at Booz Allen, Hall accomplished these goals and landed a job with Avon to help with its planned expansion in the Pacific Rim. Hall so impressed upper managers at Avon that she was able to negotiate the duties of her various roles and structure her jobs to enable herself to accomplish her goals. For example, after the birth of her first child, she decided to work in new product development, which allowed her to adopt a flexible work schedule while continuing to develop her skills.

Setting specific and challenging career goals has helped Sharon Hall make significant achievements. In trying to determine what specific experiences to concentrate on throughout her career, Hall has followed this guideline: "Always be doing something that contributes significant, positive change to the organization. That's the ultimate job security."[46]

Midcareer.   Workers in the midcareer stage have generally been in the workforce between 20 and 35 years and face the challenge of remaining productive. Many workers achieve the height of career success during the midcareer stage, as exemplified by Michael Eisner, CEO of Walt Disney Co., Anita Roddick, CEO of the Body Shop, Jack Smith, CEO of General Motors, and Lou Gerstner, CEO of IBM. Many other midcareer workers, however, need to come to terms with career plateaus, obsolescence, and major career changes.

A **career plateau** is a position from which the chances of being promoted into a higher-level position within an organization or of obtaining a position with more responsibility in another organization become very small.[47] There are several reasons workers reach a career plateau. First, because of the hierarchical nature of most organizations, there are fewer and fewer positions to be promoted into as workers advance. Second, competition for upper-level positions in organizations is intense, and the number of these positions has been reduced because of downsizing.[48] Third, if some workers delay retirement past the traditional age of 65, their positions do not open up for midcareer workers to assume.[49] Finally, changes in technology or the lack of important new skills and abilities may limit the extent to which workers can advance in organizations.[50]

How can organizations help "plateaued" workers remain satisfied, motivated, and productive? Encouraging lateral moves and job rotation is often an effective means of keeping plateaued workers motivated when they no longer have the prospect of a major promotion to work toward. Chevron is one of many organizations using this strategy.[51]

What steps can plateaued workers take to remain valuable, motivated members of the organization and maintain their job satisfaction? They might take on the role of mentor. They might become "good citizens" of their organizations by suggesting changes, improvements, and generally engaging in the various forms of organizational citizenship behavior discussed in Chapter 3. Workers in early career stages often concentrate on activities that advance their careers and do not take the time to do things that help the organization as a whole. Plateaued workers, who often have a good understanding of their organization, are sometimes in an especially good position to help start a major company-wide recycling program, establish an outreach program to encourage members of an organization to volunteer time to community causes, or organize social activities such as company picnics, for example.

Workers face obsolescence when their knowledge and skills become outmoded and prevent them from effectively performing their organizational roles. Obsolescence is caused by changes in technology or in an organization's competitive environment that alter how jobs are performed. Organizations can help prevent obsolescence by providing their members with additional training whenever possible and allowing workers time off from work to take courses in their fields to keep them up-to-date. Whenever possible, workers should seek out additional training to keep their skills current.

Late Career.   The late career stage extends as long as an individual's career is active. William Dillard, the founder of Dillard's department stores, is in his eighties and still has an active career helping his company remain one of the most profitable retailing chains in the United States.[52]

Obsolescence and other potential midcareer problems also carry over into the late career stage, and it is important for workers and organizations

Career plateau

A position from which the chances of obtaining a promotion or a job with more responsibility become very small.

to take some of the steps discussed earlier to overcome these problems and help older workers remain motivated, productive, and satisfied. Unfortunately, age-related stereotypes sometimes cause members of an organization to perceive older workers as slower, resistant to change, or less productive than younger workers although this characterization is simply not true. Organizations need to dispel these myths by educating their members about the capabilities and contributions of their most senior members.

Organizations and individual workers can do many things to manage careers. When careers are effectively managed, workers are satisfied with their jobs and careers and are motivated to perform at a high level and thereby help organizations achieve their goals.

Career Challenges for the 1990s and Beyond

In Chapter 1 we discussed contemporary challenges for organizational behavior and management. Some of these challenges are very relevant to the motivation of organizational members as they pursue their careers. When career management is effective, workers are given a series of motivating job assignments that they value and that contribute to their own development, and the organization makes good use of its human resources to accomplish its goals. In this section we discuss three career challenges that organizations face: ethical career management, career management that supports diversity, and career management in an era of dual-career couples. In Chapter 9 we discuss in more detail some of the specific steps organizations can take to meet these challenges as well as the challenges that arise when organizations downsize and lay off some of their members.

Here, workers 55 years old and over take a computer course to learn to operate IBM personal computers. By learning new skills, "plateaued" workers can increase their value to an organization and at the same time increase their job satisfaction.

ETHICAL CAREER MANAGEMENT

In Chapter 1 we defined *ethics* as rules, beliefs, and values that outline the ways that managers and workers should behave when confronted with a situation in which their actions may help or harm other people inside or outside an organization. A key challenge for organizations and their managers is to ensure that career practices are ethical and that members of the organization pursue their own careers in an ethical manner.

Ethical career practices are practices built on honesty, trust, and open communication. Honesty means that managers are frank with workers concerning their career prospects, their strengths and weaknesses, and their progress to date. As we saw earlier, honesty begins before a worker actually joins an organization, when an organization informs job applicants about the good and not-so-good things in various positions and in the organization itself. Honesty continues when managers appraise performance and give workers clear and accurate feedback, which contributes to workers' being motivated to perform at a high level. To motivate subordinates, managers should also provide honest feedback concerning how subordinates' careers are progressing and information about future career opportunities and prospects. Honesty continues into the later career stages when organizations follow through on their commitments regarding provisions for retirement.

Trust is also built on members' of an organization following through on their commitments to each other. If a manager or an organization motivates a worker by promising a certain type of career progression given adequate job performance, promised career opportunities should be forthcoming whenever possible. Likewise, if a worker promises his or her supervisor to remain on the job and vows that the organization will benefit from enrolling him or her in an expensive course to learn a new technology, trust results when the worker follows through on this commitment.

Ethical career management cannot take place without open communication between managers and subordinates. Open communication leads to a clear and shared understanding of the development of careers and career prospects.

When careers are managed in an ethical fashion, promotions are based on performance. When workers understand the link between performance and promotion and other career opportunities (such as challenging assignments and special training), they are motivated to perform at a high level, as is true of junior managers at Siemens in the opening case. Moreover, ethical career management means that supervisors do not abuse their power to make career decisions and provide career opportunities. Extreme cases of supervisors abusing this power are reflected in some instances of sexual harassment, in which subordinates are led to believe that their future careers with an organization hinge on having intimate relationships with their supervisors or tolerating demeaning or inappropriate treatment and language. Sexual harassment is not only unethical but also illegal. Workers also should not have to do things that go against their own ethical standards to advance their careers. Figure 8.5 contains a short ethics quiz that provides some examples of behaviors that supervisors may request subordinates to perform that may be unethical.[53]

CAREER MANAGEMENT THAT SUPPORTS DIVERSITY

The increasing diversity of the workforce means that managers have to make sure that diverse members of an organization are given the career opportu-

Supervisors sometimes ask subordinates to do things that may be questionable on ethical grounds. Ethical career management means that subordinates do not have to engage in unethical behaviors to advance their own careers. Which of the following behaviors would you feel comfortable performing, and which do you think are basically unethical?

1. Your supervisor asks you to sign her name on some letters.

2. Your supervisor asks you to respond to a request and send it under her name.

3. Your supervisor asks you to tell callers that she is with a customer when you know that this is not true.

4. Your supervisor asks you to delay recording expenses until the next quarter.

5. Your supervisor asks you to tell others that she hasn't made a decision yet even though you know she has.

6. Your supervisor tells you to record the purchase of office equipment as an advertising expense.

7. Your supervisor asks you to back-date invoices to last quarter.

8. Your supervisor requests that you tell people you don't know certain things that you do know.

9. Your supervisor tells you to tell top management that she is working on a project that she hasn't begun yet (if top management happens to ask you).

10. Your supervisor tells you not to report sexist language you overheard if anyone asks about it.

According to Gerald Graham, Dean of the W. Frank Barton School of Business at Wichita State University, most people would consider items 3, 4, 5, 6, 7, 8, 9, and 10 to be deceptive or unethical and probably should not be agreed to.

FIGURE 8.5

Ethics Quiz

Source: Adapted from G. Graham, "Would You Lie for Your Boss or Would You Just Rather Not," *Bryan–College Station Eagle,* October 24, 1994, p. C3. Reprinted with permission.

nities they deserve. While progress has certainly been made in the hiring of diverse types of people, somewhat less progress has been made in motivating diverse members of an organization and making sure that they are given equal career opportunities.

In Chapter 4, we discussed several reasons why people have a tendency to perceive others who are similar to themselves in gender, race, age, or cultural background more favorably than they perceive those who are different, and we described ways to overcome these biases. Problems like the similar-to-me bias may result in certain members of an organization not receiving the career opportunities they deserve because they are dissimilar to managers making career-related decisions such as which subordinate is most deserving of a promotion. This inequity can result in these workers being unmotivated because they think that they will not receive the career opportunities they deserve even if they work hard and perform at a high level. Managers who are aware of these biases and problems and ways to overcome them are in a good position to promote diversity in career management.

Organizations also can take specific steps to ensure equal career opportunities to diverse members. Pacific Bell, for example, has undertaken a number of initiatives to promote the careers of minorities—in particular, of Hispanics. Summer internships and scholarships are offered to minorities even before they join Pacific Bell, to help make sure that there are minority applicants with the college degrees necessary for management positions. Minorities without college degrees are hired into nonmanagement positions that have the potential to lead to future management roles. Pacific Bell also holds Efficacy Seminars, which typically last six days and aim to help minority employees be ready for future promotions. Another example of the active steps that Pacific Bell is taking to promote the careers of diverse employees is a special two-year development track that has been instituted for minority managers to support their career development, assist them in developing their knowledge and skills, and provide them with access to mentors.[54]

Xerox Corporation is another organization that supports diversity through career management. Xerox is careful to place women and minorities in positions that will give them the experiences they need for future promotions. Minority and female Caucus Groups at Xerox provide guidance to diverse employees on how to manage their careers. Because managers often make important decisions that impact the careers of women and minorities, Xerox's Balanced Workforce process links managers' performance appraisals and compensation to the extent to which managers try to provide women and minorities with career opportunities.[55] The Balanced Workforce process thus motivates managers to support diversity at Xerox and to use career opportunities as an important tool to motivate diverse subordinates.

CAREER MANAGEMENT IN AN ERA OF DUAL-CAREER COUPLES

In managing careers, organizations have to take into account that the dual-career couple is now the norm rather than the exception. Individual workers cannot make career decisions (such as accepting a promotion that entails relocating to another state) without considering the preferences and careers of their spouses. When dual-career couples have children, the needs of the entire family have to be taken into account as careers unfold. To help dual-career couples and other workers such as single-parents and workers taking care of elderly parents effectively manage their careers, organizations can take several steps:

1. *Organizations can limit unnecessary moves and travel as much as possible:* When workers do need to relocate in the course of their career, relocation programs can be used to help their partners find new jobs and help the families adjust to the new surroundings.
2. *Organizations can use flexible working arrangements to allow their members time off when needed:* Sometimes these arrangements may entail simply changing the hours worked (for example, from 6 a.m. to 2 p.m. instead of from 9 a.m. to 5 p.m.) as at Xerox. Sometimes they may mean that workers perform some of their assigned tasks at home. At other times they may mean that managers are understanding when workers need to take time off to, for example, take care of sick children or parents.
3. *Organizations can have on-site day care centers:* One of the most pressing concerns for dual-career couples with small children and for single parents is finding quality day care for their children. On-site day care centers are growing in popularity and give working parents the peace of mind that comes from knowing that their children are in good hands.

These are just a few of the steps that organizations can take to help members manage their careers in light of the many other demands and constraints that workers face from their personal lives. Rather than ignoring these demands and constraints, as some organizations have tried to do in the past, organizations should take steps to help workers effectively meet them.

SUMMARY

Performance appraisal, pay, and career opportunities are important motivation tools that managers can use to encourage subordinates to perform at a high level. Accurate performance appraisals are essential for a motivated workforce. Pay and career opportunities are two of the most important outcomes that managers can use to motivate subordinates to perform at a high level. In this chapter, we made the following major points:

1. The goals of performance appraisal are to encourage high levels of worker motivation and performance and to provide accurate information to be used in managerial decision making. Performance appraisal can focus on the assessment of traits, behaviors, or results, be formal or informal, and rely on objective or subjective measures. Supervisors most often appraise the performance of their subordinates.

2. Pay is an important outcome for most workers. Motivation and learning theories suggest that pay should be based on performance. When individual performance can be accurately assessed, the maximum motivational impact is obtained from basing pay on individual performance. When workers are highly interdependent, individual levels of performance cannot be accurately appraised, or if high levels of cooperation across workers are desired, it can be advantageous to base pay on group or organizational performance.

3. Merit pay in the form of bonuses generally is preferable to salary increases because salary levels have multiple determinants in addition to current performance. The ethics of pay differentials and comparable worth are important issues that managers face in using pay as a motivation tool and striving for the equitable distribution of pay in organizations.

4. A career can be defined as the sum of work-related experiences throughout one's lifetime. Effective career management helps to ensure that members of an organization are motivated to perform at a high level and receive the career opportunities they should while also ensuring that the organization is making the best use of its human resources.

5. Four general types of careers are steady-state careers, linear careers, spiral careers, and transitory careers. Linear careers usually progress through five stages. At each stage, organizations and individuals can take steps to ensure high levels of worker motivation and effective career management. The five stages are (1) preparation for work, (2) organizational entry, (3) early career, (4) mid-career, and (5) late career. The early career stage is made up of two steps: establishment and achievement. Mentors and career goals can be especially helpful to workers during the achievement step.

6. Career challenges for the 1990s and beyond include ethical career management (built on honesty, trust, and open communication), career management that supports diversity (ensures that diverse members of an organization are given the career opportunities they deserve), and career management in an era of dual-career couples (acknowledges the many demands on workers arising from their jobs and personal lives).

Organizational Behavior in Action

TOPICS FOR DISCUSSION AND ACTION

1. Why are accurate performance appraisals a key ingredient in having a motivated workforce?
2. How can performance appraisals be used to form high-performing work teams?
3. Why might workers perceive appraisals based on traits as unfair?
4. Despite the positive effects of merit pay on motivation, when might an organization not want to use it?
5. Do all workers want their pay to be based on their performance? Why or why not?
6. Why do bonuses tend to be more effective motivation tools than salary increases?
7. Why are corporations reluctant to put comparable worth into practice in establishing levels of pay?
8. Which career opportunities might be good motivation tools for an accountant in a Big Eight firm?
9. Is motivation likely to be higher at some career stages than at others? Why or why not?
10. Are career plateaus inevitable for most workers? Why or why not?

BUILDING DIAGNOSTIC SKILLS

Determining Career Aspirations and Goals

Think about the kind of career you would like to have and are trying to pursue.

1. Describe your desired career. Why do you want to have this career?
2. Describe three specific jobs that you think would be excellent for your desired career.
3. Which career stage is each of these jobs relevant to?
4. What would you find especially motivating in each of these jobs?
5. How do you think your performance should be appraised on each of these jobs to result in high levels of motivation?
6. How should pay be determined on each of these jobs to result in high levels of motivation?

RESEARCH ON THE INTERNET: A MANAGER'S TOOL

Specific Task

Like many large corporations, Amoco offers its employees a wide range of career opportunities. Two such opportunities are an internship program and a co-op program. Scan Amoco's website (www.amoco.com) to learn more about this company and its career opportunities. Then click on "Jobs at Amoco," then on "Explore the Possibilities in USA," then on "Disciplines," and then on "Intern and Co-op Opportunities."

1. What are the career advantages of the co-op program offered by Amoco?

2. What are the career advantages of the internship program offered by Amoco?

General Task

Many organizations use their pay plans to ensure that employees benefit when the organization performs highly and achieves its goals. Find the website of such a company. What steps is this company taking to ensure that employees benefit when the organization performs highly? How might these initiatives contribute to employee motivation?

TOPICS FOR DEBATE

Performance appraisal, pay, and careers are three important motivation tools that managers can use to encourage subordinates to perform at a high level. Now that you have a good understanding of these motivation tools, debate the following issues.

Debate One

Team A. Performance appraisal is a more important motivation tool than pay.

Team B. Pay is a more important motivation tool than performance appraisal.

Debate Two

Team A. Career success is best defined in terms of the highest position that a worker has attained in an organization.

Team B. Career success is best defined by how an individual feels about his or her own work experiences.

EXPERIENTIAL EXERCISE

Designing Effective Performance Appraisal and Pay Systems

Objective

Your objective is to gain experience in designing a performance appraisal and pay system to motivate employees.

Procedure

The class divides into groups of from three to five people, and each group appoints one member as spokesperson, to present the group's recommendations to the whole class. Here is the scenario.

Assume the role of a gourmet cook who has just started a catering business. You are located in a college town with approximately 150,000 residents. Sixty thousand students attend the large state university located in this town. Your customers include professors who host parties and receptions in their homes, student groups who hold parties at various locations, and local professionals such as doctors and lawyers who hold parties both in their homes and at their offices.

Your staff includes two cooks who help you prepare the food and four servers who help you set up and serve the food on location. Often, one or both cooks go to the location of a catering job to help the servers prepare food that needs some cooking on site, such as a soufflé with hot raspberry sauce.

Your business is getting off to a good start, and you want to make sure that you have an effective performance appraisal and pay system in place to motivate your cooks and your servers. It is important that your cooks are motivated to prepare high-quality and imaginative dishes, are flexible and willing to help out as needed (you often get last-minute jobs), work well with each other and with you, and are polite to customers on location. It is crucial that your servers follow your specific instructions for each job, attractively set up the food on location, provide excellent service, and are also polite and pleasant to customers.

1. Using the concepts and ideas in this chapter, design an effective performance appraisal system for the cooks.
2. Using the concepts and ideas in this chapter, design an effective performance appraisal system for the servers.
3. How should you pay the cooks to ensure that they are motivated to prepare high-quality and imaginative dishes, are flexible and willing to help out as needed, work well with each other and with you, and are polite to customers on location?
4. How should you pay the servers to ensure that they are motivated to do a good job and provide high-quality service to your customers?

When your group has completed those activities, the spokesperson will present the group's recommendations to the whole class.

MAKING THE CONNECTION

Find an example of a company that tries to manage the careers of its members effectively. What steps has this company taken to try to ensure effective career management?

CLOSING CASE

The Pros and Cons of 360-Degree Appraisals

The growing popularity of 360-degree appraisals attests to the need for more feedback in organizations, and who is in a better position to give workers feedback than all the different individuals they come into contact with on the job. Peers, for example, may have a different perspective on performance than the boss. A manager who lacks assertiveness when dealing with superiors may be too assertive and dictatorial when dealing with subordinates. Receiving feedback based on evaluations from these multiple sources has the potential to provide workers with a richer picture of their strengths and weaknesses and areas for improvement.

Farm Credit Service Southwest, a lending cooperative, relies on 360-degree appraisals for about 50 percent of its annual performance appraisal process. While chief financial officer John Barkell found the process a bit intimidating, he did receive useful feedback that he has subsequently acted upon such as the need for more communication with his subordinates. Barkell instituted weekly meetings with his staff to open lines of communication and answer questions.[56]

When Chairman and CEO of AT&T, Robert Allen, received feedback from his subordinates (his top management team), they indicated that he was too passive in executive committee meetings. In response, Allen began leading the meetings in a more proactive manner.[57]

At Public Service Electric & Gas in Newark, New Jersey, manager Gordon Smouther's 360-degree appraisal indicated that he was too controlling and defensive, which resulted in him knocking down other people's ideas without giving them a chance. Smouther and his boss put together a plan which included a course at the Center for Creative Leadership and private sessions with an executive coach. His ratings have improved dramatically.[58]

Experiences such as these point to the advantages of 360-degree appraisals. They can provide managers and other workers with valuable feedback which they can use to improve their performance. However, there are also certain potential problems with 360-degree appraisals. Some managers fear that 360-degree appraisals might turn into popularity contests with managers who are well liked being rated more highly than those who may be less popular but producing better results. Others fear that managers will be reluctant to make unpopular decisions or difficult choices as this may have a negative effect on how their subordinates evaluate them. If appraisals are anonymous (to promote honesty and openness), disgruntled subordinates may seek revenge by providing their bosses with negative evaluations. On the other hand, some bosses coach their subordinates, and sometimes even threaten them, into providing positive ratings.[59] A manager at Citibank indicated that he received a very negative appraisal from a subordinate that was almost like a personal attack; he was pretty sure it came from a poor performer.[60] At Baxter International, although workers in the information technology unit were very familiar with each other's performance, they were reluctant to provide any negative evaluations and gave each other positive ratings because they knew the ratings were being used for pay raise decisions and the evaluations were not anonymous. Baxter decided to continue using the peer evaluations but more for developmental purposes rather than decision making.[61]

Clearly, 360-degree appraisals have both advantages and disadvantages. Organizations considering using 360-degree appraisals have a number of tough decisions to make. Should the appraisals be anonymous? Who should be included in the set of individuals who will be appraising performance? Which employees should receive these appraisals? How can workers reconcile conflicting feedback? Should the appraisals be used solely for developmental purposes or should they also be used for managerial decision making? In order to successfully use 360-degree appraisals, managers need to be aware of their advantages and potential problems and carefully consider the different options they face.

Questions for Discussion
1. Do the advantages of anonymous 360-degree appraisals outweigh any potential disadvantages?
2. Should 360-degree appraisals be used solely for developmental purposes or should they also be used for decision making?

Stress and Work-Life Linkages

Balancing Work and Home Life

While increasing numbers of organizations have adopted family-friendly policies, workers continue to find balancing work and home life stressful, even workers at companies with family-friendly policies. A recent study of 12,000 employees at fifty-five companies conducted by *Business Week* found that a considerable number of workers felt that their jobs were hurting their family lives. Only about half the employees thought it was possible for them to have a good home life and still advance in their companies.[1] In many organizations, bosses continue to schedule meetings at

unusual times with little notice, employees are expected to work long hours and take work home, and work is expected to take precedence over family life.[2] Workers with children are left scrambling for last-minute child care arrangements and experience guilt over not being there for their children and missing important events such as soccer games, birthday celebrations, and school plays. Interestingly enough, single employees and employees without children are just as distressed by the difficulty of balancing home and work life as working mothers.[3] For example, an attorney in New York was asked by her boss to stay late one night to work on an important project. She had previous plans for the evening, which included going to a party being given by close friends. Her boss thought work should take precedence and told her to stay at work until the project was completed. The attorney felt differently; she needed to have a good personal life and wanted to meet someone, things that would never happen if she was working all the time. The attorney did stay late that night but has since moved on to another company. Expressing similar sentiments, a chief financial officer in a marketing organization recently indicated that "Just because I'm single and childless doesn't mean I have the will or desire to work a twelve-hour day, six days a week."[4]

A recent study conducted by Baxter Healthcare, which has instituted family-friendly policies, found that 30 percent of Baxter's employees experienced stress on a weekly basis from trying to balance work and home life, and 42 percent of employees had actually sought employment elsewhere due to conflicts they experienced between work and the rest of their lives. Employees lower down in the hierarchy were stressed by not being able to take time off when they needed to, having to put in overtime with little notice, or having their schedules unexpectedly changed at the last minute. Employees higher up in the hierarchy were stressed by having to work long hours, needing to work at night and on the weekends, and always being hooked up to the office through voice-mail.[5]

Some employees are able to effectively cope with the stress they experience from balancing work and home life by setting certain priorities and sticking to them. For example, Jay and Diane Menario, both professionals with high-powered jobs and two sons, make sure that their home life and children aren't getting short-shrift by both taking shifts at home and sometimes saying no. Diane gives the boys breakfast, drives them to school, is at her desk by around 8:30 a.m., and leaves around 6:00 p.m. Jay gets to the office earlier (often before 7:00 a.m.) and is with the boys at 5:00 p.m., driving them to extracurricular activities such as Little League and preparing dinner. The Menarios also try to squeeze in some extra hours of work at home when possible, say no to unexpected requests from work that interfere with important previous commitments they have made to their sons, and say no to home commitments that are too time-consuming, such as having a dog or playing golf. They are fortunate to have bosses who are understanding and supportive.[6]

Balancing work and home life is becoming an increasingly important concern for workers and organizations. Studies by *Business Week* and Baxter Healthcare suggest that what workers really want from their organizations and bosses is respect; they want their organizations to respect the fact that they have lives and important concerns outside the workplace. This respect includes treating workers with dignity, not making unreasonable demands, and allowing workers to have input into decisions that will affect them.[7]

Overview

In previous chapters, you learned about many of the ways in which working in an organization affects individuals. In Chapter 3 you learned how people's experiences in organizations shape important attitudes they have, such as job satisfaction and organizational commitment. In Chapters 5, 6, 7, and 8 you learned how and why different aspects of an organization—the way it designs jobs, sets goals, appraises performance, and administers rewards like pay and praise—affect motivation and performance. In this chapter, we continue to explore how working in an organization affects individuals, by focusing on stress and work-life linkages (relationships between people's work and their lives as a whole).

Stress affects how people feel and behave both on and off the job. Stress is a national concern and unfortunately an all-too-familiar problem. Most of us at one time or another have experienced some of the consequences of too much stress: sleepless nights, anxiety, nervousness, and headaches or stomachaches. A recent study found that around 40 million Americans experienced stress during a two-week period.[8] Stress costs organizations millions of dollars a year in lost productivity, absenteeism and turnover, and health care costs for stress-related illnesses. Understanding and managing stress is important not only for the well-being of the members of an organization but also for the effectiveness of the organization itself.

In this chapter, we describe the nature of stress and the consequences it has for individuals and organizations. We discuss the sources of stress and the steps that workers and their organizations can take to help workers cope effectively with stress. By the end of this chapter, you will have a good understanding of how stress affects people and organizations and the tools of organizational behavior that can be used to manage stress.

The Nature of Stress

When was the last time you felt particularly stressed? Maybe you had a paper due in a couple of days but you hadn't even started it, maybe you had three big exams on the same day, maybe you weren't getting along with your roommate, or maybe you were worried about not being able to find a good job when you graduate. You might have had a sense of being overwhelmed, of facing a problem that seemed insurmountable, or of being expected to do too many things at once. Or you may have felt uncertain about how to respond to an opportunity that had the potential to benefit you but also was very challenging.

Stress is the experience of opportunities or threats that people perceive as important and also perceive they might not be able to handle or deal with effectively.[9] Several significant aspects of stress are highlighted in this definition. First, stress can be experienced because of both opportunities and threats. An *opportunity* is something that has the potential to benefit a person. A *threat* is something that has the potential to harm a person.[10] Opportunities such as learning new skills or getting a new job can be stressful if workers lack self-efficacy (see Chapter 5) and fear that they will not be able to perform at an acceptable level. When an organization reduces the size of its workforce, employees experience stress because of the threats to their financial security, psychological well-being, or career development that downsizing creates. In the opening case, having to work long hours or having one's work schedule

Stress
The experience of opportunities or threats that people perceive as important and also perceive they might not be able to handle or deal with effectively.

changed at the last minute at Baxter Healthcare caused workers to experience stress because these factors threatened their family life.

A second aspect of stress is that the threat or opportunity experienced is important to a person. By *important* we mean that it has the potential to affect a person's well-being or the extent to which someone is happy, healthy, or prosperous. Many of the things that people encounter in their daily lives could be classified as opportunities or threats, but usually only the important ones result in stress. Driving through heavy traffic on the way to work is a threat, for example, but for many people it is not significant enough to result in stress. The threat of heavy traffic may become important enough to cause stress, however, if you are caught in a traffic jam at 7:50 a.m. and are scheduled to make a crucial presentation to upper management at 8 o'clock. In this situation, heavy traffic has the potential to affect your well-being negatively—being late for your own presentation will not make you look good in the eyes of your superiors.

A third key aspect of stress is *uncertainty:* The person who is experiencing an important opportunity or threat is not sure that he or she can effectively deal with it. When people are confident that they can effectively handle an opportunity or threat, they usually do not experience stress. An orthopedic surgeon performing a routine knee operation is not likely to experience stress if he or she has performed similar operations in the past and feels confident about doing a good job. Performing a complicated hip replacement on an elderly patient in poor health, however, might be stressful for the surgeon if he or she is uncertain about the outcome. Similarly, workers experience stress from the uncertainty of being able to have a good family life while still advancing their careers.

The last aspect of stress emphasized in our definition is that stress is rooted in perception. Whether people experience stress depends on how they *perceive* potential opportunities and threats and how they *perceive* their capabilities to deal with them. One person might perceive a job change or a promotion as an opportunity for learning and career advancement, and another person might perceive the same job change or promotion as a threat because of the potential for failure. Similarly, a person with high self-efficacy might feel well equipped to take on additional responsibility, and an equally capable worker with low self-efficacy might perceive that he or she can't handle any more responsibility.

INDIVIDUAL DIFFERENCES AND STRESS

Our definition emphasizes that an individual's experience of stress depends on a number of factors, such as how important a person thinks a given opportunity or threat is and the extent to which a person thinks he or she can deal effectively with the opportunity or threat. Above all else, stress is a very personal experience. Although it may be terrifying for some students to make a presentation in front of class, for example, others enjoy being in the spotlight and having a chance to display their knowledge and wit. Similarly, some nurses who care for AIDS patients find this duty highly stressful because of the threat of accidental infection or the emotional pain caused by the death of their patients, but other nurses consider caring for AIDS patients a professional opportunity that they have the skills and knowledge to deal with. Members of an organization must realize that individuals may respond differently to the same potential source of stress (some experience stress, but others do not) and that what might seem trivial to one worker might be a real source of stress for another.

In Chapter 2 we discussed the two major ways in which people differ from each other, in personality and ability, and their implications for understanding and managing organizational behavior. Individual differences also play a significant role in determining how members of an organization perceive and think about potential sources of stress, their ability to deal with stress effectively, and ultimately the extent to which they experience stress.

Personality. Several of the personality traits we discussed in Chapter 2 are important for understanding why workers exposed to the same potential source of stress may differ in the extent to which they actually experience stress. Workers who are high on the Big Five personality dimension of *neuroticism,* or *negative affectivity,* for example, have a general tendency to view themselves, their organizations, their jobs, and the people they work with in a negative manner. These workers are likely to view ambiguous conditions and changes at work as potential threats and to feel ill equipped to deal with both threats and opportunities. Consistent with this reasoning, workers high on negative affectivity tend to experience more stress than those low on negative affectivity.[11]

As another example, workers who are high on the Big Five dimension of *extroversion,* or *positive affectivity,* tend to be outgoing and enjoy interacting and socializing with other people. In the classroom, extroverts are less likely than introverts to experience stress when making presentations. Similarly, extroverts are less likely to experience stress in jobs requiring frequent presentations or meetings with new people on a day-to-day basis, as in many sales and service jobs.

Openness to experience, which captures the extent to which workers are daring and open to a wide range of experiences, is a final example of a personality trait from the Big Five model that is likely to affect the extent to which workers experience stress. For most people, taking risks and making frequent changes can be stressful. Even entrepreneurs are stressed by the risks of starting their own companies and the frequent changes needed to be innovative. Nevertheless, it is likely that workers who are high on openness to experience may find risk taking and frequent change less stressful than those who are low on openness to experience.

In Chapter 2 we also discussed some other, more specific personality traits that are relevant to understanding and managing organizational behavior, and it is likely that these traits also impact stress. Workers who are high on *self-esteem,* for example, are less likely to experience stress from challenging work assignments and are also more likely to think that they can deal effectively with sources of stress. As another example, *Type A workers* have stress experiences different from those of *Type B workers.* Type A's, as you recall, have a strong desire to achieve, are competitive, have a sense of time urgency, are impatient, and can be hostile. They have a strong desire to get a lot done in a short period of time. The more relaxed Type B's are not so driven. Initially, researchers thought that Type A's would experience more stress than Type B's; however, recent research suggests that only Type A's who are very hostile experience high levels of stress. A final example of a personality trait that is likely to play a role in the extent to which workers experience stress is *locus of control.* Workers with an internal locus of control may experience less stress than those with an external locus of control because they feel that they can influence what happens to them. However, when events are largely beyond a worker's control (such as when a company goes bankrupt), internals may experience stress because they are not in control of the situation.

Ability.   In addition to having different personalities, workers also differ in their abilities, which can impact stress levels. Stress can be experienced when workers lack the abilities necessary to perform their jobs. Workers at the Collins & Aikman carpet factory in Dalton, Georgia, for example, experienced stress when the factory was computerized (see Insight 2.5). Some of the workers were not able to read or perform the calculations necessary to work with the new computers and felt that their jobs were threatened. Collins & Aikman helped workers deal with this source of stress by providing extensive additional training. The training itself was a source of stress for some workers who were afraid that they would not be able to deal with this opportunity to improve their skills because of other demands on their time at work and at home.[12]

Somewhat related to ability is another factor that affects whether workers feel stressed: experience. People are more likely to feel stressed when they are doing something that they lack experience in, and they are less likely to feel stressed as they gain experience. This explains why workers starting new jobs often feel stressed and nervous. Newcomers do not have experience performing the different tasks in their jobs, and the lack of experience creates uncertainty for them. A new supervisor in a bank, for example, is uncertain about how to settle work-scheduling conflicts among his subordinates, how to run a group meeting most effectively, how to get help from his boss without seeming incompetent, and how to motivate a capable but poorly performing subordinate. These sources of uncertainty create stress for the supervisor, but the stress diminishes over time as he gains experience.

CONSEQUENCES OF STRESS

Because what a worker considers stress is highly personal, workers differ in the extent to which they experience the consequences of stress, even when they are exposed to the same sources of stress (such as making a presentation or getting laid off). At some point in their lives, however, all workers experience some of the consequences of stress. These consequences are of three main types: physiological, psychological, and behavioral. Each consequence has the potential to affect well-being, performance, and effectiveness at the individual, group, and organizational levels.

Physiological Consequences.   Were you ever unable to fall asleep or stay asleep at night when you were experiencing particularly high levels of stress during the day? Such sleep disturbances are just one of the potential physiological consequences of stress. Other potential physiological consequences range from sweaty palms, feeling flushed, trembling, a pounding heart, elevated blood pressure, headaches, dizziness, nausea, stomachaches, backaches, and hives to heart attacks and impaired immune system functioning. Rock singer Stevie Nicks, for example, says that when she experiences stress before a live performance her stomach gets upset, she breaks out in a sweat, and her asthma bothers her.[13]

The relationship between stress and physiological consequences is complicated, and researchers are still struggling to understand the dynamics involved. Two individuals experiencing the same high levels of stress may have different physiological reactions. Moreover, some people seem to experience more physiological consequences than others do. People also differ in the extent to which they complain about physical symptoms of stress such as headaches and stomachaches.[14] The most serious physiological consequences of stress are likely to occur only after considerably high levels of stress are experienced for a prolonged period of time. High blood pressure, cardiovascular disease, and heart attacks, for example, may result from excessive levels of prolonged stress.

Psychological Consequences.   One of the major psychological consequences of stress is the experience of stressful feelings and emotions. Stressful feelings and emotions can range from being in a bad mood, feeling anxious, worried, and upset to feeling angry, scornful, bitter, or hostile. Any or all of these feelings will detract from workers' well-being.[15]

Another psychological consequence of stress is that people tend to have more negative attitudes when they experience stress. Workers who are highly stressed tend to have a more negative outlook on various aspects of their jobs and organizations and are more likely to have low levels of job satisfaction and organizational commitment.

Burnout
Psychological, emotional, or physical exhaustion.

Burnout—psychological, emotional, or physical exhaustion—is a special kind of psychological consequence of stress that afflicts some workers who experience high levels of work stress day in and day out for an extended period of time. Burnout is especially likely to occur when workers are responsible for helping, protecting, or taking care of other people.[16] Nurses, doctors, social workers, teachers, lawyers, and police officers, for example, can be at risk for developing burnout due to the nature of their jobs.

Three key signs of burnout are feelings of low personal accomplishment, emotional exhaustion, and depersonalization.[17] Burned-out workers often feel that they are not helping others or accomplishing as much as they should be. Emotionally they are worn out from the constant stress of dealing with people who are sometimes in desperate need of assistance. Burned-out workers sometimes depersonalize the people they need to help, thinking about them as objects or things rather than as feeling human beings. A burned-out social worker, for example, may think about a foster child in need of a new home as a case number rather than as a very scared 12-year-old. This psychological consequence may lead to a behavioral consequence when the burned-out social worker treats the child in a cold and distant manner.

Sometimes workers experience such extreme and negative psychological consequences of stress that they end up committing violent acts in the workplace. On average, between eighteen and twenty-four workers are killed each year in the United States by excessively stressed and unhappy current or former organizational members.[18] Admittedly, workers who murder their coworkers or managers or commit other kinds of violent acts often have had a history of violent behavior, substance abuse, or other psychological problems. However, it also may be that something in the workplace is causing these already disturbed individuals to experience excessively negative psychological consequences of stress that result in their violent behavior. Understanding why there is such an unusually high incidence of violence in the U.S. Postal Service can help uncover why such extreme consequences of stress are experienced, as indicated in Insight 9.1.

Insight 9.1

Stress

Violence in the Post Office

In a four-year period, approximately 2,000 acts of violence occurred in offices of the U.S. Postal Service (www.usps.gov). Workers in post offices are three times more likely than workers in other organizations to be killed by coworkers. Post office slayings have occurred in post offices in locations ranging from Edmund, Oklahoma, and Dearborn, Michigan, to Dana Point, California.[19]

Psychologist Gwendolyn Keita, who is trying to understand why the postal tragedies are occurring, suggests that work stress is partially to blame. Postal workers have little autonomy even though the nature of their jobs has changed from the very simple repetitive kinds of tasks of twenty years ago to the more responsible and complicated tasks of today. Post offices have been characterized as autocratic work environments where punishment is used and a sense of injustice or unfairness prevails.

The U.S. Postal Service has sought the help and advice of many experts in trying to change working conditions and solve problems in post offices. Improvements in working conditions under study include ways to improve communication and increase understanding and conflict resolution by, for example, training supervisors and workers to get along better with each other, stopping some supervisors from behaving in a punitive, intimidating, or bullying manner toward their subordinates, and responding quickly to worker grievances and complaints.

Acts of violence in post offices have had serious and negative psychological consequences for workers who have witnessed the slayings of their coworkers or supervisors. Workers at the Royal Oak, Michigan, post office experienced intense levels of stress after a 31-year-old former letter carrier (Thomas McIlvane) killed five coworkers, wounded four others, and then shot himself after failing in his attempts to get his job back. A team of a hundred mental health volunteers (such as psychologists and social workers) provided counseling to workers who witnessed the shootings, to the families of these workers, and to the families of the workers killed. The team helped people deal with their sense of grief and loss and tried to come up with ways to improve things (such as by better stress management and communication).[20]

Dr. Susan Silk was one of the psychologists who helped survivors of the postal slayings in Michigan recover from their psychological trauma. She now consults for post offices in Michigan trying to improve conditions, and she suggests that the post office "must empower employees to have a little more control . . . [and] treat employees with more respect and sensitivity. The whole structure needs to become more participatory."[21]

Behavioral Consequences. The potential consequence of stress on job performance is perhaps of most interest to managers. One way to summarize the relationship between stress and performance is in terms of an inverted U (see Fig. 9.1). Up to a certain point (point A in the figure), increases in stress enhance performance. Beyond that point, further increases in stress impair performance. Stress up to point A is *positive stress* because it propels workers to perform at a high level. Stress beyond point A is *negative stress* because it impairs performance.

The fact that stress can be positive is illustrated by considering the motivational theories and tools we discussed in Chapters 6, 7, and 8. These theories and tools can be used to raise levels of motivation and job performance, but they also have the potential to increase levels of stress. For example, giving a worker a difficult goal to reach and then telling the worker that he or she will receive a hefty bonus only if the goal is attained is likely to result in a certain level of stress. In this case, however, the stress is positive because it energizes the worker to try to reach the goal. Similarly, the stress that most students experience as exams approach is positive because it propels the students to study. As a final example, many performers and athletes find that a certain amount of stress (or stage fright) gets their adrenaline pumping and helps them to do their best. As Stevie Nicks indicates, "If I wasn't really nervous before walking on stage, I'd be really worried."[22] The expression "I work best under pressure" captures the feeling that positive stress can propel people to reach their goals and perform at a high level.

Stress levels that are too high, however, can impair performance and thus are negative. Students who suffer from serious test anxiety cannot remember material they may have known quite well the day before the test. Their stress and anxiety interfere with their ability to take the test, and thoughts of how poorly they are going to do prevent them from concentrating on the questions being asked. Similarly, excessively high levels of stress may prevent workers from effectively performing their jobs. Entertainers who experience excessive levels of negative stress may avoid live performances

FIGURE 9.1

An Inverted U
Relationship Between
Stress and Performance
Stress up to point A is positive
because it prompts a worker
to perform at a high level.
Stress beyond point A is
negative because it impairs
performance.

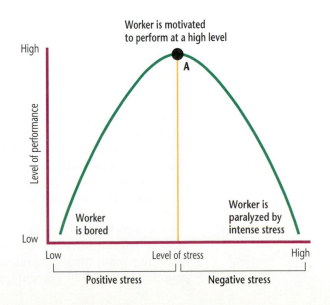

After a shooting at the Dearborn, Michigan post office, Postmaster General Marvin Runyon addressed U.S. postal workers at the Dearborn Civic Center about violence in the Postal Service. Counseling sessions were held at the meeting to help alleviate employee stress.

altogether, as Barbra Streisand did for twenty-seven years.[23] In 1994, world-renowned speed skater Dan Jansen was able to win the Olympic gold medal that had alluded him for three previous Olympic games only when he was able to relax and control his dysfunctional level of stress with the help of sports psychologist James E. Loehr.[24]

Individual differences also affect the relationship between stress and performance. Some workers, because of their personalities and abilities, are able to withstand high levels of stress that seem to propel them on to even higher levels of performance; for such workers, high levels of stress are positive. The performance levels of other workers suffer when stress becomes too high. For each worker, the point at which increases in levels of stress result in decreases in performance depends on the worker's personality traits and abilities.

Besides enhanced or diminished job performance, other potential behavioral consequences of stress include strained interpersonal relations, absenteeism, and turnover. When workers are experiencing excessively high levels of stress (negative stress), it is often hard for them to be as caring and understanding with others (coworkers, subordinates, superiors, customers) as they normally would be. A normally agreeable worker who suddenly flies off the handle may be experiencing a very high level of stress. Joseph Strickland, a vice president in charge of Amoco's Dallas plant, which has recently downsized, realized that stress levels were getting out of hand when one of the managers at the plant started giving everyone a hard time. "He was yelling at the secretaries, he was screaming at the human resources people," Strickland recalled. "It was very unlike him."[25] Workers experiencing high levels of stress may also have strained relationships with their spouses and families. This was found to be the case with some workers who were laid off at Phillips Petroleum Company.[26]

Excessively high levels of stress may also lead to absenteeism and turnover, especially when workers have other employment options. A recent study found that many nurses experience so much stress and burnout that they are planning to quit their current jobs or leave nursing altogether.[27]

In Japan, where work overload is a significant source of stress for many workers, an extreme behavioral consequence of negative stress is what the Japanese call *karoshi,* death from overwork. A recent study conducted by the Japanese government found that in 1993 about one out of six men worked a minimum of 3,100 hours a year (60 hours a week, 52 weeks a year), a schedule that physicians suggest can lead to karoshi. Karoshi is not limited to Japan; the British Medical Association has investigated claims that karoshi took the life of a young doctor who worked 86 continuous hours in England.[28] Although controversy surrounds the nature and extent of karoshi, some people think that it is unethical (and should be illegal) to stress workers to such an extent that their lives may be in danger, as indicated in Insight 9.2.

Insight 9.2   **Ethics**

An Extreme Behavioral Consequence of Stress

Twenty-seven-year-old Charles McKenzie should have had everything going for him. He graduated from the elite Yale Law School and was a first-year associate at the prestigious New York law firm of Cleary, Gottlieb, Steen, & Hamilton. McKenzie, however, cut short his career and life by jumping off a building.

Gene McKenzie, Charles's father, thinks that the excessive workloads given to new attorneys are unethical and were responsible for his son's death. Junior attorneys at top law firms claim that sometimes they are expected to work between 3,000 and 4,000 hours a year (from 60 to 80 hours per week with two weeks off for vacation and sick days). Although partners at law firms may dispute these figures, most would agree that junior attorneys do face heavy workloads. Workloads at Cleary, Gottlieb, however, do not tend to be any more excessive than those at other law firms.

Gene McKenzie sued his son's former employer, but a New York City judge dismissed the case because he thought that it did not meet New York's legal criteria for emotional harm at work—conduct that is "atrocious and intolerable in a civilized society." Gene McKenzie plans to appeal the judge's decision.[29]

Stressors
Sources of stress.

Sources of Stress

What causes stress? Four major potential **stressors,** or sources of stress, are one's personal life, one's job responsibilities, membership in work groups and organizations, and work-life linkages. Whether potential stressors become actual stressors and produce stress and whether the stress a worker experiences is positive or negative depend on how the worker perceives and interprets the stressors and on individual differences. Across these four categories of

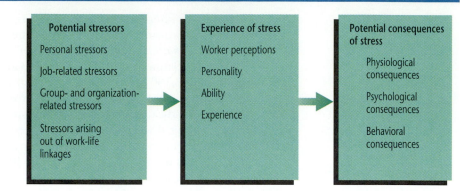

FIGURE **9.2**

Sources and Consequences
of Stress

potential stressors, an almost infinite variety of stressors may confront workers and lead to the physiological, psychological, and behavioral consequences of stress (see Fig. 9.2). The effects of these stressors combine to determine the overall level of stress a person experiences; each stressor contributes to or influences how stressed a person generally feels.

PERSONAL STRESSORS

Why are we bothering to discuss stressors from one's personal life in a book on organizational behavior? What happens to workers off the job can affect their attitudes, behaviors, and performance on the job as well as their own well-being. A normally polite and helpful salesperson may lose his temper with a disgruntled customer because he is preoccupied by the fight he had with his wife that same morning. Similarly, a marketing manager who normally has an open-door policy may avoid interacting with her colleagues because she can't get her mind off her teenage son's drug problem. Marriott International found that personal and family problems are a significant cause of the high

TO MANAGERS

The Nature of Stress

- Realize that what is stressful for one worker may not be stressful for another.
- When workers have negative attitudes toward their jobs and the organization and frequently seem on edge or in a bad mood, try to find out whether they are experiencing excessively high levels of stress by asking them about any problems or concerns they may have.
- When managing workers who help others as part of their jobs, be on the lookout for the signs of burnout—workers who feel they are not accomplishing enough, who often seem emotionally exhausted, or who depersonalize the people they are helping.
- When using motivational techniques and tools such as goal setting and contingent rewards, be sure you are not causing your subordinates to experience negative stress.
- When workers seem to be having a lot of interpersonal problems with other organizational members or with customers, clients, or patients, determine whether they are experiencing too high a level of stress.

turnover rates of workers in some of its restaurants and hotels.[30] From the opening case, it is clear that family responsibilities and home life are an important concern for workers both on and off the job.

One way of viewing these and other personal sources of stress is in terms of major and minor life events.[31] *Major life events* can have serious implications for stress and well-being and include the death of a loved one, divorce, serious illness of oneself or a loved one, and getting arrested. These are all sources of stress involving emotional or physical "threats" and are negative. Other major life events are positive "opportunities" that can be stressful, such as getting married, buying a house, having or adopting a baby, and moving to another state. Relatively *minor life events* also can be sources of stress, such as getting a speeding ticket, having trouble with your in-laws or child care provider, and even going on vacation.

How stressed a person generally feels appears to depend not only on the extent to which the stressors occur and how significant they are for the person but also on how many of them occur simultaneously during any given period.[32] New college graduates, for example, sometimes experience high levels of stress because many potentially stressful life events (both positive and negative) occur in a short period of time—moving, losing old friends, making new friends, getting married, and becoming financially independent while at the same time starting or looking for a job. Although each event might be only mildly stressful by itself, the fact that they are all happening together results in a high level of stress.

Researchers have developed questionnaires that contain checklists of stressful life events and their perceived impact. Overall stress levels are determined by the number of events that have occurred during a certain period (such as the past three years) and their significance for a person. Overall stress levels, in turn, have been shown to be related to the extent to which some of the negative consequences of stress that we discussed earlier occur.[33] Items from one of these questionnaires are listed in Table 9.1.

TABLE **9.1**

Sample Items from a Life Event Checklist to Determine Overall Stress Levels

	Happened in Last Three Years?		Current Impact on You?						
	No	**Yes**	**Negative**			**None**	**Positive**		
1. Started school or a training program after not going to school for a long time	No	Yes	−3	−2	−1	0	+1	+2	+3
2. Started work for the first time	No	Yes	−3	−2	−1	0	+1	+2	+3
3. Changed jobs for a better one	No	Yes	−3	−2	−1	0	+1	+2	+3
4. Changed jobs for a worse one	No	Yes	−3	−2	−1	0	+1	+2	+3
5. Changed jobs for one that was no better and no worse than the last one	No	Yes	−3	−2	−1	0	+1	+2	+3
6. Had trouble with boss	No	Yes	−3	−2	−1	0	+1	+2	+3
7. Demoted at work	No	Yes	−3	−2	−1	0	+1	+2	+3
8. Found out was *not* going to be promoted at work	No	Yes	−3	−2	−1	0	+1	+2	+3

(continued)

TABLE 9.1
(CONTINUED)

	Happened in Last Three Years?		Current Impact on You?						
	No	Yes	Negative			None	Positive		
9. Conditions at work got worse, other than demotion or trouble with boss	No	Yes	−3	−2	−1	0	+1	+2	+3
10. Had significant success at work	No	Yes	−3	−2	−1	0	+1	+2	+3
11. Fired from previous job	No	Yes	−3	−2	−1	0	+1	+2	+3
12. Promoted on present job	No	Yes	−3	−2	−1	0	+1	+2	+3
13. Started a business or profession	No	Yes	−3	−2	−1	0	+1	+2	+3
14. Suffered a business loss or failure	No	Yes	−3	−2	−1	0	+1	+2	+3
15. Sharply increased workload	No	Yes	−3	−2	−1	0	+1	+2	+3
16. Sharply reduced workload	No	Yes	−3	−2	−1	0	+1	+2	+3
17. Had trouble with a coworker or peer	No	Yes	−3	−2	−1	0	+1	+2	+3
18. Had trouble with a subordinate	No	Yes	−3	−2	−1	0	+1	+2	+3
19. Had trouble with a customer or client	No	Yes	−3	−2	−1	0	+1	+2	+3
20. Spouse started work for the first time	No	Yes	−3	−2	−1	0	+1	+2	+3
21. Spouse changed jobs for a worse one	No	Yes	−3	−2	−1	0	+1	+2	+3
22. Spouse promoted	No	Yes	−3	−2	−1	0	+1	+2	+3
23. Spouse demoted at work	No	Yes	−3	−2	−1	0	+1	+2	+3
24. Spouse fired	No	Yes	−3	−2	−1	0	+1	+2	+3
25. Took out a mortgage	No	Yes	−3	−2	−1	0	+1	+2	+3
26. Started buying a car, furniture, or other large purchase on an installment plan	No	Yes	−3	−2	−1	0	+1	+2	+3
27. Foreclosure of a mortgage or loan	No	Yes	−3	−2	−1	0	+1	+2	+3
28. Did not get an expected wage or salary increase	No	Yes	−3	−2	−1	0	+1	+2	+3
29. Took a cut in wage or salary without a demotion	No	Yes	−3	−2	−1	0	+1	+2	+3
30. Spouse did not get an expected wage or salary increase	No	Yes	−3	−2	−1	0	+1	+2	+3
31. Robbed	No	Yes	−3	−2	−1	0	+1	+2	+3
32. Got involved in a court case	No	Yes	−3	−2	−1	0	+1	+2	+3
33. Acquired a pet	No	Yes	−3	−2	−1	0	+1	+2	+3
34. Pet died	No	Yes	−3	−2	−1	0	+1	+2	+3
35. Was not able to take a planned vacation	No	Yes	−3	−2	−1	0	+1	+2	+3
36. Remodeled a home	No	Yes	−3	−2	−1	0	+1	+2	+3
37. Became engaged	No	Yes	−3	−2	−1	0	+1	+2	+3
38. Engagement was broken	No	Yes	−3	−2	−1	0	+1	+2	+3
39. Spouse was physically ill	No	Yes	−3	−2	−1	0	+1	+2	+3
40. Expecting a baby	No	Yes	−3	−2	−1	0	+1	+2	+3
41. Child started college	No	Yes	−3	−2	−1	0	+1	+2	+3
42. Serious family argument other than with spouse	No	Yes	−3	−2	−1	0	+1	+2	+3

Source: Adapted from R. S. Bhagat, S. J. McQuaid, H. Lindholm, and J. Segouis. "Total Life Stress: A Multimethod Validation of the Construct and Its Effects on Organizationally Valued Outcomes and Withdrawal Behaviors," *Journal of Applied Psychology,* 1985, 70, pp. 202–214; A. P. Brief, M. J. Burke, J. M. George, B. S. Robinson, and J. Webster, "Should Negative Affectivity Remain an Unmeasured Variable in the Study of Job Stress?" *Journal of Applied Psychology,* 1988, 73, pp. 193–198; B. S. Dohrenwend, L. Krasnoff, A. R. Askenasy, and B. P. Dohrenwend, "Exemplification of a Method for Scaling Life Events: The PERI Life Events Scale," *Journal of Health and Social Behavior,* 1978, 19, pp. 205–229; J. H. Johnson and I. G. Sarason, "Recent Developments in Research on Life Stress," in V. Hamilton and D. M. Warburton, eds., *Human Stress and Cognition: An Information Processing Approach* (New York: Wiley, 1979), pp. 205–236.

JOB-RELATED STRESSORS

Just as a wide variety of life events can be potentially stressful, a wide variety of potential stressors arise from a person's job. Here we consider six job-related stressors: role conflict, role ambiguity, overload, underload, promotions and challenging assignments, and conditions that impact workers' economic well-being.

In Chapter 1 we defined a *role* as a set of behaviors or tasks a person is expected to perform because of the position he or she holds in a group or organization. **Role conflict** occurs when expected behaviors or tasks are at odds with each other.[34] A social worker experiences role conflict when he is told to (1) spend more time and effort to determine whether children in foster care should be returned to their parents and (2) double the number of cases he handles each month. A middle manager experiences role conflict when her supervisor expects her to increase levels of production and her subordinates complain that they are overworked and expect her to ease up on her demands.

Role ambiguity is the uncertainty that occurs when workers are not sure about what is expected of them and how they should perform their jobs.[35] Role ambiguity can be an especially potent source of stress for newcomers to an organization, work group, or job. Newcomers are often unclear about what they are supposed to do and how they should do it. Most workers, however, experience some degree of role ambiguity at one time or another because organizations frequently change job responsibilities so that the organization can adapt to changing conditions. Ford Motor Company, for example, realized it needed to adapt to increased customer demands for high-quality automobiles and increased worker demands for more autonomy. To address the need for change, Ford reorganized some of its factories so that workers performed their jobs in teams rather than individually. Some team members experienced role ambiguity because they were unsure of their new responsibilities in the teams.

Sometimes workers experience job-related stress not because of conflicting demands (role conflict) or uncertain expectations (role ambiguity) but because of **overload**—the condition of having too many tasks to perform.[36] Robert Kakiuchi, vice president of human resources at the U.S. Bank of Washington, often works nights, weekends, and holidays to accomplish all of the tasks he is assigned. Layoffs reduced Kakiuchi's department from seventy employees to six, but the number of human resource services that he is expected to provide to other departments in the bank has not been reduced at all.[37] Kakiuchi is experiencing overload because his organization expects the remaining human resource workers to perform the tasks that used to be performed by laid-off workers.[38] Nadine Billard, a manager of export sales for the book publisher HarperCollins, experiences so much overload that she typically works fifteen-hour days and takes work home on weekends.[39] Whether the high level of stress an overloaded worker experiences is negative and impairs performance depends on the worker's personality traits and abilities.

Overload is particularly prevalent among middle and top managers. A recent study conducted by the American Management Association found that 41 percent of the middle managers surveyed had more work to do than time in which to do it. Another study conducted by the Seattle consulting firm Priority Management found that many middle managers are working much longer hours because of the extent of their overload.[40] Earlier we discussed

Role conflict

The struggle that occurs when the behaviors or tasks that a person is expected to perform are at odds with each other.

Role ambiguity

The uncertainty that occurs when workers are not sure what is expected of them and how they should perform their jobs.

Overload

The condition of having too many tasks to perform.

how overload is a significant problem in Japan and sometimes leads to the behavioral consequence of karoshi (death by overwork).

Underload
The condition of having too few tasks to perform.

Underload, not having enough work to do, can also be a source of stress for workers. When was the last time you were really bored. Maybe it was a slow day at work, maybe you were doing research for a paper at the library, maybe you were studying for an exam, or maybe you were watching a bad movie. Now imagine that you were truly bored for eight hours a day, five days a week. You would probably experience stress just because you had too little to do. As we know from the job characteristics model (see Chapter 7), most workers like to use different skills on the job and to feel that they are doing something worthwhile. More generally, a certain level of stress is positive and leads to high levels of motivation and performance, as indicated in Figure 9.1.

Promotions and challenging assignments can be a source of stress for workers who are not sure that they can perform effectively or have low self-efficacy. A worker promoted to a supervisory position who has never before had subordinates reporting to him may experience stress because he is not sure that he will able to be assertive enough. Barbra Streisand was so negatively stressed by the challenge of performing in front of 125,000 people in New York's Central Park in 1967 that she forgot the lyrics to three of her songs and avoided live performances for the next twenty-seven years. Madonna found the opportunity of singing at the 1991 Oscar presentation (which is broadcast to billions of television viewers) so stressful that her hand shook.[41]

Stressors that impact workers' *economic well-being and job security* are also powerful sources of stress.[42] More and more workers are exposed to the negative effects of stressors like losing their jobs—especially workers who have few skills, as indicated in Insight 9.3.

Insight 9.3

A Global View

Low Pay Versus Unemployment: A Cross-Cultural Comparison

Ava Bilbraut, a 33-year-old single parent with a 16-year-old son, lives in Hartford, Connecticut. Bilbraut works in a bakery during the day and has a second job at night cleaning offices. Bilbraut earns between $250 and $300 a week. She struggles to make ends meet and considers herself lucky that she doesn't get sick often because she has no health insurance. Nevertheless, a local hospital has sued her for failing to pay a bill.

Klaus Beilisch, a 30-year-old father with a wife and 16-month-old son, lives in Berlin, Germany. Beilisch's income is around $280 a week, he lives in a rent-free apartment, and his health insurance covers most of his family's medical expenses. What does Beilisch do for a living? He is unemployed.

Because of a lack of low-skill jobs in both Europe and the United States, the experiences of Ava and Klaus are not that uncommon in their respective countries. The United States has responded to this problem by trying to create new jobs and paying workers who perform them relatively low wages. Germany, in contrast, pays employed workers relatively higher wages, has higher levels of unemployment, and gives generous government benefits to workers who are unemployed.[43]

Ava and Klaus both experience stress from their economic circumstances. Ava dreams about moving somewhere else even though she feels she will never find a good job. Although the Social Security payments that her son receives because his father (Ava's first husband) is dead help out a bit, she still struggles to buy the basic necessities. Needless to say, health insurance is out of the question. When she does have some money left over, it usually amounts to no more than $1 to buy a lottery ticket, which is her only source of hope right now.

The German government takes care of Klaus's basic economic requirements, and he seems better off than Ava, but he too experiences stress. His life without work is aimless and boring. Although he occasionally looks for jobs as a security guard, salesperson, street cleaner, or postal worker, he does not want to take a job that pays the same as or less than the government unemployment benefits he receives. He also does not have much hope of improving his and his family's circumstances.[44]

Although the experiences of Ava and Klaus may seem a bit extreme to you, most, if not all, workers use the money they make from their jobs to support themselves and their loved ones. In the United States, a worker paid the minimum wage earns $8,840 a year, which is $2,300 below the national poverty level for a family of three.[45] When job-related income is very low or threatened by layoffs and downsizing, a lack of job security, or pay cuts, the well-being of workers and their families is put in jeopardy.

Numerous studies have shown that when organizations lay off employees, stress caused by the consequent unemployment can be very damaging to workers and their families and may result in physical and mental illness, depression, suicide, an increase in family violence, and a family's breakup.[46] Layoffs can also be stressful for members of an organization who do not lose their jobs or are survivors of the layoff.[47] Layoff survivors can feel guilty, angry, unhappy, lonely, or fearful that they will be the next to lose their jobs. Sometimes they become physically ill from their high levels of stress. A 46-year-old geologist who has worked for a Houston oil company for the past eleven years survived a layoff and was promoted to be the leader of a group of twelve of her close colleagues. One of her first assignments in her new supervisory role was to lay off half of the geologists in the group. Her stress levels were so high that she started to go to bed earlier and earlier at night so that she would not have to think about work.[48]

Given how important job income is to workers and their families, opportunities for increasing pay levels also can be stressful to workers who are not sure that they can meet the requirements for pay increases.[49] A car salesperson working strictly on a commission basis experiences considerable stress every day because his ability to support his family and buy them the things they need depends on how many cars he sells. He likes his job because he has a lot of autonomy and is given the opportunity to earn high commissions by his hard work. But the job is stressful because so much is riding not only on what he does but also on things that are beyond his control, such as the economy, company-sponsored discounts, and advertising.

Those are just a sampling of potential stressors that are related to a person's job. Although we discuss how workers and organizations can cope with stressors in general later in the chapter, at this point it is useful to list some of the steps managers can take to make sure that these job-related stressors do not cause workers to experience so high a level of stress that it becomes negative and impairs their well-being and performance:

- To make sure that role conflict does not get out of hand, managers should be sure not to give workers conflicting expectations and should try to ensure that what they expect subordinates to do does not conflict with what others (customers, subordinates, coworkers) expect from them.
- Role ambiguity can be kept to a manageable level by telling workers clearly what is expected of them, how they should perform their jobs, what changes are being made.
- Managers can try to make sure that none of their subordinates are overloaded and can redesign jobs that include too many tasks and responsibilities.
- When underload is a problem, managers might want to consider redesigning jobs so that they score higher on the five core dimensions in the job characteristics model (skill variety, task identity, task significance, autonomy, and feedback).
- When workers experience stress from promotions or challenging job assignments, managers should take steps to raise their self-efficacy—their belief that they can be successful. We discussed several ways to boost self-efficacy in Chapter 5, such as encouraging small successes, letting subordinates know that others like themselves have succeeded in similar kinds of situations, having high expectations, and expressing confidence in subordinates' abilities.
- Organizations should do whatever they can to minimize the negative effects of layoffs and downsizing on their employees' economic well-being by giving workers advance notice, providing counseling services, and giving workers fair and equitable severance pay. Such steps can also help reduce the stress of layoff survivors.
- When workers are experiencing stress due to, for example, a pay-for-performance plan, managers should actively work on boosting their self-efficacy.

GROUP- AND ORGANIZATION-RELATED STRESSORS

Potential stressors that can cause too high a level of stress also can arise at the work-group and organizational levels. At the work-group level, for example, misunderstandings, conflicts, and interpersonal disagreements can be sources of negative stress for group members. In Chapters 10 and 11 we discuss the benefits of using groups in organizations and some of the specific problems that work groups face and ways to alleviate them. Here, Insight 9.4 shows how misunderstandings and conflicts can cause stress among people from different cultures.

Insight 9.4

A Global View

Misunderstandings Stress Cross-Cultural Business Partners

In one of the most impressive cross-cultural business ventures to date, researchers from three competing companies—Siemens AG of Germany (www.siemens.de), Toshiba Corporation of Japan (www.toshiba.com), and IBM (www.ibm.com)—are working together at IBM's East Fishkill, New York, facility to build a new computer memory chip. The more than one hundred scientists from the three different cultures working on the project call themselves the Triad.

Managers (from all three companies) who organized this cooperative effort were originally concerned that the scientists might encounter some problems working together because of their different cultural backgrounds. Their concerns have been borne out as misunderstandings and conflicts have become a significant source of stress for many of the scientists. The German scientists from Siemens, for example, were aghast when their Japanese counterparts from Toshiba closed their eyes during meetings and appeared to be sleeping. (Apparently, overworked scientists and managers frequently do this in Japan during parts of meetings that don't relate to them.) The Japanese scientists, who are used to working in big groups, find it stressful to meet in small groups and to speak English, and some of them have tried to arrange their work so they come into contact only with fellow Japanese scientists. The American scientists from IBM experience stress because they think that the Germans spend too much time on planning, the Japanese spend too much time reviewing ideas, and neither spends enough time actually getting the project done.

Despite rumors that some scientists are withholding information from others, the project is proceeding as planned, and everyone involved is learning a great deal, not only about the technical aspects of such a joint international venture but also about its more human side. Most, if not all, of the scientists are experiencing firsthand some of the stresses involved in working in a cross-cultural team. Even making suggestions for improvements can be a source of stress. Klaus Roithner, an engineer with Siemens, claims that when he tried making suggestions to IBM engineers about how to improve some of their techniques, they accused him first of not being specific enough and then of trying to change the way IBM does things to be more like Siemens's techniques. Now, Roithner says, "I indirectly suggest an idea to IBM engineers, and let them think they have come up with it themselves." Differences in native language have also contributed to stress levels. IBM scientist Matt Wordeman indicates that although the project is still on track, the stressful misunderstandings and conflicts arising out of cultural differences may be preventing some of the creative advances the originators of the project had hoped for.[50]

International joint ventures such as the one described in Insight 9.4 have many advantages: Participants get different perspectives on a project or problem, a wide variety of skills and expertise is represented, and participants are able to benefit from their exposure to new ways of doing things. To take full advantage of these benefits of diversity (in nationality or country of origin) without experiencing too much stress from being exposed to so much that is new, individuals and groups need to be aware of and sensitive to the role that national culture plays in how people behave in groups and organizations (differences in national cultures and their effects are discussed in detail in Chapter 17).

Uncomfortable working conditions are another source of stress for groups and entire organizations. Excessive noise, temperature extremes, and poorly designed office equipment and machinery can be very stressful when workers are exposed to them day in and day out. In recent years, more than 2,000 lawsuits have been filed by workers who claim that poorly designed computer keyboards—some made by well-known companies such as Eastman Kodak, IBM, and AT&T—have resulted in high levels of stress and painful and sometimes crippling injuries to the workers' hands and wrists.[51]

Potentially dangerous or *unsafe* working conditions such as working with toxic chemicals, with dangerous machinery, in nuclear power plants, or with people who have communicable diseases like AIDS can cause stress and injuries.[52] A recent study by Circadian Technologies Inc. found that pilots who fly for United Parcel Service face dangerous working conditions between 15 percent and 31 percent of the time. The pilots' union attributes these dangerous working conditions to flights that cross several time zones and flight schedules that cause pilots to alternate between flying at night and flying during the day.[53] Dangerous working conditions can also lead to on-the-job injuries. A recent study conducted by the University of Michigan School of Public Health found that workers in Michigan missed 8.9 million days of work in a year for injuries they received while performing their jobs.[54]

When uncomfortable and unsafe working conditions are coupled with other sources of stress, such as overload, stress levels can become intolerable, as indicated in Insight 9.5.

Insight 9.5   **Ethics**

Multiple Sources of Stress Plague Lehman's Typing Pool

The federal government's Occupational Safety and Health Administration (OSHA) has recently cited a large investment banking firm, Lehman Brothers Inc. (www.lehman.com), for unsafe working conditions. At the heart of the allegations are working conditions in Lehman's Creative Arts Center, which employees indicate is a glorified typing pool. The forty typists, proofreaders, and managers employed by the center work in a large, windowless room that is open twenty-four hours a day, seven days a week.

OSHA's investigations indicate that the design of the work areas forces the typists to reach across long distances, twist their wrists, and hold their hands suspended in air without support for extended periods of time. Heavy workloads that caused workers to sit in the same position for long spells were also cited as sources of stress at the Creative Arts Center. Working conditions like these have the potential to lead to bursitis (inflammation of the shoulder or elbow), carpal-tunnel syndrome (a painful hand and arm inflammation), and other work-related injuries. Workers also indicate that a serious overcrowding problem at the center sometimes causes them to have to type on their laps because there is no desk space. Moreover, the room temperature is kept uncomfortably cold for the smooth operation of the computers, without regard for how the workers feel. Some workers feel that it is unethical for the company to expose them to these unsafe and uncomfortable working conditions. In addition, all forty workers share just two telephones.

Besides uncomfortable and unsafe working conditions, employees at the Creative Arts Center cite work overload as a major source of stress. Darlene O'Hara, a word processor at the center for around three years, likens the workplace to a sweatshop. She says that overload is so bad that word processors are not given enough time to complete typing projects and often have bankers breathing down their backs waiting for work to be completed. Another worker indicated that there is a constant push to meet unrealistic deadlines and most employees never have the time to take their fifteen-minute breaks.

A spokesman for Lehman disputes some of OSHA's allegations, but workers at the center do seem to be exposed to multiple sources of stress, and high stress levels do appear to be taking their toll. One employee indicated that Lehman was the worst place she ever worked, and Patricia Bah, who has worked at Lehman for seven years, indicated that working in the center means "a high level of stress and claustrophobic working conditions."[55]

We discuss what individuals and organizations can do to cope with stressors in general later in the chapter, but at this point it is useful to consider what managers and organizations can do to try to make sure that group and organizational-level stressors do not get out of hand. First, members of work groups can be trained to work together as a team and communicate effectively with each other (in Chapter 19, we discuss some team-building strategies). Second, organizations should make sure that workers have comfortable working conditions whenever possible. Third, organizations should ensure that workers are not exposed to any unnecessary risks on the job and that all safety precautions are in place to limit the risk of injury on the job. This is just a sampling of the steps managers and organizations can take to try to limit the extent to which these potential stressors have negative effects on the workers exposed to them.

STRESSORS ARISING OUT OF WORK-LIFE LINKAGES

People who may be employed as factory workers, receptionists, managers, nurses, or truck drivers are also often parents, spouses, children of elderly parents, volunteers in community organizations, and hobbyists. When work roles conflict with personal life, stress is often the result, as we saw in the opening case. New accountants and attorneys working in major accounting and law firms, for example, are expected to put in very long hours. Although working long hours can be stressful in its own right, it can be even more stressful when it conflicts with demands from one's personal life. Many workers have young children at home and a spouse who is putting in equally long hours. If the responsibility for taking care of an ill parent or being president of a local charity are added in, the stress can be overwhelming. Single parents often feel even more burdened because they do not have a spouse to help out with family problems and responsibilities.[56]

Even when workers do not have children, family responsibilities often cause stress when they conflict with work demands. Faith Merrens, a manager of software designers at U.S. West Communications Inc., indicates that "elder care is the biggest personal issue we face in maintaining productivity from day to day." Most of her subordinates have been absent from work to take care of elderly relatives, and Merrens herself and her boss had to take time off when their parents were in the hospital. Around 22 percent of the workforce expects to be taking care of elderly relatives in the next three or four years, and by the year 2005 around 37 percent of the workforce will be between ages 40 and 54—the ages at which these workers' elderly parents often need assistance from their middle-aged children.[57] Later in the chapter, we discuss some of the steps organizations can take to help prevent these kinds of conflicts from overwhelming their employees.

Another form of conflict between work and personal life occurs when workers are requested to do things that go against their own personal values or when they work in organizations with ethics different from their own. It is very stressful, for example, for some emergency room personnel at private hospitals to turn away potential patients because they lack medical insurance. Likewise, it is sometimes stressful for loan officers at banks to foreclose on a family's mortgage because the family cannot keep up the payments, and for insurance agents to cancel medical insurance or deny coverage for certain kinds of problems or patients. Similarly, it can be stressful for an environmentalist to work for an organization that fails to recycle paper products and protect the environment or for salespeople to sell products they know are low in quality.

Coping with Stress

Ultimately the extent to which stress is experienced and whether stress is positive or negative depends on how people *cope*—that is, manage or deal with stressors. There are two basic types of coping: problem-focused coping and emotion-focused coping. **Problem-focused coping** is the steps people take to deal directly with and act on the source of stress.[58] For example, workers facing the threat of a layoff may cope in a problem-focused manner by looking for other jobs in organizations that are not downsizing. When problem-focused coping is successful, it helps workers deal with opportunities and threats that are causing stress.

Problem-focused coping
The steps people take to deal directly with and act on the source of stress.

TO MANAGERS

Emotion-focused coping
The steps people take to deal with and control their stressful feelings and emotions.

Emotion-focused coping is the steps people take to deal with and control their stressful feelings and emotions.[59] For example, some workers facing the threat of a layoff may try to alleviate some of their stressful feelings and emotions by exercising regularly or meditating. When emotion-focused coping is successful, stressful feelings and emotions generated by threats and opportunities do not get out of hand.

Research suggests that most of the time people engage in both kinds of coping when dealing with a stressor.[60] Individuals cope with stressors in a variety of problem- and emotion-focused ways, and there are steps that organizations can take to help workers cope with the many stressors they face.

PROBLEM-FOCUSED COPING STRATEGIES FOR INDIVIDUALS

Problem-focused coping is coping directly tailored to the stressor being experienced. A college senior experiencing stress due to an upcoming job interview copes in a problem-focused way by finding out as much information as possible about the company and doing some practice interviews with a friend. When Dale Morley moved his family from London to New York so that he could assume the position of vice president of sales and marketing for

Avis International, he and his family coped with the stress of being away from relatives by periodically making audiocassettes and sending them back home.[61] In addition to such specific problem-focused coping strategies devised to manage a very specific source of stress (job interview, moving), more general strategies can be used to deal with several kinds of stressors. Here we consider three: time management, getting help from a mentor, and role negotiation.

Time Management.   One strategy for helping workers deal with problems of overload and with conflicts between work and personal life is **time management,** a series of techniques that can help workers make better use of and accomplish more with their time. Time management usually entails these steps:

- Workers make lists of all the tasks they need to accomplish during the day.
- These tasks are then prioritized in terms of those that are most important and those that are least important and can probably be put off if need be.
- Workers estimate how long it will take to accomplish these tasks and plan their workday accordingly.[62]

Time management is a coping strategy for individuals, but organizations can help their members learn effective time management techniques. Addison-Wesley Publishing Company, based in Reading, Massachusetts, for example, holds seminars on time management to help employees make better use of their time and provides them with datebooks and other aids to put into practice what they learn in the seminars.

Getting Help from a Mentor.   Recall from Chapter 4 that mentoring is a process in which a more experienced member of an organization (the mentor) provides advice and guidance to a less experienced member (the protégé). Getting help from a mentor can be an effective problem-focused coping strategy for dealing with stressors such as role conflict, role ambiguity, overload, and challenging assignments and promotions. A mentor can advise an overloaded protégé, for example, about how to prioritize tasks so the important ones get accomplished, how to determine what tasks can be put aside, when saying no to additional assignments or requests is appropriate, and in general how best to manage his or her time.

Like time management, getting help from a mentor is an individual-based problem-focused coping strategy, but organizations can take steps to help ensure that mentors are available. The Academy of Management, the professional association of management professors and researchers, implemented a mentoring program in 1994 for assistant professors of management who are ethnic minorities. Assistant professors who want to take advantage of this program are paired with a senior management scholar whose research and teaching interests (for example, in organizational behavior or human resources management) are similar to theirs. The senior scholar provides advice and guidance to the assistant professor on a wide range of issues, such as research and the publication process, teaching, and how to manage most effectively the stresses of an academic career.

 **Time management**
Prioritizing and estimating techniques that allow workers to identify the most important tasks and fit them into their daily schedule.

Role negotiation
The process through which workers actively try to change their roles in order to reduce role conflict, role ambiguity, overload, or underload.

Role Negotiation.   **Role negotiation** is the process through which workers actively try to change their roles in order to reduce role conflict, role ambiguity, overload, or underload.[63] Sometimes simply saying no to additional assignments can be an effective means of role negotiation for overloaded workers.

Role negotiation can also be an effective means of problem-focused coping for workers who are experiencing stress due to work-life linkages. Blake Ashdown, a consultant based in East Lansing, Michigan, helps resorts develop and manage exercise programs and facilities. He has engaged in role negotiation by being more selective about the assignments he takes and by turning down some resorts. Ashdown has found this strategy to be an effective means of coping with the conflict between his demanding work schedule and his responsibilities at home. By negotiating his role, Ashdown is able to spend more time with his wife and five children and avoid high levels of stress from his work.[64]

EMOTION-FOCUSED COPING STRATEGIES FOR INDIVIDUALS

In addition to trying to manage problems and opportunities that are stressful, workers also have to learn to manage the feelings and emotions that these problems and opportunities give rise to. Here we consider four emotion-focused coping strategies for individuals: exercise, meditation, social support, and clinical counseling.

Exercise.   One of the reasons why exercise is so popular today is that it is an effective means of emotion-focused coping. Jogging, aerobics, swimming, tennis, and walking are just a few of the types of exercise that workers ranging from entry-level employees to CEOs and even American presidents use to cope with stressors in an emotion-focused way. Regular exercise can reduce stress, improve cardiovascular functioning, and enhance well-being.

Meditation.   Some workers deal with stressful emotions through meditation, a mental process in which they remove themselves from the stresses of daily living for thirty minutes or so a day and just relax. There are various forms of meditation, and some of them require professional training to learn. Generally, however, meditation entails a person being in a quiet environment, sitting in a comfortable position, and tuning out everyday cares and worries by focusing mentally on some visual image or verbal phrase.[65]

Social Support.   People naturally seek help from others—social support—when they are having problems or feeling stressed. The social support of friends, relatives, coworkers, or other people who care about you and are available to discuss problems, give advice, or just be with you can be an effective means of emotion-focused coping.[66] The number of people you can turn to and the quality of the relationships you have with those people are both important in helping to alleviate stress. A sample measure that is used to determine the extent to which a person is satisfied with the social support available to him or her is provided in Fig. 9.3.

Social support can reduce stressful feelings and emotions, but sometimes it can also help workers solve problems, as indicated in Insight 9.6.

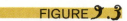

FIGURE **9.3**

A Measure of Satisfaction With Social Support

Source: Scale obtained from I. G. Sarason, Psychology Department NI-25, University of Washington, Seattle, WA 98195. Reprinted with permission. Scale described in I. G. Sarason, B. R. Sarason, E. N. Shearin, and G. R. Pierce, "A Brief Measure of Social Support: Practical and Theoretical Implications," *Journal of Social and Personal Relationships*, 1987, 4, pp. 497–510.

Instructions: The following questions ask about people in your environment who provide you with help or support. Each question has two parts. For the first part, list all the people you know, excluding yourself, whom you can count on for help or support in the manner described. Give the persons' initials, their relationship to you (see example). *Do not list more than one person next to each of the numbers beneath the question.*

For the second part, circle how *satisfied* you are with the overall support you have.

If you have had no support for a question, check the words "No one," but still rate your level of satisfaction. Do not list more than nine persons per question.

Please answer all the questions as best you can. All your responses will be kept confidential.

Example

Who do you know whom you can trust with information that could get you in trouble?

    _____ No one   **1** T.N. (brother)   **4** T.N. (father)   **7**

    2 L.M. (friend)   **5** L.M. (employer)   **8**

    3 R.S. (friend)   **6**   **9**

How satisfied?

6	⑤	4	3	2	1
very satisfied	fairly satisfied	a little satisfied	a little dissatisfied	fairly dissatisfied	very dissatisfied

---

1.   Whom can you really count on to be dependable when you need help?

    _____ No one   1   4   7

    2   5   8

    3   6   9

2.   How satisfied?

6	5	4	3	2	1
very satisfied	fairly satisfied	a little satisfied	a little dissatisfied	fairly dissatisfied	very dissatisfied

3.   Whom can you really count on to help you feel more relaxed when you are under pressure or tense?

    _____ No one

    1   4   7

    2   5   8

    3   6   9

4.   How satisfied?

6	5	4	3	2	1
very satisfied	fairly satisfied	a little satisfied	a little dissatisfied	fairly dissatisfied	very dissatisfied

5.   Who accepts you totally, including both your worst and best points?

    _____ No one   1   4   7

    2   5   8

    3   6   9

6.   How satisfied?

6	5	4	3	2	1
very satisfied	fairly satisfied	a little satisfied	a little dissatisfied	fairly dissatisfied	very dissatisfied

(continued)

FIGURE **9.3**
(CONTINUED)

7. Whom can you really count on to care about you, regardless of what is happening to you?

    _____ No one   1   4   7
                       2   5   8
                       3   6   9

8. How satisfied?

6	5	4	3	2	1
very satisfied	fairly satisfied	a little satisfied	a little dissatisfied	fairly dissatisfied	very dissatisfied

9. Whom can you really count on to help you feel better when you are feeling generally down-in-the-dumps?

    _____ No one   1   4   7
                       2   5   8
                       3   6   9

10. How satisfied?

6	5	4	3	2	1
very satisfied	fairly satisfied	a little satisfied	a little dissatisfied	fairly dissatisfied	very dissatisfied

11. Whom can you count on to console you when you are very upset?

    _____ No one   1   4   7
                       2   5   8
                       3   6   9

12. How satisfied?

6	5	4	3	2	1
very satisfied	fairly satisfied	a little satisfied	a little dissatisfied	fairly dissatisfied	very dissatisfied

Scoring: Satisfaction with social support is measured by averaging responses to the even-numbered questions (2, 4, 6, 8, 10 and 12).

Insight 9.6 A Global View

Social Support Helps Workers and Their Families Cope With Overseas Assignments

Workers in the U.S. domestic oil industry are increasingly being sent overseas by their companies for weeks at a time to teach workers in other countries how to operate equipment and machinery and drill for oil. Thirty-eight-year-old Jimmy Josey works for Bilco Tools (www.bilco-tools.com) in Houma, Louisiana, and has a wife and two sons (4 and 8 years old). Four times a year, for a month each time, he goes to the oil fields of Kazahkstan to train Kazakh, Hungarian, and Russian oil workers in how to use the oil-pipe-handling equipment manufactured by Bilco Tools. Kirby Falcon, Josey's neighbor, makes regular trips to Norway and the North Sea for his company, Hydraulic Well Control, which helps other companies drill for oil and is also based in Houma, Louisiana.

Workers in the U.S. oil industry often receive extra pay for their overseas assignments (Josey quadruples his salary when he works in Kazahkstan), but the stress of being away from their homes and families for weeks at a time takes its toll. Increasingly, workers and their families are relying on social support to help them cope. When Josey is in Kazahkstan, he often has meals with workers from Mississippi, Texas, and Oklahoma. He finds that simply having someone to talk to can help alleviate some stress while also providing tips on how to adjust to the overseas stints.

Back home, Josey's wife, Dana, copes with the stress of her husband being gone for weeks at a time by getting together with four other women in the neighborhood whose husbands are also regularly sent overseas. Social support helps Dana manage her increased responsibilities when her husband is out of the country and deal with the stress of her family being separated.[67]

Clinical Counseling.   Sometimes workers have difficulty coping on their own and seek professional help, or clinical counseling. Trained psychologists and psychiatrists can help workers learn how to cope with stressors that may seem overwhelming and at times unbearable.

Nonfunctional Strategies.   The four emotion-focused coping strategies that we have discussed are functional for individuals because they generally help to alleviate stressful feelings and emotions without creating new problems or sources of stress. Unfortunately, however, there are other emotion-focused ways of coping that are less functional for workers. Some people react to high levels of stress by eating too much, drinking too much, or taking drugs. Some workers employed by Phillips Petroleum Company, for example, started having problems with alcohol when they experienced high levels of stress from a big layoff.[68] These ways of coping are never effective in alleviating stressful feelings and emotions in the long run, and they create more problems, such as being overweight, being addicted to alcohol or drugs, and being unable to function to one's fullest capacity.

PROBLEM-FOCUSED COPING STRATEGIES FOR ORGANIZATIONS

Managers and organizations can do several things to deal with problems and opportunities that are sources of stress for employees. Some problem-focused coping strategies for organizations are job redesign and rotation, reduction of uncertainty, job security, company day care, and flexible work schedules and job sharing.

Job Redesign and Rotation.   Sometimes it is possible to redesign jobs to reduce negative stress caused by high levels of role conflict, role ambiguity, overload, or underload, or to improve working conditions. The job characteristics model (see Chapter 7) suggests which aspects of a job are especially important to consider—namely skill variety, task identity, task significance, autonomy, and feedback. Increasing autonomy can be useful to combat role conflict, and providing feedback can help cut down on role ambiguity. When overload is a problem, reducing the number of tasks a jobholder must perform is a viable option. Underload can be remedied by raising levels of skill variety, task identity, and task significance. Uncomfortable and dangerous working conditions should be remedied whenever possible. Redesigning jobs to reduce unnecessary travel and job relocations can also help reduce levels of stress, particularly for dual-career couples and single parents.

When job redesign is not a viable option, **job rotation,** assigning workers to different jobs (which themselves do not change) on a regular basis, can sometimes alleviate stress. Physicians, for example, often rotate on-call duty for hospital emergency rooms and thereby reduce the level of stress that any one physician experiences from this job assignment.

Reduction of Uncertainty.   Often, workers experience stress because they are uncertain about how to perform their assigned tasks, how to deal with conflicting goals or expectations, or how to prioritize assignments. Uncertainty also can cause stress when workers are unsure about how an organization expects or wants them to deal with competing demands from work and home. Whatever gives rise to it, uncertainty often results in stress.

One way to reduce uncertainty in organizations is by allowing workers to participate in making decisions that affect them and their jobs. When workers participate in decision making, they often have a lot more information about changes an organization makes and how to adjust to them. We discuss participation in decision making in more detail in Chapters 12 and 14. As we discuss in Chapter 14, participation can be taken one step further by empowering workers, giving them the power or authority to make decisions themselves and be responsible for outcomes of those decisions.

Another way to reduce uncertainty is to improve communication throughout an organization. Workers need clear, accurate information on a timely basis, and steps should be taken to ensure that workers understand what this information means for them and their jobs as well as for the organization as a whole. Good communication is so important in understanding and managing organizational behavior that it is the focus of Chapter 13.

Job Security.   Whenever possible, providing workers with job security so that they know they will be able to support themselves and their loved ones helps to eliminate stressors related to the economic functions of work. Workers in Japan and Europe typically have higher levels of job security than do workers in the United States.

In lean economic times, it may be hard for organizations to guarantee job security, and IBM and other companies that in the past prided themselves on high levels of security have been forced to lay off employees. Nevertheless, organizations can take steps to reduce the blow of a layoff on workers and their families. If a layoff is a real possibility, managers should provide workers with clear, honest information about their prospects in the organization. When laying off workers is necessary, it is best to give them as much advance notice as possible so they can prepare themselves and explore their options. Whenever possible, outplacement counseling should be made available to help workers find other positions or obtain additional training to increase their employment options, and workers should receive fair severance packages.

Company Day Care.   The problem of finding good, safe, affordable day care for young children is well known to many working parents, as is the problem of what to do when their children get sick. Many organizations are coming up with

Job rotation
Assigning workers to different jobs on a regular basis.

innovative ways to help workers cope with stressors arising out of this work-life linkage. For example, Tallahassee Memorial Hospital in Florida spends around $300,000 a year to run a child care center for its employees; the facility is open from 7 a.m. to midnight.[69] As another example, when four staff members, three of whom were supervisors, at the San Jose National Bank became pregnant, bank president James Kenny and human resources director Laura Graves gave the women the option of taking the standard twelve-week maternity leave allowed by San Jose National Bank or coming back to work after eight weeks with their babies in tow. Bank employees are allowed to bring their babies to work until they are six months old or are crawling.[70]

Organizations can also help workers cope with the problem of what to do when children become ill. Such assistance not only helps reduce workers' stress but also can reduce absenteeism. Schering-Plough, a pharmaceutical company in Memphis, Tennessee, has a special sick room in its child care center (run by a pediatrician), so workers' children receive proper care when they are ill. Use of the sick room by employees in its first six months of operation reduced absenteeism by 133 days. The money the company saves in six months from lower absenteeism covers the cost of operating the sick room for a whole year.[71] Time Warner has an emergency child care service for its employees. The service provides babysitters to take care of employees' sick children in their homes and also provides home care when a regular babysitter misses work.[72]

Flexible Work Schedules and Job Sharing.   Many organizations use flexible work schedules to help their employees cope with conflicts between work and personal life. Stride Rite, a shoe maker, and eight other organizations have joined together to find ways to promote flexibility in the workplace, and companies like Du Pont and Corning provide training to supervisors in how to manage workers on flexible schedules.[73] At some companies, flexible schedules allow workers to take time off or to work at home when they need to take care of a sick child or elderly parent. Workers at Xerox have this option and keep records of how they make up for their absences.[74] (For more information on flexible work schedules, see the closing case.)

When job sharing is used, two or more workers are responsible for a single job and agree on how to divide job tasks and working hours. One worker might perform the job in the mornings and another in the afternoons; workers might alternate days (one works on Mondays, Wednesdays, and Fridays and another on Tuesdays and Thursdays); or each worker might be accountable for particular tasks and assignments. Job sharing enables workers to cope with competing demands on their time from work and personal responsibilities. In order for job sharing to be effective for workers and organizations, good communication and understanding are necessities.

It is the chance for increased flexibility that causes some people to be contingent workers, hired on a temporary basis by organizations. If a contingent worker is finished with an assignment at one company and wants to take some time off before the next job, he or she is free to do so. However, this increased flexibility comes at the expense of job security, job insecurity being a source of stress itself. Art director David Debowski works on a freelance basis out of San Francisco, choosing the projects he wants to work on from ad agencies. While he enjoys the flexibility of freelance work, he initially found it stressful to not know if he would have a new project to work on when he finished his current project. He coped with this source of stress by listing himself with a temporary employment agency which specializes in his kind of work.[75]

EMOTION-FOCUSED COPING STRATEGIES FOR ORGANIZATIONS

Organizations can help workers cope effectively with stressful feelings and emotions through such things as on-site exercise facilities, organizational support, employee assistance programs, and personal days and sabbaticals.

On-Site Exercise Facilities. Realizing the benefits of exercise, many organizations such as General Foods Corporation and Digital Equipment Corporation have exercise facilities and classes that workers can use before and after work and during their lunch hours.

Organizational support
The extent to which an organization cares about the well-being of its members, tries to help them when they have a problem, and treats them fairly.

Organizational Support. **Organizational support** is the extent to which an organization cares about the well-being of its members, listens to their complaints, tries to help them when they have a problem, and treats them fairly.[76] Feeling and knowing that an organization cares about its members is likely to help reduce workers' stressful feelings and emotions. Research has found, for example, that nurses who perceive high levels of organizational support are less likely to experience negative feelings and emotions when they take care of AIDS patients.[77] Organizational support is also likely to help mitigate some of the negative feelings and emotions generated by downsizing and layoffs. An example of a measure of workers' perceptions of how supportive their organizations are is provided in Fig. 9.4.

Employee assistance programs
Company-sponsored programs that provide employees with counseling and other kinds of professional help to deal with stressors such as alcohol and drug abuse and family problems.

Employee Assistance Programs. Many organizations realize that workers sometimes face stressors that they simply cannot handle on their own. IBM, General Motors, Caterpillar, and many other organizations use **employee assistance programs** (EAPs) to provide their members with professional help to deal with stressors. Some EAPs simply provide workers with free professional counseling by trained psychologists. Others are structured to deal with particular types of stressors and problems such as alcohol or drug abuse by workers or by members of their families or problems with troubled teens. Champion International Corporation, for example, offers workshops to its employees on how to deal with potential drug abuse in their families.[78]

This on-site corporate fitness center is on the roof of an office complex in Atlanta, Georgia. More and more companies are opening fitness centers for their employees to help promote fitness and alleviate job stress.

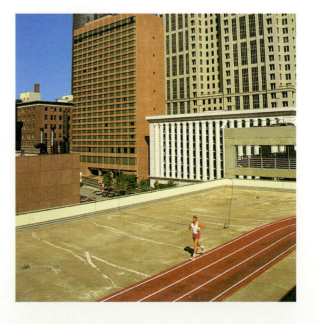

Workers indicate the extent to which they agree or disagree with each of the following statements about their organizations using the following scale:

1	2	3	4	5	6	7
Strongly *dis*agree	*Dis*agree	Slightly *dis*agree	Neither agree nor *dis*agree	Slightly agree	Agree	Strongly agree

		1	2	3	4	5	6	7
1.	The organization values my contribution to its well-being.	1	2	3	4	5	6	7
2.	If the organization could hire someone to replace me at a lower salary, it would do so.*	1	2	3	4	5	6	7
3.	The organization fails to appreciate any extra effort from me.*	1	2	3	4	5	6	7
4.	The organization strongly considers my goals and values.	1	2	3	4	5	6	7
5.	The organization would ignore any complaint from me.*	1	2	3	4	5	6	7
6.	The organization disregards my best interests when it makes decisions that affect me.*	1	2	3	4	5	6	7
7.	Help is available from the organization when I have a problem.	1	2	3	4	5	6	7
8.	The organization really cares about my well-being.	1	2	3	4	5	6	7
9.	Even if I did the best job possible, the organization would fail to notice.*	1	2	3	4	5	6	7
10.	The organization is willing to help me when I need a special favor.	1	2	3	4	5	6	7
11.	The organization cares about my general satisfaction at work.	1	2	3	4	5	6	7
12.	If given the opportunity, the organization would take advantage of me.*	1	2	3	4	5	6	7
13.	The organization shows very little concern for me.*	1	2	3	4	5	6	7
14.	The organization cares about my opinions.	1	2	3	4	5	6	7
15.	The organization takes pride in my accomplishments at work.	1	2	3	4	5	6	7
16.	The organization tries to make my job as interesting as possible.	1	2	3	4	5	6	7

Scoring: Responses to items are averaged for an overall score.
Items marked with a " * " should be scored as follows: 1 = 7, 2 = 6, 3 = 5, 5 = 3, 6 = 2, 7 = 1

FIGURE 9.4

A Measure of Perceived Organizational Support

Source: R. Eisenberger, R. Huntington, S. Hutchison, and D. Sowa, "Perceived Organizational Support," *Journal of Applied Psychology,* 1986, 71, pp. 500–507. Reprinted with permission.

In order for EAPs to be effective in reducing stressful feelings and emotions associated with various work or home problems, the workers who use them must be guaranteed confidentiality and must not be afraid that their jobs or future careers with the organization may be jeopardized because they admit they have problems and need help.

Employee health management programs (EHMPs) are a special kind of EAP designed to promote the well-being of members of an organization and encourage healthy lifestyles. EHMPs focus on helping workers improve their well-being and ability to cope with stressors by, for example, controlling their weight, quitting smoking, improving their eating habits and nutrition, and detecting potential health problems such as high blood pressure early.[79] Eighty-one percent of large organizations have at least one kind of EHMP in place.[80] Du Pont, for example, offers classes ranging from four to ten weeks long during lunch and before and after work on topics such as how to stop smoking, control one's weight and eat a healthy diet, and deal with back-related problems.[81]

Personal Days and Sabbaticals.   Providing personal days and sabbaticals can help reduce stressful feelings and emotions by allowing workers to take some time off and put their work-related stress aside for a day or two (in the case of personal days) or for a more extended period (in the case of sabbaticals). Personal days are common at many large and small organizations and are available to all employees. Sabbaticals are usually reserved for people who have been at an organization for at least several years and are in relatively high-level positions.

People usually cope with stressors in both problem-focused and emotion-focused ways. When coping is successful, it helps workers effectively deal with stressful opportunities and threats without experiencing too many stressful feelings and emotions. Figure 9.5 summarizes the various coping strategies available to individuals and organizations.

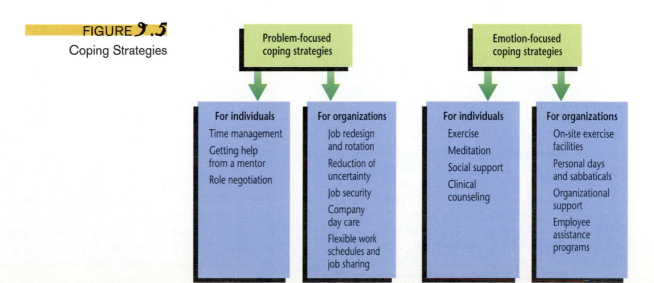

FIGURE 9.5

Coping Strategies

Problem-focused coping strategies		Emotion-focused coping strategies	
For individuals	**For organizations**	**For individuals**	**For organizations**
Time management	Job redesign and rotation	Exercise	On-site exercise facilities
Getting help from a mentor	Reduction of uncertainty	Meditation	Personal days and sabbaticals
Role negotiation	Job security	Social support	Organizational support
	Company day care	Clinical counseling	Employee assistance programs
	Flexible work schedules and job sharing		

TO MANAGERS

Coping

- When workers are experiencing too much stress and it is having negative consequences for them or for the organization, discuss with them the many possible problem-focused and emotion-focused ways of coping with stress.
- Inform workers about and encourage them to take advantage of company day care facilities, flexible work schedules, on-site exercise facilities, personal days and sabbaticals, and employee assistance programs (to the extent that these ways of coping are available at your organization).
- Let your subordinates know that you care about their well-being and are willing to help them with problems.
- Explore the viability of expanding your organization's problem- and emotion-focused coping strategies.

SUMMARY

Stress affects individual well-being and has the potential to affect the extent to which individuals and organizations achieve their goals and perform at a high level. Stress is bound up with workers' personal lives; thus the study of stress also entails exploring the nature of work-life linkages. In this chapter, we made the following major points:

1. People experience stress when they face opportunities or threats that they perceive as important and also perceive they might not be able to handle or deal with effectively. An opportunity is something that has the potential to benefit a person. A threat is something that has the potential to harm a person. Stress is a highly personal experience influenced by an individual's personality, abilities, and perceptions; what is stressful for one person might not be stressful for another.

2. Stress can have physiological, psychological, and behavioral consequences. The relationship between stress and physiological consequences is complicated, and the most serious physiological consequences (for example, cardiovascular disease and heart attack) result only after considerably high levels of stress have been experienced for a prolonged period of time. Psychological consequences of stress include negative feelings, moods, and emotions; negative attitudes; and burnout. Potential behavioral consequences of

stress include job performance, strained interpersonal relations, absenteeism, and turnover.

3. Workers who are responsible for helping others sometimes experience burnout. The three key signs of burnout are feelings of low personal accomplishment, emotional exhaustion, and depersonalization.

4. A certain level of stress is positive in that it can result in high levels of job performance. When stress levels are excessively high, negative stress is experienced, and performance suffers. Other potential behavioral consequences of high stress include strained interpersonal relations, absenteeism, and turnover.

5. Potential stressors can arise from workers' personal lives, job responsibilities, membership in work groups and organizations, and work-life linkages. Stressors from workers' personal lives include major and minor life events. Job-related stressors include role conflict, role ambiguity, overload, underload, challenging assignments and promotions, and conditions that impact workers' economic well-being. Group- and organization-related stressors include misunderstandings, conflicts, and interpersonal disagreements, uncomfortable working conditions, and dangerous or unsafe working conditions. Stressors arising out of work-life linkages result when work roles conflict with people's personal lives.

6. Coping is the steps people take to deal with stressors. Problem-focused coping is the steps people take to deal directly with the source of stress. Emotion-focused coping is the steps people take to deal with their stressful feelings and emotions. Most of the time, people engage in both types of coping when dealing with a stressor.

7. Some problem-focused coping strategies that individuals can use are time management, getting help from a mentor, and role negotiation. Some emotion-focused coping strategies for individuals are exercise, meditation, social support, and clinical counseling. Some problem-focused coping strategies that organizations can use are job redesign and rotation, reduction of uncertainty, job security, company day care, and flexible work schedules and job sharing. Some emotion-focused coping strategies for organizations are on-site exercise facilities, personal days and sabbaticals, organizational support, and employee assistance programs.

Organizational Behavior in Action

TOPICS FOR DISCUSSION AND ACTION

1. Why are opportunities such as a job promotion stressful for some people?
2. Why might excessively high levels of stress lead to turnover?
3. Should managers try to eliminate all or most role conflict and ambiguity? Why or why not?
4. Is underload as stressful as overload? Why or why not?
5. Do organizations have an ethical obligation to guarantee their members job security? Why or why not?
6. How can managers help their subordinates learn how to cope with stressors in a problem-focused way?
7. What should a manager do if he or she thinks a subordinate is using a dysfunctional form of emotion-focused coping (such as abusing drugs)?
8. Is a certain level of stress necessary to motivate workers to perform at a high level? Why or why not?
9. Why might some workers be reluctant to use an employee assistance program?
10. Why should an organization care whether its members eat well or exercise regularly?

BUILDING DIAGNOSTIC SKILLS

The Nature of Stressful Experiences

Think about the last significant stressful experience that you had on the job or at school. For the experience you have chosen, do the following:

1. Describe the experience and the surrounding circumstances.
2. Explain whether the experience was stressful because it entailed an opportunity or a threat. What was the opportunity or threat?
3. Describe your feelings when you first encountered the source of stress.
4. Describe the (a) physiological, (b) psychological, and (c) behavioral consequences of the stress.
5. Describe how you actually coped with the stressor in a problem-focused manner.
6. Describe how you actually coped with the stressor in an emotion-focused manner.
7. Describe how your employing organization or university helped you cope with the stressor. If your employing organization or university did not help you cope with the stressor, do you think it should have? How?
8. Describe the extent to which your coping efforts were successful in helping you deal with the source of stress and with your stressful feelings and emotions.

RESEARCH ON THE INTERNET: A MANAGER'S TOOL

Specific Task

Many organizations offer an array of benefits to help workers cope with stress and balance the demands they face on the job and at home. One such organization is Chevron. Scan Chevron's home page (www.chevron.com) to learn more about this company. Then click on "About Chevron," then on "College Recruiting," then on "The Company," then on "Human Resources Programs," and then on "Benefits."

1. What benefits does Chevron provide its employees to help them cope with stress?
2. What benefits does Chevron provide its employees to help them balance work and home life?

General Task

Many organizations not only take steps to help their employees cope with stress but also have initiated wellness programs to encourage healthy living and well-being. Find the website of such a company. What wellness programs does this company offer its employees? How might participating in these programs contribute to employee well-being? Why might some employees not take advantage of these programs?

TOPICS FOR DEBATE

Stress can have major impacts on people and their organizations. Now that you understand how stress affects individual workers as well as organizations, debate the following issues.

Debate One

Team A. The primary responsibility for managing work-related stress lies with the employing organization.

Team B. The primary responsibility for managing work-related stress lies with the individual worker.

Debate Two

Team A. In trying to keep stress at a manageable level, organizations should focus their efforts on eliminating sources of stress in the workplace.

Team B. In trying to keep stress at a manageable level, organizations should focus their efforts on helping workers find ways to cope with stress effectively.

EXPERIENTIAL EXERCISE

Developing Effective Coping Strategies

Objective

Your objective is to gain experience in developing effective strategies for helping members of an organization cope with stress.

Procedure

Assume the role of a supervisor of a group of twelve financial analysts for a petroleum company. Your subordinates tend to be in their late twenties and early thirties, some of them are single, others are married and have young children, and one is a single parent. Because of their job demands, they often work late and take work home on weekends.

Your company has fallen on hard times and recently downsized. You were forced to lay off three subordinates. The layoff has really shaken up the survivors, who fear that they may be next to get a "pink slip." Workloads have increased, and lately your subordinates always seem to be on edge.

Recently, four of the financial analysts got into a serious and loud argument over a project they were working on. One of the participants in this fight came to you practically in tears. She said that things had gotten so bad that members of the group always seemed to be at each other's throats, whereas in the past they used to help each other. This incident, along with your recent observations, suggested the need to take steps to help your subordinates cope effectively with the stress they seem to be experiencing.

1. Describe the steps you, as the supervisor, should take to determine which problem-focused and emotion-focused coping strategies might be effective in helping the financial analysts deal with the stress they are experiencing.
2. The class divides into groups of from three to five people, and each group appoints one member as spokesperson, to present the group's recommendations to the whole class.
3. Group members in the role of supervisor take turns describing the steps each would take to determine effective problem-focused and emotion-focused coping strategies to help subordinates deal with the stress they are experiencing.
4. Group members develop an action plan that the group as a whole thinks would best lead to the development of effective problem-focused and emotion-focused coping strategies.

When your group has completed those activities, the spokesperson will present the group's action plan to the whole class.

MAKING THE CONNECTION

Find an example of an organization that has recently taken steps to help workers cope with stressors. At which potential stressors are the organization's coping strategies directed? Are these strategies related to problem-focused coping or to emotion-focused coping?

CLOSING CASE

Flexible Working Hours Combat Stress at Xerox

At a recent annual employee meeting, Jim Edwards, controller of Xerox Corporation's (www.xerox.com) administrative center in Dallas, Texas, shocked his subordinates when he announced that from then on employees could schedule when they wanted to work. Long an advocate of the 8-to-5 workday, Edwards had come to realize that his subordinates were experiencing high levels of stress that were interfering with their ability to perform their jobs effectively and sometimes were causing them to be absent. A good proportion of these employees are dual-career couples and single parents confronted with child care dilemmas and family problems on a day-to-day basis. Their rigid 8-to-5 schedule was producing high levels of stress.

Like Xerox, more and more corporations are trying to introduce flexibility into the workplace to combat stress and increase performance.[82] Flexible work schedules allow workers to determine their own working hours so that the workday does not conflict with their other responsibilities. A father with children in elementary school, for example, might wish to start working at 6 a.m. so that he can leave at 3 p.m. and be home in time to meet his children at the school bus stop. His wife, who works in a bank, doesn't start work till 9 a.m. and thus can stay with the children in the morning before school. Other workers might prefer compressed schedules that allow them to work more hours a day and one or two fewer days a week.

Before Edwards's surprise announcement, Xerox workers had tended to think their supervisors were opposed to flexible work schedules even though flextime had always been an option for employees to discuss with their supervisors. Workers also had felt that they had to hide their personal and family problems from their bosses. Workers who needed to take time off from their jobs to deal with family problems had been afraid that doing so might hurt their future prospects with the company.

After Edwards's dramatic demonstration of Xerox's commitment to flexibility, almost half of the employees in the Dallas administrative center either changed their starting times or decided to work a compressed week. So far Xerox's experiment has proven successful. Workers continue to perform all their assigned duties, absenteeism has fallen by about 33 percent, and attitudes appear to have improved. Given its success in Dallas, Xerox is now planning to introduce flexible working hours in its headquarters at Stamford, Connecticut.[83]

Although flexible working hours have helped workers at Xerox cope with stress and the challenges of managing the relationship between their careers and home life, flexible working hours may not be the answer (or even possible) for all organizations. Some organizations have found that workers don't like compressed work schedules because ten- or twelve-hour workdays can be a source of stress. Other organizations have found that it is hard for workers on flexible schedules to work in teams because team members may have different schedules.[84] Before implementing flexible work schedules, managers need to assess the extent to which they may or may not disrupt group meetings, teamwork, and other activities essential to organizational performance. When flexible work schedules are not disruptive, they can be a potent tool, helping workers combat stress and deal effectively with work-life linkages.

Questions for Discussion
1. What are the major advantages and disadvantages of flexible work schedules?
2. In what kinds of jobs and organizations might flexible work schedules be especially appropriate and inappropriate?

The Nature of Work Groups and Teams

10

OPENING CASE

High Performing Teams at Nucor

In an industry with a multitude of problems, Nucor Corporation (www.fwi.com/nucor/) stands out as a high-performing company. Nucor is a manufacturer of steel and steel products with over $3.5 billion in revenues and 6,000 employees.[1] Nucor's success in the steel industry can, to a significant extent, be attributed to the way it uses teams to make its steel products and the ways that these teams are managed.

Nucor's production workers are organized into teams of between 8 and 40 members, depending on the nature of the team's work, such as operating the furnace or rolling the steel. The members of each team are given considerable autonomy and work together to produce an end product, such as straightened or flattened steel. While team output must meet preset quality standards and team members must abide by safety and other rules that apply to all Nucor employees (such as the company's absence policy), teams develop their own informal rules to govern behavior in the team and make their own decisions. A manager's role is to act as a coach rather than a supervisor, advising teams when they have a problem or need some outside input. Nucor's personnel manager, James M. Coblin, has found that with a little guidance and coaching, teams make good decisions and often are more stringent than managers might be.[2]

How does Nucor ensure that teams will strive to perform at a high level? Through a pay plan that links team members' weekly pay to their team's performance. Each team member receives a base wage that doesn't change from week to week. However, based on predetermined standards for the kind of work a particular team does, team members also receive a very substantial weekly bonus corresponding to the team's output. On average, weekly bonuses can be around 80 percent to as high as 150 percent of the weekly basic wage for team members.[3] With so much money at stake, team members are very motivated to perform highly, develop informal rules that will help their team to be effective, and spur each other on. Importantly, all members of a team receive the same amount of bonus money per week so that each team member develops a sense of obligation to other team members to do the best he or she can. As a result, absenteeism is low and camaraderie is high. To ensure that new employees get up to speed quickly, they are immediately assigned to an existing team to learn how to perform their work tasks on-the-job from the team's members. There is real pressure on existing team members to do a good job teaching newcomers, *and* on newcomers to learn quickly and perform highly, because the poor performance of a newcomer on a team will detract from overall team performance and reduce the team's weekly bonus. Newcomers like learning by doing at the hands of knowledgeable, experienced employees, and teaching newcomers helps experienced employees build their knowledge and expertise. If Nucor opens a new steel plant, experienced employees from its other plants are sent to help establish the new plant's work teams and to teach new employees how to perform their jobs effectively and work in teams.

As is evident from its bonus plan, Nucor is committed to the idea that teams should benefit when they perform highly and help Nucor achieve its goals.[4]

Overview

In previous chapters, we focused on how various aspects of individuals (such as personality, ability, values, attitudes, moods, perceptions, and attributions) and aspects of organizations (such as rewards, punishment, promotion, job design, goals, and performance appraisal) combine to affect how individuals feel, think, and behave in an organization, and ultimately the extent to which an organization achieves its goals. Organizations, however, are not just collections of individuals who work by themselves. Members of an organization are usually assembled or clustered into groups or teams, as at Nucor in the opening case. Organizations use groups or teams because groups can sometimes accomplish things that no one individual could accomplish working alone. For example, in a group, individuals can focus on particular tasks and become better at performing them. Performance gains that result from the use of groups have led to the popular saying "A group is more than the sum of its parts."

Groups are the basic building blocks of an organization. Individuals are clustered into groups to help organizations achieve their goals and gain a competitive advantage. Just as the effective functioning of a university depends on the performance of the various groups the university is composed of (departments such as management and psychology, student groups such as language clubs, fraternities and sororities, and governing bodies such as the student council and the faculty senate), so too does the effectiveness of Nucor and other organizations depend on the performance of groups.

Using groups in organizations, however, is not a simple process and presents managers with additional challenges as they try to understand and manage organizational behavior. People behave differently when they work in groups than when they work on their own. Although groups can sometimes work wonders for an organization, as they do at Nucor, they can wreak havoc in an organization when they function improperly. Digital Equipment Corporation, based in Maynard, Massachusetts, and one of the largest computer makers in the United States, recently disbanded a good number of its cross-functional teams (groups of workers from different areas such as marketing and engineering who are brought together to work on a product such as a minicomputer or a new computer memory chip) because the teams spent so much time in meetings trying to reach agreements that they weren't getting much work done.[5]

Given the important role that groups play in all organizations (from corporations like Nucor and Digital Equipment Corporation to hospitals, stores, restaurants, and colleges), in this and the next chapter we concentrate on the nature and functioning of work groups and teams. We start by describing what a group is, how work groups develop, key characteristics of work groups, and how being a member of a group affects individual behavior. We describe how groups control their members' behavior and turn newcomers into effective group members through the socialization process. Essentially, in this chapter we explain what work groups are like and why they are this way. In the next chapter, we build on this foundation and explore what causes some groups to perform at a high level and help an organization achieve its goals.

Introduction to Groups

Is any gathering of individuals a group? If not, what distinguishes a group from a mere collection of individuals? Two basic attributes define a group:

1. Members of a group interact with each other, so that one person's actions affect and are affected by another person's.[6]
2. Members of a group perceive that there is the potential for mutual goal accomplishment—that is, group members perceive that by belonging to the group they will be able to accomplish certain goals or meet certain needs.[7]

Group

A set of two or more people who interact with each other to achieve certain goals or to meet certain needs.

A **group,** then, is a set of two or more people who interact with each other to achieve certain goals or meet certain needs.

It is important to note at the outset that although group members may have one or more goals in common, this does not mean that all their goals are identical. For example, when a person from each of four different departments in an organization (research and development, sales, manufacturing, and engineering) is assigned to a group to work on developing a new product, all members of the group may share the common goal of developing the best product that they can devise. But research and development might define *best product* as the one that has the most innovative features; sales as the one that most appeals to price-conscious customers; manufacturing as one that can be produced the most inexpensively; and engineering as one that will be the most reliable. Although they agree on the common goal—giving the customer the best product they can devise—deciding what *best product* means can be a difficult task. A **group goal** is one that all or most members of a group can agree on as a common goal.

Group goal
A goal that all or most members of a group can agree on as a common goal.

TYPES OF WORK GROUPS

There are many types of groups in organizations, and each type plays an important role in determining organizational effectiveness. One way to classify these types is by whether they are formal or informal. Managers establish **formal work groups** to help the organization achieve its goals. The goals of a formal work group are determined by the needs of the organization. Examples of formal work groups include a product quality committee in a con-

Formal work groups
Groups established by management to help the organization achieve its goals.

A team-building exercise held at the Pecos River Learning Centers in Santa Fe is designed to help promote cooperation and unity between the members of a formal group. These team members collectively have to work out the best way to get to the top.

sumer products firm, a task force created to end sex discrimination in a law firm, and the pediatrics department in a health maintenance organization (HMO). Managers establish each of these groups to accomplish certain organizational goals, such as increasing product quality and safety in the case of the product quality committee, ending discrimination in the case of the task force, and providing health care for children who belong to the HMO in the case of the pediatrics department.

Informal work groups emerge naturally in organizations because organizational members perceive that membership in a group will help them achieve their goals or meet their needs. A group of five factory workers who go bowling every Thursday night to satisfy their common need for affiliation and friendship is an example of an informal group.

Types of Formal Work Groups.   Four important kinds of formal work groups are command groups, task forces, teams, and self-managed work teams (see Fig. 10.1). A **command group** is a collection of subordinates who report to the same supervisor. Command groups are based on the basic reporting relationships in organizations and are frequently represented on organizational charts as departments (such as marketing, sales, or accounting). The pediatrics department in an HMO, the research and development department in a pharmaceutical company, and the financial aid department in a university are all examples of command groups. Command groups are the vehicle through which much of the work in an organization gets accomplished, and thus they have profound effects on the extent to which an organization is able to achieve its goals. The supervisors or leaders of command groups can play such an important role in determining the effectiveness of these groups that we devote Chapter 12 to the topic of leadership.

A **task force** is a collection of people who come together to accomplish a specific goal. Once the goal has been accomplished, the task force is usually disbanded. The group established to end sex discrimination in a law firm and the product quality committee in a consumer products firm are examples of task forces. Sometimes when task forces address a goal or problem of long-term concern to an organization, they are never disbanded, but their membership periodically changes to provide new insights on the goal or problem as well as to not overload existing members of the task force (who have their regular job responsibilities to perform as well as their duties as members of the task force). To capture their enduring or permanent nature, these kinds of tasks forces are sometimes referred to as *standing committees* or *task groups*.

Informal work groups
Groups that emerge naturally when individuals perceive that membership in a group will help them achieve their goals or meet their needs.

Command group
A formal work group consisting of subordinates who report to the same supervisor.

Task force
A formal work group consisting of people who come together to accomplish a specific goal.

FIGURE 10.1

Types of Work Groups

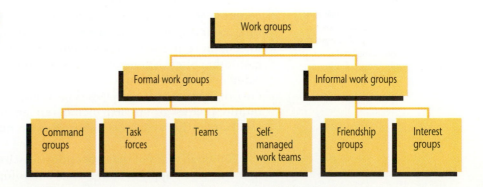

Team
A formal work group consisting of people who work intensely together to achieve a common group goal.

Self-managed work team
A formal work group consisting of people who are jointly responsible for ensuring that the team accomplishes its goals and who lead themselves.

Friendship group
An informal work group consisting of people who enjoy each other's company and socialize with each other on and off the job.

Interest group
An informal work group consisting of people who come together because they have a common goal or objective related to their organizational membership.

The consumer products firm, for example, may always have a product quality committee to ensure that quality is a foremost consideration as new products are developed and existing ones are modified.

A **team** is a formal work group with a high level of interaction among group members, who work intensely together to achieve a common group goal such as developing a new software package. When teams are effective, they draw on the abilities and experience of their members to accomplish things that could not be achieved by individuals working separately or by other kinds of work groups. Boeing, for example, uses *cross-functional teams* (groups of people from different departments such as engineering, marketing, and finance) to design and build new kinds of airplanes and has had tremendous success with them. Because of the high level of interaction in teams, however, they are tricky to manage. Digital Equipment Corporation and other organizations have run into trouble effectively managing teams because team members spend too much time trying to come to an agreement on important issues. Note that just because people work in a group does not mean that they work in a *team*, which is further characterized by *intense* interactions among group members.

A team with no manager or team member assigned to lead it is called a **self-managed work team.** Members of a self-managed work team are responsible for ensuring that the team accomplishes its goals and for performing leadership tasks such as determining how the group should go about achieving its goals, assigning tasks to individual group members, disciplining group members who are not performing at an adequate level, coordinating efforts across group members, and hiring and firing.[8] While the teams at Nucor in the opening case are not responsible for hiring and firing their members, they are still self-managing, given their high levels of autonomy. Self-managed work teams are increasing in popularity and can have a dramatic impact on organizations and their members. We discuss them in detail in the next chapter.

Types of Informal Work Groups.   Two important types of informal work groups are friendship groups and interest groups. A **friendship group** is a collection of organizational members who enjoy each other's company and socialize with each other (often both on and off the job), such as a group of factory workers who go bowling or a group of accountants at a Big Eight firm who frequently have lunch together. Friendship groups help meet workers' needs for social interaction, can be an important source of social support (see Chapter 9), and can also contribute to workers' experiencing positive moods at work and being satisfied with their jobs.

Members of an organization form an **interest group** when they have a common goal or objective (related to their organizational membership) that they are trying to achieve by uniting their efforts. Interest groups are often formed in response to pressing concerns among certain members of an organization, such as company-sponsored day care or elder care, extending existing maternity leave to cover new fathers, more actively trying to protect the environment, or proactively trying to improve conditions in the local community. Interest groups help members of an organization voice their concerns and can provide an important impetus for needed organizational changes.

Although many of the concepts we discuss in the rest of this chapter and in the next one apply to both formal and informal work groups, we mainly focus on the formal side of the organization, because this is where managers can have the most impact.

GROUP DEVELOPMENT OVER TIME: THE FIVE-STAGE MODEL

All groups change over time as group members come and go (because of turnover, new hires, and promotions, among other things), as group tasks and goals change, and as group members gain experience in interacting with each other. Noting these changes, some researchers have tried to determine the stages of group development over time. Understanding how groups change over time is important because, as we discuss later in the chapter, groups and their members face different challenges at different stages of development. In order for groups to be effective and perform at a high level, it is important for these challenges to be effectively managed. Think back to the last group project you worked on for one of your classes. It is likely that your first group meeting was dramatically different from your last group meeting or from the meetings that took place in between. At each point the group faced different challenges. Likewise, as work groups evolve from their initial inception, they too undergo important changes.

One well-known model of group development is Bruce W. Tuckman's five-stage model, outlined in Fig.10.2.[9] During stage 1, which Tuckman called *forming*, group members try to get to know each other and establish a common understanding as they struggle to clarify group goals and determine appropriate behavior within the group. Once individuals truly feel they are members of the group, the forming stage is completed.

Stage 2, called *storming*, is characterized by considerable conflict, as its name implies. Group members resist being controlled by the group and disagree about who should lead the group or how much power the leader should have. This stage is completed when group members no longer resist the group's control and there is mutual agreement about who will lead the group. Group members usually complete this stage because they see it is in their best interests to work together to achieve their goals.

In stage 3, *norming*, group members really start to feel that they belong to the group, and they develop close ties with one another. Feelings of friendship and camaraderie abound, and a well-developed sense of common purpose emerges in the group. By the end of this stage, group members agree on standards to guide behavior in the group.

FIGURE 10.2

Tuckman's Five-Stage Model of Group Development

1. Forming	2. Storming	3. Norming	4. Performing	5. Adjourning
Group members try to get to know each other and establish a common understanding.	Group is in conflict, members resist being controlled by the group, and disagreements arise concerning leadership in the group.	Group members develop close ties, feelings of friendship and camaraderie abound, and group members share a common purpose.	Group members work toward achieving their goals.	The group disbands once its goals have been achieved.

By the time stage 4, *performing*, is reached, the group is ready to tackle group tasks and work toward achieving group goals. The real work of the group gets accomplished in the performing stage. It should not take groups very long to get to this stage. Sometimes, however, it can take as long as two or three years to get to the performing stage, especially when the groups are self-managed work teams, as Saturn Corporation has discovered (see Insight 10.1).[10]

Insight 10.1   Groups

Group Development at Saturn Corporation

When General Motors and the United Auto Workers (UAW) union became partners in an effort to develop and manufacture a high-quality, low-cost small car that could compete effectively with foreign imports, the Saturn Corporation (www.saturn.com) was born. Central to this effort was the use of self-managed work teams to make decisions and manufacture cars.

The Saturn teams typically have about fifteen members and make decisions by consensus or agreement among the members. Getting newly formed teams to become self-managing, however, is not a quick or easy process. Some of the stages that groups go through at the Saturn Corporation have been described by Richard LeFauve, president of the Saturn Corporation, and Anoldo Hax, a professor of management at Massachusetts Institute of Technology.[11]

At the *forming* stage, group members are brought together for the first time. At this stage, three individuals are crucial to the group's formation: two external advisers to the group (one from management at Saturn and the other from the UAW) and one special member of the group, the "charter team member." The charter team member is responsible for many of the activities typically performed by a supervisor or foreman in an automobile plant (for example, scheduling the work and making sure workers know how to perform their assigned tasks). The charter team member "hires" the other group members and brings them on board the team, teaches them about Saturn, and makes sure that they have the necessary skills and knowledge to accomplish the group's tasks. The two external advisers provide guidance to the charter team member in these important activities.

During the *storming* stage, group members become less dependent on the charter team member as they interact more with each other. This process continues on into the *norming* stage, at which time the charter team member ceases to direct the group's activities and becomes more like the other group members (the external advisers still interact with the group only through their interactions with the charter team member, however).

Only during the *performing* stage does the group become a truly self-managing team. At the performing stage, the charter group member is on equal footing with all other group members, and the external advisers interact with the whole group as needed. The group is now truly self-managed and does not depend on the charter group member or the advisers to lead it. It sometimes takes a self-managed work team between two and three years to reach the performing stage. When a group encounters a significant change such as adding several new members, it might need to go back to the norming stage before it can truly perform as a self-managed team.[12]

In the last stage of group development identified by Tuckman—stage 5, *adjourning*—the group disbands after having accomplished its goals. Ongoing work groups in organizations do not go through this stage and often remain at the performing stage. In contrast, a task force is likely to be adjourned after it has achieved its goals.

The five-stage "forming, norming, storming, performing, adjourning" model is intuitively appealing, but research indicates that not all groups go through each of the stages, and groups do not necessarily go through the stages one at a time or in the order specified by Tuckman. Some groups are characterized by considerable levels of conflict throughout their existence and always have elements of the storming stage present.

Organizational researcher Connie Gersick's studies of task forces found that groups with deadlines for goal accomplishment did not go through a series of stages but rather alternated between periods of inertia in which the groups did not get much accomplished and periods of frenzied activity in which major changes were made within the group and the group progressed toward its goals.[13] Interestingly enough, these studies found that the timing of these stages depended on how long the group was given to achieve its goals. All of the groups studied experienced inertia for approximately the first half of their duration. For example, a group given six months to accomplish its goal might experience an initial stage of inertia for its first three months, and a group given three months to accomplish its goals may be in an initial stage of inertia for its first month and a half.

As research into group development continues, it is probably safest to conclude that although all groups change over time, there does not seem to be a single set of stages that all groups go through in a predetermined sequence.

Characteristics of Work Groups

In addition to varying in type (such as formal or informal, command group or self-managed work team) and stage of development, work groups vary in many other respects. Here we examine four characteristics of groups that have major effects on the way members behave in a group and the extent to which a group is able to reach its goals and perform at a high level: group size, group composition, group function, and group status. We also discuss a characteristic effect that groups have on their members, social facilitation.

GROUP SIZE

The size of a group is measured by the number of full-time members who work together to achieve the group's goals. Groups may be composed of just two people or more than twenty. Group size is an important determinant of the way group members behave. When groups are small, members are likely to know one another and interact regularly with each other on a day-to-day basis. When groups are small, it is relatively easy for members to share information, recognize individual contributions to the group, and thus identify with the group's goals. Strong identification with the group and its goals may lead to increased motivation and commitment to group goals and to higher levels of satisfaction.

In large groups, members are less likely to know one another and may have little personal contact with each other on a day-to-day basis. The lower level of interaction among members of large groups makes sharing information difficult. In addition, individuals may consider their own contributions to the group unimportant because there are so many other members, and this view may reduce their motivation and commitment to the group. For all these reasons, people generally tend to be less satisfied in large groups than in smaller ones.[14]

The disadvantages of using larger as opposed to smaller groups have to be weighed against the advantages of increasing group size, however. On the advantage side, larger groups have a greater number of resources at their disposal to accomplish their goals. These resources include the skills, abilities, and accumulated work experience and knowledge of group members. A second advantage of larger groups is the possibility of reaping the benefits of a **division of labor,** dividing up work and assigning particular tasks to individual group members. When individual members focus on particular tasks, they generally become skilled at performing these tasks and may perform at a high level. In fact, one of the primary reasons why groups (as well as whole organizations) exist is to make a division of labor possible.

In making a decision about group size, an organization needs to balance the skill and resource advantages that large groups offer against certain disadvantages. Chief among these disadvantages of large group size are the communication and coordination problems that can arise as the number of group members increases. For example, as a group gets bigger, it is much more difficult to let group members know about a change in procedures. Imagine communicating complex changes in procedures to each member of a forty-member group and to each member of a group of four. Coordination problems also arise as group size increases. If, for example, a group of twenty students is doing a joint research project, it is much more likely that two students will inadvertently cover the same material, that different parts of the group report will not fit well together, and that some students will not do their share of the work than would be the case if five students were working on the project. In general, the larger a group is, the greater is the potential for conflict, for duplication of effort (such as two group members performing the same tasks), and for low motivation. Some of these problems are discussed in detail in the next chapter.

To determine the best size for any group, managers have to balance the advantages of increasing group size (more skills and resources at the group's disposal and greater division of labor) and the disadvantages (more communication and coordination problems). Table 10.1 summarizes some of the potential advantages of small and large group size.

Division of labor
Dividing up work and assigning particular tasks to specific workers.

TABLE 10.1

Group Size Advantages

Potential Advantages of Smaller Groups	Potential Advantages of Larger Groups
Interactions among group members are more frequent.	Group has many resources at its disposal to accomplish its goals, including members' skills, abilities, knowledge, and experience.
Information is more easily shared among group members.	
Group members recognize their contributions to the group.	Group can have a greater division of labor, so group members focus on particular tasks. When group members focus on particular tasks, they generally become skilled at performing them.
Group members are motivated and committed to the group's goals.	
Group members are satisfied.	

GROUP COMPOSITION

Homogeneous group
A group in which members have many characteristics in common.

Group composition is the degree of similarity among group members. Members of a **homogeneous group** have many characteristics in common. These characteristics can be demographic characteristics (such as gender, race, socioeconomic background, cultural origin, age, educational background, or tenure with an organization), personality traits, skills, abilities, beliefs, attitudes, values, or types of work experience. A group of white men from the northeastern United States who all attended Ivy League colleges, did a summer internship at a law firm, believe that their careers are one of the most important parts of their lives, and work for the same New York law firm is a homogeneous group. In contrast, a group of men and women of diverse

The gold-medal winning Flexperts Total Customer Service Team is one of Motorola's forty-three hundred cross-functional teams whose combined goal to improve quality and reduce costs has led to Motorola's spectacular success in recent years.

Heterogeneous group
A group in which members have few characteristics in common.

races and cultural origins who possess degrees from both large and small state and private universities, have a variety of previous work experiences and differing beliefs about the centrality of work in their lives, and work for the same New York law firm constitute a heterogeneous group. Members of a **heterogeneous group** do not have many characteristics in common. Heterogeneous groups are characterized by diversity, homogeneous groups by similarity.

The relationship between group composition and group performance and the effects of group composition on the behavior of individual members are complex and little researched. On the one hand, people tend to like and get along well with others who are similar to themselves. Thus members of homogeneous groups may find it easier to share information, may have lower levels of conflict, and may have fewer problems in communicating and coordinating than do members of heterogeneous groups. On these grounds you might expect the performance and goal attainment of homogeneous groups to be higher than that of heterogeneous groups. Because group members are more likely to get along with each other in homogeneous groups, you might also expect their motivation and satisfaction to be high as well.

On the other hand, a group that is composed of people with different backgrounds, experiences, personalities, abilities, and "views of the world" may be better able than a homogeneous group to make good decisions because more points of view are represented. A heterogeneous group may also be able to perform at a high level because the group has a variety of resources at its disposal. Because of their differences, group members may be more likely to challenge each other and existing ways of doing things, and the outcome may be valuable and needed changes and high performance. The homogeneous group of lawyers, for example, might have few disagreements and little trouble communicating with each other but might have difficulties in dealing with female clients or clients from different ethnic or racial backgrounds. The heterogeneous group of lawyers might have more disagreements and communication problems but fewer problems interacting with clients from different races and cultural backgrounds.

To reap the advantages of heterogeneity, it is important for group members to understand each other's differences and points of view and use these diverse perspectives to enable the group to perform at a high level. In Chapter 19, we discuss some specific steps groups can take to ensure that this happens. Table 10.2 summarizes some of the potential advantages of homogeneous and heterogeneous groups.

TABLE 10.2

Group Composition Advantages

Potential Advantages of Homogeneous Groups	Potential Advantages of Heterogeneous Groups
Group members like and get along well with each other.	Group makes good decisions because diverse points of view are represented.
Group members share information, have low levels of conflict, and have few coordination problems.	Group performs at a high level because the group has a variety of resources at its disposal.

Group function
The work that a group performs as its contribution to the accomplishment of organizational goals.

GROUP FUNCTION

Group function is the work that a group performs as its contribution to the accomplishment of organizational goals. A manufacturing department, for example, is a command group that has the responsibility for producing the goods (automobiles, televisions, and so on) that an organization sells. The manufacturing department's function is to produce these goods in a cost-effective manner and maintain appropriate levels of quality.

Within the manufacturing department are small groups of workers responsible for performing a specific aspect of the manufacturing process. In an automobile-manufacturing plant, for example, one group's function might be to make the automobile bodies, another's to attach the transmission to the body, and another's to paint the body. In fact, we can think of an entire organization as a series of groups linked together according to the functions they perform to help the organization achieve its goals.

The function of a group affects the behavior of group members by letting them know how their work behaviors contribute to the organization's achieving its goals. A group's function gives group members a sense of meaning and purpose. When group members see how the work of their group influences the work of other groups and the extent to which their organization achieves its goals, they may become motivated to perform at a high level. Just as task significance—the extent to which a job affects the lives and work of other people (see Chapter 7)—affects the intrinsic motivation of individuals, so does a group's function have the potential to affect the behavior of group members. To motivate group members to perform at a high level, managers should tell members how their activities, behaviors, and the group's function contribute to organizational effectiveness.

Group status
The implicitly agreed-on, perceived importance for the organization as a whole of what a group does.

GROUP STATUS

The work that some groups in an organization do is often seen as being more important to the organization's success than the work of other groups. **Group status** is the implicitly agreed-on, perceived importance for the organization as a whole of what a group does. A top-management team, for example, has very high status because it helps to set organizational goals and determine how the organization will achieve them. The work performed by a group of accountants who prepare quarterly profit-and-loss statements and balance sheets is certainly important; however, it is often seen as less central to the organization's performance as a whole than is the work performed by the top-management team. Thus the status of the group of accountants is lower than that of the top-management team. The more important the task performed by a work group or a group's function is, the higher is the group's status in the organization. Members of groups with high status are likely to be motivated to perform at a high level because they see their work as especially important for the success of the organization as a whole.

SOCIAL FACILITATION

Does a secretary type more or fewer letters when placed in a room with three other secretaries or in a private office? Does a computer programmer take more or less time to find an error in a complex program when working on the program in the presence of other computer programmers or when working alone? Research on social facilitation provides answers to questions such as these.

Social facilitation

The effects that the presence of others has on performance, enhancing the performance of easy tasks and impairing the performance of difficult tasks.

Social facilitation is the effects that the physical presence of others has on an individual's performance. The presence of other group members tends to arouse or stimulate individuals, often because the individuals feel that others will evaluate their performance and give them positive or negative outcomes dependent on how well or poorly they do.

Two types of social facilitation effects have been studied. *Audience effects* are the effects of passive spectators on individual performance. In this case, other group members are not engaged in the task itself but are present as an audience. *Co-action effects* are the effects of the presence of other group members on the performance of an individual when the other group members are performing the same task as the individual.

Research on both types of social facilitation effects has produced some contradictory results, summarized in Fig.10.3. A typist may type more letters when in the presence of other group members than when typing alone. But a computer programmer may take more time to find an error in a complex program when working in a group of other programmers than when working independently. Why is this the case?

When individuals are stimulated by the presence of other group members, their performance of well-learned tasks and behaviors that they have performed repeatedly in the past is enhanced.[15] Typing letters is a well-learned behavior for a secretary. She or he knows exactly how to do it—it doesn't require much thought. The presence of other group members enhances the secretary's performance, and she or he types more letters when in the presence of other group members than when working alone. More generally, when individuals are stimulated or aroused, their performance of well-learned tasks tends to be enhanced.

When individuals are stimulated by the presence of other group members, their performance of difficult, complex, or novel tasks and behaviors that involve considerable expenditure of effort is impaired.[16] Finding an error in a complex computer program is a difficult task that requires considerable time, effort, and attention on the part of a computer programmer. Each computer program is different, there are multiple types of errors, and locating a single error in a complex program requires a lot of thought. Thus it takes a computer programmer longer to locate an error when she or he is working in the presence of other group members than when working alone. More generally, when individuals are stimulated or aroused, their performance of difficult tasks tends to be impaired.

FIGURE 10.3

Social Facilitation

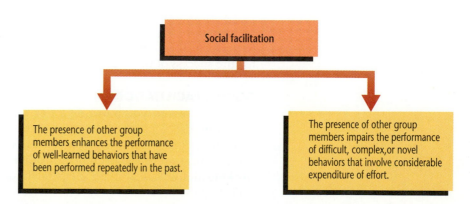

In fact, when people realize that the presence of others is interfering with their performance of a difficult task (by distracting them), they often try to isolate themselves by closing their office door, letting the answering machine take their calls, or finding a quiet place to work alone.

As indicated in Insight 10.2, organizations can buy special furniture to maximize the benefits of positive social facilitation effects and minimize the drawbacks of negative ones. Such furniture (as well as its arrangement) provides group members with the space and opportunity to meet together as a group and gives group members their own individual, private work areas.

Insight 10.2   Groups

Aetna Life's Special Group Furniture

Aetna Life & Casualty (www.aetna.com) recently reorganized workers in its home office into self-managed work teams to help gain a competitive advantage. These teams, which handle customer requests and problems, include clerks, technical writers, insurance underwriters, and financial analysts. Team members need to be able to meet with one another and coordinate their efforts. Yet at the same time their individual jobs can entail some difficult and involving tasks, such as when a financial analyst needs to perform a complicated series of analyses to come up with projected risks and returns for different types of policies. Social facilitation research suggests that individuals performing such complicated tasks perform best when they are alone.

Aetna's solution to the problem of giving team members easy access to one another and a common meeting area while at the same time allowing for individual work areas was to purchase some new "team" furniture manufactured by Steelcase. The furniture divides the total work space into areas called "neighborhoods." In each neighborhood, a central work space is created with a table, which provides a good meeting area for team members. Individual work areas are clustered around the central work space and give team members the privacy they need to perform their individual tasks. Steelcase's team furniture and the neighborhood concept allow team members the opportunity to perform difficult tasks on their own and give them ample opportunity to meet as a team and interact with each other as often as needed.[17]

How Groups Control Their Members: Roles and Rules

In order for any group (formal or informal, command group or self-managed work team, large or small, homogeneous or heterogeneous) to accomplish its goals, the group must *control*—that is, influence and regulate—its members' behavior. Controlling members' behavior is crucial whether a group's goal is

This cross-functional team at Zelium Corp., a small software company, were responsible for 23 innovations that have helped its products become market leaders.

writing superior computer programs, providing excellent customer service, raising quality levels, or cutting costs. Effective groups are groups that control their members' behavior and channel it in the direction of high performance and the attainment of group and organizational goals. A group of waiters and waitresses in a restaurant, for example, needs to ensure that group members wait on customers promptly and courteously, do not wait on each other's tables or grab each others' food orders in the kitchen, and give customers their checks in a timely fashion. This group needs to control its members' behavior to ensure that the group achieves the restaurant's goal of providing high-quality customer service. Three mechanisms through which groups control their members' behavior are roles, rules, and norms.

ROLES

The division of labor that occurs in groups and organizations necessitates the development of roles. Recall from Chapter 9 that a *role* is a set of behaviors or tasks that a person is expected to perform by virtue of holding a position in a group or organization. When a group divides up its work and assigns particular tasks to individual members, different roles are established within the group. For example, there are four roles in a group of workers responsible for the evening news program at a small television station. The local news reporter's role is to compile local stories of interest and provide on-the-scene reports as needed. The state and national news reporter's role is to cover statewide news stories and help the news anchor cover important national stories. The anchor's role is to select the stories to be covered each night (using the inputs of the local and state/national reporters) and prepare and deliver the news. The editor's role is to oversee this entire process and make sure that the time allotted for the news is efficiently and effectively used, that important stories are covered in a meaningful order, and that there is the right amount of on-the-scene reporting.

As we mentioned earlier, sometimes organizations form cross-functional teams, groups with members from different functional areas within the organization. In cross-functional teams, a team member's role is likely to be representing his or her function's perspective on the group's project, as indicated in Insight 10.3.

Insight 10.3

A Global View

Cross-Functional Team Saves Milacron from Foreign Competition

Milacron (www.milacron.com) manufactures plastic-molding machines that other companies use to make plastic products.[18] In the late 1980s, the very survival of Milacron was at stake because of foreign competition, especially from the Japanese. What saved Milacron and its employees' jobs was a cross-functional team put together by product manager Harold Faig and regional sales manager Bruce Kozak to develop a new plastic-molding machine to better meet customer needs.

The cross-functional team was composed of members from purchasing, marketing, inventory, manufacturing, and engineering. Team members' roles reflected their own areas of expertise. Team members from marketing, for example, talked with Milacron customers to determine what they were looking for in a new machine. They found out that although Milacron's existing machines had more options than similar machines made by the Japanese, they were considerably more expensive and had longer delivery times. The role of the engineers was to design the specifications for the new machine, called the Vista, so that it would be quicker and cheaper to produce while still providing customers with the options they want.

Milacron's experience with the Vista team suggests that using cross-functional teams in which group members' roles reflect their individual areas of expertise can be very beneficial for an organization. Sales of the Vista in its first year were two and a half times greater than sales of Milacron's other products, and Milacron is currently using cross-functional teams to redesign some of its other products.[19]

Associated with each role in a group are certain responsibilities and rights. All of the behaviors expected of a role occupant (the individual assigned to a role) are the role occupant's *responsibilities*. On a news team, for example, the anchor's responsibility is to prepare and deliver the news. Each role occupant also has *rights or privileges*, such as the right to use resources assigned to the role. Resources can include people, money, specialized equipment, or machinery. The local news reporter on a news team has the right to use the local camera crew and its equipment and has a monthly budget at her disposal for tracking down stories.

Roles facilitate the control of group members' behavior for several reasons. First, roles tell group members what they should be doing. Second, roles not only enable a group to hold its members accountable for their behavior but also provide the group with a standard from which to evaluate behavior. Finally, roles help managers determine how to reward group members who perform the behaviors that make up their various roles.

Role relationships
The ways in which group and organizational members interact with one another to perform their specific roles.

In establishing a set of roles in a group, group members or managers also specify **role relationships**—the ways in which group and organizational members interact with one another to perform their specific roles. Role relationships may be formally specified in a written job description that outlines how a role occupant is expected to interact with others to accomplish the group's (or organization's) goals. Role relationships may also emerge informally over time (for example, at the storming or norming stages of group development) as group members work out among themselves methods for getting the group's job done.

On a news team, the anchor's role relationships with the local and state/national reporters is formally specified in all three group members' job descriptions: The two reporters and the anchor are to work together to decide what stories will be covered each night, but the final decision is ultimately up to the anchor. The anchor has also developed with the local reporter an informal role relationship that gives this reporter considerable autonomy in determining what local news gets covered. This informal role relationship developed when the anchor realized how skilled and motivated the local news reporter was.

A large part of a person's role in a group may not be specified but may emerge over time as members interact with each other. For example, one member of a group may assume significant task responsibilities for the group and emerge as an informal group leader because she has demonstrated that she can perform these responsibilities effectively. Sometimes a manager notices that an informal leader performs certain tasks effectively and promotes the informal leader to become the new formal leader if the formal leader of the group leaves or is promoted. The process of taking the initiative to create a role by assuming certain responsibilities that are not part of an assigned role is called **role making.** In contrast, **role taking** is the performance of responsibilities that are required as part of an assigned role. Role taking is the common process of assuming a formal organizational role.

Role making
Taking the initiative to create a role by assuming responsibilities that are not part of an assigned role.

Role taking
Performing the responsibilities that are required as part of an assigned role.

On the news team, for example, the local news reporter did such a good job in covering the local scene for the evening news that the anchor always followed her suggestions for stories. Station management recognized her initiative and high performance and when the anchor left for a better position in a larger city, the local news reporter was promoted to become the new anchor. Role making can be an important process in self-managed work teams in which group members jointly try to find innovative ways of accomplishing group goals.

WRITTEN RULES

Effective groups sometimes use written rules to control their members' behavior to ensure high levels of performance and the attainment of group goals, such as the safety rules used by groups at Nucor in the opening case. Written rules specify behaviors that are required of group members and behaviors that are forbidden. Rules that a group adopts are those that best allow the group to meet its goals. The news team, for example, developed a rule that requires members of the group to determine, at the beginning of each year, when they will take their allotted three weeks of vacation and also requires them to arrange their schedules so that only one person is on vacation on any given day. The news team also developed a rule forbidding group members to take more than one week off at a time. These rules help the group achieve its goal of always providing complete news coverage. The rules also help the group achieve its goal of maintaining the continuity of the news team from the viewer's perspective. Over time, groups should experiment with their rules and try to find better ones to replace those that currently exist.

Some rules that groups develop (often called *standard operating procedures*) specify in writing the best way to perform a particular task. These rules help a group ensure that the task will be performed in the correct and most efficient manner. For example, a rule specifies exactly when and in what form the news anchor should communicate his or her plans for the evening news each night to the editor so that the editor has enough time to review the format and make any needed changes before the program airs.

Rules have several advantages in controlling and managing group members' behavior and performance:

- Rules help groups ensure that their members will perform behaviors that contribute to group and organizational effectiveness and avoid behaviors that impair performance and goal attainment.
- Rules facilitate the control of behavior because group members and managers know how and when role occupants are expected to perform their assigned tasks.
- Rules facilitate the evaluation of individual group members' performance levels because their behavior can be compared to the behavior specified in the rule.
- When the membership in a group changes, rules help newcomers learn the right way to perform their roles.

A group can develop rules at any stage of its development. Rules developed at early stages are often changed or abandoned as the nature of the group's work, group goals, or organizational goals change. A healthy group recognizes the need for change and is willing to change its rules (as well as its roles) when change is warranted.

TO MANAGERS

Roles and Rules

- Make sure members of the groups you manage clearly understand their roles and role relationships by providing clear explanations (and written documentation when necessary), being available to answer questions, and clearly communicating the reasons for and nature of any changes in roles and role relationships.
- Make sure rules are clearly written and clearly communicated to newcomers. Periodically review rules with existing group members as needed.
- Ask members of the groups you manage to let you know of any changes that they think need to be made in existing roles and written rules.

How Groups Control Their Members: Group Norms

Roles and rules help group members and managers control behavior in groups because they specify what behaviors group members should engage in so that the group will be effective, perform at a high level, and achieve its goals. Groups also control their members' behavior and channel it in the direction of high performance and group goal attainment by developing and enforcing norms.[20] Group norms tell group members how they are expected to behave. Unlike written rules, which are *formal* descriptions of actions and behaviors required by a group or organization, **group norms** are *informal* rules of conduct for behaviors that are considered important by most group members; often, they are not put in writing. Recall how the teams at Nucor in the opening case develop informal rules for controlling team members' behavior.

Group norms
Informal rules of conduct for behaviors considered important by most group members.

Groups enforce their norms by rewarding members who conform to the norm by behaving in the specified manner and punishing members who deviate from the norm.[21] Rewards for conforming to group norms can include being treated in a friendly manner by other group members, verbal praise, receiving help from members when needed, and tangible rewards. Punishments for deviating from norms can include being ignored by other group members, being criticized or reprimanded, losing certain privileges, and being expelled from the group.

Group norms are key to how groups influence and control group members' behavior to ensure that the group achieves its goals and performs at a high level. When members share a common idea of acceptable behavior, they can monitor each other's behavior to make sure they are following the group's norms.

As another example, a group of waiters and waitresses in a busy restaurant may develop informal norms that specify that group members should not steal each other's tables or orders in the kitchen and should always let each other know when they observe that customers at someone else's table are ready for their check. These norms help the group to effectively accomplish its goals of providing good service to customers and receiving maximum rewards in the form of high tips. A group member who does not follow the norm (a waiter, for example, who steals an order in the kitchen on a particularly busy day) might be reprimanded. If deviation from the norm continues, the individual might even be expelled from the group. A waitress who continually steals tables to earn more tips, for example, might be brought to the attention of the restaurant manager and eventually fired. Waiters and waitresses who conform to the group's norms are rewarded by being able to continue their membership in the group and in other ways (such as by receiving verbal praise from each other and from the restaurant manager).

Just like formal roles and rules, group norms develop to increase the ability of the group to control its members' behavior and channel their behavior in a direction that leads to the achievement of group and organizational goals.[22] When norms exist, group members do not have to waste time thinking about what to do in a particular situation; norms guide their actions and specify how they should behave. Furthermore, when people share common norms, they can predict how others will behave in certain situations and thus anticipate one another's actions. This capability improves the efficiency of interactions between group members and reduces misunderstandings.

WHY DO GROUP MEMBERS CONFORM TO NORMS?

 Compliance

Assenting to a norm in order to attain rewards or avoid punishment.

Individuals conform to group norms for three main reasons. The first and most widespread basis for conformity to group norms is **compliance**—assenting to a norm in order to attain rewards or avoid punishment.[23] When individuals comply with norms, they do not necessarily believe that the behavior specified by the norm is important for its own sake, but they believe that following the norm will bring certain benefits and ignoring it will bring certain costs. Consider how norms operate in the following example. The internal auditing department of a chemical company annually solicits contributions for the United Way, a charitable organization. Mary Kelly is a group member who doesn't really like the United Way because she has read some articles that raised questions about the United Way's use of its funds. Nevertheless, Kelly always contributes to the United Way because she is afraid that her coworkers will think less of her and perhaps avoid her if she does not.

 Identification

Associating oneself with supporters of a norm and conforming to the norm because those individuals do.

The second reason for conformity is **identification**—associating oneself with supporters of a norm and conforming to the norm because those individuals do. John Bickers, one of the newest members of the auditing department, really looks up to Ralph Diaz and Steve Cashion, who have been in the department for several years and are ripe for receiving promotions. Around the time of the United Way campaign, Bickers casually asked Diaz and Cashion over lunch how they felt about the United Way. Both Diaz and Cashion indicated that they thought it was a worthy cause, and both told Bickers that they contributed to it during the annual fund drive. This information caused Bickers to decide to contribute as well.

 Internalization

Believing that the behavior dictated by a norm is truly the right and proper way to behave.

The third and potentially most powerful basis for conformity to group norms is **internalization**—believing that the behavior dictated by the norm is truly the right and proper way to behave. Diaz and Cashion's basis for conformity is internalization: They wholeheartedly believe in the United Way's cause. Norms have the most influence on group members when the basis for conformity is internalization.

IDIOSYNCRASY CREDIT

Although most group members are expected to conform to group norms, one or a few group members sometimes are allowed to deviate from the norms without being punished. These privileged individuals are generally group members who have contributed a lot to the group in the past. Their above-average contributions to the group give them what has been termed **idiosyncrasy credit**—the freedom to violate group norms without being punished.[24]

 Idiosyncrasy credit

The freedom to violate group norms without being punished that is accorded to group members who have contributed a lot to the group in the past.

In the restaurant described earlier, John Peters, the waiter who has been with the restaurant for the longest period of time, generally takes on the responsibility of training new waiters and waitresses and settling conflicts that arise in the group. On very busy days, Peters sometimes "mistakes" other group members' orders in the kitchen for his own. However, he is never reprimanded for stealing orders. His beyond-the-call-of-duty contributions to the group give him idiosyncrasy credit, which allows him to deviate from the group's norms. Similarly, a highly skilled developer in a group of computer programmers might frequently fight with other group members and with the supervisor yet never be reprimanded. Although her behavior violates the group's norm of members' being polite and considerate to each other, the behavior is tolerated because this programmer is the one who always finds the bug in a program.

THE PROS AND CONS OF CONFORMITY AND DEVIANCE

From our discussion of group norms, you probably got the impression that conformity to group norms is always good in all situations. Conformity *is* good when norms help a group control and influence its members' behavior so that the group can accomplish its goals. But what if a group's norms are inappropriate or unethical? Or what if what was once an appropriate norm is no longer appropriate because the situation has changed? Many norms such as always behaving courteously to customers or always leaving the work area clean promote organizational effectiveness, but some group norms do not.

Studies have shown that groups of workers can develop norms that reduce levels of group performance. A group of workers might develop norms that control the pace or speed at which work is performed. A worker who works very quickly (and thus produces "too much") is called a "ratebuster." A worker who works very slowly (or below the group norm) is called a "goldbricker" or a "chiseler."[25] Chiselers and ratebusters alike are reprimanded by other members of the group for violating its norm. In the case of a ratebuster, the reprimand may cause group performance to suffer, for ratebusters generally tend to lower their levels of performance to be more in line with the group norm.

This same kind of process can occur at all levels in an organization. A group of middle managers may adopt a don't-rock-the-boat norm that dictates that the managers agree with whatever top management proposes regardless of whether they think the ideas are right or wrong. A new middle manager soon learns that it doesn't pay to rock the boat because this behavior will incur the wrath not only of coworkers but of the top manager who has been disagreed with. When such a norm exists, all middle managers might be reluctant to speak up even when they all realize that a change is sorely needed to ensure organizational effectiveness and success. In cases like this, then, conformity is not good because it maintains dysfunctional group behaviors, and deviance from the norm is appropriate.

Deviance Deviance—deviation from a norm—occurs when a member of a group violates a group norm. Groups usually respond to deviance in one of three ways.[26] First, the group might try to get the deviant to change by, for example, explaining to the deviant why the norm is so important, pointing out that the deviant is the only member of the group violating the norm, or reprimanding and punishing the deviant for violating the norm. Second, the group might try to expel the deviant, as the group of restaurant workers did when a waitress violated the group norm of not stealing tables. Third, the group might actually change the norm in question to be more in line with the deviant's behavior. When group norms are inappropriate, deviance can spark a needed change within the group.

BALANCING CONFORMITY AND DEVIANCE

As illogical as it might sound, groups need both conformity and deviance to accomplish their goals and perform at a high level. In our restaurant example, conformity to the group norms of not stealing tables or food orders and of informing group members when customers are ready for their checks helps the group meet its goals of providing good service to customers and enabling group members to make a satisfactory amount of money in tips. The norms are functional for the group because they help the group achieve its

Deviance
Deviation from a norm.

goals. A group norm for handling customer complaints, however, has recently changed.

In the past, whenever customers complained about a meal (for example, "It doesn't taste right"), the group norm was to refer the complaint to the restaurant manager. The manager would talk to the customer and invariably offer the customer an alternative selection. Then, on a particularly busy day, one of Sally Schumaker's customers had a complaint, and rather than seek out the manager, Schumaker decided to handle the problem herself. She offered the customer another meal, because that was how the manager always solved such a problem. After that, Schumaker continued to take matters into her own hands whenever one of her customers had a complaint. Over time, other members of the group noticed Schumaker's behavior and asked her why she was circumventing the restaurant manager. She explained her reasons for violating the group norm, and they made sense to the other group members: Handling problems themselves would enable them to give faster service to customers who were already somewhat dissatisfied and also would keep them from having to bother the manager every time they had a problem.

John Peters, the senior waiter, decided to check with the manager to make sure that it was all right with him if the wait staff offered a new meal to customers who had a complaint about the food. The manager thought this was a great idea and was surprised he hadn't thought of it himself. He informed group members that from then on they should handle complaints themselves (as Schumaker was already doing) but should be sure to let the cook know the nature of the complaints.

The norm of referring all complaints to the restaurant manager was dysfunctional for the group of waiters and waitresses for two reasons: (1) It meant keeping dissatisfied customers waiting (which prevented the group from achieving its good-service goal). (2) It meant seeking out the manager, which took time that could have been used to serve other customers (which prevented group members from achieving their goal of making a satisfactory amount of money in tips). Deviance from this norm was functional for the group because it stimulated the group to reexamine the norm and change it.

As this story shows, *conformity* ensures that a group can control members' behaviors to get tasks accomplished, and *deviance* forces group members to reexamine the appropriateness of group norms. Figure 10.4 depicts the relationship between levels of conformity and deviance in a group and group goal accomplishment. The group at point A has a low level of conformity and a high level of deviance. The group has difficulty controlling members' behaviors and fails to attain its goals. The group at point B has just the right balance: Conformity helps the group direct members' behaviors toward group goals, and deviance forces the group to periodically reexamine the appropriateness of group norms. In the group at point C, conformity is so high that it is stressed at the expense of the group's achieving its goals. Because group members are extremely reluctant to deviate from group norms, the group at point C retains dysfunctional norms and resists any sort of change.

Some national cultures promote excessive levels of conformity, a force that can make group members abide by norms at all costs and fear change, as indicated in Insight 10.4.

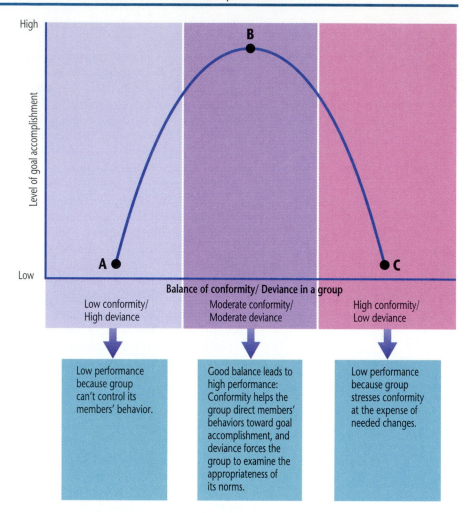

Low conformity/
High deviance

FIGURE 10.4

The Relationship Between
Levels of Conformity and
Deviance in a Group and
Group Goal Accomplishment

Low performance
because group
can't control its
members' behavior.

Good balance leads to
high performance:
Conformity helps the
group direct members'
behaviors toward goal
accomplishment, and
deviance forces the
group to examine the
appropriateness of
its norms.

Low performance
because group
stresses conformity
at the expense of
needed changes.

Insight 10.4   **A Global View**

Conformity to Group Norms in Japan

Conformity to group norms and resistance to change are prevalent in
modern-day Japan. Young children are taught the importance of conforming to group norms at an early age, and Japanese of all ages tend
to see conformity as desirable and change as threatening.

At the Tatsuta Nambu elementary school in Aichi (in central
Japan), it is a norm that little children should wear white bicycle helmets
on their way to and from school. Even children who don't ride bikes to
school but instead walk wear the helmets.

JAL Coordination Service Co. teaches female office workers how to follow norms regarding the proper ways to bow and smile. Proper bowing and smiling are deemed to be so important that companies send about 800 of their members a year to JAL for training at a cost of about $240 per person for a two-day seminar.

Another, more significant, example comes from the political arena. As Japan's Liberal Democratic party loses power and influence because of charges of corruption, and as the need for political change becomes increasingly evident, voters remain reluctant to deviate from old ways of doing things, even when it comes to voting. In one recent poll, 45 percent of the respondents indicated that they did not favor any political party, and voting turnouts have reached record lows in certain districts. Apparently, some Japanese find deviation from the norm of supporting the Liberal Democratic party threatening, fear the change that may result from it, and simply are not voting. Some Japanese seem to be waiting for the emergence of a new norm regarding which party and policies to support before they resume their involvement in politics by voting.

Sociologist Akira Fujitake suggests that change in Japan may be slow because of "a barrier called 'the group.'"[27] The Japanese stress conformity to group norms to such a great extent that harmony is sometimes valued over needed change.

ENSURING THAT GROUP NORMS ARE FUNCTIONAL FOR THE ORGANIZATION

In our restaurant example, because group goals are aligned with the restaurant's goals, the norms that are functional for the group (such as not stealing tables and food) are also functional for the organization, and norms that are dysfunctional for the group (such as referring customer complaints to the manager) are dysfunctional for the organization. When group and organizational goals are closely aligned, groups are inclined to develop norms that help the groups achieve their goals and also are functional for the organization. Likewise, to the benefit of both the groups and the organization, groups are inclined to discard norms that are inadvertently dysfunctional.

Group goals, however, are not always congruent with organizational goals. The goal of a group of workers who assemble radios, for example, might be to *minimize* the amount of effort that each member exerts on the job. To achieve this goal, the workers develop the norm of assembling no more than 50 radios a day. The group could easily assemble 75 radios each day, but this performance level would entail additional effort from group members. In this case, the group norm is clearly dysfunctional for the organization because group goals are inconsistent with organizational goals. The norm, however, is functional for the group because it helps group members achieve their goal of not having to work too hard.

How can managers ensure that group norms are functional for the organization? They can try to align group goals with organizational goals. One way to do this is to make sure that group members benefit or are rewarded when the organization achieves its goals. In our restaurant example, group members benefited from the restaurant's achieving its goal of providing good service—good service leads to more money from tips. The alignment of group and organizational goals can also be achieved by rewarding group members on the basis of individual or group performance. At Nucor in the opening case, management aligns groups' goals with organizational goals by rewarding group members with weekly bonuses based on group performance.

Conversely, the group of workers assembling radios receives no tangible benefits when the organization reaches its performance goal. Group members are paid on an hourly basis and receive the same amount of money regardless of how many radios the group assembles. Their group goal (minimizing effort expenditure) is not aligned with their organization's goal (performance) because they do not benefit if the organizational goal is met. Likewise, group norms that have developed (restricting production) are functional for the group of radio workers but dysfunctional for the organization.

The need to align group and organizational goals so that group norms will be functional for the organization has a very clear implication for how outcomes such as pay should be distributed to group members when individual contributions or performance levels cannot be readily identified or evaluated. Essentially, the outcomes that group members receive should be based on group levels of performance, so that group members benefit or are rewarded when the group is effective and contributes to the attainment of organizational goals. When group members are rewarded for high performance, high performance becomes a group goal, and norms are developed to help attain this goal. If our radio workers were able to increase their earnings by assembling more radios, it is likely that their group goal would be to increase production rather than to minimize effort, and group norms probably would develop to help the group achieve this productivity goal.

TO MANAGERS

Group Norms

- When a member of a work group behaves differently from other group members, encourage group members to consider whether existing norms are appropriate.
- To facilitate a group's development of norms that help the organization achieve its goals, make sure that group members benefit when the organization reaches its goals.
- Distribute rewards such as pay to group members on the basis of performance. When individual performance levels can be identified, base rewards on individual or group performance. When individual performance levels cannot be identified, base rewards on group performance.
- Once group and organizational goals are aligned, periodically observe group behavior in order to uncover dysfunctional norms. Discuss dysfunctional norms with group members, and suggest an alternative behavior that might help the group and organization better reach its goals.

Socialization: How Group Members Learn Roles, Rules, and Norms

The ability of a group to control its members' behaviors depends on the extent to which newcomers learn the group's roles, rules, and norms. Newcomers do not know what is expected of them and what they can and cannot do.[28] A newcomer to a group of secretaries, for example, does not know whether it is all right to take a long lunch one day and make up the time the next day by working through the lunch hour or whether it is acceptable to work from 8:30 to 4:30 instead of from 9 to 5. Newcomers are outsiders, and only when they have learned the group's roles, rules, and norms do existing group members accept them as insiders. The process by which newcomers learn the roles, rules, and norms of a group is **socialization.**

A newcomer can learn how the group controls member behavior by simply observing how existing members behave and inferring from this behavior what is appropriate and inappropriate. Though acceptable to the newcomer, this indirect method is risky from the group's perspective because newcomers might observe and learn bad habits that are unacceptable to the group. In one of our earlier examples, a computer programmer gets away with argumentative behavior that violates the group norm of being cooperative because of her idiosyncrasy credit. A newcomer to the group observing her combative behavior, however, might mistakenly assume that this behavior is acceptable to other group members—that it is in conformity with a group norm.

SOCIALIZATION AND ROLE ORIENTATION

John Van Mannen and Edgar Schein developed a model of socialization that describes the different ways in which groups can socialize their members to ensure proper learning of roles, rules, and norms. How groups socialize newcomers, in turn, influences the role orientation that newcomers adopt.[29] **Role orientation** is the characteristic way in which members of a group respond to various situations. For example, do group members react passively and obediently to commands and orders, or are group members creative and innovative in searching for solutions to problems?

Van Mannen and Schein identified six pairs of contrasting socialization tactics that influence a newcomer's learning and role orientation. The use of different combinations of these tactics leads to two different role orientations: institutionalized and individualized. In an **institutionalized role orientation,** newcomers are taught to respond to situations in the same way that existing group members respond to similar situations. An institutional orientation encourages obedience and conformity to existing roles, rules, and norms. Newcomers who have an institutionalized orientation are more likely to engage in role taking rather than in role making because this orientation emphasizes the importance of following existing ways of doing things.

In an **individualized role orientation,** individuals are taught that it is acceptable and desirable to be creative and to experiment with changing how the group does things.[30] Although group members with an individualized orientation still need to learn and follow existing roles, rules, and norms, they realize that these ways of controlling behavior are not cast in stone and that the group will consider changing them if a more effective way of behaving is identified. Members with an individualized orientation tend to engage more in role making rather than in role taking.

Socialization
The process by which newcomers learn the roles, rules, and norms of a group.

Role orientation
The characteristic way in which members of a group respond to various situations.

Institutionalized role orientation
A role orientation in which newcomers are taught to respond to situations in the same way that existing group members respond to similar situations.

Individualized role orientation
A role orientation in which newcomers are taught that it is acceptable and desirable to be creative and to experiment with changing how the group does things.

SOCIALIZATION TACTICS

The socialization tactics identified by Van Mannen and Schein are discussed below and summarized in Table 10.3. Groups or organizations can use all six tactics or a subset of the six tactics, depending on their needs and goals. Each of the six tactics actually represents a pair of contrasting tactics from which a choice can be made.

Collective Versus Individual Tactics.   When *collective* tactics are used, newcomers go through a common learning experience designed to produce standardized or highly similar responses to different situations. For example, all of the new sales associates just hired by a department store receive collective socialization by participating in the same two-week training program. They watch videotapes showing the proper way to greet customers, process a sale, return an item, and deal with customer complaints.

When *individualized* tactics are used, newcomers are taught individually how to behave. Because learning takes place on an individual basis, each newcomer's learning experiences are somewhat different, and newcomers are encouraged to behave differently in the various situations they may encounter on the job. For example, newcomers to a group of salespeople who sell cosmetics, each of whom is responsible for a different cosmetics line (such as Estée Lauder or Lancôme), receive individual socialization by company representatives to ensure that each newcomer develops the appropriate knowledge about the line and the type of customer it appeals to.

Collective tactics tend to lead to an *institutionalized* orientation; individual tactics tend to lead to an *individualized* orientation.

Formal Versus Informal Tactics.   When tactics are *formal,* newcomers are segregated from existing group members during the learning process. For example, new sales associates receive their two-week training in the department store's training room. During this period, they never interact with members of the groups they are to join once their training is complete.

When tactics are *informal,* newcomers learn on the job as members of their new work group, as is the case at Nucor in the opening case. For example, many restaurants socialize new waiters and waitresses by having them work along with and observe the behavior of experienced members of their group.

Formal tactics tend to lead to an *institutionalized* orientation; *informal* tactics tend to lead to an *individualized* orientation.

TABLE **10.3**

Socialization Tactics That Shape Group Members' Role Orientations

Tactics That Lead to an Institutionalized Orientation	Tactics That Lead to an Individualized Orientation
Collective tactics	Individual tactics
Formal tactics	Informal tactics
Sequential tactics	Random tactics
Fixed tactics	Variable tactics
Serial tactics	Disjunctive tactics
Divestiture tactics	Investiture tactics

Sequential Versus Random Tactics.   When *sequential* tactics are used, newcomers are provided with explicit information about the sequence in which they will perform new behaviors. For example, a new assistant in a veterinarians' office is told that for the first two weeks she will assist the vets with routine checkups. After that she will also weigh the animals and administer injections, and after one month on the job she will also assist the vets in surgery.

When *random* tactics are used, the order in which socialization proceeds is based on the interests and needs of individual newcomers—no set sequence is followed. For example, an apprentice wood worker who has just joined a group of custom furniture makers is told that the order in which he learns how to make different types of furniture (such as dining-room tables and rocking chairs) is up to him.

Sequential tactics tend to lead to an *institutionalized* orientation; *random* tactics tend to lead to an *individualized* orientation.

Fixed Versus Variable Tactics.   *Fixed* tactics give newcomers precise knowledge of the timetable associated with completing each stage in the learning process. The socialization of the assistant in the veterinarians' office relies on fixed tactics. The assistant knew that two weeks would have to elapse before she moved on to the next stage in her training.

Variable tactics provide no information about when newcomers will reach a certain stage in the learning process; the speed of socialization depends on the individual newcomer. The wood worker was socialized with variable tactics; he was never told how long it should take him to learn how to make different types of furniture.

Fixed tactics tend to lead to an *institutionalized* orientation; *random* tactics tend to lead to an *individualized* orientation.

Serial Versus Disjunctive Tactics.   When *serial* tactics are used, existing group members socialize newcomers, as in the case of experienced waiters and waitresses training newcomers in how to wait on customers and as is true at Nucor in the opening case.

When *disjunctive* tactics are used, newcomers must figure out and develop their own way of behaving and are not told what to do by experienced group members. For example, many new professors learn how to teach and do research through disjunctive socialization. Experienced professors in the groups or department they join often do not give them training or guidance in how to teach and do research.

Serial tactics tend to lead to an *institutionalized* orientation; *disjunctive* tactics tend to lead to an *individualized* orientation.

Divestiture Versus Investiture Tactics.   With *divestiture* tactics, newcomers receive negative interpersonal treatment from other members of the group. For example, they are ignored or taunted. Existing group members refrain from treating newcomers kindly and with respect until they learn existing roles, rules, and norms. The classic example of divestiture is in military boot camp, where new recruits are insulted and subject to a wide variety of abuse until they learn the ropes.

With *investiture* tactics, newcomers immediately receive positive social support from other group members. For example, a group of nurses goes out of its way to teach a new member how things are done in the group and to make the new member feel welcome.

Divestiture tactics tend to lead to an *institutionalized* orientation; *investiture* tactics tend to lead to an *individualized* orientation.

To summarize: Collective, formal, sequential, fixed, serial, and divestiture tactics tend to lead newcomers to develop an institutionalized orientation. Individual, informal, random, variable, disjunctive, and investiture tactics tend to lead newcomers to develop an individualized orientation.[31] What is the significance of this model for socialization in organizations?

Consider the use of socialization tactics by the military. New recruits are placed in platoons with other new recruits (*collective*), are segregated from existing group members (*formal*), go through preestablished drills and learning experiences (*sequential*), know exactly how long basic training will take and what they have to do (*fixed*), have superior officers like platoon sergeants who socialize them (*serial*), and are treated with zero respect and tolerance until they have learned their duties and "gotten with the program" (*divestiture*). As a result of their socialization experiences, new recruits develop an institutionalized role orientation in which obedience and conformity to group roles, rules, and norms are the signs of success. New members who cannot or will not perform according to these standards leave the military or are asked to leave.

No group exerts the same control over its members as the military, but other groups do use similar tactics to socialize their members. Arthur Andersen, the large accounting firm, uses socialization tactics that tend to result in an institutionalized role orientation. After new recruits are hired, they all attend a six-week course at a training center outside Chicago (*formal, fixed*). There, new employees are indoctrinated as a group (*collective*) into Arthur Andersen's way of doing business. In formal eight-hour-a-day classes (*sequential*), existing group members tell newcomers what will be expected of them (*serial*). In addition to formal classes, newcomers also learn informally during meals and recreation what it means to be working for Arthur Andersen. By the end of this socialization process, they have learned the roles, rules, and norms of the group so that they behave in expected ways when interacting with Andersen clients.

Should a group encourage an institutional role orientation in which newcomers accept the status quo? Or should a group encourage an individual role orientation in which newcomers are allowed to develop creative and innovative responses to the tasks that the group requires of them? The answer to this question depends on the goals of the group and organization. As an accounting firm, Arthur Andersen wants and needs its employees to perform auditing activities according to certain standards. Andersen's credibility and reputation with clients depend on its employees following these standards, so the organization and the various groups of which it is composed need to control and reduce variability in group members' behaviors (for example, in the procedures that are followed in an audit). Thus, at Arthur Andersen, an institutionalized orientation is desired in most workers, and socialization tactics help to ensure that this occurs.

The main benefit of an institutionalized orientation is also its main danger: the sameness it produces among group members. If all members of a group have been socialized to share the same way of looking at the world and have the same strong allegiance to existing roles, rules, and norms, the group may become resistant to change and lack the ability to come up with creative solutions to problems. As we discuss in Chapter 19, however, the very survival of groups and organizations depends on their willingness and ability to change as needed in response to changes in the environments in which they exist. Such changes include changes in customer demands, in the nature and diversity of the work force, in economic conditions, or in technology. Groups (such as marketing departments, self-managed work teams, and research and development teams) and organizations (such as consumer products firms, auto companies, and computer manufacturers) that must respond to frequent changes may benefit from an individualized orientation and should try to use individual, informal, random, variable, disjunctive, and investiture tactics whenever feasible. Microsoft, for example, tends to rely on many of these tactics to promote individualized role orientations. Microsoft takes this approach because the effectiveness of the various groups in the organization depends not on standardizing individual behavior (as is the case in Arthur Andersen) but rather on encouraging group members to come up with new and improved solutions to software problems (for more information on Microsoft, see the closing case).

Socialization helps groups achieve whatever goals they have established—to provide consistently high-quality audits, to assemble seventy-five radios a day, to develop new software—by helping them control their members' behaviors. Whether a group needs to ensure that its members closely follow established ways of doing things or wants its members to suggest new ways of doing things, the group needs to exert control over its members' behaviors and actions to make this happen. As indicated in Insight 10.5, Walt Disney Company is an organization that is aware of how important the socialization process is.

Insight 10.5 **Competitive Advantage**

Socialization at Disneyland

When you think of Disneyland, certain things come to mind: wholesome fun, cleanliness, cheerfulness, friendliness. How does an organization that employs over thirty thousand people ensure that visitors to Disneyland have a fun-filled experience—one up to Disney standards? A careful socialization process is one important means by which the Walt Disney Company ensures that all visitors to Disneyland have fun. Socialization is geared toward developing an institutionalized role orientation. Disney (www.disney.com) wants all workers at Disneyland to carefully follow Disney roles (such as their individual job duties), rules (such as no mustaches or dangling earrings), and norms (such as always taking the extra step to make sure guests have a good experience). The institutionalized orientation ensures that Disney employees will do their jobs the Disney way and thereby help Disney in its quest to gain a competitive advantage.

New recruits (or "cast members" as they are called) receive formal training at Disney University in groups of around forty-five. Their collective socialization follows a set sequence of activities. During the Traditions I program, which lasts for a day and a half, newcomers learn the Disney language and the four Disney guiding principles: safety, courtesy, show or entertainment, and efficiency. They also receive training in how to answer guests' questions no matter how difficult the questions may be.

Once cast members complete Traditions I, they move on to further socialization in the attraction areas (Adventureland, Fantasyland, and so on) that they will be joining. This session, which can last as long as a day and a half, covers rules for each specific area. Last but not least is on-the-job training by experienced cast members in the groups the newcomers will be joining (a serial tactic). This part of the socialization process can take up to two and a half weeks to complete and includes new cast members' learning their roles and their accompanying responsibilities, privileges, and role relationships.

Part of the success and competitive advantage of Disneyland lies in the fact that guests uniformly *do* have fun. How does Disney achieve this seemingly effortless outcome? Careful socialization ensures that new cast members learn how to do things the Disney way.[32]

SUMMARY

Work groups are the basic building blocks of an organization. Work groups use roles, rules, and norms to control their members' behavior, and they use several socialization tactics to turn newcomers into effective group members. Groups contribute to organizational effectiveness when group goals are aligned with organizational goals. In this chapter, we made the following major points:

1. Two attributes separate work groups from random collections of individuals in an organization. Members of a work group (a) interact with each other and (b) perceive the potential for mutual goal accomplishment. Work groups vary in whether they are formal or informal. Formal work groups include command groups, task forces, teams, and self-managed work teams. Informal work groups include friendship groups and interest groups.

2. Groups develop and change over time. The five-stage model of group development proposes that groups develop in five sequential stages: forming, storming, norming, performing, and adjourning. Research, however, has not indicated that there is a universal set of stages that all groups experience in the same order.

3. Four important characteristics of groups are size, composition, function, and status. Each has the potential to impact the extent to which a group achieves its goals, performs at a high level, and ultimately is effective in helping an organization attain its goals. Social facilitation is a characteristic effect that the presence of other group members has on individual performance such that having others present enhances performance of well-learned tasks and impairs performance of difficult tasks.

4. All groups, regardless of their type or characteristics, need to control their members' behaviors to be effective and attain their goals. Roles and rules can be used to control behavior in groups.

5. A role is a set of behaviors or tasks that a person is expected to perform by virtue of holding a position in a group or organization. Roles have rights and responsibilities attached to them. Role relationships are the ways in which group and organizational members interact with each other to perform their specific roles. Group members

acquire roles through role making and through role taking.

6. Written rules specify behaviors that are required of group members or are forbidden. They also specify how particular tasks should be performed.

7. Groups also control their members' behavior by developing and enforcing group norms. Group norms are shared expectations for behavior within a group. There are three bases for conformity to group norms: compliance, identification, and internalization.

8. To accomplish goals and perform at a high level, groups need both conformity to and deviance from norms. Whether group norms result in high levels of group performance depends on the extent to which group goals are consistent with organizational goals. To facilitate goal alignment, group members should benefit or be rewarded when the group performs at a high level and contributes to the achievement of organizational goals.

9. Group members learn roles, rules, and norms through the process of socialization. Collective, formal, sequential, fixed, serial, and divestiture socialization tactics tend to lead to an institutionalized role orientation. Individual, informal, random, variable, disjunctive, and investiture socialization tactics tend to lead to an individualized role orientation.

Organizational Behavior in Action

TOPICS FOR DISCUSSION AND ACTION

1. At what stage in the five-stage model of group development might groups exert the most control over their members' behavior?
2. Do most members of an organization want to work in teams? Why or why not?
3. In what situations might the advantages of large group size outweigh the disadvantages?
4. In what kinds of situations might it be especially important to have heterogeneous groups?
5. Why are roles an important means of controlling group members' behaviors in self-managed work teams?
6. Why do groups need rules?
7. How are rules that specify how to perform a particular task developed?
8. Why might a group keep following a dysfunctional norm or a norm that prevents the group from achieving its goals?
9. Do all groups socialize their members? Do all groups need to socialize their members? Why or why not?
10. Is socialization ever completely finished, or is it an ongoing process?

BUILDING DIAGNOSTIC SKILLS

Analyzing a "Real" Group

Choose a work group featured in a television series (for example, the group of reporters on *Murphy Brown,* the medical team on *M*A*S*H,* the crew on *The Love Boat,* the flight crew on any *Star Trek* series, or the group of decorators on *Designing Women*). For the group you have chosen, answer these questions:

1. Is this a formal or an informal group? What kind of formal or informal group is it?
2. What stage of development is this group at according to the five-stage model of group development?
3. What can you say about the size, composition, function, and status of this group?
4. What are the roles and role relationships in this group?
5. What rights and responsibilities are attached to each role in the group?
6. What rules does this group use to control its members' behavior?
7. What norms does this group use to control its members' behavior?
8. How does the group react to deviance from its norms? Do any members of this group have idiosyncrasy credit?

RESEARCH ON THE INTERNET: A MANAGER'S TOOL

Specific Task

In many organizations, interest groups are formed by employees who have common objectives or goals. One such company is Microsoft. Scan Microsoft's website (www.microsoft.com) to learn more about this company. Then click on "Company Overview," then on "Diversity," and then on "Employee Groups."

1. What kinds of interest groups have employees at Microsoft formed?
2. Why have they formed these interest groups?

General Task

Many organizations use self-managed work teams to accomplish important work tasks. Find the website of such a company. For which kinds of tasks does this company use self-managed work teams? Are these teams truly self-managing? What are the benefits of self-managed work teams for this organization?

TOPICS FOR DEBATE

Groups are the basic building blocks of organizations. Now that you have a good understanding of the nature and types of groups and how groups control and socialize their members, debate the following issues.

Debate One

Team A. Controlling group members' behaviors by using roles and rules is generally preferable to using norms.

Team B. Controlling group members' behaviors by using norms is generally preferable to using roles and rules.

Debate Two

Team A. In most organizations, an institutionalized role orientation is more desirable than an individualized role orientation.

Team B. In most organizations, an individualized role orientation is more desirable than an institutionalized role orientation.

EXPERIENTIAL EXERCISE

Developing Roles, Rules, and Norms
Objective
Your objective is to gain experience in developing roles, rules, and norms that contribute to group effectiveness.

Procedure
The class divides into groups of from three to five people, and each group appoints one member as spokesperson, to present the group's findings to the whole class. Here is the scenario.

Assume the role of a group of jazz musicians who recently started performing together. Each member of the group has had some individual success as a musician and hopes that the group will become a top-performing jazz ensemble. The immediate goals of the group are to develop a repertoire of pieces that showcase each member's individual strengths and display the energy, vitality, and creativity of the group as a whole; to play as many gigs as possible at bars and clubs within a 500-mile radius of home; and to start making contacts with recording companies. The group's long-range goal is to be a nationally visible and successful jazz group with a major-label recording contract.

The group has gotten together and played several times both with and without an audience present and thinks it has what it takes to "make it big." The group realizes, however, that it needs to get its act together to meet both its short- and long-range goals.

1. What roles should the musicians develop to help achieve group goals?
2. What rules should the musicians develop to help achieve group goals?
3. What norms should the musicians develop to help achieve group goals?
4. What steps should the musicians take to help ensure that the group has the right balance of conformity and deviance?

When your group has answered those questions, the spokesperson will describe to the rest of the class the roles, rules, and norms that your group thinks will help the jazz group achieve its goals. The spokesperson also will discuss the steps group members think should be taken to help ensure that the jazz group has the right balance of conformity and deviance.

MAKING THE CONNECTION

Find an example of a company that recently increased its use of groups or teams. Why did this company start to use groups or teams more heavily? What kinds of groups or teams is the organization using? How do the groups or teams control their members' behaviors? What effect has the increase in the use of groups or teams had on organizational performance? How do workers feel about working in the groups or teams?

CLOSING CASE

Teams Are the Heart of Microsoft

Microsoft Corporation (www.microsoft.com) is the leading company in the computer software industry both in the United States and abroad. Microsoft's annual revenues are approximately $14 billion, and the net worth of its 38-year-old founder and CEO, Bill Gates, is estimated to be near $8 billion.[33] Microsoft's success stems in part from its use of teams to manage its employees.

Microsoft employs "developers," computer programmers who write and develop software. No matter how big a project is—even a complex project such as the development of a successful operating system like Windows—the project is broken down into small parts that can be handled by teams of about twelve developers. The part of the project that each team handles is further subdivided, and each team member is assigned his or her own part of the project to work on. Developers with more experience are given more responsibilities than new members of a team, but all team members know that the success of the project depends on the sum of their individual inputs.[34]

Although each group member has his or her own part of the team project to work on, team members are expected to collaborate with each other and help each other out. Seeing two team members hunched over a computer screen is not an uncommon occurrence at Microsoft. Team members provide considerable support to each other and admiration for a job well done, but they can also be stern critics of substandard performance if a team member fails to perform at an acceptable level.

In addition to having important responsibilities, developers also have some valued privileges or rights. Principal among these is the privilege to work in a state-of-the-art computer software environment with the latest technological equipment. Practically all developers have at least two or three computer systems in their offices. Another privilege is working with some of the best computer programmers in the United States.

Developers are given considerable autonomy in how they perform their work; nevertheless, behavior at Microsoft is governed by shared informal rules that practically everyone agrees to follow. One set of informal rules covers the basic issue of working hours. Developers are free to work whatever hours suit them. If a developer has a sudden insight at midnight, it is not unusual for that person to work until the wee hours of the morning. Likewise, if a developer's child is sick, the developer can stay home a day or two to care for the child and do makeup work at some other time. Along with these "rules" on flexible working hours, almost all developers abide by another informal rule: They will put in the hours necessary to get a job done, even if they must stay up all night to work on a particularly difficult part of a program. On an informal basis, team members monitor each other's behavior, and managers may step in and call a developer they haven't seen in the office for a couple of days.

Team members are rewarded or compensated for their individual performance and for the performance of their team. Microsoft finds that this type of pay system results in high levels of motivation and performance among team members.[35] Given its worldwide strength and success in computer software, Microsoft must be doing something right in its use of teams to develop its innovative software products.

Questions for Discussion
1. Why does Microsoft divide up the work involved in developing a major software system like Windows into pieces that can be accomplished by teams of about twelve developers?
2. What motivates developers in these teams to perform at a high level?

Effective Work Groups and Teams

11

Trials and Tribulations of a FORE Systems R&D Team

FORE Systems, Inc. (www.fore.com), founded in 1990, is a growing and successful high tech company which focuses on the development of new computer software programs that enable computer networks to deliver more information more quickly to users, thus enhancing the speed of online audio and video transmission.[1] Because these computer programs are larger than any one software engineer could write on his

or her own, FORE's engineers work in research and development (R&D) teams to write its huge software programs. To manage each major project that FORE decides to pursue, an R&D team is put together and each engineer is responsible for writing a segment of the long computer codes that will then be integrated by the team into a complete program that can be over 30,000 lines long.

Writing such complex programs is a challenging task not just for technical reasons, but also because the complex interpersonal dynamics among team members must be successfully managed if a project is to be successful. FORE Systems' teams of software engineers often experience many trials and tribulations as their members work together, often for up to a year on a particular project. Take the case of the R&D team led by Matt Scott, which was charged with the development of a program code named "Maryland."[2] The Maryland project involved developing computer network software that would allow workers who might be thousands of miles apart to communicate as rapidly with each other as if they were working in the same building.

Scott's team originally had four members: Scott, Sanjaya Choudhury, Venu Moogala, and Scott Si. From the beginning, Scott and Choudhury found themselves intensely debating in team meetings about the best way to proceed with the project. As the leader, although Scott felt that Choudhury was a valuable member of the team and had good ideas, he also thought they weren't practical and shouldn't be pursued. Choudhury, for his part, felt that Scott was simply taking the upper hand in meetings and that his ideas were being ignored, leading to many acrimonious disagreements. After many team meetings were prolonged as the two argued, Scott realized that they would have to manage their interpersonal problems if the project was going to succeed and that there might always be a bit of tension between them.

After several months, during which the team managed to solve this and other interpersonal problems, the time arrived to break up the computer code writing task into separate parts, and to allocate each part to a team member, depending on his area of technical expertise. Each team member was assigned to write approximately 8,000 lines of computer code; however, they needed to be in close contact with each other because what one member wrote affected what the others wrote, and all the five pieces would eventually need to be integrated into one computer program.

As the pace of the team's work quickened, team members found themselves working nights and weekends and sometimes getting on each other's nerves. When team members eventually sat down to put together their individual sections of computer code to create an integrated program, they experienced a rude shock. The program wouldn't work because the team members each had different approaches to writing code and they hadn't worked together closely enough to make sure that their codes would mesh with each other.

Because the Maryland team was scheduled to present their complete program at a trade show in a month, Scott's boss, Steve Hand, the director of software engineering, became concerned and started checking up on the team. The pressure they were under brought the team much closer together; interpersonal problems were forgotten as they strived to meet the deadline of the trade show while showing Hand that they were on top of things. Team members worked round the clock to complete the program. They wanted to prove to everyone, especially their competitors at the trade show, that their program was superior. With only hours to spare, the program was completed, and the team members who went to the trade show confidently reported back that their program appeared to be better than their competitors' programs.

Thus, despite some mishaps along the way, the Maryland team proved to be highly effective and achieved its goal. The program has since been shipped out on CD-ROM to FORE Systems' customers and the "Maryland" team has been disbanded, its members going on to new assignments at FORE Systems.[3]

Overview

In Chapter 10 we discussed the nature of work groups, how they control their members' behavior, and how they socialize newcomers to contribute to the attainment of group and organizational goals. In this chapter, we continue our study of work groups and focus on what makes work groups like the R&D team profiled in the opening case effective. Recall from the last chapter that effective work groups perform at a high level and help an organization achieve its goals.

Numerous factors determine how effective a work group is and how well its members work together. In fact, the group characteristics we discussed in Chapter 10, the ways that groups control their members, and the socialization process all have the potential to influence how effective a work group is. In this chapter, we build on this foundation and examine why and how groups can be more than the sum of their parts and can help an organization perform at a high level. We examine the factors that can lead to problems in groups and can contribute to poor group and organizational performance. We also examine three important types of work groups in detail: top-management teams, self-managed work teams, and research and development teams. By the end of this chapter, you will have a good understanding of what makes work groups effective in organizations.

Process Losses, Process Gains, and Group Effectiveness

Effective work groups contribute to the attainment of organizational goals by providing the organization with important outputs. The outputs might be finished products such as correctly typed reports and high-quality automobiles, or less tangible but no less important outputs such as satisfied customers and patients. Desired outputs also include behaviors not related to a group's specific tasks. These behaviors include promptly reporting broken-down machinery, suggesting ways of improving work processes, going out of one's way to help customers, helping group members when they are under pressure, and other forms of organizational citizenship behavior (see Chapter 3). As you will learn below, effective work groups perform at the highest level possible by minimizing performance difficulties or process losses. Moreover, effective work groups increase their potential performance over time by achieving process gains or finding better ways to work.

POTENTIAL PERFORMANCE

Potential performance
The highest level of performance that a group is capable of achieving at a given point in time.

Managers strive to have groups perform at the highest level possible, which is called a group's **potential performance.**[4] Although potential performance is important because it reflects a work group's capabilities, it is often difficult to know in advance and can change as conditions change. When Japanese car companies were experimenting with ways to improve the productivity of groups of assembly-line workers, one innovative approach they took was to continually increase groups' expected or potential performance levels. Realizing that the capabilities of groups are often underestimated, Japanese managers strove to push groups to produce up to their true potential.

In order for an organization to achieve its goals, managers and work groups need to strive to ensure that a group's *actual* performance comes as close as possible to its *potential* performance. In many situations, however, a group's actual performance falls short of its potential performance, even though the group is capable of achieving its potential. To see what this can mean for an organization, consider the following situation. A group of six salesmen staff the men's clothing department in a small, exclusive department store. This group is fully capable of providing excellent customer service, keeping the department clean and neat, and stocking and restocking merchandise in a timely fashion. Recently, however, the group's actual performance has fallen below its potential performance. Customers wishing to return merchandise are often kept waiting unnecessarily, and counters and dressing rooms are often cluttered with clothes. Why is the actual performance of this group below its potential performance, and what can the store's management do to increase group effectiveness?

Process losses

Performance difficulties that a group experiences because of coordination and motivation problems.

PROCESS LOSSES AND PERFORMANCE

Research has shown that **process losses**—performance difficulties that a group experiences because of coordination and motivation problems—are an important factor when a group's actual performance falls short of its potential performance.[5] Coordination problems arise when group activities are divided among group members (because of the division of labor that occurs in groups) and then group members' contributions are merged or combined into some group product or output. The R&D team profiled in the opening case experienced a process loss when they tried to put their individual sections of computer code together to create a program and the codes couldn't be successfully merged. Motivation problems occur because members of a group may not always be motivated to contribute a high level of inputs to the group. Fig. 11.1 depicts the relationship between actual and potential performance and process losses (the figure also includes process gains, which we discuss in the next section).

The group of six salesmen described earlier experienced a coordination problem when they tried to keep the counters and dressing rooms clean and tidy. Often, when a salesman knew that one of his customers was coming to the store, he selected some clothes he thought the customer would like and displayed them on a counter or hung them in a dressing room. At the same time, clothing remained on the counters and in the dressing rooms from customers who had already been served and had left the store. Even though keeping counters neat and restocking shelves were among their job responsibilities, the salesmen tended to avoid these tasks because they did not want to make the mistake of restocking clothes that one of their coworkers had just picked out for a customer. As a result of this coordination problem, counters and dressing rooms were usually cluttered.

The group's motivation problem revolved around the processing of returned clothing. All group members had equal responsibility for processing

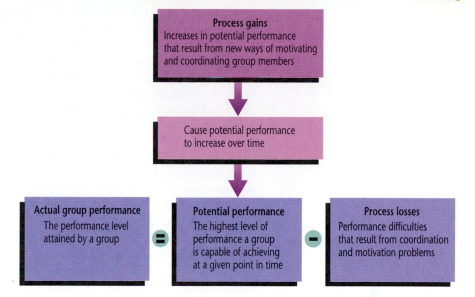

Process gains
Increases in potential performance that result from new ways of motivating and coordinating group members

Cause potential performance to increase over time

Actual group performance
The performance level attained by a group

=

Potential performance
The highest level of performance a group is capable of achieving at a given point in time

−

Process losses
Performance difficulties that result from coordination and motivation problems

FIGURE 11.1

The Relationship Between Actual and Potential Performance, Process Losses, and Process Gains

returned clothing, yet customers wishing to return an item were often kept waiting even though several of the salesmen appeared to be available to wait on them. Because the salesmen received no commission for processing returns and disliked all the paperwork involved, each one of them would wait a minute or two before volunteering to help a customer with a return in the hope that one of his colleagues would handle the transaction.

To meet the challenge of ensuring that a group's actual performance equals its potential performance, managers must try to eliminate as many process losses as possible. The manager of the men's clothing department eliminated the coordination problem by designating one counter and one dressing room to be used for displaying clothes for particular customers and by instructing all salesmen to restock the clothes they had selected once they were finished helping their customers. In addition, all salesmen were explicitly instructed to restock clothes on the remaining counters and in the other dressing rooms whenever they saw them. The manager solved the motivation problem by keeping track of the returns that each salesman processed. Once the salesmen knew that their returns were being tracked, customers were never again kept waiting.

PROCESS GAINS AND PERFORMANCE

In addition to eliminating process losses that prevent a group from performing up to its potential, managers also need to increase a group's potential performance. To increase the effectiveness of a work group, managers need to identify ways to improve the group's motivation and coordination to achieve **process gains**[6]—increases in potential performance that result from new ways of motivating and coordinating group members (see Fig. 11.1). The Japanese managers experimenting with ways to continuously improve group performance in assembly-line settings were searching for process gains: new and better ways to coordinate and motivate workers to raise levels of potential performance.

In the department store example, the department manager successfully eliminated the process losses so that the department no longer was sloppy and

Process gains
Increases in potential performance that result from new ways of motivating and coordinating group members.

returns were handled efficiently. But the manager thought that the group's potential performance could be higher. He thought that if group members pooled their skills and abilities, they could create some innovative and attractive merchandise displays that would boost sales. To achieve this process gain (and raise the group's potential level of performance), the manager needed to raise the group's motivation. Together, all of the department managers and the store manager devised a strategy to achieve process gains by raising levels of motivation in groups throughout the store. At the next store meeting, the store manager announced a quarterly competition among the sales groups for the most innovative and attractive merchandise display. Winning groups would have their picture displayed in the employee lunchroom, and each member of the winning group would receive a $75 gift certificate for store merchandise. This strategy had its intended effect: The quality of merchandise displays increased dramatically in many of the store's departments.

In the next sections, we examine various aspects of groups that can influence group performance by increasing or decreasing process gains and losses. A manager's key objectives in creating and sustaining highly effective work groups are to (1) eliminate process losses by ensuring that the actual performance of a group is as close as possible to potential performance and (2) create process gains by continually raising the level of potential performance.

Social Loafing: A Problem in Group Motivation and Performance

In some groups, any given individual's contribution to group performance cannot be easily recognized or identified by other group members or by outsiders such as supervisors. Consider a group of custodians who are jointly responsible for keeping the food court in a busy shopping mall clean. The custodians are not assigned to particular areas but work together to patrol the whole food court, picking up trash and cleaning dirty tables. Because the custodians work together, it is difficult to identify the performance of any individual custodian. When individuals work in groups where individual performances are not readily observable, there is a strong potential for **social loafing,** the tendency of individuals to exert less effort when they work in a group than when they work alone.[7]

 Social loafing
The tendency of individuals to exert less effort when they work in a group than when they work alone.

Social loafing, which can seriously impact work-group effectiveness, occurs for two reasons. First, recall from our discussion of learning and motivation in earlier chapters that motivation, effort, and performance tend to be highest when outcomes such as praise and pay are administered to workers contingent on their level of individual performance. Because the custodians are working in a group and their individual levels of performance cannot easily be identified and evaluated by a supervisor, the custodians realize that they will not receive positive outcomes (such as praise) for performing at a high level or negative outcomes (such as a reprimand) for performing at a low level.[8] As a result of this lack of a connection between inputs and outcomes, the custodians' motivation is lower than it would be if they were working individually, and they do not exert as much effort.

A second reason social loafing occurs is that workers who are performing in a group sometimes think that their own efforts are unimportant or not really needed, and this belief lowers their level of motivation.[9] For example, a custodian might not clean off many tables when he works in a group because he thinks that his input is not really necessary and that some other member of the group will clean the tables he misses.

Have you observed social loafing when you were working on a group project for one of your classes? Sometimes one or two students in a group do not do their share of the work. They think they will receive the same grade as everyone else in the group regardless of how much or little effort they exert, or they think their contributions aren't really needed for the group to do a good job.

Social loafing is a serious problem for work groups because it results in a process loss that lowers group performance. When social loafing occurs, actual group performance is lower than potential performance because some members of the group are not motivated to work as hard as they would if they were working on their own. Furthermore, social loafing by one or a few members of a group sometimes induces other members of the group to cut back on their efforts as well. This type of process loss is a result of the so-called **sucker effect.**[10] It occurs when group members who were not originally inclined to engage in social loafing reduce their efforts when they observe other group members loafing. Because they do not want to be taken advantage of or be considered suckers,[11] their motivation decreases when they see others in the group slack off. The sucker effect is consistent with the equity theory of motivation, which suggests that workers who perceive inequity are motivated to try to restore equity by bringing their outcome/input ratios back into balance with the ratios of their referents, other group members (see Chapter 6).

GROUP SIZE AND SOCIAL LOAFING

Several studies have found that the tendency for group members to put forth less effort increases as the size of the group increases.[12] This increase in social loafing occurs because larger numbers of people in a group increase the problems associated with identifying and evaluating individual performance. The more custodians a supervisor has to monitor, for example, the less time the supervisor can devote to evaluating each custodian. As group size increases, members may also be more likely to think that their own efforts are not an important part of the group's performance.

Other kinds of process losses also occur as group size increases.[13] As you learned in Chapter 10, in a large group, there is much potential for conflict and coordination problems, both of which widen the gap between potential and actual performance due to process losses.

WAYS TO REDUCE SOCIAL LOAFING

It is important to reduce the occurrence of social loafing because it can lead to process losses that lower group performance. Managers can try to reduce or eliminate social loafing by making individual contributions identifiable, by making individuals feel that they are making valuable contributions to a group, and by keeping the group as small as possible.

Making Individual Contributions Identifiable.   One way to eliminate social loafing is to make individual contributions to a group or individual performance levels identifiable so that individual performance can be evaluated.[14] For example, the contributions of individual custodians could be made identifiable and their performance evaluated by dividing the food court into separate zones and giving each custodian a separate zone to keep clean. Individual

Sucker effect
A condition in which some group members, not wishing to be considered suckers, reduce their own efforts when they see social loafing by other group members.

performance could then be evaluated by observing how clean each zone is. As indicated in Insight 11.1, the identifiability of individual contributions can sometimes be increased by increasing the level of supervision in a group.

Insight 11.1   **Ethics**

Social Loafing at the Cuyahoga Metropolitan Housing Authority

The six hundred employees of the Cuyahoga Metropolitan Housing Authority are responsible for maintaining public housing in Cleveland. When Claire E. Freeman became head of the housing authority, social loafing was at near-epidemic levels. Public housing was covered with graffiti and strewn with litter, and tenants often had to wait for weeks to get plumbing repaired or broken windows replaced. Some tenants complained that the housing authority was not treating them in an ethical manner, especially in light of the abundant evidence of social loafing. Tenants complained, for example, that they often saw groups of maintenance workers lounging under trees. When Freeman visited different housing projects, she sometimes saw no one actually working but groups of workers sitting around and drinking coffee.[15]

To compound the problem, lucrative overtime duty was assigned to workers on the basis of seniority, in accordance with union rules. As a result of this policy, many workers who lounged around all day were able to earn additional money (at a premium rate) by "working" overtime. This practice also raised questions about potential unethical conduct at the housing authority.

Freeman was able to eliminate some of the social loafing and ethics questions by increasing direct supervision.[16] Workers are now less inclined to loaf because they know that supervisors are monitoring their behavior and evaluating their performance.

Sometimes when it is difficult for supervisors to identify individual contributions, other group members can do so by using a peer evaluation or performance appraisal system (see Chapter 8). Some professors, for example, try to eliminate social loafing on group projects by having students evaluate each other's contributions to a group project and assigning grades to individual students based, in part, on these evaluations.

Making Individuals Feel That They Are Making Valuable Contributions to a Group. In some kinds of groups it is impossible for supervisors or group members to monitor individual behavior or make individual performance identifiable. For example, in a professional singing group that provides background music for commercials and movies, it is very difficult to assess the effort of any individual singer, and an individual's performance (the quality of an individual's singing) cannot be distinguished from the performance of the group as a whole.

In situations where individual performances cannot be separated from the performance of the group as a whole, managers can reduce social loafing by making each individual feel that he or she makes an important and worthwhile contribution to the group.[17] Making individuals feel like valued group members in this manner is the second way to reduce social loafing and increase work-group effectiveness. This goal could be accomplished in the group of singers by periodically reminding group members of the special contributions that each of them makes to the group. A singer with a very deep and resonant voice, for example, could be reminded that his singing adds unique richness to the group's overall sound. Another way to stress the importance of each member's value and contributions is to let group members know that the success or failure of the group sometimes hinges on their individual efforts.

Bill Walsh, former coach of the San Francisco 49ers and of the Stanford University football team, tried to make each football player feel that he made an important contribution to team performance to motivate him to do his best and eliminate any potential social loafing. As Coach Walsh put it, "You develop within the organization and the players an appreciation for the role each athlete plays on the team. You talk to each player and let each one know that, at some point, he will be in a position to win or lose a game. It may be one play in an entire career for a certain player or many plays each game for a Joe Montana. But the point is that everyone's job is essential. Everyone has a specific role and specific responsibilities. . . . You talk to each player and indicate the importance of everyone's participation in the process—that it is important for everyone to express himself, to offer ideas, explanations, solutions, formulas."[18] Walsh's insights on making each member of a team feel that his or her unique contribution is important for a team's success come from his years of experience as a football coach, but they are equally applicable to the management of research and development teams in FORE Systems Inc. and self-managed work teams.

Another way to reduce social loafing by making individuals realize the importance of their contributions to a group is by reminding them of why they were chosen to be part of the group. In forming task forces, for example, managers typically select individuals with expertise and experience in different areas in order to get the full range of perspectives that a heterogeneous group provides (see Chapter 10). By reminding members that they were selected for the task force because of the unique contributions they can make, managers can drive home the message that members can (and are expected to) make an important and worthwhile contribution to the group.

Keeping the Group as Small as Possible.   The third way to reduce social loafing is to keep the group as small as possible.[19] Social loafing is more likely as groups get bigger because individuals perceive that their own effort and performance levels are unidentifiable, unnecessary, or likely to be duplicated by others in the group. Managers should try to identify the optimal size of a group, given the tasks that members are performing. If managers sense that process losses are increasing as a group gets larger, they should take steps to reduce group size. One way to do this is to divide the work so that it is performed by two groups. In the menswear department, for example, rather

Social Loafing

- Whenever feasible, make individual contributions or individual levels of performance in a group identifiable, and evaluate these contributions.
- When work is performed in groups, let each member know that he or she can make an important and worthwhile contribution to the group.
- When you are unable to evaluate individual contributions to a group, consider having group members evaluate each other's contributions and rewarding group members on the basis of group performance.
- Keep work groups as small as possible while making sure that a group has enough resources—member knowledge, skills, experiences—to achieve its goals.

than have six different salespeople interacting to manage the whole department, two people could be given the responsibility to manage the men's designer clothes like Polo and Tommy Hilfiger, and the other four could manage the lower-priced clothing section. Indeed, one reason organizations are composed of so many different groups is to avoid the process losses that occur because of large group size and social loafing.

Interestingly enough, in the R&D team in the opening case, individual contributions were identifiable, each team member knew that he or she was playing a vital role on the team, and team size was small. Not only was there no social loafing on this team, but team members worked nights and weekends, and, towards the end of the project, almost round the clock.

Group Tasks and Group Performance: Thompson's Model of Task Interdependence

Process losses, particularly those that result from social loafing, are most prevalent when group members feel their individual contributions are not identifiable or important. In some groups, however, process losses occur because of the types of tasks that members perform. Process losses are especially likely to occur when the nature of the task itself makes it difficult to identify individual performance levels. To limit these process losses, managers need to understand what characteristics of tasks not only make identification of individual performance difficult but also increase coordination and motivation problems. Managers also need to understand the effects of different kinds of tasks on group behavior. Armed with this understanding, managers can then use outcomes or rewards (pay, bonuses, praise, or interesting assignments) to motivate group members to perform at a high level.

In earlier chapters we emphasized that outcomes should be given to workers on the basis of their individual levels of performance. But on some kinds of group tasks, individual performance cannot be identified. To determine how to distribute outcomes to group members so that they will be motivated to perform at a high level, the kinds of tasks a group performs must be understood and taken into account. James D. Thompson's model of group tasks helps managers identify (1) task characteristics that can lead to process losses and (2) the most effective ways to distribute outcomes or rewards to

Task interdependence
The extent to which the work performed by one member of a group affects what other members do.

Pooled task interdependence
The task interdependence that results when each member of a group makes a separate and independent contribution to group performance.

group members to generate high motivation. Thompson's model is based on the concept of **task interdependence**—that is, the extent to which the work performed by one member affects what other group members do. As task interdependence within a group increases, the degree and intensity of the interactions between group members who are required to perform the group's tasks also increases. Thompson identifies three types of task interdependence: pooled, sequential, and reciprocal.[20]

POOLED INTERDEPENDENCE

If a group task involves **pooled task interdependence,** each member of the group makes a separate and independent contribution to group performance. Because each member's contribution is separate, it can be readily identified and evaluated. On group tasks that involve pooled interdependence, group performance is determined by summing up the contributions or performances of individual group members.[21] Pooled interdependence is depicted in Fig. 11.2(a). Members A, B, and C make independent contributions to group performance. The total of the separate outputs of the three group members equals the group's performance.

Examples of tasks with pooled interdependence include the work performed by the members of a typing pool, by the waiters and waitresses in a restaurant, by a group of physicians in an HMO, and by a group of sales representatives for a book publisher. In each of these examples, group performance is the result of adding up the performances of individual group members: the amount of correspondence typed, the number of customers served, the number of patients treated, the number of books sold.

One common source of process losses on tasks with pooled interdependence is duplication of effort, such as when two waiters inadvertently take orders from the same table or two typists mistakenly type the same report. Duplication of effort reduces a group's performance level because members spend time and energy on tasks that another group member has already performed. This coordination problem can usually be solved by carefully and clearly assigning tasks to group members.

Motivation problems can easily be avoided on tasks with pooled interdependence by evaluating individual levels of performance and rewarding group members for their individual performance. For these kinds of tasks, distributing rewards based on individual performance is likely to result in high levels of motivation, as theories of learning and motivation suggest. In fact,

FIGURE 11.2

Three Types of Task Interdependence

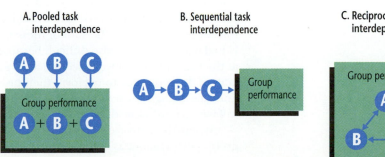

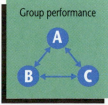

This Brazilian shoe manufacturer uses sequential interdependence to assemble inexpensive shoes that have captured a significant share of the U.S. shoe market.

because each member's contribution is separate when tasks are characterized by pooled interdependence, the potential for process losses due to a lack of motivation is relatively low.

SEQUENTIAL INTERDEPENDENCE

> **Sequential task interdependence**
>
> The task interdependence that results when group members must perform specific behaviors in a predetermined order.

A group task based on **sequential task interdependence** requires specific behaviors to be performed by group members in a predetermined order. The level of each group member's performance affects the performance of other group members later in the work cycle, and one worker's output is needed for another worker to complete his or her job. In Fig. 11.2(b), for example, the performance of member A affects the ability of member B to perform her task; in turn, the activities of member B affect the ability of member C to perform his task. Examples of sequential interdependence include all types of assembly-line work—such as the production of cars, televisions, or Subway sandwiches—where the finished product is the result of the sequential inputs of group members.

Sequential interdependence makes identifying the individual performances of group members difficult because each member makes a contribution to the same final product. (In contrast, when task interdependence is *pooled*, each member contributes his or her own final product, and group performance depends on the sum of these contributions.) Identification of individual performance is also difficult because an error made by a group member at the beginning of a work sequence can affect the ability of group members later in the sequence to perform their tasks well. If a worker on a car assembly line fails to align the axle correctly, for example, workers farther down the line will have a hard time aligning the wheels and making the brakes work properly.

When the activities of group members are sequentially interdependent, group performance is determined by the performance level of the least capable or poorest-performing member of the group. In a plant that produces televisions on an assembly line, for example, televisions move along the line at a set speed, and workers stationed along the line complete their required tasks (such as installing the on/off control) on each television that passes by. The assembly line can move only at the speed of the slowest worker along the line; thus the number of televisions produced by the group of assembly-line workers is limited by the performance capabilities of the group's poorest performer.

For those reasons, the potential for process losses is higher with sequential interdependence than with pooled interdependence. Motivation and social loafing problems are also encountered more often because all group members work on the same product and it is thus often hard to discern levels of individual performance.

How can organizations try to overcome the motivation and social loafing problems associated with sequential interdependence? One way is by closely monitoring on-the-job behaviors of group members. Assembly lines, for example, usually employ a relatively large number of supervisors to monitor the behaviors of work-group members. A second way to counteract the negative effects of sequential task interdependence is to form work groups consisting of individuals with similar levels of ability. When that is done, the talents and motivation of high performers will not be wasted because of the presence of a low performer in a group. A third way to overcome motivation problems is by rewarding group members on the basis of group levels of performance. When group members are rewarded based upon group performance, all members (including the poorest performers) may be more likely to be motivated to perform at a high level. Rewarding sequentially interdependent group members for group performance may also cause members to monitor and control each other's behavior, for social loafing by one member might impair group performance and reduce the rewards received by all members of the group.

Process losses arising from coordination problems also arise when tasks are sequentially interdependent. If a worker at the start of an assembly line comes to work late or needs to stop working during the day, for example, the whole line must be shut down unless a replacement worker is readily available. How can managers try to overcome coordination difficulties? They can reward workers for good attendance and punctuality, and they can have available a pool of multiskilled workers who can step in at different points in the production process to take over for absent group members.

RECIPROCAL INTERDEPENDENCE

▶ **Reciprocal task interdependence**
The task interdependence that results when the activities of all work-group members are fully dependent on one another.

Group tasks are characterized by **reciprocal task interdependence** when the activities of all work-group members are fully dependent on one another so that each member's performance influences the performance of every other member of the group. Figure 11.2(c) shows that not only do member A's actions affect B's, and member B's actions affect C's (as would be the case with sequential interdependence), but member C's actions also affect A's and B's, member A's actions affect C's, and member B's actions affect A's. Examples of work groups whose tasks are reciprocally interdependent include high-tech research and development teams, top-management teams, emergency-room personnel, and an operating-room team in a hospital. Members of the FORE Systems R&D team described in the opening case were reciprocally interdependent. Although they worked very closely together in the first and last stages of their project, they lost sight of the need to do so when they were writing their individual segments of computer code. The need to work closely together was hammered home to them when the individual segments couldn't be successfully combined, and from then on they worked very closely together and successfully completed the program.

The potential for process losses is highest when tasks are reciprocally interdependent because motivation and coordination problems can be particularly troublesome. Motivation problems such as social loafing arise because it is difficult, if not impossible, to identify an individual's level of performance when the final product is the result of the complex interplay of all group members' contributions.

How can managers try to minimize process losses when a group's activities are reciprocally interdependent? They should keep groups relatively small. They should emphasize that each group member can make an important and distinctive contribution to the group and should encourage group members to feel personally responsible for group goal accomplishment. To reduce the tendency for social loafing, they should reward group members for group performance, because a group reward may cause group members to monitor and control each other's behavior in order to maximize rewards to all group members.

An example of a group characterized by reciprocal interdependence is the top-management team of a small company that manufactures toys. On the team are the vice presidents in charge of marketing and sales, production, research and development, and finance. Leading the team is the president of the company. How well the company as a whole does depends on the complex interplay between those various functions, but at any point in time it is difficult to evaluate the performance of any one of the top managers. Under these circumstances, there is a high potential for social loafing, but it does not often occur because (1) the group is relatively small, (2) each vice president thinks that his or her contributions are indispensable to the success of the company because each is an expert in a particular function, and (3) group members' salaries depend on how well the firm does.

Work groups performing tasks characterized by reciprocal interdependence experience considerable coordination problems because of the inherent unpredictability of group relations and interactions. In contrast to the case of sequential interdependence, there is no set ordering of group activities in the case of reciprocal interdependence. The top-management team described above experiences coordination problems on a day-to-day basis. When sales of a dinosaur board game greatly exceeded expectations, for example, the managers in charge of marketing, production, and finance had to work out a plan to increase production runs for the game while keeping costs down and not interfering with the production of other products. But the production manager was on a month-long trip to Taiwan, China, and Singapore to evaluate the feasibility of moving some of the firm's manufacturing facilities overseas, so the group had difficulties coming up with a viable plan, and sales were lost.

How can managers alleviate coordination problems on complex tasks? One way is to keep group size relatively small, to limit the number of individuals who must coordinate their efforts. Another way is to locate group members close to one another so that whenever a group member needs input from another, that person is readily available. Because of advances in electronic forms of communication and computer software for groups, however, members in different locations can still be in constant communication with one another. If the top-management team of the toy company had been set up with such group software developed by companies such as Microsoft, the production manager scouting factory sites in East Asia could have been in communication with other group members by means of a portable personal computer.

Other coordination difficulties arising with reciprocal interdependence can also be alleviated by clear and open communication between group members (a topic discussed in detail in Chapter 13). Finally, coordination difficulties can be reduced if group members develop norms that result in group members always being available to help each other when needed.

As task interdependence moves from pooled to sequential to reciprocal interdependence, the potential for *process losses* increases because identifying individual performances becomes increasingly harder and because coordination becomes more difficult. The potential for *process gains* also increases as task interdependence becomes more complex. As the level and intensity of group members' interactions increase and the expertise and skills of group members are brought to bear on the group's tasks, the potential for **synergy** increases. Synergy (a type of process gain) occurs when members of a group acting together are able to produce more or better output than would have been produced by the combined efforts of each person acting alone.

For example, the top-management team of the toy company recently developed a new line of compact travel toys that were an instant success with children and very profitable for the company. The managers in charge of marketing, production, research and development, and finance worked closely throughout the development and launching of the new line, and their reciprocally interdependent interactions enabled them to come up with a winner. If each of the managers had worked on his or her own, the new line would never have been launched. As another example, the software engineers in the opening case were able to produce a complex computer program that could never have been written if each engineer worked on his or her own.

 Synergy
A process gain that occurs when members of a group acting together are able to produce more or better output than would have been produced by the combined efforts of each person acting alone.

 **TO MANAGERS**

Group Tasks and Group Effectiveness

- When a group task involves pooled interdependence, allocate individual tasks to group members to avoid duplication of effort, and evaluate individual levels of performance and reward group members for their individual performances.
- When a group task involves sequential interdependence, do as many of the following as feasible: (a) Monitor on-the-job behaviors of group members. (b) Reward group members for group performance. (c) Assign workers with similar ability levels to the same group. (d) Reward workers for good attendance and punctuality. (e) Have multiskilled workers available to fill in for absent group members.
- When a group task involves reciprocal interdependence, do as many of the following as feasible: (a) Keep group size relatively small. (b) Make sure that each group member realizes that he or she can make an important and distinctive contribution to the group. (c) Reward group members for group performance. (d) Increase the physical or electronic proximity of group members. (e) Encourage clear and open communication. (f) Encourage group members to help each other when needed.

Group Cohesiveness and Group Performance

Regardless of the kinds of tasks performed, work groups differ in how attractive they are to their members. When groups are very attractive to their members, individuals value their group membership and have strong desires to remain members of the group. The attractiveness of a group to its members is called **group cohesiveness.**[22] Groups high in cohesiveness are very appealing to their members; groups low in cohesiveness are not very appealing to their members. An important property of work groups, group cohesiveness affects group performance and effectiveness.

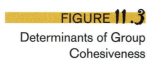
Group cohesiveness
The attractiveness of a group to its members.

FACTORS THAT CONTRIBUTE TO GROUP COHESIVENESS

A variety of factors influence a group's level of cohesiveness.[23] Here, we examine five: group size, similarity of group members, competition with other groups, success, and the exclusiveness of the group (see Fig. 11.3).

Group Size.   As you learned in Chapter 10, as groups get bigger, their members tend to be less satisfied. For this reason, large groups do not tend to be cohesive. In large groups, a few members of the group tend to dominate group discussions, and the opportunities for participation by other group members are limited. Large groups have the greatest potential for conflict, and members find it difficult to form close ties with each other. A small or medium group size (between three and fifteen people) tends to promote cohesiveness. In the closing case for Chapter 10, you saw how Microsoft Corporation helps to ensure a certain level of cohesiveness in its teams of developers by keeping group size down to about twelve members.

Similarity/Diversity of Group Members.   People generally like, get along with, and most easily communicate with others who are similar to themselves. Moreover, people tend to perceive others who are similar to themselves more positively than they perceive those who are different (because of the similar-to-me bias discussed in Chapter 4). Groups tend to be most cohesive when group members are homogeneous or share certain attitudes, values, experiences, and other characteristics. For example, a task force composed of individuals (such as engineers) with the same educational background and work experiences will tend to be more cohesive than a task force whose members (an engineer, an accountant, a financial analyst, and a biochemist) have dissimilar

FIGURE 11.3

Determinants of Group
Cohesiveness

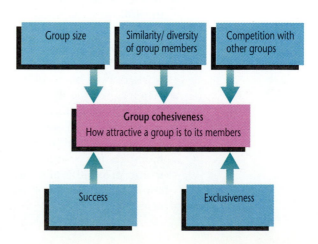

backgrounds. One caveat, however, needs to be made about the similarity or homogeneity of group members. As you saw in Chapter 10, diversity (or heterogeneity) of group members can be beneficial because it provides the group with varied resources and perspectives (such as a wider range of skills, abilities, and experiences) from which to draw. If the diversity of group members helps the group achieve its goals, then *diversity* rather than similarity is likely to facilitate group cohesiveness.

Competition with Other Groups.   Competition between groups in an organization increases group cohesiveness when it motivates members of each group to band together to achieve group goals. For this reason, organizations often promote group cohesiveness by having work groups compete against each other. Groups of salespersons compete to see which group can sell the most each month, groups of production workers compete to see which group can maintain the highest quality standards, and groups of maintenance workers compete to have the best attendance record. Healthy competition is also encouraged by giving groups names and publicizing which groups are doing especially well. Sometimes groups compete not so much with groups inside their organization, but with groups from other organizations. For example, in the opening case, the R&D team working on the Maryland project in FORE Systems became cohesive when they pulled together to create a program that would be better than their competitors' programs.

Although a certain level of competition across groups can help each group be cohesive, too much competition can be dysfunctional and impair group effectiveness. When competition is too high or intense, groups sometimes try to sabotage each other and become more concerned with "winning the battle" than with achieving organizational goals. In order for any organization to achieve its goals, different groups in the organization must be willing and able to cooperate with each other.

Success.   "Nothing succeeds like success," according to an old adage. When groups are successful in achieving their goals, they become especially attractive to their members, and group cohesiveness increases.

The Boston-based rock group Aerosmith is one of the most cohesive rock bands in the world. Although band members have had many personal disagreements and fights over the years, the basic similarity of the band members—they all share a common background and live within miles of one another—has kept them together for over 25 years.

Exclusiveness.　A group's exclusiveness is indicated by how difficult it is to become a member of the group, the extent to which outsiders look up to group members, the group's status in the organization (see Chapter 10), and the special rights and privileges accorded group members. When group members must undergo very tough initiation processes or are required to undertake extensive training to join a group, the value of their group membership increases in their eyes. For example, individuals who wish to become firefighters have to meet stringent physical criteria as well as undergo and succeed at a series of extensive training exercises. Groups of firefighters tend to be highly cohesive, in part because of how difficult it is to become a member of the group. Fraternities, sororities, football teams, and cheerleading squads at universities also tend to be high on cohesiveness. It is often difficult to become a member of these groups, outsiders look up to group members who have special rights and privileges, and these groups tend to have high status.

CONSEQUENCES OF GROUP COHESIVENESS

Is cohesiveness a group property that managers should encourage? Is there such a thing as too much cohesiveness? As we saw when discussing group norms in the preceding chapter, the consequences of group cohesiveness for an organization depend on the extent to which group goals are aligned with organizational goals. Recall how in the restaurant example in Chapter 10, the goals of the group of waiters and waitresses (providing good service and getting good tips) were aligned with the restaurant's goal of having satisfied customers. In examining the consequences of group cohesiveness, we first focus on the case in which group and organizational goals are aligned, and then we look at the case in which they are not aligned.

Consequences When Group Goals Are Aligned With Organizational Goals.　The first major consequence of group cohesiveness when group and organizational goals are aligned is *the level of participation and communication within the group*.[24] As cohesiveness increases, group members become more active participants in the group, and the level of communication within the group increases. This outcome can be beneficial for the organization. Group members will be more likely to perform behaviors necessary for the group and organization to achieve its goals, and information will be readily shared among group members. (As we discuss in Chapter 14, an exception to this consequence occurs in cohesive decision-making groups that fall victim to groupthink.)

The group of waiters and waitresses, for example, was moderately cohesive. As a result, group members performed a variety of behaviors to ensure that customers received good service. They kept the salt and pepper shakers and the sugar bowls on the tables filled, helped each other with especially large tables, and kept the restaurant clean and tidy. Moreover, information flowed through the group very quickly. When the group changed its norm of always referring complaints to the manager, for instance, the change was communicated to all group members on the very same day that it was discussed with the manager.

Consistent with the increased level of participation found in cohesive groups is the fact that cohesiveness sometimes results in low levels of turnover. This has been the experience at a Pepsi bottling company in Springfield, Missouri (Insight 11.2).

Insight 11.2

Groups

Cohesiveness at a Pepsi Bottler

The Springfield, Missouri, plant of Pepsi-Cola General Bottler, Inc., has consistently had the highest quality of the more than 200 Pepsi bottling facilities. Quality is assessed by sampling the colas that are bottled at each plant. The consistently high quality attained by the Springfield plant is attributed in part to excellent teamwork and cohesive work groups.

There is practically zero turnover at this plant. The average employee tenure is fifteen years, and not one employee in production has worked at the plant for less than eight years. Because employees at the plant work so well together and work groups are highly cohesive, turnover at this Pepsi bottler has been extraordinarily low.[25]

Although good communication within groups is important, too much communication can be dysfunctional if group members waste a lot of time talking to each other, especially about nonwork matters such as the Monday night football game or last night's episode of *Melrose Place*. Thus a moderate amount of group cohesiveness is functional for the group and the organization when it encourages group members to participate in the group and share information. Too much cohesiveness, however, can be dysfunctional if group members waste time chitchatting.

The second major consequence of group cohesiveness when group and organizational goals are aligned is *the level of conformity to group norms*.[26] As group cohesiveness increases, conformity to group norms tends to increase as well. Increased conformity can be functional for groups and the organization because it enables groups to control and direct their members' behaviors toward achieving their goals. Too much conformity, however, can be dysfunctional if a group eliminates all deviance. As we discussed in Chapter 10, deviance can benefit a group by helping it recognize and discard dysfunctional norms, but excessive conformity can make a group resistant to change.

A moderate amount of group cohesiveness gives groups the level of conformity they need to achieve their goals but still allows for some deviance. Too much cohesiveness can stifle opportunities for change and growth. The restaurant group had enough conformity to control members' behavior but not so much that a waitress was afraid to deviate from a dysfunctional norm (referring all food complaints to the manager).

The third major consequence of group cohesiveness when group and organizational goals are aligned is *group goal accomplishment*.[27] Cohesive groups tend to be very effective at achieving their goals. Group members who value their group membership are motivated to help the group achieve its goals. Such members generally work well together, help each other when needed, and perform the behaviors necessary for the group to be effective. This consequence certainly seems to be effective for the organization, and for the most part it is. If groups become too cohesive, however, group members may be so driven toward group goal accomplishment that they lose sight of the fact that the group is part of a larger organization. Excessively cohesive groups may fail to cooperate with other groups for the good of the organization because group members' sole loyalty is to their own group. Once again, a moderate amount of group cohesiveness is functional for groups and organizations because it facilitates goal accomplishment. Too much cohesiveness is dysfunctional because it can result in group members' failing to cooperate with others outside the group.

By now it should be clear that a certain level of cohesiveness contributes to group effectiveness. When that level is insufficient, group members are not motivated to participate in the group and do not effectively communicate with each other, the group has difficulty influencing its members' behavior, and the group is not very successful at achieving its goals. When that level is excessive—when groups are too cohesive—time is wasted by group members socializing on the job, conformity is stressed at the expense of needed change, and group goal accomplishment is emphasized at the expense of needed cooperation with other groups and with the organization as a whole. A moderate amount of group cohesiveness results in the most favorable group and organizational outcomes. A moderately cohesive group will have the right level of communication and participation, sufficient conformity to influence group members' behavior (while not stamping out all deviance), and a needed emphasis on group goal accomplishment (but not at the expense of other groups and the organization). Indicators or signs of the level of cohesiveness in a work group are as follows:

- *Signs that a group has a moderate level of cohesiveness.* Group members work well together, there is a good level of communication and participation in the group, the group is able to influence its members' behavior, and the group tends to achieve its goals.
- *Signs that a group has a low level of cohesiveness.* Information flows slowly within the group, the group has little influence over its members' behavior, and the group tends not to achieve its goals.
- *Signs that a group has a very high level of cohesiveness.* Group members socialize excessively on the job, there is a very high level of conformity in the group and intolerance of deviance, and the group achieves its goals at the expense of other groups.

Table 11.1 summarizes some of the advantages and potential disadvantages of a *high level* of cohesiveness when group goals are aligned with organizational goals.

Consequences When Group Goals Are Not Aligned With Organizational Goals. Our conclusions about the consequences of cohesiveness apply only when the group's goals are aligned with the organization's goals. What are the consequences when group goals are *not* aligned with the organizational goals?

When group goals are not aligned with organizational goals (recall from Chapter 10 the radio assemblers whose goal was to minimize effort expenditure), the consequences of group cohesiveness for the organization are almost always negative. In this case, group cohesiveness is dysfunctional for the organization because it helps the group achieve its goals at the expense of organizational goals.

TABLE **11.1**

Consequences of High Cohesiveness When Group Goals Are Aligned with Organizational Goals

Consequences of High Cohesiveness	Advantages	Potential Disadvantages
A high level of participation and communication within the group	Group members are more likely to perform behaviors necessary for the group and organization to achieve their goals, information flows quickly in the group, and turnover may be relatively low.	Group members may waste time socializing on the job and chatting about nonwork matters.
A high level of conformity to group norms	The group is able to control its members' behavior to achieve group goals.	Excessive conformity within the group may result in resistance to change and failure to discard dysfunctional norms.
Group goal accomplishment	The group achieves its goals and is effective.	Group members may not cooperate with other groups as much as they should.

Like the group of restaurant workers, the group of radio assemblers was moderately cohesive. However, because the radio assemblers' group goal of minimizing effort expenditure was inconsistent with the organization's performance goal, the group's moderate level of cohesiveness was dysfunctional for the organization. Within the group, there was a high level of communication, but it usually involved nonwork topics such as football and baseball scores. There also was a sufficient amount of conformity to group norms, which resulted in all members restricting their output so that the group never produced more than 50 radios a day even though it could have produced 75. Finally, the group was very effective at achieving its goal of producing no more than 50 radios.

Table 11.2 summarizes the consequences of a *high level* of cohesiveness when group goals are not aligned with organizational goals.

TABLE **11.2**

Disadvantages of High Cohesiveness When Group Goals Are Not Aligned with Organizational Goals

Consequences of High Cohesiveness	Disadvantages
A high level of participation and communication within the group	Group members waste time socializing on the job and chatting about nonwork matters.
A high level of conformity to group norms	Group members behave in ways that are dysfunctional for the organization.
Group goal accomplishment	The group achieves its goals at the expense of organizational goals.

TO MANAGERS

Group Cohesiveness

- If group and organizational goals are aligned and group cohesiveness is very low, try to increase cohesiveness by decreasing the size of the group, increasing the level of similarity of group members (but not at the expense of the benefits diversity brings to group performance), introducing some element of competition with other groups, encouraging "small successes," and giving group members special rights or privileges.
- If group and organizational goals are aligned and group cohesiveness is very high, try to lower it by increasing group size, introducing more diversity within the group, discouraging competition with other groups, and encouraging cooperation.
- If group and organizational goals are not aligned, do not try to increase cohesiveness. Try to realign group goals with organizational goals by ensuring that group members benefit when their efforts help the organization achieve its goals.

Important Organizational Groups

Now that you understand some of the problems and challenges that groups face in organizations and the factors that influence work-group effectiveness, we turn to a discussion of three types of work groups: top-management teams, self-managed work teams, and research and development teams. Although we could discuss other important types of groups in organizations (such as whole departments, assembly-line groups, or task forces), we concentrate on these three because they have the potential to dramatically affect an organization's performance.

THE TOP-MANAGEMENT TEAM

An organization's top-management team is the group of managers who report to the chief executive officer (CEO). Top-management teams (chosen by an organization's CEO or the board of directors) can have profound effects on organizational performance because they determine what an organization is trying to accomplish and develop plans for goal attainment. Because the complex nature of top management activities requires intensive interaction among team members, top-management teams are characterized by reciprocal task interdependence. What steps can a CEO take to reduce process losses associated with reciprocal task interdependence? First, team size should be kept relatively small (most top-management teams average between five and seven members). Second, members of the team need to be assured that their individual input to the group is important for the team's and the organization's success. Third, group members need to be persuaded to be honest and open in their communication with one another. Finally, a CEO should make sure that members are readily available and accessible whenever other group members need their input and expertise.

The quality of decision making in the top-management team is a function of the personal characteristics and backgrounds of team members.[28] It has been found, for example, that the best decisions are made by top-management teams that are diverse or heterogeneous, consisting of managers from different functions (such as marketing, finance, and production). Diversity in team membership ensures that the team will have the adequate complement of skills, knowledge, expertise, and experience to guide the activities of the organization as a whole. Also, when managers can bring different views and information to bear on a problem, an organization can avoid the dangerous problem of *groupthink,* a pattern of faulty decision making that occurs when like-minded people reinforce one another's tendencies to interpret events and information in similar ways (see Chapter 14).[29]

Taking the concept of the top management team one step further, some organizations do not have a single CEO but rather are headed by a team of co-CEOs or copresidents. Companies that are team managed in this way include Dayton Hudson, Dillard's, and Macy's. The prime example of team management at the top is provided by Nordstrom Inc., as indicated in Insight 11.3.

Insight 11.3

Groups

Nordstrom's Team Approach

Nordstrom Inc. (www.nordstrom-pta.com), a chain of department stores that prides itself on high-quality merchandise and excellent customer service, has never been headed by a single CEO. During the organization's rapid period of growth in the 1980s (revenues increased approximately 500 percent), the retailer was run by a team of three of the founder's grandsons: Bruce A., John N., and James F. Nordstrom. Bruce, John, and James rotated the title of president among themselves and, as a team, ran Nordstrom through this remarkable period of growth.

In the early 1990s, Nordstrom encountered serious problems ranging from sluggish sales and lower profits to union disputes and charges of discrimination. True to their team-based approach to top management, Bruce, John, and James made a change that surprised many in top-management circles. Four nonfamily members were promoted to the positions of copresident, once again running the company as a team. Bruce, John, and James promoted themselves to the positions of cochairmen and added another cochairman to their team, cousin-in-law John A. McMillan. The cochairmen focus their attention on long-term strategy, including new site selection and expansion plans. The copresidents have responsibility for running the day-to-day affairs of the company.

Critics of Nordstrom's team-based approach to top management argue that it is hard for the company to demonstrate strength and vision in its leadership when there is no single leader. Moreover, in a rapidly changing industry such as retailing, quick decision making and action are often required, and the team approach might take too long.

Although the copresidents focus on different parts of the business (each is responsible for different types of merchandise) and have a high degree of autonomy in making individual and group decisions, they are a unified team characterized by open and frequent communication and formal weekly meetings. They often disagree with each other and have lively debates, but they respect each other's opinions and try to resolve disputes by focusing on their common goal: doing what will be best for the customer.[30]

SELF-MANAGED WORK TEAMS

The team of copresidents at Nordstrom has the autonomy that characterizes self-managed work teams. Team members themselves decide on what the team will do and how it will go about doing it. Although this particular self-managed team is at the very top of the Nordstrom organization, self-managed teams can be found at all levels in an organization.

Some organizations use self-managed work teams, rather than more traditional types of groups or individuals working separately, to motivate group members to perform at a higher level and be more satisfied with their jobs. In a self-managed work team, separate tasks that in the past might have been performed by individuals led by a supervisor are brought together, and a group of workers is given the responsibility for ensuring that the group's tasks get done.[31]

As an example of how a self-managed work team operates, consider the following situation. Requests for credit from AT&T Credit Corporation used to be processed by individuals. Extending or denying credit to customers involved a number of steps: reviewing the application, verifying the customer's credit rating, notifying the customer of whether his or her request for credit had been accepted or rejected, preparing a written contract, and collecting payments from the customer. Individuals were assigned to one of these steps. Some workers focused exclusively on reviewing applications, others on checking credit ratings, others on collecting payments, and so on. AT&T president Thomas C. Wajnert noted that under this arrangement workers had little sense of how their individual jobs contributed to AT&T's organizational goal of customer satisfaction. To remedy this situation, Wajnert decided to combine these individual tasks and give teams of workers the responsibility for all activities, ranging from the initial review of an application to collecting payments from approved customers. The switch to the use of self-managed work teams resulted in customers' being notified of the acceptance or rejection of their applications several days sooner than under the old system and the daily processing of twice as many applications.[32]

The job characteristics model of job design (see Chapter 7) provides a good framework for understanding why the use of self-managed work teams can lead to higher levels of motivation, performance, and satisfaction. Recall that this model suggests that jobs will be motivating and result in high levels of performance and satisfaction when they are high in skill variety, task identity, task significance, autonomy, and feedback.[33] Often, it is difficult to design individual jobs that are high on each of these dimensions. The job of reviewing applications at AT&T Credit Corporation, for example, required a limited number of skills, was low on task identity because the worker often did not know whether the application was eventually accepted or rejected, was low on task significance because the worker did not have a sense of how the job affected the customer, and had little autonomy. Combining the tasks in this job with the tasks in the other jobs that are involved in processing applications and extending credit, and then giving a group of workers responsibility for performing all of these tasks, raises levels of each job characteristic for *each group member*. Skill variety is raised because group members use the full complement of skills necessary to perform all of the groups' varied activities. Task identity and task significance are heightened because the groups perform all the activities necessary to provide credit to customers and have a real sense of how their activities impact customer satisfaction.

A number of conditions must be present for self-managed work teams to be effective.[34]

1. The group must be truly self-managing. The group itself must have the autonomy and authority to do many of the things traditionally reserved for managers, such as setting group goals, determining how the group should go about reaching these goals, and assigning individual tasks to group members. Some managers are reluctant to give up these responsibilities. One of the advantages of using self-managed teams is that the number of middle managers needed in an organization may decrease.

2. Self-managed work teams appear to be most effective when the work performed by group members is sufficiently complex and results in some sort of finished end product. By "complex" we mean that a number of different steps and procedures must be performed to accomplish the group's goals. By "finished end product" we mean some identifiable group output such as extending or rejecting credit to customers and collecting payments.

3. Managers in the organization must support and be committed to the use of self-managed work teams. Some self-managed work teams fail because managers do not want to give up some of their authority to the teams or because managers do not support the teams by giving them the necessary guidance or coaching. Managers need to be available to the groups in an advisory capacity and provide coaching when needed as well as help groups that veer off track to get back up to speed. When members of a self-managed work team have serious disagreements, for example, managers should be available to help team members settle their differences.

4. Members of successful self-managed work teams must be carefully selected to ensure that the team has the right complement of skills and expertise to get the job done. On the kind of complex tasks that these teams are most suited for, it is important that group members have a variety of skills.

5. Team members need to have the ability to work with others and the desire to work as part of a team. Not all workers desire to work closely with others, nor do all workers desire the added levels of responsibility that go along with being a member of a self-managed work team.

Self-managed work teams have been used successfully by a number of organizations such as General Mills, Federal Express, Chaparral Steel, 3M, Aetna Life & Casualty, and Johnsonville Foods.[35] However, more research is needed to understand why they have been successful as well as why they are sometimes not so successful. One recent study suggests that members of self-managed work teams may be somewhat reluctant to discipline each other (for example, by withholding rewards or punishing a group member who is not performing acceptably),[36] a situation that may result in some team members performing at a lower level in self-managed teams. Other studies suggest that the extent to which group members value their membership in a self-managed team and the status the group has in the wider organization may contribute to the success of a self-managed work team.[37] In any case, additional research is needed to uncover the advantages and potential disadvantages of using self-managed work teams.

RESEARCH AND DEVELOPMENT TEAMS

Organizations often use research and development (R&D) teams to develop new products, especially in high-tech industries such as electronics, pharmaceuticals, and computers, as is true at FORE Systems in the opening case. Some R&D teams are cross-functional—team members represent each of the functions or capabilities necessary to develop and launch a new product. An R&D team trying to develop a sophisticated electronic notepad, for example, might include members from research and development, engineering, manufacturing, finance, marketing, and sales (see Fig. 11.4). A team on which each of these capabilities is represented is in a good position to develop a successful new product.

An R&D team that is created to expedite new product design and promote innovation in an organization is known as a **skunk works.** The group consists of members of the engineering and research departments and other support functions like finance and marketing. Skunk works often meet and work in facilities that are separated from the rest of the organization. Having

Skunk works
An R&D team that is created to expedite new product design and promote innovation in an organization.

FIGURE **11.4**

A Cross-Functional Research and Development Team

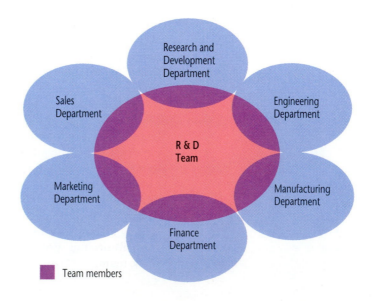

their own facilities gives group members the opportunity for the intensive interactions necessary for innovation (or other process gains) and ensures that the group will not be interrupted or distracted by the day-to-day problems of the organization. Members of skunk works often become very possessive of the products they are developing and feel completely responsible for the products' success or failure. Ford Motor Company established a skunk works to keep the dream of a new Mustang coupe and convertible alive, as indicated in Insight 11.4.

Insight 11.4

Competitive Advantage

Skunk Works Develops New Mustang

When Ford Motor Company (www.ford.com) projected that developing a new Mustang coupe and convertible would cost approximately $1 billion, top executives almost abandoned the project. But, thanks to a skunk works, the project was saved, and a new model Mustang was developed and launched. In the end, developing the new Mustang cost Ford only about $700 million and was accomplished in 25 percent less time than Ford usually takes to develop a new model, helping Ford in its quest to gain a competitive advantage.

John Coletti, one of the champions of the Mustang and founders of the skunk works, along with other team members, realized that to develop the new Mustang in a timely fashion while at the same time lowering costs, the team would need the freedom to make its own decisions and not follow Ford's usual development process. Will Boddie, the engineer who led the team, recognized the need to have everyone working on the project in close proximity to one another but distanced from Ford itself so that they would not be encumbered by Ford's prevailing procedures and norms. A furniture warehouse in Allen Park, Michigan, was converted to become the home of the skunk works, and team members—everyone from drafters to engineers and from stylists to "bean counters"—moved into cramped offices to work on the Mustang.

A turning point in the team's development occurred when an unexpected problem arose during testing of the prototype for the Mustang convertible. When chief engineer Michael Zevalkink test-drove the prototype, the car shimmied and shook. Engineers worked for a year to resolve the problem, but when Zevalkink test-drove the "corrected" model, the car still shook. Senior executives at Ford were aware of the problem but did not renege on their promise to preserve the independence and autonomy of the skunk works.

During an eight-week period, the convertible was furiously reengineered (the engineers involved slept on the floor of the warehouse at night), and the problem was solved by installing bracing in the car and redesigning the mirrors. Will Boddie, however, wasn't satisfied with these changes. When he saw a new Mercedes convertible in a parking lot, he thought, "Why shouldn't the Mustang convertible have as smooth a ride as a Mercedes convertible?" He told the skunk works engineers to purchase a Mercedes convertible and take it apart to learn the key to its smooth ride. The consequence of this research was the attachment of a 25-pound cylinder behind the front fender of the Mustang (a similar attachment on the Mercedes contributes to its smooth ride).[38]

The skunk works was successful in developing the new Mustang in record time and at a lower-than-usual cost because team members closest to the issues involved had not only the autonomy to make decisions and changes as circumstances warranted but also a high level of commitment to the team's goal of keeping the Mustang alive. The skunk works' autonomy and relative isolation from Ford itself enabled the team to respond to problems and make needed changes with timeliness and efficiency, key ingredients for gaining a competitive advantage.

As this case illustrates, a skunk works approach to R&D can be very successful in developing new products and innovations and gaining a competitive advantage. Even when new product development requires the involvement of many different people in an organization, skunk works can still be effective. The skunk works that developed the Mustang, for example, included about 400 people grouped into what were called "chunk teams," each of which worked on developing a particular aspect, or "chunk," of the car.[39]

SUMMARY

Group and organizational effectiveness hinge on minimizing process losses, achieving process gains, aligning group goals with organizational goals, and having the appropriate level of group cohesiveness. Three types of groups that are especially important in many organizations include the top management team, self-managed work teams, and research and development teams. In this chapter, we made the following major points:

1. Actual group performance often falls short of potential performance because of process losses due to coordination and motivation problems in groups. Process gains cause the potential performance of a group to rise, and they enhance group effectiveness.

2. Social loafing, a motivation problem that leads to process losses, is the tendency of individuals to exert less effort when they work in a group than when they work alone. Social loafing occurs for two reasons: (a) Individuals in a group think that they will not receive positive outcomes for performing at a high level or negative outcomes for substandard performance because individual levels of performance cannot easily be identified and evaluated. (b) Individuals think that their own efforts are unimportant or not really needed. Social loafing can be eliminated or reduced by making individual performance levels identifiable, making each individual feel that he or she can make an important and worthwhile contribution to the group, and by keeping group size down.

3. Group tasks can be characterized in terms of the nature of interdependence among group members. Thompson describes three types of task in-

terdependence: pooled, sequential, and reciprocal. The nature and causes of process losses and process gains depend on the type of task involved and the degree of interdependence among group members.

4. Group cohesiveness is the attractiveness of a group to its members. Group size, the similarity/diversity of group members, competition with other groups, success, and the exclusiveness of the group help to determine the level of group cohesiveness. Consequences of group cohesiveness are the level of participation and communication within a group, the level of conformity to group norms, and group goal accomplishment. When group goals are aligned with organizational goals, there is an optimal level of group cohesiveness that results in high levels of performance. When group goals are not aligned with organizational goals, group cohesiveness is dysfunctional for an organization.

5. Three kinds of work groups that have the potential to affect organizational performance dramatically are top-management teams, self-managed work teams, and research and development teams.

Organizational Behavior in Action

1. Give an example of (a) a process gain in a research and development team and (b) a process loss in a research and development team.
2. Give an example of (a) a process gain in a self-managed work team and (b) a process loss in a self-managed work team.
3. Why do some individuals engage in social loafing while others do not?
4. Can managers change the type of task interdependence in a work group, or is task interdependence a relatively fixed characteristic? If managers can change it, how might they do so?
5. Why is it sometimes hard to manage groups that are reciprocally interdependent?
6. Is social loafing a problem in top management teams? Why or why not?
7. What kinds of workers would probably prefer to work in a self-managed work team rather than in a traditional type of work group?
8. How can excessive group cohesiveness result in low levels of performance?
9. How can too little group cohesiveness result in low levels of performance?
10. In what kinds of organizations might it be especially important for work groups to be cohesive?

Group Effectiveness

Think of a group that you are currently a member of—a work group, a club, or any other group that you belong to and actively participate in. Briefly describe the group. Then answer each of these questions:

1. What process losses are experienced in this group? Why?
2. What process gains are experienced in this group? Why?
3. Does the actual performance of this group equal its potential performance? Why or why not?
4. How might this group raise its potential performance?
5. Is social loafing a problem in this group? Why or why not?
6. How would you characterize the major tasks performed by this group in terms of Thompson's model of task interdependence?
7. Is this a cohesive group? Why or why not?
8. Does cohesiveness help or hinder the group's performance?
9. Are group goals aligned with any larger organizational goals?

Specific Task

Many organizations use teams to increase levels of quality and customer satisfaction. One such organization is Motorola. Scan Motorola's website (www.mot.com) to learn more about this company. Then click on "Jobs," then on "Motorola Life," then on "Culture," then on "Quality, and then on "TCS Teams."

1. How are teams used at Motorola to enhance quality and customer satisfaction?
2. Do you think individuals working alone could accomplish what these teams are accomplishing? Why or why not?

General Task

Many organizations take steps to ensure that groups and teams within the organization are cohesive. Find the website of such a company. What steps are managers in this organization taking to ensure that groups and teams are cohesive? Do you think each of these steps will be effective or ineffective in terms of encouraging group cohesiveness? Why or why not?

TOPICS FOR DEBATE

Organizational effectiveness hinges on the effectiveness of the groups that make up an organization. Now that you have a good understanding of what makes for effective work groups, debate the following issues.

Debate One

Team A. Social loafing is inevitable in groups and cannot be avoided.

Team B. Social loafing is not inevitable in groups and can be avoided.

Debate Two

Team A. Process losses in work groups are more common than process gains.

Team B. Process gains in work groups are more common than process losses.

EXPERIENTIAL EXERCISE

Curtailing Social Loafing

Objective

Your objective is to gain experience in developing a strategy to reduce social loafing in an ongoing group.

Procedure

Assume the role of a manager of a home improvements/building supply store that sells a wide range of products—including lumber, plumbing fixtures, windows, and paint—to both commercial accounts and individual customers. The store is staffed by three types of employees who work in three different groups: (1) a group of six cashiers who check out purchases made by individuals on site, (2) a group of five floor workers who help customers locate items they need, stock merchandise, and reshelve returns, and (3) a group of four workers who handle commercial accounts. All the workers are paid on an hourly basis. The cashiers and floor workers earn the minimum wage; the commercial account workers earn one and a half times the minimum wage.

You are pleased with the performance of the cashiers and the commercial account workers. The floor workers, however, seem to be putting forth less effort than they should. On several occasions, customers have complained about not being able to find items, and you personally have located the items for them even though there were ample floor workers on duty. The floor workers do not seem busy, and their workloads have not increased recently; yet they have a backlog of work to be done, including stocking new merchandise and reshelving. Despite their backlog, you often see members of this group chatting with each other, taking cigarette breaks outside the back of the store, and making personal telephone calls, all outside their regularly scheduled breaks.

1. Develop a plan of action to reduce social loafing in the group of floor workers.
2. The class divides into groups of from three to five people, and each group appoints one member as spokesperson, to present the group's action plans to the whole class.
3. Group members take turns describing their action plans for reducing social loafing among the floor workers.
4. After discussing the pros and cons of each different approach, the group develops a plan of action to reduce social loafing among the floor workers.

When your group has completed these activities, the spokesperson will present the group's action plan to the whole class.

MAKING THE CONNECTION

Find an example of a company that groups many of its employees into self-managed work teams. Why does this company use self-managed work teams? What process gains (if any) occur in these teams? What process losses (if any) occur in these teams? Do the employees like working in self-managed work teams? What contributes to the level of cohesiveness in the teams?

CLOSING CASE

Self-Managed Work Teams Cause Success and Surprise at XEL

In the mid-1980s, Bill Sanko and his partners bought XEL Communications Inc. from GTE Corporation. XEL manufactures telecommunications equipment such as custom circuit boards for phone companies and corporate phone systems. In order for the small (180-employee) company to compete with industry leaders such as AT&T, Sanko realized that he would need to make some dramatic changes aimed at cutting costs and decreasing production time on custom orders to increase customer responsiveness.

After much soul searching, Sanko and John Puckett, vice president of manufacturing, with the help of a consultant, decided to reorganize the company's production workers into self-managed work teams. In the past, the firm had used a traditional hierarchy of authority to manage the work process. Factory workers reported to supervisors who reported to department managers who reported to others higher up in XEL's hierarchy. After the 1988 reorganization, factory workers, who were now members of self-managed work teams, took on many of the responsibilities and decisions that had been their supervisors' and upper managers' jobs. As a result of this major change, XEL was able to cut its supervisory and support staff by 30 percent. The changeover to self-managed work teams also reduced coordination and motivation problems, resulting in speedier and more efficient handling of custom orders. Visible signs of these improvements are brightly colored banners on the plant walls, which indicate each team's standing on everything from attendance to deliveries to team performance measures. Teams are also eligible for quarterly bonuses based on team performance.[40]

Although Sanko is not likely to complain about these impressive figures, he admits that self-managed work teams bring their fair share of surprises. Because members of self-managed work teams schedule and supervise themselves and are responsible for team performance levels, difficulties that Sanko and Puckett never imagined sometimes arise. For example, it is difficult to add new members to self-managed work teams at XEL. Much of the work performed by the teams is done along a production or assembly line that can move only as fast as the slowest member of a team can work. Because newcomers tend to work slowly while they are learning their jobs, they can hold the whole team back. Because the team is responsible for its own performance level, newcomers may have a hard time being accepted and feeling on equal footing with other group members. When they eventually fit in, newcomers generally appreciate being a member of a closely knit group complete with its own name (for example, "Catch the Wave" and "Red Team") and identity. High levels of camaraderie have resulted, among other things, in low levels of turnover at XEL.

Although the teams have taken over many of the responsibilities of supervisors and managers (they even schedule team members' vacations), supervisors are now needed for other activities such as helping team members settle disputes, helping feuding teams settle their differences, and stepping in when a team veers off track. Recently, for example, Puckett overheard disagreements in the stockroom. At the same time, other teams were complaining to him that the stockroom team was not doing its job very well (and thus was impairing the performance of teams that needed to obtain supplies). A little probing by Puckett revealed a problem: Some members of the stockroom team were clocking in more time on their timecards than they were actually working and were covering up for each other. To bring matters under control, Puckett immediately disbanded the team, fired the dishonest team members, and installed a traditional supervisor to manage the stockroom.[41] Puckett's immediate concern was to get the stockroom back in good working order because its operations affect the extent to which other teams can perform at a high level. This change does *not* mean that a self-managed team will never again run the stockroom.

Despite some problems, XEL's production times for custom orders have dropped from eight to four weeks since the changeover to self-managed work teams was made, costs have dropped 25 percent, and quality has gone up. In the 1990s, XEL's bold experiment with self-managed work teams became a well-known success story in management circles. The Association for Manufacturing Excellence chose XEL to be one of four companies showcased in a film about teams. In addition, managers from Hewlett-Packard and other major corporations toured the XEL factory in Aurora, Colorado, to learn the keys to XEL's success. XEL Communications has since joined Salient 3 Communications, Inc.[42]

Questions for Discussion
1. What are some of the benefits of using self-managed work teams?
2. What problems might managers face if they use self-managed work teams?

Leadership

12

Kenneth Lay Transforms Enron and the Energy Industry

When Kenneth Lay became CEO of Enron Corp. (www.enron.com), a Houston-based provider of energy including natural gas and electricity, the company was experiencing a tough, chaotic time, including a surplus of natural gas, declining natural gas prices, and deregulation of

the industry.[1] Lay realized that if Enron was to survive, prosper, and reach its full potential, he not only had to transform the way the company operated but also would need to transform the industry within which it operated. He succeeded. Enron is now a highly successful and widely admired company with over $20 billion in revenues; perhaps equally admired is Lay, who created the power house Enron is today, as reflected by its role as a leading player in the push to deregulate the electricity industry.[2]

Lay, who received a PhD in economics from the University of Houston, has wide ranging experience in the energy industry and in dealing with government regulation. Lay was employed by Humble Oil (now Exxon USA), Florida Gas, Transco Energy, and Houston Natural Gas prior to his current position as CEO of Enron; he also served a stint as the Deputy Under Secretary for the United States Interior Department. He is highly knowledgeable and extremely self-confident, qualities which have contributed to his willingness to take risks, risks that have paid off for Enron since he took over as CEO. Lay is also a man of high integrity who works hard and is extremely energetic; he relaxes by jogging two to three miles a day and boating off Galveston Island.[3]

Equally notable are the ways that Lay leads and motivates his subordinates. First, he clearly and enthusiastically communicates his vision both to Enron's employees and to energy industry leaders. Lay empowers his managers to make decisions; he wants them to grow and develop on the job, which will only happen if they have the autonomy to make their own decisions and learn from their mistakes. He strives to have each Enron employee feel responsible for the growth and success of the company. In his view, every employee needs to take responsibility for recognizing and solving problems as they arise, and he in turn takes steps to show his employees that he cares about them and wants them to reach their full potential. Lay visits with employees at their work sites and really listens to what they have to say. Lay treats his employees as he would want to be treated himself. As he puts it, "If you get involved in building things, you tend to like being your own boss and being responsible for it."[4]

Enron currently has the biggest market share of the wholesale electricity market, which has already been deregulated. Lay's vision is for Enron to continue to grow as a driving force in the energy industry. For example, he envisions Enron as also being a key player in the retail electricity market once it is deregulated and is a strong proponent of deregulation, which is expected to cut energy costs for consumers around the country.[5] All in all, Lay seems to be doing all the right things to ensure the continued success and growth of Enron.

Overview

When things go wrong in an organization, blame is most often laid at the leader's door. Colby Chandler, a past CEO of Kodak Corporation, for example, was commonly thought to be responsible for many of Kodak's troubles in the 1980s. Likewise, Ken Olsen, the founder of Digital Equipment Corporation, was blamed for the troubles that caused that company's earnings to plummet and many of its employees to be laid off. Similarly, when organizations are doing particularly well, people tend to think that their leaders are doing an especially good job. A classic example of this perception was the stunning turnaround of Chrysler Corporation in the 1980s, attributed to CEO Lee Iacocca. More recent examples come from Microsoft's achievements under Bill Gates and Enron's growth under Kenneth Lay. Because leaders are thought to affect organizational performance, when an organization runs into trouble, a new leader is often brought on board to turn the organization around.

In addition to being held responsible for the success or failure of whole organizations, leaders are also held responsible for the performance of the individuals and groups within an organization. The leadership capabilities of the manager of a group of car salespeople may be questioned when the group's annual sales performance becomes the lowest in a geographic region, for example. Similarly, the high sales performance of another group may be attributed to the exceptional leadership provided by that group's manager.

The common belief that leaders make a difference and can have a major impact on individuals, groups, and whole organizations has prompted organizational behavior researchers to devote considerable effort to understanding leadership. Researchers have focused primarily on two leadership issues: (1) Why some members of an organization become leaders while others do not, and (2) why some leaders are more successful or effective than others. In general, research confirms the popular belief that leadership is indeed an important ingredient of individual, group, and organizational effectiveness.[6] Good leaders spur on individuals, groups, and whole organizations to perform at a high level and achieve their goals. Conversely, a lack of effective leadership is often a contributing factor to lackluster performance.

In this chapter, we focus on the nature of leadership in organizations. We define leadership and discuss the different types of leaders found in organizations. We explore different approaches to leadership—the trait and behavior approaches, Fiedler's contingency model, path-goal theory, the Vroom and Yetton model, and leader-member exchange theory. We consider substitutes and neutralizers for leadership. We also examine some new topics in leadership theory and research: transformational and charismatic leadership, the effect of a leader's mood on his or her subordinates, and gender and leadership. The various approaches to leadership complement each other—no one theory describes the "right" or "only" way to become a leader or be a good leader. Each of the theories focuses on a different set of issues, but taken together they enable you to better understand how to become an effective leader. By the end of this chapter, you will be able to assess how and why leaders can have profound effects on organizational behavior at all levels.

Introduction to Leadership

Although you can often recognize a leader when you see one in action, coming up with a precise definition of leadership is difficult. Researchers disagree on many of the characteristics that define leadership. They generally agree, however, on two characteristics:[7]

1. *Leadership involves exerting influence over other members of a group or organization.*[8] Kenneth Lay, in the opening case, exerts considerable influence over Enron and most of its employees by, for example, enthusiastically communicating his vision for Enron, empowering employees to make decisions and feel responsible for the success of Enron, and encouraging employees to learn from their mistakes and reach their full potential.
2. *Leadership involves helping a group or organization achieve its goals.* Lay is striving to help Enron achieve its goals of being a dominant force in the energy industry and continuing to expand its activities in this market.

Leadership

The exercise of influence by one member of a group or organization over other members to help the group or organization achieve its goals.

Leaders

The individuals who influence group or organizational members to help the group or organization achieve its goals.

Formal leaders

Members of an organization who are given authority by the organization to influence other organizational members to achieve organizational goals.

Informal leaders

Organizational members with no formal authority to influence others who nevertheless exert considerable influence because of special skills or talents.

Combining these two key characteristics, we can define **leadership** as the exercise of influence by one member of a group or organization over other members to help the group or organization achieve its goals.[9] The **leaders** of a group or organization are the individuals who exert such influence.

Leaders help organizations and the individuals and groups they are made up of achieve goals that can range from achieving high levels of motivation and performance to making innovative decisions to increasing job satisfaction and organizational commitment. In fact, many aspects of organizational behavior that you have studied in previous chapters are influenced by leaders: attitudes (Chapter 3), learning (Chapter 5), motivation (Chapters 6, 7, and 8), stress (Chapter 9), and work-group effectiveness (Chapters 10 and 11). Research has shown, for example, that leaders influence their subordinates' or followers' levels of motivation, performance, absenteeism, and turnover, and the quality of their decisions (we use *followers* and *subordinates* interchangeably to refer to the members of a group or organization who are influenced by a leader).[10]

Leaders may succeed at helping groups and organizations achieve their goals, but sometimes they do not. *Leader effectiveness* is the extent to which a leader helps a group or organization to achieve its goals. An *effective* leader helps achieve goals; an *ineffective* leader does not. Kenneth Lay is an effective leader at Enron because he has helped Enron achieve its goal of being a dominant force in the energy industry. By studying leadership, you will be in a good position to understand leadership successes and failures as well as how and why leaders help groups and organizations achieve their goals.

All leaders exert influence over members of a group or organization. Some leaders, however, have formal authority to do so; others do not. **Formal leaders** are members of an organization (like Kenneth Lay in the opening case) who are given authority by the organization to influence other organizational members to achieve organizational goals.[11] Many managers are formal leaders because they have the authority to influence their subordinates and are expected to use it. Recall from Chapter 1 that leading is one of the four principal managerial functions.

Not all managers are leaders, however.[12] Some managers do not have subordinates who report to them. The accounting manager of a restaurant who does all of the accounting work for the restaurant herself is a manager but not a formal leader. In contrast, the head cook who manages the kitchen and supervises twelve other cooks is both a manager and a formal leader. The formal job description for the position of head cook specifies that the head cook is responsible for ensuring that the other cooks who work for the restaurant consistently prepare high-quality food for customers. Because this chapter is about leadership, it also is about managers who are leaders.

Informal leaders have no formal job authority to influence others but sometimes exert just as much influence in an organization as formal leaders—and sometimes more. Informal leaders' ability to influence others often arises from special skills or talents that they possess—skills that group members realize will help the group achieve its goals. Eight waiters employed in a restaurant all had the same job of serving customers, for example; but the waiter who was the most experienced and had the best interpersonal skills became the informal leader of the group. He made sure that the other waiters provided good service, and he always stepped in to help settle arguments before they got out of hand. The other waiters listened to him because his advice

about customer service helped them earn large tips and because his mediation skills made the restaurant a nice place to work.

In general, both formal leaders and informal leaders influence others in
groups and organizations. The various approaches to leadership that we describe in this chapter seek to explain why some people become leaders and
others do not and why some leaders are more effective than others.

Early Approaches to Leadership

Two of the earliest perspectives on leadership were offered by the trait approach and the behavior approach. The trait approach seeks to identify personal characteristics that effective leaders possess. The behavior approach
focuses on the behaviors that effective leaders engage in.

THE TRAIT APPROACH

Early studies of leadership sought to identify enduring personal characteristics and traits that distinguish leaders from followers and effective from ineffective leaders. Recall from Chapter 2 that *traits* are a person's particular
tendencies to feel, think, and act in certain ways. The search for leadership
traits began in the 1930s, and after nearly three hundred studies the list was
narrowed to several traits that showed the strongest relationship to effective
leadership:[13]

- *Intelligence* helps a leader solve complex problems.
- *Task-relevant knowledge* ensures that a leader knows what has to be done,
  how it should be done, what resources are required, and so on, for a
  group and organization to achieve its goals.

Tommye Jo Daves (right), a
58-year-old grandmother, is the
plant manager of a Levi's factory in
Murphy, North Carolina, that
employs 385 workers and
produces three million pairs of
jeans a year. She began as a
seamstress in the plant in 1959
and rose to the top of the hierarchy
because her job knowledge and
personal qualities earned the trust
and respect of the work force.

- *Dominance,* an individual's need to exert influence and control over others, helps a leader channel followers' efforts and abilities toward achieving group and organizational goals.
- *Self-confidence* helps a leader influence followers and persist in the face of obstacles or difficulties.
- *Energy/activity levels,* when high, help a leader deal with the many demands he or she faces on a day-to-day basis.
- *Tolerance for stress* helps a leader deal with the uncertainty inherent in any leadership role.
- *Integrity* and *honesty* ensure that a leader behaves ethically and is worthy of followers' trust and confidence.
- *Emotional maturity* ensures that a leader is not overly self-centered, can control his or her feelings, and can accept criticism.[14]

General Norman Schwarzkopf, who successfully led U.S. troops (570,000 strong) in the Gulf War under extremely difficult conditions, appears to concur with the findings of trait approach research. In his autobiography, Schwarzkopf suggests that good leaders are truthful, have the confidence and courage to say no when necessary, desire and are able to influence or manipulate others, and are knowledgeable.[15] We can also infer from the opening case that Kenneth Lay probably possesses many of these traits: He is intelligent, self-confident, and has considerable knowledge and experience in the energy industry. He also has high integrity and is energetic. Moreover, he probably is tolerant of stress given his continued success in such a high-profile position and his continued efforts to push for deregulation of the energy industry.

Before we look at other leadership factors, two points must be made about using the trait approach:

1. *For at least some traits, it is not clear which comes first, being in a leadership position or possessing the trait in question.* A new marketing manager for Goodyear Tire and Rubber Co. who formerly worked for Frito-Lay, for example, at first may know little about the marketing of tires. But after a year on the job, the manager is an expert in the marketing of tires and is in fact a competent leader of her subordinates. If a researcher assessed this manager's task-relevant knowledge and her performance as a leader, both would be rated highly. This outcome may cause the researcher to assume that the manager's high level of task-relevant knowledge contributed to her leadership effectiveness. However, what really happened was that being put in a leadership position forced the manager to acquire the necessary knowledge about marketing tires.
2. *The trait approach provides little guidance concerning what advice or training to give current or soon-to-be leaders.* With the exception of acquiring task-relevant knowledge, there is not much that existing leaders can do (on their own) to change their standing with regard to leadership traits such as intelligence or dominance. As you learned in Chapter 2, to the extent that personality traits *can* change, change only occurs over the long term (several years). Many organizations, however, cannot afford to wait several years for the development of effective leaders. As Insight 12.1 suggests, such organizations can hire executive coaches to teach leaders how to improve the way they treat their subordinates.

Insight 12.1 — Diversity

Executive Coaches to the Rescue

Some people find themselves in a precarious position when they are promoted to a leadership position because of their technical expertise and skills. These people could be successful leaders if leadership were based on skill alone, but it's not, and sometimes personality traits limit their effectiveness. A person with a Type A personality, for example, may be so impatient with his subordinates and his own boss that he always finishes their sentences for them and screams when others don't do things his way or don't understand what he is talking about. Such a leader makes subordinates feel stupid for asking questions or making suggestions and causes other members of the organization to avoid him or her as much as possible. Realizing that things are not going smoothly, the person may try to organize an office party or group lunch to lighten things up, but no one shows any interest.

Other leaders sometimes have difficulty interacting with diverse subordinates. A person who is younger than some of her subordinates may find it awkward to exert influence over people who are ten or fifteen years her senior. A person of one ethnic background or gender may feel ill at ease leading workers who are from different ethnic backgrounds or of the other gender. Such people may have had little experience interacting with diverse members of an organization, let alone leading them.

Enter the executive coach. More and more companies are hiring executive coaches to help leaders learn how to deal with diverse subordinates, coworkers, and superiors. American Express, AT&T, Citibank, Colgate, Levi Strauss, Northern Telecom, and Procter & Gamble are on the growing list of firms hiring executive coaches. Alicia Whitaker, director of career planning at Colgate (www.colgate.com), notes that although coaching may be needed, leaders are often reluctant to admit that they need help and may view such an admission as a sign of weakness. Leaders often prefer their meetings with a coach to remain a secret.

Who are these coaches, and what do they do? Many are trained and experienced psychologists or psychiatrists who are expert in helping people to change their behavior. Coaches can be freelancers who work on their own, or they can be members of a consulting firm such as Gemini Consulting, which employs about 250 senior consultants who often serve as executive coaches. Psychological training alone, however, is not enough. An executive coach must also be attuned to the business world, the realities of organizational life, and the challenge of managing diversity. Robert Mintz, director of human resources for Time Inc. Magazines, met with twenty-five psychologists and psychiatrists and failed to hire any of them to coach leaders in his company because they were all relatively ignorant about how large modern corporations operate.

Coaching approaches vary considerably, but all involve self-revelation, a process in which leaders are confronted with clear information about how they treat others, how others perceive them, and the effect they have on those around them. Once self-revelation has occurred, the coach tries to get the leader to change. Some coaches focus on behavior—although Type A leaders will probably always be Type A, they will be more effective if they learn how to listen to other people and control their impatience. Other coaches try to discover why a person is impatient or hostile. These coaches try to change individuals through an intensive and time-consuming process involving not only the leader but also his or her family and associates. Such intensive coaching is usually reserved for leaders at the top of an organization.[16] Executive coaching can be a useful way for an organization to help leaders whose traits and lack of experience are preventing them from becoming effective leaders.

Individuals who possess the traits associated with effective leadership are more likely to become effective leaders than those who do not, but the trait approach alone cannot fully explain why or how effective leadership occurs. Many individuals who possess the identified traits never become leaders, and many leaders who possess them are not effective. This observation suggests the need to move from the search for leadership traits to the consideration of other factors that contribute to leadership effectiveness. In the next stage of answering the question "What makes a good, effective leader?" researchers sought to identify specific behaviors performed by effective leaders.

THE BEHAVIOR APPROACH: CONSIDERATION AND INITIATING STRUCTURE

Rather than looking at the traits or characteristics of leaders, the behavior approach focuses on what leaders actually do. Researchers at Ohio State University in the 1940s and 1950s were at the forefront of the leader behavior approach.[17] They sought to identify what it is that effective leaders actually do—the specific behaviors that contribute to their effectiveness. The Ohio State researchers realized that one of the key ways in which leaders influence followers is through the behaviors the leaders perform. The behavior approach seeks to identify leader behaviors that help individuals, groups, and organizations achieve their multiple goals.

The Ohio State researchers developed a list of over 1,800 specific behaviors that they thought leaders might engage in, such as setting goals for followers, telling followers what to do, being friendly, and making sure that followers are happy.[18] The researchers then developed scales to measure these behaviors and administered the scales to thousands of workers. The workers were asked to indicate the extent to which their leaders performed the various leader behaviors. After analyzing the responses, the researchers found that most leader behaviors involved either *consideration* or *initiating structure*. The Ohio State results have been replicated in many studies and in other countries such as Germany.[19]

Consideration.   Behavior indicating that a leader trusts, respects, and values good relationships with his or her followers is known as **consideration.** Stanley

Consideration
Behavior indicating that a leader trusts, respects, and values good relationships with his or her followers.

Gault, for example, when hired by Goodyear Tire and Rubber as CEO to help turn around the troubled company, demonstrated consideration on his very first day on the job. He showed his followers that he trusted them. While moving into his luxurious office, he was offered a set of keys for the locked cabinets lining the office walls. Gault indicated that he didn't want the keys because he liked to keep things unlocked. The employee who offered Gault the keys urged him to reconsider because many people would be going in and out of his office every day and the cleaning staff would come in at night. Gault's response was that he didn't need the keys because, as he put it, "this company should be run on the basis of trust."[20] Other examples of consideration include a leader being friendly, treating group members as his or her equals, and explaining to group members why he or she has done certain things.

A leader who engages in consideration also shows followers that he or she cares about their well-being and is concerned about how they feel and what they think. Kenneth Lay, in the opening case, engages in consideration when he visits with his employees at their work sites, listens to their concerns, and shows them that he cares. Some company leaders learn foreign languages to be considerate to their subordinates, as indicated in Insight 12.2.

Insight 12.2 A Global View

CEO of GM Europe Engages in Consideration

General Motors (GM) Europe (www.gm.com) was already the most profitable European car maker when Louis Hughes took over as president in the early 1990s. Always a high achiever, Hughes was not content to maintain the status quo at GM Europe, however. His aim was to improve GM's European production capabilities so that they would rival the efficiency of the manufacturing operations that Japanese companies set up outside Japan. Hughes has planned many initiatives to increase sales and reduce production costs, and his attention to the human side of his leadership position has also been noteworthy.

Hughes appears to be one CEO who recognizes the importance of consideration. To be able to communicate with, and show that he cares about, the hourly paid workers in Germany who make the Opel automobile, Hughes learned German and insisted that it be used in meetings in Germany. Recognizing the need to have a good relationship with his subordinates, Hughes took his ten top managers on an Outward Bound adventure in the Swiss Alps for five days. There as they worked together as a team while sleeping in tents, crossing rivers on homemade rafts, and maneuvering around a 250-foot gorge, they learned to trust one another and get along together. Though at times terrifying, the experiences did seem to foster good relations, and one top engineer who participated in the adventure decided to take his own engineering managers on a similar trip.

In addition to engaging in consideration himself, Hughes also encourages his managers to be considerate and has taken actions to foster this behavior. He has hired a psychologist to train his managers in how to work well in groups and how to be considerate to subordinates. All in all, Hughes's efforts seem to be paying off. GM Europe continues to be a top-performing European automaker and regularly outperforms its rivals.[21]

► Initiating structure
Behavior that a leader engages in to make sure that work gets done and subordinates perform their jobs acceptably.

Initiating Structure.   Behavior that a leader engages in to make sure that work gets done and subordinates perform their jobs acceptably is known as **initiating structure.** Assigning individual tasks to followers, planning ahead, setting goals, deciding how the work should be performed, and pushing followers to get their tasks accomplished are all initiating-structure behaviors.[22]

When C. Michael Armstrong took over as CEO at Hughes Aircraft Co., he engaged in initiating structure by eliminating two layers of management, relocating top managers of international divisions from the United States to the countries in which their divisions operated, relocating the company's missile-building unit from California to Arizona to lower costs, and eliminating monthly management meetings that seemed to waste time. Moreover, he instituted a benchmarking system that required managers to compare the costs and production times of their products to those of their competitors.[23]

Armstrong, as CEO, is a leader at the top of his organizations' hierarchy, but leaders at lower levels also engage in initiating structure. The informal leader of the group of waiters in the restaurant described earlier, for example, engaged in initiating structure by developing a system in which waiters with very large parties would receive help from other waiters whose stations were not full. This leader also engaged in consideration by taking an interest in the personal lives of the other waiters and by having a cake made and a small party to celebrate the birthday of each.

Consideration and initiating structure are complementary and independent leader behaviors. They are *complementary* because leaders can engage in both types of behaviors. They are *independent* because knowing the extent to which a leader engages in consideration says nothing about the extent to which he or she engages in initiating structure and vice versa.

Other Behavior Models.   Around the same time that the Ohio State researchers were studying consideration and initiating structure, researchers at the University of Michigan were also trying to identify behaviors responsible for effective leadership. Although the specific approach and findings of the University of Michigan researchers differed from those of the Ohio State researchers, the Michigan researchers also came up with two major types of leadership behaviors: employee-centered behaviors and job-oriented behaviors.[24] They correspond to consideration and initiating structure, respectively.

Some of the leadership models that management consultants use to explain to practicing managers how to be effective also focus on consideration and initiating structure. As we discuss in Chapter 19, an approach to organizational change designed to make managers more effective as leaders (Robert Blake and Jane Mouton's Managerial Grid) focuses on the extent to which leaders are concerned about people (consideration) and production (initiating structure).[25] Paul Hersey and Kenneth Blanchard's model, which is quite popular with consultants, also focuses on consideration and initiating structure behaviors.[26]

When researchers first began examining consideration and initiating structure, they assumed that consideration would lead to high levels of job satisfaction in a leader's subordinates and initiating structure would lead to high levels of job performance. Subsequent research, however, found no firm relationship between consideration and followers' job satisfaction or initiating structure and follower performance. Sometimes initiating-structure behavior leads to high levels of performance, and sometimes it is unrelated to performance. Likewise, consideration sometimes leads to high levels of job satisfaction, but at other times it does not. In addition, initiating structure is sometimes related to job satisfaction, just as consideration sometimes affects performance. We describe the reasons for these seemingly confusing results below when we discuss what is missing in the behavior and the trait approaches. First, we describe two other important leader behaviors.

THE BEHAVIOR APPROACH: LEADER REWARD AND PUNISHING BEHAVIOR

In addition to engaging in consideration and initiating structure, leaders behave in other ways that have important effects on their followers. Recall from Chapter 5 that *reinforcement* can increase the probability of desirable behaviors and *punishment* can decrease the probability of undesirable behaviors occurring. In organizations, leaders (and managers) are responsible for administering reinforcements and punishments.

Leader reward behavior
A leader's positive reinforcement of subordinates' desirable behavior.

Leader reward behavior occurs when a leader positively reinforces subordinates' desirable behavior.[27] Leaders who notice when their followers do a good job and acknowledge it with compliments, praise, or more tangible benefits such as a pay raise or promotion are engaging in reward behavior. Leader reward behavior helps to ensure that workers perform at a high level. Gurcharan Das, past CEO of Vicks Vaporub's Indian subsidiary (which was acquired by Procter & Gamble) and currently a vice president and managing director at Procter & Gamble, recalls engaging in leader reward behavior when he was CEO by giving annual raises to all workers who met at least twenty consumers and twenty retailers or wholesalers during the year. Why did Das reward this behavior? It helped the workers keep in touch with the marketplace and come up with ways to improve the Indian company's products and services.[28]

Leader punishing behavior
A leader's negative response to subordinates' undesired behavior.

Leader punishing behavior occurs when a leader reprimands or otherwise responds negatively to subordinates who perform undesired behavior.[29] A factory foreman who docks the pay of any subordinate who fails to wear safety glasses on the job is engaging in leader punishing behavior.

Although punishing behavior can be an effective means of curtailing undesirable or potentially dangerous behavior in organizations (see Chapter 5), it is generally more effective to use reinforcement to encourage desired behavior than to use punishment to stop undesired behavior. Punishment can have unintended side effects such as resentment. The foreman mentioned above would obtain more desirable organizational results by engaging in leader reward behavior, such as giving a bonus of some sort to subordinates who wear their safety glasses every day for a three-month period. Despite the research evidence, however, leaders often engage in punishing behavior. In fact, some leaders punish their subordinates so frequently and intensely that they rank among "America's Toughest Bosses,"[30] and some people question whether their excessive use of punishment is ethical (Insight 12.3).

Insight 12.3

Ethics

Leader Punishing Behavior Taken to the Extreme

All leaders probably engage in punishing behavior from time to time, but some leaders seem to punish their subordinates almost all the time. Recently, *Fortune* magazine came up with a list of "America's Toughest Bosses"—leaders who rely on excessive levels of punishment to influence their subordinates. Steve Jobs, founder of Apple Computer and Next Computer, made the list. In a meeting with a manufacturing manager who indicated that a part needed for Next's new computer (which turned out to be a flop) would cost $200, Jobs reportedly turned bright red and started screaming at the manager that he didn't know what he was doing, that the part should cost $20, and that the manager was going to ruin the company. (The part did end up costing $200.)

Other tough bosses on *Fortune's* list include Linda Wachner (CEO of Warnaco), T. J. Rodgers (CEO of Cypress Semiconductor), Herbert Haft (CEO of the Dart Group), Jack Connors (CEO of the advertising firm Hill Holliday), and Harvey and Bob Weinstein (who lead the film distribution company Miramax). Examples of these leaders' punishing behavior abound. T. J. Rodgers has been known to hold back the paychecks of managers who temporarily fall behind on their assignments, and Herbert Haft fired his wife and son because he thought they were trying to seize power and take control of his company (see Insight 18.5). Many of these leaders are aware of their excessive use of punishment. The Weinsteins even acknowledge that their toughness isn't "healthy" for workers.

Some people think that when leaders go overboard in punishing their subordinates, the leaders are actually engaging in unethical behavior—threatening the well-being of their subordinates and not treating them with the respect and dignity they deserve. Some tough bosses have actually lost their jobs, in part because of their excessive use of punishment. Paul Kazarian's dismissal from his position as CEO of the appliance maker Sunbeam-Oster was partially due to his punishing behavior, which included throwing an orange juice container at the company controller. Why haven't the other tough bosses been fired? Despite their penchant for punishment, they have been very successful.[31] One wonders, however, if these tough bosses might be even more successful if they didn't rely so much on punishing behaviors to exert influence in their companies.

MEASURING LEADER BEHAVIORS

Considerable attention has been focused on the development of scales to measure the leader behaviors described previously. The *Leadership Behavior Description Questionnaire* asks a leader's subordinates to indicate the extent to which their leader or supervisor engages in a number of different consideration and initiating-structure behaviors. The *Leadership Opinion Questionnaire,* completed by the leaders themselves, asks leaders to indicate which of a variety of consideration and initiating-structure behaviors they think result in good leadership.[32] Researchers have also developed measures of leader reward behavior and leader punishing behavior. Figure 12.1 is an example of one of these measures, which is completed by a leader's subordinates.

WHAT IS MISSING IN THE TRAIT AND BEHAVIOR APPROACHES?

Although the trait and behavior approaches to leadership are different from each other—one focuses on what effective leaders are like, and the other on what they do—they do have something in common. Each approach essentially ignores the situation in which leadership takes place. Recall from Chapter 2 that the *interaction* of an individual's characteristics (such as traits and behaviors)

FIGURE 12.1

A Measure of Leader Reward and Punishing Behavior

Source: P. M. Podsakoff, W. D. Todor, R. A. Grover, and V. L. Huber, "Situational Moderators of Leader Reward and Punishment Behaviors. Fact or Fiction?" *Organizational Behavior and Human Decision Processes,* 1984, 34, pp. 21–63. Reprinted with permission of Academic Press, Inc.

The subordinates of a leader are asked to indicate the extent to which they agree or disagree with each of the following statements on the following scale:

1 = Strongly disagree   **5** = Slightly agree
2 = Disagree   **6** = Agree
3 = Slightly disagree   **7** = Strongly agree
4 = Neither agree nor disagree

1. My supervisor always gives me positive feedback when I perform well.

2. My supervisor gives me special recognition when my work performance is especially good.

3. My supervisor would quickly acknowledge an improvement in the quality of my work.

4. My supervisor commends me when I do a better than average job.

5. My supervisor personally pays me a compliment when I do outstanding work.

6. My supervisor informs his or her boss and/or others in the organization when I do outstanding work.

7. If I do well, I know my supervisor will reward me.

8. My supervisor would do all that she/he could to help me go as far as I would like to go in this organization if my work was consistently above average.

9. My good performance often goes unacknowledged by my supervisor.*

10. I often perform well in my job and still receive no praise from my supervisor.*

11. If I performed at a level below that which I was capable of, my supervisor would indicate his/her disapproval.

12. My supervisor shows his/her displeasure when my work is below acceptable standards.

13. My supervisor lets me know about it when I perform poorly.

14. My supervisor would reprimand me if my work was below standard.

15. When my work is not up to par, my supervisor points it out to me.

* For these items, scoring is reversed such that 1 = 7, 2 = 6, 3 = 5, 5 = 3, 6 = 2, 7 = 1.
Leader reward behavior = the sum of items 1–10
Leader punishment behavior = the sum of the items 11–15

with the organizational situation (including the amount of formal authority that leaders have and the nature of their subordinates) determines an individual's behavior (for example, leadership and performance) in an organization.

The trait approach takes into account leaders' personal aspects but ignores the situations in which they try to lead. Certain leadership traits may lead to effective leadership in certain situations and to ineffective leadership in other situations. Dominance, for example, may make a football coach a good leader for a football team. But the same trait in the head research scientist at a medical research laboratory that employs MDs and PhDs may actually detract from the leader's effectiveness because the subordinates (the MDs and PhDs) tend to be independent thinkers who work best when they are left alone.

Similarly, the behavior approach seeks to identify the behaviors responsible for effective leadership without considering how the situation affects behavior. The behavior approach implicitly assumes that regardless of the situation (such as a group's characteristics and composition or the type of task), certain leadership behaviors will result in high levels of subordinates' satisfaction and performance. However, just as the situation moderates the effects of a leader's traits, it also influences the effects of a leader's behaviors. The performance of a group of workers who are building a complicated custom-built house, for example, may be enhanced when their leader engages in initiating structure by scheduling the work so that the house is completely framed before the roof is put on, by maintaining high quality standards, and by pushing workers to perform their tasks as quickly as possible. In contrast, the performance of a group of assembly line workers who manufacture stereos and have been performing the same tasks day in and day out for several years and know exactly how to do their jobs may be unaffected by their leader's initiating structure. In fact, in this situation, initiating structure may lower levels of job satisfaction as workers become annoyed by having their leader breathing down their necks and telling them what to do when they already know exactly what needs to be done and how to do it.

The trait and behavior approaches contribute to our understanding of effective leadership by indicating what effective leaders tend to be like and what they do (see Table 12.1). A fuller understanding of leadership, however, can be gained only by also considering how the situation affects leadership.

TABLE 12.1

The Nature of Leadership: The Role of Traits and Behaviors

Approach	Premise	Drawbacks
Trait approach	Effective leaders possess certain qualities or traits that help a group or an organization achieve its goals.	Some effective leaders do not possess all of these traits, and some leaders who possess these traits are not effective. The approach ignores the situation in which leadership takes place.
Behavior approach	Effective leaders perform certain behaviors, which may include consideration, initiating structure, reward behavior, and punishing behavior.	The relationship between these behaviors and subordinate performance and satisfaction is not necessarily clear-cut. The behavior approach ignores the situation in which leadership takes place.

TO MANAGERS

Trait and Behavior Approaches to Leadership

- Make sure you know and understand the work that your subordinates perform. Also make sure any subordinates who are leaders have the appropriate task-relevant knowledge.
- Seek outside help, perhaps from an executive coach, if you are having trouble relating to your subordinates. Signs of trouble include frequent conflicts or disagreements or your subordinates avoiding you, withholding information from you, or acting fearful in your presence.
- Vary your leadership behavior according to the situation, and instruct any subordinates who are leaders to do the same. Do not require them to always engage in certain leadership behaviors such as initiating structure or consideration.
- Whenever possible, use reward behavior instead of punishing behavior, and instruct your subordinates who are leaders to do the same.

Many of the approaches that we examine in the rest of this chapter, such as Fiedler's contingency model, explicitly consider how the nature of the situation impacts leadership.

Fiedler's Contingency Theory of Leadership

The trait and behavior approaches ignore how the situation influences leadership effectiveness. Recognizing that organizational behavior is determined by the interaction of (1) individuals' characteristics and (2) the situations in which individuals find themselves, Fred Fiedler approached leadership from an interactional perspective. His **contingency theory of leadership,** one of the most popular and well-researched leadership theories, takes into account the personal characteristics of leaders and the situation, and it considers how both impact leader effectiveness.[33] Fiedler's theory sheds light on two important leadership issues: (1) Why, in a particular situation, some leaders will be effective and other leaders with equally good credentials will be ineffective, and (2) why a particular leader may be effective in one situation but not in another.

> **Contingency theory of leadership**
> The theory that leader effectiveness is determined by both the personal characteristics of leaders and by the situations in which leaders find themselves.

LEADER STYLE

Like the trait approach, Fiedler's theory acknowledges that personal characteristics influence whether leaders are effective. Fiedler was particularly interested in styles of leadership—how a person approaches being a leader. He identified two distinct leader styles—relationship-oriented and task-oriented—and proposed that all leaders are characterized by one style or the other.

Leaders who are *relationship-oriented* want to be liked by and to get along well with their subordinates. Although they want their subordinates to perform at a high level, relationship-oriented leaders' first priority is developing good relationships with their followers. Their second priority is making sure that the job gets done (task accomplishment). Ken Franklin, who manages American-owned factories (*maquiladoras*) in Mexico's Bermúdez Industrial Park in Ciudad Juárez, has learned that a relationship-oriented style is particularly important when leading Mexican subordinates. Every morning at 6 o'clock he greets factory workers personally when they start work.[34]

Leaders who are *task-oriented* want their subordinates to perform at a high level and accomplish all of their assigned tasks. Their first priority is task accomplishment, and they push subordinates to make sure that the job gets done. Having good relationships with their subordinates is their second priority.

According to Fiedler, a leader's style, whether relationship-oriented or task-oriented, is an enduring characteristic. Leader style cannot easily be changed—a relationship-oriented leader cannot be trained to be task-oriented and vice versa. A leader's style also cannot easily change with the situation—a leader will not be relationship-oriented in one situation and task-oriented in another.

Which style of leadership is most effective depends on the kind of situation the leader is dealing with. Because leaders cannot change their style, an organization must do one of two things to ensure that its leaders are able to help their subordinates and the organization as a whole attain important goals. An organization must either assign leaders to situations in which they will be effective or change the situation to fit the leader.

Fiedler devised and used a unique scale to measure leader style: the **least preferred coworker scale.** He asked leaders to think about their least preferred coworker (LPC), the coworker with whom they have the most difficulty working. The leader was then asked to rate the LPC on a number of dimensions such as the extent to which the LPC was friendly, enthusiastic, and pleasant. Relationship-oriented leaders (also called *high LPC leaders*) described their least preferred coworker in relatively positive terms. They were able to say some good things about the coworker with whom they had the most difficulty working. They were able to set aside the work-related problems they had with the LPC and see that this person had merit as another human being. In contrast, task-oriented leaders (also called *low LPC leaders*) described their least preferred coworker negatively. They believed their LPC had few redeeming qualities. Because they had difficulty working with the LPC, their overall impression of this person was very negative.

Fiedler thought that how leaders described their least preferred coworker provided a good insight into their approach to leading. Relationship-oriented leaders, he theorized, would try to think positively about others, even about the LPC, because a positive outlook would foster good relationships. Task-oriented leaders, however, would think negatively about others who were difficult to work with because their undesired behavior might hinder task accomplishment.

The least preferred coworker scale is not accepted by all researchers. Some have not been satisfied with Fiedler's use of LPC ratings to measure leader style and have questioned the meaning of these ratings.

SITUATIONAL CHARACTERISTICS

Fiedler proposed that situations vary in their favorability for leading—that is, the extent to which the situation allows the leader to easily channel subordinate behavior in the direction of high performance and goal attainment. When a situation is favorable for leading, it is easier for a leader to exert influence than it is when a situation is unfavorable. According to Fiedler, three characteristics determine how favorable situations are for leading: leader-member relations, task structure, and position power.

Least preferred coworker scale
A questionnaire that measures leader style by scoring leaders' responses to questions about the coworker with whom they have the most difficulty working.

Leader-member relations

The relationship between a leader and his or her followers.

Leader-Member Relations.   When **leader-member relations**—the relationship between the leader and his or her followers—are good, followers like, trust, and feel a certain degree of loyalty toward their leader, and the situation is favorable for leading. When leader-member relations are poor, a situation is unfavorable for leading. Two examples will illustrate the nature of leader-member relations.

Robert Holkan, as head mechanic, leads a group of mechanics in a garage. He gets along well with the mechanics, and they often go out to lunch together. In Holkan's leadership situation, leader-member relations are good. Mary Lester is head of the English department of a small liberal arts college. The other professors in the department think Lester is a snob and a bit pretentious. Leader-member relations are poor in Lester's leadership situation.

Task structure

The extent to which the work to be performed by a group is clearly defined.

Task Structure.   **Task structure** is the extent to which the work to be performed by a group is clearly defined. When a group has specific goals that need to be accomplished and every group member knows how to go about achieving the goals, task structure is high. When group goals are vague or uncertain and members are not sure how to go about performing their jobs, task structure is low. Situations are more favorable for leading when task structure is high.

Task structure is high for head mechanic Robert Holkan because the garage has the clear goal of repairing customers' cars in a timely fashion and because the highly skilled mechanics generally know exactly what needs to be done on each car. Task structure is low for Mary Lester. Within the English department there is considerable turmoil about the relative emphasis on teaching and research. The English professors are split about which is more important, and there is considerable disagreement about how to evaluate professors' research and teaching performance. A result of the uncertainty about what the "work" of the department should be (teaching or research) is low task structure.

Position power

The amount of formal authority a leader has.

Position Power.   **Position power** is the amount of formal authority a leader has. If a leader has the power to reward and punish subordinates by, for example, granting them pay raises and bonuses or docking their pay, position power is high. If a leader can do little to reward or punish subordinates, position power is low. A situation is more favorable for leading when position power is high.

At the garage, Robert Holkan has low position power because he has little control over rewards and punishments for the mechanics. The owner of the garage determines pay rates, benefits, and other rewards, and Holkan has little input into the process. Conversely, Lester has high position power as head of the English department. Each year the department has a set amount of money to be used for faculty raises, and Lester determines how to distribute the money among the English department faculty. She also determines who teaches which courses and the times at which all courses are taught. Members of the department are reluctant to disagree with her because they are afraid that she may assign them undesirable teaching times (such as from 3 to 5 p.m. on Fridays).

THE CONTINGENCY MODEL

All possible combinations of good and poor leader-member relations, high and low task structure, and high and low position power yield eight leadership situations. Fiedler applied the word *octant* to each type of situation (see Fig. 12.2).

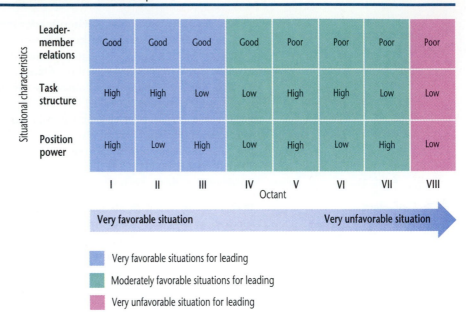

FIGURE **12.2**

Favorability of
Situations for Leading
Source: Adapted from F. E. Fiedler,
A Theory of Leadership Effectiveness
(New York: McGraw-Hill, 1967).
Reprinted with permission.

According to Fiedler's theory, octant I, II, and III situations are very favorable for leading; octant IV, V, VI, and VII situations are moderately favorable for leading; and an octant VIII situation is very unfavorable for leading.

Head mechanic Robert Holkan has good leader-member relations, high task structure, and low position power (octant II in Fig. 12.2), a very favorable situation for leading. Professor Mary Lester, in contrast, has poor leader-member relations, low task structure, and high position power (octant VII in Fig. 12.2), a moderately favorable situation for leading.

To determine whether Robert Holkan or Mary Lester will be the more effective leader, we need to look at Holkan's and Lester's leadership styles and the favorability of their situations. The impact of each of these factors on leader effectiveness depends, or is contingent, on the other. To identify their leadership style, we ask both of them to describe their least preferred coworker. Holkan describes his least preferred coworker very negatively; he thinks this mechanic is basically stupid and difficult to get along with. This description indicates that Holkan is a task-oriented or low LPC leader. Lester describes her least preferred coworker in positive terms. Even though she has trouble working with this professor, she thinks that he is intelligent and pleasant. This description indicates that Lester is a relationship-oriented or high LPC leader.

According to Fiedler's theory, task-oriented leaders are most effective in situations that are very favorable or very unfavorable, and relationship-oriented leaders are most effective in moderately favorable situations (see Table 12.2). Thus, even though Holkan's and Lester's leadership situations are different and their leader styles are different, they are actually equally effective as leaders. Holkan is a task-oriented leader in a very favorable situation, and Lester is a relationship-oriented leader in a moderately favorable situation.

Why are task-oriented leaders most effective in very favorable and in unfavorable situations, and why are relationship-oriented leaders most effective

TABLE 12.2

Fiedler's Contingency Theory of Leadership

Leader Style	Nature of Leader	Situations in Which Style Is Most Effective
Relationship-oriented	Wants to be liked by and to get along well with subordinates *First priority :* Developing good relationships with subordinates *Second priority:* Getting the job done	Moderately favorable for leading (octants IV, V, VI and VII in Fig.12.2)
Task-oriented	Wants subordinates to perform at a high level and accomplish all assigned tasks. *First priority:* Getting the job done *Second priority:* Developing good relationships with subordinates	Very favorable or very unfavorable for leading (octants I, II, III, and VIII in Fig. 12.2)

in moderately favorable situations? Recall that the first priority of task-oriented leaders is task accomplishment and their second priority is good interpersonal relations. Fiedler suggests that when leaders and people in general are under stress, they concentrate on their first priorities. A very unfavorable situation for leading is stressful for most leaders, and task-oriented leaders will focus on getting the job done because that is their first priority. This focus is likely to be effective in such situations because it increases the chances that a group will at least accomplish its tasks. In very favorable situations, task-oriented leaders, realizing that the group will achieve its goals because the situation is so good, can focus on their second priority—good interpersonal relations—because they know the job will get done. In moderately favorable situations, relationship-oriented leaders can focus on both interpersonal relations and task accomplishment.[35]

Some leadership experts have questioned these explanations and Fiedler's model. Research studies provide some support for the model but also suggest that it (like most theories) needs modifying.[36]

Recall that Fiedler considers leader style to be relatively fixed or enduring. According to contingency theory, leaders cannot be taught to be relationship-oriented or task-oriented in responding to a particular situation, nor can a leader alter his or her style according to the situation. Instead, leaders must be assigned to situations in which they will be effective because of their style, or situations must be changed to fit the leader.

For example, to improve the favorability of a situation for leading, it may be possible to increase levels of task structure by giving a leader specific goals to be accomplished and guidelines for how to channel subordinates' behavior to reach these goals. Alternatively, an organization may be able to increase position power to improve the favorability of a situation by giving a leader the formal authority to make decisions about pay raises, bonuses, and promotions for subordinates. Finally, an organization may be able to improve leader-member relations by training leaders and their followers in how best to communicate and relate to each other (a topic that we discuss in detail in Chapter 19).

TO MANAGERS

Fiedler's Contingency Model

● Do not expect leaders to change their leader style from task-oriented to relationship-oriented or vice versa.
● Assign task-oriented leaders to very unfavorable or to very favorable situations. Assign relationship-oriented leaders to moderately favorable situations.
● If you or one of your subordinates is a relationship-oriented leader in a very unfavorable situation, try to increase the favorability of the situation by improving leader-member relations, increasing task structure by clarifying goals or ways to achieve goals, or raising levels of position power.

Contemporary Perspectives on Leadership

Several other theories or approaches to leadership have been proposed. Each deals with a different aspect of leadership. Like Fiedler's contingency model, these models are interactional—that is, they take into account aspects of both the leader and the situation in trying to understand leader effectiveness. The combination of these additional perspectives with Fiedler's work, the trait approach, and the behavior approach provides a rich picture of what it takes to ensure that leaders are as effective as possible. Effective leadership, in turn, increases the likelihood that groups and organizations will achieve their goals.

Path-goal theory describes how leaders can motivate their followers to perform at a high level and can keep them satisfied. The Vroom and Yetton model deals with a specific aspect of leadership: the extent to which leaders should involve their subordinates in decision making. Leader-member exchange theory takes into account the fact that leaders often do not treat each of their subordinates equally but instead develop different kinds of relationships with different subordinates. Each of these perspectives adds to your understanding of what makes leadership effective in organizations.

PATH-GOAL THEORY: HOW LEADERS MOTIVATE FOLLOWERS

Robert House, a widely respected leadership researcher, realized that much of what leaders try to do in organizations involves motivating their followers. House's **path-goal theory** describes how leaders can motivate their followers to achieve group and organizational goals and the kinds of behaviors leaders can engage in to motivate followers (see Table 12.3).

Path-goal theory suggests that effective leaders follow three guidelines to motivate their followers. The guidelines are based on the expectancy theory of motivation (see Chapter 6). Effective leaders who follow these guidelines have highly motivated subordinates who are likely to meet their work goals and perform at a high level:

1. *Determine what outcomes subordinates are trying to obtain in the workplace.* For example, what needs are they trying to satisfy, or what goals are they trying to meet? After gaining this information, the leader must have control over those outcomes or over the ability to give or withhold the outcomes to subordinates. The new manager of a group of five attor-

Path-goal theory
A theory which describes how leaders can motivate their followers to achieve group and organizational goals and the kinds of behaviors leaders can engage in to motivate followers.

TABLE 12.3

Path-Goal Theory

Effective leaders motivate their followers to achieve group and organizational goals.

Effective leaders make sure that they have control over outcomes their subordinates desire.

Effective leaders reward subordinates for performing at a high level or achieving their work goals by giving them desired outcomes.

Effective leaders raise their subordinates' beliefs about their ability to achieve their work goals and perform at a high level.

In determining how to treat their subordinates and what behaviors to engage in, effective leaders take into account their subordinates' characteristics and the type of work they do.

neys in a large law firm determined that salary raises and the opportunity to work on interesting cases with big corporate clients were the outcomes that her subordinates most desired. She already controlled the assignment of cases and clients, but her own boss determined salary raises. After realizing the importance of salary raises for the motivation of her subordinates, the manager discussed with her boss the importance of being able to determine her own subordinates' raises. The boss gave her sole authority to determine their raises as long as she kept within the budget. In this way, the manager made sure she had control over outcomes that her subordinates desired.

2. *Reward subordinates for performing at a high level or achieving their work goals by giving them desired outcomes.* The manager in the law firm had two important goals for her subordinates: completing all assignments within the budgeted hours and winning cases. When subordinates met these goals, they were performing at a high level. To motivate her subordinates to attain these goals, the manager made sure that her distribution of interesting monthly case assignments and semiannual raises reflected the extent to which her subordinates met these two goals. The subordinate who always stayed within the budgeted hours and won all of his cases in the last six months received not only the biggest raise but also received the choicest assignments.

3. *Make sure the subordinates believe that they can obtain their work goals and perform at a high level.* Leaders can do this by showing subordinates the paths to goal attainment (hence the name path-goal theory), by removing any obstacles that might come up along the way, and by expressing confidence in subordinates' capabilities. The manager in the law firm realized that one of her subordinates had low expectations. He had little confidence in his ability to stay within budget and to win cases no matter how hard he worked. The manager was able to raise this subordinate's expectations by showing him how to allocate his billable hours among the various cases he was working on and explaining to him the key ingredients to winning a case. She also told

him to ask her for help whenever he came across a problem he thought might jeopardize his chances of winning a case. The subordinate followed her advice, and together they worked out ways to get around problems that came up on the subordinate's various cases. By clarifying the paths to goal attainment and helping to remove obstacles, the supervisor helped raise this subordinate's expectations and motivation, and he actually started to win more cases and complete them within the budgeted hours.

House identified four types of behavior that leaders can engage in to motivate subordinates:

- *Directive behavior* (similar to initiating structure) lets subordinates know what tasks need to be performed and how they should be performed.
- *Supportive behavior* (similar to consideration) lets subordinates know that their leader cares about their well-being and is looking out for them.
- *Participative behavior* enables subordinates to be involved in making decisions that affect them.
- *Achievement-oriented behavior* pushes subordinates to do their best. Such behavior includes setting difficult goals for followers, expecting high performance, and expressing confidence in subordinates' capabilities.

In determining how to motivate subordinates or which of these behaviors to engage in, a leader has to take into account the nature of his or her subordinates and the work they do. If a subordinate is experiencing a lot of stress, a leader who engages in supportive behavior might be especially effective. Directive behaviors are likely to be beneficial when subordinates work on complex and difficult projects, such as the lawyer who was having trouble winning cases. As we discussed earlier, when subordinates are performing easy tasks that they know exactly how to do, initiating structure or directive behaviors are not necessary and are likely to be resented because people do not like to be told how to do something that they already do quite well. When it is important for subordinates to accept a decision that a leader needs to make, participative leadership behavior is likely to be effective (as you will see in the description of the Vroom and Yetton model).

Path-goal theory enhances our understanding of effective leadership in organizations by specifying how leaders should motivate their followers. Motivation, as we explained in Chapters 6, 7, and 8, is one of the key determinants of performance in organizations, and the ability to motivate followers is a crucial aspect of leader effectiveness.[37]

THE VROOM AND YETTON MODEL: DETERMINING THE LEVEL OF SUBORDINATE PARTICIPATION IN DECISION MAKING

One of the most important things that leaders do in organizations is make decisions. Good decisions help the organization achieve its goals; bad decisions hinder goal attainment. The **Vroom and Yetton model,** developed in the 1970s by Victor Vroom and Philip Yetton, describes the different ways in

Vroom and Yetton model
A model that describes the different ways in which leaders can make decisions and guides leaders in determining the extent to which subordinates should participate in decision making.

which leaders can make decisions and guides leaders in determining the extent to which subordinates should participate in decision making.[38]

As many leaders have learned, allowing subordinates to participate in decision making and problem solving can enhance leadership.[39] Participation helps to ensure that subordinates will accept a decision that affects them or requires their support. Participation may result in better decisions if, for example, subordinates have information pertaining to the decision that the leader does not have. Participation can help foster subordinates' growth and development and may result in higher levels of performance and satisfaction in the future.

Participation, however, has certain disadvantages. The biggest disadvantage is time. Not only does decision making take longer when subordinates participate, but both the subordinates and the leader spend time making the decision. Another disadvantage of participation is that subordinates may want to make a decision that is good for them personally but not good for the organization. In this situation, leaders are in the awkward position of having to reject their subordinates' advice even though the subordinates were asked to participate. Given the advantages and disadvantages of subordinates' participation in decision making, the Vroom and Yetton model seeks to specify when and how much leaders should allow their subordinates to participate.

Choosing an Appropriate Decision Making Style. To identify the optimal amount of participation, the Vroom and Yetton model first requires leaders to determine whether an individual or a group decision needs to be made. Individual decisions pertain to a single subordinate. An example is the decision the law firm manager had to make about how to motivate a subordinate with low confidence in his own ability. Group decisions pertain to a group of subordinates. An example is the decision the law firm manager had to make about how to distribute raises to all subordinates.

Leaders making either individual or group decisions can choose from five different decision-making styles, which vary in the extent to which subordinates participate in making the decision. Listed and described in Table 12.4, these five styles are categorized as follows:

- Autocratic (A): The leader makes the decision without input from subordinates.
- Consultative (C): Subordinates have some input, but the leader makes the decision.
- Group (G): The group makes the decision; the leader is just another group member.
- Delegated (D): The leader gives exclusive responsibility to subordinates.

For group decisions, leaders can choose from styles AI, AII, CI, CII, and GII. For individual decisions, leaders can choose from styles AI, AII, CI, GI, and DI.

The Vroom and Yetton model instructs leaders to choose among these alternative decision styles on the basis of their answers to a series of questions concerning (1) specific aspects of the decision that needs to be made, (2) characteristics of the subordinates involved, and (3) whether the leader has the information needed to make a good decision. The questions are arrayed

TABLE 12.4

Decision Styles in the Vroom and Yetton Model

	Group Problems and Decisions		**Individual Problems and Decisions**	
Least Participative	AI.	Leader solves the problem or makes the decision using information available at the time. No outside input.	AI.	The leader solves the problem or makes the decision using information available at the time. No outside input.
	AII.	The leader obtains the necessary information from subordinates. The leader makes the decision.	AII.	The leader obtains the necessary information from the subordinate involved in the decision. The leader makes the decision.
	CI.	The leader shares the problem with the relevant subordinates individually and gets their ideas and suggestions without bringing them together as a group. The leader makes the decision.	CI.	The leader shares the problem with the subordinate and asks for ideas and suggestions. The leader makes the decision.
	CII.	The leader shares the problem with subordinates as a group, obtaining their ideas and suggestions. The leader makes the decision.	GI.	The leader shares the problem with the subordinate, and together they analyze the problem and arrive at a mutually agreeable solution.
Most Participative	GII.	The leader shares the problem with subordinates as a group, does not try to influence the group, and is willing to accept and implement any solution that has the support of the entire group.	DI.	The leader delegates the problem to the subordinate, provides any relevant information, but gives the subordinate responsibility for solving the problem.

Source: Adapted from V. H. Vroom and P. W. Yetton, *Leadership and Decision-Making* (Pittsburgh: University of Pittsburgh Press, 1973). Reprinted with permission.
Note: A = Autocratic, C = Consultative, G = Group, D = Delegated.

in a *decision tree* (see Fig. 12.3). By answering each question and following through on the tree, the leader finds the problem type which characterizes the decision which needs to be made. For each problem type, there is a feasible set which includes one or more leadership styles that are appropriate for the decision in question (or the problem type). Where multiple styles are appropriate, one style is recommended to minimize the amount of time required to make the decision (time is measured in *people-hours,* the number of people involved times the number of hours spent by each person), and other styles are recommended to further subordinates' development and growth. More specifically, the leadership style to the far left in a feasible set in Figure 12.3 is the least participative and minimizes the people-hours needed to make the decision. Subordinate development and growth, in contrast, is fostered by increasing levels of participation. The style at the far right of a feasible set involves the highest level of participation and thus allows for the most growth by subordinates.

Putting the Vroom and Yetton Model to Work: An Example.   The best way to understand this leadership model is to apply it to a specific decision that a given leader needs to make and then follow through on the decision tree shown in Figure 12.3. Amy Cantos is the head of the accounting department in the business school of a large midwestern state university. There are six secretaries in the department and twenty-four professors. Cantos has to assign each secretary to work for four professors. Some of the secretaries are more

Questions leaders ask themselves about each decision

A. Is there a quality requirement such that one solution is likely to be more rational than another?
B. Do I have sufficient information to make a high-quality decision?
C. Is the problem structured?
D. Is acceptance of decision by subordinates critical to effective implementation?
E. If I were to make the decision by myself, is it reasonably certain that it would be accepted by my subordinates?
F. Do subordinates share the organizational goals to be attained in solving this problem?
G. Is conflict among subordinates likely in preferred solutions? (This question is irrelevant to individual problems.)
H. Do subordinates have sufficient information to make a high-quality decision?

Decision tree (numbers identify problem types)

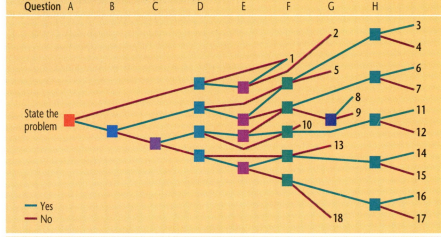

Problem types and feasible sets

Feasible sets list the appropriate decision-making styles for each problem type. Separate sets are shown for group and individual problems. Decision-making styles are categorized as autocratic (A), consultative (C), group (G), and delegated (D).

Problem type	Feasible sets		Problem type	Feasible sets	
	Group	Individual		Group	Individual
1	AI, AII, CI, CII, GII	AI, DI, AII, CI, GI	10	AII, CI, CII	AII, CI
2	GII	DI, GI	11	AII, CI, CII, GII	DI, AII, CI, GI
3	AI, AII, CI, CII, GII	AI, DI, AII, CI, GI	12	AII, CI, CII, GII	AII, CI, GI
4	AI, AII, CI, CII, GII	AI, AII, CI, GI	13	CII	CI
5	AI, AII, CI, CII,	AI, AII, CI	14	CII, GII	DI, CI, GI
6	GII	DI, GI	15	CII, GII	CI, GI
7	GII	GI	16	GII	DI, GI
8	CII	CI	17	GII	GI
9	CI, CII	CI	18	CII	CI

FIGURE 12.3

The Vroom and Yetton Decision Tree
Source: V. H. Vroom and P. W. Yetton, *Leadership and Decision-Making* (Pittsburgh: University of Pittsburgh Press, 1973). Reprinted with permission.

skilled than others, and some of the professors have heavier workloads than others, so these assignments are more complicated than they seem at first. Should Cantos make these assignments herself, or should she allow her subordinates (the secretaries and the professors) to participate in the decision-making process?

Using the decision tree shown in Figure 12.3, Cantos first asks herself question A: "Is there a quality requirement such that one solution is likely to be more rational than another?" Cantos answers yes to this question because it is important for the workload to be spread as evenly as possible among the secretaries and for professors who have heavy workloads and a lot of deadlines to have the most skilled secretaries.

Moving along on the "yes" path from question A leads to question B: "Do I have sufficient information to make a high-quality decision?" Cantos answers yes to question B because she is familiar with the skill levels of the six secretaries and with the workloads and deadlines faced by each of the twenty-four professors.

Moving along the "yes" path from question B leads to question D: "Is acceptance of decision by subordinates critical to effective implementation?" Cantos answers "yes" to question D because it is important that both the secretaries and the professors accept the secretarial assignments. Moving along the "yes" path from question D leads to question E: "If I were to make the decision by myself, is it reasonably certain that it would be accepted by my subordinates?" Cantos answers "yes" to question E because she has a good working relationship with the secretaries and the professors and she knows that all of her subordinates feel she does what is best for the department.

Moving along on the "yes" path from question E leads to question F: "Do subordinates share the organizational goals to be attained in solving this problem?" Cantos answers no to this question because the secretaries' goals are to work for the professors who are easiest to get along with but most of the professors (regardless of their workloads) have the goal of getting one of the most skilled secretaries.

Moving along the "no" path from question F leads to the number 5, which indicates that this is a number 5–type problem. Because Cantos's decision is a group rather than an individual decision, four decision styles could be appropriate for this problem. The first style in the feasible set is the most autocratic and will take the least amount of time. The last style in the set is consultative, has the most involvement by subordinates, and is good for their growth and development. Because Cantos needs to make a quick decision and doesn't want to waste the secretaries' or the professors' time, she chooses the first style in the set, AI.

Research Support.　　Research support for the Vroom and Yetton model has been mixed. Some studies support the model, and others do not. Recently Vroom and Arthur Jago extended the model by including additional questions and allowing leaders to answer the questions on 5-point scales rather than in the simple yes-no format. These extensions added to the complexity of the model, and a computer program has been developed to help managers find their way through the more complicated decision tree.[40] Not enough research has been conducted to evaluate these extensions.

Some researchers and leaders question whether it is realistic to assume that leaders will or can actually follow this model when they are making important decisions in groups or organizations. Some leaders, because of their personalities, may generally want to make decisions on their own with little input from subordinates (style AI) even if the decision tree recommends a more participative style. Leaders who are relationship-oriented may not feel comfortable making autocratic decisions.

Researchers and leaders also question how subordinates will react to leaders' using different styles depending on the situation. Subordinates allowed to participate in one decision, for example, may expect to participate in others as well and may resent it when their leader uses (correctly, according to the decision tree) a more autocratic style.

Whether leaders will actually follow the Vroom and Yetton model and whether the model actually leads to better decisions is unclear. What is clear, however, is that when and how much leaders should allow their subordinates to participate in decision making depends on aspects of the decision, the subordinates involved, and the information needed to make a good decision. Moreover, the Vroom and Yetton model may give overly autocratic leaders some needed guidance about how and when to involve their subordinates in decision making. As indicated in Insight 12.4, leaders can sometimes put themselves in a precarious position by making all decisions themselves.

Insight 12.4

Leadership

Autocratic Founder of Fast-Food Chain Flounders

In 1941, Carl Karcher borrowed money on his new Plymouth to buy a pushcart to sell hot dogs. Over the next fifty-two years, Karcher parlayed the business started into the Carl's Jr. (www.carlsjr.com.) restaurant chain, with over 600 units and sales of approximately $300 million a year. Karcher has always been an autocratic leader, making decisions on his own and not allowing his subordinates any room for participation. Although this style worked for Karcher for a while, it was ultimately responsible for his losing control of the company he founded.

Karcher's story offers a lesson in the risks of being too autocratic. Karcher was a visionary entrepreneur. He predicted the trend toward healthy food and was among the first to offer salad bars and grilled chicken sandwiches in his fast-food restaurants. But he insisted on having absolute power over his empire and making all decisions. One decision he made was that he would appear in all advertising for his restaurants, regardless of what other members of his organization or the ad agency he employed thought.

When company profits started to fall and Karcher's personal financial position began to deteriorate, he still expected to remain in charge and make decisions as he always had done. One of the last decisions that Karcher tried to railroad past the board of directors involved selling burritos in Carl's Jr. restaurants. The burritos were made by an outside company that was involved in giving Karcher a $6 million personal loan. When the board rejected his proposal and tried to come up with a compromise plan, Karcher stuck by his guns and insisted on his plan.

One by one, board members, whom Karcher himself had picked, voted to oust him as chair. The only dissenting director was his son. Board member Elizabeth Sanders, formerly an executive at Nordstrom Inc., was chosen to replace Karcher. If Karcher had not been so autocratic, his rags-to-riches story might have had a happier ending.[41]

LEADER-MEMBER EXCHANGE THEORY: RELATIONSHIPS BETWEEN LEADERS AND FOLLOWERS

Leader-member exchange theory

A theory that describes the different kinds of relationships that may develop between a leader and a follower and what the leader and the follower give to and receive back from the relationship.

Leaders do not treat all of their subordinates in exactly the same way and may develop different types of relationships with different subordinates. The **leader-member exchange theory** describes the different kinds of relationships that may develop between a leader and a follower and describes what the leader and the follower give to and receive back from the relationship.

This model focuses on the *leader-follower dyad*—that is, the relationship between the leader and the follower (a *dyad* is two individuals regarded as a pair).[42] Leader-member exchange theory proposes that each leader-follower dyad develops a unique relationship that stems from the unfolding interactions between the leader and the follower.

Although each relationship is unique, the theory suggests that two general kinds of relationships develop in leader-follower dyads (see Fig. 12.4). In some dyads, the leader develops with the subordinate a special relationship characterized by mutual trust, commitment, and involvement. In these dyads, the subordinate helps the leader, the leader helps the subordinate, and each has substantial influence over the other. The leader spends a lot of time with the subordinate, who is given latitude or freedom to use his or her own judgment on the job. In turn, the subordinate tends to be satisfied and to perform at a high level. Subordinates who develop this special kind of relationship with their leader are said to be in the *in-group*.[43]

Other subordinates develop a more traditional relationship with their leader. In these dyads, the leader relies on his or her formal authority and position in the organization to influence the subordinate and the subordinate is expected to perform his or her jobs in an acceptable manner and to follow rules and the directives of the leader. The subordinate has considerably less influence over the leader, and the leader gives the subordinate less freedom to use his or her own judgment. These dyads are characterized by an impersonal, distant, or cold relationship between the leader and the subordinate. Subordinates who develop this kind of relationship with their leaders are said to be in the *out-group*. They tend to be less satisfied and perform at a lower level than in-group subordinates.

The relationship between a leader and his or her own supervisor is also a dyad that can be classified as an in-group or out-group relationship. Leaders who have high-quality relationships with their own supervisors are more likely to develop high-quality relationships with their own subordinates. Fur-

FIGURE 12.4

Leader-Member Exchange Theory
The relationship between in-group followers and the leader is characterized by trust, commitment, and involvement. The relationship between out-group followers and the leader is based on the formal authority of the leader and obedience to rules.

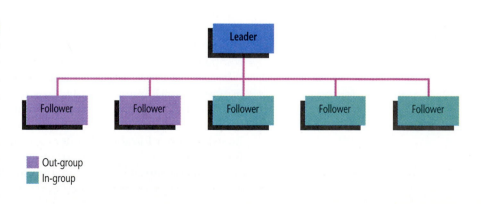

Leader

Follower | Follower | Follower | Follower | Follower

■ Out-group
■ In-group

TO MANAGERS

Contemporary Perspectives on Leadership

- Determine what outcomes your followers are trying to obtain from their jobs, and make sure that you have as much control as possible over those outcomes.
- Distribute desired outcomes to your subordinates when they attain their work goals and perform at a high level.
- Raise your followers' expectations by clarifying how they can attain their work goals, removing obstacles that hamper goal attainment and high performance, and expressing confidence in their ability to succeed.
- Tailor your leadership behaviors to the characteristics of your subordinates and to the situation.
- When determining how much to allow your subordinates to participate in decision making, consider the decision that needs to be made, the subordinates involved, and the information you need to make a good decision.
- Realize that participation in decision making can contribute to your subordinates' growth and development on the job but can also be time-consuming.
- Develop high-quality relationships with as many of your subordinates as possible—that is, have a big in-group and a small out-group.

thermore, research conducted in Japan suggests that leaders who have high-quality relationships with their own supervisors are more likely to advance quickly in an organization.[44]

Research suggests that it is desirable for leaders to develop special relationships with their subordinates, for subordinates who are in the in-group are more likely to perform at a high level and be loyal to their leaders than are subordinates in the out-group. Research further suggests that a sharp distinction between the in-group and the out-group may not be desirable because subordinates in the out-group might resent their relatively inferior status and differential treatment.[45]

Does Leadership Always Matter in Organizations?

By and large, research suggests that leaders *can* make a difference. Some researchers, however, have questioned whether leadership *always* makes a difference in helping individuals, groups, and organizations achieve goals such as high levels of job satisfaction and job performance, smoothly functioning and effective work groups, and an increase in an organization's revenues and market share. These researchers argue that although it might make people feel good and secure to think that leaders are important and in charge, leadership may be more a figment of the imagination than a fact of organizational life.[46] These researchers suggest that leaders sometimes have little effect on the attitudes and behaviors of their followers. Sometimes, no matter what a leader does, workers are dissatisfied with their jobs or fail to perform highly. At other times, subordinates are satisfied with their jobs, attain or exceed their work goals, and perform at a high level without a leader exerting much influence at all.

As an example of a worker of the latter type, consider Jason Jackson, a scriptwriter for a hit situation comedy on a major network. Jackson prefers to work at home, where he has few interruptions. He stops by his office only a couple of times a week to pick up his mail. Jackson rarely sees his supervisor outside the quarterly planning and scheduling meetings that they both attend. Nevertheless, Jackson is very satisfied with his job and by all counts is a top performer. The show is in the top 10 and Jackson has received numerous industry awards for his scripts.

Jackson's case may be a bit extreme, but it does suggest in some situations leadership might not be very important. Two organizational behavior researchers, Steven Kerr and John Jermier, realized that leadership substitutes and neutralizers sometimes act to limit the influence that leaders have in organizations.[47]

LEADERSHIP SUBSTITUTES

Leadership substitute

Something that acts in place of a formal leader and makes leadership unnecessary.

A **leadership substitute** is something that acts in place of a formal leader and makes leadership unnecessary. Characteristics of the subordinate, the work, the group, and the organization all have the potential to act as substitutes for leadership. In Jackson's case, for example, both his personal characteristics and the nature of his work serve as leadership substitutes. Jackson is intelligent, skilled, and has high levels of intrinsic motivation. (Recall from Chapter 6 that a worker who is intrinsically motivated enjoys his or her job and performs it for its own sake.) Jackson loves writing and happens to be very creative. Because he is the way he is, Jackson does not need a supervisor to push him to write good scripts; his intrinsic motivation and capabilities ensure that he performs at a high level. That Jackson's work tends to be interesting is an additional substitute for leadership: It contributes to his high performance and job satisfaction. It is not necessary for Jackson's supervisor to push him to perform, try to keep him happy, or even see him on a regular basis because of these powerful leadership substitutes. Fortunately, Jackson's supervisor realizes this and basically leaves Jackson alone, thereby freeing up some time to concentrate on his many other subordinates who *do* require leadership.

LEADERSHIP NEUTRALIZERS

Sidney Harman, CEO of Harman International Industries, realized that not seeing his subordinates on a day-to-day basis was leading them and his whole organization to imminent ruin. Harman International, located in California, manufactures audio equipment such as speakers for stereo systems. Although the company is located on the West Coast, Sidney Harman tried to lead the company from his office in Washington, D.C. How successful was he as a long-distance CEO? In 1991, Harman International lost $20 million on sales of almost $600 million. Fortunately, Harman acted quickly to improve the performance of his company. He moved to California, and the result was a stunning turnaround of the company. Rather than losing money, the next year the company had a $3.5 million profit.[48]

Why did Harman's move to California coincide with the dramatic change in his company's fortunes? Harman suggests that when he was 3,000 miles away he was unable to have as much influence on his subordinates as he needed. Not having their leader around on a day-to-day basis caused managers to tolerate and accept mediocre performance.[49] Essentially, the physical distance separating Harman from his subordinates neutralized his leadership efforts.

A **leadership neutralizer** is something that prevents a leader from having any influence and negates the leader's efforts. When neutralizers are present, there is a leadership void. The leader has little or no effect, and there is nothing to take the leader's place (there are no substitutes). Characteristics of the subordinate, the work, the group, and the organization can all serve as potential neutralizers of leadership. When subordinates lack intrinsic motivation and are performing boring tasks, for example, it is often necessary to use extrinsic rewards such as pay to motivate them to perform at a high level. Sometimes, however, the leaders of these subordinates do not have control over rewards like pay.

Elizabeth Williams, the leader of a group of ticket takers on a commuter railroad, had little at her disposal to motivate her subordinates to perform at a high level. The ticket takers' pay and benefits were based on seniority, and their employment contract specified that they could be disciplined and dismissed only for a major infraction such as coming to work intoxicated. Like Sidney Harman when he lived on the East Coast, Williams often did not see her subordinates—the ticket takers worked on the trains, but she did not. Because of those powerful neutralizers, Williams had little influence over her ticket takers, who often failed to collect tickets during rush hour because they didn't want to force their way through passenger cars crowded with commuters standing in the aisles. Leadership neutralizers contributed to the railroad losing money from lost ticket sales just as the transcontinental distance between Harman and his managers contributed to Harman International's losses in the early 1990s.

As these examples indicate, *substitutes* for leadership are actually *functional* for organizations because they free up some of a leader's time for other activities. But *neutralizers* are *dysfunctional* because a leader's influence is lacking. The fact that substitutes and neutralizers exist probably contributes to the perception that leadership is unimportant. Despite their existence, however, research suggests that leaders do in fact make a difference and can have positive effects on the attitudes and behaviors of their followers.[50]

New Topics in Leadership Research

Given the prominence of the subject of leadership in the popular press and scholarly literature, it is not surprising that there are always new developments in theorizing about and research on leadership. In this section we explore some new topics of research: transformational and charismatic leadership, the effects of a leader's moods on his or her followers, and gender and leadership.

TRANSFORMATIONAL AND CHARISMATIC LEADERSHIP

Leadership researcher Bernard Bass has proposed a theory that looks at how leaders can sometimes have dramatic effects on their followers and their organizations and literally transform them. Although several theories focus on transformational and charismatic leadership, we concentrate on Bass's theory because it has been well received by other researchers, is relatively comprehensive, and incorporates ideas from some other well-known approaches to leadership.[51]

Leadership neutralizer
Something that prevents a leader from having any influence and negates a leader's efforts.

Lou Gerstner, CEO of IBM, is well respected as a transformational leader who has revolutionized the way his company operates. He is well known for throwing away the rule book and for supporting and encouraging employees to find their own solutions to problems.

Transformational leadership

Leadership that inspires followers to trust the leader, perform behaviors that contribute to the achievement of organizational goals, and perform at a high level.

According to Bass, **transformational leadership** occurs when a leader transforms, or changes, his or her followers in three important ways that together result in followers trusting the leader, performing behaviors that contribute to the achievement of organizational goals, and being motivated to perform at a high level (see Fig. 12.5):

1. Transformational leaders increase subordinates' awareness of the importance of their tasks and the importance of performing them well.
2. Transformational leaders make subordinates aware of their needs for personal growth, development, and accomplishment.
3. Transformational leaders motivate their subordinates to work for the good of the organization rather than exclusively for their own personal gain or benefit.[52]

How do transformational leaders influence their followers and bring these changes about? Transformational leaders are **charismatic leaders.** They have a vision of how good things *could be* in an organization that contrasts with how things currently *are*. Charismatic leaders clearly communicate this vision to their followers and, through their own excitement and enthusiasm, induce their followers to enthusiastically support this vision. To convey the excitement of their vision, charismatic leaders tend to have high levels of self-confidence and self-esteem, which further encourage their followers to respect and admire them.[53] From the opening case, it is clear that Kenneth Lay enthusiastically communicates his vision for Enron to his employees as well as his vision for a deregulated energy industry.

Charismatic leader

A self-confident, enthusiastic leader able to win followers' respect and support for his or her vision of how good things could be.

FIGURE 12.5

Transformational Leadership

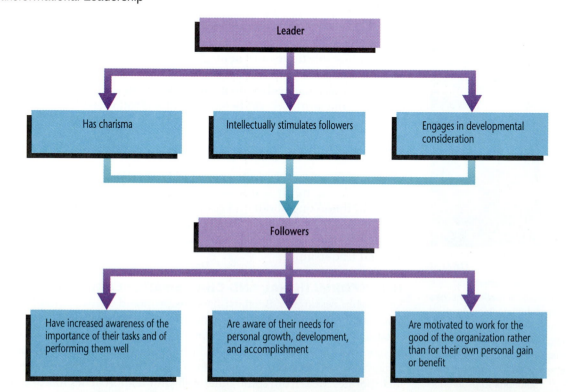

Transformational leaders influence their followers by intellectually stimulating them to become aware of problems in their groups and organization and to view these problems from a new perspective—one consistent with the leader's vision. Before the leader makes his or her influence felt, followers may not realize a problem exists, and if they do, they probably do not see the problem as something that directly concerns them. A transformational leader causes followers to view problems differently and feel some degree of responsibility for helping to solve them.[54] Recall how Lay makes his subordinates feel responsible for the growth and success of Enron as well as for recognizing and solving problems that arise.

Transformational leaders also influence their followers through developmental consideration. **Developmental consideration** includes not only the consideration behavior discussed earlier in the chapter (which indicates a leader's concern for followers' well-being) but also behavior through which a leader provides support and encouragement to followers and gives them opportunities to develop and grow on the job by acquiring new skills and capabilities.[55] At Enron, Lay strives to ensure that employees have the opportunity to grow and develop on the job and reach their full potential.

Like Kenneth Lay, Michael Walsh, past CEO of Tenneco, was a transformational leader who had dramatic effects on his followers and on Tenneco as a whole, as indicated in Insight 12.5.

Developmental consideration
Behavior that a leader engages in to provide support and encouragement to followers and give them opportunities to develop and grow on the job.

Insight 12.5

Competitive Advantage

Walsh's Transformational Leadership at Tenneco

In the early 1990s, Tenneco (www.tenneco.com) hired Michael Walsh to help turn around the troubled organization and help it gain a competitive advantage. Tenneco is an industrial and manufacturing conglomerate with businesses in the chemicals, automotive parts, shipbuilding, natural-gas pipelines, packaging, and agricultural and construction equipment industries.[56] When Walsh took over, Tenneco's sales were down 1.4 percent, and profits were down 67.2 percent over the prior year.[57]

Several of Walsh's views on leadership sound strikingly similar to what we have described as transformational leadership. Walsh stressed the importance of being enthusiastic and energetic and communicating with one's subordinates. He preferred oral communication over written memos and reports because it is more direct and involving. He thought that all members of an organization (even one as large as Tenneco) need to be aware of the problems facing the organization and need to feel that they can and should be part of the solution adopted to gain a competitive advantage.

Transformational leadership appeared to work for Walsh. After his first eighteen months on the job, profits were up, costs were down, and inefficiencies were reduced. Prior to the dramatic changes that Walsh made, for example, parts would sometimes travel 179 miles within Tenneco factories as part of the production process. This inefficiency (caused by a lack of forethought and good planning) contributed to high costs.[58]

Tenneco's recent financial performance highlights Walsh's success in transforming this company and its employees and helping Tenneco gain a competitive advantage. Perhaps even more impressive, however, is the fact that his message reached the rank-and-file workers at Tenneco. Besides holding numerous "town meetings," Walsh made videotapes urging workers to be innovative.

After watching these tapes, Alan Doran, a worker at a paper mill owned by Tenneco in Counce, Tennessee, came up with a better recipe for making liner board out of wood chips and chemicals—a change that resulted in higher quality and an annual savings of $350,000. The credit for this innovation clearly goes to Doran, but Walsh, through his transformational leadership, spurred Doran to feel responsible for making this improvement in a formula that hadn't been changed in thirty years.

Bob Evans, another paper mill worker, came up with a way to prevent mill machinery from continually breaking down—an innovation that resulted in $353,000 in annual savings. Evans indicated that "the old adage at mills like this used to be 'We hired you from the neck down.' Walsh treats us like we have minds."[59]

Walsh's transformational leadership was even in evidence when he was faced with an unfortunate and shocking personal blow. On January 20, 1993, Walsh announced that he had an inoperable form of brain cancer. Even though radiation and chemotherapy treatments were sapping his strength, Walsh's self-confidence, energy, and enthusiasm were still evident. He personally orchestrated the announcement of his illness to Tenneco employees and to the business community in an open and honest way that also made clear his intention of remaining CEO and helping Tenneco achieve his vision of proving "America's industrial might."[60] He was frank with his managers about his condition and tried to put them at ease by joking, such as when he asked the heads of the six Tenneco divisions in a regular meeting to introduce themselves because he was having trouble with his short-term memory. Walsh eventually became too weak to lead Tenneco, resigned, and died in 1994. However, his legacy as a transformational leader and as an inspiring human being will always be remembered at Tenneco and by those who knew him.[61]

Transactional leadership
Leadership that motivates followers by exchanging rewards for high performance and noticing and reprimanding subordinates for mistakes and substandard performance.

Transformational leadership is often distinguished from transactional leadership. **Transactional leadership** occurs when a leader motivates followers by exchanging rewards for high performance and noticing and reprimanding subordinates for mistakes and substandard performance.[62] Transformational leaders may also engage in transactional leadership (for example, by rewarding high performers with high salaries). But they go one step further by actually inducing followers to support their vision, put aside self-interest for the sake of the group and the organization, and take responsibility for helping to solve problems. In the process, subordinates grow and develop more than they would working under a leader who engages exclusively in transactional leadership.

Research on transformational leadership is in its early stages, so it would be premature to try to evaluate fully the merits of Bass's theory. Some preliminary studies, however, suggest that transformational leadership may spur followers on to higher levels of performance while enhancing their personal development and job satisfaction.[63] Transformational leadership may be especially important for organizations that are in trouble or failing to achieve their goals. Often, organizations in trouble bring in a CEO from outside the organization to help them transform themselves, as indicated in Insight 12.6.

Insight 12.6

Leadership

Transformational Leaders for Troubled Companies

Troubled organizations are increasingly relying on outsider CEOs to turn things around. In 1993, for example, Kodak hired George Fisher from Motorola, IBM hired Lou Gerstner from RJR Nabisco, and Westinghouse hired Michael Jordan from Clayton Dubilier & Rice. Some outsider CEOs are successful at changing the fate of the organizations, but others are not. What seems to set the most successful outsiders apart is a focus on transformational leadership.

The best outsiders spend some time learning about their organizations and then create a vision of how things can change for the better. They think big rather than small, and they implement a new approach. Mike Walsh, a past outsider CEO, dramatically changed the way things were done at Tenneco and involved everyone in the change effort, from the heads of Tenneco's six divisions to workers in Tenneco's factories and mills.

Another way that outsider CEOs transform their troubled companies is by intellectually stimulating the key players in the organization. The conventional approach advocated by those in management circles is for an outsider CEO to replace existing top managers in the company with his or her "own people." But successful outsiders realize that there are skilled and valuable managers in the companies they join, and they are able to identify these managers quickly. The successful outsider shares with these key managers his or her views of the problems facing the company and his or her vision for the future. Rather than resisting change, the managers often become the messengers of change and help spread the outsider's vision throughout the company. Finally, as outlined in transformational leadership theory, a successful outsider CEO often engages in developmental consideration with an organization's managers and actively works to develop good relationships with them.[64]

LEADER MOOD

Megan Kelly and Rachel Feinstein are two bank tellers working for a medium-size bank in New York City. They work different hours and have different supervisors but are close friends and frequently compare notes about their jobs and supervisors. Kelly recently complained to Feinstein that her boss Bob Griffith always seems so down. Even when everything is going smoothly on his shift, he rarely smiles and often looks as though the world is coming to an end. Although Griffith treats all the tellers on his shift fairly and is a capable supervisor, Kelly decides to try to switch to Feinstein's shift.

Part of the reason Kelly requested a transfer to Feinstein's shift was some of the things that Feinstein told her about her boss, Santiago Ramirez. He almost always is in a good mood, and it is nice to be around him. He frequently jokes with the tellers, and smiles and laughs are as common on his shift as they are rare on Griffith's.

Kelly's experience with her grouchy supervisor and your own intuition probably suggest that subordinates prefer to work for leaders who are in good moods rather than for those who are not. Likewise, you might expect that subordinates might even work harder when their leaders are happy and enthusiastic. Surprisingly, little research has been conducted on the effects that leader mood has on subordinates. Some preliminary research, however, suggests that leader mood may be an important factor to consider in trying to understand why some leaders are more effective than others.

One recent study explored the effects of positive leader mood in a retail setting. The leaders were store managers of branch stores belonging to a national chain. The researchers found that the managers who were in positive moods at work had stores that provided better customer service and had lower turnover rates than did the stores whose managers were not in positive moods. Although more research is needed, this initial study suggests that leader mood may be an important determinant of leader effectiveness.[65]

GENDER AND LEADERSHIP

One common stereotype in organizations is that women are supportive, nurturing, and generally good at managing interpersonal relations. The male counterpart to the stereotype of the relationship-oriented woman is the notion that men are directive and focus on getting the job done—in other words, that men tend to be task-oriented. Judging from these stereotypes, you might expect that gender would have an effect on leadership and that, for example, female leaders engage in more consideration behaviors than men do and male leaders engage in more initiating-structure behaviors than women do.

Researchers have investigated this question, and one recent review of the literature conducted by well-respected researcher Alice Eagly and a colleague suggests that when men and women have leadership positions in organizations, they tend to behave in a similar manner. Men do not engage in more initiating structure nor do women engage in more consideration.[66]

One difference did emerge in the ways that men and women lead their subordinates, however. Women tended to lead in a more democratic style, and men tended to lead in a more autocratic style.[67] When leaders are democratic, they tend to involve their subordinates in decision making and seek their subordinates' input on a variety of matters. Autocratic leaders tend to discourage subordinate participation in decision making and like to do things their own way. In terms of the Vroom and Yetton model, these results suggest that within a feasible set of decision styles for any given decision, women would be more likely to use one of the more participative styles and men would be more likely to use one of the more autocratic styles.

Why are women more democratic than men when they occupy leadership positions in organizations? Researchers have offered two potential explanations.[68] One is that women's interpersonal skills (expertise in interacting with and relating to other people) tend to be better than men's. In order to be democratic or participative, a leader needs to have good interpersonal skills. To encourage subordinates to express their opinions, for example, it is important for a leader to understand how subordinates feel. To reject subordinates' ideas or proposed solutions to problems while maintaining good relationships with subordinates, a leader needs to be sensitive to subordinates' feelings. Women may be more democratic as leaders than men simply because they are more skilled interpersonally.

The other potential explanation for the finding that women leaders tend to be more democratic than men is that women in leadership positions encounter more resistance from subordinates than do men in leadership positions. (Consistent with this reasoning is the tendency that people have to evaluate female leaders a bit more harshly than they evaluate male leaders.)[69] Gender stereotypes (see Chapter 4) may lead members of an organization to readily accept men in leadership positions but to resist women taking on these same roles. For example, a 55-year-old male executive in an engineering firm who has always had a male supervisor throughout his professional career may resist having to report to a woman. His female supervisor, recognizing his resistance and resentment, might try to overcome it by involving the subordinate in decision making and seeking his input on a variety of matters. Given that women are assuming more and more leadership positions in organizations, it is important to understand whether and why women might somehow be different from men when it comes to leadership.

TO MANAGERS

New Topics in Leadership Research

- Let your subordinates know how important the work they do is for their work groups and for the organization as a whole.
- Convey to your subordinates that it is important for them to grow and develop on the job and to feel that they are accomplishing something.
- Show your subordinates that you are concerned about them, and give them the opportunity to learn new things and acquire new skills.
- Have your own vision of how good things could be in the groups you manage and in your whole organization, and convey your vision to your subordinates.
- Be enthusiastic and excited about your vision.
- Discuss with your subordinates problems you are facing, and show them how these problems can be solved if everyone works to achieve your vision.
- Use managers who are especially good at involving subordinates in decision making to help other managers who have trouble being participative improve their interpersonal skills.

Recap of Leadership Approaches

In this chapter we have described several approaches to understanding effective leadership in organizations. These leadership approaches are complementary: Each sheds light on a different aspect of, or set of issues pertaining to, effective leadership. These approaches are recapped in Table 12.5.

TABLE 12.5

Approaches to Understanding Effective Leadership

Approach	Focus
Trait approach	Specific traits that contribute to effective leadership
Behavior approach	Specific behaviors that effective leaders engage in
Fiedler's contingency model	Characteristics of situations in which different kinds of leaders (relationship-oriented and task-oriented) are most effective
Path-goal theory	How effective leaders motivate their followers
Vroom and Yetton model	When leaders should involve their subordinates in decision making
Leader-member exchange theory	The kinds of personal relationships that leaders develop with followers
Substitutes and neutralizers	When leadership is unnecessary and when a leader is prevented from having influence
Transformational and charismatic leadership	How leaders make profound changes in their followers and organizations
Leader mood	How leaders' feelings influence their effectiveness
Gender and leadership	Similarities and differences in men and women as leaders

SUMMARY

Leaders at all levels in an organization help individuals, groups, and the organization as a whole achieve their goals and can thus have profound effects in organizations. The approaches to leadership covered in this chapter help explain how leaders influence their followers and why leaders are sometimes effective and sometimes ineffective. In this chapter, we made the following major points:

1. Leadership is the exercise of influence by one member of a group or organization over other members to help the group or organization

achieve its goals. Formal leaders have formal authority to influence others by virtue of their job responsibilities. Informal leaders lack formal authority but influence others by virtue of their special skills or talents.

2. The trait approach to leadership has found that good leaders tend to be intelligent, dominant, self-confident, energetic, able to withstand stress, honest, mature, and knowledgeable. Possessing these traits, however, does not guarantee that a leader will be effective, nor does the failure to have one or more of these traits mean that a leader will be ineffective.

3. A lot of the behaviors that leaders engage in fall into two main categories: consideration and initiating structure. Consideration includes all leadership behaviors that indicate that leaders trust, respect, and value a good relationship with their followers. Initiating structure includes all the behaviors that leaders engage in to help subordinates achieve their goals and perform at a high level. Leaders also engage in rewarding and punishing behaviors.

4. Fiedler's contingency theory proposes that leader effectiveness depends on both leader style and situational characteristics. Leaders have either a relationship-oriented style or a task-oriented style. Situational characteristics, including leader-member relations, task structure, and position power, determine how favorable a situation is for leading. Relationship-oriented leaders are most effective in moderately favorable situations. Task-oriented leaders are most effective in extremely favorable or unfavorable situations. Leaders cannot easily change their style, so Fiedler recommends changing situations to fit the leader or assigning leaders to situations in which they will be most effective.

5. Path-goal theory suggests that effective leaders motivate their followers by giving them outcomes they desire when they perform at a high level or achieve their work goals. Effective leaders also make sure their subordinates believe that they can obtain their work goals and perform at a high level, show subordinates the paths to goal attainment, remove obstacles that might come up along the way, and express confidence in their subordinates' capabilities. Leaders need to adjust the type of behavior they engage in (directive, supportive, participative, or achievement-oriented) to correspond to the nature of the subordinates they are dealing with and the type of work they are doing.

6. The Vroom and Yetton model specifies the extent to which leaders should have their subordinates participate in decision making. How much subordinates should participate depends on aspects of the decision that needs to be made, the subordinates involved, and the information needed to make a good decision.

7. Leader-member exchange theory focuses on the leader-follower dyad and suggests that leaders do not treat each of their followers the same but rather develop different kinds of relationships with different subordinates. Some leader-follower dyads have high-quality relationships. Subordinates in these dyads are members of the in-group. Other leader-follower dyads have low-quality relationships. Subordinates in these dyads form the out-group.

8. Sometimes leadership does not seem to have much of an effect in organizations because of the existence of substitutes and neutralizers. A leadership substitute is something that acts in place of a formal leader. Substitutes make leadership unnecessary because they take the place of the influence of a leader. A leadership neutralizer is something that prevents a leader from having influence and negates a leader's efforts. When neutralizers are present, there is a leadership void—the leader is having little or no effect, and nothing else is taking the leader's place.

9. Transformational leaders increase their followers' awareness of the importance of their jobs and the followers' own needs for personal growth and accomplishment and motivate followers to work for the good of the organization. Leaders transform their followers by being charismatic, intellectually stimulating their followers, and engaging in developmental consideration. Transactional leadership occurs when leaders motivate their subordinates by exchanging rewards for high performance and reprimanding instances of low performance.

10. Leader mood at work has the potential to influence leader effectiveness. Preliminary research suggests that when leaders tend to be in a good mood at work, their subordinates may perform at a higher level and be less likely to resign.

11. Women and men do not appear to differ in the leadership behaviors (consideration and initiating structure) that they perform in organizations. Women, however, appear to be more democratic or participative than men as leaders.

Organizational Behavior in Action

TOPICS FOR DISCUSSION AND ACTION

1. In what ways are the trait and behavior approaches to leadership similar?
2. Under what circumstances might leader punishing behavior be appropriate?
3. Are Fiedler's contingency model and the trait approach consistent with one another or inconsistent? Explain.
4. How might a relationship-oriented leader who manages a restaurant and is in a very unfavorable situation for leading improve the favorability of the situation so that it becomes moderately favorable?
5. In what kinds of situations might it be especially important for a leader to focus on motivating subordinates (as outlined in path-goal theory)?
6. What might be some of the consequences of a leader having a relatively small in-group and a large out-group of subordinates?
7. Can organizations create substitutes for leadership to cut down on the number of managers they need to employ? Why or why not?
8. When might having a charismatic leader be dysfunctional for an organization?
9. Do organizations always need transformational leaders, or are they needed only some of the time? Explain.
10. Are men and women equally likely to be transformational leaders? Why or why not?

BUILDING DIAGNOSTIC SKILLS

Contemporary Leaders

Choose a public figure with whom you are familiar (you personally know the individual, you have read about the person in magazines and newspapers, or you have seen him or her on TV) who is in a leadership position. Pick someone other people in your class are likely to know. The person could be a leader in politics or government (at the national, state, or local level), a leader in your community, or a leader at the college or university you attend. For the leader you have selected, answer the following questions:

1. What traits does this leader appear to possess?
2. What behaviors does this leader engage in?
3. Is this leader relationship-oriented or task-oriented? How favorable is the leadership situation according to Fiedler's contingency model?
4. How does this leader try to motivate his or her followers?
5. To what extent does this leader allow his or her followers to participate in decision making?
6. Do any substitutes or neutralizers exist with regard to this leader? What are they?
7. Is this a transformational leader? Why or why not?
8. Does this leader engage in transactional leadership?

RESEARCH ON THE INTERNET: A MANAGER'S TOOL

Specific Task

The Coca-Cola Company is a very successful organization which has benefited from effective leadership. Scan Coca-Cola's website (www.cocacola.com) to learn more about this company. Then click on the CocaCola logo and bottle, then on "About the Coca-Cola Company," and then on "To Share Owners."

1. What goals and initiatives is Chairman of the Board Roberto C. Goizueta pursuing for Coca-Cola?
2. How would you describe his leadership approach?

Specific Task

Many organizations undertake initiatives to develop their employees so that they will one day be ready to assume leadership positions within the organization. Find the website of such a company. What steps is this company taking to ensure that its employees receive the training and development they need to assume leadership positions? What qualities does this organization appear to value in its leaders?

TOPICS FOR DEBATE

Leaders can have powerful effects on their subordinates and their organizations as a whole. Now that you have a good understanding of leadership, debate the following issues.

Debate One

Team A. Managers can be trained to be effective leaders.

Team B. Managers either have what it takes to be an effective leader or they don't. If they don't, they cannot be trained to be effective leaders.

Debate Two

Team A. Transactional leadership is more important than transformational leadership for an organization's success.

Team B. Transformational leadership is more important than transactional leadership for an organization's success.

EXPERIENTIAL EXERCISE

Effectively Leading a Work Group

Objective
Your objective is to gain experience in effectively leading a group of workers who have varying levels of ability and motivation.

Procedure
Assume the role of Maria Cuellar, who has just been promoted to the position of supervisor of a group of four workers who create designs for wallpaper. The group's goal is to create creative and best-selling wallpaper designs. Cuellar is excited about assuming her first real leadership position but also apprehensive. As a former member of this group, she has had ample opportunity to observe some of her new subordinates' (and former group members') on-the-job behaviors.

Each person brings different strengths and weaknesses to his or her job. Ralph Katten can turn out highly creative (and occasionally) best-selling designs if he tries. But often he does not try; he seems to daydream a lot and not take his work seriously. Elisa Martinez is a hard worker who does an acceptable job; her designs are not particularly noteworthy but are not bad either. Karen Parker is new to the group and is still learning the ins and outs of wallpaper design. Tracy McGuire is an above-average performer; her designs are good, and she turns out a fair number of them.

1. Using the knowledge you have gained from this chapter (for example, about the behavior approach, path-goal theory, and leader-member exchange theory), describe the steps Maria Cuellar should take to effectively lead this group of wallpaper designers. Should she use the same approach with each of her subordinates, or should her leadership approach differ depending on the subordinate involved?
2. The class divides into groups of from three to five people, and each group appoints one member as spokesperson, to present the group's recommendations to the whole class.
3. Group members take turns describing the steps Cuellar should take to be an effective leader.
4. Group members compare and contrast the different leadership approaches that Cuellar might take and assess their advantages and disadvantages.
5. Group members decide what advice to give Maria Cuellar to help her be an effective leader of the four designers.

When the group has completed those activities, the spokesperson will present the group's recommendations to the whole class.

MAKING THE CONNECTION

Find an example of a leader who has recently had dramatic effects on the performance of his or her work group or organization. Describe the leader and his or her behavior. Is this leader transformational? Why or why not?

CLOSING CASE

Lou Gerstner Turns Around "Big Blue"

IBM (also known as "Big Blue") racked up losses of $2.9 billion in 1991 and $5 billion in 1992. At its height, IBM stock had reached $125 a share, but by early 1993 it was selling at less than $46 a share, its lowest price in seventeen years. Thus it came as little surprise when CEO John Akers announced in January 1993 that he would step down. Akers had been blamed for Big Blue's slowness to react to changes in the marketplace, such as the decline in demand for mainframe computers, and for his inability to move the company forward. With his departure the business community was abuzz with rumors about who would be chosen to lead the troubled giant.

In March 1993, IBM announced that Lou Gerstner, a man with no experience at IBM or in the computer industry, had agreed to become CEO of the troubled company. Could Gerstner change Big Blue's fortunes?

Gerstner has an undergraduate degree in engineering from Dartmouth College and an MBA from Harvard Business School. By the time he was 31, he was the youngest partner at the consulting firm of McKinsey & Co., and he quickly proceeded to assume a variety of leadership positions in companies that became top performers in their industries. When Gerstner was president of American Express from 1985 to 1989, that company's net income increased by 66 percent. During his tenure as CEO of RJR Nabisco from 1989 to 1993, he reduced Nabisco's debt from $26 billion to $14 billion while encouraging new product development.

Gerstner has been described as a hands-on, detail-oriented leader who likes to get involved in the day-to-day operations of the companies he leads. He is highly performance oriented, likes to make tough decisions, tends to be impatient, and can be a difficult person to work for. Top managers at IBM receive regular phone calls from Gerstner not only at work but also at home in the evening and on weekends as he works to keep track of the performance of their units. Gerstner makes decisions quickly and follows through on them. A self-confident and generally even-tempered person, he also attends to the human side of being a leader and works on fostering good relationships with the managers who report to him. Gerstner loves to go to work (he reportedly told his wife one Sunday, "I really can't wait to get to the office tomorrow"), but he also likes to play golf, work in his garden, and read.[70]

Several months into his job as IBM CEO, Gerstner made some dramatic changes at Big Blue by working from sixteen to eighteen hours a day, six days a week. Among other things, he established task forces to identify opportunities for new products and markets, moved to cut IBM's labor force and production costs, changed the organization's structure, and even changed how executives were paid. He also took the time to get to know IBM employees and their perspectives by having meals with rank-and-file workers (*without* their bosses being present) and by holding "townhall" meetings.[71] These meetings have been key to Gerstner's efforts to change IBM's traditional ways of doing things. As he suggests, "It's not something you do by writing memos. You've got to appeal to people's emotions. They've got to buy in with their hearts and their bellies, not just their minds."[72]

Gerstner has continued to cut costs, change direction, and refocus IBM's activities while bringing IBM's various units in closer contact with each other and encouraging their managers to work together.[73] His efforts have paid off in dramatically turning around the fortunes of IBM. IBM's 1997 earnings were $6.1 billion, in sharp contrast to the losses this company experienced when Gerstner first took over and its stock price has more than doubled.[74] Gerstner recently announced that he would carry on in his position as CEO of IBM for at least another five years. He thinks IBM's turnaround is only about half complete and more remains to be done.[75] No doubt, IBM will be in good hands under Gerstner's continued leadership.

Questions for Discussion

1. Why was Lou Gerstner, a man with no experience in the computer industry, chosen to lead IBM?
2. How would you characterize Gerstner's leadership approach?

Communication

13

OPENING CASE

Encouraging Good Communication at The Brownstein Group

Advertising and public relations executive Marc Brownstein used to be a big player in the New York advertising scene, representing important clients such as Hallmark Cards and American Express. However, in 1989 he decided to return to his native city, Philadelphia, and assume the position of

president of the small ad agency his father Berny (pictured here) had founded, The Brownstein Group (www .brownsteingroup .com). Months later, Marc Brownstein was confident that he had made the right decision and was leading the agency effectively because The Brownstein Group's revenues were up, it was gaining clients, and it was developing increased industry recognition.[1] Seeking to further enhance his leadership skills in order to build his agency, Brownstein decided to enroll in a short executive development course. One of his assignments for the course was to have his managers complete an anonymous questionnaire rating his job performance as president of the agency.[2]

Although the course lasted only for a couple of days, the feedback Brownstein received from the questionnaire his managers completed has had a lasting impact not only on Brownstein but on the whole agency. Brownstein was shocked to learn that his managers did not think that he was an effective leader. While they thought that he meant well, managers complained about a breakdown in communication at the agency. Managers claimed that Brownstein failed to keep them informed about important matters such as how the agency was doing and who were its new clients, and often failed to provide his managers with feedback about their own performance. Also, they claimed that Brownstein didn't seem to consider his subordinates' preferences when handing out assignments and that he was generally a poor listener. For example, when managers met with him in his office, he would often interrupt them several times to take phone calls.[3]

Despite his agency's success, Brownstein realized that he had to make some major changes quickly or he would lose some talented employees. At the time his employees completed the questionnaires, turnover at the small agency was already surprisingly high although he hadn't known why. Now, Brownstein realized that the high turnover was at least partially the result of poor communication with his subordinates, so he decided to change his communication style.

First, he decided to schedule regular meetings with all the agency's staff to open up lines of communication. Any topic was fair game for these meetings, and Brownstein would answer questions as well as inform his staff about important issues and concerns such as the agency's client base. Moreover, Brownstein made a point of really listening to his managers during these meetings, focusing his attention solely on what the person he was talking to was saying and putting phone calls on hold. As a result of these basic changes, communication has improved at The Brownstein Group to the point that various committees and groups are suggesting important changes to the ways that things are done at Brownstein, such as changes in the way the agency manages its clients and in the company's benefits plan.[4] Now that lines of communication are opening up, Brownstein knows what is really going on his employees' minds.

The lesson that Brownstein and other managers need to learn is that not only do they need to regularly communicate important information throughout their organizations, but they also need to listen to what their subordinates have to say because the feedback they receive from their employees is potentially as important as the feedback they give to them.

Overview

Communication is one of the most important processes that take place in organizations; it has major effects on individual, group, and organizational performance.[5] High-performing organizations such as Microsoft and Coca-Cola have mastered the communication process. As a result, members of the organization have the information they need when they need it to achieve their goals. In contrast, the poor performance of other organizations such as IBM in the early 1990's can be attributed in part to communication problems within the organization. Faulty communication among top managers and between top managers and workers lower in the hierarchy (for example, those in sales) prevented IBM's top managers from realizing that they needed to change IBM's focus to deemphasize the manufacturing and marketing of mainframe computers in order for the company to remain competitive. In the opening case, The Brownstein Group was at risk for losing valuable employees due to poor communication.

An organization's effectiveness hinges on good communication, and so too does the effectiveness of groups and individuals inside the organization. Groups are able to achieve their goals and perform at a high level only when group members communicate with each other and with other organizational members and groups as needed. Similarly, individual learning, motivation, and job satisfaction hinge on good communication. Even when individuals have the ability and motivation to perform at a high level, for example, communication problems can prevent them from being effective. A highly capable and motivated sales representative for a textbook publisher may fail to meet her sales goal because the publisher's editorial and marketing staffs did not properly communicate the best features of the books to be sold.

Given the significant influence that communication has on individual, group, and organizational effectiveness, this chapter focuses on the nature of communication in organizations. We define communication, outline its implications for understanding and managing organizational behavior, and describe the functions that communication serves in organizations. We provide a model of the communication process and discuss communication problems and ways to avoid them. We explore one of the key components of the communication process, the communication medium, in depth. We also examine patterns of communication that are prevalent in organizations. By the end of this chapter, you will have a good understanding of effective communication in organizations.

What Is Communication?

One of the defining features of communication is the *sharing of information with other people.*[6] An accountant for Price Waterhouse communicates with his boss when he tells him how a large auditing project is going, when he asks to take his vacation at the beginning of June, and when he requests that his boss purchase a new computer software package to help in the preparation of complicated income tax forms. A member of a self-managed work team at Rockwell Corporation, which manufactures parts for the Hellfire missiles that were used in the Gulf War, communicates when she tells another member of her team that there is a serious defect in one of the parts the team has just completed and when she suggests that another team member is letting product quality slip and thus imperiling the armed service members who are the missile's ultimate users.

The simple sharing of information is not enough for communication to take place, however. The second defining feature of communication is the *reaching of a common understanding.*[7] The sharing of information does not accomplish much in organizations unless people concur on what this information means. For example, when the accountant at Price Waterhouse tells his supervisor that he has run into some problems on the large auditing project and completing the project might take more time than was originally allocated, the supervisor might assume that the audit is a relatively standard one that is just a bit more complicated and time consuming than most others. The problems the accountant has unearthed, however, pertain to questionable (and perhaps illegal) activities that he suspects the top-management team was trying to hide from the auditor. In this situation, communication has not taken place because the supervisor does not understand the magnitude of the problems the auditor is referring to. A common understanding has not been reached. This lack of a common understanding reduces the effectiveness of both the auditor and the supervisor. The auditor does not receive the supervisor's advice and help in handling this tricky situation, and the supervisor is not performing an important role responsibility—namely, close involvement in unusual or especially difficult auditing projects.

Communication, then, is the sharing of information between two or more individuals or groups to reach a common understanding. Reaching a common understanding does *not* mean that people have to agree with each other. What it does mean is that people must have a relatively accurate idea of what a person or group is trying to tell them.

Communication is good or effective when members of an organization share information with each other and all parties involved are relatively clear about what this information means. Communication is ineffective when people either do not receive the information they need or are not quite sure what the information they do receive means. When a CEO screams at a top manager that he is an idiot, the CEO may be trying to convey that he is disappointed with the performance of the manager's division, worried about its future, and concerned that the manager has not done everything possible to help turn things around. Having been screamed at, however, the manager leaves the room thinking that his boss is unreasonable, unbalanced, and impossible to work for. The boss's use of the word *idiot* conveyed nothing of the boss's real concerns about the division and its performance. To the manager, being called an "idiot" meant only that his boss lost his temper and was dumping on him. In this case, communication is ineffective because the communicators reached no common understanding about performance of the manager's division, its future, and the steps that should have been or should now be taken to improve its performance.

Although most people assume that they will be communicating with others who speak the same language that they do, the increasingly interconnected nature of the global economy often results in people communicating with others whose first language is different from their own. In some situations, people believe they have a right to speak in their native tongue, as indicated in Insight 13.1.

Communication
The sharing of information between two or more individuals or groups to reach a common understanding.

Insight 13.1

A Global View

European Union Grapples With Multiple Languages

A forerunner of the European Union (EU) was established to normalize relations between France and Germany after World War II and to foster close economic ties between those and other European countries.

Although there have been lively discussion and debate during the drafting of EU laws to govern economic and political relations among member nations, one unexpected source of contention is the language that EU officials and delegates should use for communicating orally with each other and for law writing.

Germany is the leading economic power in the EU, and German is the single most widely spoken language among EU countries. French and English, however, are the languages that delegates use to discuss issues and draft laws. German chancellor Helmut Kohl is disappointed that German is rarely heard and that EU documents are written in French and English and are translated into German rather than being written in German in the first place. Why isn't German used instead of French or English? Representatives to the EU from non-German-speaking countries such as Greece, Portugal, Italy, and Spain usually can speak French or English but not German. Nevertheless, German delegates have been told by the German government to speak German at certain formal EU meetings and speaking engagements.

Being able to speak their native language at EU meetings has become a matter of pride to EU delegates from other countries as well. After German delegates Martin Bangemann and Peter Schmidhuber began to speak in German at formal EU meetings, the Italian delegates decided that they were going to speak in Italian at the meetings. Delegates from other countries followed suit, greatly increasing problems in communicating with each other.

From the start, it had been agreed that delegates to the EU would be able to speak in their native tongues at certain meetings. However, with more and more countries joining the EU, each of which has its own language, maintaining effective communication is becoming difficult. With 132 language combinations to be handled (translating documents from Portuguese to Finnish, Greek to Norwegian, Italian to Norwegian, and so on) and over three hundred translators translating EU discussions and documents, the urge to select one common language in which to conduct EU business is increasing.[8]

As the experience of the European Union illustrates, it is sometimes a luxury to be able to communicate in your native language to others who speak and understand it. Because Americans generally speak fewer languages than do citizens in other countries, Americans need to be sensitive to the fact that they are fortunate to be able to speak English as much as they do when communicating with people from other countries.

The Functions of Communication

Effective communication is important in organizations because it impacts practically every aspect of organizational behavior. For example, members of an organization come to understand each other's personalities, attitudes, and values (discussed in Chapters 2 and 3) only when they communicate effectively with each other. Likewise, workers are motivated to perform at a high level when someone communicates clearly what is expected and the consequences of performing at a high level and when someone expresses confidence in their ability to perform (Chapters 5–8). Finally, groups can work efficiently and effectively to accomplish their goals and leaders can influence their followers (Chapters 10–12) only when effective communication takes place.

When organizations experience problems such as unmotivated workers or excessively high turnover, poor communication is often partially to blame. A secretary may have low motivation to develop new bookkeeping skills or to take on the additional responsibility of planning conferences because he thinks he is in a dead-end job. If no one has bothered to communicate to him that secretaries do have opportunities to advance in the company, then the individual, the group of which he is a member, and the organization as a whole are deprived of the benefits a highly motivated worker can bring. Similarly, an organization that announces that it has been acquired by another company may see its turnover rate triple even though no layoffs and few internal changes will result from the change in ownership. The reason for the exodus is likely to be vague statements by upper management—statements that do little to quell workers' fears about what is going to happen to their jobs. Expecting the worst, the best performers (who have the most opportunities available to them elsewhere) decide to quit.

Good communication prevents many problems like these and serves several important functions in organizations: providing knowledge, motivating organizational members, controlling and coordinating individual efforts, and expressing feelings and emotions (see Table 13.1).

PROVIDING KNOWLEDGE

A basic function of communication is to provide knowledge to members of an organization so that they can perform their jobs effectively and achieve their goals.[9] By providing knowledge about, for example, ways to perform tasks and about decisions that have been made, an organization makes sure that members have the information they need to perform at a high level. In the opening case, Marc Brownstein realized that he needed to provide his subordinates with knowledge about the ad agency's ongoing performance and client base.

Although the knowledge function of communication is most apparent when a worker has just started a new job, it is often equally important for sea-

TABLE 13.1

Functions of Communication

Providing knowledge about company goals, how to perform a job, standards for acceptable behavior, needed changes, and so on

Motivating organizational members—for example, by determining valences, raising expectancies and instrumentalities, assigning specific and difficult goals, and giving feedback

Controlling and coordinating individual efforts—for example, by reducing social loafing, communicating roles, rules, and norms, and avoiding duplication of effort

Expressing feelings and emotions such as positive and negative moods, excitement, and anger

soned veterans. As you learned in Chapter 10, individuals starting a new job face considerable uncertainty about what they are supposed to do, how they should go about doing it, and what the standards for acceptable behavior are in the organization. Communication from coworkers, supervisors, customers, clients, and others helps to reduce this uncertainty and provides newcomers with the knowledge they need to perform their jobs effectively.

Communication is essential for the socialization of newcomers at all levels in an organization. When Stanley Gault and Mike Walsh took over as CEOs of Goodyear and Tenneco (respectively) in the early 1990s, for example, each of them spent the first couple of weeks on the job communicating with as many workers as they could to learn about the troubled companies they were hired to help turn around.[10] Walsh instituted a series of "town hall" meetings and traveled around the United States talking to employees at all levels about Tenneco's problems.

The knowledge function also is important for even the most experienced members of an organization because things change. Just as the products or services an organization provides change in response to changes in customers' desires, so does the nature of a worker's job responsibilities. Clear communication of new tasks, goals, responsibilities, and policies helps to ensure that members of an organization will continue to understand what needs to be done to achieve organizational goals.

MOTIVATING ORGANIZATIONAL MEMBERS

As you learned in Chapters 6, 7, and 8, motivation is a key determinant of performance in organizations, and communication plays a central role in motivating members of an organization to achieve their goals. Expectancy theory (see Chapter 6) proposes, for example, that managers need to do the following:

- Determine what outcomes subordinates are trying to obtain from their jobs—that is, determine the valences of various outcomes.
- Make sure that workers perceive that obtaining these outcomes is contingent on performing at a high level—that is, make sure that instrumentalities are high.
- Make sure that workers believe that they can perform at a high level—that is, make sure that expectancies are high.

The only way that a manager can determine the valences of different outcomes for any given worker is by communicating with (talking *and* listening to) that worker to find out what outcomes the worker desires. Likewise, managers need to communicate to workers that they are capable of performing at a high level and that they will receive the outcomes they desire if they do so.

As another example of the role of communication in motivating workers, consider goal-setting theory (examined in Chapter 7). It suggests that workers will perform at a high level when they have specific and difficult goals and are given feedback concerning how they are doing. Managers use communication to let workers know what goals they should be striving for and how they are progressing in their efforts to achieve those goals. Recall from the opening case how managers in The Brownstein Group complained that Marc Brownstein failed to provide them with feedback on their performance.

CONTROLLING AND COORDINATING INDIVIDUAL EFFORTS

As you learned in Chapters 10 and 11, it is essential for groups and organizations to control their members' behaviors so that they perform their jobs in an acceptable fashion. Recall, for example, that a key challenge for self-managed work teams and other kinds of work groups is to reduce social loafing, the tendency of people to exert less effort when working in groups than when working on their own. When a member of a group engages in social loafing, one of the primary ways that other members of the group can reduce it is by communicating to the loafer that his or her behavior has been observed and is not going to be tolerated. Groups and organizations exert control over their members by regularly communicating information about roles, rules, and norms to them.

In addition to controlling members' behavior, groups and organizations also need to coordinate the efforts of their individual members. In Chapter 11, we discussed how members of a group and organization are often interdependent, so that the work performed by some members affects what others do. As the interdependence between group members increases, the need for communication to coordinate their efforts in order to achieve group goals also increases.[11] Communication also helps to eliminate duplication of effort and to prevent one poorly performing member from keeping other members from achieving group goals.

EXPRESSING FEELINGS AND EMOTIONS

One of the most important functions of communication is to allow people to express their feelings and emotions.[12] These feelings and emotions can be general or specific and can originate from inside or outside the workplace.

Recall from Chapter 3 that *work moods* are the feelings people experience on a day-to-day basis as they perform their jobs. Often, individuals and groups can better achieve their goals if they can communicate their moods to others. The moods workers experience on the job influence their perceptions and evaluations of people and situations as well as their behavior.[13]

Ortho Biotech, a biopharmaceutical company with a diverse work force, is well known for the time and effort it expends communicating to its employees so that they buy into its central vision and work to achieve organizational goals.

TO MANAGERS

For example, when the manager of an electronics store snapped at a subordinate who was proposing an innovative way to increase customer traffic through the store and thus increase sales, the hurt look on the subordinate's face made the manager realize that such impatience was out of line. The manager decided to communicate his feelings to the subordinate, and he frankly told him that he was in a lousy mood and that they should wait until the next day to discuss what sounded like a promising proposal. This simple communication of feelings helped to prevent a minor incident from turning into a major problem.

Emotions such as excitement or anger are often stirred by specific events at work or at home, and it is often useful for individuals to communicate their emotions to others in an organization. A worker who has just learned that she has received a major promotion may be so elated that she can't think straight enough to have an in-depth discussion with her supervisor about finding and training her successor. Simply communicating this fact to the supervisor and postponing the conversation for a while is the sensible thing to do. Similarly, as you learned in Chapter 9, a worker who is upset and angry about his spouse's terminal illness may feel a little bit better when he communicates his emotions to others and receives their social support.[14] Moreover, supervisors, coworkers, and subordinates will be more understanding of the worker's lack of enthusiasm or recent tendency to be overly critical when they realize the tremendous strain he is under.

Communication of moods and emotions helps organizational members understand each other, and when people understand each other, they are better able to work together to perform well and achieve their goals.

The Communication Process

Effective communication involves a number of distinct steps.[15] Workers and managers who are aware of these steps can ensure that communication provides knowledge, motivates organizational members, controls and coordinates their efforts, and expresses feelings and emotions. These steps and

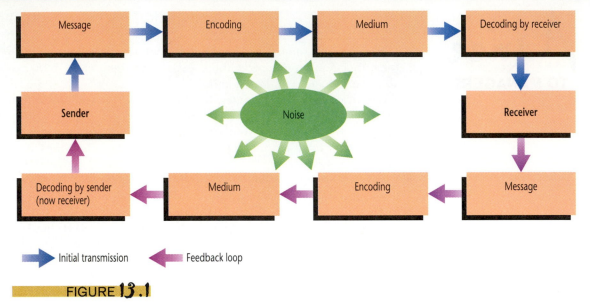

Message	→ Encoding	→ Medium	→ Decoding by receiver

Noise

Initial transmission ← Feedback loop

FIGURE **13.1**

The Communication Process

their interrelationships are indicated in the model of the communication process presented in Fig. 13.1 and are described below. Although the model is cyclical, the sender initiates the process, so we start by discussing the sender and the message.

THE SENDER AND THE MESSAGE

The **sender** is the individual, group, or organization that needs or wants to share information with some other individual, group, or organization in order to accomplish one or more of the four functions of communication described above. The **receiver** is the individual, group, or organization for which the information is intended. For example, a supervisor may wish to send information to a subordinate about his or her performance, a task force on diversity may need to communicate to top management its assessment of barriers to the promotion of minorities into management positions, or an organization may need to communicate to the Environmental Protection Agency the actions it has taken to comply with new waste disposal regulations.

The **message** is the information that the sender needs or wants to share with other people. Effective communication depends on messages that are as clear and complete as possible. Clarity is important regardless of the content of the message—that is, whether it is performance feedback to an individual worker, task-force findings and conclusions, or an organization's response to new government regulations. A message is *clear* when it contains information that is easily interpreted or understood. A message is *complete* when it contains all the information necessary to achieve a common understanding between the sender and the receiver. Sometimes, problems in the communication process crop up because the sender is vague or unsure about what the message should be. A supervisor, for example, might give vague feedback to a subordinate about performance on a recent assignment because the supervisor gave too little thought to how the subordinate actually performed or how performance could improve in the future.

 Sender
The individual, group, or organization that needs or wants to share information with some other individual, group, or organization.

Receiver
The individual, group, or organization for which information is intended.

 Message
The information that a sender needs or wants to share with other people.

Chevron CEO John Derr understands the importance of sending clear, complete messages, and when he needs to communicate with his work force, he often personally addresses them, individually or in groups, to avoid any misunderstandings that may arise.

Encoding
Translating a message into symbols or language that a receiver can understand.

ENCODING

Once the sender has decided what the message is, the next step in the process is **encoding**—translating the message into symbols or language that the receiver can understand. A supervisor who puts ideas about how a subordinate is performing and ways that performance can be improved into words, a task force that summarizes the results of its investigations and weekly meetings into words and statistics such as the number of African Americans and women in top-management positions, and a member of an organization who shows a government inspector the organization's waste disposal operations—all of these are examples of the encoding of messages.

Although encoding ideas by putting them into words seems simple enough, some organizations are finding that their employees lack the basic writing and oral communication skills needed to do this and are taking action to improve encoding. First Bank Systems Inc. in Minneapolis, Minnesota, for example, helps workers ranging from clerks to managers improve their grammar through skills-upgrading classes. Smith Corona Corporation, located in New Canaan, Connecticut, trains workers in how to answer telephone calls.[16]

For communication to be effective, the sender must translate the message into a form that the receiver can understand. When ideas are translated into words, for example, the sender must take care to use words that the receiver understands. Have you ever listened to a computer expert explain the workings of a new software package using terminology that meant nothing to you? This failed attempt at communication probably added to your confusion instead of providing you with the knowledge you needed. A visit to a doctor can also be an exercise in frustration if the doctor describes your problem and its treatment in words that you can't understand.

In both of those examples, a breakdown in communication occurs because of the use of **jargon**, specialized terminology or language that members of a profession, occupation, or other group develop to aid communication among

Jargon
Specialized terminology or language that members of a group develop to aid communication among themselves.

themselves. Computer experts have their own jargon, as do physicians, lawyers, and members of practically every other occupation or profession. Jargon facilitates communication within an occupation because it simplifies encoding. Rather than having to describe a complex array of symptoms and their likely causes, a nurse can use a single medical term such as *gastroenteritis,* and other health care providers will know the ailment the nurse is referring to.

Jargon becomes a problem only when the receiver of a jargon-laden message is outside the sender's profession or occupational group (just as a patient is not part of the group of health care providers that includes doctors, nurses, and lab technicians). Messages encoded with jargon can lead to *effective* communication when senders and receivers are members of the same occupation or profession. When receivers are outside the occupation or profession, the use of jargon leads to *ineffective* communication.

Although jargon is often used to simplify encoding, it sometimes is a source of humor in the workplace, as illustrated in Insight 13.2. Virtually all occupations and professions and sometimes even companies have their own jargon.

Insight 13.2

Communication

Send the Double Header to the Bates Motel, the Redhead Needs a Toxic Clean-up, and Run Some Lab Rats Please

The title of this Insight uses jargon from three professions. According to jargon expert John Davis, among psychiatrists a "double header" is a schizophrenic, and "the Bates motel" is a mental hospital. To some day care workers a "redhead" is a child with measles, and a "toxic clean-up" is a diaper change. "Lab rats" are focus groups, small groups of consumers that advertising agencies bring together to determine how consumers are likely to react to new products and advertising campaigns.[17]

Parents may be dismayed to learn that they are referred to as "meddlers" who engage in "ambushes" (unscheduled visits) of their children's day care centers only to find their child with a "deathgrip" (stuffed animal). Company executives may be surprised that their ad agencies use "liars for hire" (advertising copy writers) to promote the company's "cancer cures" (new products).[18]

Just as workers at day care centers and advertising agencies have their own jargon, the employees of a particular company often develop their own jargon. At Adolph Coors Company, newly developed beers are called "the liquid." At Microsoft, a worker's knowledge and ability are referred to as his or her "bandwidth." At Wal-Mart, training the employees of newly acquired companies to smile and offer extra customer service is known as being "Wal-Martized." Intel Corporation executives "Intellize" new businesses they are trying to get into, such as telecommunications.[19]

Medium
The pathway through which an encoded message is transmitted to a receiver.

Verbal communication
The sharing of information by means of words, either spoken or written.

THE MEDIUM

Once a message is encoded, it is transmitted to the receiver through some medium. The **medium** is the pathway through which an encoded message is transmitted to a receiver (*media* is the plural form). **Verbal communication** is the sharing of information by means of words, either spoken or written. For messages that are encoded into words, the media can include face-to-face oral communication, oral communication over the telephone, and written communication through the use of memos, letters, and reports that may be electronically transmitted through electronic mail or fax machines.

Each medium of verbal communication has advantages and disadvantages. Although there are no clear-cut rules about when to use one rather than another, there are two guidelines for selecting a medium.

One guideline is to select a medium that the receiver monitors—a medium that the receiver pays attention to. People differ in their preferences for communication media. Lou Gerstner, CEO of IBM, prefers to use oral face-to-face communication. Ron Shaich, president of the Boston-based fast-food chain Au Bon Pain, likes to see things in writing. The most effective communication with people such as Shaich entails written memos, reports, and letters.[20] A sender who ignores receivers' individual preferences for media is asking for trouble. A receiver may not realize the importance of your message because you deliver it in a casual conversation over lunch rather than in a formal report. Or a receiver who prefers oral communication and is inundated with memos and letters may toss your letter into the trash without reading it.

The other guideline to follow in selecting a medium is to try to select one that is appropriate to the message you are trying to convey and to use multiple media when necessary. Common sense suggests that if you are communicating a personal and important message to an individual (such as information about being fired, being promoted, receiving a raise, or being transferred to another unit), oral communication is called for, preferably face to face. Alternatively, if the message you are trying to communicate is involved and complex, such as a proposal to open a new factory in Singapore, written communication is appropriate. If the message is important, you might want to back up the written communication with oral communication as well.

Nonverbal communication
The sharing of information by means of facial expressions, body language, and mode of dress.

Words are not the only way people communicate. **Nonverbal communication** is the sharing of information by means of facial expressions (smiles and grimaces), body language (posture and gestures), and even mode of dress (elegant business attire versus jeans and a T-shirt).[21] The boss's look of disgust when you tell him the recent sales promotion you designed was a flop, your coworker slamming his door in your face after a recent argument, or the uniform worn by a police officer standing next to your illegally parked car all transmit encoded messages to you. Many organizations have informal dress days to communicate that workers and managers are partners and should trust one another (see the closing case).

Often, when people do not feel comfortable about expressing part of a message verbally, they express it nonverbally. In general, because people tend to have less control over their nonverbal than over their verbal communication, their facial expressions or body language give them away when they wish to withhold some information. A sender who compliments someone he dislikes but fails to look the receiver in the eye, for example, is not concealing his insincerity.

Nonverbal communication also can be useful for communicating support, acceptance, and a sense of camaraderie. Researchers have long noted the value of hugs as a form of communication. Hugs help reduce stress, raise self-confidence, and make people feel connected with those around them. Studies of newborns, the elderly, and children in orphanages have shown that touch is necessary for psychological well-being. Sometimes a good hug at the right time can express powerful feelings and emotions. This was the case when retiring Supreme Court justice William Brennan greeted his successor David Souter after Souter's confirmation hearings. According to Souter, "He hugged me and he hugged me, and he went on hugging me for a very, very long time."[22]

We have covered just some of the issues involved in selecting a communication medium. Given the importance of choosing the right medium and the difficulty of making the right choice, we focus on additional aspects of this step in the communication process later in this chapter, in the sections on information richness and the impact of technological advances on organizational communication.

THE RECEIVER: DECODING AND THE FEEDBACK LOOP

Just as senders have to translate their ideas or messages into a form that can be sent to the receiver, receivers have to make sense of the messages they receive. **Decoding** is interpreting or trying to make sense of a sender's message. For messages that are relatively clear-cut, such as information about a raise or about a specific goal, decoding can be straightforward. Some messages, however, are ambiguous. For example, what caused your boss's look of disgust when you told him your sales promotion was a flop? Was the look due to his displeasure with your performance or his concern over the dwindling sales of the product involved? Or was it just the result of one more piece of bad news that day? During decoding, the receiver tries to determine which interpretation of the message, of all the possible interpretations, is accurate.

When messages are ambiguous, the receiver may have difficulty with decoding or may think that the message means something other than what the sender intended. When messages are ambiguous, the likelihood increases that the receivers' own beliefs, attitudes, values, moods, perceptual biases, and so on will influence decoding.

You may be tempted to think that communication is largely complete once decoding has taken place. As indicated in Fig. 13.1, however, only about half of the communication process has occurred up to this point—the initial transmission half. Recall that communication is the sharing of information to reach a common understanding. Up until and including the point at which the receiver decodes the message, the communication process has largely been concerned with the sharing of information. Members of an organization know they have reached a common understanding and have communicated effectively by completing the feedback loop, the second half of the process illustrated in Fig. 13.1.

After decoding the message, the receiver has to respond to it and start the feedback loop. The receiver must first decide what message to pass on to the original sender. Sometimes the receiver's message is as simple as "I got your memo and agree that we need to meet to discuss this issue." At other times the receiver may provide, in a long and detailed message, the information that the

Decoding
Interpreting or trying to make sense of a sender's message.

sender requested. Or the receiver's response might be that he or she did not understand the message.

Once the receiver decides on a response, he or she *encodes* the message and transmits it, using a *medium* that the original sender monitors. The original sender *decodes* the response. If the original sender is confident that the receiver properly interpreted the initial message and a common understanding has been reached, the communication process is complete. However, if during decoding the original sender realizes that the receiver did not properly interpret or decode the message, the whole communication process needs to continue until both parties are confident that they have reached a common understanding.

The feedback loop in the communication process can be just as important as the initial transmission of the message because it confirms that the message has been received and properly understood. Thus effective communicators do whatever they can to make sure they receive feedback. For example, an advertising executive hoping to convince an automobile company to use her firm to promote a new car may send a detailed proposal to the manager in the automobile company who will make the decision. In the letter accompanying the proposal, the advertising executive makes sure she will receive feedback by telling the manager that she will be calling him in two or three weeks to answer any questions he has. During the phone conversation, the advertising executive makes sure that the manager has understood the key components of the proposal.

BARRIERS TO EFFECTIVE COMMUNICATION AND WAYS TO IMPROVE COMMUNICATION

 Noise

Anything that interferes with the communication process.

Noise is anything that interferes with the communication process. Noise can include the use of jargon, poor handwriting, a broken answering machine, a heavy workload that prevents a receiver from reading a written report, a receiver's bad mood resulting in the misinterpretation of a message, or the operation of perceptual biases (see Chapter 4). One of the key challenges for managers is to eliminate as much noise as possible. In the opening case, Marc Brownstein eliminated noise when he stopped taking phone calls while meeting with his subordinates.

Noise is a general term, but there are specific communication problems that result in ineffective communication. Here we examine five important potential communication problems in organizations and ways to overcome them so that individuals, groups, and organizations can communicate effectively and thus better achieve their goals: filtering and information distortion, poor listening, lack of or inappropriate feedback, rumors, and cross-cultural differences in linguistic styles.

 Filtering

A sender's withholding part of a message because the sender thinks the receiver does not need or will not want to receive the information.

Filtering and Information Distortion and Ways to Avoid Them. **Filtering** occurs when senders withhold part of a message because they think the receiver does not need the information or will not want to receive it. Nobody wants to be the bearer of bad news, and subordinates are particularly loath to pass negative information on to their bosses. However, if subordinates withhold negative information or filter it out of their messages, a supervisor may not even be aware of a problem until it's almost too late to resolve it and what was once a minor problem that could have been easily fixed looms as a potential disaster. Supervisors also sometimes filter information in their communications with subordinates. As a result, subordinates may have more negative attitudes, be less effective, or experience more stress. Sometimes when an organization is making major changes, such as downsizing, supervisors fail to give their subordinates information about the changes, and the result is high levels of stress as subordinates become uncertain about their future with the organization.

The magnitude of the filtering problem is underscored by the fact that subordinates are sometimes reluctant to convey negative information to their superiors even in crisis situations. For example, National Aeronautics and Space Administration (NASA) scientists who analyze commercial airline crashes have found that junior crew members are often afraid to transmit important information to the plane's captain. A tragic example of this problem is the Air Florida plane that crashed into a bridge over the Potomac River after taking off from National Airport in Washington, D.C., in 1982. Federal Aviation Administration (FAA) investigators determined that the crash resulted in part from the copilot's failure to tell the pilot about problems with engine power readings that were caused by ice on the engine sensors. As a result of this and other instances of poor communication and filtering, the FAA now has mandatory assertiveness and sensitivity training for airline crew members to make sure that they communicate effectively and do not engage in filtering.[23]

Information distortion
The change in meaning that occurs when a message travels through a series of different senders to a receiver.

Related to the problem of filtering is **information distortion,** the change in meaning that occurs when a message travels through a series of different senders to a receiver. Experiments (and the children's game "Telephone") have shown, for example, that a message that starts at one end of a chain of people is likely to become something quite different by the time it reaches the last receiver at the other end of the chain. In addition, senders may deliberately alter or distort a message to serve their own interests—to make themselves look good or to advance their own individual or group goals at the expense of the organization's goals.

Filtering and information distortion can be avoided by establishing trust in an organization. One aspect of trust is not blaming the sender for bad news. When subordinates trust their supervisors, supervisors trust their subordinates, and coworkers trust each other, and when all members of an organization are confident that they will not be blamed for problems that they are not responsible for, filtering and distortion are less likely to take place.

Poor Listening and Improving Listening Skills.   Many people enjoy hearing themselves talk more than they enjoy listening to others. Not surprisingly, poor listening is responsible for many communication problems in organizations. Consistent with this observation are findings from a recent study that suggests that managers think the voice mail they send is more important than the voice mail they receive and that senders generally think their messages are more important, urgent, and helpful than do the receivers.[24] In addition, people sometimes listen only to the part of a message they want to hear.

Members of an organization can do several things to become better listeners or receivers of messages. As Marc Brownstein learned in the opening case, being a good listener entails giving a sender your undivided attention, looking him or her in the eye, and not interrupting. Rather than thinking about what they are going to say next, good listeners focus on trying to understand what they are hearing and how the sender feels about it. Being a good listener also means asking questions and rephrasing key points to make sure you understand their meaning, avoiding distracting the sender (for example, by glancing at the clock or tapping a pencil), and accepting what the sender is telling you even if it is not what you want to hear. It is especially important for supervisors to be good listeners when communicating with their subordinates and thereby counter the natural tendency to pay more attention to information that comes from one's superiors rather than from one's subordinates. The FAA's mandatory sensitivity training for airline crews, for example, may help pilots become better listeners.

Lack of or Inappropriate Feedback and Developing Good Feedback Skills. Sometimes communication breaks down because receivers either fail to provide feedback (as was true in the opening case) or provide feedback in an inappropriate manner. This barrier to effective communication is especially likely to occur when feedback is negative, for giving negative feedback makes people feel uncomfortable. A manager at a bank, for example, may be reluctant to let one of her subordinates know that a loan application on which the subordinate worked closely with a customer is going to be turned down. The manager may avoid bringing up the issue, thus putting the subordinate in the embarrassing position of first hearing the bad news from the unhappy customer. By developing good feedback skills, managers and workers at all levels in an organization will be more likely to respond in an appropriate manner to messages they receive, whether positive or negative.

Good feedback concentrates on the message being responded to, not on the sender's personality, attitudes, capabilities, or more general performance levels. Good feedback is specific and focuses on things the sender controls. In providing feedback, the receiver should try to put himself or herself in the original sender's shoes, understand how the sender feels, and relay feedback in a manner that will convey the right message while not unnecessarily hurting the sender's feelings.

Rumor
Unofficial information on topics that are important or interesting to an organization's members.

Rumors and How to Overcome Them. A **rumor** is unofficial information on topics that are important or interesting to an organization's members. Rumors usually spread quickly and uncontrollably and, once started, are often hard to stop. Rumors are especially likely to spread when members of an organization are not informed about matters that have the potential to affect them personally, such as a takeover attempt by another company, an impending layoff, or a scandal involving a top manager. Rumors on sensational topics help relieve the everyday boredom of organizational life. Such rumors often entail gossip about the personal lives and habits of members of the organization.

How can companies try to halt the spread of inaccurate and sometimes damaging rumors as well as provide workers with up-to-date, accurate information on issues that are important to them? One way is through the use of company television systems, as indicated in Insight 13.3.

Insight 13.3

Communication

Company TVs and Rumor Control

In the past, workers often complained that they were the last to know about important events in their organizations. Top managers also complained that unfounded rumors were rampant, especially when the organization was undergoing major changes or experiencing some kind of crisis.

To avoid these problems and send accurate information to employees so that they are the first rather than the last to learn about things that will affect them, more and more companies are using their own internal TV systems. For example, in October 1992 Ford Motor Company (www.ford.com) made an announcement that came as a surprise to many outsiders: Alexander J. Trotman would be assuming the position of chairman of the board. Ford employees, however, got the news before the press did by watching some 2,300 TVs located in Ford factories and offices. These TVs are part of Ford's internal TV system, which allows virtually all employees to see and hear the same live programs simultaneously. According to the Atlanta consulting firm KJH Communications, over ninety companies have similar kinds of systems. They are used to control rumors, to communicate accurate information to large numbers of employees, and to aid in emergencies.[25]

Similarly, after Lou Gerstner took over as CEO of IBM, he appeared on IBM's internal TV system eight times during his first nine months on the job to ease workers' fears and doubts about the future of their organization. When heavy fog in Memphis, Tennessee, halted delivery of thousands of Federal Express's (www.fedex.com) overnight packages and letters, the company used its internal TV system to keep workers informed and instruct them on what to do. Federal Express also uses its TV system to communicate accurate information and halt the spread of unfounded rumors, such as those that sprang up when the company stopped making deliveries between European countries and laid off 4,000 European workers. American workers learned of these changes on Federal Express's TV system and were reassured that their own jobs were secure. The European workers who were actually let go were informed of the layoff face to face.[26]

Grapevine
A set of informal communication pathways through which unofficial information flows.

Rumors are often spread through the **grapevine,** a set of informal communication pathways through which unofficial information flows in an organization.[27] In any group, department, or division of an organization, some individuals seem to know everything about everyone and everything and pass along large quantities of unofficial information to others. Rumors spread through the grapevine can be about such topics as the private or work lives of key organizational members, the organization itself, or the future of the organization and its members. Although rumors that are spread through the grapevine are often inaccurate, sometimes information transmitted through the grapevine *is* accurate. For example, Mike O'Connell, a marketing manager in an airline company, told one of his coworkers over lunch that he was quitting his job, had given his supervisor two weeks' advance notice, and would be joining British Airways in London. By the end of the same work day, everyone in O'Connell's department knew of his plans even though O'Connell hadn't mentioned them to anyone else (nor had his supervisor).

Cross-Cultural Differences and Understanding Linguistic Styles.   When people from different cultures interact, communication difficulties sometime arise because of differences in linguistic styles. **Linguistic style** is a person's characteristic way of speaking, including tone of voice, volume, speed, use of pauses, directness or indirectness, choice of words, use of questions and jokes, and taking credit for ideas.[28] Within cultures, linguistic styles can vary between, for example, different regions of a country or between men and women. Cross-culturally, differences in linguistic style are often much greater and have the potential to lead to many misunderstandings in cross-cultural communications.

For example, in Japan, workers tend to communicate more formally and be more deferential toward their bosses than they do in the United States. Japanese don't mind lengthy pauses in a conversation while they are thinking about something that was brought up; Americans often find lengthy pauses in conversations uncomfortable and feel the need to fill in the pauses by talking. Americans are more likely to take individual credit for ideas and accomplishments in conversations, whereas Japan's more group-oriented culture makes individual credit-taking less likely.[29] These cross-cultural differences can result in many communication difficulties. For instance, U.S. workers' tendencies to take credit for their ideas and accomplishments may cause Japanese workers to think they are being boastful when this is not the case. Lengthy pauses on the part of Japanese communicators may cause U.S. communicators to feel that the Japanese aren't interested in the discussion, while U.S. communicators' tendencies to fill these pauses may cause the Japanese to think the U.S. communicators are being pushy and not giving them a chance to think.

Cultures also differ in terms of the physical distance between speakers and listeners deemed appropriate for conversations at work.[30] For example, Brazil and Saudi Arabia favor closer physical distances than the United States. Americans may feel uncomfortable when Brazilians stand "too" close to them during a conversation, while Brazilians may be wondering why Americans keep backing up and seem so standoffish.

Cross-cultural communication difficulties such as these can be overcome by understanding cross-cultural differences in linguistic styles. When interacting with people from a different culture, members of an organization should try to learn as much as possible about the linguistic style of that culture. Expatriate managers who have lived in the country in question can often be a good source of information about linguistic style because they have firsthand experience in interacting with members of the culture. Learning about more general cross-cultural differences (see Chapter 17) also is helpful because these more general differences are often linked to differences in linguistic styles.

> ◣ **Linguistic Style**
> A person's characteristic way of speaking.

TO MANAGERS

The Communication Process

- Make sure your message is clear in your own mind before you try to communicate it to others.
- Encode your message in a form that the receiver will understand. Use jargon only with members of your own profession or occupation.
- Determine which media the people you communicate with regularly prefer to use, and use those media when communicating with those people.
- Make sure the medium you use is monitored by the receiver and appropriate for your message. Use multiple media for messages that are both complex and important.
- When you communicate to others, make sure that there is a way for you to receive feedback.
- Encourage your subordinates to share bad news with you, and do not blame them for things beyond their control.
- Be a good listener, and train your subordinates to be the same.
- When interacting with people from other cultures, learn as much as you can about the linguistic styles of those cultures.

Selecting an Appropriate Communication Medium: Information Richness and New Information Technologies

That sharing information to reach a common understanding is often more difficult than it seems is evidenced by the communication difficulties experienced by many organizations, such as The Brownstein Group in the opening case. Choosing the right communication medium for any given message can help ensure that a message is received and properly understood, but selecting a medium involves tradeoffs for both the sender and the receiver. One way to examine these tradeoffs is by exploring the information richness of various media, their demands on the receiver's and the sender's time, and the paper trail they leave. In this section, we explore these issues and the implications of advances in information technology for communication in organizations.

INFORMATION RICHNESS

Information richness

The amount of information a medium of communication can carry and the extent to which it enables senders and receivers to reach a common understanding.

Communication media differ in their **information richness**—that is, the amount of information they can carry and the extent to which they enable senders and receivers to reach a common understanding.[31] Media that are high in information richness are capable of transmitting more information and are more likely to generate a common understanding than are media that are low in richness. The various media available to organizational members can be categorized into four general groups based on their information richness (see Fig. 13.2).[32]

Face-to-Face Communication. Face-to-face communication is the medium highest in information richness, for at least two reasons. The first is that it provides the receiver not only with a verbal message but also with a nonverbal message conveyed by the sender's body language and facial expressions. The nonverbal part of the communication provides receivers with additional information they can use in decoding the message. When Joan Schmitt, an en-

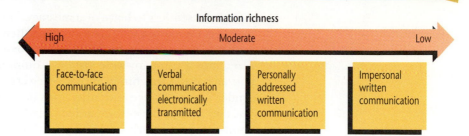

FIGURE 13.2

The Information Richness of
Communication Media

gineer for a construction firm, met with her supervisor Fred Johnston to discuss the plans for a Brazilian project the company was bidding on, Johnston got up from behind his desk to sit in a chair next to Schmitt's as she described her proposal. His action provided Schmitt with information: He respected her and wanted her to feel that they were on equal footing in their discussion of the bidding. Similarly, when Johnston mentioned that the newly hired and inexperienced son of the owner of the firm was to be a member of the team preparing the bid, his failure to look her in the eye and his pursed lips conveyed that he was not pleased with this situation.

The second reason face-to-face communication is highest in information richness is that it allows receivers to provide senders with instant feedback. Senders can clarify ambiguous information immediately, and the communication process can be cycled through as many times as needed until a common understanding is reached. At the engineering firm, Fred Johnston was quite familiar with the Brazilian clients for whom the bid was being prepared and thought it best that they be more involved in the bidding process than was normally the case. He suggested, for example, that the clients have more input into materials specifications and quality parameters than was usual. Joan Schmitt was taken aback by Johnston's suggestion. She wasn't sure why it was important and wasn't sure how to carry it out. After a twenty-minute discussion, however, Schmitt realized that what Johnston was suggesting was not unreasonable or difficult and made sense given the clients' desire to have more input into the details of the building's construction than was customary.

Verbal Communication Electronically Transmitted.   Verbal communication that is electronically transmitted over telephone lines is the communication medium next highest in information richness. Telephone conversations do not provide the receiver with nonverbal information from body language and facial expressions, but they still are a rich source of information. The receiver can hear the message, interpret the tone of voice in which it is delivered, hear clearly which parts of the message the sender emphasizes, and get a sense of the sender's general demeanor while communicating. Because this type of verbal communication is personally addressed to the receiver, the receiver is likely to pay attention to it. When Johnston was talking on the telephone with the Brazilian clients about the building they wanted, for example, he could sense their enthusiasm and was pleased that they sounded comfortable talking with him.

Telephone conversations also allow for instant feedback so misunderstandings can be cleared up quickly. Although not in common use because of its high cost, AT&T's video telephone allows callers to see on a screen the person they are talking to. That image adds to the information richness of this medium.

Also in this category of electronic verbal media is communication using voice mail and answering machines. Voice mail is a communication system that allows senders to leave oral messages for receivers who can retrieve these messages even when they are away from their offices. Answering machines are similar to voice mail in function but are based in individual offices, not organized into a company-wide system. Communication by means of voice mail and answering machines allows receivers to gather information from the sender's tone of voice and inflections in the sender's verbal communication, but they do not permit immediate feedback. Voice mail and answering machines are particularly useful media when receivers are frequently away from their offices (as is often the case for salespeople, building contractors, professors, and insurance agents). When using voice mail or answering machines to communicate with a receiver, the sender needs to make sure that the receiver monitors this medium by calling in frequently to receive messages.

Communication by means of company TV systems, which we discussed earlier, combines elements of verbal communication electronically transmitted with elements of face-to-face communication. This medium relies on electronic transmission of messages but, because of the presence of visual images, enables receivers to interpret facial expressions and body language. Communication over this medium, however, is not personally addressed to particular receivers, and as a result the audience may pay less attention to the message than the sender was hoping for.

Personally Addressed Written Communication.   Written communications (such as letters and memos) that are addressed personally to the receiver are next in information richness. Personally addressing the communication helps to ensure that the receiver will pay attention to it, and writing for one person allows the sender to write the message in such a way that the receiver is most likely to understand it. Feedback is not instantaneous, but this may not be always be a disadvantage. In some situations it is important for receivers to have time to reflect on a message and formulate a response.

Electronic mail (e-mail) is included in this category of media. Electronic mail allows people to communicate with each other through their personal computers. Senders transmit messages to receivers by typing the message on their personal computer and addressing it to the receiver's electronic address. For this form of personal communication to be effective, receivers have to check periodically to see whether they have any electronic messages. Though popular and increasing in usage in companies large and small, e-mail poses some difficult ethical issues for organizations and their members, as indicated in Insight 13.4.

Insight 13.4   **Ethics**

The Ethics of E-Mail

Few workers think their bosses have the right to eavesdrop on their telephone conversations, whether these conversations are work related or personal. Similarly, many workers who use e-mail as an alternative to phone conversations, especially when communicating with others who are hard to get hold of (for example, because they travel frequently), do not expect their bosses to read their messages. E-mail messages, however, can often be easily accessed by supervisors and other members of an organization, and many of them do not think it is unethical to read other people's e-mail without their knowledge.

Donn Parker, a computer security specialist who works for SRI International (www.sri.com) in Menlo Park, California, indicated that "A lot of our large international company clients, whether they need to or not, periodically actually do monitor some employees' e-mail at random just to maintain their right (to do so)."[33] Consistent with Parker's observations, a survey of Silicon Valley companies conducted by the *San Jose Mercury News* found that managers at a majority of the companies thought that they had the right to read their employees e-mail. Furthermore, monitoring of e-mail is sometimes done not for business reasons but out of curiosity, a desire for amusement, or boredom.

Some workers and managers think that reading other people's e-mail is unethical and violates their rights to privacy. Realizing the ethical questions raised by this activity, some organizations actually have policies against it. Some victims of e-mail eavesdropping have brought their cases to court, charging that their rights to privacy have been violated. In 1994 the California Supreme Court ruled that the need to safeguard rights to privacy outlined in the state's constitution applies not only to the government but also to business organizations and private individuals.[34] Some people believe that this ruling will help prevent the unwarranted reading of employees' e-mail because that action could be seen as a violation of rights to privacy protected by California's constitution. Given this ruling and increasing public concern, the ethics of e-mail is likely to be an issue that more and more organizations will need to grapple with in the coming years.

Impersonal Written Communication.   Lowest in information richness is written communication that is not addressed to a particular receiver. This form of communication is used when a sender needs to communicate with a large number of receivers simultaneously, such as when a company president wants to let all members of an organization know that rumors of an impending layoff are unfounded. Because this type of medium is impersonal, receiving feedback is unlikely. For this reason, it is especially important for the sender to use language that all receivers will be able to interpret correctly, so a common understanding can be reached.

This kind of medium is also useful when a large amount of information needs to be communicated, such as the monthly sales of a company's products by state, enrollment in a large state university by college and major, and the specifications and instructions for using a complicated printing press to print newspapers. When information is complicated (like the printing press instructions), some form of written communication is a necessity so that receivers can go back and review the information as needed.

The four categories of communication media were presented in order of decreasing information richness.[35] As in most attempts to classify things, however, there are exceptions to this categorization scheme, and some media do not fit neatly into one of the categories. Sometimes, for example, written communication can convey just as much (and perhaps more) information and have the same potential for creating a common understanding as verbal communication. Also, as you will see a little later in this section, some communication media (such as computers that can be used for electronically mediated group meetings) are not easily categorized into one of the four types.

TRADEOFFS IN THE CHOICE OF MEDIA

Because face-to-face communication is highest in information richness, should it always be used whenever possible? Although face-to-face communication is often the medium of choice (as evidenced by the fact that managers spend a lot of their time communicating in this way), it is not always necessary. The same information can sometimes be shared by using a medium lower in information richness. The primary reason for using a medium lower in information richness is that people must sometimes make tradeoffs between richness and other factors. One of the most significant tradeoffs is between *information richness* and the *amount of time* it takes to communicate the message by using the medium. Oral, face-to-face communication, for example, has high information richness but can be very time-consuming, so its richness has to be balanced against the time it consumes.

When messages are important (such as information about a new procedure for handling customer complaints) and the sender is not certain that a written message will be understood, then more often than not taking the time to communicate orally is worthwhile. When a message is clear-cut and sure to be understood (such as an announcement that a company will close at noon on the Friday before Memorial Day weekend), a written memo or letter may save everyone's time.

In assessments of the advantages and disadvantages of the various media for any message, another tradeoff that needs to be taken into account is the tradeoff between *information richness* and the *need for a paper trail*—that is, written documentation of a message. When messages are complicated and need to be referred to later (such as information about how to use a new piece of machinery), a paper trail is a clear advantage. At other times, written communication is advantageous not so much because the message is complex but because a sender may want proof at some time in the future that a message was sent. A patient who is denied medical insurance coverage for a particular procedure and appeals the insurance company's decision wants to be able to prove that the insurance company was notified of and approved the procedure.

As mentioned earlier, for messages that are important and complicated, senders should generally rely on multiple communication media to ensure that their messages are received and properly understood.

NEW INFORMATION TECHNOLOGIES

Recent advances in information technologies not only have given members of organizations new ways to communicate with each other but also have given them timely access to more information than ever before. New information technologies contribute primarily to the knowledge function of communication. Organizations, however, must be careful not to let their reliance on these technologies inadvertently lead them to shortchange other important functions. Motivation and expressing feelings and emotions, for example, might be difficult to accomplish solely through electronic communication.

Organizations also have to be careful not to overload their members with so much information that they spend more time reading electronic mail and bulletin boards than they do performing their jobs. Another significant danger of information overload is that receivers might overlook really important messages while attending to relatively unimportant ones.

In addition to providing greater information access, new technologies have made new communication options available to those within and outside organizations. In fact, advances in information technology may someday make traditional paper-based communication a thing of the past in certain kinds of situations, as illustrated in Insight 13.5.

Insight 13.5 — Communication

Moving Toward the Paperless Office

When Aetna Life & Casualty Company (www.aetna.com) recently gave 10,000 three-ring binders to schools throughout the United States, it signaled that it was moving one step closer to having paperless offices. Aetna no longer needs the binders because most of its training manuals, ratebooks, and other insurance documents (which used to be on paper) are now on computer. Aetna estimates that this change from paper to electronic communication results in annual cost savings of around $6 million due to, for example, the elimination of costly storage fees for extra manuals and binders (around $2,000 a month) and the 4.5 cents per page cost of updating and changing employees' manuals when procedures are altered (often involving millions of pages).

Nordstrom, Inc., the prestigious department store chain, is also saving money by relying less on paper and more on computers. Kurt Dahl, Nordstrom production services manager, estimates that his company has achieved annual savings of $1 million by changing from printed sales reports to sales reports that are available only on computer.

Managers indicate that replacing paper communication with electronic communication works best for internal documents such as memos, letters, manuals, and standard operating procedures. Communicating with people outside the organization—customers, clients, shareholders—is still most effective on paper. Schmitt Loewenberg, head of information services at Aetna, for example, indicates that written communication on paper is the medium of choice for sending customers claim checks and premium notices.[36] Although a totally paperless office may never be a reality, advances in information technology are helping companies eliminate many of the written documents on paper that clutter most workers' offices.

Computer Networks. Among the communication options made possible by new technology are worldwide computer networks. The Internet, for example, is a global system of 25,000 computer networks that provide approximately 20 million people with a vast array of information they can access through their personal computers and provide new ways of communicating with others in the system. The majority of these networks (or groupings of subscribers by, for example, company or profession) are owned by businesses, commercial research laboratories, and universities. The Internet is easy to join, is relatively inexpensive to use, and allows users to send messages to any computer with an address in the network. The Internet also provides its members with access to literally thousands of sources of information on a wide variety of topics ranging from Middle Eastern politics to chemical engineering and semiconductor manufacturing.[37]

Communication/information technology advances such as the Internet have dramatically altered the nature of communication in organizations like General Electric, IBM, J. P. Morgan, Merrill Lynch, Motorola, Schlumberger, and Xerox. Mort Meyerson, CEO of Perot Systems, for example, sends and receives over 7,000 Internet e-mail messages a month. In January 1994, workers at IBM used the Internet to send and receive over 580,000 messages outside the company. Researchers at the R&D division of General Electric send and receive approximately 5,000 electronic messages a day. Schlumberger (which provides services to the oil and gas industries and manufactures oil and gas meters) uses the Internet to exchange information across different units of the organization as well as to communicate with customers, suppliers, and university researchers. When IBM engineers work on new product development in collaboration with other companies, they often share information with one another through the Internet. Given the proprietary nature of such work, IBM goes to great lengths to secure these messages from unwanted intruders.[38]

Intranets
Company-wide computer networks.

Many organizations, using the same technology that the Internet is based on, have created their own company-wide computer networks, called **intranets,** to facilitate communication within the organization. Intranets can be accessed by all members of an organization and contain a wide variety of information ranging from directories, manuals, and product specifications to delivery schedules, minutes of meetings, and current financial performance. Organizations use intranets to efficiently communicate information to their members as well as to provide members with easy access to information that they need to perform their jobs when they need it. The growing numbers of companies using intranets to facilitate communication include Chevron, Goodyear, Levi Strauss, Pfizer, and USWest.[39]

Electronic Communication for Work Groups. Other advances in information technology allow members of a work group to communicate with each other, have electronically mediated meetings, and work together by sending and receiving messages to each other through their computers. Group members send messages to each other by typing them into their personal computers, and they receive messages by reading them on their computer screens. One advantage of this kind of electronic communication for work groups is that group members can be scattered around the globe and still meet and operate as a group. However, the use of electronic communication to motivate members of a work group, control and coordinate their individual efforts, and allow them to express their feelings appears to be inferior to traditional face-to-face communication and meetings.[40]

Personal, face-to-face communication is better than electronic communication for group meetings for several reasons:

1. Research has shown that groups that communicate electronically generally take longer to accomplish tasks (such as making a decision) than groups that meet face-to-face.[41]
2. In electronic group meetings, members lack many of the verbal and nonverbal cues (such as a raised voice, nodding of the head, and eye contact) that regulate group discussions and turn-taking.[42] Two or more participants in an electronic meeting, for example, might simultaneously transmit messages to the group by typing the messages into their computers. This situation may disrupt the flow of the discussion and overload other group members with information. In face-to-face group meetings, two or more members of a group rarely speak at the same time.
3. Electronic communication often causes group members to feel anonymous and depersonalized, two conditions that are not conducive to high motivation and the expression of feelings.

As a result of those (and other) factors, groups that communicate electronically do not tend to perform as highly as face-to-face groups, and group members are considerably less satisfied.[43]

Is face-to-face communication always preferable to electronic communication for work groups? Research shows that it is important to consider the *type of task* a group performs and the degree of *task interdependence* among group members. Recall from Chapter 11 that task interdependence is the extent to which the work performed by one member of a group affects what other group members do. In general, as the level of interdependence among group members increases, the advantages of face-to-face communication over electronic communication become more pronounced.[44]

However, for additive group tasks, in which the level of interdependence is low and the contributions of individual group members are summed to determine group performance, electronic communication has certain advantages. Members of a marketing group at a toy company who were trying to come up with a name for a new stuffed hippopotamus toy, for example, found that brainstorming electronically was a quick and effective way to generate many potential names. Each member of the group sat at his or her personal computer and typed in potential names for fifteen minutes. At the end of this time the group had over fifty different names to consider. One member of the group pointed out that a face-to-face brainstorming session probably would have taken longer because only one member could suggest a name at a time and individuals' brainstorming might have been limited by hearing others' suggested names.

Teleconferencing is a new form of electronic communication that can overcome some of the disadvantages of electronic group meetings while still allowing group members to communicate with each other when they are hundreds or thousands of miles apart. Group members who are using

Companies such as Ford, IBM, and Compaq make great use of global video teleconferencing to coordinate their marketing and research and development activities on a global basis. This communication mechanism saves countless hours of traveling time and is extremely cost effective for many purposes.

teleconferencing can actually see and talk to each other on television screens like those used on programs such as *Nightline* and the evening news. Teleconferencing is relatively high in information richness because group members can see each other face to face (on the television screens) while they communicate. The Japanese company Hitachi Limited, for example, uses teleconferencing to facilitate communication between its twenty-nine research laboratories in Japan. Scientists and engineers in the different laboratories are able to share knowledge and cooperate on joint research projects through teleconferencing. Teleconferencing is also a good choice of medium when members of a group or organization are located in different countries. Hewlett-Packard and IBM use teleconferencing when managers of their foreign and domestic divisions communicate.

Workers in countries such as the United States, Great Britain, Germany, and Japan may be inclined to take advances in information technology like voice and electronic mail and teleconferencing for granted because they are generally available. In other countries, however, options for communication media are vastly different. Consider the case of Russia. There are only twelve telephone lines per hundred people, 360,000 villages have no phone systems at all, and in many localities there are thirty-two-year waiting lists for new phone lines. Russia's international phone system can accommodate only 124 calls between Russia and the United States at one time. Communication between different units of the same company within Russia is also quite difficult. For example, when workers at the Ingersoll-Rand Company's Moscow office try to call the company's pneumatic-tool operations near Nishny Novgorod about 200 miles away, they often receive a constant busy signal and have to reserve a telephone call two and a half hours in advance. Russell D. Koxin, a manager at Conoco International Petroleum, which has facilities in northern Russia, worries that he will not be able to communicate with workers in case of an emergency.[45]

TO MANAGERS

Communication Networks in Organizations

Communication in an organization occurs in certain recurring patterns, regardless of the type of communication that takes place. The set of pathways through which information flows within a group or organization is called a **communication network.**

GROUP COMMUNICATION NETWORKS

As you learned in Chapters 10 and 11, self-managed work teams, top-management teams, and other work groups play an important role in most organizations. Among the communication networks that can develop in such groups are the wheel, the chain, the circle, and the all-channel network (see Fig. 13.3).

Wheel Network.   In a wheel network, most information travels through one central member of the group. This central member receives all messages from other group members and is the sole sender of messages to them. Essentially, all information flows to and from the central member, and the other members of the group do not communicate directly with each other.

Wheel networks are most common when there is *pooled task interdependence* among group members. Recall from Chapter 11 that when task interdependence is pooled, group members work independently and group performance is determined by summing up the performances of the members of the group. Examples of such groups are typing pools and groups of sales representatives covering different geographic regions. To perform tasks characterized by pooled interdependence, group members have little need to

> **Communication network**
> The set of pathways through which information flows within a group or organization.

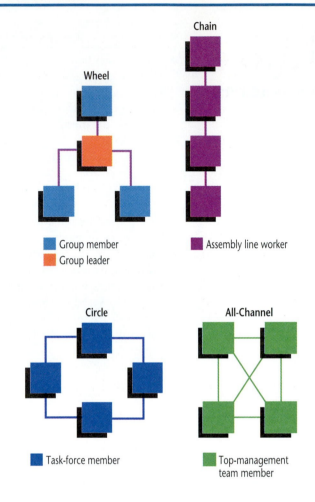

FIGURE **13.3**

Group Communication
Networks

communicate directly with each other; most communication flows to and from either the formal or the informal leader of the group. For these kinds of group tasks, the wheel is an effective communication pathway because it economizes on all members' time.

Chain Network.   In a chain network, communication flows in a predetermined sequence from one group member to the next. Group members at either end of the chain communicate only with the one group member next to them, but other group members communicate with individuals on either side of them in the chain. Chain networks are common when there is *sequential task interdependence*—members are required to perform specific behaviors in a predetermined order. Examples of such groups include all types of assembly-line work for which the finished product is the result of the sequential inputs of group members (see Chapter 11). While working on an assembly line, individuals are able to communicate only with others who are adjacent to them on the line.

Chain networks also characterize communication in some hierarchical groups. A small parking garage in New York City has a work group composed of four members: (1) the worker who parks the cars, (2) the worker who gives customers claim tickets and collects parking fees, (3) the worker who oversees management of the garage day in and day out, and (4) the manager of the organization that owns this garage and others throughout the city. The order in which we described the members of the group corresponds to their position in the group's hierarchy. The worker who parks the cars is lowest in the hierarchy and takes directives from the ticket taker. The ticket taker is next in the hierarchy and is supervised by the on-site manager, who in turn reports to the general manager. Communication in this group essentially goes up and down the hierarchy.

Circle Network.   The circle network occurs in groups whose members communicate with others who are adjacent to them—that is, members who are similar to them on some dimension ranging from experience, interests, or area of expertise to the location of their offices or where they sit when the group meets. On task forces and committees, communication sometimes flows between members who come from similar backgrounds. When groups sit at a round table, members tend to talk to those on either side of them. Workers tend to communicate with group members whose offices are located next to theirs.

All-Channel Network.   In an all-channel network, every group member communicates with every other group member. All-channel networks are prevalent when there is *reciprocal task interdependence*. Recall from Chapter 11 that when task interdependence is reciprocal, the activities of work-group members depend on one another—each group member's behaviors influence the behaviors of every other member of the group. Examples of groups that use an all-channel communication network because of the complex nature of the work they perform include high-tech research and development teams, top-management teams, emergency-room personnel, and the surgical team in an operating room in a hospital.

ORGANIZATIONAL COMMUNICATION NETWORKS

Organization charts that summarize the formal reporting relationships in an organization reflect one type of organizational communication network. Formal reporting relationships emerge from the chain of command established by an organization's hierarchy. The hierarchy determines which subordinates report to a given supervisor, whom that supervisor reports to, and so on, up and down the chain of command. A simple organization chart is provided in Fig. 13.4. When an organizational communication network is accurately described by an organization chart, communication flows up and down the hierarchy of the organization from superiors to subordinates and vice versa.

Newcomers to an organization may not see an organization chart until they have been on the job for several months. But when they see the chart, they are often surprised because the communication patterns that they have been observing bear little resemblance to the communication patterns specified by the chart. Lack of congruence between actual communication patterns and those specified in an organization chart is not uncommon. Communication in organizations often flows around issues, goals, projects, and problems rather than upward and downward from one formal reporting relationship to another. The roundabout flow ensures that members of the organization have access to the information they need to perform their jobs. Realizing this, some organizations have abandoned the organization chart altogether, as indicated in Insight 13.6.

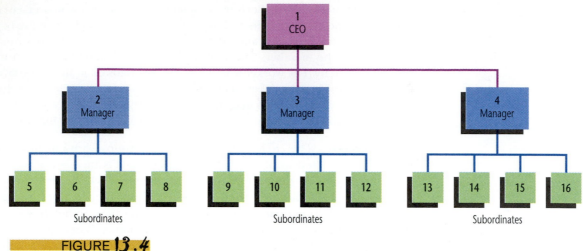

Subordinates   Subordinates   Subordinates

FIGURE 13.4

A Simple Organization Chart

Insight 13.6

Competitive Advantage

Emerson Electric Outlaws the Organization Chart

Emerson Electric (based in St. Louis, Missouri; www.emersonelectric
.com), a manufacturer of electrical products for both industrial and consumer use, has an impressive track record of high performance among
U.S. manufacturing firms. Emerson's earnings, earnings per share, and
dividends have increased from year to year for over a thirty-year period,
and the company has been ranked among the highest-performing companies in returns to investors.[46]

Charles E. Knight, CEO and chairman of the board, suggests that
one of the keys to Emerson's success and competitive advantage is good
communication. Good communication at Emerson means open communication when top managers like division presidents and plant managers meet regularly with rank-and-file workers to discuss issues and
problems such as what competitors are doing.

Communication does not just come from the top down at Emerson, however. Managers at all levels listen to subordinates and often
make changes based on their subordinates' ideas. Emerson strives to
have communication revolve around plans, projects, and problems
rather than around formal reporting relationships between managers
and subordinates. CEO Knight indicates that Emerson purposely does
not have an organization chart because an emphasis on formal reporting relationships hampers good, open communication and can para-
lyze organizations.[47]

When workers are informed about what's going on in a company and about current issues and problems, they are more likely to support needed changes in the ways that things are done. As an indicator of Emerson's commitment to good communication, Knight and other top managers claim that all Emerson employees can tell you what cost reduction initiative they are working on and who the competitors are for the products they work on; have met with management in the past six months; and understand where the profits and costs come from on the products they are working on.[48] Emerson's enviable performance for over thirty years suggests that good communication is worth striving for and a key contributor to gaining a competitive advantage.

Actual communication patterns in an organization may look more like the informal network shown in Fig. 13.5 than like the formal organization chart in Fig. 13.4. Although the relationships shown on an organization chart are somewhat stable, actual communication patterns, as in the network shown in Fig. 13.5, are likely to change as conditions in the organization change. Members of an organization develop new patterns of communication as the type of information they need changes.

Communication experts David Krackhardt and Jeffrey Hanson suggest that there are at least three informal communication networks in organizations: the advice network, the trust network, and the communication network.

FIGURE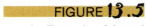

An Example of Actual
Communication Patterns
in an Organization

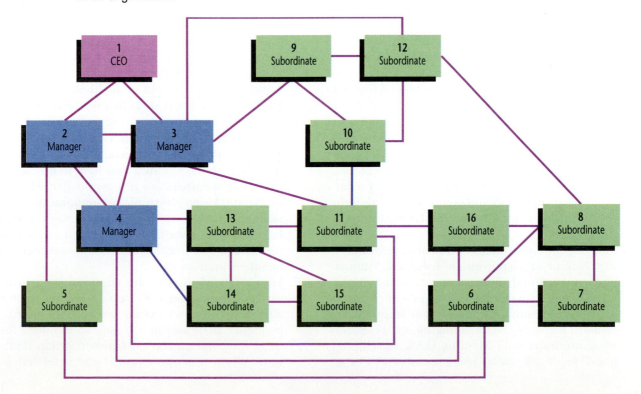

The *advice network* provides paths of communication for obtaining technical information such as which countries are the best locations for overseas low-cost manufacturing plants and for solving problems such as how to fix a complicated machine that breaks down. The *trust network* provides paths of communication for delicate information such as information pertaining to conflicts, disagreements, and power struggles, as well as the handling of potential and actual crisis situations such as a product recall. The *communication network* provides paths of communication that are used on a day-to-day basis for ordinary work-related matters such as a change in accounting procedures or the upcoming company picnic.[49]

SUMMARY

Communication is one of the most important processes that takes place in organizations. Effective communication allows individuals, groups, and organizations to achieve their goals and perform at a high level, and it affects virtually every aspect of organizational behavior. In this chapter, we made the following major points:

1. Communication is the sharing of information between two or more individuals or groups in an organization to reach a common understanding. Communication serves four major functions in organizations: providing knowledge, motivating organizational members, controlling and coordinating individual efforts, and expressing feelings and emotions.

2. The communication process entails a number of steps, including the sender's encoding of the message, selection of a medium, decoding of the message by the receiver, and completing the feedback loop. Jargon (specialized language used by members of a group) facilitates communication within the group and hinders communication outside the group.

3. Filtering and information distortion, poor listening, lack of or inappropriate feedback, rumors, and cross-cultural differences in linguistic styles can all lead to ineffective communication in organizations. Communication can be improved by establishing trust and encouraging open communication, improving listening skills, developing good feedback skills, using company TVs to spread accurate information, and understanding cross-cultural differences in linguistic styles.

4. Communication media vary in information richness (the amount of information they can carry and the potential they have for enabling senders and receivers to reach a common understanding). Face-to-face communication is the medium highest in information richness. It is followed by verbal communication electronically transmitted, personally addressed written communication, and impersonal written communication. Other factors that affect the selection of a medium include how much of the sender's and receiver's time it takes and whether it leaves a paper trail.

5. Advances in information technology, such as global computer networks like the Internet, generally tend to contribute most to the knowledge function of communication. Given the vast array of information currently available to organizational members, organizations have to be careful that their members are not overloaded with information. Using electronic communication to replace face-to-face communication in work groups has certain disadvantages that tend to increase as the level of task interdependence between group members increases.

6. Four types of work-group communication networks are the wheel, the chain, the circle, and the all-channel network. As the level of task interdependence increases in a group, so too does the need for communication between group members. When a group's task is characterized by

pooled interdependence, the wheel network is likely to be used. When a group's task is characterized by sequential interdependence, a chain network is likely to be used. When a group's task is characterized by reciprocal interdependence, an all-channel network is likely to be used. An organization's actual communication network is seldom accurately depicted in its formal organization chart. Networks change as communication needs change within the organization or group.

Organizational Behavior in Action

1. Why is reaching a common understanding a necessary condition for communication to have taken place?
2. Why are members of an organization sometimes reluctant to express their feelings and emotions?
3. Why is feedback a necessary component of the communication process?
4. What jargon have you encountered? How did it hamper or help your understanding of messages being communicated to you?
5. Is filtering always dysfunctional? Why or why not?
6. Why do almost all organizations have grapevines?
7. Why are some people annoyed by the increasing use of voice mail in many organizations (instead of having secretaries and assistants take messages for people who are away from their desks)?
8. Is using a medium that is high in information richness always desirable? Why or why not?
9. How have advances in technology changed the ways that you communicate with other people on a day-to-day basis?
10. Should organizations have organization charts? If not, why not? If so, what should they be used for?

Effective and Ineffective Communication

Think of two communication experiences you had in the last six months—one in which you felt that you communicated especially effectively with another individual or group (call it Communication Experience 1, or CE1) and one in which you felt that you had particularly poor communication with another individual or group (call it Communication Experience 2, or CE2). If you are working, try to pick experiences that occurred at work. Describe both experiences, and then answer these questions:

1. Which of the functions of communication were served in CE1 and CE2? Which of the functions of communication should have been served in CE2 but were not?
2. Which parts of the communication process worked especially well in CE1? Which parts of the communication process failed in CE2?
3. Was any jargon used in either CE1 or CE2? If not, why not? If so, did the use of jargon lead to effective or ineffective communication?
4. Did any filtering take place in CE1 or CE2? Why or why not?
5. Were rumors or the grapevine involved in CE1 or CE2?
6. Describe the information richness of the communication media that were involved in CE1 and CE2.
7. Did either CE1 or CE2 involve the use of any advances in information technology? If so, how did these advances aid or hinder good communication?

RESEARCH ON THE INTERNET: A MANAGER'S TOOL

Specific Task

Many organizations use the Internet to communicate important information to prospective employees about career opportunities. One such organization is Baker Hughes. Scan Baker Hughes' website (www.bakerhughes.com) to learn more about this company. Then click on "Baker Hughes Careers," and then on "Career Opportunities." After reading this material, click on the different areas on the menu at the left-hand side of the screen that you would be most interested in for a career.

1. What kinds of information does Baker Hughes communicate to prospective employees over the Internet?
2. Which kinds of positions at Baker Hughes would be most appealing to you personally?

General Task

Many organizations use the Internet to communicate important information to customers, prospective employees, and the general public about the organization's goals and culture. Find the website of such a company. What are this company's goals? How would you describe this company's culture? Do you think the company's home page effectively communicates this important information? Why or why not?

TOPICS FOR DEBATE

Good communication is central to the functioning and effectiveness of all organizations. Now that you have a good understanding of communication in organizations, debate the following issues.

Debate One

Team A. Technological advances in communication make it easier for members of an organization to communicate with each other and with people outside the organization.

Team B. Technological advances in communication make it more difficult for members of an organization to communicate with each other and with people outside the organization.

Debate Two

Team A. Communication networks in groups and organizations are deliberately created by members of the organization.

Team B. Communication networks in groups and organizations arise spontaneously.

EXPERIENTIAL EXERCISE

Troubling Communication

Objective

Your objective is to gain experience in communicating effectively in a troublesome situation.

Procedure

The class divides into groups of from three to five people, and each group appoints one member as spokesperson, to present the group's conclusions to the whole class. Here is the scenario.

One group member assumes the role of David Gimenez, the supervisor of a group of chemical engineers. Another group member assumes the role of Stuart Kippling, one of the chemical engineers. The remaining members of the group are observers. Once Gimenez and Kippling assume their roles, the observers take notes on the verbal and nonverbal communication they observe as well as instances of effective and ineffective communication between the two.

For the past several months, Kippling has been designing a prototype of a new waste control processing device. He has just discovered that his device does not conform to a new Environmental Protection Agency (EPA) regulation that will go into effect in one year. This is a major setback. Although some of the design work can be salvaged, at least several weeks of work will be lost. Gimenez and Kippling are meeting in Gimenez's office to discuss the problem, why it occurred, and how it can be avoided in the future. Gimenez's position is that extrapolating from recent EPA regulations, requirements, and deliberations, Kippling should have been able to anticipate EPA's most recent ruling and take it into account in his design work, or at least he should have drawn up a contingency plan in case such a ruling was put in effect. Kippling's position is that there is no way he could have known what EPA was going to do.

1. Gimenez and Kippling assume their roles. They are meeting to discuss the problem, why it occurred, and how it can be avoided in the future. Gimenez is to meet with his boss in fifteen minutes to discuss the problem, so he and Kippling have only fifteen minutes to come to some kind of resolution of this matter.
2. When Gimenez and Kippling's meeting is finished, the observers should discuss the verbal and nonverbal communication they observed as well as what was particularly effective and ineffective.
3. The entire group determines which instances of communication between Gimenez and Kippling were especially effective and why and which instances of communication were especially ineffective and why.

When the group has finished those activities, the spokesperson will present the group's conclusions to the whole class.

MAKING THE CONNECTION

Find an example of a company that has experienced communication problems. What communication problems has this company experienced? Why did these problems occur? What steps, if any, has the company taken to solve these problems?

CLOSING CASE

Good Communication Saves the Day at Georgia Power

In the late 1980s and early 1990s, Georgia Power (www.georgiapowerco.com), a utility company that provides electricity for 1.7 million customers in Georgia[50] and employs approximately 14,000 workers, was under intense pressure. Planned deregulation of utilities and rising competition were jeopardizing profits. The CEO and chairman of the board was retiring. A recent employee survey indicated that only 4 percent of the workforce knew the company's two major goals, increasing return on equity and lowering the cost of electricity. The Internal Revenue Service was auditing some of the utility's accounting practices, and questions had been raised about a corporate plane crash in which a former associate of the utility (along with the plane's two pilots) had been killed. Employees at all levels were confused about what was happening in the company, and rumors were running rampant about its future. Georgia Power seemed to have lost sight of its goals.[51]

Realizing the need to quickly salvage what appeared to be a sinking ship, new CEO Bill Dahlberg reasoned that good communication was needed not only to improve employee attitudes and knowledge of the utility's goals but also to share his vision of the company's future and ways to improve customer service. Dahlberg gave Georgia Power's nine-member communication department, whose annual budget was over $750,000, primary responsibility for spearheading the communications initiative to educate and motivate employees.

Leslie Lamkin and Emily Carmain, two of the managers in charge of the communications department, decided that a multimedia approach based on improving and expanding both written and oral communication inside Georgia Power was needed. Among the many changes they initiated in written communication were the updating and expanding of Georgia Power's weekly newsletter to employees to make it more attractive, easier to read, and more informative. Another initiative was to begin publishing the quarterly *Scoreboard* newsletter, which reported the company's current performance.

To improve oral communication, the communication managers introduced a tiered approach to convey the CEO's vision for the company and its goals of increasing profitability and lowering costs to employees at all levels in the organization. CEO Dahlberg met personally with his top-management team to instill his message. Those top managers then met with their subordinates—managers at the next level down in the hierarchy. During the meetings, the lower-level managers watched a video in which Dahlberg communicated his vision. After having points of confusion clarified and questions answered by their supervisors, these managers communicated company goals of raising profitability and lowering costs to their subordinates. In this way the message traveled down the hierarchy to first-level employees.

These efforts at improving communication in Georgia Power were successful in raising knowledge levels of the workforce. After the changes, 70 percent of the workforce knew the company's goals (as opposed to 4 percent). Workers' attitudes, however, were still negative. More had to be done.[52]

To improve attitudes, Dahlberg and the communications department undertook some additional initiatives. First, to build an atmosphere of trust and camaraderie, they instituted a monthly "jeans day" on which almost everyone in the company wears blue jeans. Second, they established the "Everybody Has a Customer" award so that rank-and-file employees could recognize each other's accomplishments and communicate appreciation of these efforts through an award and a certificate. Third, they instituted the policy that all employees would be invited to annual division meetings at which CEO Dahlberg speaks. Recent surveys suggest that these and other communication initiatives are helping to raise employees' knowledge of goals and to improve job satisfaction and other attitudes at Georgia Power.[53]

Questions for Discussion
1. Why did CEO Dahlberg think that good communication was so important for solving Georgia Power's problems?
2. What specific steps were taken at Georgia Power to improve communication?

Decision Making

14

Changing the Way Decisions Are Made at Boeing

The Boeing Company (www.boeing.com) is the global leader in airplane manufacturing; it has two thirds of the market share for large commercial planes and is also the biggest supplier of military aircraft. Furthermore, business couldn't be better. Commercial airline companies such as American Airlines and British Airways have increased their demand for new airplanes so much that Boeing has had to hire

over 35,000 additional workers in an attempt to double the number of planes it makes each year.[1]

Given that things seem to be going so well for Boeing, it seems strange that Boeing recently had to stop work on two of its key assembly lines for a month, an event that cost the company $1.6 billion due to lost production. Moreover, other production problems resulted in an approximate additional $1 billion charge against earnings.[2] The crux of Boeing's problem seems to be that the ways in which Boeing produces airplanes are inefficient and outdated.

Boeing's inefficient production process can at least partially be blamed on Boeing's policy of being responsive to customers. Boeing has traditionally offered its customers almost limitless choices in customizing the airplanes they order from Boeing; Boeing strives to produce an optimal plane for each customer depending on what the customer wants and specifies. Exteriors of planes, for example, can be painted to customer specifications, and Boeing offers over 100 shades of white paint, for starters. Many parts such as flashlights or clipboards can be located in different parts of the plane and ordered to fit different specifications. For example, on a 747, customers have a choice of whether or not to have air flow ducts in the rear cargo hold or compartment. They can have one duct, two ducts, or no ducts and have a choice of where the ducts are located. This customer choice in turn affects over 2,000 other parts that go into making a 747. Engineering has to modify the over 900 pages of drawings for this section of the plane by using a very complicated code. Purchasing and manufacturing then rely on these modified sketches to procure parts and plan how to put them together. Given their very complicated nature, more than a quarter of the modifications and codes engineering makes to the drawings have to be redone. This is only for one set of changes made to one part of a 747.[3]

Trying to optimally meet customers needs has resulted in a very cumbersome and unyielding manufacturing process, with hundreds of employees having to make multiple and complicated decisions that are not easily communicated to each other and which often result in reams of paperwork. Problems are then compounded by other inefficiencies at Boeing. For example, the company's various computer systems located in different parts of the plant are not integrated with each other into an overall system to facilitate communications across departments; Boeing has 400 different computer data banks for parts and sketches.

Top managers have set about to dramatically change and improve the production process at Boeing. Equally important, however, is a change in philosophy. Rather than making an optimal plane for each customer, Boeing plans on limiting customer choices to a set number of options packages, similar to the way car buyers order options packages for new cars. Boeing will provide customers with safe, high-quality airplanes that satisfy their needs, and not strive to manufacture an optimal plane for each customer given each customer's idiosyncratic preferences. If customers want to further customize the planes they order, they will have to pay for the additional changes. Boeing also plans on having just four integrated computer programs and data bases to facilitate decision making for design, purchasing, inventory, and production. Employees will no longer have to use complicated codes that can take two years to learn.[4] Streamlining decision making at a huge organization like Boeing is, of course, a major endeavor, but one likely to have big payoffs.

Overview

Making decisions is an integral part of behavior in organizations. Good decisions help individuals, groups, and organizations achieve their goals and perform well. Bad decisions hinder goal attainment and lower performance. Managers make decisions about a range of issues: whom to hire and what training to provide, how to motivate current employees, which leader behaviors to engage in to promote high performance and positive attitudes, and what and how to communicate with others inside and outside the organization. Workers also make decisions about a range of issues: whether to attend work or take a day off, how hard to work on the job, how to go about performing a task, how to cope with job-related stress, and whether to look for another job or stay put. In the opening case, Boeing's traditional practice of customizing planes has resulted in workers having to make many complicated decisions to respond to customer preferences.

In this chapter we discuss how members of organizations make decisions. We examine the types of decisions that need to be made in organizations and the decision-making process. We explore some biases and problems in decision making. We look at the pros and cons of using groups instead of individuals to make decisions and some of the issues involved in group decision making. We discuss one of the most sought after yet elusive decision-making processes: creativity. By the end of the chapter, you will have a good understanding of decision making in organizations and how it can be improved to help individuals, groups, and organizations achieve their goals and perform at a high level.

Types of Decisions

In previous chapters we have discussed some of the choices that members of organizations have to make, decisions ranging from how managers should motivate and reward subordinates, to what is the best way for subordinates to communicate important information to their supervisors, to how group members should respond to a deviant coworker. Making such choices is the essence of decision making. In fact, **decision making** can be defined as the process by which members of an organization choose a specific course of action to respond to both the problems and the opportunities that confront them. Good decisions result in a course of action that helps an individual, group, or organization to be effective. Bad decisions hinder effectiveness and may lead to actions that result in poor performance and negative attitudes at all organizational levels.

Decision making in response to *problems* occurs when individual, group, or organizational goal attainment and performance are threatened. A doctor's goal of providing good medical care in a rural community is threatened when the doctor lacks the financial resources to purchase medical equipment. A production group's goal of winning the monthly quality contest is threatened when two of its members engage in social loafing. An organization's goal of being profitable is threatened when the top-management team experiences communication problems. Through the decision-making process, organizational members choose how to respond to these and other kinds of problems.

Decision making in response to *opportunities* occurs when members of an organization take advantage of opportunities for benefit or gain. Such decisions

Decision making
The process by which members of an organization choose a specific course of action to respond to both problems and opportunities.

can range from an upper-level manager in a successful electronics company deciding whether to market the firm's products in Canada, to a telephone operator at the same company deciding whether to take a course in basic secretarial skills to open up new employment opportunities. Individuals, groups, and whole organizations reach their full potential only when they take advantage of opportunities like these. Andrew Grove, CEO of Intel, suggests that successful companies often fail because they get complacent and fail to take advantage of opportunities. Thus Grove and managers at Intel are constantly on the lookout for opportunities and spend a lot of time figuring out how to respond to them (see the closing case).[5]

Whether to solve a problem or choose how to respond to a potential opportunity, two basic types of decisions are made in organizations: nonprogrammed decisions and programmed decisions.

NONPROGRAMMED DECISIONS

Sometimes the problems and opportunities that confront an individual, group, or organization are relatively novel—that is, they are problems and opportunities that members of the organization have never before encountered. Novel problems and opportunities continually arise because change is a fact of organizational life (change is discussed in detail in Chapter 19). In the opening case, the way in which Boeing traditionally made airplanes resulted in workers being confronted with many novel problems and opportunities as they sought to configure planes to suit each customer's unique specifications.

When members of an organization choose how to respond to novel problems and opportunities, they engage in **nonprogrammed decision making.**[6] Nonprogrammed decision making involves a search for information.[7] Because the problem or opportunity has not been experienced before, members of the organization are uncertain about how they should respond, and thus they search for any information they can find to help them make the decision.

> **Nonprogrammed decision making**
> Decision making in response to novel problems and opportunities.

Mike Castiglioni, the manager of a successful Italian restaurant called Ciao! in a small Texas town, for example, was confronted with a novel problem when a successful Italian restaurant chain, The Olive Garden, opened a new restaurant a few blocks away. The arrival of a strong competitor posed a novel problem for Mike; previously Ciao! had been the only Italian restaurant in town. Similarly, the staff at Ciao! was provided with a potential employment opportunity when The Olive Garden advertised for waiters and waitresses.

As soon as he learned that The Olive Garden was planning to open a restaurant, Mike tried to find out as much as he could about it (its lunch and dinner menus and prices, the kinds of customers it appeals to, and the quality of its food) in order to respond to this new competition. Mike also traveled to the nearby cities of Houston and Dallas and ate in several Olive Garden restaurants to sample the food and ambience and record customer traffic. As a result of these search activities, Mike decided that the quality of the food he served at Ciao! was better and that the prices the two restaurants charged were similar. The Olive Garden, however, had a wider selection of menu items and offered a soup or salad with every entrée. Mike decided to expand his menu by adding three new items to the lunch menu and four to the dinner menu. He also decided to serve a house salad with all entrées, which would appeal to his health-conscious customers. As a result of his search for information, Mike Castiglioni was able to decide how to respond to the problem of competition in a successful way, and Ciao! continues to thrive despite The Olive Garden's presence.

PROGRAMMED DECISIONS

Although members of an organization frequently make unprogrammed decisions, they also need to engage in **programmed decision making**—making decisions in response to recurring problems and opportunities.[8] To make a programmed decision, the decision maker uses a **performance program,** a standard sequence of behaviors that organizational members follow routinely whenever they encounter a particular type of problem or opportunity.[9] Department stores develop performance programs that specify how salespeople should respond to customers who return items that have been worn and are defective. Grocery stores develop performance programs that indicate how clerks should respond when sale items are out of stock. Universities develop performance programs dictating how to deal with students who cannot complete their courses.

Organizations develop performance programs whenever the same kinds of problems or opportunities keep cropping up. Once a performance program is developed, members of the organization initiate the performance program almost automatically as soon as the problem or opportunity is encountered. They do not have to search for information or think about what they should do. Organizational rules (see Chapter 10) are types of performance programs developed to help members make programmed decisions.

Because of improvements in the local economy, Mike Castiglioni was faced with the recurring problem of Ciao!'s experienced waiters and waitresses being offered jobs at The Olive Garden and other new restaurants opening up in town. Although the waiters and waitresses at Ciao! were generally satisfied with their jobs, they interviewed at some of the new restaurants to see whether they could earn more money, get better benefits, or have better working hours. Periodically, waiters or waitresses came to Mike and told him that they had been offered better benefits or working hours by one of his competitors. The first couple of times this happened, Mike needed to make a *nonprogrammed* decision because the problem was relatively novel. Accordingly, he searched for information to help make the decision: How costly would it be to hire and train a new waiter or waitress? How important was it to have experienced waiters and waitresses who knew many of Ciao!'s regular customers? As a result of his search for information, Mike concluded that, whenever possible, he should try to retain as many of Ciao!'s waiters and waitresses as he could by matching the hourly rates, benefits, and working hours they were offered at other restaurants.

Once Mike had made this decision, whenever waiters or waitresses came to him and told him of better job offers that they had received, he matched the offers whenever he could. Mike Castiglioni essentially had decided on a standard response to a recurring problem—the essence of *programmed* decision making and the use of performance programs.

As this example illustrates, performance programs often evolve from nonprogrammed decisions. Essentially, if what was once a novel problem or opportunity keeps recurring, it becomes a programmed decision, and the organization comes up with a standard response or performance program (see Fig. 14.1). In the opening case, Boeing realized that its traditional practice of customizing each airplane it produced to unique customer specifications was inefficient and causing workers to have to make too many time-consuming nonprogrammed decisions. Boeing's plan to offer a limited number of option packages to customers is likely to turn many of these nonprogrammed decisions into programmed ones as workers follow predetermined specifications or performance programs for the kind of plane and option package they are producing.

Programmed decision making
Decision making in response to recurring problems and opportunities.

Performance program
A standard sequence of behaviors that organizational members follow routinely whenever they encounter a particular type of problem or opportunity.

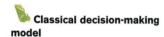

FIGURE **14.1**

Nonprogrammed and
Programmed Decision Making

Performance programs save time because they make it unnecessary for organizational members to search for information to make a decision; instead, all they need to do is follow the performance program. Managers, however, must be able to realize when performance programs need to be changed and make the appropriate changes in them. Organizations tend to be slow to change performance programs because doing things the way they have always been done is often easier than devising and implementing new procedures.

The Decision-Making Process

When people think of decision making in organizations, the kinds of decisions they usually have in mind are nonprogrammed decisions involving a search for information. Thus, in the remainder of this chapter, we focus on nonprogrammed decisions, and whenever we use the term *decision* we are referring to a *nonprogrammed* decision. Two widely studied models of the decision-making process are the classical decision-making model and James March and Herbert Simon's administrative decision-making model.

THE CLASSICAL MODEL OF DECISION MAKING

Classical decision-making model

A prescriptive approach based on the assumptions that the decision maker has all the necessary information and will choose the best possible solution or response.

The **classical decision-making model** is a *prescriptive model*; it describes how people *should* make decisions.[10] This model rests on two assumptions: (1) People have access to all the information they need to make a decision, and (2) people make decisions by choosing the best possible solution to a problem or response to an opportunity.[11] According to the classical model, a decision maker should choose how to respond to problems and opportunities by engaging in these four steps:[12]

1. Listing all alternatives from which a choice will be selected: These alternatives represent different responses to the problem or the opportunity.
2. Listing the consequences of each alternative: The consequences are what would occur if a given alternative was selected.
3. Considering his or her own preferences for each alternative or set of consequences and then ranking the sets from most preferred to least preferred.
4. Selecting the alternative that will result in the most preferred set of consequences.

According to the classical model, if members of an organization follow those four steps, they will make optimal decisions—the best decisions that can be made, given the decision maker's preferences.[13]

Do members of an organization actually make decisions according to the classical model? If they do not, could they make better decisions if they did follow those four steps? The answer to both questions is no—because of several basic problems with the classical model.

The classical model is unrealistic.[14] Its assumption that decision makers have all the information needed to make optimal decisions bears little resemblance to the conditions facing most decision makers in organizations. Even if decision makers did have all necessary information, they probably would not be able to use it all. The cognitive abilities of decision makers are limited; often they cannot take into account the large quantities of information available to them.

One way to consider the difficulties with the classical model is to compare the four steps described above to actual decision making in organizations. With regard to the first step, *decision makers often do not know all the alternatives that they can choose from.*[15] One of the defining features of nonprogrammed decisions is that they involve a considerable amount of searching for information. Even after this search is complete, it is likely that decision makers are aware of only some of all possible alternatives.

For example, the challenge facing Sarah Hunter, a marketing manager at a Fortune 500 food products company, was to solve the problem of lackluster sales of a line of frozen desserts. Hunter's search for alternatives yielded three potential solutions to the problem: (1) The company could launch a series a newspaper and magazine advertisements with coupons. (2) The company could negotiate with major grocery store chains to give the desserts a more visible location (at eye level) in the frozen foods sections. (3) The company could develop a series of expensive television ads to air during prime time. Hunter's information search failed to uncover other alternatives: (1) renaming the products, (2) changing product packaging, (3) reorienting the packaging and marketing of some of the products to appeal to certain segments of the market (for example, angel food cake to appeal to health-conscious adults and frozen yogurt bars to appeal to young children), and (4) dropping the line altogether.

In the second step of the classical model, decision makers list the consequences of each alternative. As in the first step, however, *decision makers often do not know all of the consequences that will ensue if they choose a given alternative.*[16] One reason it is hard to make decisions is that the decision maker often does not know what will happen if a given course of action is chosen. Sarah Hunter did not know whether coupons in newspapers and magazines would significantly boost sales, because her company had had mixed success with this approach in the past. She knew that television ads were likely to increase sales, but it was not clear whether the increase in sales would be temporary or long lasting or whether it would be large enough to offset the high costs of purchasing air time in prime viewing hours.

As the third step in the classical model, decision makers must consider their own preferences for sets of consequences. Once again, the classical model assumes that decision makers are able to rank sets of consequences and know their own preferences.[17] However, *decision makers don't always know for sure what they want.* Stop and think about some of the important and difficult decisions you have had to make. Sometimes these decisions were difficult to make precisely because *you weren't sure what you wanted.* A graduating senior with an accounting degree from the University of Wisconsin, for example, finds it hard to choose between a job offer from a Wisconsin bank and one from a Big Six accounting firm in New York City because he doesn't know whether he prefers the security of staying in Wisconsin where most of his family and friends are to the excitement of living in a big city and the opportunity to work for a Big Six firm. Similarly, Sarah Hunter did not know whether she preferred to focus heavily on dramatically improving the sales of frozen desserts or to boost sales just enough to maintain profitability while putting her major marketing thrust on some of the other products she was responsible for, such as frozen low-calorie dinners.

Because of these problems with the first three steps in the classical model, *it is often impossible for organizational members to make the best possible decisions.*[18] Moreover, even if members of an organization were able to collect all of the information needed for steps 1 and 2 and knew their preferences at step 3, there are at least two additional reasons for their not following the steps in the classical model. One reason is that the amount of time and effort it would take to collect all the information might not be worthwhile. The other is that once the information is collected, the limits of decision makers' cognitive abilities would probably limit their ability to take all the information into account in making the decision.[19]

Realizing the problems with the classical model, James March and Herbert Simon developed a more realistic account of decision making: the administrative decision-making model. March and Simon's approach is more useful than the classical model for understanding decision making in organizations, and Herbert Simon was awarded the Nobel Prize in economics for some of the ideas in their model.

MARCH AND SIMON'S ADMINISTRATIVE MODEL OF DECISION MAKING

Administrative decision-making model

A descriptive approach stressing that incomplete information, psychological and sociological processes, and the decision maker's cognitive abilities affect decision making and that decision makers often choose satisfactory, not optimal, solutions.

The classical model is prescriptive; it indicates how decisions should be made. In contrast, March and Simon's **administrative decision-making model** is *descriptive*; it explains how people *actually make* decisions in organizations.[20] March and Simon stress that incomplete information, psychological and sociological processes, and the decision maker's cognitive abilities affect decision making and that decision makers often choose satisfactory, not optimal, solutions.[21]

Decision makers choose how to respond to problems and opportunities on the basis of a simplified and approximate account of the situation—the decision maker's definition of the situation. Decision makers do not take into account all information relevant to a problem or opportunity, nor do they consider all possible alternatives and their consequences.

Sarah Hunter did not consider renaming or changing the packaging of the frozen desserts, reorienting them to appeal to certain segments of the market, or even recommending that the company drop the products altogether. She did not define the situation in those terms. She defined the situation in terms of increasing sales of existing products, not changing the products to make them more attractive to customers. In addition, the thought of dropping the line never entered her mind, although that is what the company ended up doing two years later.

Decision makers may follow some of the steps in the classical model, such as generating alternatives and considering the consequences of the alternatives and their own preferences. But the information they consider is based on their definition of the situation, and that is the result of psychological and sociological factors. Psychological factors include the decision maker's personality, ability, perceptions, experiences, and knowledge. Sociological factors include the groups, organization, and organizational and national culture of which the decision maker is a member.

The alternatives Sarah Hunter considered and, more generally, her definition of the situation were based in part on two factors. One was her past marketing experiences: She had always worked on improving and maintaining sales of "successful" products. The other was the marketing department in which she worked. It was quite conservative. For example, it rarely made changes to product names and packaging, had introduced few new products in the past ten years, and had not stopped selling an existing product in twelve years.

Rather than making optimal decisions, organizational members often engage in **satisficing**—that is, they search for and choose acceptable responses to problems and opportunities, not necessarily the best possible responses.[22] One way that decision makers can satisfice is by listing criteria that would lead to an acceptable choice and picking an alternative that meets these criteria. In trying to decide which of many job applicants to hire for a given position, for example, organizations often satisfice by listing criteria that an acceptable candidate would meet (such as an appropriate degree from a college or university, job-related experience, and good interpersonal skills) and then choosing a candidate who meets these criteria. If organizations were to make the optimal hiring decision rather than a satisfactory one, they would have to pick the best candidate (out of all possible candidates)—the person who had the best educational background, prior experience, and interpersonal skills. Often, it would be very difficult and time-consuming (if not impossible) to do this. In the opening case, Boeing's practice of striving to optimally satisfy customers' needs and desires by offering limitless choices in the design of planes resulted in an inefficient and time-consuming production process.[23] Top management's decision to try to provide customers with satisfactory planes that would meet their needs, but may not necessarily be optimal or the best possible plane given a customer's idiosyncratic preferences, is likely to simplify and speed up the manufacture of airplanes.

One criterion of a satisfactory decision in any organization is that it be *ethical*. Ethical decisions promote well-being and do not cause harm to members of an organization or to other people affected by an organization's activities. Although it is easy to describe what an ethical decision is, sometimes it is difficult to determine the boundary between ethical and unethical decisions in an organization. Is it ethical, for example, for a pharmaceutical company to decide to charge a high price for a life-saving drug and thus put it out of the reach of some people who need it? On the one hand, it can be argued that the drug is costly to produce and the company needs the revenues to continue producing the drug as well as to research ways to improve its effectiveness. On the other hand, it can be argued that the company has a moral or ethical obligation to make this life-saving drug available to as many people as possible.

Some people deliberately make unethical decisions to benefit themselves or their organizations, but even decision makers who strive to be ethical are sometimes faced with difficult choices or ethical dilemmas such as that faced by the pharmaceutical company. Under these circumstances, satisficing or making

 Satisficing

Searching for and choosing an acceptable response or solution, not necessarily the best possible one.

acceptable decisions that are ethical can be difficult. Realizing the importance of ethical decision making and the challenges it sometimes entails, many organizations are now taking steps to ensure that ethical decisions are made, as indicated in Insight 14.1.

Insight 14.1 Ethics

Making Ethical Decisions

Insider trading, discrimination, and unsafe working conditions are a few examples of the results of unethical decision making in organizations. In an effort to ensure that all decisions are ethical, more and more organizations have created a special position: ethics officer.[24]

Ethics officers are upper-level employees (often with the title "director" or "vice president") who usually report to the CEO of a company and earn anywhere from $90,000 to $200,000 a year. Among their many tasks, ethics officers develop ethical standards to be used in decision making, listen to employees' complaints about unethical decision making, train employees in making ethical decisions, and counsel decision makers about ethical questions. Ethics officers often provide guidance to decision makers on issues related to protecting the environment, product safety, use of expense accounts, potential conflicts of interest, receiving gifts from customers or suppliers, and honoring contracts.[25]

Richard Greeves is the ethics officer at Textron's Bell Helicopter unit (www.bhti.com). Greeves often listens to workers' complaints about what they think might be unethical decisions, and he helps managers make ethical decisions on issues ranging from the use of expense accounts to responding to potential misconduct by one's coworkers. Greeves also holds training sessions to promote ethical decision making and holds meetings of Textron's senior management ethics committee.

Ethics officers not only promote ethical decision making in organizations but also can help an organization under attack for ethical violations. In November 1992, new federal regulations were put in place that reduce the penalties for ethical violations if an organization has an ethics officer or an ethics program.

Although ethics officers certainly seem like a good idea, they are not without their critics. Peter Neary, a consultant with the Center for Creative Leadership in Colorado, thinks that having ethics officers is "a terrible idea" because it makes it seem as though ethics is the concern of just one person. Moreover, Neary thinks that the CEOs of companies should have the primary responsibility for promoting ethical decision making.[26] What everyone does agree on, however, is the need for ethical decision making throughout an organization.

A naval judge found that Admiral Frank Kelso lied when he denied being on the third floor of the Las Vegas Hilton when 15 female naval officers were assaulted by their male counterparts. This incident, which became known as Tailhook, led to many changes in Navy procedures designed to prevent such unethical behavior from occurring and to improve ethical decision making.

Bounded rationality
An ability to reason that is constrained by the limitations of the human mind itself.

Unlike the classical model, which disregards the cognitive limitations of the decision maker, March and Simon acknowledge that decision makers are constrained by **bounded rationality**—an ability to reason that is limited by the limitations of the human mind itself. March and Simon's model assumes that bounded rationality is a fact of organizational life. Members of an organization try to act rationally and make good decisions that benefit the organization, but their rationality is limited by their own cognitive abilities.[27] It is often impossible for decision makers to simultaneously consider all the information relevant to a decision (even if this information is available) and use all this information to make an optimal choice. Even though computers and advances in information technology (some of which we discussed in Chapter 12) can help members of an organization make good decisions, rationality is always limited, or bounded, by the capabilities of the human mind. Thus decision makers approach decisions on the basis of their own subjective definitions of the situation, and they usually satisfice rather than optimize.[28]

When members of an organization realize that decision making proceeds more often as described by March and Simon than as outlined in the classical model, they are better able to understand why both good and bad decisions are made in organizations and how decision making can be improved. Good decisions are often made when decision makers are able to identify and focus on the key aspects of the situation. Bad decisions may result from defining a situation improperly.

How did Sarah Hunter, in our earlier example, define the situation she was in? She believed that her challenge was to improve sales of an existing product rather than to change the product or evaluate whether it should be dropped. Her definition of the situation limited the potential solutions she considered. Only after trying two of those solutions and failing did she and

TO MANAGERS

The Decision-Making Process

- Realize that different members of an organization are going to define the same problem or opportunity in different ways depending on their personalities, abilities, knowledge, expertise, and the groups they belong to.
- Carefully examine how you define problems and opportunities. Explore the implications of defining these problems and opportunities in different ways.
- Realize there are limits to the amount of information you and your subordinates can take into account when making decisions. Focus on information that is most relevant to the decision at hand.

her company realize the need to redefine the situation and recognize that they had an unsuccessful product line that needed to be either dramatically changed or dropped.

Sources of Error in Decision Making

Given that decision makers often do not have all the information they need to make a good decision and are boundedly rational, it is not surprising that a variety of sources of error in decision making exist. Some of these sources of error are pervasive and recurring. Many decision makers succumb to the errors, and any one decision maker may continue to make less than satisfactory decisions because these sources of error are operating. Two major sources of error arise from (1) the shortcuts or rules of thumb people use to make decisions, which can lead to both good and bad decisions, and (2) the human tendency to throw good money after bad or continue involvement in unfruitful activities.

HEURISTICS AND THE BIASES THEY MAY LEAD TO

Given the number and complexity of the many decisions that people have to make at work and in their personal lives, it is not surprising that they often try to simplify things or use certain rules of thumb to help them make decisions. The rules of thumb that help people simplify decision making are called **heuristics.**[29] Heuristics are involved in much of the decision making that takes place in organizations; people tend to use them without even knowing they are doing so. Because they simplify matters, heuristics can aid in the decision-making process, but they can also lead to *biases*—systematic errors in decision making.[30] Three common rules of thumb are the availability, representativeness, and anchoring and adjustment heuristics (see Fig. 14.2).

Availability Heuristic. When making decisions, organizational members often have to judge the frequency with which different events occur and their likely causes. The **availability heuristic** reflects the tendency to determine the frequency of an event and its causes by how easy events and causes are to remember (that is, how *available* they are from memory).[31] People tend to judge an event that is easy to remember as occurring more frequently than an event that is difficult to remember. Likewise, if a potential cause of an event comes to mind very easily, people are likely to think that it is an important causal factor.

The availability heuristic can aid decision making because events and causes that actually do occur frequently come easily to mind. However, factors

 Heuristics
Rules of thumb that simplify decision making.

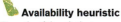 **Availability heuristic**
The rule of thumb that says an event that is easy to remember is likely to have occurred more frequently than an event that is difficult to remember.

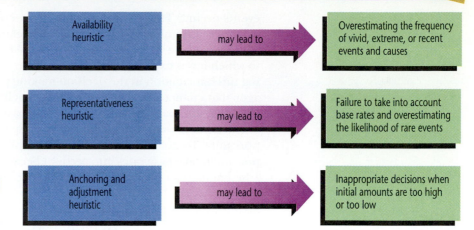

FIGURE **14.2**

Heuristics and the Biases They
May Lead To

other than frequency of occurrence also determine the availability of information from memory, so use of the availability heuristic can cause certain biases to enter into decision making. One such bias is the overestimation of the frequency of *vivid* or *extreme* events and causes because they are easy to remember.[32] Another is the overestimation of the frequency of *recent* events and causes because they also tend to be easy to remember.[33]

When Sarah Hunter was trying to decide how to increase sales of frozen desserts, for example, she remembered that one of her coworkers recently had dramatic success boosting sales of fruit drinks by using a series of advertisements and coupons in magazines and the Sunday newspaper supplements. That this instance of success with these kinds of ads was *recent* and *extreme* led Hunter to *overestimate* the extent to which this approach had increased sales. This same bias led her to ignore instances in which the same kinds of advertisements and coupons failed to increase sales of other products while increasing marketing costs. As a result of the biases emanating from the availability heuristic, Hunter decided to place advertisements and coupons in magazines and Sunday supplements in the hope of increasing sales of frozen desserts, a strategy that proved to be unsuccessful.

Representativeness Heuristic. The **representativeness heuristic** reflects the tendency to predict the likelihood of an event from the extent to which the event is typical (or *representative*) of similar kinds of events that have happened in the past.[34] A manager in the United States trying to determine whether a domestically popular hand cream will sell in Spain, for example, compares the extent to which Spain is similar to foreign countries in which the cream has sold especially well or to countries in which the cream has not sold well. The manager decides not to export the hand cream to Spain because Spain is typical of other countries in which the product was a flop (some of them were Spanish-speaking).

The representativeness heuristic can sometimes be a good shortcut to estimating the likelihood of an upcoming event because the fact that similar kinds of events happened in the past may be a good predictor of the upcoming event. Sometimes, however, this heuristic can cause decision makers to disregard important information about the frequency of events. In such cases, the representativeness heuristic leads to biased decision making.

One source of bias emanating from the representativeness heuristic is the failure to take into account the **base rate,** the actual frequency with which

Representativeness heuristic
The rule of thumb that says similar kinds of events that happened in the past are a good predictor of the likelihood of an upcoming event.

Base rate
The actual frequency with which an event occurs.

events occur.[35] The manager in the hand cream example should have considered the number of times the hand cream did not sell in a foreign country. If he had, he would have found that the product sold well in *most* countries to which it was exported and that its failure in a foreign market was rare. Using this information in the decision-making process would have told the manager that chances that the cream would sell well in Spain were pretty high. However, the manager did not take this base-rate information into account, decided not to export the hand cream to Spain, and missed out on a good opportunity. To avoid the pitfalls of the representativeness heuristic, it is important to take base rates into account because it is likely that common events (the hand cream's high sales in foreign countries) will occur again and that rare events (the product's failure in a few countries, some of which were Spanish-speaking) will not occur again.

▸ **Anchoring and adjustment heuristic**

The rule of thumb that says that decisions about how big or small an amount (such as a salary, budget, or level of costs) should be can be made by making adjustments from some initial amount.

Anchoring and Adjustment Heuristic.   The **anchoring and adjustment heuristic** reflects the tendency to make decisions based on adjustments from some initial amount (or *anchor*).[36] Decisions about salary increases are often made by choosing a percentage increase from a worker's current salary. Budget decisions are often made by deciding whether the current budget should be increased or decreased. Decisions about the degree to which costs must be cut are often based on the current level of costs. In situations like these, if the initial amounts are reasonable, then the anchoring and adjustment heuristic might be a good shortcut for decision making.

By using this heuristic, decision makers need to consider only the degree to which the current level needs to be changed. They do not, for example, need to determine a person's salary from scratch or build a budget from ground zero. But if the original amount from which a decision or adjustment is made is *not* reasonable, the anchoring and adjustment heuristic will lead to biased decision making. If workers' current salary levels are low in comparison to what they could be earning in similar kinds of jobs and companies, even a relatively large percentage increase (such as 15 percent) may still leave them underpaid. Likewise, if a department's budget is much too high, a 10 percent decrease will lead to the department still being allocated more money than it really needs.

ESCALATION OF COMMITMENT

▸ **Escalation of commitment**

The tendency to invest additional time, money, or effort into what are essentially bad decisions or unproductive courses of action.

A second source of error in decision making (in addition to biases) is **escalation of commitment,** the tendency of decision makers to invest additional time, money, or effort into what are essentially bad decisions or unproductive courses of action that are already draining organizational resources.[37] Here is a typical escalation-of-commitment scenario: (1) A decision maker initially makes a decision that results in some kind of loss or negative outcome. (2) Rather than change the course of action contained in the initial decision, the decision maker commits more time, money, or effort to the course of action. (3) Further losses are experienced because of this escalation of commitment to a failing course of action. Escalation of commitment is graphically illustrated in Fig. 14.3.

Sarah Hunter experienced escalation of commitment in her quest to improve sales of frozen desserts. First, she embarked on a series of magazine and newspaper ads. When this approach failed to boost sales and money was lost, she decided to negotiate with grocery store chains to get more visibility for the products in the frozen foods section. This was difficult to do, but she persevered and was successful in getting more visible locations for the products.

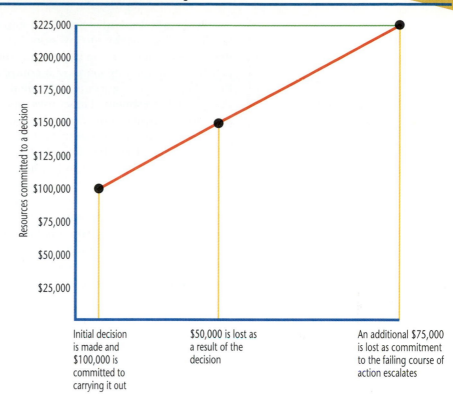

FIGURE 14.3

Escalation of Commitment

This strategy, however, also failed to boost sales. Instead of reassessing her original decision to try to boost sales of these products, Hunter persisted in her quest and gave her boss a proposal for a series of expensive television advertisements. Luckily for the organization, the boss denied her request and halted her escalation of commitment.

Escalation of commitment is common in organizations and in people's personal lives. Investors in stocks and real estate, for example, often continue to invest in losing ventures, pouring good money after bad. Even decision makers at the very top of organizations are vulnerable to the escalation of commitment, as indicated in Insight 14.2.

Insight 14.2　　**Ethics**

Escalation of Commitment at Prudential Insurance Company

Recently, some people have questioned whether Prudential Insurance Company (www.prudential.com) is as solid as "the Rock" in its famous logo. A few well-publicized scandals are shaking confidence in the largest insurer in the United States. One scandal involved the Prudential Securities (formerly called Prudential-Bache) unit of Prudential.

Brokers at Prudential Securities sold stakes in oil and gas and real estate limited partnerships to investors. Investors bought stakes in these limited partnerships with the hope of making a return on their investment just as they might buy shares of a company's stock or invest in a mutual fund. However, investors not only failed to get any return but lost a lot of their initial investment. These investors filed lawsuits against Prudential Securities, accusing brokers of misconduct ranging from unethical sales tactics to downright dishonesty and misrepresentation of the facts.

In October 1993, Prudential agreed to pay $41 million in penalties and set up a $300 million fund to be used to compensate investors who suffered losses in the limited partnerships and were victims of unethical behavior. This amount may be just the tip of the iceberg of the sum that will be needed to compensate investors. According to some estimates, compensation will cost Prudential as much as $1 billion.

How could a major insurance company have had such a potential disaster brewing in one of its subsidiaries for several years? Why did top management take so long to rectify matters? Over a nine-year period, during which George L. Ball was CEO of the subsidiary and the limited partnership fiasco took place, top managers at Prudential committed a lot of resources to Prudential Securities. Early on and throughout his tenure, there were signs that Ball was not the right person for the job. Likewise, there were signs that the subsidiary was losing money. But instead of rethinking the wisdom of their original choice of Ball and their commitment of resources to Prudential Securities, top managers at Prudential escalated their commitment to him and to the failing subsidiary. Ball remained in power, and Prudential continued to pour money into the subsidiary. By the time Ball finally left Prudential Securities, the subsidiary had lost $264 million on Prudential's investment of $1.6 billion. The company's losses were even greater when investors' and the public's loss of confidence were added in.

Recently Robert Winters, the current chairman and CEO of Prudential, was asked why the company had been so committed to Ball and why top management had been so slow to make the decision to remove him from power. Winters never directly answered the question.[38]

Why does escalation of commitment occur, even among presumably knowledgeable decision makers? There appear to be at least three causes of this type of faulty decision making:

1. *Decision makers often do not want to admit to themselves or to other people that they have made a mistake.*[39] Rather than reassess the wisdom of their original decision in light of the negative consequences they have experienced, decision makers commit more resources to the course of action in order to reconfirm the "correctness" of the original decision.

2. *Decision makers erroneously believe that an additional commitment of resources is justified, given how much has been spent already, and may help to recoup some of the losses.*[40] When the newspaper and magazine ads and the location change in the grocery stores failed to boost sales, what did Sarah Hunter do? She decided that after investing so much time, effort, and money into boosting sales, she had no alternative but to push

Sunk costs

Costs that cannot be reversed and will not be affected by subsequent decision making.

ahead with the TV ads. The costs that she had already incurred, however, were **sunk costs**—costs that could not be reversed and would not be affected by subsequent decision making—so they should not have entered into her decision making.

3. *Decision makers tend to take more risks when they frame or view decisions in negative terms (for example, as a way to get back money that has been lost) rather than in positive terms (for example, as a way to make more money).*[41] When Sarah Hunter originally thought about TV ads, she decided against them because they were too risky; they would cost too much money given the uncertainty about whether they would boost sales. At that point, Hunter had spent no resources on boosting sales, and the TV ads were framed (in her mind) in *positive* terms: as a way to boost sales. But after her first two strategies failed, the TV ads were framed in *negative* terms: as a way to recover some of the time, effort, and money she had already spent unsuccessfully trying to boost sales. Once this decision was framed negatively, Hunter was willing to risk the high cost of the ads.

Biases resulting from escalation of commitment and the use of heuristics can result in poor decision making at all levels in an organization. This problem is compounded by the fact that decision makers often use heuristics without being aware that they are doing so. Escalation of commitment also occurs without decision makers realizing that they are throwing good money after bad. No matter how knowledgeable a decision maker is, the potential for poor decision making as a result of biases and the escalation of commitment is always present.

TO MANAGERS

Sources of Error in Decision Making

- Do not give vivid or extreme instances of an event or cause too much weight in decision making. If a vivid or extreme instance comes to mind, think about the extent to which less extreme or vivid events and causes have occurred.
- When making decisions, be sure to consider events and causes beyond the most recent ones.
- When trying to estimate the likelihood of an event or cause occurring, take into account the number of times that this event or cause has actually occurred. Remember, rare events are unlikely to be repeated.
- Whenever you are making a decision based on adjusting some initial amount (such as a worker's salary or marketing expenditures), stop and determine whether the initial amount was originally set too high or too low.
- Realize that a sign of good decision making is the ability to recognize when a decision needs to be reversed.
- When deciding whether to commit resources to a course of action, take into account the costs only of the resources you are about to commit. Do not take into account costs that have already been incurred.
- If you are deciding whether to commit more resources to a course of action that has already resulted in some losses of money, time, or effort, ask yourself whether you would commit the resources if you had not already experienced the losses but had your current knowledge.

Group Decision Making

Formal and informal groups, rather than a single individual, often make decisions in organizations. These groups might have a formal leader or supervisor who oversees the decision-making process. The Vroom and Yetton model (see Chapter 12) provides leaders with guidance on when they should rely on group decision making instead of individual decision making. Self-managed work teams and other groups that do not have a formal leader also need to make decisions. In this section we consider some of the potential advantages, disadvantages, and consequences of group decision making.

ADVANTAGES OF GROUP DECISION MAKING

Advantages of using groups to make decisions include the availability and diversity of members' skills, knowledge, and expertise; enhanced memory for facts; greater ability to correct errors; and greater decision acceptance.

Availability and Diversity of Members' Skills, Knowledge, and Expertise.   When groups make decisions, each group member's skills, knowledge, and expertise can be brought into play. For certain kinds of decisions, an individual decision maker is very unlikely to have all the different capabilities needed to make a good decision. For example, when Jack Welch, CEO of General Electric (GE), needed to decide whether to invest $70 million to modernize GE's washing-machine-manufacturing facilities near Louisville, Kentucky, or buy washing machines from another company and sell them under the GE brand name, he clearly did not have all the skills, knowledge, and expertise needed to make the decision by himself. He needed input from various managers about manufacturing costs, product development costs, and quality considerations. He also needed input from union representatives about whether GE's unionized workers would agree to needed changes in their jobs to help cut costs if the company decided to go ahead with the modernization program. Relying on group decision making, Welch undertook the modernization program, which proved to be a wise choice.[42] Whenever a decision requires skills, knowledge, and expertise in several areas (such as marketing, finance, engineering, production, and research and development), group decision making has clear advantages over individual decision making.

This advantage of group decision making suggests that there should be *diversity* among group members (see Chapter 10). In addition to diversity in knowledge and expertise, it is often desirable to have diversity in age, gender, race, and ethnic background. Diversity gives a group the opportunity to consider different points of view. Traditionally, for example, groups that design new automobiles for major car companies have been all male. But some companies are now realizing that it is important to have women and foreign designers on the team. They bring new, different, and important insights on car design—insights that result in features that appeal to female car buyers and buyers in other countries around the world.[43]

NutraSweet Corp. is another company that values diversity. NutraSweet is focusing on selling more of its sugar substitute to African Americans and Hispanics, who have a relatively high incidence of diabetes compared to the general population, and to countries such as Indonesia. Given this aim, NutraSweet CEO Robert E. Flynn views a diverse workforce as a practical business necessity.[44]

Although diverse work groups can improve decision making, they can give rise to a problem: Group members who have different points of view because of their varied backgrounds sometimes find it hard to get along with each other. Many organizations are trying to respond to this challenge through diversity training programs, which aim to help members of an organization understand each other so they can work together effectively and make good decisions, as indicated in Insight 14.3.

Insight 14.3

Diversity

Helping Diverse Group Members Get Along

Increasing diversity sometimes results in conflict and disagreement when diverse members of a group or organization don't see eye to eye or fail to respect and appreciate each other's points of view. To counter this effect, many organizations are instituting diversity training programs so their employees can work well together and make good decisions. In the aftermath of the Tailhook scandal, in which some female naval officers were subject to intense sexual harassment from male officers at a social event, Acting Secretary of the Navy J. Daniel Howard gave thousands of sailors a day off to attend sensitivity training programs to help them become sensitive to diversity issues and treat others who are different from themselves with the respect they deserve. Similarly, Federal Express has a voluntary four-and-a-half-day training program available to its 5,500 managers. As evidenced by the long waiting lists for the program, managers find the program useful in managing diverse groups of employees. Pacific Gas & Electric (www.pge.com) has a mandatory four-hour diversity training for its 12,000 employees. Employees must be finding this experience valuable because the classes often run long, sometimes lasting six or eight hours.[45]

What goes on in diversity training programs? Several approaches can be used to help diverse members of a group learn to get along and respect each other's points of view. In one approach, members of a panel consisting of a few members of a diverse group (such as women, Hispanics, African Americans, or homosexuals) describe and share with an audience their own experiences and difficulties. In another approach, members of an organization work for a while with people who are different from themselves. New recruits to the San Diego Police Department, for example, are assigned a one-week tour of duty working with citizens who are very different from themselves. A white woman may be sent to work with an all-male Hispanic teenage gang to gain some understanding of how these youths view society and to learn how to relate to people who are very different from herself.

Other approaches to diversity training include self-assessment questionnaires that help members of an organization confront their own stereotypes and prejudices; role-plays that allow members of an organization to see different points of view in action; and the creation of personal action plans for which organizational members come up with specific steps that they will take to, for example, help diverse members of groups feel appreciated, respected, and have positive work experiences. A manager at Federal Express who has had a hard time keeping minority members in the groups he supervises might institute a mentoring program or might agree to come up with interesting and challenging tasks for these valued but sometimes neglected group members.[46] Regardless of how it is done, helping diverse group and organization members get along so that they can make good decisions and work together to achieve their goals is a business imperative in the 1990s.

Enhanced Memory for Facts.   When a decision requires the consideration of a substantial amount of information, groups have an advantage over individuals because of their memory for facts.[47] Most people engaged in the process of making a decision have experienced the frustrating problem of forgetting an important piece of information. Because a group can rely on the memory of each of its members, the problem of forgetfulness is minimized. Information that one member of the group forgets is likely to be remembered by another. For example, even if Jack Welch had all the information he needed to decide whether General Electric should make or buy washing machines, it is highly unlikely that he would be able to remember all of this information when the time came to make the final decision. Having a group of GE managers and workers available to participate in the decision making helped to ensure that important information was not forgotten or overlooked.

Capability of Error Detection.   No matter how experienced decision makers are, they all make mistakes. Some errors might occur in the information-gathering stage or in the evaluation of alternatives. Other errors can occur when the final decision is made. When a group makes a decision, errors made by some group members might be detected and corrected by others.[48] If, for example, a manager at GE made a mistake in calculating production costs at the new manufacturing facility that was being contemplated, there was always the chance that another manager would detect the error.

Greater Decision Acceptance.   For a decision to be implemented, it is often necessary for several members of an organization to accept the decision. When a grocery store manager decides, for example, to increase the store's hours from 18 to 24 hours a day by changing the employees' work schedules (and not hiring any new workers), store employees must accept this decision for it to work. If none of the employees is willing to work the new 10 p.m. to 6 a.m. shift, the decision cannot be implemented.

The likelihood of employee acceptance of a decision increases when employees take part in the decision-making process and the manager does not make the decision alone. The successful implementation of GE's decision to invest $70 million to modernize its washing-machine-manufacturing facilities, for example, depended on the union that represented GE employees agreeing to changes in the workers' jobs.[49] By involving the union in the decision making, Jack Welch helped ensure that union officials and members would accept and support the decision to go ahead with the modernization plan.

DISADVANTAGES OF GROUP DECISION MAKING

Group decision making has certain advantages over individual decision making (particularly when the decisions are complex, require the gathering and processing of a variety or large amount of information, and require acceptance by others for successful implementation). But there are also disadvantages to group decision making. Two of them are time and the potential for groupthink.

Time.   Have you been in the annoying situation of being in a group that seemed to take forever to make a decision that you could have made in half the time? One of the disadvantages of group decision making is the amount of time it consumes. Groups seldom make decisions as quickly as an individual can. Moreover, if you multiply the amount of time a group takes to make a group decision by the number of people in the group, you can see the extent to which group decision making consumes the time and effort of organizational members.

For decisions that meet certain criteria, individual decision making takes less time than group decision making and is likely to result in just as good a decision. Use individual and not group decision making when (1) an individual is likely to have all the capabilities that are needed to make a good decision, (2) an individual is likely to be able to gather and accurately take into account all the necessary information, and (3) acceptance by other members for successful implementation is either unnecessary or likely to occur regardless of their involvement in decision making.

The Potential for Groupthink.   Irving Janis coined the term *groupthink* in 1972 to describe a paradox that he observed in group decision making: Sometimes groups of highly qualified and experienced individuals make very poor decisions.[50] The decision made by President John F. Kennedy and his advisers to carry out the ill-fated Bay of Pigs invasion of Cuba in 1962, the decisions made by President Lyndon B. Johnson and his advisers between 1964 and 1967 to escalate the war in Vietnam, the decision made by President Richard M. Nixon and his advisers to cover up the Watergate break-in in 1972, and the

Groupthink was an important factor that contributed to the failure of decision making that resulted in the **Challenger** space shuttle disaster. Engineers were prevented from airing their fears and concerns by managers who united to tell NASA officials that all was well with the O-ring seals on the rocket boosters that caused the explosion.

decision made by NASA and Morton Thiokol in 1986 to launch the *Challenger* space shuttle, which exploded after takeoff, killing all crew members—all these decisions were influenced by groupthink. After the fact, the decision makers involved in these and other fiascoes are often shocked that they and their colleagues were involved in such poor decision making. Janis's investigations of groupthink primarily focused on government decisions, but the potential for groupthink in business organizations is just as likely.

Groupthink is a pattern of faulty decision making that occurs in cohesive groups whose members strive for agreement at the expense of accurately assessing information relevant to the decision.[51] Recall from Chapter 11 that cohesive groups are very attractive to their members. Individual members of a cohesive group value their membership and have strong desires to remain members of the group. When groupthink occurs, members of a cohesive group unanimously support a decision favored by the group leader without carefully assessing its pros and cons.

This unanimous support is often founded in the members' exaggerated beliefs about the capabilities and morality of the group. They think the group is more powerful than it is and could never make a decision that might be morally or ethically questioned. As a result, the group becomes close-minded and fails to pay attention to information that suggests that the decision might not be a good one. Moreover, when members of the group *do* have doubts about the decision being made, they are likely to discount those doubts and may decide not to mention them to other group members. As a result, the group as a whole perceives that there is unanimous support for the decision, and group members actively try to prevent any negative information pertaining to the decision from being brought up for discussion.[52] Figure 14.4 summarizes Janis's basic model of the groupthink phenomenon. It is important to note that although groupthink occurs only in cohesive groups, many cohesive groups never succumb to this faulty mode of decision making.

A group leader can take the following steps specifically to prevent the occurrence of groupthink; these steps also contribute to good decision making in groups in general:[53]

- The group leader encourages all group members to be critical of proposed alternatives, to raise any doubts they may have, and to accept criticism of their own ideas. It is especially important for a group leader to subject his or her own viewpoint to criticism by other group members.
- The group leader refrains from expressing his or her own opinion and views until the group has had a chance to consider all alternatives. A leader's opinion given too early is likely to stifle the generation of alternatives and productive debate.
- The group leader encourages group members to gather information pertaining to a decision from people outside the group and to seek outsiders' perspectives on the group's ideas.
- Whenever a group meets, the group leader assigns one or two members to play the role of **devil's advocate**—that is, to criticize, raise objections to, and identify potential problems with any decisions the group reaches. The devil's advocate should raise these problems even if he or she does not believe the points are valid.
- If an important decision is being made and time allows, after a group has made a decision, the group leader holds a second meeting during

 Groupthink
A pattern of faulty decision making that occurs in cohesive groups whose members strive for agreement at the expense of accurately assessing information relevant to the decision.

Devil's advocate
Someone who argues against a cause or position in order to determine its validity.

Symptoms of groupthink

1. **Illusion of invulnerability**
   Group members are very optimistic and take excessive risks.
2. **Belief in inherent morality of the group**
   Group members fail to consider the ethical consequences of decisions.
3. **Collective rationalizations**
   Group members ignore information that suggests they might need to rethink the wisdom of the decision.
4. **Stereotypes of other groups**
   Other groups with opposing views are viewed as being incompetent.
5. **Self-censorship**
   Group members fail to mention any doubts they have to the group.
6. **Illusion of unanimity**
   Group members mistakenly believe they are all in total agreement.
7. **Direct pressure on dissenters**
   Members who disagree with the group's decision are urged to change their views.
8. **Emergence of self-appointed mind guards**
   Some group members try to shield the group from any information that suggests that they need to reconsider the wisdom of the decision.

Defective decision-making process

Bad decisions

FIGURE 14.4

Groupthink

Source: Adapted from Irving L. Janis, *Groupthink: Psychological Studies of Policy Decisions and Fiascoes,* 2d ed. Copyright 1982 by Houghton Mifflin Company. Reprinted with permission.

which group members can raise any doubts or misgivings they might have about the course of action the group has chosen.

OTHER CONSEQUENCES OF GROUP DECISION MAKING

Three other consequences of group decision making are not easily classified as advantages or disadvantages: diffusion of responsibility, group polarization, and the potential for conflict.

Diffusion of Responsibility. Group decisions are characterized by a diffusion of responsibility[54]—that is, the group as a whole rather than any one individual is accountable for the decision. If the decision was a good one, the group gets the credit; if the decision was a poor one, a single individual is not blamed.

Sometimes when important decisions are made that entail considerable uncertainty, it can be very stressful for one individual to assume sole responsibility for the decision. Moreover, under these conditions some people are inclined to make a decision that they know will not come back to haunt them rather than the decision that they think is best for the organization. When this is the case, diffusion of responsibility can be an advantage of group decision making.

Diffusion of responsibility can also be a disadvantage if group members do not take the time and effort needed to make a good decision because they are not held individually accountable. This consequence is related to the concept of social loafing (see Chapter 11), the tendency for individuals to exert less effort when they work in a group than when they work alone.

Group Polarization.   Another consequence of group decision making is that groups tend to make more extreme decisions than do individuals. This tendency is called group polarization.[55] By *extreme decisions* we mean more risky decisions (committing a large amount of resources to developing a new product that may or may not be successful) or more conservative (deciding not to introduce any new products because of the uncertainty involved) than a middle-of-the road approach (committing a moderate amount of money to new product development).

Why are decisions made by groups more extreme than decisions made by individuals? The diffusion of responsibility is one reason.[56] But there are at least two more explanations for group polarization. First, knowing that other group members have the same views or support the same decision can cause group members to become more confident of their positions.[57] Group members who initially supported committing a moderate amount of resources to the development of a new product may become more confident in the product's potential success after learning that other members of the group also feel good about the product. As a result of this increased confidence, the group makes the more extreme decision to commit a large amount of resources. Second, as a group discusses alternatives, members of the group often come up with persuasive arguments to support their favored alternative (why the new product under consideration is "bound to be" a success).[58] As a result of these persuasive arguments, the group's confidence in the chosen alternative increases, and the decision becomes more extreme.

Potential for Conflict.   There is always the potential for conflict in decision-making groups. Group members differ in their knowledge, skills, and expertise as well as in their past experiences. These differences cause them to view problems and opportunities and responses to them in different ways. Moreover, certain group members may stand to benefit from one alternative being

TO MANAGERS

Group Decision Making

- Use groups to make decisions when the decision requires a wide range of skills, knowledge, and expertise, or more information than a single individual could be expected to consider and remember, or when acceptance by others is necessary to implement the decision. But keep in mind that group decision making is time-consuming.
- Use individuals to make decisions when an individual has all the skills and knowledge necessary to make a good decision, when an individual can gather and accurately take into account all necessary information, and when acceptance by others for successful implementation is either unnecessary or likely to occur regardless of their involvement in decision making.
- Encourage group members to be critical of each other's ideas and to raise any doubts or misgivings they may have.
- In the groups you lead, wait to express your own opinions until the group has had a chance to evaluate the different alternatives.
- Whenever a decision-making group is cohesive, follow the five steps to help prevent groupthink.
- Impress on group members that each of them is responsible for helping the group make a good decision.

chosen over another, and self-interest may cause those members to push for that alternative. Other group members may resent this pressure and disagree or push for an alternative that benefits them. Such conflict (as you will see in Chapter 18) can be both functional and dysfunctional for groups and organizations: functional when it forces group members to evaluate alternatives carefully, dysfunctional when group members are more concerned about winning the battle than about making a good decision.

Group Decision-Making Techniques

Several techniques have been developed to help groups make good decisions that promote high levels of performance and positive attitudes and avoid some of the potential disadvantages of group decision making. In this section we describe three of those techniques: brainstorming, the nominal group technique, and the Delphi technique. We also discuss some of the group decision-making techniques used in total quality management programs.

BRAINSTORMING

Sometimes groups do not consider as wide a range of alternative responses to problems and opportunities as they should. At other times, group members prematurely make a decision without adequately considering other alternatives. **Brainstorming** is a spontaneous, participative decision-making technique that groups use to generate a wide range of alternatives from which to make a decision.[59] A typical brainstorming session proceeds like this:

1. Group members sit around a table, and one member of the group describes the problem or opportunity in need of a response.
2. Group members are encouraged to share their own ideas with the rest of the group in a free and open manner without any critical evaluation of the ideas.
3. Group members are urged to share their ideas no matter how far-out they may seem, to come up with as many ideas as they can, and to build on each other's suggestions.
4. One member of the group records the ideas on a chalkboard or flip chart as they are presented.

Although it seems that brainstorming groups would come up with a wide range of alternatives, research suggests that individuals working separately tend to generate more ideas than do brainstorming groups.[60] A group of marketing managers who brainstorm to come up with a catchy name for a new convertible sports car, for example, will in all likelihood come up with fewer ideas than will individual managers who dream up ideas on their own and then pool them. Why does this outcome occur? There are at least two reasons. First, even though members of brainstorming groups are encouraged to share even the wildest or strangest idea and even though criticism is suppressed, group members tend to be inhibited from sharing all their ideas with others. Second, **production blocking** takes place. This loss of productivity in brainstorming groups has several causes.[61] Group members cannot give their full attention to generating alternatives because they are listening to other people's ideas. They forget some of their ideas while they are waiting for their turn to share them with the rest of the group. Only one person can speak at a time, so the number of ideas that can be presented is limited.

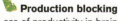 **Brainstorming**

A spontaneous, participative decision-making technique that groups use to generate a wide range of alternatives from which to make a decision.

Production blocking

Loss of productivity in brainstorming groups due to various distractions and limitations inherent to brainstorming.

Electronic brainstorming can overcome some of these problems. Group members can use personal computers to record their ideas while at the same time having access to alternatives generated by other group members on their computer screens. Electronic brainstorming is an effective means of preventing some of the production blocking that occurs when brainstorming groups meet face to face.[62]

THE NOMINAL GROUP TECHNIQUE

> **Nominal group technique**
> A decision-making technique that includes the following steps: group members generate ideas on their own and write them down, group members communicate their ideas to the rest of the group, and each idea is then discussed and critically evaluated by the group.

The **nominal group technique** (NGT) also can be used to overcome production blocking and is a way for groups that need to make a decision in a couple of hours to select an alternative.[63] Group members sit around a table, and one member of the group describes the problem or opportunity. Group members are then given a certain amount of time (perhaps twenty or thirty minutes) to come up with ideas or alternative ways to respond to the problem or opportunity and write them down on a piece of paper. Because group members come up with alternatives on their own, the NGT avoids production blocking. Moreover, when the NGT is used, group members are encouraged to write down all their ideas no matter how bizarre they may seem. Doing this individually may help to overcome the inhibition that limits some brainstorming groups.

After writing all their ideas, group members present their ideas in a round-robin fashion: Each person seated at the table presents one idea at a time. One member records the ideas on a chalkboard or flip chart, and no discussion of the ideas takes place at this point. After all the ideas are listed, the group discusses them one by one. Group members are allowed to raise questions and objections and critically evaluate each idea. After each alternative has been discussed, each group member privately ranks all of the alternatives from most preferred to least preferred. The alternative that receives the highest ranking in the group is chosen, and the decision-making process is complete.

The nominal group technique allows groups to reach a decision (sometimes in a couple of hours) and allows for the consideration of all group members' ideas. But it is not feasible for complex decisions that require the processing of large amounts of information and repeated group meetings. The NGT is also not appropriate when it is important that all or most group members agree on the alternative chosen, such as is the case when a jury deliberates.

THE DELPHI TECHNIQUE

> **Delphi technique**
> A decision-making technique in which a series of questionnaires are sent to experts on the issue at hand who never actually meet face to face.

When the **Delphi technique** is used, group members never meet face to face.[64] When a leader is faced with a problem or opportunity that needs to be responded to, the advice of experts in the area is sought through written communication. The leader describes the problem or opportunity and solicits their help by asking them to complete and return a questionnaire. After all the questionnaires have been returned, the leader compiles the responses and sends a summary of them to all group members along with additional questions that need to be answered for a decision to be made. This process is repeated as many times as needed to reach a consensus or a decision that most of the experts think is a good one.

The Delphi technique has the advantage of not requiring group members who may be scattered around the country or the globe to meet face to face. Its principal disadvantages are that it can be time-consuming and does not allow for group interaction. It also depends on the cooperation of the experts to respond promptly to the questionnaires and take the time needed to complete them carefully. These disadvantages can be overcome to some extent by using computer software for work groups that is being developed by companies such as Microsoft (see Chapter 13).

GROUP DECISION-MAKING TECHNIQUES USED IN TOTAL QUALITY MANAGEMENT

Total quality management (TQM)[65] is a philosophy and set of practices that have been developed to improve the quality of an organization's goods and services and the efficiency with which they are produced. TQM (which we discuss in detail in Chapter 19) includes two group decision-making techniques, benchmarking and empowerment, that can be used to improve group decision making in general. The objective of these techniques is to encourage group members to make suggestions and use their knowledge to come up with ways to reduce costs and waste and increase quality with the ultimate goal of pleasing the final customer. Benchmarking and empowerment can be used, for example, in manufacturing settings to reduce defects and recalls of new cars, in customer service departments to shorten the time it takes to respond to a customer complaint, and in accounting departments to make bills easier for customers to read.

Benchmarking. When groups make decisions, it is often difficult for group members to grasp exactly what they should be striving for or trying to achieve when they evaluate alternatives. A group's overall goal, for example, may be to increase performance and quality, but the level of performance or quality that the group should aim at may not be clear to group members. Benchmarking helps groups figure out what they should be trying to accomplish when they make decisions (a *benchmark* is a standard against which something can be measured or judged).

Benchmarking is selecting a high-performing group or organization that is currently providing high-quality goods or services to its customers and using this group or organization as a model. When a low-performing group needs to make a decision, members compare where their group is with where the benchmark group or organization is on some criteria of quality and try to come up with ways to reach the standard set by the benchmark group or organization. For example, when groups in express delivery organizations like DHL and Airborne Express need to decide how to improve the quality of their services to customers, they sometimes use Federal Express's guarantee of next-day delivery and continuous tracking of letters and packages as benchmarks of what they should be striving for.

Empowerment. A guiding principle of total quality management is that performance and quality improvements are the responsibility of *all* organizational members because the workers performing jobs are often in the best position to come up with ways to change their tasks or products to improve performance and quality.

Empowerment is the process of giving workers throughout an organization the authority to make decisions and be responsible for their outcomes. Empowerment often requires managers and other workers to change the way they think about decision making. Rather than managers making the decisions and the rest of an organization's employees carrying them out, empowerment requires that the responsibility for decision making be shared throughout an organization.

Getting workers and managers to change the way they think about decision making in an organization can be difficult but also can be worth the effort.

Benchmarking
Selecting a high-performing group and using this group as a model.

Empowerment
The process of giving workers throughout an organization the authority to make decisions and be responsible for their outcomes.

Empowerment helps to ensure that work groups will see it as their responsibility to come up with ways to improve performance and quality. McDonald's, Federal Express, Kmart, Citibank, and Xerox are among the growing list of companies using empowerment to improve group decision making.[66] Xerox has gone so far as to push its suppliers to use empowerment (and other TQM practices) to improve the quality of the parts Xerox buys from them.[67] Xerox, for example, purchases electromagnetic components from Trident Tools, located in Rochester, New York. Xerox helped train Trident employees in TQM techniques such as empowerment so that the quality of Trident parts would improve. As a result of this training, groups of workers at Trident have come up with ways to reduce the number of steps in the company's materials-ordering procedures from 26 to 12, reduce the lead-time needed to fill customer orders from 16 to 7 weeks, and reduce the amount of time needed to design new components from 5 years to 16 months.

The empowerment of group members often changes the nature of managers' jobs too, as indicated in Insight 14.4.

Insight 14.4

Decision Making

Managing Empowered Group Members

When work-group members are empowered, workers often make many of the decisions and have a lot of the responsibility that used to be part of middle managers' jobs. As a result, some middle managers have been laid off. What do the remaining middle managers do now that empowered work groups have taken on many of their former responsibilities? Essentially they serve as coaches, facilitators, teachers, and sponsors of the empowered groups. They are, in a sense, what some people call the "new non-manager managers."[68]

One of these new non-manager managers is 37-year-old Cindy Ransom, a middle manager in charge of a Clorox (www.clorox.com) manufacturing plant in Fairfield, California, that employs around a hundred workers. In 1990, Ransom empowered her subordinates by asking them to reorganize the entire plant. Teams of workers earning hourly wages were suddenly setting up training programs, drafting rules governing absenteeism, and redesigning the plant into five customer-focused business groups. Ransom intentionally did little to interfere with what the workers were doing; her input consisted mainly of answering questions. Two years later, Ransom's plant showed the most improvement in performance in its division. What did Ransom do as workers started taking over many of the responsibilities and tasks she used to perform? She focused on identifying and satisfying the needs of Clorox's customers and suppliers, activities on which she had not spent much time in the past.

Middle managers traditionally may have told workers what to do and how and when to do it, but managers of empowered work groups see it as their responsibility to ask the right questions and allow their work groups to decide on the answers. Dee Zalneraitis, who is a middle manager in charge of the Hudson, Massachusetts, division of the R. R. Donnelley & Sons printing company (www.rrdonnelley.com), admits that sometimes it is hard for her to let groups make decisions on their own when she already knows the answers. Group members, however, learn much more about their group's and their organization's problems and opportunities when they make decisions on their own. Zalneraitis involves her subordinates in decision making as much as possible. As a result, her own job is both more easy and more difficult. For example, budget time always used to be particularly stressful for Zalneraitis as she struggled to find ways to cut costs. Now, budgeting is easier because her empowered subordinates often come up with ways to save money that haven't occurred to her. However, as Zalneraitis puts it, "It takes a lot more time explaining things. You really have to enjoy helping them learn."[69] All in all, empowerment has changed the nature of middle managers' jobs. They have lost some of their old responsibilities, but have gained new ones.

Creativity

Many organizations value creativity and innovation, yet both are poorly understood by managers and researchers alike. Nevertheless, progress has been made in understanding the factors that foster creativity in decision making.

Creativity can be defined as a decision making process that produces novel and useful ideas.[70] By *novel*, we mean that the ideas represent new ways of thinking. By *useful*, we mean that the ideas have the potential to contribute to the performance and well-being of individuals, groups, and organizations. The idea of easy-to-use stick-on notes (Post-it note pads), the idea of offering healthy foods like salads in fast-food restaurants such as McDonald's, and the idea of flexible work schedules—all are examples of the results of creativity. Creative ideas like these are novel and useful responses to problems and opportunities and can result from individual and group decision making.

Innovation is the successful implementation of creative ideas.[71] The 3M Corporation innovated when it successfully manufactured and marketed Post-it notepads. Creativity and innovation are so important for organizations that corporate reputations often hinge on these two processes, as indicated in Insight 14.5.

 Creativity
A decision-making process that produces novel and useful ideas.

 Innovation
The successful implementation of creative ideas.

Insight 14.5 **Competitive Advantage**

Corporate Reputations Built on Creativity and Innovation

Each year *Fortune* magazine conducts an annual Corporate Reputations Survey. For the 1993 survey, more than 10,000 upper-level managers, members of boards of directors, and financial analysts rated over 400 of the largest corporations on eight aspects of corporate reputation. These aspects include the quality of an organization's management and of the goods and services the organization provides, financial soundness and use of financial and human resources to the best advantage, and concern for the community and the environment. All of these factors contribute to an organization's competitive advantage.

An examination of the ten companies with the best corporate reputations according to *Fortune*'s survey suggests that reputations are built on creativity and innovation. The ten most admired companies include Rubbermaid, Home Depot, Coca-Cola, Microsoft, 3M, Walt Disney, Motorola, J. P. Morgan, Procter & Gamble, and United Parcel Service.[72] Creative decision making and innovation are the norm rather than the exception in these companies and contribute to their gaining a competitive advantage.

Rubbermaid introduces, on average, one new product per day. Microsoft introduced almost one hundred new products in a two-year period. Walt Disney is constantly coming up with creative ideas for new characters, songs, and stories and with novel ways to exploit opportunities to merchandise and market them. In 1993 *Aladdin* and in 1994 and 1995 *The Lion King* and their characters were seen at the movies, on TV and home videos, as toys, in books, on lunchboxes, and in Disney theme parks. Home Depot, the largest chain of home improvement retail stores, has come up with and implemented creative ideas for improving the range of merchandise available in its many stores. Motorola's commitment to creativity and innovation is evidenced by its position as the world's biggest producer of cellular phones and pagers. An instance of creativity and innovation at United Parcel Service (UPS) is the use of electronic notepads by drivers to get signatures from customers who receive deliveries (UPS uses Motorola's cellular technology for the notepads). The signatures are instantly transmitted to the UPS telecommunications center in New Jersey, which can then provide customers with detailed information pertaining to the location of parcels. The message in these events is clear: A large part of an organization's reputation and competitive advantage is based on its ability to create and innovate.

THE CREATIVE PROCESS

Each instance of creativity seems unique because an individual or group has come up with a novel way of responding to a problem or opportunity. The creative process, however, usually entails a number of steps (see Fig. 14.5).[73] The first two steps are recognizing the problem or opportunity and *gathering information*. For example, when Wesley Boyd, chief executive and cofounder of Berkeley Systems, Inc., a software company known for its creativity and inno-

FIGURE **14.5**

The Creative Process

Creativity | Innovation

Recognition of a problem or an opportunity → Information gathering → Production of creative ideas → Selection of creative idea(s) → Implementation of creative idea(s)

vation, recognized an opportunity to introduce a new product, he collected information pertaining to customers' desires and programming capabilities.[74] He searched for information about how to write programs that allow users to do things they can't do with existing software and at the same time to express their own individuality and have some fun. No matter how creative they may be, decision makers such as Boyd cannot come up with good ideas if they do not have information relevant to the problem or opportunity.

The third step in the creative process is the production of ideas. Once decision makers have the information they need, they come up with potential responses to problems or opportunities. After Berkeley had collected information about what customers wanted and what, as a software company, Berkeley was able to provide them, Boyd, programmer Jack Eastman, and other Berkeley employees came up with the idea for a new software package called After Dark that allows users to choose their own screen savers and have screen savers change periodically. Screen saver programs were originally designed to protect computer screens from being damaged when computers are turned on but not in use, but now they are also used for security reasons, as a form of personal expression, and for fun. One screen saver that Berkeley has had tremendous success with is the squadron of flying toasters that flap across many personal computer monitors. After Boyd, Eastman, and other Berkeley employees had gathered the necessary information, they came up with many ideas for screen savers—tropical fish, bouncing balls, floating clocks, kaleidoscopes, urban skylines, moonscapes, and Star Trek characters.[75]

During the production of ideas, it is important that decision makers feel free to come up with ideas that seem far-fetched or off the wall. In fact, group decision-making techniques such as brainstorming and the nominal group technique were designed to encourage the production of a large number of ideas no matter how wild they may seem. As Wesley Boyd puts it, "You need to have an environment that supports creativity and allows people not to worry about getting slapped down when they come up with a good idea."[76] These ideas can emerge at any time; Jack Eastman came up with the idea of the flying toasters when he was fiddling around in his kitchen in the middle of the night.

Once the ideas have been produced, decision makers are then ready for the fourth step of the creative process: selection of the idea or ideas that they think will be useful. Sometimes decision makers assess each idea according to some criteria that they may have previously determined to be important, such as the estimated annual sales of a new type of screen saver or the amount of computer memory needed to run a program. At this step, the information gathered during the second step can be helpful in evaluating the usefulness of each idea generated.

Once one or more ideas have been selected, it is time for implementation. At this stage in the creative process innovation kicks in. Can the organization successfully implement the creative ideas it has developed and chosen to pursue? Although Berkeley Systems encourages workers to have fun on the job (a winding, plastic slide connects the first and second floors of its headquarters building in Berkeley, California), successful innovation is taken very seriously. Recent steps the company has taken to innovate include the hiring of several experienced financial analysts to help manage the financial aspects of implementing new ideas and the acquisition of funds from two venture capital firms to develop and market new products.[77] Without actions such as these, the creative ideas that decision makers come up with might be wasted because they could not be implemented.

Although the steps in the creative process are described previously and are shown in Figure 14.5 as if they always occur in a certain sequence, the order in which they occur is not fixed, nor does each step have to take place for creativity to occur. For example, the idea for screen savers that automatically change after a certain period of time originally came about when Wesley Boyd happened to notice that the screen saver on Jack Eastman's computer changed from time to time. At that point, no software companies were offering changing screen savers, and Boyd started gathering information about the viability of this idea. Once he had the information, he and other Berkeley employees started generating ideas about new designs and types of screen savers.

Creativity and the creative process, by their nature, are hard to predict. It is difficult to tell in advance, for example, which decision makers will come up with creative ideas. Some people are naturally more creative than others, but, under the right circumstances, a person who is not terribly creative may come up with a creative solution. Evidence also shows that creativity is more likely to occur in some groups and organizations than in others. Researchers who have tried to identify some of the determinants of creativity have found that characteristics of individual decision makers and of the situations in which they make decisions contribute to creativity.

CHARACTERISTICS OF DECISION MAKERS THAT CONTRIBUTE TO CREATIVITY

Numerous characteristics of decision makers have been linked to creativity, but the ones that seem to be most relevant to understanding creativity *in organizations* are personal characteristics or individual differences, task-relevant knowledge, and intrinsic motivation (see Fig. 14.6). These characteristics contribute to creativity whether decisions are made individually or in groups.

Although these factors contribute to creativity, they do not, of course, guarantee that any given decision maker or group of decision makers will be creative. And the lack (or low level) of any of these factors does not mean that a person or group will not or cannot be creative. Creativity is determined by the interaction or joint effects of a number of factors.

FIGURE 14.6

Determinants of Creativity

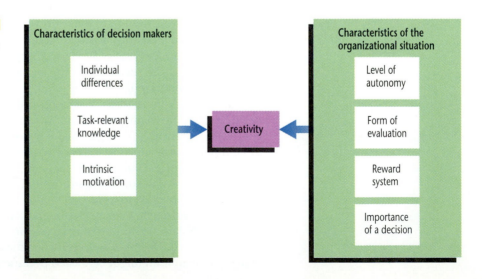

Individual Differences.   In Chapter 2 we described a variety of ways in which people differ from each other and some of the personality traits and abilities especially relevant to understanding and managing organizational behavior. At least three of the personality traits we discussed earlier are likely to contribute to creativity.[78]

Recall that one of the Big Five general personality traits is *openness to experience,* which captures the extent to which an individual is original, is open to a wide variety of stimuli, has broad interests, and is willing to take risks. How does openness to experience contribute to creativity? It helps decision makers come up with new ideas and ways of doing things, and it helps to ensure that decision makers are willing to take the risks involved in proposing unusual ideas.

Two specific personality traits that are likely to contribute to creative decision making are *locus of control* and *self-esteem* (see Chapter 2). Locus of control captures the extent to which people think that their own actions and behaviors are important in determining what happens. *Internals* believe they have a lot of control over their environment and what happens to them. *Externals* believe that outside forces determine their fate. An *internal* locus of control contributes to creativity because it results in decision makers' feeling responsible for coming up with new ideas and making good decisions. An *external* locus of control hinders creativity because decision makers believe that whatever decision they make will have little impact on performance or well-being.[79]

Self-esteem is pride in oneself and in one's capabilities.[80] Self-esteem contributes to decision makers' confidence that they can come up with creative ideas, and it gives them the confidence to take risks and suggest ideas that may seem outlandish.

In addition to personality, it also is likely that ability contributes to creativity. At the broadest level, intelligence contributes to creativity because it helps decision makers come up with new ideas, see connections between things that other people do not see, view things from different perspectives, and synthesize a lot of information. Other cognitive abilities also contribute to creativity, especially when they are relevant to the area in which a decision is being made. Numerical ability (the speed and accuracy with which a person can solve arithmetic problems), for example, is likely to contribute to creativity in a group of people who are looking at the overall cost implications of various changes to a manufacturing process.

Task-Relevant Knowledge.   Task-relevant knowledge is all of the information, skills, and expertise that an individual or group has about the decision that needs to be made.[81] Without task-relevant knowledge, it would be difficult for an architect to come up with a creative design for a new building, for a doctor to find a new way to treat arthritis, and for a secretary to discover a unique and useful filing system. To generate creative responses, the architect needs a good understanding of building design and architectural principles, the doctor needs knowledge pertaining to medicine in general and to arthritis in particular, and the secretary needs to be familiar with the kinds of information to be filed, the ways in which it needs to be accessed, and how frequently it is accessed.

Intrinsic Motivation.   In Chapter 6 we distinguished between intrinsic and extrinsic motivation. For intrinsically motivated workers, the source of motivation is the work itself. These workers enjoy performing their jobs, often love their work, and get a sense of personal satisfaction when they do a good job or come up with a creative idea. Extrinsically motivated workers may perform at a high level, but the source of their motivation is external; they are motivated by, for example, the pay they receive and the chances of receiving a bonus, raise, or promotion.

In general, workers are more likely to be creative when they are intrinsically motivated.[82] The high level of involvement in the work that intrinsic motivation brings seems to spur creativity. Wesley Boyd indicated that he was able to attract workers to his new company not by offering them high salaries but by giving them the opportunity to do the work they enjoyed and "offering them a place where they could let their imaginations run wild."[83]

CHARACTERISTICS OF THE ORGANIZATIONAL SITUATION THAT CONTRIBUTE TO CREATIVITY

Although certain individuals may be more likely than others to be creative, creativity is also more likely to occur in certain situations than in others. Four situational characteristics are likely to affect creativity: level of autonomy, form of evaluation, reward system, and the importance of a decision (see Fig. 14.6).

Level of Autonomy.   More than 70 percent of the R&D scientists who participated in a study of creativity indicated that autonomy was an important factor in instances of creativity that they were involved in or observed in their organizations.[84] Autonomy is the freedom and independence to make decisions and personal control over one's work on a day-to-day basis. The job characteristics model of task design discussed in Chapter 7 indicates that autonomy contributes to intrinsic motivation. Given that intrinsic motivation is a spur to creativity, it is not surprising that a high degree of autonomy is good for creativity. Workers at Berkeley Systems have a high level of autonomy, which contributes to their creativity in coming up with new types of screen savers and other useful computer programs. Total quality management explicitly recognizes the importance of autonomy for creative decision making with its emphasis on empowerment. Managers in some organizations have trouble encouraging creativity in their organizations because workers and managers are not used to the idea of individuals or groups being autonomous, as indicated in Insight 14.6.

Insight 14.6   **A Global View**

Increasing Autonomy in Japan to Spur Creativity

Japanese companies are well known for being able to improve existing modes of production and products, but they are not known for coming up with ideas for new products or businesses. Why do Japanese workers not come up with many creative ideas for new products? One reason is that autonomy and independent thinking have traditionally taken second place to the need for consensus and following the lead of upper management in Japanese companies. For example, Yasutaka Mori, the director of international business development for Shiseido, Japan's largest cosmetics manufacturer, admits that he has often been reluctant to make proposals for new ventures even though doing so is one of his key job responsibilities. As he puts it: "It's hard to explain just how vulnerable you are when you make a suggestion for a new business. Until recently you knew that there would have to be consensus not only among top management but also among your peers to get a proposal approved. So you'd figure it's safer just not to do anything."[85]

Top managers in Shiseido and other Japanese organizations are realizing that their future may depend on workers coming up with creative ideas and feeling comfortable expressing them. The president of Shiseido, Yoshiharu Fukuhara, instituted four-day seminars held at resorts on Mount Fuji to encourage autonomy and independence and to empower managers. He warns: "Our company cannot be like a military troop where the president gives an order and then everyone rushes to do it. Companies like that will not survive in the next era."[86] Mori was one of the managers who attended the seminar, and it seemed to work for him. After attending, he submitted a proposal for opening a division in South China. Top management approved the proposal.

Fuji Film encourages managers to read about topics such as animal behavior and the history of European cities in the hope that reading will get their creative juices flowing and start them on the road to independent thinking and the production of novel ideas. Fuji Film human resources manager Takashi Kamiya says: "You can't just tell your employees, 'Be Creative!' You have to create an environment that caters more to the individual so that employees can learn how to draw their own maps for the company's future. We've never had to do that before."[87]

Form of Evaluation.   Imagine how William Shakespeare would have felt when he was writing some of his masterpieces if a supervisor had been standing over his shoulder critiquing scenes or bits of dialogue that didn't sound quite right ("A hero who believes in ghosts, talks to himself a lot, and kills his girlfriend's father? I don't think so, Will.") and criticizing him when he took too long to complete a play. In all likelihood, these kinds of actions would have hampered some of Shakespeare's creativity.

Creative people and decision makers like to know how they are doing and to receive feedback and encouragement. But overly evaluative feedback and criticism can hamper creativity because it can make decision makers afraid to take risks.[88] If there is a strong likelihood that your boss will criticize the far-out idea you come up with, you may not risk expressing it. However, if your boss is interested in your ideas and provides constructive comments about how they may be improved and points out some of their pros and cons, you may be encouraged to come up with an even better idea.

Reward System.   People who come up with creative ideas like to be rewarded for them. But what happens if workers think that their salaries, bonuses, and chances for promotion hinge on their almost always being right, rarely or never making mistakes, and always being efficient in their use of time? Their creativity may be hampered, and they may be unlikely to take risks to come up with and choose creative responses to problems and opportunities.[89] By definition, creative responses are new, and there is always the potential that they may fail.

TO MANAGERS

To help promote creativity, an organization's reward system should recognize and reward hard work and creativity. Creative decision makers and others in the organization need to see that hard work and creativity are recognized, appreciated, and rewarded—for example, through bonuses and raises. It is important, however, that these rewards not be seen as an attempt to control behavior and that workers do not feel that they are being closely watched and that rewards are contingent on what their supervisors observe.[90] It also is important that workers *not* be punished when some of their creative ideas do not pan out.

Importance of a Decision.   Being creative is intrinsically rewarding, but it also can be hard work. Creativity is enhanced when members of an organization feel that what they are working on is important.[91] As you learned from the job characteristics model (see Chapter 7), when workers perceive that what they are doing is important (that is, when task significance is high), they are likely to be intrinsically motivated.

SUMMARY

The decisions made by workers at all levels in organizations can have a major impact on levels of performance and well-being and on the extent to which individuals, groups, and whole organizations achieve their goals. In this chapter, we made the following major points:

1. Decision making is the process by which members of an organization choose how to respond to problems and opportunities. Nonprogrammed decision making occurs when members of an organization choose how to respond to novel problems and opportunities. Nonprogrammed decision making involves a search for information. Programmed decision making occurs when members of an organization respond to recurring problems and opportunities by using standard responses (performance programs). This chapter focuses on nonprogrammed decision making.

2. The classical model of decision making is a prescriptive model that assumes that decision makers

have access to all the information they need and will make the best decision possible. A decision maker using the classical model takes these four steps: (a) listing all alternatives, (b) listing the consequences of each alternative, (c) considering his or her preferences for each alternative or set of consequences, (d) selecting the alternative that will result in the most preferred set of consequences. Decisions made according to the classical model are optimal decisions.

3. There are problems with the classical model because it is not realistic. Decision makers often do not know all the alternatives they can choose from, often do not know the consequences of each alternative, may not be clear about their own preferences, and in many cases lack the mental ability to take into account all the information required by the classical model. Moreover, the classical model can be very time-consuming.

4. March and Simon's administrative decision-making model is descriptive; it explains how decisions are actually made in organizations. March and Simon propose that decision makers choose how to respond to problems and opportunities on the basis of a simplified and approximate account of the situation called the decision maker's definition of the situation. This definition is the result of both psychological and sociological processes. Rather than making optimal decisions, decision makers often satisfice, or make an acceptable decision, not necessarily an optimal decision. Satisficing occurs because of bounded rationality.

5. Heuristics are rules of thumb that simplify decision making but can lead to errors or biases. The availability heuristic reflects the tendency to determine the frequency of an event and its causes by how easy they are to remember (how available they are from memory). The availability heuristic can lead to biased decision making when the frequency of events and causes is overestimated because they are vivid, extreme, or recent. The representativeness heuristic reflects the tendency to predict the likelihood of an event from the extent to which the event is typical (or representative) of similar kinds of events that have happened in the past. Representativeness can lead to biased decision making when decision

makers fail to take into account base rates. The anchoring and adjustment heuristic reflects the tendency to make decisions based on adjustments from some initial amount (or anchor). The anchoring and adjustment heuristic can lead to biased decision making when the initial amounts were too high or too low.

6. Escalation of commitment is the tendency of decision makers to invest additional time, money, or effort into losing courses of action. Escalation of commitment occurs because decision makers do not want to admit that they have made a mistake, view further commitment of resources as a way to recoup sunk costs, and are more likely to take risks when decisions are framed in negative rather than in positive terms.

7. The advantages of using groups instead of individuals to make decisions include the availability and diversity of members' skills, knowledge, and expertise; enhanced memory for facts; capability of error detection; and greater decision acceptance. The disadvantages of group decision making include the time it takes to make a decision and the potential for groupthink. Other consequences include diffusion of responsibility, group polarization, and the potential for conflict.

8. Group decision-making techniques used in organizations include brainstorming, the nominal group technique, and the Delphi technique. Two group decision-making techniques used in total quality management are benchmarking and empowerment.

9. Creativity is a decision making process that produces novel and useful ideas. Innovation is the successful implementation of creative ideas. The steps in the creative process are recognition of a problem or opportunity, information gathering, production of ideas, selection of ideas, and implementation. Decision makers who are high on openness to experience, have an internal locus of control, have high self-esteem, have task-relevant knowledge, and are intrinsically motivated are especially likely to be creative. Situational characteristics that are likely to impact creativity are workers' levels of autonomy, the evaluation and reward systems used in an organization, and the perceived importance of a decision.

Organizational Behavior in Action

1. Do programmed decisions and the use of performance programs always evolve from what were originally nonprogrammed decisions? Why or why not?
2. For what kinds of decisions might the classical model be more appropriate than March and Simon's model?
3. How might the anchoring and adjustment heuristic affect goal setting?
4. Can the availability and the representativeness heuristics operate simultaneously? Why or why not?
5. How might decision-making groups fall into the escalation-of-commitment trap?
6. Why do members of diverse groups sometimes find it hard to make a decision?
7. In what ways can conflict in a decision-making group be both an advantage and a disadvantage?
8. Do all workers want to be empowered and make the decisions that their bosses used to make? Why or why not?
9. What is the relationship between the anchoring and adjustment heuristic and benchmarking?
10. Is creativity important in all kinds of jobs? Why or why not?

BUILDING DIAGNOSTIC SKILLS

Analyzing Individual and Group Decisions

Think of two important decisions that you have recently made—one that you made individually and one that you made as a member of a group. Describe each decision. For each decision, answer these questions:

1. Was the process by which you made the decision more accurately described by the classical model or by March and Simon's model? Why?
2. In what ways were heuristics involved in making the decision?
3. Was escalation of commitment involved in making the decision?
4. Why did you make the individual decision on your own rather than in a group? Do you think a better decision would have been made if the decision had been made in a group? Why or why not?
5. Why did you make the other decision as a member of a group rather than on your own? Do you think that you could have made a better decision on your own? Why or why not?
6. Was any creativity involved in making the group decision? Why or why not?
7. If your answer to question 6 is yes, what factors facilitated creative decision making? If your answer is no, would creativity have led to a better decision? Why or why not?

RESEARCH ON THE INTERNET: A MANAGER'S TOOL

Specific Task

Tele-Communications Inc. (TCI) is a company which faces both a variety of opportunities and threats from the environment. Scan TCI's website (www.tci.com) to learn more about this company. Then click on "Press Releases." Review the various press releases listed.

1. What kinds of opportunities and threats does TCI face?
2. How does TCI respond to these threats and opportunities?

General Task

Many organizations strive to encourage their members to be creative. Find the website of such a company. What steps is this company taking to encourage creativity? Which kinds of employees are being encouraged to be creative? Do you think this company's creativity initiatives would be successful in other companies? Why or why not?

TOPICS FOR DEBATE

Decision making is one of the most important processes in all organizations. Now that you have a good understanding of decision making, debate the following issues.

Debate One

Team A. Individuals generally make better decisions than groups.

Team B. Groups generally make better decisions than individuals.

Debate Two

Team A. Organizations can teach their members how to be creative.

Team B. Organizations cannot teach their members how to be creative.

EXPERIENTIAL EXERCISE

Using the Nominal Group Technique
Objective
Your objective is to gain experience in using the nominal group technique.

Procedure
The class divides into groups of from three to five people, and each group appoints one member as spokesperson, to report the group's experiences to the whole class. Here is the scenario.

Assume the role of a self-managed work team. The team is one of the best-performing teams in the company, and the members like and get along well with each other. Currently team members are paid an hourly wage based on seniority. The company has decided to change the way in which members of all self-managed teams are paid and has asked each team to propose a new pay plan. One plan will be chosen from those proposed and instituted for all teams.

Use the nominal group technique to decide on a pay plan by following these steps:

1. Each team member comes up with ideas for alternative pay plans on his or her own and writes them down on a piece of paper.
2. Team members present their ideas one by one while one member records them on a piece of paper. There is no discussion of the merits of the different alternatives at this point.

3. Team members discuss the ideas one by one and raise any questions or objections. Critical evaluation takes place at this step.
4. Each team member privately ranks all the alternatives from most preferred to least preferred.
5. The team chooses the alternative that receives the highest ranking.

After the decision has been made, team members discuss the pros and cons of using the nominal group technique to make a decision like this one.

When your group has completed the exercise, the spokesperson will report back to the whole class on the decision the group reached as well as the group's assessment of the pros and cons of the nominal group technique.

MAKING THE CONNECTION

Find an example of a company that has recently made and successfully implemented one or more creative decisions and thus has been innovative. Do decisions in this organization tend to be made by individuals or by groups? Which of the determinants of creativity appear to play a role in decision making in this company?

CLOSING CASE

Making Decisions at Intel

Today, most personal computers (PCs) bear the catchy "Intel Inside" trademark indicating that they use at least one of the chips made by Intel Corporation (www.intel.com), one of the largest producers of semiconductors and microprocessors used in PCs and other electronic products.[92] Intel's profits have soared, and its future looks rosier than ever. In the mid-to-late 1980s, however, Intel was losing money, and it looked as though the company might be going down the tubes. The transformation came about through a series of good, creative decisions.

Andrew Grove, Intel's CEO and one of its founders, is credited with spearheading a decision-making process that resulted in the spending of billions of dollars on innovative research and development and on the construction of new, advanced manufacturing plants. Grove has given a lot of thought to effective decision making in organizations.

Grove maintains that decision makers should always be on the lookout for new opportunities and be at least one step ahead of competitors. In an industry in which technology changes so rapidly, decision makers need to make quick decisions and take advantage of new opportunities as they arise. Intel is constantly coming up with new kinds of computer chips (such as the Pentium) in its attempt to stay one step ahead of its competitors.

Grove believes that decision makers need to take risks and be creative but must be willing to admit when they have made mistakes and move quickly to cut their losses. In late 1992, for example, Intel decided that three projects in which the company had invested around $35 million should be dropped. Grove and other managers at Intel acknowledge their bad decisions and abandon projects that show no signs of paying off. As the dramatic rises in the price of Intel stock attest, however, Intel is making many more good decisions than bad.

Grove's approach to decision making emphasizes the need for change in response to changes inside an organization (such as changes in an organization's employees) and outside an organization (such as changes in what customers want or in available technology). Decision making should take into account the need for change, and decision makers should try to change their ways of viewing problems and opportunities to mirror the dynamics of the marketplace. For example, ten years ago Intel was primarily manufacturing semiconductor memories and selling them to a few major customers. Now, Intel makes microprocessors and views its customer base as including all 100 million end users of PCs. When making decisions now, Intel managers try to figure out what these customers will need in ten years and how Intel can design microprocessors to help satisfy those needs.

Grove acknowledges that making decisions involving millions of dollars can be stressful, especially when the future is uncertain. He says: "The pace of work these days isn't easy to live with, but welcome to the Nineties. Intel didn't create this world; we're just supplying the tools with which we can all work ourselves to death. Exhausting as it is, it's highly preferable to being unemployed."[93]

Questions for Discussion
1. Why do decisions sometimes need to be made quickly?
2. Is change an important aspect of decision making in all organizations or only in those in rapidly changing industries like the semiconductor industry?

Organizational Structure and Culture

15

Campbell Soup Is Red Hot

Under its hard-driving, charismatic CEO David W. Johnson, the Campbell Soup Company (www.campbellsoups.com) has been achieving record performance in the 1990s. All its different businesses or divisions, such as its soup, snack foods, frozen foods, entrées, and fruits and vegetables

divisions, have been enjoying booming sales and profits. To a large degree Campbell's continuing success can be attributed to the methods Johnson uses to motivate and coordinate Campbell's employees and to encourage them to perform at a high level.

First, Johnson created a structure of work roles and

reporting relationships that allows the company to make the most efficient use of its resources. To encourage the development of new kinds of products, in each division he groups employees into customer-driven teams, armed with the latest technologies, which are instructed to focus on finding new kinds of products that will best satisfy customers' needs. Johnson sets ambitious goals for each team of employees to achieve, such as finding specific ways to reduce costs or to increase the number of new products to be developed and brought to market. He then delegates to team members the authority they need to make all the decisions necessary for meeting these challenging goals. Finally, he monitors the teams' performance, and each team is rewarded according to the success it has had with using its resources to meet its goals. For example, in 1996 one team in Campbell's food services division created a chicken pot-pie for the Kentucky Fried Chicken fast food chain that became a runaway success and the best selling product ever for the division. The members of this team received substantial bonuses, and many members were promoted to become the leaders of other teams. With hundreds of similar teams throughout Campbell's many food divisions, the number of new and improved products that Campbell's has introduced has soared in the 1990s—hence its superior performance.

The other method Johnson uses to motivate his employees and get them to perform at a high level is to lead by example and to establish strong values and norms about the importance of people to the company. An easygoing and approachable Australian, he once donned a red cape and dubbed himself "Souperman" in leading a rally to energize his employees. His goal is to instill in Campbell employees strong beliefs about their importance to the organization and about how he wants them to take risks and go out on a limb to find ways to reduce costs and raise quality to improve the company's performance. He has created a culture at Campbell's based on values and norms that state that people are the source of the company's competitive advantage, and as noted earlier, he makes sure that employees are rewarded for the contributions that they make.

Working with formal roles and reporting relationships and informal values and norms, Johnson has fashioned an organization that has become a master at giving customers what they want, and doing it efficiently. Currently, Johnson is working on making Campbell a global leader, so that it can tap into the huge global demand for its high-quality food products. Imagine, for example, the potential market for Campbell's soup, goldfish crackers, or Pepperidge Farm cookies in China or India if Johnson can get Campbell's products established there.

Overview

As the opening case on Campbell Soup suggests, managing the relationship among the individuals and teams that make up an organization can be a difficult task. In this chapter we look at how organizations can create and use organizational structure and culture to effectively manage individuals and, most important, intergroup relations—the relationships between different functions and divisions. We examine the relationship between organizational structure, culture, and design. We look at the different ways in which managers can group people and resources to create organizational structures that allow workers to achieve organizational goals. We examine the mechanisms organizations use to integrate people and groups and ensure that they work together to meet organizational goals. We examine the nature of organizational culture and discuss how organizational values and norms influence intergroup relationships and organizational effectiveness. By the end of the chapter you will understand how to create and use organizational structure and culture to manage intergroup relationships effectively.

In the remaining chapters we then look at the various factors and processes that affect organizational structure and culture. In Chapter 16 we examine the way in which three factors—the environment, technology, and strategy—impact organizational structure and culture. In Chapter 17 we examine how the decision to compete internationally and become a global organization affects the way an organization operates. In Chapter 18 we examine conflict and politics and their effect on organizations and their members. In Chapter 19 we examine the issues and problems surrounding changing organizational structure and culture to enhance an organization's ability to meet its goals. By the end of Chapter 19 you will understand how the total organizational context affects the performance and well-being of an organization and the individuals and groups inside it.

Organizational Structure, Culture, and Design

As we noted in Chapter 1, organizations are composed of people who work together to achieve a wide variety of goals. One of the main reasons people work together in organizations is to enjoy the gains in productivity that arise from the division of labor and specialization. Adam Smith (see Appendix 1) noted that when people work together in organizations, they can divide an organization's task (in Smith's example the task was making pins) into narrow, very specific tasks (such as putting the point on the pin). Smith, and many others since his death over two centuries ago, confirmed that when different people specialize in different tasks, they become more productive and can perform at a higher level, which helps an organization to achieve its goals.[1]

Organizational design is the process by which managers select and manage various dimensions and components of organizational structure and culture so that an organization can achieve its goals. **Organizational structure** is the *formal* system of task and reporting relationships that controls, coordinates, and motivates employees so that they cooperate to achieve an organization's goals. The basic building blocks of organizational structure are differentiation and integration, discussed below. **Organizational culture** is the *informal* set of values and norms that controls the way people and groups in an organization interact with each other and with people outside the organization, such as customers and suppliers. Organizations can also attempt to influence the behavior of their members by encouraging the development of supportive kinds of values and norms.

In all organizations, managers must try to create an organizational structure and culture that (1) encourage employees to work hard and to develop supportive work attitudes and (2) allow people and groups to cooperate and

Organizational design
The process by which managers select and manage various dimensions and components of organizational structure and culture so that an organization can achieve its goals.

Organizational structure
The formal system of task and reporting relationships that controls, coordinates, and motivates employees so that they cooperate and work together to achieve an organization's goals.

Organizational culture
The informal set of values and norms that controls the way people and groups in an organization interact with each other and with people outside the organization.

work together effectively.[2] As we saw in the Apple Computer example, structure and culture affect the way people behave: their motivation, their desire to perform well or engage in supportive kinds of citizenship behaviors. Structure and culture also affect intergroup relationships and the motivation of different functions and divisions to work together and share resources in order to increase organizational performance.

What bearing does organizational design have on organizational behavior? The way a structure or culture is designed or evolves over time affects the way people and groups behave within the organization. Once an organization decides how it wants its members to behave, what attitudes it wants to encourage, and what it wants its members to accomplish, it can then design its structure and encourage the development of the cultural values and norms to obtain these desired attitudes, behaviors, and goals.

How does an organization determine which attitudes and behaviors to encourage? An organization bases these design decisions on the *contingencies* it faces (a *contingency* is any event that might possibly occur and thus must be taken into account in planning). Contingency theory is the theory that organizations design their structures and cultures to allow them to effectively respond to and manage events, whether expected or unexpected.[3] In Chapter 16 we examine the three major contingencies that determine what kind of structure and culture an organization designs: the organization's environment, the technology an organization uses, and the organization's strategy. First, however, we must describe the different kinds of structure that organizations can use to coordinate and motivate their members, and the way in which organizational culture is established and develops over time.[4] Figure 15.1 illustrates the nature of the organizational design process.

FIGURE **15.1**

The Nature of
Organizational Design

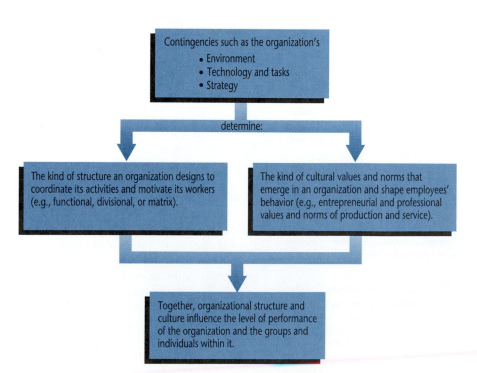

Contingencies such as the organization's
- Environment
- Technology and tasks
- Strategy

determine:

The kind of structure an organization designs to coordinate its activities and motivate its workers (e.g., functional, divisional, or matrix).

The kind of cultural values and norms that emerge in an organization and shape employees' behavior (e.g., entrepreneurial and professional values and norms of production and service).

Together, organizational structure and culture influence the level of performance of the organization and the groups and individuals within it.

Differentiation: Grouping Organizational Activities

Differentiation is the grouping of people and tasks into functions and divisions to produce goods and services.[5] A **function** is a set of people who work together and perform the same types of tasks or hold similar positions in an organization. For example, the salespeople in a car dealership belong to the sales function. Together, car sales, car repair, car parts, and accounting are the set of functions that allow a car dealership to sell and maintain cars. Similarly, product design, software programming, and manufacturing are crucial functions that allow Compaq and Dell Computer to develop innovative products.

As organizations grow and their division of labor into various functions increases, they typically differentiate further into divisions. As Campbell Soup started to produce different kinds of products, it created separate product divisions, each of which had its own food research, quality, and manufacturing functions. A **division** is a group of functions created to allow an organization to produce and dispose of its goods and services to customers. In developing an organizational structure, managers must decide how to differentiate and group an organization's activities by function and division in a way that achieves organizational goals effectively.[6] The result of this process can be most easily seen in an organizational chart that shows the relationship between an organization's functions and divisions, as at PepsiCo in Insight 15.1.

Differentiation
The grouping of people and tasks into functions and divisions to produce goods and services.

Function
A set of people who perform the same types of tasks or hold similar positions in an organization.

Division
A group of functions created to allow an organization to produce and dispose of its goods and services to customers.

Insight 15.1

Structure

PepsiCo's Organizational Chart

PepsiCo (www.pepsico.pcy.mci.net) is one of the most successful companies in the United States. Its famous soft drink was developed in 1890, and by 1945 Pepsi-Cola had developed a national following. The turning point for the Pepsi-Cola Company, however, came in 1964, when it decided to expand into new business areas and started this process by merging with the snack maker Frito-Lay of Dallas to become PepsiCo. Soon after, the company became involved in the restaurant business, so it operated in three different businesses: snack foods, restaurants, and soft drinks. The problem PepsiCo faced was how to manage its different businesses effectively.

Top management, guided by CEO Wayne Calloway, developed three principal operating divisions: the Snack Foods, Restaurant, and Soft Drinks divisions (see Fig. 15.2). Each operating division is composed of several subdivisions selling specific products. The Restaurant Division, for example, consists of three product divisions: KFC, Pizza Hut, and Taco Bell. Each product division has the functions necessary to manage its business effectively. So far, this grouping of organizational activities has allowed PepsiCo to manage its growth spectacularly well. The company made record profits in 1995, and each of the three operating divisions is thriving under the control of its management team. Calloway gives each team wide autonomy to run its division as it thinks best.

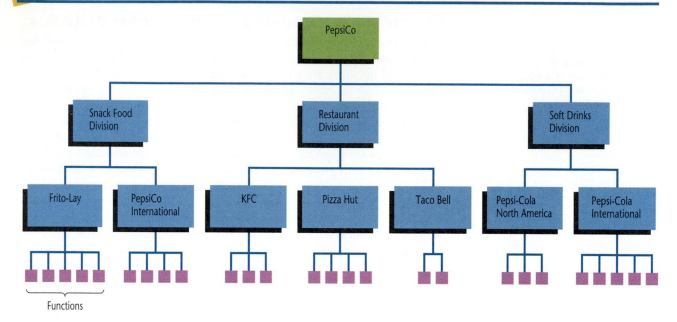

Functions

FIGURE 15.2

PepsiCo's Organizational Chart

Organizations can choose from among many kinds of structure to group their activities. Associated with each kind are specific advantages and disadvantages. We first discuss differentiation by function and examine the advantages and disadvantages of a functional structure. We then look at differentiation by division, which results in the creation of complex types of divisional structure: product, market, and geographic structures. Finally, we examine matrix structure, a special kind of structure used when an organization is changing quickly.

FUNCTIONAL STRUCTURE

Functional structure

An organizational structure that groups together people who hold similar positions, perform a similar set of tasks, or use the same kinds of skills.

A **functional structure** groups people together because they hold similar positions in an organization, perform a similar set of tasks, or use the same kinds of skills. This division of labor and specialization allows an organization to become more effective. Dell Computer Company, a personal computer manufacturer based in Austin, Texas, provides a good example of how a company develops a functional structure.

Dell Computer was founded in 1984 by Michael Dell, who used $1,000 of his savings to begin an operation to assemble personal computers. At first, he and three employees assembled computers on a six-foot-square table. But spectacular demand for his product, a cheap IBM clone, led to huge growth of his company. By 1995 he was employing over 4,500 workers, and his company had sales of over $2 billion. To effectively control the activities of his employees as his company grew, Dell created the functional structure illustrated in Fig. 15.3.

Dell groups all employees who perform tasks related to assembling personal computers into the manufacturing function and all employees who handle Dell's telephone sales into the sales function. Engineers responsible for designing Dell's computers are grouped into the product development function, and employees responsible for obtaining supplies of hard disks, chips, and other inputs are grouped into the materials management function. The functional structure suits the needs of Dell's growing company as it battles with Compaq and IBM for control of the personal computer market.

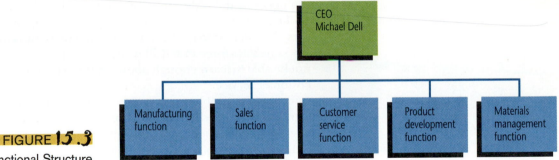

FIGURE 15.3

Dell's Functional Structure

ADVANTAGES OF A FUNCTIONAL STRUCTURE

A functional structure offers several advantages for the managing of organizational activities, and all organizations (even relatively small ones) group their activities by function to gain the productivity benefits that result from the division of labor and specialization.

Coordination Advantages. People grouped together according to similarities in their positions can easily communicate and share information with each other. As we saw in Chapter 13 on communication and Chapter 14 on decision making, people who approach problems from the same perspective can often make decisions more quickly and effectively than can people whose perspectives differ. A functional grouping also makes it easier for people to learn from one another's experiences. Thus a functional structure helps employees improve their skills and abilities and thereby enhances individual and organizational performance.

Motivation Advantages. Differentiation by function improves an organization's ability to motivate employees. When employees are grouped together by function, supervisors are in a good position to monitor individual performance, reward high performance, and discourage social loafing. Functional supervisors find monitoring easy because they usually possess high levels of skill in the particular function. Differentiation by function also allows group members to monitor and control one another's behavior and performance levels. Functional grouping can also lead to the development of norms, values, and group cohesiveness that promote high performance (see Chapter 11). Finally, grouping by function creates a career ladder to motivate employees: Functional managers and supervisors are typically workers who have been promoted because of their superior performance.

DISADVANTAGES OF A FUNCTIONAL STRUCTURE

To manage the increasing division of labor and specialization, most organizations develop a functional structure because of its coordination and motivation advantages. But as an organization continues to grow and its activities become more diverse and complex, a functional structure may no longer allow the organization to coordinate its activities effectively. Functional structure may become a disadvantage for any one of three reasons:

1. When the range of products or services that a company produces increases, the various functions can have difficulty efficiently servicing

the needs of the wide range of products. Imagine the coordination problems that would arise, for example, if a company started to make cars, then went into computers, and then went into clothing but used the same sales force to sell all three products. Most salespeople would not be able to learn enough about all three products to provide good customer service.

2. Coordination problems may arise. As organizations attract customers with different needs, they may find it hard to service these different needs by using a single set of functions. The needs of individual customers, for example, are often very different from the needs of large corporate customers, although each group requires a high level of personalized service.

3. As companies grow, they often expand their operations nationally, and servicing the needs of different regional customers by using a single set of manufacturing, sales, or purchasing functions becomes very difficult.

To solve these coordination problems, organizations typically further differentiate their activities by adopting a divisional structure.

DIVISIONAL STRUCTURES: PRODUCT, MARKET, AND GEOGRAPHIC

A divisional structure that overlays functional groupings allows an organization to coordinate intergroup relationships more effectively than does a functional structure. Companies can choose from three kinds of divisional structure: product, market, and geographic structures (see Fig. 15.4). Each is suited to a particular kind of coordination problem facing an organization.

Product structure

A divisional organizational structure that groups functions by types of product so that each division contains the functions it needs to service the products it produces.

Product Structure.   When an organization chooses to group people and functions so that it can produce a wide variety of different products, it moves to a **product structure.** Each product division contains the functions necessary to service the specific goods or services it produces. Figure 15.4(a) shows the product structure used by a company such as General Electric or Westinghouse. The organization has separate product divisions—computer, aerospace, and appliance—and each division has its own set of functions (such as accounting, marketing, and research and development).

What are the advantages of a product structure? It allows a company to increase its division of labor so that it can produce an increased number of *similar products* (such as a wider variety of appliances like stoves, refrigerators, or ovens) or expand into new markets and produce totally *new kinds of products* (such as when an appliance maker starts to produce computers or airplanes). General Electric, for example, currently has over a hundred divisions producing a huge number of products ranging from washing machines to light bulbs to electric turbines to television programs.

Market structure

A divisional organizational structure that groups functions by types of customers so that each division contains the functions it needs to service a specific segment of the market.

Market Structure.   Sometimes the most pressing problem facing an organization is to deliver products to customers in a way that best meets customer needs. To accomplish this goal, an organization is likely to choose a **market structure** and group functions into divisions that can be responsive to the needs of particular types of customers. The large computer maker Digital Equipment Corporation, for example, serves individual customers, but the organization also has business and government customers who buy in large quantities and want personal computers designed to suit their particular needs

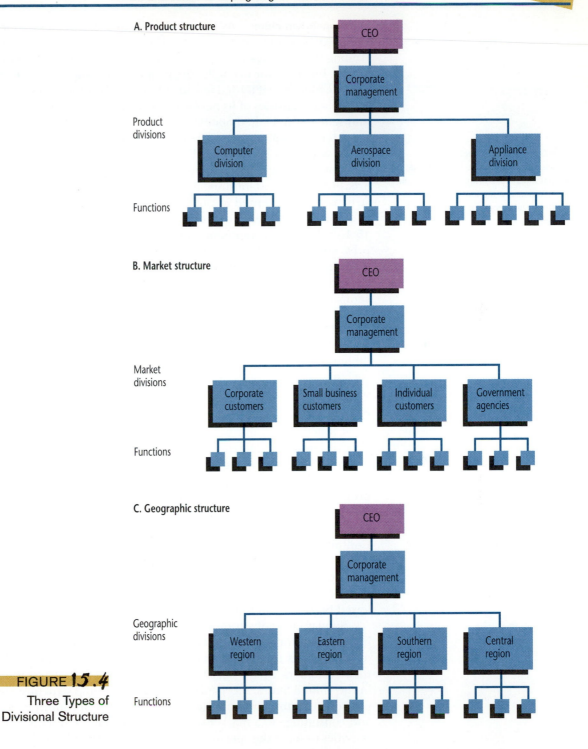

A. Product structure

B. Market structure

C. Geographic structure

FIGURE 15.4

Three Types of
Divisional Structure

and loaded with their specific choice of software. To allow its divisions to tailor or modify computers to suit the specific needs of each group of customers, Digital moved from a product structure to a market structure. Figure 15.4(b) shows the market structure that Digital created.[7]

Geographic Structure.   As an organization grows, it begins to operate in many different areas of a country or in different countries and has difficulty controlling the activities of employees in locations far away from one central location. Imagine, for example, the problems a company like Federal Express would experience if it tried to control from its headquarters in Memphis, Tennessee, the activities of its personnel who are spread through every large city and state in the United States.

🔖 **Geographic structure**
A division organizational structure that groups functions by region so that each division contains the functions it needs to service customers in a specific geographic area.

An organization facing the problem of controlling its activities on a national or international level is likely to use a **geographic structure** and group functions into regional divisions to service customers in different geographic areas (details on establishing and managing an international organizational structure are presented in Chapter 17). Each geographic division has access to a full set of the functions it needs to provide its goods and services. Figure 15.4(c) shows the geographic structure that Federal Express uses. Federal Express created four different regional divisions to control its activities. Each region has the set of functions needed to meet Federal Express's goal of providing reliable next-day delivery, and managers in each region are responsible for controlling the company's operations in their region.

ADVANTAGES OF A DIVISIONAL STRUCTURE

Divisional structures—whether product, market, or geographic—have coordination and motivation advantages that overcome many of the problems associated with a functional structure as the size and complexity of an organization increase.

Coordination Advantages.   Because each division contains its own set of functions, functions are able to focus their activities on a specific kind of good, service, or customer. This narrow focus helps a division to create high-quality products and provide high-quality customer service. Each product division, for example, has its own sales force that specializes in selling its particular product. This specialization allows salespeople to perform effectively.

A divisional structure also facilitates communication between functions and can improve decision making, thereby increasing performance. Both Conrail and Burlington Northern, large railroad companies, began dividing up their shipping operations into product divisions that reflected the specific shipping needs of the products the companies ship—cars, chemicals, food products, and so on. The change from a functional to a product structure allowed both of them to reduce costs and make better use of their resources.[8]

Similar kinds of advantages result from using a market structure. Grouping different functions together in a market division to serve one type of customer enables the functions to coordinate their activities and better serve their customers. KPMG Peat Marwick, the fourth largest accounting company in the United States, reorganized from a functional structure (in which people were organized into traditional functions like accounting, auditing, taxes, and consulting) to a market structure (in which all functions combine their activities to serve the specific needs of service, manufacturing, financial, and other types of industry.[9] KPMG moved to a market structure to make better use of its human and other resources.

A geographic structure puts managers closer to the scene of operations than are managers at central headquarters. Regional managers are well positioned to be responsive to local situations such as the needs of regional customers and to fluctuations in resources. Thus regional divisions are often able to find solutions to region-specific problems and to use available resources more effectively than are managers at corporate headquarters.

Finally, on an individual level, people who are grouped together into divisions are sometimes able to pool their skills and knowledge and brainstorm new ideas for products or improved customer service. As divisions develop a common identity and approach to solving problems, their cohesiveness increases, and the result is improved decision making.

Motivation Advantages.   Differentiation into divisions offers organizations a wide range of motivation advantages. First, a divisional structure gives rise to a new level of management: **corporate management** (see Fig. 15.4). The responsibility of corporate management is to supervise and oversee the managers of the various divisions. Corporate managers coordinate and motivate divisional managers and reward them on the basis of the performance of their individual divisions. Thus a divisional structure makes it relatively easy for organizations to evaluate and reward the performance of individual divisions and their managers and to assign rewards in a way that is closely linked to their performance. Recall from Chapter 8 that this clear connection between performance and reward increases motivation. Corporate managers can also evaluate one regional operation against another and thus share ideas between regions and find ways to improve performance.

A second motivation advantage is that divisional managers are close to their employees and are in a good position to monitor and evaluate their performance. Furthermore, divisional managers enjoy a large measure of autonomy because they, not corporate managers, are responsible for operations. Their autonomy promotes positive work attitudes and boosts performance. Another motivation advantage of a divisional structure is that regional managers and employees are close to their customers and may develop personal relationships with them—relationships that may give those managers and employees extra incentive to perform well. Finally, on an individual level, employees' close identification with their division can increase their commitment, loyalty, and job satisfaction.

DISADVANTAGES OF A DIVISIONAL STRUCTURE

Although divisional structures offer large, complex organizations a number of coordination and motivation advantages over functional structures, they have certain disadvantages as well. Some of these disadvantages can be avoided by good management, but some are simply the result of the way a divisional structure works.

First, because each division has its own set of functions, **operating costs—** the costs associated with managing an organization—increase. The number of managers in an organization, for example, increases, because each division has its own set of sales managers, manufacturing managers, and so on. There is also a completely new level of management, the corporate level, to pay for.

Second, as we discuss below, communication may suffer. Because divisional structures normally have more managers and more levels of management than functional structures have, communications problems can arise as various managers at various levels in various divisions attempt to coordinate their activities.

Third, divisions may start to compete for organizational resources and may start to pursue divisional goals and objectives at the expense of organizational ones. These conflicts reduce cooperation and can cause the organization to

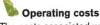
Corporate management
The set of managers whose responsibility is to supervise and oversee the divisional managers.

Operating costs
The costs associated with managing an organization.

lose any advantages it gained from the divisional structure (such as the sharing of information and knowledge between divisions or improved customer service and improved product development).

In summary, divisional structures have many coordination and motivation advantages over functional structures, but they have disadvantages as well. An organization must compare the benefits and costs of using a functional or a divisional structure, and when the benefits exceed the costs, it should move to a divisional structure. Even with a divisional structure, however, an organization must manage the structure to reduce its disadvantages and must keep divisions and functions coordinated and motivated.

MATRIX STRUCTURE

Matrix structure
An organizational structure that simultaneously groups people by function and by product team.

A complex form of differentiation that some organizations use to control their activities results in the **matrix structure,** which simultaneously groups people in two ways: by the *function* of which they are a member and by the *product team* on which they are currently working.[10] In practice, the employees who are members of the product teams in a matrix structure have two bosses—a functional boss and a product boss.

In Fig. 15.5, which illustrates a matrix structure, the vertical lines show the functions of an organization, and the horizontal lines show the product teams responsible for developing or manufacturing the organization's products. At the intersection of the lines are employees who report to both a functional boss and a product boss and are members of a team developing a specific product. One team in Figure 15.5 is composed of the employees who work on the new Alpha computer workstation for small businesses, and another team

FIGURE **15.5**

A Matrix Structure

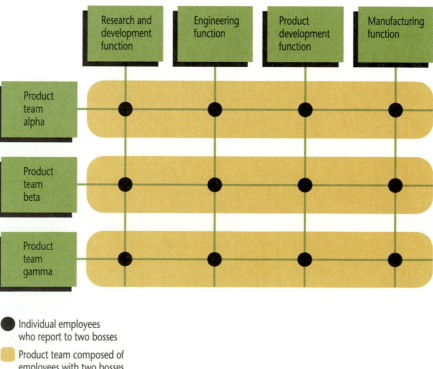

● Individual employees who report to two bosses

▬ Product team composed of employees with two bosses

works on the Beta project to design a workstation to meet the needs of large corporate customers.

Coordination Advantages.   Typically, a company uses a matrix structure (rather than an ordinary divisional structure) for three reasons: (1) It needs to develop new products very rapidly. (2) It needs to maximize communication and cooperation between team members. (3) Innovation and creativity are the key to the organization's competitive advantage.[11] Product teams permit face-to-face problem solving and provide a work setting in which managers with different functional expertise can cooperate to solve nonprogrammed decision-making problems.

Membership in the product teams of a matrix structure is not fixed. Two-boss employees are transferred from team to team as their functional expertise is needed. For example, three electrical engineers work in the Alpha team to design the most efficient system to link the electronic components. When they solve the Alpha design problem, they may then move to the Beta team if it requires their expertise. The flexibility of a matrix structure allows an organization to make best use of its human resources and thus provides great coordination and efficiency advantages.

Motivation Advantages.   To understand the matrix's role in motivation, it is important to understand that the members of the product teams in a matrix structure are generally highly qualified and skilled employees who possess advanced degrees and are experts in their chosen field. The matrix structure provides a work setting in which such employees are given the freedom and autonomy to take responsibility for their work activities. As we saw in Chapter 7, job design is important in determining work attitudes and behaviors, and many people enjoy jobs with a high motivating potential score. Matrix structures provide such jobs and as a result encourage work behaviors that lead individuals to be concerned with quality and innovation.

Disadvantages of a Matrix Structure.   As you might expect, matrix structures have some disadvantages. They have several properties that can produce job dissatisfaction; thus many people do not like working in them.[12] One reason for this increase in job dissatisfaction is that matrix structures increase role conflict and role ambiguity (see Chapter 9) and can cause high levels of work stress. Two bosses making conflicting demands on a two-boss employee cause role conflict, and the very loose system of role and reporting relationships in the matrix makes employees vulnerable to role ambiguity. This conflict and ambiguity can increase feelings of stress. Another source of discomfort is the difficulty employees have in demonstrating their personal contributions to team performance because they move so often from one team to another. In addition, opportunities for promotion are limited because most movement is lateral, from team to team, not vertical to upper management positions.

Of all the types of differentiation that we have discussed so far, the matrix is associated with the most complex coordination and motivation issues. On the one hand, it has enormous coordination advantages; on the other hand, it can cause complex motivational problems. The extent of these problems explains why matrix structures are used only by companies that depend on rapid product development for their survival and that manufacture products designed to meet specific customer needs. Matrix structures are especially common in high-tech and biotechnology companies.

TO MANAGERS

SUMMARY

Differentiation, the grouping of tasks into functions and divisions, allows an organization to effectively manage an increase in the division of labor and specialization as it grows. Large organizations are more complex than small organizations. They have a greater number and variety of functions and divisions because they produce a greater number and variety of goods and services. As organizations grow and differentiate, they can use several different organizational structures. Each structure offers coordination and motivation advantages and disadvantages, and each is suited to addressing a particular problem facing the organization. Differentiation by function is the most common way to group organizational tasks. Product, market, geographic, and matrix structures offer advantages for organizations facing specific problems in managing their products and customers as they grow and differentiate.

Integration: Mechanisms for Increasing Coordination

Integration
Coordinating the activities of different functions and divisions

The higher the level of differentiation, the greater are the problems of **integration**—that is, coordinating the activities of different functions and divisions. Integration becomes a problem because each function and division develops a different orientation toward the whole organization. Each function or division starts to pursue its own goals and objectives and to view the problems facing the organization from its own particular perspective.[13] Different functions, for example, may develop different orientations toward time, toward the major goals facing an organization, or toward other functions.

The manufacturing function typically has a very short-term orientation. It evaluates its performance on an hour-to-hour or daily basis, and its major goal is to keep costs under control and get the goods out the factory door on time. By contrast, the research and development function has a long-term orientation. New product development is a slow process, and R&D is often concerned more with innovation and improving product quality than with cost. Such differences in orientation may reduce coordination between functions and lower their motivation to integrate their activities to meet organizational goals.

In an organization with a product structure, employees may become concerned more with the interests of their own divisions than with the interests of the whole organization and may refuse or simply not see the need to cooperate or share information or knowledge with other divisions. In a market structure, each division can become focused on its own set of customers and lose sight of whether its activities could benefit other divisions. In a geographic structure, the goal of satisfying the needs of regional customers can come to outweigh the needs of the whole organization.

As discussed earlier, Digital Equipment Corporation adopted a market structure and organized its activities around its different customer groups—small business accounts, large corporate accounts, and so on. By 1994, however, CEO Robert Palmer realized that this structure was not working. Each division was developing its own research program to develop new computer systems to benefit each kind of customer. Because R&D is so expensive, Digital's costs were increasing dramatically. To add insult to injury, the divisions were not pooling their research findings, so Digital Equipment Corporation essentially was a collection of five separate organizations, each of which was doing its own thing. Palmer decided to move from a market structure to a product structure and focus the organization's activities on developing a few, specific products that could be tailored later to meet the needs of different kinds of customers.

The problem of integrating the activities of different functions and divisions becomes more and more acute as the number of functions and divisions increases and their activities become more diverse. For this reason, organizations must find ways to integrate their activities if they are to be effective as they grow and differentiate. In practice, organizations use three principal tools to increase integration among functions and divisions: the hierarchy of authority, mutual adjustment, and standardization.[14]

THE HIERARCHY OF AUTHORITY

When problems of coordinating and motivating intergroup relationships emerge, one of the first steps that organizations take is to create an organizational hierarchy that reflects the authority that each role or jobs possesses. **Authority** is the power that enables a person in a higher position to hold a person in a lower position accountable for his or her actions. Authority carries with it the responsibility for using organizational resources effectively. Positions

Authority
The power that enables one person to hold another person accountable for his or her actions.

Almost all organizations have well-established organizational hierarchies, and the larger and older an organization is, the taller the hierarchy is likely to be. This picture of the opening of the synod of African bishops illustrates the hierarchical nature of the Roman Catholic church. The bishops sit by rank around Pope John Paul II.

at the top of an organization's hierarchy possess more authority and responsibility than do positions farther down in the hierarchy. In a hierarchy, each lower position is under the supervision of a higher one; as a result, authority integrates the activities of managers and workers across hierarchical levels.

Recall from the last section, for example, how the position of divisional manager emerges when an organization splits apart into divisions and how the level of corporate manager emerges to integrate the activities of divisional managers. Similarly, a hierarchy emerges inside each function to integrate the activities of workers within each function.

As an organization grows and the problem of integrating activities within and between functions and divisions increases, the organization typically increases the number of levels in its hierarchy. As it does so, the **span of control**—the number of subordinates who report to a manager—narrows.[15]

Compare the hierarchies shown in Figs. 15.6(a) and 15.6(b). The CEO in Figure 15.6(a) supervises six different functions, so the CEO's span of control

Span of control
The number of employees who report to a manager.

FIGURE **15.6**

Using the Hierarchy to Manage Intergroup Relations

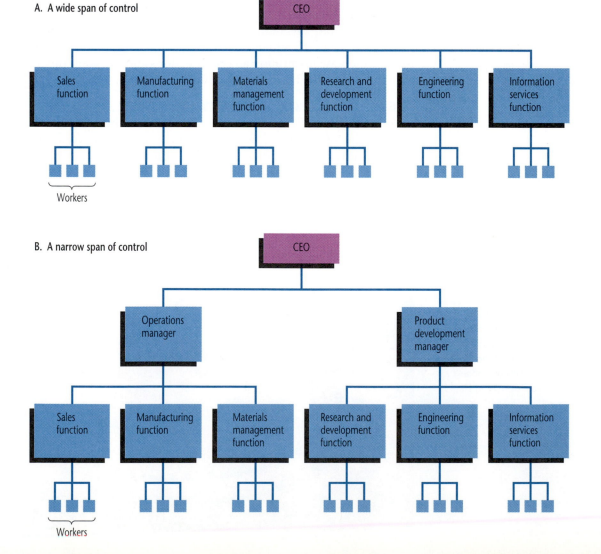

A. A wide span of control

Workers

B. A narrow span of control

Workers

is six subordinates. There are three levels in the hierarchy—the CEO, the subordinate managers in charge of each function, and the workers who report to each functional manager. Suppose the CEO decides that he can no longer effectively integrate the activities of the six functions because they are growing so rapidly. One way of solving this problem is to create a new level in the hierarchy. So the CEO adds a level to the hierarchy by creating the positions of operations manager and product development manager, as shown in Figure 15.6(b). Each of the new managers supervises three functions. These two managers and the CEO then work together as a team to integrate the activities of all six functions. The organization now has four levels in the hierarchy, the CEO's span of control narrows from six to two, and the span of control of the two new managers is three.

Increasing the number of levels in an organization's hierarchy increases integration between the activities of different functions and increases control *inside* each function. In general, as the number of levels in the organizational hierarchy increases, the span of control narrows. As the span of control narrows, managers' ability to coordinate and motivate subordinates' activities increases.

Tall and Flat Hierarchies.   The number of levels in a hierarchy varies from organization to organization. In general, the larger and more complex an organization is, the taller is its hierarchy. Tall organizations have many levels in the hierarchy relative to their size; flat organizations have few (see Fig. 15.7).

Just as problems of integrating the activities of different functions increase as the number of functions increases, problems of integrating between hierarchical levels emerge when an organization's hierarchy becomes too tall. More specifically, communication and decision-making problems start to occur. As the number of management levels increases, the time it takes to send messages up and down the hierarchy increases and decision making slows. In addition, information passed from person to person can be distorted or filtered as messages become garbled and managers naturally

FIGURE 15.7

Examples of Flat and Tall Hierarchies

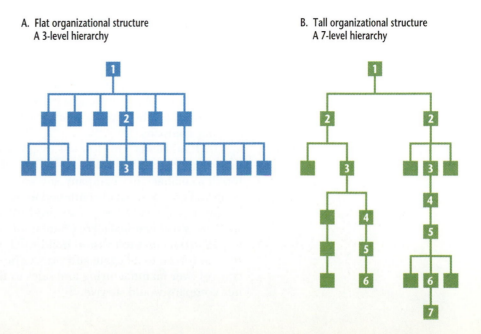

A. Flat organizational structure
   A 3-level hierarchy

B. Tall organizational structure
   A 7-level hierarchy

interpret messages according to their own interests. These problems further reduce the quality of decision making. In fact, all the communications problems discussed in Chapter 13 increase as the height of an organization's hierarchy increases.

Decentralizing Authority.   To reduce the communication and decision-making problems that accompany a hierarchy's growth, organizations may prefer **decentralization** to **centralization,** choosing to distribute authority to managers at all levels of the hierarchy and giving them responsibility for making decisions. Authority is said to be *centralized* when only managers at the top of an organization can make important decisions. Authority is *decentralized* when managers throughout the hierarchy are allowed to make significant decisions.[16] The decentralization of authority offers two benefits. It solves communication and decision-making problems because lower-level managers do not have to continually consult or report up the hierarchy to their superiors. At the same time, greater job responsibilities can increase motivation by making lower-level jobs more interesting and rewarding. The experience of Heida Thurlow shows how important it is for managers to decentralize and delegate authority to lower-level employees as the complexity of an organization grows. (See Insight 15.2.)

Decentralization

The distribution of authority and responsibility for decision making to managers at all levels of an organization's hierarchy.

Centralization

The concentration of authority and responsibility for decision making in the hands of managers at the top of an organization's hierarchy.

Insight 15.2

Integration

Decentralizing Authority Solves a Crisis

In 1979 Heida Thurlow, a German-born mechanical engineer, patented a device that keeps the handles of saucepans and other kinds of cookware cool to the touch even when food has been cooking for hours. To exploit her invention, she created a company, Chantal Cookware Inc., to manufacture high-quality, high-priced enamel cookware, which she sells through stores like Bloomingdale's and Dillard's and catalogues like Williams-Sonoma. By 1994 Thurlow had built her company into a $10 million a year business, employing 42 people who produce over 70 different kinds of cookware sold in over 2,000 different stores. Along this road to success, however, a crisis arose that almost cost Heida her life and her company.[17]

In 1986 Heida Thurlow was diagnosed with breast cancer and endured months of chemotherapy to fight off the disease. All of a sudden, too ill to manage her company, she was faced with a crisis. As her company had grown, she had continued to make all important decisions herself and personally had supervised all of her employees. She also personally had handled all of Chantal's major sales accounts, visiting customers from coast to coast to build the business. Now, unable to work, she was forced to delegate authority to her employees and decentralize control over manufacturing and sales to them. She wondered whether her company would survive.

The results of the forced decentralization astounded Thurlow. Her subordinates, who had been watching her make decisions over the years and had learned her approach to doing business, successfully assumed many of her responsibilities. One employee, comptroller Cathy Korndorffer, effortlessly took control of purchasing and accounts receivable. Eventually, when Thurlow was well again, Korndorffer was promoted to general manager. Other employees took control of Chantal's major sales accounts and serviced the needs of the company's major customers, who were very understanding of the changes taking place.

When Thurlow eventually returned full-time to work, she found that she had no need to take back control of many of these activities. As a result of the decentralization of many of her former responsibilities, she found she had more time to engage in planning the company's future. She began to design new kinds of cookware to expand the company's product line, and she had more time to spend meeting prospective customers to find new outlets for Chantal's widening range of products.

Thurlow found that Chantal's culture had changed too. Her employees welcomed their new responsibilities and were more committed to the company. The crisis had forged them into a closely knit team of people who shared the values of promoting Chantal's success and supporting Heida Thurlow through her crisis. Changes in the organization's structure and culture changed the attitudes and behaviors of its members and made Chantal a much stronger company.

Even though decentralizing authority can lessen the problems associated with tall hierarchies, organizations still must try to prevent their hierarchies from becoming too tall. In recent years, the poor performance of GM, IBM, Westinghouse, and many other organizations has been attributed to the slow communication and poor decision making that resulted when the companies allowed their hierarchies to grow out of control. These companies became slow to respond to changes in their competitive environment and were outmaneuvered by flatter and more agile competitors. At one time, for example, GM had over nineteen levels in its hierarchy compared to Toyota's seven.

The design of the organizational hierarchy is one of the most important decisions an organization faces as it attempts to integrate its functions and divisions and direct their efforts toward achieving organizational goals. Managers need to constantly scrutinize the hierarchy to make sure it meets organizational needs, and they must change it if it does not. The terms *restructuring* and *reengineering*, discussed in Chapter 1, refer to the process of changing organizational task and reporting relationships to improve coordination and motivation. We discuss issues and problems in changing organizational structure in detail in Chapter 19.

MUTUAL ADJUSTMENT

The organizational hierarchy integrates organizational activities because it gives higher-level managers the power to control the actions of lower-level managers. The operations manager in Fig. 15.6(b), for example, can tell the sales, manufacturing, and materials management managers what to do and how to coordinate their activities. However, the operations manager cannot tell the product development manager what to do because the operations manager and product development manager are at the same level in the hierarchy. Furthermore, the operations manager cannot tell anybody in R&D, engineering, or information systems what to do *even though they are at a lower hierarchical level,* because they do not report to the operations manager. These functions report to the product development manager, who is responsible only to the CEO. Ultimately, only the CEO, the person at the top of the hierarchy, has the authority to tell everybody in the organization what to do, and that is why an organization's top manager is so powerful.

Because managers at the same level or in different functions have no power over each other, organizations need to use tools other than the organizational hierarchy to integrate their activities. One important integration mechanism is **mutual adjustment,** the ongoing informal communication among different people and functions that is necessary for an organization to achieve its goals. Mutual adjustment makes an organization's structure work smoothly, and managers must constantly make efforts to promote it and do all they can to facilitate communication and the free flow of information among functions. Mutual adjustment, for example, prevents the emergence of different orientations that can cause significant communication and decision-making problems between functions and divisions.

An organization has to build into its structure integrating mechanisms that facilitate mutual adjustment and make it easy for managers and employees in different functions and divisions to meet and coordinate their activities. We discuss direct contact, liaison roles, and several other integrating mechanisms in increasing order of their ability to promote mutual adjustment.[18]

Direct Contact. In using direct contact, managers from different functions try to establish face-to-face working relationships that allow them to solve common problems informally, without having to go through the formal channels of authority in the hierarchy. In a functional structure, for example, managers in sales try to develop good informal working relationships with managers in manufacturing so that both can make decisions that allow them to achieve their goals simultaneously. Reaching agreement may not be easy because manufacturing and sales goals are not always identical. Manufacturing's goal is to keep costs at a minimum, and to do this it is often necessary to keep production on a particular schedule running smoothly and to manufacture goods in large batches. Sales' goal is to respond to the needs of customers, and sales often needs to ask manufacturing to change production schedules on short notice to accommodate unexpected customer requests. Because such sales-dictated changes raise manufacturing's costs, the potential for conflict arises. A high level of direct contact between sales and manufacturing managers, however, can lead to a give-and-take relationship that fosters interfunctional cooperation.

Liaison Roles. Recognizing the importance of direct contact, organizations often establish liaison roles that give specific functional managers the formal responsibility of maintaining a high level of direct contact with managers in another function. To facilitate communication and effective decision making, managers in liaison roles meet regularly to exchange information, and mem-

▸ Mutual adjustment
The ongoing informal communication among different people and functions that is necessary for an organization to achieve its goals.

bers of one function transmit requests to other functions through these liaison personnel. Over time, the personal working relationships that develop among managers performing liaison roles enhance coordination and integration throughout the organization.

Teams and Task Forces. When two or more functions are involved in decision making, organizations often create interfunctional teams and task forces to facilitate communication and cooperation. A *team* is a permanent group made up of representatives from two or more functions that meets regularly to discuss important ongoing problems facing the organization, set goals, and review progress toward those goals. A *task force* is a temporary (or ad hoc) group set up to solve a specific problem. An organization may set up a task force to study problems that it expects to encounter as it expands its operations into Argentina, for example. When the task force has come up with a solution to its assigned problem, it is disbanded. In contrast, an organization may use a team to increase coordination between functions (see Fig. 15.8). Because developing the organizational budget is an ongoing activity, an organization is likely to create a permanent team composed of members from several functions whose job is to constantly monitor and oversee the budget process and make recommendations for allocating funds to different functions and divisions.

The importance of interdepartmental teams and task forces for promoting mutual adjustment cannot be overemphasized. It has been estimated that managers spend over 70 percent of their time in face-to-face meetings with other managers to make decisions and solve problems that cannot be dealt with through the formal hierarchy of authority or in any other way.[19]

Cross-Functional Teams. Recently, many organizations have moved to promote mutual adjustment by using cross-functional teams. *Cross-functional teams* are composed of people from different functions who are permanently assigned to work full-time on a team to bring a new good or service to the market. Cross-functional teams are different from ordinary teams in several ways. Members of an ordinary team are full-time members of a *function* or *division* who meet together regularly to share information. Members of cross-functional

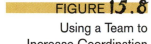

FIGURE **15.8**

Using a Team to Increase Coordination Between Functions

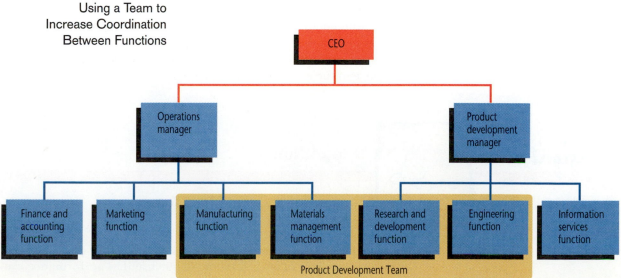

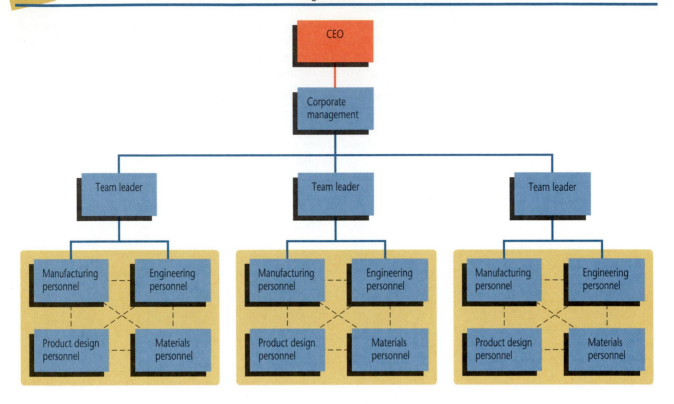

Cross-functional teams

FIGURE **15.9**

A Cross-Functional
Team Structure
Cross-functional teams are
composed of functional
personnel who are assigned
full-time to work in the team.

teams are full-time members of the team and report to the leader of the team. Figure 15.9 shows the cross-functional team structure that results when cross-functional teams are used to promote mutual adjustment.

Hallmark Cards moved to a cross-functional team structure when it decided to organize its tasks according to specific types of cards—birthday cards, Christmas cards, Mother's Day cards, and so on. Rather than having card designers, rhyme writers, and others work in separate functions, Hallmark assigned them to cross-functional teams to reduce the need to coordinate among functions. The new structure greatly improved efficiency and speeded product development. A new card used to take a year to get to the market; now it takes only a few months. Chrysler Corporation was a pioneer in the use of cross-functional teams, which have greatly contributed to its current strong performance in the car market (Insight 15.3).

Insight 15.3   Integration

Teams, Teams, and More Teams

After almost going bankrupt in the early 1990s, Chrysler (www.chrysler .com) made a profit of over $2 billion in 1993, and its performance has continued to improve. This profit is the result not of cost cutting but of producing the kinds of cars that customers want, such as the cab-forward LH cars introduced in 1993 and a newly redesigned minivan in 1996. Chrysler and its top managers—Robert Eaton, chairman, and Robert Lutz, president—attribute a lot of Chrysler's success to its fortuitous development and use of cross-functional teams in 1988.

In 1988 Chrysler acquired American Motors (AMC) and its 700 design engineers. Rather than distributing these engineers among Chrysler's different engineering functions—transmission, exhaust, brakes, engines, and so on—Chrysler made a radical decision. It chose to keep the engineers together and have all 700 of them work together in a cross-functional team devoted to redesigning the Jeep Grand Cherokee, infamous among consumers for its poor reliability.

The 700 engineers from all areas of design engineering worked together on a single huge work floor and were joined by marketing, finance, purchasing, and other functional experts, who provided information about customers' needs, input costs, and so on. Top management gave the team a target price for the car. The team was told to design a car that could be made for that price. The result was astounding. The design was finished in two years, and the Jeep Cherokee was an instant success when it was introduced in 1992. Chrysler was so pleased with the results of its use of a cross-functional team that it decided to move from its old functional structure to a cross-functional team structure throughout the organization.

Functional personnel are assigned to four major teams—small cars, large cars, minivans, and Jeep/truck—and Chrysler built a $1 billion new technology center with separate floors to house each team. The cross-functional team structure allows functional experts to meet and share ideas to speed the development process. It allows for the intense kinds of interactions among people that are necessary for successful innovation and product development. Each team has its own vice president, and the biggest challenge Chrysler now faces is to transfer new product information from one team to another so that each team can quickly capitalize on the advances made by the others. To allow for integration between teams, Chrysler developed a system of integrating roles that allows team members to go from floor to floor, meeting with members of other teams to share information.

The cross-functional team structure differs from a matrix structure because members do not move between product teams but stay with their team permanently. It also differs from a product structure. In a product structure, people are assigned to different functions, and then regular teams or liaison roles are used to coordinate between functions. The use of cross-functional teams is increasing as organizations discover how much they can enhance performance.

Integrating Roles. Organizations can promote mutual adjustment by creating **integrating roles,** permanent managerial positions in which the manager's only role is to coordinate the activities of different divisions (in contrast, integration is just one of the many responsibilities of a manager in a liaison role). Managers in integrating roles are *outside* the divisions they coordinate. As at Chrysler, their full-time responsibility is to increase the flow of information

Integrating role
A permanent managerial position in which the manager's only role is to coordinate the activities of different divisions.

between divisions and teams and to help people share ideas and otherwise improve the quality of decision making across an organization.

Integrating roles are used only when organizations have a great need to promote integration among divisions. Most commonly found in product structures, integrating roles coordinate the activities of different product divisions so that they can share resources. Such coordination leads to increased performance and a quickened pace of innovation and product development. Figure 15.10 shows the use of integrating roles in a product structure.

Matrix Structure.   The matrix structure, discussed earlier in this chapter, contains many of the complex integrating mechanisms we have described. The team members in a matrix play an integrating role between their function and the product team to which they are assigned, and cross-functional teams are the principal way in which people are grouped to coordinate work activities. The matrix is the most flexible of all organizational structures because it promotes the highest level of mutual adjustment. As we discussed earlier, however, the lack of formal task and reporting relationships that promote flexibility and adaptability can cause major coordination and motivation problems. For these reasons, a matrix structure is used only when very high levels of integration among functions are needed; otherwise, the cross-functional team structure is likely to be preferable.

STANDARDIZATION

The third principal tool that organizations can use to control their activities and integrate functions and divisions is **standardization**—the development of routine responses to recurring problems or opportunities that specify how individuals and functions are to coordinate their actions to accomplish organizational goals. Standardized performance programs (discussed in Chapter 14) lower the need for mutual adjustment and for complex integrating mechanisms.

As a mechanism for coordinating work activities, standardization is less costly than using the hierarchy of authority or mutual adjustment. The latter two, unlike standardization, require a great deal of managerial time and effort. In practice, an organization can develop performance programs to standardize inputs, throughput or conversion processes, and outputs. How the

Standardization
The development of routine responses to recurring problems or opportunities.

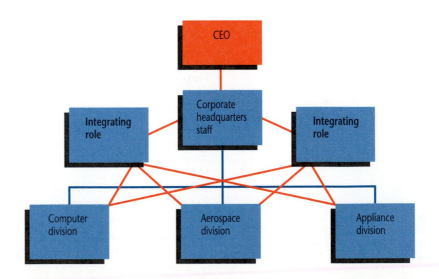
FIGURE **15.10**

Using Integrating Roles in a Product Structure to Increase Integration organization creates these performance programs determines how effectively its organizational structure works.[20]

Standardizing Inputs.   Organizational inputs include the skills and capabilities of managers and workers, the quality of the raw materials and component parts used to make products, and the machinery and computers used in the production process. Organizations can, for example, develop performance programs that specify in advance the standards or targets (such as quality or reliability) that inputs must reach before they can be used as inputs. Japanese car companies, for example, are renowned for the stringent specifications that they require suppliers of car components such as engine blocks to meet. Japanese and, increasingly, U.S. companies recognize that inputs that conform to high standards are easier to use than are merely adequate inputs, and that they result in a higher-quality final product.

Organizations can standardize the skills of their managers and workers by requiring them to have certain qualifications and experiences. An assembly-line worker might be required to have a high school diploma, an R&D scientist might be required to have a PhD from a prestigious research university, and a CEO might be required to have shown that he or she has successfully managed similar kinds of businesses in the past. Organizations that recruit and select workers who meet stringent criteria can be relatively confident that their employees will respond in appropriate ways to uncertain events. This is why many organizations, ranging from large accounting firms to Fortune 500 companies to government agencies, spend so much time recruiting and selecting employees.

Standardizing Throughputs.   To standardize throughputs (the conversion processes that an organization uses to convert inputs into outputs), organizations develop performance programs that specify the behaviors they expect from their employees. When behaviors are specified, both individuals and groups act consistently in ways that allow an organization to achieve its goals. The principal way in which organizations standardize behaviors is by the use of rules and standard operating procedures (SOPs) (see Chapter 10).[21] Because rules and SOPs specify the series of actions or decisions that employees are expected to perform in a given situation, they *standardize* employee responses to the situation.

Formalization is the use of rules and standard operating procedures to control an organization's activities. The more an organization can rely on formalization to specify required behaviors, the less it needs to use either direct supervision from the hierarchy or mutual adjustment. Formalization can result in lower operating costs and thus increased organizational performance. Once rules have been developed, they are inexpensive to use and cost little to implement and maintain. All that is required is that new employees be taught the appropriate rules to follow in certain situations. (Recall from Chapter 10 that socialization is the process by which employees learn organizational rules and SOPs.) All organizations make extensive use of rules because they are inexpensive and effective ways of coordinating activities both within and between functions and divisions.

Although some rules are necessary to the smooth running of an organization, too many rules can give rise to a number of problems:

- Excessive formalization can straitjacket employees and prevent them from responding creatively and flexibly to new situations.

Formalization
The use of rules and standard operating procedures to control an organization's activities.

- Employees' inclination to obey rules without thinking about their consequences can reduce the quality of organizational decision making.
- Too much emphasis on the use of existing rules and performance programs can make it especially difficult for an organization to make changes and develop new rules.

Standardizing Outputs.   Organizations can standardize outputs, the goods and services they produce, by specifying the level of performance they require from their employees and setting standards by which to measure actual employee outputs. Instead of specifying the *behaviors* the organization can expect from its employees (as rules and SOPs do), the organization specifies what the *outputs* of its employees must be for the organization to achieve its goals.[22]

Output standards are also an effective way to control behavior. Imagine, for example, how difficult it is for a manager to monitor the behavior of employees such as salespeople or R&D scientists. It is impossible to watch a scientist to see how well he or she "does research," and the costs of following around salespeople would be exorbitant. So organizations try to standardize an employee's output by specifying sales goals for salespeople, such as how much they should sell each month or how many customers they should visit each day. Specifying goals for researchers is more difficult because their work is so long-term and complex, but an R&D function can be measured by the number of new products it develops or the number of new patents it files.

By using specific goals and targets to measure the performance of individuals and groups, an organization increases control over its activities, and that increased control allows the organization to better achieve its goals. Performance goals and targets can also be developed to measure the quality of finished goods and services—for example, the number and quality of toaster ovens produced or the degree to which defective electric blankets are returned by customers. The more ways an organization can devise to measure its performance, the more effective it becomes.

Employees of Corning Inc. of New York inspect ceramic substrates at the end of the production line to ensure their uniform quality and reliability. This is an example of how to standardize the outputs of the manufacturing process.

What Is Organizational Culture?

An organization's structure—the *formal* system of task and reporting relationships—embodies a number of decisions the organization makes about how it wants and needs to coordinate and motivate individuals and groups to perform at a high level and to achieve organizational goals. In creating an organizational structure, managers first decide how to group people and tasks into functions and divisions. Then they decide how to use the hierarchy of authority, mutual adjustment, and standardization to integrate individual, group, functional, and divisional activities. Earlier, we defined *organizational culture* as the *informal* values and norms that control how individuals and groups in an organization interact with each other and with people outside the organization. Just as the formal task and reporting relationships specified by an organization's structure can control the behavior of people and groups in the organization, the values and norms embodied in an organization's culture can also shape and control individual and group attitudes and behavior and the quality of intergroup relationships. Organizational culture is another, less formal means by which an organization can influence and control its members to help achieve organizational goals.

VALUES, NORMS, AND ORGANIZATIONAL CULTURE

Organizational cultures include two kinds of values: terminal and instrumental.[23] A **terminal value** is a desired goal that an organization seeks to achieve. Organizations might adopt any or all of the following as terminal values: excellence, stability, predictability, profitability, innovation, economy, morality, and quality. An **instrumental value** is a desired mode of behavior that an organization wants its members to observe. Organizations might encourage workers to adopt instrumental values such as working hard, respecting traditions and authority, being conservative and cautious, being frugal, being creative and courageous, being honest, taking risks, and maintaining high standards.

An organization's culture consists of both the goals an organization seeks to achieve (its *terminal values*) and the modes of behavior the organization encourages (its *instrumental values*). Ideally, an organization's instrumental values help the organization achieve its terminal values. For example, a new computer company whose culture has a *terminal* value of excellence through innovation may try to attain this value by encouraging workers to adopt the *instrumental* values of working hard, being creative, and taking risks (this combination of terminal and instrumental values leads to an *entrepreneurial culture* in an organization). Similarly, an insurance company that desires stability and predictability as its terminal values may emphasize cautiousness and obedience to authority (the result of adopting these values would be a *conservative culture* in the organization).

To encourage members to adopt certain terminal and instrumental values and, as a result, behave in certain ways as they pursue organizational goals, an organization develops specific norms. In Chapter 10 we defined a norm as a shared expectation for behavior. Norms are *informal* rules of conduct that emerge over time to regulate behaviors that are considered important in an organization. So, for example, the specific norms of being courteous and keeping the work area clean or being a "team player" will develop in an organization whose more general terminal or instrumental values include being helpful and hard working or cooperative.

Terminal value
A desired goal that an organization seeks to achieve.

Instrumental value
A desired mode of behavior that an organization wants its members to observe.

Over time, organizational members learn from each other how to interpret various situations and respond to them in ways that reflect the organization's shared values and norms. Eventually, members of an organization behave in accordance with the organization's values and norms often without realizing they are doing so. The way in which United Parcel Service develops and maintains a system of norms and values demonstrates the power of organizational culture to shape workers' attitudes and behavior (see Insight 15.4).

Insight 15.4

Competitive Advantage

Does UPS Value Economy and Efficiency Too Much?

United Parcel Service (UPS) (www.ups.com) controls more than three-fourths of the ground parcel service in the United States, delivering 10 million packages a day in its fleet of 128,000 trucks. It is also the most profitable company in its industry. In 1993 its profits were almost $900 million. UPS employs over 250,000 people, and since its founding as a bicycle-messenger service in 1907 by James E. Casey, UPS has developed a system of instrumental and terminal values that has been a model for competitors such as Federal Express and the United States Postal Service. From the beginning, Casey made efficiency and economy the company's driving terminal values, and he made loyalty, humility, discipline, dependability, and intense effort the company's instrumental values.

UPS goes to extraordinary lengths to develop and maintain these values in its workforce. First, its work systems from the top of the company down to its trucking operations are the subject of intense scrutiny by the company's 3,000 industrial engineers. These engineers time every part of employees' jobs and are constantly introducing the latest in electronic and computer technology into the company's operations. They are constantly on the lookout for ways to improve efficiency.

Truck drivers, for example, are instructed in extraordinary detail how to perform their tasks: They must step from their truck with their right foot first, fold their money face up, carry packages under their left arm, walk at a pace of three feet per second, and slip the key ring holding their truck keys over their third finger.[24] Employees are not allowed to wear beards, must be carefully groomed, and are instructed in how to deal with customers. Drivers who perform below average receive visits from training supervisors who accompany them on their delivery routes and instruct them on how to raise their performance level. Not surprisingly, as a result of this intensive training and close supervision, UPS employees internalize very strong norms about the appropriate ways to behave to help the organization achieve its terminal values of economy and efficiency.

UPS encourages employees to share the organization's terminal and instrumental values of efficiency and hard work by making it worthwhile for them personally. UPS is owned by its managers, almost all of whom joined the company as truck drivers and worked their way up the ranks. Each year, all managers receive shares in the company based on UPS's and their own performance. When managers retire, they sell their shares back to the company, a transaction that normally makes millionaires out of long-service managers. Truck drivers earn an average salary of from $40,000 to $50,000 a year, making them the most highly paid truck drivers in the world.

In 1994, however, UPS's continuing attempts to increase efficiency caused the first strike in its history. Walkouts, employee lawsuits, and federal fines became common as UPS workers rebelled against the company's continuing efforts to raise productivity through, in their view, means that threatened safety and lowered the quality of service. Increasingly, delivery workers are being asked to perform more and more complex tasks that take more time to perform. At the same time they are being asked to make more deliveries each day—up to 220 a day from 160 a few years ago. The weight of the packages they are expected to deliver has also increased sharply, and the use of a new electronic delivery system that allows supervisors to track a driver's progress in intimate detail makes employees feel as though they are being watched all the time. These changes have increased stress levels among drivers and other employees, who claim they are being pushed to the limit.

Kent Nelson, CEO of UPS, believes that the company has been fair in what it is asking its employees to achieve. But UPS's recent troubles have caused managers to reexamine UPS's values and recognize that although the drive to increase efficiency may be desirable, the costs associated with it may be too high.

Socialization is the process by which newcomers learn an organization's values and norms and develop the work behaviors and attitudes necessary to perform their specific organizational roles. To encourage group members to learn certain organizational values and norms and to adopt specific role orientations, organizations like UPS use specific socialization tactics.[25] Over time, as a result of socialization, organizational members internalize an organization's values and norms (see Chapter 10). Recall that internalization is evident when organizational members behave in accordance with values and norms not just because they think they have to but because they think that these norms and values describe the right and proper way to behave.[26]

We have discussed what an organizational culture is, what it can do for an organization, and how employees learn an organization's culture. But we have said nothing about where culture comes from or who "designs" it. Where does culture come from, and what determines the kind of values and norms present in an organization's culture? Two important sources of terminal and instrumental values are the founder of an organization and ethical values.

THE ROLE OF THE FOUNDER

The founder of an organization and his or her personal values and beliefs have a substantial influence on an organization's culture and the norms, stories, myths, and legends that develop in a company.[27] Founders set the scene for the way a culture develops because they establish organizational values and hire members of a new organization. Presumably, organizational founders select people who have values and interests similar to theirs, and these people are probably attracted to an organization because of the founder's values.[28] Thus organizational culture develops in accordance with the attraction-selection-attrition (ASA) framework discussed in Chapter 2.

Over time, organizational members buy into the founder's vision of what his or her company is going to achieve—its terminal values. These values become more distinct and powerful as strong instrumental values and organizational norms develop to support the organization's efforts to obtain its terminal values. Microsoft founder Bill Gates, for example, has pioneered an entrepreneurial culture in Microsoft based on the values of creativity and hard work. John Dryden, founder of the Prudential Insurance Company, pioneered the concept that an insurance company should be operated in the interests of its policyholders, a terminal value that gave rise to a philanthropic, caring culture. We also saw earlier how James Casey established UPS's values of efficiency and economy, which company managers still strive to maintain.[29]

ETHICAL CULTURES

An organization can purposefully develop some kinds of cultural values to control the way its members behave. One important class of values that fall into this category is **ethical values,** the moral values and norms that establish the appropriate way for an organization and its members to deal with each other and with those outside the organization. Ethical values rest on principles that stress the importance of treating everyone affected by an organization's activities with respect, in a fair manner, and in a way that promotes (and does not hurt) their well-being.

In developing cultural values that will control the interactions of organizational members with each other and with those outside the organization, top management must constantly make choices about the right or appropriate thing to do. A company such as IBM or Sears might wonder whether it should develop procedural guidelines for giving advance notice to its employees and middle managers about big impending layoffs or plant closings. Traditionally, companies have been reluctant to do so because they fear employee hostility and apathy. Similarly, a company has to decide whether to allow its managers to pay bribes to government officials in foreign countries where such payoffs are an accepted way of doing business although they are illegal.[30]

To make these decisions, managers rely on ethical instrumental values embodied in an organization's culture.[31] Such ethics outline the right and wrong ways to behave when confronted with a situation in which an action may help one person or stakeholder group but hurt another.[32] Ethical values, and the rules and norms that reflect them, are an integral part of an organization's culture because they help to determine how organizational members will manage situations and make decisions.

STRONG AND WEAK CULTURES

Several researchers have sought to identify what differentiates organizations with strong cultures from those with weak cultures. Organizations with strong cultures have cohesive sets of values and norms that bind organizational members together and foster commitment from employees to achieve orga-

Ethical values
The moral values and norms that establish the appropriate way for an organization and its members to deal with each other and with those outside the organization.

nizational goals. Weak cultures provide little guidance to organizational employees about how they should behave. Organizations with weak cultures use formal organizational structure, rather than values and norms, to coordinate organizational behavior.

Understanding the foundations of strong cultures is important because some authors claim that strong cultures generate high performance and give an organization a competitive advantage. Thomas Peters and Robert Waterman, Jr., have provided a well-known account of the values and norms that characterize successful organizations and their cultures.[33] Peters and Waterman argue that successful organizations share three sets of values.

First, successful companies have values promoting what Peters and Waterman call a "bias for action." Successful companies emphasize the values of autonomy and entrepreneurship, and they encourage employees to take risks—for example, to find new ways to provide high-quality products or customer service. Top managers are closely involved in the day-to-day operations of a successful company and do not simply make decisions isolated in some "ivory tower." Employees are also committed to instrumental values and norms that encourage a "hands-on, value-driven approach."

The second set of values stems from the nature of an organization's mission—that is, what the organization does and how it tries to do it. Peters and Waterman believe that management should cultivate values so that an organization sticks to what it does best and maintains control over its core activities. An organization can easily get sidetracked into pursuing activities outside its area of expertise just because they seem to promise a quick return. General Mills, for example, developed restaurant chains (Red Lobster and the Olive Garden), businesses that had nothing to do with its core cereal business. In 1995 with profits in its cereal business falling, General Mills announced that it would spin off its restaurant businesses into a separate company so that it could focus all its attention on its core cereal business. Peters and Waterman stress that a company needs to "stick to the knitting," which means staying with the businesses it knows best. It also means establishing close relations with customers and adopting customer-oriented norms as a way of improving the organization's competitive position. Organizations that emphasize customer-oriented values are able to learn customer needs and improve their ability to develop products and services that customers desire. These kinds of values are strongly represented in companies such as IBM, Hewlett-Packard, and Toyota, which focus on their core business and take constant steps to maintain and develop it.

The third set of values bears on the operation of an organization. A company should try to establish values and norms that motivate employees to do their best. These values develop out of a belief that productivity is obtained through people and that respect for the individual is the primary means by which a company can create the right culture for productive behavior. Some organizations, for example, seek to develop values that demonstrate their commitment to investing in their human resources, to increase their worth and promote the success of the organization.[34] Encouraging employees to learn new skills or better utilize existing skills, increasing spending on education and training, and investing in the long-term development of workers are all ways in which organizations can increase the value of their human resources. As William Ouchi has noted (see Appendix 1), this attitude toward employees pervades the culture of Japanese companies.[35]

PROFESSIONAL AND PRODUCTION CULTURES

Organizations that invest in their employees develop a *professional culture,* which reflects the desire to increase the value of human resources to promote long-term effectiveness. These organizations adopt employment practices and procedures that demonstrate their commitment to their members, and they encourage members to return this commitment in the form of supportive work attitudes and high performance. Microsoft, Intel, and Motorola, for example, emphasize the long-term nature of the employment relationship and try to avoid layoffs. These companies develop career paths and invest heavily in training and development to increase employees' value to the organization. In these ways, terminal and instrumental values pertaining to the worth of human resources encourage the development of supportive work attitudes.

In professional cultures, employees often receive rewards linked directly to their performance and to the performance of the company as a whole. Sometimes, employee stock ownership plans (ESOPs) are developed in which workers as a group are allowed to buy a significant percentage of their company's stock. Workers who are owners of the company have additional incentive to develop skills that allow them to perform highly and search actively for ways to improve quality, efficiency, and performance.

Some organizations develop cultures with values that do not include protecting and increasing the worth of their human resources as a major goal. These organizations have a *production culture,* and their employment practices are based on short-term employment according to the needs of the organization and on minimal investment in employees who perform simple, routine tasks. In organizations with a production culture, employees are not often rewarded for their performance and thus have little incentive to improve their skills or otherwise invest in the organization to help it to achieve goals. The lack of commitment the organization shows to its employees is returned in full measure by workers. In production cultures, antagonistic relationships frequently develop between the organization and its workers, and instrumental values of noncooperation, laziness, and loafing and work norms of output restriction are common.

In a professional culture, an emphasis on entrepreneurship and respect for the employee allows the use of organizational structures, such as the cross-functional team structure, that give employees the latitude to make decisions and motivate them to succeed. Because a flat structure best allows values of autonomy and cooperation to develop, an organization seeking to establish a professional culture should be designed with only the number of managers and hierarchical levels that are necessary to get the job done. The organization also should be sufficiently decentralized to encourage employee participation, but centralized enough for management to make sure that the organization pursues its central mission.

By using structure to encourage the development of values and norms, an organization can create a culture that reinforces the way its structure operates so that the two work together to help the organization achieve its goals. Organizations can harness both the formal and the informal aspects of the work situation to build a strong culture, increase performance, and enhance their competitive advantage.

ORGANIZATIONAL CEREMONIES, RITES, AND LANGUAGE

One way of building a strong culture is to develop organizational ceremonies, rites, and language to help people learn about an organization's values and norms.[36] Ceremonies and rites are formal actions or rituals that recognize events of importance to organizations and their members. Graduation from high school and college, for example, is accompanied by a ceremony in which graduates, wearing formal academic robes, receive their diplomas and degrees in front of their peers, families, and friends. This ceremony recognizes the graduates' achievements and marks their passage into a new sphere of their life. Companies also hold ceremonies and rites that mark significant events. Southwest Airlines, for example, holds ceremonies to recognize high-performing employees. In addition, the way employees dress up for special occasions, the weekly cookouts with top managers, and managers' periodic stints at performing low-level organizational jobs are special acts that reinforce and communicate Southwest's cultural values to its members.

Table 15.1 summarizes four kinds of rites that organizations use to communicate cultural norms and values to their members: rites of passage, of integration, of enhancement, and of degradation.[37]

Rites of passage, such as graduation, determine how individuals enter, move up in, or leave an organization. The socialization programs developed by the army or by large accounting firms such as Arthur Andersen, which we described in Chapter 10, are rites of passage, as are the ways in which an organization grooms people for promotion or retirement.

Rites of integration, such as office parties, company cookouts, and shared announcements of organizational successes, build and reinforce common bonds between organizational members. A company's annual meeting, for example, is often used to communicate the organization's values to its managers, employees, and shareholders. Wal-Mart's annual stockholders' meeting is an extravagant ceremony that celebrates the company's success. In 1994 Wal-Mart flew 3,000 of its highest performers to its annual meeting at corporate headquarters in Fayetteville, Arkansas, for a show that included performers such as exercise guru Richard Simmons and singers Reba McIntyre and Andy Williams. Wal-Mart believes that expensive entertainments that reward its supporters reinforce its high-performance values and culture. The proceedings are even shown live in all Wal-Mart stores so that all employees can participate in the rites celebrating the company's achievements.[38]

TABLE **15.1**

Organizational Rites

Type of Rite	Example of Rite	Purpose of Rite
Rites of passage	Induction and basic training	Learn and internalize norms and values
Rites of integration	Annual office party	Build common norms and values
Rites of enhancement	Presentation of annual award	Motivate commitment to norms and values
Rites of degradation	Firing of top executive	Change or reaffirm norms and values

Rites of enhancement, such as awards dinners, newspaper releases, and employee promotions, give an organization the opportunity to publicly acknowledge and reward employees' contributions and thereby to enhance employees' commitment to organizational values.

As Insight 15.5 shows, Triad Systems uses its annual trade show to integrate employees into, and to enhance, its organizational culture.

Insight 15.5   Culture

Triad Systems Builds a Culture Based on Success

Triad Systems Corp. (www.triadhc.com) is a 20-year-old computer company based in Livermore, California, with annual sales of $140 million. Each year Triad Systems holds a trade show in which all its major divisions and many of its suppliers are represented. At these shows employees receive awards for excellent service to the company. With much hoopla, employees receive the Grindstone Award for "individuals who most consistently demonstrate initiative, focus, dedication, and persistence," the Innovator Award for those who "conceive and carry out innovative ideas," and the Busting the Boundaries Award for "those who work most effectively across functional and divisional boundaries to accomplish their work."[39] Of Triad's 1,500 employees, over 700 win awards annually!

The goal of Triad's trade show and awards ceremony is to develop organizational folklore to support Triad's work teams and build a productive culture. Triad believes that giving praise and recognition to its employees builds a community of people who share similar values and who will jointly strive for organizational success. Also, providing members with organizational experiences in common promotes the development of a common corporate language across functional groups—a language that bonds people together and allows them to better coordinate their activities. So far, Triad has been successful with its approach: It has received a national award for quality, and its sales have exceeded its forecasts in every quarter to date.

Stories and the language of an organization are other important vehicles for the communication of organizational culture. Stories (whether fact or fiction) about organizational heroes and villains and the actions that led them to be so categorized provide important clues about cultural values and norms. Some people suggest that studying these stories can guide organizational employees by revealing the kinds of behaviors that are valued by the organization and the kinds of practices that are frowned on.[40]

Because language is the principal medium of communication in organizations, the characteristic phrases that people use to frame and describe

Bill Gates, the CEO of the giant software company Microsoft, goes to great lengths to develop values, norms, and a company culture in which people feel motivated to take risks and perform highly to benefit both themselves and the company.

events provide important clues about norms and values. In the past, if any manager in IBM's laptop computer division, for example, used the phrase "I non-concur" to disagree with a proposed plan of action, that plan was abandoned because one of IBM's instrumental values was achieving consensus. But after divisions were given the authority to control their activities, the language changed, and a manager who tried to use that phrase during a meeting was told by other managers, "We no longer recognize that phrase," indicating that the division had adopted new terminal values.

The concept of organizational language extends beyond spoken language to include nonverbal communication—how people dress, the offices they occupy, and cars they drive. Casual dress supports Microsoft's entrepreneurial culture and values that encourage employees to be different, to be creative, and to take risks to speed the development of new products. By contrast, formal business attire supports Arthur Andersen's conservative culture, which emphasizes the importance of conforming to organizational norms, such as respect for authority and staying within one's prescribed role. When people understand the language of an organization's culture, they know how to behave in the organization and what attitudes are expected of them.

Many organizations have particular "technical" organizational languages that they use to facilitate mutual adjustment between organizational members. At 3M Corporation, entrepreneurs have to emphasize the relationship between their product and 3M's terminal values in order to get their ideas pushed through the product development committee. Because many 3M products are flat—compact disks, Post-it notes, floppy disks, paper, transparencies—"flatness" is often a winning theme in 3M's corporate language. At Microsoft, employees have developed a corporate language full of technical software phrases to overcome communication problems. Such languages and jargon are found in many specialized work contexts—the military, sports teams, hospitals, and so on—and we discussed in Chapter 13 the important role they play in enhancing organizational communication. Like an organization's socialization practices, organizational ceremonies, jargon, stories, and language help people learn the cultural ropes in the organizational setting.

Advice TO MANAGERS

Culture

- Always study the culture of your organization, and identify the terminal and instrumental values on which it is based in order to assess how it affects organizational behavior.
- Assess whether organizational norms are effectively transmitting the values of your organization's culture to organizational members. Analyze how norms could be improved.
- Examine how your organization socializes new members. Assess whether socialization practices are effective in helping newcomers to learn the organization's culture, and look for ways to improve the process.
- Try to identify ceremonies or rites that your organization can use to help employees to learn cultural values, enhance employee commitment, and bond employees to the organization.

SUMMARY

Organizational culture is an important means through which organizations coordinate and motivate the behavior of their members. Organizational structure and culture work together to shape employee behavior so that employees work to achieve organizational goals. The values in an organization's culture strongly reflect the values of the founder and top managers, and the importance they place on employees is evident in the work setting they create through the design of its culture. An organization can shape work attitudes and behaviors by its employment practices, by the way it invests in and rewards its workforce over time, and by its attempts to encourage values of excellence. Organizational culture and structure combine to produce a work setting in which people are (or perhaps are not) motivated to perform.

Over time, both structure and culture may be taken for granted by employees who do not notice the many important ways in which the work situation around them influences their behavior. Structure and especially culture are often very difficult to change. People become used to acting in a certain way. So even when management changes task and role relationships or attempts to change organizational values and norms, organizational members do not always change in response. Thus it is not surprising that organizations are often slow to change and that when they do change, significant restructuring and upheaval are necessary to change the organization and its members behavior.

We have more to say about these issues in Chapter 19, where we look in depth at the nature of organizational change and development. But first we must examine the factors that cause organizations to choose different kinds of structure and culture. The determinants of organizational structure and culture are discussed in the next chapter.

SUMMARY

Organizational structure and culture affect how people and groups behave in an organization. Together they provide a framework that shapes attitudes, behaviors, and performance. Organizations need to create a structure and culture that allow them to manage individuals and intergroup relations effectively. In this chapter, we made the following major points:

1. Organizational structure is the formal system of task and reporting relationships that controls, coordinates, and motivates employees so that they cooperate to achieve an organization's goals. Differentiation and integration are the basic building blocks of organizational structure.

2. Five structures that organizations use to differentiate their activities and to group people into functions or divisions are functional, product, market, geographic, and matrix structures. Each of these is suited to a particular purpose and has specific coordination and motivation advantages and disadvantages associated with it.

3. As organizations grow and differentiate, problems of integrating activities inside and particularly between functions and divisions arise. Organizations can use the hierarchy of authority, mutual adjustment, and standardization to increase integration.

4. To integrate their activities, organizations develop a hierarchy of authority and decide how to allocate decision-making responsibility. Two important choices that they must make are how many levels to have in the hierarchy, and how much authority to decentralize to managers throughout the hierarchy and how much to retain at the top.

5. To promote integration, organizations develop mechanisms for promoting mutual adjustment (the ongoing informal communication and interaction among people and functions). Mechanisms

that facilitate mutual adjustment include direct contact, liaison roles, teams and task forces, cross-functional teams and cross-functional team structures, integrating roles, and matrix structures.

6. Organizations that use standardization to integrate their activities develop performance programs that specify how individuals and functions are to coordinate their actions to accomplish organizational objectives. Organizations can standardize their input, throughput, and output activities.

7. Organizational culture is the set of informal values and norms that control the way individuals and groups interact with each other and with people outside the organization. Organizational cultures are collections of two kinds of values: terminal and instrumental. Norms encourage members to help adopt organizational values and behave in certain ways as they pursue organizational goals.

8. The values of the founder of the organization and the ethical values the organization develops to inform its employees about appropriate ways to behave have a significant impact on organizational culture. Strong cultures have cohesive sets of values and norms that bind organizational members together and foster commitment from employees to achieve organizational goals. Strong cultures can be built through an organization's socialization process and from the informal ceremonies, rites, stories, and language that develop in an organization over time.

Organizational Behavior in Action

TOPICS FOR
DISCUSSION
AND ACTION

1. What is differentiation, and why does it occur?
2. How do a matrix structure and a cross-functional team structure differ?
3. What kind of organizational structure would you expect to find in (a) a fast food restaurant, (b) a company like General Electric or General Motors, (c) a biotechnology company?
4. What kind of structure does your college or business use? Why?
5. Why is integration a problem for an organization?
6. What are the main issues in deciding on the design of an organization's hierarchy of authority?
7. Why is mutual adjustment an important means of integration in most organizations?
8. What kinds of organizational activities are easiest to standardize? Most difficult?
9. What is organizational culture? What role does the founder of an organization play in the development of organizational culture over time? What role does ethics play?

**BUILDING
DIAGNOSTIC
SKILLS**

Understanding Organizational Structure and Culture

Think of an organization that you are familiar with—a university, restaurant, church, department store, or an organization that you have worked for—and answer these questions:

1. What form of differentiation does the organization use to group people and resources? Draw a diagram showing the major functions. Why do you think the organization uses this form of differentiation? Would another form be more appropriate?
2. How many levels are there in the organization's hierarchy? Draw a diagram showing the levels in the hierarchy and the job titles of the people at each level. Do you think this organization has the right number of levels in its hierarchy? How centralized or decentralized is authority in the organization?
3. To what degree does the organization use mutual adjustment and standardization to coordinate its activities? What mechanisms does it use to increase mutual adjustment? Does it use teams or cross-functional teams? What kinds of rules and standard operating procedures does it use?
4. What are the organization's principal terminal and instrumental values? What kinds of norms has it developed to shape the behavior of its members? How would you characterize the organization's culture?
5. How does the organization socialize its members? Are you aware of any ceremonies, stories, or other means the organization uses to transmit its culture to its members?

RESEARCH ON THE INTERNET: A MANAGER'S TOOL

Specific Task

Each organization needs to develop the right structure and culture to manage its activities effectively. Enter Xerox Corporation's website (www.xerox.com), click on facts about Xerox, and then click on business groups.

1. What kind of structure do you think Xerox uses to manage the various activities of its business groups?
2. Why do you think Xerox uses this structure?

General Task

Search for the website of a company that describes in detail either the nature of its structure or culture. What is the nature of its structure or culture? Why did it choose it?

TOPICS FOR DEBATE

Different organizational structures and cultures prompt organizational members to behave in different ways. Now that you understand the kinds of choices that organizations face when they create their organizational structures and cultures, debate the following issues.

Debate One

Team A. Organizational structure is more important than organizational culture in coordinating and motivating individuals and functions to achieve an organization's goals.

Team B. Organizational culture is more important than organizational structure in coordinating and motivating individuals and functions to achieve an organization's goals.

Debate Two

Team A. Standardization is more important than mutual adjustment in helping an organization to integrate its activities.

Team B. Mutual adjustment is more important than standardization in helping an organization to integrate its activities.

EXPERIENTIAL EXERCISE

Analyzing Organizations

For this chapter you will analyze the structure and culture of a real organization such as a department store, restaurant, hospital, fire station, or police department. In the next chapter you will identify the contingencies that have influenced the development of the organization's structure and culture.

Objective

Your objective is to gain experience in analyzing and diagnosing an organization.

Procedure

The class divides into groups of from three to five people. Group members discuss the kind of organization the group will analyze and then explore the possibility of gaining access to the organization by using a personal contact or by calling and going to see the manager in charge of the organization. After the group gains access to the organization, each member of the group interviews one or more members of the organization. Use the questions listed below to develop an interview schedule to guide your interview of the organization's employees, but be sure to ask additional questions to probe more deeply into issues that you think are interesting and reveal how the organization's structure and culture work.

After all of the groups complete the assignment, the instructor either will allocate class time for each group to make a presentation of its findings to the whole class or will request a written report.

1. Draw an organizational chart showing the major roles and functions in your organization.
2. What kind of structure does your organization use? Why does it use this structure? What are the advantages and disadvantages of this structure?
3. How does your organization integrate and coordinate its activities?
   a. Describe the organization's hierarchy of authority. Is it tall or flat? Is it centralized or decentralized? How wide a span of control does the top manager have?
   b. What integrating mechanisms does the organization use to coordinate its activities?
   c. To what degree does the organization standardize its activities, and how does it do this?
4. Summarizing this information, would you say the organization is highly differentiated? Highly integrated? Is there a balance between differentiation and integration?
5. What kinds of values and norms guide people's behavior in this organization? (Hint: During the interview, ask for examples of ceremonies, rites, or stories that seem to describe organizational values.) Where do these values and norms come from? How does this organization socialize new employees? What kinds of ethical values govern employees' behavior?

MAKING THE CONNECTION

Find an example of an organization that has been changing its structure or culture recently. What changes did the organization make, why did it make them, and what does it hope to achieve from them?

CLOSING CASE

Change and Change Again at Apple Computer

Incorporated in 1977, Apple computer designs, manufactures, and markets personal computers for use in business, education, and the home. Apple Computer was created in 1976, when two engineers, Steven Jobs and Steven Wozniak, collaborated to produce a computer designed for personal use.[41] As early orders for their computer increased, Jobs and Wozniak soon realized that they could not do everything themselves. They needed to employ more people to produce Apple's goods and services.

To produce more effectively, Jobs and Wozniak structured their company so that different people were grouped together to perform specific business functions (such as sales and marketing, purchasing, engineering, and manufacturing), thus creating a functional structure. Jobs and Wozniak also kept their organization flat so that it had few levels of managers. This structure encouraged employees to be creative, flexible, and responsive to the uncertainty that characterized the new personal computer industry. With few rules and few managers, Apple operated on the basis of personal contact among people in different functions who were members of teams and task forces.

As a result of their decisions about how to organize and run their company, Jobs and Wozniak created an entrepreneurial culture at Apple characterized by intensely loyal members who were committed to developing innovative products. Values and norms that emphasized cooperation, encouraged the sharing of information and ideas, and led to high employee commitment to the organization developed.

By 1982 Apple's structure had become taller, and levels of management had increased. A new chief executive, John Sculley, had been hired to take control of the management side of the business. Fast growth and the introduction of a wider range of products, including the Macintosh computer, had led to many communication and coordination problems among the different functions. Sculley decided that Apple would change from a structure based on functions to one based on products—a product structure. Each product would be manufactured by a separate division, each of which would have its own set of functions such as marketing, research and development, and product engineering.

Problems arose with this product structure. Jobs, now the head of the Macintosh Division, began to champion the development of his project, the Macintosh computer, over other types of computers, triggering hostile competition for resources among Apple's divisions. The organization's values began to change as cooperation fell, and people began to become more loyal to their division than to the organization as a whole. Moreover, the costs of running the company rose dramatically because functions were duplicated in each division.

By 1985 recession in the computer industry had worsened these problems and made reorganization imperative. Jobs was ousted from the company, and Sculley took total control. Faced with increasing competition from computer clone makers, Sculley searched for ways to change Apple's structure to reduce costs.[42] Apple moved back to a functional structure in which, once again, one set of functions served the needs of all the different kinds of computers Apple produced. For example, all computers were now manufactured in one central production function where one management team had overall control, rather than in separate product divisions headed by different teams of managers. Sculley also began to downsize Apple's workforce, laying off employees and flattening the organization's hierarchy by getting rid of layers of management.

The layoffs poisoned relationships between managers and workers and destroyed Apple's entrepreneurial cultural values.[43] Apple's loyal employees were furious about these layoffs. After all they had contributed to the company, employees could not believe that Apple would behave toward them in this way. Fired employees engaged in a very visible demonstration for several weeks outside Apple headquarters, norms of cooperation changed into confrontational norms, and morale and employee commitment fell.

Despite Sculley's changes, Apple's situation continued to deteriorate as competition from low-cost clone manufacturers increased, and in 1994 Sculley himself was ousted as CEO because of Apple's poor performance. He was replaced as CEO by Michael Spindler, who championed the development of a new kind of low-cost, user-friendly computer—the Apple Performa—and continued to reduce Apple's workforce and simplify its organizational structure.

In 1994 and 1995, with its new Performa computers selling well and its stream-lined structure in place, Apple was fighting back, and its managers continued to look for new ways to organize Apple's activities to cut costs and maintain its technological edge in its fierce battle with companies like Compaq, Dell, IBM, and AST.

Discussion Questions
1. Why did Apple move from a functional to a product structure and back again?
2. How and why did Apple's culture change over time?

Determinants of Organization Structure and Culture

16

OPENING CASE

Up the Amazon.com

Amazon.com (www.amazon.com), the first company to sell books over the Internet, was formed by Jeffrey Bezos, a computer science and electronics engineering graduate from Princeton University. In July 1995 Bezos launched his venture on the Internet from a 400-square-foot office; six weeks later he moved the company to a 2,000-square-foot building; six months later the company moved again to a

17,000-square-foot warehouse.[1] In its first year of operation the company's revenues were over $5 million, and in 1997 after continuing success the company went public

with a share offering that has made Bezos a multimillionaire. Why has the company performed so well? Because of Bezos's ability to choose the right strategy and technology for his company's new venture, and to fashion an organizational structure and culture that has allowed him to use his company's resources to the maximum advantage.[2]

Bezos's strategy is based on Amazon.com's ability to make accessible to customers virtually every book in print in the world today via Amazon.com's vast electronic library, and to provide an ongoing electronic forum whereby customers can comment on and discuss books, and even ask one another for book recommendations. Amazon is able to pursue this strategy of differentiation, a strategy based on providing customers with a unique service, because of the company's' innovative use of technology. It uses some of the most powerful computer servers possible, and its programmers have developed efficient customized software that allows customers to connect easily with the company and makes book purchasing easy and problem free.

From the beginning, Bezos saw the need to develop an operating structure that would allow him to use Amazon.com's information technology most efficiently, and which allowed the company to be as responsive to customers as possible. The structure Bezos chose, one which most small companies adopt, was a functional structure, in which people and resources are grouped together because they perform similar tasks. Thus, employees who answered customers' e-mail inquiries and took their Internet orders were grouped together in the operations department; employees responsible for developing and managing software were grouped together in the development department. A functional structure enabled Bezos to exercise adequate supervision over Amazon.com's growing business. Finally, Bezos fostered an entrepreneurial culture for Amazon.com, one in which employees are encouraged to experiment to find ways to do things better—which basically means finding new and better ways to serve customers—and are rewarded for doing so. Employees frequently work from 8:00 to 8:00 and on weekends, many employees own stock in the company, and Bezos has deliberately kept the organization's structure as flat as possible to encourage the high level of flexibility and communication a growing company needs.

So far, Amazon.com has been successful, and it is the biggest Internet book seller. However, in 1997, the two biggest book sellers in the United States, Barnes & Noble (www.barnesandnoble.com) and Borders (www.borders.com) started their own Internet publishing ventures, so the environment is becoming much more competitive. The question is, does Amazon.com have the right strategy and structure in place that will allow it to continue to dominate the Internet book selling market, or will it become an "also ran?"

Overview

Jeffrey Bezos faced the challenge of creating a strategy and structure that would allow his company to capitalize on the opportunities presented by new technology that made it possible to sell books over the Internet. This challenge is the essence of organizational design (see Chapter 15), the process by which managers select and manage various dimensions and components of organizational structure and culture so that an organization can achieve its goals. Having discussed the various dimensions and components of organizational structure and culture, we can turn to the issue of how contingencies (events that might possibly occur and thus must be taken into account in an organization's planning) determine the kind of structure and culture an organization chooses to coordinate its activities.

In this chapter we examine three crucial contingencies that affect the organizational design process: the organization's environment, the technology an organization uses, and the organization's strategy. We discuss a fourth contingency, international or global competition, in Chapter 17. By the end of this chapter you will understand how these contingencies determine the choice of organizational structure and culture and why managing these contingencies is such a crucial task in today's increasingly competitive environment.

The Organization's Environment

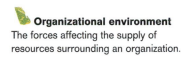

Organizational environment
The forces affecting the supply of resources surrounding an organization.

The **organizational environment** is the set of forces surrounding an organization that determine its ability to obtain resources. These resources include inputs such as the raw materials and skilled employees that an organization needs to produce goods and services; resources such as the computers, buildings, and machinery used to transform inputs into outputs of goods and services; and resources such as customers who are willing to buy an organization's goods and services.

An organization depends on its environment for the resources it needs to produce goods and services for customers. Because resources are often scarce and because many organizations compete for the same resources, obtaining resources is a difficult and uncertain process. McDonald's, Burger King, Taco Bell, and Pizza Hut all compete to acquire the customers' fast food dollars, for example. Similarly, Dell, IBM, Apple, and Gateway compete for personal computer customers and for high-quality inputs such as Intel's microprocessors or Microsoft's software to build their computers. In attempting to deal effectively with the many components of its uncertain environment, an organization must design its structure and culture in a way that allows organizational members to secure and protect the organization's access to the resources it needs to achieve its goals. For this reason the environment is a determinant of organizational structure and culture.

FORCES THAT AFFECT THE SUPPLY OF RESOURCES

Perhaps the best way to understand how the environment affects organizational design is to examine the various forces present in an environment that affect an organization's ability to obtain resources. When we have identified these forces, we can look at how an organization can design its structure and culture to encourage the development of attitudes and behaviors that encourage and allow members to obtain these resources and meet their goals. Figure 16.1 identifies the most important of the many forces in an organization's environment.

Suppliers.   To obtain required inputs, an organization must develop and manage relationships with its suppliers. Harley-Davidson, for example, the famous motorcycle maker, has over a thousand different suppliers of inputs such as tires, windshields, light bulbs, electronic components, and radios. Harley's goal is to secure high-quality input resources at reasonable prices. To accomplish this goal, Harley has developed many ways of managing supplier

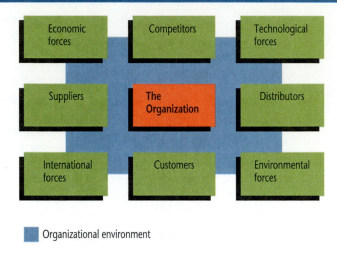

FIGURE 16.1

Forces in an Organization's Environment

■ Organizational environment

relationships. Harley has long-term contracts with many suppliers in which it agrees to purchase from them certain quantities of inputs at certain prices. If a particular input is crucial, an organization might take stronger measures to protect its access to the input by buying its suppliers. Harley, for example, owns the company that supplies most of its important electronic components, so it has a guaranteed supply of that input. Other inputs that Harley requires include skilled workers and experienced supervisors and managers. (See the Closing Case for more information.)

Distributors. On the output side, an organization must establish channels of distribution that give it access to customers. Distributors are the various organizations that help an organization sell its products. Harley and all other motorcycle companies distribute and sell their products through franchised dealerships. Franchised dealerships can develop personalized relationships with customers and devise ways to offer customers good-quality sales and service. Companies that sell less complex products like televisions or stereos sell through stores or even directly to customers. But no matter how an organization distributes its products, it has to develop and manage relationships with its distributors in order to have the best chance of securing the resources (such as customers' dollars) it needs to buy more inputs and pay its employees.

Competitors. Another important environmental force that affects an organization's ability to obtain resources is competitors. Competitors are organizations that compete for the same set of resources: inputs such as the best microprocessors for Compaq or Dell, or carburetors for Harley bikes; outputs such as customers; or even the best channels of distribution for outputs. Large soft-drink companies such as Coca-Cola and PepsiCo, for example, actively compete for shelf space in supermarkets—a very scarce resource—because more shelf space will attract greater numbers of customers to their products. The more competitive an environment is, the more difficult it is to obtain access to resources, as Amazon.com discovered when Barnes & Noble and Borders began to steal away its Internet customers.

Customers. Relationships with customers affect the supply of resources. Organizations try to manage these relationships in several ways. They engage in massive advertising campaigns to bring their products to the notice of customers. They also polish and protect their reputation. If customers trust a company's products, they will stay with a company, and Amazon.com claims its has many repeat customers because of its high level of customer service. On the other hand, the Big Three automakers (GM, Ford, and Chrysler) experienced many problems in the 1970s and 1980s because prospective customers did not believe that their cars were as reliable or of as high a quality as cars being manufactured by their Japanese competitors. In the 1990s, however, sales of American cars have increased as the quality of the vehicles has increased.

Other Forces. Other forces indirectly affect an organization's access to resources:

- Economic forces such as the rate of interest or state of the economy, which determine overall demand for a company's products.
- International or global forces such as the presence of strong foreign competitors or cheap foreign inputs or tariffs on foreign goods (see Chapter 17).
- Technological forces such as the emergence of new technologies that can make a company's products or methods of production out of date or less reliable.
- Environmental forces such as a country's desire to reduce air pollution or hazardous waste or to reduce health risks by discouraging smoking. The Big Three automakers, for example, have been under increasing pressure to develop an electric car and to develop other ways to reduce pollution and increase gas mileage.
- Government forces such as regulations concerning antitrust, equal employment opportunity, occupational health and safety, and changes to the tax code.

UNCERTAINTY, DIFFERENTIATION, AND INTEGRATION

An organization has to manage all of the above forces in its environment to obtain the resources it needs to achieve its goals. The major problem facing an organization is the uncertainty of its environment. It is difficult for managers to predict or control the availability of needed resources. The more uncertain the environment is, the more important it is for organizational members to be able to react quickly to changes that take place. The level of uncertainty in the environment is the first major contingency that an organization must prepare for as it designs its structure and culture.

To deal with this uncertainty, an organization must choose a level of differentiation that gives its members flexibility to react to and manage the various forces in the environment.[3] In general, the number and nature of the functions an organization develops and the kinds of people an organization employs reflect the nature of the forces in the environment that cause uncertainty. For example, all organizations create functions to manage the uncertainty associated with the availability of materials and inputs: The purchasing and materials management function is created to handle relationships with suppliers. The sales and marketing function is created to handle relationships with distributors and customers. The research and development function is created to track new technological developments

FIGURE 16.2

Using a Functional Structure to Manage Environmental Forces

and develop new or improved products for customers. Figure 16.2 shows how an organization can use a functional structure (see Chapter 15) to manage the demands of its environment.

The greater the number of different forces an organization has to deal with in its environment, the greater is the level of functional differentiation. Similarly, the greater the uncertainty surrounding any specific force (due, perhaps, to rapid changes), the larger the function will become. As the technology involved in making cars changed rapidly in the 1980s, for example, the size of the functions that manage technology—R&D and product engineering—increased dramatically as the Big Three U.S. automakers hired significant numbers of new scientists and engineers.

The argument that the design of an organization's structure needs to match the uncertainty of the environment in which the organization operates was taken further by Paul Lawrence and Jay Lorsch. According to Lawrence and Lorsch, an organization faces an important challenge in managing the environment: It has to create a structure with the right levels of both differentiation and integration to match the uncertainty of the environment in which it operates.[4]

Uncertainty and Differentiation.   In Lawrence and Lorsch's model, differentiation measures the degree to which a function or division develops orientations (attitudes, values and norms, and ways of doing things) that allow its members to manage the specific environmental force that each function or division is dealing with. The role of research and development personnel, for example, is to monitor the technological environment and to help an organization adjust to changes in technology that will affect the goods and services the organization produces. Because technological change typically takes place over the long run, people in R&D need to develop a long-term attitude toward product development that allows them to anticipate organizational needs five or even ten years in advance. They also need to develop values that support risk taking and creativity. In contrast, sales personnel face the immediate problem of disposing of an organization's goods and services, so they need to develop attitudes that allow them to take quick action to sell products and values that emphasize meeting short-run goals and objectives.

In their research, Lawrence and Lorsch found that, in effective organizations, differentiation—the degree of differences in attitudes and orientations between functions—increased as the environment became more uncertain. The reason for this was that higher differentiation gave functional personnel more ability and opportunity to understand and respond to the specific environment for which they were responsible. This greater depth of understanding enabled the functional employees to move quickly to take corrective action when changes occurred in their part of the organizational environment.

Uncertainty and Integration.   Lawrence and Lorsch also found that as the degree of differentiation increased (the result of increased uncertainty), organizations had to increase the level of integration between functions if people in different functions were to be able to work together effectively (see Fig. 16.3). Lawrence and Lorsch defined integration as the degree of coordination or mutual adjustment between functions.[5] Recall from Chapter 15 that organizations use liaison roles, integrating roles, and even matrix or cross-functional team structures to increase the level of mutual adjustment and integration between functions and divisions.

Lawrence and Lorsch found that because differentiation makes it more difficult for people in different functions to communicate and share ideas, organizations need to increase integration to manage their environments effectively and achieve their goals. When environmental uncertainty is low, differentiation is low; as a result, functions have similar attitudes and orientations toward organizational goals and how to achieve them, and the need for integration is reduced. When uncertainty is low, the hierarchy of authority and standardization provide sufficient integration to control cross-functional activities. As uncertainty increases, however, the level of differentiation increases, and organizations must increase their level of integration if they are to be effective.

In summary, the level of uncertainty determines what kind of structure will best allow an organization to manage the environment. The more uncertain the environment is, the more an organization must allow functions to

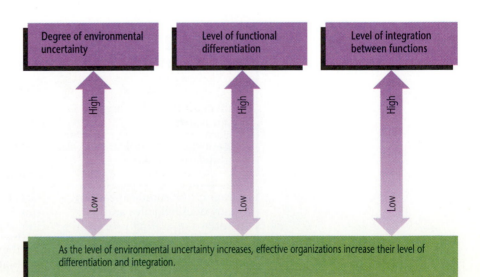

FIGURE 16.3

The Effect of Uncertainty on Differentiation and Integration

Degree of environmental uncertainty

Level of functional differentiation

Level of integration between functions

High — Low

As the level of environmental uncertainty increases, effective organizations increase their level of differentiation and integration.

develop their own approaches to solving problems, and the more an organization must find ways to integrate activities, improve coordination, and motivate the different functions to work together to achieve organizational goals.

MECHANISTIC AND ORGANIC STRUCTURES

Lawrence and Lorsch's research supported the conclusions of an earlier study by Tom Burns and G. M. Stalker, which also investigated the way in which organizations design their structures to allow them to manage their environments.[6] Burns and Stalker found that effective organizations operating in stable, low-uncertainty environments tended to develop a mechanistic structure, and organizations operating in changing, high-uncertainty environments tended to develop an organic structure. Table 16.1 summarizes the differences between these two structures.

A **mechanistic structure** is designed so that individuals and functions behave in predictable ways and can be held accountable for their actions. Mechanistic structures have several characteristic design features. They have tall organizational hierarchies, and decision making is centralized at the top of the organization. Communication and decision making flow from the top down, and people at lower levels in the hierarchy simply follow orders passed down from the top. Mechanistic structures are also characterized by a high level of standardization and rely heavily on detailed and extensive use of rules and standard operating procedures to control the activities of their members. Mechanistic structures develop a rigid division of labor; people are assigned to clearly specified tasks and roles so that they can be held directly accountable for their actions.

Because a mechanistic structure is designed so that individuals and functions behave in predictable ways, organizational activities can be programmed in advance to achieve predictable outcomes. A mechanistic structure suits a stable environment.

In contrast, an **organic structure** is designed so that individuals and functions can behave flexibly and respond quickly to frequently changing and unusual situations. Organic structures tend to be relatively flat, and authority is

Mechanistic structure
An organization structure that is designed so that individuals and functions behave in predictable ways and can be held accountable for their actions.

Organic structure
An organizational structure that is designed so that individuals and functions can behave flexibly and respond quickly to frequently changing and unusual situations.

TABLE 16.1

Characteristics of Mechanistic and Organic Structures

Mechanistic Structures	Organic Structures
Tall, centralized hierarchy of authority	Flat, decentralized hierarchy of authority
Top-down communication and decision making	Lateral communication and decision making between people in different departments
Great use of standardization: many detailed rules and standard operating procedures	Great use of mutual adjustment: much face-to-face communication in taskforces and teams
Clearly specified tasks and roles and a defined division of labor	Deliberately ill-defined tasks and roles and a loose division of labor

decentralized to the people who are most in touch with changes in the environment on a day-to-day basis. As a result, a greater amount of decision making and communication takes place laterally between people in different functions, rather than vertically from the top of the hierarchy down. This speeds the decision-making process. In an organic structure, mutual adjustment rather than standardization becomes the principal method of integration, further facilitating communication and cooperation among functions. The division of labor is deliberately kept ill defined, and workers are encouraged to act outside their roles and assume new responsibilities as the need arises. An organic structure is also higher on dimensions such as skill variety, task identity, autonomy, and feedback, all important motivating characteristics of jobs discussed in Chapter 8, and this also encourages people to perform highly and develop supportive work attitudes.

In an organic structure, employees unfettered by rigid rules and SOPs become used to acting flexibly to solve problems. Organic structures facilitate the sharing and pooling of ideas and allow for the timely formation of task forces and cross-functional teams that can make effective decisions in an uncertain situation.

ORGANIZATIONAL CULTURE AND THE ENVIRONMENT

As the research by Lawrence and Lorsch and by Burns and Stalker indicates, the level of uncertainty in the environment affects how organizations should design their structures. In more uncertain environments, organizations should adopt organic structures in which employees are given freedom and autonomy to make decisions. The more stable and predictable the environment is, the more organizations should develop a mechanistic structure in which roles and responsibilities are clearly prescribed. These two kinds of structures, in turn, have important implications for the kinds of cultures that emerge in organizations operating in different kinds of environments.

Organizations with organic structures develop cultures very different from the cultures of organizations with mechanistic structures. Because people have little autonomy in a mechanistic structure, they are likely to develop instrumental values that stress being cautious, obeying superior authority, and the importance of staying inside one's role and respecting traditions. Such instrumental values give rise to a culture in which predictability and stability are the desired terminal values that will help the organization achieve its goals. Organizations operating in a stable environment do not need and often do not want innovative responses from their employees.

In contrast, in organic structures—in which people are given more freedom, and cooperation between functions is encouraged—instrumental values of being creative, taking risks, and challenging established traditions and opinions are likely to develop. These are exactly the kinds of values that organizations in uncertain environments want to encourage because they need to respond and adapt quickly to changing conditions. Innovation is likely to flourish and an entrepreneurial culture is likely to develop when organizations use an organic structure.

Organizations in different kinds of environments develop different kinds of cultures. The way in which an organization's structure and culture need to match its environment is put in focus by the challenges facing George Fisher, the former head of Motorola, as he went about changing the design of Eastman Kodak. (see Insight 16.1).

Insight 16.1

Environment

A New Plan for Kodak

In the early 1990s the performance of Eastman Kodak (www.kodak .com) was falling rapidly. The company was suffering from the effects of a changing environment in which chemical imaging was giving way to electronic imaging in photography, copying, and other means of transmitting information. Kodak had no particular research capability in the electronic imaging field, and over the years it had developed a mechanistic structure and a conservative culture that prevented it from reacting quickly enough to the rapid changes that were taking place in its environment. In 1993 the company's board of directors reacted to Kodak's deteriorating situation by firing CEO Kay Whitmore and replacing him with the former CEO of Motorola, George Fisher, who had made Motorola a leader in electronic products.

Fisher was confronted with the huge challenge of changing Kodak's structure and culture to allow the organization to regain control over its environment. Industry analysts advised him to lay off 25,000 of the company's 110,000 managers and workers to demolish the conservative values that plagued the company.[7] Most of Kodak's management was inbred, and managers were used to guaranteed life-time employment. To break the mold and change the company's instrumental and terminal values, Fisher was advised to establish a tougher, more efficiency-oriented culture with a concern for both innovation and the bottom line.

On the subject of how to change Kodak's structure, analysts advised Fisher to take a radical approach to changing task and reporting relationships. Over the years, the different divisions in Kodak's product structure had carved out separate fiefdoms for themselves and operated independently. As a result, the divisions competed for resources to develop their own projects and neglected to share ideas and information that might have helped other divisions develop innovative products that would allow the company as a whole to compete effectively in its environment. Moreover, Kodak's hierarchy of authority had become tall and unwieldy, and top management found it very difficult to coordinate the company's resources. Fisher was advised to flatten Kodak's structure, wipe out over 50 percent of its corporate staff, and restructure activities to focus on Kodak's core product lines. Then, to force the divisions to cooperate, he was advised to develop integrating roles to make the most of the company's resources.

No one is underestimating the difficulty of the task facing Fisher. Big questions remain about the company's ability to change quickly enough to be able to survive in the quickly changing electronic information environment. If Fisher cannot change Kodak's structure and culture fast enough, Kodak may just shrink and focus on its core business: high-quality photographic products.

Environment

- Analyze the set of forces in the environment surrounding your organization and the degree of uncertainty associated with each force.
- Evaluate the way your organizational structure and culture are designed to manage these forces. Are the levels of differentiation and integration appropriate? Is your organization sufficiently mechanistic or organic?
- Implement organizational design changes that will improve your organization's ability to respond to its environment.

SUMMARY

Organizational design is influenced by the nature of the environment in which an organization operates. In an uncertain environment, an organization needs to be able to respond quickly and creatively to unexpected events and must design a structure and a culture that allow people to behave flexibly and innovatively. Such a design allows an organization to perform at a high level when uncertainty is high. In a stable environment, an organization can design a structure and a culture that give managers more control over employees and encourage the development of cultural values and norms that make employee attitudes and behaviors more predictable. This type of design allows an organization to perform at a high level when uncertainty is low.

The Organization's Technology and Tasks

In Chapter 7, we defined job design as the process of linking specific tasks to specific jobs. The purpose of job design is to create a system of interrelated jobs that motivate workers to contribute their skills and knowledge and allow them to use those inputs to help the organization achieve its goals. At the organizational level, **technology** is the term used to describe the combination of human resources (skills, knowledge, abilities, techniques) and raw materials and equipment (machines, computers, tools) that workers use to convert raw materials into finished goods and services. Each job or function in an organization is part of an organization's technology.

In selecting a type of technology to produce goods and services, an organization chooses a way to use resources to achieve its goals. After the organizational environment, technology is the second major design contingency that an organization faces. An organization must design its structure and culture to allow the efficient operation of its technology.

WOODWARD'S MODEL OF TECHNOLOGY

One of the first research studies to find a relationship between an organization's technology and its structure was conducted by Joan Woodward in England in the 1950s.[8] At the beginning of her research, Woodward was not focusing on technology. Her original interest was to find whether certain organizational structures were more effective than others. She began by measuring several characteristics of structure, such as the number of levels in the hierarchy, the span of control of managers at different levels, whether authority was centralized or decentralized, and the degree of formalization and mutual adjustment.

Technology
The combination of human resources and raw materials and equipment that workers use to convert raw materials into finished goods and services.

Woodward also analyzed how these factors were related to measures of the organization's effectiveness such as its profitability or market share.

When she analyzed her data, Woodward found no relationships between effectiveness and these measures of organizational structure until she classified her organizations according to the kind of technology they used (data she had collected earlier). When she did this, she found some interesting relationships between technology, structure, and organizational effectiveness. In the following pages we discuss the relationship between the three of the types of technology that Woodward identified and the structures associated with each technology.

Small-Batch Technology. **Small-batch technology** relies primarily on the skills and knowledge of individual workers to produce one-of-a-kind, customized goods and services or small quantities of goods and services. Examples of products that are made by means of small-batch technology include Rolls Royce cars, custom-designed clothing or furniture, and personalized services for customers such as financial planning, legal work, or surgery. Although machines can be an important part of small-batch technology, it is the individual worker who decides how and when machines should be used in the process of converting inputs (such as patients in need of surgery) to outputs (healthy people).

The use of small-batch technology allows an organization to tailor its use of people and resources to the demands of different customers. Each customer of a famous clothes designer like Dior, Armani, or Anne Klein, for example, may request a specific kind of suit or dress to be made from a particular kind of fabric. The clothing designer custom-designs clothes to suit each customer's specific request and then gives the design to workers who have the skills to tailor the clothes according to the designs. The result is custom-tailored clothing, which is expensive because the organization had to organize tasks to be able to respond to unique customer requests—the main contingency associated with small-batch technology.

> **Small-batch technology**
> Technology that relies on the skills and knowledge of individual workers to produce one-of-a-kind, customized goods and services or small quantities of goods and services.

Skilled workers at Steinway and Sons wrap a 22-foot-long maple rim around the press that will shape it into the case for a Model D grand piano, an example of small-batch production in action. Roughly 200 people are involved in making and assembling the piano, which has twelve thousand parts and costs about $60,000 to buy.

The organizational structure that best matches the needs of small-batch technology is one that allows workers to be flexible in the way they perform their tasks. Such flexibility allows workers to organize and combine their skills and knowledge in different ways to satisfy various specific customer requests. The structure must also allow different functions to work closely together to respond quickly to new requests. Thus an organic structure, which decentralizes authority and permits a high level of mutual adjustment between people and functions, best matches the needs of small-batch technology. The cross-functional team structure, a type of organizational structure that allows people from different functions to work together (see Chapter 15), is appropriate because it allows people to cooperate and develop common values and norms as they work to help the organization achieve its goals.

Mass Production Technology.   **Mass production technology** is a manufacturing process that results in the production of large numbers of identical products. The key characteristic of this kind of technology, used in making cars and tin cans among thousands of other things, is that tasks are standardized and performed in a sequence so that each worker's task builds on the tasks that come before it. All the tasks that go into making a specific kind of product can be repeated endlessly so that all cars or bottles produced are identical. To manufacture a different kind of car or bottle, the production line is stopped and retooled—that is, the machines, computers, and workers' tasks are reprogrammed to produce the new product. When retooling is completed, large volumes of the new product are produced in a standardized, sequential fashion.

The Big Three automakers use mass production technology to produce cars. The cars are assembled sequentially: The car body is attached to the transmission; then the doors are attached to the body, and so on. These companies have found that mass production technology leads to low production costs and, as a result, to low prices that attract customers. In contrast, Rolls Royce, Lamborghini, and other small, specialized automakers use small-batch technology—small teams of workers pool their skills to produce each car separately. Because this way of organizing tasks is much more expensive than mass production, a Rolls Royce Silver Shadow costs over $165,000 versus around $18,000 for a mass-produced Ford Taurus sedan. Rolls Royce and Lamborghini are not concerned with reducing costs, however. Their goal is to attract affluent customers who want and can afford high-priced, unique, luxury products.

As you might expect, because mass production technology is very different from small-batch technology, the organizational design choices necessary to operate it are quite different from those that are needed for small-batch technology. The latter requires a flexible arrangement of tasks that allows people and functions to respond flexibly to the needs of different customers. In contrast, the goal of mass production technology is to reduce costs to a minimum and produce standardized products. Woodward found that organizations operating a mass production technology typically choose a mechanistic structure. Managers create a tall hierarchy in which control is centralized at the top of the organization. Formalization through written rules and standard operating procedures is high to standardize and program tasks and to give managers easy access to information about changes in product costs or quality, and tasks are designed to give workers little freedom and autonomy. In fact, typically the skills required of mass production workers are low, and jobs are low on task variety and task identity.

Mass production technology
Technology that results in the production of large numbers of identical products.

Continuous-process technology
Technology in which the manufacturing process is entirely mechanized and the workers' role is to monitor the machines and computers that actually produce the goods.

Continuous Process Technology.   The third type of technology that Woodward identified, **continuous-process technology,** is one in which the manufacturing process is entirely mechanized and the workers' role is confined to monitoring the machines and computers that actually produce the goods.[9] Examples of products produced by continuous-process technology are electricity, gasoline, bulk chemical products, soft drinks, and beer and wine. The technology is called continuous because it does not stop. Inputs constantly enter the manufacturing process and are continuously transformed into outputs.

Given its continuous, programmed nature, we might expect that organizations using continuous process technology would adopt a mechanistic structure, and in part they do. However, the main contingency that organizations must plan for when using this technology is the possibility of the catastrophe that will occur if their sophisticated, large-scale machinery and computers break down. Periodically, large chemical complexes such as paint factories or oil refineries explode and cause significant loss of life and damage to property. In 1984, for example, a Union Carbide chemical plant in Bhopal, India, exploded; the result was a huge loss of life and multi-billion-dollar damages that almost bankrupted the company. Similarly, accidents have occurred at nuclear power stations like Chernobyl and Three Mile Island, which also used a continuous-process technology. To operate continuous-process technology safely and effectively, an organization must be able to respond quickly to unexpected events and prevent catastrophes from occurring. Thus an organization needs an organic structure that will allow managers to work together quickly and flexibly to deal with problems as they arise.

Jobs in continuous-process technology are typically high on task identity and task significance because of the vital importance of maintaining machinery and equipment in peak operating order. Autonomy and feedback characteristics are also important because managers at all levels and in all functions must work together to share information and knowledge to keep the system in first-class order and deal with emergencies smoothly and effectively.

THOMPSON'S TECHNOLOGICAL TYPES

Another model of technology that has implications for the design of an organization's structure was developed by James D. Thompson.[10] In Chapter 11, we discussed Thompson's model of task interdependence and examined how different levels of task interdependence lead to coordination and motivation problems that affect group performance. Thompson linked each form of task interdependence—pooled, sequential, and reciprocal—to a type of technology and argued that the level of task interdependence associated with a technology should lead organizations to make different organizational design choices. In the following sections we discuss the three types of technology that Thompson identified and their effect on organizational design decisions (see Fig. 16.4).

Mediating technology
Technology that links independent but standardized tasks.

Mediating Technology.   A **mediating technology** links independent but standardized tasks. It is based on pooled task interdependence (individuals and functions working independently to produce goods and services). Each person and function makes a separate contribution to the group performance necessary to convert inputs into outputs, and a mediating technology links the various tasks together.

When a mediating technology is used, organizations standardize work activities among functions to eliminate the need for mutual adjustment. As a result, standardization is the mechanism used to integrate work activities and link

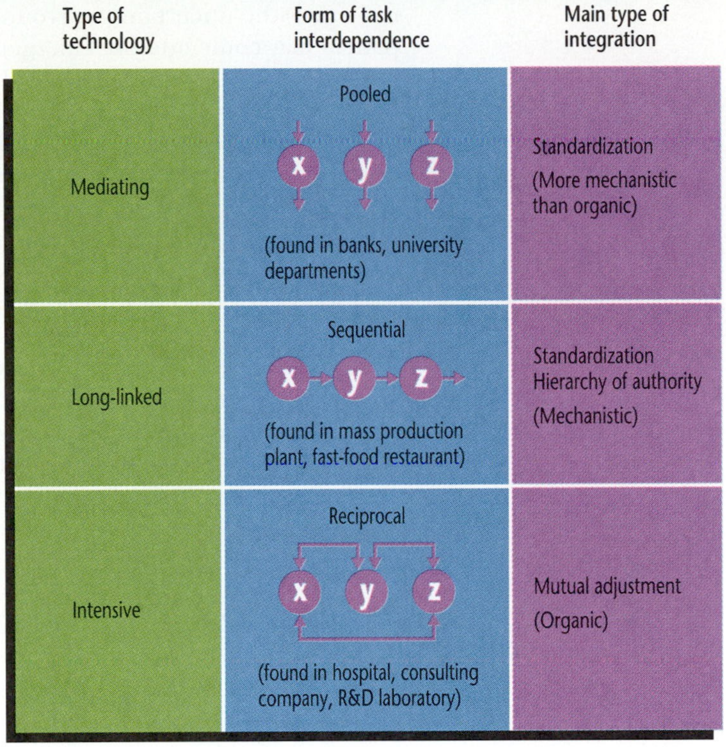

Type of technology	Form of task interdependence	Main type of integration
Mediating	Pooled (found in banks, university departments)	Standardization (More mechanistic than organic)
Long-linked	Sequential (found in mass production plant, fast-food restaurant)	Standardization Hierarchy of authority (Mechanistic)
Intensive	Reciprocal (found in hospital, consulting company, R&D laboratory)	Mutual adjustment (Organic)

FIGURE 16.4

Types of Technology
Identified by Thompson

people and functions together. Task and role relationships are clearly defined to facilitate integration between functions, and an organization develops a mechanistic structure. In a bank, for example, the activities of the checking and the lending functions are separate from one another, but the performance of the bank as a whole depends on how well each performs. Is checking attracting enough new accounts? Is lending using legal loan practices? Banks use standardization and formalization to ensure that each function performs its assigned role so that the organization as a whole works effectively.

Long-linked technology
Technology that is applied to a series of programmed tasks performed in a predetermined order.

Long-Linked Technology.   **Long-linked technology** is applied to a series of programmed tasks performed in a predetermined order. It is based on sequential task interdependence (individuals and groups contributing their efforts in a programmed, predetermined order to produce identical goods and services). Mass production technology is a long-linked technology, so the design implications of long-linked technology are similar to those noted for mass production technology: Organizations develop a mechanistic structure in which rules and SOPs clearly specify how the tasks of the various functions are to be coordinated, and the hierarchy of authority is used to monitor and closely supervise interfunctional activities.

Intensive technology
Technology that is applied to tasks that are performed in no predetermined order.

Intensive Technology.   **Intensive technology** is applied to tasks that are performed in no predetermined order. It is based on reciprocal task interdependence (individuals and functions working jointly and flexibly, in no predetermined order, to produce goods and services). The sequence in which individuals and functions perform their tasks is determined by the nature of the goods or services they produce. The way a hospital works is a good example of intensive technology in action. The main problem a hospital has to manage is the uncertainty surrounding clients' problems. At any moment, a patient may come into the emergency room with a broken leg, cardiac arrest, or food poisoning, and the hospital has to have the resources available to treat the specific problem. It must have on hand doctors, nurses, radiologists, an operating theater, and so on, to deal with any problem that may arise, and the sequence in which these resources are used depends on the nature of the problem. An intensive technology is needed to deal with unique customer requests (surgery or custom-designed clothing) or with the uncertainty surrounding the process of inventing a new drug or designing a new car.

Because of the high need for cross-functional coordination, an intensive technology requires an organizational structure with a high degree of integration. Because standardization and the hierarchy of authority do not provide enough integration between individuals or functions to allow an organization to respond flexibly and quickly to solve the problem, mutual adjustment becomes the primary means of integration. Thus task forces, teams, and other mechanisms are required to operate intensive technology effectively. For this reason organizations use an organic structure, and cross-functional teams are becoming increasingly important in operating this technology.

PERROW'S MODEL OF TECHNOLOGY

Charles Perrow developed a model of technology to explain why organizations make different design choices.[11] He was interested in what makes some tasks more complicated or difficult to perform than others. Perrow identified four types of technology—routine manufacturing, craftswork, nonroutine research, and engineering production—and he identified two dimensions on which tasks differ—task variety and task analyzability—and linked them to the use of different kinds of organizational structure.

Task variety is the number of new and different demands that a task places on an individual or a function. When task variety is high, tasks are unpredictable, often because new problems are continuously arising or new or different demands are being made of a worker. When tasks are repetitious or identical, task variety is low. **Task analyzability** is the degree to which standardized solutions are available to solve problems that arise. If task analyzability is high, then finding a solution and developing a performance program to solve a problem is easy. Task analyzability is low when individuals and functions must engage in an extensive search process to find a solution to a problem or demand.

Figure 16.5 shows correspondence between the four types of technology and task variability and task analyzability. In quadrant 1, routine manufac-

Task variety
The number of new and different demands that a task places on an individual or a function.

Task analyzability
The degree to which standardized solutions are available to solve problems that arise.

FIGURE **16.5**

Perrow's Model of Technology
Source: Adapted from C. Perrow, *Organizational Analysis: A Sociological View* (Belmont, Calif.: Wadsworth, 1970), p. 78.

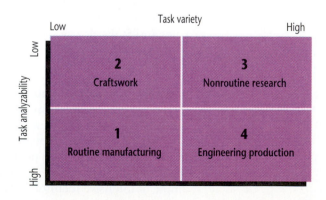

turing, tasks are simple, task variety is low (tasks are repetitious), and task analyzability is high (standardized solutions are available). The technology that McDonald's uses to produce hamburgers, that supermarkets use to check out customers, and that manufacturing plants use to produce tin cans is what Perrow called routine manufacturing technology. At the opposite extreme in quadrant 3, nonroutine research, tasks are complex and nonroutine, task variety is high (many new or different problems or demands are encountered), and task analyzability is low (finding a solution to a problem is hard). Tasks of this nature include pharmaceutical research and development, high-tech design of products, and the activities of top-management team members who must devise new strategies for an organization to follow. The organizational structure required to deal with nonroutine research is by necessity complex—for example, a matrix or cross-functional team structure.

Between those two extremes are the other two types of technology identified by Perrow. Craftswork (quadrant 2) is characterized by low task analyzability and low task variety: The range of new problems encountered is small, but each problem requires some search activity to find a solution to it. An accountant who prepares tax returns, for example, becomes used to the range of problems she must solve, but each client's account is different and each client needs personal attention. In quadrant 4, engineering production, task variety is high but analyzability is low: Many new problems are constantly occurring, but each is relatively easy to solve. Examples of companies that use an engineering production technology are large civil engineering companies, such as Bechtel, which build bridges and design road systems or even cities, and engineering companies that custom build machines or cars to order.

When an organization's tasks and technology are routine and oriented toward mass production, the organization is likely to design a mechanistic structure, in which integration takes place through established hierarchical channels of authority and through formal rules and standard operating procedures. As tasks and technology become more complex and nonroutine, the organization needs to design a more organic structure (such as a cross-functional team structure) to increase the level of mutual adjustment both within and between functions. Increasing the level of face-to-face communication allows individuals and functions to manage nonroutine tasks and to be more creative in problem solving and decision making. The way in which McKinsey & Co. developed an organic structure to manage its people and resources illustrates many of the issues surrounding the management of nonroutine, intensive, and small-batch technology (see Insight 16.2).

Insight 16.2   Technology

McKinsey & Co.

McKinsey & Co. (www.mckinsey.com) is the largest and most profitable management consulting company in the world. The organization has over $1 billion in annual revenues, 58 offices worldwide, and 3,000 consultants who work with prestigious companies such as AT&T, GM, IBM, American Express, and Johnson & Johnson. Each of its client companies comes to McKinsey with a unique problem that it needs help in solving. Because every company and every problem is different, task variety is very high. The fact that the managers of these companies cannot find a solution to their problem (or at least need confirmation of their own solution) means that task analyzability is low. McKinsey's clients are willing to pay the company $200,000 a month plus all expenses to find a solution to their problems, and frequently the problem-solving process takes months.

How does McKinsey find a solution to a client's problem? McKinsey operates with a nonroutine and small-batch technology. It assembles a handpicked team of consultants who have the specific skills needed to find a solution to a particular client's problem. The members of the team are reciprocally interdependent—each possesses a skill that the other team members depend on, such as in marketing, operations research, or competitive analysis. Because of the degree of interdependence, McKinsey also operates an intensive technology that allows for mutual adjustment between team members as they custom-design a solution for each client.

Typically, at the end of a project each client receives the team's solution to the problem in a nuts-and-bolts, no-holds-barred oral presentation and in written form in McKinsey's famous blue binder. The company is then left to implement McKinsey's solution, the consulting team is dissolved, and its members are reassigned to other teams and other clients.

To allow its teams to operate in the most effective way, McKinsey designed an organic structure that allows its consultants the freedom to work on projects for which they can best use their skills. However, McKinsey has also developed values based on excellence in serving clients and norms about the importance of teamwork and cooperation, both of which allow its teams of consultants to work effectively together. At the same time, there is intense competition in the firm. Only one out of every ten junior associates is promoted to partner, so each associate must demonstrate his or her personal excellence.[12] Individual competence, creativity, and the ability to be a team player are key values in McKinsey's culture. These cultural values reinforce McKinsey's organic structure and provide the setting that allows the company to operate its technology so effectively and dominate the consulting environment.

TECHNOLOGY AND ORGANIZATIONAL CULTURE

Perrow's, Woodward's, and Thompson's models of technology point to the same kinds of design solution: The more routine a technology is (Perrow), the more a manufacturing process depends on machinery (Woodward) and on a sequential, programmed arrangement of tasks (Thompson), the more mechanistic is the structure the organization should adopt. The more nonroutine a technology is (Perrow), the more a manufacturing process depends on the skills and knowledge of people (Woodward) and on a reciprocal arrangement of tasks (Thompson), the more likely is the organization to use an organic structure.

TO MANAGERS

Technology

- Use Woodward's, Thompson's, and Perrow's frameworks to identify the main contingencies associated with operating the technologies in your organization.
- Decide whether your organization's current structure and culture are matched to the needs of your technology.
- Implement any changes in organizational design, such as decentralizing authority or raising the level of integration by empowering workers, that may allow you to operate your technology more effectively.

What implications does technology have for the type of cultural values and norms that an organization is likely to encourage and develop? Are different kinds of technologies associated with different kinds of organizational cultures? In general, as an organization's technology becomes more nonroutine and the development of new goods and services depends more on creative decision making than on programmed solutions, an organization becomes more likely to adopt terminal values of innovation and quality and instrumental values of being creative and taking risks. The development of these values is encouraged and facilitated by designing an organic structure that gives people the freedom and autonomy to experiment with finding new ways to solve problems and to work together to make creative decisions. The culture of McKinsey & Co. illustrates this well.

As technology becomes more routine, programmed, and dependent on machines and computers, an organization becomes more likely to adopt terminal values of stability and predictability and instrumental values of economy and being conservative, cautious, and obedient. Recall from Chapter 15 that UPS, which operates with a very programmed, routine technology, developed just such a set of values (see Insight 15.4). As at UPS, these values are facilitated by the use of a mechanistic structure, which gives managers control over people and tasks and standardizes how people should behave to achieve organizational goals.

Thus, different cultures emerge in different functions and organizations because of differences in technology. These cultural values and norms, if managed effectively, help organizations operate their technologies by facilitating cooperation both inside and between functions.

The Organization's Strategy

An organization pursues a strategy—a plan of action—to develop the skills, knowledge, and capabilities that will allow it to compete successfully in its environment for resources and gain a competitive advantage, outperforming its competitors. The primary resources that any organization needs to survive and thrive are customers and the revenues they provide. To attract customers, organizations can pursue one or more of the following strategies[13] (see Fig. 16.6):

- **Cost-leadership strategy:** Organizations strive to lower their costs and then attract customers with lower prices (made possible by lower costs).
- **Differentiation strategy:** Organizations attract customers by offering them unique or distinctive goods and service.[14]

Cost-leadership strategy
A strategy that aims to attract customers with low prices that are made possible by low costs.

Differentiation strategy
A strategy that aims to attract customers with unique or distinctive goods and services.

FIGURE 16.6

Types of Organizational
Strategies

**Focused cost-leadership
strategy**

A strategy that aims to attract one kind
of customer or group of customers with
a low-cost product.

**Focused differentiation
strategy**

A strategy that aims to attract one kind
of customer or group of customers with
a differentiated product.

- **Focused cost-leadership strategy:** Organizations focus on one kind of customer or group of customers and produce a low-cost product for that group.[15]
- **Focused differentiation strategy:** Organizations focus on one kind of customer or group of customers and produce a differentiated product for that group.[16]

Founder Sam Walton decided that Wal-Mart, for example, would pursue a cost-leadership strategy. To serve the needs of large numbers of rural consumers who were being ignored by urban retailers like Sears and Kmart, Walton located his first stores in rural areas where land was cheap. He pioneered the development of low-cost materials management technology that allowed Wal-Mart to purchase, distribute, and sell products at a cost lower than its competitors'. This low-cost competence allowed Wal-Mart to sell items at low prices. Wal-Mart attracted enough customers away from stores like Sears and Kmart to become the largest and most profitable retail store in the world. Through the development of a cost-leadership strategy, Wal-Mart triumphed.

In contrast to Wal-Mart, stores like Neiman Marcus, Nordstrom, and Saks Fifth Avenue serve an affluent clientele that is interested in high-quality, personalized service and unique goods. To attract and hold this type of customer, these stores pursue a differentiation strategy by offering designer clothes, high-priced and unique gadgets, and highly personalized service.

Finally, local clothing stores or copy shops that select a group of customers, like students, and focus on attracting them with a low-cost product are pursuing a focused cost-leadership strategy. An exclusive clothes designer like Calvin Klein or Christian Dior that focuses on producing clothing for customers who are very rich is pursuing a focused differentiation strategy. Amazon.com is also pursuing a focused differentiation strategy by concentrating on the groups of customers who want to buy books over the Internet.

How can organizational design help an organization pursue cost-leadership and differentiation strategies (either the focused or the general kind)? Organizational design can help an organization achieve increases in efficiency, quality, innovation and creativity, and responsiveness to customers—improvements in four areas crucial to gaining a competitive advantage (as we outlined in Chapter 1). Increasing efficiency is most closely associated with a cost-leadership strategy. Increases in quality, innovation, and customer re-

Many companies pursuing a cost-leadership strategy have opened discount stores such as the WalMart store shown here. WalMart stores buy in bulk and offer little service in order to provide customers with products at rock bottom prices.

sponsiveness are most closely associated with a differentiation strategy. An organization that attempts to simultaneously pursue a low-cost *and* a differentiation strategy has to attempt the difficult task of increasing its performance in all four areas.[17] In the remainder of this chapter we examine how organizational design can help an organization pursue its chosen strategy.

HOW ORGANIZATIONAL DESIGN CAN INCREASE EFFICIENCY

Good organizational design can increase efficiency by helping to lower the costs of operating the organization. Managers and workers cost money, not just in salary but also in benefits, offices, computers, and so on. A middle manager can cost an organization over $300,000 a year, top managers can cost millions, and the costs associated with maintaining whole functions such as sales or research and development can run into tens or even hundreds of millions of dollars a year. By making careful choices, organizations can use organizational design to reduce operating costs, just as Amazon.com did.

Designing Structure. As we saw in Chapter 15, the number of levels in an organizational hierarchy typically increases as organizations grow and become more complex. Because every level in a hierarchy adds considerably to operating costs, an organization can increase efficiency by keeping its structure as flat as possible. If an organization becomes too tall, it needs to take steps to flatten its hierarchy. In 1985, for example, General Motors' hierarchy had over nineteen levels. Since then, GM has shrunk its hierarchy to thirteen levels, a number that is still too high according to industry analysts who point out that there are only seven levels in Toyota's hierarchy.

Another way to keep a hierarchy relatively flat is to decentralize authority by giving lower-level employees more responsibility and allowing them to make important decisions. This strategy of empowerment (see Chapter 14), which gives employees more control over their activities, is being used increasingly by organizations that want to keep their hierarchies as flat as possible. Empowerment reduces the need for extra managers but also raises a job's motivating potential score by increasing characteristics such as task identity, autonomy, and feedback. Insight 16.3 shows how John Deere, a maker of agricultural equipment, took advantage of empowering employees to reinvent its organizational structure.

Insight 16.3 Competitive Advantage

John Deere Empowers Its Employees

In the early 1990s John Deere (www.deere.com) was losing millions of dollars; by 1994 its profit exceeded $400 million and has been increasing since. How has Deere's startling turnaround been achieved? According to CEO Hans W. Becherer, Deere has taken advantage of the skills and capabilities of its workers to increase efficiency and raise quality. Many of Deere's problems stemmed from a competitive environment. Caterpillar and Komatsu were ruthlessly cutting prices to battle with Deere for a share of the dwindling agricultural machinery market. To survive, Deere was forced to downsize. After laying off managers and employees, Deere realized it had to find a way to make better use of the skills of the employees who remained.

Deere undertook to teach its manufacturing workers new skills. It installed sophisticated, computerized production-line technology and trained workers to operate it. Deere also sought to improve its manufacturing by grouping workers into teams whose goal included finding new ways to reduce costs and increase quality.

Deere was not content merely with improving workers' skills in manufacturing; it also began to teach them new skills that would help them to find ways to increase efficiency and improve performance. For example, Deere realized that manufacturing workers, with their detailed knowledge about how Deere products work, could become persuasive salespeople. So groups of production workers were given training in sales techniques and sent to visit Deere customers to explain to them how to operate and service the organization's new products. While speaking with customers, these new "salespeople" were able to collect information to help Deere further reduce costs and develop new products that will appeal to customers. The new sales jobs are temporary. Workers go on assignment but then return to the production line, where they use their new knowledge to find ways to improve efficiency and quality.

These moves to empower employees have been so successful that Deere recently negotiated a new agreement with its workers (who are members of the United Auto Workers union). The agreement specifies that pay increases will be based on workers' learning new skills and completing college courses in areas such as computer programming that will help the company increase efficiency and quality. No longer will seniority be the main determinant of pay, as it is in some unionized workplaces.[18]

> Deere's new policy of empowering its workforce has benefits for workers and for the organization as a whole. Workers recognize the connection between these changes and their job security. The increases in efficiency and quality enable Deere to regain control of its share of the agricultural machinery market. Moreover, the satisfaction that workers feel when they have the opportunity to utilize new skills and develop new capabilities increases their commitment to the company and to helping it succeed.

Functions are also extremely expensive to maintain, and it is important for an organization to constantly evaluate the appropriateness of the form of differentiation it has chosen. Is it suited to the type of goods and services the organization produces, to its current environment, and to its technology? A company using functional differentiation might need to move to a geographic structure to sell goods to customers more efficiently. Or a company that is using a market structure might need to switch to a product structure to reduce operating costs.

The more complex an organization is, the higher is the level of integration it needs to coordinate and control interfunctional activities. Integration, however, is expensive, so using proper design for achieving it is essential to an organization's efficiency. The most expensive integrating mechanisms are mutual adjustment and a hierarchy of authority to integrate activities within and between functions. The least expensive mechanism of integration is standardization, because once rules and SOPs are developed they provide a stable organizing framework to control and direct behavior. Organizations seeking to increase their efficiency must constantly evaluate the types of integrating mechanisms they are using and must evaluate whether the benefits of using them exceed the costs. If rules and SOPs can be used in place of direct supervision, for example, organizations should do so to reduce their costs.

Wal-Mart, McDonald's, and other organizations that seek to outperform competitors by increasing efficiency and charging customers low prices are always evaluating the design of their organizational structure and taking steps to change it to reduce costs. Unfortunately, many organizations do not continually perform this evaluation and thus fail to recognize how costly their structure is to operate. Poorly managed companies develop bloated hierarchies and employ thousands more employees than they need. When a new, more efficient competitor comes along and profits drop, shareholders and top managers quickly realize how inefficient the organization has become. Management then moves swiftly to prune the organizational hierarchy, laying off thousands of people and causing hardship and distress to the employees who remain. Careful attention to organizational design could have warded off many problems, but managers failed to see the problems in time. In Chapter 19, we examine in detail the reasons that many organizations are slow to change their structure and their culture.

Managing Culture.   An organization's culture has an important impact on the organization's efficiency. In Chapter 15, we discussed how organizations can try to encourage the development of instrumental values that encourage employees to be frugal and economical with organizational resources. When Stanley Gault took over at Goodyear Rubber and Tire, for example, he was concerned about the previous management's free-spending ways and sent signals to his managers about his new, more frugal values by such actions as selling off the company's fleet of corporate jets and removing light bulbs in his office to save electricity. In contrast, even while IBM was losing billions of dollars and laying off thousands of people, management still maintained a fleet of corporate jets, organized conferences at expensive luxury resorts, and paid little attention to reducing costs.

Organizations that pursue a cost-leadership strategy pay considerable attention to creating terminal and instrumental values that lead to a cost-cutting culture. These organizations develop rules and procedures that lay out their philosophy on ways to reduce costs (for example, by always turning out the lights when they are not in use). They encourage instrumental values of hard work and being frugal, and they socialize new employees into these values and norms so that they become a taken-for-granted part of the organization. Wal-Mart's managers, for example, routinely meet on Saturday mornings to review the week's business and find new ways to reduce costs. The high level of performance that low-cost organizations expect of their members is one of their defining characteristics, and we saw in Insight 16.3 how John Deere is trying to develop new values of efficiency and economy by empowering its workforce.

HOW ORGANIZATIONAL DESIGN CAN INCREASE QUALITY

Quality is a measure of the degree to which goods and services are reliable and perform as intended over long periods of time. High quality is one characteristic that clearly differentiates one organization's goods and services from another's. The quality of a Japanese car or a custom-made suit is measured by its ability to stand up to wear and tear and provide customers with consistent service. Just as organizational design can help to increase efficiency, it can also help to improve quality and thus allow an organization to pursue a differentiation strategy. Total quality management (TQM), the collective term for the many ways in which organizations attempt to manage their activities to increase the level of quality of their goods and services, is discussed at length in Chapter 19.[19] In general, TQM involves creating an organizational structure and culture that encourage a concern for quality.

Designing Structure.   As we saw in the John Deere example, workers who perform specific functional tasks, such as manufacturing, sales, or research and development, possess detailed knowledge about the best way to perform these tasks. An organization can take advantage of this knowledge to increase quality if employees are given the freedom and autonomy to experiment and find better ways to produce, sell, or design goods and services. To help provide this freedom, an organization can keep its hierarchy as flat as possible and decentralize control to lower-level employees. This design choice gives employees more input into the decision-making process and allows an organization to take greater advantage of the skills and experience of its members.

This method of increasing quality can be taken even further if employees from different functions are grouped together into cross-functional teams to pool their knowledge and share ideas. Materials management, for example, might know of a company that makes a new, higher-quality starter motor, but it also knows that changing to the new motor would require a redesign of the engine, which would in turn entail a change in the manufacturing process. In a cross-functional structure, members from different functions can meet to discuss whether changing to the new starter motor would be worthwhile and how the changeover could be accomplished efficiently and painlessly. Organizations can improve the quality and reliability of their products by designing task and role relationships that allow people to cooperate and put their skills and knowledge to the best use for achieving organizational goals.

Standardization is another very important mechanism for increasing quality (see Chapter 15). Although standardization indicates that an organization has found the current best way to perform a task, the organization must continually experiment with ways of improving its rules and SOPs to increase quality. The way in which a Texaco refining and marketing plant in Kansas went about implementing a total quality management program illustrates many of the issues in designing a structure to promote quality (see Insight 16.4).

Insight 16.4   **Strategy**

Texaco's TQM Program

In 1985 managers at Texaco's (www.texaco.com) refinery and marketing plant in El Dorado, Kansas, were in a quandary. The plant was experiencing record absenteeism, the gasoline it produced was of poor quality, and its safety record was dismal (a major deficiency in an organization operating a continuous-process technology). Richard Masica, the refinery's new plant manager, decided that something had to be done. Aware of the potential benefits of total quality management, Masica hired a consultant to help him and his management team implement a TQM program.

The consultant began by having Masica and his managers define their goals and vision for the plant in terms of the quality, safety, and efficiency targets they wanted the plant to reach. The next step was to begin a program to involve the plant's employees in the implementation of the TQM process and get their input into setting appropriate goals. This step required managers to share with workers cost and profit figures on the plant's performance. Many middle managers worried that sharing these figures with workers would lessen their authority: This information, they feared, would put workers in a position to question the way things were done.

Sharing information and allowing workers to have input into the decision-making process, however, are hallmarks of TQM. So workers and managers at Texaco met regularly to discuss progress toward goals and over time learned to trust one another. This learning process was aided by a change in the reward system—paying workers and managers performance bonuses based on improvements in the plant's performance (evident each time the plant met one of its established goals). In fact, the enthusiastic cooperation of the workforce with management caused a potential problem when the workers' union feared it would lose its authority over the workforce. Masica solved this problem by bringing the union into the decision-making process and involving it in setting performance goals.

The plant's TQM program has been successful. The plant's performance as measured by increases in quality, safety, and efficiency soared. Moreover, according to Masica, the culture of the plant is now totally different. Conflict between workers and management has given way to instrumental values of cooperation and involvement and to terminal values of quality and product excellence. The plant has become a showcase recognized throughout its industry as an example of how to implement a successful TQM program, and Texaco has implemented the program in its other refineries. Masica was also rewarded for his efforts. He is now a vice president of the whole Texaco chemical division.

Managing Culture.   Creating a culture that encourages a concern for quality is another way to use organizational design to promote quality. Texaco, Xerox, Ford, Campbell Soup, and other organizations have gone to great lengths to create organizational values that put a premium on increasing quality and to teach those values to employees through TQM programs. At Xerox, for example, the total quality management started from the top down. All of Xerox's top managers attended a TQM program to learn TQM values and techniques and how to implement them. Top managers then returned to their organizations and taught their subordinates these values and techniques. In turn, lower-level managers taught total quality values to their subordinates. Xerox employees have adopted terminal values of excellence through improved product quality and instrumental values that encourage them to experiment and to share information and knowledge to increase quality. Developing a culture for quality is central to TQM.

HOW ORGANIZATIONAL DESIGN CAN INCREASE INNOVATION AND CREATIVITY

Innovation is the development of new or improved goods and services or new processes that reduce the costs of production. For organizations pursuing a differentiation strategy, the technological edge resulting from superior skills in innovation is often a source of competitive advantage. Why are Mercedes-Benz cars so desired? The company is the leader in developing new and improved systems that increase the performance and safety of its vehicles. Why is Merck & Co., the pharmaceutical maker, one of the most respected companies in the United States? It has developed many of the most successful new drugs and has done so at a speed that is the envy of many other companies.

Designing Structure.   Companies that depend on creativity and innovation to maintain their competitive advantage face the task of designing an organizational structure and culture that foster those processes. As we discussed in Chapter 15, organizations that depend on innovation to keep themselves competitive fashion structures that allow for a high level of integration between different functions to speed communication and decision making.

Many high-tech companies, for example, have adopted a matrix structure to increase their ability to utilize and enhance their research and development skills. A matrix structure allows for the intensive cross-functional integration necessary to speed product development, and it is built on mechanisms, such as task forces, teams, and integrating roles, that facilitate mutual adjustment.

Although matrix structure is the structure most often used by companies that develop new products and processes, several disadvantages are associated with its use (see Chapter 15), not the least of which is its high cost. Because of those disadvantages, many companies that are concerned with making improvements to existing products (rather than inventing new ones) are increasingly adopting cross-functional team structures to speed product development and improve decision making. This structure also permits a high degree of cross-functional integration but is easier and costs less to operate than a matrix.

Both of these structures are flat and decentralize authority to technical specialists in the various functions who are able to make quick decisions. Flat, organic, cross-functional team structures provide an ideal setting for encouraging attitudes and behaviors that lead to high-quality research and development. In fact, organic structures in general not only speed innovation but also provide employees with greater freedom and autonomy, which, in turn, increase their motivation to perform and foster the creativity that is necessary for successful innovation.

Managing Culture. Creating values and norms that encourage creativity and innovation is also an important organizational design task. This process begins when an organization recognizes and rewards employee behaviors that demonstrate commitment to terminal and instrumental values that promote creativity and innovation. Hewlett-Packard, 3M, Microsoft, Apple Computer, and IBM are all companies that take special steps to promote instrumental values of risk taking and exploration. The founders of these companies played an important role in establishing terminal values of being creative and

As part of its strategy to develop new products to increase its revenues, Armstrong World Industries, a manufacturer of vinyl flooring, innovated these fast-selling decorated ceiling tiles, which are meant to distract children in doctors' offices and hospitals.

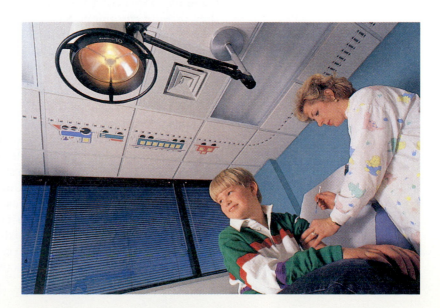

innovative. The founders of both Hewlett-Packard and 3M, for example, established informal norms that encourage employees to spend 16 percent of their time using organizational resources to work on projects of their own choosing. At both organizations, successful innovators are heralded as organizational champions and are given special status and prerogatives, including huge research budgets and freedom to experiment on projects of their own choosing. New recruits are socialized into these values. An entrepreneurial atmosphere pervades these companies, and research and development takes center stage in both organizations. The development of an organic structure fosters values of innovation, and, with culture and structure reinforcing one another, a company like 3M or Hewlett-Packard can retain a leading position in its industry over the long term.

Pursuing a differentiation strategy based on innovation is one of the most difficult things to do. Only a handful of companies have done so successfully over the long term. Microsoft founder Bill Gates, for example, went to great lengths to establish a culture for innovation and used small teams to foster creative decision making and promote the introduction of new software products. In 1994, however, worried that Microsoft's growing size and complexity would reduce innovation and creativity, Gates totally reorganized the company. He chose a product structure to allow each division to focus its energies on one task and thus avoid the bureaucratic problems that seem to go with large size. Gates recognizes that if Microsoft loses its competitive advantage as the leading innovator of software products, his company will lose everything.

HOW ORGANIZATIONAL DESIGN CAN INCREASE RESPONSIVENESS TO CUSTOMERS

An organization that attempts to pursue a differentiation strategy based on responsiveness to customers attempts to build a competitive advantage by staying attuned to changing customer needs and by developing techniques to keep employees focused on providing customers with the best possible service. IBM, Nordstrom, Xerox, Four Seasons Hotels, Eastman Kodak, and Dell Computer are among the organizations renowned for the level of service they provide customers. Salespeople at Nordstrom, for example, develop long-term relationships with their customers, keep them informed about the arrival of new clothes that might appeal to their personal tastes, and offer attentive, personalized service every time they walk into the store. This high level of service breeds loyal, repeat customers and has made Nordstrom a very profitable operation.

Designing Structure.   Geographic and market structures stand out as choices for organizations that seek a high level of responsiveness to customers. A geographic structure allows an organization to respond to the needs of regional customers and to stock goods that cater to their needs. Regional managers can become attuned to customers' needs, and because they are close to regional employees, it is easy for them to oversee the level of service that employees give to customers. A market structure, which groups people and functions according to needs of different kinds of customers, clearly has a high level of responsiveness to customers as its major goal. In a market structure, the activities of different functions are combined to provide personalized service for a particular group of customers. The likely outcome is intense customer loyalty.

Managing Culture.   Creating a culture for service is also a major priority for organizations pursuing a differentiation strategy based on responsiveness to customers. Instrumental values of caring for customers, attentive service, and speedy after-sales support must be developed to create a culture for service. A culture for service can also be encouraged by developing evaluation and reward practices linked to attitudes and behaviors that demonstrate instrumental values of being helpful and responsive to customers. The Mary Kay Cosmetics Company, for example, holds yearly awards shows at which successful salespeople are singled out as organizational heroes and are rewarded with pink Cadillacs. Mary Kay Cosmetics goes to great lengths to demonstrate its support of terminal values of high-quality customer service.

Many companies are increasingly using rewards such as gifts and free travel for employees who show their commitment to providing good customer service. Managers whose goal is a culture for service must build values and norms that support customer-oriented attitudes and behaviors and then must reinforce them with rewards linked to desired performance. Denny's has recently attempted to increase its responsiveness to the needs of its minority customers (see Insight 16.5).

Insight 16.5   **Diversity**

Denny's Changes Its Ways

The Denny's restaurant chain, convicted of discriminating against its African American customers in 1994, agreed as part of its settlement with the National Association for the Advancement of Colored People (NAACP) to give African Americans a larger role in the company's management and to increase minority ownership of its franchises. One franchisee, Donald J. Bohana, an African American entrepreneur in the predominantly black Watts-Willowbrook area of Los Angeles, decided, without telling Denny's, to customize the menu of his restaurants to become more responsive to the preferences of African American customers.[20] Besides the standard Denny's meatballs, roast beef, and french fries, Bohana's menus now include "soul food" such as chitterlings, oxtails, hot wings, black-eyed peas, collard greens, and candied yams.

After learning about Bohana's moves to customize the menu to suit local tastes, Denny's decided that such customization might not be a bad strategy for the whole Denny's chain. So in 1994, in an effort to increase flagging sales—due in part to negative publicity generated by the organization's discriminatory activities—Denny's decided to allow all of its restaurant franchisees to customize their menus to suit the tastes of different ethnic groups and customers in different regions of the country. Bohana, for one, is now selling more soul food than standard Denny's fare. Because Denny's gets a 4 percent royalty on whatever food is sold in its restaurants, the company is happy that its franchisees are offering popular ethnic and regional dishes. Denny's is also allowing franchisees to play music that suits the tastes of their customers and to develop restaurant policies that meet customers' needs. The Denny's organization is learning how to be responsive to the needs of its diverse customers, and the hope is that this effort will help change the culture and values of the company.

SUMMARY

Similar to managing the environment and managing technology, managing an organization's strategy requires close and continuous attention to the work setting in which behavior takes place. Workers' attitudes and behavior are shaped by the work setting, which is created by the design of organizational structure and culture. Different strategies require the use of different forms of differentiation and integration, the development of different kinds of rules and SOPs, and the evolution of different systems of norms and values. Managing the relationship between strategy and structure is one of the most difficult and crucial tasks of managers in an organization.

Advice TO MANAGERS

Strategy

- Evaluate the way you are currently pursuing your strategy, and decide how you might improve efficiency, quality, innovation, or customer responsiveness to increase performance.
- Consider implementing a TQM program to discover ways to increase performance.
- Evaluate how your organization's structure and culture are helping or hurting organizational performance, and implement any organizational design changes that will help to increase your competitive advantage.

SUMMARY

Organizational design creates the context in which behavior in organizations takes place. It is a crucial managerial activity that sets the scene for managing individuals and groups in organizations. Organizations design their structures and cultures to allow them to manage pressures from an uncertain and changing environment, their technologies, and the type of strategy they are using. In this chapter, we made the following major points:

1. Organizational design is the process by which managers select and manage various dimensions and components of organizational structure and culture so that an organization can achieve its goals.
2. The organizational environment is the set of resources surrounding an organization. The level of uncertainty associated with obtaining resources from its environment is the first major contingency confronting an organization.

3. In a highly uncertain environment, an organization should have high levels of differentiation and integration and a structure tending toward the organic. When levels of uncertainty are low, an organization should have low levels of differentiation and integration and a structure tending toward the mechanistic.

4. Technology is the combination of skills, knowledge, abilities, techniques, materials, machines, computers, tools, and equipment that workers use to convert inputs into outputs. The uncertainty surrounding the operation of a technology is the second contingency that an organization faces.

5. The more a technology depends on machines (Woodward's model), the more sequential and programmed the tasks (Thompson's model), and the more routine the technology (Perrow's model), the more an organization should use a mechanistic structure because the uncertainty surrounding the operation of the technology is low.

6. Organizations can pursue two main kinds of strategy to obtain resources such as customer revenue: a cost-leadership strategy or a differentiation strategy. To pursue either or both of these strategies, they need to develop superior skills in increasing efficiency, quality, innovation and creativity, or responsiveness to customers. The design of an organization's structure and culture is an important factor in determining whether the organization is successful in pursuing its chosen strategy.

Organizational Behavior in Action

TOPICS FOR ACTION AND DISCUSSION

1. Why do the different forces in the environment cause uncertainty for organizations?
2. According to Lawrence and Lorsch, why do levels of differentiation and integration increase as uncertainty increases?
3. What specific contingencies make it necessary for an organization to use a mechanistic structure and an organic structure?
4. Pick an organization with which you are familiar, and describe its environment and technology in terms of Woodward's, Thompson's, and Perrow's models. Next, describe the organization's structure. Is there a fit between its structure and its environment and technology?
5. Which one of Thompson's technological types and Perrow's technological types do you think is the most difficult to manage? Why?
6. Pick five clothing stores in your local mall, and discuss the similarities and differences in their strategies.
7. How can good organizational design lower costs and help differentiate an organization's products?
8. Describe the environment, technology, and strategy that you would expect to affect a typical biotechnology company. What kinds of cultural values and norms that shape its employees' behavior would you expect to find?

BUILDING DIAGNOSTIC SKILLS

Designing Organizations

Think of an organization that you are familiar with—a fast-food restaurant, church, department store, or an organization that you have worked for. (The organization that you selected for this assignment in Chapter 15 may be an appropriate choice.) Then answer these questions:

1. What are the most important environmental forces that this organization has to manage? How uncertain is the environment surrounding the organization?
2. In what ways are the structure and culture of the organization a response to its environment?
3. Using all three models of technology (Woodward's, Thompson's, and Perrow's), describe the technology used by the organization. In what ways are its structure and culture a response to its technology?
4. What strategy does the organization pursue? In what ways do its structure and culture allow it to pursue its strategy effectively?
5. On the basis of this analysis, would you say that the organization's structure and culture fit the contingencies the organization faces? Why or why not?

RESEARCH ON THE INTERNET: A MANAGER'S TOOL

Specific Task

An organization's strategy should match its structure. Enter Marriott Corporation's website (www.marriott.com), and click on "Marriott at a Glance," which lists the Marriott's major businesses and activities.

1. Given the nature of Marriott's businesses, what kind of strategy or strategies do you think Marriott is pursuing?
2. Given the nature of these strategies, what kind of structure do you think that Marriott should use to control its activities?

General Task

Search for the website of a company that describes in detail one or more of the factors (e.g. strategy or technology) that influence its choice of organizational structure or culture. How does this factor or factors influence the way it operates?

TOPICS FOR DEBATE

Different contingencies—the environment, technology, and strategy—cause organizations to design their structures and cultures in different ways. Now that you understand the contingencies facing an organization, debate the following issues.

Debate One

Team A. An organization can never be too organic because the environment constantly changes and an organization has to be able to respond to change quickly.

Team B. A structure that is too organic can be a problem because ill-defined task and authority relationships can slow decision making and responses to change.

Debate Two

Team A. Efficiency and quality are the most important sources of competitive advantage.

Team B. Innovation and responsiveness to customers are the keys to competitive success.

EXPERIENTIAL EXERCISE

Analyzing Organizations II
Objectives

Your objective is to identify the contingencies that have influenced the development of an organization's structure and culture over time—specifically, to analyze the organization's environment, technology, and strategy.

Procedures

Incorporate the following questions into your interview schedule:

1. Which forces in the environment are most difficult to manage? Why? In what ways does the need to manage these forces influence (a) the organization's structure and (b) the organization's culture?
2. On the basis of the answers to the preceding question and the information gathered during the first part of this exercise (in Chapter 15), indicate whether the organization has a mechanistic or an organic structure.

3. How does the organization produce its goods and services? (Hint: To identify the kind of technology the organization uses, (a) describe Woodward's three types of technology, and ask which is most characteristic of the way the organization produces its goods and services, and (b) describe pooled, sequential, and reciprocal task interdependence to see whether the organization's technology is principally mediating, long-linked, or intensive.)

4. How does the way the organization produces goods and services influence the organization's structure and culture?

5. What kinds of skills, knowledge, or capabilities does the organization possess that give it a competitive advantage (for example, superior efficiency, quality, responsiveness to customers, or innovation)? (If the organization is a not-for-profit enterprise, ask in what ways does the organization try to excel at what it does.) Use this information to identify the organization's strategy.

6. How does the organization's strategy affect its structure and culture?

MAKING THE CONNECTION

Find an example of a company that has been experiencing a change in its environment, technology, or strategy, and discuss how it used its structure and culture to respond to the change.

CLOSING CASE

Harley-Davidson Goes Hog Wild

In the early 1980s Harley-Davidson, the famous maker of large motorcycles, was in a crisis because of intense competition from Japanese manufacturers like Honda and Kawasaki, which were sending increasing numbers of large bikes into the U.S. market. Before the entry of the Japanese, Harley had 100 percent of the large-bike market in the United States. By 1985 its share of the motorcycle market had dropped to 23 percent because the Japanese, as a result of using modern manufacturing methods, were able to offer customers high-quality, reliable bikes at prices that Harley could not match.

Because its management team was not used to facing competition, Harley was slow to respond to the Japanese challenge. Harley's organizational structure featured a tall, centralized hierarchy of authority, and managers communicated mainly along formal lines of authority. As a result, decision making at Harley-Davidson was slow and ponderous. In addition, the way Harley manufactured its bikes had changed little for years even though product quality was a problem. Harley employed many quality control inspectors to fix faults after the bikes were assembled but did nothing to address the problems at earlier stages in the assembly process that were responsible for the defects. Even after quality control had "fixed" the bikes, Harley dealers had to cover the floors of their showrooms with cardboard to soak up the oil that leaked from the brand-new Harleys.

Manufacturing problems were not the only problems that haunted Harley. The design of the bikes had changed little for years, although in the past the company had been an industry innovator. Harley had 185,000 loyal supporters in the Harley Owners Group (HOG), but the company had lost sight of its customers and what they wanted in a large bike. Harley-Davidson was verging on bankruptcy when it appealed to the U.S. government for protection from Japanese manufacturers, accusing them of selling bikes in the United States for less money than it cost to produce them in Japan. In 1982 the U.S. government imposed an import tariff on Japanese bikes, which raised their price and gave Harley a chance to regain its strength.[21] Given this chance, Harley had to face a big challenge: how to reorganize and manage its resources so that it could reduce costs, increase innovation, and compete effectively with the Japanese manufacturers.

To face its competitors head on, Harley's management decided to change its organizational structure and forge a culture whose terminal and instrumental values were focused on quality. Harley designed a flatter, more flexible, and more integrated structure organized around cross-functional teams whose members were jointly responsible for manufacturing and quality control decisions. The company demolished its old functional structure, which had separated functions such as marketing and manufacturing, and created three organization-wide teams that spanned all functions to promote Harley's new quality values. Harley called these teams the create-demand team, the production team, and the product-support team. Teams were charged with implementing a total quality management program in which all functions would cooperate to continuously improve the performance of their activities. Their goals were to boost quality, efficiency, innovation, and responsiveness to customers.

In the old structure, Harley middle managers had been forced to go back and forth from the manager of one function to the manager of another to get approval for changes. This process slowed communication and decision making and created a conservative, timid culture. In the new structure, teams respond flexibly to one another's needs, and managers can better cooperate and make quicker decisions. CEO Richard F. Teerlink, who has led Harley's turnaround, attributes much of the upturn in the company's fortunes to two things: (1) the way the new structure and culture allows Harley to respond to and control the various forces in its environment and (2) the total quality management program, which has allowed Harley to operate its manufacturing process more effectively. In Teerlink's words, Harley's new quality values have resulted in "more responsive product development, manufacturing excellence, and marketing innovation."[22] Harley's market share has grown from 25 to 64 percent and is limited only by the organization's ability to manufacture bikes fast enough to meet customer demand.

Discussion Questions

1. In what ways did Harley's structure change after the import tariff was imposed?
2. Why did the new structure and culture help Harley to regain control over its environment?

Managing Global Organizations

17

OPENING CASE

Daimler-Benz Learns Lessons from Abroad

Daimler-Benz (www.daimler-benz.com), maker of the famous German Mercedes-Benz cars, has been undergoing a rapid transformation in the nineties under its hard-driving CEO Juergen Schrempp. By 1995 Daimler-Benz's global car sales were falling, its costs were rising, and the company was in trouble. Schrempp's job was to turn the company around. To find out how to do this, he looked abroad, to the lessons to be learned from other global carmakers.

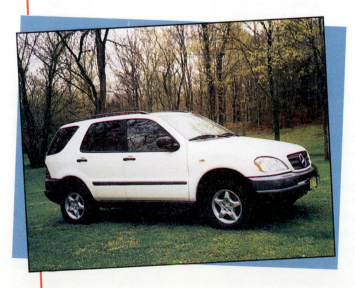

First, Schrempp looked to Japanese carmakers, like Toyota and Honda, to learn the techniques of lean production, which result in more efficient and higher-quality car production, and computer aided design, which allow car designers to bring new cars models to the market faster. Schrempp drove Mercedes designers and engineers to adopt these innovations, and within a few years the results were seen as new models started rolling off the production line.

Schrempp also learned the lesson from the Japanese that it is important to make cars where costs are low. For the first time in history, Daimler-Benz began making a new model, its first sports utility vehicle, in another country—the United States. The first sports utility vehicles produced in Alabama in 1997 were sold out for a year, in part due to their low relative cost and exceptional quality and design. Although the German managers and engineers transplanted to Alabama to oversee Mercedes operations were frequently heard to complain about homesickness and the culture shock that comes from living in a foreign country, Daimler-Benz learned many new lessons.[1] In fact, to reduce costs and respond to foreign markets, Daimler-Benz is planning new car plants in other countries. A plant that opened in France in 1997 will produce a revolutionary, inexpensive, two-seat model for less than $9,000 for city dwellers.

Schrempp also looked to the United States for lessons that Daimler-Benz could use. Following the lead of U.S. car manufacturers, who had experienced problems similar to Daimler-Benz's in the 1980s, Schrempp tried to transform his organization's stodgy structure and culture. He laid off 40,000 employees, eliminated a layer of top managers, and tried to increase the pace of innovation by paying managers stock options and awarding workers bonuses based on their contribution to overall profits, something that Chrysler had pioneered. However, in keeping with Germany's cultural values, which have always recognized the need to protect the rights of employees (there are nine worker-directors on Daimler-Benz's board of directors), he guaranteed workers that there would be no more layoffs until 2000 to gain their commitment to his new global approach.

These lessons from the global environment have paid off for Schrempp and for Daimler-Benz. Worldwide sales of Mercedes vehicles have increased by almost 20 percent and are continuing to grow, profits are soaring, and its employees are enjoying the job security and higher income that comes when a company operates successfully at the global level.

Overview

As the experiences of Daimler-Benz suggest, organizations that look abroad and examine the ways that other global companies operate can learn many valuable lessons. This chapter examines why a company expands globally and how differences between countries pose challenges to managing organizations effectively. We examine the way an organization manages the global environment and the kinds of global strategies, structures, and cultures that organizations adopt to allow them to use people and resources effectively. We examine how operating in a global environment gives rise to new challenges in managing human resources because of the need to manage and integrate the activities of people from different countries. By the end of this chapter you will understand why for all organizations, large and small, understanding and managing the global environment is a major challenge. In fact, along with the domestic environment, technology, and strategy, the global environment is the fourth main contingency influencing the design of an organization's structure and the kind of values and norms that evolve in an organization over time.

Developing Global Understanding

Global organization
An organization that produces or sells goods or services in more than one country.

A **global organization** is an organization that produces or sells goods or services in more than one country. Many U.S. organizations have long been global organizations. Since colonial days, merchants have shipped tobacco, sugar, coal, metals, and other products to Europe. After World War I, large consumer products companies like H. J. Heinz Company, Ford, General Motors, Procter & Gamble, and Kellogg Company began establishing foreign divisions all over the world to manufacture and sell their products. Today, so common is the presence of U.S. organizations in the rest of the world that people in other countries often consider the foreign divisions of U.S. companies like Ford and Procter & Gamble to be domestic or home companies—the links of those organizations to U.S. parent companies are forgotten or ignored. Similarly, few American consumers realize that companies like Burger King, Howard Johnson, Shell Oil, and Philips are now foreign-owned companies. Many American consumers *are* aware that companies such as Toyota, Sony, and Honda are Japanese companies, but few know that Sony owns Columbia Records and CBS Records and is a major player in the U.S. entertainment industry.

Global companies such as Daimler-Benz, Sony, Ford, Nestlé, and Philips treat the world as one large market. Products such as the Sony Walkman, Seiko watches, Ford's new global car, the Contour, Waterford crystal, Wedgwood china, Perrier water, and Philips light bulbs are global products that appeal to customers worldwide.[2]

WHY ORGANIZATIONS ENTER THE GLOBAL ENVIRONMENT

Organizations expand into the global environment (see Fig. 17.1) to gain access to valuable resources that are found throughout the world. Many U.S. organizations, as well as organizations based in other countries, obtain inputs abroad because foreign inputs may cost less or be of higher quality than those same inputs bought at home. In Malaysia, Thailand, the Dominican Republic, and Mexico, for example, labor costs can be less than 10 percent of labor costs in the United States. The North American Free Trade Agreement (NAFTA) signed in 1993 paved the way for cooperation among Canada, the United States, and Mexico by eliminating many trade barriers. Many companies in these three countries have taken advantage of NAFTA to find new markets for their products and new sources of cheap labor and other inputs.

Organizations also obtain inputs abroad because foreign suppliers possess certain skills that allow them to make high-quality inputs.[3] Ford and General Motors buy the design skills of Italian companies like Ferrari and Lamborghini, electronic components from Japanese companies like NEC and Matsushita (well known for their quality), and machine tools and manufacturing equipment from German companies like Daimler-Benz and BASF (well known for their excellent engineering skills).

On the output side, a major motivation of companies to expand their operations globally is to attract more customers (a crucial resource) for their goods and services. For example, the potential size of the U.S. market for hamburgers

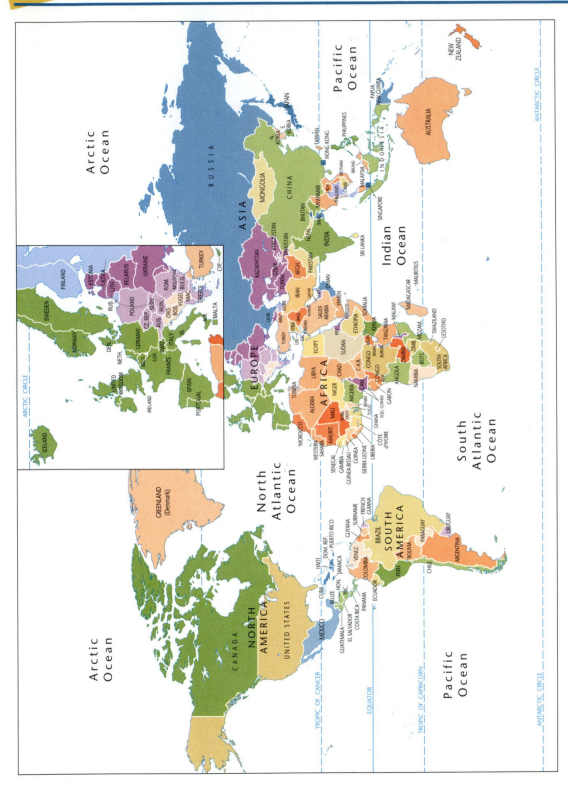

FIGURE 17.1
The Global Environment
Copyright 1994.

is 265 million people, but there are 3 billion potential burger-eaters in Asia alone. Thus, it is not surprising that McDonald's has expanded globally, opening restaurants throughout Asia and the rest of the world to take advantage of the huge global appetite for hamburgers, french fries, and milk shakes.[4]

When an organization expands globally and begins to buy its inputs abroad, sell its products abroad, or set up operations in foreign countries, it faces the task of learning to understand how countries, or national cultures, differ from one another. A **national culture** is the particular set of economic, political, and social values that exist in a particular nation. U.S. national culture, for example, is based on capitalistic economic values, democratic political values, and individualistic, competitive social values—all of which characterize the way people in the United States live and work.

National culture
The particular set of economic, political, and social values that exist in a particular nation.

HOFSTEDE'S MODEL OF NATIONAL CULTURE

Culture, whether organizational or national, is a product of the values and norms that people use to guide and control their behavior. Recall from Chapters 3 and 15 that values determine what people think are the good, right, or appropriate goals that they should pursue. Values also specify the norms that prescribe the appropriate behaviors for reaching these desired goals.[5] On a national level, a country's values and norms determine what kinds of attitudes and behaviors are acceptable or appropriate. Members of a particular national culture are socialized into these values as they grow up, and norms and social guidelines prescribe the way people in a given culture should behave toward one another and, often, toward people of different cultures.

Researchers have spent considerable time and effort identifying similarities and differences between the cultural values and norms of different countries. A model of national culture developed by Geert Hofstede argues that differences in the values and norms of different countries are captured by five dimensions of culture.[6] As part of his job as a psychologist for IBM, Hofstede collected data on employee values and perceptions of the work situation from more than 100,000 IBM employees in sixty-four countries. Based on his research, Hofstede identified five dimensions along which national cultures can be placed.

Häagen-Dazs, a U.S. company, invented its Dutch-sounding name to make American consumers believe they were buying a premium foreign ice cream. It now sells its ice cream in Asia and elsewhere around the world to take advantage of global consumers' taste for its product.

Individualism Versus Collectivism.   The dimension that Hofstede called *individualism versus collectivism* focuses on the values that govern the relationship between individuals and groups. In countries where individualism prevails, values of individual achievement, freedom, and competition are stressed. In countries where collectivism prevails, values of group harmony, cohesiveness, and consensus are very strong, and the importance of cooperation and agreement between individuals is stressed. In collectivist cultures, the group is more important than the individual, and group members follow norms that stress group rather than personal interests. Japan epitomizes a country where collectivist values dominate, and the United States epitomizes a country where individualist values prevail.[7]

Power distance

The degree to which a country accepts the fact that differences in its citizens' physical and intellectual capabilities give rise to inequalities in their well-being.

Power Distance.   Hofstede used **power distance** to refer to the degree to which a country accepts that differences in its citizens' physical and intellectual capabilities give rise to inequalities in their well-being. This concept also measures the degree to which countries accept economic and social differences in wealth, status, and well-being as natural. Countries that allow inequalities to persist or increase are said to have *high power distance*. Professionally successful workers in high-power-distance countries amass wealth and pass it on to their children. In these countries, inequalities increase over time; the gap between rich and poor, with all the attendant political and social consequences, grows very large. In contrast, countries that dislike the development of large inequalities among their citizens are said to have *low power distance*. Such countries use taxation or social welfare programs to reduce inequality and improve the lot of the least fortunate members of society. Low-power-distance countries are more interested in preventing a wide gap between rich and poor and discord between classes.

Advanced Western countries such as the United States, Germany, the Netherlands, and the United Kingdom score relatively low on power distance and are high on individualism. Poor Latin American countries such as Guatemala and Panama and Asian countries such as Malaysia and the Philippines score high on power distance and low on individualism.[8] These findings suggest that the cultural values of richer countries emphasize protecting the rights of individuals and, at the same time, providing a fair chance of success to every member of society. But even among Western countries there are differences. Both the Dutch and the British see their countries as more protective of the poor and disadvantaged than are Americans, who believe that people have the right to be rich as well as the right to be poor.

Achievement Versus Nurturing Orientation.   Countries that are *achievement oriented* value assertiveness, performance, success, and competition and are results oriented. Countries that are *nurturing oriented* value the quality of life, warm personal relationships, and service and care for the weak. Japan and the United States tend to be achievement oriented. The Netherlands, Sweden, and Denmark tend to be nurturing oriented.

Uncertainty Avoidance.   Just as people differ in their tolerance for uncertainty and willingness to take risks, so do countries. Countries low on uncertainty avoidance (such as the United States and Hong Kong) are easygoing, value diversity, and are tolerant of differences in what people believe and do. Countries high on uncertainty avoidance (such as Japan and France) tend to be rigid and intolerant. In high-uncertainty-avoidance cultures, conformity to the values of the social and work groups to which a person belongs is the norm, and structured situations are preferred because they provide a sense of security. Insight 17.1 illustrates the different attitudes that organizations in France and Germany have toward diversity and toward the treatment of their employees.

Insight 17.1

Diversity

How Cultural Values Shape Attitudes Toward Employees

French and German organizations admire the entrepreneurial drive of American managers and the American work ethic but treat their managers and workers in different ways than do U.S. organizations. French and German organizations are far less concerned with issues of equity and opportunity in managing their diverse workforces than are U.S. organizations. In France, for example, social class still determines the gender, ethnicity, and background of employees who will successfully climb the organizational hierarchy. Women and minorities occupy far fewer managerial positions in France and Germany than in the United States. Moreover, U.S. companies employ far more foreign nationals in their top-management ranks than do German and French companies.[9] In part, this difference reflects differences in these countries' cultural values. Both Germany and France (unlike the United States) are relatively high on uncertainty avoidance, and France in particular wishes its citizens to conform to the norms and values of French culture, which does not encourage diverse behavior.

Although concern for diversity is not a top priority in France and Germany, French and German organizations do seem to be more concerned than U.S. organizations with employees' well-being. The workforce in both France and Germany is far more stable than it is in the United States, and French and German employees tend to work for many years for the same company. As a result, organizations in France and Germany are more concerned with protecting and nurturing the workforce than are U.S. organizations. For example, in France and Germany the average manager and worker get at least six weeks of paid vacation (most U.S. employees get two weeks). French and German employees also enjoy a much wider range of benefits, such as paid maternity leave and layoff payments whose value increases as the number of years a person has worked for an organization increases. Indeed, both France and Germany regard the U.S. system of hiring and firing as harsh and exploitative.[10] Nevertheless, decision making is highly centralized in French and German organizations, which, unlike U.S. companies, operate in accordance with strict, mechanistic, and bureaucratic principles. A relatively high need for achievement and strong desire to avoid uncertainty lead French and German managers to closely monitor and supervise their employees.

Long-Term Versus Short-Term Orientation.   The last dimension that Hofstede identified concerns whether citizens of a country have a long- or a short-term orientation toward life and work.[11] A *long-term orientation* derives from values that include thrift (saving) and persistence in achieving goals. A *short-term orientation* derives from values that express a concern for maintaining personal stability or happiness and for living for the present. Japan and Hong Kong, well known for their high rate of per capita savings, have long-term orientations. The United States and France, which tend to spend more and save less, have a short-term orientation.

Table 17.1 lists the ways people in ten countries score on Hofstede's five dimensions of national culture.

SYMBOLS, CEREMONIES, STORIES, AND LANGUAGE: EXPRESSIONS OF CULTURAL VALUES

A nation's rites, ceremonies, and symbols reflect the values of the nation's culture.[12] Ceremonies and rites are collective events that unite people. In Japan, for example, the ceremonial exchange of business cards reflects that country's interest in social status and a person's relative position in a social or work group. When meeting for the first time, Japanese business people exchange carefully engraved cards that specify their status in their respective organizations. Those who discover from the card exchange that they are lower down in the hierarchy are appropriately respectful to those higher up. Business cards are a visible symbol of a person's place in a group. Without a card, a manager has no status; thus business travelers to Japan are advised to take along a large supply of cards to hand to each businessperson they meet.

TABLE 17.1

Culture Dimension Scores for Ten Countries

	Power Distance	Individualism	Achievement Orientation	Uncertainty Avoidance	Long-Term Orientation
United States	L	H	H	L	L
Germany	L	H	H	M	M
Japan	M	M	H	H	H
France	H	H	M	H	L
Netherlands	L	H	L	M	M
Hong Kong	H	L	H	L	H
Indonesia	H	L	M	L	L
West Africa	H	L	M	M	L
Russia	H	M	L	H	L
China	H	L	M	M	H

Note: H = top third
      M = medium third } among 53 countries and regions for the first four dimensions; among 23 countries for the fifth
      L = bottom third

Source: Adapted from G. Hofstede, "Cultural Constraints in Management Theories," *Academy of Management Executive,* 1993, 7, p. 91.

Global companies must be careful to recognize and not misuse symbols that are important to ethnic or religious groups in the host country. In 1994, for example, McDonald's ran into problems in the United Kingdom. As part of its promotion of the soccer World Cup competition, the company printed the flags of all World Cup nations including Saudi Arabia on throwaway hamburger bags. Because McDonald's did not realize that the flag of Saudi Arabia contains a verse from the Koran—"There is no God but Allah, and Mohammed is his Prophet"—the organization inadvertently offended thousands of Muslims, who thought it sacrilegious to throw away the bag that contained this scripture. Because of this error, McDonald's had to destroy 2 million bags.

Stories and language also reflect cultural values and reveal the things that have most significance in a culture. The Inuit, who live in northern-most Canada, Alaska, and Siberia, have twenty-four different words for *snow*. The Inuit language distinguishes between powder snow, wet snow, drifting snow, and so on. English, in contrast, has only one word because the impact of snow on the lives and culture of English-speakers is relatively small.

There are lots of stories about organizations translating the names of products into a foreign language only to find that the words have a completely different connotation in the foreign language. For example, when Ford introduced the Cliente into Mexico, the car was slow to sell because *cliente* is slang for "streetwalker" in Mexico. The first attempt to translate *Coca-Cola* into Chinese characters was not successful, yielding an expression that meant "Bite the Head Off a Dead Tadpole."[13]

Body language is another important manifestation of a nation's culture. An interesting cultural phenomenon is the amount of personal space that people of different nationalities think is appropriate in face-to-face dealings. Americans and Brazilians, for example, have quite different notions about how far apart from each other two speakers should stand. Thus, when an American has a conversation with a Brazilian, both speakers may seem to dance across the room. While the American backs away from the Brazilian to maintain what the American feels is a comfortable personal distance, the Brazilian moves forward to maintain what the Brazilian feels is a comfortable personal distance. Responding to what seems like encroachment, the American retreats. Responding to what seems like aloofness, the Brazilian advances. Most often, this dance is totally involuntary, and the parties are aware only of being uneasy.

Similarly, Japanese and Americans are notoriously offended by body odor and are often discomfited when in contact with people from cultures in which the elimination of body odor is not high priority.

CULTURE SHOCK

People who move to a foreign country and find themselves confused and bewildered by the meaning and significance of objects and events taken for granted in that country are victims of culture shock—like the Daimler-Benz managers profiled in the opening case. Customs that might induce culture shock include siesta hour in hot climates where shops close in the afternoon, the tendency for dinner to be eaten at 10 p.m. or later in Spain and Mexico, and the custom of butchers in different cultures to cut meat in such a way that an American customer in a foreign supermarket might scan the various cuts of beef and not recognize most of them.

Pictured is a familiar McDonald's restaurant with a not so familiar logo. This McDonalds is located in Moscow and illustrates McDonald's drive to be the largest and most successful fast food provider.

Although many people can adapt to the ways of a new culture, many people cannot. Foreign assignments, especially for whole families, can be particularly stressful when different family members experience different kinds of culture shock, such as when children are placed in a foreign school system, a parent goes to a foreign supermarket, or a manager experiences a foreign approach to work. Together, these shocks can combine to create a feeling of homesickness, which is one reason foreign McDonald's, Burger King, and Pizza Hut restaurants are frequented by Americans living abroad and why the British tend to buy their national newspapers when they are in other countries even for just a few days.

To successfully manage the global environment, organizations and their managers have to learn to deal with the different values, norms, and attitudes

TO MANAGERS

Managing the Global Environment

- If you become an expatriate manager, spend considerable time learning about the national culture of the country in which you are located. Involve your family in this process.
- Analyze the economic, political, and social values of the country, particularly the way the country does business.
- Use Hofstede's model to analyze the country's cultural values, and contrast these values with U.S. values to isolate major differences.
- Spend considerable time talking with other expatriate managers in your host country and with its citizens to identify the norms and etiquette of the country that you should be aware of when dealing with residents on both a business and a social level.
- Be adaptable, and embrace the opportunity to use your experiences in foreign countries to learn more about your own national culture and its cultural values.

that characterize different national cultures. Managers have to recognize, for example, that although organizations in the United States may reward and encourage values of entrepreneurship and risk taking, important decisions are made by the group in Japan, and respect for superiors and for established channels of authority is the norm in Mexico.

Global organizations have to decide how to adapt their operations to the various political, economic, and social values that they encounter as they expand into the global environment. The greater an organization's global presence—that is, the greater the number of different countries in which an organization operates—the greater is the range of national cultural differences the organization will confront and need to manage. In the next section, we consider what organizations can do to manage the global environment.

Managing the Global Environment

Many of the most significant problems that global organizations encounter in the international environment relate to choices about where to buy inputs, produce goods and services, and sell the final product. Global organizations have to make complex choices about which activities to perform at home and which to perform abroad. In this section we look at the choices organizations face in managing their activities at all stages of the production process. Figure 17.2 shows the sequence of stages in the process of manufacturing and distributing goods and services. At each stage, the global environment can impact an organization.

THE RAW-MATERIALS STAGE

The raw-materials stage is the stage at which an organization obtains supplies of the basic commodities it needs to begin its manufacturing process. Many organizations reduce the uncertainty surrounding the supply of raw materials—such as aluminum, copper, wood, and oil—by expanding to other countries to obtain them. Many large chemical companies, for example, own oil fields and explore and refine oil in countries throughout the world to obtain secure supplies of oil, the major input in many chemical and plastic products. McDonald's, to protect its supply of cheap beef, raises cattle on its huge ranches in Brazil. Alicia (Aluminum Company of America), the giant aluminum company, controls much of the world's supply of bauxite (the ore from which aluminum is smelted). De Beers, the world's largest supplier of diamonds, controls diamond production in South Africa and diamond distribution throughout the world.

THE INTERMEDIATE-MANUFACTURING AND ASSEMBLY STAGES

After deciding whether to expand globally to control its supply of raw materials, an organization must decide whether to locate its intermediate-manufacturing

FIGURE 17.2

Managing the Flow
of Global Resources

| Raw-materials stage | Intermediate-manufacturing stage | Assembly stage | Distribution stage | Final-customer stage |

Intermediate manufacturing
The conversion of raw materials into supplies of component parts.

and assembly operations at home or abroad. **Intermediate manufacturing** is the conversion of raw materials into supplies of component parts such as electronic components, tires, or microprocessors. At the assembly stage, an organization assembles components into finished goods or services.

Organizations often expand into other countries to find low-cost locations for intermediate manufacturing and assembly. The low price of labor in Mexico, China, and Malaysia, for example, has driven many U.S. companies to send leather, plastic, and other raw materials to companies in these countries for conversion into components such as shoe soles or shoe uppers, which are assembled into the final product (shoes) by other companies in the same country or elsewhere.

In the 1980s, for example, AT&T found itself at a competitive disadvantage compared with Japanese electronics manufacturers in selling phones, answering machines, and fax machines in the United States because it was using relatively high-priced U.S. labor and components. To compete effectively, AT&T was forced to find foreign suppliers for its components. Today, the antennas on AT&T answering machines are made in Taiwan, the message recording tapes are made in Japan, the cordless batteries are made in Hong Kong, and the answering machines are assembled in China.

China, with its vast supply of cheap labor, has become a preferred assembly point for many of the largest global organizations. Many of the toys sold in the United States, for example, are assembled in China, and increasingly China is acquiring the technology to make component parts like memory chips and plastic parts for toys. Very often, U.S. manufacturers (like AT&T) have no choice but to go abroad to buy components or assemble their products because if they do not, they will be priced out of the marketplace. The cost to the United States, however, is the loss of relatively high-paying U.S. manufacturing jobs and the layoff of large numbers of U.S. workers.

THE DISTRIBUTION AND FINAL-CUSTOMER STAGES

Coordinating the shipping, marketing, and sale of products to distributors and final customers is an especially complicated issue for a global organization. Many different problems arise, depending on the nature of the goods and services that an organization provides. For example, customer needs or tastes for some goods are similar the world over, as they are for Levi's blue jeans or McDonald's hamburgers. But some goods—such as electronic products, cars, and computers—must be tailored to suit the needs and tastes of customers in different countries. The more customer needs for a particular product differ from one country to another, the more an organization has to alter, modify, or adapt its products to suit the needs of customers in each country. Though often necessary for an organization's international survival, customization is a complicated and expensive process.

MANAGING MANUFACTURING AND DISTRIBUTION

Depending on the level of customization that is necessary, an organization can choose several methods to manufacture and distribute its products to customers.[14]

Exporting.   If products have a truly universal appeal—if customers the world over have similar needs for the product—exporting is likely to be the preferred distribution strategy. An organization that chooses to export produces goods and services at home or at the lowest-cost global location and simply ships the products to customers in different countries. In each country, independent distributors then take care of the final distribution of products to stores or to final customers. Exporting can be very expensive if shipping costs are high, as they are for heavy, bulk products like chemicals, or if import tariffs are high in the country to which the goods are shipped. Another potential problem with exporting is that the foreign distributor may do a poor job of marketing the product or may provide poor after-sales service. Either shortfall will alienate foreign customers.

Licensing.   If any of the problems associated with exporting arise, or if the preferences of consumers in several countries diverge, an alternative distribution strategy available to an organization is **licensing,** formally granting to a company located in a foreign country the right to make and distribute the organization's product. Du Pont, for example, may license the German chemical company Hoechst to use Du Pont's patented process to produce a range of plastic products in Germany for distribution to countries throughout the European Union. Du Pont receives a licensing fee from Hoechst for the use of its patent and has none of the problems of physically shipping and marketing the product abroad. Similarly, a service organization like McDonald's or the Hilton Hotel Company might allow an Asian company to purchase the right to use its name and operating procedures and open up a chain of restaurants or hotels in a country in the Pacific Rim. The Tokyo Disney theme park, for example, is owned by a Japanese company that pays a licensing fee to the Walt Disney Company for the use of the Disney name.

Licensing allows foreign companies to customize a product to suit the tastes of local customers relatively easily. Being on the spot, foreign companies are sensitive to local tastes and familiar with local channels of distribution. In Japan, for example, distribution is a very centralized activity controlled by a few huge companies that can keep foreign products out of the market if they choose to.

There is a major drawback to licensing, however. Although the company that grants the license avoids the problems of global distribution, it cedes profit to the licensee.

Joint Ventures.   An increasingly common way for organizations to distribute and sell their products abroad is by entering into joint ventures with foreign companies. A **joint venture** is a strategic alliance in which organizations agree to pool their skills and resources and produce and distribute a product together. A global organization enters into an international joint venture to take advantage of a foreign company's close knowledge of local customer tastes, sources of low-cost inputs, and the best channels of distribution for the product. In return, the foreign organization can take advantage of the global organization's technology or skill in designing and making the product, such as Microsoft's skills in producing world-class software or Toyota's skills in low-cost car manufacturing. By pooling their skills in a joint venture, each organization offers the other something that would otherwise be very expensive to obtain, so both organizations gain by establishing a long-term relationship. In 1994, for example, Adolph Coors Company formed a joint venture with Korea's Jingo Ltd. to produce and sell Coors beer in South Korea. Both companies will pool their resources to construct the Jingo-Coors Brewing Co., which will produce 1.8 million barrels of beer a year.[15]

Many U.S. companies are adopting innovative ways of allying with their suppliers and assemblers to take advantage of lower prices. Often, an organization has many foreign suppliers, each of which produces one of the many components that are assembled into the final product. To manage this

Licensing
Formally granting the right to do something, such as making and distributing a product.

Joint venture
A strategic alliance in which organizations agree to pool their skills and resources and produce and distribute a product together.

Network organization
A set of organizations linked by contracts or alliances.

complex network of joint ventures, a global organization may create a **network organization** to link all its venture partners together and facilitate the production and assembly of component parts into the final product.

AT&T, for example, created a network organization and linked its joint-venture partners together so that it could produce answering machines at low cost. AT&T electronically sends designs for new component parts and assembly instructions for new products to its network of venture partners, who coordinate their activities to produce the components in the desired quantities and then ship them to the final assembly point. From there, the answering machines are sent back to the United States and other countries for distribution to AT&T customers. In 1994 AT&T announced that it was marketing a new telephone videoconferencing system to allow business customers to meet face to face to integrate their activities on a global basis. AT&T's development of this product was spurred by its own experiences in attempting to find the most effective ways to coordinate its joint-venture activities.

Wholly Owned Foreign Subsidiaries.   When global organizations want to retain complete control over their activities, they establish wholly owned foreign divisions, or subsidiaries, to manufacture and distribute their products in foreign countries. Foreign subsidiaries are most commonly created when a global organization wants to protect product quality or the manufacturing methods that go into making its products.[16] In a joint venture, the global organization shares its skills with the foreign company, and there is a danger that the foreign company may take this knowledge to go it alone in its home country.

To protect their technology or their product's reputation, many companies, such as IBM and Daimler-Benz, establish foreign subsidiaries so that they have complete control over the distribution, sale, and after-sale service of their products. In this way, they can guarantee product and service quality, something that is particularly important for complex products like mainframe computers and cars, which require high-quality after-sales service.

Like joint ventures, foreign subsidiaries give companies access to local knowledge about customer preferences so that products can be fully customized to suit local tastes. In many cases, however, companies establish foreign subsidiaries to reap the advantages of lower labor costs. As indicated in Insight 17.2, some U.S. car companies have established foreign manufacturing subsidiaries, called maquiladoras, in Mexico.

Insight 17.2   **A Global View**

Assembled in Mexico

Since the passage of the North American Free Trade Agreement in 1993, many U.S. and Japanese car companies have taken advantage of low labor costs in Mexico by establishing both component parts factories and assembly plants in the region around Monterrey and Saltillo, about 200 miles south of the U.S.–Mexico border. At Ford's assembly plant in Hermosillo, for example, the average worker earns $6.35 an hour in wages and benefits, whereas a comparable Ford worker in Michigan earns around $40 an hour in wages and benefits.[17] Mexican workers are still among the best-paid factory workers in the Monterrey-Saltillo region even though they earn considerably less than their U.S. counterparts.

Other car companies have moved to the Monterrey-Saltillo region to take advantage of low labor costs. Chrysler built a huge new assembly plant in Saltillo, Nissan built an engine and transmission plant in 1986 and added an assembly operation in 1992, and GM currently has two plants in operation. As the large car companies have arrived, they have been followed by a host of car component manufacturers, which have located their operations near to the carmakers to respond to their needs. Many of these component manufacturers are linked in strategic alliances to carmakers. Nissan, in particular, has developed a network organization with its suppliers, and Honda and Toyota are beginning to follow suit.

As a result of the presence of the carmakers, other U.S. companies, such as Xerox and IBM, have been attracted to the area surrounding Saltillo and Monterrey, and the economy of northern Mexico is booming. The growth in employment in Mexico is expected to eventually reduce the flow of illegal immigrants to the United States. Moreover, although most cars presently being made in Mexico are shipped back to the United States, as the incomes of Mexican workers grow, they will start buying more new cars. In addition, U.S. and Japanese carmakers view their Mexican plants as the regional base from which they will export cars to all of Latin America. From their maquiladoras, the automakers are poised to take advantage of economic growth in the emerging markets of countries throughout the Americas.

The biggest problem with establishing subsidiaries in foreign countries is that the more manufacturing plants an organization has, the more it costs to operate them.[18] Nevertheless, the high cost is often offset by the lower price of labor and the huge revenues that organizations receive from selling products in foreign markets.

GLOBAL LEARNING

Global learning—learning how to manage suppliers and distributors and to respond to the needs of customers all over the world—is a difficult and complex task.[19] How can global organizations and expatriate managers learn about the characteristics of different countries and exploit this knowledge to increase organizational performance?

First, expatriate managers can learn about the sources of low-cost inputs and the best places to assemble their products throughout the world. Expatriate managers are responsible for developing relationships with organizations in different countries and for taking advantage of various economic, political, and cultural conditions to effectively produce and sell the parent organization's goods and services.[20]

Second, expatriate managers in functions such as research and development, manufacturing, and sales can take advantage of their presence in a foreign country to learn the skills and techniques that companies in that country use. They can apply this knowledge to improve the performance not only of their foreign subsidiaries but also of their domestic or home divisions. After

Global learning
Learning how to manage suppliers and distributors and to respond to the needs of customers all over the world.

World War II, for example, many of Toyota's manufacturing managers visited the U.S. car plants of GM and Ford to learn how these companies assembled cars. Those Japanese managers took that manufacturing knowledge back to Japan, where they improved on the American techniques and developed the flexible manufacturing technology that gave Toyota and other Japanese automakers their competitive advantage over U.S. companies in the 1980s. Recognizing the lead Japanese companies had gained in quality manufacturing techniques, GM, Ford, Xerox, Motorola, and many other U.S. companies sent their managers to Japan in the 1980s and 1990s to learn about the new techniques. These U.S. companies then incorporated the Japanese techniques into their manufacturing operations, often improving on them in the process.

Motorola, Xerox, and other U.S. companies have become experts in total quality management (TQM) and have divisions that sell their TQM skills to other U.S. and European companies that want to learn TQM techniques. In this way, global learning continually takes place as companies compete with one another worldwide for customers. To stay up to speed in the game of global competition, all global organizations are forced to learn the most recent developments in manufacturing technology, research and development, and other functional areas. The CEOs and top managers of many organizations reached their present lofty positions because their experiences as expatriate managers gave them the opportunity to engage in global learning.

One reason that has been put forth to explain the Japanese lead in low-cost, high-quality manufacturing in the 1970s and 1980s is that after World War II the Japanese sent a lot of their managers abroad, particularly to the United States, to learn new techniques and gain access to state-of-the-art technology. In the 1970s, however, U.S. companies did *not* send their managers to Japan or Europe, so they were unaware of the low-cost, high-quality developments that were taking place abroad. The harmful effect of this failure to take advantage of global learning by the Big Three U.S. automakers in the 1970s is the subject of Insight 17.3.

Insight 17.3 A Global View

A Failure of Global Learning

Until 1970 the Big Three U.S. automakers—General Motors, Ford, and Chrysler—were used to a stable domestic environment in which they had complete dominance over customers; a mass production technology that had changed little in thirty years; and a strategy based on producing large, luxurious, high-priced and not very reliable cars. In the early 1970s, however, the Big Three were caught unawares by several unexpected events associated with the entry of Japanese carmakers into the U.S. market.

First, the Big Three were confronted with Japanese competitors that had developed a new, more efficient manufacturing technology.

Second, the domestic environment changed because the entry of new Japanese competitors increased the level of competition for customers. Third, the Japanese used their improved technology to pursue a strategy based on producing small, high-quality, low-priced cars—a combination the Big Three had dismissed as unimportant, believing that "small cars mean small profits."

Were the Big Three ready to confront these developments? Did they have in place the organizational structures that would allow them to respond quickly to these changes, to adopt new technologies and develop new small, high-quality, fuel-efficient cars to fight off the Japanese challenge? The answer was no. The Big Three were totally unprepared because they had not engaged in global learning. Moreover, they had become very inwardly focused, believing that they were the world leaders and feeling confident that although the Japanese might come to them for advice, they needed no advice from anyone.

Over time, each of the Big Three had developed a tall, centralized hierarchy, which did not facilitate global learning. Each was very bureaucratic, was slow to make decisions, and could not respond to Japanese competition. Like Harley-Davidson (see Chapter 16), both Chrysler and Ford nearly went bankrupt. GM lost billions of dollars and survived only because its huge size and long dominance of the U.S. car market had allowed the organization to accumulate a lot of resources.

By the end of the 1970s, managers in the Big Three realized that they had lost control of their respective organizations and that they needed to change them to meet and survive the Japanese challenge. They also realized that they needed to change the attitudes and behaviors of their members and encourage the development of a new global orientation that would allow them to compete effectively with foreign companies. They began this change in the 1980s by sending teams of managers to Japan to learn how Toyota and other Japanese companies were operating their technologies.

To facilitate organizational learning, the Big Three redesigned their structures and cultures. They shrank their hierarchies, ruthlessly laying off hundreds of thousands of managers and workers. They altered their form of differentiation. With Chrysler leading the way, all three began to adopt a product team structure and use cross-functional teams to speed global learning and the development of new car models. They also tried to develop new kinds of values and norms (exemplified by Ford's "Quality Is Job 1" campaign) to change workers' attitudes and behaviors and to introduce Japanese values of teamwork and group decision making.

What has been the result of these attempts to open the Big Three to global learning? By 1993 all three companies had started to make a profit. By 1995, as a result of their new strategies and structures, they had regained significant market share from the Japanese. Moreover, in 1994 it was announced that Chrysler had become the lowest-cost carmaker in the world. By the year 2000 these companies hope to dominate their Japanese competitors at a global level, and they are now constantly alert to ways to use global learning to enhance their performance.

Global Strategy and Structure

In today's global environment, competition is everywhere. Global organizations confront foreign competitors not only abroad but also at home, when foreign competitors enter their home markets. In the tire industry, for example, Goodyear Tire & Rubber, a U.S. company, competes in almost every country in the world against the French company Michelin, the Italian company Pirelli, and the Japanese company Bridgestone. These four competitors go head to head to try to attract customers for their products, and each organization views its environment in global terms—that is, managers treat the world as a single market and nations as subparts of a global market. In this section we examine some strategies that organizations use to expand globally and the organizational structures and cultures they can use to manage their strategies to take advantage of global learning.

GLOBALIZATION VERSUS CUSTOMIZATION

These days there is much discussion about the globalization of world markets, and expressions such as "global village" and "global products" abound. These terms reflect that consumers the world over are developing similar tastes for products such as Coca-Cola, BMW or Mercedes-Benz cars, or Levi's blue jeans. Organizations are increasingly organizing their activities on a global basis to be able to take advantage of worldwide demand for their products.[21] Nevertheless, consumers in different countries do have different tastes. To be successful, global organizations have to be responsive to the needs of foreign consumers and tailor or customize their products to suit local tastes. Thus, for example, the formula and name for Coca-Cola was altered to meet the tastes of consumers in China, the sizes of clothes differ to match the different statures of customers in the United States and Asia, and even the colors of cars or refrigerators reflect local tastes.

This tension between *globalization* (the need to view the world as a single market) and *customization* (the need to be responsive to consumer tastes in individual countries) is one of the main challenges facing global organizations.[22] This challenge influences the strategies they use to compete in the global market, their organizational structure, their culture, and the way they manage their workforce in different countries. The strategy that a company uses to compete globally depends on the way the organization decides to respond to the pressures for globalization and the pressures for customization. Historically, there has been a pattern in the strategies that U.S. companies have used to expand globally and in the kinds of structures they adopt to manage their strategies.[23]

INTERNATIONAL STRATEGY AND INTERNATIONAL DIVISIONAL STRUCTURE

Many of the largest U.S. companies, such as Kellogg, H. J. Heinz, and Procter & Gamble, adopted an international strategy when they began their program of global expansion. Companies with an **international strategy** retain important functional activities like research and development and product design in their home countries to protect their competitive advantage, and they establish wholly owned subsidiaries abroad to manufacture and distribute their products in foreign markets. Sometimes the foreign subsidiary is just responsible for distributing domestically manufactured products in the foreign country.

International strategy
A strategy in which a company retains important functional activities at home to protect its competitive advantage and establishes wholly owned subsidiaries abroad to manufacture and distribute its products in foreign markets.

Microsoft uses the latter kind of international strategy. For example, all Microsoft software products are produced in the United States, where they are customized (in their language, for example) for customers in each foreign country and then are exported abroad and distributed and sold to software distributors in the foreign country. Honda Motor Co., in contrast, decided to manufacture cars in the United States as part of its international strategy (see Insight 17.4).

Insight 17.4   A Global View

Honda of America

In 1982, to offset U.S. threats of trade sanctions against Japanese car companies, Honda (www.honda.jp) became the first Japanese car company to produce cars in the United States, establishing a plant in Marysville, Ohio, to produce the Honda Accord. Since then, over 6 million Hondas have been produced at the Marysville plant and are exported to over eighteen countries including Japan. Quality levels at the plant have been almost as high as they are in Japan, and costs are also in line with those in Japan.[24]

In establishing the plant, Honda pursued an international strategy. At first, the cars were designed and many components were made in Japan by Honda and other Japanese companies. As time has passed, however, Honda has begun to transfer more of its design and research activities to the United States to capitalize on American design expertise. It is also buying more of its component parts from U.S. manufacturers that have learned to meet Honda's stringent quality requirements.

In fact, the 1997 Honda Accord was designed jointly in Japan by Japanese and U.S. engineers. Seventy of Honda's American engineers took their families to live in Japan for two years, at an average cost to Honda (including housing and schooling) of more than $600,000 per family. So far the venture appears to have paid off. Sales of the new Accord have been brisk. At a time when U.S. car companies are regaining market share, Honda is maintaining its part of the U.S. car market.

International divisional structure

An organizational structure in which an international division manages global operations, coordinating between managers in domestic divisions and managers in foreign subsidiaries.

To manage an international strategy, a global organization is likely to adopt an **international divisional structure,** an organizational structure in which an international division manages global operations.[25] This structure is depicted in Fig. 17.3, which shows how the international division takes the responsibility for coordinating between managers in domestic divisions (that supply either finished products or essential product knowledge) and managers in foreign subsidiaries (who manufacture or distribute the products). The use of a foreign division allows for the effective supervision of expatriate and local managers of the foreign subsidiaries.

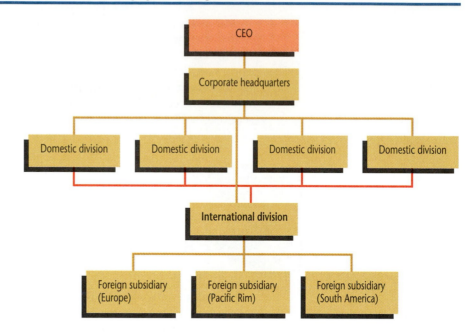

FIGURE 17.3

International Divisional
Structure

As we saw in Chapter 15, one of an organization's major decisions involves how much authority to centralize at the top of the hierarchy and how much to decentralize to divisional managers. For a global organization, the choice is how much authority to centralize at home with domestic managers and how much authority to decentralize to foreign managers. Companies pursuing an international strategy usually centralize most important product decisions (such as design) at home but give managers in foreign subsidiaries responsibility for customizing products to local tastes and marketing them in the foreign country. As we saw in the Honda example, however, as time goes on, more decision-making authority may be decentralized to the foreign subsidiaries.

MULTIDOMESTIC STRATEGY AND GLOBAL GEOGRAPHIC STRUCTURE

Over time, many U.S. companies find that as the size of their global presence and operations increases, they have difficulty pursuing an international strategy and controlling the operations of their foreign subsidiaries with an international divisional structure. As we saw in Chapter 15, problems with a functional structure arise when it is unable to handle the needs of different products or regional customers. These same problems start to occur as a company's global presence increases. Moreover, as managers in the foreign subsidiaries become more and more expert in responding to the needs of customers in their countries, they begin to demand more authority and responsibility over their operations. As a result, when a company becomes very large, it often adopts a **multidomestic strategy:** It decentralizes authority for making all significant product decisions to managers in each foreign subsidiary so that they can develop the range of products that best appeal to the tastes of local customers. Each subsidiary is given all the functions and autonomy it needs to produce its products; often, the only link among subsidiaries is the flow of profits back to the parent.

As the Ford Motor Company, for example, expanded into Europe, it pursued an international strategy. As it realized that European consumers pre-

Multidomestic strategy
A strategy in which a company decentralizes to managers in each foreign subsidiary the authority for making all significant product decisions.

ferred cars that were less expensive and better suited to narrow roads than were Fords designed for use in the United States, it decided to decentralize control to its foreign subsidiary, Ford of Europe, headquartered in the United Kingdom. Ford of Europe became Europe's biggest and most successful car manufacturer. When Ford of America almost went bankrupt in the early 1990s because of Japanese competition, only the flow of profits from its European subsidiary kept Ford of America afloat. One result of this experience is that British-born Alex Trotman, the person who spearheaded Ford's success in Europe, is now Ford of America's CEO.

To manage a multidomestic strategy, an organization adopts a **global geographic structure:** The company replicates all of its functions in each country in which it operates. This structure is depicted in Fig. 17.4, which shows a company with five foreign subsidiaries, each of which has all the functions it needs to produce and distribute products to customers in the country or region in which it is located.

A company that establishes a foreign subsidiary in the United Kingdom might give that subsidiary the responsibility for supplying its products to the whole of the European Union. Compaq Computer, for example, manufactures computers in England and Ireland that it distributes throughout Europe. Similarly, Toyota, Honda, and Nissan have car plants in England that sell to every country in the European Union.

The combination of a multidomestic strategy and a global geographic structure has both advantages and disadvantages. The biggest advantage is that it allows a global organization to respond to local customer needs through customized products. One disadvantage is that the strategy is very expensive to operate because each subsidiary has its own set of functions. Another disadvantage is that the global geographic structure does not facilitate global learning because managers in each autonomous subsidiary learn nothing from one another. Managers do not move from one country or subsidiary to another and are far away from managers in the organization's home divisions. As a result, subsidiaries cannot benefit from the sharing of information about vital matters such as the location of the lowest-cost source of inputs or product assembly or the most recent developments in product design or manufacturing technology.[26]

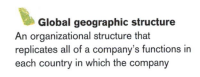

Global geographic structure
An organizational structure that replicates all of a company's functions in each country in which the company

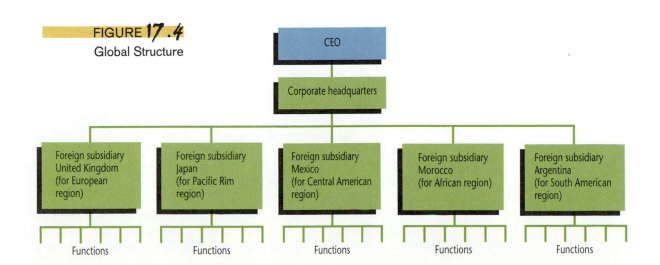

FIGURE 17.4
Global Structure

TRANSNATIONAL STRATEGY AND GLOBAL MATRIX STRUCTURE

Given those disadvantages, and especially given the emergence of competition from low-cost foreign competitors, many U.S. companies that were pursuing multidomestic strategies have been forced to search for a new combination of strategy and structure that allows them to make better use of global resources. Increasingly, U.S. companies have turned to a **transnational strategy:** The organization locates foreign subsidiaries to produce inputs and assemble products in countries where costs are lowest, and it locates foreign subsidiaries in a few select countries to customize and manufacture products to meet the needs of customers in a particular world region, such as Europe, Africa, or Asia. All of the subsidiaries of a transnational company are linked together in a global network organization to facilitate the transfer of resources on a global basis. Each foreign subsidiary is expected to build particular functional skills (such as in manufacturing or product development) and then share these skills with the other subsidiaries so that the organization as a whole is able to achieve the gains from global learning. Levi Strauss & Co. is one organization pursuing a transnational strategy (see Insight 17.5).

Transnational strategy
A strategy in which a company locates foreign subsidiaries both in low-cost countries to produce inputs and assemble products and in a few select countries to customize and manufacture products to meet the needs of customers in a particular region.

Insight 17.5   **A Global View**

Levi's Transnational Strategy

Levi Strauss & Co., the U.S. company that produces blue jeans that are famous throughout the world, has a strong incentive to increase its global presence: The jeans that retail in the United States for $30 sell in places like London, Paris, and Tokyo for $80 or more! The wholesale price of Levi's jeans in Europe and Japan is $31.99, more than their retail price in the United States.[27] Outside the United States, Levi's jeans are a status symbol and command a premium price from young European and Asian consumers, even though in the United States their status has been eroded by competition from manufacturers like Guess and Ralph Lauren.

To take advantage of its popularity in foreign markets and at the same time increase profit margins at home, Levi Strauss has increasingly pursued a transnational strategy. The organization has located its raw materials, intermediate manufacturing, and assembly operations in places where costs are lowest. It buys much of its cotton from Texas. At El Paso the cotton is turned into denim, dyed, and stone-washed. The denim fabric is then sent to the Dominican Republic, the Philippines, and elsewhere to be tailored into jeans. In fact, Levi Strauss currently has no U.S. assembly operations for its jeans—it closed them all to take advantage of low-cost labor abroad.

To pursue its transnational strategy, Levi Strauss created a number of foreign subsidiaries to handle its marketing throughout the world and to allow it to customize its jeans to the needs of different countries or world regions. Asian customers have a somewhat smaller stature than Americans, for example, so it is important for a greater variety of smaller-sized jeans to be available to increase sales in Asian countries. Popular colors for jeans also differ from country to country. Levi Strauss's European division handles distribution and marketing throughout Europe and is responsible for identifying the demands of customers in different European countries. This information is then transmitted to Levi's input suppliers and assembly plants, to ensure that they produce and tailor jeans that suit the demands of European consumers.

Levi Strauss is also taking advantage of its transnational strategy to transfer abroad the marketing skills it has developed in the United States. It is currently introducing Docker's, its successful line of casual clothes, into Europe and Asia, using the experience it gained in introducing Docker's to the U.S. market. The organization is also making a big push to introduce wrinkle-free cotton slacks to U.S. consumers, a concept first developed in Europe. Levi Strauss and other companies that pursue transnational strategies are constantly on the lookout for ways to exploit their organizational strengths to better serve the needs of their global customers and increase their profits.

Global matrix structure

An organizational structure that simultaneously groups organizational activities in two ways, by product and by world area.

An organization pursuing a transnational strategy is likely to choose a **global matrix structure,** grouping its activities in two ways—by the products it produces and by the world areas in which it competes.[28] The company shown in Fig. 17.5, for example, has three product groups (computers, consumer electronics, and appliances) selling products in three regions (the Americas, Europe, and Asia). At the intersection of the axes are foreign subsidiaries, such as APB Industries, which is based in São Paulo, Brazil. The foreign subsidiaries, which are located throughout the world, make the components and assemble each product. The managers of the subsidiaries report to two bosses: the boss of their product group, who is responsible for controlling costs, and the boss of the world area in which they are located, who is responsible for customizing products to the needs of customers in that world area.

APB Industries assembles washing machines for the South American market. The managers of APB report to the head of the Appliance Product Group, who is located in Berlin, Germany, and to the head of the Americas Region, who is located in Houston, Texas. The Berlin-based Appliance Product Group is responsible for providing the São Paulo plant with the most modern technology and for shipping it the lowest-cost components that can be obtained throughout the world. The Houston-based Americas Region group is responsible for providing the São Paulo operation with information about the demand for washing machines in the various South American countries and about the various tastes that consumers have (such as their preferences for specific colors and features).

A global matrix structure is very complicated to operate. Global organizations like Nestlé, Ford, and APB Industries have hundreds of subsidiaries operating in almost every country of the world. Despite the complexity of the reporting relationships that have to be managed, more and more large organizations are operating global matrix structures to obtain the benefits of pursuing a transnational strategy.

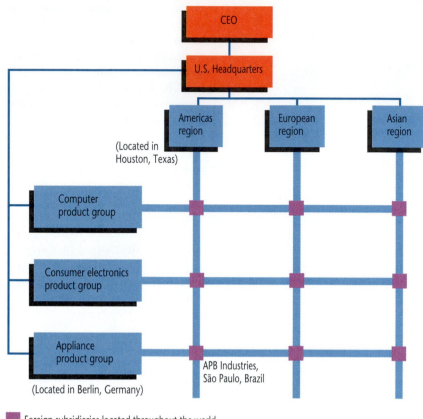

FIGURE **17.5**
Global Matrix Structure

FIGURE **17.5**
Global Matrix Structure

Table 17.2 summarizes the advantages and disadvantages associated with the three strategies for managing the global environment.

INTEGRATING THE GLOBAL ORGANIZATION

As we discussed in Chapter 16, as the organizational environment becomes more complex, an organization needs to increase its level of differentiation, and doing so requires the organization to increase its level of integration. This same principle holds true at the global level. As the strategy of a global organization becomes more complex and the organization operates in more and more countries (environments) and adopts a more complex structure such as a global matrix structure (higher differentiation), the organization needs to increase integration between its subsidiaries and domestic divisions. Organizations use various means to increase integration, some of which have been discussed in previous chapters.

Electronic Communication Media. Managing the relationships between domestic divisions and foreign subsidiaries through electronic means is becoming an increasingly important way of integrating global organizations. Global teleconferencing (which allows managers in different countries to communicate face to face in real time to coordinate their activities), faxes, e-mail, and conference calls are all used by organizations to speed global communication, learning, and decision making. Manufacturers of inexpensive clothing, for example, often wait for Anne Klein, Armani, or some other de-

TABLE 17.2
Advantages and Disadvantages of Three Global Strategies

Strategy	Advantages	Disadvantages
International	Ability to protect important functional skills at home, such as R&D knowledge Relatively low operating costs	Limited ability to customize products to suit needs of local market
Multidomestic	Ability to customize products to suit needs of local market	High operating costs
Transnational	Ability to locate operations where costs are lowest Ability to customize products	Very high operating costs Problems of coordinating global activities

signer of high-priced clothes to come out with a new spring or fall line. They then copy the couturier design and electronically transmit specifications for color, fabric, and style to foreign manufacturers, who reproduce the design within weeks and ship the garments to the United States for the manufacturer to distribute to stores under its own brand name. Figure 17.6 shows how Ford uses global communication to design cars.

Global Networks. To encourage managers from different countries and different product areas to communicate, and to facilitate global learning, global organizations are increasingly moving their managers from one foreign subsidiary

FIGURE 17.6

Ford's Well-Developed Global Network

"Long Distance Design," 8/29/93. Copyright 1993 by the New York Times Company. Reprinted with permission.

• Design sites of the new Ford Corporate Design organization

in their global network to another to help them develop a global outlook. This practice ensures that expatriate managers build up a network of contacts throughout the world that they can use to increase integration.[29] When a specific problem arises, such as in maintaining manufacturing quality, a manufacturing manager with a global network can call a contact in Hong Kong or Germany to help find a solution to the problem.

Global Teams.   Sometimes organizations use global teams—groups of managers from foreign subsidiaries and domestic divisions who go from subsidiary to subsidiary to facilitate global learning and to integrate global organizations. Team members act as consultants and transfer new skills to foreign subsidiaries to help them reduce costs and improve quality. At the same time, team members learn new foreign techniques that they can bring back to the home country in which the organization is based. For example, when the Big Three U.S. automakers wanted to learn total quality management techniques from Japanese car companies, they sent a global team of managers to Japan.

GLOBAL ORGANIZATIONAL CULTURE

National cultures vary widely, as do the values and norms that guide the way people think and act. When an organization expands into foreign countries, it employs citizens whose values reflect those of their national culture. The fact that national culture is a determinant of organizational culture poses some interesting problems for an organization seeking to manage its global operations.[30]

If differences in values between countries cause differences in attitudes and behaviors between workers in different subsidiaries, an organization will find it difficult to obtain the benefits of global learning. If different subsidiaries develop different organizational cultures, they will develop their own orientations toward the problems facing the company. They will become concerned more with their own problems than with the problems facing the company as a whole, and integration will decline.

To prevent the emergence of different national subcultures within a global organization, an organization must take steps to create a **global organizational culture** that is stronger than the cultures within its various subsidiaries. Managers must take steps to create organization-wide values and norms that foster cohesiveness among global divisions. How can managers create a global organizational culture?

Electronic communication media, global networks, and global teams can be used to transmit values to the organization's divisions and subsidiaries. Global networks can socialize managers into the values and norms of the global organization. The transfer of managers from one subsidiary to another enables managers to internalize global norms and understand that they are members of a global organization, not just members of a U.S-owned subsidiary in a foreign country. Global teams can also facilitate the development of shared values.

Many large companies attempt to develop a cohesive set of values and norms throughout a global organization by transferring top managers from the domestic divisions or functions to head the foreign subsidiaries. When Nissan, Honda, and Sony, for example, expand abroad, the whole top-management team of the foreign subsidiary is composed of Japanese

Global organizational culture
Organization-wide values and norms that foster cohesiveness among the divisions of a global organization.

managers whose job is to transplant Japanese values of teamwork and co-operation to the subsidiary. The Japanese have been very successful at maintaining control of the organizational culture of their plants in the United States and England. Quality levels at Japanese auto plants in the United States frequently are close to levels in Japan. One downside of this process is that "foreign" (for example, American or English) managers who join these Japanese subsidiaries often claim that getting promoted is difficult. Some believe that they, like many women in corporate America (see the opening case in Chapter 4), hit a sort of glass ceiling beyond which future promotion is impossible, not because of their gender but because they are not Japanese. Many U.S. companies, however, are increasingly promoting their foreign managers to high-level positions to foster a global culture within their organizations.

SUMMARY

To compete around the world, global organizations develop strategies for using their resources effectively at the global level. The challenge they face is to balance the need for a global approach to reduce costs with the need to customize products for customers in different regions. To meet this challenge, global organizations have been developing global structures to facilitate global learning. When a company adopts a more complex strategy, it needs a more complex structure to allow it to manage its worldwide activities. Similarly, to facilitate the sharing of information and ideas, global organizations have been trying to develop global cultures and encourage global learning by transferring managers from one country to another. In the future, the pressures for globalization are likely to increase, thereby increasing the organizational design challenges facing the managers of global organizations.

Advice TO MANAGERS

Managing the Global Environment

- To exploit and manage global resources effectively, choose the best method to manage manufacturing and distribution. Recognize that creating foreign subsidiaries is expensive and that joint ventures and network organizations can avoid the costs of global expansion while providing the benefits.
- Be open to the opportunities presented by global learning, and develop a global rather than a national orientation.
- When you plan the path of your company's expansion abroad, choose an appropriate strategy for expansion.
- Match your strategy to the appropriate organizational structure. Increase your use of electronic information media, and rotate managers to develop a global network to encourage global learning and increase your level of integration.
- When you require a high level of communication and integration among foreign subsidiaries, take steps to develop a strong global organizational culture. A strong global culture can smooth over differences among people from different national cultures.

Managing Global Human Resources

Now that you are aware of the challenges facing global organizations and the kinds of strategies and structures they adopt to meet these challenges, we can focus on some of the issues involved in managing members of global organizations. In this section, we discuss some topics covered in earlier chapters, such as motivation, leadership, and group processes, but in a global context.

PERSONALITY AND ABILITY

Are there reasons to believe that personality and ability differ among countries, just as they differ among people, so that different nations have different personality types or different sets of abilities? For example, is the Big Five model of personality (extroversion, neuroticism, agreeableness, conscientiousness, openness to experience) that we discussed in Chapter 2 generally applicable to people the world over? Just as Hofstede's model of national culture suggests that five dimensions differentiate the cultures of different countries and that different nations fall at different points on these dimensions, so it seems reasonable to believe that the Big Five traits and specific traits such as locus of control, need for power, and need for affiliation will be applicable across countries. However, there may be differences in the relative positions of citizens of different countries on these personality traits because of the effects of nurture, which accounts for almost half of the differences in personality (see Chapter 2).

For organizational behavior, the central message is that personality does not change in the short term. Thus, effective global managers are those who learn to understand, work with, and tolerate the differences in people's personalities that are due to national culture. These managers accept diversity and develop strategies to understand foreign nationals' points of view and to respond to their needs. This is no easy task. Teams composed of workers from different countries often find it difficult to deal with one another, in part because of differences in their national personalities. The promotion of many top managers to the position of CEO may be due to their ability to interact well with people of all nationalities.

Personality is also likely to affect organizational culture. Recall from Chapter 15 that the values of an organization's founder and the type of people who are selected by the organization are major sources of organizational culture. At a national level, we might expect some sort of national personality profile to describe the cultures of a nation's organizations, showing, for example, that the cultures of Japanese organizations are more similar to each other than they are to the cultures of U.S. or German organizations.[31]

As far as ability is concerned, most of the differences among countries are probably explained by nurture. For example, the level of education in a country goes far toward explaining differences in verbal and numerical ability, as does the support that children and adults receive at home and from their peers. As we saw in Insight 2.6, the United States is far behind some countries in the resources it devotes to education. Training and such programs are vital to successful competition in a global economy where workers are being asked to perform increasingly complex tasks, operate computer-controlled machinery, and learn new skills.

VALUES AND ATTITUDES

Research such as Hofstede's has found that despite differences between the values of different countries, the same five dimensions (individualism versus collectivism and so on) can be used to describe and differentiate between the value systems of countries across the world. Where a country falls along these value dimensions is in part the result of conditions within the country. We have pointed out, for example, why advanced Western nations are oriented toward individualism and low power distance—because they are relatively rich and have the luxury of choosing whether to be concerned more with protecting the rights of others or with providing some measure of equal opportunity for their citizens. We also have discussed how the personality profile of a nation affects organizational culture, and we expect that national values also feed into organizational culture.

Do the attitudes of people in different countries toward organizational commitment and job satisfaction (see Chapter 3) differ? For example, are U.S. workers likely to be more satisfied with their jobs than are workers in Japan? Evidence suggests that there are differences in attitude among countries, and many researchers believe that many of these differences are due to differences in opportunity resulting from a variety of economic, political, and cultural conditions. For example, a U.S. manager might be very unhappy with his job because he is slow to be promoted, but a manager in France may consider himself lucky to have the same type of job because of France's relatively high unemployment rate. To a large extent, people's feelings about an organization are affected by conditions within their society.

PERCEPTION AND LEARNING

The culture of a country (its language, symbols, beliefs, values, norms, stereotypes, and so on) shapes its members' perceptions of the world. Anthropologists have extensively studied the effect of national culture on perception. In Japanese companies, for example, women are typically perceived as less capable and deserving than men; consequently, they have low status and quickly bump into the glass ceiling because of cultural stereotypes. Similarly, in many Muslim countries, the presence of women in commercial or business situations is considered inappropriate because of religious beliefs.

Global organizations face a dilemma: They need to respond with sensitivity to differences in the national cultures of the countries in which they do business while they struggle to maintain core organizational values. Expatriate managers who understand how people in different countries perceive situations will be in a good position to appreciate other points of view and make decisions that conform to the organization's values (see Chapter 4). Notions about ethical behavior, for example, diverge widely around the world. In some countries, corruption is taken for granted and perceived as normal. A U.S. subsidiary operating in such a country must decide whether its managers should be guided by the ethical values of the host country or the values of the United States. (U.S. companies expect their managers to act as if they were in the United States.)

We have discussed the importance of global learning to a global organization, and in Chapter 5 we examined various theories and approaches that organizations can use to facilitate learning. We noted, for example, that individuals differ in what they regard as positive and negative reinforcers. Some workers, for example, view money as a positive reinforcer, but others view challenging job assignments as a positive reinforcer. At a global level, managers need to develop an appreciation for the preferences of their workers and develop approaches toward positive (or negative) reinforcement that are adapted to the national culture of the countries in which they are located.

The principles of organizational behavior modification (see Chapter 5) can also be applied at the global level to encourage employees to learn appropriate behaviors. Social learning theory also becomes particularly important in a global context where, through processes like vicarious learning, workers in other countries can learn from observing global managers. Moreover, managers can take steps to raise workers' feelings of self-efficacy, especially when an organization enters a host country less technologically advanced than its home country and the organization has to teach workers new skills to allow them to perform at a high level.

MOTIVATION

As we discussed in Chapter 6, motivation determines the direction of workers' behavior in organizations, their levels of effort, and their persistence. Are there reasons to believe that workers' motivation differs across countries, or even that workers in different countries are motivated by different intrinsic and extrinsic rewards? Do workers in different countries have different sets of needs, for example, that they are trying to satisfy at work?

Many studies have attempted to assess differences in needs between countries. The general conclusion seems to be, as with Hofstede's model, that although workers the world over have similar needs, the average strength of these needs varies by country.[32] For example, the need for security is more pronounced in Japan than it is in the United States. The strength of the need for security and self-actualization is related to economic, political, and cultural conditions within a country. The more advanced a country is and the higher its standard of living, the more likely are its workers to seek to satisfy on the job needs that are related to personal growth and accomplishment.

At a global level, expectancy theory, which focuses on how workers decide what specific behaviors to perform at work and how much effort to exert, is clearly influenced by national culture. The valence of work outcomes such as pay, job security, and the opportunities for interesting work is probably affected by national culture. Pay, for example, may have a very high valence for workers in poor, undeveloped countries where job-related income determines whether a worker can feed, clothe, immunize, and house his or her family.

Beyond determining the magnitude of valences for workers, however, the process by which workers decide what level of effort to expend at work can also depend on the values in national culture. For example, we talked in Chapter 10 about the free-rider tendency that can emerge in groups. There is some evidence that this tendency is linked to a collectivist versus an individualist orientation, so that, for example, free riding is more prevalent in cultures that are more attuned to the needs of the individual rather than of the group.[33] In countries that have a collectivist orientation, the need to associate with and be a part of the group curbs any incentive to free-ride. Similarly, it might be argued that in countries with high power distance, where inequalities between people are accepted, workers have less assurance that their level of performance will be linked to desired outcomes like promotion. Research on these issues is in its infancy, however, and although it seems clear that motivation is influenced by national culture, little is known about the nature of this relationship.

GROUPS AND TEAMS

Groups and teams are becoming an increasingly important tool that organizations use to increase their level of performance (see Chapters 10 and 11). Top-management teams, task forces, cross-functional teams, and self-managed work teams are all types of groups and teams that we have talked about in earlier chapters. In this chapter, we have discussed the importance of developing cross-cultural teams to facilitate global learning, as well as the communications problems that can emerge in such teams. Some researchers argue that teams function more effectively in some countries than in others because of differences in value systems among countries. As you might expect, groups in countries with collectivist values are likely to be more cohesive than are groups composed of members with individualistic orientations.[34]

In Japan, for example, children are socialized to collectivist values in school and in their neighborhoods, where the importance of conforming to group norms is taught from a very early age. When Japanese people join an organization, they already know how to behave in a group situation, and this knowledge facilitates the use of teams by the organization. In individualistic cultures, organizations need to teach people how to behave in groups and socialize them to group norms. A global organization that cultivates a culture that encourages cooperation rather than competition among workers in different countries may overcome the individualistic orientation of the national culture and improve group performance.

LEADERSHIP

Do leaders differ the world over? Are different styles of leadership appropriate in some countries but not in others? Do subordinates in different countries respond better to some leadership styles than to others? Research on this issue is in its infancy. However, as we discussed in Chapter 12, different styles of leadership work better in some contexts than in others. Because national culture (through its effect on organizational culture) is an important determinant of work context, it follows that expatriate managers need to carefully monitor the effect of their leadership style on their subordinates and modify it accordingly.

One research study found that a participative leadership style works best in a collectivist context with low power distance. However, it also found that the participative style is applicable to most contexts. According to another study, workers who live in countries where power distance is high and who accept inequality prefer a directive leadership style where the leader makes the decision and gives the orders.[35] In Mexico, for example, where power distance is high, a centralized, directive leadership style is preferred.[36]

COMMUNICATION AND DECISION MAKING

Global expansion greatly increases the problems associated with organizational communication and decision making. Basic language differences make encoding and decoding messages difficult, and physical distances and differences in time zones further complicate the communication process. We discussed earlier (see Chapter 13) how teleconferencing and other advanced technology can be used to increase coordination among divisions. Global networks can also be developed to speed the transfer of information around the world.

Given the communications problems experienced by global organizations, it is not surprising that global decision making is difficult. Different decision-making styles have been associated with different cultures. In collectivist cultures, group decision making is common and the group bears collective responsibility for the result of the decision. In individualistic, achievement-oriented cultures, one person typically makes the decision and is responsible for the outcome. Individual decision making is quicker than group decision making. Decisions made by a group, however, can be of a higher quality because more viewpoints and perspectives get shared, providing the group is diverse, of course (see Chapter 14).

We saw in Chapter 10 that the level of diversity can be a determinant of effective decision making in top-management teams and a lack of diversity can lead to groupthink. To avoid groupthink, it has been reported that Japanese organizations, with their collectivist orientations, typically first give a problem to be solved to the newest members of the group, because they are the ones least likely to be affected by groupthink.[37] Then the group as a whole meets to discuss the new members' recommendations.

Earlier in this chapter we discussed how organizations can design their structure to speed decision making. Decentralizing decision-making responsibility to lower-level managers in foreign countries is one important choice that an organization has to make in managing its global operations. Similarly, a strong global organizational culture and managers who share a common orientation help to promote effective decision making.

SUMMARY

The people who manage global organizations face the same set of challenges as the people who manage domestic operations. The global challenges, however, are often more difficult to meet because of differences in national culture. Some managers enjoy the challenge of global management and relish the prospect of going abroad to experience managing in new cultures. Others prefer to remain at home and let expatriate or foreign managers run operations abroad. Whatever their preference, in today's increasingly global environment, most managers at some point in their careers will encounter the need to enter the global environment, and then they will experience firsthand the motivation, leadership, communications, and other challenges of managing a global organization.

SUMMARY

Understanding and managing global organizational behavior begins with understanding the nature of the differences between national cultures and then tailoring an organization's strategy and structure so that the organization can manage its activities as it expands abroad. To succeed, global companies must help their managers to develop the skills that will allow them to work effectively in foreign contexts and deal with differences in national culture. In this chapter, we made the following major points:

1. A global organization is an organization that produces or sells goods or services in more than one country.
2. According to Hofstede's model of national culture, differences in the values and norms of different countries are captured by five dimensions of culture: individualism versus collectivism, power distance, achievement versus nurturing orientation, uncertainty avoidance, and long-term versus short-term orientation. Symbols, ceremonies, stories, and language are important means through which values are communicated to the members of a national culture.
3. To exploit the advantages of the global environment, an organization has to manage activities at the raw-materials, intermediate-manufacturing, assembly, distribution, and final-customer stages. Methods an organization can use to control these activities include exporting, licensing, joint ventures, and wholly owned foreign subsidiaries.
4. Global learning is learning how to manage suppliers and distributors and to respond to the needs of customers all over the world.
5. Global organizations can use three principal strategies to manage global expansion, each of which is associated with a type of global organizational structure: an international strategy and international divisional structure, a multidomestic strategy and global geographic structure, and a transnational strategy and global matrix structure. The more complex the strategy, the greater is the need to integrate the global organizational structure, and the stronger the global culture needs to be.
6. All the challenges associated with understanding and managing individual and group behavior that are found at a domestic level, such as motivating and leading workers and managing groups and teams, are found at a global level. Expatriate managers must adapt their management styles to suit differences in national culture if they are to be effective.

Organizational Behavior in Action

**TOPICS FOR
ACTION AND
DISCUSSION**

1. Why do organizations expand globally, and how would you expect differences in national culture to affect the choices organizations make about which countries to locate in?
2. In what ways do you think the culture of the United States may have changed on the five dimensions of Hofstede's model in the last twenty-five years?
3. What kinds of interpersonal or situational factors do you think are likely to trigger culture shock?
4. What are the advantages of joint ventures for global organizations?
5. Why is global learning so important in today's global environment?
6. What is the tension between globalization and customization?
7. When and why does a company move from an international to a multidomestic to a transnational strategy?
8. Why is a global geographic structure easier than a global matrix structure to manage?
9. How might a global organization go about developing a strong global organizational culture?
10. What factors might make it easier to motivate workers, manage teams, and make decisions in some national cultures than in others?

**BUILDING
DIAGNOSTIC
SKILLS**

Going Global

Pick a foreign company to study that has been in the news recently, or pick one you have some particular interest in, perhaps because its products appeal to you. Go to the library and, using magazines like *Business Week* or *Fortune,* locate some articles about this company and the country in which it is located. Then answer these questions:

1. Describe the culture of the country in which the company is based, using Hofstede's model to analyze its cultural values.
2. What kinds of goods or services does the company produce? What advantages does this company receive from its global activities?
3. What kind of strategy does this company use to expand globally? Has the strategy been successful? Why or why not?
4. What kind of structure does the company use to manage its strategy?
5. Did the company form any joint ventures with U.S. companies?
6. Has the company been experiencing any kinds of problems in the global arena?
7. Has the company encountered any problems in managing its global human resources?
8. What challenges do you think the company will face in the future on a global level?
9. Would you like to join the company? Why or why not?

RESEARCH ON THE INTERNET: A MANAGER'S TOOL

Specific Task

Every large organization usually needs to develop a viable global strategy to allow it to grow and prosper. Enter VIACOM Corporation's website (www. viacom.com/forbes.tin), and click on CEO Sumner M. Redstone's speech about "Innovative Strategies for the 21st Century."

1. What kind of opportunities and threats does Redstone think the global environment poses for VIACOM?
2. Why does Redstone think that VIACOM will prosper in the global environment?

General Task

Search for the website of a company that describes in detail the global challenges confronting the company and the way it is proposing to deal with them.

TOPICS FOR DEBATE

Differences in national culture cause problems for global organizations. Now that you understand the issues that global organizations and their managers confront, debate the following issues.

Debate One

Team A. Because the differences among national cultures are so great, an organization should let foreign managers run its foreign subsidiaries.

Team B. An organization should train expatriate managers to run foreign subsidiaries; otherwise, the organization may lose control over its foreign operations.

Debate Two

Team A. Moving the jobs of U.S. workers to foreign countries to reduce costs is unethical and will hurt the United States in the long run.

Team B. Moving the jobs of U.S. workers to foreign countries is necessary for companies to compete in a global market and will help the United States in the long run.

EXPERIENTIAL EXERCISE

Challenges for Expatriate Managers

Objective

Your objective is to help gain an understanding of the opportunities and problems facing expatriate managers and their families as they face the challenge of adjusting to the demands of a long-term foreign assignment.

Procedure

The class divides into groups of from three to five people, and each group appoints one member as spokesperson, to report the group's findings to the whole class.

Here is the scenario. You are a group of managers who are responsible for the construction of a new power station near Madras, India. The assignment will last for two years, and your families will join you one month after your arrival in India. You are meeting to brainstorm the opportunities and problems you will encounter during your stay abroad and to develop a plan that will allow you and your families to adjust successfully to your foreign assignment. As a first step you have identified three main challenges associated with planning for the Indian assignment: understanding the Indian culture; having successful interpersonal interactions with Indian managers, workers, and citizens; and finding ways to help your families adjust to India.

1. For each of the three challenges, list specific opportunities and problems that you think you will have to manage to make a successful adjustment to India. Which challenge do you think will be the most difficult to deal with? Which will be the easiest?
2. Outline the steps that you can take to ease your transition to India (a) before your arrival, (b) after your arrival, and (c) before and after your families' arrival.
3. What kinds of assistance and support do you expect your organization to provide as you plan for the Indian assignment?

When asked by your instructor, the spokesperson should be ready to describe your group's action plan. After all groups have reported, the class as a whole works to design the prototype of a plan that organizations can use to make the transition to a foreign country as smooth and productive as possible.

MAKING THE CONNECTION

Find an example of an organization that has been expanding its activities abroad and has been experiencing problems in managing its global activities. What is the nature of the problems it has encountered?

CLOSING CASE

How a Culture Clash Broke a Joint Venture

In 1992, Pittsburgh-based Corning Glass Works and Vitro, a Mexican glass-making company, formed a joint venture to share technology and market one another's glass products throughout the United States and Mexico. They formed their alliance to take advantage of the opportunities presented by the North American Free Trade Agreement (NAFTA), which opened up the markets of both countries to one another's products. At the signing of the joint venture, both companies were enthusiastic about the prospects for their alliance. Managers in both companies claimed that they had similar organizational cultures. Both companies had a top-management team that was still dominated by members of the founding families; both were global companies with broad product lines; and both had been successful in managing alliances with other companies in the past. Nevertheless, two years later Corning Glass terminated the joint venture and gave Vitro back the $150 million it had given Corning for access to Corning's technology. Why had the venture failed? The cultures and values of the two companies were so different that Corning managers and Vitro managers could not work together.

Vitro, the Mexican company, did business the Mexican way, in accordance with values prevailing in Mexican culture. In Mexico, business is conducted at a slower pace than in the United States. Used to a protected market, Mexican companies are inclined to sit back and make their decisions in a "very genteel," consensual kind of way.[38] Managers typically come to work at 9 a.m., spend two or more hours at lunch, often at home with their families, and then work late, often until 9 p.m. Mexican managers and their subordinates are intensely loyal and respectful to their superiors, the corporate culture is based on paternalistic, hierarchical values, and most important decision making is centralized in a small team of top managers. This centralization slows decision making because middle managers may come up with a solution to a problem but will not take action without top-management approval. In Mexico, building relationships with new companies takes time and effort because trust develops slowly. Thus personal contacts that develop slowly between managers in different companies are an important prerequisite for doing business in Mexico.

Corning, the American company, did business the American way, in accordance with values prevailing in American culture. Managers in the United States take short lunch breaks or work through lunch so they can leave early in the evening. In many American companies, decision-making authority is decentralized to lower-level managers, who make important decisions and commit their organization to certain courses of action. U.S. managers like to make decisions quickly and worry about the consequences later.

Aware of the differences in their approaches to doing business, managers from Corning and from Vitro tried to compromise and find a mutually acceptable working style. Managers from both companies agreed to take long working lunches together. Mexican managers agreed to forgo going home at lunchtime, and U.S. managers agreed to work a bit later at night so that they could talk to Vitro's top managers and thus speed decision making. Over time, however, the differences in management style and approach to work became a source of frustration for managers from both companies. The slow pace of decision making was frustrating for Corning's managers. The pressure by Corning's managers to get everything done quickly was frustrating for Vitro's managers. In the end, the Americans withdrew from what had seemed to be a promising venture. Corning's managers working in Mexico discovered that the organizational cultures of Vitro and Corning were not so similar after all, and they decided to go home. Vitro's managers also realized that it was pointless to prolong the venture when the differences were so great.

Corning and many other U.S. companies that have entered into global agreements have found that doing business in Mexico or in any other country is different from doing business at home. American managers living abroad should not expect to do business the American way. Because values, norms, customs, and etiquette differ from one country to another, expatriate managers must learn to understand the differences between their national culture and the culture of the host country if they are to manage global organizational behavior successfully.

Discussion Questions
  1. Why did Corning's managers and Vitro's managers experience culture shock when dealing with each other?
  2. What could have been done to overcome the culture shock and make the joint venture succeed?

Power, Politics, and Conflict

18

OPENING CASE

A Breakup at CIC Industries

Until the summer of 1997, the story of CIC Corp. (www. cicagency.com), located in College Station, Texas, was one of continuing success. CIC was founded in 1984 by two partners, David Hickson and Glenn S. Collins, III, who each took a 50-50 stake in the small business. CIC's strategy was to maintain and service high-tech equipment, such as CT scanners, X-rays, and lasers, in hospitals and universities

across the United States. Hickson's and Collin's new venture proved very successful, business increased very rapidly, and by 1997 the company had 150 employees. In 1997 they upgraded their service program so that all maintenance transactions could be handled electronically over the Internet using the company's in-house software programs. Since CIC's new Internet service could save hospitals up to 20 percent of their maintenance costs, savings that would amount to millions of dollars a year, hospitals flocked to join the program and CIC's future looked bright indeed.[1]

Imagine then the impact of the bombshell that occurred in July 1997. Hickson, on vacation with his family, returned to College Station to find that in his absence Collins had staged a coup. He found that he had been replaced as president by a CIC manager who was one of Collins's closest friends, that CIC managers and workers who had been loyal to Hickson had been fired, and that all the keys and security codes to CIC buildings had been changed so that he had no access to his office. Hickson immediately sought and obtained a legal restraining order from a judge that allowed him back into the company and reinstated fired employees. The judge also issued an order preventing the two men from taking any actions that were not part of their normal job duties.

Apparently this extraordinary situation had arisen because the two owners had not been able to agree on the company's future direction, a problem that had resulted in a deteriorating personal relationship between them. Since they both were equal owners, neither had power over the other to resolve the conflict, which as a result had become worse over time. Because of the conflict, different camps had formed in the organization, with different CIC managers being a member of one camp or the other and loyal either to Collins or Hickson.

In the months following this episode it became clear that the two men would be unable to resolve the conflicts and problems between them. The only solution to the conflict seemed to be for one person to buy out the other, and they each searched for bank financing to do so. Finally, in October 1997 it was announced that Hickson had purchased Collin's share of the business. However, the problems between the two men will apparently not be resolved there.[2] Collins immediately announced that he would use the money from his share of CIC to start his own company, Asset Management Technologies Corp., which would essentially provide the same kind of service as CIC. Thus, the two companies may become competitors in the years to come.

Overview

At CIC Industries Collins and Hickson battled for control of the company and used their power and positions in the organization to lobby for the support of managers. Essentially, both men were in conflict and were using their power to engage in politics to gain control of the whole company. In this chapter we explore power, politics, and conflict in organizations.

We discuss the nature of power and politics, how they can help and harm an organization, and where the power of individuals, functions, and divisions comes from. We survey the political tactics that managers can use to gain control of organizational resources. We then turn our attention to organizational conflict, examining its sources, the way a typical conflict plays out in an organization, and the strategies that can be used to manage conflict so that it helps rather than harms an organization. By the end of this chapter you will understand that power, politics, and conflict play central roles in organizational life and that one of a manager's important tasks is to learn how to manage these processes to increase organizational effectiveness.

The Nature of Power and Politics

Whenever people come together in an organization, their activities must be directed and controlled so that they can work together to achieve their common purpose and goals. **Power,** the ability of one person or group to cause another person or group to do something they otherwise might not have done, is the principal means of directing and controlling organizational goals and activities.[3]

Power

The ability of one person or group to cause another person or group to do something that they otherwise might not have done.

Managers often disagree about what an organization's goals should be and what the best ways of achieving them are. One way in which managers can attempt to control the decision-making process so that the organization pursues goals that support their interests is to use their power to engage in politics.[4] **Organizational politics** is activities in which managers engage to increase their power and to pursue goals that favor their individual and group interests.[5] Managers at all levels may engage in political behavior to gain promotion or to influence organizational decision making in their favor.

Organizational politics

Activities in which managers engage to increase their power and to pursue goals that favor their individual and group interests.

Is the use of power and politics to promote personal or group interests over organizational interests necessarily a bad thing? There are various answers to this question.

On the one hand, the terms *power* and *politics* often have negative connotations because people associate them with attempts to use organizational resources for personal advantage and to achieve personal goals at the expense of other goals. When Jacques Attali took over as head of the European Bank for Reconstruction and Development, for example, he took advantage of his power as head of the bank to make personal use of its resources. Attali spent over $1.5 million to change the marble in the bank's new London offices to suit his taste, and he spent almost the same amount to hire private planes for his personal use. During his reign at the bank, the organization spent $310 million on itself, twice the amount it invested or lent to countries in Eastern Europe and the former Soviet Union.[6] Managers who use (or, more correctly, abuse) power and politics to promote their own interests are likely to harm the interests of others—in this case, countries that were to receive aid from the bank.

On the other hand, power and politics can help organizations in a number of ways. First, when different managers or groups champion different solutions to a problem and use their power to promote these solutions, the ensuing debates over the appropriate course of action can help improve the quality of organizational decision making. In other words, **political decision making**—decision making characterized by active disagreement over which organizational goals to pursue and how to pursue them—can lead to a more efficient use of organizational resources. Second, different managerial perspectives can promote the change that allows an organization to adapt to its changing environment. When a **coalition,** a group of managers who have similar interests, lobbies for an organization to pursue new strategies or change its structure, the use of power can move the organization in new directions.[7]

Political decision making

Decision making characterized by active disagreement over which organizational goals to pursue and how to pursue them.

Coalition

A group of managers who have similar interests and join forces to achieve their goals.

We have more to say about organizational politics later in the chapter. For now, the main point is that power and politics can help an organization in two main ways: (1) Managers can use power to control people and other resources so that they cooperate and help to achieve an organization's current goals. (2) Managers can also use power to engage in politics and influence the decision-making process to help promote new, more appropriate organizational goals. An organization has to guard continually and vigilantly against managers who might use power to harm the organization.

Power-hungry managers are people to be feared and avoided. Nevertheless, power is necessary for the efficient functioning of organizations, and in any group of people the question of how to distribute power and establish a power structure is an important one. An organization's power structure—partially revealed by the organizational chart—derives from the formal and informal sources of the power that managers, functions, and divisions possess, which determines how the organization makes decisions and whose interests those decisions favor.

To see how power can be acquired formally and informally, it is necessary to examine where organizational power comes from. When managers at the top of an organization understand the sources of power, it is easy for them to manage power and politics to gain the benefits while minimizing the negative effects. Indeed, a prerequisite of managerial success is the ability to analyze and chart an organization's power structure accurately. Such an analysis enables managers to develop coalitions and build a power base from which they can influence organizational decision making.

Sources of Individual Power

Most individuals in an organization have some ability to control the behavior of other individuals or groups, but some have more power than others. From where do individuals in an organization get their power, and how do they get it? Researchers distinguish between the formal and informal power that individuals possess (see Fig. 18.1).[8]

SOURCES OF FORMAL INDIVIDUAL POWER

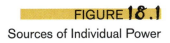 **Formal individual power**
Power that originates from a person's position in an organization.

Formal individual power is the power that stems from a person's position in an organization's hierarchy. When individuals accept a position in an organization, they accept the formal responsibility to carry out agreed-on tasks and duties. In return, the organization gives them formal authority to use its people and other resources to accomplish job-related tasks and duties.

FIGURE **18.1**

Sources of Individual Power

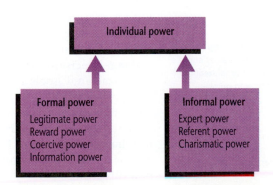

Formal power is a reflection of an individual's *legitimate, reward, coercive,* and *information* power.

Legitimate power
The power to control and use organizational resources to accomplish organizational goals.

Legitimate Power. **Legitimate power** confers on an individual the legal authority to control and use organizational resources to accomplish organizational goals.[9] The legitimate power of a CEO, for example, is granted by the organization's board of directors, which gives the CEO authority over all organizational resources. The CEO, in turn, has the right to confer legitimate power on managers lower down in the organization's hierarchy. Down through the hierarchy, upper-level managers give lower-level managers the authority to hire, fire, monitor, and oversee the behavior of subordinates. The CEO and lower-level managers also possess the power to withdraw authority from their subordinates, by firing, demotion, or otherwise stripping away a subordinate's authority to control organizational resources.

Legitimate power is the ultimate source of an individual's power in an organization. One day a CEO like Louis Gerstner of IBM may have a personal staff of 500 people, a private jet, a chauffeur-driven limousine, and the right to use a company's New York penthouse. But if a CEO is removed from office by the board of directors, the next day all of his or her authority and privileges are gone. The greater a manager's legitimate power is, the greater is the manager's responsibility and the more accountable is the person for his or her performance and use of organizational resources. This is why CEOs who perform poorly are quickly replaced, as the former CEOs of Westinghouse, Digital, General Motors, and many other badly performing companies have discovered.

Reward power
The power to give pay raises, promotion, praise, interesting projects, and other rewards to subordinates.

Reward Power. **Reward power** is the power to give pay raises, promotion, praise, interesting projects, and other rewards to subordinates. As long as subordinates value the rewards, a manager can use reward power to influence and control their behavior. In Chapter 5 on learning, we discussed how important positive reinforcement can be in influencing behavior, and in Chapters 6 and 7 we discussed how rewards can influence motivation.

The amount of rewards that an organization can give is limited. When extrinsic rewards such as raises and promotions are scarce, intrinsic rewards like praise and interesting job assignments can become more important. One challenge that managers face is motivating their subordinates when their ability to confer tangible rewards is limited.

Coercive power
The power to give or withhold punishment.

Coercive Power. **Coercive power** is the power to give or withhold punishment. Punishments range from suspension to demotion, termination, unpleasant job assignments, or even the withholding of praise and goodwill.

The ability to reward or punish subordinates gives supervisors great power, which is sometimes abused. As we discussed in Chapter 5, punishment has negative side effects and should be used with caution. It is for this reason that most organizations have clearly defined rules concerning when and how employees are to be rewarded or punished. Clearly specified rules and procedures that govern how coercive power and reward power are used prevent superiors from arbitrarily using their legitimate power to benefit their supporters and hurt opponents or people they simply dislike or disagree with.[10] The function of review boards and promotion committees in organizations, for example, is to ensure that people are promoted on the basis of merit and *what* they know, not *whom* they know.

In Chapter 6 we discussed the importance of perceptions of equity in determining motivation in organizations. No matter what rewards or punishments people actually receive, they compare their rewards or punishments to those received by referent others. If they feel inequitably treated, they may perform poorly, be dissatisfied with their jobs, or quit. The ability to confer rewards and punishments fairly and equitably is a crucial managerial skill, and organizations usually provide managers with written guidelines to help them perform this function.

 Information power

The power that stems from access to and control over information.

Information Power.   **Information power** is power stemming from access to and control over information.[11] The greater a manager's access to and control over information, the greater is his or her information power. The more information a manager possesses, the better able that person is to solve problems facing subordinates, and, as a result, the greater the subordinates' dependence on the manager. Some managers are reluctant to share information with subordinates. They fear that if subordinates know as much as the manager knows, the manager will lose the power to control and shape a subordinate's behavior.

Although individual managers sometimes benefit from keeping information to themselves and away from subordinates, the most effective organizations are those in which organizational members share, not hoard, information. Indeed, in organizations that recognize the value of empowering employees (see Chapter 14), managers deliberately decentralize authority to subordinates and make information easily available so that they can assume more responsibility for organizational activities and thus be more motivated.[12]

SOURCES OF INFORMAL INDIVIDUAL POWER

Several managers in a group or department may be at the same level in the organizational hierarchy or hold the same position, but some will have more power than others. Similarly, some lower-level managers may seem to have as much power and authority as higher-level managers—or even more. What accounts for this paradox? Power comes not only from an individual's formal position in an organization but also from a person's personality, skills, and capabilities. Power stemming from personal characteristics is **informal individual power**.[13] Researchers have identified several sources of it: *expert, referent,* and *charismatic* power.

Informal individual power

Power that stems from personal characteristics such as personality, skills, and capabilities.

Expert Power.   In any group, some individuals have skills or talents that allow them to perform at a higher level than others. In a group of engineers, there may be one or two individuals who always seem to find a simple or inexpensive design solution to a problem. In a group of salespeople, there may be a few individuals who always seem to land large new accounts. Group members often consult and look to such individuals for advice and in doing so come to depend on them. This dependence gives these individuals expert power over the others.

Expert power

Informal power that stems from superior ability or expertise.

Expert power is informal power that stems from superior ability or expertise in performing a task. Generally, people who possess expert power are promoted up the hierarchy of authority so that their informal power eventually becomes formal. Sometimes, however, individuals with expert power are mavericks: They have little ability or desire to assume formal authority over others. When that is the case, managers with formal power must take pains to develop good working relationships with subordinates who have expert power; otherwise, conflict may arise as formal leaders and informal leaders with expert power battle for control over people and resources. Insight 18.1 shows how powerful an informal leader can be.

Insight 18.1   Power

A Split in a Law Firm

In 1994 attorney Mark Dombroff and his team of 28 lawyers broke away from the 350-member law firm of Katten, Muchin & Zavis to form the independent firm of Dombroff & Gilmore in Washington, D.C. Dombroff, a powerful member of the larger firm's executive committee, left that company because of a power struggle with its comanaging partners—Muchin, Katten, and Zavis—over customer billing. Although Muchin, Katten, and Zavis were the formal leaders of the firm, Dombroff and his lawyers brought in over $12 million of revenues, 10 percent of the larger firm's gross receipts. Dombroff's legal expertise put him in a powerful position in the firm because of his group's ability to generate income. When the managing partners told Dombroff to increase the rate at which he billed his clients, however, he refused because of his belief that clients were paying as much as they could afford. In addition, Dombroff wanted to introduce some novel billing practices of his own, such as a form of "frequent client bonus" through which any client who spent $500,000 in fees with Dombroff could accrue points toward free legal services.

The managing partners of the firm did not like Dombroff's refusal to increase prices or his new billing proposals. Recognizing Dombroff's expert power and their inability to control him and his group if it came to a showdown, Muchin, Katten, and Zavis agreed to let Dombroff and his group split off to found their own firm. The split was so amicable that the partners of the larger firm lent the new firm $500,000 to start up. They wisely recognized that they would probably do business with Dombroff in the future and that it was best to maintain a good working relationship with a lawyer as powerful as he.

Referent power
Informal power that stems from being liked, admired, and respected.

Referent Power.   People who gain power and influence in a group because they are liked, admired, and respected are said to possess **referent power.** Individuals who are high on the personality traits of agreeableness, extraversion, or even conscientiousness are often liked or admired (see Chapter 2). Willingness to help others may also lead to someone's being liked or admired. Fame is one sign that a person has acquired referent power. Why are famous film stars and athletes paid to endorse goods and services? Advertisers expect their referent power to attract their admirers to buy the companies' products. People with referent power are liked because of who they are, not just because of their expertise or their ability to influence people, obtain resources, or secure their own ends.

Charismatic Power.   **Charismatic power** is an intense form of referent power stemming from an individual's personality or physical or other abilities, which induce others to believe in and follow that person.[14] In Chapter 12, we discussed how charismatic leaders—that is, leaders who possess charismatic power—often inspire awe in their followers, who buy into the leader's vision and work with excitement and enthusiasm toward goals set by the leader.[15] When charismatic power exists, legitimate power, reward power, and coercive power lose their significance because followers give the charismatic leader the right to hold the reins of power and to make the significant decisions that define the goals of an organization and its members.

> **Charismatic power**
> An intense form of referent power that stems from an individual's personality or physical or other abilities, which induce others to believe in and follow that person.

Many charismatic leaders can excite a whole organization and propel it to new heights, as have Michael Walsh at Tenneco, Lee Iacocca at Chrysler, and Bill Gates at Microsoft. But charismatic power can have a dark side, evident when followers of the charismatic leader blindly follow the leader and fail to take personal responsibility for their actions because they think the leader knows what is best for the organization. When charismatic power is abused by a leader who has a mistaken or an evil vision, no checks or balances exist to resist the leader's directives, no matter how outrageous they may be.

Some researchers have argued that charismatic leadership is an advantage only when a formal hierarchy of authority places some checks on the power of a charismatic leader.[16] Thus, only when the power of a charismatic CEO is balanced by the power of the board of directors is the CEO a force for good and someone who can stir people to work together to pursue common goals. An interesting contest between two charismatic people occurred at the Fox Broadcasting Network (see Insight 18.2).

Dreamworks, the new motion picture studio, was founded by three of the most charismatic and powerful people in Hollywood— Stephen Spielberg, the famous director, and the powerful movie moguls David Geffen and Jeffrey Katzenberg.

Insight 18.2

Power

A Clash of Charisma

In July 1994, the most powerful woman in television broadcasting, Lucie Salhany, was fired from her job as head of Fox Broadcasting by Rupert Murdoch, the owner of the network. The charismatic Murdoch, a multibillionaire, is arguably the most powerful person in global news and television broadcasting and is renowned for his ability to sense a business opportunity and capitalize on it. His knowledge of the telecommunications business is encyclopedic, and he is always ready to challenge his managers to stand up to him and disagree with him if they think he is wrong. The managers who cannot do so are the ones to go.

Standing up to Murdoch, however, was not Salhany's problem, for she is charismatic in her own right. According to reports, she is a genuinely nice person, and few people can withstand her intense charm and ability to convey to people that she fervently cares about them and their interests. But she also has the reputation of being the iron fist in a velvet glove. Until she clashed with Murdoch, she had consistently gotten her way.

One of Salhany's claims to fame is that, before she went to Fox, she syndicated the hugely successful television program *Star Trek: The Next Generation.* According to executives at Fox (who were stunned by her firing), her problem was that Murdoch likes executives to stand up to him only if they are doing well. Soon after Salhany's arrival at Fox, she made the decision to launch *The Chevy Chase Show,* which turned out to be spectacularly unsuccessful. Murdoch apparently never forgave her for this series (which bombed to the tune of $40 million) or for her support of a highbrow rather than a lowbrow approach to television programming.[17] Apparently, in a bottom-line business where performance is measured by Neilsen ratings and advertising dollars, charisma goes only so far. Even charismatic leaders have to be able to demonstrate their success, especially when they are dealing with a charismatic leader who has legitimate power.

Sources of Functional and Divisional Power

Although formal individual power, particularly legitimate power, is the primary source of power in organizations, managers in particular functions or divisions can take advantage of other sources of power to enhance their individual power. A division or function becomes powerful when the tasks that it performs give it the ability to control the behavior of other divisions or

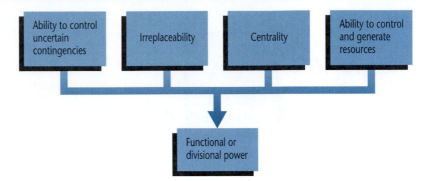

FIGURE **18.2**

Sources of Functional
and Divisional Power

functions, to make them dependent on it, and thus to increase its share of organizational resources (see Fig. 18.2).[18]

ABILITY TO CONTROL UNCERTAIN CONTINGENCIES

A contingency is an event or problem that must be planned for; an organization must have in place the people and resources to solve the problem. A function or division has power over others if it can reduce the uncertainty they experience or manage the contingency that is troubling them.[19] The marketing function, for example, often has power over the manufacturing function because it can forecast potential demand for a product (the contingency facing manufacturing). This ability reduces the uncertainty that manufacturing faces because it enables manufacturing to plan production runs so as to minimize costs. Similarly, the public relations department and legal function are able to manage problems for other functions after those problems have occurred, and in doing so they reduce uncertainty for those other functions and gain power over them. In general, functions or divisions that can solve the organization's problems and reduce the uncertainty it experiences are the ones that have the most power in the organization.[20]

IRREPLACEABILITY

A function or division gains power when it is irreplaceable—that is, when no other function or division can perform its activities.[21] In one study of a French tobacco plant, for example, Michael Crozier found that the relatively low-status repair engineers had great power in the plant. The plant managers were very respectful toward them.[22] The source of the engineers' power, Crozier discovered, was their irreplaceability. Although the engineering function was low in the formal hierarchy, the engineers as a group were the only employees who knew how to fix the plant's machines when they broke down. If they chose to, the engineers could cause problems for the manufacturing function. To maintain their status as irreplaceable employees, the engineers jealously hoarded their knowledge and refused to write it down.

All functions and divisions are irreplaceable to a certain degree. How irreplaceable they are depends on how easy it is to find a replacement for them. For example, many organizations assemble their products in low-cost foreign locations and thus reduce the power of the domestic manufacturing function relatively easily. Because it is difficult for an organization to gain access to high-quality research and development information, the R&D function in many companies is more irreplaceable than is manufacturing.

CENTRALITY

The power of a function or division also stems from its importance, or centrality, to the organization—that is, how central it is to the organization's operations and the degree to which it is at the center of information flows.[23] Central functions, whose activities are needed by many other functions, have access to a lot of information, which gives them power in their dealings with others.[24] The product development department, for example, has a high degree of centrality because R&D, engineering, marketing, and manufacturing all need product specifications in order to plan their activities. In the course of its dealings with other functions, product development acquires a lot of valuable information about many aspects of organizational activities—information that it can use to make other functions dependent on it.

ABILITY TO CONTROL AND GENERATE RESOURCES

The ability to control and generate resources for an organization is another source of functional and divisional power. The ability to control resources is, for example, a principal source of power for corporate headquarters managers.[25] These managers control the purse strings of the organization and have the ability to give or withhold rewards—money and funding—to functions and divisions. This ability is important because the more money a division is given, the more people it can hire and the more advanced facilities it can build so that it increases its chance of success. In contrast, when divisions are starved for funds, they cannot buy new technology to increase their efficiency, and this lack reduces their efficiency in the long run.

Although controlling resources is important, the ability to generate them is also important. The division whose goods and services provide the organization with the most profits will be the most important division in the organization. Very often, new CEOs and corporate headquarters staff are promoted from the divisions that have been most successful in generating resources. Most of IBM's current or past top managers came from its mainframe division, which until recently had provided most of IBM's revenues and profits. Similarly, most of General Motors' top managers came from its most important car divisions.

To fully understand the power structure of an organization, a manager needs to analyze all sources of power. The sources of individual power, such as position in the hierarchy, are the most important determinants of power. But a manager must also take into consideration the sources of functional and divisional power when determining the relative power of functional and divisional managers in the organization.

Organizational Politics: The Use of Power

Organizational politics are activities that managers engage in to increase their power. Once they acquire it, they can use power to influence decision making so that the organization pursues goals that favor their individual, functional, and divisional interests.

One reason many people engage in organizational politics is that jobs are a scarce resource.[26] The higher a manager rises in a hierarchy, the more difficult it is to continue to rise because fewer and fewer jobs are available at the upper levels. To compete for these scarce jobs and to increase their chance of promotion and their share of organizational resources, people try to increase their power and influence.[27] Without constant vigilance, organizational politics can get out of hand and prevent the organization from achieving its goals. For this reason, organizations must try to manage organizational politics to promote positive effects and prevent destructive effects.

To understand how organizations can manage politics, we need to look at the tactics that managers use to increase their individual power and the power of their functions and divisions.

TACTICS FOR INCREASING INDIVIDUAL POWER

Managers can use many kinds of political tactics to increase their power, to become expert at political decision making, and to increase their chance of obtaining their goals.[28] In the following pages we describe some commonly used tactics (see Fig. 18.3).

Tapping the Sources of Functional and Divisional Power.   The way in which functions and divisions gain informal power suggests several tactics that managers can use to increase their individual power. First, managers can try to make themselves irreplaceable.[29] For example, they may develop specialized skills such as knowledge of computers or special relationships with key customers that allow them to solve problems or limit uncertainty for other managers in the organization. Second, managers may specialize in an area of increasing concern to the organization so that they eventually control a crucial contingency facing the organization. Third, managers can try to make themselves more central in an organization by deliberately accepting responsibilities that bring them into contact with many functions or managers. Politically astute managers cultivate both people and infor-

FIGURE 18.3

Political Tactics for Increasing
Individual Power

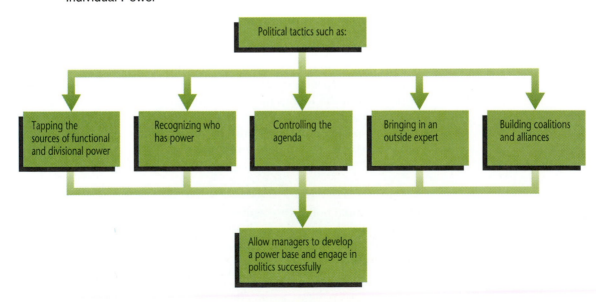

mation, and they are able to build up a personal network of contacts in the organization—contacts that they can use to pursue personal goals such as promotion.

Recognizing Who Has Power. Another way to increase individual power is to develop the ability to recognize who has power in the organization. With this knowledge a person knows whom to try to influence and impress. By supporting a powerful manager and being indispensable to him or her, it is possible to rise with that person up the organizational ladder. There are five factors to assess in order to determine the relative power of different managers in an organization.[30]

1. *Sources of Power:* Power has many sources in an organization. The power of a manager or subunit may come from legitimate authority, from the possession of scarce resources, or from expertise. A manager who assesses the source of various managers' power will learn whom to influence to obtain his or her objectives.
2. *Consequences of Power:* The people who have the most power can be identified by an assessment of who benefits the most from the decisions made in an organization. For example, managers compete for resources through the budgeting process, and obtaining access to scarce resources is a measure of how much power a manager has.
3. *Symbols of Power:* Many symbols of prestige and status are generally associated with power in an organization. Job titles, for example, are a prized possession, and titles such as "chief executive officer" and "president" confer great prestige on the officeholder. The use of a corporate jet or a chauffeured car, occupying a corner office with a wonderful view, and having a reserved parking place are other signs of power.
4. *Personal Reputations:* A person's reputation within an organization is likely to indicate the person's power to influence decision making.
5. *Representational Indicators:* The organizational roles a person or subunit plays and the responsibilities a person or subunit possesses are indications of power. A manager's membership on an influential committee, such as a company's operations committee, is a sign of the person's influence in organizational decision making. Managers who occupy central administrative roles have access to important information and derive power from this access. It strengthens their ability to make sound decisions and to alter the bargaining process in their favor.

By focusing on those five factors, a person new to an organization can assess which people or groups have the most power. Armed with this knowledge, the newcomer can make certain predictions about which groups will be favored by the decision-making process to receive a large share of organizational resources or will be protected from cutbacks if resources are scarce.

Once managers have accurately assessed the power structure of an organization and have obtained some individual power, they can use several other tactics to enhance their power.

Controlling the Agenda. An important tactic for influencing decision making is to control the agenda—that is, to determine what issues and problems decision makers will consider. The ability to control the agenda is one reason managers like to be members of or in charge of committees. By controlling the agenda, managers can limit the consideration of alternatives in the course of decision making. Powerful managers, for example, can prevent formal discussion of any issue they do not support by not putting the issue on the agenda.

Bringing in an Outside Expert.   When a major disagreement over goals emerges, as it often does when an organization is undergoing change or restructuring, managers know that every subunit is fighting to safeguard its own interests. Managers in charge of different functions want the ax to fall on functions other than theirs and want to benefit from whatever change takes place. Knowing that one function or one person's preferred alternative will be perceived by others as politically motivated and self-interested, a manager may bring in an outside expert who is considered to be a neutral observer. The manager then uses the "objective" views of this expert to support his or her position.

Building Coalitions and Alliances.   Managers may form a coalition with other managers to obtain the power they need to influence the decision-making process in their favor. Many coalitions result from agreements to trade support: Function A agrees to support function B on an issue of interest to function B, and in return function B supports function A on an issue of interest to function A. Skills in coalition building are important in organizational politics because functional interests frequently change as the organizational environment changes. Because of such changes, coalitions must be actively managed by their members.

The ability to forge coalitions and alliances with the managers of the most important divisions provides aspiring top managers with a power base from which they can promote their personal agenda. Having many friends enhances a manager's claims to power in the organization, but there is a downside to alliances: the possibility that individual members will request alliance support for losing propositions. It is particularly important for top-level managers to build personal relationships with members of the board of directors. CEOs need the support of the board in any contest between top managers; without it CEOs might lose their job to another top-level manager.

MANAGING ORGANIZATIONAL POLITICS

The exercise of power is an essential ingredient of organizational life, so it is important for an organization to manage organizational politics and harness it to support organizational interests. The management of organizational politics falls primarily to the CEO because only the CEO possesses legitimate power over all other managers. This power allows the CEO to control political contests so that they help rather than harm the organization. If the CEO is perceived as being weak, however, other top managers (who may possess their own stock of expert, referent, or charismatic power) will lobby for their own interests and compete among themselves for control of resources.

Power struggles sap the strength of an organization, waste resources, and distract the organization from achieving its goals. To avoid power struggles, an organization must have a strong CEO who can balance and manipulate the

TO MANAGERS

Managing Power and Politics

- Recognize that power and politics influence all behavior in organizations and that it is necessary to develop the skills to be able to understand and manage them.
- Analyze the sources of power in the function, division, and organization in which you work to identify powerful people and the organization's power structure.
- To influence organizational decision making and your chances of promotion, try to develop a personal power base to increase your visibility and individual power.

power structure so that no manager or coalition of managers becomes strong enough to threaten organizational interests. When there is a balance of power, the decisions that result from the political process are more likely to favor the long-term interests of the organization.

What Is Organizational Conflict?

Organizational politics gives rise to conflict as people or groups attempt to influence the goals and decision making of an organization to advance their own interests, usually at the expense of some other people or groups. **Organizational conflict** is the struggle that arises when the goal-directed behavior of one person or group blocks the goal-directed behavior of another person or group.[31]

▶ **Organizational conflict**
The struggle that arises when the goal-directed behavior of one person or group blocks the goal-directed behavior of another person or group.

The effect of conflict on organizational performance has received considerable attention. In the past, researchers viewed conflict as always bad or dysfunctional for an organization because they thought it led to lower organizational performance.[32] According to this view, conflict occurs because managers have not designed an organizational structure that allows people, functions, or divisions to cooperate to achieve corporate objectives. The current view of conflict is that, although it is unavoidable, it can often increase organizational performance if it is carefully managed.[33]

Figure 18.4 illustrates the effect of conflict on organizational performance. At first, conflict increases organizational performance. It exposes

FIGURE 18.4

The Effect of Conflict on
Organizational Performance

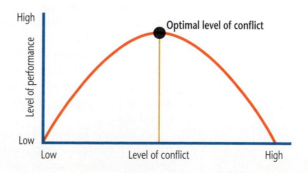

weaknesses in organizational decision making and design and prompts the organization to make changes. Managers realign the organization's power structure and shift the balance of power in favor of the group that can best meet the organization's needs. At some point—point A in Fig. 18.4—an increase in conflict leads to a decline in performance. Conflict gets out of control, and the organization fragments into competing interest groups.

The job of top managers is to prevent conflict from going beyond point A and to channel conflict to increase organizational performance. Thus managing conflict, like managing politics, is a way to improve organizational decision making and resource allocation to increase organizational effectiveness.

SOURCES OF ORGANIZATIONAL CONFLICT

Conflict, both between individuals and between groups, has many sources, and managers need to be aware of them so that when it occurs they can either control or resolve it. Three major sources of interpersonal and intergroup conflict are differentiation, task relationships, and scarcity of resources.[34]

DIFFERENTIATION

Recall from Chapter 15 that differentiation is the grouping of people and tasks into functions and divisions to produce goods and services. The splitting of the organization into functions or divisions may produce conflict because it brings to the surface differences in functional orientations and status inconsistencies.

Differences in Functional Orientations.   Different functions commonly develop different orientations toward the organization's major priorities. Their views of what needs to be done to increase organizational performance differ because their tasks differ. Manufacturing generally has a short-term, cost-directed efficiency orientation. Research and development is oriented toward long-term, technical goals, and sales is oriented toward satisfying customer needs. Thus manufacturing may see the solution to a problem as one of reducing costs, research and development as one of promoting product innovation, and sales as one of increasing demand.

Because of differences in functional orientation, functions have different views of organizational priorities. The differences can lead to conflict that does considerable harm because it undermines group cohesiveness and functional integration and thus lowers corporate performance.

Status Inconsistencies.   Over time some functions or divisions come to see themselves as more vital than others to an organization's operations and believe that they have higher status or greater prestige in the organization. In this situation, high-status functions make little attempt to adapt their behaviors to the needs of other functions, thus blocking the goals of other functions.[35] Similarly, functions that are most central to the company's operations may come to see themselves as more important than other functions and attempt to achieve their goals at the expense of the less central functions.

A dispute between Harvard professors and the editors of the *Harvard Business Review* provides an interesting example of conflict due to differences in functional orientation and status (see Insight 18.3).

Insight 18.3

Conflict

Magazine Trouble

In 1993 the task of managing the *Harvard Business Review* (*HBR*), a highly respected management publication, was removed from the direct control of the Harvard Business School and given to a company called the Harvard Business School Publishing Corp. (www.hbsp.harvard.edu). The reason for the change was to try to increase the circulation and revenues earned from *HBR*. A professional publishing staff was recruited to manage the journal, which in the past had been managed by the business school's own professors. Ruth M. McMullin was made chief executive of the holding company charged with directing the policy of *HBR*.

From the beginning, the venture seems to have been in trouble. Harvard Business School professors had traditionally seen themselves as having higher status (because they were the main contributors to the journal) than the magazine staff that edited their articles. But under McMullin, *Harvard Business Review* began to reflect a new vision. The review began to publish fewer articles by Harvard professors and to pursue ventures in which the professors had no stake and over which they had little control.

As conflict between professors and *HBR* over control of the journal increased, the editor was changed three times in twenty-two months, many members of the editorial staff left, and the editing and publication process slowed down. Many professors were annoyed that the salaries of many top staffers of the Harvard Business School Publishing Corp. were higher than their own. McMullin, for example, earned $400,000 a year, triple the salary of a typical Harvard professor.[36] The policy of publishing fewer articles written by Harvard professors and paying staffers such high salaries resulted in such a high level of conflict that McMullin resigned in 1994. She claimed that her views on running a professional publishing organization had diverged too far from those of the professors.

TASK RELATIONSHIPS

Task relationships generate conflict between people and groups because organizational tasks are interrelated and affect one another. Overlapping authority, task interdependence, and incompatible evaluation systems may stimulate conflict among functions and divisions.[37]

Overlapping Authority.   If two different functions or divisions claim authority for the same task, conflict may develop. Such confusion often arises when a growing organization has not yet fully worked out relationships between different groups. As a result, functions or divisions fight for control of a resource and thus spawn conflict, as happened at Harvard Business School. At the individual level too, managers can come into conflict over the boundaries of their authority, especially when one manager attempts to seize another's authority and resources. If a young manager starts to upstage his or her boss, for example, the boss may react by assigning the subordinate to relatively unimportant projects or by deliberately withholding the resources the person needs to do a good job.

Task Interdependencies.   The development or production of goods and services depends on the flow of work from one function to another; each function builds on the contributions of other functions.[38] If one function does not do its job well, the ability of the function next in line to perform is compromised, and the outcome is likely to be conflict. For example, the ability of manufacturing to reduce costs on the production line depends on how well research and development has designed the product for cheap manufacture and how well sales has attracted large, stable customer accounts. When one function fails to perform well, all functions suffer, as professors at Harvard Business School found when their articles were taking months to edit because of changes in staff.

The potential for conflict increases as the interdependence of functions or divisions increases. Thus, as task interdependence increases from pooled, to sequential, to reciprocal interdependence (see Chapter 11), the potential for conflict among functions or divisions increases.[39]

Incompatible Evaluation Systems.   Inequitable performance evaluation systems that reward some functions but not others sometimes create conflict.[40] Typical problems include finding ways to jointly reward sales and production to avoid scheduling conflicts that lead to higher costs or dissatisfied customers. Also, the more complex the task relationships between functions are, the harder it is to evaluate each function's individual contribution to performance and reward it appropriately, which also increases the likelihood of conflict.

SCARCITY OF RESOURCES

Competition for scarce resources produces conflict.[41] Conflict over the allocation of capital occurs among divisions and between divisions and corporate headquarters. Budget fights can be fierce when resources are scarce. Other organizational groups also have an interest in the way a company allocates scarce resources. Shareholders care about the size of the dividends. Employees want to maximize their salaries and benefits. Managers in competition for scarce resources may fight over who should get the biggest pay raise. The high salaries paid to *Harvard Business Review* staffers are an example of competition over scarce resources (money).

Pondy's Model of Organizational Conflict

Because conflict of one kind or another is inevitable in organizations, it is an important influence on behavior. One of the most widely accepted models of organizational conflict was developed by Louis Pondy.[42] Pondy viewed conflict as a dynamic process that consists of five sequential stages (see Fig. 18.5). No

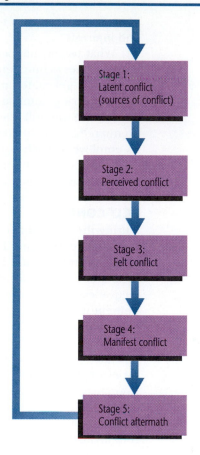

FIGURE 18.5

Pondy's Model of
Organizational Conflict

matter how or why conflict arises in an organization, managers can use Pondy's model to analyze a conflict and guide their attempts to manage it.

LATENT CONFLICT

In the first stage of Pondy's model there is no actual conflict. The potential for conflict to arise is present, though latent, because of the sources of conflict that we just examined.

PERCEIVED CONFLICT

The stage of perceived conflict begins when one party becomes aware that its goals are being thwarted by the actions of another party. Each party searches for the origins of the conflict, defines why the conflict is emerging, analyzes the events that led to its occurrence, and constructs a scenario that accounts for the problems it is experiencing with other parties. For example, the manufacturing function of a company may trace its production problems to defective inputs used in the assembly process. Manufacturing managers wonder why the inputs are substandard and after an investigation discover that the materials management function chooses to buy inputs from the lowest-cost sources of supply rather than paying for high-quality inputs. This decision reduces input costs and improves materials management's performance but raises production costs and worsens manufacturing's performance.

Manufacturing comes to see materials management as thwarting its goals and interests.

What usually happens at the stage of perceived conflict is that the conflict escalates as functions start to battle over the cause of the problem. In an attempt to get materials management to change its purchasing practices, manufacturing complains about materials management to the CEO or to anyone else who will listen. Materials management argues that low-cost inputs do not reduce quality and claims that manufacturing does not properly train its employees. Each party perceives the conflict and its causes differently. Thus, although both functions share the same goal of superior product quality, they attribute the cause of poor quality very differently.

FELT CONFLICT

During the stage of felt conflict the parties in conflict develop negative feelings about each other. Typically, each group closes ranks, develops an us-versus-them attitude, and blames the other group for the problem. As conflict escalates, cooperation between groups declines, as does organizational effectiveness. For example, it is almost impossible to speed new product development if materials management and manufacturing are fighting over the quality of inputs and final products.

As the parties in conflict battle and argue for their points of view, the significance of the disputed issue is likely to be blown out of proportion. Consider, for example, a relatively simple kind of conflict: conflict between roommates. Roommate A consistently neglects to put his dirty dishes in the dishwasher and clean the kitchen counters. To get the sloppy roommate to clean up, roommate B first makes a joke about the messy kitchen. If no change occurs in roommate A's behavior, roommate B starts to complain. If there is still no improvement, the roommates begin fighting and develop such antagonistic feelings toward each other that they not only cease to be friends but also start to look for other living arrangements. The original problem was relatively minor, but when roommate A did nothing to solve it, the problem escalated into something that became increasingly difficult to manage.

To avoid a loss of effectiveness, organizations want to prevent conflict from escalating and prefer managers, functions, or divisions to collaborate on a solution. People or groups can handle conflict with others in five basic ways: compromise, collaboration, accommodation, avoidance, and competition (see Fig. 18.6).[43] The horizontal axis of Fig. 18.6 measures the degree to which one party is concerned with obtaining its own goals. The vertical axis measures the extent to which the party is concerned with helping some other party achieve its goals. Using this model, it is possible to compare the different way of handling conflict during the felt stage.

At the middle of the figure is *compromise*. Compromise usually involves bargaining and negotiation to reach a solution that is acceptable to both parties. Sometimes, the parties in dispute use *collaboration* to find a solution: Each side tries to satisfy not only its own goals but also the goals of the other side. Collaboration can benefit an organization because the parties work together to find a solution that leaves them both better off. Compromise and collaboration enable the parties in dispute to solve their differences.

Accommodation is a style of handling conflict in which one party simply allows the other to achieve its goals. With *avoidance,* both parties refuse to rec-

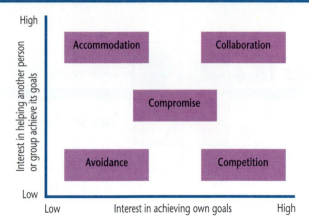

FIGURE 18.6

Ways of Handling Conflict

ognize the real source of the problem and act as if there were no problem. Both of these conflict solutions are unsatisfactory from the organization's perspective and from the perspective of one or both of the parties in conflict. Accommodation means that one group uses its power to force the other to submit—to accommodate to its demands. This solution is unlikely to lead to cooperation; furthermore, the weaker party is likely to become resentful and be on the lookout for any opportunity to get back at the stronger party. Similarly, avoidance means that the conflict will smolder and the parties will remain uncooperative or uncommunicative.

Competition leads to the greatest and most visible conflict. Each party is looking out for its own interests and has little interest in understanding the other's position or taking the other's needs into account. When a conflict is handled competitively, or when accommodation or avoidance are typical styles of handling conflict, the conflict escalates to the next stage in Pondy's model.

MANIFEST CONFLICT

In the stage of manifest conflict, one party decides how to react to or deal with the party that it sees as the source of the conflict, and both parties try to hurt each other and thwart each other's goals.

Manifest conflict can take many forms. Open aggression or even violence between people and groups may occur. There are many stories and myths in organizations about boardroom fights in which managers actually came to blows as they sought to promote their interests. Infighting in the top-management team is a more indirect form of aggression that occurs as managers seek to promote their own careers at the expense of others in the organization. When Lee Iacocca was at Ford, for example, Henry Ford II decided to bring in the head of General Motors as the new Ford CEO. Within one year, Iacocca engineered the new CEO's downfall to clear his own path to the top. Eventually, he lost the battle when Henry Ford forced him out because he feared that Iacocca would take his power.

The story of a fight between a father and son for control of a major corporation because of the son's desire to supplant his aged father shows how destructive manifest conflict can be if nothing is done to stop it (see Insight 18.4).

Insight 18.4

Diversity

The Darts Are Being Thrown

The $1.3 billion Dart Group, which owns large stakes in Crown Books, the nation's third largest book merchant, and Track Auto, a discount auto parts chain, is headed by 72-year-old Herbert Haft, chairman. Haft, who earned a reputation as a corporate raider from his attempts to take over Safeway and Eckerd Corporation, keeps close control over his company and is known for his centralized management style.[44] In 1977 his son, Robert Haft, joined him as a manager in the Dart Group after leaving Harvard Business School. Later Robert became chairman of Crown Books and his father's heir apparent as chairman of the Dart Group.

By 1993, tired of waiting for his father to retire as chairman and pass the reins of power to him, Robert formed a plan to remove his father as head of the Dart Group. With the support of his mother and sister (large stockholders) he devised a succession plan to take his father's position—a plan he thought would benefit his whole family in the long run. When his father discovered the plan, he was outraged by his son's audacity and reacted in a way that Robert had not foreseen. The elder Haft took immediate steps to reduce the power his son had developed in the corporation and to consolidate his own position. He started by relieving Robert of his duties as chairman of Crown and then fired him after the details of his plot and the extent of the involvement of other family members became more apparent.

Robert Haft admitted his mistake and attempted a reconciliation, commenting that "my heart is always open to my father."[45] Herbert Haft, however, had no desire to welcome Robert back into the family business, and the anger between him and his wife led them to begin divorce proceedings. As part of the divorce settlement, she demanded her share of the Dart Group, which then presumably she would hand over to her son. The Haft family is totally estranged because of Herbert Haft's desire to keep his power and control of the corporation that he founded.

Manifest conflict between groups such as teachers and parents, prisoners and guards, and unions and managers is also common. In the past, for example, in industrial disputes managers often obtained their goals by using tactics such as sabotage, strikebreaking, hiring new workers as permanent replacements for striking workers, and physical intimidation.

Manifest conflict also takes the form of a lack of cooperation between people or functions, a result that can seriously hurt an organization. If organizational members do not cooperate, integration falls and an organization cannot achieve its goals. One particularly dysfunctional kind of manifest conflict occurs when parties accommodate to or avoid managing a conflict. In this situation, one party might try to frustrate the goals of its opponent by passivity—that is, by doing nothing. Suppose there is a history of conflict between sales and production but sales desperately needs a rush order for an important client. What might manufacturing do? One strategy is to agree informally to sales' requests and then do nothing. When sales comes banging on the door looking for its products, manufacturing says: "Oh, you meant *last* Friday. I thought you meant *this* Friday." In general, the stronger manifest conflict is, the more organizational effectiveness suffers because coordination and integration between managers and subunits fall.

Managers need to do all they can to prevent manifest conflict from becoming dysfunctional and to intervene as early as possible in this stage. If they cannot prevent the breakdown in communication and coordination that usually occurs in this stage, the conflict advances to the last stage: the conflict aftermath.

CONFLICT AFTERMATH

Sooner or later conflict in an organization is resolved in one way or another—someone gets fired, a CEO tells a division to shape up, the organization gets reorganized, or the conflict becomes so bad that the organization fails. Regardless of the outcome, it is almost certain that the causes of the conflict will arise again in another context. Suppose that sales, still angry over the earlier "mix-up" with manufacturing, approaches manufacturing with a new request. How will these functions behave? Probably their wariness and lack of trust will make it hard for them to agree on anything. Now suppose that after the earlier encounter sales and manufacturing were able to solve their dispute amicably through compromise and collaboration. In that case, when sales next has a special request for manufacturing, the two departments will be able to sit down together and work out a joint plan that suits the needs of both functions.

Every conflict episode leaves a conflict aftermath that affects the way both parties perceive and respond to a future conflict episode. If conflict can be resolved by compromise or collaboration before it progresses to the manifest stage, the conflict aftermath will promote good future working relationships. But if conflict is not resolved until late in the process, the competition that takes place will result in a conflict aftermath that sours future working relationships and leads to an organizational culture poisoned by the presence of permanently uncooperative relationships.

Conflict Management Techniques

One of management's major responsibilities is to help parties in conflict—subordinates, functions, or divisions—cooperate in resolving their disputes. Indeed, much of a manager's time can be spent in managing conflict. Many conflict management techniques exist to help managers handle conflict in ways that lead to cooperative, functional outcomes rather than competitive, dysfunctional outcomes. Some of these techniques are aimed at changing the attitudes and behavior of individuals in conflict. Some are aimed at changing troublesome task relationships between people or groups. Some are aimed at changing the structure of the organization and the situation that caused the conflict.

INDIVIDUAL-LEVEL CONFLICT MANAGEMENT

The management of conflict between individuals is accomplished by techniques designed to change the attitudes or behavior of those involved in the conflict.[46] If the conflict is due to a clash of personalities and the parties in conflict simply do not understand one another's point of view, the organization can help the people involved by bringing in outside help to give advice and counsel. Education and sensitivity and awareness training help people learn to understand and to deal with those who are not like themselves. If the conflict is due to workforce diversity—such as when a young person supervises older, more experienced workers or a female manager supervises an all-male work group—the organization can use education and training to help employees appreciate the differences in their attitudes and avoid or successfully resolve conflict.

If the conflict is the result of dispute between a few key organizational members and education and training do not help, another solution is to move people around. Managers can transfer people to new positions in which they can learn to appreciate others' points of view. Job rotation and temporary assignments to new departments or even to new countries help people to develop fresh perspectives on issues in dispute. Promotion can also be used to change attitudes. Management might deal with troublesome union shop stewards by making them supervisors and with troublesome manufacturing managers by promoting them sideways into a position in training, plant security, or elsewhere. In this way parties to the conflict are permanently removed from the conflict situation. As a last resort, an organization can fire the people involved and replace them with others who have no history of dysfunctional conflict. Replacing the CEO or other top managers is one common method of eliminating conflict.

GROUP-LEVEL CONFLICT MANAGEMENT

Group-level techniques are aimed at changing the attitudes and behaviors of groups and departments in conflict.[47] Managers can physically separate work groups, deny them the opportunity to interact face to face, and thus eliminate the potential for direct conflict. Coordination between separate groups is then made possible by using integrating roles (see Chapter 15) and giving some people the full-time responsibility to coordinate the groups' activities while keeping them physically separate. Sometimes, managers can develop rules and standard operating procedures to coordinate the groups' activities or can give them common goals, which allow them to achieve goals simultaneously.

Often, techniques to reduce direct conflict between work groups provide only a temporary solution to the problem. If the underlying causes are not addressed, the conflict is never truly solved, and the level of integration in the organization falls as does performance. Because few organizations can afford this outcome, most usually try to resolve the conflict at its source. One strategy that organizations pursue is to adopt individual-level conflict management techniques and fire, transfer, or replace people. Another strategy is to get the groups in conflict to sit down and work out a joint solution.

Negotiation is a process in which groups with conflicting interests meet together to make offers, counteroffers, and concessions to each other in an effort to resolve their differences.[48] Direct negotiations between groups are held either with or without a **third-party negotiator**—an outsider who is

Negotiation
A process in which groups with conflicting interests meet together to make offers, counteroffers, and concessions to each other in an effort to resolve their differences.

Third-party negotiator
An outsider skilled in handling bargaining and negotiation.

Mediator

A neutral third party who tries to help parties in conflict reconcile their differences.

Arbiter

A third party who has the authority to impose a solution to a dispute.

skilled in handling bargaining and negotiation. The third party facilitates the bargaining process and helps the parties in dispute find a solution to their problem.[49] Sometimes the common superior of the parties in conflict acts as the third party. If the third party plays the role of **mediator,** he or she takes a neutral stance and helps the parties to reconcile their differences. If the parties cannot find an equitable solution, the third party may act as **arbiter,** or judge, and impose a solution. The way Gerald Levin solves conflicts between top managers at Time Warner shows that a CEO can handle conflict and politics in a way that helps an organization build a competitive advantage (see Insight 18.5).

Competitive Advantage

Managing Conflict at Time Warner

In 1993 Gerald M. Levin took full control of Time Warner (www. pathfinder.com) after the death of its charismatic CEO, Steven Ross. Ross had been well known for his flamboyant style and social contacts with entertainment giants like Steven Spielberg and Barbra Streisand. He whisked the Warner studio's stars around on corporate jets, used his homes in Aspen and Acapulco to entertain them, and did all he could to maintain their commitment to Time Warner and his company's competitive position. The introverted Levin has a different, low-key style. His focus is internal, and he uses his expert power to manage Time Warner's far-flung empire and reduce the company's huge debt.

Levin adopted a very decentralized style to manage the Time Warner empire. Time Warner's five major divisions are Time Inc. Magazines, HBO, Warner Brothers Motion Pictures, Warner Music, and Time Warner Cable. With such highly interrelated activities there is always the potential for interdivisional conflict. When divisions do come into conflict, Levin's strategy has been to act as mediator: He helps the divisions solve their problems but ultimately lets them find the solution. One continuing source of conflict is the price HBO should pay Warner Brothers Motion Pictures for the rights to show Warner Brothers movies. Obviously, the less HBO pays, the bigger its profits are, and the less Warner Brothers receives, the lower its profits are. Levin allows the divisions to negotiate their own solution to this recurring problem.

Divisional managers at Time Warner are fiercely loyal to Levin because of his decentralized management approach and his recognition that, for the best long-run result the divisions must be allowed to find their own solutions. Levin's low-key style has been less well received by people outside Time Warner, in the flamboyant entertainment business. They perceive his conciliatory style to be a sign of weakness, and they compare Levin unfavorably with charismatic Steve

Ross, who was known for rushing in and imposing his own solution on managers in conflict.

There have been persistent rumors that Time Warner's big shareholders neither like nor understand Levin's style. According to one rumor, Edgar Bronfman, Jr., heir to the Seagram fortune, is interested in taking control of Time Warner (Seagram already owns 15 percent of Time Warner shares). Bronfman would then install as CEO one of his high-profile friends—perhaps Michael Ovitz, the charismatic head of Creative Artists Agency, a company that manages the interests of many famous entertainers.

Reacting to the need to raise his visibility and to demonstrate that he really is in control, Levin has been taking steps to increase his profile and to demonstrate his power. He has begun to visit movie stars like Kevin Costner and Clint Eastwood on the sets of their Warner movies and has been increasing his wining and dining of the entertainment industry's most important players. Clearly, the CEO of an entertainment giant like Time Warner needs to be able to manage people and groups inside and outside the organization to promote the company's competitive advantage. To maintain his position, his power, and his ability to resolve conflict in the huge Time Warner empire, Levin needs to increase his referent power and use all of the resources of his position to his advantage.

Conflict management through negotiation involves influencing people's attitudes. In any bargaining situation, two different processes go on simultaneously: (1) distributive bargaining, in which the parties divide the resources, deciding who gets what and how much (Warner Brothers and HBO, in Insight 18.5, are engaging in distributive bargaining), and (2) attitudinal structuring, in which the parties try to influence their opponent's attitudes, try to appear aggressive in order to increase their share of the resources, or perhaps act in a conciliatory manner to preserve long-term working relationships, save face, or demonstrate how much power they have should they choose to use it.[50]

One of the most common types of negotiation and bargaining takes place between unions and management during contract talks. Suppose this year management is in a strong position because the economy is in recession. When management and the union sit down to negotiate, management crushes the union, which goes back to its members empty-handed. Next year, the economy has recovered, and the negotiations begin again. What will be the attitude of the union this time? Management probably will confront a no-holds-barred attempt to beat management and get everything the union thought it should have gotten last year.

When two parties are in continual negotiation with one another, they realize that, for the survival of the organization, they need to adopt a long-term perspective that emphasizes their joint objectives and minimizes differences. Union and management negotiators often develop long-term relationships with one another and try to cooperate because they know that stalemates and attempts to destroy each other result in an antagonistic, destructive conflict aftermath in which everybody loses. Negotiation and bargaining are difficult and delicate processes in which the art of give-and-take and posturing for position is finely developed. Negotiations typically take place over a period of months as the parties discover what they can and cannot get. This is true of negotiations not only between management and unions but also between corporate headquarters managers and divisional managers and between managers and subordinates as they discuss pay and promotion.

ORGANIZATIONAL-LEVEL CONFLICT MANAGEMENT

Conflict management at the organization level involves modifying the organizational structure and culture to resolve ongoing conflicts and to lessen the occurrence of conflict. By clarifying task and reporting relationships, good organizational design reduces the potential for latent conflict to arise in the first place. There are many ways to change organizational structure and culture to reduce conflict.[51]

Managers can change the level of differentiation and integration in the organization. Recall from Chapter 15 that conflict can arise if a growing organization continues to use a functional structure when some form of divisional structure is more appropriate. Manufacturing managers may complain that R&D managers are working too slowly on essential product developments and come into conflict with R&D managers, who complain that they are being forced to work on too many different products at the same time. If the company moves to a product structure and assigns different R&D managers to develop different products, the speed of product development will increase, and the level of conflict will be reduced.

Another way to manage conflict at the organizational level is to increase the level of integration between functions or divisions by employing more complex kinds of integrating mechanisms. Suppose managers from sales, R&D, manufacturing, and product design are coming into conflict because they have different ideas about the kinds of goals the organization should be pursuing. One way to solve this problem is to put the managers in a team and increase the intensity of their interaction so that they can learn about each other's different perspectives or orientations. A matrix structure offers another way to prevent or manage conflict by providing for intense interactions among people. But, although the lack of barriers in a matrix structure decreases conflict, conflict due to role ambiguity is a potential source of conflict that must be carefully managed.

Organizational culture also has an important role to play in reducing the potential for conflict in an organization. If a strong set of organizational values and norms exists, people in different functions or divisions share a vision of the organization. A common vision helps reduce conflict and makes conflict much easier to manage when it occurs. Despite the disputes between managers and workers at UPS, discussed in Insight 15.4, both groups were strongly committed to the success of their organization, and their joint commitment helped them to patch up their differences.

Organizations use all three types of conflict management techniques to resolve and manage conflict in the work setting. Conflict can never be eliminated because differences in interests and in attitudes, as well as competition over resources, are integral to the way organizations operate. For the outcome of conflict to be beneficial, organizational members have to learn how to deal with conflict when it occurs and to adopt the appropriate way of resolving it.

Understanding and managing conflict is an important part of a manager's job and an important aspect of organizational behavior at all levels.

Managing Conflict

- Recognize that conflict is an enduring part of organizational behavior, and develop the skills to be able to analyze and manage it.
- When conflict occurs, try to identify its source and move quickly to intervene to find a solution before the problem escalates.
- Whenever you make an important change to role and task relationships, always consider whether the change will create conflict. Recognize that good organizational design can prevent conflict from emerging.
- Recognize that the appropriateness of a conflict management strategy depends on the source of the conflict.

SUMMARY

Understanding and managing power, politics, and conflict is an integral part of a manager's job. Organizations are composed of people who come together to achieve their common goals. When resources are scarce, people and groups have to compete for them; some achieve their goals while others do not. In an organization, managers have the primary responsibility to ensure that competition for resources is free and fair and that people who obtain power over resources do so because they possess skills and abilities that will, in the long run, benefit all members of the organization. Managers also have the responsibility to manage conflicts as they arise to ensure the long-term success of the organization and to maintain a balance of power to ensure that politics and conflict benefit rather than harm the organization. In this chapter, we made the following major points:

1. Power is the ability of one person or group to cause another person or group to do something they otherwise might not have done. Politics is activities in which managers engage to increase their power and to pursue goals that favor their indi-

vidual and group interests. Power and politics can benefit or harm an organization.

2. Sources of formal individual power include legitimate power, reward power, coercive power, and information power. Sources of informal individual power include expert power, referent power, and charismatic power.

3. Sources of functional and divisional power include the ability to control uncertain contingencies, irreplaceability, centrality, and the ability to control and generate resources.

4. Managers can use many kinds of political tactics to increase their individual power. These tactics include making oneself irreplaceable and central, controlling contingencies and resources, recognizing who has power, controlling the agenda, bringing in an outside expert, and building coalitions and alliances. Managing politics to obtain its positive effects requires a balance of power in an organization and a strong CEO who has the ability to keep powerful people and groups in check.

5. Conflict is the struggle that arises when the goal-directed behavior of one person or group blocks the goal-directed behavior of another person or

group. Whether conflict benefits or harms an organization depends on how it is managed.

6. The three main sources of conflict are differentiation, task relationships, and the scarcity of resources. When conflict occurs, it typically moves through a series of stages. In Pondy's model of conflict, these stages are latent conflict, perceived conflict, felt conflict, manifest conflict, and the conflict aftermath.

7. Various techniques are available to manage conflict. Conflict management techniques can be used at the individual, group, and organizational levels.

Organizational Behavior in Action

TOPICS FOR DISCUSSION AND ACTION

1. In what ways can the use of power and politics help or harm an organization?
2. What are the principal sources of a manager's formal power and informal power? How does the way a manager exercises power affect subordinates?
3. Think of a manager you have worked under or a leader you have been in close contact with. What were the main sources of this person's individual power? What was your reaction to the way this person exercised power?
4. What are the main sources of functional and divisional power?
5. Why is it important to have a power balance in an organization?
6. In what ways can the manager of a function deliberately set out to gain power inside an organization?
7. Why may conflict be good or bad for an organization?
8. What are the main sources of conflict between functions?
9. Why is it important for managers to try to reduce manifest conflict and create a good conflict aftermath?
10. What are the main conflict resolution strategies?

BUILDING DIAGNOSTIC SKILLS

Understanding Conflict and Politics

Think of the last time you came into conflict with another person or group, such as a manager you worked for or even a friend or family member. Then answer these questions:

1. Was this the first time you came into conflict with this party, or was the conflict one in a series of conflicts?
2. What was the source of the conflict? Did you and the other party see the source of the conflict differently? If so, why?
3. How would you describe the way you both reacted to the conflict?
4. Did the conflict reach the stage of manifest conflict? If it did not, how did you manage to avoid coming into manifest conflict? If it did, what form did the manifest conflict take?
5. How was the conflict resolved?
6. What kind of conflict aftermath resulted from the way you or the other party managed the conflict?
7. How well do you think you managed the conflict with the other party?
8. Given what you know now, how could you have handled the conflict more effectively?

RESEARCH ON THE INTERNET: A MANAGER'S TOOL

Specific Task

All organizations need to manage their relationships with their stakeholders effectively, but they can do this in different ways. Enter Cypress Semiconductor's website (www.cypress.com), click on news at Cypress semiconductor, and look at the letter Cypress's CEO, T. J. Rodgers, wrote to Doris Gormley, a Cypress shareholder.

1. What is the source of the conflict between Gormley and Rodgers?
2. What is Rodgers' approach to managing the source of the conflict? How does his management style affect his approach?

General Task

Search for the website of a company that has been experiencing one of the types of conflict discussed in the chapter. What is the source of the conflict and how are the parties involved in the conflict trying to manage it?

TOPICS FOR DEBATE

Organizational politics and conflict are part of the fabric of behavior in organizations. Now that you understand how these processes work in organizations, debate the following issues.

Debate One

Team A. The use of power by self-interested managers and groups has the potential to do an organization more good than harm.

Team B. The use of power by self-interested managers and groups has the potential to do an organization more harm than good.

Debate Two

Team A. The most effective way to manage conflict is to change the people involved rather than to change the situation.

Team B. The most effective way to manage conflict is to change the situation rather than to change the people involved.

EXPERIENTIAL EXERCISE

Managing Conflict Successfully

Objective

Your objective is to gain an appreciation of the conflict process and to understand the difficulties involved in managing conflict successfully.

Procedure

The class divides into groups of from three to five people, and each group appoints one member as spokesperson, to report on the group's findings to the whole class. Here is the scenario.

You are a group of top managers who have been charged with resolving an escalating conflict between manufacturing and sales managers in a large company that manufactures office furniture. The company's furniture can be customized to the needs of individual customers, and it is crucial that sales provides manufacturing with accurate information about each customer's specific requirements. Over the last few months, however, manufacturing has been complaining that sales provides this information too late for it to make the most efficient use of its resources, that sales is increasingly making errors in describing each customer's special needs, and that sales demands unreasonably quick turnaround for its customers. For its part, sales is complaining about sloppy workmanship in the final product, which has led to an increased level of customer complaints, about increasing delays in delivery of the furniture, and about manufacturing's unwillingness to respond flexibly to unexpected last-minute customer requests. Problems are increasing, and in the last meeting between senior manufacturing and sales managers harsh words were spoken during a bitter exchange of charges and counter charges.

1. As a group, use the concepts discussed in this chapter (particularly Pondy's model) to analyze the nature of the conflict between manufacturing and sales. Try to identify the sources of the conflict and ascertain how far the conflict has gone.
2. Devise a detailed action plan for resolving the conflict. Pay particular attention to the need to create a good conflict aftermath. In devising your plan, be sure to analyze (a) the obstacles to resolving the conflict, (b) the appropriate conflict management techniques to use, and (c) ways to design a new control and reward system to help eliminate such conflict in the future.

When asked by your instructor, the spokesperson will describe your group's analysis of this conflict between functions and the action plan for resolving it.

MAKING THE CONNECTION

Find an example of an organization in which two or more managers, functions, or divisions have been coming into conflict or have been engaged in a power struggle for control of organizational resources. What was the source of the problem, how are they behaving toward one another, and how is the problem being managed?

CLOSING CASE

A Power Struggle in a Power Company

Virginia Power, a regulated utility company based in Richmond, Virginia, is owned by Dominion Resources, an unregulated corporation. Virginia Power, which accounts for 90 percent of Dominion's profits, is headed by James T. Rhodes, a former nuclear engineer whose low-key, conservative management style endears him to the management team of engineers who run Virginia Power. Rhodes reports to Thomas E. Capps, the chairman of Dominion Resources, a flamboyant lawyer and financier who has no interest in the workings of a utility and is mainly concerned with finding ways to increase the return of the power company to its shareholders by, for example, finding tax advantages to exploit.

Since 1992, when the two men assumed their present positions, they have been engaged in a bitter power struggle that has escalated as each month has gone by. Capps, a consummate deal maker, has alienated Rhodes by attempting to reduce Rhodes's power: He centralized support functions at Dominion's headquarters and tried to engineer mergers with other utility companies, which would lessen Rhodes's power by making Virginia Power less central and important to Dominion.

Rhodes has resisted Capps's attempts to interfere in Virginia Power's affairs. He sees Capps as someone looking for a quick fix and not at the long-term interests of Virginia Power. Although Rhodes reports to Capps, Virginia Power's status as a regulated utility makes the question of how much power Capps has over Rhodes ambiguous; much of Rhodes's power derives from state regulations. Rhodes has exploited Virginia Power's regulated status to resist Capps's attempts to influence and control what he does.

In fact, for several months in 1993 not only did Capps lose control over Rhodes but Rhodes gained control over Capps. Rhodes used his power as the major generator of Dominion's resources and threatened that he and his top-management team would leave the utility unless the board of directors agreed to ask Capps to resign. Capps, 58 years old, believing that he had lost the support of the board, agreed to resign at age 60. The board of directors appointed James Betts, a senior member of the board, to keep the peace between Rhodes and Capps until Capps left.

Still in a position of power, Capps began to lobby individual board members to regain their support. He accused Rhodes of being disloyal to the board and pointed out the many ways in which he (Capps) had helped Dominion. With some board members wavering, Capps, who was still Dominion's CEO, then increased the number of board members from twelve to fifteen and appointed supporters. Before Rhodes could stop him, Capps had regained control of the board and the company. The result of Capps's lobbying effort was that in May 1994 the board voted to recommend a search to replace Rhodes as head of Virginia Power.

Rhodes, using the power he has from Virginia Power's central and regulated status, fought back, and the state of Virginia obtained an agreement from the board not to fire Rhodes without advance notice. Rhodes found new ways to protect his position, and once again lobbied the board against Capps.

In the summer of 1994 the company was in a stalemate. The two men were deadlocked and would not talk to one another. The board and managers throughout the company were totally split, and a person appointed to mediate between them was forced to resign after the stress of his job resulted in his being hospitalized with chest pains. The company remains in chaos and disarray, and no end to the power struggle is in sight because each man has his own base of power and is maneuvering to retain it. As Capps is reported to have told analysts at a recent meeting, "Jim and I have found a new way to make electricity."[52]

Discussion Questions

1. What factors caused the political infighting between Rhodes and Capps?
2. How should these managers try to resolve their conflict?

Organizational Change and Development

19

Sears Transforms Itself

Sears, the well-known department store chain, has experienced huge problems in the 1990s that have caused it to transform itself. In the early 1990s Sears was losing billions of dollars because sales at its stores were falling and because the captial needs of its financial services businesses, such as Allstate Insurance and Dean Witter brokerage, were greater than the corporation could provide. The company was searching desperately for a new strategy

to allow it to compete successfully, and for the first time in its history Sears board of directors selected an outsider, Arthur C. Martinez, a senior executive at the upscale store Sak's Fifth Avenue to become its new CEO.

Martinez moved quickly to change Sears strategy and structure to improve the company's performance. First, he decided to spin Allstate and Dean Witter off to shareholders and sell Coldwell Banker in order to focus the company on its core department store business. He even closed the famous Sears catalog, which had been losing money for years. Then, he crafted a new look for Sears stores.

Martinez decided that Sears should be a moderate-price department store chain with a focus on the target customer of the "middle-American mom." He flooded the stores with women's apparel under the advertising theme "The Softer Side of Sears." At the same time he restructured Sears's operations, cutting 50,000 positions, flattening the company's huge bureaucracy, closing 113 unprofitable stores, discontinuing the catlaog, and eliminating several unprofitable businesses. Martinez's new strategy worked wonders for Sears's bottom line. Within three years losses of billions a year were changed into profits of hundreds of millions as Sears reinvented itself and once again developed a loyal customer base.

Martinez, however, has not been content to change Sears only once. Recognizing that the department store industry is highly competitive because of cost–efficient rivals like Wal-Mart and Target, and that customer tastes and preferences also change rapidly, he has been working to craft a new strategy for Sears.

Martinez has decided that Sears should take advantage of its brand names such as Craftsman tools, the new top-selling brand of tools in the United States, and its Kenmore line of appliances, and that he needs to transform Sears into a top-of-the-line, consumer-brands company that appeals to different kinds of people. Thus, while keeping its focus on the middle-American mom in its flagship department stores, Martinez is proposing that Sears open thousands of new small stores that specialize, for example in Craftsman tools or Kenmore appliances.[1]

By adopting this new multi-store strategy, and by continuing to emphasize efficiency and cost-cutting, Martinez hopes to position Sears for the department store environment of the 20th century.[2] Clearly, under Martinez, Sears is a company that will continue to be alert to the need to change and reinvent itself to meet the changing demands of its customers so that it will never have to experience the problems of the early 1990s.

Overview

An increase in competition from stores like Wal-Mart and Target caused managers at Sears to reevaluate the way their organization worked and to make changes to keep it profitable. Sears is only one of many organizations, large and small, that have been under increasing pressure to change in order to survive and prosper. In the turbulent 1990s, most organizations are confronting the need to learn new ways to reduce costs and provide better goods and services for customers. The need to change is a fact of life that most organizations have to deal with. Indeed, in today's environment, organizations cannot afford to change only when their performance is deteriorating; they need continuously to predict and anticipate the need for change.

Organizations change for many reasons, and they pursue many types of change, including the changes that restructuring, reengineering, innovation, and total quality management bring about. In this chapter we complete our analysis of organizational behavior by examining the nature and process of organizational change. We look at forces for and resistance to change; we examine different types of change in organizations; and we look at action research, a method organizations can use to plan, implement, and ease the change process. We examine various techniques that managers can use to overcome resistance to change and facilitate the change process.[3] By the end of this chapter you will understand why managing change successfully is a vital part of the manager's job.

Forces for and Resistance to Organizational Change

Organizational change
The movement of an organization away from its present state and toward some desired future state to increase its effectiveness.

Organizational change is the movement of an organization away from its present state and toward some desired future state to increase its effectiveness. Why does an organization need to change the way it performs its activities? The organizational environment is constantly changing, and an organization must adapt to these changes in order to survive.[4] Table 19.1 lists the most important forces for and impediments to change that confront an organization and its managers.

FORCES FOR CHANGE

Recall from Chapter 16 that many forces in the environment have an impact on an organization and that recognizing the nature of these forces is one of a manager's most important tasks.[5] If managers are slow to respond to competitive, economic, political, global, and other forces, the organization will lag behind its competitors and its effectiveness will be compromised.

TABLE **19.1**

Forces for and Impediments to Change

Forces for Change	Impediments to Change
Competitive forces	*Organizational impediments*
	Power and conflict
Economic and political forces	Differences in functional orientation
	Mechanistic structure
Global forces	Organizational culture
Demographic and social forces	*Group impediments*
	Group norms
	Group cohesiveness
Ethical forces	Groupthink and escalation of commitment
	Individual impediments
	Uncertainty and insecurity
	Selective perception and retention
	Habit

Competitive Forces.   Organizations are constantly striving to achieve a competitive advantage. Competition is a force for change because unless an organization matches or surpasses its competitors on at least one of the dimensions of competitive advantage—efficiency, quality, innovation, or responsiveness to customers—it will not survive.[6]

To lead on the dimensions of *efficiency* or *quality,* an organization must constantly adopt the latest technology as it becomes available. The adoption of new technology usually brings a change to task relationships as workers learn new skills or techniques to operate the new technology.[7] Later in this chapter we discuss total quality management and reengineering, two change strategies that organizations can use to achieve superior efficiency or quality.

To lead on the dimension of *innovation* and obtain a technological advantage over competitors, a company must possess skills in managing the process of innovation, another source of change that we discuss later. Central to the ability to obtain and sustain a competitive advantage is the ability to lead on the most important dimension of all: *responsiveness to customers.*

Economic, Political, and Global Forces.   As we saw in Chapter 17, economic and political forces continually affect organizations and compel them to change how and where they produce goods and services. Economic and political unions between countries are becoming an increasingly important force for change.[8] The North American Free Trade Agreement (NAFTA), signed in 1993, paved the way for cooperation among Canada, the United States, and Mexico. Many organizations in these countries have taken advantage of NAFTA to find new markets for their products and new sources of inexpensive labor and inputs.

The European Union (EU)—an alliance of European countries that traces its origin to the end of World War II—includes over twenty members eager to exploit the advantages of a large protected market. Poland and many other formerly communist countries of eastern Europe, and Georgia and other former republics of the Soviet Union, are seeking to join the European Union to foster their own economic and political development.

Japan and other fast-growing Asian countries such as Malaysia, Thailand, and China, recognizing that economic unions protect member nations and create barriers against foreign competitors, have moved to increase their presence in foreign countries. Many Japanese companies, for example, have opened new manufacturing plants in the United States and Mexico and in European countries such as Spain and the United Kingdom so that they can share in the advantages offered by NAFTA and the European Union. Toyota, Honda, and Nissan have all opened large car plants in England to supply cars to EU member countries. These firms have taken advantage of low labor costs in England (compared to costs in France, Germany, or Japan), and their products made in England are not subject to EU import tariffs because they are produced within the European Union, not exported to it from Japan.

Similarly, in the Far East, the countries of the Pacific Rim—China, Japan, Thailand, Taiwan, Malaysia, Singapore—face the problem of how to develop an economic union of their own as the world divides into three distinct economic spheres: North America, Europe, and Asia. By the year 2001, trade between countries within these three spheres is expected to be many times greater than trade between spheres.

No organization can afford to ignore the effects of global economic and political forces on its activities. The rise of low-cost foreign competitors, the development of new technology that can erode a company's competitive advantage, and the failure to exploit low-cost sources of inputs abroad can all doom an organization that does not change and adapt to the realities of the global marketplace.[9]

Other global challenges facing organizations include the need to change an organizational structure to allow expansion into foreign markets, the need to adapt to a variety of national cultures, and the need to help expatriate managers adapt to the economic, political, and cultural values of the countries in which they are located.[10] Mercedes, for example, is sending thirty managers already experienced in both U.S.- and Japanese-style manufacturing methods to head its new operations in the United States.

Demographic and Social Forces.   Managing a diverse workforce is one of the biggest challenges to confront organizations in the 1990s and beyond.[11] We have discussed in previous chapters how changes in the composition of the workforce and the increasing diversity of employees have presented organizations with many challenges and opportunities. Increasingly, changes in the demographic characteristics of the workforce have led managers to change their styles of managing all employees and to learn how to understand, supervise, and motivate minority and female organizational members effectively. Managers have had to abandon the stereotypes they unwittingly may have used in making promotion decisions and have had to accept the importance of equity in the recruitment and promotion of new hires. They also have had to acknowledge the baby-busters' desire for a lifestyle that strikes an acceptable balance between work and leisure. As more and more women have entered the workforce, companies have had to accommodate to the needs of dual-career and single-parent families, to provide child care, and to allow their members to adopt work schedules that allow them to manage work-life linkages.[12]

Many companies have helped their workers keep up with changing technology by providing support for advanced education and training. Increasingly, organizations are coming to realize that the ultimate source of competitive advantage and organizational effectiveness lies in fully utilizing the skills of their members, by, for example, empowering employees to make important and significant decisions.[13] As we discuss later in this chapter, reengineering and total quality management are change strategies that aim to alter how an organization views its activities and the workers who perform them.

Ethical Forces.   Just as it is important for an organization to take steps to change in response to changing demographic and social forces, it also is important for an organization to take steps to promote ethical behavior in the face of increasing government, political, and social demands for more responsible and honest corporate behavior.[14] Many companies have created the role of ethics officer, a person to whom employees can report ethical lapses by an organization's managers or workers and can turn for advice on difficult ethical questions. Organizations are also trying to promote ethical behavior by giving employees more direct access to important decision makers and by protecting whistle-blowers who turn the organization in when they perceive ethical problems with the way certain managers behave.

In 1994, for example, Lucky Stores and Safeway's Pak 'N Save reached a settlement with the government to pay millions of dollars (Lucky $5 million and Safeway $6 million) in penalties, restitution to consumers, donations to food banks, and investigators' costs because employees had reported that these companies were routinely selling old meat as new meat and were calling ground chicken, pork, or turkey "ground beef."[15] As part of the settlement, these companies agreed to set up a system to make it easy for employees to report unethical and illegal practices and to not penalize whistle-blowers who reported such incidents.

Many organizations need to make changes to allow managers and workers at all levels to report unethical behavior so that an organization can move quickly to eliminate such behavior and protect the general interests of its members and customers.[16] Similarly, if organizations operate in countries that pay little attention to human rights or to the well-being of organizational members, they have to learn how to change these standards and to protect their foreign employees. Levi Strauss is a good example of an organization that has changed its ethical practices to protect its employees in foreign countries and to improve the quality of their work lives (see Insight 19.1).

Insight 19.1   Ethics

Levi Strauss Protects Its Workforce

Levi Strauss has been reassessing its ethical practices and its relationship with its workforce. In the early 1990s, to compete against low-cost foreign clothing manufacturers, the company shut down many of its relatively costly U.S. manufacturing plants and contracted with inexpensive foreign suppliers to produce its clothing. Today over 50 percent of Levi's clothes are manufactured overseas.[17] After transferring much of its manufacturing overseas, however, managers at Levi Strauss were shocked by charges that some of the foreign manufacturers were using forced labor and that in many countries women and children were being forced to work long hours and were being paid a pittance for their efforts.

Top managers established a task force to investigate these charges. The task force found that unethical practices were taking place in the 600 suppliers that were audited. As a result, Levi Strauss broke off relations with thirty suppliers and decided to completely pull out of China because of pervasive human rights violations among its Chinese suppliers, including the use of convicts to produce clothes. In addition, the task force was charged with devising a series of ethical guidelines concerning factors such as pay and working conditions in specific countries, guidelines for Levi Strauss to use in its negotiations with foreign suppliers. The company wants to protect its foreign workers and its reputation and image as it expands in the global environment.

IMPEDIMENTS TO CHANGE

From customer design preferences to the issue of where clothes should be produced to the question of whether economic or political unrest will affect the availability of raw materials, the forces of change bombard organizations from all sides. Effective organizations are agile enough to adjust to these forces. But many forces internal to an organization make the organization resistant to change and thus threaten its effectiveness and survival.

In the last decade many of America's best-known and formerly strongest and most successful companies—Digital Equipment, General Motors, IBM, Ford, Chrysler, Eastman Kodak, TWA, Macy's, Texas Instruments, Westinghouse—have seen their fortunes decline. Some, such as Macy's and TWA, have gone bankrupt; some, such as Westinghouse and Digital Equipment, are still in deep trouble; and some, such as General Motors and IBM, seem to have reversed their decline and started a recovery. How did such former powerhouses lose their effectiveness? The main explanation for such decline is almost always an organization's inability to change in response to changes (such as an increase in competition) in its environment. Research suggests that one of the main reasons for some organizations' inability to change is **organizational inertia,** the tendency of an organization to maintain the status quo. Resistance to change lowers an organization's effectiveness and reduces its chances of survival.[18] Impediments to change that cause inertia are found at the organization, group, and individual levels[19] (see Table 19.1).

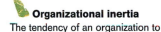

Organizational inertia
The tendency of an organization to maintain the status quo.

ORGANIZATION-LEVEL RESISTANCE TO CHANGE

Many forces inside an organization make it difficult for the organization to change in response to changing conditions in its environment.[20] The most powerful organization-level impediments to change include power and conflict, differences in functional orientation, mechanistic structure, and organizational culture.

Power and Conflict.   Change usually benefits some people, functions, or divisions at the expense of others. When change causes power struggles and organizational conflict, an organization is likely to resist it.[21] Suppose that a change in purchasing practices will help materials management to achieve its goal of reducing input costs but will harm manufacturing's ability to reduce manufacturing costs. Materials management will push for the change, but manufacturing will resist it. The conflict between the two functions will slow the process of change and perhaps prevent change from occurring at all.

If powerful functions can prevent change, an organization will not change. It is this kind of resistance that many large companies have experienced. At IBM, for example, managers in the mainframe computer division were the most powerful in the corporation. To preserve their established prestige and power in the organization, they fought off attempts to redirect IBM's resources to produce the personal computers or minicomputers that customers wanted. This failure to change in response to customer demands severely reduced IBM's speed of response to its competitors. As a result, IBM lost billions of dollars in the early 1990s.

Differences in Functional Orientation.   Differences in functional orientation are another major impediment to change and source of organizational inertia. Different functions and divisions often see the source of a problem differently because they see an issue or problem primarily from their own viewpoint. This "tunnel vision" increases organizational inertia because the organization must spend time and effort to secure agreement about the source of a problem before it can even consider how the organization needs to change to respond to the problem.

Mechanistic Structure. Recall from Chapter 16 that a mechanistic structure is characterized by a tall hierarchy, centralized decision making, and the standardization of behavior through rules and procedures. In contrast, organic structures are flat and decentralized and rely on mutual adjustment between people to get the job done.[22] Which structure is likely to be more resistant to change?

Mechanistic structures are more resistant to change. People who work within a mechanistic structure are expected to act in certain ways and do not develop the capacity to adjust their behavior to changing conditions. The extensive use of mutual adjustment and decentralized authority in an organic structure fosters the development of skills that allow workers to be creative, responsive, and able to find solutions for new problems. A mechanistic structure typically develops as an organization grows and is a principal source of inertia, especially in large organizations.

Organizational Culture. The values and norms in an organization's culture can be another source of resistance to change. Just as role relationships result in a series of stable expectations between people, so values and norms cause people to behave in predictable ways. If organizational change disrupts taken-for-granted values and norms and forces people to change what they do and how they do it, an organization's culture will cause resistance to change. For example, many organizations develop conservative values that support the status quo and make managers reluctant to search for new ways to compete. As a result, if the environment changes and a company's products become obsolete, the company has nothing to fall back on, and failure is likely.[23] Sometimes, values and norms are so strong that even when the environment is changing and it is clear that a new strategy needs to be adopted, managers cannot change because they are committed to the way they presently do business.

GROUP-LEVEL RESISTANCE TO CHANGE

As we discussed in Chapters 10 and 11, much of an organization's work is performed by groups, and several group characteristics can produce resistance to change. Here we consider four: group norms, group cohesiveness, groupthink, and escalation of commitment.

Group Norms. Many groups develop strong informal norms that specify appropriate and inappropriate behaviors and govern the interactions between group members (see Chapter 10). Often, change alters task and role relationships in a group; when it does, it disrupts group norms and the informal expectations that group members have of one another. As a result, members of a group may resist change because a whole new set of norms may have to be developed to meet the needs of the new situation.

Group Cohesiveness. Group cohesiveness, the attractiveness of a group to its members, affects group performance (see Chapter 11). Although some level of cohesiveness promotes group performance, too much cohesiveness may actually reduce performance because it stifles opportunities for the group to change and adapt. A highly cohesive group may resist attempts by management to change what it does or even who is a member of the group. Group members may unite to preserve the status quo and to protect their interests at the expense of other groups.

Groupthink and Escalation of Commitment.   Groupthink is a pattern of faulty decision making that occurs in cohesive groups when members discount negative information in order to arrive at a unanimous agreement. Escalation of commitment worsens this situation because even when group members realize that their decision is wrong, they continue to pursue it because they are committed to it. These group processes (discussed in Chapter 14) make changing a group's behavior very difficult. The more important the group's activities are to the organization, the greater is the impact of these processes on organizational performance.

INDIVIDUAL-LEVEL RESISTANCE TO CHANGE

Individuals within an organization may be inclined to resist change because of uncertainty, selective perception, and force of habit.[24]

Uncertainty and Insecurity.   People tend to resist change because they feel uncertain and insecure about what its outcome will be.[25] Workers might be given new tasks. Role relationships may be reorganized. Some workers might lose their jobs. Some people might benefit at the expense of others. Workers' resistance to the uncertainty and insecurity surrounding change can cause organizational inertia. Absenteeism and turnover may increase as change takes place, and workers may become uncooperative, attempt to delay or slow the change process, and otherwise passively resist the change in an attempt to quash it.

Selective Perception and Retention.   Perception and attribution play a major role in determining work attitudes and behaviors (see Chapter 4). There is a general tendency for people to selectively perceive information that is consistent with their existing views (or schemas) of their organizations. Thus, when change takes place, workers tend to focus only on how it will personally affect them or their function or division. If they perceive few benefits, they may reject the purpose behind the change. Not surprisingly, it can be difficult for an organization to develop a common platform to promote change across an organization and get people to see the need for change in the same way.

Habit.   Habit, people's preference for familiar actions and events, is another impediment to change. The difficulty of breaking bad habits and adopting new styles of behavior indicates how resistant habits are to change. Why are habits hard to break? Some researchers have suggested that people have a built-in tendency to return to their original behaviors, a tendency that stymies change.

LEWIN'S FORCE-FIELD THEORY OF CHANGE

As you have seen, a wide variety of forces make organizations resistant to change, and a wide variety of forces push organizations toward change. Researcher Kurt Lewin developed a theory about organizational change.

Forces for and Resistances to Change

- Periodically analyze the organizational environment and identify forces for change.
- Analyze how the change in response to these forces will affect people, functions, and divisions inside the organization.
- Using this analysis, decide what type of change to pursue, and develop a plan to overcome possible resistance to change and to increase the forces for change.

Force-field theory
The theory that organizational change occurs when forces for change strengthen, resistance to change lessens, or both occur simultaneously.

According to his **force-field theory,** these two sets of forces are always in opposition in an organization.[26] When the forces are evenly balanced, the organization is in a state of inertia and does not change. To get an organization to change, managers must find a way to increase the forces for change, *reduce* resistance to change, or do both simultaneously. Any of these strategies will overcome inertia and cause an organization to change.

Figure 19.1 illustrates Lewin's theory. An organization at performance level P1 is in balance: Forces for change and resistance to change are equal. Management, however, decides that the organization should strive to achieve performance level P2. To get to level P2, managers must *increase* the forces for change (the increase is represented by the lengthening of the up-arrows), *reduce* resistance to change (the reduction is represented by the shortening of the down-arrows), or do both. If they pursue any of the three strategies successfully, the organization will change and reach performance level P2.

Before we look in more detail at the techniques that managers can use to overcome resistance and facilitate change, we need to look at the types of change they can implement to increase organizational effectiveness.

FIGURE 19.1

Lewin's Force-Field
Theory of Change

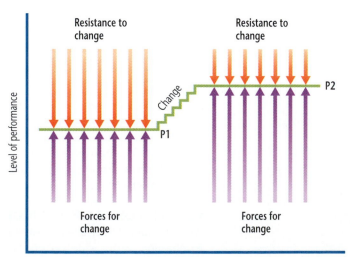

Evolutionary and Revolutionary Change in Organizations

Managers continually face choices about how best to respond to the forces for change. They can adopt several types of change to help their organizations achieve desired future states. In general, types of change fall into two broad categories: evolutionary change and revolutionary change.[27]

Evolutionary change is gradual, incremental, and narrowly focused. Evolutionary change involves not a drastic or sudden altering of the basic nature of an organization's strategy and structure but a constant attempt to improve, adapt, and adjust strategy and structure incrementally to accommodate to changes taking place in the environment.[28] Socio-technical systems theory and total quality management are two instruments of evolutionary change that organizations use in their attempt to make incremental improvements in the way work gets done. Such improvements might be a better way to operate a technology or to organize the work process.

Evolutionary change is accomplished gradually, incrementally. Some organizations, however, need to make major changes quickly. They do not want to take the time to set up and implement programs that foster evolutionary change or wait for the performance results that such programs can bring about. Faced with drastic, unexpected changes in the environment (for example, a new technological breakthrough) or with impending disaster resulting from years of inaction and neglect, an organization needs to act quickly and decisively. Revolutionary change is called for.

Revolutionary change is rapid, dramatic, and broadly focused. Revolutionary change involves a bold attempt to quickly find new ways to be effective. It is likely to result in a radical shift in ways of doing things, new goals, and a new structure. It has repercussions at all levels in the organization—corporate, divisional, functional, group, and individual. Reengineering, restructuring, and innovation are three important instruments of revolutionary change.

EVOLUTIONARY CHANGE I: SOCIO-TECHNICAL SYSTEMS THEORY

Socio-technical systems theory was one of the first theories that proposed the importance of changing role and task or technical relationships to increase organizational effectiveness.[29] It emerged from a study of changing work practices in the British coal-mining industry.[30]

After World War II, new technology that changed work relationships among miners was introduced into the British mining industry. Before the war, coal mining was a small-batch or craft process. Teams of skilled miners dug coal from the coal face underground and performed all the other activities necessary to transport the coal to the surface. Work took place in a confined space where productivity depended on close cooperation among team members. Workers developed their own routines and norms to get the job done and provided each other with social support to help combat the stress of their dangerous and confining working conditions.

This method of coal mining, called the "hand got method," approximated small-batch technology (see Chapter 16). To increase efficiency, managers decided to replace it with the "long wall method." This method utilized

---

Evolutionary change
Change that is gradual, incremental, and narrowly focused.

Revolutionary change
Change that is rapid, dramatic, and broadly focused.

Socio-technical systems theory
Ideas about how organizations should choose specific kinds of control systems that match the technical nature of the work process.

a mechanized, mass production technology. Coal was now cut by miners using powered drills, and it was transported to the surface on conveyer belts. Tasks became more routine as the work process was programmed and standardized. On paper, the new technology promised impressive increases in mining efficiency. After its introduction at the mines, however, efficiency rose only slowly, and absenteeism among miners, which had always been high, increased dramatically. Consultants were called to the mines to figure out why the expected gains in efficiency had not occurred.

The researchers pointed out that, to operate the new technology efficiently, management had changed the task and role relationships among the miners. The new task and role relationships had destroyed informal norms and social support, disrupted long-established informal working relationships, and reduced group cohesiveness. To solve the problem, the researchers recommended linking the new technology with the old social system by recreating the old system of tasks and roles and decentralizing authority to work groups. When management redesigned the production process, productivity improved and absenteeism fell.

This study showed the importance of the need to fit, or "jointly optimize," the workings of an organization's technical and social systems. The lesson to take from socio-technical systems theory is that when managers change task and role relationships, they must recognize the need to gradually adjust the technical and social systems so that group norms and cohesiveness are not disrupted. By taking this gradual approach, an organization can avoid the group-level resistance to change that we discussed earlier in this chapter.

EVOLUTIONARY CHANGE II: TOTAL QUALITY MANAGEMENT

Total quality management
An ongoing and constant effort by all of an organization's functions to find new ways to improve the quality of the organization's goods and services.

Total quality management (TQM) is an ongoing and constant effort by all of an organization's functions to find new ways to improve the quality of the organization's goods and services.[31] In many companies, the initial decision to adopt a TQM approach signals a radical change in the way they organize their activities. Once TQM is adopted by an organization, however, it leads to continuous, incremental change, and all functions are expected to cooperate with each other to improve quality.

First developed by a number of American business consultants such as W. Edwards Deming and Joseph Juran, total quality management was eagerly embraced by Japanese companies after World War II. For Japanese companies, with their tradition of long-term working relationships and cooperation between functions, the implementation of the new TQM system was an incremental step. Shop-floor workers in Japan, for example, had long been organized into **quality circles,** groups of workers who met regularly to discuss the way work is performed in order to find new ways to increase performance.[32]

Quality circles
Groups of workers who meet regularly to discuss the way work is performed in order to find new ways to increase performance.

Changes frequently inspired by TQM include altering the design or type of machines used to assemble products and reorganizing the sequence of activities—either within or between functions—necessary to provide a service to a customer. As in socio-technical systems theory, the emphasis in TQM is on the fit between technical and social systems. That emphasis is evident in Deming's fourteen principles of TQM, listed in Table 19.2.

TABLE **19.2**

Deming's Principles of Total Quality Management

1. Create constancy of purpose toward improvement of product and service, with the aim of becoming competitive, staying in business, and providing jobs.
2. Adopt the new philosophy. We are in a new economic age. Western management must awaken to the challenge, learn its responsibilities, and take on leadership for change.
3. Cease dependence on inspection to achieve quality. Eliminate the need for inspection on a mass basis by building quality into the product in the first place.
4. End the practice of awarding business on the basis of price tag. Instead, minimize total cost.
5. Improve constantly and forever the system of production and service, to improve quality and productivity and thus constantly decrease costs.
6. Institute training on the job.
7. Institute leadership. The aim of leadership should be to help people, machines, and gadgets do a better job. Management leadership, as well as leadership of production workers, needs overhauling.
8. Drive out fear, so that everyone may work effectively for the company.
9. Break down barriers between departments. People in research, design, sales, and production must work as a team, to foresee problems in production and in use that may be encountered with the product or service.
10. Eliminate slogans, exhortations, and targets for the work force asking for zero defects and new levels of productivity. Such exhortations only create adversarial relationships. The bulk of the causes of low quality and low productivity belong to the system and thus lie beyond the power of the work force.
11. (a) Eliminate work standards on the factory floor; substitute leadership.
    (b) Eliminate management by objective, management by numbers, and numerical goals; substitute leadership.
12. (a) Remove barriers that rob the hourly workers of their right to pride of workmanship. The responsibility of supervisors must be changed from sheer numbers to quality.
    (b) Remove barriers that rob people in management and in engineering of their right to pride of workmanship.
13. Institute a vigorous program of education and self-improvement.
14. Put everybody in the company to work to accomplish the transformation. The transformation is everybody's job.

Source: From Andrea Gabor, *The Man Who Discovered Quality.* Copyright © 1990 by Andrea Gabor. Reprinted by permission of Times Books, a division of Random House, Inc.

Changing cross-functional relationships to help improve quality is very important in TQM. Poor quality often originates at crossover points or after handoffs—when people turn over the work they are doing to people in different functions. The job of intermediate manufacturing, for example, is to assemble inputs that are assembled into a final product. Coordinating the design of the various inputs so that they fit together smoothly and operate effectively together is one area that TQM focuses on. Members of the different functions work together to find new ways to reduce the number of inputs needed or to suggest design improvements that will enable inputs to be assembled more easily and reliably. Such changes increase quality and lower costs. Note that the changes associated with TQM (as with socio-technical systems theory) are changes in task, role, and group relationships.

The results of TQM activities can be dramatic. Analysts attribute a doubling of sales and a quadrupling of export earnings at Eastman Chemical Company to the TQM program begun in 1981 (see Insight 19.2).

Insight 19.2

Total Quality Management

Eastman Chemical Wins the Baldridge Award for Quality

In 1993 Eastman Chemical was the only large company to win the Malcolm Baldridge National Quality Award, and it is the only chemical company that has ever won this award. The company, which supplies more than 400 types of chemicals to over 7,000 customers worldwide, is rated as the number-one supplier by over 70 percent of its customers.[33] How does Eastman Chemical achieve this impressive feat?

In 1981, with some early help from W. Edwards Deming and Joseph Juran, the company began to put in place a TQM program that now extends throughout the organization. At the top of the company, president Ernest W. Davenport Jr. chairs a weekly all-day meeting of the company's top TQM team, consisting of the highest-ranking managers. In their own divisions, these managers are the leaders of quality teams composed of the division's most senior managers. The divisional managers head quality teams composed of functional managers, and the functional managers head quality teams composed of a mixture of workers and supervisors. Thus Eastman Chemical has literally thousands of quality teams that are jointly responsible for finding and implementing improvements that are shared with other teams throughout the organization. Each team is also responsible for systematically assessing the results of its efforts over time.

The TQM program has had considerable success in improving all aspects of the company's business—from reducing costs to raising quality to finding new ways to train and make better use of employees. In the early years of the TQM program, however, management encountered pockets of resistance from professional employees. Many of the company's 350 PhDs did not believe that concerted efforts by TQM teams could lead to increased effectiveness, until they were shown the bottom-line improvements in quality and cost that TQM can achieve.

More and more companies are embracing the continuous, incremental type of change that results from the implementation of TQM programs. Many companies have found, however, that implementing a TQM program is not always easy, because it requires workers and managers to adopt new ways of viewing their roles in an organization. As Table 19.2 suggests, management must be willing to decentralize control of decision making, empower workers, and assume the role of facilitator rather than supervisor. The "command and control" model gives way to an "advise and support" model. It is important that workers, as well as managers, share in the increased profits that successful TQM programs can provide. In Japan, for example, performance bonuses frequently account for 30 percent or more of workers' and managers' salaries, and salaries can fluctuate widely from year to year as a result of changes in organizational performance.

Resistance to the changes a TQM program requires can be serious unless management explicitly recognizes the many ways that TQM affects relationships between functions and even divisions. We discuss ways to deal with resistance to change at length later in this chapter.

Despite the success that organizations like Xerox, Harley-Davidson, and Ford have had with TQM, other organizations, such as Florida Power and Light and McDonell Douglas, did not obtain the increases in quality and reductions in cost that are often associated with TQM. As a result, these companies abandoned their TQM programs. Two reasons for a lack of success with TQM are underestimates of the degree of commitment from people at all levels in the organization that is necessary to implement a TQM program and the long time frame that is necessary for TQM efforts to succeed and show results. TQM is not a quick fix that can turn an organization around overnight. It is an evolutionary process that bears fruit only when it becomes a way of life in an organization.[34]

REVOLUTIONARY CHANGE I: REENGINEERING

Reengineering involves the "fundamental rethinking and radical redesign of business processes to achieve dramatic improvements in critical, contemporary measures of performance such as cost, quality, service, and speed."[35] Change resulting from reengineering requires managers to go back to the basics and pull apart each step in the work process to identify a better way to coordinate and integrate the activities necessary to provide customers with goods and services. Instead of focusing on an organization's *functions,* the managers of a reengineered organization focus on business processes. (The closing case describes how Hallmark Cards undertook a total reengineering of its vital design process.)

A **business process** is any activity (such as order processing, inventory control, or product design) that is vital to the quick delivery of goods and services to customers or that promotes high quality or low costs. Business processes are not the responsibility of any one function; they involve activities across functions. Because reengineering focuses on business processes and not on functions, a reengineered organization always adopts a new approach to organizing its activities.

Organizations that take up reengineering ignore the existing arrangement of tasks, roles, and work activities. Management starts the reengineering process with the customer (not with the product or service) and asks the question "How can we reorganize the way we do our work, our business processes, to provide the best-quality, lowest-cost goods and services to the customer?" Frequently, when companies ponder this question, they discover better ways to organize their activities. For example, a business process that currently involves members of ten different functions working sequentially to provide goods and services might be performed by one person or a few people at a fraction of the cost after reengineering. Because reengineering often results in such changes, job enlargement and enrichment (discussed in Chapter 7) are common results of reengineering. Individual jobs become increasingly complex, and people are grouped into

Business process
Any activity that is vital to the quick delivery of goods and services to customers or that promotes high quality or low costs.

cross-functional teams as business processes are reengineered to reduce costs and increase quality.

Reengineering and TQM are highly interrelated and complementary. After revolutionary reengineering has taken place and the question "What is the best way to provide customers with the goods or service they require?" has been answered, evolutionary TQM takes over with its focus on "How can we now continue to improve and refine the new process and find better ways of managing task and role relationships?" Successful organizations examine both questions simultaneously, and they continuously attempt to identify new and better processes for meeting the goals of increased efficiency, quality, and responsiveness to customers. At Eastman Chemical, for example, the TQM process began with a major reengineering plan that decentralized authority for business processes to teams of managers low in the organization and reduced the number of levels in the hierarchy to four. Another example of a reengineering change, at IBM Credit, is described in Insight 19.3.

Insight 19.3

Reengineering

A New Approach at IBM Credit

IBM Credit, a wholly owned division of IBM, manages the financing and leasing of IBM computers, particularly mainframes, to IBM customers. Before reengineering took place, a financing request received by the division's headquarters in Old Greenwich, Connecticut, went through a five-step approval process that involved five different functions. First, the IBM salesperson called up the credit department, which logged the request and took details about the potential customer. This information then went to the credit-checking department, where a credit check on the potential customer was made. When the credit check was complete, the request went to the contracts department, which wrote the contract. From there, the request went to the pricing department, which determined the actual financial details of the loan, such as the interest rate and the duration of the loan. Finally, the whole package of information went to the dispatching department, which assembled it and delivered it to the sales representative, who gave it to the customer.

This series of cross-functional activities took an average of seven days to complete. Sales representatives constantly complained that this procedure resulted in a low level of responsiveness to customers, reduced customer satisfaction, and gave potential customers time to shop around not only for other sources of financing but also for competitors' machines. The delay in closing the deal caused uncertainty for all concerned.

When two senior IBM credit managers reviewed the finance approval process, they found that the time actually spent by the different specialists in the different functions amounted to only ninety minutes.

The approval process took seven days to complete because of the delays that resulted as the loan application made its way from one department to another. The managers saw that the activities taking place in each department were not complex. Each department had its own computer system containing its own work procedures, but the work done in each department was pretty routine.

Armed with this information, the IBM managers realized that the five-step approval process could be reengineered into a process that one person working with a computer system containing all the necessary information could handle. A team of experts was available to help process complex applications. After the reengineering effort, a typical application could be processed in four hours. A sales rep could get back to a customer quickly to close a deal, and most of the uncertainty surrounding the transaction was removed. This dramatic increase in performance was brought about by a radical change to the process as a whole.[36]

REVOLUTIONARY CHANGE II: RESTRUCTURING

Organizations experiencing a rapid deterioration in performance may try to turn things around by restructuring. An organization that resorts to restructuring reduces its level of differentiation and integration by eliminating divisions, departments, or levels in the hierarchy and downsizes by getting rid of employees to lower operating costs. For example, in 1989 when William F. Malec took over as the head of the federally administered Tennessee Valley Authority (TVA), the organization had over fourteen levels in its hierarchy of 37,000 employees, and its customers had experienced an average increase in their utility rates of over 10 percent per year. Describing TVA as a top-heavy bureaucracy, Malec quickly moved to slash costs and restructure the organization. By 1994 he had reduced the levels in the hierarchy to nine and the employees to 18,500, and he had guaranteed to freeze utility rates for ten years.

Change in the relationships between divisions or functions is a common outcome of restructuring. In the opening case, Sears streamlined its operations in order to implement its reengineering effort. Similarly, IBM, in an effort to cut development costs and speed cooperation between engineers, created a new division in 1994 to take control of the production of microprocessors and memory systems. This restructuring move pulled engineers from IBM's thirteen divisions and grouped them together in brand-new headquarters in Austin, Texas, to increase their effectiveness.

Why does restructuring become necessary, and why may an organization need to downsize its operations? Sometimes, an unforeseen change in the environment occurs: Perhaps a shift in technology makes the company's products obsolete, or a worldwide recession reduces demand for its products. Sometimes an organization has excess capacity when customers no longer want the goods and services it provides because they are outdated or offer poor value for money. Sometimes organizations downsize because they have grown too tall and bureaucratic and their operating costs have become much too high. Sometimes, like Sears and Microsoft, organizations restructure even when they are in a strong position, simply to stay on top.

All too often, companies are forced to downsize and lay off employees because they have not continually monitored the way they operate—their basic business processes—and have not made the incremental changes to their strategies and structures that would have allowed them to contain costs and adjust to changing conditions. Paradoxically, because they have not paid attention to the need to reengineer themselves, they are forced into a position where restructuring becomes the only way they can survive and compete in an increasingly competitive environment.

Restructuring, like reengineering, TQM, and other change strategies, generates resistance to change. Often, the decision to downsize will require the establishment of new task and role relationships. Because this change may threaten the jobs of some workers, they resist the changes taking place. Many plans to introduce change, including restructuring, take a long time to implement and fail because of the high level of resistance that they encounter at all levels of the organization.

REVOLUTIONARY CHANGE III: INNOVATION

Restructuring is often necessary because changes in technology make the technology an organization uses to produce goods and services, or the goods and services themselves, obsolete. For example, changes in technology have made computers much cheaper to manufacture and more powerful and have changed the type of computers customers want. If organizations are to avoid being left behind in the competitive race to produce new goods and services, they must take steps to introduce new products or develop new technologies to produce those products reliably and at low cost. Innovation, as we dis-

Bill Gates tries to promote creativity and innovation at Microsoft by allowing employees to dress and to decorate their office spaces as they like. Shown here is software designer Sean Selitrennikoff, clearly pleased with his personal work space at Microsoft.

cussed in Chapter 14, is the successful use of skills and resources to create new technologies or new goods and services so that an organization can change and better respond to the needs of customers.[37] Innovation can result in spectacular success. Apple Computer changed the face of the computer industry when it introduced its personal computer. Honda changed the face of the small motor bike market when it introduced small 50cc motorcycles. Mary Kay changed the way cosmetics are sold to customers when it introduced at-home cosmetics parties and personalized selling.

Although innovation does bring about change, it is also associated with a high level of risk because the outcomes of research and development activities are often uncertain.[38] It has been estimated that only from 12 to 20 percent of R&D projects result in products that get to market.[39] Thus innovation can lead not only to change of the sort that organizations want—the introduction of profitable new technologies and products—but also to the kind of change that they want to avoid—technologies that are inefficient and products that customers don't want. In 1993, for example, Synergen, the biotechnology company, was riding high on the promise of its new drug Antril as an effective treatment for severe blood infections. By 1994 tests of the drug had revealed that it had no promise, and Synergen announced that it was laying off 375 people, about 60 percent of its Boulder, Colorado, workforce, and was looking for a prospective buyer.[40]

Innovation is one of the most difficult instruments of change to manage. Recall from previous chapters that when organizations rely on innovation as the source of their competitive advantage, they need to adopt organic, flexible structures such as matrix or cross-functional team structures that give people the freedom to experiment and be creative.[41] As in reengineering, the need for functions to coordinate their activities and to work together is important for successful innovation, and companies that rely on innovation have to facilitate the change effort and support the efforts of their members to be creative. For example, the term *skunk works* was coined at Lockheed Corporation when that company set up a specialized unit, separate from its regular functional organization, to pioneer the development of the U-2 spy plane. In Insight 11.6 we discussed how Ford created a skunk works to develop its new model Mustang and how research and development teams work. To try to increase the success rate of innovation and new product development, many high-tech organizations have developed the role of **product champion,** an expert manager appointed to head a new product team and lead a new product from its beginning to commercialization.[42] Many of the techniques for managing change that we discuss in the next section were developed to help facilitate innovation. Of all the instruments of revolutionary change, innovation offers the prospect for the greatest long-term success but also the greatest risk.

> **Product champion**
> An expert manager appointed to head a new product team and lead a new product from its beginning to commercialization.

Managing Change: Action Research

No matter what type of evolutionary or revolutionary change an organization adopts, managers face the problem of getting the organization to change. Kurt Lewin, whose force-field theory argues that organizations are balanced between forces for change and resistance to change, has a related perspective on how managers can bring change to their organization (see Fig. 19.2).

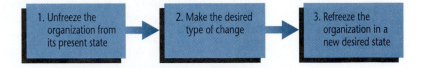

1. Unfreeze the organization from its present state → 2. Make the desired type of change → 3. Refreeze the organization in a new desired state

FIGURE 19.2

Lewin's Three-Step Change Process

In Lewin's view, implementing change is a three-step process: (1) unfreezing the organization from its present state, (2) making the change, and (3) refreezing the organization in the new desired state so that its members do not revert to their previous work attitudes and role behaviors.[43] Lewin warns that resistance to change will quickly cause an organization and its members to revert to their old ways of doing things unless the organization actively takes steps to refreeze the organization with the changes in place. It is not enough to make some changes in task and role relationships and expect the changes to be successful and to endure. To get an organization to remain in its new state, managers must actively manage the change process.

Action research is a strategy for generating and acquiring knowledge that managers can use to define an organization's desired future state and to plan a change program that allows the organization to reach that state.[44] The techniques and practices of action research, developed by experts, help managers to unfreeze an organization, move it to its new desired position, and refreeze it so that the benefits of the change are retained. Figure 19.3 identifies the main steps in action research.

Action research

A strategy for generating and acquiring knowledge that managers can use to define an organization's desired future state and to plan a change program that allows the organization to reach that state.

FIGURE 19.3

The Steps in Action Research

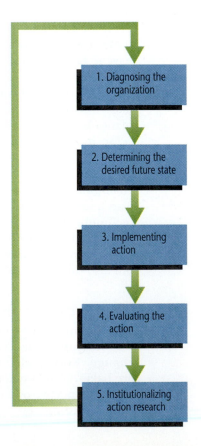

1. Diagnosing the organization
2. Determining the desired future state
3. Implementing action
4. Evaluating the action
5. Institutionalizing action research

DIAGNOSIS OF THE ORGANIZATION

The first step in action research requires managers to recognize the existence of a problem that needs to be solved and acknowledge that some type of change is needed to solve it. In general, recognition of the need for change arises because somebody in the organization perceives a gap between desired performance and actual performance. Perhaps customer complaints about the quality of goods or services have increased. Perhaps profits have recently fallen, or operating costs have been escalating. Perhaps turnover among managers or workers has been excessive. In the first stage of action research, managers need to analyze what is going on and why problems are occurring. Recall that an increase in competition caused managers at Sears, in the opening case, to reevaluate the organization's present state.

Diagnosing the organization can be a complex process. Like a doctor, managers have to distinguish between symptoms and causes. For example, there is little point in introducing new technology to reduce production costs if the problem is that demand is falling because customers do not like the design of the product. Managers have to carefully collect information about the organization to diagnose the problem correctly and get employees committed to the change process. At this early stage of action research it is important for managers to collect information from people at all levels in the organization and from outsiders such as customers and suppliers. Questionnaire surveys given to employees, customers, and suppliers, and interviews with workers and managers at all levels, can provide information that is essential to a correct diagnosis of the organization's present state.

DETERMINING THE DESIRED FUTURE STATE

After identification of the present state, the next step is to identify where the organization needs to be—its desired future state. This step also involves a difficult planning process as managers work out various alternative courses of action that could move the organization to where they would like it to be and determine what type of change to implement. Identifying the desired future state involves deciding what the organization's strategy and structure should be (as Sears's managers did). Should the organization focus on reducing costs and increasing efficiency? Or are raising quality and responsiveness to customers the keys to future success? What is the best kind of organizational structure to adopt to realize organizational goals, a product structure or perhaps a cross-functional team structure?

IMPLEMENTING ACTION

Implementing action is the third step of action research.[45] It is a three-step process. First, managers need to identify possible impediments to change that they will encounter as they go about making changes—impediments at the organization, group, and individual levels.[46] Suppose managers choose to reengineer the company from a functional to a cross-functional team structure to speed product development and reduce costs. They must anticipate the obstacles they will encounter when they unfreeze the organization and make the changes. Functional managers, for example, are likely to strongly resist efforts to change the company because the change will reduce their power and prestige in the organization. Similarly, members of each function who have grown accustomed to working with the same people and to stable task and role relationships will resist being assigned to a new team where tasks and roles have to be worked out again and new interpersonal relationships have to be learned.

The more revolutionary the change that is adopted, the greater will be the problem of implementing it. Managers need to find ways to minimize, control, and co-opt resistance to change. They also need to devise strategies to bring organizational members on board and foster their commitment to the change process. Managers must also look to the future and seek ways to refreeze the changes that they have made so that people cannot slide back into old behaviors.

The second step in implementing action is deciding who will be responsible for actually making the changes and controlling the change process. The choices are to employ **external change agents,** outside consultants who are experts in managing change; **internal change agents,** managers from within the organization who are knowledgeable about the situation; or some combination of both.[47]

External change agent
An outside consultant who is an expert in managing change.

The principal problem with using internal change agents is that other members of the organization may perceive them as being politically involved in the changes and biased toward certain groups. External change agents, in contrast, are likely to be perceived as less influenced by internal politics (although recall from Chapter 18 that one political tactic is to bring in an outside expert to provide support for one's own view of what needs to be changed). Another reason for employing external change agents is that as outsiders they have a detached view of the organization's problems and can distinguish between the "forest and the trees." Insiders can be so involved in what is going on that they cannot see the true source of the problems. In Chapter 16, we mentioned that management consultants from McKinsey & Co. are frequently brought in by large organizations to help the top-management team diagnose the organization's problems and suggest solutions. Many consultants specialize in certain types of organizational change, such as restructuring, reengineering, or implementing total quality management.

Internal change agent
A manager from within an organization who is knowledgeable about the situation to be changed.

The third step in implementing action is deciding which specific change strategy will most effectively unfreeze, change, and refreeze the organization. Specific techniques for implementing change are discussed later in this chapter. The types of change that these techniques give rise to fall into two categories: top-down and bottom-up.[48]

Top-down change is change that is implemented by managers at a high level in the organization. The result of radical organizational restructuring and reengineering is top-down change. Managers high up in the organization decide to make a change, realizing full well that it will reverberate at all organizational levels. The managers choose to manage and solve problems as they arise at the divisional, functional, or individual levels.

Top-down change
Change that is implemented by managers at a high level in the organization.

Bottom-up change is change that is implemented by employees at low levels in the organization and gradually rises until it is felt throughout the organization. When an organization wants to engage in bottom-up change, the first step in the action research process—diagnosing the organization—becomes pivotal in determining the success of the change. Managers involve employees at all levels in the change process, to obtain their input and to lessen their resistance. By reducing the uncertainty employees experience, bottom-up change facilitates unfreezing and increases the likelihood that employees

Bottom-up change
Change that is implemented by employees at low levels in the organization and gradually rises until it is felt throughout the organization.

will retain the new behaviors that they learn during the change process. Top-down change proceeds rapidly and forces employees to keep up with the pace of change, troubleshooting to solve problems as they arise.

In general, bottom-up change is easier to implement than top-down change because it provokes less resistance. Organizations that have the time to engage in bottom-up change are generally well-run organizations that pay attention to change, are used to change, and change often. Poorly run organizations, those that rarely change or postpone change until it is too late, are forced to engage in top-down restructuring simply to survive. Neither Digital Equipment nor Chrysler had the luxury of being able to use bottom-up change when their performance declined precipitously. Digital CEO Robert Palmer and Chrysler CEO Lee Iacocca had to take immediate action to reduce costs and develop new products that would allow their companies to survive. In contrast, Microsoft CEO Bill Gates is constantly searching for ways to improve his organization's performance, even though Microsoft dominates its competitors. In 1994, while Microsoft was earning record profits, Gates announced a program to change Microsoft continuously so that it would still be on top of its industry into the next century.

Organizations that change the most are able to exploit the advantages of evolutionary bottom-up change because their managers are always open to the need for change and constantly use action research to find new and better ways to operate and increase effectiveness. Organizations in which change happens rarely are likely candidates for revolutionary top-down change. Because their managers do not use action research on a continuing basis, they attempt change so late that their only option is some massive restructuring or downsizing to turn their organization around.

EVALUATING THE ACTION

The fourth step in action research is evaluating the action that has been taken and assessing the degree to which the changes have accomplished the desired objectives. Armed with this evaluation, management decides whether more change is needed to reach the organization's desired future state or whether more effort is needed to refreeze the organization in its new state.[49]

The best way to evaluate the change process is to develop measures or criteria that allow managers to assess whether the organization has reached its desired objectives. When criteria developed at the beginning of action research are used consistently over time to evaluate the effects of the change process, managers have ample information to assess the impact of the changes they have made. They can compare costs before and after the change to see whether efficiency has increased. They can survey workers to see whether they are more satisfied with their jobs. They can survey customers to see whether they are more satisfied with the quality of the organization's products. Managers at Sears carefully surveyed their customers to see if they liked Sears's new clothing lines, for example. That information helped them to evaluate the success of their change effort.

Assessing the impact of change is especially difficult because the effects of change may emerge slowly. The action research process that we have been describing may take several years to complete. Typically, reengineering and restructuring take months or years, and total quality management, once under

Designing a Plan for Change

- Develop criteria to evaluate whether change is necessary, and use these criteria systematically throughout the change process to assess progress toward the ideal future state.
- After analyzing resistances to change, carefully design a plan that both reduces resistance to and facilitates change.
- Recognize that change is easiest to manage when an organization and its members are used to change, and consider using a total quality management program as a way of keeping the organization attuned to the need for change.

way, never stops. Consequently, managers need valid and reliable measures that they can use to evaluate performance. All too often poorly performing organizations fail to develop and consistently apply criteria that allow them to evaluate their performance. For those organizations, the pressure for change often comes from the outside, as shareholders complain about poor profits, parents complain about their children's poor grades, or state inspectors find high rates of postsurgery infection in hospitals.

INSTITUTIONALIZING ACTION RESEARCH

The need to manage change is so vital in today's quickly changing environment that organizations must institutionalize action research—that is, make it a required habit or a norm adopted by every member of an organization. The institutionalization of action research is as necessary at the top of the organization (where the top management team plans the organization's future strategy) as it is on the shop floor (where workers meet in quality circles to find new ways to increase efficiency and quality). Because change is so difficult and requires so much thought and effort to implement, members at all levels of the organization must be rewarded for being part of successful change efforts. Top managers can be rewarded with stock options and bonus plans linked to organizational performance. Lower-level members can be rewarded through an employee stock ownership plan and by performance bonuses and pay linked to individual or group performance. Indeed, tangible rewards are one way of helping to refreeze the organization in its new state because, as we discussed in Chapter 8, pay is an important motivation tool for helping people learn and sustain desired organizational behaviors.

Organizational Development

Organizational development
A series of techniques and methods that managers can use in their action research program to increase the adaptability of their organization.

Organizational development (OD) is a series of techniques and methods that managers can use in their action research program to increase the adaptability of their organization.[50] In the words of organizational theorist Warren Bennis, OD refers to a "complex educational strategy intended to change beliefs, attitudes, values, and structure of organizations so that they can better adapt to new technologies, markets, and challenges and the dizzying rate of change itself."[51] The goal of OD is to improve organizational effectiveness and to help people in organizations reach their potential and realize their goals and objectives. As action research proceeds, managers need to continually unfreeze, change, and refreeze managers' and workers' attitudes and behaviors. Many OD techniques have been developed to help managers do this. We first look at OD techniques to help managers unfreeze an organization and overcome resistances to change. We then look at OD techniques to help managers change and refreeze an organization in its new desired state.

OD TECHNIQUES TO DEAL WITH RESISTANCE TO CHANGE

Resistance to change occurs at all levels of an organization. It manifests itself as organizational politics and power struggles between individuals and groups, differing perceptions of the need for change, and so on. Tactics that managers can use to reduce resistance to change include education and communication, participation and empowerment, facilitation, bargaining and negotiation, manipulation, and coercion.[52]

Education and Communication. One of the most important impediments to change is uncertainty about what is going to happen. Through education and communication, internal and external agents of change can provide organizational members with information about the change and how it will affect them. Change agents can communicate this information in formal group meetings, by memo, in one-on-one meetings, and, increasingly, through electronic means such as e-mail and videoconferencing. Wal-Mart, for example, has a state-of-the-art videoconferencing system. Managers at corporate headquarters put on presentations that are beamed to all Wal-Mart stores so that both managers and workers are aware of the changes that will be taking place.

As part of his action research program, Michael Walsh, former CEO of Union Pacific and Tenneco (see Insight 12.5), was famous for conducting "town meetings" to tell employees about the changes they would be experiencing, to get their input, and to help them to accept change. A master at organizational change, Walsh successfully restructured two large companies.

Even when plant closures or massive layoffs are planned, it is still best—from both an ethical and a change standpoint—to inform employees about what will happen to them as downsizing occurs. Many organizations fear that disgruntled employees may try to hurt the organization as it closes or sabotage the closing process. Most often, however, employees are cooperative until the end. As organizations become more and more aware of the benefits offered by incremental change, they are increasing communication with the workforce to gain workers' cooperation and to overcome their resistance to change.

Participation and Empowerment. Inviting workers to participate in the change process is becoming a popular method of reducing resistance to change. Participation complements empowerment (see Chapter 14), increasing workers' involvement in decision making and giving them greater autonomy to change work procedures to improve organizational performance. In addition, to encourage workers to share their skills and talents, organizations are opening up their books to inform workers about the organization's financial condition. Some organizations use employee stock ownership plans

(ESOPs) to motivate and reward employees and to harness their commitment to change. Wal-Mart, for example, has an ESOP for its ordinary store employees and encourages their continual input into decision making. Participation and empowerment are two key elements of most TQM programs. The way in which General Electric implemented a major change in its appliance division illustrates how empowerment can work in practice to create a competitive advantage (Insight 19.4).

Insight 19.4

Competitive Advantage

GE's Empowered Workforce

In 1992 when GE's huge washing machine complex in Appliance Park outside Louisville, Kentucky, posted another huge loss of over $40 million, GE was on the point of shutting it down and getting out of the washing machine business. With a history of poor labor relations and poor product quality, GE's managers were about to give up, but management and unions sat down in one last attempt to find a solution to the problem that would save the workers' jobs and GE's washing machine business.

Together, management and the union worked out a program to reengineer the way the washing machine factory operated. Previously, the union had insisted on strict job definitions to protect its members. Each worker had been responsible for performing a specific task and had been paid on a piece-rate basis. The new 43-point agreement threw this work system to the winds. Workers expressed their willingness to make radical changes in the work process, assuming new job duties and responsibilities.[53]

Workers now move around the factory freely from job to job when their services are needed. To broaden their job definitions, they have learned the skills to perform many jobs, and they have been organized into teams that have the responsibility for raising quality and increasing productivity. The number of supervisors has been cut dramatically, which has also saved costs. When workers spot defective parts, rather than report the problem to their now-more-distant superiors, they can complain directly to the parts supplier.

The effects of these changes have been dramatic. In 1995 Appliance Park made a large profit. GE has increased employment there by over a thousand workers and has decided to invest over $1 billion to upgrade the products and production facilities. Workers' jobs are secure, and a new spirit of optimism pervades the workplace as workers look forward to sharing in the returns that the changed work system and newly acquired competitive advantage have made possible. However, it took the threat of plant closure to bring about this momentous change.

Facilitation.   Both managers and workers find change stressful because established task and role relationships alter as it takes place. As we discussed in Chapter 9, organizations have several ways to help their members manage stress: providing them with training to help them learn how to perform new tasks, providing them with time off from work to recuperate from the stressful effects of change, or even giving senior members sabbaticals to allow them to recuperate and plan their future work activities. Companies such as Microsoft and Apple Computer, for example, give their most talented programmers time off from ordinary job assignments to think about ways to create new kinds of products.

Many companies employ psychologists and consultants who specialize in helping employees to handle the stress associated with change. During organizational restructuring, when large layoffs are common, many organizations employ consultants to help laid-off workers deal with the stress and uncertainty of being laid off and having to find new jobs. Some companies pay consultants to help their CEOs manage the responsibilities associated with their own jobs, including the act of laying off workers, which CEOs find particularly stressful, for they understand the impact that layoffs have on employees and their families.

Bargaining and Negotiation.   Bargaining and negotiation are important tools that help managers manage conflict (see Chapter 18). Because change causes conflict, bargaining is an important tool in overcoming resistance to change. By using action research, managers can anticipate the effects of change on interpersonal and intergroup relationships. Managers can use this knowledge to help different people and groups negotiate their future tasks and roles and reach compromises that will lead them to accept change. Negotiation also helps individuals and groups understand how change will affect others so that the organization as a whole can develop a common perspective on why change is taking place and why it is important.

Manipulation.   When it is clear that change will help some individuals and groups at the expense of others, senior managers need to intervene in the bargaining process and manipulate the situation to secure the agreement, or at least the acceptance, of various people or groups to the results of the change process. As we discussed in Chapter 18, powerful managers have considerable ability to resist change, and in large organizations infighting among divisions can slow or halt the change process unless it is carefully managed. Politics and political tactics like co-optation and building alliances become important as ways of overcoming the opposition of powerful functions and divisions that feel threatened by the changes taking place.

Coercion.   The ultimate way to eliminate resistance to change is to coerce the key players into accepting change and threaten dire consequences if they choose to resist. Workers and managers at all levels can be threatened with reassignment, demotion, or even termination if they resist or threaten the change process. Top managers attempt to use the legitimate power at their disposal to quash resistance to change and to eliminate it. The advantage of coercion can be the speed at which change takes place. The disadvantage is that it can leave people angry and disenchanted and can make the refreezing process difficult.

Small-group interaction in a training workshop held in Poughkeepsie, New York. This workshop was held to improve understanding of how people interpret what takes place in a mediation or bargaining situation.

Managers should not underestimate the level of resistance to change. Organizations work because they reduce uncertainty by means of predictable rules and routines that people can use to accomplish their tasks. Change wipes out the predictability of rules and routines and perhaps spells the end of the status and prestige that accompany some positions. It is not surprising that people resist change and that organizations themselves, as collections of people, are so difficult to change.

OD TECHNIQUES TO PROMOTE CHANGE

Many OD techniques are designed to make changes and to refreeze them. These techniques can be used at the individual, group, and organization levels. The choice of techniques is determined by the type of change. In general, the more revolutionary a change is, the more likely is an organization to use OD techniques at all three levels. Counseling, sensitivity training, and process consultation are OD techniques directed at changing the attitudes and behavior of individuals. Different techniques are effective at the group and organization levels.

Counseling, Sensitivity Training, and Process Consultation.   Recall from Chapter 2 that the personalities of individuals differ and that the differences lead individuals to interpret and react to other people and events in a variety of ways. Even though personality cannot be changed significantly in the short run, people can be helped to understand that their own perceptions of a situation are not necessarily the correct or the only possible ones. People can also be helped to understand that they should learn to tolerate differences in perception and to embrace and accept human diversity. Counseling and sensitivity training are techniques that organizations can use to help individuals understand the nature of their own and other people's personalities and to use that knowledge to improve their interactions with others.[54] The highly motivated, driven boss, for example, must learn that his or her subordinates are not disloyal, lazy, or afflicted with personality problems because they are content to go home at 5 o'clock and want unchallenging job assignments. Instead, they have their own set of work values, and they value their leisure time. Traditionally, one of OD's main efforts has been to improve the quality of the work life of organizational members and increase their well-being and satisfaction with the organization.

Organizational members who are perceived by their superiors or peers to have certain problems in appreciating the viewpoints of others or in dealing with certain types of organizational members are counseled by trained professionals such as psychologists. Through counseling they learn how to more effectively manage their interactions with other people in the organization. Recall from Chapter 1, for example, that one challenge facing growing numbers of white male managers is learning how to manage female and minority employees effectively. Similarly, a female manager might receive counseling because her peers find her too aggressive or ambitious and her drive to succeed is poisoning work relationships in a group.

> **Sensitivity training**
> An OD technique that consists of intense counseling in which group members, aided by a facilitator, learn how others perceive them and may learn how to deal more sensitively with others.

Sensitivity training is an intense type of counseling.[55] Organizational members who are perceived as having problems in dealing with others meet in a group with a trained facilitator to learn more about how they and the other group members view the world. Group members are encouraged to be forthright about how they view themselves and other group members, and through discussion they learn the degree to which others perceive them in similar or different ways. Through examining the source of differences in perception, members of the group may reach a better understanding of the way others perceive them and may learn how to deal more sensitively with others.

Participation in sensitivity training is a very intense experience because a person's innermost thoughts and feelings are brought to light and dissected in public. This process makes many people very uncomfortable, so certain ethical issues may be raised by an organization's decision to send "difficult" members for sensitivity training in the hope that they will learn more about themselves.

> **Process consultation**
> An OD technique in which a facilitator works closely with a manager on the job to help the manager improve his or her interaction with other group members.

Is a manager too directive, too demanding, or too suspicious of subordinates? Does a manager deliberately deprive subordinates of information in order to keep them dependent? **Process consultation** provides answers to such questions. Process consultation bears a resemblance to both counseling and sensitivity training.[56] A trained process consultant, or facilitator, works closely with a manager on the job, to help the manager improve his or her interaction with other group members. The outside consultant acts as a sounding board so that the manager can gain a better idea about what is going on in the group setting and can discover the interpersonal dynamics that are determining the quality of work relationships within the group.

Process consultation, sensitivity training, and counseling are just three of the many OD techniques that have been developed to help individuals learn to change their attitudes and behavior so that they can function effectively both as individuals and as organizational members. It is common for many large organizations to provide their higher-level managers with a yearly budget to be spent on individual development efforts such as these or on more conventional knowledge-gaining events such as executive education programs.

Team Building and Intergroup Training. To manage change within a group or between groups, change agents can employ three different kinds of OD

Team building
An OD technique in which a facilitator first observes the interactions of group members and then helps them become aware of ways to improve their work interactions.

techniques. **Team building,** a common method of improving relationships within a group, is similar to process consultation except that all the members of a group participate together to try to improve their work interactions.[57] For example, group members discuss with a change agent who is a trained group facilitator the quality of the interpersonal relationships among team members and between the members and their supervisor. The goal of team building is to improve the way group members work together—to improve group processes to achieve process gains and reduce process losses that are occurring because of social loafing (discussed in Chapter 11). Team building does *not* focus on what the group is trying to achieve.

Team building is important when reengineering reorganizes the way people from different functions work together. When new groups are formed, team building can help group members quickly establish task and role relationships so that they can work effectively together. Team building facilitates the development of functional group norms and values and helps members develop a common approach to solving problems.

The change agent begins the team-building process by watching group members interact and identifying the way the group currently works. Then the change agent talks with some or all of the group members one on one to get a sense of the problems that the group is experiencing or just to identify where the group process could be improved. In a subsequent team-building session that normally takes place at a location away from the normal work context, the change agent discusses with group members the observations he or she has made and asks for their views on the issues brought to their attention. Ideally, through this discussion team members develop a new appreciation about the forces that have been affecting their behavior. Group members may form small task forces to suggest ways of improving group process or to discuss specific ways of handling the problems that have been arising. The goal is to establish a platform from which group members themselves, with no input from the change agent, can make continuous improvements in the way the group functions.

Intergroup training
An OD technique that uses team building to improve the work interactions of different functions or divisions.

Intergroup training takes team building one step further and uses it to improve the ways different functions or divisions work together. Its goal is to improve organizational performance by focusing on a function's or division's joint activities and output. Given that cross-functional coordination is especially important in reengineering and total quality management, intergroup training is an important OD technique that organizations can exploit to implement change.

Organizational mirroring
An OD technique in which a facilitator helps two interdependent groups explore their perceptions and relations in order to improve their work interactions.

A popular form of intergroup training is called **organizational mirroring,** an OD technique designed to improve the effectiveness of interdependent groups.[58] Suppose that two groups are in conflict or simply need to learn more about each other and one of the groups calls in a consultant to improve intergroup cooperation. The consultant begins by interviewing members of both groups to understand how each group views the other and to uncover possible problems the groups are having with each other. The groups are then brought together in a training session, and the consultant tells them that the goal of the session is to explore perceptions and relations in order to improve work relationships. Then, with the consultant leading the discussion, one group describes its perceptions of what is happening and its problems with the other group, while the other group sits and listens. Then the consultant reverses the situation—hence the term *organizational mirroring*—and the group that was listening takes its turn discussing its perceptions of what is happening and its problems, while the other group listens.

As a result of that initial discussion, each group appreciates the other's perspective. The next step is for members of both groups to form task forces to discuss ways of dealing with the issues or problems that have surfaced. The goal is to develop action plans that can be used to guide future intergroup relations and provide a basis for follow-up. The change agent guiding this training session needs to be skilled in intergroup relations because both groups are discussing sensitive issues. If the process is not managed well, intergroup relations can be further weakened by this OD technique.

Organizational confrontation meeting

An OD technique that brings together all of the managers of an organization to confront the issue of whether the organization is effectively meeting its goals.

Total Organizational Interventions. A variety of OD techniques can be used at the organization level to promote organization-wide change. One is the **organizational confrontation meeting**.[59] At this meeting, all of the managers of an organization meet to confront the issue of whether the organization is effectively meeting its goals. At the first stage of the process, again with facilitation by a change agent, top management invites free and open discussion of the organization's situation. Then the consultant divides the managers into groups of seven or eight, ensuring that the groups are as heterogeneous as possible and that no bosses and subordinates are members of the same group (so as to encourage free and frank discussion). The small groups report their findings to the total group, and the sorts of problems confronting the organization are categorized. Top management uses this statement of the issues to set organizational priorities and plan group action. Task forces are formed from the small groups to take responsibility for working on the problems identified, and each group reports back to top management on progress that has been made. The result of this process is likely to be changes in the organization's structure and operating procedures. Restructuring, reengineering, and total quality management often originate in organization-wide OD interventions that reveal the kinds of problems that an organization needs to solve.

Managerial Grid®

A matrix that OD facilitators use to characterize an organization's managerial style in terms of its managers' concern for people and concern for production.

Another organization-wide OD technique is the use of the **Managerial Grid**® developed by Robert Blake and Jane Mouton, two famous OD researchers who were instrumental in developing intergroup training techniques as well.[60] The Managerial Grid® is a matrix that was designed to facilitate changing an organization's management style and its norms and values to establish what Blake and Mouton called a "team management" style. In an organization using this style of management, managers act to build commitment from employees and to develop organizational values based on mutual trust and respect.

Blake and Mouton identified five styles of management ("team management" is one of them) and two factors—*concern for people* and *concern for production* (broadly similar, respectively, to the leadership dimensions of *consideration* and *initiating structure* discussed in Chapter 12)—that characterize the values of most organizations. In Blake and Mouton's view, effective organizations exhibit a strong concern for both people and production, and organizations that shortchange one or the other or both of them need to implement an organization-wide OD intervention program to teach managers how to develop the team management style.

Using questionnaires completed by an organization's managers, Blake and Mouton assess an organization's concern for people and concern for production. "Impoverished" is the word they use to describe the management style of organizations that score low on both factors. Managers in such organizations exert minimum effort to get required work done. In contrast, the management style in organizations in which managers score high on concern for production and low on concern for people Blake and Mouton call "task management." "Country club management" is the term they use for a management style that emphasizes a concern for people but not for production.

In Blake and Mouton's view, an organization that does not score high on both concern for people and concern for production should embark on an organization-wide training program to raise managerial concern for these factors and achieve a "team management" style as the preferred choice. After the training program is completed, managers should be reassessed to determine how effective the OD training was in moving their style in the direction of team management.

SUMMARY

Organizational change is an ongoing process that has important implications for organizational performance and for the well-being of an organization's members. An organization and its members must be constantly on the alert for changes from within the organization and from the outside environment, and they must learn how to adjust to change quickly and effectively. Often, the revolutionary types of change that result from restructuring and reengineering are necessary only because an organization and its managers ignored or were unaware of changes in the environment and did not make incremental changes as needed. The more an organization changes, the easier and more effective the change process becomes. Developing and managing a plan for change are vital to an organization's success. In this chapter, we made the following major points:

1. Organizational change is the movement of an organization away from its present state and toward some future state to increase its effectiveness. Forces for organizational change include competitive forces, economic, political, and global forces, demographic and social forces, and ethical forces. Organizations are often reluctant to change because resistance to change at the organization, group, and individual levels has given rise to organizational inertia.

2. Sources of organization-level resistance to change include power and conflict, differences in functional orientation, mechanistic structure, and organizational culture. Sources of group-level resistance to change include group norms, group cohesiveness, and groupthink and escalation of commitment. Sources of individual-level resistance to change include uncertainty and insecurity, selective perception and retention, and habit.

3. According to Lewin's force-field theory of change, organizations are balanced between forces pushing for change and forces resistant to change. To get an organization to change, managers must find a way to increase the forces for change, reduce resistance to change, or do both simultaneously.

4. Types of changes fall into two broad categories: evolutionary and revolutionary. The main instruments of evolutionary change are socio-technical systems theory and total quality management. The main instruments of revolutionary change are reengineering, restructuring, and innovation.

5. Action research is a strategy that managers can use to plan the change process. The main steps in action research are (1) diagnosis and analysis of the organization, (2) determining the desired future state, (3) implementing action, (4) evaluating the action, and (5) institutionalizing action research.

6. Organizational development (OD) is a series of techniques and methods to increase the adaptability of organizations. OD techniques can be used to overcome resistance to change and to help the organization to change itself.

7. OD techniques for dealing with resistance to change include education and communication, participation and empowerment, facilitation, bargaining and negotiation, manipulation, and coercion.

8. OD techniques for promoting change include, at the individual level, counseling, sensitivity training, and process consultation; at the group level, team building and intergroup training; and at the organization level, organizational confrontation meetings and use of the Managerial Grid®.

Organizational Behavior in Action

TOPICS FOR DISCUSSION AND ACTION

1. What are the main forces for and impediments to change?
2. How do evolutionary change and revolutionary change differ?
3. What is the main purpose of total quality management?
4. What is a business process, and why is reengineering a popular instrument of change today?
5. Why is restructuring sometimes necessary for reengineering to take place?
6. Which type of change is likely to encounter the greatest resistance?
7. What are the main steps in action research?
8. What is organizational development, and what is its goal?
9. In what ways can team building and intergroup training promote organizational effectiveness?

BUILDING DIAGNOSTIC SKILLS

Coping with Change

Imagine that you are the manager of a design group that is soon to be reengineered into a cross-functional team composed of people from several different functions that have had little contact with one another.

1. Discuss the resistance to change at the organization and individual levels that you will likely encounter.
2. Using action research, chart the steps that you will use to manage the change process.
   a. How will you diagnose the work group's present state?
   b. How will you determine the cross-functional team's desired future state?
   c. What will be the most important implementation choices you will face? For example, how will you manage resistance to change?
   d. What criteria will you use to evaluate the change process?
3. How might you use team building and other organizational development techniques to implement the change.

RESEARCH ON THE INTERNET: A MANAGER'S TOOL

Specific Task

Many organizations have been undergoing major kinds of change in the 1990s. Kmart is one such company. Enter Kmart Corporation's website (www.kmart.com), and click on "The Kmart Story," which gives a brief account of the changes that have occurred at Kmart historically.

1. What kinds of forces for change have been operating on Kmart that have been affecting the way it operates?
2. Search for some recent articles on Kmart that bring the Kmart story up to date. What is happening at Kmart now and how well is the company

doing? What change strategy is the company using to improve its performance?

General Task
Search for the website of a company that has been experiencing one of the types of changes discussed in the chapter. What kind of changes has the company been undergoing, and what forces and resistances to change are working on the company?

TOPICS FOR DEBATE

Organizational change alters role and task relationships at all levels of an organization. Now that you understand the nature and process of organizational change, debate the following issues:

Debate One
Team A. The most effective way to change an organization is to use evolutionary change.

Team B. The most effective way to change an organization is to use revolutionary change.

Debate Two
Team A. Changing people's attitudes and behavior is easier than changing organizational structure and culture.

Team B. Changing organizational structure and culture is easier than changing people's attitudes and behavior.

EXPERIENTIAL EXERCISE

Analyzing Forces for and Impediments to Change
Objectives
Your objective is to understand the complex problems surrounding organizational change.

Procedure
The class divides into groups of from three to five people. Each member of the group assumes the role of supervisor of a group of manufacturing workers who assemble mainframe computers. Here is the scenario.

The workers' jobs are changing because of the introduction of a new, computer-controlled manufacturing technology. Using the old technology, workers stationed along a moving conveyor belt performed a clearly defined set of operations to assemble the computers. The new, computerized technology makes it possible to produce many different models of computers simultaneously.

To operate the technology effectively, workers have to learn new, more complex skills, and they also have to learn how to work in teams because the new technology is based on the use of flexible work teams. In the new work teams, the workers themselves, not a supervisor, will be responsible for product quality and for organizing work activities. The new role of the supervisor will be to facilitate, not direct, the work process. Indeed, a major part of the change to flexible work teams involves introducing a total quality management program to improve quality and reduce costs.

1. Chart the main impediments to change at the organization, group, and individual levels that you, as internal change agents, are likely to encounter as you assign workers to flexible work teams.
2. Discuss some ways to overcome resistance to change in order to help the organization move to its future desired state.
3. Discuss the pros and cons of top-down change and bottom-up change, and decide which of them should be used to implement the change in the work system.
4. Which specific organizational development techniques might be most useful in helping to implement the change smoothly?

MAKING THE CONNECTION

Find an example of a company that has recently gone through a major change. What type of change was it? Why did the organization make the change, and what does it hope to achieve from it?

CLOSING CASE

A Revolution at Hallmark Cards

Hallmark Cards, based in Kansas City, Missouri, sells 44 percent of the 7.3 billion birthday, Christmas, and other kinds of cards sold each year in the United States. In the 1990s it has come under increasing attack from smaller and more agile competitors who pioneered new kinds of specialty greeting cards and sell them, often at discount prices, in supermarkets and discount stores. Hallmark's top managers realized that they needed to respond to these changes in their environment if they were to keep Hallmark on top of its market into the next century. So they decided to examine how things were currently being done at Hallmark, in order to determine what changes needed to be made.

Top management began this evaluation by placing a hundred managers into teams to analyze Hallmark's competitors, the changing nature of customer needs, the organizational structure the company was using to coordinate its activities, and the ways the company was developing, distributing, and marketing its cards—its basic business processes. What the teams found startled managers from the top down and showed that there was a need for change.

Managers discovered that although Hallmark had the world's largest creative staff—over 700 artists and writers who design over 24,000 new cards each year—it was taking over three years to get a new card to market. Once an artist designed a new card and a writer came up with an appropriate rhyme or message, it took an average of three years for the card to be produced, packaged, and shipped to retailers. Information on changing customer needs, a vital input into decisions about what cards should be designed, took many months to reach artists. That delay made it difficult for Hallmark to respond quickly to its competitors.

Armed with this information, the hundred team managers presented top management with a hundred recommendations for changes that would allow the company to do its work more quickly and effectively. The recommendations called for a complete change in the way the company organized its basic business processes. The managers proposed a complete reengineering and restructuring of the company's activities to achieve certain goals: to get new cards to market in under a year, to create new kinds of products to appeal to changing customer desires, and to achieve those two goals while continuously improving quality and reducing costs. How was the company to achieve these ambitious goals?

Hallmark began by completely restructuring its activities. The organization had been using a functional structure. Artists worked separately from writers, and both artists and writers worked separately from materials management, printing, and manufacturing personnel. These functions were often located far apart from each other. From the time a card went from the creative staff to the printing department, twenty-five handoffs (work exchanges between functions) were needed to produce the final product, and 90 percent of the time work was simply sitting in somebody's in- or out-basket. Taking the advice of the teams, Hallmark changed to a cross-functional team structure. People from different functions—artists, writers, editors, and so on—were grouped into teams responsible for producing a specific kind of card, such as Christmas cards, get-well cards, or new lines of specialty cards.

To eliminate the need for handoffs between departments, each team is responsible for all aspects of the design process. To reduce the need for handoffs within a team, all team members work together from the beginning to plan the steps in the design process, and all are responsible for reviewing the success of their efforts. To help each team evaluate its efforts and to give each team the information it needs about customer desires, Hallmark introduced a computerized point-of-sales merchandising system in each of its Hallmark Card stores, so each team has instant feedback on what and how many kinds of cards are selling. Each team can now continuously experiment with new card designs to attract more customers.

The effects of these changes have been dramatic. Not only are cards introduced in less than one year, but some reach the market in a matter of months. Quality has increased as each team focuses on improving its cards, and costs have fallen because the new work system is so efficient. The new streamlined, more flexible Hallmark is now able to keep up with smaller competitors. It continually creates new cross-functional teams to speed the introduction of new lines of cards and to keep up the pace of change.

Discussion Questions
1. What were the main steps in Hallmark's change process?
2. Do you think Hallmark's designers like the changed work system? Why or why not?

Appendix: Research Methods in Organizational Behavior

Overview

Research methods is a broad term that refers to the set of techniques used to acquire knowledge or learn about something of interest. In organizational behavior, research methods are the techniques used to learn about how individuals and groups respond to and act in organizations and how organizations respond to their environments.

An understanding of research methods is important for several reasons:

1. It allows researchers, managers, and other members of organizations to learn about why people feel and behave as they do in organizations.
2. It helps people to solve problems in organizations and, more generally, come up with ways to increase performance and well-being.
3. It can help managers and other members of an organization use findings from research done by others to improve conditions in their organizations.
4. It can help members of an organization properly evaluate advice and recommendations provided by others such as consultants.
5. It allows people to evaluate the various theories of organizational behavior.[1]

Our discussion of research methods proceeds as follows. We present a general model of the scientific process used to learn about organizational behavior. We discuss how researchers develop theories to explain some aspect of organizational behavior and how theories can be evaluated. We move on to the actual testing of theories. We discuss the different types of research designs that are used throughout the scientific process. We conclude with a discussion of ethical considerations.

The Scientific Process

A basic model of the scientific process is provided in Fig. A.1.[2] Because the model is cyclical, we could start describing the process at any point. For convenience, we start at point A, the observation of organizational behavior. At point A, a researcher notices something about organizational behavior that she or he wishes to learn more about. The researcher may observe, for example, that levels of absenteeism are higher in some groups than in others,

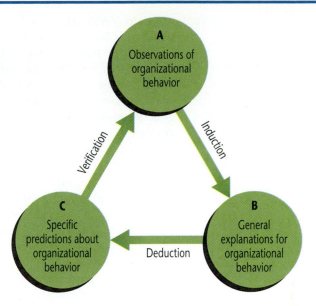

FIGURE A.1

The Scientific Process

that workers performing some jobs experience much higher levels of stress than do those performing other jobs, or that some workers put forth much more effort than others.

After making observations like these, the researcher tries through induction to come up with a general explanation for what she or he has observed (point B in Fig. A.1). Induction is the process that researchers use to come up with general ways to account for or explain specific observations or instances of organizational behavior. Researchers who observed that individuals varied in the amounts of effort they exerted on the job, for example, tried to come up with some general explanations for what they observed. The outcome was theories of work motivation.

Once a researcher has a general explanation to account for a phenomenon, then, through deduction, she or he makes specific predictions that seem likely to be true if the general explanation was a good one. Deduction is the process of making specific predictions (point C in Fig. A.1) from general explanations. A general explanation for absenteeism (arrived at through induction), for example, might be that workers are most likely to be absent from their jobs when they are dissatisfied and have many personal responsibilities in addition to their work responsibilities. Having made this general explanation from induction, the researcher might use deduction to predict that nurses who are dissatisfied with their jobs and have children will have higher levels of absence from work during a year than will nurses who are satisfied and do not have children.

Once a researcher has made a prediction, the next step in the scientific process is to test this prediction and determine the extent to which it is true. Verification is the process by which researchers determine whether their predictions are accurate by making specific observations about organizational behavior. The researcher might ask 150 nurses employed by a large hospital to complete a questionnaire that includes measures of job satisfaction and also asks them how many children they have. The researcher might also ask the hospital to supply the number of days each nurse is absent for one year. These observations allow the researcher to verify whether her predictions are accurate. Verification completes the cycle of the scientific process and the researcher is back at point A in Fig. A.1.

Because human behavior in organizations is complex and determined by many factors, it is often the case that at least part of the predictions researchers make are not verified or found to be true by observations of actual organizational behavior. When this occurs, a new cycle of induction and deduction begins. Researchers cycle through the process again and try to come up with another general explanation for what they observed, make predictions from this explanation, and then test these predictions through verification.

Research in organizational behavior, as in all fields of study, is a cooperative undertaking. Several different researchers might all be studying the same phenomenon and learning from each other's research. One researcher who studies absenteeism, for example, might come up with a new explanation for absenteeism. Based on this explanation, another researcher might make certain predictions and test them in several organizations. Some of these predictions might be verified, and others might not be. A third researcher then might seek to modify the original explanation to account for these new observations.

Researchers cooperate with each other or learn and build from each other's research in several ways. Researchers who already know each other often share ideas and research findings informally as well as ask for each other's advice. At professional meetings and conferences researchers present their work to other researchers who are interested in the same topic. Moreover, researchers write up their ideas and findings and publish them in journals and books for others to read.

Coming Up With General Explanations: The Role of Theory Building

A theory is a general explanation of some phenomenon. Theories are arrived at through induction. When researchers build theories, they are moving from point A to point B in the scientific process shown in Fig. A.1. Theories summarize and organize what researchers have already learned about some phenomenon as well as provide direction for future research. Theories can never be proved to be "correct" because there is always the possibility that a future study will not support the theory. When research findings are consistent with or support a theory, confidence in the theory increases. Above all else, theories should be useful. Theories should help us understand organizational behavior as well as provide direction for future research in organizational behavior.

Four basic criteria that researchers can use to determine a theory's usefulness are correspondence, coherence, parsimony, and pragmatism.[3] *Correspondence* is the extent to which a theory is congruent with what is actually observed in organizations. One way to determine correspondence is to see whether predictions derived from the theory are verified or found to be true. *Coherence* is the extent to which the logic in the theory is straightforward and the theory is free of any logical contradictions. *Parsimony* is the extent to which a theory is free of concepts or relationships that are not necessary to provide a good explanation. Suppose there are two theories of absenteeism, one includes five concepts and the other ten, and each does an equally good job of explaining absenteeism. The simpler theory is preferred because of its greater parsimony. *Pragmatism* is the extent to which a theory stimulates further research. A minimal condition for pragmatism is that the theory is able to be tested. No matter how eloquent a theory is, if no one is able to test it, the theory is not very useful at all.

Developing Specific Predictions: Formulating Hypotheses

Once a theory is in place, researchers need to make specific predictions based on the theory—or, through deduction move from point B to point C in Fig. A.1. Specific predictions in organizational behavior are often stated in the form of hypotheses. A hypothesis is a statement about the relationship between two or more variables.[4] A variable is a dimension along which some aspect of individuals, groups, or organizations differs or varies. Variables pertaining to individuals include age, gender, job satisfaction, organizational commitment, motivation, and job performance. Variables pertaining to groups include group size, group norms, and group cohesiveness. Variables pertaining to organizations include organizational structure, technology, and culture.

Some hypotheses simply state that two or more variables are related to each other. Other hypotheses state how variables affect each other—that is, they describe a causal relationship between variables. Ultimately, researchers always prefer to be able to state their hypotheses in causal terms; causal relationships provide explanations for why things happen. When hypotheses are not stated in causal terms, the reason often is that the researcher is very uncertain about what causal relationship to expect or knows that she or he will not be able to conduct research to test a causal relationship.

When hypotheses do describe a causal relationship between variables, the variables can be categorized into four types: independent variables, dependent variables, mediator variables, and moderator variables. An *independent variable* is a variable that causes another variable to change when it varies or changes. The variable that changes in response to the independent variable is called the *dependent variable* (see Fig. A.2). A hypothesis might state, for example, that when the payment of production workers changes from an hourly basis to a piece-rate basis, levels of performance or production increase. In this example, the method of pay is the independent variable, and performance is the dependent variable.

FIGURE A.2

A Casual Relationship

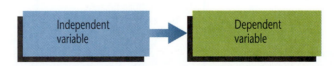

Sometimes independent variables do not directly affect dependent variables but rather operate through a third variable. A **mediator variable** is a mechanism through which an independent variable has an effect on a dependent variable (see Fig. A.3). In organizational behavior, mediator variables often refer to something that is hard to observe directly, such as motivation. In our previous example, a mediator of the relationship between method of pay and performance may be motivation. Method of pay impacts motivation such that workers are more motivated to perform at a high level when their pay is based on their performance rather than on an hourly rate. When motivation increases, performance increases (assuming all else is equal).

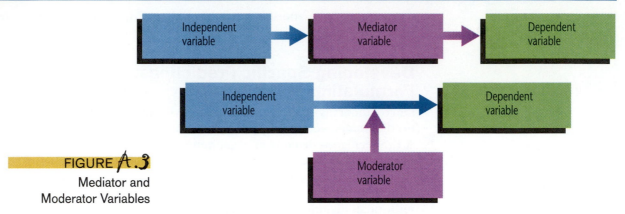

Mediator and
Moderator Variables

A **moderator variable** is a variable that, when it changes, changes the nature of the relationship between the independent and the dependent variables (see Fig. A.3). When the moderator variable changes, for example, it can turn strong positive relationships into weaker positive relationships, into negative relationships, or into no relationships at all. Positive, negative, and no relationships are depicted graphically in Fig. A.4. An example of a moderator of the relationship between method of pay and performance is financial need. A hypothesis might state that there is a strong, positive relationship between method of pay and performance for workers who have high financial needs and a weak positive relationship for workers who have low financial needs.

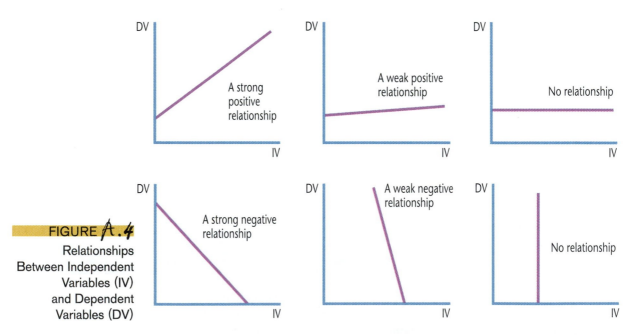

FIGURE A.4

Relationships
Between Independent
Variables (IV)
and Dependent
Variables (DV)

Testing Hypotheses: Operationalizing Variables

Once researchers have specific predictions or hypotheses, they then have to test them through the process of verification—that is, they must move from point C to point A in the scientific process illustrated in Fig. A.1. In order to test hypotheses, researchers need to find ways to measure the variables in the hypotheses. Many of the variables of interest in organizational behavior are abstract. Job satisfaction, motivation, stress, culture, and organizational structure, for example, are abstract terms that are sometimes hard to define, let alone measure. Nevertheless, finding measures for these variables is necessary in order to test hypotheses.

As a first step, researchers need to have clear conceptual definitions of the variables or be certain about what exactly they are trying to measure. Then they need to find ways of operationalizing, or measuring, these variables. A specific measure of a variable is sometimes called an operational definition of the variable.

There are two important criteria by which to judge whether a good operational definition or measure of a variable is being used in a research study: reliability and validity. *Reliability* is the extent to which a measure of a variable is free of error. Suppose you are weighing people but the scale you are using is not reliable. Each time you weigh them their weight varies by three or four pounds even though their actual weight has not changed. Your measure of weight lacks reliability because it contains a significant amount of error.

Measures of job satisfaction, performance, and other organizational behavior variables need to be reliable in order for researchers to be able to have good tests of their hypotheses. For some organizational behavior variables, such as job satisfaction, reliable measures have already been created in the past and used in many research studies. These measures typically ask workers to answer a number of questions about their current jobs. Sample items from two of these measures are provided in Fig. 3.6 in Chapter 3. When using an existing measure of a variable, researchers should always determine how reliable or free of error the measure is in their own particular study.

There are several ways to assess the reliability of a measure. For example, if a questionnaire measure of job satisfaction asks workers to answer ten questions about their current job, each of the questions should be assessing job satisfaction. One way to determine whether the measure is reliable is to assess the extent to which each person's answers to the questions are consistent with each other. If each question taps job satisfaction, but on some questions people indicate that they are very satisfied and on others that they are very dissatisfied, then there is a lot of error in the measure and it is not reliable. This technique assesses internal consistency reliability.

Another way of determining reliability is assessing the extent to which repeated measures of a variable agree with each other (assuming that the variable itself has not changed). This technique assesses test-retest reliability. For example, the height of adults should not change from day to day, and a way to assess the reliability of a measure of height is to use the measure to determine people's height on several different days and assess the extent to which the measures of height are the same from day to day.

The second criterion by which to judge an operational definition or measure is validity. *Validity* is the extent to which an operational definition of a variable is actually measuring the variable in question. Given that many of the variables in organizational behavior research are abstract, it is essential that measures of variables are valid or that the measures are actually measuring what the researcher wants to measure. A measure of job satisfaction, for example, is not valid if it is simply measuring the extent to which people tend to have a positive outlook on life in general and not how they feel about their current jobs. Reliability is a necessary but not sufficient condition for validity. In order for a measure to be valid, at a minimum the measure has to be free of error. However, the measure also has to be tapping into the right variable.

Determining the validity of measures in organizational behavior is an ongoing and complicated process. Researchers cannot be sure from one research study that their measures are valid. Only through repeated use of measures can researchers be confident in the validity of their measures. Moreover, there are multiple indicators of validity. One indicator is the extent to which experts in an area think that the measure is adequately gauging the variable in question. Another indicator is the extent to which the measure is related to measures of other variables in expected ways and is different from other measures of different variables. Only through using a measure many times and relying on multiple indicators of validity can researchers be confident in the validity of their measures.

Research Designs

The design of a specific research study is geared toward what the researcher wishes to accomplish from the study. Different research designs or ways of conducting research are well suited to different stages in the research process. Here, we discuss three types of research designs: qualitative research, cross-sectional research, and experimental research.[5] Qualitative research can help researchers move from point A to B and from point B to C in the scientific process (see Fig. A.1). Cross-sectional and experimental research can help researchers move from point B to C and from point C to A. Each research design can be helpful in other ways as well. Cross-sectional research, for example, sometimes helps researchers move from point A to point B.

QUALITATIVE RESEARCH

One hallmark of qualitative research is the careful observation of actual behavior in organizations. Researchers watch what members of an organization do and listen to what they say in the hopes of getting an accurate picture of what naturally occurs in an organization. Researchers keep careful records of what they have observed. Qualitative research can provide researchers with a rich description of organizational life and the many factors that affect it.

There are two basic ways of doing qualitative research: participant observation and direct observation. In participant observation, the researcher actually becomes a member of the organization that he or she is observing, and often other members of the organization do not realize that the newest member of the department or team is conducting research. Participant observation gives the researcher the opportunity to experience firsthand what it is like to be a member of the organization, and it helps the researcher gain the confidence and trust of other members of the organization. In direct observation, the researcher enters an organization as an observer and records what he or she sees (often as it occurs). Direct observation can be less time-consuming than participant observation.

Because qualitative research entails detailed observations, it is often conducted in one or a few organizations. A key question that arises from this kind of research design pertains to the generalizability of the findings—the extent to which what researchers discover in one organization is true of other organizations.

CROSS-SECTIONAL RESEARCH

When using a cross-sectional design, researchers develop and test specific hypotheses about relationships between variables. To do so, they must develop or use existing measures of variables that are both reliable and valid. Questionnaires and interviews are often used to gather measures of variables. Although qualitative designs are well suited for making observations and coming up with general explanations for them, cross-sectional designs are well-suited for testing specific hypotheses because the researcher is actually collecting measures of variables. However, researchers cannot test hypotheses that state causal relationships between variables by using cross-sectional designs because they have no control over the many other factors that might impact a dependent variable in addition to the independent variable. Hence, with cross-sectional designs, researchers can test only hypotheses that state that certain variables are related to each other.

EXPERIMENTAL RESEARCH

The hallmark of experimental research designs is the controlled manipulation, or changing, of an independent variable to determine what effect it has on a dependent variable. There are two types of experimental research designs: true experiments and quasi-experiments.

True experiments are the only kind of research design that allows researchers to test causal hypotheses and draw conclusions about causal relationships. True experiments allow researchers to do this by controlling for everything else that might affect a dependent variable besides changes in the independent variable. Two features of true experiments provide this control: a control group and random assignment of participants to the experimental and the control groups.

Suppose a researcher is interested in the relationship between method of pay and performance and decides to do an experiment. The researcher hypothesizes that switching from an hourly pay plan to a piece-rate pay plan results in an increase in performance. He or she takes a group of workers who are currently being paid on an hourly rate and switches them to a piece-rate plan and measures their performance before and after the change. Performance does increase after the change. Can the researcher conclude that the change in pay plan caused the change in performance? No, and the reason is that the researcher did not control for other things—in addition to the change in pay plan—that might have been responsible for a change in performance, such as the fact that the workers have gained more job experience and thus their performance would have increased regardless of the change in pay plan.

By having a control group—a group of participants for whom the researcher does not change the independent variable (in this case, the pay plan)—the researcher is able to control for, or take into account, other things besides the pay plan that might affect performance because the control group also will be exposed to these things. By randomly assigning participants to the experimental and control groups, the researcher guarantees that these groups start out at an equivalent position. Because the experimental and control groups start out in equivalent positions (because of random assignment), the only difference between the groups is the change in pay plan. Thus, if the performance level of the control group stays the same but rises for the experimental group, the researcher can confidently conclude that the change in pay plan caused the change in performance. Conversely, if the performance levels of both groups stay the same or increase, then the change in pay plan is not having the hypothesized effect.

For practical reasons it is very difficult to conduct true experiments in real organizations. Manipulating variables like pay and randomly assigning workers to experimental and control groups is often very disruptive to the ongoing activities of an organization, and few managers are willing to tolerate these disruptions. Partially for this reason, true experiments are often conducted in laboratory settings at universities using college students as participants rather than workers. The logic behind this practice is that if a researcher is studying some fundamental aspect of human functioning like motivation, she or he should be able to observe its operation in a laboratory with students or in an organization with workers. Although this assumption makes sense, it might also be the case that conditions in organizations are so different from conditions in the lab (or that some differences between workers and college students are so fundamental) that results from the lab do not generalize to the field or to real organizations. In other words, what might occur in the laboratory might not occur in an organization and vice versa. To be on the safe side, researchers need to supplement laboratory research with field research whenever possible. Some of the problems associated with conducting field experiments were revealed by the famous Hawthorne experiments.

Insight A.1

Organizational Behavior

The Hawthorne Studies

From 1924 to 1932 a series of experiments was conducted at the Hawthorne Works of the Western Electric Company, which became a part of AT&T.[6] These experiments, which became known as the Hawthorne studies, were started as an attempt to investigate how the characteristics of the work setting, specifically the level of lighting or illumination, affects worker fatigue and performance. The researchers conducted an experiment in which they systematically varied the level of illumination and attempted to measure its effects on worker productivity. However, the experiment produced some very strange results. The researchers found that whether they raised or lowered the level of illumination, productivity increased. In fact, productivity only began to fall when the level of illumination had dropped to the level of moonlight, a level at which presumably workers could no longer see well enough to do their work efficiently.

As you can imagine, the researchers were very puzzled with these results. They called on a noted Harvard psychologist, Elton Mayo, to help them and Mayo proposed to start another series of experiments to solve the mystery. These experiments, which became known as the Relay Assembly Test Experiments, were designed to investigate the effects of other aspects of the work context on job performance, such as the number and length of rest periods and hours of work on fatigue and monotony with the goal of raising productivity.[7] During a two-year study of a small group of female workers, the researchers once again observed that productivity increased over time but, once again, the increases could not be solely attributed to the effects of changes in the work setting. Gradually, the researchers came to realize that, to some degree, the results the researchers were obtaining were due to the fact that they themselves had become part of the experiment. In other words, the involvement of the researchers was affecting the results because the workers actually enjoyed receiving attention and being the subject of study and were willing to cooperate with the researchers to give them the results the researchers wanted.

Subsequently, it was found that many other factors also influenced worker behavior. However the importance of this effect, the famous "Hawthorne effect," was that it seemed to suggest that the attitudes of workers towards their jobs affect the level of their performance. In particular, that the style of management and supervision could affect performance. One of the main implications of the Hawthorne studies was that the characteristics of the social setting or group in which behavior takes place is as important as the technical aspects of the task in explaining the level of performance. The Hawthorne studies demonstrated the importance of understanding how the feelings, thoughts, and behavior of work group members and managers affect performance. It was becoming increasingly clear to researchers that understanding behavior in organizations is a complex process and that simple solutions to increasing performance are hard to come by.[8]

Similar to a true experiment, quasi-experiments also involve the manipulation of an independent variable. The major difference is that in a quasi-experiment a researcher does not have a control group or does not randomly assign participants to experimental and control groups. Quasi-experiments are often a practical necessity when researchers want to conduct experiments in real organizations. For example, a researcher might find an organization that currently operates six factories that employ a hundred workers each. The organization wants to experiment with changing from an hourly pay plan to a piece-rate pay plan. Management decides to make the change in three of the factories and leave the other three (to be used as a control group) on the existing hourly plan. In this quasi-experiment, there is a control group but no random assignment because of the practical problem that all workers in a single factory need to be working under the same pay system.

Because of the lack of a control group or random assignment, researchers cannot test causal hypotheses or arrive at causal conclusions from quasi-experiments. Nevertheless, quasi-experiments can provide valuable insights into organizational behavior.

TRADEOFFS IN THE CHOICE OF RESEARCH DESIGNS

By this time, it should be clear to you that multiple tradeoffs affect the choice of a research design. Qualitative designs have the advantage of providing researchers with a rich account of the many factors that influence organizational behavior. True experiments have the advantage of allowing researchers to test causal relationships. Researchers cannot come to causal conclusions from qualitative designs, and they might be neglecting important organizational behavior variables in true experiments. No one design is preferable over another, and each one is well suited to different stages in the scientific process. Moreover, research on any topic in organizational behavior benefits from research using all three types of designs.

Ethical Considerations In Organizational Behavior Research

Researchers have ethical obligations to research participants. There is disagreement about the exact nature of these obligations, but here are some guidelines that many researchers would agree with:[9]

1. The researcher should obtain the informed consent of research participants. When consent is informed, participants know that they are taking part in a research study and do so voluntarily. Obtaining informed consent becomes troublesome in a participant observation design because an integral feature of this design is that members of an organization do not realize that research is actually being conducted.
2. Participants should not be harmed in any way by the research being conducted.
3. Participants' rights to privacy should be respected.
4. Participants in a control group should not be denied treatment that the researcher knows would benefit them. This guideline is most clearly relevant to medical research. However, there are instances when it might be relevant to organizational behavior research, such as the case when a researcher knows that a certain type of training benefits workers yet gives only some of the workers the training (that is, those in the experimental group).
5. Participants should be debriefed. Once researchers have completed a study, they should let participants know what the study was about and that they are available to answer questions.
6. Data should be treated confidentially.

Summary

Only through conducting research on organizational behavior can progress be made in understanding how individuals and groups respond to and act in organizations and how organizations respond to their environments.

REFERENCES

CHAPTER 1

1. T. A. Stewart, "Brain Power: Who Owns It . . . How They Profit From It." *Fortune,* March 17, 1997, pp. 104–110.
2. S. N. Chakravarty, "How an Outsider's Vision Saved Kodak." *Forbes,* January 13, 1997, pp. 45–47.
3. "Return of the Stopwatch," *The Economist,* January 23, 1993, p. 69.
4. H. Fayol, *Industrial and General Administration* (London: Pitman, 1949); P. F. Drucker, *Management Tasks, Responsibilities, Practices* (New York: Harper and Row, 1974).
5. L. S. Richman, "Reengineering Under Fire," *Fortune,* April 18, 1994, p. 186.
6. H. Mintzberg, *The Nature of Managerial Work* (New York: Harper and Row, 1963).
7. R. L. Katz, "Skills of an Effective Administrator," *Harvard Business Review,* September-October 1974, pp. 90–102.
8. C.W.L. Hill and G. R. Jones, *Strategic Management: An Integrated Approach,* 4th ed. (Boston: Houghton Mifflin, 1998).
9. L. S. Richman, "Reengineering Under Fire," *Fortune,* April 18, 1994, p. 186.
10. R. Edward Freeman, *Business Ethics: The State of the Art* (New York: Oxford University Press, 1991).
11. R. C. Soloman, *Ethics and Excellence* (New York: Oxford University Press, 1992).
12. L. K. Trevino, "Ethical Decision Making in Organizations: A Person-Situation Interactionist Model," *Academy of Management Review,* 1986, 11, pp. 601–617.
13. H. Mintzberg, "The Case for Corporate Social Responsibility," *Journal of Business Strategy,* December 1983, pp. 3–15; J. J. Chrisman and A. B. Carroll, "Corporate Responsibility—Reconciling Economic and Social Goals," *Sloan Management Review,* 1984, 25, pp. 59–65.
14. H. Mintzberg, "The Case for Corporate Social Responsibility," *Journal of Business Strategy,* Winter 1973, pp. 3–15.
15. T. M. Jones, "Ethical Decision Making by Individuals in Organizations: An Issue Contingent Model," *Academy of Management Review,* 1991, 16, pp. 366–395; G. R. Shea, *Practical Ethics* (New York: American Management Association, 1988).
16. L. I. Kessler, *Managing Diversity in an Equal Employment Opportunity Workplace* (Washington, D.C.: National Foundation for the Study of Employment Policy, 1990).
17. W. B. Johnson and A. H. Packer, *Workforce 2000: Work and Workers in the 21st Century* (Indianapolis: Hudson Institute, 1987); M. Galen and A. T. Palmer, "White, Male and Worried," *Newsweek,* January 31, 1994, pp. 50–55.
18. Johnson and Packer; Galen and Palmer.
19. H. W. Fullerton, Jr., "New Labor Force Projections Spanning 1988–2000," *Monthly Labor Review,* November 1989, pp. 3–12.
20. M. Fine, F. Johnson, and M. S. Ryan, "Cultural Diversity in the Workforce," *Public Personnel Management,* 1990, 19, pp. 305–319.
21. T. Cox, Jr., *Cultural Diversity in Organizations* (San Francisco: Berrett Koehler, 1994).
22. D. Jamieson and J. O'Mara, *Managing Workforce 2000: Gaining the Diversity Advantage* (San Francisco: Jossey-Bass, 1991).
23. C. Hall, "Hoechst Celanese Diversifying Its Ranks," *Dallas Morning News,* September 27, 1992, pp. 1H, 7H.
24. S. Jackson and Associates, *Diversity in the Workplace: Human Resource Initiatives* (New York: Guildford Press, 1992).
25. Lennie Copeland, "Learning to Manage a Multicultural Workforce," *Training,* 1988, 25, pp. 48–56; B. Geber, "Managing Diversity," *Training,* 1990, 27, pp. 23–30.
26. J. R. Fulkerson and R. S. Schuler, "Managing Worldwide Diversity at Pepsi-Cola International," in Jackson and Associates, *Diversity in the Workplace,* pp. 248–278.
27. C. K. Prahalad and Y. L. Doz, *The Multinational Mission: Balancing Local Demands and Global Vision* (New York: Free Press, 1987); C. A. Bartlett and S. Ghoshal, *Transnational Management* (Homewood, Ill.: Irwin, 1992).
28. P. J. Dowling and R. S. Schuler, *International Dimensions of Human Resource Management* (Boston: PWS-Kent, 1990).
29. N. Adler, *International Dimensions of Organizational Behavior* (Boston: Kent, 1991).
30. G. Hofstede, "The Cultural Relativity of Organizational Practices and Theories," *Journal of International Business Studies,* Fall 1983, pp. 75–89.
31. R. L. Tung, "Selection and Training in U.S., European, and Japanese Multinationals," *California Management Review,* 1982, 25, pp. 57–71.
32. J. Keebler, "Ford Merges World Design," *Automotive News,* July 1993, p. 1.
33. J. Jarboe, "A Boy and His Airline," *Texas Monthly,* April 1989, pp. 98–104.
34. K. Labich, "Is Herb Kelleher America's Best CEO?" *Fortune,* May 2, 1994, pp. 45–52.
35. Labich, "Is Herb Kelleher America's Best CEO?"

CHAPTER 2

1. A. Reinhardt, "Intel's Dreamers Make Room for a Details Man," *Business Week,* 1997, May 26, pp. 125, 128.
2. A. Reinhardt, "Intel's Dreamers,".
3. Reinhardt, "Intel's Dreamers." D. E. Walsh, "Chip-Making Technique Called Breakthrough," *The Bryan-College Station Eagle,* 1997, September 8, p. B8. D. Takahashi, "Intel's Top Chip Architect to Unveil His Latest Creation," *Wall Street Journal,* October 10, 1997, pp. B1, B6.
4, 5. A. Tellegen, D. T. Lykken, T. J. Bouchard, K. J. Wilcox, N. L. Segal, and S. Rich, "Personality Similarity in Twins Reared Apart and Together," *Journal of Personality and Social Psychology,* 1988, 54, pp. 1031–1039.
6. J. M. George, "The Role of Personality in Organizational Life: Issues and Evidence," *Journal of Management,* 1992, 18, pp. 185–213.
7. R. D. Arvey, T. J. Bouchard, N. L. Segal, and L. M. Abraham, "Job Satisfaction: Environmental and Genetic Components," *Journal of Applied Psychology,* 1989, 74, pp. 187–192. A. P. Brief, M. J. Burke, J. M. George, B. Robinson, and J. Webster, "Should Negative Affectivity Remain an Unmeasured Variable in the Study of Job Stress?" *Journal of Applied Psychology,* 1988, 73, pp. 193–198. J. L. Holland, *Making Vocational Choices: A Theory of Careers* (Englewood Cliffs, N.J.: Prentice-Hall, 1973); R. J. House, W. D. Spangler, and J. Woycke, "Personality and Charisma in the U.S. Presidency: A Psychological Theory of Leader Effectiveness," *Administrative Science Quarterly,* 1991, 36, pp. 364–396.
8. M. R. Barrick, M. K. Mount, and J. P. Strauss, "Conscientiousness and Performance of Sales Representatives: Test of the Mediating Effects of Goal Setting," *Journal of Applied Psychology,* 1993, 78, pp. 715–722.
9. A. Davis-Blake and J. Pfeffer, "Just a Mirage: The Search for Dispositional Effects in Organizational Research," *Academy of Management Review,* 1989, 14, pp. 385–400.
10. R. C. Carson, "Personality," *Annual Review of Psychology,* 1989, 40, pp. 227–248. D. T. Kenrick and D. C. Funder, "Profiting from Controversy: Lessons from the Person-Situation Debate," *American Psychologist,* 1988, 43, pp. 23–34. D. C. Rowe, "Resolving the Person-Situation Debate: Invitation to an Interdisciplinary Dialogue," *American Psychologist,* 1987, 42, pp. 218–227.
11. B. Schneider, "The People Make the Place," *Personnel Psychology,* 1987, 40, pp. 437-453.
12. "Who Hires at Small Concerns? Often, It Is the Head Honcho," *Wall Street Journal,* November 17, 1992, p. A1.
13. J. M. Digman, "Personality Structure: Emergence of the Five-Factor Model," *Annual Review of Psychology,* 1990, 41, pp. 417–440. R. R. McCrae and P. T. Costa, "Validation of the Five-Factor Model of Personality Across Instruments and Observers," *Journal of Personality and Social Psychology,* 1987, 52, pp. 81–90; R. R. McCrae and P. T. Costa, "Discriminant Validity of NEO-PIR Facet Scales," *Educational and Psychological Measurement,* 1992, 52, pp. 229–237.
14. L. Bird, "Lazarus's IBM Coup Was All About Relationships," *Wall Street Journal,* May 26, 1994, pp. B1, B7.
15. Bird, "Lazarus's IBM Coup."
16. M. R. Barrick and M. K. Mount, "The Big Five Personality Dimensions and Job Performance: A Meta-Analysis," *Personnel Psychology,* 1991, 44, pp. 1–26. Barrick, Mount, and Strauss, "Conscientiousness and Performance of Sales Representatives."
17. J. O'C. Hamilton, "Roger Salquist," *Business Week, Reinventing America,* 1992, p. 186.
18. "A Gallery of Risk Takers," *Business Week, Reinventing America,* 1992, p. 183.
19. J. Saddler, "Young Risk-Takers Push the Business Envelope," *Wall Street Journal,* May 12, 1994, pp. B1, B2.
20. Saddler, "Young Risk-Takers."
21. M. A. Burke, A. P. Brief, and J. M. George, "The Role of Negative Affectivity in Understanding Relationships Between Self-Reports of Stressors and Strains: A Comment on the Applied Psychology Literature," *Journal of Applied Psychology,* 1993, 78, pp. 402–412.
22. Barrick and Mount, "The Big Five Personality Dimensions and Job Performance." J. M. George, "Mood and Absence," *Journal of Applied Psychology,* 1989, 74, pp. 317–324. J. M. George, "Time Structure and Purpose as a Mediator of Work-Life Linkages," *Journal of Applied Social Psychology,* 1991, 21, pp. 296–314.
23. J. B. Rotter, "Generalized Expectancies for Internal vs. External Control of Reinforcement," *Psychological Monographs,* 1966, 80, pp. 1-28; P. Spector, "Behavior in Organizations as a Function of Employees' Locus of Control," *Psychological Bulletin,* 1982, 91, pp. 482-497.
24. M. Snyder, "Self-Monitoring of Expressive Behavior," *Journal of Personality and Social Psychology,* 1974, 30, pp. 526–537. M. Snyder, "Self-Monitoring

Processes," in L. Berkowitz, ed., *Advances in Experimental Social Psychology,* 1979, 12, pp. 85–128.

25. J. Brockner, *Self-Esteem at Work* (Lexington, Mass.: Lexington Books, 1988).

26. D. C. Ganster, J. Schaubroeck, W. E. Sime, and B. T. Mayes, "The Nomological Validity of the Type A Personality Among Employed Adults," *Journal of Applied Psychology,* 1991, 76, pp. 143–168. R. H. Rosenman, "Current and Past History of Type A Behavior Pattern," in T. Schmidt, J. M. Dembrowski, and G. Blumchen, eds., *Biological and Psychological Factors in Cardiovascular Disease* (New York: Springer-Verlag).

27. R. A. Baron, "Personality and Organizational Conflict: Effects of the Type A Behavior Pattern and Self-Monitoring," *Organizational Behavior and Human Decision Processes,* 1989, 44, pp. 281-297.

28. D. C. McClelland, Human Motivation (Glenview, Ill.: Scott, Foresman, 1985). D. C. McClelland, "How Motives, Skills, and Values Determine What People Do," *American Psychologist,* 1985, 40, pp. 812–825. D. C. McClelland, "Managing Motivation to Expand Human Freedom," *American Psychologist,* 1978, 33, pp. 201–210.

29. D. C. McClelland, "Achievement and Entrepreneurship: A Longitudinal Study," *Journal of Personality and Organizational Behavior,* 1965, 1, pp. 389–392.

30. D. G. Winter, *The Power Motive* (New York: Free Press, 1973).

31. R. J. House, W. D. Spangler, and J. Woycke, "Personality and Charisma in the U.S. Presidency: A Psychological Theory of Leader Effectiveness," *Administrative Science Quarterly,* 1991, 36, 364–396.

32. M. Pacelle, "Noted Architects' Firm Falls Apart in Fight over Control, Clients," *Wall Street Journal,* September 2, 1992, pp. A1, A9.

33. M. J. Stahl, "Achievement, Power, and Managerial Motivation: Selecting Managerial Talent with the Job Choice Exercise," *Personnel Psychology,* 1983, 36, pp. 775–789.

34. D. C. McClelland and D. H. Burnham, "Power Is the Great Motivator," *Harvard Business Review,* 1976, 54, pp. 100–110.

35. L. M. Hough, N. K. Eaton, M. D. Dunnette, J. D. Kamp, and R. A. McCloy, "Criterion-Related Validities of Personality Constructs and the Effect of Response Distortion on Those Validities," *Journal of Applied Psychology,* 1990, 75, pp. 581–595.

36. D. Lubinski and R. V. Dawis, "Aptitudes, Skills, and Proficiencies," in M. D. Dunnette and L. M. Hough, eds., *Handbook of Industrial and Organizational Psychology,* 2d ed., vol. 3. (Palo Alto, Calif.: Consulting Psychologists Press, 1992), pp. 1–59.

37. Lubinski and Dawis.

38. J. C. Nunnally, *Psychometric Theory,* 2d ed. (New York: McGraw-Hill, 1978). T. G. Thurstone, "Primary Mental Abilities & Children," *Educational and Psychological Measurement,* 1941, 1, pp. 105–116.

39. M. D. Dunnette, "Aptitudes, Abilities, and Skills," in M. D. Dunnette, ed., *Handbook of Industrial and Organizational Psychology* (Chicago: Rand McNally, 1976), pp. 473–520.

40. E. A. Fleishman, "The Description and Prediction of Perceptual-Motor Skill Learning," in R. Glaser, ed., *Training Research and Education* (Pittsburgh: University of Pittsburgh Press, 1962). E. A. Fleishman, "On the Relation Between Abilities, Learning, and Human Performance," *American Psychologist,* 1972, 27, pp. 1017–1032.

41. H. M. Chipuer, M. Rovine, and R. Plomin, "LISREL Modeling: Genetic and Environmental Influences on IQ Revisited," *Intelligence,* 1990, 14, pp. 11–29. N. L. Pedersen, R. Plomin, J. R. Nesselroade, and G. E. McClearn, "A Quantitative Genetic Analysis of Cognitive Abilities During the Second Half of the Life Span," *Psychological Science,* 1992, 3, pp. 346–353.

42. L. McGinley, " 'Fitness' Exams Help to Measure Worker Acuity," *Wall Street Journal,* April 21, 1992, pp. B1, B6.

43. D. Goleman, *Emotional Intelligence* (New York: Bantam Books, 1994). J. D. Mayer and P. Salovey, "The Intelligence of Emotional Intelligence," *Intelligence,* 1993, 17, pp. 433–442. J. D. Mayer and P. Salovey, "What is Emotional Intelligence?," in P. Salovey and D. Sluyter, eds., *Emotional Development and Emotional Intelligence: Implications for Education* (New York: Basic Books, 1997). P. Salovey and J. D. Mayer, "Emotional Intelligence," *Imagination, Cognition, and Personality,* 1989-1990, 9, pp. 185–211.

44, 45. A. Farnham, "Are You Smart Enough to Keep Your Job?," *Fortune,* 1996, January 15, pp. 34–48. M. E. P. Seligman, *Learned Optimism* (New York, A. A. Knopf, 1990).

46. Farnham, "Are You Smart Enough."

47. K. Miller, "At GM, the Three R's Are the Big Three," *Wall Street Journal,* July 3, 1992, pp. B1, B6.

48. H. Cooper, "Carpet Firm Sets Up an In-House School to Stay Competitive," *Wall Street Journal,* October 5, 1992, pp. A1, A5.

49. Cooper, "Carpet Firm Sets Up an In-House School."

50. R. Henkoff, "Where Will the Jobs Come From?" *Fortune,* October 19, 1992, pp. 58–64.

51. A. Bernstein, "Replenishing Our Human Capital," *Business Week, Reinventing America,* 1992, pp. 78–79.

52. A. Bernstein, "Teaching Business How to Train," *Business Week, Reinventing America,* 1992, pp. 82–90.

53. G. E. Schares, "Experts in Overalls," *Business Week, Reinventing America,* 1992, p. 90.

54. C. Hymowitz and G. Stern, "At Procter & Gamble, Brands Face Pressure and So Do Executives," *Wall Street Journal,* May 10, 1993, pp. A1, A8.

55. Z. Schiller, "Ed Artzt's Elbow Grease Has P&G Shining," *Business Week,* October 10, 1994, pp. 84–86.

56. Hymowitz and Stern, "At Procter & Gamble, Brands Face Pressure and So Do Executives."

57. Schiller, "Ed Artzt's Elbow Grease Has P&G Shining."

58. G. Stern, "Two Mismatched Men Compete for the One Big Job," *Wall Street Journal,* July 15, 1994, pp. B1, B6. R. Narisetti, "How Two Ex-Rivals Work Together at P&G," *Wall Street Journal,* August 6, 1997, pp. B1, B6.

59. R. Narisetti, "How Two Ex-Rivals Work Together at P&G."

CHAPTER 3

1, 2. G. P. Zachary, "The New Search for Meaning in 'Meaningless' Work," *Wall Street Journal,* January 9, 1997, pp. B1, B7.

3. M. Jackson, "Leaders in Laughter: Corporate America Is Spending Thousands to Keep the Giggles Coming from Employees," *The Bryan-College Station Eagle,* April 27, 1997, p. D6.

4. W. R. Nord, A. P. Brief, J. M. Atieh, and E. M. Doherty, "Work Values and the Conduct of Organizational Behavior," in B. M. Staw and L. L. Cummings, eds., *Research in Organizational Behavior,* vol. 10 (Greenwich, Conn.: JAI Press, 1988), pp. 1–42.

5. M. Rokeach, *The Nature of Human Values* (New York: Free Press, 1973).

6. Nord, Brief, Atieh, and Doherty, "Work Values and the Conduct of Organizational Behavior."

7. M. Fishbein and I. Ajzen, "Attitudes and Opinions," *Annual Review of Psychology,* 1972, 23, pp. 487–544.

8. "Job Satisfaction: Made in the U.S.A.," *Business Week,* October 28, 1991, p. 45. "Office Labor Woes: If You Think Morale Is Bad Here, Try Working in Japan," *Wall Street Journal,* November 19, 1991, p. A1.

9. D. Watson and A. Tellegen, "Toward a Consensual Structure of Mood," *Psychological Bulletin,* 1985, 98, pp. 219–235.

10. J. M. George and A. P. Brief, "Feeling Good-Doing Good: A Conceptual Analysis of the Mood at Work-Organizational Spontaneity Relationship," *Psychological Bulletin,* 1992, 112, pp. 310–329.

11, 12. J. M. George, "Mood and Absence," *Journal of Applied Psychology,* 1989, 74, pp. 317–324. J. M. George, "State or Trait: Effects of Positive Mood on Prosocial Behaviors at Work," *Journal of Applied Psychology,* 1991, 76, pp. 299–307.

13. J. M. George and K. Bettenhausen, "Understanding Prosocial Behavior, Sales Performance, and Turnover: A Group Level Analysis in a Service Context," *Journal of Applied Psychology,* 1990, 75, pp. 698–709.

14. A. M. Isen and R. A. Baron, "Positive Affect as a Factor in Organizational Behavior," in B. M. Staw and L. L. Cummings, eds., *Research in Organizational Behavior,* vol. 13 (Greenwich, Conn.: JAI Press, 1991), pp. 1–53. R. C. Sinclair, "Mood, Categorization Breadth, and Performance Appraisal: The Effects of Order of Information Acquisition and Affective State on Halo, Accuracy, Informational Retrieval, and Evaluations," *Organizational Behavior and Human Decision Processes,* 1988, 42, pp. 22–46.

15. J. M. George, "The Role of Personality in Organizational Life: Issues and Evidence," *Journal of Management,* 1992, 18, pp. 185–213.

16. J. M. George, "Time Structure and Purpose as Mediator of Work-Life Linkages," *Journal of Applied Social Psychology,* 1991, 21, pp. 296–314.

17. R. D. Arvey, T. J. Bouchard, N. L. Segal, and L. M. Abraham, "Job Satisfaction: Environmental and Genetic Components," *Journal of Applied Psychology,* 1989, 74, pp. 187–192.

18. T. DeAngelis, "The 'Who Am I' Question Wears a Cloak of Culture," *APA Monitor,* October 1992, pp. 22–23.

19. DeAngelis, "The 'Who Am I' Question."

20. S. Shellenberger, "More Job Seekers Put Family Needs First," *Wall Street Journal,* November 15, 1991, pp. B1, B6.

21, 22. Shellenberger, "More Job Seekers Put Family Needs First."

23. R. W. Rice, K. Markus, R. P. Moyer, and D. B. McFarlin, "Facet Importance and Job Satisfaction: Two Experimental Tests of Locke's Range of Affect Hypothesis," *Journal of Applied Social Psychology,* 1991, 21, pp. 1977–1987.

24. D. Milbank, "More Business Graduates Snap Up Jobs in Rust Belt That Promise Them Clout," *Wall Street Journal,* July 21, 1992, pp. B1, B6.

25. F. Herzberg, *Work and the Nature of Man* (Cleveland: World, 1966).

26. N. King, "Clarification and Evaluation of the Two-Factor Theory of Job Satisfaction," *Psychological Bulletin,* 1970, 74, pp. 18–31. E. A. Locke, "The Nature and Causes of Job Satisfaction," in M. Dunnette, ed., *Handbook of Industrial and Organizational Psychology* (Chicago: Rand McNally, 1976), pp. 1297–1349.

27. D. B. McFarlin and R. W. Rice, "The Role of Facet Importance as a Moderator in Job Satisfaction Processes," *Journal of Organizational Behavior,* 1992, 13, pp. 41–54. R. A. Katzell, "Personal Values, Job Satisfaction, and Job Behavior," in H. Borow, ed., *Man in a World of Work* (Boston: Houghton Mifflin, 1964).

28. T. Lee, "What Kind of Job Are You Likely to Find?" *National Business Employment Weekly,* Spring 1992, pp. 5–6.

29. Lee, "What Kind of Job Are You Likely to Find?"

30. McFarlin and Rice, "The Role of Facet Importance as a Moderator in Job Satisfaction Processes."

31. F. J. Landy, "An Opponent Process Theory of Job Satisfaction," *Journal of Applied Psychology,* 1978, 63, pp. 533–547.

32. B. M. Staw and J. Ross, "Stability in the Midst of Change: A Dispositional Approach to Job Satisfaction," *Journal of Applied Psychology,* 1985, 70, 469–480.

33. R. W. Griffin, "Effects of Work Redesign on Employee Perceptions, Attitudes, and Behaviors: A Long-Term Investigation," *Academy of Management Journal,* 1991, 34, pp. 425–435.

34. D. J. Weiss, R. V. Dawis, G. W. England, and L. H. Lofquist, *Manual for the Minnesota Satisfaction Questionnaire, Minnesota Studies in Vocational Rehabilitation,* vol. 22, 1967.

35. R. B. Dunham and J. B. Herman, "Development of a Female Faces Scale for Measuring Job Satisfaction," *Journal of Applied Psychology,* 1975, 60, pp. 629–631. T. Kunin, "The Construction of a New Type of Attitude Measure," *Personnel Psychology,* 1955, 8, pp. 65–78.

36. P. C. Smith, L. M. Kendall, and C. L. Hulin, *The Measurement of Satisfaction in Work and Retirement* (Chicago: Rand McNally, 1969).

37. M. T. Iaffaldano and P. M. Muchinsky, "Job Satisfaction and Performance: A Meta-Analysis," *Psychological Bulletin,* 1985, 97, pp. 251–273.

38. D. R. Dalton and D. J. Mesch, "On the Extent and Reduction of Avoidable Absenteeism: An Assessment of Absence Policy Provisions," *Journal of Applied Psychology,* 1991, 76, pp. 810–817. D. R. Dalton and C. A. Enz, "Absenteeism in Remission: Planning, Policy, and Culture," *Human Resource Planning,* 1987, 10, pp. 81–91. D. R. Dalton and C. A. Enz, "New Directions in the Management of Employee Absenteeism: Attention to Policy and Culture," in R. S. Schuler and S. A. Youngblood, eds., *Readings in Personnel and Human Resource Management* (St. Paul: West, 1988), pp. 356–366. "Expensive Absenteeism," *Wall Street Journal,* July 7, 1986, p. 1.

39. R. M. Steers and S. R. Rhodes, "Major Influences of Employee Attendance: A Process Model," *Journal of Applied Psychology,* 1978, 63, pp. 391–407.

40. George, "Mood and Absence."

41. W. H. Mobley, "Intermediate Linkages in the Relationship Between Job Satisfaction and Employee Turnover," *Journal of Applied Psychology,* 1977, 62, pp. 237–240.

42. George and Brief, "Feeling Good-Doing Good." D. W. Organ, *Organizational Citizenship Behavior: The Good Soldier Syndrome* (Lexington, Mass.: Lexington Books, 1988).

43. W. M. Bulkeley, "Study Finds Hidden Costs of Computing," *Wall Street Journal,* November 2, 1992, p. B5.

44. Bulkeley, "Study Finds Hidden Costs of Computing."

45. George and Brief, "Feeling Good-Doing Good."

46. Organ, *Organizational Citizenship Behavior.*

47. "Finding Motivation in the Little Things," *Wall Street Journal,* November 2, 1992, p. B1.

48. "We Caught You Doing Something Right," *Texas A&M University Human Resources Newsletter,* October 1992, p. 6.

49. N. Schmitt and A. G. Bedeian, "A Comparison of LISREL and Two-Stage Least Squares Analysis of a Hypothesized Job Satisfaction-Life Satisfaction Reciprocal Relationship," *Journal of Applied Psychology,* 1982, 67, pp. 806–817.

50. N. J. Allen and J. P. Meyer, "Affective, Continuance, and Normative Commitment to the Organization: An Examination of Construct Validity," *Journal of Vocational Behavior,* 1996, vol. 49, pp. 252–276.

51. S. Alexander, "Life's Just a Bowl of Cherry Garcia for Ben & Jerry's," *Wall Street Journal,* July 15, 1992, p. B3.

52. B. Davis and D. Milbank, "If the U.S. Work Ethic Is Fading, Alienation May Be Main Reason," *Wall Street Journal,* February 7, 1992, p. A1.

53. A. Farnham, "The Trust Gap," *Fortune,* December 4, 1989, pp. 56–78.

54. Farnham, "The Trust Gap."

55. N. J. Allen and J. P. Meyer, "Affective, Continuance, and Normative Commitment to the Organization: An Examination of Construct Validity"; J. E. Mathieu and D. M. Zajac, "A Review and Meta-Analysis of the Antecedents, Correlates, and Consequences of Organizational Commitment," *Psychological Bulletin,* 1990, 108, pp. 171–194.

56. Allen and Meyer, "Affective, Continuance, and Normative Commitment to the Organization"; Mathieu and Zajac, "A Review and Meta-Analysis of the Antecedents, Correlates, and Consequences of Organizational Commitment."

57, 58. A. Deutschman, "What 25-Year-Olds Want," *Fortune,* August 27, 1990, pp. 42–50.

CHAPTER 4

1. A. B. Fisher, "When Will Women Get to the Top?" *Fortune,* September 21, 1992, pp. 44–56.

2. L. Himelstein and S. A. Forest, "Breaking Through," *Business Week,* February 17, 1997, pp. 64–70.

3. L. Himelstein and S. A. Forest, "Breaking Through,". J. B. White and C. Hymowitz, "Watershed Generation of Women Executives Is Rising to the Top," *Wall Street Journal,* February 10, 1997, A1, A6.

4, 5. S. Hamm, "Why Women Are So Invisible," *Business Week,* August 25, 1997, p. 136.

6. A. B. Fisher, "When Will Women Get to the Top."

7. S. Hamm, "Why Women Are So Invisible."

8. S. Hamm, "Can Marimba's CEO Keep the Beat?," *Business Week,* September 1, 1997, p. 86.

9. A. Miller, K. Springen, and D. Tsiantar, "Now: The Brick Wall," *Newsweek,* August 24, 1992, pp. 54–56.

10. "Investment Manager Profiles," *Nelson's Directory of Investment Managers* (Port Chester, N.Y.: Nelson Publications, 1993), pp. 1–3.

11. S. Hamm, "Why Women Are So Invisible."

12. Fisher, "When Will Women Get to the Top?" Miller, Springen, and Tsiantar, "Now: The Brick Wall."

13. H. R. Schiffmann, *Sensation and Perception: An Integrated Approach* (New York: Wiley, 1990).

14. S. T. Fiske and S. E. Taylor, *Social Cognition* (Reading, Mass.: Addison-Wesley, 1984).

15. J. S. Bruner, "Going Beyond the Information Given," in H. Gruber, G. Terrell, and M. Wertheimer, eds., *Contemporary Approaches to Cognition* (Cambridge, Mass.: Harvard University Press, 1957). Fiske and Taylor, *Social Cognition.* G. R. Jones, R. Kosnik, and J. M. George, "Internalization and the Firm's Growth Path: On the Psychology of Organizational Contracting," in R. W. Woodman and W. A. Pasmore, eds., *Research in Organizational Change and Development* (Greenwich, Conn.: JAI Press, 1993), pp. 105–135.

16. Fiske and Taylor, *Social Cognition.*

17. D. J. Schneider, "Social Cognition," *Annual Review of Psychology,* 1991, 42, pp. 527–561.

18. Fiske and Taylor, *Social Cognition.*

19, 20. S. Shellenbarger, "As Population Ages, Older Workers Clash with Younger Bosses," *Wall Street Journal,* June 13, 1994, pp. A1, A8.

21. D. C. McClelland and J. W. Atkinson, "The Projective Expression of Needs: The Effect of Different Intensities of the Hunger Drive on Perception," *Journal of Psychology,* 1948, 25, pp. 205–222.

22. J. M. George and A. P. Brief, "Feeling Good-Doing Good: A Conceptual Analysis of the Mood at Work-Organizational Spontaneity Relationship," *Psychological Bulletin,* 1992, 112, pp. 310–329. A. M. Isen and R. A. Baron, "Positive Affect as a Factor in Organizational Behavior," in B. M. Staw and L. L. Cummings, eds., *Research in Organizational Behavior,* vol. 13 (Greenwich, Conn.: JAI Press, 1991), pp. 1–54.

23, 24. J. E. Ellis, "Monsanto's New Challenge: Keeping Minority Workers," *Business Week,* July 8, 1991, pp. 60–61.

25. M. R. Leery and R. M. Kowalski, "Impression Management: A Literature Review and Two-Component Model," *Psychological Bulletin,* 1990, 107, pp. 34–47.

26. Leery and Kowalski, "Impression Management."

27. C. N. Alexander, Jr., and G. W. Knight, "Situated Identities and Social Psychological Experimentation," *Sociometry,* 1971, 34, pp. 65–82. Fiske and Taylor, *Social Cognition.* K. J. Gergen and M. G. Taylor, "Social Expectancy and Self-Presentation in a Status Hierarchy," *Journal of Experimental Social Psychology,* 1969, 5, pp. 79–92.

28. J. Stephenson, "Business Etiquette's More Than Minding Peas, Queues," *The Bryan-College Station Eagle,* February 8, 1993, pp. A1, A3.

29. Leery and Kowalski, "Impression Management."

30. Fiske and Taylor, *Social Cognition.*

31. Fiske and Taylor, *Social Cognition.* R. M. Kanter, *Men and Women of the Corporation* (New York: Basic Books, 1977).

32. J. E. Rigdon and C. Hymowitz, "For Black Men, Success Resolves Few Problems," *Wall Street Journal,* May 12, 1992, pp. B1, B3.

33. A. Cuneo, "Diverse by Design," *Business Week, Reinventing America,* 1992, p. 72.

34. S. A. Fisicaro, "A Reexamination of the Relation Between Halo Errors and Accuracy," *Journal of Applied Psychology,* 1988, 73, pp. 239–244.

35. E. D. Pulakos and K. N. Wexley, "The Relationship Among Perceptual Similarity, Sex, and Performance Ratings in Manager-Subordinate Dyads," *Academy of Management Journal,* 1983, 26, pp. 129–139.

36. "Racial Differences Discourage Mentors," *Wall Street Journal,* October 29, 1991, p. B1.

37. J. S. Lublin, "Rights Law to Spur Shifts in Promotions," *Wall Street Journal,* December 30, 1991, pp. B1, B4.

38. E. S. Browning, "Computer Chip Project Brings Rivals Together, but Cultures Clash," *Wall Street Journal,* May 3, 1994, pp. A1, A8.

39. R. K. Merton, *Social Theory and Social Structure* (New York: Free Press, 1957).

40. R. Rosenthal and L. F. Jacobson, *Pygmalion in the Classroom* (New York: Holt, Rinehart and Winston, 1968).

41. C. O. Wood, M. P. Zanna, and J. Cooper, "The Nonverbal Mediation of Self-Fulfilling Prophecies in Interracial Interaction," *Journal of Experimental Social Psychology,* 1974, 10, pp. 109–120.

42. F. Heider, *The Psychology of Interpersonal Relations* (New York: Wiley, 1958). L. Ross, "The Intuitive Psychologist and His Shortcomings: Distortions in the Attribution Process," in L. Berkowitz, ed., *Advances in Experimental Social Psychology,* vol. 10 (New York: Academic Press, 1977).

43. E. E. Jones and R. E. Nisbett, "The Actor and the Observer: Divergent Perceptions of the Causes of Behavior," in E. E. Jones, D. E. Kanouse, H. H. Kelley, R. E. Nisbett, S. Valins, and B. Weiner, eds., *Attribution: Perceiving the Causes of Behavior* (Morristown, N.J.: General Learning Press, 1972).

44. J. A. Knight and R. R. Vallacher, "Interpersonal Engagement in Social Perception: The Consequence of Getting into the Action," *Journal of Personality and Social Psychology,* 1981, 40, pp. 990–999. M. Zuckerman, "Attribution of Success and Failure Revisited, or: The Motivational Bias Is Alive and Well in Attribution Theory," *Journal of Personality,* 1979, 47, pp. 245–287.

45. D. T. Miller and M. Ross, "Self-Serving Biases in Attribution of Causality: Fact or Fiction?" *Psychological Bulletin,* 1975, 82, pp. 213–225.

46. Fiske and Taylor, *Social Cognition.*

47. J. M. Burger, "Motivational Biases in the Attribution of Responsibility for an Accident: A Meta-Analysis of the Defensive-Attribution Hypothesis," *Psychological Bulletin,* 1981, 90, pp. 496–512. Fiske and Taylor, *Social Cognition.*

48. J. A. Hall and S. E. Taylor, "When Love Is Blind: Maintaining Idealized Images of One's Spouse," *Human Relations,* 1976, 29, pp. 751–761.

49. F. Rice, "How to Make Diversity Pay," *Fortune,* August 8, 1994, pp. 78–86.

50, 51. Rice, "How to Make Diversity Pay."

52. S. Gelston, "The '90s Work Force Faces Diverse Challenges," *Boston Herald,* January 25, 1994, p. N18.

53. M. Lee, "Diversity Training Brings Unity to Small Companies," *Wall Street Journal,* September 2, 1993, p. B2.

54, 55. Rice, "How to Make Diversity Pay."

56. Rutkowski and Associates, *Employment Law Update,* September 1991, pp. 1–12.

57. E. Klee, L. Hayes, and G. W. Childress, "A Kentucky Response to the ADA," *Training & Development,* April 1994, pp. 48–49.

58. S. M. Shafer, "Sexual Harassment Exists at All Levels, Army Says," *The Bryan-College Station Eagle,* September 12, 1997, p. A4.

59. "Chevron Settles Claims of 4 Women at Unit as Part of Sex Bias Suit," *The Wall Street Journal,* January 22, 1995, p. B12.

60. R. L. Paetzold and A. M. O'Leary-Kelly, "Organizational Communication and the Legal Dimensions of Hostile Work Environment Sexual Harassment," in G. L. Kreps (ed.), *Sexual Harassment: Communication Implications* (Cresskill, NJ: Hampton Press, 1993).

61. A. M. O'Leary-Kelly, R. L. Paetzold, and R. W. Griffin, "Sexual Harassment as Aggressive Action: A Framework for Understanding Sexual Harassment" (Paper presented at the annual meeting of the Academy of Management, Vancouver, August 1995).

62. "Chevron Settles Claims of 4 Women at Unit as Part of Sex Bias Suit."

63. E. Jensen and J. Lippman, "NBC's Problem: Gifted Executive Who Drank," *The Wall Street Journal,* December 13, 1996, pp. B1, B19.

64. S. J. Bresler and R. Thacker, "Four-Point Plan Helps Solve Harassment Problems," *HR Magazine,* May, 1993, pp. 117–124.

65. Du Pont's Solution, *Training,* March, 1992, p. 29. E. Jensen and J. Lippman, "NBC's Problem: Gifted Executive Who Drank." J. S. Lublin, "Sexual Harassment Moves Up Agenda in Many Executive Education Programs," *The Wall Street Journal,* December 2, 1991, B1, B4. "Navy Is Teaching Sailors What Proper Conduct Is," *The Bryan-College Station Eagle,* April 19, 1993, A2.

66. M. France and T. Smart, "The Ugly Talk On the Texaco Tape," *Business Week,* November 18, 1996, p. 58. J. S. Lublin, "Texaco Case Causes a Stir in Boardrooms," *The Wall Street Journal,* November 22, 1996, pp. B1, B6. T. Smart, "Texaco: Lessons from a Crisis-In-Progress, *Business Week,* December 2, 1996, p. 44.

67–69. Lublin, "Texaco Case Causes a Stir In Boardrooms."

70. L. E. Wynter, "Allstate Rates Managers On Handling Diversity," *The Wall Street Journal,* October 1, 1997, p. B1.

CHAPTER 5

1. S. Browder, "Starbucks Does Not Live by Coffee Alone," *Business Week,* August 5, 1995. M. A. Schilling, "Starbucks Corporation: Still Perking," in C.

W. L. Hill and G. R. Jones, *Strategic Management: An Integrated Approach* (Boston: Houghton Mifflin Company, 1998). "Starbucks: Making Values Pay," *Fortune,* September 29, 1997, pp. 261-265. H. Schultz and D. J. Yang, *Pour Your Heart Into It* (Hyperion, 1997). S. Williams, "Starbucks' Growth Is an Open Book," *Seattle Times,* June 29, 1993.

2, 3. Browder; Schilling; "Starbucks: Making Values Pay"; Schultz and Yang; Williams.

4. W. C. Hamner, "Reinforcement Theory and Contingency Management in Organizational Settings," in H. Tosi and W. C. Hamner, eds. *Organizational Behavior and Management: A Contingency Approach* (Chicago: St. Clair Press, 1974).

5. B. F. Skinner, *Contingencies of Reinforcement* (New York: Appleton-Century-Crofts, 1969).

6. F. Luthans and R. Kreitner, *Organizational Behavior Modification and Beyond* (Glenview, Ill.: Scott, Foresman, 1985).

7. J. L. Komaki, "Applied Behavior Analysis and Organizational Behavior: Reciprocal Influence of the Two Fields," in B. M. Staw and L. L. Cummings, eds., *Research in Organizational Behavior,* vol. 8 (Greenwich, Conn.: JAI Press, 1986), pp. 297–334.

8. H. M. Weiss, "Learning Theory and Industrial and Organizational Psychology," in M. D. Dunnette and L. M. Hough, eds., *Handbook of Industrial and Organizational Psychology,* 2nd ed., vol. 1 (Palo Alto, Calif: Consulting Psychologists Press, 1990), pp. 171-221.

9. S. Overman, "When It Comes to Managing Diversity, a Few Companies Are Linking Pay to Performance," *HRMagazine,* December 1992, pp. 38–40.

10. J. Flynn, C. Del Valle, and R. Mitchell, "Did Sears Take Other Customers for a Ride?" *Business Week,* August 3, 1992, pp. 24–25. K. Kelly and E. Schine, "How Did Sears Blow This Gasket?" *Business Week,* June 29, 1992, p. 38. G. A. Patterson, "Distressed Shoppers, Disaffected Workers Prompt Stores to Alter Sales Commissions," *Wall Street Journal,* July 1, 1992, p. B1, B5.

11. G. A. Patterson, "Sears' Brennan Accepts Blame for Auto Flap," *Wall Street Journal,* August 5, 1992, pp. B1, B12.

12. Weiss, "Learning Theory and Industrial and Organizational Psychology."

13. J. P. Houston, *Fundamentals of Learning and Memory,* 3d ed. (New York: Harcourt Brace Jovanovich, 1986); Weiss, "Learning Theory and Industrial and Organizational Psychology."

14. J. Stinson, "Company Policy Attends to Chronic Absentees," *Personnel Journal,* August 1991, pp. 82–85.

15. R. D. Arvey and J. M. Ivancevich, "Punishment in Organizations: A Review, Propositions, and Research Suggestions," *Academy of Management Review,* 1980, 5, pp. 123–132.

16. R. L. Rose, "After Turning Around Giddings and Lewis, Fife Is Turned Out Himself," *Wall Street Journal,* June 22, 1993, p. A1.

17, 18. Luthans and Kreitner, *Organizational Behavior Modification and Beyond.*

19. A. Bandura, *Social Learning Theory* (Englewood Cliffs, N.J.: Prentice-Hall, 1977).

20. A. Bandura, *Principles of Behavior Modification* (New York: Holt, Rinehart and Winston, 1969). Bandura, *Social Learning Theory.* T.R.V. Davis and F. Luthans, "A Social Learning Approach to Organizational Behavior," *Academy of Management Review,* 1980, 5, pp. 281–290.

21. Bandura, *Social Learning Theory.* T.R.V. Davis and F. Luthans, "A Social Learning Approach to Organizational Behavior," in Luthans and Kreitner, *Organizational Behavior Modification and Beyond.*

22. A. P. Goldstein and M. Sorcher, *Changing Supervisor Behavior* (New York: Pergamon Press, 1974). Luthans and Kreitner, *Organizational Behavior Modification and Beyond.*

23. R. M. Kanter, "Six Certainties for CEOs," *Harvard Business Review,* March–April 1992, pp. 7–8. N. Stone, "Building Corporate Character: An Interview with Stride Rite Chairman Arnold Hiatt," *Harvard Business Review,* March–April 1992, pp. 95–104.

24. A. Bandura, "Self-Reinforcement: Theoretical and Methodological Considerations," *Behaviorism,* 1976, 4, pp. 135–155.

25. M. Moravec, K. Wheeler, and B. Hall, "Getting College Hires on Track Fast," *Personnel,* May 1989, pp. 56–59.

26. M. E. Gist and T. R. Mitchell, "Self-Efficacy: A Theoretical Analysis of Its Determinants and Malleability," *Academy of Management Review,* 1992, 17, pp. 183–211.

27, 28. A. Bandura, "Self-Efficacy Mechanism in Human Agency," *American Psychologist,* 1982, 37, pp. 122–147.

29. D. Eden and A. B. Shani, "Pygmalion Goes to Boot Camp: Expectancy, Leadership, and Trainee Performance," *Journal of Applied Psychology,* 1982, 67, pp. 194–199.

30. Bandura, "Self-Efficacy Mechanism in Human Agency."

31, 32. P. Senge, *The Fifth Discipline: The Art and Practice of the Learning Organization* (New York: Doubleday, 1990).

33. S. E. Prokesch, "Unleashing the Power of Learning: An Interview with

British Petroleum's John Browne," *Harvard Business Review,* September–October, 1997, p. 148.

34. C. Power, L. Driscoll, and E. Bohn, "Smart Selling: How Companies Are Winning Over Today's Tough Customer," *Business Week,* August 3, 1992, pp. 46–52.

35. G. Anders, "More Managed Health-Care Systems Use Incentive Pay to Reward 'Best' Doctors," *Wall Street Journal,* January 25, 1993, pp. B1, B6.

CHAPTER 6

1–3. K. Miyazawa, "Jumping Ship," *Forbes,* April 8, 1996, p. 14. "PlayStation's Final Fantasy VII Has Sold More Than Half a Million Copies to Date; Sales Momentum for Most Anticipated Videogame of the Year Continues," *Business Wire,* September 25, 1997. N. Weinberg, "Playing for Keeps," *Forbes,* November 6, 1995, p. 248–249.

4. "It's Hip to be Square," *Hawaii Business,* June 1997, p. 17.

5. Square USA, Inc. Home Page (www.sqla.com).

6. F. J. Landy and W. S. Becker, "Motivation Theory Reconsidered," in B. M. Staw and L. L. Cummings, eds., *Research in Organizational Behavior,* vol. 9 (Greenwich, Conn.: JAI Press, 1987), pp. 1–38.

7. J. P. Campbell and R. D. Pritchard, "Motivation Theory in Industrial and Organizational Psychology," in M. D. Dunnette, ed., *Handbook of Industrial and Organizational Psychology* (Chicago: Rand McNally, 1976), pp. 63–130.

8, 9. R. Kanfer, "Motivation Theory and Industrial and Organizational Psychology," in M. D. Dunnette and L. M. Hough, eds., *Handbook of Industrial and Organizational Psychology,* vol. 1 (Palo Alto, Calif.: Consulting Psychologists Press, 1990), pp. 75–170.

10. A. P. Brief and R. J. Aldag, "The Intrinsic-Extrinsic Dichotomy: Toward Conceptual Clarity," *Academy of Management Review,* 1977, 2, pp. 496–499.

11. Brief and Aldag, "The Intrinsic-Extrinsic Dichotomy."

12, 13. J. O'C. Hamilton, "Trials of a Cyber-Celebrity," *Business Week,* February 22, 1993, pp. 95–97.

14. D. Gunsch, "Award Programs at Work," *Personnel Journal,* September 1991, pp. 85–89.

15. A. H. Maslow, *Motivation and Personality* (New York: Harper and Row, 1954). C. P. Alderfer, *Existence, Relatedness, and Growth: Human Needs in Organizational Settings* (New York: Free Press, 1972).

16, 17. V. H. Vroom, *Work and Motivation* (New York: Wiley, 1964).

18. Adams, "Toward an Understanding of Inequity," *Journal of Abnormal and Social Psychology,* 1963, 67, pp. 422-436.

19. Maslow, *Motivation and Personality*; Campbell and Pritchard, "Motivation Theory in Industrial and Organizational Psychology."

20. V. Anderson, "Kudos for Creativity," *Personnel Journal,* September 1991, pp. 90–93.

21. Maslow, *Motivation and Personality*; Campbell and Pritchard, "Motivation Theory in Industrial and Organizational Psychology."

22. C. P. Alderfer, "An Empirical Test of a New Theory of Human Needs," *Organizational Behavior and Human Performance,* 1969, 4, pp. 142–175. Alderfer, *Existence, Relatedness, and Growth.* Campbell and Pritchard, "Motivation Theory and Industrial and Organizational Psychology."

23. Kanfer, "Motivation Theory and Industrial and Organizational Psychology."

24–26. Vroom, *Work and Motivation.*

27. Campbell and Pritchard, "Motivation Theory in Industrial and Organizational Psychology". T. R. Mitchell, "Expectancy-Value Models in Organizational Psychology," in N. T. Feather, ed., *Expectations and Actions: Expectancy-Value Models in Psychology* (Hillsdale, N.J.: Erlbaum, 1982), pp. 293–312.

28, 29. D. C. Boyle, "Employee Motivation That Works," *HRMagazine,* October 1992, pp. 83–89.

30–32. P. A. Galagan, "Training Keeps the Cutting Edge Sharp for the Andersen Companies," *Training & Development,* January 1993, pp. 30–35.

33. M. J. Stahl and A. M. Harrell, "Modeling Effort Decisions with Behavioral Decision Theory: Toward an Individual Differences Model of Expectancy Theory," *Organizational Behavior and Human Performance,* 1981, 27, pp. 303–325.

34. Campbell and Pritchard, "Motivation Theory in Industrial and Organizational Psychology"; Kanfer, "Motivational Theory and Industrial and Organizational Psychology."

35–38. J. S. Adams, "Toward an Understanding of Inequity," *Journal of Abnormal and Social Psychology,* 1963, 67, pp. 422–436.

39. "Japanese Women Hit the Streets to Protest Work Discrimination," *Bryan–College Station Eagle,* July 28, 1994, p. A5.

40–42. L. N. Spiro, "The Angry Voices at Kidder," *Business Week,* February 1, 1993, pp. 60–63.

43. J. Greenberg, "Approaching Equity and Avoiding Inequity in Groups and Organizations," in J. Greenberg and R. L. Cohen, eds., *Equity and Justice in Social Behavior* (New York: Academic Press, 1982), pp. 389–435. J. Greenberg, "Equity and Workplace Status: A Field Experiment," *Journal of Applied Psychology,* 1988, 73, pp. 606–613. R. T. Mowday, "Equity Theory

Predictions of Behavior in Organizations," in R. M. Steers and L. W. Porter, eds., *Motivation and Work Behavior* (New York: McGraw-Hill, 1987), pp. 89–110.

44. R. Folger and M. A. Konovsky, "Effects of Procedural and Distributive Justice on Reactions to Pay Raise Decisions," *Academy of Management Journal,* 1989, 32, pp. 115–130. J. Greenberg, "Organizational Justice: Yesterday, Today, and Tomorrow," *Journal of Management,* 1990, 16, pp. 399–432.

45. Greenberg, "Organizational Justice: Yesterday, Today, and Tomorrow."

46. Greenberg, "Organizational Justice: Yesterday, Today, and Tomorrow." T. R. Tyler, "What Is Procedural Justice?" *Law and Society Review,* 1988, 22, pp. 301–335.

47. J. Greenberg, "Organizational Justice: Yesterday, Today, and Tomorrow." E. A. Lind and T. Tyler, *The Social Psychology of Procedural Justice* (New York: Plenum, 1988).

48. R. J. Bies, "The Predicament of Injustice: The Management of Moral Outrage," in L. L. Cummings and B. M. Staw, eds., *Research in Organizational Behavior,* vol. 9 (Greenwich, Conn.: JAI Press, 1987), pp. 289–319. R. J. Bies and D. L. Shapiro, "Interactional Fairness Judgments: The Influence of Causal Accounts," *Social Justice Research,* 1987, 1, pp. 199–218. J. Greenberg, "Looking Fair vs. Being Fair: Managing Impressions of Organizational Justice," in B. M. Staw and L. L. Cummings, eds., *Research in Organizational Behavior,* vol. 12 (Greenwich, Conn.: JAI Press, 1990), pp. 111–157. T. R. Tyler and R. J. Bies, "Beyond Formal Procedures: The Interpersonal Context of Procedural Justice," in J. Carroll, ed., *Advances in Applied Social Psychology: Business Settings* (Hillsdale, N.J.: Erlbaum, 1989), pp. 77–98.

49. *Systems* (A newsletter for employees and retirees of the Texas A&M System), November–December 1994, pp. 1, 4.

50. J. Greenberg, "Reactions to Procedural Injustice in Payment Distributions: Do the Means Justify the Ends?" *Journal of Applied Psychology,* 1987, 72, pp. 55–61.

51. R. Wartzman, "A Whirlpool Factory Raises Productivity—And Pay of Workers," *Wall Street Journal,* May 4, 1992, pp. A1, A4.

CHAPTER 7

1, 2. S. Baker and L. Armstrong, "The New Factory Work," *Fortune,* September 30, 1996, pp. 59–68.

3. S. H. Mehta, "Cell Manufacturing Gains Acceptance at Smaller Plants," *Wall Street Journal,* September 15, 1994, p. B2. M. Williams, "Back to the Past," *Wall Street Journal,* October 24, 1994, P. A1.

4. Baker and Armstrong, "The New Factory Work."

5. F. W. Taylor, *The Principles of Scientific Management* (New York: Harper and Brothers, 1911).

6. R. W. Griffin, *Task Design: An Integrative Approach* (Glenview, Ill.: Scott, Foresman, 1982).

7. A. C. Filley, R. J. House, and S. Kerr, *Managerial Process and Organizational Behavior* (Glenview, Ill.: Scott, Foresman, 1976). C. R. Walker, "The Problem of the Repetitive Job," *Harvard Business Review,* 1950, 28, pp. 54–58.

8. Griffin, *Task Design.*

9. L. M. Grossman, "Truck Cabs Turn into Mobile Offices as Drivers Take on White-Collar Tasks," *Wall Street Journal,* August 3, 1993, pp. B1, B9.

10. J. R. Hackman and G. R. Oldham, "Motivation Through the Design of Work: Test of a Theory," *Organizational Behavior and Human Performance,* 1976, 16, pp. 250–279. J. R. Hackman and G. R. Oldham, *Work Redesign* (Reading, Mass.: Addison-Wesley, 1980). A. N. Turner and P. R. Lawrence, *Industrial Jobs and the Worker* (Boston: Harvard School of Business, 1965).

11. Hackman and Oldham, "Motivation Through the Design of Work"; Hackman and Oldham, *Work Redesign.*

12. A. Ehrbar, "Re-Engineering Gives Firms New Efficiency, Worker the Pink Slip," *Wall Street Journal,* March 16, 1993, pp. A1, A11. R. Jacob, "Thriving in a Lame Economy," *Fortune,* October 5, 1992, pp. 44–54.

13. Jacob, "Thriving in a Lame Economy."

14, 15. Hackman and Oldham, *Work Redesign.*

16, 17. M. W. Brauchli, "When in Huangpu . . .," *Wall Street Journal,* December 10, 1993, p. R3.

18. Y. Fried and G. R. Ferris, "The Validity of the Job Characteristics Model: A Review and Meta-Analysis," *Personnel Psychology,* 1987, 40, pp. 287–322.

19. B. T. Loher, R. A. Noe, N. L. Moeller, and M. P. Fitzgerald, "A Meta-Analysis of the Relation of Job Characteristics to Job Satisfaction," *Journal of Applied Psychology,* 1985, 70, pp. 280–289.

20. G. R. Salancik and J. Pfeffer, "A Social Information Processing Approach to Job Attitudes and Task Design," *Administrative Science Quarterly,* 1978, 23, pp. 224–253.

21, 22. S. Nolen, "Contingent Employment," in *The Blackwell Encyclopedic Dictionary of Human Resource Management,* ed. L. H. Peters, C. R. Greer, and S. A Youngblood (Oxford: Blackwell Publishers, 1997), pp. 59-60.

23. R. W. Griffin, "Objective and Social Sources of Information in Task Redesign: A Field Experiment," *Administrative Science Quarterly,* 1983, 28, pp.

184–200. J. Thomas and R. Griffin, "The Social Information Processing Model of Task Design: A Review of the Literature," *Academy of Management Review,* 1983, 8, pp. 672–682.

24. E. A. Locke and G. P. Latham, *A Theory of Goal Setting and Task Performance* (Englewood Cliffs, N.J.: Prentice-Hall, 1990).

25. Locke and Latham. M. E. Tubbs, "Goal Setting: A Meta-Analytic Examination of the Empirical Evidence," *Journal of Applied Psychology,* 1986, 71, pp. 474–483.

26. P. C. Earley, "Supervisors and Shop Stewards as Sources of Contextual Information in Goal Setting: A Comparison of the U.S. with England," *Journal of Applied Psychology,* 1986, 71, pp. 111–117. M. Erez and I. Zidon, "Effect of Goal Acceptance on the Relationship of Goal Difficulty to Performance," *Journal of Applied Psychology,* 1984, 69, pp. 69–78. G. P. Latham and H. A. Marshall, "The Effects of Self-Set, Participatively Set and Assigned Goals on the Performance of Government Employees," *Personnel Psychology,* 1982, 35, pp. 399–404. T. Matsui, T. Kakkuyama, and M. L. Onglatco, "Effects of Goals and Feedback on Performance in Groups," *Journal of Applied Psychology,* 1987, 72, pp. 407–415. B. J. Punnett, "Goal Setting: An Extension of the Research," *Journal of Applied Psychology,* 1986, 71, pp. 171–172.

27. E. A. Locke, K. N. Shaw, L. M. Saari, and G. P. Latham, "Goal Setting and Task Performance: 1969–1980," *Psychological Bulletin,* 1981, 90, pp. 125–152.

28. P. M. Wright, J. M. George, S. R. Farnsworth, and G. C. McMahan, "Productivity and Extra-Role Behavior: The Effects of Goals and Incentives on Spontaneous Helping," *Journal of Applied Psychology,* 1993, 78, pp. 374–381.

29. P. C. Earley, T. Connolly, and G. Ekegren, "Goals, Strategy Development, and Task Performance: Some Limits on the Efficacy of Goal Setting," *Journal of Applied Psychology,* 1989, 74, pp. 24–33. R. Kanfer and P. L. Ackerman, "Motivation and Cognitive Abilities: An Integrative/Aptitude–Treatment Interaction Approach to Skill Acquisition," *Journal of Applied Psychology,* 1989, 74, pp. 657–690.

30. Kanfer and Ackerman, "Motivation and Cognitive Abilities."

31. S. J. Carroll and H. L. Tosi, *Management by Objectives: Applications and Research* (New York: Macmillan, 1973). P. F. Drucker, *The Practice of Management* (New York: Harper and Row, 1954). C. D. Fisher, L. F. Schoenfeldt, and J. B. Shaw, *Human Resource Management* (Boston: Houghton Mifflin, 1990). R. Rodgers and J. E. Hunter, "Impact of Management by Objectives on Organizational Productivity," *Journal of Applied Psychology,* 1991, 76, pp. 322–336.

32. Fisher, Schoenfeldt, and Shaw, *Human Resource Management.*

33. D. D. Moesel, R. F. Elliott, and G. R. Jones, "The Upjohn Company," in C. W. L. Hill and G. R. Jones, *Strategic Management* (Boston: Houghton Mifflin, 1989). C. C. Highlander, "Six Steps to Unit Productivity Improvement: A Corporatewide Effort at Upjohn," *National Productivity Review,* Winter 1986–1987, pp. 20–27.

34. www.dovercorporation.com; P. L. Zweig, J. P. Kline, S. A. Forest, and K. Gudridge, "The Case Against Mergers," *Business Week,* October 30, 1995, pp. 122-130.

35. P. L. Zweig, "Who Says the Conglomerate Is Dead?" *Business Week,* January 23, 1995, pp. 92–92.

36. J. Mendes, "Motivate and Get Out of the Way," *Fortune,* December 14, 1992, pp. 94, 98.

37, 38. P. L Zweig, "Who Says the Conglomerate Is Dead?"

CHAPTER 8

1. G. E. Schares, J. B. Levine, and P. Coy, "The New Generation at Siemens," *Business Week,* March 9, 1992, pp. 46–48.

2. G. Schares and N. Gross, "Siemens Is Starting to Look Like a Chipmaker," *Business Week,* February 7, 1994, pp. 43–44. Schares, Levine, and Coy, "The New Generation at Siemens." A. Sulkin, "PBX Vendors Start Smiling—A Little," *Business Communications Review,* January 1994, pp. 40–45.

3, 4. C. D. Fisher, L. F. Schoenfeldt, and J. B. Shaw, *Human Resource Management* (Boston: Houghton Mifflin, 1990).

5. Fisher, Schoenfeldt, and Shaw. G. P. Latham and K. N. Wexley, *Increasing Productivity Through Performance Appraisal* (Reading, Mass.: Addison-Wesley, 1982).

6. R. Henkoff, "Make Your Office More Productive," *Fortune,* February 25, 1991, pp. 72–84.

7. R. S. Schuler, *Managing Human Resources* (New York: West, 1992).

8. T. A. DeCotiis, "An Analysis of the External Validity and Applied Relevance of Three Rating Formats," *Organizational Behavior and Human Performance,* 1977, 19, pp. 247–266. Fisher, Schoenfeldt, and Shaw.

9. Schuler, *Managing Human Resources.*

10. E. E. Lawler III, *Pay and Organization Development* (Reading, Mass.: Addison-Wesley, 1981).

11. A. Bennett, "Paying Workers to Meet Goals Spreads, but Gauging Performance Proves Tough," *Wall Street Journal,* September 10, 1991, pp. B1, B8.

12. M. Oneal, "Does New Balance Have an American Soul," *Business Week,* December 12, 1994, pp. 86, 90.

13. J. Pereira, "New Balance Disproves Myths About Urban Workers," *Wall Street Journal,* June 9, 1992, p. B4.

14. "Just Deserts," *The Economist,* January 29, 1994, p. 71.

15, 16. Lawler, *Pay and Organization Development.*

17. L. N. Spiro, "What's in the Cards for Harvey Golub?" *Business Week,* June 15, 1992, pp. 112–114.

18, 19. Spiro, "What's in the Cards for Harvey Golub?" G. Levin, "Feisty AmEx Deals Card for Corp. Buying," *Advertising Age,* January 17, 1994, pp. 3, 45.

20. J. F. Lincoln, *Incentive Management* (Cleveland: Lincoln Electric Company, 1951). R. Zager, "Managing Guaranteed Employment," *Harvard Business Review,* 1978, 56, pp. 103–115.

21. Lawler, *Pay and Organization Development.*

22, 23. J. Carlton, "Commission Clash: A Real-Estate Chain Riles Its Competitors by Breaking the Rules," *Wall Street Journal,* September 10, 1991, pp. A1, A6.

24. Fisher, Schoenfeldt, and Shaw. B. E. Graham-Moore and T. L. Ross, *Productivity Gainsharing* (Englewood Cliffs, N.J.: Prentice-Hall, 1983). A. J. Geare, "Productivity from Scanlon Type Plans," *Academy of Management Review,* 1976, 1, pp. 99–108.

25. J. Labate, "Deal Those Workers In," *Fortune,* April 19, 1993, p. 26.

26. D. Duston, "Women Tend to Pay More in Marketplace, Author Claims," *Bryan–College Station Eagle,* May 18, 1993, p. A1. F. C. Whittelsey, *Why Women Pay More* (Washington, D.C.: Center for Responsive Law, 1993).

27. Fisher, Schoenfeldt, and Shaw.

28. D. J. Treiman and H. I. Hartmann, *Women, Work, and Wages: Equal Pay for Jobs of Equal Value* (Washington, D.C.: National Academy Press, 1981).

29. J. H. Greenhaus, *Career Management* (New York: Dryden Press, 1987).

30–32. M. J. Driver, "Careers: A Review of Personal and Organizational Research," in C. L. Cooper and I. Robertson, eds., *International Review of Industrial and Organizational Psychology* (New York: Wiley, 1988).

33. C. Hymowitz and G. Stern, "At Procter & Gamble, Brands Face Pressure and So Do Executives," *Wall Street Journal,* May 10, 1993, pp. A1, A8.

34. L. S. Richman, "How to Get Ahead in America," *Fortune,* May 16, 1994, pp. 46–54.

35, 36. Driver, "Careers: A Review of Personal and Organizational Research."

37, 38. Greenhaus, *Career Management.*

39. J. L. Holland, *Making Vocational Choices: A Theory of Careers* (Englewood Cliffs, N.J.: Prentice-Hall, 1973).

40. J. P. Wanous, "Realistic Job Previews: Can a Procedure to Reduce Turnover Also Influence the Relationship Between Abilities and Performance?" *Personnel Psychology,* 1978, pp. 249–258. J. P. Wanous, *Organizational Entry: Recruitment, Selection and Socialization of Newcomers* (Reading, Mass.: Addison-Wesley, 1980).

41. Greenhaus, *Career Management.*

42. G. Dreher and R. Ash, "A Comparative Study of Mentoring Among Men and Women in Managerial, Professional, and Technical Positions," *Journal of Applied Psychology,* 1990, 75, pp. 525–535. T. A. Scandura, "Mentorship and Career Mobility: An Empirical Investigation," *Journal of Organizational Behavior,* 1992, 13, pp. 169–174. W. Whitely, T. W. Dougherty, and G. F. Dreher, "Relationship of Career Mentoring and Socioeconomic Origin to Managers' and Professionals' Early Career Success," *Academy of Management Journal,* 1991, 34, pp. 331–351.

43. D. B. Turban and T. W. Dougherty, "The Role of Protégé Personality in Receipt of Mentoring and Career Success," *Academy of Management Journal,* 1994, 37, pp. 688–702.

44. L. Clyde, Jr., "Would You Make a Good Protégé," *National Business Employment Weekly: Managing Your Career,* Spring–Summer 1993, pp. 15–17.

45. Greenhaus, *Career Management.*

46. Richman, "How to Get Ahead in America."

47. T. P. Ference, J. A. F. Stoner, and E. K. Warren, "Managing the Career Plateau," *Academy of Management Review,* 1977, 2, pp. 602–612.

48. B. T. Abdelnor and D. T. Hall, *Career Development of Established Employees* (New York: Center for Research in Career Development, Columbia University, 1981). J. M. Bardwick, "Plateauing and Productivity," *Sloan Management Review,* 1983, 24, pp. 67–73.

49. Abdelnor and Hall, *Career Development of Established Employees*; J. Sonnenfeld, "Dealing with the Aging Workforce," *Harvard Business Review,* 1978, 56, pp. 81–92.

50. Ference, Stoner, and Warren, "Managing the Career Plateau."

51. J. Fierman, "Beating the Midlife Career Crisis," *Fortune,* September 6, 1993, pp. 52–62.

52. B. Ortega, "Nearing 80, Founder of Dillard Stores Seeks to Keep on Growing," *Wall Street Journal,* May 11, 1994, pp. A1, A5.

53. G. Graham, "Would You Lie for Your Boss or Would You Just Rather Not?" *Bryan–College Station Eagle,* October 24, 1993, p. C3.

54. L. S. Gottfredson, "Dilemmas in Developing Diversity Programs," in S. E. Jackson and Associates, eds., *Diversity in the Workplace: Human Resources Initiatives* (New York: Guilford Press, 1992).

55. Gottfredson, "Dilemmas in Developing Diversity Programs."

56. H. Lancaster, "Performance Reviews Are More Valuable When More Join In," *Wall Street Journal*, July 9, 1996, p. B1.

57. J. S. Lublin, "Turning the Tables: Underlings Evaluate Bosses," *Wall Street Journal*, October 4, 1994, p. B1.

58. H. Lancaster, "Performance Reviews Are More Valuable When More Join In."

59. H. Lancaster, "Performance Reviews Are More Valuable When More Join In." J. S. Lublin, "Turning the Tables: Underlings Evaluate Bosses." J. S. Lublin, "It's Shape-Up Time for Performance Reviews," *Wall Street Journal*, October 3, 1994, p. B1. S. Shellenbarger, "Reviews From Peers Instruct—and Sting," *Wall Street Journal*, October 4, 1994, pp. B1, B4.

60. J. S. Lublin, "Turning the Tables: Underlings Evaluate Bosses."

61. S. Shellenbarger, "Reviews From Peers Instruct—and Sting."

CHAPTER 9

1–3. K. H. Hammonds, R. Furchgott, S. Hamm, and P.C. Judge, "Work and Family," *Business Week*, September 15, 1997, pp. 96-99.

4, 5. S. Shellenbarger, "Work-Family Issues Go Way Beyond Missed Ball Games," *Wall Street Journal*, May 28, 1997, B1.

6. S. Shellenbarger, "These Two Bosses May Signal Move To More Family Time," *Wall Street Journal*, April 30, 1997, p. B1.

7. Hammonds, Furchgott, Hamm, and Judge. S. Shellenbarger, "Work-Family Issues Go Way Beyond Missed Ball Games."

8. "Negative Feelings Afflict 40 Million Adults in U.S.," *Wall Street Journal*, November 26, 1993, p. B1.

9. R. S. Lazarus, *Psychological Stress and Coping Processes* (New York: McGraw-Hill, 1966). R. S. Lazarus and S. Folkman, *Stress, Appraisal, and Coping* (New York: Springer, 1984). R. S. Lazarus, "Psychological Stress in the Workplace," *Journal of Social Behavior and Personality*, 1991, 6(7), pp. 1–13.

10. Lazarus and Folkman, *Stress, Appraisal, and Coping.*

11. M. J. Burke, A. P. Brief, and J. M. George, "The Role of Negative Affectivity in Understanding Relations Between Self-Reports of Stressors and Strains: A Comment on the Applied Psychology Literature," *Journal of Applied Psychology*, 1993, 78, pp. 402–412. D. Watson and L. A. Clark, "Negative Affectivity: The Disposition to Experience Aversive Emotional States," *Psychological Bulletin*, 1984, 96, pp. 465–490.

12. H. Cooper, "Carpet Firm Sets Up an In-House School to Stay Competitive," *Wall Street Journal*, October 5, 1992, pp. A1, A5.

13. J. Seligmann, T. Namuth, and M. Miller, "Drowning on Dry Land," *Newsweek*, May 23, 1994, pp. 64–66.

14. D. Watson and J. W. Pennebaker, "Health Complaints, Stress, and Distress: Exploring the Central Role of Negative Affectivity," *Psychological Review*, 1989, 96, pp. 234–254.

15. D. Watson and A. Tellegen, "Toward a Consensual Structure of Mood," *Psychological Bulletin*, 1985, 98, pp. 219–235.

16. C. Maslach, *Burnout: The Cost of Caring* (Englewood Cliffs, N.J.: Prentice-Hall, 1982).

17. R. T. Lee and B. E. Ashforth, "On the Meaning of Maslach's Three Dimensions of Burnout," *Journal of Applied Psychology*, 1990, 75, pp. 743–747.

18. J. M., "It's Murder in the Workplace," *Business Week*, August 9, 1993, p. 12. J. Solomon and P. King, "Waging War in the Workplace," *Newsweek*, July 19, 1993, pp. 30–34.

19–21. T. DeAngelis, "Psychologists Aid Victims of Violence in Post Office," *APA Monitor*, October 1993, pp. 1, 44–45.

22, 23. Seligmann, Namuth, and Miller, "Drowning on Dry Land."

24. D. Jansen, "Winning: How the Olympian Quit Trying Too Hard—and Finally Won," *USA Weekend*, July 15–17, 1994, pp. 4–5.

25. A. B. Fisher, "Welcome to the Age of Overwork," *Fortune*, November 30, 1992, pp. 64–71.

26. "Stress Busters: Employers Fight Anxiety as Staffs Shrink and Work Increases," *Wall Street Journal*, December 1, 1992, p. A1.

27. "A Nurse Shortage May Be Easing, but Stress Persists," *Wall Street Journal*, January 5, 1993, p. A1.

28, 29. A. Stevens, "Suit over Suicide Raises Issue: Do Associates Work Too Hard?" *Wall Street Journal*, April 15, 1994, pp. B1, B7.

30. S. Shellenbarger, "Keeping Workers by Reaching Out to Them," *Wall Street Journal*, June 1, 1994, p. B1.

31. J. M. George and A. P. Brief, "Feeling Good–Doing Good: A Conceptual Analysis of the Mood at Work–Organizational Spontaneity Relationship," *Psychological Bulletin*, 1992, 112, pp. 310–329.

32. T. H. Holmes and M. Masuda, "Life Change and Illness Susceptibility," in B. S. Dohrenwend and B. P. Dohrenwend, eds., *Stressful Life Events: Their Nature and Effects* (New York: Wiley, 1974), pp. 45–72. T. H. Holmes and

R. H. Rahe, "Social Readjustment Rating Scale," *Journal of Psychosomatic Research*, 1967, 11, pp. 213–218.

33. R. S. Bhagat, S. J. McQuaid, H. Lindholm, and J. Segovis, "Total Life Stress: A Multimethod Validation of the Construct and Its Effect on Organizationally Valued Outcomes and Withdrawal Behaviors," *Journal of Applied Psychology*, 1985, 70, pp. 202–214. A. P. Brief, M. J. Burke, J. M. George, B. Robinson, and J. Webster, "Should Negative Affectivity Remain an Unmeasured Variable in the Study of Job Stress?" *Journal of Applied Psychology*, 1988, 73, pp. 193–198. B. S. Dohrenwend, L. Krasnoff, A. R. Askenasy, and B. P Dohrenwend, "Exemplification of a Method for Scaling Life Events: The PERI Life Events Scale," *Journal of Health and Social Behavior*, 1978, 19, pp. 205–229. J. H. Johnson and I. G. Sarason, "Recent Developments in Research on Life Stress," in V. Hamilton and D. M. Warburton, eds., *Human Stress and Cognition: An Information Processing Approach* (New York: Wiley, 1979), pp. 205–236.

34, 35. R. L. Kahn and P. Byosiere, "Stress in Organizations," in M. D. Dunnette and L. M. Hough, eds., *Handbook of Industrial and Organizational Psychology*, 2d ed., vol. 3 (Palo Alto, Calif.: Consulting Psychologists Press, 1992), pp. 571–650. S. Jackson and R. Schuler, "A Meta-Analysis and Conceptual Critique of Research on Role Ambiguity and Role Conflict in Work Settings," *Organizational Behavior and Human Decision Processes*, 1985, 36, pp. 16–78.

36. Kahn and Byosiere, "Stress in Organizations."

37. Fisher, "Welcome to the Age of Overwork."

38. J. A. Byrne, "The Pain of Downsizing," *Fortune*, May 9, 1994, pp. 60–68.

39, 40. Fisher, "Welcome to the Age of Overwork."

41. Seligmann, Namuth, and Miller, "Drowning on Dry Land."

42. A. P. Brief and J. M. Atieh, "Studying Job Stress: Are We Making Mountains Out of Molehills?" *Journal of Occupational Behaviour*, 1987, 8, pp. 115–126.

43. D. Wessel and D. Benjamin, "In Employment Policy, America and Europe Make a Sharp Contrast," *Wall Street Journal*, March 14, 1994, pp. A1, A6.

44. Wessel and Benjamin, "In Employment Policy, America and Europe Make a Sharp Contrast."

45. T. Horwitz, "Minimum-Wage Jobs Give Many Americans Only a Miserable Life," *Wall Street Journal*, November 12, 1993, pp. A1, A8.

46. Brief and Atieh, "Studying Job Stress"; R. L. Kahn, *Work and Health* (New York: Wiley, 1981). S. V. Kasl and S. Cobb, "Blood Pressure Changes in Men Undergoing Job Loss: A Preliminary Report," *Psychosomatic Medicine*, 1970, 32, pp. 19–38.

47. J. Brockner, "The Effects of Work Layoffs on Survivors: Research, Theory, and Practice," in B. M. Staw and L. L. Cummings, eds., *Research in Organizational Behavior* (Greenwich, Conn.: JAI Press, 1988).

48. J. Fierman, "Beating the Midlife Career Crisis," *Fortune*, September 6, 1993, pp. 52–62.

49. Brief and Atieh, "Studying Job Stress." L. Levi, "Psychological and Physiological Reaction to and Psychomotor Performance During Prolonged and Complex Stressor Exposure," *Acta Medica Scandinavica*, Supplement no. 528, 1972, 191, p. 119. M. Timio and S. Gentili, "Adrenosympathetic Overactivity Under Conditions of Work Stress," *British Journal of Preventive and Social Medicine*, 1976, 30, pp. 262–265.

50. E. S. Browning, "Computer Chip Project Brings Rivals Together, but the Cultures Clash," *Wall Street Journal*, May 3, 1994, pp. A1, A8.

51. K. Pope, "Keyboard Users Say Makers Knew of Problems," *Wall Street Journal*, May 4, 1994, pp. B1, B5.

52. J. M. George, T. F. Reed, K. A. Ballard, J. Colin, and J. Fielding, "Contact with AIDS Patients as a Source of Work-Related Distress: Effects of Organizational and Social Support," *Academy of Management Journal*, 1993, 36, pp. 157–171.

53. "Cargo Pilots Say They Are Flying Tired, and Seek Tougher Schedule Rules," *Wall Street Journal*, April 5, 1994, p. A1.

54. "Workplace Injuries May Be Far Worse Than Government Data Suggest," *Wall Street Journal*, February 2, 1993, p. A1.

55. A. Peers, "Lehman in Hot Water over Typing Pool," *Wall Street Journal*, June 1, 1994, pp. C1, C25.

56. S. Shellenbarger, "Single Parenting Boosts Career Stress," *Wall Street Journal*, June 1, 1994, p. B1.

57. S. Shellenbarger, "The Aging of America Is Making 'Elder Care' a Big Workplace Issue," *Wall Street Journal*, February 16, 1994, pp. A1, A8.

58–60. S. Folkman and R. S. Lazarus, "An Analysis of Coping in a Middle-Aged Community Sample," *Journal of Health and Social Behavior*, 1980, 21, pp. 219–239. S. Folkman and R. S. Lazarus, "If It Changes It Must Be a Process: Study of Emotion and Coping During Three Stages of a College Examination," *Journal of Personality and Social Psychology*, 1985, 48, pp. 150–170. S. Folkman and R. S. Lazarus, "Coping as a Mediator of Emotion," *Journal of Personality and Social Psychology*, 1988, 54, pp. 466–475.

61. D. Dunn, "For Globetrotting Execs en Famille," *Business Week*, January 11, 1993, pp. 132–133.

62. A. Lakein, *How to Get Control of Your Time and Your Life* (New York: Peter H. Wyden, 1973). J. C. Quick and J. D. Quick, *Organizational Stress and Preventive Management* (New York: McGraw-Hill, 1984).

63. W. L. French and C. H. Bell, Jr., *Organizational Development: Behavioral Science Interventions for Organization Improvement* (Englewood Cliffs, N.J.: Prentice-Hall, 1990).

64. S. Shellenbarger, "Work and Family: Men Find More Ways to Spend Time at Home," *Wall Street Journal*, February 12, 1992, p. B1.

65. Quick and Quick, *Organizational Stress and Preventive Management*.

66. S. Cohen and T. A. Wills, "Stress, Social Support, and the Buffering Hypothesis," *Psychological Bulletin*, 1985, 98, pp. 310–357. I. G. Sarason, H. M. Levine, R. B. Basham, and B. R. Sarason, "Assessing Social Support: The Social Support Questionnaire," *Journal of Personality and Social Psychology*, 44, pp. 127–139.

67. A. Salpukas, "Striking Oil but Straining Families," *New York Times*, July 7, 1994, pp. D1–D2.

68. "Stress Busters."

69. B. Ash, "Companies Say Yes to Child-Care Services," *Bryan–College Station Eagle*, May 29, 1994, p. C5.

70. M. D. Fefer, "Babes in Work Land," *Fortune*, April 18, 1994, pp. 31–32.

71. S. Shellenbarger, "Firms Help Employees Work with Sick Kids," *Wall Street Journal*, May 11, 1994, p. B1.

72. "Work-Family Problems Get Their Own Managers," *Wall Street Journal*, April 14, 1992, p. B1.

73, 74. "Training Workers to Be Flexible on Schedules," *Wall Street Journal*, February 10, 1993, p. 1. "Workplace Flexibility Is Seen as Key to Business Success," *Wall Street Journal*, November 23, 1993, p. A1.

75. J. Aley, "The Temp Biz Boom: Why It's Good," *Fortune*, October 16, 1995, pp. 53-55.

76. R. Eisenberger, P. Fasolo, and V. Davis-LaMastro, "Perceived Organizational Support and Employee Diligence, Commitment, and Innovation," *Journal of Applied Psychology*, 1990, 75, pp. 51–59. R. Eisenberger, R. Huntington, S. Hutchinson, and D. Sowa, "Perceived Organizational Support," *Journal of Applied Psychology*, 1986, 71, pp. 500–507.

77. George, Reed, Ballard, Colin, and Fielding, "Contact with AIDS Patients as a Source of Work-Related Distress."

78. B. Oliver, "How to Prevent Drug Abuse in Your Workplace," *HRMagazine*, December 1993, pp. 78–81.

79. R. A. Wolfe and D. F. Parker, "Employee Health Management: Challenges and Opportunities," *Academy of Management Executive*, 1994, 8(2), pp. 22–31.

80. U.S. Department of Health and Human Services, *1992 National Survey of Worksite Health Promotion Activities: A Summary Report* (Washington, D.C.: U.S. Department of Health and Human Services, 1992).

81. Wolfe and Parker, "Employee Health Management: Challenges and Opportunities."

82. K. H. Hammonds, "Case Study: One Company's Delicate Balancing Act," *Business Week*, September 15, 1997, pp. 102-104; http://www.xerox.com/; S. Shellenbarger, "Some Top Executives Are Finding a Balance Between Job and Home," *Wall Street Journal*, April 23, 1997, p. B1.

83, 84. S. Shellenbarger, "More Companies Experiment with Workers' Schedules," *Wall Street Journal*, January 13, 1994, pp. B1, B6.

CHAPTER 10

1. S. Baker, "The Minimill That Acts Like A Biggie," *Business Week*, September 30, 1996, pp. 100–104. S. Baker, "Nucor," *Business Week*, February 13, 1995, p. 70. www.fwi.com/nucor/

2. S. Overman, "No-Frills HR at Nucor," *HRMagazine*, July, 1994, pp. 56–60.

3. www.fwi.com/nucor/.

4. S. Overman, "No-Frills HR at Nucor." www.fwi.com/nucor/.

5. B. Dumaine, "The Trouble with Teams," *Fortune*, September 5, 1994, pp. 86–92.

6. M. E. Shaw, *Group Dynamics*, 3d ed. (New York: McGraw-Hill, 1981).

7. T. M. Mills, *The Sociology of Small Groups* (Englewood Cliffs, N.J.: Prentice-Hall, 1967).

8. J. A. Pearce II and E. C. Ravlin, "The Design and Activation of Self-Regulating Work Groups," *Human Relations*, 1987, 11, pp. 751–782.

9. B. W. Tuckman, "Developmental Sequences in Small Groups," *Psychological Bulletin*, 1965, 63, pp. 384–399. B. W. Tuckman and M. C. Jensen, "Stages of Small Group Development," *Group and Organizational Studies*, 1977, 2, pp. 419–427.

10–12. R. G. LeFauve and A. C. Hax, "Managerial and Technological Innovations at Saturn Corporation," *MIT Management*, Spring 1992, pp. 8–19.

13. C.J.G. Gersick, "Time and Transition in Work Teams: Toward a New Model of Group Development," *Academy of Management Journal*, 1988, 31, pp. 9–41. C.J.G. Gersick, "Marking Time: Predictable Transitions in Task Groups," *Academy of Management Journal*, 1989, 32, pp. 274–309.

14. G. R. Jones, "Task Visibility, Free Riding, and Shirking: Explaining the Effect of Structure and Technology on Employee Behavior," *Academy of Management Review*, 1984, 9, pp. 684–695.

15. C. F. Bond, Jr., and L. J. Titus, "Social Facilitation: A Meta-Analysis of 241 Studies," *Psychological Bulletin*, 1983, 94, pp. 265–292. Shaw, *Group Dynamics*.

16. Bond and Titus, "Social Facilitation: A Meta-Analysis." Shaw, *Group Dynamics*.

17. B. Dumain, "Who Needs a Boss?" *Fortune*, May 7, 1990, pp. 52–60.

18. C. Farrell and Z. Schiller, "Stuck! How Companies Cope When They Can't Raise Prices," *Business Week*, November 15, 1993, pp. 146–155. J. R. Koelsch, "On the Money," *Manufacturing Engineering*, March 1994, pp. 67–72. D. Smock, "Milacron Places Its Bets on Electric Machines," *Plastics World*, July 1994, pp. 6–7.

19. P. Nulty, "The Soul of an Old Machine," *Fortune*, May 21, 1990, pp. 67–69.

20, 21. J. R. Hackman, "Group Influences on Individuals in Organizations," in *Handbook of Industrial and Organizational Psychology*, 2d ed., vol. 3, ed. M. D. Dunnette and L. M. Hough (Palo Alto, Calif.: Consulting Psychologists Press, 1992), pp. 199–267.

22. D. C. Feldman, "The Development and Enforcement of Group Norms," *Academy of Management Review*, 1984, 9, pp. 47–53.

23. Hackman, "Group Influences on Individuals in Organizations."

24. E. P. Hollander, "Conformity, Status, and Idiosyncrasy Credit," *Psychological Review*, 1958, 65, pp. 117–127.

25. M. Dalton, "The Industrial Ratebuster: A Characterization," *Applied Anthropology*, 1948, 7, 5–18.

26. Hackman, "Group Influences on Individuals in Organizations."

27. M. Williams and Y. Ono, "Japanese Cite Need for Bold Change, but Not at the Expense of 'Stability,'" *Wall Street Journal*, June 29, 1993, p. A10.

28. G. R. Jones, "Psychological Orientation and the Process of Organizational Socialization: An Interactionist Perspective," *Academy of Management Review*, 1983, 8, pp. 464–474.

29. J. Van Mannen and E. H. Schein, "Towards a Theory of Organizational Socialization," in *Research in Organizational Behavior*, vol. 1, ed. B. M. Staw (Greenwich, Conn.: JAI Press, 1979), pp. 209–264.

30. G. R. Jones, "Socialization Tactics, Self-Efficacy, and Newcomers' Adjustments to Organizations," *Academy of Management Review*, 1986, 29, pp. 262–279.

31. Jones, "Socialization Tactics." J. Van Mannen and E. H. Schein, "Toward & Theory of *Organizational Socialization*."

32. M. N. Martinez, "Disney Training Works Magic," *HRMagazine*, May 1992, pp. 53–57.

33. R. Brandt and A. Cortese, "Bill Gates's Vision," *Business Week*, June 27, 1994, pp. 57–62. S. Hamm, A. Cortese, and S. B. Garland, "Microsoft's Future," *Business Week*, January 19, 1998, pp. 58-68. K. Rebello, "Inside Microsoft," *Business Week*, July 15, 1996, pp. 56-67.

34, 35. B. Filipczak, "Beyond the Gates at Microsoft," *Training*, September 1992, pp. 37–44.

CHAPTER 11

1. A. Barrett, "Hot Growth Companies," *Business Week*, May 22, 1995, pp. 68–70. D. Leonhardt, "Good Things In Small Packages," *Business Week*, March 25, 1996, pp. 94–95. M. Murray, "A Software Engineer Becomes a Manager, With Many Regrets," *Wall Street Journal*, May 14, 1997, pp. A1, A14.

2, 3. Murray, "A Software Engineer Becomes a Manager."

4. I. D. Steiner, *Group Process and Productivity* (New York: Academic Press, 1972).

5, 6. R. A. Guzzo and G. P. Shea, "Group Performance and Intergroup Relations in Organizations," in *Handbook of Industrial and Organizational Psychology*, 2d ed., vol. 3, ed. M. D. Dunnette and L. M. Hough (Palo Alto, Calif.: Consulting Psychologists Press, 1992), pp. 269–313. Steiner, *Group Process and Productivity*.

7. P. C. Earley, "Social Loafing and Collectivism: A Comparison of the United States and the People's Republic of China," *Administrative Science Quarterly*, 1989, 34, pp. 565–581. J. M. George, "Extrinsic and Intrinsic Origins of Perceived Social Loafing in Organizations," *Academy of Management Journal*, 1992, 35, pp. 191–202. S. G. Harkins, B. Latane, and K. Williams, "Social Loafing: Allocating Effort or Taking It Easy," *Journal of Experimental Social Psychology*, 1980, 16, pp. 457–465. B. Latane, K. D. Williams, and S. Harkins, "Many Hands Make Light the Work: The Causes and Consequences of Social Loafing," *Journal of Personality and Social Psychology*, 1979, 37, pp. 822–832. J. A. Shepperd, "Productivity Loss in Performance Groups: A Motivation Analysis," *Psychological Bulletin*, 1993, 113, pp. 67–81.

8. George, "Extrinsic and Intrinsic Origins of Perceived Social Loafing in Organizations." G. R. Jones, "Task Visibility, Free Riding, and Shirking: Explaining the Effect of Structure and Technology on Employee Behavior," *Academy of Management Review*, 1984, 9, pp. 684–695. K. Williams, S. Harkins, and B. Latane, "Identifiability as a Deterrent to Social Loafing:

Two Cheering Experiments," *Journal of Personality and Social Psychology,* 1981, 40, pp. 303–311.

9. M. A. Brickner, S. G. Harkins, and T. M. Ostrom, "Effects of Personal Involvement: Thought-Provoking Implications for Social Loafing," *Journal of Personality and Social Psychology,* 1986, 51, pp. 763–769. S. G. Harkins and R. E. Petty, "The Effects of Task Difficulty and Task Uniqueness on Social Loafing," *Journal of Personality and Social Psychology,* 1982, 43, pp. 1214–1229. N. L. Kerr and S. E. Bruun, "Dispensability of Member Effort and Group Motivation Losses: Free-Rider Effects," *Journal of Personality and Social Psychology,* 1983, 44, pp. 78–94.

10. N. L. Kerr, "Motivation Losses in Small Groups: A Social Dilemma Analysis," *Journal of Personality and Social Psychology,* 1983, 45, pp. 819–828.

11. J. M. Jackson and S. G. Harkins, "Equity in Effort: An Explanation of the Social Loafing Effect," *Journal of Personality and Social Psychology,* 1985, 49, pp. 1199–1206.

12. B. Latane, "Responsibility and Effort in Organizations," in P. S. Goodman, ed., *Designing Effective Work Groups* (San Francisco: Jossey-Bass, 1986). Latane, Williams, and Harkins, "Many Hands Make Light the Work." Steiner, *Group Process and Productivity.*

13. M. E. Shaw, *Group Dynamics,* 3d ed. (New York: McGraw-Hill, 1981).

14. S. Harkins and J. Jackson, "The Role of Evaluation in Eliminating Social Loafing," *Personality and Social Psychology Bulletin,* 1985, 11, pp. 457–465. N. L. Kerr and S. E. Bruun, "Ringelman Revisited: Alternative Explanations for the Social Loafing Effect," *Personality and Social Psychology Bulletin,* 1981, 7, pp. 224–231. Williams, Harkins, and Latane, "Identifiability as a Deterrent to Social Loafing."

15, 16. J. S. Lublin, "Trying to Increase Worker Productivity, More Employers Alter Management Style," *Wall Street Journal,* February 13, 1992, pp. B1, B7.

17. Brickner, Harkins, and Ostrom, "Effects of Personal Involvement." Harkins and Petty, "The Effects of Task Difficulty and Task Uniqueness on Social Loafing."

18. R. Rapaport, "To Build a Winning Team: An Interview with Head Coach Bill Walsh," *Harvard Business Review,* January–February 1993, pp. 111–120.

19. Latane, "Responsibility and Effort in Organizations." Latane, Williams, and Harkins, "Many Hands Make Light the Work." Steiner, *Group Process and Productivity.*

20. J. D. Thompson, *Organizations in Action* (New York: McGraw-Hill, 1967).

21. Steiner, *Group Process and Productivity.*

22. L. Festinger, "Informal Social Communication," *Psychological Review,* 1950, 57, pp. 271–282. Shaw, *Group Dynamics.*

23. D. Cartwright, "The Nature of Group Cohesiveness," in *Group Dynamics,* 3d ed., ed. D. Cartwright and A. Zander (New York: Harper and Row, 1968). L. Festinger, S. Schacter, and K. Black, *Social Pressures in Informal Groups* (New York: Harper and Row, 1950). Shaw, *Group Dynamics.*

24. Shaw, *Group Dynamics.*

25. K. Denton, "Quality Is Pepsi's Challenge," *Personnel Journal,* June 1988, pp. 143–147.

26. J. R. Hackman, "Group Influences on Individuals in Organizations," in *Handbook of Industrial and Organizational Psychology,* pp. 199–267.

27. Shaw, *Group Dynamics.*

28. S. Finkelstein and D. C. Hambrick, "Top-Management Team Tenure and Organizational Outcomes: The Moderating Role of Managerial Discretion," *Administrative Science Quarterly,* 1990, 35, pp. 484–503.

29. I. L. Janis, *Victims of Groupthink,* 2d ed. (Boston: Houghton Mifflin, 1982).

30. D. J. Yang, "Nordstrom's Gang of Four," *Business Week,* June 15, 1992, pp. 122–123.

31. J. A. Pearce II and E. C. Ravlin, "The Design and Activation of Self-Regulating Work Groups," *Human Relations,* 1987, 11, pp. 751–782.

32. A. R. Montebello and V. R. Buzzotta, "Work Teams That Work," *Training and Development,* March 1993, pp. 59–64.

33. J. R. Hackman and G. R. Oldham, *Work Redesign* (Reading, Mass.: Addison-Wesley, 1980).

34, 35. B. Dumain, "Who Needs a Boss?" *Fortune,* May 7, 1990, pp. 52–60. Pearce and Ravlin, "The Design and Activation of Self-Regulating Work Groups."

36. T. D. Wall, N. J. Kemp, P. R. Jackson, and C. W. Clegg, "Outcomes of Autonomous Workgroups: A Long-Term Field Experiment," *Academy of Management Journal,* 1986, 29, pp. 280–304.

37. R. D. O'Keefe, J. A. Kernaghan, and A. H. Rubenstein, "Group Cohesiveness: A Factor in the Adoption of Innovations Among Scientific Work Groups," *Small Group Behavior,* 1975, 6, pp. 282–292. C. A. O'Reilly and K. H. Roberts, "Task Group Structure, Communication, and Effectiveness in Three Organizations," *Journal of Applied Psychology,* 1977, 62, pp. 674–681.

38. J. B. White and O. Suris, "How a 'Skunk Works' Kept the Mustang Alive—on a Tight Budget," *Wall Street Journal,* September 21, 1993, pp. A1, A12.

39. White and Suris, "How a 'Skunk Works' Kept the Mustang Alive."

40. H. Gleckman, S. Atchison, T. Smart, and J. A. Byrne, "Bonus Pay: Buzzword or Bonanza?," *Business Week,* November 14, 1994, pp. 62-64.

41. J. Case, "What the Experts Forgot to Mention," *Inc.,* September 1993, pp. 66–77.

42. www.xel.com.

CHAPTER 12

1. G. McWilliams, "The Quiet Man Who's Jolting Utilities," *Business Week,* June 9, 1997, pp. 84–88.

2. www.enron.com. E. A. Robinson, "America's Most Admired Companies," *Fortune,* March 3, 1997, pp. 68–75. "The Top Managers of 1996," *Business Week,* January 13, 1997, pp. 56–70. "Where Companies Rank in Their Own Industries," *Fortune,* March 3, 1997, pp. F1–F6.

3, 4. McWilliams, "The Quiet Man Who's Jolting Utilities."

5. www.enron.com.

6. G. Yukl and D. D. Van Fleet, "Theory and Research on Leadership in Organizations," in *Handbook of Industrial and Organizational Psychology,* 2d ed., vol. 3, ed. M. D. Dunnette and L. M. Hough (Palo Alto, Calif: Consulting Psychologists Press, 1992), pp. 147–197.

7. R. M. Stogdill, *Handbook of Leadership: A Survey of the Literature* (New York: Free Press, 1974).

8. G. Yukl, "Managerial Leadership: A Review of Theory and Research," *Journal of Management,* 1989, 15, pp. 251–289.

9. G. Yukl, *Leadership in Organizations,* 2d ed. (New York: Academic Press, 1989).

10. L. Coch and J. R. P. French, "Overcoming Resistance to Change," *Human Relations,* 1948, 1, pp. 512–532. G. Graen, F. Dansereau, Jr., T. Minami, and J. Cashman, "Leadership Behaviors as Cues to Performance Evaluation," *Academy of Management Journal,* 1973, 16, pp. 611–623. G. Graen and S. Ginsburgh, "Job Resignation as a Function of Role Orientation and Leader Acceptance: A Longitudinal Investigation of Organizational Assimilation," *Organizational Behavior and Human Performance,* 1977, 19, pp. 1–17. R. J. House and M. L. Baetz, "Leadership: Some Empirical Generalizations and New Research Directions," in B. M. Staw and L. L. Cummings, eds., *Research in Organizational Behavior,* vol. 1 (Greenwich, Conn.: JAI Press, 1979), pp. 341–423. N. R. F. Maier, *Problem Solving and Creativity in Individuals and Groups* (Belmont, Calif.: Brooks-Cole, 1970). K. N. Wexley, J. P. Singh, and G. A. Yukl, "Subordinate Personality as a Moderator of the Effects of Participation in Three Types of Appraisal Interviews," *Journal of Applied Psychology,* 1973, 58, pp. 54–59.

11. House and Baetz, "Leadership."

12. Yukl, "Managerial Leadership."

13. Stogdill, *Handbook of Leadership.* House and Baetz, "Leadership."

14. B. M. Bass, *Bass and Stogdill's Handbook of Leadership: Theory, Research, and Managerial Applications,* 3d ed. (New York: Free Press, 1990). House and Baetz, "Leadership." S. A. Kirpatrick and E. A. Locke, "Leadership: Do Traits Matter?" *Academy of Management Executive,* 1991, 5(2), pp. 48–60. Yukl, *Leadership in Organizations.* Yukl and Van Fleet, "Theory and Research on Leadership in Organizations."

15. B. Dumaine, "Management Lessons from the General," *Business Week,* November 2, 1992, p. 143.

16. L. Smith, "The Executive's New Coach," *Fortune,* December 27, 1993, pp. 126–134.

17. E. A. Fleishman, "The Description of Supervisory Behavior," *Personnel Psychology,* 1953, 37, pp. 1–6. A. W. Halpin and B. J. Winer, "A Factorial Study of the Leader Behavior Descriptions," in *Leader Behavior: Its Description and Measurement,* ed. R. M. Stogdill and A. E. Coons (Columbus: Bureau of Business Research, Ohio State University, 1957).

18. E. A. Fleishman, "Performance Assessment Based on an Empirically Derived Task Taxonomy," *Human Factors,* 1967, 9, pp. 349–366.

19. D. Tscheulin, "Leader Behavior Measurement in German Industry," *Journal of Applied Psychology,* 1971, 56, pp. 28–31.

20. P. Nulty, "The Bounce Is Back at Goodyear," *Fortune,* September 7, 1992, pp. 70–72.

21. A. Taylor III, "Why GM Leads the Pack in Europe," *Fortune,* May 17, 1993, pp. 83–86.

22. E. A. Fleishman and E. F. Harris, "Patterns of Leadership Behavior Related to Employee Grievances and Turnover," *Personnel Psychology,* 1962, 15, pp. 43–56.

23. J. Cole, "New CEO at Hughes Studied Its Managers, Got Them on His Side," *Wall Street Journal,* March 30, 1993, pp. A1, A8.

24. R. Likert, *New Patterns of Management* (New York: McGraw-Hill, 1961). N. C. Morse and E. Reimer, "The Experimental Change of a Major Organizational Variable," *Journal of Abnormal and Social Psychology,* 1956, 52, pp. 120–129.

25. R. R. Blake and J. S. Mouton, *The New Managerial Grid* (Houston: Gulf, 1978).

26. P. Hersey and K. Blanchard, *Management of Organizational Behavior: Utilizing Human Resources* (Englewood Cliffs, N.J.: Prentice-Hall, 1982).

27. P. M. Podsakoff, W. D. Todor, R. A. Grover, and V. L. Huber, "Situational Moderators of Leader Reward and Punishment Behaviors: Fact or Fiction?"

Organizational Behavior and Human Performance, 1984, 34, pp. 21–63. P. M. Podsakoff, W. D. Todor, and R. Skov, "Effects of Leader Contingent and Noncontingent Reward and Punishment Behaviors on Subordinate Performance and Satisfaction," *Academy of Management Journal,* 1982, 25, pp. 810–821.

28. G. Das, "Local Memoirs of a Global Manager," *Harvard Business Review,* March–April 1993, pp. 38–47.

29. Podsakoff, Todor, Grover, and Huber, "Situational Moderators of Leader Reward and Punishment Behaviors." Podsakoff, Todor, and Skov, "Effects of Leader Contingent and Noncontingent Reward and Punishment Behaviors on Subordinate Performance and Satisfaction."

30, 31. B. Dumaine, "America's Toughest Bosses," *Fortune,* October 18, 1993, pp. 38–50.

32. E. A. Fleishman, *Leadership Opinion Questionnaire* (Chicago: Science Research Associates, 1960).

33. F. E. Fiedler, *A Theory of Leadership Effectiveness* (New York: McGraw-Hill, 1967). F. E. Fiedler, "The Contingency Model and the Dynamics of the Leadership Process," in *Advances in Experimental Social Psychology,* ed. L. Berkowitz (New York: Academic Press, 1978).

34. M. Mofflet, "Culture Shock," *Wall Street Journal,* September 24, 1992, pp. R13–R14.

35. House and Baetz, "Leadership."

36. House and Baetz, "Leadership." L. H. Peters, D. D. Hartke, and J. T. Pohlmann, "Fiedler's Contingency Theory of Leadership: An Application of the Meta-Analysis Procedures of Schmidt and Hunter," *Psychological Bulletin,* 1985, 97, pp. 274–285.

37. J. C. Wofford and L. Z. Liska, "Path-Goal Theories of Leadership: A Meta-Analysis," *Journal of Management,* 1993, 19, pp. 857–876.

38. V. H. Vroom and P. W. Yetton, *Leadership and Decision-Making* (Pittsburgh: University of Pittsburgh Press, 1973).

39. J. Templeman, "Bob Eaton Is No Lee Iacocca—but He Doesn't Need to Be," *Business Week,* November 9, 1992, p. 96.

40. V. H. Vroom and A. G. Jago, *The New Leadership: Managing Participation in Organizations* (Englewood Cliffs, N.J.: Prentice Hall, 1988).

41. D. J. Jefferson, "Dumped, Carl Karcher Vows Fight to Retake His Fast-Food Empire," *Wall Street Journal,* October 7, 1993, pp. A1, A4.

42. R. M. Dienesch and R. C. Liden, "Leader-Member Exchange Model of Leadership: A Critique and Further Development," *Academy of Management Review,* 1986, 11, pp. 618–634. G. Graen, M. Novak, and P. Sommerkamp, "The Effects of Leader-Member Exchange and Job Design on Productivity and Satisfaction: Testing a Dual Attachment Model," *Organizational Behavior and Human Performance,* 1982, 30, pp. 109–131.

43. G. Graen and J. Cashman, "A Role-Making Model of Leadership in Formal Organizations: A Development Approach," in *Leadership Frontiers,* ed. J. G. Hunt and L. L. Larson (Kent, Oh.: Kent State University Press, 1975), pp. 143–165.

44. M. Wakabayashi and G. B. Graen, "The Japanese Career Progress Study: A Seven-Year Follow-Up," *Journal of Applied Psychology,* 1984, 69, pp. 603–614.

45. W. E. McClane, "Implications of Member Role Differentiation: Analysis of a Key Concept in the LMX Model of Leadership," *Group and Organization Studies,* 1991, 16, pp. 102–113. Yukl, *Leadership in Organizations.* Yukl and Van Fleet, "Theory and Research on Leadership in Organizations."

46. J. R. Meindl, "On Leadership: An Alternative to the Conventional Wisdom," in *Research in Organizational Behavior,* vol. 12, ed. B. M. Staw and L. L. Cummings (Greenwich, Conn.: JAI Press, 1990), pp. 159–203.

47. S. Kerr and J. M. Jermier, "Substitutes for Leadership: Their Meaning and Measurement," *Organizational Behavior and Human Performance,* 1978, 22, pp. 375–403.

48, 49. L. Killian, "California, Here We Come," *Forbes,* November 23, 1992, pp. 146–147.

50. P. M. Podsakoff, B. P. Niehoff, S. B. MacKenzie, and M. L. Williams, "Do Substitutes for Leadership Really Substitute for Leadership? An Empirical Examination of Kerr and Jermier's Situational Leadership Model," *Organizational Behavior and Human Decision Processes,* 1993, 54, pp. 1–44.

51. B. M. Bass, *Leadership and Performance Beyond Expectations* (New York: Free Press, 1985).

52. Bass, *Leadership and Performance Beyond Expectations.* Bass, *Bass and Stogdill's Handbook of Leadership.* Yukl and Van Fleet, "Theory and Research on Leadership in Organizations."

53. J. A. Conger and R. N. Kanungo, "Behavioral Dimensions of Charismatic Leadership," in *Charismatic Leadership,* J. A. Conger, R. N. Kanungo, and Associates (San Francisco: Jossey-Bass, 1988).

54, 55. Bass, *Leadership and Performance Beyond Expectations.* Bass, *Bass and Stogdill's Handbook of Leadership.* Yukl and Van Fleet, "Theory and Research on Leadership in Organizations."

56. R. Johnson, "Tenneco Hired a CEO from Outside, and He Is Refocusing the Firm," *Wall Street Journal,* March 29, 1993, pp. A1, A14.

57. N. E. Field, "'Success Depends on Leadership,'" *Fortune,* November 18, 1991, pp. 153–154.

58, 59. Johnson, "Tenneco Hired a CEO from Outside."

60. W. Zellner, "The Fight of His Life," *Business Week,* September 20, 1993, pp. 55–64.

61. Field, "'Success Depends on Leadership.'" Johnson, "Tenneco Hired a CEO from Outside." Zellner, "The Fight of His Life."

62. Bass, *Leadership and Performance Beyond Expectations.*

63. B. M. Bass, B. J. Avolio, and L. Goodheim, "Biography and the Assessment of Transformational Leadership at the World Class Level," *Journal of Management,* 1987, 13, pp. 7–20. J. J. Hater and B. M. Bass, "Superiors' Evaluations and Subordinates' Perceptions of Transformational and Transactional Leadership," *Journal of Applied Psychology,* 1988, 73, pp. 695–702. J. Seltzer and B. M. Bass, "Transformational Leadership: Beyond Initiation and Consideration," *Journal of Management,* 1990, 16, pp. 693–703. D. A. Waldman, B. M. Bass, and W. O. Einstein, "Effort, Performance, and Transformational Leadership in Industrial and Military Service," *Journal of Occupational Psychology,* 1987, 60, pp. 1–10.

64. B. Dumaine, "What's So Hot About Outsiders?" *Fortune,* November 29, 1993, pp. 63–67.

65. J. M. George and K. Bettenhausen, "Understanding Prosocial Behavior, Sales Performance, and Turnover: A Group-Level Analysis in a Service Context," *Journal of Applied Psychology,* 1990, 75, pp. 698–709.

66–68. A. H. Eagly and B. T. Johnson, "Gender and Leadership Style: A Meta-Analysis," *Psychological Bulletin,* 1990, 108, pp. 233–256.

69. A. H. Eagly, M. G. Makhijani, and B. G. Klonsky, "Gender and the Evaluation of Leaders: A Meta-Analysis," *Psychological Bulletin,* 1992, 111, pp. 3–22.

70. C. Arnst, J. Dobrzynski, and B. Ziegler, "Faith in a Stranger: As an Outsider and Non-Techie, Lou Gerstner Breaks the Mold," *Business Week,* April 5, 1993, pp. 18–21.

71. Arnst, Dobrzynski, and Ziegler, "Faith in a Stranger." J. Dobrzynski, "An Exclusive Account of Lou Gerstner's First Six Months," *Business Week,* October 4, 1993, pp. 87–97.

72. S. Lohr, "On the Road with Chairman Lou," *New York Times,* June 26, 1994, Business section, pp. 1, 6.

73. B. Morris, "Big Blue," *Fortune,* April 14, 1997, pp. 68-81. R. Narisetti, "IBM's Gerstner to Stay Five More Years," *Wall Street Journal,* November 21, 1997, pp. A3, A4.

74. www.ibm.com.

75. R. Narisetti, "IBM's Gerstner to Stay Five More Years."

CHAPTER 13

1. "Ultimate Vision," *ADWEEK Eastern Edition,* November 10, 1997, p. 54.

2. www.brownsteingroup.com. "Pennsylvania," *ADWEEK Eastern Edition,* September 9, 1996, p. 57. H. Stout, "Self-Evaluation Brings Change to a Family's Ad Agency," *Wall Street Journal,* January 6, 1998, p. B2.

3, 4. Stout, "Self-Evaluation Brings Change to a Family's Ad Agency."

5. L. W. Porter and K. H. Roberts, "Communication in Organizations," in *Handbook of Industrial and Organizational Psychology,* ed. M. D. Dunnette (Chicago: Rand McNally, 1976), pp. 1553–1589.

6, 7. C. A. O'Reilly and L. R. Pondy, "Organizational Communication," in *Organizational Behavior,* ed. S. Kerr (Columbus, Oh.: Grid, 1979).

8. "Building Babel in Brussels," *The Economist,* August 6, 1994, p. 44.

9. P. P. Le Breton, *Administrative Intelligence-Information Systems* (Boston: Houghton Mifflin, 1963). W. G. Scott and T. R. Mitchell, *Organization Theory* (Homewood, Ill.: Irwin, 1976).

10. B. Dumaine, "What's So Hot About Outsiders?" *Fortune,* November 29, 1993, pp. 63–67.

11. O. W. Baskin and C. E. Aronoff, *Interpersonal Communication in Organizations* (Santa Monica, Calif.: Goodyear, 1989).

12. F. Fearing, "Toward a Psychological Theory of Human Communication," *Journal of Personality,* 1953–1954, 22, pp. 73–76. Scott and Mitchell, *Organization Theory.*

13. J. M. George, "Mood and Absence," *Journal of Applied Psychology,* 1989, 74, pp. 317–324. J. M. George, "State or Trait: Effects of Positive Mood on Prosocial Behaviors at Work," *Journal of Applied Psychology,* 1991, 76, pp. 299–307. J. M. George and A. P. Brief, "Feeling Good–Doing Good: A Conceptual Analysis of the Mood at Work–Organizational Spontaneity Relationship," *Psychological Bulletin,* 1992, 112, pp. 310–329.

14. S. Cohen and T. A. Wills, "Stress, Social Support, and the Buffering Hypothesis," *Psychological Bulletin,* 1985, 98, pp. 310–357. J. M. George, T. F. Reed, K. A. Ballard, J. Colin, and J. Fielding, "Contact with AIDs Patients as a Source of Work-Related Distress: Effects of Organizational and Social Support," *Academy of Management Journal,* 1993, 36, pp. 157–171.

15. E. M. Rogers and R. Agarwala-Rogers, *Communication in Organizations* (New York: Free Press, 1976).

16. "Employers Struggle to Teach Their Workers Basic Communication

Skills," *Wall Street Journal,* November 30, 1993, p. A1.

17, 18. J. Davis, *Buzzwords* (New York: Crown, 1993). "Insider Talk," *The Economist,* October 9, 1993, p. 100.

19. "Corporate Jargon: If You Don't Know the Inside Skinny, It Can Be a Jumble," *Wall Street Journal,* February 15, 1994, p. A1.

20. "Managing Your Boss," *Harvard Business Review Video Series No. 4.*

21. J. T. Malloy, *Dress for Success* (New York: Warner Books, 1975).

22. J. Sandberg, "People Are Hugging a Lot More Now and Seem to Like It," *Wall Street Journal,* March 15, 1993, pp. A1, A5.

23. J. Carey, "Getting Business to Think About the Unthinkable," *Business Week,* June 24, 1991, pp. 104–106.

24. Briefings from the Editors, "The New Communications: Don't Fax Me, I'll Fax You," *Harvard Business Review,* March–April 1993, pp. 8–9.

25, 26. N. Templin, "Companies Use TV to Reach Their Workers," *Wall Street Journal,* December 7, 1993, pp. B1, B16.

27. Baskin and Aronoff, *Interpersonal Communication in Organizations.*

28–30. D. Tannen, "The Power of Talk," *Harvard Business Review,* September-October, 1995, pp. 138-148. D. Tannen, *Talking from 9 to 5* (New York: Avon Books, 1995).

31. R. L. Daft, R. H. Lengel, and L. K. Trevino, "Message Equivocality, Media Selection, and Manager Performance: Implications for Information Systems," *MIS Quarterly,* 1987, 11, pp. 355–366. R. L. Daft and R. H. Lengel, "Information Richness: A New Approach to Managerial Behavior and Organization Design," in *Research in Organizational Behavior,* ed. B. M. Staw and L. L. Cummings (Greenwich, Conn.: JAI Press, 1984).

32. R. L. Daft, *Organization Theory and Design* (New York: West, 1992).

33. M. Ewell, "Who's Reading Your E-Mail? More People Than You Think," *Bryan–College Station Eagle,* April 20, 1994, p. A2.

34. Ewell, "Who's Reading Your E-Mail?"

35. Daft, *Organization Theory and Design.*

36. W. M. Bulkeley, "Advances in Networking and Software Push Firms Closer to Paperless Office," *Wall Street Journal,* August 5, 1993, pp. B1, B6.

37, 38. R. Tetzeli, "The Internet and Your Business," *Fortune,* March 7, 1994, pp. 86–96.

39. A. L. Sprout, "The Internet Inside Your Company," *Fortune,* November 27, 1995, pp. 161-168.

40. S. G. Straus and J. E. McGrath, "Does the Medium Matter? The Interaction of Task Type and Technology on Group Performance and Member Reactions," *Journal of Applied Psychology,* 1994, 79, pp. 87–97.

41. S. Kiesler, D. Zubrow, A. Moses, and V. Geller, "Affect in Computer-Mediated Communication: An Experiment in Synchronous Terminal-to-Terminal Discussion," *Human-Computer Interaction,* 1985, 1, pp. 77–104; T. W. McGuire, S. Kiesler, and J. Siegel, "Group and Computer-Mediated Discussion Effects in Risk Decision Making," *Journal of Personality and Social Psychology,* 1987, 52, pp. 917–930; J. Siegel, V. Dubrovsky, S. Kiesler, and T. W. McGuire, "Group Processes in Computer-Mediated Communication," *Organizational Behavior and Human Decision Processes,* 1986, 37, pp. 157–187; S. P. Weisband, "Group Discussion and First Advocacy Effects in Computer-Mediated and Face-to-Face Decision Making Groups," *Organizational Behavior and Human Decision Processes,* 1992, 53, pp. 352–380.

42. M. Argyle, M. Lalljee, and M. Cook, "The Effects of Visibility of Interaction in a Dyad," *Human Relations,* 1968, 21, pp. 3–17. D. K. Brotz, "Message System Mores: Etiquette in Laurel," *ACM Transactions in Office Systems,* 1983, 1, pp. 179–192. J. E. McGrath, "Time Matters in Groups," in *Intellectual Teamwork: Social and Technological Foundations of Cooperative Work,* ed. J. Galegher, R. E. Kraut, and C. Egido (Hillsdale, N.J.: Erlbaum, 1990), pp. 23–61. D. R. Rutter and G. M. Stephenson, "The Role of Visual Communication in Synchronizing Conversation," *European Journal of Social Psychology,* 1975, 7, pp. 29–37.

43, 44. Straus and McGrath, "Does the Medium Matter?"

45. D. Stead, R. Ihnatowycz, and P. Coy, "Why Ivan Can't Place a Call," *Business Week,* December 14, 1992, pp. 92–93.

46–48. C. F. Knight, "Emerson Electric: Consistent Profits, Consistently," *Harvard Business Review,* January–February 1992, pp. 57–70.

49. D. Krackhardt and J. R. Hanson, "Informal Networks: The Company," *Harvard Business Review,* July–August 1993, pp. 104–111.

50. www.georgiapowerco.com.

51, 52. L. Lamkin and E. W. Carmain, "Crisis Communication at Georgia Power," *Personnel Journal,* January 1991, pp. 35–37.

53. M. Blodgett, "Telecommuting Boosts Utility's Productivity," *Computerworld,* May 19, 1997, pp. 59-60. Lamkin and Carmain, "Crisis Communication at Georgia Power."

CHAPTER 14

1. S. Crock, "Aerospace Prognosis 1998," *Business Week,* January 12, 1998, p. 106. R. Henkoff, "Boeing's Big Problem," *Fortune,* January 12, 1998, pp. 96–103.

2. J. Flynn, J. Carey, and R. Crockett, "A Fierce Downdraft at Boeing," *Business Week,* January 26, 1998, pp. 34–35. R. Henkoff, "Boeing's Big Problem."

3, 4. R. Henkoff, "Boeing's Big Problem."

5. A. Grove, "How Intel Makes Spending Pay Off," *Fortune,* February 22, 1993, pp. 56–61.

6. J. G. March and H. A. Simon, *Organizations* (New York: Wiley, 1958). H. A. Simon, *The New Science of Management Decision* (New York: Harper and Row, 1960).

7. March and Simon, *Organizations.*

8, 9. March and Simon, *Organizations.* Simon, *The New Science of Management Decision.*

10. M. K. Stevenson, J. R. Busemeyer, and J. C. Naylor, "Judgment and Decision-Making Theory," in *Handbook of Industrial and Organizational Psychology,* 2d ed., vol. 1, ed. M. D. Dunnette and L. M. Hough (Palo Alto, Calif.: Consulting Psychologists Press, 1990), pp. 283–374.

11. W. Edwards, "The Theory of Decision Making," *Psychological Bulletin,* 1954, 51, pp. 380–417. H. A. Simon, "A Behavioral Model of Rational Choice," *Quarterly Journal of Economics,* 1955, 69, pp. 99–118.

12. Edwards, "The Theory of Decision Making." Simon, "A Behavioral Model of Rational Choice."

13. Edwards, "The Theory of Decision Making." Stevenson, Busemeyer, and Naylor, "Judgment and Decision-Making Theory."

14. Simon, "A Behavioral Model of Rational Choice."

15–17. March and Simon, *Organizations.*

18. Edwards, "The Theory of Decision Making." March and Simon, *Organizations.* Simon, "A Behavioral Model of Rational Choice."

19. March and Simon, *Organizations.* Simon, "A Behavioral Model of Rational Choice."

20. Stevenson, Busemeyer, and Naylor, "Judgment and Decision-Making Theory."

21. March and Simon, *Organizations.* Simon, "A Behavioral Model of Rational Choice."

22. March and Simon, *Organizations.*

23. Henkoff, "Boeing's Big Problem."

24. C. Kleiman, "Ethics Officers Doing It Right for Business," *Bryan–College Station Eagle,* December 12, 1993, p. C3.

25. Kleiman, "Ethics Officers Doing It Right for Business." J. Ambrose, "More Big Businesses Set Up Ethics Offices," *Wall Street Journal,* May 10, 1993, p. B1.

26. Ambrose, "More Big Businesses Set Up Ethics Offices."

27, 28. Simon, *The New Science of Management Decision.*

29. M. H. Bazerman, *Judgment in Managerial Decision Making* (New York: Wiley, 1994). D. Kahneman and A. Tversky, "Subjective Probability: A Judgment of Representativeness," *Cognitive Psychology,* 1972, 3, pp. 430–454. A. Tversky and D. Kahneman, "Judgment Under Uncertainty: Heuristics and Biases," *Science,* 1974, 185, pp. 1124–1131.

30–32. Bazerman, *Judgment in Managerial Decision Making.* Tversky and Kahneman, "Judgment Under Uncertainty."

33. Bazerman, *Judgment in Managerial Decision Making.*

34, 35. Bazerman, *Judgment in Managerial Decision Making.* Tversky and Kahneman, "Judgment Under Uncertainty."

36. Tversky and Kahneman, "Judgment Under Uncertainty."

37. B. M. Staw, "The Escalation of Commitment to a Course of Action," *Academy of Management Review,* 1981, 6, pp. 577–587. B. M. Staw and J. Ross, "Understanding Behavior in Escalation Situations," *Science,* 1986, 246, pp. 216–220.

38. T. P. Pare, "Scandal Isn't All That Ails the Pru," *Fortune,* March 21, 1994, pp. 52–60.

39, 40. Staw and Ross, "Understanding Behavior in Escalation Situations."

41. D. Kahneman and A. Tversky, "Prospect Theory: An Analysis of Decision Under Risk," *Econometrica,* 1979, 47, pp. 263–291. Staw and Ross, "Understanding Behavior in Escalation Situations."

42. Z. Schiller, "GE's Appliance Park: Rewire, or Pull the Plug?" *Business Week,* February 8, 1993, p. 30.

43. J. Martin, "Detroit's Designing Women," *Fortune,* October 18, 1993, pp. 10–11.

44. M. Galen and A. T. Palmer, "White, Male, and Worried," *Business Week,* January 31, 1994, pp. 50–55.

45, 46. A. Rossett and T. Bickham, "Diversity Training: Hope, Faith and Cynicism," *Training,* January 1994, pp. 41–45.

47. D. W. Johnson and F. P. Johnson, *Joining Together: Group Theory and Group Skills* (Boston: Allyn and Bacon, 1994). V. Villasenor, *Jury: The People vs. Juan Corona* (New York: Bantam, 1977).

48. M. Shaw, "A Comparison of Individuals and Small Groups in the Rational Solution of Complex Problems," *American Journal of Psychology,* 1932, 44, pp. 491–504. R. Ziller, "Group Size: A Determinant of the Quality and Stability of Group Decision," *Sociometry,* 1957, 20, pp. 165–173.

49. Schiller, "GE's Appliance Park."

50–53. I. L. Janis, *Groupthink*, 2d ed. (Boston: Houghton Mifflin, 1982).

54. J. M. Darley and B. Latane, "Bystander Intervention in Emergencies: Diffusion of Responsibility," *Journal of Personality and Social Psychology*, 1968, 8, pp. 377–383. M. E. Shaw, *Group Dynamics* (New York: McGraw-Hill, 1981).

55. S. Moscovici and M. Zavalloni, "The Group as a Polarizer of Attitudes," *Journal of Personality and Social Psychology*, 1969, 12, pp. 125–135. Shaw, *Group Dynamics*.

56. M. A. Wallach, N. Kogan, and D. J. Bem, "Group Influence on Individual Risk Taking," *Journal of Abnormal and Social Psychology*, 1962, 65, pp. 75–86. M. A. Wallach, N. Kogan, and D. J. Bem, "Diffusion of Responsibility and Level of Risk Taking in Groups," *Journal of Abnormal and Social Psychology*, 1964, 68, pp. 263–274.

57. L. Festinger, "A Theory of Social Comparison Processes," *Human Relations*, 1954, 7, pp. 117–140.

58. A. Vinokur and E. Burnstein, "Effects of Partially Shared Persuasive Arguments on Group-Induced Shifts: A Group Problem-Solving Approach," *Journal of Personality and Social Psychology*, 1974, 29, pp. 305–315. Shaw, *Group Dynamics*.

59. A. F. Osborn, *Applied Imagination* (New York: Scribners, 1957).

60. T. J. Bouchard, Jr., J. Barsaloux, and G. Drauden, "Brainstorming Procedure, Group Size, and Sex as Determinants of the Problem-Solving Effectiveness of Groups and Individuals," *Journal of Applied Psychology*, 1974, 59, pp. 135–138.

61. M. Diehl and W. Stroebe, "Productivity Loss in Brainstorming Groups: Toward the Solution of a Riddle," *Journal of Personality and Social Psychology*, 1987, 53, pp. 497–509.

62. R. B. Gallupe, L. M. Bastianutti, and W. H. Cooper, "Unblocking Brainstorms," *Journal of Applied Psychology*, 1991, 76, pp. 137–142.

63. D. H. Gustafson, R. K. Shulka, A. Delbecq, and W. G. Walster, "A Comparative Study of Differences in Subjective Likelihood Estimates Made by Individual, Interacting Groups, Delphi Groups, and Nominal Groups," *Organizational Behavior and Human Performance*, 1973, 9, pp. 280–291.

64. N. Dalkey, *The Delphi Method: An Experimental Study of Group Decisions* (Santa Monica, Calif.: Rand Corporation, 1969).

65. S. M. Young, "A Framework for the Successful Adoption and Performance of Japanese Manufacturing Practices," *Academy of Management Review*, 1992, 17, pp. 677–700. M. Walton, *The Deming Management Method* (New York: Perigee Books, 1990).

66. "How Does Service Drive the Service Company?" *Harvard Business Review*, November–December 1991, pp. 146–158.

67. A. Gabor, "Rochester Focuses: A Community's Core Competences," *Harvard Business Review*, July–August 1991, pp. 116–126.

68, 69. B. Dumaine, "The New Non-Manager Managers," *Fortune*, February 22, 1993, pp. 80–84.

70. T. M. Amabile, "A Model of Creativity and Innovation in Organizations," in *Research in Organizational Behavior*, vol. 10, ed. B. M. Staw and L. L. Cummings (Greenwich, Conn.: JAI Press, 1988), pp. 123–167.

71. Amabile, "A Model of Creativity and Innovation in Organizations."

72. T. Welsh, "Best and Worst Corporate Reputations," *Fortune*, February 7, 1994, pp. 58–66.

73. Amabile, "A Model of Creativity and Innovation in Organizations."

74–77. T. L. O'Brien, "Thriving on Quirkiness: Software Firm Saves Screens While Entertaining Users," *Wall Street Journal*, April 11, 1994, pp. B1–B2.

78. F. B. Barron and D. M. Harrington, "Creativity, Intelligence, and Personality," *Annual Review of Psychology*, 1981, 32, pp. 439–476. R. W. Woodman, J. E. Sawyer, and R. W. Griffin, "Toward a Theory of Organizational Creativity," *Academy of Management Review*, 1993, 18, pp. 293–321.

79. R. W. Woodman and L. F. Schoenfeldt, "Individual Differences in Creativity: An Interactionist Perspective," in *Handbook of Creativity*, ed. J. A. Glover, R. R. Ronning, and C. R. Reynolds (New York: Plenum Press, 1989), pp. 77–92.

80. Barron and Harrington, "Creativity, Intelligence, and Personality."

81. Amabile, "A Model of Creativity and Innovation in Organizations."

82. Amabile, "A Model of Creativity and Innovation in Organizations." Woodman, Sawyer, and Griffin, "Toward a Theory of Organizational Creativity."

83. O'Brien, "Thriving on Quirkiness."

84. Amabile, "A Model of Creativity and Innovation in Organizations."

85–87. E. Thornton, "Japan's Struggle to Be Creative," *Fortune*, April 19, 1993, pp. 129–134.

88–91. Amabile, "A Model of Creativity and Innovation in Organizations."

92. L. DiCarlo, "Intel to Boost PC, Server Management," *PC Week*, January 5, 1998, pp. 1-2. A. Grove, "How Intel Makes Spending Pay Off," *Fortune*, February 22, 1993, pp. 56-61. "Intel's Mood Swings," *Business Week*, January 26, 1988, p. 41. E. Scannell and D. Pendery, "Answering the 64-Bit Question," *InfoWorld*, January 12, 1998, pp. 1-2.

93. A. Grove, "How Intel Makes Spending Pay Off," *Fortune*, February 22, 1993, pp. 56–61.

CHAPTER 15

1. R. H. Hall, *Organizations: Structure and Process* (Englewood, Cliffs, N.J.: Prentice-Hall, 1972). R. Miles, *Macro Organizational Behavior* (Santa Monica, Calif.: Goodyear, 1980).

2. J. Child, *Organization: A Guide for Managers and Administrators* (New York: Harper and Row, 1977).

3. J. D. Thompson, *Organizations in Action* (New York: McGraw-Hill, 1967). J. Pfeffer, *Organizations and Organizational Theory* (Boston: Pitman, 1982).

4. R. Duncan, "What Is the Right Organizational Structure," *Organizational Dynamics*, Winter 1979, pp. 59–80.

5. Child, Organization, pp. 52–70.

6. G. R. Jones, *Organizational Theory: Text and Cases* (Reading, Mass.: Addison-Wesley, 1995).

7. G. McWilliams, "How DEC's Minicompanies Led to Major Losses," *Business Week*, February 7, 1994, pp. 62–63.

8. D. Machalaba, "Burlington Northern Executives Retire, Raising Speculation About CEO Search," *Wall Street Journal*, June 2, 1994, p. B8.

9. L. Berton and M. Selz, "Peat Marwick Cuts U.S. Staff of Professionals," *Wall Street Journal*, June 2, 1994, p. A4.

10. S. M. Davis and P. R. Lawrence, *Matrix* (Reading, Mass.: Addison-Wesley, 1977). J. R. Galbraith, "Matrix Organizational Designs: How to Combine Functional and Project Forms," *Business Horizons*, 1971, 14, pp. 29–40.

11. L. R. Burns, "Matrix Management in Hospitals: Testing Theories of Matrix Structure and Development," *Administrative Science Quarterly*, 1989, 34, pp. 349–368.

12. S. M. Davis and P. R. Lawrence, "Problems of Matrix Organization," *Harvard Business Review*, May–June 1978, pp. 131–142.

13. P. R. Lawrence and J. R. Lorsch, *Organization and Environment* (Boston: Division of Research, Harvard Business School, 1967).

14. H. Mintzberg, *The Structuring of Organizations* (Englewood Cliffs, N.J.: Prentice-Hall, 1979).

15. P. M. Blau, "A Formal Theory of Differentiation in Organizations," *American Sociological Review*, 1970, 35, pp. 201–218.

16. H. Fayol, *General and Industrial Management*, rev. ed. (New York: IEEE Press, 1984).

17. A. B. Fisher, "Profiting from Crisis," *Business Week*, February 7, 1994, p. 166.

18. J. Galbraith, *Designing Complex Organizations* (Reading, Mass: Addison-Wesley, 1973).

19. H. Mintzberg, *The Nature of Managerial Work* (New York: Harper and Row, 1973).

20. Mintzberg, *The Structuring of Organizations*, Ch. 1.

21. Thompson, *Organizations in Action*.

22. M. Rokeach, *The Nature of Human Values* (New York: Free Press, 1973).

23. R. Frank, "As UPS Tries to Deliver More to Its Customers Labor Problems Grow," *Wall Street Journal*, May 23, 1994, A1, A5.

24. J. Van Maanen, "Police Socialization: A Longitudinal Examination of Job Attitudes in an Urban Police Department," *Administrative Science Quarterly*, 1975, 20, pp. 207–228.

25. P. L. Berger and T. Luckman, *The Social Construction of Reality* (Garden City, N.Y.: Anchor Books, 1967).

26. E. H. Schein, "The Role of the Founder in Creating Organizational Culture," *Organizational Dynamics*, 1983, 12, pp. 13–28.

27. J. M. George, "Personality, Affect, and Behavior in Groups," *Journal of Applied Psychology*, 1990, 75, pp. 107–116.

28. George, "Personality, Affect, and Behavior in Groups." D. Miller and J. M. Toulouse, "Chief Executive Personality and Corporate Strategy and Structure in Small Firms," *Management Science*, 1986, 32, pp. 1389–1409.

29. R. E. Goodin, "How to Determine Who Should Get What," *Ethics*, July 1975, pp. 310–321.

30. T. M. Jones, "Ethical Decision Making by Individuals in Organizations: An Issue Contingent Model," *Academy of Management Review*, 1991, 2, pp. 366–395.

31. T. L. Beauchamp and N. E. Bowie, eds., *Ethical Theory and Business* (Englewood Cliffs, N.J.: Prentice-Hall, 1979). A. MacIntyre, *After Virtue* (Notre Dame, Ind.: University of Notre Dame Press, 1981).

32. T. J. Peters and R. H. Waterman, Jr., *In Search of Excellence: Lessons from America's Best-Run Companies* (New York: Harper and Row, 1982).

33. G. R. Jones, "Transaction Costs, Property Rights, and Organizational Culture: An Exchange Perspective," *Administrative Science Quarterly*, 1983, 28, pp. 454–467.

34. W. G. Ouchi, Theory Z: *How American Business Can Meet the Japanese Challenge* (Reading, Mass.: Addison-Wesley, 1981).

35. H. M. Trice and J. M. Beyer, "Studying Organizational Culture Through Rites and Ceremonials," *Academy of Management Review*, 1984, 9, pp. 653–669.

36. H. M. Trice and J. M. Beyer, *The Cultures of Work Organizations* (Englewood Cliffs, N.J.: Prentice-Hall, 1993).

37. B. Ortega, "Wal-Mart's Meeting Is a Reason to Party," *Wall Street Journal,* June 3, 1994, p. A1.
38. M. Ramundo, "Service Awards Build Culture of Success," *Human Resources Magazine,* August 1992, pp. 61–63.
39. Trice and Beyer, "Studying Organizational Cultures Through Rites and Ceremonials."
40. A. M. Pettigrew, "On Studying Organizational Cultures," *Administrative Science Quarterly,* 1979, 24, pp. 570–582.
41. B. Uttal, "Behind the Fall of Steve Jobs," *Business Week,* January 31, 1983, pp. 20–24.
42. Uttal, "Behind the Fall of Steve Jobs."
43. B. Dumaine, "Creating a New Company Culture," *Business Week,* January 15, 1990, pp. 127–131.

CHAPTER 16

1. S. Kotha and E. Dooley, "Amazon.com," in C.W.L. Hill and G. R. Jones, *Strategic Management: An Integrated Approach* (Boston, Mass.: Houghton Mifflin Co., 1998).
2. "Reading the Market: How a Wall Street Wiz Found a Niche Selling Books on the Internet," *Wall Street Journal,* 1996, May 16, p.A1.
3–5. This section is based heavily on P. R. Lawrence and J. W. Lorsch, *Organization and Environment: Managing Differentiation and Integration* (Boston: Graduate School of Business Administration, Harvard University, 1967).
6. T. Burns and G. M. Stalker, *The Management of Innovation* (London: Tavistock, 1961).
7. M. Maremont and L. Therrien, "To: George Fisher, Re: How to Fix Kodak," *Business Week,* November 8, 1993, p. 37.
8. J. Woodward, *Management and Technology* (London: Her Majesty's Stationery Office, 1958).
9. Woodward, *Management and Technology.*
10. J. D. Thompson, *Organizations in Action* (New York: McGraw-Hill, 1967).
11. C. Perrow, *Organizational Analysis: A Sociological View* (Belmont, Calif.: Wadsworth, 1970).
12. J. Huey, "How McKinsey Does It," *Fortune,* November 1, 1993, pp. 56–81.
13, 14. M. E. Porter, *Competitive Strategy* (New York: Free Press, 1980).
15, 16. G. R. Jones and J. R. Butler, "Costs, Revenue, and Business-Level Strategy," *Academy of Management Review,* 1988, 14, pp. 202–213.
17. C.W.L. Hill and G. R. Jones, *Strategic Management: An Integrated Approach,* 3d ed. (Boston: Houghton Mifflin, 1995).
18. K. Kelly, "The New Soul of John Deere," *Business Week,* January 31, 1994, pp. 64–66.
19. W. E. Deming, *Out of the Crisis* (Cambridge, Mass.: MIT CAES, 1986).
20. C. Sims, "Giving Denny's a Menu for Change," *New York Times,* January 2, 1994, p. B1.
21. T. Gelb, "Overhauling Corporate Engine Drives Winning Strategy," *Journal of Business Strategy,* November–December 1989, pp. 8–12.
22. B. S. Moskal, "Born to Be Real," *Industry Week,* August 2, 1993, pp. 14–18.

CHAPTER 17

1. A. Taylor, III, "Revolution at Daimler-Benz," *Fortune,* 1997, November 10, pp. 144–152.
2. T. Leavitt, "The Globalization of Markets," *Harvard Business Review,* May–June 1983, pp. 92–102.
3, 4. C.W.L. Hill and G. R. Jones, *Strategic Management: An Integrated Approach* (Boston: Houghton Mifflin, 1995).
5. M. Rokeach, *The Nature of Human Values* (New York: Free Press, 1973).
6. G. Hofstede, B. Neuijen, D. D. Ohayv, and G. Sanders, "Measuring Organizational Cultures: A Qualitative and Quantitative Study Across Twenty Cases," *Administrative Science Quarterly,* 1990, 35, pp. 286–316.
7. W. G. Ouchi, *Theory Z: How American Business Can Meet the Challenge of Japanese Management* (Reading, Mass.: Addison-Wesley, 1981).
8. G. Hofstede, "The Cultural Relativity of Organizational Practices and Theories," *Journal of International Business Studies,* Fall 1983, pp. 75–89.
9. "Big-Company CEOs Exemplify Diversity," *HR Magazine,* August 1994, pp. 25–26.
10. "Tips for Negotiations in Germany and France," *HR Focus,* July 1994, p. 18.
11, 12. Hofstede, Neuijen, Ohayv, and Sanders, "Measuring Organizational Cultures."
13. D. A. Ricks, *Big Business Blunders: Mistakes in Multinational Marketing* (Homewood, Ill.: Irwin, 1983).
14. C.W.L. Hill, P. Hwang, and W. C. Kim, "An Eclectic Theory of the Choice of International Entry Mode," *Strategic Management Journal,* 1990, 11, pp. 117–128.
15. J. Leib, "Coors, S. Korean Firm in Brewery Venture," *Denver (Colorado) Post,* November 27, 1994, p. C14.
16. D. G. Bradley, "Managing Against Expropriation," *Harvard Business Review,* July–August 1977, pp. 75–83.

17. N. Templin, "Mexican Industrial Belt Is Beginning to Form as Car Makers Expand," *Wall Street Journal,* June 29, 1994, pp. A1, A10.
18. G. R. Jones and C.W.L. Hill, "Transaction Cost Analysis of Strategy-Structure Choice," *Strategic Management Journal,* 1988, 9, pp. 159–172.
19, 20. C. A. Bartlett and S. Ghoshal, *Managing Across Borders* (Boston: Harvard Business School Press, 1989).
21. Leavitt, "The Globalization of Markets."
22. C. K. Prahalad and Y. L. Doz, *The Multinational Mission: Balancing Local Demands and Global Vision* (New York: Free Press, 1987).
23. This discussion on types of strategy draws heavily from Bartlett and Ghoshal, *Managing Across Borders.*
24. R. Schreffler, "A Decade of Progress," *Automotive Industries,* November 1992, pp. 46–49.
25. S. M. Davis, *Managing and Organizing Multinational Corporations,* in C. A. Bartlett and S. Ghoshal, eds., *Transnational Management* (Homewood, Ill.: Irwin, 1992).
26. C.W.L. Hill, *International Business* (Homewood, Ill.: Irwin, 1994).
27. N. Munk, "The Levi Straddle," *Forbes,* January 17, 1994, pp. 44–45.
28. C. A. Bartlett and Ghoshal, *Transnational Management.*
29. G.R. Jones, *Organizational Theory: Text and Cases, 2nd ed.* (Reading, Mass.: Addison-Wesley, 1998).
30. G. Hofstede, "The Cultural Relativity of Organizational Practices and Theories," *Journal of International Business Studies,* Fall 1983, pp. 75–89.
31. G. Hofstede, "Motivation, Leadership, and Organization: Do American Theories Apply Abroad," *Organizational Dynamics,* Summer 1980, pp. 42–63.
32. S. Ronan, "An Underlying Structure of Motivational Need Taxonomies: A Cross-Cultural Confirmation," in H. C. Triandis, M. D. Dunnette, and L. M. Hough, eds., *Handbook of Industrial and Organizational Psychology,* vol. 4 (Palo Alto, Calif.: Consulting Psychologists Press, 1994), pp. 241–269. N. Adler, *International Dimensions of Organizational Behavior* (Boston: Kent, 1991).
33. Hill, *International Business.*
34. Y. Kashima and V. J. Callan, "The Japanese Work Group," in Triandis, Dunnette, and Hough, eds., *Handbook of Industrial and Organizational Psychology,* pp. 609–646.
35. Adler, *International Dimensions of Organizational Behavior.*
36. Hofstede, "Motivation, Leadership, and Organization."
37. Ouchi, *Theory Z.*
38. A. DePalma, "It Takes More Than a Visa to Do Business in Mexico," *New York Times,* June 26, 1994, p. F5.

CHAPTER 18

1. CIC Corp. website (www.cicagency.com).
2. B. Fannin, "CIC workers Ask Judge to Void Noncompliance Pact," *The Eagle,* October 23, 1997. p. 1
3. R. A. Dahl, "The Concept of Power," *Behavioral Science,* 1957, 2, pp. 210–215. R. M. Emerson, "Power Dependence Relations," *American Sociological Review,* 1962, 27, pp. 31–41.
4. J. Pfeffer, *Power in Organizations* (Boston: Pitman, 1981).
5. A. M. Pettigrew, *The Politics of Organizational Decision Making* (London: Tavistock, 1973). R. H. Miles, *Macro Organizational Behavior* (Santa Monica, Calif.: Goodyear, 1980).
6. "Making Ends Meet," *The Economist,* April 7, 1993, p. 3.
7. J. G. March, "The Business Firm as a Coalition," *Journal of Politics,* 1962, 24, pp. 662–678. D. J. Vrendenburgh and J. G. Maurer, "A Process Framework of Organizational Politics," *Human Relations,* 1984, 37, pp. 47–66.
8. This section draws heavily on J.R.P. French, Jr., and B. Raven, "The Bases of Social Power," in D. Cartwright, ed., *Studies in Social Power* (Ann Arbor: University of Michigan, Institute for Social Research, 1959), pp. 150–167.
9, 10. M. Weber, *The Theory of Economic and Social Organization* (New York: Free Press, 1947).
11. Pettigrew, *The Politics of Organizational Decision Making.* G. Yukl and C. M. Falbe, "Importance of Different Power Sources in Downward and Lateral Relations," *Journal of Applied Psychology,* 1991, 76, pp. 416–423.
12. J. A. Conger and R. N. Kanungo, "The Empowerment Process: Integrating Theory and Practice," *Academy of Management Review,* 1988, 13, pp. 471–481.
13. French and Raven, "The Bases of Social Power."
14. M. Weber, *Economy and Society* (Berkeley: University of California Press, 1978). H. M. Trice and J. M. Beyer, "Charisma and Its Routinization in Two Social Movement Organizations," *Research in Organizational Behavior,* 1986, 8, pp. 113–164.
15. B. M. Bass, "Leadership: Good, Better, Best," *Organizational Dynamics,* 1985, 13, pp. 26–40.
16. Weber, *Economy and Society.*
17. R. Marin and C. Fleming, "Leaving Rupert's World," *Newsweek,* July 18, 1994, p. 65.
18. This section draws heavily on D. J. Hickson, C. R. Hinings, C. A. Lee, R. E. Schneck, and D. J. Pennings, "A Strategic Contingencies Theory of

Intraorganizational Power," *Administrative Science Quarterly,* 1971, 16, pp. 216–227, and C. R. Hinings, D. J. Hickson, J. M. Pennings, and R. E. Schneck, "Structural Conditions of Interorganizational Power," *Administrative Science Quarterly,* 1974, 19, pp. 22–44.

19. Hickson, Hinings, Lee, Schneck, and Pennings, "A Strategic Contingencies Theory of Intraorganizational Power."

20, 21. M. Gargiulo, "Two Step Leverage: Managing Constraint in Organizational Politics," *Administrative Science Quarterly,* 1993, 38, pp. 1–19.

22, 23. M. Crozier, "Sources of Power of Lower Level Participants in Complex Organizations," *Administrative Science Quarterly,* 1962, 7, pp. 349–364.

24. A. M. Pettigrew, "Information Control as a Power Resource," *Sociology,* 1972, 6, pp. 187–204.

25. G. R. Salancik and J. Pfeffer, "The Bases and Uses of Power in Organizational Decision Making," *Administrative Science Quarterly,* 1974, 19, pp. 453–473. J. Pfeffer and G. R. Salancik, *The External Control of Organizations: A Resource Dependence View* (New York: Harper and Row, 1978).

26. T. Burns, "Micropolitics: Mechanisms of Institutional Change," *Administrative Science Quarterly,* 1961, 6, pp. 257–281.

27. E. Jennings, *The Mobile Manager* (New York: McGraw-Hill, 1967).

28. This discussion draws heavily on Pfeffer, *Power in Organizations,* Ch. 5.

29. Hickson, Hinings, Lee, Schneck, and Pennings, "A Strategic Contingencies Theory of Intraorganizational Power."

30. This section draws heavily on Pfeffer, *Power in Organizations,* Ch. 2.

31. J. A. Litterer, "Conflict in Organizations: A Reexamination," *Academy of Management Journal,* 1966, 9, pp. 178–186. S. M. Schmidt and T. A. Kochan, "Conflict: Towards Conceptual Clarity," *Administrative Science Quarterly,* 1972, 13, pp. 359–370; Miles, *Macro-Organizational Behavior.*

32. Miles, *Macro-Organizational Behavior.*

33. S. P. Robbins, *Managing Organizational Conflict: A Nontraditional Approach* (Englewood Cliffs, N.J.: Prentice-Hall, 1974). L. Coser, *The Functions of Social Conflict* (New York: Free Press, 1956).

34. This discussion owes much to the seminal work of the following authors: Lou R. Pondy, "Organizational Conflict: Concepts and Models," *Administrative Science Quarterly,* 1967, 2, pp. 296–320; R. E. Walton and J. M. Dutton, "The Management of Interdepartmental Conflict: A Model and Review," *Administrative Science Quarterly,* 1969, 14, pp. 62–73.

35. M. Dalton, *Men Who Manage* (New York: Wiley, 1959); Walton and Dutton, "The Management of Interdepartmental Conflict."

36. G. Putka, "At the Elite Harvard Business Review, Business and Academics Aren't Mixing," *Wall Street Journal,* March 25, 1994, p. B1.

37. Walton and Dutton, "The Management of Interdepartmental Conflict." J. McCann and J. R. Galbraith, "Interdepartmental Relationships," in P. C. Nystrom and W. H. Starbuck, eds., *Handbook of Organizational Design* (New York: Oxford University Press, 1981).

38. J. D. Thompson, *Organizations in Action* (New York: McGraw-Hill, 1967).

39. Walton and Dutton, "The Management of Interdepartmental Conflict," p. 65.

40. Walton and Dutton, "The Management of Interdepartmental Conflict," p. 68.

41. Pondy, "Organizational Conflict," p. 300.

42. Pondy, "Organizational Conflict," p. 310.

43. K. Thomas, "Conflict and Negotiation Processes in Organizations," in M. D. Dunnette and L. M. Hough, eds., *Handbook of Industrial and Organizational Psychology,* 2d ed., vol 3 (Palo Alto, Calif.: Consulting Psychologists Press, 1992), pp. 651–717.

44. M. Lewyn, "Behind the Bloody Battle of Dart's Boardroom," *Business Week,* June 28, 1993, pp. 96–97.

45. A. Miller, F. Chadeya, and B. Shenitz, "Dysfunctional Discounters," *Newsweek,* July 12, 1993, p. 47.

46, 47. E. E. Neilsen, "Understanding and Managing Intergroup Conflict," in J. F. Veiga and J. N. Yanouzas, eds., *The Dynamics of Organizational Theory* (St. Paul, Minn.: West, 1979), pp. 290–296. Miles, *Macro-Organizational Behavior.*

48. J. Z. Rubin and B. R. Brown, *The Social Psychology of Bargaining and Negotiation* (New York: Academic Press, 1975).

49. R. E. Walton, "Third Party Roles in Interdepartmental Conflict," *Industrial Relations,* 1967, 7, pp. 29–43.

50. R. E. Walton and R. B. McKersie, *A Behavioral Theory of Labor Relations* (New York: McGraw-Hill, 1965).

51. P. R. Lawrence, L. B. Barnes, and J. W. Lorsch, *Organizational Behavior and Administration* (Homewood, Ill.: Irwin, 1976).

52. R. Frank, "Clashing Executives Tear a Company Apart," *Wall Street Journal,* July 19, 1994, pp. B1, B6.

CHAPTER 19

1. P. Sellers, "SEARS: The Turnaround Is Ending, The Revolution Has Begun,' *Fortune,* 1997, April 28, pp. 106–118.

2. Sears Annual Reports, 1995, 1996, 1997, and information from website (www.sears.com).

3. J. P. Kotter, L. A. Schlesinger, and V. Sathe, *Organization* (Homewood, Ill.: Irwin, 1979), p. 487.

4. C. Argyris, R. Putman, and D. M. Smith, *Action Science* (San Francisco: Jossey-Bass, 1985).

5. R. M. Kanter, *The Change Masters: Innovation for Productivity in the American Corporation* (New York: Simon & Schuster, 1984).

6. C.W.L. Hill and G. R. Jones, *Strategic Management: An Integrated Approach,* 3d ed. (Boston: Houghton Mifflin, 1995).

7. G. R. Jones, *Organizational Theory: Text and Cases* (Reading, Mass.: Addison-Wesley, 1995).

8. C.W.L. Hill, *International Business* (Chicago, Ill.: Irwin, 1994).

9. C. A. Bartlett and S. Ghoshal, *Managing Across Borders* (Boston: Harvard Business School Press, 1989).

10. C. K. Prahalad and Y. L. Doz, *The Multinational Mission: Balancing Local Demands and Global Vision* (New York: Free Press, 1987).

11. D. Jamieson and J. O'Mara, *Managing Workforce 2000: Gaining a Diversity Advantage* (San Francisco: Jossey-Bass, 1991).

12. T. H. Cox and S. Blake, "Managing Cultural Diversity: Implications for Organizational Competitiveness," *Academy of Management Executive,* August 1991, pp. 49–52.

13. S. E. Jackson and Associates, *Diversity in the Workplace: Human Resource Initiatives* (New York: Guilford Press, 1992).

14. W. H. Shaw and V. Barry, *Moral Issues in Business,* 6th ed. (Belmont, Calif.: Wadsworth, 1995).

15. "Tossing the Whole Barnyard in the Meat Grinder," *Consumer Reports,* July 1994, p. 431.

16. T. Donaldson, *Corporations and Morality* (Englewood Cliffs, N.J., Prentice-Hall, 1982).

17. J. Impoco, "Working for Mr. Clean Jeans," *U.S. News and World Report,* August 2, 1993, pp. 19–20.

18. M. Hannan and J. Freeman, "Structural Inertia and Organizational Change," *American Sociological Review,* 1989, 49, pp. 149–164.

19. L. E. Greiner, "Evolution and Revolution as Organizations Grow," *Harvard Business Review,* July–August 1972, pp. 37–46.

20. R. M. Kanter, *When Giants Learn to Dance: Mastering the Challenges of Strategy* (New York: Simon and Schuster, 1989).

21. J. P. Kotter and L. A. Schlesinger, "Choosing Strategies for Change," *Harvard Business Review,* March–April 1979, pp. 106–114.

22. T. Burns and G. M. Stalker, *The Management of Innovation* (London: Tavistock, 1961).

23. P. R. Lawrence and J. W. Lorsch, *Organization and Environment* (Boston: Harvard Business School Press, 1972).

24. R. Likert, *The Human Organization* (New York: McGraw-Hill, 1967).

25. C. Argyris, *Personality and Organization* (New York: Harper and Row, 1957).

26. This section draws heavily on K. Lewin, *Field Theory in Social Science* (New York: Harper and Row, 1951).

27. D. Miller, "Evolution and Revolution: A Quantum View of Structural Change in Organizations," *Journal of Management Studies,* 1982, 19, pp. 11–151. D. Miller, "Momentum and Revolution in Organizational Adaptation," *Academy of Management Journal,* 1980, 2, pp. 591–614.

28. C. E. Lindblom, "The Science of Muddling Through," *Public Administration Review,* 1959, 19, pp. 79–88. P. C. Nystrom and W. H. Starbuck, "To Avoid Organizational Crises, Unlearn," *Organizational Dynamics,* 1984, 12, pp. 53–65.

29. E. L. Trist, G. Higgins, H. Murray, and A. G. Pollock, *Organizational Choice* (London: Tavistock, 1965). J. C. Taylor, "The Human Side of Work: The Socio-Technical Approach to Work Design," *Personnel Review,* 1975, 4, pp. 17–22.

30. E. L. Trist and K. W. Bamforth, "Some Social and Psychological Consequences of the Long Wall Method of Coal Mining," *Human Relations,* 1951, 4, pp. 3–38. F. E. Emery and E. L. Trist, *Socio-Technical Systems* (London: Proceedings of the 6th Annual International Meeting of the Institute of Management Sciences, 1965), pp. 92–93.

31. W. Edwards Deming, *Out of the Crisis* (Cambridge, Mass.: MIT Press, 1989). M. Walton, *The Deming Management Method* (New York: Perigee Books, 1990).

32. J. McHugh and B. Dale, "Quality Circles," in R. Wild, ed., *International Handbook of Production and Operations Research* (London: Cassel, 1989).

33. T. M. Rohan, "Culture Change Wins the Baldridge," *Industry Week,* January 4, 1994, pp. 41–43.

34. S. M. Young, "A Framework for the Successful Adoption and Performance of Japanese Manufacturing Techniques in the United States," *Academy of Management Review,* 1992, 17, pp. 677–700.

35, 36. M. Hammer and J. Champy, *Reengineering the Corporation* (New York: HarperCollins, 1993).

37. Jones, *Organizational Theory*. R. A. Burgelman and M. A. Maidique, *Strategic Management of Technology and Innovation* (Homewood, Ill.: Irwin, 1988).

38. G. R. Jones and J. E. Butler, "Managing Internal Corporate Entrepreneurship: An Agency Theory Perspective," *Journal of Management*, 1992, 18, pp. 733–749.

39. E. Mansfield, J. Rapoport, J. Schnee, S. Wagner, and M. Hamburger, *Research and Innovation in the Modern Corporation* (New York: Norton, 1971).

40. "Synergen Inc.," *Wall Street Journal*, August 2, 1994, p. B6.

41. R. A. Burgelman, "Designs for Corporate Entrepreneurship in Established Firms," *California Management Review*, 1984, 26, pp. 154–166.

42. D. Frey, "Learning the Ropes: My Life as a Product Champion," *Harvard Business Review*, September–October 1991, pp. 46–56.

43. Lewin, *Field Theory in Social Science*, pp. 172–174.

44. This section draws heavily on P. A. Clark, *Action Research and Organizational Change* (New York: Harper and Row, 1972); L. Brown, "Research Action: Organizational Feedback, Understanding and Change," *Journal of Applied Behavioral Research*, 1972, 8, pp. 697–711; N. Margulies and A. P Raia, eds., *Conceptual Foundations of Organizational Development* (New York: McGraw-Hill, 1978).

45. W. L. French and C. H. Bell, *Organizational Development* (Englewood Cliffs, N.J.: Prentice-Hall, 1990).

46. L. Coch and J.R.P. French, "Overcoming Resistance to Change," *Human Relations*, 1948, 1, pp. 512–532.

47, 48. French and Bell, *Organizational Development*.

49. W. L. French, "A Checklist for Organizing and Implementing an OD Effort," in W. L. French, C. H. Bell, and R. A. Zawacki, *Organizational Development and Transformation* (Homewood, Ill.: Irwin, 1994), pp. 484–495.

50. Kotter, Schlesinger, and Sathe, *Organization*, p. 487.

51. W. G. Bennis, *Organizational Development: Its Nature, Origins, and Perspectives* (Reading, Mass.: Addison-Wesley, 1969).

52. Kotter and Schlesinger, "Choosing Strategies for Change."

53. Z. Schiller and T. Smart, "If You Can't Stand the Heat, Upgrade the Kitchen," *Business Week*, April 25, 1994, p. 35.

54. E. H. Schein, *Organizational Psychology* (Englewood Cliffs, N.J.: Prentice-Hall, 1980).

55. R. T. Golembiewski, "The Laboratory Approach to Organization Change: Schema of a Method," in Margulies and Raia, eds., *Conceptual Foundations of Organizational Development*, pp. 198–212. J. Kelley "Organizational Development Through Structured Sensitivity Training;" Schein, *Organizational Psychology*, pp. 213–228.

56. E. H. Schein, *Process Consultation* (Reading, Mass.: Addison-Wesley, 1969).

57. M. Sashkin and W. Warner Burke, "Organization Development in the 1980s," *Journal of Management*, 1987, 13, pp. 393–417. D. Eden, "Team Development: Quasi-Experimental Confirmation Among Combat Companies," *Group and Organization Studies*, 1986, 5, pp. 133–146. K. P. DeMeuse and S. J. Liebowitz, "An Empirical Analysis of Team Building Research," *Group and Organization Studies*, 1981, 6, pp. 357–378.

58. French and Bell, *Organization Development*.

59. R. Beckhard, "The Confrontation Meeting," *Harvard Business Review*, March–April 1967, pp. 159–165.

60. R. R. Blake and J. S. Mouton, *The New Managerial Grid* (Houston: Gulf, 1978).

APPENDIX

1. E. F. Stone, *Research Methods in Organizational Behavior* (Santa Monica, Calif.: Goodyear, 1978).

2. C. G. Hempel, *Aspects of Scientific Explanation* (New York: Free Press, 1965); Stone, *Research Methods in Organizational Behavior*.

3. A. Kaplan, *The Conduct of Inquiry* (New York: T. Y. Crowell, 1964).

4. M. Cohen and E. Nagel, *An Introduction to Logic and Scientific Method* (New York: Harcourt, Brace, 1934). F. Kerlinger, *Foundations of Behavioral Research* (New York: Holt, Rinehart and Winston, 1973). Stone, *Research Methods in Organizational Behavior*.

5. Some of the material in this section draws from the following sources: T. D. Cook and D. T. Campbell, "The Design and Conduct of Quasi-Experiments and True Experiments in Field Settings," in *Handbook of Industrial and Organizational Psychology*, ed. M. D. Dunnette, pp. 223-326 (Chicago: Rand McNally, 1976). P. J. Runkel and J. E. McGrath, *Research on Human Behavior* (New York: Holt, Rinehart and Winston, 1972). Stone, *Research Methods in Organizational Behavior*.

6. E. Mayo, *The Human Problems of Industrial Civilization* (New York: MacMillan, 1933). F.J. Roethlisberger and W.J. Dickson, *Management and the Worker* (Cambridge, Mass.: Harvard University Press, 1947).

7. D. W. Organ, "Review of *Management and the Worker* by F. J. Roethlisberger add W. J. Dickson," *Academy of Management Review*, 1986, 13, 460–464.

8. For an analysis of the problems in determining cause from effect in the Hawthorne Studies and in social settings in general see A. Carey, "The Hawthorne Studies: A Radical Criticism," *American Sociological Review*, 1967, 33, 403–416.

9. S. W. Cook, "Ethical Issues in the Conduct of Research in Social Relations," in *Research Methods in Social Relations*, ed. C. Selltiz, L. S. Wrightsman, and S. W. Cook (New York: Holt, Rinehart and Winston, 1976). H. C. Kelman, *A Time to Speak: On Human Values and Social Research* (San Francisco: Jossey Bass, 1968). Runkel and McGrath, *Research on Human Behavior*. Stone, *Research Methods in Organizational Behavior*.

PHOTO CREDITS

SUBJECT INDEX

NAME INDEX

COMPANY INDEX